SOUTHEASTERN SEC CONFERENCE

1994 Football Guide
Volume XLVI

SEC FOOTBALL GUIDE 1994

Official Yearbook of the Most Powerful Conference in College Football

SOUTHEASTERN CONFERENCE

TRIUMPH BOOKS
Chicago

© copyright 1994 the Southeastern Conference. All rights reserved.

For more information on the SEC, contact:

Southeastern Conference
2201 Civic Center Boulevard
Birmingham, Alabama 35203-1103

The book is available in quantity at special discounts for your group or organization. For further information contact the publisher:

Triumph Books
644 S. Clark Street, Suite 2000
Chicago, IL 60605
312/939-3330
FAX 312/663-3557

Printed in the United States of America

Editorial Staff:
SEC Media Relations Department
  Mark Whitworth, Assistant Commissioner
  Graham Edwards, Director
  Karen Frascona, Associate Director
  Gina Estes, Administrative Assistant
  Glenn Thackston, Assistant

Special Assistance:
Information and photographs furnished by the Sports Information Departments of the member institutions.

Typesetting and Printing:
Ambrose Printing Company
Nashville, Tennessee

Graphic Artist:
FitzMartin Design Partners
Birmingham, Alabama

Table of Contents

INTRODUCTION
Media Services....2
1994 SEC Headlines....4-5
1994 SEC Championship Game....6
SEC Bowl Agreements/JP Sports....7
Year-by-Year Champions....8

SOUTHEASTERN CONFERENCE....9
SEC History....10-11
SEC Year in Review....12-14
National Champions/1993-94 NCAA Finishes....15
SEC Headquarters/Executive Committee....16
Commissioner....17
SEC Staff....18-19
SEC Programs/Divisions....20
SEC Awards....21
Mailing Directory/Athletic Department Directory....22

ALABAMA....23
Team Information/1994 & 1995 Schedules/Stadium....24
1993 Results/Statistics....25
Coach Gene Stallings....26
All-Star Candidates....27
Roster....28
Depth Chart/Signees....29
Year-By-Year Record....30
Record vs. All Opponents/Bowl Results....31
School Records....32
Players in the NFL....33
Media List....34

ARKANSAS....35
Team Information/1994 & 1995 Schedules/Stadium....36
1993 Results/Statistics....37
Coach Danny Ford....38
All-Star Candidates....39
Roster....40
Depth Chart/Signees....41
Year-By-Year Record....42
Record vs. All Opponents/Bowl Results....43
School Records....44
Players in the NFL....45
Media List....46

AUBURN....47
Team Information/1994 & 1995 Schedules/Stadium....48
1993 Results/Statistics....49
Coach Terry Bowden....50
All-Star Candidates....51
Roster....52
Depth Chart/Signees....53
Year-By-Year Record....54
Record vs. All Opponents/Bowl Results....55
School Records....56
Players in the NFL....57
Media List....58

FLORIDA....59
Team Information/1994 & 1995 Schedules/Stadium....60
1993 Results/Statistics....61
Coach Steve Spurrier....62
All-Star Candidates....63
Roster....64
Depth Chart/Signees....65
Year-By-Year Record....66
Record vs. All Opponents/Bowl Results....67
School Records....68
Players in the NFL....69
Media List....70

GEORGIA....71
Team Information/1994 & 1995 Schedules/Stadium....72
1993 Results/Statistics....73
Coach Ray Goff....74
All-Star Candidates....75
Roster....76
Depth Chart/Signees....77
Year-By-Year Record....78
Record vs. All Opponents/Bowl Results....79
School Records....80
Players in the NFL....81
Media List....82

KENTUCKY....83
Team Information/1994 & 1995 Schedules/Stadium....84
1993 Results/Statistics....85
Coach Bill Curry....86
All-Star Candidates....87
Roster....88
Depth Chart/Signees....89
Year-By-Year Record....90
Record vs. All Opponents/Bowl Results....91
School Records....92
Players in the NFL....93
Media List....94

LSU....95
Team Information/1994 & 1995 Schedules/Stadium....96
1993 Results/Statistics....97
Coach Curley Hallman....98
All-Star Candidates....99
Roster....100
Depth Chart/Signees....101
Year-By-Year Record....102
Record vs. All Opponents/Bowl Results....103
School Records....104
Players in the NFL....105
Media List....106

OLE MISS....107
Team Information/1994 & 1995 Schedules/Stadium....108
1993 Results/Statistics....109
Coach Billy Brewer....110
All-Star Candidates....111
Roster....112
Depth Chart/Signees....113
Year-By-Year Record....114
Record vs. All Opponents/Bowl Results....115
School Records....116
Players in the NFL....117
Media List....118

MISSISSIPPI STATE....119
Team Information/1994 & 1995 Schedules/Stadium....120
1993 Results/Statistics....121
Coach Jackie Sherrill....122
All-Star Candidates....123
Roster....124
Depth Chart/Signees....125
Year-By-Year Record....126
Record vs. All Opponents/Bowl Results....127
School Records....128
Players in the NFL....129
Media List....130

SOUTH CAROLINA....131
Team Information/1994 & 1995 Schedules/Stadium....132
1993 Results/Statistics....133
Coach Brad Scott....134
All-Star Candidates....135
Roster....136
Depth Chart/Signees....137
Year-By-Year Record....138
Record vs. All Opponents/Bowl Results....139
School Records....140
Players in the NFL....141
Media List....142

TENNESSEE....143
Team Information/1994 & 1995 Schedules/Stadium....144
1993 Results/Statistics....145
Coach Phillip Fulmer....146
All-Star Candidates....147
Roster....148
Depth Chart/Signees....149
Year-By-Year Record....150
Record vs. All Opponents/Bowl Results....151
School Records....152
Players in the NFL....153
Media List....154

VANDERBILT....155
Team Information/1994 & 1995 Schedules/Stadium....156
1993 Results/Statistics....157
Coach Gerry DiNardo....158
All-Star Candidates....159
Roster....160
Depth Chart/Signees....161
Year-By-Year Record....162
Record vs. All Opponents/Bowl Results....163
School Records....164
Players in the NFL....165
Media List....166

1993 IN REVIEW....167
Standings/Non-conference Record/Bowl Results/Stat Leaders....168
SEC Championship Game....169
Team Statistics....170-171
Individual Statistics....172-174
Superlatives....175
Top Performances....176
SEC in the NFL Draft....177
NCAA Attendance Leaders....178

THROUGH THE YEARS....179
Year-by-Year Champions/Undefeated Teams....180
National Champions....181
All-Time Standings/Rivalries/Intra-Conference Record....182
Record vs. Other Conferences/Non-Conference Record....183
Year-By-Year Standings....184-191
National Statistical Champions....192
Year-By-Year Statistical Leaders....193-197
All-Time Television Appearances....198-203
National Attendance Leaders....204-206

RECORD BOOK....207
Individual Records....208-227
Longest Plays....228-232
Team Records....233-242
SEC Championship Game Individual Superlatives....243
SEC Championship Game Team Superlatives....244

HONORS....245
Hall of Fame Members....246
SEC Heisman Trophy Winners....247-248
SEC Players in Heisman Vote....249-252
National Award Winners....253
SEC All-Americas....254-259
SEC Academic All-Americas....260
NFF Scholar-Athletes/CFA Academic Awards....261
Individual SEC Awards....262-263
All-SEC Teams....264-281
Academic All-SEC Teams....282-288
Freshman All-SEC Teams....289
SEC Players of the Week....290
SEC Players of the Week/50-Year All-SEC....291
Quarter Century Team/SEC All-Decade Teams....292

BOWLS & POLLS....293
1994-95 Bowl Directory....294-295
Records/Appearances/Wins/Notes....296
Bowl Games of SEC Members....297-299
Results of Major Bowls....300-303
Bowl Most Valuable Players....304
All-Time AP Poll....305
AP Polls....306-308
No. 1 AP Rankings/UPI Polls....309-311
USA Today/CNN Polls....312

COACHES....313
All-Time Coaching Records....314-316
Coach of the Year....317
Winningest SEC Coaches (All Games)....318
Winningest SEC Coaches (SEC Games)....319
Winningest Division I Coaches....320-321

1994 SEC Football 3

SEC FOOTBALL

As college football celebrates its 125th anniversary in 1994, the Southeastern Conference looks to build upon the contributions its members have made to this grand game.

National championship teams, Heisman Trophy winners, All-America performers and legendary coaches have given loyal SEC fans plenty to celebrate since the formation of the conference in 1933.

With such a storied past, it is no wonder the SEC established the all-time NCAA attendance mark in 1993. A total of 4,897,564 fans attended a game at an SEC stadium last year, representing almost one/fifth of all Division IA spectators last season.

SEC fans have come to expect great things from their league: almost twice as many bowl appearances as any other conference in the nation and the best non-conference winning percentage for 10 of the last 14 years.

SEC IN PRESEASON POLLS

Seven of the SEC's 12 schools have been mentioned in at least one 1994 preseason poll.

Football Writers
1. Florida
8. Alabama
9. Tennessee
16. Auburn

Football News
2. Florida
9. Alabama
13. Tennessee
19. Auburn

The Sporting News
4. Florida
8. Alabama
9. Tennessee
16. Auburn

Athlon
8. Florida
10. Tennessee
12. Auburn
16. Alabama
20. Georgia
25. Mississippi State

BEST FOOT FORWARD

The SEC is the only conference in the nation to return three different placekickers who earned first-team All-America honors during the 1993 season. In addition, the conference also boasts the returning consensus All-America punter from a year ago.

Florida's Judd Davis (UPI All-America) received the 1993 Lou Groza Award, given annually to the nation's top placekicker. Alabama's Michael Proctor (*Football News* All-America) led the nation with an average of 1.83 field goals per game. Tennessee senior John Becksvoort (Football Writers and Scripps Howard All-America) won the league scoring title last year with a mark of 8.6 points per game.

Auburn punter Terry Daniel enjoyed a record-breaking year in 1993 and finished second in the nation with an average of 46.9 yards per kick.

1994 HEADLINES

ENCORE PERFORMANCES

Five offensive and three defensive players named first-team All-SEC in 1993 by at least one group (Coaches or Associated Press) return for the 1994 campaign. A list of returning all-stars and team(s) they were selected to follows:

PK - John Becksvoort (Tennessee)
Associated Press
DB - Alundis Brice (Ole Miss)
Associated Press
P - Terry Daniel (Auburn)
Coaches, Associated Press
ILB - Randall Godfrey (Georgia)
Coaches
OT - Reggie Green (Florida)
Coaches, Associated Press
WR - Brice Hunter (Georgia)
Associated Press
PK - Michael Proctor (Alabama)
Coaches
OG - Jeff Smith (Tennessee)
Coaches, Associated Press

IN A LEAGUE OF THEIR OWN

The SEC has long been known for its great coaches through the years: Bryant, Dooley, Vaught, Jordan and Neyland to name a few.

In 1992 and 1993 the SEC produced the consensus National Coach of the Year. This marked the second time in league history the honor was received by a conference coach in consecutive seasons (1970-Charlie McClendon, LSU and 1971-Paul "Bear" Bryant, Alabama).

Auburn head coach Terry Bowden concluded a story-book inaugural season by becoming the only first-year Division I coach to go undefeated. Bowden earned Coach of the Year honors after guiding the Tigers to a perfect 11-0 record in 1993.

Alabama's Gene Stallings, who led the Crimson Tide to a 13-0 worksheet and the 1992 National Championship, became the SEC's eighth coach to capture national honors.

Two other coaches patrolling the SEC sidelines in 1994 have distinguished themselves as the National Coach of the Year during their career: Arkansas skipper Danny Ford (1981) and Mississippi State's Jackie Sherrill (1980).

STATE OF THE SEC

Four schools have won or shared the SEC football title over the last five years, while a sixth captured two league crowns before joining the conference. A comparison of SEC teams over the last five and 10 years follows:

Last 5 Years (1989-93)

	W-L-T	Pct	Conference Championships	Bowl Games	Final AP Poll	AP Top 10
Alabama	50-11	.820	2	5	4	3
Tennessee	47-11-3	.795	2	5	5	2
Florida	46-15	.754	2	4	4	3
Auburn	39-16-2	.702	2	2	3	2
Ole Miss	36-22	.621	0	3	2	0
Georgia	34-24	.586	0	3	2	1
Arkansas	27-28-2	.491	1	2	1	0
Miss. State	27-28-2	.491	0	2	1	0
S. Carolina	24-28-3	.464	0	0	0	0
Kentucky	23-33	.411	0	1	0	0
LSU	21-34	.382	0	0	0	0
Vanderbilt	15-40-1	.277	0	0	0	0

Last 10 Years (1984-93)

	W-L-T	Pct	Conference Championships	Bowl Games	Final AP Poll	AP Top 10
Alabama	90-20-2	.813	2	9	7	4
Auburn	85-29-4	.737	4	7	7	5
Tennessee	85-29-7	.731	3	9	7	3
Florida	83-33-2	.719	2	6	6	5
Georgia	74-41-3	.640	0	8	4	1
Arkansas	72-43-3	.623	2	7	4	0
LSU	65-47-3	.578	2	5	5	2
Ole Miss	60-51-3	.539	0	4	2	0
S. Carolina	58-50-5	.535	0	3	2	0
Kentucky	52-59-1	.469	0	2	1	0
Miss. State	47-63-2	.429	0	2	1	0
Vanderbilt	31-78-1	.287	0	0	0	0

Note: First SEC season for Arkansas and South Carolina was 1992. Previously Arkansas was member of Southwest Conference and South Carolina was independent in football. Final AP Poll consisted of 20 teams 1984-88 and 25 teams 1989-93.

SEC Championship Game
December 3

The SEC's Eastern and Western Division winners will meet in Atlanta's Georgia Dome to battle for the league championship and the right to represent the conference in the USF+G Insurance Sugar Bowl. The third-annual title game is set for December 3 and will again be nationally televised by ABC Sports at 3:30 p.m. ET.

The game is a result of conference expansion, which saw Arkansas and South Carolina become the first members added in SEC history. Under NCAA regulations, a conference with 12 members may play a 12th football game to determine its champion, provided the regular season is played in divisions.

The participants of the game are determined each year during the eight-game regular-season conference schedule as the teams with the best overall SEC winning percentage in each division.

The SEC Championship Game is also the only Division IA football contest in the nation which may be decided by a tie-breaking system. In the event of a tie at the end of regulation, the SEC will implement NCAA Rule 3-1-3 (Extra Periods) which was altered by the NCAA Football Rules Committee to allow teams to have a tie breaker with as few exceptions as possible to rules in regular periods.

An extra period shall consist of two series with both teams putting the ball in play at their opponent's 25-yard line. Each team retains the ball until it scores or fails to make a first down. The team scoring the greater number of points during regulation and the extra period(s) shall be declared the winner.

Championship Game Quick Facts

Date: Saturday, December 3
Site: Georgia Dome; Atlanta, Ga.
Capacity: 71,500
Time: 3:30 p.m (ET)
Television: ABC Sports

For Tickets:
SEC Championship Game
2201 Civic Center Blvd.
Birmingham, AL 35203
(205) 458-3015

Georgia Dome Contract: Through 1995 game
ABC Sports Contract: Through 1995 game
Highest TV Rating: 9.8 (23.8 million viewers) - 1992
Largest Crowd: 83,091 (Alabama vs. Florida, Legion Field) - 1992
Top Passer: Shane Matthews, Florida (30-49-2, 287 yds, 2 TDs) - 1992
Top Rusher: Derrick Lassic, Alabama (21 for 117 yds, 2 TDs) - 1992
Most Valuable Players: 1992 - DB Antonio Langham (Alabama)
1993 - QB Terry Dean (Florida)

Atlanta's Georgia Dome (71,500) will be the site of the SEC Football Championship through the 1995 season.

Divisional Representative Tie-Breaker

In the event of a tie for the division championship, the following procedures will be used to break all ties to determine the SEC Football Championship Game representative:

All Conference versus Conference Games (both division and non-division) will be counted in the Conference Standings.

A. TWO TEAM TIE
1. Head-to-head competition between the two tied teams.
2. Records of the tied teams within the division.
3. Head-to-head competition versus the team within the division with the best overall (divisional and non-divisional) Conference record and proceeding through the division. Multiple ties within the division will be broken from first to last.
4. Overall record versus non-division teams.
5. Combined record versus all common non-divisional teams.
6. Record versus common non-divisional team with the best overall Conference (divisional and non-divisional) record and proceeding through other common non-divisional teams based on their order of finish within their division.
7. Vote of the Athletic Directors whose institution is not involved in the tie.

B. THREE (OR MORE) TEAM TIE
(Once the tie has been reduced to two teams, go to the two team tie breaker format)
1. Combined head-to-head record among the tied teams.
2. Record of the tied teams within the division.
3. Head-to-head competition versus the team within the division with the best overall (divisional and non-divisional) Conference record and proceeding through the division. Multiple ties within the division will be broken from first to last.
4. Overall record versus non-division teams.
5. Combined record versus all common non-divisional teams.
6. Record versus common non-divisional team with the best overall Conference (divisional and non-divisional) record and proceeding through other common non-divisional teams based on their order of finish within their division.
7. Vote of the Athletic Directors whose institution is not involved in the tie.

1994 SEC Football

SEC Bowl Agreements

The Southeastern Conference has agreements to send five of its member institutions to postseason bowl games following the 1994 season.

The winner of the SEC Football Championship Game will continue to serve as the host team for the USF+G Insurance Sugar Bowl in New Orleans, La. The SEC began its long-standing agreement with the Sugar Bowl on January 1, 1977, when Georgia battled Pittsburgh.

The CompUSA Florida Citrus Bowl has the second selection in the SEC bowl process. The three-year agreement was announced January 29, 1992. The Orlando, Fla., bowl is allowed to select an SEC representative from the following: (A) SEC Championship Game runner-up; (B) Conference team that has an equal or better overall record as the SEC Championship Game runner-up; (C) Conference team ranked within five places in the *USA Today/CNN Coaches* Poll of either participant in the SEC Championship Game as of the first Monday after the regular season ends. If presented with more than one option, the bowl will designate which team it will select that same day.

The Outback Steakhouse Gator Bowl joined the SEC bowl mix on May 15, 1992, with a three-year agreement to select third to secure a conference team to play in the Jacksonville, Fla., bowl. The Peach Bowl in Atlanta, Ga., announced May 4, 1993, it would select fourth in the SEC bowl process. The Carquest Bowl released June 1, 1993, it opted to pick fifth for filling its Ft. Lauderdale, Fla., event.

Under NCAA postseason football requirements, all teams in bowl games must win a minimum of six games against Division IA opponents during the regular season. (A complete directory of bowl games may be found on pages 294-295).

USF+G INSURANCE SUGAR BOWL
Date: Monday, January 2
Time: 7:30 p.m. (CST)
Site: New Orleans, La.
Stadium: Superdome (73,520)
Television: ABC
Teams: SEC Champion vs. Coalition Team

CompUSA FLORIDA CITRUS BOWL
Date: Monday, January 2
Time: 1:00 p.m. (EST)
Site: Orlando, Fla.
Stadium: Citrus Bowl (70,000)
Television: ABC
Teams: SEC 2 vs. Big 10 2

OUTBACK STEAKHOUSE GATOR BOWL
Date: Sunday, January 1
Time: 7:30 p.m. (EST)
Site: Gainesville, Fla.
Stadium: Ben Hill Griffin Stadium (83,000)
Television: TBS
Teams: SEC 3 vs. Coalition Team

PEACH BOWL
Date: Sunday, January 1
Time: 8:00 p.m. (EST)
Site: Atlanta, Ga.
Stadium: Georgia Dome (71,000)
Television: ESPN
Teams: SEC 4 vs. ACC 3

CARQUEST BOWL
Date: Monday, January 2
Time: 1:30 p.m. (EST)
Site: Ft. Lauderdale, Fla.
Stadium: Joe Robbie Stadium (73,000)
Television: CBS
Teams: SEC 5 vs. Big East 3

SEC Football On JP Sports

The Southeastern Conference signed an agreement with Jefferson Pilot Sports (JP Sports) on February 27, 1992, to televise SEC football through the 1995 season. The Charlotte, N.C., company holds the rights to televise 12 or 13 games annually throughout the nine-state SEC area on a syndicated basis for the next two years.

In 1992, the first year of airing SEC football, JP Sports secured 52 markets in the nine-state area and averaged 1.04 million households. Another 350,000+ homes were reached through cable and over-the-air distribution.

JP Sports, which has also extended its agreement to broadcast SEC Basketball through 1995-96, will air a conference football game in the early Saturday afternoon time period (12:40 p.m. Eastern) as allowed by the College Football Association. Games will be selected 12 days in advance beginning with contests scheduled for September 24.

Bob Carpenter and Tim Foley return to the broadcast booth, while Bob Kesling will again handle halftime, post-game and sideline coverage. Carpenter, who will describe the play-by-play, has been associated with ESPN since 1988. He served as play-by-play announcer on that network's prime-time college football schedule in 1988 and host of "College Game Day" in 1989. Since 1990 Carpenter has been an announcer mainstay on ESPN's major league baseball coverage.

Foley, an All-American defensive back at Purdue, is back for his 10th season of SEC football analysis. He played 11 seasons with the Miami Dolphins before retiring in 1981. Foley was recently named to the 25th Anniversary All-Dolphin Team.

Kesling is sports director at WBIR-TV in Knoxville, Tenn., and has worked numerous SEC events through the years including both the men's and women's basketball tournaments.

Carpenter 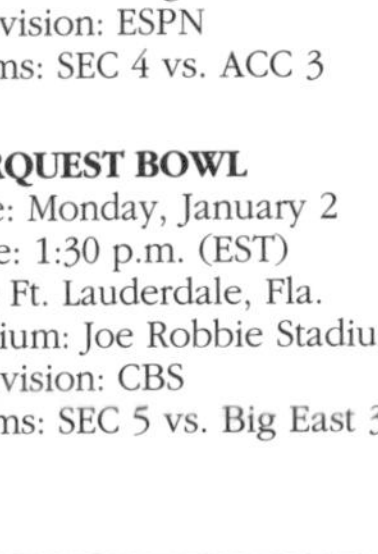   **Foley**    **Kesling**

1994 SEC Football

SEC Football Champions

Year - Champion	SEC	Overall	Coach
1933 - Alabama	5-0-1	7-1-1	Frank Thomas
1934 - Tulane	8-0	10-1	Ted Cox
Alabama	7-0	10-0	Frank Thomas
1935 - LSU	5-0	9-2	Bernie Moore
1936 - LSU	6-0	9-1-1	Bernie Moore
1937 - Alabama	6-0	9-1	Frank Thomas
1938 - Tennessee	7-0	11-0	Bob Neyland
1939 - Tennessee	6-0	10-1	Bob Neyland
Georgia Tech	6-0	8-2	Bill Alexander
Tulane	5-0	8-1-1	"Red" Dawson
1940 - Tennessee	5-0	10-1	Bob Neyland
1941 - Mississippi State	4-0-1	8-1-1	Allyn McKeen
1942 - Georgia	6-1	11-1	Wally Butts
1943 - Georgia Tech	3-0	7-4	Bill Alexander
1944 - Georgia Tech	4-0	9-2	Bill Alexander
1945 - Alabama	6-0	10-0	Frank Thomas
1946 - Georgia	5-0	11-0	Wally Butts
Tennessee	5-0	9-2	Bob Neyland
1947 - Ole Miss	6-1	9-2	John Vaught
1948 - Georgia	6-0	9-2	Wally Butts
1949 - Tulane	5-1	7-2-1	Henry Frnka
1950 - Kentucky	5-1	11-1	Paul Bryant
1951 - Georgia Tech	7-0	11-0-1	Bobby Dodd
■Tennessee	5-0	10-1	Bob Neyland
1952 - Georgia Tech	6-0	12-0	Bobby Dodd
1953 - Alabama	4-0-3	6-3-3	Red Drew
1954 - Ole Miss	5-1	9-2	John Vaught
1955 - Ole Miss	5-1	10-1	John Vaught
1956 - Tennessee	6-0	10-1	Bowden Wyatt
1957 - ■Auburn	7-0	10-0	Ralph Jordan
1958 - ■LSU	6-0	11-0	Paul Dietzel
1959 - Georgia	7-0	10-1	Wally Butts
1960 - ■Ole Miss	5-0-1	10-0-1	John Vaught
1961 - ■Alabama	7-0	11-0	Paul Bryant
LSU	6-0	10-1	Paul Dietzel
1962 - Ole Miss	6-0	10-0	John Vaught
1963 - Ole Miss	5-0-1	7-1-2	John Vaught
1964 - ■Alabama	8-0	10-1	Paul Bryant
1965 - ■Alabama	6-1-1	9-1-1	Paul Bryant
1966 - Alabama	6-0	11-0	Paul Bryant
Georgia	6-0	10-1	Vince Dooley
1967 - Tennessee	6-0	9-2	Doug Dickey
1968 - Georgia	5-0-1	8-1-2	Vince Dooley
1969 - Tennessee	5-1	9-2	Doug Dickey
1970 - LSU	5-0	9-3	Charlie McClendon
1971 - Alabama	7-0	11-1	Paul Bryant
1972 - Alabama	7-1	10-2	Paul Bryant
1973 - ■Alabama	8-0	11-1	Paul Bryant
1974 - Alabama	6-0	11-1	Paul Bryant
1975 - Alabama	6-0	11-1	Paul Bryant
1976 - Georgia	5-1	10-2	Vince Dooley
Kentucky	5-1	9-3	Fran Curci
1977 - Alabama	7-0	11-1	Paul Bryant
1978 - ■Alabama	6-0	11-1	Paul Bryant
1979 - ■Alabama	6-0	12-0	Paul Bryant

Year - Champion	SEC	Overall	Coach
1980 - ■Georgia	6-0	12-0	Vince Dooley
1981 - Georgia	6-0	10-2	Vince Dooley
Alabama	6-0	9-2-1	Paul Bryant
1982 - Georgia	6-0	11-1	Vince Dooley
1983 - Auburn	6-0	11-1	Pat Dye
1984 - Vacated			
1985 - Tennessee	5-1	9-1-2	Johnny Majors
1986 - LSU	5-1	9-3	Bill Arnsparger
1987 - Auburn	5-0-1	9-1-2	Pat Dye
1988 - Auburn	6-1	10-2	Pat Dye
LSU	6-1	8-4	Mike Archer
1989 - Alabama	6-1	10-2	Bill Curry
Tennessee	6-1	11-1	Johnny Majors
Auburn	6-1	10-2	Pat Dye
1990 - Tennessee	5-1-1	9-2-2	Johnny Majors
1991 - Florida	7-0	10-2	Steve Spurrier
1992 - ■Alabama	8-0	13-0	Gene Stallings
1993 - Florida	7-1	11-2	Steve Spurrier

■*National Champion NOTE: Overall records include bowl games*

CHAMPIONSHIPS BY SCHOOL:

Alabama - 20	('33-34t-37-45-53-61t-64-65-66t-71-72-73-74-75-77-78-79-81t-89t-92)	
Tennessee - 11	('38-39t-40-46t-51t-56-67-69-85-89t-90)	
Georgia - 10	('42-46t-48-59-66t-68-76t-80-81t-82)	
LSU - 7	('35-36-58-61t-70-86-88t)	
Ole Miss - 6	('47-54-55-60-62-63)	
Auburn - 5	('57-83-87-88t-89t)	
* Georgia Tech - 5	('39t-43-44-51t-52)	
* Tulane - 3	('34-39t-49)	
Kentucky - 2	('50-76t)	
Florida - 2	('91-93)	
Mississippi State - 1	('41)	

* Denotes former member of the SEC

SEC CHAMPIONSHIP COACHES:

Paul Bryant (14) - Kentucky (1) 1950; Alabama (13) 1961-64-65-66-71-72-73-74-75-77-78-79-81
Johnny Vaught (6) - Ole Miss 1947-54-55-60-62-63
Vince Dooley (6) - Georgia 1966-68-76-80-81-82
Bob Neyland (5) - Tennessee 1938-39-49-46-51
Frank Thomas (4) - Alabama 1933-34-37-45
Wally Butts (4) - Georgia 1942-46-48-59
Pat Dye (4) - Auburn 1983-87-88-89
Bill Alexander (3) - Georgia Tech 1939-43-44
Johnny Majors (3) - Tennessee 1985-89-90
Bernie Moore (2) - LSU 1935-36
Bobby Dodd (2) - Georgia Tech 1951-52
Paul Dietzel (2) - LSU 1958-61
Doug Dickey (2) - Tennessee 1967-69
Steve Spurrier (2) - Florida 1991-93
Ted Cox (1) - Tulane 1934
Red Dawson (1) - Tulane 1939
Allyn McKeen (1) - Mississippi State 1941
Henry Frnka (1) - Tulane 1949
Red Drew (1) - Alabama 1953
Bowden Wyatt (1) - Tennessee 1956
Ralph Jordan (1) - Auburn 1957
Charlie McClendon (1) - LSU 1970
Fran Curci (1) - Kentucky 1976
Bill Arnsparger (1) - LSU 1986
Mike Archer (1) - LSU 1988
Bill Curry (1) - Alabama 1989
Gene Stallings (1) - Alabama 1992

SOUTHEASTERN CONFERNCE

SEC Commissioner Roy Kramer is joined by 1993-94 H. Boyd McWhorter SEC Scholar-Athletes Tammy Newlon of Mississippi State and Peter Duitsman of South Carolina. The two award winners were honored at the 1994 SEC Spring Meeting and will each receive a $10,000 postgraduate scholarship through funds provided by the SEC and the USF+G Sugar Bowl.

History of the Southeastern Conference

Throughout its 62-year history the Southeastern Conference has been a leader in the integration of athletic competition and higher education.

Since its formation in 1933, the SEC has achieved both stature and stability by designating governing/voting power to the presidents of the member institutions. They have determined the policies of the conference and through the years this involvement has been the principal source of strength in the evolution of the SEC.

Intercollegiate athletics has encountered many challenges in the 1990s and again the SEC provided guidance. In 1993, the member institutions adopted The Principles of Gender Equity. Committed to increasing the quantity and quality of women's athletic opportunities, each school will provide at least two more women's intercollegiate programs than the number of men's.

Faced with the task of conference realignment after competing with 10 members since 1966, the SEC welcomed the University of Arkansas on Aug. 1, 1990, and the University of South Carolina on Sept. 25, 1990. Joining charter members Alabama, Auburn, Florida, Georgia, Kentucky, LSU, Mississippi, Mississippi State, Tennessee and Vanderbilt, on July 1, 1991, Arkansas and South Carolina became the first schools added in conference history.

Fully incorporated into conference competition by 1992, Arkansas and South Carolina participated in SEC championships for all sports except football during the 1991-92 academic year. The SEC was again at the forefront, introducing football, basketball and baseball divisional play and the nation's first ever Division I football championship game.

SEC schools began athletic competition with one another almost 100 years ago as members of the Southern Intercollegiate Athletic Association.

Seven institutions (Alabama, Auburn, Georgia, Georgia Tech, North Carolina, Sewanee and Vanderbilt) attended the SIAA organizational meeting of faculty representatives, called by Dr. William L. Dudley of Vanderbilt, in Atlanta Dec. 22, 1894.

Student teams from the schools began meeting in various sports with little pattern to their contests. Baseball was the most popular campus sport, but the American adaptation of the English game rugby, called "football" was drifting down from the East and Midwest. Southerners were quickly attracted to this sport formalized in 1869.

The first football game in the Southeast was played April 9, 1880, on the ground now called Old Stoll Field at the University of Kentucky. Kentucky, then known as Kentucky A&M, was host to the contest in which Transylvania College, then called Kentucky University, upset Centre College 13 3/4 to 0. Kentucky A&M (now UK) organized a team and in November 1881, played Transylvania a three-game series (winning 7 1/2 to 1, then losing 1 to 2 and 2 1/2 to 3 3/4). By 1895 11 current SEC members were playing football.

Basketball moved quickly to the South as Vanderbilt was playing at the Nashville YMCA in 1893, just two years after Dr. James Naismith originated the game at Springfield (Mass.) College. The Commodores won 9-6 in a game with nine players on each team. Basketball becamean intercollegiate sport in 1901 and in 1908 Vanderbilt was meeting Columbia and Yale intersectionally.

Track was organized on a conference level at the 1895 SIAA meeting presided over by President Dudley who served until his death in 1914. The first championship meet was held at Vanderbilt May 15, 1896. By 1900 eight of the 13 charter SEC members were participating.

The seven-member SIAA expanded to 19 institutions in 1895 (Alabama, Auburn, Central, Clemson, Cumberland, Georgia, Georgia Tech, Kentucky, LSU, Mercer, Mississippi State, Nashville, North Carolina, Sewanee, Southwestern Presbyterian, Tennessee, Texas, Tulane and Vanderbilt) and by 1920 there were 30 members.

The larger schools reorganized as the Southern Conference at a meeting in Gainesville Dec. 12-13, 1920. Professor S.V. Sanford of Georgia called the meeting and served as the first president. Charter members of the Southern Conference included: Alabama, Auburn, Clemson, Georgia, Georgia Tech, Kentucky, Maryland, Mississippi State, North Carolina, North Carolina State, Tennessee, Virginia, Virginia Tech and Washington & Lee.

Despite an original limit of 16, the membership grew to 23 by 1928. In 1922 Florida, Louisiana State, Mississippi, South Carolina, Tulane, Vanderbilt and Virginia Military joined, while Sewanee and Duke became members in 1923 and 1928 respectively. At one time or another the SIAA and the SC included most of the Southern colleges from Virginia to Texas.

The 13 members west and south of the Appalachian Mountains reorganized as the Southeastern Conference at the annual SC meeting of Dec. 8-9, 1932, in Knoxville. The 10 coast members remained in the Southern Conference. Dr. Frank L. McVey of Kentucky was elected president of the new conference whose charter members were: Alabama, Auburn, Florida, Georgia, Georgia Tech, Kentucky, Louisiana State, Mississippi, Mississippi State, Sewanee, Tennessee, Tulane and Vanderbilt. (Sewanee withdrew Dec. 13, 1940, Georgia Tech on June 1, 1964 and Tulane on June 1, 1966). McVey held an informal meeting of the school presidents in Birmingham Feb. 16, 1933, then the first full meeting in Atlanta Feb. 27.

The Office of the Commissioner was formed in 1940 in Jackson due to the great amount of detail work developing, especially in recruiting and eligibility. Former Mississippi Governor Martin S. Conner took office as commissioner Aug. 21, 1940, as an extension of the authority of the presidents. Conner later became ill and the secretary of the conference, Dean N.W. Dougherty of Tennessee, served as acting commissioner during the fall of 1946.

The office moved to Birmingham with the appointing of Bernie H. Moore as the second full-time commissioner on Feb. 21, 1948. Moore, a former LSU coach, guided the SEC to national respect in his 18-year tenure.

A.M. (Tonto) Coleman succeeded Moore upon his retirement April 1,1966. The Alabama native, who was reared in Texas and experienced in athletic coaching and administration, served six and a half years.

Dr. H. Boyd McWhorter, then Dean of Arts and Sciences at Georgia and secretary of the league since 1967, accepted the position upon the retirement of Coleman Aug. 1, 1972. Under his leadership the SEC experienced unparalleled growth. In McWhorter's first year the SEC distributed $1.57 million and 14 years later (1986) the league distributed $15 million in revenue to the member institutions.

Dr. Harvey W. Schiller, an Air Force colonel and faculty chair at the U.S. Air Force Academy, followed McWhorter

10 Southeastern Conference

upon retirement, taking office Sept. 15, 1986. Under his guidance the SEC established itself as a leader in the areas of athletic scholarship and marketing.

Roy F. Kramer succeeded Schiller on Jan. 10, 1990. Kramer, who has served on numerous NCAA committees, joined the league office after spending 12 years as athletic director at Vanderbilt.

The first SEC champions were crowned in 1933 in four sports (baseball, basketball, football and outdoor track). The league's inaugural championship event was a basketball tournament in Atlanta Feb. 24-28, 1933. Records show the first men's team title for cross-country was awarded in 1935, while golf and swimming were added in 1937. The league later began hosting championships in tennis (1953) and indoor track (1957). A men's all-sports champion (Bernie Moore Trophy) has been awarded every year since 1973-74.

In the 1979-80 academic year SEC championships for women were recognized in basketball, tennis and volleyball. The following year golf, gymnastics, swimming and track and field were added. The administration of women's athletics officially came under the auspices of the conference office on Sept. 1, 1984. A women's all-sports champion has been awarded every year since 1983-84.

The SEC currently regulates nine men's and 10 women's sports:

Men - baseball, basketball, football, golf, swimming, tennis and track (cross country, indoor and outdoor).

Women - basketball, golf, gymnastics, soccer, swimming, tennis, track (cross country, indoor and outdoor) and volleyball.

SEC Commissioners

MARTIN S. CONNER
1940-46

BERNIE H. MOORE
1948-66

A.M. (Tonto) COLEMAN
1966-72

DR. H. BOYD McWHORTER
1972-86
Commissioner Emeritus

DR. HARVEY W. SCHILLER
1986-89

ROY F. KRAMER
1990-Present

SEC MILESTONES

December 8-9, 1932
At the annual Southern Conference meeting in Knoxville, Tenn., the 13 members west and south of the Appalachian Mountains reorganized as the Southeastern Conference.

November 30, 1933
Alabama defeats Vanderbilt 7-0 to finish 5-0-1 in the conference and capture the SEC's first football title.

August 21, 1940
Martin S. Conner, former governor of Mississippi, takes office as the first commissioner of the SEC in Jackson, Miss.

February 21, 1948
Former LSU coach Bernie H. Moore appointed the SEC's second commissioner and conference office moves to Birmingham, Ala.

April 1, 1966
A.M. (Tonto) Coleman succeeds Moore as the conference's third commissioner.

August 1, 1972
Dr. H. Boyd McWhorter becomes the league's fourth commissioner.

January 1, 1977
The SEC begins its long-standing agreement with the Sugar Bowl to send its champion to New Orleans as Georgia faced Pittsburgh.

July, 1983
The SEC signs agreement with the Turner Broadcasting System to begin airing a "Game of the Week" beginning in the fall of 1984.

September 15, 1986
Dr. Harvey W. Schiller succeeds McWhorter as SEC Commissioner.

January 10, 1990
Roy F. Kramer becomes the conference's sixth commissioner.

May 31, 1990
SEC presidents unanimously recommend that the commissioner be authorized to enter discussions with interested institutions for the purpose of expansion.

August 1, 1990
Arkansas accepts invitation to become the SEC's 11th member.

September 25, 1990
South Carolina accepts invitation to become 12th member of the SEC.

November 29, 1990
SEC presidents announce divisions and vote to adopt an eight-game football schedule to begin in 1992.

May 30, 1991
SEC presidents award the SEC Football Championship Game to the city of Birmingham.

January 29, 1992
SEC and the Florida Citrus Bowl announce the Orlando, Fla., game will feature a conference team (No. 2) vs. the Big 10 runner-up each of the next three years.

February 27, 1992
SEC signs agreement with Jefferson Pilot Sports to televise SEC football games annually through the 1995 season.

April 15, 1992
ABC Sports announces a four-year contract to nationally televise the SEC Football Championship Game.

May 15, 1992
SEC signs an agreement with the Gator Bowl to send one of its top teams (No. 3) to the Jacksonville, Fla., game for the next three seasons.

December 5, 1992
SEC hosts the nation's first Division IA conference football championship game at Legion Field. Alabama defeats Florida 28-21 to win the 1992 SEC crown and the league's USF&G Sugar Bowl berth. The national telecast by ABC Sports draws a 9.8 rating.

May 4, 1993
SEC and the Peach Bowl announce the Atlanta, Ga., game will feature a conference team (No. 4) vs. the third-place ACC squad for the next two years.

June 1, 1993
SEC and the Carquest Florida Sunshine Classic formerly announce the Ft. Lauderdale, Fla., game will feature an SEC team (No. 5) vs. Big East's third-place squad for the next two years.

Febuary 11, 1994
SEC announces multi-sport television agreement with CBS Sports to televise SEC football (1996-2000), men's basketball and women's basketball (1994-95 through 2000-2001).

February 25, 1994
The 1994 and 1995 SEC Football Championship Games will be played at the Georgia Dome in Atlanta.

June 2, 1994
SEC announces it will distribute a league-record $34.36 million back to the 12 member institutions under the 1993-94 revenue sharing plans, more than double the amount it distributed just four years earlier.

1994 SEC Football

The Southeastern Conference
"The Standard For Excellence"

Providing a balance between athletics and academics, the Southeastern Conference has long been a national leader both on the field of competition and in the classroom. Since the conference's formation in 1933, the SEC's member institutions have built perhaps the greatest tradition of intercollegiate competition of any league in the country.

The 1993-94 academic year will be recorded as another highly successful chapter in the 61-year history of the conference. SEC squads captured seven national team titles during the course of 1993-94, just two crowns off the record-setting pace of a year ago. In all, the SEC has won 28 national team championships over the past four years for an average of seven per season.

The 1993-94 national champions for the SEC included: Arkansas men's basketball, men's cross country, men's indoor track and men's outdoor track; Georgia women's tennis; LSU women's indoor track and women's outdoor track.

Overall, the SEC placed at least one team in the top 13 nationally in 18 of 19 conference sports and in the top five in 16 of 19 sports. The 19-sport breakdown included seven national champions, two NCAA runners-up as well as two third place, one fourth place and one 13th place NCAA finish. The SEC also boasted an NCAA semifinal squad in three sports as well as a No. 4 final poll ranking in football and two NCAA College World Series berths.

The NCAA runners-up were Arkansas women's cross country and Alabama gymnastics. In addition, the league posted one-two national showings in men's indoor track (Arkansas and Tennessee) and women's indoor track (LSU and Alabama).

The SEC established a new high for NCAA Championship participation during the 1993-94 season with 100 teams advancing to their respective national tournament. SEC student-athletes earned an all-time best 41 individual national titles, while All-America honors were bestowed on an SEC-high 427 individuals as the league provided at least one All-America in 17 of 19 sports.

Additionally, the SEC Academic Honor Roll recipient record was shattered for the sixth-straight year as 660 student-athletes were honored for their work in the classroom.

Florida won it's third-straight Bernie Moore All-Sports Trophy, symbolic of the conference's premier men's athletic program. Georgia won the Women's All-Sports Trophy for the third time in the last five years and the sixth time overall. The Gator program collected five SEC titles while Georgia picked up three overall. The remaining SEC championships were won by Arkansas (five), Alabama (two), Tennessee (two), Auburn (one) and Vanderbilt (one). Both the Bernie Moore and Women's All-Sports Trophies were discontinued following the 1993-94 academic year.

On the national level, the SEC was tied for third among all conferences with four programs ranked in the inaugural Sears/NACDA Director's Cup rankings. Florida headlined all SEC squads with a fourth-place showing. Tennessee finished 13th, Alabama was 15th and Georgia rounded out the SEC's showing at 21st. Points are awarded for a team's finish in 10 men's core sports (basketball, cross country, tennis, baseball, golf, track and field, football, soccer, swimming and wrestling as well as two wildcard sports) and 10 women's core sports (basketball, cross country, tennis, volleyball, track and field, softball, swimming, golf, soccer, field hockey and two wildcard sports). The Pac-10 led all leagues with six teams ranked in the Top 25.

A brief sport-by-sport summary of the 1993-94 year follows:

Baseball - The SEC sent multiple teams to the College World Series for the fourth time overall, the third time in the last five years, and extended its string of four-straight years leading the nation in NCAA Tournament bids (Auburn, Florida, LSU, Tennessee). Tennessee won its first SEC title since 1951 as well as the Eastern Division crown, while LSU picked up the Western Division title.

Men's Basketball - SEC Champion Arkansas won the league's first NCAA Championship since 1978, while Eastern Division Champion Florida gave the SEC two Final Four teams for the first time in history. The SEC led all leagues with a .800 NCAA Tournament winning percentage. The league sent half its teams to

---

1993-94 SEC National Champions

Arkansas .... Men's Basketball
Arkansas .... Men's Cross Country
Arkansas .... Men's Indoor Track
Arkansas ...... Men's Outdoor Track
Georgia .... Women's Tennis
LSU .... Women's Indoor Track
LSU .... Women's Outdoor Track

• The SEC placed at least one team in the Top 5 nationally in 16 of 19 sports.

• Last year, an SEC-record 100 league teams participated in NCAA Championships. SEC student-athletes earned an all-time best 41 individual national titles, while All-America honors were bestowed on an SEC-high 427 individuals as the league provided at least one All-America in 17 of 19 sports.

postseason action for the 16th-straight year as Alabama and Kentucky rounded out the league's NCAA entries and Miss. State and Vanderbilt (finals) appeared in the NIT. The SEC finished with a nation-high three teams ranked in the USA Today/CNN/Coaches Top 13. Arkansas' Nolan Richardson was National Coach of the Year.

Women's Basketball - Alabama became the fifth different SEC squad to reach the NCAA Final Four, giving the league a national semifinal squad in 12 of 13 seasons under the NCAA, while the league's six entries led the nation for the 12th time in the last 13 years. The SEC also kept alive its streak of at least four teams ranked in the final Associated Press poll for the 13th-straight season with SEC Champion Tennessee (first), Vanderbilt (12th), Alabama (16th), Florida (20th) and Ole Miss (23rd) appearing in the rankings. Tennessee's Pat Summitt was Naismith National Coach of the Year.

Men's Cross Country - Arkansas began its quest for a third-straight SEC and NCAA Triple Crown by winning both men's cross country titles. The NCAA title was the fourth-straight for the Hogs and the seventh in the last 10 years, while the league championship was the third-straight for the program.

Women's Cross Country - For the fifth time in the last six years, the SEC had a team finish first or second at the NCAA Championships as conference winner Arkansas garnered its third-straight runner-up finish. The Razorback sweep of the men's and women's SEC crowns was the fifth time in the last six years the same school has claimed both trophies.

Football - Florida defeated Alabama in a rematch of the 1992 SEC Championship game for the SEC title and Sugar Bowl berth as the league sent four squads overall to bowls (Alabama - Gator, Kentucky - Peach, Tennessee - Citrus). SEC schools established the NCAA single-season attendance record as 4,897,564 fans visited league stadiums in 1993. The SEC led the nation in non-conference winning percentage for the 10th time in the last 14 seasons and Auburn's Terry Bowden was consensus National Coach of the Year.

Men's Golf - Three SEC squads finished in the NCAA Tournament Top 10 for the 3rd time in league history as SEC Champion Florida (third), Arkansas (fourth) and Auburn (seventh) completed the league's top 10 entries. LSU (22nd) rounded out the league's tourney field and gave the SEC four NCAA teams for the fifth time in the last seven years.

Women's Golf - Georgia won the SEC crown but did not advance beyond NCAA regional play. Tennessee (13th) and Florida (15th) gave the SEC at least two NCAA teams for the 10th-straight year. The league has now had a top five NCAA team finish and at least one top five individual finish in 11 of 12 seasons.

Gymnastics - The league continued its dominance of the sport, placing four teams in the NCAA top 10 and winning all five individual titles for the second-straight year. Alabama finished second while SEC Champion Georgia placed third. Florida (sixth) and LSU (eighth) rounded out the league's NCAA entries. Kentucky earned its share of the spotlight as its at-large qualifier won three individual national crowns.

Men's Indoor Track - Arkansas continued on the road to the track triple crown winning its 11th-straight NCAA Indoor Track title to pace nine SEC entries in the field. The Hogs' 54-point margin of victory over second-place Tennessee was the largest ever in the event. The SEC's four Top 10 finishes (Georgia, tie-sixth; Kentucky, tie-ninth) marked the most in league history. Other NCAA team finishes included: Ole Miss (t19th), South Carolina (t19th), Alabama (t30th), Florida (t30th), LSU (t53rd). Individually, the league won one of 14 events.

Women's Indoor Track - The SEC boasted five Top 20 finishes, including a one-two finish as defending national champion LSU won the league's sixth title in the last eight years and SEC Champion Alabama finished runner-up. The title was the fifth for LSU since 1987. Tennessee (11th), Arkansas (t20th), Kentucky (t20th), Georgia (t27th), Ole Miss (t43rd) and Auburn (49th) rounded out the SEC's scoring. The league won 11 of 16 individual titles.

Men's Outdoor Track - Arkansas completed its quest for the SEC and NCAA track triple crowns by winning both meets. It marked the sixth-straight year the national champion hailed from the SEC. League teams secured four NCAA Top 10 showings, marking the third-straight year the SEC has had at least four Top 10 squads with Tennessee (third), LSU (sixth) and Georgia (eighth). Florida (t13th), Kentucky (t13th), Alabama (15th),

Nicole Haislett, Florida
1993-94 SEC Female
Athlete of the Year

Corliss Williamson, Arkansas
1993-94 SEC Male
Athlete of the Year

1994 SEC Football 13

Mississippi State (20th), Ole Miss (32nd) and South Carolina (65) rounded out the SEC's scoring. League competitors won four of 19 individual titles and Arkansas' John McDonnell was named National Coach of the Year for both indoor and outdoor track.

Women's Outdoor Track - LSU won its eighth-straight NCAA title with a 43-point margin of victory. Tennessee (fifth) was the league's only other Top 10 squad. SEC Champion Alabama (12th), Arkansas (23rd), Auburn (t42nd), Florida (t42nd), Ole Miss (50th) and South Carolina (55th) finished the SEC's scoring. Individually, the SEC captured four of 19 titles at the meet. LSU's Pat Henry was the indoor and outdoor track National Coach of the Year.

Women's Soccer - Vanderbilt captured the inaugural SEC Championship and all four league squads finished at or above .500. Arkansas and Vanderbilt both ranked among the Southern Region's Top 10.

Men's Swimming - For only the third time in SEC history, four league teams finished in the Top 10 at the NCAA Championships, led by SEC Champion Auburn's fourth-place showing. Florida (eighth), Tennessee (ninth) and Alabama (t10th) rounded out the group. Georgia (16th), South Carolina (19th) and Arkansas (t20th) gave the league at least five Top 20 appearances for the third-straight year and the fifth time since 1986. LSU (t29th) was the SEC's final placer as the league took three of 21 individual titles and 78 All-America honors.

Women's Swimming - Fresh off its ninth-consecutive SEC Championship, Florida finished third at the NCAA meet, marking the Lady Gators' 13th-straight NCAA top-three showing. Auburn (fifth) and Alabama (ninth) gave the SEC a trio of Top 10 teams for the third-straight year and the fourth time since 1985. Overall eight SEC teams placed at the NCAA Championship including: Tennessee (14th), Georgia (15th), LSU (18th), Kentucky (19th) and South Carolina (28th). It marked the ninth-straight time at least six SEC schools scored at nationals as conference performers won five of 21 individual NCAA crowns.

Men's Tennis - The SEC led all conferences in NCAA Tournament bids for the fifth time in the last six seasons as nine squads (Arkansas, Auburn, SEC and SEC Tournament Champion Florida, Georgia, Kentucky, Ole Miss, Mississippi State, South Carolina, Tennessee) participated in the 46-team field, including three of the top eight seeds. Mississippi State paced all SEC squads, reaching the national semifinals. The league boasted eight of the Top 15 teams in the final ITA poll including: Mississippi State (third), Georgia (fifth), Florida (tie-eighth, Ole Miss (t10th), Tennessee (13th), Kentucky (14), Auburn (t15th) and South Carolina (t15th). LSU (22nd) rounded out the Top 25. Individually, the SEC won the NCAA singles and doubles titles for the second-straight year. The final Top 25 ITA individual rankings featured nine SEC singles players and eight SEC doubles tandems.

Women's Tennis - SEC and SEC Tournament Champion Georgia won the school's first NCAA tennis title and led the league's three tournament entries (Florida and Kentucky). An SEC player won the league's third-straight NCAA singles title while a conference doubles team finished runner-up for the NCAA title. Final ITA Top 25 team rankings included: Georgia (first), Florida (fifth), Kentucky (12th), Ole Miss (16th) and South Carolina (24th). Individually, the league accounted for five of the Top 25 singles, including a best of No. 3 and five of the Top 25 doubles (high of first) in the final ITA poll.

Volleyball - SEC and SEC Tournament Champion Florida extended the league's streak of NCAA Final Four appearances to four-straight years with its second-consecutive berth as the SEC tied its record of four teams (Georgia, Kentucky, Tennessee) in the 32-team field.

1993-94 SEC Review

Sport	SEC Champion	SEC Tournament Champion(s)	NCAA Teams	Best National Finish (NCAAs and/or Poll)	$All-Americas	Individual National Champions
Baseball	Tennessee	Tennessee/LSU	4	LSU/Auburn (CWS/tie-seventh)	6	—
Men's Basketball	Arkansas	Kentucky	4	Arkansas (Champion)	1	—
Women's Basketball	Tennessee	Tennessee	6	Alabama (Final Four/Fourth USA poll)	3	—
Men's Cross Country	Arkansas	—	3	Arkansas (Champion)	5	0 of 1
Women's Cross Country	Arkansas	—	2	Arkansas (Second)	6	0 of 1
Football	Florida	—	4#	Auburn (Fourth AP Poll)	9	—
Men's Golf	Florida	—	4	Florida (Third)	1	0 of 1
Women's Golf	Georgia	—	2	Tennessee (13th)	0	0 of 1
Women's Gymnastics	Georgia	—	4	Alabama (Second)	22	5 of 5
Men's Indoor Track	Arkansas	—	9	Arkansas (Champion)	40	1 of 14
Women's Indoor Track	Alabama	—	8	LSU (Champion)	39	11 of 16
Men's Outdoor Track	Arkansas	—	10	Arkansas (Champion)	63	9 of 21
Women's Outdoor Track	Alabama	—	8	LSU (Champion)	42	4 of 19
Women's Soccer	Vanderbilt	—	0	—	0	—
Men's Swimming	Auburn	—	8	Auburn (Fourth)	78	3 of 21
Women's Swimming	Florida	—	8	Florida (Third)	82	5 of 21
Men's Tennis	Florida	Florida	9	Mississippi State (Semifinals/Third ITA poll)	17	2 of 2
Women's Tennis	Georgia	Georgia	3	Georgia (Champion)	11	1 of 2
Volleyball	Florida	Florida	4	Florida (Final Four)	2	—
TOTALS	**100**		**7**	**National Champions**	**427**	**41**

Bowl Teams
$ First team members only

SEC In 1993-94 NCAA Championships

MEN

BASEBALL
LSU	College World Series
Auburn	College World Series
Tennessee	Mideast Region
Florida	Atlantic I Region

BASKETBALL
Arkansas	National Champion
Florida	Final Four
Kentucky	SE Region 2nd Round
Alabama	SE Region 2nd Round

CROSS COUNTRY
Arkansas	National Champion	31
Tennessee	18th	409
Florida	21st	459

FOOTBALL (AP Poll - Bowl)
Auburn	(4th)
Florida	(5th Sugar)
Tennessee	(12th Citrus)
Alabama	(14th Gator)
Kentucky	(NR Peach)

GOLF
Florida	3rd	1,136
Arkansas	4th	1,138
Auburn	7th	1,145
LSU	22nd	

INDOOR TRACK
Arkansas	National Champion	94
Tennessee	2nd	40
Georgia	6th (tie)	21
Kentucky	9th (tie)	17
Ole Miss	19th (tie)	10
South Carolina	19th (tie)	10
Alabama	30th (tie)	7
Florida	30th (tie)	7
LSU	53rd (tie)	1

OUTDOOR TRACK
Arkansas	National Champion	83
Tennessee	3rd	38
LSU	6th	27
Georgia	8th	24
Florida	13th (tie)	17
Kentucky	13th (tie)	17
Alabama	15th	16
Miss. State	20th	12
Ole Miss	32nd	8
South Carolina	65th	2

SWIMMING
Auburn	4th	301.5
Florida	8th	171.5
Tennessee	9th	150.5
Alabama	10th (tie)	146
Georgia	16th	71
South Carolina	19th	42
Arkansas	20th (tie)	38
LSU	29th (tie)	20

TENNIS
Mississippi State	Semifinals
Georgia	Quarterfinals
Florida	First Round
Ole Miss	First Round
Arkansas	Region VI
Auburn	Region III
Kentucky	Region III
South Carolina	Region II
Tennessee	Region III

WOMEN

BASKETBALL
Alabama	Final Four
Vanderbilt	East Region Semis
Tennessee	Mideast Region Semis
Auburn	E Region 2nd Round
Ole Miss	ME Region 2nd Round
Florida	W Region 1st Round

CROSS COUNTRY
Arkansas	2nd	71
Alabama	13th	326

GOLF
Tennessee	13th	1,258
Florida	15th	1,266

GYMNASTICS
Alabama	2nd	196.40
Georgia	3rd	196.350
Florida	6th	194.850
LSU	8th	193.225

INDOOR TRACK
LSU	National Champion	48
Alabama	2nd	29
Tennessee	11th	17
Arkansas	20th (tie)	9
Kentucky	20th (tie)	9
Georgia	27th (tie)	7
Ole Miss	43rd (tie)	2
Auburn	49th (tie)	1

OUTDOOR TRACK
LSU	National Champion	86
Tennessee	5th	30
Alabama	12th	18
Arkansas	23rd	10
Auburn	42nd (tie)	4
Florida	42nd (tie)	4
Ole Miss	50th	3
South Carolina	55th	2

SWIMMING
Florida	3rd	387.5
Auburn	5th	242
Alabama	9th	153
Tennessee	14th	96
Georgia	15th	85
LSU	18th	56
Kentucky	19th	45
South Carolina	28th	25

TENNIS
Georgia	National Champion
Florida	Quarterfinals
Kentucky	Second Round

VOLLEYBALL
Florida	Final Four
Georgia	South Region Semis
Kentucky	Second Round
Tennessee	Second Round

SEC All-Time National Champions

MEN

Baseball
1990 Georgia (52-19)
1991 LSU (55-18)
1993 LSU (53-17-1)

Basketball
1948 Kentucky (36-3)
1949 Kentucky (32-2)
1951 Kentucky (32-2)
1958 Kentucky (23-6)
1978 Kentucky (30-2)
1994 Arkansas (31-3)

Boxing
1949 LSU (20)

Cross Country
1972 Tennessee (134)
1991 Arkansas (52)
1992 Arkansas (46)
1993 Arkansas (31)

Football
1951 Tennessee (10-1/AP, UPI)
1957 Auburn (10-0/AP)
1958 LSU (11-0/AP, UPI)
1960 Ole Miss (10-0-1/FWAA)
1961 Alabama (11-0/AP, UPI)
1964 Alabama (10-1/AP, UPI)
1965 Alabama (9-1-1/AP, FWAA)
1973 Alabama (11-1/UPI)
1978 Alabama (11-1/AP, FWAA)
1979 Alabama (12-0/ AP, UPI, FWAA)
1980 Georgia (12-0/AP, UPI, FWAA)
1992 Alabama (13-0/AP, UPI, USA Today, FWAA)

Golf
1940 LSU (601-tie)
1942 LSU (590-tie)
1947 LSU (606)
1955 LSU (574)
1968 Florida (1154)
1973 Florida (1149)
1993 Florida (1145)

Indoor Track
1992 Arkansas (53)
1993 Arkansas (66)
1994 Arkansas (94)

Outdoor Track
1933 LSU (58)
1974 Tennessee (60)
1989 LSU (53)
1990 LSU (44)
1991 Tennessee (51)
1992 Arkansas (60)
1993 Arkansas (69)
1994 Arkansas (83)

Swimming
1978 Tennessee (307)
1983 Florida (238)
1985 Florida (287.5)

Tennis
1985 Georgia
1987 Georgia

WOMEN

Basketball
1987 Tennessee (28-6)
1989 Tennessee (35-2)
1991 Tennessee (30-5)

Cross Country
1988 Kentucky (75)

Golf
1985 Florida (1218)
1986 Florida (1180)

Gymnastics
1987 Georgia (187.90)
1988 Alabama (190.05)
1989 Georgia (192.65)
1991 Alabama (195.125)
1993 Georgia (198.00)

Indoor Track
1987 LSU (49)
1989 LSU (61)
1991 LSU (48)
1992 Florida (50)
1993 LSU (49)
1994 LSU (48)

Outdoor Track
1987 LSU (62)
1988 LSU (61)
1989 LSU (86)
1990 LSU (53)
1991 LSU (78)
1992 LSU (87)
1993 LSU (93)
1994 LSU (86)

Swimming
1982 Florida (505)

Tennis
1992 Florida
1994 Georgia

1994 SEC Football   15

SEC Headquarters

The Southeastern Conference office moved to its current headquarters in downtown Birmingham October 15, 1991.

The two-story structure was designed specifically to house the SEC's 25-person staff as well as accommodate the needs of the various committees, coaches and administrative groups which meet at the conference office on a regular basis. In addition, the office building includes displays honoring the current champion in each of the 19 conference sports, exhibits featuring the 12 member institutions and the league's history as well as a research library.

The multi-faceted operation of the SEC Office includes certifying the eligibility of all student-athletes, managing championship events, enhancing academic opportunities for student-athletes, monitoring NCAA and SEC compliance, coordinating officiating assignments, negotiating television contracts, distributing conference revenue, cultivating corporate sponsorships and coordinating media and public relations efforts.

The SEC headquarters, which contains more than 30,000-square feet of working space, was provided by the city of Birmingham. It is located two blocks from Interstate 59-20, adjacent to the Birmingham-Jefferson Civic Center, and is a five-minute drive from the airport.

The office of the commissioner, formed in 1940, was originally located in Jackson, Miss. Upon the appointment of Bernie Moore as commissioner in 1946, the SEC headquarters relocated to Birmingham's Redmont Hotel. In October 1967 the conference office moved to the Central Bank Building in downtown Birmingham, before moving to the Riverchase Galleria Tower in May 1988.

The SEC Office (above) spans half a block and was provided by the city of Birmingham. It is located at 2201 Civic Center Boulevard within the newly-developed City Center. The foyer entrance (left) is highlighted by a two-story glass rotunda. It features school banners, championship pedestals and links the two galleries which display the member institutions' exhibits.

SEC Officers

DR. CHARLES WETHINGTON
(Kentucky)
President

DR. JOHN LOMBARDI
(Florida)
Vice President

DR. MAX WILLIAMS
(Ole Miss)
Secretary

Executive Committee

DR. CHARLES WETHINGTON (Kentucky)

DR. JOHN LOMBARDI (Florida)

DR. MAX WILLIAMS (Ole Miss)

DR. JOE JOHNSON (Tennessee)

DR. JANE MOORE (Auburn)

DR. MIKE McGEE (South Carolina)

MRS. BEV LEWIS (Arkansas)

16 Southeastern Conference

ROY KRAMER
SEC Commissioner

A prominent leader in intercollegiate athletics, Roy Foster Kramer became the sixth commissioner of the Southeastern Conference January 10, 1990.

During his tenure at the helm of the SEC, the conference has experienced unparalleled growth. In 1993-94 alone, the SEC won seven national championships and distributed an all-time high $34.36 million to the member institutions, more than double the amount ($16.3 million) distributed in his first year as commissioner. Most recently, Kramer negotiated a multi-sport national television package with CBS Sports, featuring men's and women's basketball from 1994-95 through 2000-2001 and football from 1996 to 2000.

Within seven months of his appointment, the conference announced plans for expansion, adding Arkansas and South Carolina officially on July 1, 1991. Following expansion, Kramer guided the league in formulating divisional play and the first Division IA conference football championship game. He has since also helped secure football bowl agreements for the SEC's top five teams through the 1994 season. In addition, he has been instrumental in the creation of new scheduling formats for all sports as well as the implementation of coaches educational seminars.

On the national level, Kramer served two terms on the prestigious NCAA Men's Basketball Committee which selects the 64-team field for the NCAA Tournament and administrates all tournament games. He was chairman of the committee for the 1992 NCAA Tournament. Kramer served a four-year term (1989-93) on the NCAA Basketball Television Negotiating Committee that was responsible for securing the seven-year $1 billion contract with CBS Sports.

Kramer, a member of the NACDA Executive Committee, also serves on the NCAA Committee on Infractions. During his career he has distinguished himself as a member of several other NCAA committees including, the Special Advisory Committee to Review Distribution of Revenue, the Committee for National Drug Testing Policy, the Investment Committee and the Select Committee to Study Intercollegiate Athletics, which proposed the President's Commission. He also served as chairman of the NCAA Men's Committee on Committees in 1987 and 1988.

During his 12 years (1978-90) as athletic director at Vanderbilt University, Kramer was a leader in establishing conference policies. He is a past chairman of the league's athletic directors and was influential in bringing the SEC Basketball Tournament to Nashville in 1984, the first sellout in tournament history. In addition Kramer helped land the 1991 SEC Tournament for Vanderbilt, as well as the first and second rounds of the 1982 and 1989 NCAA Tournaments.

Other highlights of his Vanderbilt tenure include a $6 million addition and renovation of McGugin Center, which houses the complete Commodore athletic program and the construction of Vanderbilt Stadium in 1981. He was inducted into the Tennessee Sports Hall of Fame in February, 1989.

After a nine-year stint as a high school head football coach in Michigan, which included three state championships, Kramer joined the coaching staff at Central Michigan University. Just two years later he became the head coach at CMU and compiled an 83-32-2 (.718) record in 11 seasons. In 1974 he was tabbed NCAA National Coach of the Year after guiding the Chippewas to a 12-1 record and the Division II National Championship.

Kramer obtained his bachelor's degree from Maryville (Tenn.) College in 1953 following a standout career as a football lineman and wrestler. He received the school's Distinguished Alumnus Award in 1982. He added a master's at the University of Michigan in 1954 and then spent three years in the U.S. Army, rising from a non-commissioned officer to a first lieutenant in the European NATO Command.

The Maryville, Tenn., native was born October 30, 1929. He is married to the former Sara Jo Emert. They have three children (Steve, Sara Gray Cassell and Jane House) and six grandchildren.

Experience
1990 -	Commissioner, Southeastern Conference
1978 - 1990	Athletic Director, Vanderbilt University
1967 - 1977	Head Football Coach, Central Michigan University
1965 - 1966	Assistant Football Coach, Central Michigan University
1956 - 1964	Head High School Football Coach
	1956 - Hudson, Mich.
	1957 - Dowagiac, Mich.
	1958-59 - Benton Harbor, Mich.
	1960-64 - East Lansing, Mich.
1954 - 1955	Assistant Football Coach Battle Creek (Mich.) High School

SEC Highlights
- Instrumental in SEC expansion movement which included addition of Arkansas and South Carolina
- Guided SEC efforts to establish divisions, new scheduling formats and Division IA's first conference championship football game
- Negotiated a multi-sport televison package with CBS Sports, featuring football (1996-2000) and men's and women's basketball (1994-95 through 2000-2001)
- Administered a distribution of more than $133 million to the member institutions during his first five years
- Led SEC negotiations resulting in bowl agreements with the Citrus, Gator, Peach and Carquest
- Spearheaded negotiations for new SEC headquarters building

Committees
- NACDA Executive Committee (1993-present)
- NCAA Committee on Infractions (1988 - present)
- NCAA Basketball Television Negotiating Committee (1989 - 1993)
- NCAA Special Advisory Committee to Review Distribution of Revenue (1989 - 1993)
- NCAA Men's Basketball Committee (1987-92, Chair 1992)
- NCAA Men's Committee on Committees (1985-88, Chair 1987-88)
- NCAA Committee for National Drug Testing Policy (1984-1989)
- NCAA Select Committee to Study Intercollegiate Athletics (1984-86)
- NCAA Investment Committee (1983-86)

Vanderbilt Highlights
- $6 million addition and renovation of McGugin Center, Vanderbilt's athletic complex
- Construction of 41,000-seat Vanderbilt Stadium

Coaching Highlights
- Posted an overall record of 83-32-2 (.718) in 11 seasons at CMU (1967-77)
- Named National Coach of the Year after leading Central Michigan to 12-1 mark and 1974 NCAA Division II National Championship
- Compiled a 58-14-3 (.793) record, including three state championships (Class C - Hudson, Class B - Dowagiac, Class A - East Lansing), in nine years at four Michigan high schools

Honors
- Tennessee Sports Hall of Fame (February 1989)
- Contribution to Football Award by the Middle Tennessee Chapter of the National Football Foundation and Hall of Fame (1982)
- Maryville College Distinguished Alumnus Award (1982)

Mark Womack
Executive Associate Commissioner

Responsibilities:
  Finance, Administration,
  Television, Bowl Relations
Education:
  Alabama, 1978, Bachelor's
Joined SEC Staff: 1978

John Guthrie
Associate Commissioner

Responsibilities:
  Coordinator Men's
  Basketball Officials, Baseball
Education:
  Oglethorpe University, Bachelor's;
  Middle Tennessee State, Masters
Joined SEC Staff: 1981

Jim McCullough
Associate Commissioner

Responsibilities:
  Eligibility, Financial Aid,
  NCAA Rule Interpretations
Education:
  Clarion State, 1954, Bachelor's
  Westminster, 1961, Masters
Joined SEC Staff: 1982

Patricia Wall
Associate Commissioner

Responsibilities:
  Championships, Women's Sports
Education:
  MacMurray College, Bachelor's
  MacMurray College, Master's
Joined SEC Staff: 1987

John Gerdy
Associate Commissioner

Responsibilities:
  Compliance, Academic Affairs,
  Rule Interpretations
Education:
  Davidson, 1979, Bachelor's
  Ohio, 1983, Master's;
  Ohio, 1986, Doctorate
Joined SEC Staff: 1989

Brad Davis
Associate Commissioner

Responsibilities:
  Special Projects, Basketball
  Tournament, Building Operations
Education:
  Auburn, 1978, Bachelor's
Joined SEC Staff: 1988

Sharon Gaunt
Assistant Commissioner

Responsibilities:
  Coordinator of Officiating for
  Women's Sports
Education:
  James Madison, Bachelor's
  Indiana, Master's
  Eastern Kentucky, Education
  Specialist's
  Indiana, Doctorate
Joined SEC Staff: 1993

Mark Whitworth
Assistant Commissioner

Responsibilities:
  Communications and Public Affairs
Education:
  Asbury College, 1984, Bachelor's;
  Tennessee, 1987, Master's
Joined SEC Staff: 1988

Graham Edwards
Director of Media Services

Responsibilities:
  Men's Basketball, Baseball and
  Football Media Contact
Education:
  Georgia, 1988, Bachelor's
Joined SEC Staff: 1989

Karen Frascona
Associate Director of Media Services

Responsibilities:
  Women's Basketball, Olympic Sports
  and Football Media Contact
Education:
  Villanova, 1989, Bachelor's
Joined SEC Staff: 1993

Bobby Gaston
Coordinator of Football Officials

Responsibilities:
    Oversee SEC Football Officiating Crews
Education:
    Georgia Tech, 1948, Bachelor's
Joined SEC Staff: 1989

Peggy Blake
Director of Business Operations

Education:
    American Institute of Banking
Joined SEC Staff: 1990

Jackie Posey
Executive Assistant

Education:
    Georgia, Bachelor's
Joined SEC Staff: 1974

Debbie Corum
Director of Championship Marketing

Education:
    Vanderbilt, Bachelor's
Joined SEC Staff: 1989

Gina Estes
Administrative Assistant
(Media Relations)

Katrice Upshaw
Administrative Assistant
(Championship Marketing)

Sylvia Hagan
Administrative Assistant
(Basketball Officiating/Baseball)

Brenda Gray
Receptionist

Dauna Koonce
Administrative Assistant
(Compliance)

Damon Evans
Compliance Assistant

Vickie McCormack
Administrative Assistant
(Football and Women's Officiating)

Marie Robbins
Championships Assistant

Lelia Staples
Administrative Assistant
(Eligibility)

Glenn Thackston
Media Relations Assistant

1994 SEC Football   19

Service Education Commitment

The Southeastern Conference will distribute approximately $34.36 million to the 12 member institutions in the revenue sharing plans for the 1993-94 fiscal year, which ends Aug. 31, 1994.

The $34.36 million is the highest total ever distributed in SEC history, edging the $34.34 million distributed to the schools in 1992-93.

The revenue sharing plans include money generated by football television, bowls, the SEC Football Championship, basketball television, the SEC Basketball Tournament and the NCAA Basketball Tournament.

Broken down by categories and rounded off, the $34.36 million was derived from $13.7 million for football television, $4.5 million from bowls, $4.9 million from the SEC Football Championship, $3.8 million from basketball television, $2.6 million from the SEC Basketball Tournament and $4.86 million from the NCAA Basketball Tournament.

The amount distributed to each school which participated in all revenue sharing ranged from a high of $2.9 million to a low of $2.7 million.

Not included in the $34.36 million was $2.7 million redistributed to the institutions by the CFA for participation in the 1993 television package, $3.7 million retained by the institutions participating in bowls and $360,000 divided among all 12 institutions by the NCAA for academic enhancement.

Other yearly money distributions, since 1980, are as follows: 1980 ($4.1 million); 1981 ($5.57 million); 1982 ($7.54 million); 1983 ($9.53 million); 1984 ($18.4 million); 1985 ($9.34 million); 1986 ($13.1 million); 1987 ($13.56 million); 1988 ($14.34 million); 1989 ($13.85 million); 1990 ($16.3 million); 1991 ($20.6 million), 1992 (27.7 million) and 1993 (34.34 million).

The SEC's financial support of its institutions ensures the continued quality of academic and athletic opportunities for student-athletes. The Conference has developed the following programs to better serve its membership:

• The SEC conducts Coaches Orientation Programs twice yearly at the SEC headquarters to supplement existing institutional orientation programs and to enhance the professional development of coaches. The one-day programs, which began June 15, 1993, were developed with input from Conference Compliance Coordinators, Faculty Athletics Representatives, Athletics Directors and the SEC Student-Athlete Advisory Committee. Topics of discussion range from the role of the SEC and NCAA to the role of athletics in higher education.

• The SEC was the first conference in the nation to assemble a Student-Athlete Advisory Committee. Two representatives from each of the SEC's member schools are selected to serve on the committee which meets twice a year to discuss issues of concern to the student-athlete.

• The annual SEC Summer Workshop is designed to review administrative procedures of the Conference. Topics of discussion include how to fill out all required forms, due dates for submitting materials to the Conference office, eligibility rules, financial aid, criteria for satisfactory progress and transmission of squad lists. Participants include: Faculty Athletics Representatives, Senior Women's Administrators, Directors of Financial Aid, Directors of Admissions, Registrars and Compliance Coordinators.

• The SEC hosts youth clinics each year in conjunction with the men's basketball, women's basketball and volleyball tournaments. These clinics provide children from host cities the opportunity to receive instruction from SEC and other area coaches.

• The 12 member institutions of the SEC provide over $23 million in scholarships for more than 3,300 student-athletes each year.

The SEC, in conjunction with the USF&G Sugar Bowl, annually awards post-graduate scholarships totaling $70,000 to 12 student-athletes.

The top male and female nominee each receive the H. Boyd McWhorter Scholar Athlete Award, named for the league's fourth commissioner and a $10,000 scholarship. Ten additional student-athletes (five male and five female) are each awarded $5,000 to continue their education.

The SEC television contract with Jefferson-Pilot for men's basketball and football also guarantees at least $80,000 to be distributed to the participating schools through the JP Player of the Game program. This money is allocated for the general scholarship fund of each institution.

SEC Divisions

The 5-2-1 schedule format, implemented in 1992, allows each school to play all five division opponents along with two permanent and one rotating non-division opponent each year. Schools will play each rotating non-division opponent two years (home and away) before the next opponent appears on its schedule. This ensures every SEC member plays at least twice during an eight-year period.

Division alignment and schedule format follows:

Eastern Division
Florida
Georgia
Kentucky

South Carolina
Tennessee
Vanderbilt

Western Division
Alabama
Arkansas
Auburn

LSU
Ole Miss
Miss. State

Alabama
Permanent Non-Division (2): Tennessee, Vanderbilt
Rotating Non-Division (1):
1994/95 UG/at UG   1998/99 UF/at UF
1996/97 UK/at UK   2000/01 USC/at USC

Arkansas
Permanent Non-Division (2): South Carolina, Tennessee
Rotating Non-Division (1):
1994/95 VU/at VU   1998/99 UK/at UK
1996/97 UF/at UF   2000/01 UG/at UG

Auburn
Permanent Non-Division (2): Florida, Georgia
Rotating Non-Division (1):
1994/95 UK/at UK   1998/99 UT/at UT
1996/97 USC/at USC   2000/01 VU/at VU

Florida
Permanent Non-Division (2): Auburn, LSU
Rotating Non-Division (1):
1994/95 at UM/UM   1998/99 at UA/UA
1996/97 at AR/AR   2000/01 at MSU/MSU

Georgia
Permanent Non-Division (2): Auburn, Ole Miss
Rotating Non-Division (1):
1994/95 at UA/UA   1998/99 at LSU/LSU
1996/97 at MSU/MSU   2000/01 at AR/AR

Kentucky
Permanent Non-Division (2): LSU, Miss. State
Rotating Non-Division (1):
1994/95 at AU/AU   1998/99 at AR/AR
1996/97 at UA/UA   2000/01 at UM/UM

LSU
Permanent Non-Division (2): Florida, Kentucky
Rotating Non-Division (1):
1994/95 USC/at USC   1998/99 UG/at UG
1996/97 VU/at VU   2000/01 UT/at UT

Ole Miss
Permanent Non-Division (2): Georgia, Vanderbilt
Rotating Non-Division (1):
1994/95 UF/at UF   1998/99 USC/at USC
1996/97 UT/at UT   2000/01 UK/at UK

Mississippi State
Permanent Non-Division (2): Kentucky, South Carolina
Rotating Non-Division (1):
1994/95 UT/at UT   1998/99 VU/at VU
1996/97 UG/at UG   2000/01 UF/at UF

South Carolina
Permanent Non-Division (2): Arkansas, Miss. State
Rotating Non-Division (1):
1994/95 at LSU/LSU   1998/99 at UM/UM
1996/97 at AU/AU   2000/01 at UA/UA

Tennessee
Permanent Non-Division (2): Alabama, Arkansas
Rotating Non-Division (1):
1994/95 at MSU/MSU   1998/99 at AU/AU
1996/97 at UM/UM   2000/01 at LSU/LSU

Vanderbilt
Permanent Non-Division (2): Alabama, Ole Miss
Rotating Non-Division (1):
1994/95 at AR/AR   1998/99 at MSU/MSU
1996/97 at LSU/LSU   2000/01 at AU/AU

SEC Awards

The Bernie Moore and Women's All-Sports Trophies

The Bernie Moore and the Women's All-Sports Trophies, presented annually by the Southeastern Conference, are symbolic of the league's premier men's and women's athletic programs.

The SEC officially began tabulating points for the Bernie Moore All-Sports Trophy, named for former SEC Commissioner Bernie Moore, following the 1973-74 season. The tabulation of points for the Women's All-Sports Trophy began following the 1983-84 school year. Both trophies were discounted following the 1994 academic year.

Points for the two trophies were awarded on a 12-11-10-9-8-7-6-5-4-3-2-1 basis for all sports. However, beginning in 1991-92 only the top six finishes counted toward an institution's total. If a team was on probation in a sport, the institution was required to count that sport's vacated position among its six. In the event of a tie for a position, the points for the number of places involved were added together, divided by the number of teams involved in the tie and awarded to those teams equally.

Bernie Moore Trophy Winners

1973-74	Alabama	65.5
1974-75	Tennessee	60.0
1975-76	Alabama	66.5
1976-77	Alabama	62.5
1977-78	Auburn	59.5
1978-79	LSU	61.0
1979-80	Tennessee	56.5
1980-81	Tennessee	50.0
1981-82	Alabama	55.0
	Tennessee	55.0
1982-83	Alabama	50.0
1983-84	Auburn	51.0
1984-85	Georgia	56.0
1985-86	LSU	56.0
1986-87	LSU	55.5
1987-88	LSU	57.5
1988-89	LSU	59.0
1989-90	Tennessee	55.5
1990-91	LSU	54.5
1991-92	Florida	65.0
1992-93	Florida	61.0
1993-94	Florida	67.0

Women's All-Sports Trophy Winners

1983-84	Georgia	58.0
1984-85	Florida	59.0
1985-86	Georgia	58.5
1986-87	Georgia	59.5
1987-88	Florida	53.5
1988-89	Florida	56.5
1989-90	Georgia	54.5
1990-91	Georgia	59.0
1991-92	Florida	65.5
1992-93	Florida	63.5
1993-94	Georgia	63.5

H. Boyd McWhorter Scholar-Athlete Awards

Each year the SEC, in conjunction with the USF+G Sugar Bowl, provides the league's male and female H. Boyd McWhorter Scholar-Athlete Award winners with a $10,000 post-graduate scholarship. In addition, five other male and female student-athletes each receive $5,000 post-graduate scholarships.

The award recipients are chosen by a committee of Faculty Athletics Representatives from the 12 SEC institutions.

The award is named for former SEC Commissioner H. Boyd McWhorter.

1985-86	John Young (Track)	Tennessee
	Virginia Diederich (Swimming)	Georgia
1986-87	Jeff Noblin (Football)	Ole Miss
	Julie Estin (Gymnastics)	Alabama
1987-88	Danny Hoskins (Football)	Ole Miss
	Linda Leith (Swimming)	Georgia
1988-89	Mikael Olander (Track)	LSU
	Deanne Burnett (Swimming)	Georgia
1989-90	Burke Masters (Baseball)	Miss. State
	Janice Kerr (Gymnastics)	Florida
1990-91	Al Parker (Tennis)	Georgia
	Patty Wiegand (Track)	Tennessee
1991-92	Jeff Laubenthal (Baseball)	Alabama
	Jenifer Kleyn (Volleyball)	Auburn
1992-93	Lang Wiseman (Basketball)	Tennessee
	Aimee York (Volleyball)	Miss. State
1993-94	Peter Duitsman (Soccer)	South Carolina
	Tammy Newlon (Basketball)	Miss. State

SEC Athlete of the Year

Each year the SEC selects a male and female athlete of the year by a vote of the league's athletic directors.

1975-76	Harvey Glance (Track)	Auburn
1976-77	Larry Sievers (Football)	Tennessee
1977-78	Jack Givens (Basketball)	Kentucky
1978-79	Reggie King (Basketball)	Alabama
1979-80	Kyle Macy (Basketball)	Kentucky
1980-81	Rowdy Gaines (Swimming)	Auburn
1981-82	Buck Belue (Football/Baseball)	Georgia
1982-83	Herschel Walker (Football/Track)	Georgia
1983-84	Terry Hoage (Football)	Georgia
	Tracy Caulkins (Swimming)	Florida
1984-85	Will Clark (Baseball)	Miss. State
	Penney Hauschild (Gymnastics)	Alabama
1985-86	Bo Jackson (Football)	Auburn
	Jennifer Gillom (Basketball)	Ole Miss
1986-87	Cornelius Bennett (Football)	Alabama
	Lillie Leatherwood-King (Track)	Alabama
1987-88	Will Perdue (Basketball)	Vanderbilt
	Dara Torres (Swimming)	Florida
1988-89	Derrick Thomas (Football)	Alabama
	Bridgette Gordon (Basketball)	Tennessee
1989-90	Alec Kessler (Basketball)	Georgia
	Dee Dee Foster (Gymnastics)	Alabama
1990-91	Shaquille O'Neal (Basketball)	LSU
	Daedra Charles (Basketball)	Tennessee
1991-92	Shaquille O'Neal (Basketball)	LSU
	Vicki Goetze (Golf)	Georgia
1992-93	Jamal Mashburn (Basketball)	Kentucky
	Nicole Haislett (Swimming)	Florida
1993-94	Corliss Williamson (Basketball)	Arkansas
	Nicole Haislett (Swimming)	Florida

1994 SEC Football

National Football Outlets

Networks

ABC Sports
47 West 66th Street,
13th Floor
New York, NY 10023
(212) 887-4867

CBS Sports
51 West 52nd Street,
30th Floor
New York, NY 10019
(212) 975-4907

ESPN
ESPN Plaza
Bristol, CT 06010
(203) 584-8477

Jefferson Pilot Sports
One Julian Price Place
Charlotte, NC 28208
(704) 374-3669

NBC Sports
30 Rockefeller Plaza
New York, NY 10112
(212) 664-5407

Wire Services

Associated Press
Rick Warner
50 Rockefeller Plaza
New York, NY 10020
(212) 621-1640
           OR
Ed Shearer
1 CNN Center
500 South Tower
Atlanta, GA 30303
(404) 522-8971

United Press International
220 East 42nd Street
New York, NY 10017
(212) 560-1100

National Publications

Sporting News
P.O. Box 56
1212 N. Lindbergh Boulevard
St. Louis, MO 63166
(314) 997-7111

Sports Illustrated
Time & Life Building
Rockefeller Center
New York, NY 10020
(212) 522-3124

USA Today
1000 Wilson Boulevard
Arlington, VA 22229
(703) 276-3735 or 3400

Associations

American Football Coaches
   Association
5900 Old McGregor Road
Waco, TX 76712
(817) 776-5900

College Football Association
6688 Gunpark Drive, Ste. 201
Boulder, CO 80301-3339
(303) 530-5566

Football Writers Association
   of America
Box 1022
Edmond, OK 73083
(405) 341-4731

National Football Foundation
   and Hall of Fame
1865 Palmer Avenue, Ste. 103
Larchmont, NY 10538
(914) 834-0474

NCAA
6201 College Boulevard
Overland Park, KA 66211-2422
(913) 339-1906

Bowls

A complete Bowl Directory can be found on pages 290-291.

SEC Athletic Department Directory

ALABAMA — (205) 348-3600
P.O. Box 870323
Tuscaloosa, AL 35487-0323
323 Bryant Drive
Tuscaloosa, AL 35486

ARKANSAS — (501) 575-2000 (men)
Broyles Athletic Complex
Maple @ Razorback Road
Fayetteville, AR 72701
Broyles Athletic Complex
Maple @ Razorback Road
Fayettville, AR 72701

(Women's Department) — (501) 575-4957
215 Barnhill Arena
Fayetteville, AR 72701
Street Address - same

AUBURN — (205) 844-4750
P.O. Box 351
Auburn, AL 36831-0351
Donahue Drive
Auburn, AL 36830

FLORIDA — (904) 375-4683
P.O. Box 14485
Gainesville, FL 32604
Stadium West
North/South Drive
Gainesville, FL 32611

GEORGIA — (706) 542-1515
P.O. Box 1472
Athens, GA 30613-2199
Butts-Mehre Heritage Building
One Selig Circle
Athens, GA 30602

KENTUCKY — (606) 257-8000
Memorial Coliseum
Euclid Avenue
Lexington, KY 40506-0019
Street Address - same

LSU — (504) 388-6606
P.O. Box 25095
Baton Rouge, LA 70894-5095
North Stadium Drive
Baton Rouge, LA 70894

OLE MISS — (601) 232-7241
Athletic Department
Fraternity Row
University, MS 38677
Street Address - same

MISSISSIPPI STATE — (601) 325-2808
P.O. Drawer 5327
Mississippi State, MS 39762
Humphrey Coliseum
Collegeview Street
Mississippi State, MS 39762

SOUTH CAROLINA — (803) 777-4202
Rex Enright Athletic Center
1300 Rosewood Drive
Columbia, SC 29208
Street Address - same

TENNESSEE — (615) 974-1220 (men)
P.O. Box 15016
Knoxville, TN 37901-5016
1720 Volunteer Boulevard
Knoxville, TN 37996-3100

(Women's Department) — (615) 974-0001
115 Stokley Athletics Center
1720 Volunteer Boulevard
Knoxville, TN 37996-3100
Street Address - same

VANDERBILT — (615) 322-4727
P.O. Box 120158
Nashville, TN 37212
2601 Jess Neely Drive
Nashville, TN 37212

ALABAMA

DR. ROGER SAYERS
President

DR. THOMAS JONES
Faculty Representative

CECIL "Hootie" INGRAM
Athletic Director

University of Alabama

PRESIDENT:
Dr. Roger Sayers (Illinois 1958)
FACULTY REPRESENTATIVE:
Dr. Thomas Jones (Kentucky 1959)
ATHLETIC DIRECTOR:
Cecil "Hootie" Ingram (Alabama 1955)
HEAD COACH:
Gene Stallings (Texas A&M 1957)
LOCATION: Tuscaloosa, Alabama
FOUNDED: 1831
ENROLLMENT: 20,000
NICKNAME: Crimson Tide
COLORS: Crimson and White
STADIUM: Bryant-Denny Stadium (70,123) — Grass
Legion Field (83,091) — Artificial (Birmingham)

Crimson Tide Quick Facts

1993 RECORD: 9-3-1
(5-1-1 Home, 3-1 Away, 1-1 Neutral)
1993 SEC RECORD (FINISH): 5-2-1 (1st-Western)
(2-1-1 Home, 3-1 Away)
BOWL: Outback Steakhouse Gator
Alabama 24, North Carolina 10
ALL-TIME RECORD: 691-237-44 (.734)
SEC RECORD: 284-103-21 (.721) — Regular Season Games
SEC CHAMPIONSHIPS: 20
(1933, 34t, 37, 45, 53, 6lt, 64, 65, 66t,
71, 72, 73, 74, 75, 77, 78, 79, 81t, 89t, 92)
BOWL APPEARANCES: 46
BOWL RECORD: 26-17-2 (.589)
LAST APPEARANCE: 1993 Outback Steakhouse Gator
(Alabama 24, North Carolina 10)

ALABAMA Team Information

OFFENSIVE SYSTEM: Pro-I

DEFENSIVE SYSTEM: 3-4

LETTERMEN RETURNING: 53
- 23 Offense
- 27 Defense
- 3 Specialists

LETTERMEN LOST: 34
- 18 Offense
- 15 Defense
- 1 Specialists

STARTERS RETURNING: 14
  OFFENSE (5)
  - RG   Jon Stevenson (6-3, 275, Sr.)
  - TE   Tony Johnson (6-5, 248, Jr.)
  - QB   Jay Barker (6-3, 210, Sr.)
  - FB   Tarrant Lynch (6-1, 224, Sr.)
  - RB   Sherman Williams (5-10, 193, Sr.)

  DEFENSE (6)
  - DE   Elverett Brown (6-5, 266, Sr.)
  - ILB Michael Rogers (6-1, 232, Sr.)
  - OLB Darrell Blackburn (6-4, 224, So.)
  - CB   Tommy Johnson (5-10, 180, Sr.)
  - CB   Willie Gaston (5-11, 183, Sr.)
  - SS   Sam Shade (6-1, 190, Sr.)

  SPECIALISTS (3)
  - P   Bryne Diehl (6-3, 215, Sr.)
  - PK   Michael Proctor (5-10, 183, Jr.)
  - K   William Watts (6-1, 180, So.)

STARTERS LOST: 13
  OFFENSE (7)
  - SE   Kevin Lee (6-1, 183, Sr.)
  - LT   Matt Hammond (6-3, 270, Sr.)
  - LG   John Clay (6-2, 273, Sr.)
  - C   Tobie Sheils (6-3, 250, Sr.)
  - RT   Roosevelt Patterson (6-4, 290, Sr.)
  - FL   David Palmer (5-8, 170, Jr.)
  - RB   Chris Anderson (5-9, 187, Sr.)

  DEFENSE (5)
  - NT   James Gregory (6-4, 280, Sr.)
  - DE   Jeremy Nunley (6-5, 254, Sr.)
  - OLB Lemanski Hall (6-1, 227, Sr.)
  - CB   Antonio Langham (6-1, 170, Sr.)
  - FS   Chris Donnelly (6-0, 180, Sr.)

  SPECIALISTS (1)
  - SN   Matthew Pine (6-3, 221, Jr.)

Bryant-Denny Stadium: (70,123)
Record: 164-18-3 (.895)
First Game: Oct. 4, 1929 - Alabama 22, Ole Miss 7
Largest Crowd: 70,123 (20 times)
  Last: Nov. 13, 1993 - Alabama 36, Miss. State 25

1994 Alabama Schedule

Date	Opponent	Location
Sept. 3	UT-CHATTANOOGA	BIRMINGHAM
Sept. 10	VANDERBILT	TUSCALOOSA
Sept. 17	at Arkansas	Fayetteville, Ark.
Sept. 24	TULANE	BIRMINGHAM
Oct. 1	GEORGIA	TUSCALOOSA
Oct. 8	SOUTHERN MISS	TUSCALOOSA
Oct. 15	at Tennessee	Knoxville, Tenn.
Oct. 22	OLE MISS	TUSCALOOSA
Nov. 5	at LSU	Baton Rouge, La.
Nov. 12	at Miss. State	Starkville, Miss.
Nov. 19	AUBURN	BIRMINGHAM

1995 Alabama Schedule

Date	Opponent	Location
Sept. 2	at Vanderbilt	Nashville, Tenn.
Sept. 9	SOUTHERN MISS	BIRMINGHAM
Sept. 16	ARKANSAS	TUSCALOOSA
Sept. 30	at Georgia	Athens, Ga.
Oct. 7	N.C. STATE	TUSCALOOSA
Oct. 14	TENNESSEE	BIRMINGHAM
Oct. 21	at Ole Miss	Oxford, Miss.
Oct. 28	LOUISIANA TECH	BIRMINGHAM
Nov. 4	LSU	TUSCALOOSA
Nov. 11	MISS. STATE	TUSCALOOSA
Nov. 25	at Auburn	Auburn, Ala.

1993 Alabama Individual Leaders

RUSHING	Atts	Yards	Avg	TDs	Yds/Game
SHERMAN WILLIAMS	168	738	4.4	9	67.1
Chris Anderson	90	314	3.5	3	28.5
TARRANT LYNCH	67	276	4.1	3	25.1
BRIAN STEGER	46	249	5.4	2	24.9
David Palmer	42	278	6.6	0	23.2

PASSING	Atts	Comp	Ints/TDs	Pct	Yds
JAY BARKER	171	98	7/4	.573	1525
BRIAN BURGDORF	84	48	3/4	.571	533

RECEIVING	Rec	Yds	Avg	TDs	Yds/Game
David Palmer	61	1000	16.4	7	83.3
Kevin Lee	26	510	19.6	1	42.5
TARRANT LYNCH	19	171	9.0	2	15.5
CHAD KEY	17	269	15.8	0	22.4
TONY JOHNSON	12	117	9.8	1	9.8

SCORING	G	TDs	PAT	2-Pt. FGs	FGs Tot	Tot Avg	Avg
MICHAEL PROCTOR	12	0	31	0	22	97	8.1
SHERMAN WILLIAMS	11	9	0	0	0	54	4.9
David Palmer	12	7	0	1	0	44	3.7
TARRANT LYNCH	11	5	0	0	0	30	2.7
Chris Anderson	11	3	0	0	0	18	1.6
BRIAN STEGER	10	2	0	0	0	12	1.2

PUNTING	No	Yds	Avg	Long
BRYNE DIEHL	56	2441	43.6	68

KICKOFF RETURNS	No	Yds	Avg	TDs	Avg/Game	Long
David Palmer	20	439	21.9	0	36.6	50

PUNT RETURNS	No	Yds	Avg	TDs	Avg/Game	Long
David Palmer	31	244	7.9	0	20.3	34

TACKLES	Total	Sk(Yds)	TL(Yds)	Ints
Lemanski Hall	76	2 (-14)	8 (-19)	2
SAM SHADE	73	0	5 (-31)	2
MICHAEL ROGERS	72	2 (-16)	8 (-17)	0
Jeremy Nunley	72	10 (-60)	6 (-14)	0
WILLIE GASTON	57	0	2 (-17)	4

INTERCEPTIONS	No	Yds	TDs	Int/Game	Long
Antonio Langham	7	67	1	0.6	44
WILLIE GASTON	4	13	0	0.3	13
TOMMY JOHNSON	4	18	0	0.3	18

Returning Players in All Capitals

Bryne Diehl  • Michael Rogers  • Sam Shade

1993 Alabama Team Statistics

	UA	OPP
FIRST DOWNS	226	170
Rushing	113	92
Passing	97	72
Penalty	16	6
NET YARDS RUSHING	2119	1565
Yards Gained	2614	1967
Yards Lost	495	402
Rushing attempts	535	428
Average per rush	3.96	3.66
Average per game	176.5	130.4
NET YARDS PASSING	2569	1539
Average per game	214.1	128.3
Passes attempted	300	310
Passes completed	169	144
Had intercepted	16	22
TOTAL OFFENSIVE YARDS	4688	3104
Average per game	390.7	258.7
Total plays	835	738
Average per play	5.6	4.2
NUMBER PUNTS/YARDS	56/2441	88/3230
Punting average	43.6	36.7
Net punting average	38.1	33.6
PUNT RETURNS/YARDS	32/270	29/311
Punt return average	8.4	10.7
KICKOFF RETURNS/YARDS	30/589	53/956
Kickoff return average	19.6	18.1
PENALTIES/YARDS	83/702	79/675
Penalty yards per game	58.5	56.3
FUMBLES/LOST	26/10	17/7
INTERCEPTION RETURNS/YARDS	22/213	16/167
Interception return average	9.7	10.4
TOUCHDOWNS	36	19
Rushing	20	10
Passing	13	9
Return	3	0
FIELD GOALS MADE/ATTEMPTED	22/29	8/11
KICK EXTRA POINTS MADE/ATTEMPTED	32/33	16/17
SAFETY	0	1
TWO-POINT CONVERSIONS	1/3	1/2
TOTAL POINTS	316	158
Average per game	26.3	13.2

1993 Alabama Results

9-3-1 Overall • 5-2-1 SEC (1st-Western)

Date	Opponent		Result	Att
Sept. 4	TULANE (B'ham)	W	31-17	83,001
Sept. 11	at Vanderbilt [JP]	W	17-6	41,000
Sept. 18	ARKANSAS [JP]	W	43-3	70,123
Sept. 25	LOUISIANA TECH (B'ham)	W	56-3	83,091
Oct. 2	at South Carolina [ESPN]	W	17-6	74,718
Oct. 16	TENNESSEE (B'ham) [ABC]	T	17-17	83,091
Oct. 23	at Ole Miss	W	19-14	43,500
Oct. 30	SOUTHERN MISS - HC	W	40-0	70,123
Nov. 6	LSU [JP]	L	13-17	70,123
Nov. 13	MISSISSIPPI STATE [ABC]	W	36-25	70,123
Nov. 20	at Auburn	L	14-22	85,214
Dec. 4	Florida (B'ham) [ABC] (SEC Championship Game)	L	13-28	76,345
Dec. 31	North Carolina [ESPN] (Outback Steakhouse Gator Bowl • Jacksonville, Fla.)	W	24-10	67,205

1994 SEC Football

Gene Stallings

HOMETOWN:
Paris, Texas

ALMA MATER (YEAR):
Texas A&M (1957)

PLAYING CAREER:
Texas A&M end 1954-56 (All Southwest Conference 1955; Tri-Captain 1956)

COACHING CAREER:
Texas A&M Student Assistant 1957; Alabama Assistant 1958-64; Texas A&M Head Coach 1965-71; Dallas Assistant (NFL) 1972-85; St. Louis Head Coach (NFL) 1986-87; Phoenix Head Coach (NFL) 1988-89; Alabama Head Coach 1990-present.

COACHING ACHIEVEMENTS:
1967 SWC Champions; 1992 National, SEC and Western Division Champions; 1992 National and SEC Coach of the Year; 1993 SEC Western Division Champions

BORN:
March 2, 1935

WIFE:
Ruth Ann

CHILDREN:
Anna Lee 35, Laurie 34, John Mark 31, Jacklyn 29, Martha Kate 23

ASSISTANT COACHES:
MIKE DUBOSE (Alabama 1975) - Defensive Line
JIM FULLER (Alabama 1967) - Offensive Centers/Guards
WOODY McCORVEY (Alabama State 1972) - Receivers
BILL OLIVER (Alabama 1963) - Defensive Coordinator/Secondary
DANNY PEARMAN (Clemson 1987) - Offensive Tackles
RANDY ROSS (St. Bernard College 1975) - Recruiting Coordinator
JEFF ROUZIE (Alabama 1974) - Linebackers
HOMER SMITH (Princeton 1954) - Offensive Coordinator/Quarterbacks
IVY WILLIAMS (Xavier 1971) - Running Backs

SUPPORT STAFF:
LEBARON CARUTHERS (North Carolina State 1977) - Strength & Conditioning Coach
BILL McDONALD (Alabama 1967) - Athletic Trainer

Year-By-Year Record

Year	School	Conf.	All	Bowl
1965	Texas A&M	1-6 (t7th)	3-7	
1966	Texas A&M	4-3 (4th)	4-5-1	
1967	Texas A&M	6-1 (1st)	7-4	Cotton
1968	Texas A&M	2-5 (t6th)	3-7	
1969	Texas A&M	2-5 (6th)	3-7	
1970	Texas A&M	0-7 (8th)	2-9	
1971	Texas A&M	4-3 (4th)	5-6	
1986	St. Louis (NFL)		4-11-1	
1987	St. Louis (NFL)		7-8	
1988	Phoenix (NFL)		7-9	
1989	Phoenix (NFL)		5-6	
1990	Alabama	5-2 (t2nd)	7-5	Fiesta
1991	Alabama	6-1 (2nd)	11-1	Blockbuster
1992	Alabama	8-0 (1st)	13-0	Sugar
1993	Alabama	5-2-1 (1-W)	9-3-1	Gator

OVERALL RECORD	43-35-1 (.551)	90-88-3 (.506)	15 Years
College Record	43-35-1 (.551)	67-54-2 (.553)	11 Years
NFL RECORD		23-34-1 (.405)	4 Years
Alabama Record	24-5-1 (.817)	40-9-1 (.810)	4 Years
Texas A&M Record	19-30	27-45-1	7 Years

26 Alabama

Alabama All-Star Candidates

TOMMY JOHNSON
Senior • Cornerback
5-10 • 180 • Niceville, Fla.

• Emerged as a leader in the Crimson Tide secondary, starting every game of junior campaign and recording a career-high four interceptions, including two in the SEC Championship Game versus Florida.
• Finished the 1993 season with 43 total tackles, eight pass break-ups and one blocked punt.
• Currently boasts seven career interceptions, including one for a touchdown, 89 total tackles and 11 pass break-ups.

JON STEVENSON
Senior • Center
6-3 • 280 • Memphis, Tenn.

• Alabama's only returning starter on the offensive line. Will play the third different position of his career, at center, in 1994. Began as an offensive tackle, moved to right guard last season, and won the top spot at center in 1994's spring drills.
• Played 1,405 career snaps and missed last half of of 1993 campaign due to knee injury.
• A former freshman All-America and All-SEC honoree.

JOHNSON STATS

Year	Tackles	Int (Yds)	PBU	FC	FR
1991	12	1 (92)	2	0	0
1992	34	2 (17)	1	1	1
1993	43	4 (18)	8	0	0
Career	89	7 (127)	11	1	1

MICHAEL PROCTOR
Junior • Placekicker
5-10 • 183 • Pelham, Ala.

• Earned finalist honors for the Lou Groza Award, All-America honors from *Football News*, and first-team Coaches' All-SEC acclaim last season. Tallied 97 points and a new school record for longest field goal without a kicking tee (53 yarder vs. Ole Miss).
• Led the Tide in scoring the past two seasons, compiling 191 career points, and has converted a string of 66-consecutive PATs. Connected on 41 of 56 field goals and 68 of 69 PATs throughout Alabama career.
• Ranked on per game averages, finished the 1993 season as both the SEC's and nation's top field goal kicker, hitting 22 of 29 attempts (76 percent).

SHERMAN WILLIAMS
Senior • Tailback
5-10 • 193 * Mobile, Ala.

• Despite being hampered by injuries in 1993, started eight of 12 regular-season games and posted a career-high 738 yards and team-high nine touchdowns, returning as the Tide's leading rusher.
• Opened the season with five-straight 100-plus yard rushing games, becoming only the third Tide player to accomplish the feat. During that stint, rushed for 148 yards and one touchdown versus Arkansas, a career-best performance.
• Posted 1,145 yards throughout three-year career to go with 19 touchdowns and a per carry average of 4.7 yards.

PROCTOR STATS

Year	FGM	FGA	Pct	Long	PAT	Pct	Pts	Avg
1992	19	27	.704	47	37-38	.974	94	7.8
1993	22	29	.760	53	31-31	1.000	97	8.1
Career	41	56	.732	53	68-69	.986	191	7.9

WILLIAMS STATS

Year	Atts	Yds	Avg	TD	Rec	Yds	Avg	TD
1991	12	108	9.0	2	0	0	0	0
1992	64	299	4.5	8	9	120	13.3	0
1993	168	738	4.4	9	8	79	9.9	0
Career	244	1145	4.7	19	17	199	11.7	0

1994 SEC Football

1994 Alabama Roster

No.	Name	Pos.	Ht.	Wt.	Class	Exp.	Hometown (High School/JC)
26*	Carl Albright	H	5-9	135	Jr.	SQ	Tuscaloosa, Ala. Tuscaloosa Academy)
32	Curtis Alexander	RB	6-1	195	Fr.	SQ	Memphis, Tenn. (Whitehaven)
26	Michael Ausmus	FS	5-9	178	Jr.	2L	Mobile, Ala. (Murphy)
7	Jay Barker	QB	6-3	210	Sr.	3L	Trussville, Ala. (Trussville)
66	Tim Barnett	LT	6-5	287	Jr.	SQ	Bear Creek, Ala. (Phillips)
64	Maurice Belser	LG	6-2	289	Jr.	2L	Cordova, Ala. (Cordova)
44	Darrell Blackburn	RDE	6-4	224	So.	1L	Huntsville, Ala. (Butler)
97	Vann Bodden	LDE	6-4	248	Jr.	1L	Moss Point, Miss. (Moss Point)
85	Curtis Brown	SE	6-3	189	Jr.	2L	John's Island, S.C. (St. John's)
76	Elverett Brown	RDT	6-5	266	Sr.	3L	Montgomery, Ala. (Jeff Davis)
75	Shannon Brown	LDT	6-5	263	Jr.	2L	Millbrook, Ala. (Stanhope-Elmore)
92	Tyrell Buckner	LLB	6-1	235	So.	1L	Denison, Texas (Denison)
14	Brian Burgdorf	QB	6-2	190	Jr.	2L	Cedartown, Ga. (Cedartown)
94	Kendrick Burton	LDT	6-6	290	Jr.	1L	Hartselle, Ala. (Hartselle)
24	Blair Canale	FS	6-3	199	So.	1L	Memphis, Tenn. (Christian Brothers)
71	John Causey	C	6-1	260	So.	1L	Hayneville, Ala. (Lowndes Academy)
33	Hunter Christian	LOB	6-1	210	Jr.	SQ	Tuscaloosa, Ala. (Tuscaloosa Christian Academy)
84	Roman Colburn	SE	6-0	180	Sr.	2L	Ft. Payne, Ala. (Ft. Payne)
40	Mickey Conn	LCB	5-10	175	Sr.	2L	Snellville, Ga. (South Gwinnett)
29	Tracy Cummings	FB	6-0	235	Fr.	SQ	Jonesboro, Ga. (Forest Park)
35	Derek Cunningham	RCB	5-8	150	Fr.	SQ	Pelham, Ala. (Pelham)
27	Danny Davis	SS	6-2	213	Sr.	2L	Memphis, Tenn. (Christian Brothers)
55	Fernando Davis	LLB	6-3	225	So.	1L	Aberdeen, Miss. (Aberdeen)
12	Bryne Diehl	P	6-3	215	Sr.	2L	Oakman, Ala. (Oakman)
72	Pete DiMario	RG	6-5	270	So.	1L	Tuscaloosa, Ala. (Central)
54	Anthony Dowdell	RDE	6-1	226	So.	SQ	Columbus, Ga. (Shaw)
57	Lamont Floyd	LLB	6-2	240	So.	1L	Orange Park, Fla. (Orange Park)
49	Jeff Foshee	FB	5-9	207	Sr.	3L	Millbrook, Ala. (Stanhope Elmore)
68	Will Friend	LG	6-3	270	Fr.	SQ	Philadelphia, Miss. (Neshoba Central)
22	Willie Gaston	RCB	5-11	183	Sr.	2L	Mobile, Ala. (Murphy)
37	Rhondi Gibson	CB	5-10	185	Jr.	SQ	Brewton, Ala. (T.R. Miller)
38	Patrick Hape	TE	6-4	240	So.	1L	Killen, Ala. (Brooks)
60	Joey Harville	LT	6-5	285	Sr.	3L	Moulton, Ala. (Hatton)
8	Tracy High	RCB	5-9	175	Jr.	1L	Pontotoc, Miss. (Pontotoc)
50	Joel Holliday	LT	6-4	275	Fr.	SQ	Six Mile, S.C. (Daniel)
91	Dameian Jeffries	LDE	6-4	274	Sr.	3L	Sylacauga, Ala. (B.B. Comer)
10	Tommy Johnson	LCB	5-10	180	Sr.	3L	Niceville, Fla. (Niceville)
5	Tony Jonson	TE	6-5	248	Jr.	2L	Como, Miss. (North Panola)
56	Chris Jordan	RT	6-6	290	Fr.	SQ	Jackson, Ala. (Jackson)
19	Chad Key	SE	6-4	210	Jr.	1L	Parrish, Ala. (Walker)
9	Freddie Kitchens	QB	6-3	200	So.	1L	Attalla, Ala. (Etowah)
83	Will Knowlton	LLB	6-3	217	Jr.	SQ	Fayette, Ala. (Fayette County)
36	Kevin Komisar	LLB	6-0	200	Jr.	SQ	Nashville, Tenn. (Hillwood)
81*	Chester Lewis	SN/TE	6-4	236	So.	SQ	Tuscaloosa, Ala. (Tuscaloosa Academy)
45	Tarrant Lynch	FB	6-1	224	Sr.	3L	Town Creek, Ala. (Hazlewood)
74	Kareem McNeal	RT	6-5	287	Jr.	2L	Tuskegee, Ala. (Alabama Christian)
80	Toderick Malone	Fla.	6-0	185	Jr.	1L	Attalla, Ala. (Etowah)
95	Kelvin Moore	RDE	6-3	240	So.	1L	Daphne, Ala. (Daphne)
16	Josh Niblett	TE	6-2	208	Jr.	1L	Demopolis, Ala. (Dempolis Academy)
79	Jeremy Pennington	RG	6-3	270	So.	1L	Vernon, Ala. (Lamar County)
42	Paul Pickett	LLB	6-3	230	Fr.	SQ	LaGrange, Ga. (LaGrange)
78	Ozell Powell	RDT	6-5	275	So.	1L	Greenville, Ala. (Greenville)
3	Michael Proctor	PK	5-11	183	Jr.	2L	Pelham, Ala. (Pelham)
34	Marlon Reyes	LCB	5-10	176	Fr.	SQ	Mexico, Ala. (Darlington)
52	Michael Rogers	RLB	6-1	232	Sr.	3L	Luverne, Ala. (Luverne)
13	Cedric Samuel	RCB	5-9	170	So.	1L	Dempolis, Ala. (Dempolis)
31	Sam Shade	SS	6-1	190	Sr.	3L	Birmingham, Ala. (Wenonah)
23	Andre Short	SS	5-11	205	Fr.	SQ	LaGrange, Ga. (LaGrange)
53	Darrell Smith	C	6-2	265	So.	SQ	Munford, Ala. (Munford)
41	Ralph Staten	RLB	6-3	200	So.	1L	Semmes, Ala. (Mary Montgomery)
28	Brian Steger	RB	6-3	210	So.	1L	New Market, Ala. (Buckhorn)
69	Jon Stevenson	RG	6-3	275	Sr.	3L	Memphis, Tenn. (Christian Brothers)
46	John Tanks	RLB	6-2	226	Jr.	1L	Butler, Ala. (Choctaw County)
93	Steve Thompson	LDT	6-5	270	Fr.	SQ	Birmingham, Ala. (Berry)
96	Bryan Thornton	RDT	6-7	280	Jr.	2L	Mobile, Ala. (LeFlore)
6	Lance Tucker	QB	6-0	175	Fr.	SQ	Fayette, Ala. (Fayette County)
39	Eric Turner	SS	6-1	200	Jr.	2L	Ft. Payne, Ala. (Ft. Payne)
30	Taurus Turner	FB	6-1	200	So.	1L	Ft. Payne, Ala. (Ft. Payne)
25	Dameian Vallery	RB	6-2	200	Fr.	SQ	Aldine, Texas (MacArthur)
81	Edgar Walker	LDE	6-4	240	Fr.	SQ	Dothan, Ala. (Dothan)
90	John Walters	LLB	6-2	225	Jr.	2L	Dallas, Texas (Lake Highlands)
15	William Watts	PK	6-1	180	So.	1L	Pleasant Grove, Ala. (Pleasant Grove)
1	Marcell West	Fla.	5-11	177	So.	1L	Niceville, Fla. (Niceville)
4	Matt Wethington	PK	5-11	176	Sr.	1L	Titusville, Fla. (Titusville)
51	Laron White	C	6-2	272	So.	1L	Courtland, Ala. (Courtland)
20	Sherman Williams	RB	5-10	193	Sr.	3L	Mobile, Ala. (Blount)

*Duplicate Number

Numerical Roster

No.	Name	Pos.
1	Marcell West	Fla.
3	Michael Proctor	PK
4	Matt Wethington	PK
5	Tony Johnson	TE
6	Lance Tucker	QB
7	Jay Barker	QB
8	Tracy High	RCB
9	Freddie Kitchens	QB
10	Tommy Johnson	LCB
12	Bryne Diehl	P
13	Cedric Samuel	RCB
14	Brian Burgdorf	QB
15	William Watts	PK
16	Josh Niblett	TE
19	Chad Key	SE
20	Sherman Williams	RB
22	Willie Gaston	RCB
23	Andre Short	SS
24	Blair Canale	FS
25	Dameian Vallery	RB
26	Michael Ausmus	FS
26*	Carl Albright	H
27	Danny Davis	SS
28	Brian Steger	RB
29	Tracy Cummings	FB
30	Taurus Turner	FB
31	Sam Shade	SS
32	Curtis Alexander	RB
33	Hunter Christian	LOB
34	Marlon Reyes	LCB
35	Derek Cunningham	RCB
36	Kevin Komisar	LLB
37	Rhondi Gibson	CB
38	Patrick Hape	TE
39	Eric Turner	SS
40	Mickey Conn	LCB
41	Ralph Staten	RLB
42	Paul Pickett	LLB
44	Darrell Blackburn	RDE
45	Tarrant Lynch	FB
46	John Tanks	RLB
49	Jeff Foshee	FB
50	Joel Holliday	LT
51	Laron White	C
52	Michael Rogers	RLB
53	Darrell Smith	C
54	Anthony Dowdell	RDE
55	Fernando Davis	LLB
56	Chris Jordan	RT
57	Lamont Floyd	LLB
60	Joey Harville	LT
64	Maurice Belser	LG
66	Tim Barnett	LT
68	Will Friend	LG
69	Jon Stevenson	RG
71	John Causey	C
72	Pete DiMario	RG
74	Kareem McNeal	RT
75	Shannon Brown	LDT
76	Elverett Brown	RDT
78	Ozell Powell	RDT
79	Jeremy Pennington	RG
80	Toderick Malone	FL
81	Edgar Walker	LDE
81*	Chester Lewis	SN/TE
83	Will Knowlton	LLB
84	Roman Colburn	SE
85	Curtis Brown	SE
90	John Walters	LLB
91	Dameian Jeffries	LDE
92	Tyrell Buckner	LLB
93	Steve Thompson	LDT
94	Kendrick Burton	LDT
95	Kelvin Moore	RDE
96	Bryan Thornton	RDT
97	Vann Bodden	LDE

*Duplicate Number

Alabama

1994 Alabama Depth Chart

OFFENSE

SE:	85	Curtis Brown
	19	Chad Key
LT:	60	Joey Harville
	74	Kareem McNeal
LG:	64	Maurice Belser
	79	Jeremy Pennington
C:	69	JON STEVENSON
	53	Darrell Smith
RG:	51	Laron White
	72	Pete DiMario
RT:	50	Joel Holliday
	56	Chris Jordan
TE:	38	Patrick Hape
	5	TONY JOHNSON
WR:	80	Toderick Malone
	37	Rhondi Gibson
QB:	7	JAY BARKER
	14	Brian Burgdorf
RB:	20	SHERMAN WILLIAMS
	28	Brian Steger
FB:	45	TARRANT LYNCH
	30	Taurus Turner

DEFENSE

LE:	91	Dameian Jeffries
	97	Vann Bodden
LT:	75	Shannon Brown
	94	Kendrick Burton
RT:	78	Ozell Powell
	96	Bryan Thornton
RE:	76	ELVERETT BROWN
	95	Kelvin Moore
OLB:	42	Paul Pickett
	55	Fernando Davis
MLB:	52	MICHAEL ROGERS
	90	John Walters
OLB:	41	Ralph Staten
	46	John Tanks
LCB:	10	TOMMY JOHNSON
	40	Mickey Conn
SS:	31	SAM SHADE
	39	Eric Turner
FS:	24	Blaire Canale
	26	Michael Ausmus
RCB:	22	WILLIE GASTON
	13	Cedric Samuel

SPECIALISTS

PK:	3	MICHAEL PROCTOR
	15	William Watts
P:	12	BRYNE DIEHL
	6	Hayden Stockton

Returning Starters In All Capitals

1994 Alabama Signees

Name	Pos.	Ht.	Wt.	Hometown/High School
Michael Coleman	DB	5-11	195	Nashville, Tenn./Stratford
Chris Edwards	LB	6-2	215	Bessemer, Ala./Jess Lanier
Brad Ford	DB	5-10	170	Dadeville, Ala./Fresno City CC
Warren Foust	QB	6-3	205	Midwest City, Okla./Midwest City
Calvin Hall	WR	6-4	190	Gallatin, Tenn./Gallatin
Steven Harris	LB	6-2	215	Town Creek, Ala./Hazlewood
Matt Harrison	OL	6-5	260	Dadeville, Ala./Dadeville
Chris Hood	LB	6-3	240	Town Creek, Ala./Hazlewood
Eddie Hunter	LB	6-2	215	LeFlore, Ala./LeFlore
Eric Kerley	DL	6-2	280	Hoover, Ala./Berry
Montoya Madden	RB	5-9	205	Town Creek, Ala./Hazlewood
Franz Odom	LB	6-1	240	Semmes, Ala./Mary Montgomery
Matt Parker	DL	6-4	260	Lawton, Okla./NE Okla. JC
John David Phillips	QB	6-4	195	Anniston, Ala./Anniston
Dennis Riddle	RB	6-0	195	Tuscaloosa, Ala./Central
Dwayne Rudd	LB	6-3	240	Batesville, Miss./S. Panola
Rod Rutledge	TE	6-5	230	Birmingham, Ala./Erwin
Kenneth Scissum	RB	6-1	210	Attalla, Ala./Etowah
Chris Sign	OL	6-2	250	Arlington, Texas/Lamar
Tito Smith	LB	6-3	200	Birmingham, Ala./Shades Valley
Sage Spree	OL	6-4	275	Eutaw, Ala./Warrior Academy
Josh Swords	OL	6-3	275	Brentwood, Tenn./Brentwood Academy
Deshea Townsend	DB	5-10	170	Batesville, Miss./S. Panola
Granison Wagstaff	LB	6-2	225	Enterprise, Ala./Enterprise
Owen Winston	DB	6-0	175	Montgomery, Ala./Carver

Tarrant Lynch

Jay Barker

1994 SEC Football 29

Alabama Year-By-Year Records

Year	Coach	SEC	SEC Finish	Overall	Bowls
1892	E.N. Beaumont			2-2	
1893	Eli Abbott			0-4	
1894	Eli Abbott			3-1	
1895	Eli Abbott			0-4	
1896	Otto Wagonhurst			2-1	
1897	Allen McCants			1-0	
1898	No Team				
1899	W.A. Hartin			3-1	
1900	M. Griffin			2-3	
1901	M.H. Harvey			2-1-2	
1902	Eli Abbott, J.O. Heyworth			4-4	
1903	W.B. Blount			3-4	
1904	W.B. Blount			7-3	
1905	Jack Leavenworth			6-4	
1906	J.W.H. Pollard			5-1	
1907	J.W.H. Pollard			5-1-2	
1908	J.W.H. Pollard			6-1-1	
1909	J.W.H. Pollard			5-1-2	
1910	Guy S. Lowman			4-4	
1911	D.V. Graves			5-2-2	
1912	D.V. Graves			5-3-1	
1913	D.V. Graves			6-3	
1914	D.V. Graves			5-4	
1915	Thomas Kelly			6-2	
1916	Thomas Kelly			6-3	
1917	Thomas Kelly			5-2-1	
1918	No Team				
1919	Xen C. Scott			8-1	
1920	Xen C. Scott			10-1	
1921	Xen C. Scott			5-4-2	
1922	Xen C. Scott			6-3-1	
1923	Wallace Wade			7-2-1	
1924	Wallace Wade			8-1	
1925	Wallace Wade			10-0	Rose
1926	Wallace Wade			9-0-1	Rose
1927	Wallace Wade			5-4-1	
1928	Wallace Wade			6-3	
1929	Wallace Wade			6-3	
1930	Wallace Wade			10-0	Rose
1931	Frank W. Thomas			9-1	
1932	Frank W. Thomas			8-2	
1933	Frank W. Thomas	5-0-1	1	7-1-1	—
1934	Frank W. Thomas	7-0-0	1t	10-0-0	Rose
1935	Frank W. Thomas	4-2-0	5	6-2-1	—
1936	Frank W. Thomas	5-0-1	2	8-0-1	—
1937	Frank W. Thomas	6-0-0	1	9-1-0	Rose
1938	Frank W. Thomas	4-1-1	2t	7-1-1	—
1939	Frank W. Thomas	2-3-1	8	5-3-1	—
1940	Frank W. Thomas	4-2-0	4	7-2-0	—
1941	Frank W. Thomas	5-2-0	3	9-2-0	Cotton
1942	Frank W. Thomas	4-2-0	5	8-3-0	Orange
1943	No Team				
1944	Frank W. Thomas	3-1-2	3t	5-2-2	Sugar
1945	Frank W. Thomas	6-0-0	1	10-0-0	Rose
1946	Frank W. Thomas	4-3-0	6	7-4-0	—
1947	H.D. "Red" Drew	6-2-0	3	8-3-0	Sugar
1948	H.D. "Red" Drew	4-4-1	6t	6-4-1	—
1949	H.D. "Red" Drew	4-3-1	6	6-3-1	—
1950	H.D. "Red" Drew	6-2-0	3	9-2-0	—
1951	H.D. "Red" Drew	3-5-0	7t	5-6-0	—
1952	H.D. "Red" Drew	4-2-0	4	4-2-0	Orange
1953	H.D. "Red" Drew	4-0-3	1	6-3-3	Cotton
1954	H.D. "Red" Drew	3-3-2	6t	4-5-2	—
1955	J.B. "Ears" Whitworth	0-7-0	12	0-10-0	—
1956	J.B. "Ears" Whitworth	2-5-0	8t	2-7-1	—
1957	J.B. "Ears" Whitworth	1-6-1	11	2-7-1	—
1958	Paul "Bear" Bryant	3-4-1	6t	5-4-1	—
1959	Paul "Bear" Bryant	4-1-2	4	7-2-2	Liberty
1960	Paul "Bear" Bryant	5-1-1	3	8-1-2	Bluebonnet
1961	Paul "Bear" Bryant	7-0-0	1t	11-0-0	Sugar
1962	Paul "Bear" Bryant	6-1-0	2	10-1-0	Orange
1963	Paul "Bear" Bryant	6-2-0	3	9-2-0	Sugar
1964	Paul "Bear" Bryant	8-0-0	1	10-1-0	Orange
1965	Paul "Bear" Bryant	6-1-1	1	9-1-1	Orange
1966	Paul "Bear" Bryant	6-0-0	1t	11-0-0	Sugar
1967	Paul "Bear" Bryant	5-1-0	2	8-2-1	Cotton
1968	Paul "Bear" Bryant	4-2-0	3t	8-3-0	Gator
1969	Paul "Bear" Bryant	2-4-0	8	6-5-0	Liberty
1970	Paul "Bear" Bryant	3-4-0	7t	6-5-1	Bluebonnet
1971	Paul "Bear" Bryant	7-0-0	1	11-1-0	Orange
1972	Paul "Bear" Bryant	7-1-0	1	10-2-0	Cotton
1973	Paul "Bear" Bryant	8-0-0	1	11-1-0	Sugar
1974	Paul "Bear" Bryant	6-0-0	1	11-1-0	Orange
1975	Paul "Bear" Bryant	6-0-0	1	11-1-0	Sugar
1976	Paul "Bear" Bryant	5-2-0	3	9-3-0	Liberty
1977	Paul "Bear" Bryant	7-0-0	1t	11-1-0	Sugar
1978	Paul "Bear" Bryant	6-0-0	1	11-1-0	Sugar
1979	Paul "Bear" Bryant	6-0-0	1	12-0-0	Sugar
1980	Paul "Bear" Bryant	5-1-0	2t	10-2-0	Cotton
1981	Paul "Bear" Bryant	6-0-0	1t	9-2-1	Cotton
1982	Paul "Bear" Bryant	3-3-0	6t	8-4-0	Liberty
1983	Ray Perkins	4-2-0	3t	8-4-0	Sun
1984	Ray Perkins	2-4-0	7t	5-6-0	—
1985	Ray Perkins	4-1-1	2t	9-2-1	Aloha
1986	Ray Perkins	4-2-0	2t	10-3-0	Sun
1987	Bill Curry	4-2-0	4t	7-5-0	Hall of Fame
1988	Bill Curry	4-3-0	4t	9-3-0	Sun
1989	Bill Curry	6-1-0	1t	10-2-0	Sugar
1990	Gene Stallings	5-2-0	2t	7-5-0	Fiesta
1991	Gene Stallings	6-1-0	2	11-1-0	Blockbuster
1992	Gene Stallings	8-0-0	1	13-0-0	Sugar
1993	Gene Stallings	5-2-1	1-W	9-3-1	Gator

Bowl Results (26-17-3)

Bowl	Opponent	Result	Date
Rose	Washington	W 20-19	1-1-26
Rose	Stanford	T 7-7	1-1-27
Rose	Washington State	W 24-0	1-1-31
Rose	Stanford	W 29-13	1-1-35
Cotton	Texas A&M	W 29-21	1-1-42
Orange	Boston College	W 37-21	1-1-43
Sugar	Duke	L 26-29	1-1-45
Rose	Southern Cal	W 34-14	1-1-46
Sugar	Texas	L 7-27	1-1-48
Orange	Syracuse	W 61-6	1-1-53
Cotton	Rice	L 6-28	1-1-54
Liberty	Penn State	L 0-7	12-9-59
Bluebonnet	Texas	T 3-3	12-17-60
Sugar	Arkansas	W 10-3	1-1-62
Orange	Oklahoma	W 17-0	1-1-63
Sugar	Ole Miss	W 12-7	1-1-64
Orange	Texas	L 17-21	1-1-65
Orange	Nebraska	W 39-28	1-1-66
Sugar	Nebraska	W 34-7	1-2-67
Cotton	Texas A&M	L 16-20	1-1-68
Gator	Missouri	L 10-35	12-28-68
Liberty	Colorado	L 33-47	12-13-69
Bluebonnet	Oklahoma	T 24-24	12-31-70
Orange	Nebraska	L 6-38	1-1-72
Cotton	Texas	L 13-17	1-1-73
Sugar	Notre Dame	L 23-24	1-1-74
Orange	Notre Dame	L 11-13	1-1-75
Sugar	Penn State	W 13-6	12-31-75
Liberty	UCLA	W 36-6	12-20-76
Sugar	Ohio State	W 35-6	1-2-78
Sugar	Penn State	W 14-7	1-1-79
Sugar	Arkansas	W 24-9	1-1-80
Cotton	Baylor	W 30-2	1-1-81
Cotton	Texas	L 12-14	1-1-82
Liberty	Illinois	W 21-15	12-29-82
Sun	Southern Methodist	W 28-7	12-24-83
Aloha	Southern Cal	W 24-3	12-28-85
Sun	Washington	W 28-6	12-25-86
Hall of Fame	Michigan	L 24-28	1-2-88
Sun	Army	W 29-28	12-29-88
Sugar	Miami (Florida)	L 25-33	1-1-90
Fiesta	Louisville	L 7-35	1-1-91
Blockbuster	Colorado	W 30-25	12-28-91
Sugar	Miami (Florida)	W 34-13	1-1-93
Gator	North Carolina	W 24-10	12-31-93

Alabama

Alabama vs. All Opponents

Opponent	W	L	T
Arkansas	4	0	0
Arkansas State	1	0	0
Army	1	0	0
Auburn	33	24	1
Baylor	2	0	0
Birmingham	2	3	0
Birmingham-Southern	11	0	0
Boston College	1	3	0
Bryson College	1	0	0
California	1	1	0
Carlisle	0	1	0
Case College	1	0	0
Centre	2	1	0
Chattanooga	9	0	0
Cincinnati	5	0	0
Clemson	11	3	0
Cumberland	0	1	0
Colorado	1	1	0
Davidson	1	0	0
Delta State	1	0	0
Duke	1	1	0
Duquesne	3	0	0
*Florida	17	9	0
Florida State	3	0	1
Fordham	1	1	0
Furman	5	0	0
George Washington	3	0	0
Georgia	33	22	4
Georgia Tech	28	21	3
Haskell	1	0	0
Houston	7	0	0
Illinois	1	0	0
Kentucky	30	1	1
LSU	37	15	5
Louisiana Tech	3	0	0
Louisville	2	1	0
Loyola (New Orleans)	1	0	0
Marion Institute	9	0	0
Maryland	2	1	0
Maryville	3	0	0
Memphis State	6	1	0
Mercer	2	0	0
Michigan	0	1	0
Miami	14	3	0
Millsaps	3	0	0
Mississippi	33	6	2
Mississippi College	7	0	0
Mississippi State	64	11	3
Missouri	1	2	0
Nashville	1	0	0
Nebraska	3	2	0
North Carolina	1	0	0
North Carolina State	3	0	0
Notre Dame	1	5	0
Oglethorpe	2	0	0
Ohio State	2	0	0
Oklahoma	1	0	1
Pennsylvania	1	0	0
Penn State	8	5	0
Richmond	1	0	0
Rice	0	3	0
Rutgers	2	0	0
St. Mary's	1	0	0
Samford	20	0	1
Sewanee	17	10	3
South Carolina	9	0	0
Southern Cal	5	2	0
Southern Methodist	2	0	0
Southern Mississippi	23	4	2
Southwestern	2	0	0
Southwestern Louisiana	7	0	0
Spring Hill	3	0	0
Stanford	1	0	1
Syracuse	1	1	0
Tampa	1	0	0
Temple	3	0	0
Tennessee	41	27	8
Texas	0	7	1
Texas A&M	3	1	0
Texas Christian	2	3	0
Tulane	26	10	3
Tulsa	3	0	0
UCLA	1	0	0
Union	4	0	0
Vanderbilt	49	18	4
Villanova	0	1	0
Virginia Tech	10	0	0
Washington	4	0	0
Washington & Lee	1	0	0
Washington State	1	0	0
Wichita State	1	0	0
Wisconsin	0	1	0

*disagreement between school about series record

Alabama's dramatic goal line stand in the 1979 Sugar Bowl gave the Crimson Tide a 14-7 victory over Penn State and coach Paul "Bear" Bryant his sixth national championship.

1994 SEC Football

Alabama School Records

Individual

Game
Total Offense	457	Scott Hunter vs. Auburn	(1969)
Yards Rushing	284	Bobby Humphrey vs. Miss. State	(1986)
Rushing Attempts	42	Johnny Musso vs. Auburn	(1970)
Yards Passing	484	Scott Hunter vs. Auburn	(1969)
Pass Attempts	55	Scott Hunter vs. Auburn	(1969)
Pass Completions	32	Gary Hollingsworth vs. Tennessee	(1989)
Yards Receiving	217	David Palmer vs. Vanderbilt	(1993)
Receptions	12	David Bailey vs. Auburn	(1969)

Season
Total Offense	2,329	Walter Lewis	(1983)
Yards Rushing	1,471	Bobby Humphrey	(1986)
Rushing Attempts	238	Bobby Humphrey	(1987)
Yards Passing	2,379	Gary Hollingsworth	(1989)
Pass Attempts	339	Gary Hollingsworth	(1989)
Pass Completions	205	Gary Hollingsworth	(1989)
Touchdown Passes	16	Mike Shula	(1985)
Yards Receiving	1000	David Palmer	(1993)
Receptions	61	David Palmer	(1993)
Touchdown Catches	10	Al Lary	(1950)
Interceptions	10	Hootie Ingram	(1952)
Points	108	Siran Stacy	(1989)

Career
Total Offense	5,690	Walter Lewis	(1980-83)
Yards Rushing	3,228	Bobby Humphrey	(1985-88)
Rushing Attempts	615	Bobby Humphrey	(1985-88)
Yards Passing	4,899	Scott Hunter	(1968-70)
Pass Attempts	672	Scott Hunter	(1968-70)
Pass Completions	382	Scott Hunter	(1968-70)
Touchdown Passes	35	Mike Shula	(1983-86)
Yards Receiving	2,070	Ozzie Newsome	(1974-77)
Receptions	132	David Bailey	(1969-71)
Touchdown Catches	18	Dennis Homan	(1965-67)
Interceptions	19	Antonio Langham	(1990-93)
Points	312	Van Tiffin	(1983-86)

Team

Game
Points	89	vs. Delta State	(1951)
Total Offense	833	vs. Virginia Tech	(1973)
Yards Rushing	748	vs. Virginia Tech	(1973)
Yards Passing	484	vs. Auburn	(1969)
First Downs	34	vs. Penn State	(1983)
Total Defense	-5	vs. Vanderbilt	(1945)
Rushing Defense	16	vs. Auburn	(1971)
Passing Defense	0	vs. Tulane	(1957)
		vs. Chattanooga	(1959)

Season
Points	454	(1973)
Total Offense	5,288	(1973)
Yards Rushing	4,027	(1973)
Yards Passing	2,707	(1969)
First Downs	263	(1979)
Fewest Points Allowed	15	(1933)
Total Defense	596	(1938)
Rushing Defense	305	(1938)
Passing Defense	291	(1938)
Consecutive Wins	28	(Twice, last Sept. 21, 1991 to October 2, 1993)

David Palmer

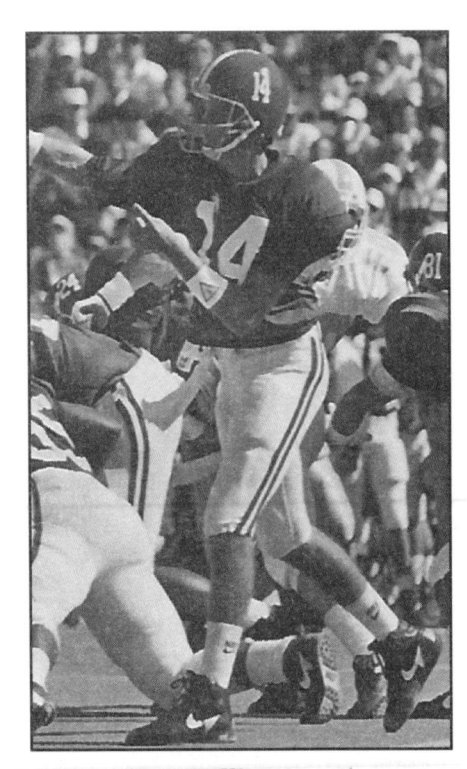

Gary Hollingsworth

Alabama

Alabama in the NFL

Ray Abruzzese, DB
Buffalo Bills 1962-64; NY Jets 1965-66
Butch Avinger, B
New York Giants 1953
Buddy Aydelette, G
Green Bay Packers 1980; Pittsburgh Steelers 1987
Bob Baumhower, DT
Miami Dolphins 1977-84, 1986
Jesse Bendross, SE
San Diego Chargers 1984-85
Cornelius Bennett, LB
Buffalo Bills 1987-93
George Bethune, DL
LA Rams 1989-90
Lew Bostick, G
LA Rams 1939-42
Jim Bowdoin, G
Green Bay Packers 1928-31; NY Giants 1932
Steve Bowman, B
NY Giants 1966
Thomas Boyd, LB
Detroit Lions 1987
Byron Braggs, DT
Green Bay Packers 1981-83; Tampa Bay Buccaneers 1984-85
Tommy Brooker, TE-K
Kansas City Chiefs 1962-66
Dave Brown, B
NY Giants 1943, 1946-47
Phillip Brown, B
Atlanta Falcons 1988
Bill Buckler, G
Chicago Bears 1926-28, 1931-33
Jim Cain, E
St. Louis Cardinals 1949; Detroit Lions 1950, 1953-55
Tom Calvin, B
Pittsburgh Steelers 1952-54
Paul Ott Carruth, RB
Green Bay Packers 1986-88
Joe Carter, RB
Miami Dolphins 1984-86
Jeremiah Castille, DB
Tampa Bay Buccaneers 1983-86; Denver Broncos 1987-88
Thornton Chandler, TE
Dallas Cowboys 1986-89
Jackie Cline, DL
Miami Dolphins 1987-89; Atlanta Falcons 1990
Ted Cook, E
Detroit Lions 1947; Green Bay Packers 1948-50
John Copeland, DL
Cincinnati Bengals 1993
Russ Craft, B
Philadelphia Eagles 1946-53; Pittsburgh Steelers 1954
Paul Crane, LB
NY Jets 1966-72
Sylvester Croom, C
New Orleans Saints 1975
Howard Cross, TE
NY Giants 1989-93
Bob Cryder, G
New England Patriots 1978-83; Seattle Seahawks 1984-86; Detroit Lions 1987-88
Ed Culpepper, G
St. Louis Cardinals 1958-60; Minnesota Vikings 1961; Houston Oilers 1962-63
Eric Curry, DL
Tampa Bay Buccaneers 1993
Fred Davis, T
Washington Redskins 1941-42, 1945; Chicago Bears 1946-51
Johnny Davis, RB
Tampa Bay Buccaneers 1978-80; San Francisco 49ers 1981-82; Cleveland Browns 1983-86
Ricky Davis, S
Cincinnati Bengals 1975; Tampa Bay Buccaneers 1976; Kansas City Chiefs 1977
Wayne Davis, LB
St. Louis Cardinals 1987; Phoenix Cardinals 1988
Chuck DeShane, B
Detroit Lions 1945-49
Joe Dommanovich, C
Boston Yankees 1948-50; NY Yankees 1950-51
Philip Doyle, Pk
NY Giants, 1991
Randy Edwards, DT
Seattle Seahawks 1984-86
Leon Fichman, T
Detroit Lions 1946-47

Greg Gantt, P
NY Jets 1974-75
Woody Gerber, G
Philadelphia Eagles 1941-42
Harry Gilmer, QB
Washington Redskins 1948-52, 1954; Detroit Lions 1955-56
Chris Goode, DB
Indianapolis Colts 1987-93
Kerry Goode
Tampa Bay Buccaneers 1988
Preston Gothard, TE
Pittsburgh Steelers 1985-88
Jon Hand, DT
Indianapolis Colts 1986-93
Charley Hannah, T-DE
Tampa Bay Buccaneers 1977-82; LA Raiders 1983-88
Herb Hannah, T
NY Giants 1951
John Hannah, G
New England Patriots 1973-85
Paul Harris, LB
Tampa Bay Buccaneers 1977-78
Tony Holm, B
St. Louis Cardinals 1932; Pittsburgh Steelers 1933
Dennis Homan, WR
Dallas Cowboys 1968-70; Kansas City Chiefs 1971-72
Dixie Howell, B
Washington Redskins 1937
Bobby Humphrey, RB
Denver Broncos 1989-90; Miami Dolphins 1992
Scott Hunter, QB
Green Bay Packers 1971-73; Buffalo Bills 1974; Atlanta Falcons 1976-78; Detroit Lions 1979
Tom Hupke, G
Detroit Lions 1934-37; Cleveland Rams 1938-39
Don Hutson, E-K
Green Bay Packers 1935-45
Billy Jackson, RB
Kansas City Chiefs 1981-86
Bobby Jackson, B
Philadelphia Eagles 1960; Chicago Bears 1961
Wilbur Jackson, RB
San Francisco 49ers 1974-79; Washington Redskins 1980-82
Curt Jarvis, NG
Tampa Bay Buccaneers 1987-90
Bruce Jones, G
Green Bay Packers 1927-28
Joey Jones, WR
Atlanta Falcons 1986-87
Ralph Jones, E
Detroit Lions 1946; Baltimore Colts 1947
Robbie Jones, LB
NY Giants 1984-88
Terry Jones, DT
Green Bay Packers 1978-86
Lee Roy Jordan, LB
Dallas Cowboys 1963-76
E.J. Junior, LB
St. Louis Cardinals 1981-87; Phoenix Cardinals 1988; Miami Dolphins 1989-91; Seattle Seahawks 1993
Les Kelley, LB
New Orleans Saints 1967-69
Emanuel King, LB
Cincinnati Bengals 1985-88; LA Raiders 1989-90
Barry Krauss, LB
Baltimore Colts 1979-83; Indianapolis Colts 1984-88; Miami Dolphins 1989-90
Derrick Lassic, TB
Dallas Cowboys 1993
Larry Lauer, C
Green Bay Packers 1956-57
Bill Lee, T
Green Bay Packers 1937-42, 1946
Tony Leon, G
Washington Redskins 1943
Walter Lewis, QB
New England Patriots 1987
Antonio London, LB
Detroit Lions 1993

Woodrow Lowe, LB
San Diego Chargers 1976-87
Bobby Luna, B
San Francisco 49ers 1955; Pittsburgh Steelers 1959
Marty Lyons, DE
NY Jets 1979-90
Ken MacAfee, E
NY Giants 1954-58; Philadelphia Eagles 1959; Washington Redskins 1959
Vaughn Mancha, C
Boston Yankees 1948
John Mangum, CB
Chicago Bears 1990-93
Frank Martin, B
Chicago Bears 1941; NY Giants 1945
Keith McCants, LB
Tampa Bay Buccaneers 1990-92; Houston Oilers 1993
Joel McCoy, B
Detroit Lions 1946
Curtis McGriff, DT
NY Giants 1980-86
Mark McMillian, CB
Philadelphia Eagles 1992-93
Don McNeal, CB
Miami Dolphins 1980-89
Chris Mohr, P
Tampa Bay Buccaneers 1989; Buffalo Bills 1991-93
Ricky Moore, RB
Buffalo Bills 1986
Norm Mosley, B
Pittsburgh Steelers 1948
Russ Mosley, B
Green Bay Packers 1945-46
Steve Mott, C
Detroit Lions 1983-89
Johnny Musso, RB
Chicago Bears 1975-77
Joe Namath, QB
NY Jets 1965-76; LA Rams 1977
Tony Nathan, RB
Miami Dolphins 1979-87
Billy Neighbors, G
New England Patriots 1962-65; Miami Dolphins 1966-69
Benny Nelson, S
Houston Oilers 1964
Ozzie Newsome, TE
Cleveland Browns 1978-90
Derrick Oden, LB
Philadelphia Eagles 1993
Ray Ogden, TE
St. Louis Cardinals 1965-66; New Orleans Saints 1967; Atlanta Falcons 1967-68; Chicago Bears 1969-71
Mitchell Olenski, T
Detroit Lions 1947
Norman Olsen, T
Cleveland Rams 1944
Ray Perkins, WR
Baltimore Colts 1967-71
Benny Perrin, DB
St. Louis Cardinals 1982-85
Claude Perry, T
Green Bay Packers 1927-35
Mike Pitts, LB
Atlanta Falcons 1983-86; Philadelphia Eagles 1987-92; New England Patriots 1993
Mike Raines, DT
San Francisco 49ers 1974
David Ray, K-WR
Los Angeles Rams 1969-74
Thomas Rayam, DT/OT
Washington Redskins 1991; Cincinnati Bengals 1992
Greg Richardson, WR
Minnesota Vikings 1987
Jess Richardson, T
Philadelphia Eagles 1953-61; New England Patriots 1962-64
Larry Roberts, DE
San Francisco 49ers 1986-92
Freddie Robinson, DB
Indianapolis Colts 1987-89; Washington Redskins 1990

Jeff Rutledge, QB
LA Rams 1979-81; NY Giants 1982-89; Washington Redskins 1990-92
Ed Salem, B
Washington Redskins 1951
Haywood (Sandy) Sanford, E
Washington Redskins 1940
Randy Scott, LB
Green Bay Packers 1981-86
Willie Shelby, KR-RB
Cincinnati Bengals 1976-77; St. Louis Cardinals 1978
Billy Shipp, T
NY Giants 1954
Mike Shula, QB
Tampa Bay Buccaneers 1987
Steve Sloan, QB
Atlanta Falcons 1966-67
Ben Smith, E
Green Bay Packers 1933; Pittsburgh Steelers 1934-35; Washington Redskins 1937
Riley Smith, B
Washington Redskins 1936-38
Brent Sowell, OL
Chicago Bears 1987
Ken Stabler, QB
Oakland Raiders 1970-79; Houston Oilers 1980-81; New Orleans Saints 1982-84
Siran Stacy, RB
Philadelphia Eagles 1992
Bart Starr, QB
Green Bay Packers 1956-71
Rebel Steiner, E
Green Bay Packers 1950-51
Dwight Stephenson, C
Miami Dolphins 1980-87
Vaughan Stewart, C
Chicago Cardinals 1943
George Teague, DB
Green Bay Packers 1993
Corky Tharp, DB
NY Jets 1960
Derrick Thomas, LB
Kansas City Chiefs 1989-93
George Thornton
San Diego Chargers 1991-92; NY Giants 1993
Van Tiffin, PK
Miami Dolphins 1987
Richard Todd, QB
NY Jets 1976-83; New Orleans Saints 1984-85; NY Jets 1986
Tommy Tolleson, WR
Atlanta Falcons 1966
Wayne Trimble, DB
San Francisco 49ers 1967
Paul Tripoli, DB
Tampa Bay Buccaneers 1987
Bob Trocolor, B
NY Giants 1942-44
Kevin Turner, FB
New England Patriots 1992-93
Mike Washington, DB
Tampa Bay Buccaneers 1976-84
Jerry Watford, E
Chicago Cardinals 1953-54
Cecil (Bull) Wesley, C
NY Giants 1928
Wayne Wheeler, WR
Chicago Bears 1974
Art (Tarzan) White, G
NY Giants 1937-39, 1945
Butch Wilson, E
Baltimore Colts 1963-67; NY Giants 1968-69
Rich Wingo, LB
Green Bay Packers 1979-84
Bob Wood, T
Chicago Cardinals 1940
Steve Wright, T
Green Bay Packers 1964-66; NY Giants 1968-69; Washington Redskins 1970; Chicago Bears 1971; St. Louis Cardinals 1972
Willie Wyatt, NG
Tampa Bay Buccaneers 1990
John Wyhonic, G
Philadelphia Eagles 1946-47
Bill Young, T
Washington Redskins 1937-42, 1946
Sid Youngelman, T
San Francisco 49ers 1955; Philadelphia Eagles 1956-58; Cleveland Browns 1959; NY Jets 1960-61; Buffalo Bills 1962-63

1994 SEC Football — 33

Alabama Media Information

Alabama Assistant Athletic Director
Larry White

Alabama Sports Information
P.O. Box 870391
Tuscaloosa, AL 35487-0391
(205) 348-6084
FAX: (205) 348-8841

White (Home): 333-1640

Football Beat Writers
Cecil Hurt
Tuscaloosa News (PM)
P.O. Drawer 1
Tuscaloosa, AL 35401
(205) 345-0505

Doug Segrest
Birmingham News (PM)
P.O. Box 2553
Birmingham, AL 35202
(205) 325-2427

Ray Melick
Birmingham Post-Herald (AM)
P.O. Box 2553
Birmingham AL 35202
(205) 325-2420

Tommy Sims
Montgomery Advertiser (AM)
P.O. Box 950
Montgomery, AL 36102
(205) 262-1611

Bill Bryant
Huntsville Times
P.O. Box 1487 West Station
Huntsville, AL 35807
(205) 532-4430

P. M. Black
Huntsville News
P.O. Box 1007
Huntsville, AL 35801
(205) 532-4430

Glenn Gilbeau
Mobile Press-Register
304 Government Street
Mobile, AL 36601
(205) 433-1551

Jimmy Smothers
Gadsden Times
P.O. Box 188
Gadsden, AL 35902
(205) 547-7521

Phillip Tutor
Anniston Star (AM)
P.O. Box 189
Anniston, AL 36201
(205) 236-1550

Other Daily Newspapers
Mark Edwards
Decatur Daily
P.O. Box 1527
Decatur, AL 35601
(205) 353-4612

Jon Johnson
Dothan Eagle
203 N. Oates Street
Dothan, AL 36301
(205) 792-3141

Jerry Felts
Times Daily
P.O. Box 797
Florence, AL 35631
(205) 766-8405

Specialty Publications
Kirk McNair
Bama Magazine
P.O. Box 6104
Tuscaloosa, AL 35486
(205) 345-5074

Wire Services
Phil Jenkins
United Press International
P.O. Box 1306
Montgomery, AL 36104
(205) 262-1951

Kendall Weaver
Associated Press
P.O. Box 1000
Montgomery, AL 36101

Television Broadcasters
Rick Karle, Mike Raita
WBRC-TV
P.O. Box 6
Birmingham, AL 35201
(205) 323-2822

Ken Lass, William Jenkins
WVTM-TV
P.O. Box 10502
Birmingham, AL 35202
(205) 328-6883

Doug Bell, Mike Dubberly
WBMG-TV
P.O. Box 6146
Birmingham, AL 35259
(205) 322-4200

Doug Holten, David Lamb
WCFT-TV
P.O. Box 5239
Tuscaloosa, AL 35401
(205) 553-1333

Gus Hergert
WAAY-TV
1000 Monte Sano Blvd.
Huntsville, AL 35801
(205) 533-3131

Steve Johnson
WHNT-TV
P.O. Box 19
Huntsville, AL 35804
(205) 533-1919

Mark Thornhill
WAFF-TV
P.O. Box 2116
Huntsville, AL 35804
(205) 533-6397

Scott Hunter
WKRG-TV
P.O. Box 160587
Mobile, AL 36616
(205) 479-5555

Eric McClendon
WALA-TV
P.O. Box 1548
Mobile, AL 36601
(205) 433-3754

Jerome Hand
WSFA-TV
P.O. Box 2566
Montgomery, AL 36105
(205) 281-2902

Chad Gentey
WAKA-TV
3020 E. Blvd.
Montgomery, AL 36116

Alabama Network
Eli Gold
2124 Rockland Dr.
Birmingham, AL 35226
(205) 979-1492

Doug Layton
119 Euclid Ave.
Birmingham, AL 35213
(205) 967-2383

Jerry Duncan
417 North 20th Street #700
Birmingham, AL 35203

Stations Carrying Games
Originator is WFFX, Tuscaloosa
Network includes more than 70 stations.

Radio Stations
WERC Radio
P.O. Box 10904
Birmingham, AL 35202
(205) 942-9600

WZZK Radio
530 Beacon Parkway W. #303
Birmingham, AL 35209
(205) 942-4566

WUAL Radio
P.O. Box 100
University, AL 35486
(205) 348-6644

WAPI Radio
2146 Highland Ave, South
Birmingham, AL 35205
(205) 933-9274

Doug Layton
WVOK Radio
Goodwin Crest Drive #500
Birmingham, AL 35209
(205) 945-4646

Campus Media
Sports Editor
Crimson White
P.O. Box A
University, AL 35486
(205) 348-6144

Alabama

ARKANSAS

DR. DANIEL FERRITOR
Chancellor

AL WITTE
Faculty Representative

FRANK BROYLES
Athletic Director

University of Arkansas

CHANCELLOR:
 Dr. Daniel Ferritor (Rockhurst 1962)
FACULTY REPRESENTATIVE:
 Al Witte (Wisconsin 1955)
ATHLETIC DIRECTOR:
 Frank Broyles (Georgia Tech 1947)
HEAD COACH:
 Danny Ford (Alabama 1970)
LOCATION: Fayetteville, Arkansas
FOUNDED: 1871
ENROLLMENT: 14,408
NICKNAME: Razorbacks
COLORS: Cardinal and White
STADIUM: Razorback Stadium (50,019) — Artificial
 War Memorial Stadium (53,727) — Little Rock - Artificial

Razorback Quick Facts

1993 RECORD: 5-5-1
 (2-3-1 Home, 3-2 Away)
1993 SEC RECORD (FINISH): 3-4-1 (2nd-Western)
 (1-2-1 Home, 2-2 Away)
BOWL: None
ALL-TIME RECORD: 550-361-40 (.599)
SEC RECORD: 5-7-2 (.429) — Regular Season Games
SEC CHAMPIONSHIPS: 0
BOWL APPEARANCES: 27
BOWL RECORD: 9-15-3 (.389)
LAST APPEARANCE: 1991 Independence Bowl
 (Georgia 24, Arkansas 15)

ARKANSAS
Team Information

OFFENSIVE SYSTEM: Multiple

DEFENSIVE SYSTEM: 4-3

LETTERMEN RETURNING: 43
- 18 Offense
- 22 Defense
- 3 Specialists

LETTERMEN LOST: 18
- 8 Offense
- 7 Defense
- 0 Specialists

STARTERS RETURNING: 13

OFFENSE (9)
- OG Pat Baker (6-3, 275, Sr.)
- FB Oscar Gray (6-2, 245, Sr.)
- QB Barry Lunney, Jr. (6-2, 190, Jr.)
- TB Oscar Malone (5-9, 180, Jr.)
- FL J.J. Meadors (5-8, 152, Jr.)
- OT Verl Mitchell (6-3, 270, Jr.)

DEFENSE (5)
- DE Marcus Adair (6-2, 225, Jr.)
- FS Carl Kidd (6-1, 200, Sr.)
- CB Dean Peevy (5-11, 185, Sr.)
- NG Junior Soli (6-1, 275, Jr.)
- DT Vernon Wade (6-4, 260, Sr.)

SPECIALISTS (2)
- K Lance Ellison (6-5, 230, Sr.)
- P Doyle Preston (6-2, 190, So.)

STARTERS LOST: 10

OFFENSE (5)
- TE Kirk Botkin (6-3, 225, Sr.)
- SE Tracy Caldwell (5-11, 182, Sr.)
- OG Isaac Davis (6-3, 295, Sr.)
- OT Chris Oliver (6-5, 275, Sr.)
- C   Don Struebing (6-3, 264, Fr.)

DEFENSE (5)
- OLB Tyrone Chatman (5-9, 220, Sr.)
- OLB Darwin Ireland (6-1, 225, Sr.)
- DE   Henry Ford (6-3, 260, Sr.)
- SS   Alfred Jackson (6-0, 190, Sr.)
- CB   Orlando Watters (5-11, 176, Sr.)

SPECIALISTS (0)

Razorback Stadium (50,019)
Record: 113-54-2 (.675)
First Game: Oct. 8, 1938 — Baylor 9, Arkansas 6
Largest Crowd: 51,496 (Nov. 7, 1987) — Arkansas 10, Baylor 7

1994 Arkansas Schedule

Sept.	3	SMU	LITTLE ROCK
Sept.	10	at South Carolina	Columbia, S.C.
Sept.	17	ALABAMA	FAYETTEVILLE
Sept.	24	at Memphis State	Memphis, Tenn.
Oct.	1	VANDERBILT	LITTLE ROCK
Oct.	8	at Tennessee	Knoxville, Tenn.
Oct.	15	OLE MISS	FAYETTEVILLE
Oct.	29	at Auburn	Auburn, Ala.
Nov.	5	at Mississippi State	Starkville, Miss.
Nov.	12	NORTHERN ILLINOIS	FAYETTEVILLE
Nov.	26	LSU	LITTLE ROCK

1995 Arkansas Schedule

Sept.	2	at SMU	Dallas, Texas
Sept.	9	SOUTH CAROLINA	FAYETTEVILLE
Sept.	16	at Alabama	Tuscaloosa, Ala.
Sept.	23	MEMPHIS STATE	LITTLE ROCK
Sept.	30	at Vanderbilt	Nashville, Tenn.
Oct.	7	TENNESSEE	FAYETTEVILLE
Oct.	14	Ole Miss	TBA
Oct.	28	AUBURN	LITTLE ROCK
Nov.	4	MISSISSIPPI STATE	LITTLE ROCK
Nov.	11	SW LOUISIANA	FAYETTEVILLE
Nov.	25	at LSU	Baton Rouge, La.

Arkansas

1993 Arkansas Individual Leaders

RUSHING	Atts.	Yards	Avg	TDs	Yds/Game
OSCAR MALONE	89	555	6.2	5	69.4
MARIUS JOHNSON	116	554	4.8	3	50.4
CARLTON CALVIN	76	350	4.6	2	31.8
OSCAR GRAY	56	243	4.3	0	22.1
DEXTER HEBERT	57	207	3.6	2	25.9

PASSING	Att	Comp	Ints/TDs	Pct	Yds
BARRY LUNNEY	202	104	7/6	.515	1241
MIKE CHERRY	14	7	1/0	.500	75
JASON ALLEN	17	3	2/0	.177	38

RECEIVING	Rec	Yds	Avg	TDs	Yds/Game
J.J. MEADORS	28	429	15.3	3	39.0
Kirk Botkin	23	257	11.2	0	25.7
OSCAR GRAY	18	173	9.6	2	15.7
Tracy Caldwell	13	176	13.5	1	19.6
KOTTO COTTON	11	131	11.9	0	19.6

SCORING	G	TDs	PAT	FGs	Tot	Avg
OSCAR MALONE	8	5	0	0	30	3.8
MARIUS JOHNSON	11	3	0	0	18	1.6
J.J. MEADORS	11	3	0	0	18	1.6
LANCE ELLISON	8	0	5	4-10	17	2.1
DAVID BOULWARE	4	0	13	1-1	16	4.0

PUNTING	No	Yds	Avg	Long
DOYLE PRESTON	56	2109	37.7	59

KICKOFF RETURNS	No	Yds	Avg	TDs	Avg/Game	Long
Orlando Watters	18	392	21.8	0	35.6	42
J.J. MEADORS	5	106	21.2	0	9.6	32
KOTTO COTTON	3	50	16.7	0	5.0	21
MIKE NUNNERLY	3	29	9.7	0	2.6	11

PUNT RETURNS	No	Yds	Avg	TDs	Avg/Game	Long
Orlando Watters	28	157	5.6	0	14.3	20

TACKLES	Total	Sk(Yds)	TL(Yds)	Ints
Darwin Ireland	93 (37-56)	1(-7)	3(-10)	0
Henry Ford	68 (42-26)	14(-85)	23(-116)	0
Orlando Watters	57 (40-17)	0	3(-9)	6
Tyrone Chatman	56 (28-28)	0	2(-3)	2
MARCUS ADAIR	54 (26-28)	7(-57)	11(-65)	0

INTERCEPTIONS	No	Yds	TDs	Int/Game	Long
Orlando Watters	6	185	2	0.6	99
Alfred Jackson	3	3	0	0.3	3

Returning Players in All Capitals

1993 Arkansas Team Statistics

	AR	OPP
FIRST DOWNS	200	223
Rushing	126	115
Passing	62	101
Penalty	12	7
NET YARDS RUSHING	2123	1853
Yards rushing	2320	2187
Yards lost	197	334
Rushing attempts	498	463
Average per rush	4.3	4.0
Average per game	193.0	168.5
NET YARDS PASSING	1354	2072
Average per game	123.1	188.4
Passes attempted	233	302
Passes completed	114	171
Had intercepted	10	13
TOTAL OFFENSIVE YARDS	3477	3925
Average per game	316.1	356.8
Total plays	731	765
Average per play	4.8	5.1
NUMBER PUNTS/YARDS	56/2109	48/1877
Punting average	37.7	39.1
Net punting average	35.7	35.8
PUNT RETURNS/YARDS	28/157	20/110
Punt return average	5.6	5.5
KICKOFF RETURNS/YARDS	36/640	29/529
Kickoff return average	17.8	18.2
PENALTIES/YARDS	49/424	72/590
Penalty yards per game	38.6	53.6
FUMBLES/LOST	25/15	23/6
INTERCEPTION RETURNS/YARDS	13/194	10/166
Interception return average	14.9	16.6
TOUCHDOWNS	22	21
Rushing	14	13
Passing	6	6
Return	2	2
FIELD GOALS MADE/ATTEMPTED	5/11	18/22
KICK EXTRA POINTS MADE/ATTEMPTED	18	21
SAFETY	0	0
TWO-POINT CONVERSIONS	0	0
TOTAL POINTS	165	208
Average per game	15.0	18.9

Marcus Adair   Barry Lunney   Oscar Malone

1993 Arkansas Results

5-5-1 Overall • 3-4-1 SEC (2nd - Western)

Date	Opponent	W/L	Score	Attendance
Sept. 4	at SMU	W	10-6	26,163
Sept. 11	SOUTH CAROLINA	W	18-17	47,321
Sept. 18	at Alabama [JP]	L	3-43	70,123
Sept. 25	MEMPHIS STATE (Little Rock)	L	0-6	51,733
Oct. 2	at Georgia	W	20-10	73,825
Oct. 9	TENNESSEE (Little Rock) [JP]	L	14-28	54,120
Oct. 16	at Ole Miss (Jackson) [JP]	L	0-19	37,000
Oct. 30	AUBURN - HC	L	21-31	50,100
Nov. 6	MISS. STATE (Little Rock)	T	13-13	50,075
Nov. 13	TULSA	W	24-11	28,525
Nov. 27	at LSU [ESPN]	W	42-24	54,239

1994 SEC Football

Danny Ford

HOMETOWN:
Gadsden, Alabama

ALMA MATER (YEAR):
Alabama (1970)

PLAYING CAREER:
Alabama offensive tackle 1967 - 69 (All-SEC 1969; Academic All-SEC 1969; Alabama Team Captain 1969)

COACHING CAREER:
Alabama Graduate Assistant 1970-71; Alabama Assistant 1972-73; Virginia Tech Assistant 1974-76; Clemson Assistant Head Coach 1977-78; Clemson Head Coach 1978-1989; Arkansas Assistant 1992; Arkansas Head Coach 1993-present.

COACHING ACHIEVEMENTS:
1981 National Coach of the Year (Walter Camp, UPI, Football Writers, Football Coaches); 1981 ACC Coach of the Year; 1981 National Champion; 1981 ACC Champion; 1982 ACC Champion; 1983 ACC Coach of the Year; 1986 ACC Champion; 1987 ACC Champion; 1988 ACC Champion.

BORN:
April 2, 1948

WIFE:
Deborah Anderson

CHILDREN:
Jennifer 21, Ashleigh 18, Mary Elizabeth 13, Daniel Lee 8

ASSISTANT COACHES:
LOUIS CAMPBELL (Arkansas 1973) - Secondary
ROCKEY FELKER (Mississippi State 1975) - Quarterbacks
FITZ HILL (Ouachita Baptist 1987) - Wide Receivers
BUDDY KING (Clemson 1973) - Offensive Line
JOE KINES (Jacksonville State 1966) - Defensive Coordinator
DAVID MITCHELL (Arkansas State 1974) - Running Backs
JOE PATE (Alabama 1968) - Linebackers
LARRY VAN DER HEYDEN (Iowa State 1964) - Offensive Line
JIM WASHBURN (Gardner Webb 1973) - Defensive Line

SUPPORT STAFF:
HAROLD HORTON (Arkansas 1962) - Director of Football Operations
VIRGIL KNIGHT (Northeastern State College 1970) - Strength Coach
DEAN WEBER (Bridgewater 1967) -Trainer

Year-By-Year Record

Year	School	Conf.	All	Bowl
1978	Clemson	—	1-0	Gator
1979	Clemson	4-2 (t2nd)	8-4	Peach
1980	Clemson	2-4 (t4th)	6-5	
1981	Clemson	6-0 (1st)	12-0	Orange
1982	Clemson	6-0 (1st)	9-1-1	
1983	Clemson	—	9-1-1	
1984	Clemson	—	7-4	
1985	Clemson	4-3 (t3rd)	6-6	Independence
1986	Clemson	5-1-1 (1st)	8-2-2	Gator
1987	Clemson	6-1 (1st)	10-2	Citrus
1988	Clemson	5-1 (1st)	10-2	Citrus
1989	Clemson	5-2 (3rd)	10-2	Gator
1993	Arkansas	3-4-1 (2nd-W)	5-5-1	

OVERALL RECORD	46-18-2 (.712)	101-34-5 (.739)	13 Years
Arkansas Record	3-4-1	5-5-1	1 Year
Clemson Record	43-14-1	96-29-4	12 Years
Bowl Record	6-2	(6-2 Clemson)	

Arkansas

Arkansas All-Star Candidates

PAT BAKER
Senior • Offensive Guard
6-3 • 310 • Owasso, Okla.

• Started all 11 games last season after transferring from Northeast Oklahoma Junior College where he earned All-America and All-Conference status.
• Improved dramatically as the season progressed and is being projected as an All-SEC player by the Arkansas coaching staff for the 1994 season.
• Earned the starting nod in 1993 despite having suffered a broken leg in the first two days of his first spring practice.

CARL KIDD
Senior • Free Safety
6-1 • 198 • Pine Bluff, Ark.

• Recorded 53 tackles, the second-highest number among the Arkansas defensive backs last season. Also posted six pass break-ups.
• Earned All-America honors in 1992 at Northeast Oklahoma Junior College before transferring to Arkansas.
• Started all 11 games at free safety last season.

KIDD STATS

Year	Tackles	Solos	Assists	TFL-Yds	Sacks-Yds	PBU
1993	53	22	31	0	0	6

J.J. MEADORS
Junior • Flanker
5-6 • 153 • Ruston, La.

• Emerged as Arkansas' biggest playmaker in 1993, averaging 15.3 yards on 28 receptions and making the team's longest play of the season, a 72-yard TD catch versus Georgia.
• Recorded two 72-yard receiving games, versus Georgia and Auburn. Also caught six passes for 70 yards against Ole Miss.
• Averaged 21.2 yards on five kickoff returns and ran the reverse once for five yards.

DEAN PEEVY
Senior • Cornerback
5-11 • 185 • Montgomery, Ala.

• Has quietly been one of Arkansas' most solid performers, earning the starting position prior to the first game of 1992 and starting 18 games over the past two campaigns.
• Posted five interceptions during the 1992 season and has seven career thefts, just three shy of the Razorbacks' all-time top 10.
• Registered 25 tackles last year, including 15 unassisted stops, and has 66 career stops. Also has six career pass breakups.

MEADORS STATS

Year	Rec	Yds	Avg	TD
1992	1	25	25.0	0
1993	28	429	15.3	3
Career	29	453	15.6	3

PEEVY STATS

Year	Tackles	Solos	Assists	TFL(-Yds)	PBU	INT
1990	2	2	0	0	0	0
1992	39	23	16	2(-7)	4	5
1993	25	15	10	0	2	2
Career	66	40	26	2(-7)	6	7

1994 SEC Football

1994 Arkansas Roster

No.	Name	Pos.	Ht.	Wt.	Class	Exp.	Hometown (High School/JC)
50	Marcus Adair	DE	6-3	221	Jr.	1L	Memphis, Tenn. (East/Air Force)
76	Winston Alderson	OG	6-4	298	So.	SQ	El Dorado, Ark. (El Dorado)
	Bobby Aldridge	LB	5-11	206	So.	SQ	Springdale, Ark. (Springdale)
13	Jason Allen	QB	6-1	196	Sr.	3L	Edmond, Okla. (Edmond)
87	Ken Anderson	DE	6-4	298	Fr.	RS	Shreveport, La. (Captain Shreve)
	Polo Arellano-Friar	SS	5-8	165	Fr.	HS	Fayetteville, Ark.
19	Lawrence Arnold	CB	5-9	184	So.	SQ	Crossett, Ark. (Crossett)
	Ed Baker	WR	5-10	162	Jr.	HS	St. Paul, Minn. (St. Paul)
83	Mark Baker	TE	6-2	255	Fr.	RS	Osceola, Ark. (Osceola)
61	Pat Baker	OG	6-3	310	Sr.	1L	Owasso, Okla. (Owasso/NEO)
6	Alan Behrman	K	5-7	158	Fr.	RS	Montgomery, Ala. (Jeff Davis)
91	Geno Bell	NG	6-2	290	So.	1L	Columbia, S.C. (Columbia)
15	David Boulware	K	5-8	150	So.	1L	Matthews, N.C. (Sun Valley)
42	Vincent Bradford	LB	6-2	221	So.	1L	Malvern, Ark. (Malvern)
51	Sam Brooks	LB	5-11	234	Fr.	RS	Odessa, Ark. (Permian)
32	Spencer Brown	CB	5-11	178	Jr.	2L	Morrilton, Ark. (Morrilton)
39	Carlton Calvin	FB	6-0	236	Sr.	3L	Keller, Texas (Keller)
4	Marcus Campbell	CB	6-0	181	Fr.	RS	North Little Rock, Ark. (N. Little Rock)
21	Tracy Cantlope	CB	5-10	179	Jr.	2L	Dothan, Ala. (Northview)
18	Mike Cherry	QB	6-4	219	So.	1L	Texarkana, Ark. (Arkansas)
20	Leon Clark	TB	5-10	185	Fr.	RS	South Garland, Texas (S. Garland)
	Ponce Clark	TB	5-11	196	So.	RS	Evanston, Ill. (Township)
94	Steven Conley	DE	6-5	217	Jr.	2L	Chicago, Ill. (Luther South)
23	Jessie Cornelius	FB	6-0	204	So.	SQ	Dallas, Texas (Carter)
69	Bryan Cornish	OT	6-4	304	Sr.	3L	Warren, Ark. (Warren)
5	Kotto Cotton	SE	6-0	187	Sr.	3L	North Little Rock, Ark. (N. Little Rock)
96	Darius Cummings	DE	6-2	246	Sr.	SQ	Ft. Smith, Ark. (Southside)
	Mike Davis	OLB	6-0	205	Fr.	HS	Arlington, Texas (Arlington)
3	Del Delco	FS	6-0	208	Jr.	2L	Houston, Texas (Mayde Creek)
	Jason DeWitt	CB	6-0	200	Fr.	RS	Siloam Springs, Ark. (Siloam Springs)
74	Derek Don de'Ville	OG	6-2	270	So.	SQ	Kirkwood, Mo. (Vianney)
14	Lance Ellison	K	6-5	242	Sr.	3L	Conway, Ark. (Conway)
9	Anthony Eubanks	SE	6-2	190	Fr.	RS	Spiro, Okla. (Spiro)
67	Zach Finger	C	6-4	263	Fr.	RS	Fayetteville, Ark. (Fayetteville)
	Matthew Freedman	P	5-9	165	Fr.	RS	Laredo, Texas (United High)
	Cody Gildon	CB	5-10	177	Fr.	RS	Texarkana, Texas (Pleasant Grove)
31	Oscar Gray	FB	6-2	270	Sr.	2L	Houston, Texas (Smiley)
	Bryan Hantes	QB	6-1	190	Fr.	RS	Red Oak, Texas (Red Oak)
	Alex Harris	TB	5-11	208	Fr.	RS	Hot Springs, Texas (Hot Springs)
35	Dexter Hebert	TB	5-7	204	So.	1L	Beaumont, Texas (Kelly)
8	Anthony Hicks	OLB	6-2	217	So.	1L	Arkadelphia, Ark. (Arkadelphia)
82	Kevin Hile	TE	6-3	230	Jr.	1L	Lee's Summitt, Mo. (Lee's Summitt)
65	Bryan Hudson	OT	6-5	270	Fr.	RS	Alexander, Ark. (Bryant)
84	Carl Johnson	TE	6-2	240	Jr.	2L	Pine Bluff, Ark. (Dollarway)
24	Cordale Johnson	TB	5-10	195	Sr.	2L	Denver, Colo. (Mullen)
22	Marius Johnson	TB	5-8	179	Jr.	2L	Houston, Texas (Austin)
40	Willie Johnson	OLB	6-0	228	Sr.	3L	Lufkin, Texas (Lufkin)
	Pat Kenning	DE	6-3	236	Fr.	RS	Dunwoody, Ga. (Bolles)
2	Carl Kidd	SS	6-1	198	Jr.	1L	Pine Bluff, Ark. (Dollarway/NEO)
98	Chris Kinnebrew	NG	5-11	310	Sr.	2L	Ansonia, Conn. (Ansonia)
56	Trent Knapp	LB	6-0	230	Sr.	2L	Houston, Texas (Clements)
	Chris Labbe	OT	6-6	305	Fr.	HS	Waterfall, Texas (Mesalaskee)
89	Chad Lairamore	TE	6-4	232	Fr.	RS	Ozark, Ark. (Ozark)
38	Duane Lawson	FB	6-0	220	So.	SQ	Richardson, Texas (Berkner)
7	Barry Lunney, Jr.	QB	6-2	187	Jr.	2L	Ft. Smith, Ark. (Southside)
30	Oscar Malone	TB	5-8	192	Jr.	2L	Gadsden, Ala. (Gadsden)
1	J.J. Meadors	FL	5-6	153	Jr.	2L	Ruston, La. (Ruston)
62	Chris Miller	C	6-1	278	So.	1L	Angleton, Texas (Angleton)
72	Verl Mitchell	OT	6-3	282	Jr.	2L	Paragould, Ark. (Paragould)
80	Eddie Mosley	DT	6-4	269	So.	SQ	Memphis, Tenn. (Trezevant)
68	Tony Nagy	C	6-5	277	Jr.	1L	Tulsa, Okla. (Union)
	Saint Nelson	CB	5-8	184	So.	RS	Arlington, Texas (Arlington)
27	Mike Nunnerley	SS	6-1	203	Jr.	2L	North Little Rock, Ark. (N. Pulaski)
63	Jason Ogden	OG	6-2	303	So.	SQ	Friendswood, Texas (Friendswood)
10	Dean Peevy	CB	5-11	185	Sr.	3L	Montgomery, Ala. (Lee)
25	James Perry	SE	5-8	173	So.	1L	Houston, Texas (Northbrook)
59	Cole Plafcan	OG	6-4	270	Jr.	SQ	Little Rock, Ark. (Catholic)
17	Doyle Preston	P	6-2	190	Jr.	2L	Saltillo, Texas (Mt. Vernon)
	William Price	FB	5-10	210	Fr.	RS	League City, Texas (Clear Brook)
26	Brian Proud	TB	5-7	172	So.	SQ	Springdale, Ark. (Shiloh Christian)
70	Scott Rivers	OT	6-5	260	So.	SQ	Benton, Ark. (Benton)
95	David Sanders	DE	6-4	279	Fr.	RS	Jackson, Miss. (Provine)
66	Earl Scott	C	6-2	272	Jr.	2L	North Little Rock, Ark. (N. Little Rock)
	William Sharp	K	5-9	165	So.	TR	Waco, Texas (Midway)
73	Shannon Shelby	OT	6-5	257	So.	1L	Houston, Texas (Worthing)
71	Carlos Showers	OT	6-5	278	So.	SQ	Morrilton, Ark. (Morrilton)
	Shannon Sidney	FL	6-1	170	Fr.	RS	Russellville, Ark. (Russellville)
	Andre Simmons	LB	5-9	248	Fr.	RS	Hughes, Ark. (Hughes)
	Mike Simmons	FS	6-2	216	Fr.	RS	Houston, Texas (Clear Brook)
46	Demetrius Smith	OLB	6-2	230	Sr.	2L	Little Rock, Ark. (Mills)
44	Mark Smith	OLB	6-3	230	So.	1L	Webb City, Mo. (Webb City)
	Tracey Smith	TB	6-0	192	Fr.	RS	Forrest City, Ark. (Forrest City)
90	Junior Soli	NG	6-1	289	Jr.	2L	Columbus, Ga. (Spencer)
79	Anthony Swartz	OG	6-3	301	So.	SQ	Dickinson, Texas (Dickinson)
99	Curtis Thomas	DT	6-3	270	Jr.	2L	Baytown, Texas (Lee)
	Dan Thompson	FL	5-11	163	Fr.	RS	Westlake Village, Calif.
37	Derrick Thompson	SE	5-9	160	Sr.	1L	Ft. Worth, Texas (Dunbar)
33	Tate Turner	FB	6-0	217	Fr.	RS	Camdenton, Mo. (Camdenton)
93	Vernon Wade	DT	6-3	270	Sr.	2L	Lufkin, Texas (Lufkin)
11	Matt Wait	P	6-0	226	Fr.	RS	Hot Springs, Ark. (Lake Hamilton)
	Zach Weatherford	OLB	6-1	209	So.	HS	North Little Rock, Ark. (N. Little Rock)
85	Waylon Wishon	DE	6-0	248	Jr.	2L	Rogers, Ark. (Rogers)

Numerical Roster

No.	Name	Pos.
1	J. J. Meadors	FL
2	Carl Kidd	SS
3	Del Delco	FS
4	Marcus Campbell	CB
5	Kotto Cotton	SE
6	Alan Behrman	K
7	Barry Lunney, Jr.	QB
8	Anthony Hicks	OLB
9	Anthony Eubanks	SE
10	Dean Peevy	CB
11	Matt Wait	P
13	Jason Allen	QB
14	Lance Ellison	K
15	David Boulware	K
17	Doyle Preston	P
18	Mike Cherry	QB
19	Lawrence Arnold	CB
20	Leon Clark	TB
21	Tracy Cantlope	CB
22	Marius Johnson	TB
23	Jessie Cornelius	FB
24	Cordale Johnson	TB
25	James Perry	SE
26	Brian Proud	TB
27	Mike Nunnerley	SS
30	Oscar Malone	TB
31	Oscar Gray	FB
32	Spencer Brown	CB
33	Tate Turner	FB
35	Dexter Hebert	TB
37	Derrick Thompson	SE
38	Duane Lawson	FB
39	Carlton Calvin	FB
40	Willie Johnson	OLB
42	Vincent Bradford	LB
44	Mark Smith	OLB
46	Demetrius Smith	OLB
50	Marcus Adair	DE
51	Sam Brooks	LB
56	Trent Knapp	LB
59	Cole Plafcan	OG
61	Pat Baker	OG
62	Chris Miller	C
63	Jason Ogden	OG
65	Bryan Hudson	OT
66	Earl Scott	C
67	Zach Finger	C
68	Tony Nagy	C
69	Bryan Cornish	OT
70	Scott Rivers	OT
71	Carlos Showers	OT
72	Verl Mitchell	OT
73	Shannon Shelby	OT
74	Derek Don de'Ville	OG
76	Winston Alderson	OG
79	Anthony Swartz	OG
80	Eddie Mosley	DT
82	Kevin Hile	TE
83	Mark Baker	TE
84	Carl Johnson	TE
85	Waylon Wishon	DE
87	Ken Anderson	DE
89	Chad Lairamore	TE
90	Junior Soli	NG
91	Geno Bell	NG
93	Vernon Wade	DT
94	Steven Conley	DE
95	David Sanders	DE
96	Darius Cummings	DE
98	Chris Kennebrew	NG
99	Curtis Thomas	DT

1994 Arkansas Depth Chart

OFFENSE

SE:	26	Kotto Cotton
	25	James Perry
	or 9	Anthony Eubanks
LT:	72	VERL MITCHELL
	71	Carlos Showers
LG:	61	PAT BAKER
	59	Cole Plafcan
C:	66	Earl Scott
	68	Tony Nagy
RG:	76	Winston Alderson
	79	Tony Swartz
RT:	70	Scott Rivers
	73	Shannon Shelby
TE:	84	Carl Johnson
	82	Kevin Hile
FL:	1	J. J. MEADORS
	19	Shannon Sidney
QB:	18	Mike Cherry
	13	Jason Allen
	7	BARRY LUNNEY, JR.
TB:	30	OSCAR MALONE
	22	Marius Johnson
FB:	39	CARLTON CALVIN
	31	Oscar Gray

DEFENSE

RE:	50	MARCUS ADAIR
	87	Ken Anderson
T:	99	Curtis Thomas
	93	VERNON WADE
NG:	90	JUNIOR SOLI
	91	Geno Bell
E:	85	Waylon Wishon
	94	Steve Conley
WLB:	40	Willie Johnson
	8	Anthony Hicks
MLB:	56	Trent Knapp
	42	Vincent Bradford
SLB:	44	Mark Smith
	46	Demetrius Smith
LC:	32	Spencer Brown
	21	Tracy Cantlope
RC:	10	DEAN PEEVY
		Saint Nelson
SS:	2	CARL KIDD
	27	Mike Nunnerley
FS:	3	Del Delco
		Mike Simmons

SPECIALISTS

K:	15	David Boulware
	14	LANCE ELLISON
P:	11	Matt Wait
		Matthew Freedman

Returning Starters In All Capitals

1994 Arkansas Signees

Name	Pos.	Ht.	Wt.	Hometown/High School
Chad Abernathy	L	6-5	250	Mountain View, Ark./Mountain View
Melvin Bradley	LB	6-2	235	Barton, Ark./Barton
Don Bray	LB	6-2	220	Carrollton, Ga./NE Okla. A&M
Anthony Brightman	L	6-5	265	Memphis, Tenn./Houston
Russ Brown	L	6-2	265	Bristow, Okla./Bristow
Marvin Caston	LB	6-3	224	Winnsboro, La./Winnsboro
Nathan Cole	OLB	6-5	213	Albertville, Ala./Albertville
Glen Davidson	L	6-5	250	Tupelo, Miss./Tupelo
Grant Garrett	OC	6-4	270	Lake Hamilton, Ark./Lake Hamilton
Quinn Guidry	PK	5-10	155	Boutte, La./Hahnville
Ryan Hale	L	6-5	265	Rogers, Ark./Rogers
DeAnthony Hall	CB	5-11	190	Tuscaloosa, Ala./Central
Derrick Harrell	LB/FB	6-3	235	Dumas, Ark./Dumas
Tyrone Henry	B	6-0	216	Wilson, Ark./Rivercrest
Al Heringer	TE/LB	6-5	222	Jonesboro, Ark./Jonesboro
Madre Hill	B	6-1	182	Malvern, Ark./Malvern
Mike Higgins	WR	6-3	205	Carrollton, Ga./NE Okla. A&M
Brad Houston	PK	5-10	165	Brandon, Miss./NW Rankin Attn.
Jeremy Irons	WR	6-3	185	Park Forest, Ill./Rich East
Fred Johnson	L	6-3	265	Dallas, Texas/H. Grady Spruce
Norman Nero	DB	6-3	195	Atmore, Ala./Escambia County
Zac Painter	DB	5-10	184	Jonesboro, Ark./Jonesboro
Robert Reed	QB	6-2	200	Brandon, Miss./NW Rankin Attn.
Chad Row	L	6-5	245	Flower Mound, Texas/Flower Mound

Barry Lunney, Jr.   **Oscar Malone**

1994 SEC Football

Arkansas Year-By-Year Records

Year	Coach	Conf	Finish	Overall	Bowls
1894	John C. Futrall			2-1	
1895	John C. Futrall			1-0	
1896	John C. Futrall			2-1	
1897	B.N. Wilson			2-0-1	
1898	B.N. Wilson			2-1	
1899	Colbert Searles			3-1-1	
1900	Colbert Searles			2-1-1	
1901	Charles Thomas			3-5	
1902	Charles Thomas			6-3	
1903	D.A. McDaniel			3-4	
1904	A.D. Brown			4-5	
1905	A.D. Brown			2-6	
1906	F.C. Longman			2-4-2	
1907	F.C. Longman			3-4-1	
1908	Hugo Bezdek			5-4	
1909	Hugo Bezdek			7-0	
1910	Hugo Bezdek			7-1	
1911	Hugo Bezdek			6-2-1	
1912	Hugo Bezdek			4-6	
1913	E.T. Pickering			7-2	
1914	E.T. Pickering			4-5	
1915	T.T. McConnell	1-1	2t	4-2-1	
1916	T.T. McConnell	0-2	5t	4-4	
1917	Norman Paine	0-1-1	6	5-1-1	
1918	Norman Paine	0-1	6t	3-2	
1919	J.B. Craig	1-2	5	3-4	
1920	G.W. McLaren	2-0-1	2	3-2-2	
1921	G.W. McLaren	2-1	3	5-3-1	
1922	Francis Schmidt	1-3	6	5-4	
1923	Francis Schmidt	2-2	4t	6-2-1	
1924	Francis Schmidt	1-2-1	7	7-2-1	
1925	Francis Schmidt	2-2-1	4t	4-4-1	
1926	Francis Schmidt	2-2	3t	5-5	
1927	Francis Schmidt	3-1	3	8-1	
1928	Francis Schmidt	3-1	2	7-2	
1929	Fred Thomsen	3-2	3	7-2	
1930	Fred Thomsen	2-2	5	3-6	
1931	Fred Thomsen	0-4	7	3-5-1	
1932	Fred Thomsen	1-4	7	1-6-2	
1933	Fred Thomsen	4-1	1	7-3-1	Dixie
1934	Fred Thomsen	2-3-1	5	4-4-2	—
1935	Fred Thomsen	2-4	5	5-5	—
1936	Fred Thomsen	5-1	1	7-3	—
1937	Fred Thomsen	3-2-1	3	6-2-2	—
1938	Fred Thomsen	1-5	6t	2-7-1	—
1939	Fred Thomsen	2-3-1	5	4-5-1	—
1940	Fred Thomsen	1-5	6	4-6	—
1941	Fred Thomsen	0-6	7	3-7	—
1942	George Cole	0-6	7	3-7	—
1943	John Tomlin	1-4	5t	2-7	—
1944	Glen Rose	2-2-1	3	5-5-1	—
1945	Glen Rose	1-5	7	3-7	—
1946	John Barnhill	5-1	1t	6-3-2	Cotton
1947	John Barnhill	1-4-1	5t	6-4-1	Dixie
1948	John Barnhill	2-4	5	5-5	—
1949	John Barnhill	2-4	6	5-5	—
1950	Otis Douglas	1-5	7	2-8	—
1951	Otis Douglas	2-4	6	5-5	—
1952	Otis Douglas	1-5	7	2-8	—
1953	Bowden Wyatt	2-4	5	3-7	—
1954	Bowden Wyatt	5-1	1	8-3	Cotton
1955	Jack Mitchell	3-2-1	4	5-4-1	—
1956	Jack Mitchell	3-3	4	6-4	—
1957	Jack Mitchell	2-4	5t	6-4	—
1958	Frank Broyles	2-4	5t	4-6	—
1959	Frank Broyles	5-1	1t	9-2	Gator
1960	Frank Broyles	6-1	1	8-3	Cotton

Year	Coach	Conf	Finish	Overall	Bowl
1961	Frank Broyles	6-1	1t	8-3	Sugar
1962	Frank Broyles	6-1	2	9-2	Sugar
1963	Frank Broyles	3-4	4	5-5	—
1964	Frank Broyles	7-0	1	11-0	Cotton
1965	Frank Broyles	7-0	1	10-1	Cotton
1966	Frank Broyles	5-2	2t	8-2	—
1967	Frank Broyles	3-3-1	5	4-5-1	—
1968	Frank Broyles	6-1	1t	10-1	Sugar
1969	Frank Broyles	6-1	2	9-2	Sugar
1970	Frank Broyles	6-1	2	9-2	—
1971	Frank Broyles	5-1-1	2	8-3-1	Liberty
1972	Frank Broyles	3-4	4t	6-5	—
1973	Frank Broyles	3-3-1	4t	5-5-1	—
1974	Frank Broyles	3-3-1	4t	6-4-1	—
1975	Frank Broyles	6-1	1t	10-2	Cotton
1976	Frank Broyles	3-4-1	6	5-5-1	—
1977	Lou Holtz	7-1	2	11-1	Orange
1978	Lou Holtz	6-2	2t	9-2-1	Fiesta
1979	Lou Holtz	7-1	1t	10-2	Sugar
1980	Lou Holtz	3-5	6t	7-5	Hall of Fame
1981	Lou Holtz	5-3	4	8-4	Gator
1982	Lou Holtz	5-2-1	3	9-2-1	Bluebonnet
1983	Lou Holtz	4-4	5	6-5	—
1984	Ken Hatfield	5-3	3t	7-4-1	Liberty
1985	Ken Hatfield	6-2	2t	10-2	Holiday
1986	Ken Hatfield	6-2	2t	9-3	Orange
1987	Ken Hatfield	5-2	2t	9-4	Liberty
1988	Ken Hatfield	7-0	1	10-2	Cotton
1989	Ken Hatfield	7-1	1	10-2	Cotton
1990	Jack Crowe	1-7	7	3-8	—
1991	Jack Crowe	5-3	2t	6-6	Independence
1992	Jack Crowe/Joe Kines	3-4-1	4-W	3-7-1	—
1993	Danny Ford	3-4-1	2-W	5-5-1	—

Bowl Results (9-15-3)

Date	Bowl	Opponent	Result	
1-1-34	Dixie	Centenary	T	7-7
1-1-47	Cotton	LSU	T	0-0
1-1-48	Dixie	William & Mary	W	21-19
1-1-55	Cotton	Georgia Tech	L	6-14
1-1-60	Gator	Georgia Tech	W	14-7
1-1-61	Cotton	Duke	L	6-7
1-1-62	Sugar	Alabama	L	3-10
1-1-63	Sugar	Ole Miss	L	13-17
1-1-65	Cotton	Nebraska	W	10-7
1-1-66	Cotton	LSU	L	7-14
1-1-69	Sugar	Georgia	W	16-2
1-1-70	Sugar	Ole Miss	L	22-27
12-20-71	Liberty	Tennessee	L	13-14
1-1-76	Cotton	Georgia	W	31-10
1-2-78	Orange	Oklahoma	W	31-6
12-25-78	Fiesta	UCLA	T	10-10
1-1-80	Sugar	Alabama	L	9-24
12-27-80	Hall of Fame	Tulane	W	34-15
12-28-81	Gator	North Carolina	L	27-31
12-31-82	Bluebonnet	Florida	W	28-24
12-27-84	Liberty	Auburn	L	15-21
12-22-85	Holiday	Arizona State	W	18-17
1-1-87	Orange	Oklahoma	L	8-42
12-29-87	Liberty	Georgia	L	17-20
1-2-89	Cotton	UCLA	L	3-17
1-1-90	Cotton	Tennessee	L	27-31
12-29-91	Independence	Georgia	L	15-24

Arkansas

Arkansas vs. All Opponents

Opponent	W	L	T
Abilene Christian	1	0	0
Air Force	1	0	0
Alabama	0	4	0
Arkansas A&M	1	0	0
Arizona State	2	0	0
Auburn	0	2	1
Austin College	2	0	0
Barksdale Field	1	0	0
Baylor	35	33	2
California	1	0	0
Camp Pike	0	1	0
Centenary	3	1	2
Central Arkansas	2	0	0
Central Missouri State	1	0	0
Central Oklahoma State	1	0	0
Chicago	0	0	1
Chiloco College	1	1	0
Citadel	0	1	0
College of the Ozarks	8	0	0
Colorado State	3	0	0
Dallas Medics	0	1	0
Detroit	2	0	0
Drury College	13	5	2
Duke	0	1	0
East. Central Oklahoma	4	0	0
East Texas State	1	0	0
Fairmont College	2	0	0
Florida	1	0	0
Fordham	0	1	0
Ft. Scott High	2	2	0
Ft. Smith High	8	0	0
George Washington	0	1	1
Georgia	3	3	0
Georgia Tech	1	1	0
Hardin-Simmons	3	0	0
Haskell College	1	0	1
Hawaii	1	0	0
Henderson State	6	0	0
Hendrix College	15	0	2
Houston	12	6	0
Iowa	0	1	0
Iowa State	1	0	0
Joplin High	1	0	1
Kansas	0	2	0
Kansas City Medics	1	1	0
Kansas State	1	3	0
Kentucky	0	1	0
Kingfisher College	1	0	0
Little Rock High	0	1	0
Louisiana State	14	23	2
Louisiana Tech	1	0	0
Memphis State	0	2	0
Miami (Fla.)	0	3	0
Mississippi	20	19	1
Mississippi State	0	3	1
Missouri	1	2	0
Missouri-Rolla	15	4	0
Monticello Navy	0	1	0
Navy	2	0	0
Nebraska	1	0	0
Neosho High	1	0	0
New Mexico	2	0	0
New Mexico State	3	0	0
NE Oklahoma	1	0	0
Norman Navy	0	1	0
North Carolina	0	1	0
North Texas St.	7	0	0
NW Louisiana St.	3	0	0
Northwestern	1	0	0
Oklahoma	4	9	1
Oklahoma Baptist	2	1	0
Oklahoma Mine	1	0	0

Opponent	W	L	T
Oklahoma State	30	15	1
Ouachita College	6	2	1
Pacific	1	0	0
Phillips College	4	0	1
Pierce City College	1	2	0
Pittsburg State	4	0	0
Rice	35	29	3
Santa Clara	0	2	0
St. Louis University	1	2	1
SE Missouri State	1	0	1
South Carolina	2	0	0
Southern California	1	2	0
Southern Methodist	34	28	5
Southwestern Louisiana	1	0	0
SW Missouri State	3	2	0
Stanford	0	1	0
Tahlequah Seminary	1	0	0
Tennessee	1	4	0
Texas	19	54	0
Texas A&M	38	24	3
Texas Christian	43	23	2
Texas-El Paso	1	0	0
Texas Southwestern	3	0	1
Texas Tech	28	7	0
Tulane	3	0	0
Tulsa	51	15	3
UCLA	0	1	1
Utah State	2	0	0
Vanderbilt	2	1	0
Villanova	0	1	0
Washington (St. Louis)	4	1	0
Webb City High	1	0	0
Wichita State	6	0	0
William & Mary	1	2	0
Wisconsin	0	1	0

Current athletic director Frank Broyles is the winningest coach in Arkansas history, having guided the Razorbacks to a 144-58-5 mark including seven conference titles and the 1964 National Championship.

1994 SEC Football

Arkansas School Records

Individual

Game
Total Offense	360	Bill Montgomery vs. Ole Miss	(1970)
Yards Rushing	271	Dickey Morton vs. Baylor	(1973)
Rushing Attempts	38	David Dickey vs. Southern Methodist	(1966)
Yards Passing	345	Joe Ferguson vs. Texas A&M	(1971)
Pass Attempts	51	Joe Ferguson vs. Texas A&M	(1971)
Pass Completions	31	Joe Ferguson vs. Texas A&M	(1971)
Yards Receiving	204	Mike Reppond vs. Rice	(1971)
Receptions	13	Wear Schoonover vs. Baylor	(1929)
		James Shibest vs. Southern Methodist	(1984)

Season
Total Offense	2,212	Quinn Grovey	(1990)
Yards Rushing	1,298	Dickey Morton	(1973)
Rushing Attempts	242	Dickey Morton	(1972)
Yards Passing	2,203	Joe Ferguson	(1971)
Pass Attempts	271	Joe Ferguson	(1971)
Pass Completions	160	Joe Ferguson	(1971)
Touchdown Passes	18	Quinn Grovey	(1990)
Yards Receiving	986	Mike Reppond	(1971)
Receptions	56	Mike Reppond	(1971)
Touchdown Catches	8	Chuck Dicus	(1968)
		Derek Russell	(1990)
Interceptions	9	Jim Rinehart	(1949)
Points	120	Bill Burnett	(1969)

Career
Total Offense	5,916	Quinn Grovey	(1987-90)
Yards Rushing	3,570	Ben Cowins	(1975-78)
Rushing Attempts	635	Ben Cowins	(1975-78)
Yards Passing	4,802	Brad Taylor	(1981-84)
Pass Attempts	644	Brad Taylor	(1981-84)
Pass Completions	337	Bill Montgomery	(1968-70)
Touchdown Passes	29	Bill Montgomery	(1968-70)
		Quinn Grovey	(1987-90)
Yards Receiving	1,920	James Shibest	(1983-86)
Receptions	118	Chuck Dicus	(1968-70)
Touchdown Catches	16	Chuck Dicus	(1968-70)
		Derek Russell	(1987-90)
Interceptions	14	Steve Atwater	(1985-88)
Points	294	Bill Burnett	(1968-70)

Team

Game
Points	100	vs. Southwest Missouri State	(1911)
Total Offense	658	vs. Texas Christian	(1970)
Yards Rushing	520	vs. Texas Tech	(1978)
Yards Passing	372	vs. Oklahoma State	(1943)
First Downs	37	vs. Texas Christian	(1980)
Total Defense	17	vs. Pittsburg State	(1936)
		vs. Kansas	(1936)
Rushing Defense	-25	vs. Texas Tech	(1981)
Passing Defense	0	Six Times	
		Last: vs. Southern Methodist	(1975)

Season
Points	402	(1970)
Total Offense	4,926	(1989)
Yards Rushing	3,523	(1975)
Yards Passing	2,448	(1970)
First Downs	269	(1971)
Fewest Points Allowed	57	(1964)
Total Defense	1,774	(1961)
Rushing Defense	756	(1965)
Passing Defense	538	(1954)
Consecutive Wins	22	(November 23, 1963 to January 1, 1966)

Quinn Grovey

Dickey Morton

Arkansas

Arkansas in the NFL

Gary Adams
Philadelphia Eagles
O'Neal Adams
New York Giants, Brooklyn
Lance Alworth
San Diego Chargers, Dallas Cowboys
Gary Anderson
San Diego Chargers, Tampa Bay Buccaneers
Rick Apolskis
New York Giants
Steve Atwater
Denver Broncos
Herman Bagby
Brooklyn, Cleveland Browns
Alton Baldwin
Buffalo Bills, Green Bay Packers
Hubert Barker
New York Giants
Mike Bender
Atlanta Falcons
Jim Benton
Cleveland Browns, Chicago Bears, Los Angeles
Danny Brabham
Houston Oilers, Cincinnati Bengals
Maurice Britt
Detroit Lions
Jon Brittenum
San Diego Chargers
Williams Brooks
Detroit Lions
Richard Brothers
Chicago Bears
Bill Brown
Washington Redskins, Green Bay Packers
Trent Bryant
Kansas City Chiefs, Washington Redskins
Wes Bryant
Minnesota Vikings
Scott Bull
San Francisco 49ers
Dick Bumpas
Pittsburgh Steelers
Bobby Burnett
Buffalo Bills, Denver Broncos
Ravin Caldwell
Washington Redskins
Leon Campbell
Chicago Bears, Pittsburgh Steelers
Lewis Carpenter
Detroit Lions, Cleveland Browns
Preston Carpenter
Cleveland Browns, Washington Redskins, Miami Dolphins, Minnesota Vikings
Albert Casey
St. Louis Browns
Daryl Cato
Miami Dolphins
Ronnie Caveness
Houston Oilers, Kansas City Chiefs
Freddie Childress
Cincinnati Bengals, Oakland Raiders, Dallas Cowboys, New England Patriots, Cleveland Browns
Jessie Clark
Green Bay Packers, Detroit Lions, Phoenix Cardinals
Thomas Cobb
Kansas City Chiefs, Cleveland Browns, Detroit Lions, Chicago Bears
Raymond Cole
Milwaukee
James Collier
New York Giants, Washington Redskins
Anthoney Cooney
Chicago Bears

Charles Corgan
Kansas City Chiefs, Hartford, New York Giants
Ben Cowins
Philadelphia Eagles, Kansas City Chiefs
Steve Cox
Cleveland Browns, Washington Redskins
Reggie Craig
Kansas City Chiefs, Cleveland Browns
Elbert Crawford
Los Angeles Rams, New England Patriots, Denver Broncos
Milan Creighton
Chicago Cardinals
Bobby Crockett
Buffalo Bills
Dick Cunningham
Philadelphia Eagles, Houston Oilers, Detroit Lions, Buffalo Bills
Chuck Dicus
San Diego Chargers, Pittsburgh Steelers
Freddie Douglas
Pittsburgh Steelers, Tampa Bay Buccaneers
Bobby Duckworth
San Diego Chargers, Los Angeles
Paul Dudley
New York Giants, Philadelphia Eagles
Kay Eakin
New York Giants, Miami Dolphins
Jerry Eckwood
Tampa Bay Buccaneers
Bobby Joe Edmonds
Seattle Seahawks, Tampa Bay Buccaneers, Detroit Lions
Ron Faurot
New York Jets
Joe Ferguson
Buffalo Bills, Detroit Lions, Tampa Bay Buccaneers
Milton Fields
Washington Redskins
Ike Forte
New York Giants
Barry Foster
Pittsburgh Steelers
Aubrey Fowler
Baltimore Colts
Tom Ginn
Detroit Lions
Bob Griffin
Los Angeles, Detroit Lions
Ray Hamilton
Cleveland Browns, Detroit Lions, Los Angeles
Dan Hampton
Chicago Bears
Dave Hanner
Green Bay Packers
LaSalle Harper
New York Giants
Leotis Harris
Green Bay Packers
Ken Hayden
Philadelphia Eagles, Washington Redskins
Chuck Herman
Atlanta Falcons
Howard Hickey
Cleveland Browns, Los Angeles
Glen Ray Hines
Houston oilers, New Orleans Saints, Pittsburgh Steelers
Bill Hix
Philadelphia Eagles
John Hoffman
Chicago Bears
Derek Holloway
Washington Redskins

Greg Horne
Cincinnati Bengals, St. Louis Cardinals, Washington Redskins
Jim Lee Howell
New York Giants, Tampa Bay Buccaneers
Charles Jamerson
Hartford
Ray Lee Johnson
San Diego Chargers
Harry Jones
Philadelphia Eagles
Allen Keen
Philadelphia Eagles
Keith Kidd
Minnesota Vikings
Mike Kirkland
Baltimore Colts
Steve Korte
New Orleans Saints
Greg Koch
Green Bay Packers, Miami Dolphins
Jerry Lamb
Kansas City Chiefs
Greg Lasker
New York Giants
Chester Ledbetter
Chicago Cardinals
Jim Lindsey
Minnesota Vikings
Steve Little
St. Louis Cardinals
Kenneth Lunday
New York Giants
Vaughn Lusby
Chicago Bears, Cincinnati Bengals
Brison Manor
Denver Broncos
Wayne Martin
New Orleans Saints
Gino Mazzanti
Baltimore Colts
Bruce Maxwell
Detroit Lions
Bill McClard
New Orleans Saints, San Francisco 49ers
Lamar McHan
Chicago Cardinals, San Francisco 49ers
Peter Merloni
Boston Braves
Nick Miller
Cleveland Browns
Charles Moore
Washington Redskins
Henry Moore
New York Giants, Baltimore Colts
Jerry Moore
Chicago Bears, New Orleans Saints
Jim Mooty
Dallas Cowboys
Dickey Morton
Pittsburgh Steelers
Lock Morton
Neward
Tom Murphy
Chicago Cardinals
Tony Ollison
Indianapolis Colts
Kerry Owens
Cincinnati Bengals, Cleveland Browns
Leon Pense
Pittsburgh Steelers
Loyd Phillips
Chicago Bears, New Orleans Saints
Joyce Pipkin
New York Giants, Los Angeles
David Reavis
Pittsburgh Steelers, Tampa Bay Buccaneers
Danny Rhodes
Baltimore Colts

Jack Robbins
Chicago Cardinals
James Rouse
Chicago Bears
Coy Ernest Ruple
Pittsburgh Steelers
Derek Russell
Denver Broncos
Floyd Sagely
Chicago Bears
Howard Sampson
Green Bay Packers
Clyde Scott
Philedelphia Eagles, Detroit Lions
Milt Simington
Cleveland Browns, Pittsburgh Steelers
Gerald Skinner
Green Bay Packers
Dwight Sloan
Chicago Cardinals, Detroit Lions
Billy Ray Smith, Sr.
Baltimore Colts, Pittsburgh Steelers, Los Angeles
Billy Ray Smith, Jr.
San Diego Chargers
Rollen Smith
St. Louis Cardinals
Ronny South
New Orleans Saints
Ray Spillers
Philadelphia Eagles
Bob Stankovitch
Kansas City Chiefs
George Stewart
Kansas City Chiefs
Donnie Stone
Denver Broncos
Pat Summerall
Detroit Lions, Chicago Cardinals, New York Giants
R.C. Thielemann
Atlanta Falcons, Washington Redskins
Wilfred Thorpe
Cleveland Browns
Curtis Townsend
St. Louis Cardinals, San Diego Chargers
Kendall Trainor
Phoenix Cardinals
Ron Underwood
Chicago Bears
Clyde Van Sickle
Green Bay Packers
Danny Walters
San Diego Chargers
Tim Webster
Green Bay Packers
Marsh White
New York Giants
Fred Williams
Chicago Bears, Washington Redskins
Patrick Williams
New York Jets
Ben Winkelman
Milwaukee
Bill Winston
New York Jets
Dennis Winston
Pittsburgh Steelers, New Orleans Saints
Don Wunderly
Pittsburgh Steelers
Kevin Wyatt
Miami Dolphins, San Diego Chargers
Harry Wynne
Boston Yanks, New York Giants
Theo Young
Pittsburgh Steelers

NOTE: No positions and years available.

1994 SEC Football 45

Arkansas Media Information

Arkansas SID
Rick Schaeffer

Arkansas Sports Information
Broyles Athletic Complex
Fayetteville, AR 72701
(501) 575-2751
FAX: (501) 575-7481

Schaeffer (Home): 521-7393

Football Beat Writers

Dudley Dawson
Northwest Arkansas Times
Drawer D
Fayetteville, AR 72702
(501) 442-1720

Nate Allen
Donrey Media
453 East Prospect
Fayetteville, AR 72701
(501) 444-7167

Steve Caldwell
Arkansas Democrat-Gazette
3210 Navajo Court
Fayetteville, AR 72701
(501) 444-8084

Bob Holt
Arkansas Democrat-Gazette
629 East Lafayette
Fayetteville, AR 72701
(501) 582-2412

Bob Stephens
Morning News
P.O. Box 7
Springdale, AR 72764
(501) 751-6200

Other Newspapers

Wally Hall, Sports Editor
Arkansas Democrat-Gazette
115 East Capitol
Little Rock, AR 72201
(501) 378-3411

Orville Henry
Arkansas Democrat-Gazette
509 Cherry Ave.
Malvern, AR 72104
(501) 442-3932

Grant Tolley
Southwest Times Record
P.O. Box 1359
Fort Smith, AR 72901
(501) 785-7752

Bill Conners, Sports Editor
Tulsa World
P.O. Box 1770
Tulsa, OK 74102
(918) 581-8355

Al Dunning
Memphis Commercial Appeal
495 Union Avenue
Memphis, TN 38103
(901) 529-2211

Specialty Publications

Clay Henry
Hawgs Illustrated
Suite 217
17 1/2 E. Center
Fayetteville, AR 72762
(501) 582-2332

Wire Service

Harry King
Associated Press
1101 West Second
Little Rock, AR 72201
(501) 374-5536

Television

Mike Irwin
KFSM-TV
P.O. Box 1568
Fayetteville, AR 72702
(501) 521-1378

Kevin Barnes
KHOG-TV
P.O. Box 1029
Fayetteville, AR 72702
(501) 521-1010

Paul Eells
KATV-TV
P.O. Box 77
Little Rock, AR 72203
(501) 324-7544

Steve Sullivan
KARK-TV
P.O. Box 748
Little Rock, AR 72203
(501) 376-1610

Ray Tucker
KHTV-TV
P.O. Box 269
Little Rock, AR 72203
(501) 376-0364

Chuck Carney
KFSM-TV
Box 369
Fort Smith, AR 72902
(501) 783-1191

Bob Healey
KTUL-TV
P.O. Box 8
Tulsa, OK 74101
(918) 446-3719

John Walls
KOTV-TV
P.O. Box 6
Tulsa, OK 74101
(918) 582-9554

Al Jerkens
KJRH-TV
P.O. Box 2
Tulsa, OK 74101
(918) 742-6397

Harold Graeter, Jarvis Greer, Mike Fleming
WMC-TV
1960 Union Avenue
Memphis, TN 38104
(901) 726-0408

Glenn Carver, John Koski
WHBQ-TV
485 South Highland
Memphis, TN 38111
(901) 320-1345

Les Smith, Johnny Dark
WREG-TV
803 Channel 3 Drive
Memphis, TN 38103
(901) 577-0117

Radio Network

For information contact:

Mark Renner
Razorback Network
KATV
P.O. Box 77
Little Rock, AR 72203

Paul Eells (Play-By-Play)
KATV-TV
P.O. Box 77
Little Rock, AR 72203
(501) 324-7544

Rick Schaeffer (Color Analyst)
Broyles Athletic Complex
Fayetteville, AR 72701
(501) 575-2751

Campus Media
Arkansas Traveler
Hill Hall
Fayetteville, AR 72701

AUBURN

DR. WILLIAM V. MUSE
President

DR. JANE MOORE
Faculty Representative

DAVID HOUSEL
Athletic Director

Auburn University

PRESIDENT:
Dr. William V. Muse (Northwestern State 1960)
FACULTY REPRESENTATIVE:
Dr. Jane Moore (Judson 1957)
ATHLETIC DIRECTOR:
David Housel (Auburn 1969)
HEAD COACH:
Terry Bowden (West Virginia 1978)
LOCATION: Auburn, Alabama
FOUNDED: 1856
ENROLLMENT: 21,500
NICKNAME: Tigers
COLORS: Burnt Orange and Navy Blue
STADIUM: Jordan-Hare Stadium (85,214) - Natural

Tiger Quick Facts

1993 RECORD: 11-0
(7-0 Home, 4-0 Away)
1993 SEC RECORD (FINISH): 8-0 (Not Eligible for title)
(4-0 Home, 4-0 Away)
BOWL: None
ALL-TIME RECORD: 553-329-46 (.621)
SEC RECORD: 203-167-17 (.547) — Regular Season Games
SEC CHAMPIONSHIPS: 5
(1957, 83, 87, 88t, 89t)
BOWL APPEARANCES: 23
BOWL RECORD: 12-9-2 (.565)
LAST APPEARANCE: 1990 Peach Bowl
(Auburn 27, Indiana 23)

AUBURN
Team Information

OFFENSIVE SYSTEM: Pro I

DEFENSIVE SYSTEM: 4-3

LETTERMEN RETURNING: 46
- 18 Offense
- 25 Defense
- 3 Specialists

LETTERMEN LOST: 21
- 12 Offense
- 7 Defense
- 2 Specialists

STARTERS RETURNING: 18
- **OFFENSE** (6)
  - WR Thomas Bailey (6-0, 196, Sr.)
  - WR Frank Sanders (6-2, 200, Sr.)
  - TE Andy Fuller (6-3, 243, Jr.)
  - OG Todd Boland (6-3, 257, Sr.)
  - C   Shannon Roubique (6-1, 295, Jr.)
  - OG Jason Taylor (6-1, 295, Jr.)
- **DEFENSE** (9)
  - DE Willie Whitehead (6-3, 231, Sr.)
  - DE Alonzo Etheridge (6-4, 255, Sr.)
  - DT Mike Pelton (6-3, 262, Sr.)
  - LB Terry Solomon (6-2, 224, Jr.)
  - LB Jason Miska (6-2, 202, Jr.)
  - LB Anthony Harris (6-2, 221, Jr.)
  - CB Chris Shelling (5-10, 180, Sr.)
  - SS Otis Mounds (6-0, 194, Sr.)
  - FS Brian Robinson (6-3, 194, Jr.)
- **SPECIALISTS** (2)
  - P   Terry Daniel (6-1, 226, Sr.)
  - SN Brian Brinsfield (6-1, 201, Sr.)

STARTERS LOST: 7
- **OFFENSE** (5)
  - OT Anthony Redmon (6-5, 288, Sr.)
  - OT Wayne Gandy (6-5, 275, Sr.)
  - QB Stan White (6-3, 202, Sr.)
  - FB Tony Richardson (6-2, 219, Sr.)
  - TB James Bostic (6-0, 224, Jr.)
- **DEFENSE** (2)
  - DT Damon Primus (6-3, 278, Sr.)
  - CB Calvin Jackson (5-10, 179, Jr.)
- **SPECIALISTS** (1)
  - PK Scott Etheridge (5-11, 153, Sr.)

Jordan-Hare Stadium (85,214)
Record: 187-41-7 (.811)
First Game: Nov. 30, 1939 — Auburn 7, Florida 7
Largest Crowd: 85,319 (Dec. 2, 1989)
   Auburn 30, Alabama 20

1994 Auburn Schedule

Sept.	3	at Ole Miss	Oxford, Miss.
Sept.	10	NE LOUISIANA	AUBURN
Sept.	17	LSU	AUBURN
Sept.	24	EAST TENNESSEE STATE	AUBURN
Sept.	29	KENTUCKY	AUBURN
Oct.	8	at Mississippi State	Starkville, Miss.
Oct.	15	at Florida	Gainesville, Fla.
Oct.	29	ARKANSAS	AUBURN
Nov.	5	EAST CAROLINA	AUBURN
Nov.	12	GEORGIA	AUBURN
Nov.	19	at Alabama	Birmingham, Ala.

1995 Auburn Schedule

Sept.	2	OLE MISS	AUBURN
Sept.	16	at LSU	Baton Rouge, La.
Sept.	23	NE LOUISIANA	AUBURN
Sept.	30	at Kentucky	Lexington, Ky.
Oct.	7	MISSISSIPPI STATE	AUBURN
Oct.	14	FLORIDA	AUBURN
Oct.	21	SOUTHERN MISS	AUBURN
Oct.	28	at Arkansas	Fayetteville, Ark.
Nov.	4	WESTERN MICHIGAN	AUBURN
Nov.	11	at Georgia	Athens, Ga.
Nov.	25	ALABAMA	AUBURN

1993 Auburn Individual Leaders

RUSHING	Atts	Yards	Avg	TDs	Yds/Game
James Bostic	199	1205	6.1	12	109.6
STEPHEN DAVIS	87	480	5.5	3	53.3
Tony Richardson	58	249	4.3	4	22.6
Reid McMilion	38	232	6.1	1	21.1
ROYMON MALCOLM	15	113	7.5	1	11.3

PASSING	Atts	Comp	Ints/TDs	Pct	Yds
Stan White	271	164	8/13	.605	2057
PATRICK NIX	15	10	0/2	.667	131

RECEIVING	Rec	Yds	Avg	TDs	Yds/Game
FRANK SANDERS	48	842	17.5	6	76.5
Tony Richardson	28	273	9.8	2	24.8
THOMAS BAILEY	27	427	15.8	4	38.8
DERRICK DORN	12	122	10.2	0	11.1
Reid McMilion	12	94	7.8	0	8.5

SCORING	G	TDs	PAT	FGs	Tot	Avg
Scott Etheridge	11	0	45-45	12-15	81	7.4
James Bostic	11	13	0-0	0-0	78	7.1
FRANK SANDERS	11	7	0-0	0-0	42	3.8
Tony Richardson	11	6	0-0	0-0	36	3.3

PUNTING	No	Yds	Avg	Long
TERRY DANIEL	51	2393	46.9	71

KICKOFF RETURNS	No	Yds	Avg	TDs	Avg/Game	Long
THOMAS BAILEY	26	504	19.4	0	45.8	31

PUNT RETURNS	No	Yds	Avg	TDs	Avg/Game	Long
THOMAS BAILEY	27	210	7.8	0	19.1	30

TACKLES	Total	Sk(Yds)	TL(Yds)	Ints
JASON MISKA	125(68-57)	2(-9)	4(-6)	0
ANTHONY HARRIS	123(53-70)	7(-32)	8(-17)	1
TERRY SOLOMON	77(42-35)	1(-10)	1(-2)	0
BRIAN ROBINSON	74(43-31)	0	1(-1)	5
CHRIS SHELLING	74(46-28)	0	2(-14)	4

INTERCEPTIONS	No	Yds	TDs	Int/Game	Long
BRIAN ROBINSON	5	131	2	0.5	45
CHRIS SHELLING	4	169	1	0.4	73
Calvin Jackson	2	104	1	0.2	96

Returning Players in All Capitals

1993 Auburn Team Statistics

	AU	OPP
FIRST DOWNS	248	166
Rushing	133	72
Passing	99	82
Penalty	16	12
NET YARDS RUSHING	2432	1406
Yards rushing	2714	1686
Yards lost	282	280
Rushing attempts	513	350
Average per rush	4.7	4.0
Average per game	221.1	127.8
NET YARDS PASSING	2188	2039
Average per game	198.9	185.4
Passes attempted	288	349
Passes completed	174	153
Had intercepted	8	15
TOTAL OFFENSIVE YARDS	4620	3445
Average per game	420.0	313.2
Total plays	800	698
Average per play	5.8	4.9
NUMBER PUNTS/YARDS	51/2393	73/2921
Punting average	46.9	40.0
Net punting average	38.73	32.2
PUNT RETURNS/YARDS	33/264	26/418
Punt return average	8.0	16.1
KICKOFF RETURNS/YARDS	31/537	40/889
Kickoff return average	17.3	22.2
PENALTIES/YARDS	66/551	69/639
Penalty yards per game	50.1	58.1
FUMBLES/LOST	23/14	17/10
INTERCEPTION RETURNS/YARDS	15/423	8/49
Interception return avg	28.2	6.1
TOUCHDOWNS	45	24
Rushing	26	7
Passing	15	15
Return	4	1
FIELD GOALS MADE/ATTEMPTED	12/15	8/13
KICK EXTRA POINTS MADE/ATT	45/45	20/20
SAFETY	1	0
TWO-POINT CONVERSIONS	0	2/4
TOTAL POINTS	353	192
Average per game	32.1	17.5

1993 Auburn Results

11-0 Overall • 8-0 SEC (Not Eligible)

Date	Opponent		Score	Att.
Sept. 2	OLE MISS	W	16-12	78,246
Sept. 11	SAMFORD	W	35-7	68,936
Sept. 18	at LSU	W	34-10	71,936
Sept. 25	SOUTHERN MISSISSIPPI	W	35-24	83,476
Oct. 2	at Vanderbilt	W	14-10	40,527
Oct. 9	MISSISSIPPI STATE	W	31-17	84,222
Oct. 16	FLORIDA	W	38-35	85,214
Oct. 30	at Arkansas	W	31-21	50,100
Nov. 6	NEW MEXICO STATE - HC	W	55-14	82,128
Nov. 13	at Georgia	W	42-28	85,434
Nov. 20	ALABAMA	W	22-14	85,214

James Bostic   Jason Miska   Stan White

1994 SEC Football

Terry Bowden

HOMETOWN:
Birmingham, Alabama

ALMA MATER:
West Virginia (1978); Law Degree - Florida State (1981)

PLAYING CAREER:
West Virginia running back 1977-78 (Two-year letterman)

COACHING CAREER:
Florida State Graduate Assistant 1979-81; Florida State Assistant 1982; Salem Head Coach 1983-85; Akron Assistant 1986; Samford Head Coach 1987-92; Auburn Head Coach 1993-present.

COACHING ACHIEVEMENTS:
1987 NCAA Division III National Coach of the Year; 1993 SEC Coach of the Year; 1993 Consensus NCAA Coach of the Year.

BORN:
February 24, 1956

WIFE:
Former Shryl Lambert

CHILDREN:
Tera Dawn 12, Jordan Leigh 4, Erin Renee 3, Cori Ann 2

ASSISTANT COACHES:
 WAYNE HALL (Alabama 1974) - Assistant Head Coach/Defensive Coordinator/Linebackers
 TOMMY BOWDEN (West Virginia 1977) - Offensive Coordinator/Wide Receivers
 JIMBO FISHER (Salem College 1988) - Quarterbacks
 RICK TRICKETT (Glenville State 1972) -Offensive Line
 RODNEY ALLISON (Texas Tech 1978) - Running Backs
 RODNEY GARNER (Auburn 1990) - Tight Ends
 JOE WHITT (Alabama State 1972) - Defensive Ends
 KURT CRAIN (Auburn 1988) - Defensive Tackles
 JACK HINES (West Virginia 1972) -Defensive Backs

SUPPORT STAFF:
 HERB WALDROP (Auburn 1960) - Head Trainer
 REED WAINWRIGHT (Auburn 1989) - Conditioning Coach
 JERRY FUQUA (Auburn 1988) - Strength Coach

Year-By-Year Record

Year	School	Conf.	All	Bowl
1983	Salem		3-7	
1984	Salem		8-3	NAIA Playoffs
1985	Salem		8-3	NAIA Playoffs
1987	Samford		9-1	
1988	Samford		5-6	
1989	Samford		5-6	
1990	Samford		6-4-1	
1991	Samford		12-2	IAA Playoffs
1992	Samford		9-3	IAA Playoffs
1993	Auburn	8-0	11-0	
OVERALL RECORD		**8-0**	**76-35-1 (.683)**	10 Years
Auburn Record		**8-0**	**11-0**	1 Year
Samford Record		0-0	46-22-1 (.674)	6 Years
Salem Record		0-0	19-12 (.594)	3 Years
Bowl Record		0-0		

50 Auburn

Auburn All-Star Candidates

TERRY DANIEL
Senior • Punter
6-1 • 226 • Valley, Ala.

• Earned All-America honors and first-team All-SEC distinction after averaging 46.9 yards per punt to lead the SEC and finish second nationally in punting as a junior.
• Established new Auburn records for highest punting average in a single season (46.9 in 1993) and career (44.5 in 1992-93).
• Posted 16 punts of 50 or more yards, three punts of 60 or more yards and a career-long 71 yard punt versus Florida. Did not average less than 40 yards per punt in any game.

DANIELS STATS

Year	Punts	Yds.	Avg.	LP
1992	65	2771	42.6	68
1993	51	2393	46.9	71
Career	116	5164	44.5	71

FRANK SANDERS
Senior • Wide Receiver
6-2 • 200 • Ft. Lauderdale, Fla.

• Auburn leader in receptions with 48 for 842 yards and six TDs, finishing third in SEC in catches and fourth in the league in receiving yards.
• On receiving end of 4th-and-15, 35-yard TD pass from Patrick Nix in Alabama game and of Stan White's passing record breaker at LSU. Also scored Auburn's final TD against Florida on a reverse.
• His 48 catches is third-highest single-season total in Auburn history, as is his 842 yards receiving. Moved to 10th on Auburn career reception list with 63 total.

SANDERS STATS

Year	Rec.	Yds.	Avg.	TD	LG
1991	2	42	21.0	0	29
1992	13	204	15.7	2	33
1993	48	842	17.5	6	57
Career	63	1088	17.3	8	57

SHANNON ROUBIQUE
Junior • Center
6-1 • 278 • Denham Springs, La.

• As a sophomore, established himself as one of the top centers in the SEC and was an all-conference selection by the *Birmingham News*.
• Started all 11 games in 1993 and has now started 21 of 22 contests in Auburn career, 11 at center and 10 at guard. Played 730 of Auburn's 800 total snaps in 1993.
• Graded 75-percent for the season, including 84 percent versus Mississippi State and 82 percent versus Alabama. Had only six missed assignments all season, only two in last eight games and one in last five games.

CHRIS SHELLING
Senior • Cornerback
5-10 • 180 • Columbus, Ga.

• First-team *Birmingham News* All-SEC selection and second-team Coaches All-SEC recipient after recording 74 tackles and four interceptions as a junior. Led Auburn defensive backs and ranked among SEC secondary leaders in tackles.
• His 65-yard interception return against Florida set up Auburn's final touchdown, and his 73-yard interception return versus Georgia is among top 10 longest in Auburn history. Averaged 42.3 yards per interception return, an Auburn record for that category in a single season.
• Has now started 22 consecutive games at Auburn, 11 at strong safety in 1992 and 11 more at corner in 1993. Named SEC Defensive Player of the Week for his performance against Mississippi State after posting six tackles, one interception and causing a fumble.

SHELLING STATS

Year	Tackles	TFL	Sack	Int	FR
1991	18 (10-8)	0	1	0	0
1992	74 (42-32)	2	0	4	1
1993	74 (46-28)	2	0	4	0
Career	166 (98-68)	4	1	8	1

1994 SEC Football

1994 Auburn Roster

No.	Name	Pos.	Ht.	Wt.	Class	Exp.	Hometown (High School/JC)
64	Brian Adcock	OL	6-3	256	So.	SQ	Tampa, Fla. (Chamberlain)
68	Shay Allen	OG	6-4	267	So.	SQ	Prattville, Ala. (Prattville)
9	Ken Alvis	SS	6-3	196	Fr.	RS	Demopolis, Ala. (Demopolis)
71	Willie Anderson	OG	6-6	320	So.	1L	Whistler, Ala. (Vigor)
59	Toby Anderson	LB	5-8	213	Jr.	SQ	Eufaula, Ala. (Eufaula)
18	Thomas Bailey	WR	6-0	196	Sr.	3L	Enterprise, Ala. (Enterprise)
19	Allen Barnett	QB	6-2	202	So.	SQ	Alex City, Ala. (Benjamin Russell)
1	Lewis Battle	WR	5-10	162	So.	1L	Roanoke, Ala. (Handley)
57	Dwight Beard	LB	6-2	233	So.	SQ	Warrior, Ala. (Warrior)
52	Todd Boland	OG	6-3	257	Sr.	2L	New Brockton, Ala. (New Brockton)
62	Brian Brinsfield	SN	6-1	201	Sr.	3L	Spanish Fort, Ala. (Fairhope)
72	Jeff Bryan	OG	6-4	302	Jr.	SQ	Leesburg, Ga. (Lee Co.)
97	Myron Burton	DE	6-5	266	So.	1L	Columbus, Ga. (Shaw)
15	John Cooley	QB	6-2	212	So.	TR	Sarasota, Fla. (C. Mooney)
16	Dameyune Craig	QB	6-0	177	Fr.	RS	Prichard, Ala. (Blount)
30	Kelsey Crook	CB	5-9	164	Sr.	1L	Ohatchee, Ala. (Ohatchee)
79	Bobby Daffin	DE	6-3	218	Fr.	RS	Prichard, Ala. (Vigor)
36	Terry Daniel	P	6-1	226	Sr.	2L	Valley, Ala., Ala. (Valley)
48	Stephen Davis	TB	6-2	222	Jr.	1L	Spartanburg, S.C. (Spartanburg)
83	Matt DeValk	TE	6-5	214	So.	1L	Daphne, Ala. (Daphne)
49	Derrick Dorn	TE	6-4	211	Jr.	2L	Daleville, Ala. (Daleville)
91	Alonzo Etheridge	DE	6-4	255	Sr.	3L	Selma, Ala. (Selma)
35	Demond Fields	FB	6-0	229	So.	SQ	Spartanburg, S.C. (Spartanburg)
75	John Franklin	OT	6-9	252	So.	1L	Graceville, Fla. (Graceville)
5	Joe Frazier	LB	6-0	212	Sr.	3L	Montgomery, Ala. (Lanier)
82	Andy Fuller	TE	6-3	243	Jr.	2L	Huntsville, Ala. (Johnson)
14	Tyrone Goodson	WR	6-3	180	Fr.	RS	Brooksville, Fla. (Central)
32	Willie Gosha	WR	6-1	161	So.	1L	Ft. Walton, Fla. (Choctawhatchee)
53	Anthony Harris	LB	6-2	221	Jr.	2L	Ft. Pierce, Fla. (Westwood)
26	Matt Hawkins	P	5-11	172	Jr.	1L	Pensacola, Fla. (Washington)
52	James Kiger	OG	6-3	259	Fr.	RS	Daleville, Ala. (Daleville)
46	John Kolen	LB	6-0	200	So.	1L	Montgomery, Ala. (Trinity)
93	Ramon Luster	DT	6-2	279	Jr.	2L	Birmingham, Ala. (Ensley)
29	Roymon Malcolm	TB	6-3	222	Jr.	2L	Ruston, La. (Ruston)
27	David McClinton	CB	5-9	172	Fr.	RS	Montgomery, Ala. (Trinity)
80	Jessie McCovery	TE	6-3	258	So.	1L	St. Elmo, Ala. (Theodore)
24	Dell McGee	CB	5-8	181	Jr.	2L	Columbus, Ga. (Kendrick)
95	Andre Miller	DE	6-2	246	Jr.	2L	Meridian, Miss. (MeridianS)
45	Jason Miska	LB	6-2	202	Jr.	2L	Bridgeport, Ct. (ND Catholic)
12	Harold Morrow	TB	6-0	198	Jr.	2L	Maplesville, Ala. (Maplesville)
47	Marcellus Mostella	LB	6-3	206	So.	1L	Gadsden, Ala. (Gadsden)
2	Otis Mounds	SS	6-0	194	Sr.	3L	Ft. Lauderdale, Fla. (Dillard)
10	Patrick Nix	QB	6-2	188	Jr.	2L	Rainbow City, Ala. (Etowah)
51	LaDerrick Odom	LB	6-3	210	Fr.	RS	Beatrice, Ala. (J.F. Sheilds)
78	Brian Osborn	OT	6-5	293	Sr.	3L	Plant City, Fla. (Plant City)
50	Mike Pelton	DT	6-3	262	Sr.	3L	Goshen, Ala. (GoshenS)
61	Eric Reebals	LB	5-11	192	So.	1L	Homewood, Ala. (Homewood)
23	Adrian Reese	FB	6-1	210	So.	SQ	Auburn, Ala. (Auburn)
25	Darryl Riggins	CB	6-1	182	So.	1L	Ft. Pierce, Fla. (Central)
20	Brian Robinson	FS	6-3	194	Jr.	2L	Ft. Lauderdal, Fla. (Dillard)
58	Derrick Robinson	LB	6-3	221	So.	1L	Denham Springs, La. (Denham Springs)
73	Jim Roe	OT	6-5	281	So.	1L	Mauldin, S.C. (Mauldin)
31	Charles Rose	CB	5-11	177	Jr.	1L	Leeds, Ala. (Leeds)
56	Shannon Roubique	C	6-1	278	Jr.	2L	Denham Springs, La. (Denham Springs)
70	Daryl Sanders	OT	6-3	306	So.	SQ	Roanoke, Ala. (Handley)
81	Frank Sanders	WR	6-2	200	Sr.	3L	Ft. Lauderdale, Fla. (Dillard)
3	Robert Scott	WR	5-10	160	So.	1L	Winter Haven, Fla. (Winter Haven)
4	Chris Shelling	SS	5-10	180	Sr.	3L	Columbus, Ga. (Baker)
6	Fred Smith	CB	5-9	190	Sr.	2L	Eufaula, Ala. (Eufaula)
94	Nate Smith	DT	6-5	226	Fr.	RS	Shalimar, Fla. (Choctawhatchee)
44	Terry Solomon	LB	6-2	224	Jr.	2L	Cairo, Ga. (Cairo)
54	Scott Stacy	DE	6-2	245	Jr.	TR	Prattville, Ala. (Prattville)
17	Patrick Sullivan	QB	6-3	200	So.	1L	Birmingham, Ala. (Mountain Brook)
87	Shannon Suttle	DE	6-4	241	Fr.	RS	LaFayette, Ala. (LaFayette)
66	Jason Taylor	OG	6-1	295	Jr.	2L	Mobile, Ala. (Shaw)
60	Leonard Thomas	OG	6-2	270	So.	1L	Columbus, Ga. (Kendrick)
55	Carlos Thornton	LB	6-1	233	Sr.	3L	Pacelli, Ala. (Holy Trinity)
96	Gary Walker	DE	6-3	258	So.	1L	Lavonia, Ga. (Franklin Co.)
76	Ricardo Walker	DT	6-2	275	So.	1L	Darlington, S.C. (St. John's)
90	Willie Whitehead	DE	6-3	231	Sr.	3L	Tuskegee, Ala. (Tuskegee)
13	Jamie Williams	DB	5-11	187	So.	1L	Union Springs, Ala. (Bullock Mem.)
19	Ben Williamson	DB	5-10	169	So.	1L	Eufaula, Ala. (Eufaula)

Numerical Roster

No.	Name	Pos.
1	Lewis Battle	WR
2	Otis Mounds	SS
3	Robert Scott	WR
4	Chris Shelling	SS
5	Joe Frazier	LB
6	Fred Smith	CB
9	Kenny Alvis	SS
10	Patrick Nix	QB
11	Alan Barnett	QB
12	Harold Morrow	TB
13	Jamie Williams	DB
14	Tyrone Goodson	WR
15	John Cooley	QB
16	Dameyune Craig	QB
17	Patrick Sullivan	QB
18	Thomas Bailey	WR
19	Ben Williamson	DB
20	Brian Robinson	FS
22	Tyreece Williams	WR
23	Adrian Reese	FB
24	Dell McGee	CB
25	Daryl Riggins	CB
26	Matt Hawkins	P
27	David McClinton	CB
29	Roymon Malcolm	TB
30	Kelsey Crook	CB
31	Charles Rose	CB
32	Willie Gosha	WR
35	Demond Fields	FB
36	Terry Daniel	P
44	Terry Solomon	LB
45	Jason Miska	LB
46	John Kolen	LB
47	Marcellus Mostella	CB
48	Steve Davis	TB
49	Derrick Dorn	TE
50	Mike Pelton	DT
51	LaDerrick Odom	LB
52	James Kiger	OG
53	Anthony Harris	LB
54	Scott Stacy	DE
56	Shannon Roubique	C
57	Dwight Beard	LB
58	Derrick Robinson	LB
59	Toby Anderson	LB
60	Leonard Thomas	OG
61	Eric Reebals	LB
62	Brian Brinsfield	SN
64	Brian Adcock	OL
65	Kevin Cummings	OL
66	Jason Taylor	OG
68	Shay Allen	OG
70	Daryl Sanders	OT
71	Willie Anderson	OG
72	Jeff Bryan	OG
73	Jim Roe	OT
75	John Franklin	OT
78	Brian Osborn	OT
80	Jesse McCovery	TE
81	Frank Sanders	WR
82	Andy Fuller	TE
83	Matt DeValk	TE
87	Andy Swafford	WR
90	Willie Whitehead	DE
91	Alonzo Etheridge	DE
92	Bobby Daffin	DE
93	Ramon Luster	DT
94	Nate Smith	DT
95	Andre Miller	DE
96	Gary Walker	DE
97	Myron Burton	DE
99	Shannon Suttles	DE

52 Auburn

1994 Auburn Depth Chart

OFFENSE

WR:	81	FRANK SANDERS
	32	Willie Gosha
WR:	18	THOMAS BAILEY
	14	Tyrone Goodson
TE:	82	ANDY FULLER
	49	Derrick Dorn
TT:	71	Willie Anderson
	73	Jim Roe
TG:	60	Leonard Thomas
	70	Daryl Sanders
C:	56	SHANNON ROUBIQUE
	59	James Kiger
SG:	66	JASON TAYLOR
	72	Jeff Bryan
ST:	75	John Franklin
	78	Brian Osborn
QB:	10	Patrick Nix
	16	Dameyune Craig
FB:	12	Harold Morrow
	5	Joe Frazier
TB:	48	Stephen Davis
	29	Roymon Malcolm

DEFENSE

DE:	90	WILLIE WHITEHEAD
	95	Andre Miller
LT:	96	Gary Walker
	93	Ramon Luster
RT:	50	MIKE PELTON
	93	Ramon Luster
DE:	91	ALONZO ETHERIDGE
	97	Myron Burton
SLB:	53	ANTHONY HARRIS
	51	LaDerrick Odom
MLB:	45	JASON MISKA
	58	Derrick Robinson
WLB:	44	TERRY SOLOMON
	47	Marcellus Mostella
FC:	8	CALVIN JACKSON
	24	Dell McGee
BC:	4	CHRIS SHELLING
	6	Fred Smith
SS:	2	OTIS MOUNDS
	9	Ken Alvis
FS:	25	Darryl Riggins
	20	BRIAN ROBINSON

SPECIALISTS

PK:	26	Matt Hawkins
P:	36	TERRY DANIEL

Returning Starters In All Capitals

1994 Auburn Signees

Name	Pos.	Ht.	Wt.	Hometown/High School
Adam Bailey	DL/OL	6-5	280	Snellville, Ga./S. Gwinnett
Derrick Balkcorn	OL	6-6	305	Chipley, Fla./Chipley
Fred Beasley	RB	6-2	200	Montgomery, Ala./Robert E. Lee
Jason Bray	DB	5-11	175	LaGrange, Ga./LaGrange
Marcus Camp	LB	6-2	225	Lithonia, Ga./Lithonia
Terrance Crowder	LB	6-3	200	Carrollton, Ga./Carrollton
DeMarcus Curry	OT	6-5	295	Columbus, Ga./Kendrick
Tyrone Dillard	TE	6-3	230	Riverdale, Ga./Riverdale
Charles Dorsey	DT	6-2	270	Ft. Lauderdale, Fla./Dillard
Douglas Forrester	OL	6-4	280	High Springs, Fla./Alachua-Santa Fe
Kevin Gentle	K/P	6-1	180	Guntersville, Ala./Guntersville
Karl Lavine	DL	6-3	270	Ft. Walton Beach, Fla./Choctowatchee
Kendall Mack	DL	6-5	280	Pineville, S.C./St. Stephens
LaFonzo McLean	DB	6-0	185	Lumber City, Ga./Telfair Co.
Kevin McLeod	FB	6-2	222	Clarkston, Ga./Clarkston
Larry Melton	DB	5-10	180	Valdosta, Ga./Valdosta
Richard Neal	LB	6-0	211	Daytona Beach, Fla./Seabreeze
Patterson Owens	DE	6-5	258	Mobile, Ala./LeFlore
Victor Riley	OL	6-6	295	Swansea, S.C./Swansea
Andre Rone	WR	5-11	170	Daytona Beach, Fla./Seabreeze
James Roscoe	DE	6-5	225	Ft. Lauderdale, Fla./Dillard
Scott Stacey	DE/LB	6-2	245	Prattville, Ala./Hines CC
Dale Terrell	FB	6-1	222	Lakeland, Fla./Lakeland

Stephen Davis

Anthony Harris

1994 SEC Football

Auburn Year-By-Year Records

Year	Coach	SEC	SEC Finish	Overall	Bowls
1892	Dr. G. Petrie			2-2-0	
1893	G. H. Harvey				
	D. M. Balliet			3-0-2	
1894	F. M. Hall			1-3-0	
1895	J. W. Heisman			2-1-0	
1896	J. W. Heisman			3-1-0	
1897	J. W. Heisman			2-0-1	
1898	J. W. Heisman			2-1-0	
1899	J. W. Heisman			3-1-1	
1900	Billy Watkins			4-0-0	
1901	Billy Watkins			2-2-1	
1902	R. S. Kent				
	Mike Harvey			2-4-1	
1903	Billy Bates			4-3-0	
1904	Mike Donahue			5-0-0	
1905	Mike Donahue			2-4-0	
1906	Mike Donahue			1-5-1	
1907	W. S. Keinholz			6-2-1	
1908	Mike Donahue			6-1-0	
1909	Mike Donahue			5-2-0	
1910	Mike Donahue			6-1-0	
1911	Mike Donahue			4-2-1	
1912	Mike Donahue			6-1-0	
1913	Mike Donahue			8-0-0	
1914	Mike Donahue			8-0-1	
1915	Mike Donahue			6-2-0	
1916	Mike Donahue			6-2-0	
1917	Mike Donahue			6-2-1	
1918	Mike Donahue			2-5-0	
1919	Mike Donahue			8-1-0	
1920	Mike Donahue			7-2-0	
1921	Mike Donahue			5-3-0	
1922	Mike Donahue			8-2-0	
1923	Boozer Pitts			3-3-3	
1924	Boozer Pitts			4-4-1	
1925	Dave Morey			5-3-1	
1926	Dave Morey			5-4-0	
1927	Dave Morey			0-3-0	
	Boozer Pitts			0-4-2	
1928	George Bohler			1-8-0	
1929	George Bohler				
	John Floyd			2-7-0	
1930	Chet Wynne			3-7-0	
1931	Chet Wynne			5-3-1	
1932	Chet Wynne			9-0-1	
1933	Chet Wynne	2-2-0	6t	5-5-0	—
1934	Jack Meagher	1-6-0	10	2-8-0	—
1935	Jack Meagher	5-2-0	4	8-2-0	—
1936	Jack Meagher	4-1-1	3	7-2-2	Bacardi
1937	Jack Meagher	4-1-2	3	6-2-3	Orange
1938	Jack Meagher	3-3-1	7t	4-5-1	—
1939	Jack Meagher	3-3-1	5t	5-5-1	—
1940	Jack Meagher	3-2-1	5	6-4-1	—
1941	Jack Meagher	0-4-1	11	4-5-1	—
1942	Jack Meagher	3-3-0	7	6-4-1	—
1943	NO TEAM				
1944	Carl Voyles	0-4-0	10t	4-4-0	—
1945	Carl Voyles	2-3-0	7t	5-5-0	—
1946	Carl Voyles	1-5-0	10	4-6-0	—
1947	Carl Voyles	1-5-0	11	2-7-0	—
1948	Earl Brown	0-7-0	12	1-8-1	—
1949	Earl Brown	2-4-2	8	2-4-3	—
1950	Earl Brown	0-7-0	12	0-10-0	—
1951	Ralph "Shug" Jordan	3-4-0	6	5-5-0	—
1952	Ralph "Shug" Jordan	0-7-0	12	2-8-0	—
1953	Ralph "Shug" Jordan	4-2-1	5	7-3-1	Gator
1954	Ralph "Shug" Jordan	3-3-0	6t	8-3-0	Gator
1955	Ralph "Shug" Jordan	5-1-0	2	8-2-1	Gator
1956	Ralph "Shug" Jordan	4-3-0	5	7-3-0	—
1957	Ralph "Shug" Jordan	7-0-0	1	10-0-0	—

Year	Coach	SEC	SEC Finish	Overall	Bowls
1958	Ralph "Shug" Jordan	6-0-1	2	9-0-1	—
1959	Ralph "Shug" Jordan	4-3-0	5	7-3-0	—
1960	Ralph "Shug" Jordan	5-2-0	4	8-2-0	—
1961	Ralph "Shug" Jordan	3-4-0	7	6-4-0	—
1962	Ralph "Shug" Jordan	4-3-0	6	6-3-1	—
1963	Ralph "Shug" Jordan	6-1-0	2	9-2-0	Orange
1964	Ralph "Shug" Jordan	3-3-0	6	6-4-0	—
1965	Ralph "Shug" Jordan	4-1-1	2	5-5-1	Liberty
1966	Ralph "Shug" Jordan	1-5-0	8	4-6-0	—
1967	Ralph "Shug" Jordan	3-3-0	7	6-4-0	—
1968	Ralph "Shug" Jordan	4-2-0	3t	7-4-0	Sun
1969	Ralph "Shug" Jordan	5-2-0	3	8-3-0	Bluebonnet
1970	Ralph "Shug" Jordan	5-2-0	3	9-2-0	Gator
1971	Ralph "Shug" Jordan	5-1-0	2t	9-2-0	Sugar
1972	Ralph "Shug" Jordan	6-1-0	2	10-1-0	Gator
1973	Ralph "Shug" Jordan	2-5-0	8t	6-6-0	Sun
1974	Ralph "Shug" Jordan	4-2-0	2t	10-2-0	Gator
1975	Ralph "Shug" Jordan	2-4-0	6t	4-6-1	—
1976	Doug Barfield	3-3-0	6t	4-7-0	—
1977	Doug Barfield	5-1-0	3	6-5-0	—
1978	Doug Barfield	3-2-1	3	6-4-1	—
1979	Doug Barfield	4-2-0	3t	8-3-0	—
1980	Doug Barfield	0-6-0	9t	5-6-0	—
1981	Pat Dye	2-4-0	6t	5-6-0	—
1982	Pat Dye	4-2-0	3t	9-3-0	Citrus
1983	Pat Dye	6-0-0	1	11-1-0	Sugar
1984	Pat Dye	4-2-0	3t	9-4-0	Liberty
1985	Pat Dye	3-3-0	5	8-4-0	Cotton
1986	Pat Dye	4-2-0	2t	10-2-0	Citrus
1987	Pat Dye	5-0-1	1	9-1-2	Sugar
1988	Pat Dye	6-1-0	1t	10-2-0	Sugar
1989	Pat Dye	6-1-0	1t	10-2-0	Hall of Fame
1990	Pat Dye	4-2-1	4	8-3-1	Peach
1991	Pat Dye	2-5-0	8	5-6-0	—
1992	Pat Dye	2-5-1	5-W	5-5-1	—
1993	Terry Bowden	8-0	—	11-0	—

Bowl Results (12-9-2)

Bowl	Opponent	Result	Date
Barcardi	Villanova	T 7-7	1-1-37
Orange	Michigan State	W 6-0	1-1-38
Gator	Texas Tech	L 13-35	1-1-54
Gator	Baylor	W 33-13	12-31-54
Gator	Vanderbilt	L 13-25	12-31-55
Orange	Nebraska	L 7-13	1-1-64
Liberty	Ole Miss	L 7-13	12-18-65
Sun	Arizona	W 34-10	12-28-68
Bluebonnet	Houston	L 7-36	12-31-69
Gator	Ole Miss	W 35-28	1-2-71
Sugar	Oklahoma	L 22-40	1-1-72
Gator	Colorado	W 24-3	12-30-72
Sun	Missouri	L 17-34	12-29-73
Gator	Texas	W 27-3	12-30-74
Tangerine	Boston College	W 33-26	12-18-82
Sugar	Michigan	W 9-7	1-2-84
Liberty	Arkansas	W 21-15	12-27-84
Cotton	Texas A&M	L 16-36	1-1-86
Citrus	Southern Cal	W 16-7	1-1-87
Sugar	Syracuse	T 16-16	1-1-88
Sugar	Florida State	L 7-13	1-2-89
Hall of Fame	Ohio State	W 31-14	1-1-90
Peach	Indiana	W 27-23	12-29-90

Auburn

Auburn vs. All Opponents

Opponent	W	L	T
Akron	1	0	0
Alabama	24	33	1
Arizona	2	1	0
Arkansas	2	0	1
Army	0	2	0
Baylor	1	2	1
Birmingham-Southern	13	3	0
Boston College	1	2	0
Cal-State Fullerton	1	0	0
Centre	1	2	0
Chattanooga	19	0	0
Cincinnati	2	0	0
Clemson	31	11	2
Colorado	1	0	0
Davidson	0	2	0
Detroit	1	0	0
Duke	3	3	0
East Carolina	2	0	0
Erskine	1	0	0
Florida	38	30	2
Florida State	13	4	1
Furman	3	0	0
Georgia	46	44	7
Georgia Southern	1	0	0
Georgia Tech	47	39	4
Georgetown	0	0	1
George Washington	0	1	0
Hardin-Simmons	1	0	0
Houston	5	1	0
Indiana	1	0	0
Kansas	2	0	0
Kansas State	2	0	0
Kentucky	20	5	1
Louisiana College	1	0	0
LSU	12	15	1
Louisiana Tech	5	0	1
Louisville	1	0	0
Loyola (New Orleans)	1	0	0
Manhattan	0	1	0
Marion	6	0	0
Maryland	2	1	0
Maryville	1	0	1
Marquette	0	1	0
Memphis State	0	2	0
Mercer	11	0	0
Miami (Florida)	7	4	0
Michigan	1	0	0
Michigan State	1	0	0
Mississippi	12	6	0
Mississippi State	47	18	2
Missouri	0	1	0
Nashville	3	1	0
Nebraska	0	3	0
New Mexico State	1	0	0
North Carolina	2	3	0
North Carolina State	1	1	0
North Texas State	1	0	0
Oglethorpe	4	0	0
Ohio State	1	0	1
Oklahoma	0	1	0
Oregon State	1	0	0
Pacific	1	0	0
Presbyterian	1	0	0
Rice	0	2	0
Richmond	1	0	0
Rutgers	1	0	0
St. Louis	1	0	0
Samford	25	0	1
Santa Clara	0	1	0
Sewanee	4	6	2
South Carolina	2	1	1
Southeastern Louisiana	0	1	0
Southern Cal	1	0	0
Southern Methodist	0	3	0
Southern Mississippi	16	5	0
Southwestern Louisiana	4	0	0
Spring Hill	5	0	0
Stetson	1	1	0
Syracuse	0	0	1
Tennessee	22	18	3
Texas	3	5	0
Texas A&M	0	2	0
Texas Christian	3	0	0
Texas Tech	0	1	0
Tulane	14	17	6
Vanderbilt	14	19	1
Villanova	4	1	2
Virginia Tech	2	1	1
Wake Forest	6	2	0
Washington & Lee	1	0	0
Western Carolina	1	0	0
Wisconsin	0	0	1
Wofford	3	1	0

Auburn's winningest coach, Ralph "Shug" Jordan, directed the Tigers to a 176-83-6 record in his 25-year career, including 12 bowl appearances.

1994 SEC Football

Auburn School Records

Individual

Game
Total Offense	384	Pat Sullivan vs. Florida	(1970)
Yards Rushing	307	Curtis Kuykendall vs. Miami-Florida	(1944)
Rushing Attempts	38	Bo Jackson vs. Ole Miss	(1985)
		Stacy Danley vs. Georgia	(1988)
Yards Passing	366	Pat Sullivan vs. Florida	(1970)
Pass Attempts	58	Stan White vs. Tennessee	(1990)
Pass Completions	30	Jeff Burger vs. Georgia Tech	(1987)
		Stan White vs. Tennessee	(1990)
Yards Receiving	263	Alexander Wright vs. Pacific	(1989)
Receptions	11	Terry Beasley vs. Southern Mississippi	(1971)

Season
Total Offense	2,856	Pat Sullivan	(1970)
Yards Rushing	1,786	Bo Jackson	(1985)
Rushing Attempts	278	Bo Jackson	(1985)
Yards Passing	2,586	Pat Sullivan	(1970)
Pass Attempts	338	Stan White	(1990)
Pass Completions	180	Stan White	(1990)
Touchdown Passes	20	Pat Sullivan	(1971)
Yards Receiving	1,051	Terry Beasley	(1970)
Receptions	55	Terry Beasley	(1971)
Touchdown Catches	12	Terry Beasley	(1971)
Interceptions	9	Buddy McClinton	(1969)
Points	102	Bo Jackson	(1985)

Career
Total Offense	7,920	Stan White	(1990-93)
Yards Rushing	4,303	Bo Jackson	(1982-85)
Rushing Attempts	657	Joe Cribbs	(1976-79)
Yards Passing	8,016	Stan White	(1990-93)
Pass Attempts	1,231	Stan White	(1990-93)
Pass Completions	661	Stan White	(1990-93)
Touchdown Passes	53	Stan White	(1990-93)
Yards Receiving	2,507	Terry Beasley	(1969-71)
Receptions	141	Terry Beasley	(1969-71)
Touchdown Catches	29	Terry Beasley	(1969-71)
Interceptions	18	Buddy McClinton	(1967-69)
Points	274	Bo Jackson	(1982-85)

Team

Game
Points	94	vs. Georgia Tech	(1894)
Total Offense	695	vs. Southwestern Louisiana	(1985)
Yards Rushing	565	vs. Southwestern Louisiana	(1985)
Yards Passing	442	vs. Florida	(1970)
First Downs	39	vs. Ole Miss	(1985)
Total Defense	-30	vs. Tennessee	(1958)
Rushing Defense	-85	vs. Miami-Florida	(1968)
Passing Defense	-10	vs. Alabama	(1952)

Season
Points	379	(1986)
Total Offense	4,923	(1984)
Yards Rushing	3,438	(1985)
Yards Passing	2,885	(1970)
First Downs	N/A	
Fewest Points Allowed	0	(1914)
Total Defense	1,330	(1957)
Rushing Defense	674	(1957)
Passing Defense	528	(1956)
Consecutive Wins	17	(November 10, 1956 to October 11, 1958)

Terry Beasley

Stan White

Auburn

Auburn in the NFL

Tommie Agee, RB
Seattle Seahawks 1987-88; Kansas City Chiefs 1989; Dallas Cowboys 1990-93
Mike Alford, C
St. Louis Cardinals 1965; Detroit Lions 1966
William Andrews, RB
Atlanta Falcons 1979-83, 1986
Billy Atkins, B
San Francisco 49ers 1958-59; Buffalo Bills 1960-61, 1963; NY Titans 1962; NY Jets 1963; Denver Broncos 1964
George Atkins, G
Detroit Lions 1955
Dowe Aughtman, OT
Dallas Cowboys 1984-85
Tom Banks, C
St. Louis Cardinals 1971-80
Corey Barlow, CB
Philadelphia Eagles 1992-93
Fred Baxter, TE
NY Jets 1993-93
Terry Beasley, WR
San Francisco 49ers 1972-75
Ken Bernich, LB
NY Jets 1975
David Beverly, P
Houston Oilers 1974; Green Bay Packers 1975-80
Eddie Blake, UG
Miami Dolphins 1992-93
Forrest Blue, C
San Francisco 49ers 1968-74; Baltimore Colts 1975-78
Scott Bolton, WR
Green Bay Packers 1988
M.L. Brackett, T
Chicago Bears 1956-57; NY Giants 1958
James Brooks, RB
San Diego Chargers 1981-83; Cincinnati Bengals 1984-91; Cleveland Browns 1992-93
Aundray Bruce, OLB
Atlanta Falcons 1988-91; LA Raiders 1992-93
Chet Bulger, T
Chicago Cardinals 1942-43; 1945-49; Pittsburgh Steelers 1944; Detroit Lions 1950
Jackie Burkett, LB
Baltimore Colts 1961-66; New Orleans Saints 1967, 1970; Dallas Cowboys 1968-69
Jimmy Burson, DB
St. Louis Cardinals 1963-67; Atlanta Falcons 1968
Gregg Carr, LB
Pittsburgh Steelers 1985-88
Lloyd Cheatham, B
Chicago Cardinals 1942
Carlo Cheattum, DB
Buffalo Bills 1989
Richard Cheek, G
Buffalo Bills 1970; Houston Oilers 1972
Joe Childress, RB
Chicago Cardinals 1956-59; St. Louis Cardinals 1960-65
Tom Cochran, B
Washington Redskins 1949
Bill Cody, LB
Detroit Lions 1966; New Orleans Saints 1967-70; Philadelphia Eagles 1972
Lewis Colbert, P
Kansas City Chiefs 1986-88
Kurt Crain, ILB
Houston Oilers 1988
Ted Cremer, E
Detroit Lions 1946-48; Green Bay Packers 1948
Joe Cribbs, RB
Buffalo Bills 1980-83; San Francisco 49ers 1986-87; Miami Dolphins 1988
Frank D'Agostino, G
Philadelphia Eagles 1956; NY Titans 1960

Ernie Danjean, G
Green Bay Packers 1957
Rufus Deal, B
Washington Redskins 1942
Al Del Greco, PK
Green Bay Packers 1984-86; Pheonix Cardinals 1988-90; Houston Oilers 1992-93
Dave Edwards, LB
Dallas Cowboys 1963-75
Eric Floyd
San Diego Chargers 1990-91; Philadelphia Eagles 1992-93
Byron Franklin, WR
Buffalo Bills 1981-84; Seattle Seahawks 1985-87
Wayne Frazier, C
San Diego Chargers 1962; Houston Oilers 1965; Kansas City Chiefs 1966-67; Buffalo Bills 1967
Tucker Frederickson, RB
NY Giants 1965-71
Bob Freeman, B
Cleveland Browns 1957-58; Green Bay Packers 1959; Philadelphia Eagles 1960-61; Washington Redskins 1962
Mike Fuller, S
San Diego Chargers 1975-80; Cincinnati Bengals 1981-82
Brent Fullwood, RB
Green Bay Packers 1987-90
Vern Ghersanich, G
Chicago Cardinals 1943
Robert Goff, DT
Tampa Bay Buccaneers 1988-90; New Orleans Saints 1991
Chris Gray, OT
Miami Dolphins 1993-93
Kevin Greene, DE
LA Rams 1985-92
Andy Gross, G
NY Giants 1967-68
George Gross, DT
San Diego Chargers 1963-67
Lee Gross, C
New Orleans Saints 1975-77; Baltimore Colts 1979
Bob Harris, LB
St. Louis Cardinals 1983-86
Max Harrison, E
NY Giants 1940
Hal Herring, C
Cleveland Browns 1950-52
Dave Hill, T
Kansas City Chiefs 1963-74
Nate Hill, DT
Green Bay Packers 1988
John Hudson, C
Philadelphia Eagles 1990-91; 1993
Donnie Humphrey, DT
Green Bay Packers 1984-86
Bobby Hunt, DB
Dallas Texans 1962; Kansas City Chiefs 1963-67; Cincinnati Bengals 1968-69
Chuck Hurston, DE
Kansas City Chiefs 1965-70; Buffalo Bills 1970-71
Fred Hyatt, WR
St. Louis Cardinals 1968-72; New Orleans Saints 1973; Washington Redskins 1973
Bo Jackson, RB
LA Raiders 1987-90
Jeff Jackson, LB
Atlanta Falcons 1984-86
Lionel James, RB
San Diego Chargers 1984-89
Tim Jessie, RB
Washington Redskins 1987
Chuckie Johnson, DT
Phoenix Cardinals 1993
David Jordan, OT
NY Giants 1984-87
James Joseph
Philadelphia Eagles 1991-92

Jon Kilgore, P
LA Rams 1965-67; Chicago Bears 1968; San Francisco 49ers 1969
David King, CB
San Diego Chargers 1985
Ed King
Cleveland Browns 1991-93
Mike Kolen, LB
Miami Dolphins 1970-75, 1977
Reese McCall, TE
Baltimore Colts 1978-82; Detroit Lions 1983-85
John McGeever, DB
Denver Broncos 1962-65; Miami Dolphins 1966
Secdrick McIntyre, RB
Atlanta Falcons 1977
Chris Martin, LB
New Orleans Saints 1983; Minnesota Vikings 1984-88; Kansas City Chiefs 1988-92
Dave Middleton, E
Detroit Lions 1955-60; Minnesota Vikings 1961
Bob Meeks, OG
Denver Broncos 1992-93
Ron Middleton, TE
Atlanta Falcons 1986-87; Washington Redskins 1988, 1990-94; Cleveland Browns 1989
Edmund Nelson, DT
Pittsburgh Steelers 1982-87
Dan Nugent, G
Washington Redskins 1976-80
Neil O'Donoghue, K
Buffalo Bills 1977; Tampa Bay Buccaneers 1978-79; St. Louis Cardinals 1980-84
Craig Ogletree, LB
Cincinnati Bengals 1990
Jeff Parks, TE
Houston Oilers 1986-87; Green Bay Packers 1988
George Peoples, RB
Dallas Cowboys 1982; New England Patriots 1983
Jim (Red) Phillips, WR
LA Rams 1958-64; Minnesota Vikings 1965-67
Kevin Porter, CB
Kansas City Chiefs 1988-92; NY Jets 1993
Jim Price, LB
NY Jets 1963; Denver Broncos 1964
Walter Reeves, TE
Phoenix Cardinals 1989-93
Ken Rice, T
Buffalo Bills 1961, 1963; Oakland Raiders 1964-66; Miami Dolphins 1966-67
Gerald Robinson, DE
Minnesota Vikings 1986-88; San Diego Chargers 1989-90; LA Rams 1991-92
David Rocker, DT
LA Rams 1992-93
Tracy Rocker, DT
Washington Redskins 1989-90
Lamar Rogers
Cincinnati Bengals 1991-93
Benji Roland, DT
Minnesota Vikings 1989; Tampa Bay Buccaneers 1990
George Rose, CB
Minnesota Vikings 1964-66; New Orleans Saints 1967
Herb (Bummy) Roton, E
Philadelphia Eagles 1937
Torrance (Bo) Russell, T
Washington Redskins 1939-40
Stacy Searels, OT
San Diego Chargers 1988-89
Rob Selby
Philadelphia Eagles 1991-93

Jimmy Sidle, TE-RB
Atlanta Falcons 1966
Howard Simpson, T
Minnesota Vikings 1961-65
Ralph Sivell, G
NY Giants 1944-45
Reggie Slack, QB
Houston Oilers 1990-92
Brian Smith, LB
LA Rams 1989-90
Doug Smith, DT
Houston Oilers 1986-93
Zeke Smith, LB
Baltimore Colts 1960; NY Giants 1961-62
Ron Stallworth, DT
NY Jets 1989-90
Curtis Stewart, RB
Chicago Bears 1988
Pat Sullivan, QB
Atlanta Falcons 1972-75
Ricky Sutton, DE
Pittsburgh Steelers 1993-93
Mickey Sutton, S
Houston Oilers 1966
Ben Tamburello, OG
Philadelphia Eagles 1987-91
Ben Thomas, DT
New England Pats 1985; Green Bay Packers 1986-87; Atlanta Falcons 1988
Jack Thornton, LB
Miami Dolphins 1966
Travis Tidwell, QB
NY Giants 1950-51
Lawyer Tillman, WR
Cleveland Browns 1989-93
Keith Uecker, T
Denver Broncos 1982-84; Green Bay Packers 1985-92
Steve Wallace, OT
San Francisco 49ers 1986-93
Reggie Ware, RB
LA Raiders 1988
Frank Warren, DE
New Orleans Saints 1981-89
Ed West, TE
Green Bay Packers 1984-93
Freddy Weygand, WR
Chicago Bears 1989
Gerald Williams, DE
Pittsburgh Steelers 1986-91
John (Tex) Williams, G
Philadelphia Eagles 1942
Quency Williams, DE
LA Raiders 1984
Larry Willingham, DB
St. Louis Cardinals 1971-72
Chester Willis, RB
Oakland Raiders 1981; LA Raiders 1982-84
James Willis, LB
Green Bay Packers 1993
Jerry Wilson, E
Philadelphia Eagles 1959-60; San Francisco 49ers 1960
Dick Wood, QB
Denver Broncos 1962; San Diego Chargers 1962; NY Jets 1963-64; Oakland Raiders 1965; Miami Dolphins 1966
Chris Woods, WR
LA Raiders 1987-90
Alexander Wright, WR
Dallas Cowboys 1990-91; LA Raiders 1992-93
Mickey Zofko, RB
Detroit Lions 1971-74; NY Giants 1974

Auburn Media Information

*Auburn Assistant AD/
Media and Public Relations*
Kent Partridge

Auburn Sports Information
P.O. Box 351
Auburn, AL 36831-0351
(205) 844-9800
FAX: (205) 844-9807

Partridge (Home): 826-1034

Football Beat Writers
Neal Sims
Birmingham News (PM)
Box 2553
Birmingham, AL 35202
(205) 325-2222

Richard Scott
Birmingham Post-Herald (AM)
Box 2553
Birmingham, AL 35202
(205) 325-2222

Dave Mundee
Opelika-Auburn News (AM)
Drawer 2208
Opelika, AL 36801
(205) 749-6271

Brian Bourke
Montgomery Advertiser (AM)
Box 1000
Montgomery, AL 36102
(205) 262-1611

Mike Griffith
Anniston Star (PM)
216 W. 10th St.
Anniston, AL 36210
(205) 236-1550

Mark Rice
Ledger-Enquirer
17 W. 12th St.
Columbus, GA 31902
(404) 571-8502

Phillip Marshall
Huntsville Times (PM)
2317 Memorial Parkway
Huntsville, AL 35801
(205) 532-4430

Other Daily Newspapers
Tony Barnhart
Atlanta Journal-Constitution
Box 4689
Atlanta, GA 30302
(404) 526-5331

LeBron Miles
Decatur Daily (PM)
Box 1527
Decatur, AL 35602
(205) 353-4612

Jon Johnson
Dothan Eagle (AM)
Box 1968
Dothan, AL 36302
(205) 792-3141

Tom Smith
Florence Times (PM)
Box 797
Florence, AL 35631
(205) 766-8405

Jimmy Smothers
Gadsden Times (PM)
401 Locust St.
Gadsden, AL 35901
(205) 547-7521

Alan Clemons
Huntsville News (AM)
Box 1007
Huntsville, AL 35804
(205) 532-4536

Kim Shugart
Mobile Press/Register
304 Government St.
Mobile, AL 36601
(205) 433-1551

Tuscaloosa News (PM)
2001 Sixth St.
Tuscaloosa, AL 35401
(205) 345-0505

Scott Adamson
Daily Home
P.O. Box 977
Talladega, AL 35106

Specialty Publications
Mark Murphy
Inside the Auburn Tigers
Box 2666
Auburn, AL 36830
(205) 745-4370

Wire Services
Kendall Weaver/Paul Newberry
Associated Press
107 S. Lawrence
Montgomery, AL 36104
(205) 262-5947

Play-by-Play Broadcasters
Jim Fyffe
WLWI Radio
Box 4999
Montgomery, AL 36195
(205) 240-9274

Charlie Trotman
Rt. 4, Box 223
Woodley Rd.
Montgomery, AL 36116
(205) 288-4121

Quentin Riggins
Auburn Network
P.O. Box 351
Auburn, AL 36831

Stations Carrying Games
Originating station is
The Auburn Network

Network consists of over 70 stations in Alabama, Georgia and Tennessee. For additional information, contact Mike Hubbard at (205) 844-0545

Television Broadcasters
Mike Scruggs
WJSU-TV
Box 40
Anniston, AL 36202
(205) 237-8651

Doug Bell
WBMG-TV
2075 Golden Crest Dr.
Birmingham, AL 35209

Ken Lass, Jim Dunaway
WVTM-TV
Box 10502
Birmingham, AL 35202
(205) 328-6883

Rick Karle, Mike Raita
WBRC-TV
Box 6
Birmingham, AL 35201
(205) 323-2822

Dave Platta
WTVM-TV
1909 Wynnton Rd.
Columbus, GA 31906
(404) 324-6471

Mark Haggard
WRBL-TV
Box 270
Columbus, GA 31906
(404) 323-3333

Steve Johnson
WHNT-TV
200 Holmes Ave.
Huntsville, AL 35801
(205) 533-1919

Bruce Cunningham
WAFF-TV
Box 2116
Huntsville, AL 35804
(205) 533-4848

Gus Hergert
WAAY-TV
Box 2555
Huntsville, AL 35804
(205) 533-3131

Randy Patrick
WKRG-TV
Box 160587
Mobile, AL 36616
(205) 479-5555

Rennie Knott
WALA-TV
Box 1548
Mobile, AL 36633
(205) 434-1010

Phil Snow
WSFA-TV
Box 250251
Montgomery, AL 36125-0251
(205) 281-2902

Brian Corbett
WAKA-TV
P.O. Box 230667
Montgomery, AL 36123-0667

Sheldon Haygood
WHOA-TV
Channel 32
P.O. Box 3236
Montgomery, AL 36193
(205) 271-6330

Radio Stations
Andy Burcham
WKKR
P.O. Box 2329
Opelika, AL 36801
(205) 745-4657

Rod Bramblett
WAUD
Gentry Building
Auburn, AL 36830
(205) 887-3401

Bud Smith
WJHO
2009 Pepperell Parkway
Opelika, AL 36801
(205) 745-6484

Campus Media
Sports Editor
The Auburn Plainsman
Foy Union
Auburn University, AL 36849
(205) 844-4130

Sports Director
WEGL-FM 91.1
Haley Center
Auburn University, AL 36849
(205) 826-5184

FLORIDA

DR. JOHN LOMBARDI
President

DR. NICHOLAS CASSISI
Faculty Representative

JEREMY FOLEY
Athletic Director

University of Florida

PRESIDENT:
Dr. John Lombardi (Pamona College 1963)
FACULTY REPRESENTATIVE:
Dr. Nicholas Cassisi (John Carroll 1954)
ATHLETIC DIRECTOR:
Jeremy Foley (Hobart College 1974)
HEAD COACH:
Steve Spurrier (Florida 1967)
LOCATION: Gainesville, Florida
FOUNDED: 1853
ENROLLMENT: 36,000
NICKNAME: Gators
COLORS: Orange and Blue
STADIUM: Ben Hill Griffin Stadium at Florida FielD (83,000) - Natural

Gator Quick Facts

1993 RECORD: 11-2
(5-1 Home, 3-1 Away, 3-0 Neutral)
1993 SEC RECORD (FINISH): 7-1 (1st)
(3-0 Home, 3-1 Away, 1-0 Neutral)
BOWL: USF+G Insurance Sugar
Florida 41, West Virginia 7
ALL-TIME RECORD: 491-332-38 (.592)
SEC RECORD: 174-170-15 (.506) - Regular Season Games
SEC CHAMPIONSHIPS: 2
(1991, 1993)
BOWL APPEARANCES: 21
BOWL RECORD: 10-11 (.476)
LAST APPEARANCE: 1994 USF+G Insurance Sugar Bowl
(Florida 41, West Virginia 7)

FLORIDA
Team Information

OFFENSIVE SYSTEM: Pro-Set (multiple formations)

DEFENSIVE SYSTEM: 4-4-3

LETTERMEN RETURNING: 49
- 23 Offense
- 23 Defense
- 3 Specialists

LETTERMEN LOST: 18
- 12 Offense
- 4 Defense
- 2 Specialists

STARTERS RETURNING: 15
OFFENSE (5)
QB	Terry Dean (6-2, 204, Sr.)
QB	Danny Wuerffel (6-2, 201, So.)
OT	Jason Odom (6-5, 288, Jr.)
OT	Reggie Green (6-7, 296, Jr.)
OG	Dean Golden (6-6, 278, Sr.)

DEFENSE (8)
DE	Kevin Carter (6-6, 271, Sr.)
DT	Ellis Johnson (6-3, 276, Sr.)
LB	Dexter Daniels (6-2, 235, Jr.)
BB	Ben Hanks (6-2, 213, Jr.)
CB	Larry Kennedy (5-10, 184, Sr.)
FS	Michael Gilmore (5-11, 180, Sr.)
CB	Anthone Lott (5-9, 189, So.)

SPECIALISTS (2)
P	Shayne Edge (5-11, 171, Sr.)
PK	Judd Davis (6-1, 185, Sr.)

STARTERS LOST: 10
OFFENSE (7)
WR	Willie Jackson (6-1, 202, Sr.)
WR	Harrison Houston (5-9, 175, Sr.)
OG	Jim Watson (6-3, 289, Sr.)
TE	Charlie Dean (6-2, 245, Sr.)
RB	Errict Rhett (5-11, 214, Sr.)
FB	Kelvin Randolph (5-10, 234, Sr.)
C	Gantt Crouch (6-3, 263, Sr.)

DEFENSE (3)
ILB	Ed Robinson (6-0, 240, Sr.)
GB	Monty Grow (6-3, 222, Sr.)
DT	William Gaines (6-5, 293, Sr.)

SPECIALISTS (0)

Ben Hill Griffin Stadium at Florida Field (83,000)
First Game: 1930 — Alabama 20, Florida 0
Largest Crowd: 85,507 (Nov. 27, 1993)
Florida State 33, Florida 21

1994 Florida Schedule

Sept.	3	NEW MEXICO STATE	GAINESVILLE
Sept.	10	KENTUCKY	GAINESVILLE
Sept.	17	at Tennessee	Knoxville, Tenn.
Oct.	1	at OLE MISS	Oxford, Miss.
Oct.	8	LSU	GAINESVILLE
Oct.	15	AUBURN	GAINESVILLE
Oct.	29	GEORGIA	GAINESVILLE
Nov.	5	SOUTHERN MISS - HC	GAINESVILLE
Nov.	12	SOUTH CAROLINA	GAINESVILLE
Nov.	19	at Vanderbilt	Nashville, Tenn.
Nov.	26	at Florida State	Tallahassee, Fla.

1995 Florida Schedule

Sept.	2	HOUSTON	GAINESVILLE
Sept.	9	at Kentucky	Lexington, Ky.
Sept.	16	TENNESSEE	GAINESVILLE
Sept.	30	OLE MISS	GAINESVILLE
Oct.	7	at LSU	Baton Rouge, La.
Oct.	14	at Auburn	Auburn, Ala.
Oct.	28	at Georgia	Athens, Ga.
Nov.	4	NORTHERN ILLINOIS	GAINESVILLE
Nov.	11	at South Carolina	Columbia, S.C.
Nov.	18	VANDERBILT	GAINESVILLE
Nov.	25	FLORIDA STATE	GAINESVILLE

1993 Florida Individual Leaders

RUSHING	Atts	Yards	Avg	TDs	Yds/Game
Errict Rhett	247	1,289	5.2	11	107.4
TERENCE FOY	14	104	7.4	2	20.8
Kelvin Randolph	11	49	4.5	1	4.9
Daryl Frazier	5	49	9.8	0	4.5

PASSING	Atts	Comp	Ints/TDs	Pct	Yds
DANNY WUERFFEL	273	159	10 / 22	.582	2,230
TERRY DEAN	200	118	10 / 17	.590	1,651

RECEIVING	Rec	Yds	Avg	TDs	Yds/Game
JACK JACKSON	51	949	18.6	11	79.1
Willie Jackson	49	675	13.8	6	75.0
CHRIS DOERING	43	553	12.9	7	46.1
Errict Rhett	36	271	7.5	0	22.6
Harrison Houston	35	643	18.4	7	53.6

SCORING	G	TDs	PAT	FGs	Tot	Avg
JUDD DAVIS	12	0	51-53	15-19	96	8.0
JACK JACKSON	12	12	0	0	72	6.0
Errict Rhett	12	11	0	0	66	5.5
CHRIS DOERING	12	7	0	0	42	3.5
Harrison Houston	12	7	0	0	42	3.5

PUNTING	No	Yds	Avg	Long
SHAYNE EDGE	43	1,837	42.7	61

KICKOFF RETURNS	No	Yds	Avg	TDs	Avg/Game	Long
JACK JACKSON	17	480	28.2	1	40.0	100
Harrison Houston	11	238	21.6	0	19.8	40

PUNT RETURNS	No	Yds	Avg	TDs	Avg/Game	Long
LARRY KENNEDY	19	165	8.7	0	13.8	34
SOROLA PALMER	13	129	9.9	0	12.9	33

TACKLES	Total	Sk(Yds)	TL(Yds)	Ints
Ed Robinson	117 (59-58)	0.5 (-11)	5 (-18)	0
DEXTER DANIELS	86 (47-39)	0.5 (-6)	2 (-10)	1
BEN HANKS	83 (45-38)	0	6 (-15)	1
William Gaines	73 (50-23)	2.5 (-23)	11.5 (-33)	0
LARRY KENNEDY	67 (47-20)	0	1 (-1)	0

INTERCEPTIONS	No	Yds	TDs	Int/Game	Long
MICHAEL GILMORE	4	0	0	0.3	0
ANTHONE LOTT	3	20	0	0.25	20

Returning Players in All Capitals

1993 Florida Team Statistics

	UF	OPP
FIRST DOWNS	298	225
Rushing	103	88
Passing	182	116
Penalty	13	21
NET YARDS RUSHING	1647	1334
Yards gained	1977	1678
Yards lost	330	344
Rushing attempts	400	417
Average per rush	4.1	3.2
Average per game	137.3	111.2
NET YARDS PASSING	4072	2705
Average per game	339.3	225.4
Passes attempted	488	419
Passes completed	284	233
Had intercepted	21	16
TOTAL OFFENSIVE YARDS	5719	4039
Average per game	476.6	336.6
Total plays	888	836
Average per play	6.44	4.83
NUMBER PUNTS/YARDS	44/1837	72/2905
Punting average	41.8	40.3
Net punting average	38.5	36.2
PUNT RETURNS/YARDS	36/298	20/142
Punt return average	8.3	7.1
KICKOFF RETURNS/YARDS	37/828	63/1250
Kickoff return average	22.4	19.8
PENALTIES/YARDS	109/846	71/577
Penalty yards per game	70.5	48.1
FUMBLES/LOST	18/9	25/14
INTERCEPTION RETURNS/YARDS	16/112	21/297
Interception return average	7.0	14.1
TOUCHDOWNS	61	28
Rushing	18	9
Passing	41	17
Return	1	2
FIELD GOALS MADE/ATTEMPTED	15/19	15/23
KICK EXTRA POINTS MADE/ATTEMPTED	53/56	22/24
SAFETY	1	0
TWO-POINT CONVERSION	3/5	1/4
TOTAL POINTS	472	237
Average per game	39.3	19.8

Dexter Daniels   **Judd Davis**   **Chris Doering**

1993 Florida Results
11-2 Overall • 7-1 SEC Champion

Date	Opponent	Result	Score	Att.
Sept. 4	ARKANSAS STATE	W	44-6	84,051
Sept. 11	at Kentucky	W	24-20	58,175
Sept. 18	TENNESSEE [ABC]	W	41-34	85,247
Oct. 2	MISS. STATE [JP]	W	38-24	84,738
Oct. 9	at LSU [ESPN]	W	58-3	60,060
Oct. 16	at Auburn	L	35-38	85,214
Oct. 30	Georgia (J'ville) [ABC]	W	33-26	80,392
Nov. 6	SW LOUISIANA - HC	W	61-14	83,711
Nov. 13	at South Carolina [JP]	W	37-26	70,188
Nov. 20	VANDERBILT [JP]	W	52-0	83,818
Nov. 27	FLORIDA STATE [ABC]	L	21-33	85,507
Dec. 4	Alabama (Birmingham) [ABC]	W	28-13	76,345
	(SEC Championship Game)			
Jan. 1	West Virginia [ABC]	W	41-7	75,437
	(USF&G Insurance Sugar Bowl • New Orleans)			

1994 SEC Football   61

Steve Spurrier

Year-By-Year Record

Year	School	Conf.	All	Bowl
1983	Tampa Bay	(USFL)	11-7	Playoffs
1984	Tampa Bay	(USFL)	14-4	Playoffs
1985	Tampa Bay	(USFL)	10-8	
1987	Duke	2-5 (7th)	5-6	
1988	Duke	3-3-1 (6)	7-3-1	
1989	Duke	6-1 (t1st)	8-4	All American
1990	Florida	6-1	9-2	
1991	Florida	7-0 (1st)	10-2	Sugar
1992	Florida	6-2 (t1E)	9-4	Gator
1993	Florida	7-1 (1st)	11-2	Sugar
OVERALL RECORD		37-13-1 (.735)	94-42-1 (.689)	10 years
College Record		37-13-1 (.735)	59-23-1 (.717)	7 Years
USFL Record			35-19 (.648)	3 Years
Florida Record		26-4 (.867)	39-10 (.796)	4 Years
Duke Record		11-9-1	20-13-1	3 Years
Bowl Record		1-2	(0-1 Duke, 1-1 Florida)	

HOMETOWN:
Johnson City, Tennessee

ALMA MATER (YEAR):
Florida (1967)

PLAYING CAREER:
Florida starting quarterback 1964-66 (All-SEC and All-America 1965, 1966; SEC Most Valuable Player and Heisman Trophy winner 1966); San Francisco (NFL) 1967-75; Tampa Bay (NFL) 1976; National Football Foundation Hall of Fame 1986.

COACHING CAREER:
Florida Assistant 1978; Georgia Tech Assistant 1979; Duke Assistant 1980-82; Tampa Bay Head Coach (USFL) 1983-85; Duke Head Coach 1987-89; Florida Head Coach 1990-Present (also serves as offensive coordinator and quarterbacks coach).

COACHING ACHIEVEMENTS:
USFL Playoffs 1983, 1984; 1988 and 1989 ACC Coach of the Year; 1989 ACC Co-Champions; 1990 AP and UPI SEC Coach of the Year; 1991 Nashville Banner SEC Coach of the Year; 1991 SEC Champions; 1993 SEC Champion; 1994 USF+G Sugar Bowl Champions.

BORN:
April 20, 1945

WIFE:
Jeri Starr

CHILDREN:
Lisa 26, Amy 24, Steve 22, Scotty 6

ASSISTANT COACHES:
JIM COLLINS (Elon 1974) - Recruiting Coordinator/Tight Ends
DWAYNE DIXON (Florida 1985) - Wide Receivers
CARL FRANKS (Duke 1982) - Inside Linebackers
BOBBY PRUETT (Marshall 1965) - Defensive Coordinator/Defensive Backs
JOHN REAVES (Florida 1972) - Offensive Backfield
BOB SANDERS (Davidson 1976) - Defensive Line Coordinator/Defensive Ends
JIMMY RAY STEPHENS (Florida 1977) - Offensive Line
CHARLIE STRONG (Central Arkansas 1982) - Assistant Head Coach/Defensive Tackles
RON ZOOK (Miami-Ohio 1976) - Special Teams/Nicklebackers

SUPPORT STAFF:
RICH TUTEN (Clemson 1976) - Strength Coach
MIKE WASIK (Florida 1987) - Athletic Trainer for Football

Florida

Florida All-Star Candidates

JACK JACKSON
Junior • Wide Receiver
5-9 • 171 • Moss Point, Miss.

• Led Florida in receptions in 1993 with 51 for 949 yards, the third-highest seasonal total in Gator history. Also posted 11 touchdown catches, the SEC's top number. Earned second-team *Football News* Sophomore All-America and second-team All-SEC acclaim in 1993.
• Ranked among the top five national leaders in kickoff returns, averaging 28.2 yards per return, the highest average in the Florida record book and the SEC's second-best mark on the season.
• Averaged 18.6 yards per reception, the best in school history for a receiver who caught 50 or more passes.

JACKSON STATS

Receiving					Kickoff Returns					
Year	Rec	Yds	Avg	TD	Long	Year	No.	Yds	Avg	TD	Long
1992	35	462	13.2	3	53	1992	7	149	21.3	0	33
1993	51	949	18.6	11	73	1993	17	480	28.2	1	100
Career	86	1411	16.4	14	73	Career	24	629	26.2	1	100

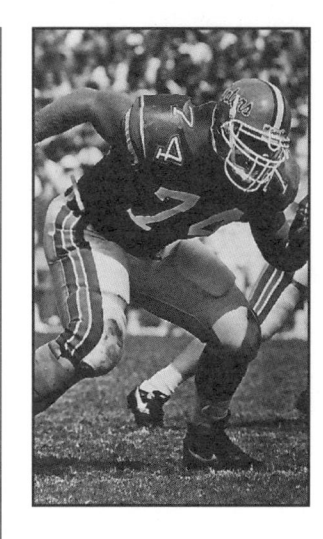

JASON ODOM
Junior • Offensive Tackle
6-5 • 297 • Bartow, Fla.

• Has started 23-consecutive games at right tackle, earning the top early in his true freshman season in 1992.
• Earned second-team *Football News* Sophomore All-America honors and second-team All-SEC honors last year.
• Considered Florida's, most consistent offensive lineman last season, earning the squad's 1993 Offensive Lineman of the Year award.

ELLIS JOHNSON
Senior • Defensive Tackle
6-3 • 282 • Wildwood, Fla.

• Earned Florida's 1994 spring Defensive MVP award following a dominating performance throughout spring drills. Will serve as a defensive co-captain this fall.
• As a junior, led the team in quarterback sacks with seven and tackles for loss with 15 for -76 yards.
• Posted 38 defensive "Big Plays," the team's second-highest total: 15 tackles for loss, 17 quarterback hurries, four pass deflections, one fumble recovery and one caused fumble. Also recorded four pass deflections on the season.

JOHNSON STATS

Year	Tackles	Solos	Assists	Sacks (Yds)
1991	16	10	6	0
1992	32	22	10	3 (-23)
1993	55	39	16	7 (-47)
Career	103	71	32	10 (-70)

KEVIN CARTER
Senior • Defensive End
6-6 • 266 • Tallahassee, Fla.

• Recorded 59 total tackles in 1993, the second-highest number for a Florida defensive lineman. Also posted the squad's third-best "Big Play" total with 30.5 on the season: 11.5 tackles for loss, 12 quarterback hurries, one fumble recovery, three forced fumbles and one blocked kick.
• Started 25 of the last 26 games at defensive end, earning second-team *Football News* Sophomore All-America and second-team All-SEC honors in 1992.
• Ranked second on the team in quarterback sacks with 6.5 in 1993.

CARTER STATS

Year	Tackles	Solos	Assists	Sacks (Yds)
1991	14	5	9	0
1992	64	38	26	3.5 (-53)
1993	59	33	26	6.5 (-57)
Career	137	76	61	10 (110)

1994 SEC Football

1994 Florida Roster

No.	Name	Pos.	Ht.	Wt.	Class	Exp.	Hometown (High School/JC)
91	Tremayne Allen	TE	6-2	217	Jr.	SQ	Antioch, Tenn. (Brentwood Academy)
22	Tyrone Baker	TB	5-9	175	Fr.	SQ	Gainesville, Fla. (Buchholz)
97	David Barnard	DT	6-1	295	Jr.	2L	Miami, Fla. (Miami Sr.)
45	Jason Bartley	ILB	5-11	221	Jr.	2L	Jacksonville, Fla. (Fletcher)
44	James Bates	ILB	6-1	220	So.	1L	Sevierville, Tenn. (Sevier Co.)
15	Ronnie Battle	WR	5-8	166	Fr.	SQ	Ft. Myers, Fla. (Cypress Lakes)
39	Chris Bilkie	FB	6-2	236	Sr.	3L	Holmes Beach, Fla. (Manatee)
87	Chris Braun	TE	6-3	245	Sr.	1L	Gainesville, Fla. (Buchholz)
68	Elijah Brown	DT	6-3	298	Fr.	SQ	Jacksonville, Fla. (University Christian)
67	Mark Campbell	DE	6-3	287	Jr.	2L	Miami, Fla. (Sunset)
57	Kevin Carter	DE	6-6	265	Sr.	3L	Tallahassee, Fla. (Lincoln)
40	Johnie Church	DE	6-3	255	Jr.	2L	Ft. Myers, Fla. (Cypress Lakes)
66	Keith Council	DT	6-4	264	Fr.	SQ	Orlando, Fla. (Evans)
48	Dexter Daniels	ILB	6-2	240	Jr.	2L	Valdosta, Ga. (Valdosta)
56	Cameron Davis	DE	6-4	251	So.	1L	Lauderhill, Fla. (St. Thomas Aquinas)
6	Judd Davis	PK	6-1	185	Sr.	2L	Ocala, Fla. (Forest)
12	Terry Dean	QB	6-2	207	Jr.	2L	Naples, Fla. (Collier)
28	Chris Doering	WR	6-4	181	Jr.	1L	Gainesville, Fla. (P.K. Yonge)
14	Shayne Edge	P	5-11	174	Sr.	3L	Lake City, Fla. (Columbia)
19	Bart Edmiston	PK	5-10	176	So.	1L	Pensacola, Fla. (Washington)
34	Jerome Evans	FB	6-1	228	So.	SQ	Arcadia, Fla. (DeSoto Co.)
99	McDonald Ferguson	DT	6-1	242	So.	SQ	Miami, Fla. (N. Miami)
5	Terrence Foy	TB	5-9	195	So.	1L	Orlando, Fla. (Winter Park)
36	Kevin Freeman	ILB	6-0	224	Sr.	3L	Palmetto, Fla. (Manatee)
35	Michael Gilmore	FS	5-11	180	Sr.	3L	Chipley, Fla. (Chipley)
62	Dean Golden	OG	6-6	283	Sr.	3L	Plantation, Fla. (South Plantation)
78	Reggie Green	OT	6-6	298	Jr.	2L	Bradenton, Fla. (Southeast)
42	Darren Hambrick	NB	6-2	205	So.	1L	Lacoochee, Fla. (Dade City-Pasco)
11	Ben Hanks	NB	6-2	224	Jr.	2L	Miami, Fla. (Miami Senior)
13	Mike Harris	FS	6-2	191	Fr.	SQ	Gainesville, Fla. (Buchholz)
69	P.J. Harrison	OT	6-6	296	Jr.	1L	Bushnell, Fla. (South Sumter)
82	Aubrey Hill	WR	5-11	175	Sr.	3L	Miami, Fla. (Carol City)
51	Anthony Ingrassia	C	6-2	296	Sr.	1L	Watchung, N.J. (Watchung Hills)
27	Demetric Jackson	FS	6-0	175	So.	1L	Ft. White, Fla. (Columbia)
1	Jack Jackson	WR	5-9	171	Jr.	2L	Moss Point, Miss. (Moss Point)
61	Ellis Johnson	DT	6-3	283	Sr.	3L	Wildwood, Fla. (Wildwood)
77	Eric Johnson	OT	6-6	297	Fr.	SQ	Pace, Fla. (Pace)
53	Kevin Johnson	C	6-3	270	Jr.	1L	Vero Beach, Fla. (Vero Beach)
3	Larry Kennedy	CB	5-10	186	Sr.	3L	Sarasota, Fla. (Riverview)
10	Eric Kressler	QB	6-2	206	So.	1L	Palm Beach Gardens, Fla. (Palm Beach Gardens)
18	Eddie Lake	SS	5-10	185	Sr.	2L	Tarpon Springs, Fla. (Tarpon Springs)
9	Anthone Lott	CB	5-9	189	So.	1L	Jacksonville, Fla. (Raines)
8	Pat Lowe	NB	6-3	221	Fr.	SQ	Ft. Lauderdale, Fla. (Dillard)
32	Kedra Malone	CB	5-8	175	Sr.	3L	Niceville, Fla. (Niceville)
20	Sam McCorkle	FS	5-9	176	Jr.	1L	Ft. Pierce, Fla. (Central)
46	Xavier McCray	SS	5-11	208	Fr.	SQ	Miami, Fla. (Carol City)
76	Keith McMahon	OT	6-6	298	Fr.	SQ	Bradenton, Fla. (Manatee)
60	Henry McMillian	DT	6-3	276	Sr.	2L	Folkston, Ga. (Charlton Co.)
29	Thomas Miller	CB	5-11	174	Fr.	SQ	Tampa, Fla. (Hillsborough)
71	Jeff Mitchell	OG	6-5	278	So.	1L	Clearwater, Fla. (Countryside)
23	Dwayne Mobley	FB	5-10	219	So.	1L	Brooksville, Fla. (Hernando)
90	Mike Moten	DE	6-5	255	Fr.	Sq	Daytona Beach, Fla. (Mainland)
80	Shawn Nunn	TE	6-3	246	So.	1L	Ocala, Fla. (Vanguard)
74	Jason Odom	OT	6-5	297	Jr.	2L	Bartow, Fla. (Bartow)
17	Sorola Palmer	WR	6-0	173	Jr.	2L	Lacombe, La. (Mandeville)
47	Matt Pearson	ILB	6-2	235	Jr.	2L	Mayo, Fla. (Lafayette Co.)
98	Anthony Riggins	DE	6-4	222	Jr.	1L	Ft. Pierce, Fla. (Central)
59	Wyley Ritch	C	6-5	249	Fr.	SQ	Ft. White, Fla. (Sante Fe)
54	Willie Rodgers	ILB	6-1	232	Fr.	SQ	Miami, Fla. (Hialeah)
88	Taras Ross	TE	6-3	241	Fr.	SQ	Dade City, Fla. (Dade City-Pasco)
16	Brian Schottenheimer	QB	6-2	195	So.	SQ	Overland Park, Kan. (Blue Valley)
2	Shea Showers	CB	5-11	170	So.	1L	Alachua, Fla. (Sante Fe)
52	David Swain	C	6-3	270	Sr.	3L	Altamonte Springs, Fla. (Lake Brantley)
26	Dwayne Thomas	NB	6-3	223	Fr.	SQ	Jacksonville, Fla. (Lee)
65	Derek Walker	OG	6-5	277	So.	1L	Rockledge, Fla. (Rockledge)
50	Kavin Walton	ILB	6-1	221	Fr.	SQ	Miami, Fla. (Carol City)
24	Fred Weary	CB	5-11	176	Fr.	SQ	Jacksonville, Fla. (Mandarin)
25	Elijah Williams	TB	5-10	178	Fr.	SQ	Milton, Fla. (Milton)
4	Lawrence Wright	SS	6-1	191	So.	1L	Miami, Fla. (N. Miami)
7	Danny Wuerffel	QB	6-2	206	So.	1L	Ft. Walton, Fla. (Ft. Walton Beach)
75	Donnie Young	OG	6-3	294	So.	1L	Venice, Fla. (Venice)

NB = NICKLEBACKER

Numerical Roster

No.	Name	Pos.
1	Jack Jackson	WR
2	Shea Showers	CB
3	Larry Kennedy	CB
4	Lawrence Wright	SS
5	Terrence Foy	TB
6	Judd Davis	PK
7	Danny Wuerffel	QB
8	Pat Lowe	NB
9	Anthone Lott	CB
10	Eric Kressler	QB
11	Ben Hanks	NB
12	Terry Dean	QB
13	Mike Harris	FS
14	Shayne Edge	P
15	Ronnie Battle	WR
16	Brian Schottenheimer	QB
17	Sorola Palmer	WR
18	Eddie Lake	SS
19	Bart Edmiston	PK
20	Sam McCorkle	FS
22	Tyrone Baker	TB
23	Dwayne Mobley	FB
24	Fred Weary	CB
25	Elijah Williams	TB
26	Dwayne Thomas	NB
27	Demetric Jackson	FS
28	Chris Doering	WR
29	Thomas Miller	CB
32	Kedra Malone	CB
34	Jerome Evans	FB
35	Michael Gilmore	FS
36	Kevin Freeman	ILB
39	Chris Bilkie	FB
40	Johnie Church	DE
42	Darren Hambrick	NB
44	James Bates	ILB
45	Jason Bartley	ILB
46	Xavier McCray	SS
47	Matt Pearson	ILB
48	Dexter Daniels	ILB
50	Kavin Walton	ILB
51	Anthony Ingrassia	C
52	David Swain	C
53	Kevin Johnson	C
54	Willie Rodgers	ILB
56	Cameron Davis	DE
57	Kevin Carter	DE
59	Wyley Ritch	C
60	Henry McMillian	DT
61	Ellis Johnson	DT
62	Dean Golden	OG
65	Derek Walker	OG
66	Keith Council	DT
67	Mark Campbell	DE
68	Elijah Brown	DT
69	P.J. Harrison	OT
71	Jeff Mitchell	OG
74	Jason Odom	OT
75	Donnie Young	OG
76	Keith McMahon	OT
77	Eric Johnson	OT
78	Reggie Green	OT
80	Shawn Nunn	TE
82	Aubrey Hill	WR
87	Chris Braun	TE
88	Taras Ross	TE
90	Mike Moten	DE
91	Tremayne Allen	TE
97	David Barnard	DT
98	Anthony Riggins	DE
99	McDonald Ferguson	DT

Florida

1994 Florida Depth Chart

OFFENSE

WR:	1	Jack Jackson
	17	Sorola Palmer
WR:	82	Aubrey Hill
	28	Chris Doering
TE:	80	Shawn Nunn
	88	Taras Ross
LT:	78	REGGIE GREEN
	77	Eric Johnson
LG:	71	Jeff Mitchell
	62	DEAN GOLDEN
C:	52	David Swain
	53	Kevin Johnson
	51	Anthony Ingrassia
RG:	75	Donnie Young
	65	Derek Walker
RT:	74	JASON ODOM
	76	Keith McMahon
QB:	12	TERRY DEAN
	7	DANNY WUERFFEL
FB:	39	Chris Bilkie
	23	Dwayne Mobley
RB:	25	Elijah Williams
	22	Tyrone Baker

DEFENSE

LE:	57	KEVIN CARTER
	56	Cameron Davis
LT:	61	ELLIS JOHNSON
	97	David Barnard
RT:	60	Henry McMillian
	99	McDonald Ferguson
RE:	67	Mark Campbell
	40	Johnie Church
ILB:	48	DEXTER DANIELS
	50	Kavin Walton
ILB:	44	James Bates
	47	Matt Pearson
LC:	3	LARRY KENNEDY
	2	Shea Showers
RC:	9	ANTHONE LOTT
	29	Thomas Miller
SS:	4	Lawrence Wright
	18	Eddie Lake
FS:	35	MICHAEL GILMORE
	13	Mike Harris
NB:	11	BEN HANKS
	42	Darren Hambrick

SPECIALISTS

PK:	6	JUDD DAVIS
	19	Bart Edmiston
P:	14	SHAYNE EDGE
	6	Judd Davis

Returning Starters In All Capitals

1994 Florida Signees

Name	Pos.	Ht.	Wt.	Hometown/High School
Reidel Anthony	WR	6-0	165	South Bay, Fla./Glades Central
Teako Brown	DB	5-11	185	Miami, Fla./Carol City
Ed Chester	DL	6-4	270	Springhill, Fla./Springstead
Tony Cochran	DL	6-4	240	Montezuma, Ga./Macon County
Willie Cohens	LB	6-3	215	Starke, Fla./Bradford County
Mo Collins	OL	6-5	287	Charlotte, N.C./West Charlotte
Tony George	DB	6-0	175	Cincinnati, Ohio/Winton Woods
Jacquez Green	WR	5-9	165	Ft. Valley, Ga./Peach County
Ike Hilliard	WR	6-0	185	Patterson, La./Patterson
Mike Jackson	DL	6-5	230	Wrightsville, Ga./Johnson County
Terry Jackson	DB	6-0	195	Gainesville, Fla./P.K. Yonge
Nafis Karim	WR	5-11	165	Marietta, Ga./Pope
Travis McGriff	WR	5-9	170	Gainesville, Fla./P.K. Yonge
Mike Peterson	DB	6-2	195	Alachua, Fla./Santa Fe
Jamie Richardson	WR	5-11	165	Tallahassee, Fla./Godby
Dossy Robbins	FB	6-1	235	Marathon, Fla./Marathon
Deac Story	OL	6-5	275	Winter Park, Fla./Winter Park
Fred Taylor	RB	6-1	215	Belle Glade, Fla./Glades Central

Larry Kennedy

Reggie Green

1994 SEC Football

Florida Year-By-Year Records

Year	Coach	SEC	SEC Finish	Overall	Bowls
1906	Jack Forsythe	5-3-0			
1907	Jack Forsythe	4-1-1			
1908	Jack Forsythe	5-2-1			
1909	G.E. Pyle	6-1-1			
1910	G.E. Pyle	6-1-0			
1911	G.E. Pyle	5-0-1			
1912	G.E. Pyle	5-2-1			
1913	G.E. Pyle	4-3-0			
1914	Charles McCoy	5-2-0			
1915	Charles McCoy	4-3-0			
1916	Charles McCoy	0-5-0			
1917	A.L. Busser	2-4-0			
1918	A.L. Busser	0-1-0			
1919	A.L. Busser	5-3-0			
1920	William Kline	6-3-0			
1921	William Kline	6-3-2			
1922	William Kline	7-2-0			
1923	J.A. VanFleet	6-1-2			
1924	J.A. VanFleet	6-2-2			
1925	H.L. Sebring	8-2-0			
1926	H.L. Sebring	2-6-2			
1927	H.L. Sebring	7-3-0			
1928	Charles Bachman	8-1-0			
1929	Charles Bachman	8-2-0			
1930	Charles Bachman	6-3-1			
1931	Charles Bachman	2-6-2			
1932	Charles Bachman	3-6-0			
1933	D.K. Stanley	2-3-0	9t	5-3-1	—
1934	D.K. Stanley	2-2-1	7	6-3-1	—
1935	D.K. Stanley	1-6-0	12	3-7-0	—
1936	Josh Cody	1-5-0	11	4-6-0	—
1937	Josh Cody	3-4-0	8	4-7-0	—
1938	Josh Cody	2-2-1	7	4-5-1	—
1939	Josh Cody	0-3-1	12	5-5-1	—
1940	Thomas Lieb	2-3-0	8t	5-5-0	—
1941	Thomas Lieb	1-3-0	10	4-6-0	—
1942	Thomas Lieb	1-3-0	9	4-5-0	—
1943	NO TEAM				
1944	Thomas Lieb	0-3-0	10t	4-3-0	—
1945	Thomas Lieb	1-3-1	10t	4-5-1	—
1946	Raymond Wolf	0-5-0	12	0-9-0	—
1947	Raymond Wolf	0-3-1	12	4-5-1	—
1948	Raymond Wolf	1-5-0	10t	5-5-0	—
1949	Raymond Wolf	1-4-1	10t	4-5-1	—
1950	Bob Woodruff	2-4-0	10	5-5-0	—
1951	Bob Woodruff	2-4-0	9t	5-5-0	—
1952	Bob Woodruff	3-3-0	6	7-3-0	Gator
1953	Bob Woodruff	1-3-2	9	3-5-2	—
1954	Bob Woodruff	5-2-0	3t	5-5-0	—
1955	Bob Woodruff	3-5-0	10	4-6-0	—
1956	Bob Woodruff	5-2-0	3	6-3-1	—
1957	Bob Woodruff	4-2-1	3t	6-2-1	—
1958	Bob Woodruff	2-3-1	8t	6-4-1	Gator
1959	Bob Woodruff	2-4-0	9	5-4-1	—
1960	Ray Graves	5-1-0	2	9-2-0	Gator
1961	Ray Graves	3-3-0	6	4-5-1	—
1962	Ray Graves	4-2-0	5	7-4-0	Gator
1963	Ray Graves	3-3-1	7	6-3-1	—
1964	Ray Graves	4-2-0	2t	7-3-0	—
1965	Ray Graves	4-2-0	3	7-4-0	Sugar
1966	Ray Graves	5-1-0	3	9-2-0	Orange
1967	Ray Graves	4-2-0	3t	6-4-0	—
1968	Ray Graves	3-2-1	6t	6-3-1	—
1969	Ray Graves	3-1-1	4	9-1-1	Gator
1970	Doug Dickey	3-3-0	5t	7-4-0	—
1971	Doug Dickey	1-6-0	8t	4-7-0	—
1972	Doug Dickey	3-3-1	6	5-5-1	—
1973	Doug Dickey	3-4-0	5t	7-5-0	Tangerine
1974	Doug Dickey	3-3-0	4t	8-4-0	Sugar
1975	Doug Dickey	5-1-0	2t	9-3-0	Gator
1976	Doug Dickey	4-2-0	4	8-4-0	Sun
1977	Doug Dickey	3-3-0	5	6-4-1	—
1978	Doug Dickey	3-3-0	4t	4-7-0	—
1979	Charley Pell	0-6-0	9t	0-10-1	—
1980	Charley Pell	4-2-0	4t	8-4-0	Tangerine
1981	Charley Pell	3-3-0	4t	7-5-0	Peach
1982	Charley Pell	3-3-0	6t	8-4-0	Bluebonnet
1983	Charley Pell	4-2-0	3t	9-2-1	Gator
1984	Charley Pell/Galen Hall	5-0-1	*	9-1-1	—
1985	Galen Hall	5-1-0	*	9-1-1	—
1986	Galen Hall	2-4-0	7t	6-5-0	—
1987	Galen Hall	3-3-0	6	6-6-0	Aloha
1988	Galen Hall	4-3-0	4t	7-5-0	All-American
1989	Galen Hall/Gary Darnell	4-3-0	4t	7-5-0	Freedom
1990	Steve Spurrier	6-1-0	—	9-2-0	—
1991	Steve Spurrier	7-0-0	1	10-2-0	Sugar
1992	Steve Spurrier	6-2-0	1t-E	9-4-0	Gator
1993	Steve Spurrier	7-1-0	1	11-2-0	Sugar

*position vacated in standings

Bowl Results (10-11)

Bowl	Opponent	Result	Date
Gator	Tulsa	W 14-13	1-1-53
Gator	Ole Miss	L 3-7	12-27-58
Gator	Baylor	W 13-12	12-31-60
Gator	Penn State	W 17-7	12-28-62
Sugar	Missouri	L 18-20	1-1-66
Orange	Georgia Tech	W 27-12	1-2-67
Gator	Tennessee	W 14-13	12-27-69
Tangerine	Miami-Ohio	L 7-16	12-22-73
Sugar	Nebraska	L 10-13	12-31-74
Gator	Maryland	L 0-13	12-29-75
Sun	Texas A&M	L 14-37	1-2-77
Tangerine	Maryland	W 35-20	12-20-80
Peach	West Virginia	L 6-26	12-31-81
Bluebonnet	Arkansas	L 24-28	12-31-82
Gator	Iowa	W 14-6	12-30-83
Aloha	UCLA	L 16-20	12-25-87
All-American	Illinois	W 14-10	12-29-88
Freedom	Washington	L 7-34	12-30-89
Sugar	Notre Dame	L 28-39	1-1-92
Gator	N.C. State	W 27-10	12-31-92
Sugar	West Virginia	W 41-7	1-1-94

66 Florida

Florida vs. All Opponents

Opponent	W	L	T
Air Force	1	0	0
Akron	1	0	0
*Alabama	9	17	0
Arkansas	0	1	0
Arkansas State	2	0	0
Army	1	2	0
Auburn	30	38	2
Baylor	1	0	0
Boston College	1	1	0
California	2	0	0
Cal-State Fullerton	1	0	1
Chicago	1	1	0
Cincinnati	1	0	0
Citadel	12	0	0
Clemson	9	3	1
College of Charleston	3	0	0
Columbia College	3	0	0
Davidson	0	1	0
Drake	1	0	0
Duke	3	2	0
Duquesne	1	0	0
East Carolina	1	0	0
Florida Southern	13	1	0
Florida State	23	12	1
Furman	6	2	0
George Washington	2	0	0
*Georgia	26	43	2
Georgia A&M	2	0	0
Georgia Southern	1	0	0
Georgia Tech	9	23	6
Hampden-Sydney	1	0	1
Harvard	0	2	0
Houston	2	1	0
Illinois	2	0	0
Indiana	0	1	0
Indiana State	2	0	0
Iowa	1	0	0
Kansas State	2	0	0
Kentucky	27	17	0
Kent State	1	0	0
Kings College	1	0	0
LSU	19	18	3
Louisiana Tech	1	0	0
Louisville	2	0	0
Loyola (New Orleans)	1	0	0
Maryland	11	6	0
Maryville	1	0	0
Memphis State	1	1	0
Mercer	10	6	1
Miami (Florida)	25	24	0
Miami (Ohio)	0	1	0
Mississippi	7	9	1
Mississippi College	1	0	1
Mississippi State	30	16	2
Missouri	0	1	0
Montana State	1	0	0
Nebraska	0	1	0
Newberry	1	0	0
New Mexico	1	0	0
North Carolina	2	7	1
North Carolina State	9	4	1
Northern Illinois	1	0	0
Northwestern	2	0	0
North Texas State	0	1	0
Notre Dame	0	1	0
Oglethorpe	3	1	0
Oklahoma State	1	0	0
Oregon	1	0	0
Penn State	1	0	0
Pittsburgh	0	0	1
Presbyterian	1	0	0
Randolph Macon	2	0	0
Rice	3	4	1
Richmond	2	0	0
Rollins	13	2	1
Rutgers	1	0	1
Samford	2	0	0

Opponent	W	L	T
San Jose State	1	0	0
Sewanee	7	2	0
South Carolina	8	3	3
Southern Cal	1	0	1
Southern Methodist	2	2	0
Southern Mississippi	1	0	0
Southwestern Louisiana	3	0	0
Stetson	15	2	2
Syracuse	1	2	0
Tampa	5	0	0
Temple	1	2	0
Tennessee	8	15	0
Texas A&M	1	1	0
Texas	0	2	1
Tulane	13	6	2
Tulsa	4	1	0
UCLA	2	3	0
Utah	1	0	0
Vanderbilt	16	9	2
Villanova	0	4	0
Virginia	1	0	0
Virginia Tech	1	0	0
Washington	0	1	0
West Virginia	1	0	0
West Texas State	1	0	0

* disagreement between schools about series record

Gator quarterback Kerwin Bell, a 1985 All-SEC honoree, passed for 7,585 yards and 56 touchdowns in his career.

Florida School Records

Individual

Game
Total Offense	428	Danny Wuerffel vs. Miss. State	(1993)
Yards Rushing	316	Emmitt Smith vs. New Mexico	(1989)
Rushing Attempts	41	Errict Rhett vs. Georgia	(1993)
Yards Passing	449	Danny Wuerffel vs. Miss. State	(1993)
Pass Attempts	66	John Reaves vs. Auburn	(1969)
Pass Completions	33	John Reaves vs. Auburn	(1969)
	33	John Reaves vs. Miami	(1971)
Yards Receiving	238	Carlos Alvarez vs. Miami-Florida	(1969)
Receptions	15	Carlos Alvarez vs. Miami-Florida	(1969)

Season
Total Offense	3,176	Shane Matthews	(1992)
Yards Rushing	1,599	Emmitt Smith	(1989)
Rushing Attempts	284	Emmitt Smith	(1989)
Yards Passing	3,205	Shane Matthews	(1992)
Pass Attempts	463	Shane Matthews	(1992)
Pass Completions	275	Shane Matthews	(1992)
Touchdown Passes	28	Shane Matthews	(1991)
Yards Receiving	1,329	Carlos Alvarez	(1969)
Receptions	88	Carlos Alvarez	(1969)
Touchdown Catches	12	Carlos Alvarez	(1969)
Interceptions	7	John Clifford	(1970)
		Randy Talbot	(1974)
		Will White	(1990)
Points	110	Tommy Durrance	(1969)

Career
Total Offense	9,241	Shane Matthews	(1989-92)
Yards Rushing	4,163	Errict Rhett	(1990-93)
Rushing Attempts	873	Errict Rhett	(1990-93)
Yards Passing	9,287	Shane Matthews	(1990-92)
Pass Attempts	1,202	Shane Matthews	(1990-92)
Pass Completions	722	Shane Matthews	(1990-92)
Touchdown Passes	74	Shane Matthews	(1990-92)
Yards Receiving	2,563	Carlos Alvarez	(1969-71)
Receptions	172	Carlos Alvarez	(1969-71)
Touchdown Catches	24	Willie Jackson	(1990-93)
Interceptions	14	Will White	(1989-92)
Points	222	Emmitt Smith	(1987-89)

Team

Game
Points	77	vs. West Texas State	(1982)
Total Offense	774	vs. West Texas State	(1982)
Yards Rushing	531	vs. Utah	(1977)
Yards Passing	512	vs. SW Louisiana	(1993)
First Downs	35	vs. SW Louisiana	(1993)
Total Defense	32	vs. Georgia Tech	(1963)
Rushing Defense	-18	vs. Florida State	(1969)
Passing Defense	0	vs. Furman	(1947)
		vs. Mississippi State	(1958)

Season
Points	387	(1990)
Total Offense	5,719	(1993)
Yards Rushing	3,326	(1975)
Yards Passing	4,072	(1993)
First Downs	298	(1993)
Fewest Points Allowed	70	(1957)
Total Defense	1,942	(1963)
Rushing Defense	884	(1965)
Passing Defense	420	(1955)
Consecutive Wins	11	(1927-28; Three in 1927, Eight in 1928)

Emmitt Smith

John Reaves

Florida in the NFL

Neal Anderson, RB
Chicago Bears 1986-93
Trace Armstrong, DT
Chicago Bears 1989-93
Ephesians Bartley, OLB
Philadelphia Eagles 1992
Jim Beaver, G
Philadelphia Eagles 1962
Kerwin Bell, QB
Atlanta Falcons 1988; Tampa Bay Buccaneers 1989
Michael Brandon, DE
Indianapolis Colts 1993
Scot Brantley, LB
Tampa Bay Buccaneers 1980-87
Larry Brinson, RB
Dallas Cowboys 1977-79; Seattle Seahawks 1980
Barry Brown, E
Baltimore Colts 1966-67; NY Giants 1968; Boston Patriots 1969-70
Lomas Brown, OT
Detroit Lions 1985-93
Carl Brumbaugh, QB
Chicago Bears 1930-34, 1936, 1938; Cleveland Rams 1937
Glenn Cameron, LB
Cincinnati Bengals 1975-85
Earl Carr, RB
San Francisco 49ers 1978; Philadelphia Eagles 1979
Rick Casares, RB
Chicago Bears 1955-64; Washington Redskins 1965; Miami Dolphins 1966
Don Chandler, K
NY Giants 1956-64; Green Bay Packers 1965-67
Wes Chandler, WR
New Orleans Saints 1978-81; San Diego Chargers 1981-87
Clifford Charlton, LB
Cleveland Browns 1988-89; Miami Dolphins 1990
Brian Clark, K
Tampa Bay Buccaneers 1982
Mike Clark, DE
Washington Redskins 1981
Hagood Clarke, DB
Buffalo Bills 1964-68
Cris Collinsworth, WR
Cincinnati Bengals 1981-88
Ray Criswell, P
Tampa Bay Buccaneers 1988
Brad Culpepper, DT
Minnesota Vikings 1992-93
Al Darby, WR
Houston Oilers 1976; Tampa Bay Buccaneers 1978
Floyd Dean, LB
San Francisco 49ers 1963-64
Frank Dempsey, G
Chicago Bears 1950-53
Guy Dennis, G
Cincinnati Bengals 1969-72; Detroit Lions 1973-75
Cal Dixon, C
NY Jets 1992-93
Dwayne Dixon, WR
Tampa Bay Bucs 1984
Everett Douglas, T
NY Giants 1953
Jimmy DuBose, RB
Tampa Bay Buccaneers 1976-78
Paul Duhart, B
Green Bay Packers 1944; Pittsburgh Steelers 1945
Ricky Easmon, DB
Dallas Cowboys & Tampa Bay Buccaneers 1985-86
Richard Fain, DB
Cincinnati Bengals 1991; Chicago Bears 1992

Chris Faulkner, TE
LA Rams, 1984; San Diego Chargers 1985
Dan Fike, OG
Cleveland Browns 1985-93
Don Fleming, B
Cleveland Browns 1960-62
Derrick Gaffney, WR
NY Jets 1978-84
Larry Gagner, G
Pittsburgh Steelers 1966-69; Kansas City Chiefs 1972
David Galloway, DT
Phoenix Cardinals 1982-89; Denver Broncos 1990
Lewis Gilbert, TE
Atlanta Falcons 1978-79; Philadelphia Eagles 1980; San Francisco 49ers 1980; LA Rams 1981
Chip Glass, TE
NY Giants 1974
Clark Goff, T
Pittsburgh Steelers 1940
Tim Golden, LB
New England Patriots 1982-84; Philadelphia Eagles 1985
Bobby Joe Green, P
Chicago Bears 1962-73
Sammy Green, LB
Seattle Seahawks 1976-79; Houston Oilers 1980
Tony Green, RB
Washington Redskins 1978; Seattle Seahawks 1979; NY Giants 1979
Mal Hammack, RB
Chicago Cardinals 1955, 1957-59; St. Louis Cardinals 1960-66
Lorenzo Hampton, RB
Miami Dolphins 1985-89
Jack Harper, RB
Miami Dolphins 1967-68
James Harrell, LB
Detroit Lions 1979-86; Kansas City Chiefs 1987
Roy Harris, DT
Atlanta Falcons 1984-85
Joe Hergert, HB
Buffalo Bills 1960-61
Bob Hewko, QB
Tampa Bay Buccaneers 1983
Billy Hinson, OG
Denver Broncos 1985; Atlanta Falcons 1986
Chuck Hunsinger, B
Chicago Bears 1950-52
John Hunt, C
Dallas Cowboys, 1984
Scott Hutchinson, DE
Buffalo Bills 1978-80; Tampa Bay Buccaneers 1981-83
Randy Jackson, T
Chicago Bears 1967-74
John James, P
Atlanta Falcons 1972-81; Detroit Lions 1982; Houston Oilers 1983-84
Alonzo Johnson, LB
Philadelphia Eagles 1986-87
James Jones, FB
Detroit Lions 1983-88; Seattle Seahawks 1989-91
Jimmy Jordan, RB
New Orleans Saints 1967
Vince Kendrick, RB
Atlanta Falcons 1974; Tampa Bay Buccaneers 1976
Crawford Ker, OG
Dallas Cowboys 1985-90; Denver Broncos 1991
Floyd Konetsky, E
Cleveland Rams 1944-45; Baltimore Colts 1947
Frank Lasky, T
NY Giants 1964-65

Burton Lawless, G
Dallas Cowboys 1975-79; Detroit Lions 1980; Miami Dolphins 1981
Terry LeCount, WR
San Francisco 49ers 1978; Minnesota Vikings 1979-83
Tony Lilly, S
Denver Broncos 1984-87
David Little, LB
Pittsburgh Steelers 1981-91
Buford Long, B
NY Giants 1953-55
Tony Lomack, WR
LA Rams 1990
Shane Matthews, QB
Chicago Bears 1993
Tony McCoy, DT
Indianapolis Colts 1992-93
Vito McKeever, DB
Tampa Bay Buccaneers 1986-87
Lee McGriff, WR
Tampa Bay Buccaneers 1976
Dexter McNabb, FB
Green Bay Packers 1992-93
Wilber Marshall, LB
Chicago Bears 1984-87; Washington Redskins 1988-92; Houston Oilers 1993
Patrick Miller, LB
San Diego Chargers 1988
Ernie Mills, WR
Pittsburgh Steelers 1991-93
Alonzo Mitz, DE
Seattle Seahawks 1986-90; Cincinnati Bengals 1991-93
Nat Moore, WR
Miami Dolphins 1974-86
Mike Mularkey, TE
Minnesota Vikings 1984-88; Pittsburgh Steelers 1989-91
Dennis Murphy, DT
Chicago Bears 1965
Godfrey Myles, LB
Dallas Cowboys 1991-93
Ricky Nattiel, WR
Denver Broncos 1987-91
Tim Newton, MG
Minnesota Vikings 1985-88; Tampa Bay Buccaneers 1989-91; Kansas City Chiefs 1993
Jack O'Brien, E
Pittsburgh Steelers 1954-56
Louis Oliver, DB
Miami Dolphins 1989-93
Ralph Ortega, LB
Atlanta Falcons 1975-78; Miami Dolphins 1979-80
Joel Parker, WR
New Orleans Saints 1974-77
Bernie Parrish, DB
Cleveland Browns 1959-66; Houston Oilers 1966
Anton Peters, T
Denver Broncos 1963
David Posey, K
New England Patriots 1978
John Reaves, QB
Philadelphia Eagles 1972-75; Cincinnati Bengals 1975-78; Minnesota Vikings 1979; Houston Oilers 1981
Larry Rentz, DB
San Diego Chargers 1969
Huey Richardson, LB
Pittsburgh Steelers 1991
Stacey Simmons, WR
Indianapolis Colts 1990
Jack Simpson, B
Baltimore Colts 1958-60; Pittsburgh Steelers 1961-62
Cedric Smith, FB
Minnesota Vikings 1990; New Orleans Saints 1991
Emmitt Smith, RB
Dallas Cowboys 1990-93

Jack Smith, T
Philadelphia Eagles 1945
Larry Smith, RB
LA Rams 1969-73; Washington Redskins 1974
Del Speer, DB
Cleveland Browns 1993
Jimmy Spencer, DB
New Orleans Saints 1992-93
Steve Spurrier, QB-P
San Francisco 49ers 1967-75 QB, Tampa Bay Buccaneers 1976
Bruce Starling, DB
Denver Broncos 1963-64
Kay Stephenson, QB
San Diego Chargers 1967; Buffalo Bills 1968
John Symank, B
Green Bay Packers 1957-62; St. Louis Cardinals 1963
Steve Tannen, CB
NY Jets 1970-74
Allen Trammell, S
Houston Oilers 1966
Richard Trapp, E
Buffalo Bills 1968; San Diego Chargers 1969; NY Jets 1970; Philadelphia Eagles 1971-72
Scott Trimble, OT
San Diego Chargers 1985
Harmon Wages, RB
Atlanta Falcons 1968-71, 1973
Dale Waters, E
Washington Redskins 1932-33
Rhondy Weston, DT
Tampa Bay Buccaneers 1989; Cleveland Browns 1990
Adrian White, DB
NY Giants 1987-91; Green Bay Packers 1992; New England Patriots 1993
Broughton Williams, T
Chicago Bears 1947
David Williams, OT
Houston Oilers 1989-93
Jarvis Williams DB
Miami Dolphins 1988-93
John L. Williams, FB
Seattle Seahawks 1986-93
Jim Yarbrough, T
Detroit Lions 1969-77
Jason Yeats, TE
Houston Oilers 1960
Tyrone Young, TE
New Orleans Saints 1983-84
Jack Youngblood, DE
LA Rams 1971-84
Jeff Zimmerman, OG
Dallas Cowboys 1987-91

Neal Anderson

1994 SEC Football 69

Florida Media Information

Florida Assistant AD/ Communications
Norm Carlson

Florida Assistant AD/ Sports Information
John Humenik

Florida Sports Information
P.O. Box 14485
Gainesville, FL 32604
(904) 375-4683, Ext 6102 or 6103
FAX: (904) 375-4809

Humenik (Home): 377-1908

Football Writers
Mike Bianchi, Robbie Andreau
Gainesville Sun
P.O. Box 147147
Gainesville, FL 32614-7147
(904) 374-5055

Gene Fernette
Florida Times Union
P.O. Box 1949
Jacksonville, FL 32201
(904) 359-4246

John Oesher
Florida Times Union
4839 Gopher Circle
Middleburg, FL 32068
(904) 282-6716

David Alfonso
Tampa Tribune
P.O. Box 191
Tampa, FL 33601
(813) 272-7655

Chris Harry
Tampa Tribune
1740 N.W. 6th Ave.
Gainesville, FL 32607
(904) 338-7829

Larry Guest
Orlando Sentinel
P.O. Box 2833
Orlando, FL 32802
(407) 420-5000

Mike Dame
Orlando Sentinel
309 N.E. 8th Ave.
Gainesville, FL 32601
(904) 372-6460

Hubert Mizell, John Romano
St. Petersburg Times
P.O. Box 1121
St. Petersburg, FL 33731
(813) 893-8123

Willie Hiatt
Bradenton Herald
P.O. Box 921
Bradenton, FL 33506
(813) 748-0411

Brent Woronoff
Daytona News Journal
901 Sixth Street
Daytona Beach, FL 32017
(904) 252-1511

David Jones
Florida Today
P.O. Box 41900
Melbourne, FL 32941-9000
(407) 242-3612

Andre Christopher
The Miami Herald
1 Herald Plaza
Miami, FL 33101
(305) 376-3700

Mic Huber
Sarasota Herald-Tribune
P.O. Box 1719
Sarasota, FL 33578
(813) 953-7755

Mike Cobb
Lakeland Ledger
P.O. Box 408
Lakeland, FL 33802
(813) 687-7010

Sports Editor
Ft. Lauderdale News
123 NW 20th Terrace
Gainesville, FL 32603
(904) 373-7916

Jeff Snook
Palm Beach Post
P.O. Box 24700
West Palm Beach, FL 33416
(407) 820-4100

Sports Editor
Tallahassee Democrat
P.O. Box 990
Tallahassee, FL, 32302
(904) 599-2100

Cesar Brioso
Ocala Star-Banner
P.O. Box 490
Ocala, FL 32670
(904) 867-4010

Specialty Publications
Marty Cohen
Gator Bait
P.O. Box 14022
Gainesville, FL 32604
(904) 372-1215

Wire Service
Ron Word
Associated Press
1 Riverside Ave.
Jacksonville, FL 32220
(904) 356-2829

Fred Goodall
Associated Press
P.O. Box 191
Tampa, FL 33601
(813) 223-3270

Play-By-Play Broadcasters
Mick Hubert — Radio
P.O. Box 14485
Gainesville, FL 32604
(904) 375-4683, Ext. 6600

Lee McGriff — Radio
3501 W. University Ave.
Gainesville, FL 32605

Lynn Mixson
SportsChannel Florida
Executive Court 1
2295 Corporate Blvd. NW
Suite 140
Boca Raton, FL 33431

David Steele
3205 Mallard Circle
Winter Park, FL 32989

Jim Yarbrough
1692 Joline Court
Winter Park, FL 32789

Television Broadcasters
John Cornell
WCJB-TV
P.O. Drawer WCJB
Gainesville, FL 32604
(904) 372-3545

Sports Director
WTLV-TV
1070 East Adams Street
Jacksonville, FL 32202
(904) 354-1212

Sports Director
WJXT-TV
P.O. Box 5270
Jacksonville, FL 32207
(904) 389-4000

Sports Director
WJKS-TV
P.O. Box 17000
Jacksonville, FL 32216
(904) 641-1700

Radio Stations
Sports Director
WYKS
4908 NW 34th St.
Gainesville, FL 32604
(904) 375-2200

Sports Director
WKTK Radio
1440 NE Waldo Road
Gainesville, FL 32609
(904) 377-0985

Sports Director
WGGG Radio
900 NW 8th Avenue
Gainesville, FL 32601
(904) 376-1230

Campus Media
Larry Vettel
WRUF Radio
P.O. Box 1444
Gainesville, FL 32604
(904) 392-0771

Sports Editor
Florida Alligator
P.O. Box 14257
Gainesville, FL 32604

Sports Director
WUFT-TV
P.O. Box 13375
Gainesville, FL 32604
(904) 392-4311

GEORGIA

DR. CHARLES KNAPP
President

DR. GARY COUVILLON
Faculty Representative

VINCE DOOLEY
Athletic Director

University of Georgia

PRESIDENT:
Dr. Charles Knapp (Iowa State 1968)
FACULTY REPRESENTATIVE:
Dr. Gary Couvillon (SW Louisiana 1961)
ATHLETIC DIRECTOR:
Vince Dooley (Auburn 1954)
HEAD COACH:
Ray Goff (Georgia 1978)
LOCATION: Athens, Georgia
FOUNDED: 1785
ENROLLMENT: 28,750
NICKNAME: Bulldogs
COLORS: Red and Black
STADIUM: Sanford Stadium (85,434) - Natural

Bulldog Quick Facts

1993 RECORD: 5-6
   (3-3 Home, 2-2 Away, 0-1 Neutral)
1993 SEC RECORD (FINISH): 2-6 (4th - Eastern)
   (1-3 Home, 1-2 Away; 0-1 Neutral)
BOWL: None
ALL-TIME RECORD: 589-335-53 (.630)
SEC RECORD: 212-146-13 (.589) — Regular Season Games
SEC CHAMPIONSHIPS: 10
   (1942, 46t, 48, 59, 66t, 68, 76, 80, 81t, 82)
BOWL APPEARANCES: 31
BOWL RECORD: 15-13-3 (.532)
LAST APPEARANCE: 1993 Florida Citrus Bowl
   (Georgia 21, Ohio State 14)

GEORGIA
Team Information

OFFENSIVE SYSTEM: Multiple

DEFENSIVE SYSTEM: Multiple

LETTERMEN RETURNING: 45
- 19 Offense
- 23 Defense
- 3 Specialists

LETTERMEN LOST: 19
- 8 Offense
- 8 Defense
- 3 Specialists

STARTERS RETURNING: 16
  OFFENSE (8)
  - TB   Terrell Davis (6-1, 211, Sr.)
  - WR   Hason Graham (5-11, 166, Sr.)
  - WR   Brice Hunter (6-0, 197, Jr.)
  - OT   Adam Meadows (6-7, 261, So.)
  - OG   Steve Roberts (6-3, 270, Sr.)
  - OG   Troy Stark (6-6, 260, So.)
  - C   David Weeks (6-6, 263, Jr.)
  - QB   Eric Zeier (6-2, 200, Jr.)

  DEFENSE (6)
  - DT   Phillip Daniels (6-6, 245, Jr.)
  - ILB Randall Godfrey (6-3, 226, Jr.)
  - SS   Buster Owens (6-0, 196, Jr.)
  - DT   Matt Storm (6-6, 290, Sr.)
  - FS   Ralph Thompson (6-1, 193, Sr.)
  - CB   Carlos Yancey (6-2, 186, Sr.)

  SPECIALISTS (2)
  - P   Scot Armstrong (6-2, 192, Sr.)
  - SN   Dan Rogers (6-4, 285, Sr.)

STARTERS LOST: 10
  OFFENSE (3)
  - RB   Earl Fouch (6-2, 210, Sr.)
  - TE   Shannon Mitchell (6-3, 235, Sr.)
  - OT   Bernard Williams (6-9, 310, Sr.)

  DEFENSE (5)
  - OLB Carlo Butler (6-2, 207, Sr.)
  - ILB Charlie Clemons (6-2, 226, Sr.)
  - OLB Mitch Davis (6-3, 240, Sr.)
  - NG   Bill Rosenberg (6-3, 275, Sr.)
  - CB   Greg Tremble (5-11, 185, Sr.)

  SPECIALISTS (2)
  - PK   Kanon Parkman (5-11, 171, Jr.)
  - SN   Drew David (6-1, 212, Sr.)

Sanford Stadium (85,434)
Record: 230-74-10 (.748)
First Game: Nov. 12, 1929 — Georgia 12, Yale 0
Largest Crowd: 85,434 (Seven times)
  Last: Nov. 13, 1993 - Auburn 42, Georgia 28

1994 Georgia Schedule

Sept.	3	at South Carolina	Columbia, S.C.
Sept.	10	TENNESSEE	ATHENS
Sept.	17	NE LOUISIANA	ATHENS
Sept.	24	OLE MISS	ATHENS
Oct.	1	at Alabama	Tuscaloosa, Ala.
Oct.	8	CLEMSON	ATHENS
Oct.	15	VANDERBILT	ATHENS
Oct.	22	at Kentucky	Lexington, Ky.
Oct.	29	at Florida	Gainesville, Fla.
Nov.	12	at Auburn	Auburn, Ala.
Nov.	26	GEORGIA TECH	ATHENS

1995 Georgia Schedule

Sept.	2	SOUTH CAROLINA	ATHENS
Sept.	9	at Tennessee	Knoxville, Tenn.
Sept.	16	NEW MEXICO STATE	ATHENS
Sept.	23	at Ole Miss	Oxford, Miss.
Sept.	30	ALABAMA	ATHENS
Oct.	7	at Clemson	Clemson, S.C.
Oct.	14	at Vanderbilt	Nashville, Tenn.
Oct.	21	KENTUCKY	ATHENS
Oct.	28	FLORIDA	ATHENS
Nov.	11	AUBURN	ATHENS
Nov.	25	Georgia Tech	Atlanta, Ga.

1993 Georgia Individual Leaders

RUSHING	Atts	Yards	Avg	TDs	Yds/Game
TERRELL DAVIS	167	824	4.9	5	74.9
Frank Harvey	36	146	4.1	3	13.3
BILL MONTGOMERY	45	144	3.2	3	3.2
Earl Fouch	11	40	3.6	0	3.6
STERLING BOYD	16	29	1.8	0	4.8

PASSING	Atts	Comp	Ints/TDs	Pct	Yds
ERIC ZEIER	425	269	24 / 7	.633	3525

RECEIVING	Rec	Yds	Avg	TDs	Yds/Game
BRICE HUNTER	76	970	12.8	9	88.2
Shannon Mitchell	49	539	11.0	2	49.0
JEFF THOMAS	39	469	12.0	1	42.6
HASON GRAHAM	36	699	19.4	5	63.5
Brian Bohannon	20	260	13.0	2	23.6

SCORING	G	TDs	PAT	FGs	Tot	Avg
KANON PARKMAN	11	0	35-36	19-27	92	8.4
BRICE HUNTER	11	9	1-1	0	56	5.1
TERRELL DAVIS	11	8	0	0	48	4.4
HASON GRAHAM	11	5	0	0	30	2.7
Frank Harvey	11	3	0	0	18	1.6
BILL MONTGOMERY	11	3	0	0	18	1.6

PUNTING	No	Yds	Avg	Long
Scot Armstrong	37	1419	38.4	57

KICKOFF RETURNS	No	Yds	Avg	TDs	Avg/Game	Long
JERRY JERMAN	18	398	22.1	0	39.8	73
HASON GRAHAM	13	261	20.1	0	23.7	47
CHRIS McCRANIE	5	109	21.8	0	21.8	36

PUNT RETURNS	No	Yds	Avg	TDs	Avg/Game	Long
CHRIS McCRANIE	14	202	14.4	1	40.4	45
JEFF THOMAS	11	61	7.6	0	7.6	10

TACKLES	Total (S-A)	Sk (Yds)	TL (Yds)	Ints
RANDALL GODFREY	114 (71-43)	1 (-5)	4 (-5)	1
Charlie Clemons	90 (50-40)	0	2 (-3)	3
Mitch Davis	87 (49-38)	13 (-74)	6 (-12)	1
Greg Tremble	80 (56-24)	0	3 (-7)	3
Bill Rosenberg	79 (35-44)	1 (-1)	6 (-10)	0

INTERCEPTIONS	No	Yds	TDs	Int/Game	Long
BUSTER OWENS	3	23	0	.27	23
Greg Tremble	3	20	1	.27	20
Charlie Clemons	3	14	0	.27	11

Returning Players in All Capitals

1993 Georgia Team Statistics

	UG	OPP
FIRST DOWNS	232	217
Rushing	77	113
Passing	139	92
Penalty	16	12
NET YARDS RUSHING	1181	2171
Yards rushing	1491	2441
Yards lost	310	270
Rushing Attempts	344	488
Average per rush	3.4	4.5
Average per game	107.4	197.4
NET YARDS PASSING	3552	2029
Average per game	322.9	184.5
Passes attempted	432	297
Passes completed	272	153
Had intercepted	7	17
TOTAL OFFENSIVE YARDS	4733	4200
Average per game	430.3	381.8
Total plays	776	785
Average per play	6.1	5.4
NUMBER PUNTS/YARDS	48/1802	53/2034
Punting average	37.5	38.4
Net punting average	34.3	33.4
PUNT RETURNS/YARDS	25/263	32/158
Punt return average	10.5	4.9
KICKOFF RETURNS/YARDS	43/861	59/1140
Kickoff return average	20.0	19.3
PENALTIES/YARDS	78/631	67/535
Penalty yards per game	57.4	48.5
FUMBLES/LOST	20/12	18/9
INTERCEPTION RETURNS/YARDS	17/157	7/108
Interception return average	9.2	15.4
TOUCHDOWNS	39	37
Rushing	12	21
Passing	24	14
Return	3	2
FIELD GOALS MADE/ATTEMPTED	19/27	10/16
SAFETY	0	0
TWO-POINT CONVERSIONS	1	1
TOTAL POINTS	328	289
Average per game	29.8	26.3

1993 Georgia Results

5-6 Overall • 2-6 SEC (4th - Eastern)

Date	Opponent	W/L	Score	Att.
Sept. 4	SOUTH CAROLINA	L	21-23	84,912
Sept. 11	at Tennessee [ESPN]	L	6-38	96,228
Sept. 18	TEXAS TECH	W	52-37	74,511
Sept. 25	at Ole Miss	L	14-31	38,000
Oct. 2	ARKANSAS	L	10-20	73,825
Oct. 9	SOUTHERN MISS	W	54-24	68,458
Oct. 16	at Vanderbilt	W	41-3	28,554
Oct. 23	KENTUCKY - HC [JP]	W	33-28	81,307
Oct. 30	Florida (Jacksonville) [ABC]	L	26-33	80,392
Nov. 13	AUBURN	L	28-42	85,434
Nov. 25	at Georgia Tech [ABC]	W	43-10	46,018

Randall Godfrey   **Brice Hunter**   **Eric Zeier**

1994 SEC Football

Ray Goff

Year-By-Year Record

Year	School	Conf.	All	Bowl
1989	Georgia	4-3 (t4th)	6-6	Peach
1990	Georgia	2-5 (t6th)	4-7	
1991	Georgia	4-3 (t4th)	9-3	Independence
1992	Georgia	6-2 (t1st-E)	10-2	Citrus
1993	Georgia	2-6 (4th-E)	5-6	
OVERALL RECORD		18-19 (.486)	34-24 (.586)	5 Years
Georgia Record		18-19 (.486)	34-24 (.586)	5 Years
Bowl Record		2-1	(2-1 Georgia)	

HOMETOWN:
Moultrie, Georgia

ALMA MATER:
Georgia (1978)

PLAYING CAREER:
Georgia starting quarterback 1975-76 (All-SEC, SEC Player of the Year, Seventh in Heisman Trophy balloting, 1976); Number two quarterback 1974; Freshman team quarterback 1973.

COACHING CAREER:
Georgia Graduate Assistant 1977; South Carolina Head Junior Varsity Coach 1978-79; South Carolina Assistant Coach 1980; Georgia Recruiting Coordinator 1981-82; Georgia Assistant Coach 1983-88; Georgia Head Coach 1989-present.

COACHING ACHIEVEMENTS:
1992 SEC Eastern Division Co-Champion

BORN:
July 10, 1955

WIFE:
Stephanie Ferguson of Lithonia, Georgia

CHILDREN:
Lindsey 10, Allison 7

ASSISTANT COACHES:
WAYNE McDUFFIE (Florida State 1968)-Assistant Head Coach/Offensive Coordinator/Offensive Line
MARION CAMPBELL (Georgia 1952)-Defensive Coordinator/Defensive Line
DICKY CLARK (Georgia 1977)-Force Unit Coordinator/Outside Linebackers
GREG DAVIS (McNeese State, 1973)-Quarterbacks
STEVE DENNIS (Georgia, 1979)-Defensive Backs
DARRYL DRAKE (Western Kentucky 1980)-Wide Receivers
DAVID KELLY (Furman 1979)-Running Backs
MAC McWHORTER (Georgia 1974)-Offensive Line/Tight Ends
FRANK ORGEL (Georgia 1961)-Inside Linebackers

SUPPORT STAFF:
STEVE BRYANT (Georgia 1981)-Assistant Trainer
MIKE DILLON (South Carolina 1981)-Assistant Trainer
JOHN KASAY (Georgia 1967)-Director of Strength and Conditioning
ROBBY STEWART-Defensive Line Strength

Georgia

Georgia All-Star Candidates

RANDALL GODFREY
Junior • Inside Linebacker
6-3 • 226 • Valdosta, Ga.

- First team Coaches All-SEC in 1993, leading Georgia in tackles for second-straight season (114 total stops).
- Posted a career-high 16 tackles in win over Kentucky and had three other 12-tackle games on the season. In all last season, posted seven double-digit tackle performances with seven outings of 5+ solo hits.
- Returned his only interception of 1993 into a 46-yard touchdown vs. Southern Miss.
- Freshman All-America and SEC Defensive Freshman of the Year in 1992 after leading Bulldogs with 114 total tackles that year as well in addition to a sack and three tackles for loss.

TRAVIS JONES
Senior • Defensive Tackle
6-3 • 257 • Irwinton, Ga.

- Converted from inside linebacker to starting defensive tackle prior to 1993 season, but missed entire campaign with kidney disorder.
- Saw spot duty at inside linebacker during career with best season coming in 1992 (44 total tackles, 4 sacks and 1 tackle for loss).
- Received Georgia's outstanding player award following 1994 spring practice.
- One of 11 players named to the 1993 CFA Good Works Team which recognizes student-athletes' contributions to community service.

GODFREY STATS

Year	Tackles	Sk (Yds)	TFL (Yds)	Int	PBU	FR
1992	114 (69-45)	1 (-16)	3 (-5)	1	3	1
1993	114 (71-43)	1 (-5)	4 (-5)	1	1	0
Career	228 (140-88)	2 (-21)	7 (-10)	2	4	1

JONES STATS

Year	Tackles	Sk (Yds)	TFL (Yds)	Int	PBU	FR
1990	18 (10-8)	0	1 (-2)	0	0	0
1991	18 (13-5)	0	0	0	0	0
1992	44 (27-17)	4 (-15)	1 (-1)	0	0	0
Career	80 (42-38)	4 (-15)	2 (-3)	0	0	0

BRICE HUNTER
Junior • Wide Receiver
6-0 • 197 • Valdosta, Ga.

- Led the SEC and shattered the Georgia single-season record with 76 receptions last season en route to first-team AP and *Football News* All-SEC honors.
- Also set the Bulldog single-season marks for receiving yardage (970) and touchdown receptions (9) in 1993.
- Earned sophomore All-America honors from *Football News*.
- Had at least five catches in 10 of 11 outings last season with a season-high 10 on two occasions (Southern Miss and Auburn).
- Best overall games came vs. Southern Miss (10 for 179 yards, 2 TDs) and Florida (9 for 109 yards, 1 TD) in 1993.

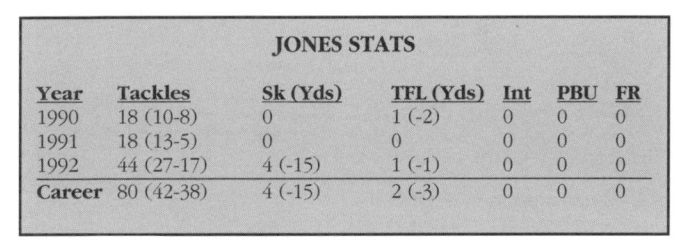

ERIC ZEIER
Senior • Quarterback
6-2 • 207 • Marietta, Ga.

- A 1994 *Playboy* preseason All-America and the most prolific passer in Georgia history, Zeier owns 61 Bulldog and 11 SEC passing records entering his senior season.
- Holds the distinction of being the only player in SEC history to pass for more than 500 yards in a single game (544 vs. Southern Miss, 1993).
- Also the only SEC player to throw for 400+ yards more than once in a career (three times in 1993).
- Set SEC marks for single-season passing yardage (3,525) and single-season total offense (3,482) in 1993, while his 7,757 career passing yards are just 1,530 shy of the SEC career passing standard.
- One of 24 players in the nation to be named to the 1993 Hitachi/CFA Scholar-Athlete team.

HUNTER STATS

Year	Rec	Yds	Avg	TD
1992	3	30	10.0	0
1993	76	970	12.8	9
Career	79	1000	12.7	9

ZEIER STATS

Year	Atts	Comp	Int	Pct	Yds	TD
1991	286	159	4	.556	1984	7
1992	258	151	12	.585	2248	12
1993	425	269	7	.633	3525	24
Career	969	579	23	.598	7757	43

1994 SEC Football

1994 Georgia Roster

No.	Name	Pos.	Ht.	Wt.	Class	Exp.	Hometown (High School/JC)
	Ronald Bailey	CB	6-0	190	RFr.	SQ	Folkston, Ga. (Charlton County)
70	Resty Beadles	TG	6-3	280	So.	SQ	Atlanta, Ga. (Westlake)
93	Herman Bell	SG	6-3	258	So.	SQ	Bartow, Fla. (Bartow)
14	Mike Bobo	QB	6-2	207	RFr.	SQ	Thomasville, Ga. (Thomasville)
15	Larry Bowie	RB	6-0	218	Jr.	SQ	Anniston, Ala. (Anniston)
2	Sterling Boyd	SB	5-11	189	So.	1L	Sherman, Texas (Sherman)
92	Greg Bright	OLB	6-2	214	RFr.	SQ	Moultrie, Ga. (Colquitt County)
50	Scott Brownholtz	C	6-3	260	Sr.	1L	San Diego, Calif. (Mt. Carnek)
91	Derrick Byrd	OLB	6-5	235	So.	1L	Box Springs, Ga. (Central)
32	Selma Calloway	RB	5-11	208	RFr.	SQ	Colquitt, Ga. (Miller County)
	Jon Carper	P	6-2	200	So.	SQ	Statesboro, Ga. (Statesboro)
76	Damian Carson	NG	6-2	265	RFr.	SQ	Calhoun, Ga. (Calhoun)
72	Chad Chosewood	ST	6-7	288	Jr.	2L	Alto, Ga. (Habersham)
	Lee Clarke	SE	6-0	186	Sr.	SQ	Hephzibah, Ga. (Hephzibah)
12	Juan Daniels	FLK	6-2	190	So.	1L	Norcross, Ga. (Norcross)
89	Phillip Daniels	OLB	6-6	255	Jr.	2L	Donalsonville, Ga. (Seminole County)
31	Drew David	SN	6-1	212	Sr.	3L	Cairo, Ga. (Cairo)
	Brent Davis	TE	6-3	235	So.	SQ	Duluth, Ga. (Duluth)
33	Terrell Davis	SB	6-1	211	Sr.	2L	San Diego, Calif. (Lincoln Prep)
	Matt Dickson	WR	5-10	180	Sr.	SQ	Cohutta, Ga. (NW Whitfield)
47	Robert Edwards	CB	6-2	202	So.	1L	Tennille, Ga. (Washington County)
	Jim Exley	OLB	6-2	215	Jr.	SQ	Springfield, Ga. (Effingham County)
69	Antonio Fleming	TT	6-4	280	RFr.	SQ	Edison, Ga. (Calhoun County)
42	Randall Godfrey	MLB	6-3	226	Jr.	2L	Valdosta, Ga. (Lowndes County)
4	Hason Graham	SE	6-0	166	Sr.	2L	Decatur, Ga. (SW DeKalb)
7	Scott Greer	CB/SN	5-11	195	So.	TR	Rome, Ga. (W. Rome)
49	Maurice Harrell	TE	6-3	245	Sr.	3L	Eastman, Ga. (Dodge County)
88	Brice Hunter	FLK	6-0	197	Jr.	2L	Valdosta, Ga. (Valdosta)
67	Tracy Huzzie	NG	6-4	310	Sr.	1L	LaGrange, Ga. (Troup County)
17	Jerry Jerman	SE	5-10	181	Sr.	1L	Richmond, Va. (Huguenot)
27	Corey Johnson	FS	5-11	183	So.	1L	Forest Park, Ga. (Forest Park)
54	D.J. Johnson	RLB	6-3	235	RFr.	SQ	Memphis, Tenn. (Craigmont)
61	Travis Johnson	C	6-4	242	RFr.	SQ	Charlotte, N.C. (Myers Park)
56	Bryan Jones	MLB	6-0	208	So.	1L	Jacksonville, Fla. (The Bolles School)
51	Travis Jones	DT	6-3	255	Sr.	3L	Irwinton, Ga. (Wilkinson County)
99	Jeff Kaiser	NG	6-4	265	Jr.	1L	Statesboro, Ga. (Statesboro)
1	Andy Kardian	PK	6-2	170	RFr.	SQ	Martinez, Ga. (Lakeside)
36	Whit Marshall	RLB	6-2	232	Jr.	2L	Atlanta, Ga. (Lovett)
23	Chris McCranie	FLK	5-11	170	So.	1L	Moultrie, Ga. (Colquitt County)
94	Deshay McKever	DT	6-2	265	Jr.	2L	Hazelhurst, Ga. (Jeff Davis)
71	Adam Meadows	ST	6-7	272	So.	1L	Powder Springs, Ga. (McEachern)
59	Matt Messer	SN	6-0	185	Sr.	SQ	Athens, Ga. (Clarke Central)
13	Bill Montgomery	SB	6-0	190	Sr.	3L	Bowdon, Ga. (Bowdon)
30	Will Muschamp	SS	6-0	190	Sr.	3L	Rome, Ga. (Darlington School)
3	Buster Owens	SS	6-0	202	Jr.	2L	LaGrange, Ga. (LaGrange)
6	Kanon Parkman	PK	5-11	171	Jr.	2L	Stone Mountain, Ga. (Stone Mountain)
90	Brett Pellock	P	5-11	178	Jr.	SQ	Savannah, Ga. (Windsor Forest)
78	David Powell	TT	6-7	295	So.	SQ	Roebuck, S.C. (Dorman)
82	Kojara Ransom	TE	6-3	232	RFr.	SQ	St. Petersburg, Fla. (Boca Ciego)
79	Steve Roberts	SG	6-3	270	Sr.	3L	Dalton, Ga. (Dalton)
29	Erik Robinson	CB	6-1	211	RFr.	SQ	Orlando, Fla. (West Orange)
97	Walter Rouse	NG	6-4	289	So.	1L	Cordele, Ga. (Crisp County)
	Ryan Sanderson	PK	6-1	165	So.	SQ	Valdosta, Ga. (Valdosta)
	Landon Schenck	PK	6-0	170	RFr.	SQ	Dublin, Ga. (Dublin)
43	Marisa Simpson	RB	5-11	225	So.	SQ	Norcross, Ga. (Norcross)
22	Alandus Sims	FS	6-1	195	So.	TR	Orlando, Fla. (Evans)
45	Trey Sipe	CB	6-0	182	RFr.	SQ	Bonaire, Ga. (Warner Robins)
11	Brian Smith	QB	6-3	202	So.	SQ	Spartanburg, S.C. (Spartanburg)
57	Derrick Smith	OLB	6-3	238	Jr.	2L	Memphis, Tenn. (Whitehaven)
38	Marcus Smith	FS	6-3	181	RFr.	SQ	Kathleen, Ga. (Warner Robins)
75	Troy Stark	TG	6-6	271	Jr.	2L	Canandaigua, N.Y. (Canandaigua)
98	Matt Storm	DT	6-6	305	Sr.	1L	Edmonds, Wash. (Woodway)
85	Michael Taylor	TE	6-3	240	RFr.	SQ	Columbus, Ga. (Kendrick)
52	Paul Taylor	TT	6-5	275	Jr.	2L	Rome, Ga. (West Rome)
8	Jeff Thomas	SE	6-2	192	Sr.	3L	Valdosta, Ga. (Lowndes County)
26	Ralph Thompson	FS	6-1	193	Sr.	3L	Nashville, Tenn. (Hillwood)
35	Mike Thornton	RB	5-10	229	Sr.	2L	Albany, Ga. (Albany)
83	Brandon Tolbert	OLB	6-2	213	RFr.	SQ	Villa Rica, Ga. (Villa Rica)
25	Gene Toodle	RLB	6-3	213	So.	1L	Atlanta, Ga. (Cross Keys)
68	Sean Tremblay	DT	6-3	275	RFr.	SQ	Port Jefferson, N.Y. (Comsewogue)
87	James Warner	TE	6-4	239	Sr.	3L	Newnan, Ga. (Newnan)
58	Frank Watts	OLB	6-2	245	Jr.	SQ	Columbus, Ga. (Baker)
55	David Weeks	C	6-6	266	Jr	2L	Atlanta, Ga. (Marist)
9	Marcus Williams	MLB	6-1	211	So.	1L	Valdosta, Ga. (Valdosta)
20	Carlos Yancy	CB	6-2	190	Sr.	1L	Sarasota, Fla. (Sarasota)
10	Eric Zeier	QB	6-2	205	Sr.	3L	Marietta, Ga. (Marietta)

Numerical Roster

No.	Name	Pos.
1	Andy Kardian	PK
2	Sterling Boyd	SB
3	Buster Owens	SS
4	Hason Graham	SE
6	Kanon Parkman	PK
7	Scott Greer	CB/SN
8	Jeff Thomas	SE
9	Marcus Williams	MLB
10	Eric Zeier	QB
11	Brian Smith	QB
12	Juan Daniels	FLK
13	Bill Montgomery	SB
14	Mike Bobo	QB
15	Larry Bowie	RB
17	Jerry Jerman	SE
20	Carlos Yancy	CB
22	Alandus Sims	FS
23	Chris McCranie	FLK
25	Gene Toodle	RLB
26	Ralph Thompson	FS
27	Corey Johnson	FS
29	Erik Robinson	CB
30	Will Muschamp	SS
31	Drew David	SN
32	Selma Calloway	RB
33	Terrell Davis	SB
35	Mike Thornton	RB
36	Whit Marshall	RLB
38	Marcus Smith	FS
42	Randall Godfrey	MLB
43	Marisa Simpson	RB
45	Trey Sipe	CB
47	Robert Edwards	CB
49	Maurice Harrell	TE
50	Scott Brownholtz	C
51	Travis Jones	DT
52	Paul Taylor	TT
54	D.J. Johnson	RLB
55	David Weeks	C
56	Bryan Jones	MLB
57	Derrick Smith	OLB
58	Frank Watts	OLB
59	Matt Messer	SN
61	Travis Johnson	C
67	Tracy Huzzie	NG
68	Sean Tremblay	DT
69	Antonio Fleming	TT
70	Resty Beadles	TG
	Jim Exley	OLB
71	Adam Meadows	ST
72	Chad Chosewood	ST
75	Troy Stark	TG
76	Damian Carson	NG
78	David Powell	TT
79	Steve Roberts	SG
82	Kojara Ransom	TE
83	Brandon Tolbert	OLB
85	Michael Taylor	TE
87	James Warner	TE
88	Brice Hunter	FLK
89	Phillip Daniels	OLB
90	Brett Pellock	P
91	Derrick Byrd	OLB
92	Greg Bright	OLB
93	Herman Bell	SG
94	Deshay McKever	DT
97	Walter Rouse	NG
98	Matt Storm	DT
99	Jeff Kaiser	NG

Georgia

1994 Georgia Depth Chart

OFFENSE

SE:	4	Hason Graham
	8	JEFF THOMAS
ST:	71	ADAM MEADOWS
	72	Chad Chosewood
SG:	79	STEVE ROBERTS
		Randy White
C:	50	Scott Brownholtz
	55	DAVID WEEKS
TG:	70	Resty Beadles
	75	TROY STARK
TT:	69	Antonio Fleming
	52	Paul Taylor
TE:	87	James Warner
	49	Maurice Harrell
FL:	88	BRICE HUNTER
	12	Juan Daniels
QB:	10	ERIC ZEIER
	14	Mike Bobo
SB:	2	Sterling Boyd
	13	Bill Montgomery
RB:	15	Larry Bowie
	32	Selma Calloway

DEFENSE

LT:	98	MATT STORM
	68	Sean Tremblay
NG:	97	Walter Rouse
	76	Damien Carson
RT:	51	Travis Jones
	94	Deshay McKever
OLB:	89	PHILLIP DANIELS
	91	Derrick Byrd
MLB:	42	RANDALL GODFREY
	9	Marcus Williams
ROV:	36	Whit Marshall
	54	D.J. Johnson
OLB:	57	Derrick Smith
	58	Frank Watts
LCB:	20	CARLOS YANCY
	29	Erick Robinson
SS:	30	Will Muschamp
	3	BUSTER OWENS
FS:	27	Corey Johnson
	22	Alandus Sims
RCB:	47	Robert Edwards
	45	Trey Sipe

SPECIALISTS

PK:	6	KANON PARKMAN
		Ryan Sanderson
P:	90	Brett Pellock
		Jon Carper
SN:	31	DREW DAVID
	59	Matt Messer

Returning Starters In All Capitals

1994 Georgia Signees

Name	Pos.	Ht.	Wt.	Hometown/High School
Corey Allen	WR	6-3	180	Riverdale, Ga./North Clayton
Phillip Benton	LB	6-2	245	Covington, Ga./NW Miss. CC
Larry Bowie	RB	6-0	218	Anniston, Ala./NE Oklahoma JC
Brooks Brodie	OL	6-3	255	Tifton, Ga./Tift County
Larry Brown	TE	6-5	235	Decatur, Ga./Crim
*Al Davis	WR	5-9	165	Louisville, Tenn./Alcoa
Glenn Ford	DB	5-8	165	Columbus, Ga./Carver
Adrian Goodman	LB	6-2	195	Jackson, Ga./Jackson
Gilbert Grantlin	WR	6-1	180	Belle Glade, Fla./Mesa JC
Cletidus Hunt	DL	6-4	268	Memphis, Tenn./Whitehaven
Marcus Hunter	DL	6-3	270	Daphne, Ala./Daphne
Dax Langley	PK/P	6-2	170	Conyers, Ga./Heritage
*George Lombard	RB	6-0	195	Atlanta, Ga./Lovett
Armin Love	DB	6-1	185	Houston, Texas/MacArthur
Hugh Mack	OL	6-2	285	Houston, Texas/C.E. King
Emmett Mitchell	DB	6-1	190	Memphis, Tenn./Whitehaven
Alandus Sims	DB	6-1	195	Orlando, Fla./Marshall University
Kirby Smart	DB	6-0	165	Bainbridge, Ga./Bainbridge
Kenshun Smith	RB	5-11	185	Atlanta, Ga./Southside
Paul Snellings	DL	6-4	255	LaGrange, Ga./Troup County
Travis Stroud	DL	6-3	258	Atlanta, Ga./Dunwoody
Chris Terry	OLB	6-7	225	Jacksonville, Fla./Ribault
Hines Ward	QB	6-1	185	Rex, Ga./Forest Park
Allen Weathers	OL	6-6	290	Cambridge, Mass./Fresno City College
Dave Williams	RB	6-1	192	Friendswood, Texas/Friendswood
Peppi Zellner	TE/DL	6-5	230	Forsyth, Ga./Mary Persons

*Drafted in the 1994 Major League Baseball amateur draft and signed professional contracts.

Terrell Davis

Steve Roberts

1994 SEC Football   77

Georgia Year-By-Year Records

Year	Coach	SEC	SEC Finish	Overall	Bowls
1892	Dr. Charles Herty			1-1-0	
1893	Ernest Brown			2-2-1	
1894	Robert Winston			5-1-0	
1895	Glenn "Pop" Warner			3-4-0	
1896	Glenn "Pop" Warner			4-0-0	
1897	Charles McCarthy			2-1-0	
1898	Charles McCarthy			4-2-0	
1899	Gordon Saussy			2-3-1	
1900	E. E. Jones			2-4-0	
1901	Billy Reynolds			1-5-2	
1902	Billy Reynolds			4-2-1	
1903	M. M. Dickinson			3-4-0	
1904	Charles A. Barnard			1-5-0	
1905	M. M. Dickinson			1-5-0	
1906	W. S. Whitney			2-4-1	
1907	W. S. Whitney			4-3-1	
1908	Branch Bocock			5-2-1	
1909	J. Coulter			1-4-2	
	Frank Dobson				
1910	W. A. Cunningham			6-2-1	
1911	W. A. Cunningham			7-1-1	
1912	W. A. Cunningham			6-1-1	
1913	W. A. Cunningham			6-2-0	
1914	W. A. Cunningham			3-5-1	
1915	W. A. Cunningham			5-2-2	
1916	W. A. Cunningham			6-3-0	
1919	W. A. Cunningham			4-2-3	
1920	H. J. Stegeman			8-0-1	
1921	H. J. Stegeman			7-2-1	
1922	H. J. Stegeman			5-4-1	
1923	George Woodruff			5-3-1	
1924	George Woodruff			7-3-0	
1925	George Woodruff			4-5-0	
1926	George Woodruff			5-4-0	
1927	George Woodruff			9-1-0	
1928	Harry Mehre			4-5-0	
1929	Harry Mehre			6-4-0	
1930	Harry Mehre			7-2-1	
1931	Harry Mehre			8-2-0	
1932	Harry Mehre			2-5-2	
1933	Harry Mehre	3-1-0	3	8-2-0	—
1934	Harry Mehre	3-2-0	5	7-3-0	—
1935	Harry Mehre	2-4-0	11	6-4-0	—
1936	Harry Mehre	3-3-0	6	5-4-1	—
1937	Harry Mehre	1-2-2	10	6-3-2	—
1938	Joel Hunt	1-2-1	9	5-4-1	—
1939	Wally Butts	1-3-0	9	5-6-0	—
1940	Wally Butts	2-3-1	7	5-4-1	—
1941	Wally Butts	3-1-1	4	9-1-1	Orange
1942	Wally Butts	6-1-0	1	11-1-0	Rose
1943	Wally Butts	0-3-0	4t	6-4-0	—
1944	Wally Butts	4-2-0	3	7-3-0	—
1945	Wally Butts	4-2-0	4	9-2-0	Oil
1946	Wally Butts	5-0-0	1t	11-0-0	Sugar
1947	Wally Butts	3-3-0	4t	7-4-1	Gator
1948	Wally Butts	6-0-0	1	9-2-0	Orange
1949	Wally Butts	1-4-1	10t	4-6-1	—
1950	Wally Butts	3-2-1	6	6-2-3	Presidential
1951	Wally Butts	2-4-0	9t	5-5-0	—
1952	Wally Butts	4-3-0	5	7-4-0	—
1953	Wally Butts	1-5-0	10t	3-7-0	—
1954	Wally Butts	3-2-1	5	6-3-1	—
1955	Wally Butts	2-5-0	11	4-6-0	—
1956	Wally Butts	1-6-0	12	3-6-1	—
1957	Wally Butts	3-4-0	9	3-7-0	—
1958	Wally Butts	2-4-0	10	4-6-0	—
1959	Wally Butts	7-0-0	1	10-1-0	Orange
1960	Wally Butts	4-3-0	6	6-4-0	—
1961	Johnny Griffith	2-5-0	9	3-7-0	—
1962	Johnny Griffith	2-3-1	7t	3-4-3	—
1963	Johnny Giffith	2-4-0	9	4-5-1	—
1964	Vince Dooley	4-2-0	2t	7-3-1	Sun
1965	Vince Dooley	3-3-0	6t	6-4-0	—
1966	Vince Dooley	6-0-0	1t	10-1-0	Cotton
1967	Vince Dooley	4-2-0	3t	7-4-0	Liberty
1968	Vince Dooley	5-0-1	1	8-1-2	Sugar
1969	Vince Dooley	2-3-1	6	5-5-1	Sun
1970	Vince Dooley	3-3-0	5t	5-5-0	—
1971	Vince Dooley	5-1-0	2t	11-1-0	Gator
1972	Vince Dooley	4-3-0	5	7-4-0	—
1973	Vince Dooley	3-4-0	5t	7-4-1	Peach
1974	Vince Dooley	4-2-0	2t	6-6-0	Tangerine
1975	Vince Dooley	5-1-0	2t	9-3-0	Cotton
1976	Vince Dooley	5-1-0	1t	10-2-0	Sugar
1977	Vince Dooley	2-4-0	7	5-6-0	—
1978	Vince Dooley	5-0-1	2	9-2-1	Bluebonnet
1979	Vince Dooley	5-1-0	2	6-5-0	—
1980	Vince Dooley	6-0-0	1	12-0-0	Sugar
1981	Vince Dooley	6-0-0	1t	10-2-0	Sugar
1982	Vince Dooley	6-0-0	1	11-1-0	Sugar
1983	Vince Dooley	5-1-0	2	10-1-1	Cotton
1984	Vince Dooley	4-2-0	3t	7-4-1	Citrus
1985	Vince Dooley	3-2-1	4	7-3-2	Sun
1986	Vince Dooley	4-2-0	2t	8-4-0	Hall of Fame
1987	Vince Dooley	4-2-0	4t	9-3-0	Liberty
1988	Vince Dooley	5-2-0	3	9-3-0	Gator
1989	Ray Goff	4-3-0	4t	6-6-0	Peach
1990	Ray Goff	2-5-0	6t	4-7-0	—
1991	Ray Goff	4-3-0	4t	9-3-0	Independence
1992	Ray Goff	6-2-0	1t-E	10-2-0	Citrus
1993	Ray Goff	2-6-0	4-E	5-6-0	—

Bowl Results (15-13-3)

Bowl	Opponent	Result	Date
Orange	Texas Christian	W 40-26	1-1-42
Rose	UCLA	W 9-0	1-1-43
Oil	Tulsa	W 20-6	1-1-46
Sugar	North Carolina	W 20-10	1-1-47
Gator	Maryland	T 20-20	1-1-48
Orange	Texas	L 28-41	1-1-49
Presidential	Texas A&M	L 20-40	12-9-50
Orange	Missouri	W 14-0	1-1-60
Sun	Texas Tech	W 7-0	12-26-64
Cotton	Southern Methodist	W 24-9	12-31-66
Liberty	North Carolina State	L 7-14	12-16-67
Sugar	Arkansas	L 2-16	1-1-69
Sun	Nebraska	L 6-45	12-20-69
Gator	North Carolina	W 7-3	12-31-71
Peach	Maryland	W 17-16	12-28-73
Tangerine	Miami-Ohio	L 10-21	12-20-74
Cotton	Arkansas	L 10-31	1-1-76
Sugar	Pittsburgh	L 3-27	1-1-77
Bluebonnet	Stanford	L 22-25	12-31-78
Sugar	Notre Dame	W 17-10	1-1-81
Sugar	Pittsburgh	L 20-24	1-1-82
Sugar	Penn State	L 23-27	1-1-83
Cotton	Texas	W 10-9	1-2-84
Citrus	Florida State	T 17-17	12-22-84
Sun	Arizona	T 13-13	12-28-85
Hall of Fame	Boston College	L 24-27	12-23-86
Liberty	Arkansas	W 20-17	12-29-87
Gator	Michigan State	W 34-27	1-1-89
Peach	Syracuse	L 18-19	12-30-89
Independence	Arkansas	W 24-15	12-29-92
Citrus	Ohio State	W 21-14	1-1-93

Georgia

Georgia vs. All Opponents

Opponent	W	L	T
Alabama	22	33	4
Arizona	0	0	1
Arkansas	3	3	0
Auburn	44	46	7
Baylor	4	0	0
Boston College	2	1	0
Brigham Young	1	0	0
California	2	0	0
Cal State Fullerton	2	0	0
Centre	1	1	1
Chattanooga	8	0	1
Chicago	0	1	0
Cincinnati	2	0	0
Citadel	9	0	1
Clemson	37	17	4
Columbia	1	1	0
Cumberland	0	1	0
Dartmouth	1	1	0
Davidson	2	2	1
Duke	1	0	0
Duquesne	1	0	0
East Carolina	1	0	0
*Florida	44	27	2
Florida State	5	4	1
Fordham	0	1	0
Furman	21	2	0
George Washington	1	0	0
Georgia Southern	1	0	0
Georgia Tech	48	33	5
Hardin-Simmons	1	0	0
Harvard	0	1	0
Holy Cross	0	3	0
Houston	0	2	1
Kentucky	36	9	2
LSU	7	12	1
Maryland	2	3	0
Memphis State	2	0	0
Mercer	22	0	0
Miami (Florida)	7	4	1
Miami (Ohio)	0	1	0
Michigan	1	1	0
Michigan State	1	0	0
Mississippi	21	10	1
Mississippi State	12	5	0
Missouri	1	0	0
Murray State	1	0	0
Navy	0	2	0
Nebraska	0	1	0
New York University	3	3	0
North Carolina	15	11	2
North Carolina State	6	1	1
Notre Dame	1	0	0
Oglethorpe	7	1	0
Ohio State	1	0	0
Oklahoma State	2	0	0
Oregon	1	0	0
Oregon State	3	0	0
Penn	1	0	0
Penn State	0	1	0
Pittsburgh	0	3	1
Presbyterian	3	0	0
Rice	0	1	0
Richmond	3	0	0
St. Mary's	0	0	1
Samford	1	0	0
Sewanee	5	7	1
South Carolina	34	10	2
South Carolina State	1	0	0
Southern Cal	0	3	0
Southern Methodist	1	0	0
Southern Miss	3	1	0

Opponent	W	L	T
Stanford	0	1	0
Stetson	1	0	0
Syracuse	0	1	0
Temple	4	0	0
Tennessee	10	11	2
Tennessee Tech	1	0	0
Texas	1	2	0
Texas A&M	1	3	0
Texas Christian	3	0	0
Texas Tech	2	0	0
Tulane	14	10	1
Tulsa	1	0	0
UCLA	2	0	0
Vanderbilt	36	16	2
Villanova	1	0	0
Virginia	7	6	3
Virginia Military	4	0	0
Virginia Tech	1	1	0
Wake Forest	1	2	0
Western Carolina	1	0	0
William & Mary	1	0	0
Wofford	3	0	0
Yale	6	5	0

* disagreement between schools about series record

All-America quarterback Fran Tarkenton, who later guided the Minnesota Vikings to three Super Bowls, led Georgia to the 1959 SEC Championship, a 10-1 mark and a No. 5 national ranking.

1994 SEC Football

Georgia School Records

Individual

Game
Total Offense	527	Eric Zeier vs. Southern Miss	(1993)
Yards Rushing	283	Herschel Walker vs. Vanderbilt	(1980)
Rushing Attempts	47	Herschel Walker vs. Florida	(1981)
Yards Passing	544	Eric Zeier vs. Southern Miss	(1993)
Pass Attempts	65	Eric Zeier vs. Florida	(1993)
Pass Completions	36	Eric Zeier vs. Florida	(1993)
Yards Receiving	198	Lamar Davis vs. Cincinnati	(1942)
Receptions	15	Shannon Mitchell vs. Florida	(1993)

Season
Total Offense	3,482	Eric Zeier	(1993)
Yards Rushing	1,891	Herschel Walker	(1981)
Rushing Attempts	385	Herschel Walker	(1981)
Yards Passing	3,525	Eric Zeier	(1993)
Pass Attempts	425	Eric Zeier	(1993)
Pass Completions	269	Eric Zeier	(1993)
Touchdown Passes	24	Eric Zeier	(1993)
Yards Receiving	970	Brice Hunter	(1993)
Receptions	76	Brice Hunter	(1993)
Touchdown Catches	9	Brice Hunter	(1993)
Interceptions	12	Terry Hoage	(1982)
Points	126	Garrison Hearst	(1992)

Career
Total Offense	7,384	Eric Zeier	(1991-active)
Yards Rushing	5,259	Herschel Walker	(1980-82)
Rushing Attempts	994	Herschel Walker	(1980-82)
Yards Passing	7,757	Eric Zeier	(1991-active)
Pass Attempts	969	Eric Zeier	(1991-active)
Pass Completions	579	Eric Zeier	(1991-active)
Touchdown Passes	43	Eric Zeier	(1991-active)
Yards Receiving	2,098	Lindsay Scott	(1978-81)
Receptions	131	Lindsay Scott	(1978-81)
Touchdown Catches	13	Andre Hastings	(1990-92)
Interceptions	16	Jake Scott	(1967-68)
Points	353	Kevin Butler	(1981-84)

Team

Game
Points	81	vs. Mercer	(1941)
Total Offense	667	vs. Southern Miss	(1993)
Yards Rushing	502	vs. South Carolina	(1974)
Yards Passing	544	vs. Southern Miss	(1993)
First Downs	35	vs. Vanderbilt	(1981)
Total Defense	39	vs. The Citadel	(1953)
Rushing Defense	-49	vs. Virginia Military	(1967)
Passing Defense	0	vs. Alabama	(1946)
		vs. Mississippi State	(1967)

Season
Points	372	(1946)
Total Offense	4,954	(1992)
Yards Rushing	3,337	(1971)
Yards Passing	3,525	(1993)
First Downs	271	(1981)
Fewest Points Allowed	17	(1920)
Total Defense	1,429	(1941)
Rushing Defense	596	(1941)
Passing Defense	673	(1958)
Consecutive Wins	17	(November 4, 1945 to September 19, 1947)

Jake Scott

Andre Hastings

Georgia in the NFL

Scott Adams, OL
Minnesota Vikings 1992-93
Harry Babcock, E
San Francisco 49ers 1953-55
Sam Bailey, E
Boston Yanks 1946
Zeke Bratkowski, QB
Chicago Bears 1954, 1957-60; Los Angeles Rams 1961-63; Green Bay Packers 1963-68, 1971
John Brantley, LB
Houston Oilers 1989; Washington Redskins 1992; Cincinnati Bengals 1993
Charley Britt, S
Los Angeles Rams 1960-63; Minnesota Vikings 1964; San Francisco 49ers 1964
Fred Brown, HB
Buffalo Bills 1961, 1963
Norris Brown, TE
Minnesota Vikings 1983
Bob Burns, RB
New York Jets 1974
Kevin Butler, K
Chicago Bears 1985-92
Jim Cagle, DT
Philadelphia Eagles 1974
Marion Campbell
San Francisco 49ers 1954-55; Philadelphia Eagles 1956-61
Johnny Carson, SE
Washington Redskins 1954-59; Houston Oilers 1960
Dale Carver, LB
Cleveland Browns 1983
Pete Case, G
Philadelphia Eagles 1962-64; New York Giants 1965-70
Edgar Chandler, LB
Buffalo Bills 1968-72; New England Patriots 1973
Bob Clemens, HB
Green Bay Packers 1955
George Collins, G
St. Louis Cardinals 1978-82
Dick Conn, S
Pittsburgh Steelers 1974; New England Patriots 1975-79
Van Davis, E
New York Yankees 1947-1949
Art DeCarlo, HB-SE-DB
Pittsburgh Steelers 1953; Washington Redskins 1956-57; Baltimore Colts 1957-60
Bucky Dilts, P
Denver Broncos 1977-78; Baltimore Colts 1979
John Donaldson, HB
Chicago Hornets 1949; Los Angeles Dons 1949
Ray Donaldson, C
Baltimore/Indianapolis Colts 1980-92; Seattle Seahawks 1993
Andy Dudish, HB
Buffalo Bisons 1946; Baltimore Colts 1947; Brooklyn Dodgers 1948; Detroit Lions 1948
Dan Edwards, E
Brooklyn Dodgers 1948; Chicago Hornets 1949; New York Yankees 1950-51; Dallas Texans 1952; Baltimore Colts 1953-54
Clyde Ehrhardt, C
Washington Redskins 1946, 1948-49
Gene Ellenson, T
Miami (AAFC), 1946
Nick Feher, G
San Francisco 49ers 1951-54; Pittsburgh Steelers 1955
Paul Fersen, T
New Orleans Saints 1973-74
Jim Fordham, FB
Chicago Bears 1944-45
Mike Garrett, P
Baltimore Colts 1981

Joe Geri, HB
Pittsburgh 1949-51; Chicago Cardinals 1952
Freddie Gilbert, DE
Denver Broncos 1986-89
Bill Goldberg, DT
Los Angeles Rams 1990; Atlanta Falcons 1992-93
Bill Goodwin, C
Boston Yanks 1947-48
Carl Grate
New York Giants 1945
Riley Gunnels, DT
Philadelphia Eagles 1960-64; Pittsburgh Steelers 1965-66
Rodney Hampton, RB
New York Giants 1990-93
Bill Hartman, QB
Washington Redskins 1938
Andre Hastings
Pittsburgh Steelers 1993
Len Hauss, C
Washington Redskins 1964-77
Keith Henderson, RB
San Francisco 49ers, 1989-92; Minnesota Vikings 1992
Craig Hertwig, T
Detroit Lions 1975-1977
Claude Hipps, HB
Pittsburgh Steelers 1952-53
Terry Hoage, S
New Orleans Saints 1984-85; Philadelphia Eagles 1985-90; Washington Redskins 1991-93; Houston Oilers 1993
Homer Hobbs, G
San Francisco 49ers 1949-50
Pat Hodgson, SE
Washington Redskins 1966
Winford Hood, T
Denver Broncos 1984-87
Nat Hudson, G
New Orleans Saints 1981-82
Dennis (Country) Hughes, TE
Pittsburgh Steelers 1970-71
Andy Johnson, QB
New England Patriots 1974-76, 1978-81
Howard (Smiley) Johnson, G
Green Bay Packers 1940-41
Randy Johnson, G
Tampa Bay Buccaneers 1977-78
Daryll Jones, S
Green Bay Packers 1984-86
Preston Jones
Philadelphia Eagles 1993
Spike Jones, P
Houston Oilers 1970; Buffalo Bills 1971-74; Philadelphia Eagles 1975-77
John Kasay, K
Seattle Seahawks 1991-93
Clarence Kay, TE
Denver Broncos 1984-92
Gordon Kelley
San Francisco 49ers 1960-61; Washington Redskins 1962-64
Horace King, RB
Detroit Lions 1975-83
Lafeyette (Dolly) King, E
Buffalo Bisons 1946-47; Chicago Rockets 1948; Chicago Hornets 1949
Kent Lawrence, WR
Philadelphia 1969; Atlanta Falcons 1970
Milt Leathers, G
Philadelphia Eagles 1933
Allan Leavitt, K
Atlanta Falcons 1977; Tampa Bay Buccaneers
Morris Lewis, LB
New York Jets 1991-93
Nate Lewis, WR/KR
San Diego Chargers 1989-93; Los Angeles Rams 1993
Dave Lloyd, LB-K
Cleveland Browns 1959-61; Detroit Lions 1962; Philadelphia Eagles 1963-70

Tommy Lyons, G-C
Denver Broncos 1971-78
Arthur Marshall, WR
Denver Broncos 1992-93
Willie McClendon, RB-KR
Chicago Bears 1979-82
Hurdis McCrary, HB-FB
Green Bay Packers 1929-33
Guy McIntyre, G
San Francisco 49ers 1984-93
Alec Millen
N.Y. Jets 1993; San Francisco 49ers 1993
Billy Mixon, HB
San Francisco 49ers 1953-54
Norm (Buster) Mott, HB
Green Bay Packers 1933; Pittsburgh 1934; Cincinnati 1934
Tom Nash, E
Green Bay Packers 1929-32; Brooklyn Dodgers 1933-34
Ulysses Norris, TE
Detroit 1979-83; Buffalo Bills 1984-85
Joe O'Malley, E
Pittsburgh Steelers 1955-56
Jimmy Orr, FL
Pittsburgh Steelers 1958-60; Baltimore Colts 1961-70
Dunwood Pennington, K
Dallas Texans 1962
Todd Peterson
N.Y. Giants 1993; Atlanta Falcons 1993
Wayne Radloff, C
Atlanta Falcons 1985-88; San Francisco 49ers 1989-90
Larry Rakestraw, QB
Chicago Bears 1964, 1966-68
Johnny Rauch, QB
New York Bulldogs 1949; New York Yankees 1950-51; Philadelphia 1951
Andy Reed, RB
Buffalo Bills 1976
Floyd (Breezy) Reid, HB
Chicago Bears 1950, Green Bay Packers 1950-56
Owen Reynolds, E-FB
New York Giants 1925; Brooklyn 1926
Frank Richter, LB
Denver Broncos 1967-69
Preston Ridlehuber, RB
Atlanta Falcons 1966; Oakland Raiders 1968; Buffalo Bills 1968
Ray Rissmiller, T
Philadelphia Eagles 1966; New Orleans Saints 1967; Buffalo Bills 1968
Jack Roberts, HB/FB
Boston Yanks 1932, Staten Island Stapletons 1932, Philadelphia Eagles 1933-34; Pittsburgh Steelers 1934
Matt Robinson, QB
New York Jets 1977-79; Denver 1980; Buffalo Bills 1981-82
Rex Robinson, K
New England 1982
Herb St. John, G
Brooklyn Dodgers 1948; Chicago Hornets 1949
Troy Sadowski, TE
Atlanta Falcons 1989; Kansas City Chiefs 1990-91; New York Jets 1992
Theron Sapp, FB
Philadelphia 1959-63; Pittsburgh Steelers 1963-65
Jake Scott, S-KR
Miami Dolphins 1970-75; Washington Redskins 1976-78
Lindsay Scott, WR
New Orleans Saints 1982-85
Bob Sedlock, T
Buffalo Bills 1960
Frankie Sinkwich, HB
Detroit Lions 1943-44; New York Yankees 1946-47; Baltimore 1947

Ben Smith, CB
Philadelphia Eagles 1990-93
Charles (Rabbit) Smith, HB
Chicago Cardinals 1947
Gene Smith, G
Portsmouth 1930; Frakford Yellowjackets 1930
Royce Smith, G
New Orleans Saints 1972-73; Atlanta Falcons 1974-76
Bill Stanfill, DE
Miami Dolphins 1969-76
Wibur Strozier, TE
Seattle Seahawks 1987-89
Wayne Swinford, DB
San Francisco 49ers 1965-67
Hamp Tanner, T
San Francisco 49ers 1951; Dallas Texans 1952
Richard Tardits, LB
Phoenix Cardinals 1989; New England Patriots 1990-92
Fran Tarkenton, QB
Minnesota Vikings 1961-66, 1972-78; New York Giants 1967-71
Lars Tate, RB
Tampa Bay Buccaneers 1988-89; Chicago Bears 1990
Joe Tereshinski, E-DE
Washington Redskins 1947-54
Pete Tinsley, G
Green Bay Packers 1938-45
Bobby Towns, DB-RB
St. Louis Cardinals 1960; Boston Patriots 1960
Charley Trippi, HB-QB-DB
Chicago Cardinals 1947-55
Herschel Walker, RB
Dallas Cowboys 1986-89; Minnesota Vikings 1989; Philadelphia Eagles 1992-93
Bobby Walston, E-TE-K
Philadelphia Eagles 1951-62
Kirk Warner, TE
New England Patriots 1990-91
Bobby Welden, P
Minnesota Vikings 1964-67; Pittsburgh Steelers 1968-77
Gene Washington, WR
New York Giants 1979
Todd Wheeler, C
New Orleans Saints 1989-90
John Whire, FB
Philadelphia Eagles 1933
Gene White, DE
Green Bay Packers 1954
Garland Williams, T
Brooklyn Dodgers 1947-48; Chicago Hornets 1949
Scott Williams, FB
Detroit Lions 1986-88
Jim Wilson, G
San Francisco 49ers 1965-66; Atlanta Falcons 1967; LA Rams 1968
Mike Wilson, T
Cincinnati 1979-85; Seattle Seahawks 1986-87
Steve Wilson, C-T
Tampa Bay Buccaneers 1976-86
Scott Woerner, S-KR
Atlanta Falcons 1981
Tim Worley, RB
Pittsburgh Steelers 1989-91
Dick Yelvington, T
New York Giants 1952-57
George Young, DE
Cleveland Browns 1946-53

1994 SEC Football

Georgia Media Information

*Georgia Associate AD/
Sports Information*
Claude Felton

Georgia Sports Information
P.O. Box 1472
Athens, GA 30613
(706) 542-1621
FAX: (706) 542-9339

Felton (Home): 543-3910

Football Writers

Al Muskewitz
Anderson Independent
P.O. Box 2507
Anderson, SC 29622
(803) 224-4321

Chip Towers
Athens Daily News
P.O. Box 912
Athens, GA 30613
(706) 549-0123

Billy Harper, Executive Sports Editor
Athens Daily News-Banner Herald
P.O. Box 912
Athens, GA 30613
(706) 549-0123

Tony Barnhart
Atlanta Journal
P.O. Box 4689
Atlanta, GA 30302
(404) 526-5331

Scott Reid
Atlanta Constitution
P.O. Box 1792
Athens, GA 30603
(706) 354-1951

Kamon Simpson
Macon Telegraph
P.O. Box 4167
Macon, Ga. 31213

Joe Posnansky
Augusta Chronicle
715 Broad Street
Augusta, GA 30902
(706) 724-0851

Anthony Stastny, Sports Editor
Savannah Morning News
P.O. Box 1088
Savannah, GA 31402
(912) 236-4141

Harley Bowers
Executive Sports Editor
Macon Telegraph
P.O. Box 4167
Macon, GA 31213
(912) 744-4275

Chuck Williams
Columbus Enquirer
P.O. Box 711
Columbus, Ga. 31902-0711
(706) 324-5526

Sports Editor
Marietta Journal
580 Fairfield Street
Marietta, GA 30060
(404) 428-9411

Sports Editor
Athens Observer
264 1/2 North Lumpkin Street
Athens, GA 30601
(706) 548-9300

John Byrwa
Sportsbeat
810 Baxter Street
#D-4
Athen, Ga. 30605

Jeff Butler
Gainesville Times
P.O. Box 838
Gainesville, GA 30501
(706) 532-1234

Rob Cook
Dublin Courier Herald
P.O. Box BCSS
Dublin, GA 31040
(912) 272-5522

Murray Poole, Sports Editor
Brunswick News
P.O. Box 1557
Brunswick, GA 31520
(912) 265-8320

Sports Editor
Florida Times Union
P.O. Box 1949
Jacksonville, FL 32201
(904) 359-4111

Wire Service

Ed Shearer, Sports Editor
Associated Press
500 Omni International Blvd
Atlanta, GA 30335-0701
(404) 522-8971

Play-By-Play Broadcasters

Larry Munson
WSB Radio
1601 West Peachtree Street, NE
Atlanta, GA 30309
(404) 897-7000

Scott Howard, Sports Director
WGAU-WNGC Radio
850 Bobbin Mill Road
Athens, GA 30605
(706) 549-1340

Phil Schaefer
3770 North Decatur Road
Decatur, GA 30032
(404) 296-2000

Neil Williamson
WSB Radio
1601 West Peachtree Street, NE
Atlanta, GA 30309
(404) 897-7000

Television Stations

Kevin Gerke, Sports
WSB-TV
1601 West Peachtree Street, NE
Atlanta, GA 30309
(404) 897-7587

Chip Zeller, Sports
WAGA-TV
P.O. Box 4207
Atlanta, GA 30302
(404) 875-5551

Roger Manis, Sports
WXIA-TV
1611 West Peachtree Street, NE
Atlanta, GA 30309
(404) 892-1611

Steve Taylor, Sports
WGNX-TV
P.O. Box 98097
Atlanta, GA 30329
(404) 325-4646

Radio Stations

Dave Johnston
WRFC Radio
255 Milledge Avenue
Athens, GA 30605
(706) 549-6222

Matt Stewart
Georgia Network
550 Pharr Road
Atlanta, GA 30363
1-800-282-7283

Campus Media

Sports Director
WUOG Radio
P.O. Box 2065
Athens, GA 30601
(706) 542-7100

Sports Editor
Red and Black
123 North Jackson Street
Athens, GA 30601
(706) 543-1809

KENTUCKY

DR. CHARLES WETHINGTON
President

DR. VIRGINIA ATWOOD
Faculty Representative

C.M. NEWTON
Athletic Director

University of Kentucky

PRESIDENT:
　Dr. Charles Wethington (Eastern Kentucky 1956)
FACULTY REPRESENTATIVE:
　Dr. Virginia Atwood (Northwestern State 1957)
ATHLETIC DIRECTOR:
　C.M. Newton (Kentucky 1952)
HEAD COACH:
　Bill Curry (Georgia Tech 1965)
LOCATION: Lexington, Kentucky
FOUNDED: 1865
ENROLLMENT: 24,200
NICKNAME: Wildcats
COLORS: Blue and White
STADIUM: Commonwealth Stadium (57,800) - Natural

Wildcat Quick Facts

1993 RECORD: 6-6
　(4-2 Home, 2-3 Away, 0-1 Neutral)
1993 SEC RECORD (FINISH): 4-4 (3rd-Eastern)
　(2-2 Home, 2-2 Away)
BOWL: Peach Bowl
　Clemson 14, Kentucky 13
ALL-TIME RECORD: 488-445-44 (.522)
SEC RECORD: 117-238-12 (.335) — Regular Season Games
SEC CHAMPIONSHIPS: 2
　(1950, 76t)
BOWL APPEARANCES: 8
BOWL RECORD: 5-3 (.625)
LAST APPEARANCE: 1993 Peach Bowl
　(Clemson 14, Kentucky 13)

KENTUCKY
Team Information

OFFENSIVE SYSTEM: Multiple

DEFENSIVE SYSTEM: 4-3

LETTERMEN RETURNING: 49
- 26 Offense
- 20 Defense
- 3 Specialists

LETTERMEN LOST: 26
- 11 Offense
- 13 Defense
- 2 Specialists

STARTERS RETURNING: 13
OFFENSE (6)
- OT   Mark Askin (6-5, 295, Sr.)
- FB   Damon Hood (6-2, 230, Sr.)
- OT   Chris Page (6-7, 305, Jr.)
- OT   Aaron Purdie (6-4, 275, Jr.)
- TB   Moe Williams (6-2, 205, So.)
- SE   Randy Wyatt (5-10, 170, Sr.)

DEFENSE (5)
- DE   Howard Carter (6-4, 245, Sr.)
- CB   Steven Hall (6-2, 205, Jr.)
- FS   Melvin Johnson (5-11, 196, Sr.)
- LB   David Snardon (6-2, 229, Jr.)
- DT   Robert Stinson (6-4, 283, Sr.)

SPECIALISTS (2)
- P   Dan Ariza (5-10, 180, Sr.)
- PK   Nicky Nickels (6-0, 180, So.)

STARTERS LOST: 13
OFFENSE (7)
- WB   Alfonzo Browning (6-3, 203, Sr.)
- SE   Mark Chatmon (5-8, 168, Sr.)
- C   Wes Jackson (6-3, 284, Sr.)
- QB   Pookie Jones (6-1, 196, Jr.)
- OG   David Parks (6-2, 262, Sr.)
- OG   Barry Rich (6-1, 273, Sr.)
- TE   Terry Samuels (6-2, 253, Sr.)

DEFENSE (6)
- DE   Zane Beehn (6-4, 260, Sr.)
- CB   Willie Cannon (5-11, 186, Sr.)
- SS   Marcus Jenkins (6-2, 195, Sr.)
- LB   Marty Moore (6-1, 238, Sr.)
- CB   Don Robinson (6-1, 190, Sr.)
- LB   Duce Williams (6-0, 196, Sr.)

SPECIALISTS (0)

Commonwealth Stadium (57,800)
Record: 75-53-3 (.584)
First Game: Sept. 15, 1973 — Kentucky 31, Virginia Tech 26
Largest Crowd: 58,450 (Sept. 19, 1992)
   Kentucky 37, Indiana 25

1994 Kentucky Schedule

Sept.	3	LOUISVILLE	LEXINGTON
Sept.	10	at Florida	Gainesville, Fla.
Sept.	17	INDIANA	LEXINGTON
Sept.	24	SOUTH CAROLINA	LEXINGTON
Sept.	29	at Auburn	Auburn, Ala.
Oct.	15	at LSU	Baton Rouge, La.
Oct.	22	GEORGIA	LEXINGTON
Oct.	29	MISSISSIPPI STATE	LEXINGTON
Nov.	5	VANDERBILT	LEXINGTON
Nov.	12	NORTHEAST LOUISIANA	LEXINGTON
Nov.	19	at Tennessee	Knoxville, Tenn.

1995 Kentucky Schedule

Sept.	2	LOUISVILLE	LEXINGTON
Sept.	9	FLORIDA	LEXINGTON
Sept.	16	at Indiana	Bloomington, Ind.
Sept.	23	at South Carolina	Columbia, S.C.
Sept.	30	AUBURN	LEXINGTON
Oct.	14	LSU	LEXINGTON
Oct.	21	at Georgia	Athens, Ga.
Oct.	28	at Mississippi State	Starkville, Miss.
Nov.	4	at Vanderbilt	Nashville, Tenn.
Nov.	11	CINCINNATI	LEXINGTON
Nov.	18	TENNESSEE	LEXINGTON

84   Kentucky

1993 Kentucky Individual Leaders

RUSHING	Atts	Yards	Avg	TDs	Yds/Game
MOE WILLIAMS	164	928	5.7	5	84.4
DAMON HOOD	93	367	4.0	3	33.4
Pookie Jones	130	288	2.2	6	28.8
ANTONIO O'FERRAL	39	157	4.0	0	19.6
RANDY WYATT	17	123	7.2	1	11.2

PASSING	Atts	Comp	Ints/TDs	Pct	Yds
Pookie Jones	85	163	7/8	.522	1,071
ANTONIO O'FERRAL	20	44	4/1	.455	221

RECEIVING	Rec	Yds	Avg	TDs	Yds/Game
Alfonzo Browning	20	335	16.8	4	30.5
Mark Chatmon	20	294	14.7	1	29.4
Tim Calvert	9	131	14.6	0	13.1
Terry Samuels	14	139	9.9	3	12.6
RANDY WYATT	13	64	4.9	0	5.8

SCORING	G	TDs	PAT	FGs	Tot	Avg
Juha Leonoff	8	0	20-20	5-12	35	4.4
Pookie Jones	10	6	0	0	36	3.6
MOE WILLIAMS	11	5	1-1	0	32	2.9
Alfonzo Browning	11	4	0	0	24	2.2
Terry Samuels	11	3	1-1	0	20	1.8

PUNTING	No	Yds	Avg	Long
NICKY NICKELS	28	1073	38.3	68
DAN ARIZA	27	976	36.2	49

KICKOFF RETURNS	No	Yds	Avg	TDs	Avg/Game	Long
CLYDE RUDOLPH	10	209	20.9	0	26.1	44
DONNELL GORDON	6	106	17.7	0	11.8	23
RANDY WYATT	4	87	21.8	0	7.9	23

PUNT RETURNS	No	Yds	Avg	TDs	Avg/Game	Long
Matt Riazzi	26	140	5.4	0	12.7	22
Troy Hobbs	2	14	7.0	0	1.4	11

TACKLES	Total(S-A)	Sk (Yds)	TL (Yds)	Ints
Marty Moore	116 (81-35)	0	2 (-7)	3
Marcus Jenkins	67 (59-8)	0	2 (-2)	6
Duce Williams	62 (45-17)	0	3 (-15)	2
STEVEN HALL	54 (47-7)	0	0	2
MELVIN JOHNSON	49 (38-11)	0	2 (-2)	0

INTERCEPTIONS	No	Yds	TDs	Int/Game	Long
Marcus Jenkins	6	45	0	0.6	19
Marty Moore	3	55	0	0.3	35
STEVEN HALL	2	35	0	0.2	28
Adrian Sherwood	2	45	0	0.2	35

Returning Players in All Capitals

Steven Hall    Damon Hood    Moe Williams

1993 Kentucky Team Statistics

	UK	OPP
FIRST DOWNS	192	182
Rushing	121	89
Passing	56	85
Penalty	15	8
NET YARDS RUSHING	2315	1707
Yards rushing	2635	1944
Yards lost	320	237
Rushing attempts	545	385
Average per rush	4.3	4.4
Average per game	210.5	155.2
NET YARDS PASSING	1305	2089
Average per game	118.6	189.9
Passes attempted	214	344
Passes completed	108	177
Had intercepted	11	20
TOTAL OFFENSIVE YARDS	3620	3796
Average per game	329.1	345.1
Total plays	759	729
Average per play	4.8	5.2
NUMBER PUNTS/YARDS	55/2049	58/2219
Punting average	37.3	38.3
Net punting average	34.7	35.6
PUNT RETURNS/YARDS	30/153	21/139
Punt return average	5.1	6.6
KICKOFF RETURNS/YARDS	33/577	38/613
Kickoff return average	17.5	16.1
PENALTIES/YARDS	38/320	75/703
Penalty yards per game	29.1	63.9
FUMBLES/LOST	25/12	21/9
INTERCEPTION RETURNS/YARDS	20/234	11/91
Interception return average	11.7	8.3
TOUCHDOWNS	26	23
Rushing	17	11
Passing	9	11
Return	0	1
FIELD GOALS MADE/ATTEMPTED	7/16	11/16
KICK EXTRA POINTS MADE/ATTEMPTED	22/23	18/18
SAFETY	1	1
TWO-POINT CONVERSIONS	3-3	2-4
TOTAL POINTS	207	195
Average per game	18.8	17.7

1993 Kentucky Results

6-6 Overall • 4-4 SEC (3rd - Eastern)

Date	Opponent	Result	Attendance
Sept. 4	KENT	W 35-0	55,800
Sept. 11	FLORIDA	L 20-24	58,175
Sept. 18	at Indiana	L 8-24	43,545
Sept. 23	at South Carolina [ESPN]	W 21-17	65,326
Oct. 2	OLE MISS - HC	W 21-0	57,075
Oct. 16	LSU	W 35-17	54,750
Oct. 23	at Georgia [JP]	L 28-33	81,307
Oct. 30	at Mississippi State	W 26-17	28,607
Nov. 6	at Vanderbilt	L 7-12	35,500
Nov. 13	EAST CAROLINA	W 6-3	34,500
Nov. 20	TENNESSEE	L 0-48	57,878
Dec. 31	Clemson [ESPN] (Peach Bowl)	L 13-14	63,416

1994 SEC Football

Bill Curry

HOMETOWN:
College Park, Georgia

ALMA MATER (YEAR):
Georgia Tech (1965)

PLAYING CAREER:
Georgia Tech Center 1962-64 (Captain 1964); Green Bay Packers 1965-66 (Super Bowl I); Baltimore Colts 1967-72 (Super Bowl III & V, All-Pro 1971-72) Los Angeles Rams 1973; Houston Oilers 1974.

COACHING CAREER:
Georgia Tech Assistant 1976; Green Bay Assistant 1977-79; Georgia Tech Head Coach 1980-86; Alabama Head Coach 1987-89; Kentucky Head Coach 1990-present.

COACHING ACHIEVEMENTS:
1987 UPI SEC Coach of the Year; 1989 SEC Co-Champions; 1989 AP SEC Coach of the Year; 1989 Nashville Banner SEC Coach of the Year.

BORN:
October 21, 1942

WIFE:
Carolyn Newton

CHILDREN:
Kristin 25, Billy 22

ASSISTANT COACHES:
MIKE ARCHER (Miami, Fla. 1975) - Defensive Coordinator/Linebackers
DARYL DICKEY (Tennessee 1985) - Offensive Coordinator/Quarterbacks
RAY DORR (West Virginia Wesleyan 1965) - Runningbacks
BILL GLASER (Bellarmine 1965) - Special Teams Coordinator/Defensive Tackles
TOMMY LIMBAUGH (Alabama 1967) - Assistant Head Coach/Tight Ends
JOKER PHILLIPS (Kentucky 1986) - Receivers
DON RILEY (East Tennessee State 1956) - Offensive Line
RICK SMITH (Florida State 1971) - Defensive Backs
DAVID TURNER (Davidson 1985) - Defensive Ends

SUPPORT STAFF:
AL GREEN (Michigan 1973) - Trainer
JACK FLIGG (Oglethorpe 1955) - Assistant AD for Football Operations
MIKE FLORENCE (Kentucky 1979) - Strength Coach

Year-By-Year Record

Year	School	Conf.	All	Bowl
1980	Georgia Tech		1-9-1	
1981	Georgia Tech		1-10	
1982	Georgia Tech		6-5	
1983	Georgia Tech	3-2 (3rd)	3-8	
1984	Georiga Tech	2-2-1 (5th)	6-4-1	
1985	Georgia Tech	5-1 (2nd)	9-2-1	All American
1986	Georgia Tech	3-3 (4th)	5-5-1	
1987	Alabama	4-2 (t4th)	7-5	Hall of Fame
1988	Alabama	4-3 (t4th)	9-3	Sun
1989	Alabama	6-1 (t1st)	10-2	Sugar
1990	Kentucky	3-4 (5th)	4-7	
1991	Kentucky	0-7 (10th)	3-8	
1992	Kentucky	2-6 (t5thE)	4-7	
1993	Kentucky	4-4 (3rdE)	6-6	Peach
OVERALL RECORD		**36-35-1** (.507)	**74-81-4** (.478)	**14 Years**
Kentucky Record		**9-21** (.300)	**17-28** (.378)	**4 Years**
Alabama Record		14-6	26-10	3 Years
SEC Record		23-27		
Georgia Tech Record		13-8-1	31-43-4	7 Years
Bowl Record		2-3	(1-2 Alabama, 1-0 Georgia Tech, 0-1 Kentucky)	

Kentucky

Kentucky All-Star Candidates

MARK ASKIN
Senior • Offensive Tackle
6-5 • 295 • Louisville, Ky.

• Kentucky's most experienced returning offensive lineman, having started every game over last two seasons and several games as a freshman.
• As one of three returning starters on the offensive line, helped pave way for Wildcat rushing attack which ranked third in the SEC and 24th in the nation (210.5 yards per game) in 1993.
• Opened holes which allowed Wildcat backs to gain 200+ yards rushing six times and 300+ yards twice last season.
• Received *Knoxville News-Sentinel* All-SEC Freshman honors in 1991 in addition to being named to the SEC Academic Honor Roll for three-straight years.

MOE WILLIAMS
Sophomore • Halfback
6-2 • 205 • Columbus, Ga.

• SEC's leading returning rusher at 84.4 yards per game as a freshman in 1993, which ranked fourth nationally among his class.
• UK's all-time freshman rushing leader, gaining 928 yards on 164 carries.
• Recorded sixth-best rushing season in UK history and posted four 100+ yard performances to become only the second freshman in Wildcat history to accomplish the feat.
• Set UK freshman single-game rushing record with 159 yards against Georgia, the seventh-best rushing total in the SEC in 1993.
• Received second-team AP All-SEC accolades and *Knoxville News-Sentinel* SEC All-Freshman team honors last season.

WILLIAMS STATS

Year	Atts	Yds	Avg	TD	Long	Rec	Yds	Avg	TD	Long
1993	164	928	5.7	5	70	7	41	5.9	0	12

MELVIN JOHNSON
Senior • Free Safety
5-11 • 196 • Cincinnati, Ohio

• Kentucky's second-leading returning tackler with 49 total hits a year ago even though he missed the first five games of the 1993 campaign with a broken forearm.
• One of the hardest hitters in the SEC, Johnson earned UK's "Big-Hitter" award following 1994 spring drills after sidelining six Wildcat players with bone-crushing hits during spring practice.
• Started last six contests for Wildcats in 1993, recording double-digit tackles in three of last four games.
• Best game came vs. Tennessee when he was credited with a career-high 13 tackles.
• Also recorded 12 tackles vs. Vanderbilt and Clemson.

RANDY WYATT
Senior • Split End
5-10 • 170 • Paducah, Ky.

• Kentucky's leading returning receiver from a season ago, posting 13 catches for 64 yards, the team's fourth-best catch total in 1993.
• Ignited the Wildcats to a come-back win at South Carolina with a 64-yard TD run from the tailback slot with 11:47 remaining in the contest.
• Used primarily in passing situations after Moe Williams settled in at halfback.
• His 7.2 yards per carry average led Kentucky a year ago.
• Sat out 1992 season after transferring from Louisville.

JOHNSON STATS

Year	Tackles	TFL(Yds)	Sacks	Int	FF
1991	38 (NA)	0	0	0	0
1992	10 (NA)	0	0	0	0
1993	49 (38-11)	2 (-2)	0	0	1
Career	96	2 (-2)	0	0	1

WYATT STATS

Year	Atts	Yds	Avg	TD	Long	Rec	Yds	Avg	TD	Long
1990*	3	21	7.0	0	8	1	14	14.0	0	14
1991*	2	-14	-7.0	0	20	11	204	18.5	2	45
1993	17	123	7.2	1	64	13	64	4.9	0	9
Career	22	130	5.9	1	64	25	282	11.3	2	45

*University of Louisville

1994 SEC Football

1994 Kentucky Roster

No.	Name	Pos.	Ht.	Wt.	Class	Exp.	Hometown (High School/JC)
18	Dan Ariza	P	5-9	176	Sr.	1L	Miami, Fla. (Christopher Columbus)
76	Mark Askin	OT	6-5	295	Sr.	3L	Louisville, Ky. (St. Xavier)
73	Cliff Bailey	OT	6-4	280	Fr.	RS	Trezevant, Tenn. (McKenzie)
37	Shane Ball	LB	6-2	233	Sr.	1L	Henderson, Ky. (Henderson County)
15	Leman Boyd	SS	6-1	200	So.	1L	Bowling Green, Ky. (Bowling Green)
38	Brent Brasher	HB	6-2	185	Fr.	RS	Providence, Ky. (Webster County)
66	Andy Britt	OG	6-4	270	Jr.	2L	Russellville, Ky. (Russellville)
53	Howard Carter	DE	6-4	245	Sr.	2L	Dodge City, Kan. (Coffeyville CC)
57	Dan Caruthers	C	6-4	265	Sr.	1L	West Hills, Calif. (Pasadena City College)
88	Darrin Clark	TE	6-6	230	Fr.	RS	Coldiron, Ky. (Bell County)
20	Carlos Collins	CB	6-1	203	Sr.	2L	Cincinnati, Ohio (Moeller)
68	Thad Corbin	DT	6-3	245	Fr.	RS	Springfield, Tenn. (Springfield)
60	Scott Crosley	OT	6-4	268	Jr.	1L	Carmel, Ind. (Carmel)
85	Isaac Curtis	FL	6-4	203	So.	1L	Cincinnati, Ohio (Roger Bacon)
51	Kareem Dailey	LB	6-5	218	Fr.	RS	Louisville, Ky. (Jeffersontown)
37	Carl Daley	FB	5-9	188	So.	TR	Louisville, Ky. (Dayton)
82	Chris Davis	TE	6-7	273	So.	1L	Roanoke, Ala. (Handley)
67	Trent DiGiuro	OG	6-2	277	Jr.	1L	Goshen, Ky. (South Oldham)
91	Jebron Farah	SE	5-11	176	Sr.	SQ	Carlisle, Ky. (Nicholas County)
22	Pierce Foster	HB	5-11	207	Jr.	TR	Dayton, Ohio (Georgia)
83	John Gibson	DE	6-7	252	Fr.	RS	Independence, Ky. (Simon Kenton)
44	David Ginn	LB	6-5	205	Fr.	RS	Cincinnati, Ohio (Elder)
28	Donnell Gordon	HB	6-0	185	So.	1L	Pewee Valley, Ky. (South Oldham)
14	Steven Hall	CB	6-2	205	Jr.	3L	New Haven, Ind. (New Haven)
77	Dude Harper	C	6-0	250	Sr.	3L	Clemson, S.C. (Daniel)
8	George Harris	FS	5-11	180	Jr.	JC	Oakland, Calif. (City College of San Francisco)
92	Robert Harris	DE	6-4	243	Sr.	1L	Brooksville, Fla. (City College of San Francisco)
7	Billy Jack Haskins	QB	5-11	190	Fr.	RS	Paducah, Ky. (Tilghman)
17	Van Hiles	CB	6-0	175	So.	1L	Baton Rouge, La. (Episcopal)
12	Matt Hobbie	QB	5-11	180	Fr.	RS	Sarasota, Fla. (Sarasota)
61	DeAnthony Honaker	C	6-1	272	So.	SQ	Pikeville, Ky. (Pikeville)
31	Damon Hood	FB	6-2	230	Sr.	3L	Bowling Green, Ky. (Warren Central)
50	Chad Hudson	LB	6-3	240	Fr.	RS	Lilburn, Ga. (Brookwood)
75	Brandon Jackson	OT	6-4	305	Fr.	RS	Massilon, Ohio (Washington)
90	Nicholas Jerdon	TE	6-2	221	Jr.	SQ	West Chester, Ohio (Lakota)
25	Melvin Johnson	FS	5-11	196	Sr.	3L	Cincinnati, Ohio (St. Xavier)
69	Barry Jones	OG	6-5	295	Jr.	2L	Fort Mitchell, Ky. (Covington Catholic)
46	Raymond Jones	LB	5-11	190	So.	1L	Lexington, Ky. (Bryan Station)
63	Adam Kane	C	6-5	270	So.	SQ	Osceola, Ind. (Notre Dame)
87	Donte' Key	LB	6-3	220	Jr.	2L	Franklin, Ky. (Franklin-Simpson)
39	Rob Manchester	SS	6-1	190	Jr.	2L	Paducah, Ky. (Tilghman)
84	Mark Mason	FL	5-10	165	Fr.	RS	Mayfield Village, Ohio (Walsh Jesuit)
21	Raymond McLaurin	FB	6-1	202	So.	1L	Radcliff, Ky. (North Hardin)
62	Quincy Murdock	OG	6-3	284	So.	SQ	Amelia, Ohio (Amelia)
56	Matt Neuss	LB	6-2	223	Jr.	1L	Bellport, N.Y. (Bellport)
19	Nicky Nickels	PK	6-0	180	So.	1L	Lexington, Ky. (Dunbar)
5	Antonio O'Ferral	QB	5-10	180	Jr.	2L	East Patchogue, N.Y. (Bellport)
45	Evan O'Ferral	FB	5-11	200	Fr.	RS	East Patchogue, N.Y. (Bellport)
72	Aaron Purdie	OT	6-4	275	Jr.	3L	Toledo, Ohio (E.L. Bowsher)
23	Donnie Redd'	SE	5-7	178	Sr.	1L	Danville, Ky. (Danville)
78	J.D. Reed	OG	6-3	260	Fr.	RS	Springfield, Ky. (Washington County)
89	Corey Reeves	TE	6-3	237	Sr.	3L	Corbin, Ky. (Corbin)
26	William Renuart	FS	6-2	178	So.	1L	Coral Gables, Fla. (Gulliver)
71	Rob Reynolds	OT	6-6	282	Fr.	RS	Fort Thomas, Ky. (Highlands)
27	Clyde Rudolph	FL	5-7	173	Sr.	3L	Pensacola, Fla. (B.T. Washington)
6	Kio Sanford	SE	5-11	155	Fr.	RS	Lexington, Ky. (Bryan Station)
58	Mike Schellenberger	LB	6-0	236	So.	1L	Louisville, Ky. (St. Xavier)
65	John Schlarman	OG	6-2	280	Fr.	RS	Fort Thomas, Ky. (Highlands)
97	Mike Schlegel	DT	6-4	250	Jr.	2L	Harahan, La. (Jesuit)
22	Tom Shropshire	SS	6-1	195	Fr.	RS	Winchester (George Rogers Clark)
86	Tyler Siddens	SE	5-11	150	Fr.	RS	Louisville, Ky. (Ballard)
9	Jaysuma Simms	FL	5-10	170	So.	1L	Providence, Ky. (Webster County)
41	Brian Sivinski	PK	5-10	168	Jr.	1L	Lexington, Ky. (Indiana)
13	Leon Smith	FL	5-10	175	Jr.	1L	Louisville, Ky. (Trinity)
48	David Snardon	LB	6-2	229	Jr.	2L	Louisville, Ky. (Male)
11	Jeff Speedy	QB	6-2	186	So.	1L	Franklin, Tenn. (Brentwood Academy)
94	Robert Stinson	DT	6-4	283	Sr.	3L	Cadiz, Ky. (Trigg County)
64	Isreal Stone	OT	6-2	255	So.	SQ	Bardstown, Ky. (Nelson County)
98	Roger Sullivan	DT	6-3	270	Sr.	3L	McKeesport, Pa. (McKeesport)
54	Kurt Supe	DE	6-3	231	So.	1L	Cincinnati, Ohio (LaSalle)
55	Jeff Tanner	DE	6-3	225	Fr.	RS	Marianna, Fla. (Marianna)
32	James Tucker	LB	6-2	210	Jr.	2L	Arlington, Texas (Lamar)
93	Bill Verdonk	DT	6-3	240	Fr.	RS	Lake Forest, Ill. (Lake Forest)
47	Chris Ward	DE	6-5	252	So.	1L	Decatur, Ga. (Southwest DeKalb)
4	Littleton Ward	CB	5-10	155	Fr.	RS	Lexington, Ky. (Bryan Station)
10	Moe Williams	HB	6-2	205	So.	1L	Columbus, Ga. (Spencer)
1	Kiyo Wilson	CB	6-1	192	So.	1L	Paducah, Ky. (Tilghman)
43	Michael Woodfork	FB	6-1	208	So.	1L	Paducah, Ky. (Tilghman)
42	Eric Wright	LB	5-10	185	So.	1L	Massillon, Ohio (Washington)
3	Randy Wyatt	SE	5-10	170	Sr.	1L	Paducah, Ky. (Louisville)

Numerical Roster

No.	Name	Pos.
1	Kiyo Wilson	CB
3	Randy Wyatt	TB
4	Littleton Ward	CB
5	Antonio O'Ferral	QB
6	Kio Sanford	SE
7	Billy Jack Haskins	QB
8	George Harris	FS
9	Jaysuma Simms	SE
10	Moe Williams	HB
11	Jeff Speedy	QB
12	Matt Hobbie	QB
13	Leon Smith	FL
14	Steven Hall	CB
15	Leman Boyd	SS
17	Van Hiles	CB
18	Dan Ariza	P
19	Nicky Nickels	PK
20	Carlos Collins	CB
21	Raymond McLaurin	HB
22	Pierce Foster	HB
23	Donnie Redd	SE
25	Melvin Johnson	FS
26	William Renuart	FS
27	Clyde Rudolph	FL
28	Donnell Gordon	TB
31	Damon Hood	FB
32	James Tucker	LB
37	Shane Ball	LB
38	Brent Brasher	HB
39	Rob Manchester	SS
41	Brian Sivinski	PK
42	Eric Wright	LB
43	Michael Woodfork	FB
44	David Ginn	LB
45	Evan O'Ferral	FB
46	Raymond Jones	LB
47	Chris Ward	DE
48	David Snardon	LB
50	Chad Hudson	LB
51	Kareem Dailey	LB
53	Howard Carter	DE
54	Kurt Supe	DE
55	Jeff Tanner	DE
56	Matt Neuss	LB
57	Dan Caruthers	C
58	Mike Schellenberger	LB
60	Scott Crosley	OT
61	DeAnthony Honaker	C
62	Quincy Murdock	OG
63	Adam Kane	C
64	Isreal Stone	OT
65	John Schlarman	OG
66	Andy Britt	OG
67	Trent DiGiuro	OG
68	Thad Corbin	DT
69	Barry Jones	OG
71	Rob Reynolds	OT
72	Aaron Purdie	OT
73	Cliff Bailey	OG
75	Brandon Jackson	OT
76	Mark Askin	OT
77	Dude Harper	C
78	J.D. Reed	OG
82	Chris Davis	TE
83	John Gibson	DE
84	Mark Mason	FL
85	Isaac Curtis	FL
86	Tyler Siddens	SE
87	Donte' Key	LB
88	Darrin Clark	TE
89	Corey Reeves	TE
90	Nicholas Jerdon	TE
91	Jebron Farah	SE
92	Robert Harris	DE
93	Bill Verdonk	DT
94	Robert Stinson	DT
97	Mike Schlegel	DT
98	Roger Sullivan	DT

Kentucky

1994 Kentucky Depth Chart

OFFENSE

Pos	#	Name
SE:	3	RANDY WYATT
	9	Jaysuma Simms or
	27	Clyde Rudolph
LT:	72	AARON PURDIE
	71	Rob Reynolds
LG:	69	Barry Jones
	65	John Schlarman
C:	57	Dan Caruthers
	61	DeAnthony Honaker
RG:	67	Trent DiGiuro
	66	Andy Britt or
	75	Brandon Jackson
RT:	76	MARK ASKIN
	62	Quincy Murdock
TE:	89	Corey Reeves
	82	Chris Davis
QB:	11	Jeff Speedy
	5	Antonio O'Ferral
FB:	31	DAMON HOOD
	43	Michael Woodfork
HB:	10	MOE WILLIAMS
	28	Donnell Gordon
WB:	21	Ray McLaurin
	38	Brent Brasher or
	85	Isaac Curtis
FL:	80	Leon Smith
	91	Jebron Farah or
	6	Kio Sanford

DEFENSE

Pos	#	Name
LE:	54	Kurt Supe
	47	Chris Ward
LT:	98	Roger Sullivan
	97	Mike Schlegel or
	68	Thad Corbin
RT:	94	ROBERT STINSON
	93	Bill Verdonk
RE:	53	HOWARD CARTER
	92	Robert Harris
BLB:	87	Donte' Key
	48	DAVID SNARDON
MLB:	56	Matt Neuss
	58	Mike Schellenberger
WLB:	42	Eric Wright
	32	James Tucker
SC:	17	Van Hiles
	20	Carlos Collins
SS:	15	Leman Boyd
	8	George Harris
FS:	25	MELVIN JOHNSON
	39	Rob Manchester
WC:	14	STEVEN HALL
	1	Kiyo Wilson

SPECIALISTS

Pos	#	Name
PK:	41	Brian Sivinski
	12	NICKY NICKELS
P:	18	DAN ARIZA
	19	Nicky Nickels

Returning Starters In All Capitals

1994 Kentucky Signees

Name	Pos.	Ht.	Wt.	Hometown/High School
Carey Barlow	L	6-3	280	Apopka, Fla./Apopka
David Berringer	L	6-4	270	Ft. Thomas, Ky./Highlands
Daymon Carter	B	6-2	220	Henderson, Ky./CCSF
Doug Clark	K	5-9	170	Seymour, Tenn./Seymour
Kris Comstock	L	6-8	270	Apopka, Fla./Apopka
Marcus Cross	L	6-4	225	Paducah, Ky./Tilghman
Chris Ford	B	6-1	175	Tallahassee, Fla./FAMU
George Harris	B	5-11	180	Oakland, Calif./CCSF
John Harris	L	6-4	220	Jacksonville, Fla./Raines
Trevor Hypolite	B	6-2	195	Rockledge, Fla./Rockledge
Mark Jacobs	L	6-3	235	Shalimar, Fla./Choctawatchee
Jonas Liening	L	6-7	270	Minster, Ohio/Minster
Marvin Major	L	6-3	267	Elyria, Ohio/Elyria
Tremayne Martin	B	6-1	180	Apopka, Fla./Apopka
Jason McDonough	L	6-3	260	Pittsburgh, Pa./Woodland Hills
Victor Rivers	L	6-4	285	Atlanta, Ga./Douglass
Reggie Rusk	B	6-2	190	Texas City, Texas/CCSF
Joey Sackett	L	6-3	265	Tallahassee, Fla./North Florida Christian
Andre' Smith	L	6-2	215	Decatur, Ga./Southwest DeKalb
Lamont Smith	L	6-2	215	Middletown, Ohio/Lakota
Shawn Smith	B	6-3	195	Tallahassee, Fla./North Florida Christian
Jeremy Streck	L	6-5	265	Cincinnati, Ohio/Anderson
Jason Thomas	L	6-5	255	Jacksonville, Fla./Terry Parker
Miguel Viera	B	6-2	227	Medina, Ohio/Cloverleaf
Ryan Wassil	L	6-6	290	Orlando, Fla./Edgewater
Mike Webster	L	6-6	220	Independence, Ky./Simon Kenton
Maurece Williams	B	6-2	205	Columbus, Ga./Spencer

Howard Carter

Damon Hood

1994 SEC Football

Kentucky Year-By-Year Records

Year	Coach	SEC	SEC Finish	Overall	Bowls
1881	Unknown			1-2-0	
1891	Unknown			1-1-0	
1892	Prof. A. M. Miller			2-4-1	
1893	John A. Thompson			5-2-1	
1894	W. P. Finney			5-2-0	
1895	Charles Mason			4-5-0	
1896	Dudley Short			3-6-0	
1897	Lyman B. Eaton			2-4-0	
1898	W. R. Bass			7-0-0	
1899	W. R. Bass			5-2-2	
1900	W. H. Kiler			4-6-0	
1901	W. H. Kiler			2-6-1	
1902	E. W. McLeod			3-5-1	
1903	C. A. Wright			7-1-0	
1904	F. E. Schact			9-1-0	
1905	F. E. Schact			6-3-1	
1906	J. White Guyn			4-3-0	
1907	J. White Guyn			9-1-1	
1908	J. White Guyn			4-3-0	
1909	E. R. Sweetland			9-1-0	
1910	E. R. Sweetland			7-2-0	
1911	P. P. Douglass			7-3-0	
1912	E. R. Sweetland			7-2-0	
1913	Alpha Brumage			6-2-0	
1914	Alpha Brumage			5-3-0	
1915	J. J. Tigert			6-1-1	
1916	J. J. Tigert			4-1-2	
1917	S. A. Boles			3-5-1	
1918	Andy Gill			2-1-0	
1919	Andy Gill			3-4-1	
1920	W. J. Juneau			3-4-1	
1921	W. J. Juneau			4-3-1	
1922	W. J. Juneau			6-3-0	
1923	J. J. Winn			4-3-2	
1924	Fred J. Murphy			4-5-0	
1925	Fred J. Murphy			6-3-0	
1926	Fred J. Murphy			2-6-1	
1927	Harry Gamage			3-6-1	
1928	Harry Gamage			4-3-1	
1929	Harry Gamage			6-1-1	
1930	Harry Gamage			5-3-0	
1931	Harry Gamage			5-2-2	
1932	Harry Gamage			4-5-0	
1933	Harry Gamage	2-3-0	9t	5-5-0	—
1934	C.A. Wynne	1-3-0	9	5-5-0	—
1935	C.A. Wynne	3-3-0	6t	5-4-0	—
1936	C.A. Wynne	1-3-0	10	6-4-0	—
1937	C.A. Wynne	0-5-0	11t	4-6-0	—
1938	A.D. Kirwan	0-4-0	12t	2-7-0	—
1939	A.D. Kirwan	2-2-1	5t	6-2-1	—
1940	A.D. Kirwan	1-2-2	9	5-3-2	—
1941	A.D. Kirwan	0-4-0	12	5-4-0	—
1942	A.D. Kirwan	0-5-0	11t	3-6-1	—
1943	NO TEAM				
1944	A.D. Kirwan	1-5-0	9	3-6-0	—
1945	Bernie Shivley	0-5-0	12	2-8-0	—
1946	Paul "Bear" Bryant	2-3-0	8	7-3-0	—
1947	Paul "Bear" Bryant	2-3-0	9t	8-3-0	Great Lakes
1948	Paul "Bear" Bryant	1-3-1	9	5-3-2	—
1949	Paul "Bear" Bryant	4-1-0	2	9-3-0	Orange

Year	Coach	SEC	SEC Finish	Overall	Bowl
1950	Paul "Bear" Bryant	5-1-0	1	11-1-0	Sugar
1951	Paul "Bear" Bryant	3-3-0	5	8-4-0	Cotton
1952	Paul "Bear" Bryant	1-3-2	9	5-4-2	—
1953	Paul "Bear" Bryant	4-1-1	2t	7-2-1	—
1954	Blanton Collier	5-2-0	3t	7-3-0	—
1955	Blanton Collier	3-3-1	6t	6-3-1	—
1956	Blanton Collier	4-4-0	6t	6-4-0	—
1957	Blanton Collier	1-7-0	12	3-7-0	—
1958	Blanton Collier	3-4-1	6t	5-4-1	—
1959	Blanton Collier	1-6-0	10	4-6-0	—
1960	Blanton Collier	2-4-1	9	5-4-1	—
1961	Blanton Collier	2-4-0	8	5-5-0	—
1962	Charlie Bradshaw	2-3-1	7t	3-5-2	—
1963	Charlie Bradshaw	0-5-1	11	3-6-1	—
1964	Charlie Bradshaw	4-2-0	2t	5-5-0	—
1965	Charlie Bradshaw	3-3-0	6t	6-4-0	—
1966	Charlie Bradshaw	2-4-0	7	3-6-1	—
1967	Charlie Bradshaw	1-6-0	8	2-8-0	—
1968	Charlie Bradshaw	0-7-0	10	3-7-0	—
1969	John Ray	1-6-0	9	2-8-0	—
1970	John Ray	0-7-0	10	2-9-0	—
1971	John Ray	1-6-0	8t	3-8-0	—
1972	John Ray	2-5-0	7t	3-8-0	—
1973	Fran Curci	3-4-0	5t	5-6-0	—
1974	Fran Curci	3-3-0	4t	6-5-0	—
1975	Fran Curci	0-6-0	9t	2-9-0	—
1976	Fran Curci	5-1-0	1t	9-3-0	Peach
1977	Fran Curci	7-0-0	*	10-1-0	—
1978	Fran Curci	2-4-0	7t	4-6-1	—
1979	Fran Curci	3-3-0	5t	5-6-0	—
1980	Fran Curci	1-5-0	8	3-8-0	—
1981	Fran Curci	2-4-0	6t	3-8-0	—
1982	Jerry Claiborne	0-6-0	9t	0-10-1	—
1983	Jerry Claiborne	2-4-0	7	6-5-1	Hall of Fame
1984	Jerry Claiborne	3-3-0	5t	9-3-0	Hall of Fame
1985	Jerry Claiborne	1-5-0	8	5-6-0	—
1986	Jerry Claiborne	2-4-0	7t	5-5-1	—
1987	Jerry Claiborne	1-5-0	7t	5-6-0	—
1988	Jerry Claiborne	2-5-0	8t	5-6-0	—
1989	Jerry Claiborne	2-5-0	7t	6-5-0	—
1990	Bill Curry	3-4-0	5	4-7-0	—
1991	Bill Curry	0-7-0	10	3-8-0	—
1992	Bill Curry	2-6-0	5t-E	4-7-0	—
1993	Bill Curry	4-4-0	3E	6-6-0	Peach

*did not count in standings due to NCAA probation period.

Bowl Results (5-3)

Bowl	Opponent	Result	Date
Great Lakes	Villanova	W 24-14	12-6-47
Orange	Santa Clara	L 13-21	1-2-50
Sugar	Oklahoma	W 13-7	1-1-51
Cotton	Texas Christian	W 20-7	1-1-52
Peach	North Carolina	W 21-0	12-31-76
Hall of Fame	West Virginia	L 16-20	12-22-83
Hall of Fame	Wisconsin	W 20-19	12-29-84
Peach	Clemson	L 13-14	12-31-93

Kentucky vs. All Opponents

Opponent	W	L	T
Alabama	1	30	1
Auburn	5	20	1
Baldwin-Wallace	1	0	0
Baylor	2	2	0
Berea College	5	0	0
Bethany	1	0	0
Boston College	0	1	0
Bowling Green	2	1	0
Butler College	4	0	0
Carson-Newman	2	0	0
Central Michigan	4	0	0
Central University	4	10	1
Centre	11	18	1
Chicago	0	1	0
Cincinnati	21	8	3
Citadel	1	0	0
Clemson	7	4	0
Cumberland	1	0	0
Cynthiana	2	0	0
Dayton	1	0	0
DePauw	0	1	0
Detroit	4	0	0
Duke	0	4	0
Earlham	3	0	0
East Carolina	1	0	0
East Tennessee State	1	0	0
Evansville	1	0	0
Florida	17	27	0
Florida State	3	1	1
Georgetown	22	1	0
George Washington	3	0	0
Georgia	9	36	2
Georgia Tech	7	11	1
Hanover	2	0	0
Hawaii	1	0	0
Houston	0	2	0
Illinois	1	1	0
Indiana	8	15	1
Kansas	0	3	1
Kansas State	3	1	0
Kent State	5	0	0
Kentucky Military	4	0	0
Kentucky Wesleyan	5	1	0
LSU	12	31	1
Louisville	6	0	0
Manhattan	1	1	0
Marietta	1	1	0
Marquette	2	1	0
Marshall College	6	0	0
Maryland	2	3	2
Maryville	19	0	1
Memphis State	4	0	0
Miami (Florida)	5	3	0
Miami (Ohio)	6	4	1
Michigan	0	1	0
Michigan State	2	2	0
Mississippi	12	23	1
*Mississippi State	14	7	0
Missouri	2	0	0
Morris-Harvey	2	0	0
Nashville	0	1	0
North Carolina	5	5	0
North Carolina State	1	1	0
North Dakota	1	0	0
North Texas State	3	0	0
Northwestern	0	1	0
Oglethorpe	2	0	0
Ohio Northern	1	0	0
Ohio State	0	3	0

Opponent	W	L	T
Ohio University	2	1	0
Oklahoma	1	2	0
Oregon State	2	0	0
Penn State	2	2	0
Purdue	1	2	0
Rice	2	0	0
Rose Poly	2	0	0
Rutgers	2	2	1
St. Mary's	1	0	0
St. Louis	0	2	0
Santa Clara	0	1	0
Sewanee	7	3	3
South Carolina	3	1	1
Southern Illinois	1	0	0
Southern Methodist	0	1	0
Southern Mississippi	2	0	0
Southwestern	3	0	0
Tennessee	23	57	9
Tennessee Tech	1	0	0
Texas	0	1	0
Texas A&M	1	1	0
Texas Christian	1	0	0
Transylvania	14	6	1
Tulane	9	6	0
Utah State	2	1	0
Vanderbilt	29	33	4
Villanova	7	1	1
Virginia	1	0	0
Virginia Military	12	4	0
Virginia Tech	11	6	2
Washington & Lee	11	7	2
West Virginia	11	8	1
West Virginia Wesleyan	0	1	0
Wilmington	2	0	0
Wisconsin	1	0	0
Xavier (Ohio)	18	2	0

* disagreement between schools about series record

Defensive end Art Still, a consensus All-America selection, anchored a Wildcat defense which led the SEC in rushing, scoring and total defense in 1977.

1994 SEC Football

Kentucky School Records

Individual

Game
Total Offense	405	Pookie Jones vs. Mississippi State	(1992)
Yards Rushing	238	Ivy Joe Hunter vs. Vanderbilt	(1986)
Rushing Attempts	35	Marc Logan vs. Mississippi State	(1985)
Yards Passing	373	Rick Norton vs. Houston	(1965)
Pass Attempts	56	Bill Ransdell vs. Vanderbilt	(1985)
Pass Completions	30	Bill Ransdell vs. Vanderbilt	(1985)
Yards Receiving	185	Rick Kestner vs. Ole Miss	(1964)
Receptions	11	Jim Campbell vs. Bowling Green	(1980)

Season
Total Offense	1,729	Pookie Jones	(1992)
Yards Rushing	1,278	Mark Higgs	(1987)
Rushing Attempts	253	George Adams	(1984)
Yards Passing	1,823	Rick Norton	(1965)
Pass Attempts	266	Bill Ransdell	(1984)
Pass Completions	151	Bill Ransdell	(1986)
Touchdown Passes	23	Babe Parilli	(1950)
Yards Receiving	727	Felix Wilson	(1978)
Receptions	47	Neal Clark	(1991)
Touchdown Catches	10	Al Bruno	(1950)
Interceptions	9	Jerry Clairborne	(1949)
Points	84	George Adams	(1984)

Career
Total Offense	5,456	Bill Ransdell	(1983-86)
Yards Rushing	3,835	Sonny Collins	(1972-75)
Rushing Attempts	777	Sonny Collins	(1972-75)
Yards Passing	5,564	Bill Ransdell	(1983-86)
Pass Attempts	816	Bill Ransdell	(1983-86)
Pass Completions	469	Bill Ransdell	(1983-86)
Touchdown Passes	50	Babe Parilli	(1949-51)
Yards Receiving	1,508	Felix Wilson	(1977-79)
Receptions	94	Tom Hutchinson	(1960-62)
Touchdown Catches	17	Steve Meilinger	(1951-53)
Interceptions	14	Darryl Bishop	(1971-73)
Points	246	Joey Worley	(1984-87)

Team

Game
Points	83	vs. North Dakota	(1950)
Total Offense	646	vs. Tennessee Tech	(1951)
Yards Rushing	446	vs. Tennessee Tech	(1951)
Yards Passing	440	vs. Tennessee	(1969)
First Downs	31	vs. Tennessee Tech	(1951)
		vs. Virginia Tech	(1975)
		vs. Vanderbilt	(1980)
		vs. Indiana	(1984)
Total Defense	1	vs. The Citadel	(1949)
Rushing Defense	-93	vs. Kansas State	(1970)
Passing Defense	-1	vs. LSU	(1953)

Season
Points	380	(1950)
Total Offense	4,082	(1950)
Yards Rushing	3,124	(1974)
Yards Passing	2,318	(1985)
First Downs	219	(1986)
Fewest Points Allowed	53	(1949)
Total Defense	1,692	(1949)
Rushing Defense	788	(1949)
Passing Defense	479	(1955)
Consecutive Wins	12	(October 28, 1909 to November 5, 1910)

(All Records 1946-93)

Sonny Collins

Bill Ransdell

Kentucky

Kentucky in the NFL

George Adams, RB
New York Giants 1985-89; New England Patriots 1990
Ermal Allen, QB
Cleveland Browns 1947
Sam Ball, T
Baltimore Colts 1966-70
Oliver Barnett, DT
Atlanta Falcons 1990-92; Buffalo Bills 1993
Rodger Bird, DB
Oakland Raiders 1967-71
George Blanda, QB
Chicago Bears 1949-58; Baltimore Colts 1950; Houston Oilers 1960-66; Oakland Raiders 1967-75
Jerry Blanton, LB
Kansas City Chiefs 1979-85
Jeff Brady, OLB
Pittsburgh Steelers 1991
Green Bay Packers 1992
Chuck Bradley, OT
Cincinnati 1993
Warren Bryant, T
Atlanta Falcons 1978-84; Los Angeles Raiders 1985
Cornell Burbage, WR
Dallas Cowboys 1987-89
Randy Burke, WR
Baltimore Colts 1978-81
Bob Butler, G
Philadelphia Eagles 1962; New York Jets 1963
Sonny Collins, RB
Atlanta Falcons 1976
Bob Davis, B
Philadelphia Eagles 1942
Doug Davis, T
Minnesota Vikings 1966-72
Dermontti Dawson, OG
Pittsburgh Steelers 1988-93
Gene Donaldson, G
Cleveland Browns 1953
Thom Dornbrook, OT
Pittsburgh Steelers 1978
Bob Dougherty, LB
Los Angeles Rams 1957; Pittsburgh Steelers 1958; Oakland Raiders 1960-63
Maurice Douglass, DB
Chicago Bears 1986-93
John Dumbauld, DE
Philadelphia Eagles 1987; New Orleans Saints 1986, 1988
Tom Ehlers, LB
Philadelphia Eagles 1975-77
Buffalo Bills 1978
John Eibner, T
Philadelphia Eagles 1941-42, 1946
Joe Federspiel, LB
New Orleans Saints 1972-80; Baltimore Colts 1981
Don Fielder, DE
Tampa Bay Buccaneers 1982-86
Bob Fry, T
Los Angeles Rams 1953-59; Dallas Cowboys 1960-64
Dom Fucci, B
Detroit Lions 1955
Frank Fuller, DT
Los Angeles Rams 1953-58; Chicago Cardinals 1959; St. Louis Cardinals 1960-62; Philadelphia Eagles 1963
Bob Gain, T
Cleveland Browns 1952, 1954-64
Irv Goode, C
St. Louis Cardinals 1962-71; Buffalo Bills 1972; Miami Dolphins 1973-74
Will Grant, C
Buffalo Bills 1978-85; Seattle Seahawks 1986

John Grimsley, LB
Houston Oilers 1984-89
Dick Hensley, E
New York Giants 1949; Pittsburgh Steelers 1952; Chicago Bears 1953
Mark Higgs, TB
Dallas Cowboys 1988; Philadelphia Eagles 1989; Miami Dolphins 1990-93
Ivy Joe Hunter, TB
Indianapolis Colts 1989-90
New England Patriots 1991
Tom Hutchison, E
Cleveland Browns 1963-65
Bert Johnson, B
Philadelphia Eagles 1942
Clyde Johnson, T
Los Angeles Rams 1946-47
David Johnson, CB
Pittsburgh Steelers 1989-92; Atlanta Falcons 1993
Shipwreck Kelly, RB
New York Giants 1932; Brooklyn Dodgers 1933-34, 1937
Ralph Kercheval, RB-K
Brooklyn Dodgers 1933-38
Don King, T
Cleveland Browns 1954; Green Bay Packers 1956; Philadelphia Eagles 1956; Denver Broncos 1960
Kelly Kirchbaum, LB
Kansas City Chiefs 1980
Doug Kotar, RB
New York Giants 1974-81
Jim Kovach, LB
New Orleans Saints 1979-85; San Francisco 49ers 1985
Frank LeMaster, LB
Philadelphia Eagles 1974-83
Luther Lindon, T
Detroit Lions 1944-45
Jim Little, T
New York Giants 1945
Marc Logan, RB
Cincinnati Bengals 1987-88; Miami Dolphins 1989-91; San Francisco 49ers 1993
Dicky Lyons, S
New Orleans Saints 1970
Pete Marcus, E
Washington Redskins 1944
Rick Massie, SE
Denver Broncos 1987-88
Tony Mayes, DB
St. Louis Cardinals 1987
Bubba McCollum, DT
Houston Oilers
Lloyd McDermott, T
Detroit Lions 1950; Chicago Cardinals 1950-51
Steve Meilinger, E
Washington Redskins 1956-57; Green Bay Packers 1958-60; Pittsburgh Steelers 1961; St. Louis Cardinals 1961
Lou Michaels, DE-K
Los Angeles Rams 1958-60; Pittsburgh Steelers 1961-63; Baltimore Colts 1964-69; Green Bay Packers 1971
Noah Mullins, B
Chicago Bears 1946-48; New York Giants 1949
Dan Neal, C
Baltimore Colts 1973-74; Chicago Bears 1975-83
Rick Norton, QB
Miami Dolphins 1966-69
Rick Nuzum, C
Los Angeles Rams 1977; Green Bay Packers 1978-79

Dick Palmer, LB
Miami Dolphins 1970; Buffalo Bills 1972; New Orleans Saints 1973; Atlanta Falcons 1974
Babe Parilli, QB
Green Bay Packers 1952-53, 1956-58; Cleveland Browns 1956; Oakland Raiders 1960; Boston Patriots 1961-67; New York Jets 1968-69
Doug Pelfrey, PK
Cincinnati 1993
Todd Perry, OG
Chicago 1993
Wally Pesuit, T
Miami Dolphins 1977-78; Detroit Lions 1979-80
Don Phelps, B
Cleveland Browns 1950-52
Joe Phillips, WR
Washington Redskins 1985-87
Jim Ramey, DE
St. Louis Cardinals 1979
Derrick Ramsey, TE
Oakland Raiders 1978-81; Los Angeles Raiders 1982-83; New England Patriots; 1984-85; Detroit Lions 1987
Bill Ransdell, QB
New York Jets 1987; Indianapolis Colts 1988
Jerry Reese, DT
Pittsburgh Steelers 1988
Jay Rhodemyre, C
Green Bay Packers 1948-52
Dave Roller, DT
New York Giants 1971-74; Green Bay Packers 1975-78
Larry Seiple, P
Miami Dolphins 1967-77
Washington Serini, G
Chicago Bears 1948-51; Green Bay Packers 1952
John Shannon, DG
Chicago Bears 1988-89
Glenn Shaw, HB
Chicago Bears 1960; Minnesota Vikings 1961; Los Angeles Rams 1962; Oakland Raiders 1963-64
Larry Smith, LB
Houston Oilers 1987
Art Still, DE
Kansas City Chiefs 1978-87; Buffalo Bills 1988-89
Bob Talamini, G
Houston Oilers 1960-67; New York Jets 1968
Herschel Turner, G
St. Louis Cardinals 1964-65
Harry Ulinski, C
Washington Redskins 1950-51, 1953-56
Jeff Van Note, C
Atlanta Falcons 1969-86
Dean Wells, LB
Seattle 1993
Ken Willis, PK
Dallas Cowboys 1990-91; Tampa Bay Buccaneers 1992; New York Giants 1992
Earl Wilson, DE
San Diego Chargers 1985-87
Bob Windsor, TE
San Francisco 49ers 1967-71; Boston Patriots 1972-75
Bob Winkel, DT
New York Jets 1979-80
Cal Withrow, C
San Diego Chargers 1970; Green Bay Packers 1971-73; St. Louis Cardinals 1974
Walt Yowarsky, E
Washington Redskins 1951-54; Detroit Lions 1955; New York Giants 1955-57; San Francisco 49ers 1958

Bob Gain

Jeff Van Note

Doug Pelfrey

Oliver Barnett

1994 SEC Football 93

Kentucky Media Information

Kentucky SID
Tony Neely

Kentucky Sports Information
Memorial Coliseum
Room 23
Lexington, KY 40506
(606) 257-3838
FAX: (606) 323-4310

Football Writers
John Clay, Chuck Culpepper
Lexington Herald-Leader
Main and Midland
Lexington, KY 40507
(606) 231-3226

Rick Bozich, Pat Forde
Louisville Courier-Journal
525 W. Broadway
Louisville, KY 40201
(502) 582-4361

Mark Coomes
Louisville Courier-Journal
400 Old Vine Street
Suite 201
Lexington, KY 40507
(606) 254-7888

Oscar Combs, Mike Estep
Cats' Pause
P.O. Box 7297
Lexington, KY 40502
(606) 278-3474

Larry Vaught
Danville Advocate-Messenger
330 S. Fourth Street
Danville, KY 40422
(606) 236-2551

Darrell Bird
Elizabethtown News-Enterprise
P.O. Box 430
Elizabethtown, KY 42701
(502) 769-2312

Brian Rickerd
Frankfort State-Journal
P.O. Box 368
Frankfort, KY 40501
(502) 227-4556

Tom Gamble, Janet Graham
Kentucky Post
125 East Court Street
Cincinnati, OH 45202
(513) 352-2767

Rich Suwanski
Owensboro Messenger & Inquirer
1401 Frederica Street
Owensboro, KY 42301
(502) 926-0123

Nick Nicholas
Richmond Register
380 Big Hill Avenue
Richmond, KY 40391
(606) 623-1669

Jeff Neal
Somerset Commonwealth-Journal
102 North Maple
Somerset, KY 42501
(606) 678-8191

Jeff Kerr
Winchester Sun
20 Wall Street
Winchester, KY 40391
(606) 744-3123

Other Daily Newspapers
Mark Maynard
Ashland Daily Independent
226 S. 17th Street
Ashland, KY 41101
(606) 329-1717

Joe Medley
Bowling Green Daily News
813 College
Bowling Green, KY 42101
(502) 843-4321

Corbin Times-Tribune
201 N. Kentucky Avenue
Corbin, KY 40701
(606) 528-2464

Glasgow Daily Times
301 S. Green Street
Glasgow, KY 42141
(502) 651-5171

Harlan Daily Enterprise
Central Street
Harlan, KY 40831
(606) 573-4510

Jim Kirk
Henderson Gleaner-Journal
455 Klutey Park Plaza
Henderson, KY 42420
(502) 827-2000

Scott Burnside
Kentucky New Era
1618 E. Ninth Street
Hopkinsville, KY 42240
(502) 886-4444

Mike Boaz
Madisonville Messenger
Box 529
Madisonville, KY 42431
(502) 821-6833

Maysville Ledger-Independent
41 W. 2nd Street
Maysville, KY 40156
(606) 564-9091

Neil Morgan
Middlesboro Daily News
Box 579
Middlesboro, KY 40965
(606) 248-1010

Kevin Stewart
Paducah Sun
408 Kentucky Avenue
Paducah, KY 42001
(502) 442-7389

Wire Services
Mike Embry
Associated Press
Herald-Leader Building
Main and Midland
Lexingtron, KY 40507
(606) 254-2070

Play-By-Play Broadcasters
Ralph Hacker, WVLK-Radio
(play-by-play)
Box 559
Lexington, KY 40501

Charlie McAlexander (color)
Host Communications
120 Kentucky Avenue
Lexington, KY 40502
(606) 253-3230
(606) 253-5900

Dave Baker, WKYT-TV (color)
Box 655
Lexington, KY 40501

Stations Carrying Games
Originating station is WVLK AM-FM in Lexington. Network consists of 90 stations. Distribution is through the services of rights holder Host Communications.

Television Broadcasters
Alan Cutler
WLEX-TV
Box 1457
Lexington, KY 40501
(606) 255-4404

Rob Bromley
WKYT-TV
Box 55037
Lexington, KY 40555
(606) 299-0411

Kenny Rice
WTVQ-TV
Box 5590
Lexington, KY 40501
(606) 233-3600

Bob Domine
WAVE-TV
725 S. Floyd
Louisville, KY 40203
(502) 585-2201

Gary Gupton
WHAS-TV
Box 1084
Louisville, KY 40116
(502) 582-7840

Fred Cowgill
WLKY-TV
Box 6218
Louisville, KY 40116
(502) 893-3671

TV43
P.O. Box 4300
Hopkinsville, KY 42240
(502) 885-4300

David Sullivan
WDRB-TV
624 W. Muhammad Ali Boulevard
Louisville, KY 40203
(502) 584-6441

Terry Bumgarner
WOWK-TV
555 5th Avenue
Huntington, WV 25701
(304) 525-7661

Kenny Bass
WSAZ-TV
645 5th Avenue
Huntington, WV 25701
(304) 697-4780

Larry McIntosh
WPSD-TV
P.O. Box 1197
Paducah, KY 42002
(502) 442-8214

Radio Stations
Tom Leach
WVLK-FM
Box 559
Lexington, KY 40501
(606) 253-5900

Scott Pierce
WLXG-AM
1300 Greendale Road
Lexington, KY 40578
(606) 233-1515

Van Vance
WHAS
Box 1084
Louisville, KY 40116
(502) 582-7840

Doug Ormay
Kentucky Network
11001 Bluegrass Parkway
Louisville, KY 40299

Mark Durbin
WCKY-AM
219 McFarland Street
Cincinnati, OH 45202

Doug Flynn
WLAP-AM
3549 Russell Cave Rd.
Lexington, KY 40511

Campus Outlet
Kentucky Kernel
University of Kentucky
Lexington, KY 40506
(606) 257-1915

LSU

DR. WILLIAM "Bud" DAVIS
Chancellor

DR. PAT CULBERTSON
Faculty Representative

JOE DEAN
Athletic Director

Louisiana State University

CHANCELLOR:
Dr. William "Bud" Davis (Colorado 1951)
FACULTY REPRESENTATIVE:
Dr. Pat Culbertson (LSU 1963)
ATHLETIC DIRECTOR:
Joe Dean (LSU 1955)
HEAD COACH:
Curley Hallman (Texas A&M 1970)
LOCATION: Baton Rouge, Louisiana
FOUNDED: 1860
ENROLLMENT: 23,589
NICKNAME: Tigers or Fighting Tigers
COLORS: Purple and Gold
STADIUM: Tiger Stadium (80,150) - Natural

Tiger Quick Facts

1993 RECORD: 5-6
 (3-3 Home, 2-3 Away)
1993 SEC RECORD (FINISH): 3-5 (T3rd - Western)
 (1-3 Home, 2-2 Away)
BOWL: None
ALL-TIME RECORD: 574-325-46 (.632)
SEC RECORD: 202-153-21 (.565) — Regular Season Games
SEC CHAMPIONSHIPS: 7
 (1935, 36, 58, 61t, 70, 86, 88t)
BOWL APPEARANCES: 28
BOWL RECORD: 11-16-1 (.411)
LAST APPEARANCE: 1989 Hall of Fame Bowl
 (Syracuse 23, LSU 10)

LSU Team Information

OFFENSIVE SYSTEM: Multiple

DEFENSIVE SYSTEM: 4-3

LETTERMEN RETURNING: 43
- 19 Offense
- 23 Defense
- 1 Specialists

LETTERMEN LOST: 17
- 8 Offense
- 7 Defense
- 2 Specialists

STARTERS RETURNING: 13
OFFENSE (6)
- SE Brett Bech (6-1, 185, Sr.)
- LG Ben Bordelon (6-5, 287, So.)
- QB Jamie Howard (6-1, 205, Jr.)
- RT Marcus Price (6-6, 308, Sr.)
- FB Robert Toomer (5-11, 220, Jr.)
- FL Sheddrick Wilson (6-1, 195, Jr.)

DEFENSE (6)
- MLB Mike Calais (6-1, 230, So.)
- LE James Gillyard (6-2, 244, Jr.)
- SS Ivory Hilliard (6-0, 192, Jr.)
- RCB Tory James (6-2, 182, Jr.)
- LT Nate Miller (6-4, 305, Sr.)
- LCB Rodney Young (6-2, 201, Sr.)

SPECIALISTS (1)
- PK Andre' Lafleur (5-11, 178, Jr.)

STARTERS LOST: 11
OFFENSE (5)
- TE Harold Bishop (6-6, 260, Sr.)
- TB Jay Johnson (5-9, 184, So.)
- C Kevin Mawae (6-4, 270, Sr.)
- LT Ross Setters (6-5, 283, Sr.)
- RG Ronnie Simnicht (6-5, 291, Sr.)

DEFENSE (5)
- ILB Robert Deshotel (6-3, 227, Jr.)
- FS Anthony Marshall (6-2, 203, Sr.)
- RT Ike Pullett (6-4, 257, Sr.)
- ILB Ricardo Washington (6-4, 218, Sr.)
- RE Corey White (6-3, 238, Sr.)

SPECIALISTS (1)
- P Scott Holstein (6-5, 209, Sr.)

Tiger Stadium (80,140)
Record: 289-116-18 (.704)
First Game: Nov. 25, 1924 — Tulane 13, LSU 0
Largest Crowd: 82,390 (Sept. 24, 1983)
LSU 40, Washington State 14

1994 LSU Schedule

Sept.	3	TEXAS A&M	BATON ROUGE
Sept.	10	MISSISSIPPI STATE	BATON ROUGE
Sept.	17	at Auburn	Auburn, Ala.
Oct.	1	SOUTH CAROLINA	BATON ROUGE
Oct.	8	at Florida	Gainesville, Fla.
Oct.	15	KENTUCKY	BATON ROUGE
Oct.	29	at Ole Miss	Oxford, Miss.
Nov.	5	ALABAMA	BATON ROUGE
Nov.	12	SOUTHERN MISS	BATON ROUGE
Nov.	19	at Tulane	New Orleans, La.
Nov.	27	at Arkansas	Little Rock, Ark.

1995 LSU Schedule

Sept.	2	at Texas A&M	College Station, Texas
Sept.	9	at Mississippi State	TBA
Sept.	16	AUBURN	BATON ROUGE
Sept.	23	RICE	BATON ROUGE
Sept.	30	at South Carolina	Columbia, S.C.
Oct.	7	FLORIDA	BATON ROUGE
Oct.	14	at Kentucky	Lexington, Ky.
Oct.	28	NORTH TEXAS	BATON ROUGE
Nov.	4	at Alabama	Tuscaloosa, Ala.
Nov.	11	OLE MISS	BATON ROUGE
Nov.	25	ARKANSAS	BATON ROUGE

1993 LSU Individual Leaders

RUSHING	Atts	Yards	Avg	TDs	Yds/Game
Jay Johnson	106	558	5.3	6	50.7
ROBERT TOOMER	82	295	3.6	4	26.8
Germaine Williams	58	226	3.9	2	20.6
JERMAINE SHARP	45	199	4.4	0	28.4
DAVID BUTLER	24	84	3.5	0	7.6

PASSING	Atts	Comp	Ints/TDs	Pct	Yds
JAMIE HOWARD	248	106	12 / 7	.427	1319
Chad Loup	92	55	4 / 2	.598	683

RECEIVING	Rec	Yds	Avg	TDs	Yds/Game
BRETT BECH	30	429	14.3	3	39.0
EDDIE KENNISON	28	466	16.6	3	42.4
Scott Ray	25	366	14.6	1	33.3
CHRIS HILL	20	913	9.7	1	21.4
SHEDDRICK WILSON	15	182	12.1	0	16.6

SCORING	G	TDs	PAT	FGs	Tot	Avg
ANDRE' LAFLEUR	10	0	17-19	14-17	59	5.9
Jay Johnson	11	6	0	0	36	3.3
ROBERT TOOMER	11	4	0	0	24	2.2
BRETT BECH	11	3	0	0	18	1.6
EDDIE KENNISON	11	3	0	0	18	1.6

PUNTING	No	Yds	Avg	Long
Scott Holstein	56	2233	39.9	65

KICKOFF RETURNS	No	Yds	Avg	TDs	Avg/Game	Long
EDDIE KENNISON	18	410	22.8	0	37.3	44
DAVID BUTLER	11	270	24.6	0	24.6	61
GARY PEGUES	8	104	13.0	0	9.5	46

PUNT RETURNS	No	Yds	Avg	TDs	Avg/Game	Long
EDDIE KENNISON	20	256	12.8	0	23.3	55

TACKLES	Total (S-A)	Sk (Yds)	TL (Yds)	Ints
Ricardo Washington	76 (43-33)	0	1 (-1)	0
Anthony Marshall	72 (45-27)	1 (-6)	1 (-6)	5
MIKE CALAIS	69 (41-28)	0	4 (-6)	0
Robert Deshotel	69 (45-24)	3 (-20)	5 (-25)	0
Corey White	62 (39-23)	3 (-26)	7 (-33)	0

INTERCEPTIONS	No	Yds	TDs	Int/Game	Long
Anthony Marshall	5	7	0	0.5	4
TORY JAMES	4	87	0	0.4	59
IVORY HILLIARD	2	18	0	0.2	12
RODNEY YOUNG	2	23	0	0.2	23

Returning Players In All Capitals

1993 LSU Team Statistics

	LSU	OPP
FIRST DOWNS	202	230
Rushing	90	122
Passing	102	90
Penalty	10	18
NET YARDS RUSHING	1449	2149
Yards rushing	1814	2338
Yards lost	365	189
Rushing attempts	418	434
Average per rush	3.5	5.0
Average per game	131.7	195.4
NET YARDS PASSING	2002	2204
Average per game	182.0	200.4
Passes attempted	341	300
Passes completed	161	176
Had intercepted	16	13
TOTAL OFFENSIVE YARDS	3451	4353
Average per game	313.7	395.7
Total plays	759	734
Average per play	4.6	5.9
NUMBER PUNTS/YARDS	56/2233	50/1957
Punting average	39.9	39.1
Net punting average	36.9	34.0
PUNT RETURNS/YARDS	20/256	22/166
Punt return average	12.8	7.6
KICKOFF RETURNS/YARDS	46/901	44/690
Kickoff return average	19.6	15.7
PENALTIES/YARDS	67/606	75/564
Penalty yards per game	55.1	51.3
FUMBLES/LOST	25/9	26/7
INTERCEPTION RETURNS/YARDS	13/135	16/267
Interception return average	10.4	16.7
TOUCHDOWNS	21	41
Rushing	12	20
Passing	9	20
Return	0	1
FIELD GOALS MADE/ATTEMPTED	15/21	8/12
KICK EXTRA POINTS MADE/ATTEMPTED	17/21	38/41
SAFETY	0	0
TWO-POINT CONVERSIONS	0-2	0-2
TOTAL POINTS	190	308
Average per game	17.3	28.0

Mike Calais   **Jamie Howard**   **Robert Toomer**

1993 LSU Results

5-6 Overall • 3-5 SEC (t3rd - Western)

Sept. 4	at Texas A&M [ABC]	L	0-24	61,307
Sept. 11	at Mississippi State [ABC]	W	18-16	33,324
Sept. 18	AUBURN	L	10-34	71,936
Sept. 25	at Tennessee [JP]	L	20-42	95,931
Oct. 2	UTAH STATE	W	38-17	57,316
Oct. 9	FLORIDA [ESPN]	L	3-58	60,060
Oct. 16	at Kentucky	L	17-35	54,750
Oct. 30	OLE MISS - HC	W	19-17	61,470
Nov. 6	at Alabama [JP]	W	17-13	70,123
Nov. 20	TULANE	W	24-10	58,190
Nov. 27	ARKANSAS [ESPN]	L	24-42	54,239

1994 SEC Football

Curley Hallman

HOMETOWN:
Tuscaloosa, Alabama

ALMA MATER:
Texas A&M (1970)

PLAYING CAREER:
Texas A&M Defensive Back 1966-68 (All Southwest Conference 1968)

COACHING CAREER:
Texas A&M Graduate Assistant 1969; Texas A&M Volunteer Coach 1970; Orange State H.S. Assistant 1971-72; Alabama Assistant 1973-76; Memphis State Assistant 1977-78; Clemson Assistant 1979-81; Texas A&M Assistant 1982-87; Southern Mississippi Head Coach 1988-90; LSU Head Coach 1991-present.

COACHING ACHIEVEMENTS:
1988 Independence Bowl Association Coach of the Year, 1988 Kodak Regional Coach of the Year, 1988 Metro Conference Coach of the Year.

BORN:
September 3, 1947

WIFE:
Barbara Dale Tomlinson

CHILDREN:
Jennifer Dale 17, Jessica Leigh 12

ASSISTANT COACHES:
PHIL BENNETT (Texas A&M 1978) - Assistant Head Coach/Defensive Coordinator/Defensive Backs
JERRY BALDWIN (Mississippi Valley State 1975) - Assistant Head Coach/Linebackers
LYNN AMEDEE (LSU 1962) - Offensive Coordinator/Quarterbacks
STEVE BUCKLEY (Southern Miss 1985) - Running Backs
LARRY EDMONDSON (Texas A&M 1983) - Wide Receivers
RICK VILLARREAL (Southern Miss 1990) - Tight Ends/Recruiting
LARRY ZIERLEIN (Fort Hays State 1971) - Offensive Line
LEE FOBBS (Grambling State 1972) - Defensive Ends
PETE FREDENBURG (Southwest Texas State 1970) - Defensive Tackles

SUPPORT STAFF:
JOHN PURDY (St. Mary's 1972) - Trainer
CHRIS SEROKA (Southern Miss 1988) - Strength Coach
SAM NADER (Auburn 1967) - Administrative Assistant

Year-By-Year Record

Year	School	Conf.	All	Bowl
1988	Southern Mississippi		10-2	Independence
1989	Southern Mississippi		5-6	
1990	Southern Mississippi		8-3	All American
1991	LSU	3-4 (16th)	5-6	
1992	LSU	1-7 (6thW)	2-9	
1993	LSU	3-5 (t3rdW)	5-6	
OVERALL RECORD		7-16 (.304)	35-32 (.522)	6 Years
LSU Record		7-16 (.304)	12-21 (.364)	3 Years
Southern Miss Record			23-11	
SEC Record		7-16		
Bowl Record		1-1	(1-1 Southern Mississippi)	

LSU All-Star Candidates

IVORY HILLIARD
Senior • Free Safety
6-0 • 192 • Patterson, La.

• Moves to free safety in 1994 after logging second-most tackles for a Tiger defensive back (58) from the strong safety position a year ago.
• Named National Player of the Week by *Sports Illustrated* and SEC Defensive Player of the Week following win at Alabama where he registered nine tackles, intercepted two passes and tallied two sacks.
• Closed 1993 season with 27 tackles, four sacks, five tackles for loss, two interceptions and a pass break up in last four games.
• Posted season-high 13 stops (six solo) in season-opener at Texas A&M with one caused fumble and a fumble recovery.

HILLARD STATS

Year	Tackles	TFL (Yds)	Sk (Yds)	FR	Int
1991	58 (32-26)	0	0	0	0
1992	64 (34-30)	1 (-1)	0	0	2
1993	58 (38-20)	7 (-50)	4 (-47)	1	2
Career	180 (104-76)	8 (-51)	4 (-47)	1	4

GABE NORTHERN
Junior • Defensive End
6-3 • 235 • Baton Rouge, La.

• Moved from middle linebacker to defensive end for last four contests of the year, starting two games at that position late last season, both Tiger victories (Ole Miss and Alabama).
• Tallied 41 tackles (24 solos), including one sack and three tackles for loss, including a 10-stop effort vs. Auburn.
• Had an outstanding spring practice at defensive end and was dominant in several full-scale scrimmages, excelling in LSU's four-man front.

NORTHERN STATS

Year	Tackles	TFL (Yds)	Sk (Yds)	FR	Int
1992	21 (12-9)	0	0	0	0
1993	41 (24-17)	3 (-11)	1 (-6)	0	0
Career	62 (36-26)	3 (-11)	1 (-6)	0	0

EDDIE KENNISON
Sophomore • Flanker
6-0 • 184 • Lake Charles, La.

• Named to the *Knoxville News-Sentinel* SEC All-Freshman team in 1993 at the all-around position designated "athlete."
• Big play threat every time he touches the ball, returning punts and kickoffs in addition to wide receiver duties.
• Ranked third in the SEC and sixth in the nation in punt returns, sixth in the league in kickoff returns and eighth in all-purpose yards.
• Honored as LSU's ABC-TV MVP for play vs. Miss. State last season: two catches for 45 yards, four punt returns for 78 yards and two kickoff returns for 70 yards.

KENNISON STATS

Year	Rec	Yds	Avg	TD	LP	PR	Yds	Avg	TD	LP	KOR	Yds	Avg	TDs	LP
1993	28	466	16.6	3	74	20	256	12.8	0	55	18	410	22.8	0	44

MARCUS PRICE
Senior • Offensive Tackle
6-6 • 308 • Port Arthur, Texas

• One of SEC's top pass blockers, Price will be expected to fill leadership role after loss of three starters from last season's line.
• Started every game at right tackle in 1993, participating in 679 offensive plays, second only to All-SEC center Kevin Mawae.
• As a special teams performer, participated in 717 total plays, more than any other LSU player.

1994 SEC Football

1994 LSU Roster

No.	Name	Pos.	Ht.	Wt.	Class	Exp.	Hometown (High School/JC)
94	Doug Admire	DT	6-2	265	So.	SQ	Rockwall, Texas (Rockwall)
58	Pete Ballis	DT	6-2	262	Jr.	1L	Chickamaunga, Ga. (Gordon Lee)
22	Derrick Beavers	TB	5-6	176	Fr.	RS	Carencro, La. (Carencro)
87	Brett Bech	SE	6-1	184	Sr.	2L	Slidell, La. (Slidell)
31	John Bell	SS	6-0	198	Jr.	SQ	LaPorte, Texas (LaPorte)
67	Mike Blanchard	C	6-0	267	Sr.	3L	Baton Rouge, La. (Catholic)
68	Ben Bordelon	OG	6-6	297	So.	1L	Matthews, La. (Central Lafourche)
85	Josh Bradley	TE	6-7	241	So.	1L	Oak Grove, La. (Oak Grove)
44	Kimojha Brooks	MLB	6-1	228	Jr.	2L	DeRidder, La. (DeRidder)
27	Hunter Bullard	FS	5-10	174	Fr.	RS	Bossier City, La. (Airline)
24	Todd Burks	SE	5-11	174	Jr.	1L	Denham Springs, La. (Fork Union Academy)
40	David Butler	TB	5-9	179	Jr.	2L	Houma, La. (South Terrebone)
56	Mike Calais	MLB	6-1	237	So.	1L	Patterson, La. (Patterson)
75	David Carmona	DT	6-0	272	Fr.	RS	Richardson, Texas (Richardson)
50	Marcus Carmouche	C	6-3	281	So.	SQ	Lafayette, La. (Carencro)
70	Trey Champagne	OT	6-7	295	Jr.	TR	Covington, La. (Vanderbilt)
9	Talvi Crawford	SS	6-0	210	Sr.	1L	Orlando, Fla.(Garden City CC)
97	William Crowell	DT	6-0	290	Sr.	3L	Meridian, Miss. (Meridian)
46	Robert Deshotel	ILB	6-3	245	Sr.	3L	Lake Charles, La. (LaGrange)
81	Jonny Fayard	TE	6-4	242	Sr.	2L	Marrero, La. (Archbishop Shaw)
21	Kevin Franklin	TB	5-9	160	So.	1L	Baton Rouge, La. (Catholic)
7	James Gillyard	DE	6-3	242	Jr.	2L	Shreveport, La. (Woodlawn)
28	Chris Green	ILB	6-1	188	Fr.	RS	Hahnville, La. (Hahnville)
48	Jeff Hampton	ILB	6-4	227	Fr.	RS	Clear Lake, Texas (Clear Lake)
90	Furnell Hankton	DE	6-5	257	Fr.	RS	New Orleans, La. (B.T. Washington)
89	Chris Hill	FL	6-5	225	Jr.	2L	Mansfield, La. (Mansfield)
3	Ivory Hilliard	FS	6-0	192	Sr.	3L	Patterson, La. (Patterson)
63	Todd Holland	OT	6-7	278	Fr.	RS	Orlando, Fla. (Boone)
26	Casey Howard	SS	6-3	193	So.	1L	Stonewall, La. (North Desoto)
4	Jamie Howard	QB	6-1	206	Jr.	2L	Lafayette, La. (St. Thomas More)
10	Matt Huerkamp	PK	6-1	185	Jr.	1L	Shalimar, Fla. (Choctawhatchee)
35	Tim Hutton	DT	6-4	253	Fr.	RS	Slidell, La. (Slidell)
8	Tory James	CB	6-2	182	Jr.	2L	Marrero, La. (Archbishop Shaw)
78	Kerry Jenkins	OT	6-6	270	So.	SQ	Tuscaloosa, Ala. (Holt)
2	Eddie Kennison	FL	6-0	184	So.	1L	Lake Charles, La. (Washington-Marion)
80	Chad Kessler	P	6-1	194	Fr.	RS	Lake Mary, Fla. (Lake Mary)
62	Mark King	OG	6-4	283	Jr.	2L	Houma, La. (Terrebonne)
23	Andre Lafleur	PK	5-11	178	Jr.	1L	Lafayette, La. (Acadiana)
47	David LaFleur	TE	6-7	268	So.	1L	Westlake, La. (Westlake)
18	Clarence Lenton	CB	5-11	184	Sr.	SQ	Memphis, Tenn. (Westwood)
52	Brandon Michel	MLB	6-1	228	Fr.	RS	Lutcher, La. (Lutcher)
98	Nate Miller	DT	6-4	310	Sr.	3L	Tuscaloosa, Ala. (Central East)
93	Robert Miller	DT	6-5	300	So.	1L	Hattiesburg, Miss. (Hattiesburg)
57	Kenny Mixon	DE	6-4	247	Fr.	RS	Pineville, La. (Pineville)
88	Gabe Northern	DE	6-3	235	Jr.	2L	Baton Rouge, La. (Glen Oaks)
11	Gary Pegues	SS	5-8	170	Sr.	3L	Shalimar, Fla. (Choctawhatchee)
76	Adam Perry	OG	6-3	284	Fr.	RS	Covington, La. (Covington)
79	Marcus Price	OT	6-6	308	Sr.	3L	Port Arthur, Texas (Lincoln)
82	Pat Rogers	ILB	5-11	215	So.	1L	Shreveport, La. (Fair Park)
66	Brian Sharp	OG	6-3	301	Fr.	RS	Covington, La. (Covington)
1	Jermaine Sharp	TB	5-10	186	So.	SQ	Monroe, La. (Quachita Christian)
5	Eric Smith	SE	5-11	183	Jr.	TR	Vero Beach, Fla. (NW Miss. JC)
64	Jason Smothers	OG	6-0	297	Jr.	1L	Destrehan, La. (Destrehan)
43	Allen Stansberry	ILB	6-1	220	So.	1L	Baton Rouge, La. (Broadmoor)
60	Roman Starns	OT	6-3	271	Sr.	SQ	Baton Rouge, La. (Texas)
69	Jason Stein	DT	6-3	248	Fr.	RS	Luling, La. (Hahnville)
83	Brandon Stelly	FB	6-3	227	Jr.	2L	Opelousas, La. (Opelousas Catholic)
61	Jerome Sterling	C	6-3	271	Jr.	SQ	River Ridge, La. (John Curtis)
12	Casey Taber	QB	6-1	200	Fr.	RS	Schulenburg, Texas (Schulenburg)
29	Jimmy Taylor	CB	5-11	188	Fr.	RS	Shreveport, La. (Northwood)
95	Robert Thibodeaux	DT	6-2	262	Jr.	2L	River Ridge, La. (John Curtis)
36	Robert Toomer	TB	5-11	218	Jr.	2L	Sylvester, Ga. (County)
71	Tom Turner	OT	6-5	298	Jr.	2L	Bastrop, La. (Bastrop)
99	Eric Valentino	DE	6-5	233	Jr.	2L	Houston, Texas (Clear Lake)
33	Denard Walker	CB	6-1	180	So.	1L	Garland, Texas (South Garland)
72	Brian Ward	OG	6-3	286	Jr.	SQ	Linden, Ala. (Marengo Academy)
74	Sean Wells	OT	6-5	278	So.	1L	Jenks, Okla. (Jenks)
55	Chuck Wiley	DT	6-4	255	Fr.	RS	Baker, La. (Southern Lab)
30	Bobby Williams	ILB	6-2	228	Sr.	3L	Ruston, La. (Ruston)
6	Sheddrick Wilson	FL	6-2	203	Jr.	2L	Thomasville, Ga. (Thomasville)
42	Rodney Young	CB	6-2	212	Sr.	3L	Grambling, La. (Ruston)

Numerical Roster

No.	Name	Pos.
1	Jermaine Sharp	TB
2	Eddie Kennison	FL
3	Ivory Hilliard	FS
4	Jamie Howard	QB
5	Eric Smith	SE
6	Sheddrick Wilson	FL
7	James Gillyard	DE
8	Tory James	CB
9	Talvi Crawford	SS
10	Matt Huerkamp	PK
11	Gary Pegues	SS
12	Casey Taber	QB
18	Clarence Lenton	CB
21	Kevin Franklin	TB
22	Derrick Beavers	TB
23	Andre Lefleur	PK
24	Todd Burks	SE
26	Casey Howard	SS
27	Hunter Bullard	FS
28	Chris Green	ILB
29	Jimmy Taylor	CB
30	Bobby Williams	ILB
31	John Bell	SS
33	Denard Walker	CB
35	Tim Hutton	DT
36	Robert Toomer	TB
40	David Butler	TB
42	Rodney Young	CB
43	Allen Stansberry	ILB
44	Kimojha Brooks	MLB
46	Robert Deshotel	ILB
47	David LaFleur	TE
48	Jeff Hampton	ILB
50	Marcus Carmouche	C
52	Brandon Michel	MLB
55	Chuck Wiley	DT
56	Mike Calais	MLB
57	Kenny Mixon	DE
58	Pete Ballis	DT
60	Roman Starns	OT
61	Jerome Sterling	C
62	Mark King	OG
63	Todd Holland	OT
64	Jason Smothers	OG
66	Brian Sharp	OG
67	Mike Blanchard	C
68	Ben Bordelon	OG
69	Jason Stein	DT
70	Trey Champagne	OT
71	Tom Turner	OT
72	Brian Ward	OG
74	Sean Wells	OT
75	David Carmona	DT
76	Adam Perry	OG
78	Kerry Jenkins	OT
79	Marcus Price	OT
80	Chad Kessler	P
81	Jonny Fayard	TE
82	Pat Rogers	ILB
83	Brandon Stelly	FB
85	Josh Bradley	TE
87	Brett Bech	SE
88	Gabe Northern	DE
89	Chris Hill	FL
90	Furnell Hankton	DE
93	Robert Miller	DT
94	Doug Admire	DT
95	Robert Thibodeaux	DT
97	William Crowell	DT
98	Nate Miller	DT
99	Eric Valentino	DE

1994 LSU Depth Chart

OFFENSE

SE:	87	BRETT BECH
	24	Todd Burks or
	5	Eric Smith
LT:	74	Sean Wells
	71	Tom Turner
LG:	68	BEN BORDELON
	62	Mark King
C:	50	Marcus Carmouche
	67	Mike Blanchard
RG:	64	Jason Smothers
	76	Adam Perry
RT:	79	MARCUS PRICE
	78	Kerry Jenkins
TE:	47	David LaFleur
	85	Josh Bradley
QB:	4	JAMIE HOWARD
	12	Casey Taber
TB:	36	ROBERT TOOMER (at FB)
	40	David Butler
FB:	83	Brandon Stelly
	45	Andre Guerin
FL:	6	SHEDDRICK WILSON
	89	Chris Hill or
	2	Eddie Kennison

DEFENSE

DE:	7	JAMES GILLYARD
	57	Kenny Mixon or
	90	Furnell Hankton
LDT:	98	NATE MILLER
	93	Robert Miller or
	43	Allen Stansberry
SILB:	43	Allen Stansberry
	30	Bobby Williams
MLB:	56	MIKE CALAIS
	44	Kimojha Brooks
WILB:	82	Pat Rogers
	28	Chris Green
RDT:	97	William Crowell
	58	Pete Ballis or
	75	David Carmona
DE:	88	Gabe Northern
	99	Eric Valentino
LCB:	42	RODNEY YOUNG
	18	Clarence Lenton
SS:	11	Gary Pegues
	9	Talvi Crawford or
	26	Casey Howard
FS:	3	IVORY HILLIARD (at SS)
	27	Hunter Bullard
RCB:	8	TORY JAMES
	33	Denard Walker

SPECIALISTS

PK:	23	ANDRE' LAFLEUR
	4	Mark Walker
P:	14	Leon Wilson
	6	Burt Barrere
SN:	65	Marc Workman
	51	Brady Bell

Returning Starters In All Capitals

1994 LSU Signees

Name	Pos.	Ht.	Wt.	Hometown/High School
Aaron Adams	SS	6-2	215	Metairie, La./East Jefferson
Rusty Barrilleaux	C	6-3	275	Amite, La./Amite
Jeremy Baye	OG	6-6	265	Marrero, La./Shaw
Chris Beard	FL	6-0	175	Shreveport, La./Byrd
Trupania Bonner	DE	6-3	240	New Orleans, La./Jesuit
Josh Booty	QB	6-3	210	Shreveport, La./Evangel
Kendall Cleveland	TB	6-0	205	West Orange, Texas/Stark
Chris Cummings	SE	5-9	180	Dothan, Ala./Dothan
Alja Delaney	ILB	6-2	210	Haughton, La./Haughton
Chad Ducre	TE	6-4	235	Mandeville, La./Mandeville
Alan Faneca	OT	6-4	295	Rosenberg, Texas/Lamar Consolidated
Benaderyl Franklin	ILB	6-4	228	Moss Point, Miss./Moss Point
Eric Griffin	OG	6-5	250	Galliano, La./South Lafourche
Melvin Hill	QB	6-0	210	Mansfield, La./Mansfield
Raion Hill	FS	6-2	205	New Orleans, La./Brother Martin
Brian Humke	OT	6-6	260	Bossier City, La./Airline
Arnold Miller	DE	6-4	220	New Orleans, La./Carver
Matt Newchurch	MLB	6-3	245	Thibodaux, La./E.D. White
Wade Richey	PK	6-3	190	Carencro, La./Carencro
Edward Singleton	TE	6-4	280	Cecilia, La./Cecilia
Lee Stromberg	OT	6-5	256	Monroe, La./Ouachita
Mike Sutton	DE	6-5	220	New Orleans, La./Salmen
Troy Twillie	CB	6-1	170	Slidell, La./Slidell

Jamie Howard   **David LaFleur**

1994 SEC Football   101

LSU Year-By-Year Records

Year	Coach	SEC	SEC Finish	Overall	Bowl
1893	C.E. Coates			0-1-0	
1894	A.P. Simmons			2-1-0	
1895	A.P. Simmons			3-0-0	
1896	A.W. Jeardeau			6-0-0	
1897	A.W. Jeardeau			1-1-0	
1898	E.A. Chavanne			1-0-0	
1899	J.P. Gregg			1-4-0	
1900	E.A. Chavanne			2-2-0	
1901	W.S. Borland			5-1-0	
1902	W.S. Borland			6-1-0	
1903	W.S. Borland			4-5-0	
1904	D.A. Killian			3-4-0	
1905	D.A. Killian			3-0-0	
1906	D.A. Killian			2-2-2	
1907	Edgar R. Wingard			7-3-0	
1908	Edgar R. Wingard			10-0-0	
1909	J.G. Pritchard/J.W. Mayhew			6-2-0	
1910	J.W. Mayhew			1-5-0	
1911	J.K. Dwyer			6-3-0	
1912	J.K. Dwyer			4-3-0	
1913	J.K. Dwyer			6-1-2	
1914	E.T. McDonald			4-4-1	
1915	E.T. McDonald			6-2-0	
1916	E.T. McDonald/I.R. Pray/D.X. Bible			7-1-2	
1917	W. Sutton			3-5-0	
1918	No Games, World War I				
1919	Irving R. Pray			6-2-0	
1920	Branch Bocock			5-3-1	
1921	Branch Bocock			6-1-1	
1922	Irving R. Pray			3-7-0	
1923	Mike Donahue			3-5-1	
1924	Mike Donahue			5-4-0	
1925	Mike Donahue			5-3-1	
1926	Mike Donahue			6-3-0	
1927	Mike Donahue			4-4-1	
1928	Russ Cohen			6-2-1	
1929	Russ Cohen			6-3-0	
1930	Russ Cohen			6-4-0	
1931	Russ Cohen			5-4-0	
1932	Biff Jones			6-3-1	
1933	L.M. "Biff" Jones	3-0-2	2	7-0-3	—
1934	L.M. "Biff" Jones	4-2-0	4	7-2-2	—
1935	Bernie Moore	5-0-0	1	9-2-0	Sugar
1936	Bernie Moore	6-0-0	1	9-1-1	Sugar
1937	Bernie Moore	5-1-0	2	9-2-0	Sugar
1938	Bernie Moore	2-4-0	10	6-4-0	—
1939	Bernie Moore	1-5-0	10	4-5-0	—
1940	Bernie Moore	3-3-0	6	6-4-0	—
1941	Bernie Moore	2-2-2	7	4-4-2	—
1942	Bernie Moore	3-2-0	6	7-3-0	—
1943	Bernie Moore	2-2-0	3	6-3-0	Orange
1944	Bernie Moore	2-3-1	6	2-5-1	—
1945	Bernie Moore	5-2-0	3	7-2-0	—
1946	Bernie Moore	5-1-0	3	9-1-1	Cotton
1947	Bernie Moore	2-3-1	8	5-3-1	—
1948	Gaynell Tinsley	1-5-0	10t	3-7-0	—
1949	Gaynell Tinsley	4-2-0	5	8-3-0	Sugar
1950	Gaynell Tinsley	2-3-2	8	4-5-2	—
1951	Gaynell Tinsley	4-2-1	3t	7-3-1	—
1952	Gaynell Tinsley	2-5-0	10	3-7-0	—
1953	Gaynell Tinsley	2-3-3	8	5-3-3	—
1954	Gaynell Tinsley	2-5-0	9	5-6-0	—
1955	Paul Dietzel	2-3-1	9	3-5-2	—
1956	Paul Dietzel	1-5-0	11	3-7-0	—
1957	Paul Dietzel	4-4-0	7	5-5-0	—
1958	Paul Dietzel	6-0-0	1	11-0-0	Sugar
1959	Paul Dietzel	5-1-0	2t	9-2-0	Sugar
1960	Paul Dietzel	2-3-1	8	5-4-1	—
1961	Paul Dietzel	6-0-0	1t	10-1-0	Orange
1962	Charlie McClendon	5-1-0	3	9-1-1	Cotton
1963	Charlie McClendon	4-2-0	5	7-4-0	Bluebonnet
1964	Charlie McClendon	4-2-1	5	8-2-1	Sugar
1965	Charlie McClendon	3-3-0	6t	8-3-0	Cotton
1966	Charlie McClendon	3-3-0	6	5-4-1	—
1967	Charlie McClendon	3-2-1	6	7-3-1	Sugar
1968	Charlie McClendon	4-2-0	3t	8-3-0	Peach
1969	Charlie McClendon	4-1-0	2	9-1-0	—
1970	Charlie McClendon	5-0-0	1	9-3-0	Orange
1971	Charlie McClendon	3-2-0	6	9-3-0	Sun
1972	Charlie McClendon	4-1-1	3	9-2-1	Bluebonnet
1973	Charlie McClendon	5-1-0	2	9-3-0	Orange
1974	Charlie McClendon	2-4-0	9	5-5-1	—
1975	Charlie McClendon	2-4-0	6t	5-6-0	—
1976	Charlie McClendon	3-3-0	6t	7-3-1	—
1977	Charlie McClendon	4-2-0	4	8-4-0	Sun
1978	Charlie McClendon	3-3-0	4t	8-4-0	Liberty
1979	Charlie McClendon	4-2-0	3t	7-5-0	Tangerine
1980	Jerry Stovall	4-2-0	4t	7-4-0	—
1981	Jerry Stovall	1-4-1	8t	3-7-1	—
1982	Jerry Stovall	4-1-1	2	8-3-1	Orange
1983	Jerry Stovall	0-6-0	9t	4-7-0	—
1984	Bill Arnsparger	4-1-1	2	8-3-1	Sugar
1985	Bill Arnsparger	4-1-1	2t	9-2-1	Liberty
1986	Bill Arnsparger	5-1-0	1	9-3-0	Sugar
1987	Mike Archer	5-1-0	2	10-1-1	Gator
1988	Mike Archer	6-1-0	1t	8-4-0	Hall of Fame
1989	Mike Archer	2-5-0	7t	4-7-0	—
1990	Mike Archer	2-5-0	6t	5-6-0	—
1991	Curley Hallman	3-4-0	6t	5-6-0	—
1992	Curley Hallman	1-7-0	6-W	2-9-0	—
1993	Curley Hallman	3-5-0	3t-W	5-6-0	—

Bowl Results (11-16-1)

Bowl	Opponent	Result	Date
Sugar	Texas Christian	L 2-3	1-1-36
Sugar	Santa Clara	L 14-21	1-1-37
Sugar	Santa Clara	L 0-6	1-1-38
Orange	Texas A&M	W 19-14	1-1-44
Cotton	Arkansas	T 0-0	1-1-47
Sugar	Oklahoma	L 0-35	1-2-50
Sugar	Clemson	W 7-0	1-1-59
Sugar	Ole Miss	L 0-21	1-1-60
Orange	Colorado	W 25-7	1-1-62
Cotton	Texas	W 13-0	1-1-63
Bluebonnet	Baylor	L 7-14	12-21-63
Sugar	Syracuse	W 13-10	1-1-65
Cotton	Arkansas	W 14-7	1-1-66
Sugar	Wyoming	W 20-13	1-1-68
Peach	Florida State	W 31-27	12-30-68
Orange	Nebraska	L 12-17	1-1-71
Sun	Iowa State	W 33-15	12-18-71
Bluebonnet	Tennessee	L 17-24	12-30-72
Orange	Penn State	L 9-16	1-1-74
Sun	Stanford	L 14-24	12-31-77
Liberty	Missouri	L 15-20	12-23-78
Tangerine	Wake Forest	W 34-10	12-22-79
Orange	Nebraska	L 20-21	1-1-83
Sugar	Nebraska	L 10-28	1-1-85
Liberty	Baylor	L 7-21	12-27-85
Sugar	Nebraska	L 15-30	1-1-87
Gator	South Carolina	W 30-13	12-31-87
Hall of Fame	Syracuse	L 10-23	1-2-89

LSU vs. All Opponents

Opponent	W	L	T
Alabama	15	37	5
Arizona	1	0	0
Arkansas	23	14	2
Arkansas State	1	0	0
Army	0	1	0
Auburn	15	12	1
Baylor	8	3	0
Boston College	2	0	0
Cal-State Fullerton	1	0	0
Centenary	3	1	1
Chattanooga	1	0	0
Cincinnati	0	1	0
Clemson	1	0	0
Colorado	5	1	0
Colorado State	1	1	0
Cumberland	0	1	0
Duke	1	1	0
East Carolina	1	0	0
Florida	18	19	3
Florida State	2	7	0
Fordham	2	0	0
George Washington	1	0	0
Georgia	12	7	1
Georgia Tech	15	12	0
Hardin-Simmons	1	0	0
Haskell	1	1	0
Havana University	1	0	0
Holy Cross	2	1	0
Indiana	2	1	0
Iowa State	1	0	0
Jefferson College	6	0	0
Kentucky	31	12	1
Louisiana College	2	0	0
Louisiana Tech	15	1	0
Loyola (New Orleans)	4	1	0
Manhattan	1	0	0
Maryland	0	3	0
Mercer	1	0	0
Miami (Florida)	8	3	0
Miami (Ohio)	1	1	0
Millsaps	2	1	0
Mississippi	46	32	4
Mississippi College	9	0	1
Mississippi State	52	32	3
Missouri	0	1	0
Nebraska	0	5	1
North Carolina	5	1	0
Northwestern Louisiana	10	0	0
Notre Dame	3	3	0
Ohio State	0	1	1
Ohio	1	0	0
Oklahoma	0	1	0
Oklahoma State	1	0	0
Oregon	2	1	0
Oregon State	3	0	0
Pacific	3	0	0
Penn State	0	1	0
Rice	36	13	5
Rutgers	0	1	0
Samford	1	0	0
Santa Clara	0	2	0
Sewanee	3	6	0
South Carolina	12	1	0
South Dakota Wesleyan	1	0	0
Southeastern Louisiana	1	0	0
Southern Cal	1	1	0
Southern Methodist	0	1	1
Southern Mississippi	1	0	0
Southwestern Louisiana	19	0	0
Southwestern Tennessee	1	0	0
Southwestern Texas	0	1	0
Spring Hill	8	0	0
Stanford	0	1	0
Syracuse	1	1	0
Texas Christian	5	2	1
Tennessee	3	18	3
Texas	7	8	1
Texas A&M	26	18	3
Texas Tech	2	0	0
Transylvania	1	0	0
Tulane	62	22	7
Utah	2	0	0
Utah State	1	0	0
Vanderbilt	16	7	1
Wake Forest	3	0	0
Washington	1	0	0
Wichita State	1	0	0
Wisconsin	2	0	0
Wyoming	3	0	0

LSU placekicker David Browndyke, a three-time All-SEC selection, converted a conference record 14 of 14 field goals and was perfect on 29 PATs, ending his career streak at 109, during the 1989 season.

1994 SEC Football

LSU School Records

Dalton Hilliard

Wendell Davis

Individual

Game
Total Offense	433	Tommy Hodson vs. Tennessee	(1989)
Yards Rushing	237	Charles Alexander vs. Oregon	(1977)
Rushing Attempts	43	Charles Alexander vs. Wyoming	(1977)
Yards Passing	438	Tommy Hodson vs. Tennessee	(1989)
Pass Attempts	51	Jeff Wickersham vs. Mississippi State	(1983)
Pass Completions	33	Jeff Wickersham vs. Mississippi State	(1983)
Yards Receiving	248	Todd Kinchen vs. Mississippi State	(1991)
Receptions	14	Wendell Davis vs. Ole Miss	(1986)

Season
Total Offense	2,604	Tommy Hodson	(1983)
Yards Rushing	1,686	Charles Alexander	(1977)
Rushing Attempts	311	Charles Alexander	(1977)
Yards Passing	2,655	Tommy Hodson	(1989)
Pass Attempts	346	Jeff Wickersham	(1985)
Pass Completions	209	Jeff Wickersham	(1985)
Touchdown Passes	22	Tommy Hodson	(1989)
Yards Receiving	1,244	Wendell Davis	(1986)
Receptions	80	Wendell Davis	(1986)
Touchdown Catches	11	Wendell Davis	(1986)
Interceptions	8	Craig Burns	(1970)
		Chris Williams	(1978)
Points	104	Charles Alexander	(1977)

Career
Total Offense	8,938	Tommy Hodson	(1986-89)
Yards Rushing	4,050	Dalton Hilliard	(1982-85)
Rushing Attempts	882	Dalton Hilliard	(1982-85)
Yards Passing	9,115	Tommy Hodson	(1986-89)
Pass Attempts	1,163	Tommy Hodson	(1986-89)
Pass Completions	674	Tommy Hodson	(1986-89)
Touchdown Passes	69	Tommy Hodson	(1986-89)
Yards Receiving	2,708	Wendell Davis	(1984-87)
Receptions	183	Wendell Davis	(1984-87)
Touchdown Catches	19	Wendell Davis	(1984-87)
Interceptions	20	Chris Williams	(1977-80)
Points	302	Dalton Hilliard	(1982-85)

Team

Game
Points	77	vs. Rice	(1977)
Total Offense	746	vs. Rice	(1977)
Yards Rushing	503	vs. Oregon	(1977)
Yards Passing	438	vs. Tennessee	(1989)
First Downs	35	vs. Mississippi State	(1969)
Total Defense	26	vs. Mercer	(1940)
Rushing Defense	-50	vs. Ole Miss	(1982)
Passing Defense	0	Nine times	
		Last: vs. Alabama	(1971)

Season
Points	375	(1977)
Total Offense	4,843	(1987)
Yards Rushing	3,352	(1977)
Yards Passing	2,839	(1989)
Fewest Points Allowed	27	(1937)
Total Defense	1,236	(1937)
Rushing Defense	389	(1969)
Passing Defense	524	(1959)
Consecutive Wins	19	(November 30, 1957 to October 31, 1959)

104 LSU

LSU in the NFL

Charles Alexander, RB
Cincinnati Bengals 1979-85
Dan Alexander, G
New York Jets 1977-86
Eric Andolsek, OG
Detroit Lions 1988-91
Mitch Andrews, TE
Denver Broncos 1987-88
Roland Barbay, DE
Seattle Seahawks 1987-88
Walter (Piggy) Barnes, G
Philadelphia Eagles 1948-51
Ken Bordelon, LB
New Orleans Saints 1976-83
Marc Boutte, DT
Los Angeles Rams 1992-93
Mel Branch, DE
Kansas City Chiefs 1960-65; Miami Dolphins 1966-68
James Britt, DB
Atlanta Falcons 1983-86
Red Brodnax, B
Denver Broncos 1960
Michael Brooks, LB
Denver Broncos, 1987-92
New York Giants 1993
Jeff Burkett, E
Chicago Cardinals 1947
Shawn Burks, LB
Washington Redskins 1986
Clinton Burrell, S
Cleveland Browns 1980-85
Young Bussey, QB
Chicago Bears 1940-41
Billy Cannon, RB-TE
Houston Oilers 1960-63; Oakland Raiders 1964-69; Kansas City Chiefs 1970
Warren Capone, LB
Dallas Cowboys 1975; New Orleans Saints 1976
Carlos Carson, WR
Kansas City Chiefs 1980-88
Tommy Casanova, S
Cincinnati Bengals 1972-77
Jim Cason, DB
San Francisco 49ers 1948-52, 1954; Los Angeles Rams 1955-56
Toby Caston, LB
Houston Oilers 1987-92
Ed Champagne, T
Los Angeles Rams 1947-50
Ray Coates, B
New York Giants 1948-49
Pat Coffee, B
Chicago Cardinals 1937-38
Albin (Rip) Collins, B
Baltimore Colts 1950; Green Bay Packers 1951
Ray Collins, DT
San Francisco 49ers 1950-52; New York Giants 1954; Dallas Texans 1960-61
Bill Crass, B
Chicago Cardinals 1937
Jeffery Dale, S
San Diego Chargers 1985-86
Eugene Daniel, CB
Indianapolis Colts 1984-93
Ramsey, Dardar, DT
St. Louis Cardinals 1984
Kenny Davidson, DE
Pittsburgh Steelers 1990-92
Brad Davis, RB
Atlanta Falcons 1975
Tommy Davis, P-K
San Francisco 49ers 1959-69
Wendell Davis, WR
Chicago Bears 1988-93
John Demarie, G
Cleveland Browns 1967-75; Seattle Seahawks 1976
A.J. Duhe, DE-LB
Miami Dolphins 1977-84
Karl Dunbar, DE
Pittsburgh Steelers 1990

Bill Elko, DE
San Diego Chargers 1983-84
Don Estes, G
San Diego Chargers 1966
Herman Fontenot, WR
Cleveland Browns 1985-88
Sid Fournet, DT
Los Angeles Rams 1955-56; Pittsburgh Steelers 1957; Dallas Texans 1960-61; New York Titans 1962-63
Eddie Fuller, RB
Buffalo Bills 1990-93
Tom Fussell, DE
Boston Patriots 1967
Hokie Gajan, RB
New Orleans Saints 1982-86
John Garlington, LB
Cleveland Browns 1968-77
Dennis Gaubatz, LB
Detroit Lions 1963-64; Baltimore Colts 1965-69
Joe Glamp, B
Pittsburgh Steelers 1947-49
Walt Gorinski, B
Pittsburgh Steelers 1946
White Graves, DB
Boston Patriots 1965-67; Cincinnati Bengals 1968
Earl Gros, B
Green Bay Packers 1962-63; Philadelphia Eagles 1964-66; Pittsburgh Steelers 1967-69; New Orleans Saints 1970
Andy Hamilton, WR
Kansas City Chiefs 1973-74; New Orleans Saints 1975
Rudy Harmon, LB
San Francisco 49ers 1989
Bo Harris, LB
Cincinnati Bengals 1975-83
Wendell Harris, DB
Baltimore Colts 1962-65; New York Giants 1966-67
Eric Hill, LB
Phoenix Cardinals 1989-93
Dalton Hilliard, RB
New Orleans Saints 1986-93
Liffort Hobley, S
St. Louis Cardinals 1985; Miami Dolphins 1987-93
Norm Hodgins, S
Chicago Bears 1974
Tommy Hodson, QB
New England Patriots 1990-92
Greg Jackson, DB
New York Giants 1989-93
Rusty Jackson, P
Los Angeles Rams 1976; Buffalo Bills 1978-79
Steve Jackson, DB
Oakland Raiders 1977
Clint James, DE
New York Giants 1990
Garry James, RB
Detroit Lions 1986-88
Norman Jefferson, CB
Green Bay Packers 1987
Tim Joiner, LB
Houston Oilers 1983-85
Bert Jones, QB
Baltimore Colts 1973-81; Los Angeles Rams 1982
Victor Jones, RB
Denver Broncos 1991-92
Ken Kavanaugh, E
Chicago Bears 1940-41, 1945-50
Brian Kinchen, TE
Miami Dolphins 1988-91; Cleveland Browns 1992-93
Todd Kinchen
Los Angeles Rams 1992-93
Wayne Kingery, B
Baltimore Colts 1949
Ken Konz, B
Cleveland Browns 1953-59

Greg LaFleur, TE
St. Louis Cardinals 1981-86; Indianapolis Colts 1986
Fred Land, T
San Francisco 49ers 1948
Gene Lang, RB
Denver Broncos 1984-88
Buddy Lee, QB
Chicago Bears 1971
Earl Leggett, T
Chicago Bears 1957-60, 1962-65; Los Angeles Rams 1966; New Orleans Saints 1967-68
Rydell Malancon, LB
Atlanta Falcons 1984-85
Leonard Marshall, DE
New York Giants 1983-93
Eric Martin, WR
New Orleans Saints 1985-93
Sammy Martin, WR
New England Patriots 1988-91
Billy Masters, TE
Buffalo Bills 1967-69; Denver Broncos 1970-74; Kansas City Chiefs 1975-76
Bill May, B
St. Louis Cardinals 1937-38
Mike Mayes, DB
New Orleans Saints 1989
Dave McCormick, T
San Francisco 49ers 1966; New Orleans Saints 1967-68
Blake Miller, OL
Detroit Lions 1992
Fred Miller, DT
Baltimore Colts 1963-72
Paul Miller, DT
Los Angeles Rams 1954-57; Dallas Texans 1960-61; San Diego Chargers 1962
Bill Montgomery, B
Chicago Cardinals 1946
Doug Moreau, TE
Miami Dolphins 1966-69
Mike Morgan, LB
Philadelphia Eagles 1964-67; Washington Redskins 1968; New Orleans Saints 1969-70
Jesse Myles, RB
Denver Broncos 1983-84
Ed Neal, G
Chicago Bears 1951
Tommy Neck, B
Chicago Bears 1962
Ralph Norwood, OT
Atlanta Falcons 1989
R.B. Nunnery, DT
Dallas Texans 1960
Sammy Odom, LB
Houston Oilers 1964
Tracy Porter, WR
Detroit Lions 1981-82; Baltimore Colts 1983; Indianapolis Colts 1984
Remi Prudhomme, C
Buffalo Bills 1966-67, 1972; Kansas City Chiefs 1968-69; New Orleans Saints 1971
Marcus Quinn
New Orleans Saints 1982
Warren Rabb, QB
Detroit Lions 1960; Buffalo Bills 1961-62
Eddie Ray, RB-P
New England Patriots 1970; San Diego Chargers 1971; Atlanta Falcons 1972-74; Buffalo Bills 1976
Corey Raymond, DB
New York Giants 1992-93
Joe Reed, B
St. Louis Cardinals 193?, 1939
Joe Reid, C
Los Angeles Rams 1951
M.C. (Mack) Reynolds, QB
Chicago Cardinals 1958; St. Louis Cardinals 1959; Washington Redskins 1960; Oakland Raiders 1961
George Rice, DT
Houston Oilers 1966-70

Bobby Richards, E
Philadelphia Eagles 1962-65; Atlanta Falcons 1966-67
Alan Risher, QB
Tampa Bay Buccaneers 1985-86; Green Bay Packers 1987-88
Johnny Robinson, S
Dallas Texans 1960-62; Kansas City Chiefs 1963-71
Terry Robiskie, RB
Oakland Raiders 1977-79; Miami Dolphins 1980-81
Steve Rogers, RB
New Orleans Saints 1975; New York Jets 1976
Ron Sancho, LB
Denver Broncos 1989
Dan Sandifer, T
Washington Redskins 1948-49; San Francisco 49ers 1950; Philadelphia Eagles 1950-51; Green Bay Packers 1952-53; Chicago Cardinals 1953
Bill Schroll, B
Detroit Lions 1950; Green Bay Packers 1951
Malcolm Scott, TE
New York Giants 1983
Hubert Shurtz, T
Pittsburgh Steelers 1948
Lance Smith, OG
St. Louis /Phoenix Cardinals 1985-93
Jerry Stovall, DB
St. Louis Cardinals 1963-71
Gene Sykes, DB
Buffalo Bills 1963-65; Denver Broncos 1967
George Tarasovic, E
Pittsburgh Steelers 1952-53, 1956-63; Philadelphia Eagles 1963-65; Denver Broncos 1966
Jim Taylor, B
Green Bay Packers 1958-66; New Orleans Saints 1967
Willie Teal, CB
Minnesota Vikings 1980-86
Henry Thomas, NG
Minnesota Vikings 1987-93
Gaynell Tinsley, E
Chicago Cardinals 1937-38, 1940
Jess Tinsley, T
Chicago Cardinals 1929-33
Y.A. Tittle, QB
Baltimore Colts 1948-50; San Francisco 49ers 1951-60; New York Giants 1961-64
Zollie Toth, RB
Baltimore Colts 1953-54
Billy Truax, TE
Los Angeles Rams 1964-70; Dallas Cowboys 1971-73
Ebert Van Buren, B
Philadelphia Eagles 1951-53
Steve Van Buren, B
Philadelphia Eagles 1944-51
Lyman White, LB
Atlanta Falcons 1981-82
Blake Whitlatch, LB
New York Jets 1978
Chris Williams, CB
Buffalo Bills 1981-83
Mike Williams, CB
San Diego Chargers 1975-83
Harvey Williams, RB
Kansas City Chiefs 1991-93
Karl Wilson, DE
San Diego Chargers, 1987-93
Abner Wimberly, E
Green Bay Packers 1950-52
Roy Winston, LB
Minnesota Vikings 1962-76
David Woodley, QB
Miami Dolphins 1980-83; Pittsburgh Steelers 1984-85
Godfrey Zaunbrecher, C
Minnesota Vikings 1971-73

1994 SEC Football 105

LSU Media Information

LSU Associate AD/ Communications
Herb Vincent

LSU Sports Information
P.O. Box 25095
Baton Rouge, LA 70894-5095
(504) 388-8226
FAX: (504) 388-1861

Vincent (Home): 336-4781

Morning Newspapers
Sam King, Sports Editor
The Advocate
P.O. Box 588
Baton Rouge, LA 70821
(504) 383-1111

Dave Moorman, Sports
The Advocate
P.O. Box 588
Baton Rouge, LA 70821
(504) 383-1111

Scott Rabalais, Sports*
The Advocate
P.O. Box 588
Baton Rouge, LA 70821
(504) 383-1111

Sports Editor
LSU Daily Reveille
B-1 Coates Hall
Louisiana State Univ.
Baton Rouge, LA 70893
(504) 388-8676

Bob Roesler, Sports Editor
Times-Picayune/States-Item
3800 Howard Avenue
New Orleans, LA 70140
(504) 826-3405

Peter Finney, Sports
Times-Picayune/States-Item
3800 Howard Avenue
New Orleans, LA 70140
(504) 826-3405

John Reid
Times Picayune/States-Item
4944 So. Sherwood Forest #212
Baton Rouge, LA 70816
(504) 753-7368

Scooter Hobbs, Sports
American Press
P.O. Box 2893
Lake Charles, LA 70602
(318) 494-4075

Mike Lough, Sports
Daily Town Talk
P.O. Box 7558
Alexandria, LA 71301
(318) 487-6351

Kent Heitholt, Sports
Shreveport Times
222 Lake Street
Shreveport, LA 71130
(318) 459-3300

Greg Hilburn, Sports
News Star
411 North Fourth Street
Monroe, LA 71201
(318) 322-5161

Herman Fusilier, Sports Editor
Opelousas Daily World
P.O. Box 1179
Opelousas, LA 70570
(318) 942-4971

Wire Service
Mary Foster, Sports Editor
Associated Press
1001 Howard Avenue
Suite 200-A
New Orleans, LA 70113
(504) 523-3931

Television Stations
Mike Rhodes
WBRZ-TV Sports
1650 Highland Road
Baton Rouge, LA 70802
(504) 336-2360

Steve Schneider
WAFB-TV Sports
P.O. Box 2671
Baton Rouge, LA 70821
(504) 383-9999

Jim Gallagher
WVUE-TV
1025 S. Jefferson Davis
New Orleans, LA 70125
(504) 486-6161

Doug Greengard
WWL-TV Sports
1024 N. Rampart Street
New Orleans, LA 70176
(504) 529-4444

Skip Baldwin
WDSU-TV Sports
520 Royal Street
New Orleans, LA 70130
(504) 527-0666

Radio Stations
Jim Hawthorne
LSU Athletic Dept.
P.O. Drawer V
Baton Rouge, LA 70894-9008

Matt Kennedy
WJBO Radio Sports
444 Florida Street
Baton Rouge, LA 70801
(504) 383-5271

Jim Nasium
WFMF-FM Radio Sports
444 Florida Street
Baton Rouge, LA 70801
(504) 383-5271

Jim Engster, Sports
Louisiana Network
224 Florida Street
Baton Rouge, LA 70801
(504) 383-8695

Sports Director
KLSU-FM Radio
102 East Stadium Drive
Louisiana State Univ.
Baton Rouge, LA 70893
(504) 388-5911

Buddy Diliberto
WWL Radio Sports
1024 N. Rampart Street
New Orleans, LA 70176
(504) 529-4444

Specialty Publications
J.R. Ball, Editor
Tiger Rag
3609 Perkins Road
Suite G
Baton Rouge, LA 70808
(504) 343-4578

OLE MISS

DR. R. GERALD TURNER
Chancellor

DR. MAX WILLIAMS
Faculty Representative

WARNER ALFORD
Athletic Director

University of Mississippi

CHANCELLOR:
Dr. R. Gerald Turner (Abilene Christian 1968)
FACULTY REPRESENTATIVE:
Dr. Max Williams (Ole Miss 1961)
ATHLETIC DIRECTOR:
Warner Alford (Ole Miss 1961)
INTERIM HEAD COACH:
Joe Lee Dunn (UT-Chattanooga 1968)
LOCATION: Oxford, Mississippi
FOUNDED: 1848
ENROLLMENT: 10,369
NICKNAME: Rebels
COLORS: Cardinal Red and Navy Blue
STADIUM: Vaught-Hemingway (42,577) - Natural

Rebel Quick Facts

1993 RECORD: 5-6
(5-1 Home, 0-5 Away)
1993 SEC RECORD (FINISH): 3-5 (T3rd-Western)
(3-1 Home, 0-4 Away)
BOWL: None
ALL-TIME RECORD: 498-371-35 (.570)
SEC RECORD: 189-159-15 (.541) — Regular Season Games
SEC CHAMPIONSHIPS: 6
(1947, 54, 55, 60, 62, 63)
BOWL APPEARANCES: 25
BOWL RECORD: 14-11 (.560)
LAST APPEARANCE: 1992 Liberty Bowl
(Ole Miss 13, Air Force 0)

OLE MISS
Team Information

OFFENSIVE SYSTEM: Multiple

DEFENSIVE SYSTEM: 3-4

LETTERMEN RETURNING: 45
- 22 Offense
- 18 Defense
- 5 Specialists

LETTERMEN LOST: 26
- 13 Offense
- 11 Defense
- 2 Specialists

STARTERS RETURNING: 11
OFFENSE (4)
- OG Chris May (6-2, 265, Jr.)
- C   Darrell Moncus (6-2, 280, Jr.)
- WR Roell Preston (5-11, 180, Sr.)
- TE Chris Turner (6-3, 245, Sr.)

DEFENSE (5)
- CB Alundis Brice (5-11, 183, Sr.)
- DT Norman Hand (6-4, 295, Sr.)
- LB Abdul Jackson (6-0, 234, Jr.)
- CB Derek Jones (5-9, 160, So.)
- FS Michael Lowery (6-1, 200, Jr.)

SPECIALISTS (2)
- PK Walter Grant (5-7, 177, Sr.)
- P   Chris McCardle (5-9, 185, Jr.)

STARTERS LOST: 13
OFFENSE (7)
- QB Lawrence Adams (5-10, 185, Jr.)
       Moved to DB
- OT Clint Conlee (6-4, 290, Sr.)
- TB Marvin Courtney (6-0, 197, Sr.)
- OG Joel Jordan (6-2, 275, Sr.)
- OT Wesley Melton (6-5, 277, Sr.)
- WR Eddie Small (6-1, 200, Sr.)
- FB Jeremy Veasley (6-2, 232, Sr.)

DEFENSE (6)
- ILB Gary Abide (6-1, 235, Sr.)
- DT Tim Bowens (6-5, 315, Jr.)
- CB Tony Collier (5-10, 185, Sr.)
- SS Johnny Dixon (6-0, 210, Sr.)
- LB Dewayne Dotson (6-2, 260, Sr.)
- LB Cassius Ware (6-0, 240, Sr.)

SPECIALISTS (0)

Vaught-Hemingway Stadium (42,577)
Record: (177-38-8) (.812)
First Game: Oct. 1, 1915—Arkansas Aggies 10, Ole Miss 0
Largest Crowd: 43,500 (Oct. 23, 1993)
       Alabama 19, Ole Miss 14

1994 Ole Miss Schedule

Sept.	3	AUBURN	OXFORD
Sept.	10	SOUTHERN ILLINOIS	OXFORD
Sept.	17	at Vanderbilt	Nashville, Tenn.
Sept.	24	at Georgia	Athens, Ga.
Oct.	1	FLORIDA	OXFORD
Oct.	15	at Arkansas	Fayetteville, Ark.
Oct.	22	at Alabama	Tuscaloosa, Ala.
Oct.	29	LSU	OXFORD
Nov.	5	MEMPHIS	OXFORD
Nov.	12	at Tulane	New Orleans, La.
Nov.	26	MISSISSIPPI STATE	OXFORD

1995 Ole Miss Schedule

Sept.	2	at Auburn	Auburn, Ala.
Sept.	9	INDIANA STATE	OXFORD
Sept.	23	GEORGIA	OXFORD
Sept.	30	at Florida	Gainesville, Fla.
Oct.	7	TULANE	OXFORD
Oct.	14	ARKANSAS	OXFORD
Oct.	21	ALABAMA	OXFORD
Oct.	28	VANDERBILT	OXFORD
Nov.	4	at Memphis	Memphis, Tenn.
Nov.	11	at LSU	Baton Rouge, La.
Nov.	25	at Mississippi State	Starkville, Miss.

1993 Ole Miss Individual Leaders

RUSHING	Atts	Yards	Avg	TDs	Yds/Game
Marvin Courtney	71	343	4.8	3	34.3
Jeremy Veasley	78	342	4.4	0	31.1
MARK SMITH	56	300	5.4	2	30.0
RENARD BROWN	49	265	5.4	1	24.1
LAWRENCE ADAMS	108	165	1.5	2	15.0

PASSING	Atts	Comp	Ints/TDs	Pct	Yds
LAWRENCE ADAMS	195	110	12 / 13	.564	1415
Roger Reed	39	18	0 / 0	.462	191
PAUL HEAD	21	15	2 / 1	.714	172

RECEIVING	Rec	Yds	Avg	TDs	Yds/Game
Eddie Small	33	624	18.9	6	56.7
ROELL PRESTON	35	455	13.0	3	41.4
Ta'Boris Fisher	13	118	9.1	2	10.7
MARK SMITH	14	101	7.2	0	10.1
RENARD BROWN	10	76	7.6	1	6.9

SCORING	G	TDs	PAT	FGs	Tot	Avg
WALTER GRANT	11	0	23-24	12-20	59	5.4
Eddie Small	11	6	0	0	36	3.3
Marvin Courtney	10	3	0	0	18	1.8
ROELL PRESTON	11	3	0	0	18	1.6
TA'BORIS FISHER	11	3	0	0	18	1.6

PUNTING	No	Yds	Avg	Long
CHRIS McCARDLE	65	2256	34.7	53

KICKOFF RETURNS	No	Yds	Avg	TDs	Avg/Game	Long
MARK SMITH	11	290	26.4	0	29.0	55
ROELL PRESTON	3	67	22.3	0	6.1	34
Deano Orr	1	21	21.0	0	1.9	21

PUNT RETURNS	No	Yds	Avg	TDs	Avg/Game	Long
MICHAEL LOWERY	1	20	20.0	0	1.8	20
Eddie Small	5	59	11.8	0	5.4	20
TA'BORIS FISHER	29	330	11.4	1	30.0	77

TACKLES	Total (S-A)	Sk (Yds)	TL (Yds)	Ints
ABDUL JACKSON	140 (65-75)	0	5 (-19)	0
Gary Abide	93 (46-47)	4 (-20)	3 (-5)	1
Dewayne Dotson	92 (44-48)	5 (-36)	10 (-38)	0
Cassius Ware	83 (57-26)	9 (-74)	12 (-58)	1
Johnny Dixon	75 (49-26)	3 (-28)	8 (-22)	2

INTERCEPTIONS	No	Yds	TDs	Int/Game	Long
ALUNDIS BRICE	7	98	2	0.6	45
MICHAEL LOWERY	2	13	0	0.2	13
Johnny Dixon	2	0	0	0.2	0

Returning Players in All Capitals

1993 Ole Miss Team Statistics

	UM	OPP
FIRST DOWNS	180	164
Rushing	60	75
Passing	83	67
Penalty	9	22
NET YARDS RUSHING	1569	1127
Yards rushing	1911	1584
Yards lost	342	457
Rushing Attempts	427	463
Average per rush	3.7	2.4
Average per game	142.6	102.5
NET YARDS PASSING	1778	1453
Average per game	161.6	132.1
Passes attempted	255	261
Passes completed	143	117
Had intercepted	14	15
TOTAL OFFENSIVE YARDS	3347	2580
Average per game	304.3	234.6
Total plays	682	724
Average per play	4.9	3.6
NUMBER PUNTS/YARDS	66/2256	67/2622
Punting average	34.2	39.1
Net punting average	31.8	32.9
PUNT RETURNS/YARDS	37/420	26/159
Punt return average	11.4	6.1
KICKOFF RETURNS/YARDS	37/773	32/648
Kickoff return average	20.9	20.3
PENALTIES/YARDS	81/677	67/573
Penalty yards per game	61.5	52.1
FUMBLES/LOST	9/3	22/16
INTERCEPTION RETURNS/YARDS	15/190	14/167
Interception return average	12.7	11.9
TOUCHDOWNS	28	14
Rushing	9	8
Passing	14	5
Return	5	1
FIELD GOALS MADE/ATTEMPTED	15/25	14/20
KICK EXTRA POINTS MADE/ATTEMPTED	25/26	10/12
SAFETY	2	1
TWO-POINT CONVERSIONS	0/2	2/2
TOTAL POINTS	242	142
Average per game	22.0	12.9

Lawrence Adams  **Abdul Jackson**  **Mark Smith**

1993 Ole Miss Results

5-6 Overall • 3-5 SEC (t3rd - Western)

Sept. 2	at Auburn	L	12-16	78,246
Sept. 11	UT-CHATTANOOGA	W	40-7	24,500
Sept. 18	VANDERBILT	W	49-7	32,500
Sept. 25	GEORGIA	W	31-14	38,000
Oct. 2	at Kentucky	L	0-21	57,075
Oct. 16	ARKANSAS (Jackson) [JP]	W	19-0	37,000
Oct. 23	ALABAMA [ABC]	L	14-19	43,500
Oct. 30	at LSU	L	17-19	61,470
Nov. 6	at Memphis State	L	3-19	34,026
Nov. 13	N. ILLINOIS - HC	W	44-0	20,500
Nov. 27	at Mississippi State	L	13-20	40,238

1994 SEC Football

Joe Lee Dunn

Interim Head Coach

Year-By-Year Record

Year	School	Conf.	All	Bowl
1983	New Mexico	4-3 (4th)	6-6	
1984	New Mexico	1-7 (t8th)	4-8	
1985	New Mexico	2-6 (t7th)	3-8	
1986	New Mexico	2-5 (t7th)	4-8	
OVERALL RECORD		9-21 (.300)	17-30 (.362)	4 Years

HOMETOWN:
Columbus, Ga.

ALMA MATER (YEAR):
UT-Chattanooga (1968)

PLAYING CAREER:
Quarterback, tailback, defensive back, flanker at UT-Chattanooga (1964-1968)

COACHING CAREER:
UT-Chattanooga Assistant 1971-73; UT-Chattanooga Assistant Head Coach/Defensive Coordinator 1974-79; New Mexico Assistant Head Coach/Defensive Coordinator 1980-82; New Mexico Head Coach 1983-86; South Carolina Assistant Head Coach/Defensive Coordinator 1987-88; Memphis State Defensive Coordinator 1989-91; Ole Miss Defensive Coordinator 1992-93; Ole Miss Interim Head Coach 1994.

BORN:
July 14, 1946

WIFE:
Susie Sparks

CHILDREN:
Kacey Jayne 3

ASSISTANT COACHES:
JIM CARMODY (Tulane 1956) - Assistant Head Coach/Defensive Line
KEITH DANIELS (Mississippi College 1969) - Running Backs
FREEMAN HORTON (Southern Mississippi 1979) - Defensive Ends
LARRY KUECK (Stephen F. Austin 1975) - Offensive Coordinator/Quarterbacks
JOHN NEAL (Brigham Young 1980) - Defensive Backs
MELVIN SMITH (Millsaps 1982) - Wide Receivers
JOE WICKLINE (Florida 1983) - Offensive Line
GARY WITHROW (Pittsburg State 1964) - Tight Ends

SUPPORT STAFF:
CHUCK OKEY (Presbyterian 1986) - Strength Coach
LEROY MULLINS (Eastern Kentucky 1965) - Trainer

Ole Miss All-Star Candidates

ALUNDIS BRICE
Senior • Cornerback
5-11 • 180 • Brookhaven, Miss.

• First team AP All-SEC selection in 1993 after leading the SEC and ranking second in the nation with seven interceptions.
• Earned the Chucky Mullins Courage Award during spring drills and will wear the late Mullins' No. 38 during his senior campaign.
• Had a season-high 12 stops vs. Kentucky and a season-high two interceptions vs. Vanderbilt last year.
• Credited with 58 tackles on the year (42 solo), one fumble recovery and a team-high 13 pass break ups.
• Returned to the defensive back position in 1993 after spending 1992 at wide receiver.
• Clocked at 4.3 seconds in the 40 during the 1993 team testing period.

BRICE STATS

Year	Tackles	Sk (Yds)	TFL (Yds)	Int	PBU	CF	FR
1991	22 (10-12)	0	0	0	0	0	0
1992	1 (1-0)	0	0	0	0	0	0
1993	58 (42-16)	0	0	7	13	0	1
Career	81 (53-28)	0	0	7	13	0	1

ABDUL JACKSON
Senior • Linebacker
6-1 • 236 • Atlanta, Ga.

• SEC's leading tackler in 1993 when he was credited with 140 total hits and only returning Ole Miss linebacker with extensive game experience.
• Second-team All-SEC selection last season on a team which had two first-team All-SEC linebackers in Dewayne Dotson and Cassius Ware.
• Posted nine double-digit tackle outings last season and owns 255 total stops during three-year career.
• Called the "Best Kept Defensive Secret in the SEC" by Sports Illustrated.
• Returned only fumble recovery of the year for a 47-yard touchdown in win vs. Georgia.
• Posted 1993 Rebel season-high with 18 stops in opener vs. Auburn.

JACKSON STATS

Year	Tackles	Sk (Yds)	TFL (Yds)	Int	PBU	CF	FR
1991	4 (2-2)	0	0	0	0	0	0
1992	111 (55-56)	0	2 (-5)	0	2	0	1
1993	140 (65-75)	0	5 (-19)	0	2	1	1
Career	255 (122-133)	0	7 (-24)	0	4	1	1

JAMES HOLCOMBE
Senior • Offensive Tackle
6-2 • 287 • TyTy, Ga.

• A 1993 preseason All-SEC pick who returns for 1994 season after missing last year due to a neck injury.
• One of the strongest Rebel players, Holcombe has the ability to play all five interior line positions and is listed on the preseason depth chart at tackle and center.
• Ended spring as No. 1 tackle, but could move to guard slot by end of preseason drills.

ROELL PRESTON
Senior • Wide Receiver
5-11 • 180 • Miami, Fla.

• Rebels' leading returning receiver after pacing team with 35 catches and finishing second on squad with 455 yards receiving last season.
• Was the only Rebel receiver to catch at least one pass in every outing a year ago, and finished second on the team with three touchdown grabs.
• His 4.38 time in the 40 this spring was a team best.
• Best game of 1993 came vs. Georgia when he caught three passes for 105 yards, including a 49-yard touchdown pass from Lawrence Adams.

PRESTON STATS

Year	Rec	Yds	Avg	TD	PR	Yds	Avg	TD	Long
1993	35	455	13.0	3	2	11	5.5	0	7

1994 SEC Football 111

1994 Ole Miss Roster

No.	Name	Pos.	Ht.	Wt.	Class	Exp.	Hometown (High School/JC)
17	Lawrence Adams	DB	5-10	185	Jr.	2L	Jackson, Miss. (Callaway)
91	Neil Alford	NG	6-0	230	Jr.	SQ	New Orleans, La. (St. Stanislaus)
7	Eli Anding	QB	6-1	195	Fr.	RS	Etta, Miss. (New Albany-W.P. Daniel)
81	Andy Berger	WR	6-0	180	Sr.	SQ	Hendricks, Pa. (Souderton)
45	Eddie Bibbins	DB	6-4	180	HS		Harvey, La. (John Curtis)
89	Damon Bilbrew	WR	5-11	160	So.	SQ	Memphis, Tenn. (Whitehaven)
36	Bubba Bonds	WR	5-9	165	Jr.	1L	Oxford, Miss. (Oxford)
8	Antonious Bonner	FS	6-0	200	Sr.	1L	Greenwood, Miss. (Greenwood; Miss. Delta CC)
38	Alundis Brice	CB	5-11	180	Jr.	3L	Brookhaven, Miss. (Brookhaven)
40	Renard Brown	FB	6-0	220	Jr.	2L	Brookhaven, Miss. (Brookhaven)
65	Eric Bubrig	OG	6-1	280	Fr.	RS	Harvey, La. (Jesuit)
73	Terrell Burks	OT	6-3	290	Jr.	SQ	Memphis, Tenn. (Whitehaven)
39	Lonny Calicchio	P-K	6-2	235	Jr.	JC	Plantation, Fla. (South Plantation, Northwest CC)
9	Keith Campbell	SS	5-10	175	Jr.	2L	Pensacola, Fla. (Washington)
23	Sidney Carmichael	DE	6-3	220	Sr.	1L	Monroeville, Ala. (Miss. Delta CC)
79	Jonathan Casey	OL	6-3	330	Jr.	JC	Woodruff, S.C. (Itawamba CC)
87	Devon Coburn	DT	6-3	260	Fr.	RS	Noxapater, Miss. (Noxapater)
66	Jody Coulter	OG	6-2	275	Fr.	RS	Calhoun, Ga. (Calhoun)
88	Wendell Davis	TE	6-2	225	Fr.	HS	Moss Point, Miss. (Moss Point)
49	Jon Desler	CB	6-0	175	So.	1L	Potomac, Md. (Fork Union Military)
55	Chris Eaves	DE	5-10	205	Fr.	RS	Memphis, Tenn. (Harding Academy)
54	Omar Edwards	OG	6-2	280	Fr.	RS	Bradenton, Fla. (Southeast)
60	David Evans	OG	6-1	305	So.	1L	West Point, Miss. (West Point)
52	John Evans	LB	6-3	250	Jr.	JC	Pasadena, Calif. (Pasadena CC)
94	Troy "Huck" Ferguson	NG	6-0	285	Sr.	1L	Willows, Calif. (Butte JC)
10	Ta'Boris Fisher	WR	5-8	170	So.	1L	Jackson, Miss. (Provine)
92	Ed Fortson	DL	6-3	265	Jr.	JC	St. Louis, Mo. (Highland CC)
57	Otis Fox	DT	6-3	247	So.	SQ	Memphis, Tenn. (Whitehaven)
99	Darryl Gibbs	DE	6-2	255	Fr.	HS	Yazoo City, Miss. (Madison Ridgeland)
46	Jerry Graeber	FS	5-10	180	Sr.	2L	Yazoo City, Miss. (Manchester Academy)
16	Walter Grant	K	5-7	177	Sr.	1L	Ft. Lauderdale, Fla. (Southwest CC)
20	Randall Green	P-K	6-1	210	Fr.	RS	Tuscaloosa, Ala. (Central)
31	Malikia Griffin	DB	5-9	180	Fr.	HS	Batesville, Miss. (South Panola)
90	Norman Hand	DT	6-3	310	Sr.	1L	Waltersboro, S.C. (Itawamba CC)
13	Paul Head	QB	6-0	195	So.	1L	Birmingham, Ala. (Vestavia Hills)
85	Alvin Herman	DE	6-3	225	Jr.	1L	Pahokee, Fla. (Pahokee)
77	Kendrick Hickman	OT	6-4	320	Fr.	RS	Louisville, Miss. (Louisville)
69	James Holcombe	OT-C	6-2	300	Sr.	2L	Ty Ty, Ga. (Worth County)
86	Andre Hollis	WR	5-11	180	So.	SQ	Morton, Miss. (Morton)
22	Dou Innocent	FB	6-1	210	Jr.	2L	Pompano Beach, Fla. (Ely)
53	Abdul Jackson	LB	6-2	236	Sr.	3L	Atlanta, Ga. (Therrell)
64	Woody Janssen	OT	6-5	280	Jr.	1L	Holly Springs, Miss. (Northwest CC)
24	Derek Jones	CB	5-9	165	So.	1L	Woodruff, S.C. (Woodruff)
63	Johnny Jones	DE	6-1	212	Fr.	HS	Batesville, Miss. (South Panola)
29	Walker Jones	DB	6-4	205	Fr.	HS	Jackson, Miss. (Jackson Academy)
76	Skip Joyce	C	6-1	285	So.	1L	Trenton, Tenn. (Trenton-Peabody)
78	Boyd Kitchen	OT	6-4	270	So.	1L	New Orleans, La. (Jesuit)
35	John Knight	DB	6-0	180	Jr.	JC	Leland, Miss. (Mississippi Delta CC)
32	David Knott	FS	6-2	195	Jr.	JC	Brandon, Miss. (Hinds CC)
14	Broc Kreitz	QB	5-11	195	Fr.	RS	Naperville, Ill. (Waubonsie Valley)
21	Steve Lindsey	P-K	6-0	164	So.	1L	Hattiesburg, Miss. (North Forrest)
2	Michael Lowery	SS	6-0	208	Jr.	2L	McComb, Miss. (South Pike)
26	Nakia Magee	CB	5-9	190	Fr.	RS	Franklinton, La. (Franklinton)
82	Kris Mangum	TE	6-5	244	So.	TR	Magee, Miss. (Alabama)
59	Chris May	OG	6-2	270	Jr.	2L	Roanoke, Ala. (Handley)
4	Chris McCardle	P	5-9	185	Jr.	1L	Laurel, Miss. (Jones CC)
13	David McCay	WR	5-8	165	Sr.	SQ	Germantown, Tenn. (Evangelical Christian)
84	David McGowan	DT	6-2	240	So.	1L	Utica, Miss. (Raymond)
67	Alex McRee	C	6-0	200	Fr.	HS	Birmingham, Ala. (Berry)
70	Jeff Miller	OT	6-3	300	Sr.	1L	Vero Beach, Fla. (Northwest CC)
56	Darrell Moncus	C	6-1	275	Jr.	2L	Trussville, Ala. (Hewitt-Trussville)
48	Tim Montz	K	5-11	182	So.	SQ	Marietta, Ga. (Marietta)
28	Artie Moore	TB	5-8	180	So.	TR	Wiggins, Miss. (LSU)
96	Jeremy Morris	DT	6-4	245	So.	SQ	Moss Point, Miss. (Moss Point)
51	Kyron Motton	LB	5-11	210	Jr.	JC	Gardena, Calif. (Santa Monica JC)
68	Michael Myers	DL	6-3	240	Fr.	HS	Vicksburg, Miss. (Vicksburg)
15	Josh Nelson	QB	6-0	200	Jr.	JC	Anaheim, Calif. (Fullerton JC)
27	Moine Nicholson	RB	5-9	190	Fr.	HS	Louisville, Miss. (Louisville)
93	Anthony Panzarella	DT	6-2	270	Sr.	1L	Marco Island, Fla. (Fork Union)
12	Stewart Patridge	QB	6-1	200	So.	JC	Morgan City, Miss. (Miss. Delta CC)
37	Mike Peters	TB	5-9	185	Sr.	1L	Lakewood, Calif. (Fullerton)
1	Roell Preston	WR	5-11	180	Sr.	1L	Miami, Fla. (Northwest CC)
61	Shannon Provencher	OG	6-0	260	So.	SQ	Dunedin, Fla. (Dunedin)
33	Rich Robich	LB	6-2	228	Fr.	HS	Bradenton, Fla. (Southeast)
95	Morris Scott	DE	6-2	200	Fr.	HS	Louisville, Miss. (Louisville)
75	Ahmed Shahid	OT	6-3	290	Sr.	1L	Ft. Lauderdale, Fla. (Miss. Delta CC)
11	Mark Smith	TB	5-9	185	Jr.	2L	Wesson, Miss. (Wesson)
74	Scott Sumner	OG	6-2	305	So.	SQ	Atlanta, Ga. (Abilene Christian)
6	Fred Thomas	CB	5-11	175	Jr.	JC	Bruce, Miss. (Northwest CC)
5	LeMay Thomas	WR	5-10	175	Jr.	2L	Delhi, La. (Delhi)
72	Orlando Trainer	NG	6-0	270	So.	SQ	Starkville, Miss. (Starkville)
30	Trafton Trotter	FB	6-1	225	Sr.	1L	Jacksonville, Ark. (Northwest CC)
71	Ross Tucker	C	6-2	265	Fr.	HS	Brandon, Miss. (Brandon)
83	Chris Turner	TE	6-2	250	Sr.	3L	Water Valley, Miss. (Water Valley)
50	Flint Ussery	LB	5-11	225	Sr.	SQ	Oxford, Miss. (Northwest CC)
58	David Vinson	C	5-11	220	Sr.	1L	Oxford, Miss. (Northwest CC)
41	Nate Wayne	LB	6-1	225	Fr.	RS	Macon, Miss. (Noxubee County)
43	Kyle Wicker	LB	6-3	230	So.	1L	Liberty, Miss. (Centreville Academy)
44	Trey Wicker	DE	6-2	227	Fr.	1L	Liberty, Miss. (Centreville Academy)
80	Frank Wilson	TE	6-1	230	Jr.	1L	Ft. Lauderdale, Fla. (Ft. Lauderdale)
97	Stacy Wilson	DE	6-3	240	Sr.	3L	Tupelo, Miss. (Tupelo)
25	Paul Winfield	SS	6-0	200	SQ		Vicksburg, Miss. (Morris Brown)
3	Joe Woods	WR	5-9	160	Jr.	2L	Union, S.C. (Union)
42	Mike Worley	SS	6-0	185	Jr.	2L	Morrow, Ga. (Morrow)

Numerical Roster

No.	Name	Pos.
1	Roell Preston	WR
2	Michael Lowery	SS
3	Joe Woods	WR
4	Chris McCardle	P
5	LeMay Thomas	WR
6	Fred Thomas	CB
7	Eli Anding	QB
8	Antonious Bonner	FS
9	Keith Campbell	SS
10	Ta'Boris Fisher	WR
11	Mark Smith	TB
12	Stewart Patridge	QB
13	Paul Head	QB
13*	David McCay	WR
14	Broc Kreitz	QB
15	Josh Nelson	QB
16	Walter Grant	K
17	Lawrence Adams	DB
20	Randall Green	P-K
21	Steve Lindsey	P-K
22	Dou Innocent	FB
23	Sidney Carmichael	DE
24	Derek Jones	CB
25	Paul Winfield	SS
26	Nakia Magee	CB
27	Moine Nicholson	RB
28	Artie Moore	TB
29	Walker Jones	DB
30	Trafton Trotter	FB
31	Malikia Griffin	DB
32	David Knott	FS
33	Rich Robich	LB
35	John Knight	DB
36	Bubba Bonds	WR
37	Mike Peters	TB
38	Alundis Brice	CB
39	Lonny Calicchio	P-K
40	Renard Brown	FB
41	Nate Wayne	LB
42	Mike Worley	SS
43	Kyle Wicker	LB
44	Trey Wicker	DE
45	Eddie Bibbins	DB
46	Jerry Graeber	FS
48	Tim Montz	K
49	Jon Desler	CB
50	Flint Ussery	LB
51	Kyron Motton	LB
52	John Evans	LB
53	Abdul Jackson	LB
54	Omar Edwards	OG
55	Chris Eaves	DE
56	Darrell Moncus	C
57	Otis Fox	DT
58	David Vinson	C
59	Chris May	OG
60	David Evans	OG
61	Shannon Provencher	OG
63	Johnny Jones	DE
64	Woody Janssen	OT
65	Eric Bubrig	OG
66	Jody Coulter	OG
67	Alex McRee	C
68	Michael Myers	DL
69	James Holcombe	OT-C
70	Jeff Miller	OT
71	Ross Tucker	C
72	Orlando Trainer	NG
73	Terrell Burks	OT
74	Scott Sumner	OG
75	Ahmed Shahid	OT
76	Skip Joyce	C
77	Kendrick Hickman	OT
78	Boyd Kitchen	OT
79	Jonathan Casey	OL
80	Frank Wilson	TE
81	Andy Berger	WR
82	Kris Mangum	TE
83	Chris Turner	TE
84	David McGowan	DT
85	Alvin Herman	DE
86	Andre Hollis	WR
87	Devon Coburn	DT
88	Wendell Davis	TE
89	Damon Bilbrew	WR
90	Norman Hand	DT
91	Neil Alford	NG
92	Ed Fortson	DL
93	Anthony Panzarella	DT
94	Troy "Huck" Ferguson	NG
95	Morris Scott	DE
96	Jeremy Morris	DT
97	Stacy Wilson	DE
99	Darryl Gibbs	DE

* Duplicate Number

112 Ole Miss

1994 Ole Miss Depth Chart

OFFENSE
- SE: 1 ROELL PRESTON
- 10 Ta'Boris Fisher
- LT: 69 James Holcombe
- 70 Jeff Miller
- LG: 59 CHRIS MAY
- 66 Jody Coulter
- C: 76 Skip Joyce
- 56 DARRELL MONCUS
- RG: 61 Shannon Provencher
- 60 David Evans
- RT: 75 Ahmed Shahid
- 64 Woody Janssen
- TE: 82 Kris Mangum
- 83 CHRIS TURNER
- FL: 3 Joe Woods
- 5 LeMay Thomas
- QB: 15 Josh Nelson
- 13 Paul Head
- FB: 22 Dou Innocent
- 30 Trafton Trotter
- TB: 11 Mark Smith
- 37 Mike Peters

DEFENSE
- DE: 97 Stacy Wilson
- 44 Trey Wicker
- LT: 90 NORMAN HAND
- 87 Devon Coburn
- ILB: 53 ABDUL JACKSON
- 41 Nate Wayne
- NG: 94 Troy "Huck" Ferguson
- 72 Orlando Trainer
- ILB: 43 Kyle Wicker
- 51 Kyron Motton
- RT: 84 David McGowan
- 93 Anthony Panzarella
- DE: 23 Sidney Carmichael
- 85 Alvin Herman
- LCB: 38 ALUNDIS BRICE
- 49 Jon Desler
- SS: 2 MICHAEL LOWERY
- 9 Keith Campbell
- FS: 8 Antonious Bonner
- 46 Jerry Graeber
- RCB: 24 DEREK JONES
- 6 Fred Thomas

SPECIALISTS
- PK: 48 Tim Montz
- 16 WALTER GRANT
- P: 20 Randall Green
- 1 Robby Carr

Returning Starters In All Capitals

1994 Ole Miss Signees

Name	Pos.	Ht.	Wt.	Hometown/High School
Eddie Bibbins	DB	6-4	180	Harvey, La./John Curtis
Lonny Calicchio	P-K	6-2	235	Plantation, Fla./South Plantation
Johnathan Casey	OL	6-3	330	Woodruff, S.C./Woodruff
Devon Coburn	DT	6-3	260	Noxapater, Miss./Noxapater
Wendell Davis	TE	6-2	225	Moss Point, Miss./Moss Point
John Evans	LB	6-3	250	Pasadena, Calif./Pasadena CC
Ed Fortson	DL	6-3	265	St. Louis, Mo./Highland, Kan., CC
Darryl Gibbs	DE	6-2	255	Yazoo City, Miss./Madison Ridgeland
Malikia Griffin	DB	5-9	180	Batesville, Miss./South Panola
Johnny Jones	OLB	6-1	212	Batesville, Miss./South Panola
Walker Jones	DB	6-4	205	Jackson, Miss./Jackson Academy
John Knight	DB	6-0	180	Leland, Miss./Leland
David Knott	DB	6-2	195	Brandon, Miss./Hinds CC
David Lloyd	WR	6-2	190	Greenville, Miss./Miss. Delta CC
Kris Mangum	TE	6-5	244	Magee, Miss./Alabama
Alex McRee	C	6-0	200	Birmingham, Ala./Berry
Artie Moore	RB	5-8	180	Wiggins, Miss./LSU
Kyron Motton	LB	6-0	210	Gardena, Calif./Santa Monica JC
Michael Myers	DL	6-3	240	Vicksburg, Miss./Vicksburg
Josh Nelson	QB	6-3	200	La Habra Heights, Calif./Fullerton JC
Moine Nicholson	RB	5-9	190	Louisville, Miss./Louisville
Stewart Patridge	QB	6-1	200	Morgan City, Miss./Miss. Delta CC
Chris Peery	LB	6-1	240	Los Angeles, Calif./East Miss. CC
Rich Robich	LB	6-2	228	Bradenton, Fla./Southeast
Morris Scott	DE	6-2	200	Louisville, Miss./Louisville
Fred Thomas	DB	5-10	175	Bruce, Miss./Northwest CC

Norman Hand

Dou Innocent

1994 SEC Football

Ole Miss Year-By-Year Records

Year	Coach	SEC	SEC Finish	Overall	Bowl
1893	Dr. A.L. Bondurant			4-1-0	
1894	C. D. Clark			6-1-0	
1895	H. L. Fairbanks			2-1-0	
1896	J. W. Hollister			1-2-0	
1897	NO TEAM				
1898	T. G. Scarbrough			1-1-0	
1899	W. H. Lyon			3-4-0	
1900	Z. N. Estes, Jr.			0-3-0	
1901	William Sibley, Daniel S. Martin			2-4-0	
1902	Daniel S. Martin			4-3-0	
1903	Mike Harvey			2-1-1	
1904	Mike Harvey			4-3-0	
1905	None			0-2-0	
1906	T. S. Hammond			4-2-0	
1907	Frank Mason			0-6-0	
1908	Frank Kyle			3-5-0	
1909	Dr. N. P. Stauffer			4-3-2	
1910	Dr. N. P. Stauffer			7-1-0	
1911	Dr. N. P. Stauffer			6-3-0	
1912	Leo DeTray			5-3-0	
1913	William Driver			6-3-1	
1914	William Driver			5-4-1	
1915	Fred Robbins			2-6-0	
1916	Fred Robbins			3-6-0	
1917	C. R. (Dudy) Noble			1-4-1	
1918	C. R. (Dudy) Noble			1-3-0	
1919	R. L. Sullivan			4-4-0	
1920	R. L. Sullivan			4-3-0	
1921	R. L. Sullivan			3-6-0	
1922	R. A. Cowell			4-5-1	
1923	R. A. Cowell			4-6-0	
1924	Chester Barnard			4-5-0	
1925	Homer Hazel			5-5-0	
1926	Homer Hazel			5-4-0	
1927	Homer Hazel			5-3-0	
1928	Homer Hazel			5-4-0	
1929	Homer Hazel			1-6-2	
1930	Ed Walker			3-5-1	
1931	Ed Walker			2-6-1	
1932	Ed Walker			5-6-0	
1933	Ed Walker	2-2-1	6t	6-3-2	—
1934	Ed Walker	2-3-1	8	4-5-1	—
1935	Ed Walker	3-1-0	3	9-3-0	Orange
1936	Ed Walker	0-3-1	11	5-5-2	—
1937	Ed Walker	0-4-0	10t	4-5-1	—
1938	Harry Mehre	3-2-0	4	9-2-0	—
1939	Harry Mehre	2-2-0	5t	7-2-0	—
1940	Harry Mehre	3-1-0	3	9-2-0	—
1941	Harry Mehre	2-1-1	5	6-2-1	—
1942	Harry Mehre	0-5-0	11t	2-7-0	—
1943	NO TEAM				
1944	Harry Mehre	2-3-0	7	2-6-0	—
1945	Harry Mehre	3-3-0	5t	4-5-0	—
1946	H.W. "Red" Drew	1-6-0	11	2-7-0	—
1947	Johnny Vaught	6-1-0	1	9-2-0	Delta
1948	Johnny Vaught	6-1-0	2	8-1-0	—
1949	Johnny Vaught	2-4-0	9	4-5-1	—
1950	Johnny Vaught	1-5-0	11	5-5-0	—
1951	Johnny Vaught	4-2-1	3t	6-3-1	—
1952	Johnny Vaught	4-0-2	3	8-1-2	Sugar
1953	Johnny Vaught	4-1-1	2t	7-2-1	—
1954	Johnny Vaught	5-0-0	1	9-2-0	Sugar
1955	Johnny Vaught	5-1-0	1	10-1-0	Cotton
1956	Johnny Vaught	4-2-0	4	7-3-0	—
1957	Johnny Vaught	5-0-1	2	9-1-1	Sugar
1958	Johnny Vaught	4-2-0	3	9-2-0	Gator
1959	Johnny Vaught	5-1-0	2t	10-1-0	Sugar
1960	Johnny Vaught	5-0-1	1	10-0-1	Sugar
1961	Johnny Vaught	5-1-0	3	9-2-0	Cotton
1962	Johnny Vaught	6-0-0	1	10-0-0	Sugar
1963	Johnny Vaught	5-0-1	1	7-1-2	Sugar
1964	Johnny Vaught	2-4-1	7	5-5-1	Bluebonnet
1965	Johnny Vaught	5-3-0	5	7-4-0	Liberty
1966	Johnny Vaught	5-2-0	4	8-3-0	Bluebonnet
1967	Johnny Vaught	4-2-1	5	6-4-1	Sun
1968	Johnny Vaught	3-2-1	6t	7-3-1	Liberty
1969	Johnny Vaught	4-2-0	5	8-3-0	Sugar
1970	Johnny Vaught	4-2-0	4	7-4-0	Gator
1971	Billy Kinard	4-2-0	4t	10-2-0	Peach
1972	Billy Kinard	2-5-0	7t	5-5-0	—
1973	Kinard/Vaught	4-3-0	3	6-5-0	—
1974	Ken Cooper	0-6-0	10	3-8-0	—
1975	Ken Cooper	5-1-0	2t	6-5-0	—
1976	Ken Cooper	4-3-0	5t	6-5-0	—
1977	Ken Cooper	3-4-0	6	6-5-0	—
1978	Steve Sloan	2-4-0	7t	5-6-0	—
1979	Steve Sloan	3-3-0	5t	4-7-0	—
1980	Steve Sloan	2-4-0	7t	3-8-0	—
1981	Steve Sloan	1-4-1	8t	4-6-1	—
1982	Steve Sloan	0-6-0	9t	4-7-0	—
1983	Billy Brewer	4-2-0	3t	7-5-0	Independence
1984	Billy Brewer	1-5-0	9t	4-6-1	—
1985	Billy Brewer	2-4-0	6	4-6-1	—
1986	Billy Brewer	4-2-0	2t	8-3-1	Independence
1987	Billy Brewer	1-5-0	7t	3-8-0	—
1988	Billy Brewer	3-4-0	6t	5-6-0	—
1989	Billy Brewer	4-3-0	4t	8-4-0	Liberty
1990	Billy Brewer	5-2-0	2t	9-3-0	Gator
1991	Billy Brewer	1-6-0	9	5-6-0	—
1992	Billy Brewer	5-3-0	2-W	9-3-0	Liberty
1993	Billy Brewer	3-5-0	3t-W	5-6-0	—

Bowl Results (14-11)

Bowl	Opponent	Result	Date
Orange	Catholic University	L 19-20	1-1-36
Delta	Texas Christian	W 13-9	1-1-49
Sugar	Georgia Tech	L 7-24	1-1-53
Sugar	Navy	L 0-21	1-1-55
Cotton	Texas Christian	W 14-13	1-2-56
Sugar	Texas	W 39-7	1-1-58
Gator	Florida	W 7-3	12-27-58
Sugar	LSU	W 21-0	1-1-60
Sugar	Rice	W 14-6	1-2-61
Cotton	Texas	L 7-12	1-1-62
Sugar	Arkansas	W 17-13	1-1-63
Sugar	Alabama	L 7-12	1-1-64
Bluebonnet	Tulsa	L 7-14	12-19-64
Liberty	Auburn	W 13-7	12-18-65
Bluebonnet	Texas	L 0-19	12-17-66
Sun	Texas-El Paso	L 7-14	12-30-67
Liberty	Virginia Tech	W 34-17	12-14-68
Sugar	Arkansas	W 27-22	1-1-70
Gator	Auburn	L 28-35	1-2-71
Peach	Georgia Tech	W 41-18	12-30-71
Independence	Air Force	L 3-9	12-10-83
Independence	Texas Tech	W 20-17	12-20-86
Liberty	Air Force	W 42-29	12-28-89
Gator	Michigan	L 3-35	1-1-91
Liberty	Air Force	W 13-0	12-31-92

Ole Miss

Ole Miss vs. All Opponents

Opponent	W	L	T
Air Force	2	1	0
Alabama	6	33	2
Arkansas	20	19	1
Arkansas State	12	1	2
Auburn	6	12	0
Baylor	0	1	0
Boston College	3	0	1
Catholic	1	1	0
Centenary	4	3	0
Central University	1	0	0
Centre	1	1	0
Chattanooga	14	1	0
Clemson	2	0	0
Cumberland	2	1	0
Drake	0	1	0
Duquesne	1	0	0
Florida	9	7	1
Florida State	1	0	0
Furman	0	1	0
George Washington	2	0	1
Georgetown	0	2	0
Georgia	10	21	1
Georgia Tech	1	2	0
Hardin-Simmons	2	0	0
Havana	0	1	0
Henderson-Brown	1	0	1
Hendrix	3	1	1
Holy Cross	2	0	0
Houston	15	3	0
Kentucky	23	12	1
Long Beach State	1	0	0
Louisiana Tech	7	1	0
Loyola (Chicago)	1	1	0
Loyola (New Orleans)	2	1	0
LSU	32	46	4
Marquette	2	3	0
Maryland	1	1	0
Maryville	1	0	0
Memphis	38	7	2
Mercer	1	0	0
Miami (Florida)	2	1	0
Michigan	0	1	0
Millsaps	5	0	0
Minnesota	0	1	0
Mississippi College	8	4	1
Mississippi State	52	32	6
Missouri	1	3	0
Missouri Normal	3	1	0
Nashville	1	1	0
Navy	0	1	0
North Texas State	4	0	0
Northern Illinois	1	0	0
Notre Dame	1	1	0
Ohio	1	0	0
Ouachita	1	1	1
Purdue	0	1	0
Rice	1	0	0
Samford	1	1	0
Sewanee	6	8	1
South Carolina	4	5	0
Southern Methodist	0	1	0
Southern Mississippi	18	6	0
Southwest (Memphis)	20	1	2
Southwest Texas	0	1	0
Southwestern Louisiana	2	0	0
St. Louis	4	1	0
Tampa	3	0	0
Temple	0	1	1
Tennessee	18	39	1
Texas	1	5	0
Texas A&M	0	4	0
Texas Christian	5	1	0
Texas-El Paso	0	1	0
Texas Tech	1	0	0
Transylvania	0	1	0
Trinity (Texas)	2	0	0
Tulane	36	28	0
Tulsa	0	3	0
Union	14	0	1
Vanderbilt	35	31	2
Villanova	2	0	0
Virginia Tech	1	1	0
Virginia Military	0	1	0
Western Kentucky	2	0	0

Quarterback John Darnell set school records for passing yards (2,326) and total offense (2,401) in guiding the Rebels to an 8-4 worksheet and a Liberty Bowl victory in 1989.

1994 SEC Football

Ole Miss School Records

Individual

Game
Total Offense	540	Archie Manning vs. Alabama .... (1969)
Yards Rushing	241	Randy Baldwin vs. Tulane .... (1990)
Rushing Attempts	40	John Dottley vs. Mississippi State .... (1949)
Yards Passing	436	Archie Manning vs. Alabama .... (1969)
Pass Attempts	56	Archie Manning vs. Southern Miss .... (1970)
Pass Completions	37	Kent Austin vs. Tennessee .... (1982)
Yards Receiving	200	Pat Coleman vs. Arkansas State .... (1989)
Receptions	13	Barney Poole vs. Chattanooga .... (1947)
		Floyd Franks vs. Alabama .... (1969)

Season
Total Offense	2,401	John Darnell .... (1989)
Yards Rushing	1,312	John Dottley .... (1949)
Rushing Attempts	215	Steve Hindman .... (1967)
Yards Passing	2,326	John Darnell .... (1989)
Pass Attempts	312	Mark Young .... (1988)
Pass Completions	186	Kent Austin .... (1982)
Touchdown Passes	18	Charles Conerly .... (1947)
Yards Receiving	816	Willie Green .... (1989)
Receptions	54	Floyd Franks .... (1969)
Touchdown Catches	9	Ken Toler .... (1980)
Interceptions	10	Bobby Wilson .... (1949)
Points	86	Archie Manning .... (1969)

Career
Total Offense	6,713	John Fourcade .... (1978-81)
Yards Rushing	2,654	John Dottley .... (1947-50)
Rushing Attempts	478	John Dottley .... (1947-50)
Yards Passing	6,179	Kent Austin .... (1981-85)
Pass Attempts	981	Kent Austin .... (1981-85)
Pass Completions	566	Kent Austin .... (1981-85)
Touchdown Passes	31	Archie Manning .... (1968-70)
		Kent Austin .... (1981-85)
		Mark Young .... (1985-88)
Yards Receiving	2,274	Willie Green .... (1986-89)
Receptions	127	Floyd Franks .... (1968-70)
Touchdown Catches	13	J.R. Ambrose .... (1984-87)
Interceptions	20	Bobby Wilson .... (1946-49)
Points	207	Brian Lee .... (1989-92)

Team

Game
Points	92	vs. West Tennessee Teachers .... (1935)
Total Offense	623	vs. Auburn .... (1951)
Yards Rushing	515	vs. Auburn .... (1951)
Yards Passing	436	vs. Alabama .... (1969)
First Downs	36	vs. Chattanooga .... (1971)
Total Defense	0	vs. Sewanee .... (1938)
Rushing Defense	-16	vs. Auburn .... (1992)
Passing Defense	0	Eight Times
		Last: vs. Alabama .... (1988)

Season
Points	329	(1959)
Total Offense	4,286	(1980)
Yards Rushing	3,063	(1957)
Yards Passing	2,426	(1989)
First Downs	245	(1980)
Fewest Points Allowed	21	(1959)
Total Defense	1,221	(1963)
Rushing Defense	610	(1962)
Passing Defense	500	(1957)
Consecutive Wins	13	(October 1, 1955 to October 13, 1956)

Kent Austin

Randy Baldwin

Ole Miss

Ole Miss in the NFL

Buddy Alliston, LB
Denver Broncos 1960
J.R. Ambrose, WR
Green Bay Packers 1988
Tyji Armstrong, TE
Tampa Bay Buccaneers 1992-93
Kent Austin, QB
St. Louis Cardinals 1986
Randy Baldwin, RB
Minnesota Vikings 1991; Cleveland Browns 1991-93
Ken Barfield, T
Washington Redskins 1954
Ed Beatty, C
San Francisco 49ers 1955-56; Pittsburgh Steelers 1957-61; Washington Redskins 1961
Tony Bennett, OLB
Green Bay Packers 1990-93
Dave Bernard, B
Cleveland Rams 1944-45
Jon Bilbo, T
Chicago Cardinals 1938-39
Dwight Bingham, DE
Atlanta Falcons 1987
George Blair, DB-K
San Diego Chargers 1961-64
Rex Boggan, T
New York Giants 1955
Bookie Bolin, G
New York Giants 1962-67; Minnesota Vikings 1968-69
Billy Brewer, B
Washington Redskins 1960
Johnny Brewer, LB
Cleveland Browns 1961-67; New Orleans Saints 1968-70
Lester Brinkley
Dallas Cowboys 1990
Oscar Britt, G
Washington Redskins 1946
Allen Brown, E
Green Bay Packers 1966-67
Chad Brown, DT
Phoenix Cardinals, 1993
Melvin Brown, DB
Minnesota Vikings 1984-85
Ray Brown, DB
Baltimore Colts 1958-60
Don Churchwell, T
Washington Redskins 1959; Oakland Raiders 1960
Bill Clay, B
Washington Redskins 1966; New Orleans Saints 1967
Eddie Cole, LB
Detroit Lions 1979-80
Dennis Coleman, LB
New England Patriots 1971
Kem Coleman, LB
New England Patriots 1978-79
Pat Coleman, WR
New England Patriots 1990 ;Houston Oilers 1990-93
Chuck Commiskey, OG
Philadelphia Eagles 1981-82; New Orleans Saints 1986-88
Charley Conerly, QB
New York Giants 1948-61
Paige Cothren, K
Los Angeles Rams 1957-58; Philadelphia Eagles 1959
Ed Crawford, B
New York Giants 1957
Bob Crespino, E
Cleveland Browns 1961-63; New York Giants 1964-68
Doug Cunningham, RB
San Francisco 49ers 1967-73; Washington Redskins 1974

Roland Dale, E
Washington Redskins 1950
Lee Davis, DB
Cincinnati Bengals 1985; Seattle Seahawks 1985-86; Indianapolis Colts 1987
Eagle Day, QB
Washington Redskins 1959-60
Mike Dennis, RB
Los Angeles Rams 1968-69
Les Dodson, B
Pittsburgh Steelers 1941
John Dottley, B
Chicago Bears 1951-53
Jim Dunaway, DT
Buffalo Bills 1963-71; Miami Dolphins 1972
Perry Lee Dunn, RB
Dallas Cowboys 1964-65; Atlanta Falcons 1966-68; Baltimore Colts 1969
Doug Elmore, B
Washington Redskins 1962
Bill Erickson, G
New York Giants 1948
Julian Fagan, P
New Orleans Saints 1970-72; New York Jets 1973
Hap Farber, LB
Minnesota Vikings 1970; New Orleans Saints 1970
Ken Farragut, C
Philadelphia Eagles 1951-54
Charley Flowers, RB
Los Angeles Chargers 1960; San Diego Chargers 1961; New York Titans 1962
Artis Ford, DT
Cincinnati Bengals, 1993
John Fourcade, QB
New Orleans Saints 1987-90
Keith Fourcade, LB
New Orleans Saints 1987
Bobby Franklin, DB
Cleveland Browns 1960-66
Kline Gilbert, T
Chicago Bears 1953-57
Larry Grantham, LB
New York Titans 1960-62; New York Jets 1963-72
Allen Green, PK
Dallas Cowboys 1961
Willie Green, WR
Detroit Lions 1990-93
Wade Griffin, T
Baltimore Colts 1977-81
Glynn Griffing, QB
New York Giants 1963
Louis Guy, B
New York Giants 1963; Oakland Raiders 1964
Mac Haik, WR
Houston Oilers 1968-71
Parker Hall, B
Cleveland Rams 1939-41; San Francisco 49ers 1946
Merle Hapes, B
New York Giants 1942, 1946
James Harbour, WR
Indianapolis Colts 1985-86
Michael Harmon, WR
New York Jets 1983
Jim Harvey, G
Oakland Raiders 1966-71; Houston Oilers, 1972
Jimmy Heidel, DB
St. Louis Cardinals 1966; New Orleans Saints 1967
Jeff Herrod, LB
Indianapolis Colts 1988-93
Gene Hickerson, G
Cleveland Browns 1958-60, 1962-73
Stan Hindman, DE
San Francisco 49ers 1966-71, 1973-74

Chuck Hinton, C
New York Giants 1967-69
Paul Hofer, RB
San Francisco 49ers 1976-81
John (Junie) Hovious, B
New York Giants 1945
Earl (Dixie) Howell, RB
Los Angeles Dons 1949
Fuzzy Huddleston, LB
New Orleans Saints 1987
Joe Johnson, B
New York Giants 1948
Charlie Kempinski, G
San Diego Chargers 1960
Jimmy Keyes, LB-K
Miami Dolphins 1968-69
Bob Khayat, K
Washington Redskins 1960, 1962-63
Billy Kinard, B
Cleveland Browns 1956; Green Bay Packers 1957-58; Buffalo Bills 1960
Frank (Bruiser) Kinard, T
Brooklyn Dodgers 1938-44; New York Yankees 1946-47
George Kinard, C
Brooklyn Dodgers 1941-42; New York Yankees 1947
Ken Kirk, C
Chicago Bears 1960-61; Pittsburgh Steelers 1962; Los Angeles Rams 1963
Chet Kozel
Buffalo Bisons 1947-48; Chicago Rockets 1948
Frank Lambert, P
Pittsburgh Steelers 1965-66
Skip Lane, DB
Washington Redskins 1987
Everett Lindsay, OT
Minnesota Vikings 1993
Billy Lott, B
New York Giants 1958; Oakland Raiders 1960; Boston Patriots 1961-63
Tommy Luke, DB
Denver Broncos 1968
Robert McCain, E
Brooklyn Dodgers 1946
Wayne (Mac) McClure, LB
Cincinnati Bengals 1968, 1970
Buford McGee, RB
San Diego Chargers 1984-85; Los Angeles Rams 1987-91; Green Bay Packers 1992
Pete Mangum, LB
New York Giants 1954, 1956-57; Denver Broncos 1960
Archie Manning, QB
New Orleans Saints 1971-75, 1977-82; Houston Oilers 1982-83; Minnesota Vikings 1983-84
Joe Mickles, RB
Washington Redskins 1989; San Diego Chargers 1990
Jim Miller, P
San Francisco 49ers 1980-82; Dallas Cowboys 1983-84
Chris Mitchell, DB
Philadelphia Eagles 1991-92
Russell Mitchell, C
New York Giants, 1987
Timmy Moffett, WR
Los Angeles Raiders 1985-86; San Diego Chargers 1987
Tyrone Montgomery, RB
Los Angeles Raiders, 1993
Stevon Moore, DB
New York Jets 1989; Miami Dolphins 1990-91; Cleveland Browns 1992-93
Freddie Joe Nunn, DE
St. Louis Cardinals 1985-88; Phoenix Cardinals 1989-93
Darrick Owens, WR
San Francisco 49ers 1993
Jim Patton, DB
New York Giants 1955-66

Leon Perry, RB
New York Giants 1980-82
Barney Poole, E
New York Yankees 1949-51; Dallas Texans 1952; Baltimore Colts 1953; New York Giants 1954-55
Jim Poole, E
New York Giants 1937-41, 1946; Chicago Cardinals 1945
Oliver Poole, E
New York Yankees 1947; Baltimore Colts 1948; Detroit Lions 1949
Ray Poole, E
New York Giants 1947-52
Kelvin Pritchett, DT
Detroit Lions 1991-93
Benton Reed, DL
New England Patriots 1987
Bill Reynolds, B
Chicago Cardinals 1945
Lake Roberson, E
Detroit Lions 1945
Dan Sartin, C
San Diego Chargers 1969
Bill Schneller, B
Philadelphia Eagles 1940
Jonathan Shelley, CB
San Francisco 49ers 1987
Jackie Simpson, LB
Denver Broncos 1961; Oakland Raiders 1962-64
Allen Smith, E
Chicago Bears 1947-48
Ralph Smith, E
Philadelphia Eagles 1962-64; Cleveland Browns 1965-68; Atlanta Falcons 1969
Bill Stribling, E
New York Giants 1951-53; Philadelphia Eagles 1955-57
Vernon Studdard, WR-KR
New York Jets 1971
Marvin (Bo) Terrell, G
Kansas City Chiefs 1960-63
Ray Terrell, B
Cleveland Browns 1946-47; Baltimore Colts 1947
Andre Thomas, FB
Minnesota Vikings 1987
Marquise Thomas, DE
Indianapolis Colts 1993
Ken Toler, WR
New England Patriots 1981-82
Andre Townsend, DT
Denver Broncos 1984-90
Guy Turnbow, T
Philadelphia Eagles 1933-34
Jim Urbanek, DT
Miami Dolphins 1968
Bob Vaughan, G
Denver Broncos 1968
Wesley Walls, TE
San Francisco 49ers 1989-93
Curtis Weathers, LB
Cleveland Browns 1979-86
Norris Weese, QB
Denver Broncos 1976-79
Barry Wilburn, DB
Washington Redskins 1985-89; Cleveland Browns 1992
Ben Williams, DE
Buffalo Bills 1976-85
Wimpy Winther, C
Green Bay Packers 1971; New Orleans Saints 1972-73
Lee (Cowboy) Woodruff, B
Washington Redskins 1932; Philadelphia Eagles 1933
Nathan Wonsley, RB
Tampa Bay Buccaneers 1986-87
Bill Yelverton, E
Denver Broncos 1960

1994 SEC Football 117

Ole Miss Media Information

Ole Miss Assistant AD/Sports Information
Langston Rogers

Ole Miss Sports Information
P.O. Box 217
University, MS 38677
(601) 232-7522
FAX: (601) 232-7006

Rogers (Home): 236-3535

Football Writers
Rick Cleveland
The Clarion Ledger
Post Office Box 40
Jackson, MS 39205
(601) 961-7294

Rusty Hampton
The Clarion Ledger
Post Office Box 40
Jackson, MS 39205
(601) 961-7294

Bobby Hall
The Commercial Appeal
495 Union Avenue
Memphis, TN 38103
(901) 529-2360

Don Whitten
The Oxford Eagle
Post Office Box 866
Oxford, MS 38655
(601) 234-4331

Gene Phelps
N.E. Miss. Daily Journal
Post Office Box 909
Tupelo, MS 38801
(601) 842-2611

Ricky Hazel
The Meridian Star
Post Office Box 1591
Meridian, MS 39301
(601) 693-1551

Chuck Hathcock
Daily Sentinel-Star
Post Office Box 907
Grenada, MS 38901

Henry Matuszak
Commercial Dispatch
Post Office Box 511
Columbus, MS 39701
(601) 328-2424

Other Daily Newspapers
The Bolivar Commercial
Post Office Drawer 820
Cleveland, MS 38732
(601) 843-4241

Chuck Abadie
Hattiesburg American
Post Office Box 1111
Hattiesburg, MS 39401
(601) 582-4326

Starkville Daily News
Post Office Drawer 1068
Starkville, MS 39759
(601) 323-1642

Slim Smith
The Sun/Daily Herald
Post Office Box 4567
Biloxi, MS 39531

Tom Goetz
The Daily Leader
Post Office Box 551
Brookhaven, MS 39601
(601) 833-6961

Calvin Stevens
The Vicksburg Evening Post
920 South Street
Vicksburg, MS 39180
(601) 636-4545

Danny Smith
West Point Times-Leader
Post Office Box 1176
West Point, MS 39773
(601) 494-1422

Howard Bailey
Press Register
Post Office Box 1119
Clarksdale, MS 38614
(601) 226-4321

Mitch Ariff
The Delta Democrat-Times
Post Office Box 1618
Greenville, MS 38701
(601) 335-1155

Greenwood Commonwealth
Post Office Box 549
Greenwood, MS 38930
(601) 453-5312

Specialty Publications
Chuck Rounsaville
Ole Miss Spirit
1603 University Avenue
Oxford, MS 38655
(601) 236-2667

Play-by-Play Broadcasters
David Kellum, WQLJ-FM
Play-by-Play
P.O. Drawer 1077
Oxford, MS 38655
(601) 234-5107

Lyman Hellums
Color Analyst
Route 3, Box 276
Saltillo, MS 38866
(601) 869 2166

Stan Sandroni
Sideline Reporter
Post Office Drawer 1077
Oxford, MS 38655
(601) 234-5107

Stations Carrying Games
Over 50 radio stations including WKLJ in Oxford, WJDX in Jackson, and WMC in Memphis. For complete information, contact Steve Davenport, Miss. Network, 6310 I-55 North, Jackson, MS 39211, (601) 957-1700.

Television Broadcasters
Mike Rowe
WAPT-TV
Post Office Box 10297
Jackson, MS 39289
(601) 922-1652

Clay Hall
WLBT-TV
Post Office Box 1712
Jackson, MS 39215
(601) 960-4428

Rick Whitlow
WJTV-TV
1820 TV Road
Jackson, MS 39204
(601) 372-6311

Glen Carver
WREG-TV
803 Channel 3 Drive
Memphis, TN 38103
(901) 577-0100

Mike Fleming
WMC-TV
1960 Union Avenue
Memphis, TN 38103
(901) 726-0416

Ron Savage
WHBQ-TV
Post Office Box 11407
Memphis, TN 38111
(901) 320-1345

A.J. Giardina
WLOX-TV
Post Office Box 4596 WBS
Biloxi, MS 39535-4596
(601) 896-1313

Chuck Stinson
WABG-TV
849 Washington Avenue
Greenville, MS 38701
(601) 332-0949

Lindsey Hall
Sports Director
WTOK-TV
Post Office Box 2988
Meridian, MS 39302
(601) 693-1441

John DeLuca
WCBI-TV
Post Office Box 271
Columbus, MS 38930
(601) 328-1224

Will Kollmeyer
WTVA-TV
P.O. Box 350
Tupelo, MS 38852
(601) 842-7620

Radio Stations
David Kellum
WQLJ
Post Office Drawer 1077
Oxford, MS 38655
(601) 234-5107

WXVT-TV
3015 East Reed Road
Greenville, MS 38701
(601) 334-1500

WWMS-WSUH
Post Office Box 1056
Oxford, MS 38655
(601) 234-6881

Sports Director
WOXD
2211 S. Lamar
Oxford, MS 38655
(601) 234-7100

WSLI
Post Office Box 8887
Jackson, MS 39204
(601) 372-6311

WHBQ
484 South Highland
Memphis, TN 38111
(901) 329-1313

Campus Media
Daily Mississippian
University of Mississippi
Farley Hall
University, MS 38677
(601) 232-7118

UMTV
University of Mississippi
Farley Hall
University, MS 38677
(601) 234-5508

WUMS-Radio
University of Mississippi
Farley Hall
University, MS 38677
(601) 232-5395

Wire Services
Stephen Hawkins
Associated Press
125 S. Congress
Ste. 11-170
Jackson, MS 39201
(601) 948-5897

MISSISSIPPI STATE

DR. DONALD ZACHARIAS
President

DR. WALT NEWSOM
Faculty Representative

LARRY TEMPLETON
Athletic Director

Mississippi State University

PRESIDENT:
Dr. Donald Zacharias (Georgetown, Kentucky 1957)

FACULTY REPRESENTATIVE:
Dr. Walt Newsom (Michigan 1959)

ATHLETIC DIRECTOR:
Larry Templeton (Mississippi State 1969)

HEAD COACH:
Jackie Sherrill (Alabama 1966)

LOCATION: Starkville, Mississippi

FOUNDED: 1878

ENROLLMENT: 13,651

NICKNAME: Bulldogs

COLORS: Maroon and White

STADIUM: Scott Field (40,656) - Natural

Bulldog Quick Facts

1993 RECORD: 3-6-2
(2-3-1 Home, 1-3-1 Away)

1993 SEC RECORD (FINISH): 2-5-1 (5th - Western)
(2-2 Home, 0-3-1 Away)

BOWL: None

ALL-TIME RECORD: 406-429-39 (.487)

SEC RECORD: 116-245-12 (.327) — Regular Season Games

SEC CHAMPIONSHIPS: 1
(1941)

BOWL APPEARANCES: 8

BOWL RECORD: 4-4 (.500)

LAST APPEARANCE: 1993 Peach Bowl
(North Carolina 21, Mississippi State 17)

MISSISSIPPI STATE
Team Information

OFFENSIVE SYSTEM: Pro I

DEFENSIVE SYSTEM: 3-4

LETTERMEN RETURNING: 48
- 27 Offense
- 20 Defense
- 1 Specialists

LETTERMEN LOST: 18
- 7 Offense
- 9 Defense
- 4 Specialists

STARTERS RETURNING: 18
  OFFENSE (10)
  - TE   Kendell Watkins (6-2, 293, Sr.)
  - WR   Bernard Euell (5-10, 179, Jr.)
  - OT   Henry McCann (6-6, 308, So.)
  - OG   Jason Wisner (6-3, 327, Sr.)
  - C   Brian Anderson (6-5, 278, Jr.)
  - OG   Melvin Hayes (6-6, 316, Sr.)
  - OT   Jesse James (6-5, 310, Sr.)
  - WR   Chris Jones (6-3, 202, Jr.)
  - TB   Michael Davis (6-1, 239, Sr.)
  - FB   Fred McCrary (6-0, 210, Sr.)

  DEFENSE (8)
  - DE   Wesley Leasy (6-3, 237, Sr.)
  - DT   Jimmie Myles (6-2, 285, Sr.)
  - ILB Dwayne Curry (6-3, 237, So.)
  - OLB Mike James (6-1, 207, Sr.)
  - CB   Walt Harris (6-1, 187, Jr.)
  - CB   Charlie Davidson (5-11, 168, Sr.)
  - FS   Andre Bennett (6-0, 193, Sr.)
  - SS   Johnnie Harris (6-2, 210, Sr.)

STARTERS LOST: 7
  OFFENSE (1)
  - QB   Todd Jordan (6-4, 230, Sr.)

  DEFENSE (4)
  - DE   Herman Carroll (6-4, 265, Sr.)
  - NT   Arleye Gibson (6-2, 264, Sr.)
  - ILB Juan Long (6-2, 245, Sr.)
  - OLB Lateef Travis (6-3, 252, Sr.)

  SPECIALISTS (2)
  - P   Todd Jordan (6-4, 230, Sr.)
  - PK   Tom Burke (5-11, 156, Sr.)

Scott Field (40,656)
Record: 172-78-13 (.679)
First Game: Oct. 3, 1914 — Mississippi State 54, Marion Military Institute 0
Largest Crowd: 42,700 (Two Times)
Last: Nov. 1, 1986 — Alabama 38, Mississippi State 3

1994 Mississippi State Schedule

Sept.	3	at Memphis	Memphis, Tenn.
Sept.	10	at LSU	Baton Rouge, La.
Sept.	24	TENNESSEE	STARKVILLE
Oct.	1	ARKANSAS STATE	STARKVILLE
Oct.	8	AUBURN	STARKVILLE
Oct.	15	at South Carolina	Columbia, S.C.
Oct.	22	TULANE	STARKVILLE
Oct.	29	at Kentucky	Lexington, Ky.
Nov.	5	ARKANSAS	STARKVILLE
Nov.	12	ALABAMA	STARKVILLE
Nov.	26	at Ole Miss	Oxford, Miss.

1995 Mississippi State Schedule

Sept.	2	MEMPHIS	STARKVILLE
Sept.	9	LSU	STARKVILLE
Sept.	16	at Baylor	Waco, Texas
Sept.	23	at Tennessee	Knoxville, Tenn.
Sept.	30	NE LOUISIANA	STARKVILLE
Oct.	7	at Auburn	Auburn, Ala.
Oct.	14	SOUTH CAROLINA	STARKVILLE
Oct.	28	KENTUCKY	STARKVILLE
Nov.	4	at Arkansas	Little Rock, Ark.
Nov.	11	at Alabama	Tuscaloosa, Ala.
Nov.	25	OLE MISS	STARKVILLE

1993 Miss. State Individual Leaders

RUSHING	Atts	Yards	Avg	TDs	Yds/Game
MICHAEL DAVIS	205	883	4.3	7	80.3
KEVIN BOUIE	115	505	4.4	3	56.1
Karl Williamson	36	252	7.0	0	22.9
DERRICK TAITE	22	100	4.5	1	16.7
BERNARD EUELL	5	37	7.4	0	3.4

PASSING	Atts	Comp	Ints/TDs	Pct	Yds
Todd Jordan	294	131	9 / 11	.446	1,935
DERRICK TAITE	34	12	1 / 2	.353	176

RECEIVING	Rec	Yds	Avg	TDs	Yds/Game
CHRIS JONES	24	541	22.5	2	49.2
Eric Moulds	17	398	23.4	4	39.8
BERNARD EUELL	17	192	11.3	1	17.5
KENNY CAUSEY	16	319	19.9	1	29.0
FRED McCRARY	16	98	6.1	2	8.9
KEVIN BOUIE	13	158	12.2	2	17.6
MICHAEL DAVIS	8	72	9.0	0	7.2

SCORING	G	TDs	PAT	FGs	Tot	Avg
Tom Burke	11	0	18	17	69	6.3
MICHAEL DAVIS	11	7	1	0	44	4.0
KEVIN BOUIE	9	5	1	0	32	3.6
ERIC MOULDS	10	4	0	0	24	2.4
CHRIS JONES	11	2	3	0	18	1.6
FRED McCRARY	11	2	0	0	12	1.1

PUNTING	No	Yds	Avg	Long
Todd Jordan	56	2403	42.9	62
ANDY RUSS	7	269	38.4	54

KICKOFF RETURNS	No	Yds	Avg	TDs	Avg/Game	Long
KENNY CAUSEY	8	163	20.4	0	14.8	29
ERIC MOULDS	7	143	20.4	0	14.3	38
BERNARD EUELL	10	126	12.6	0	11.5	24

PUNT RETURNS	No	Yds	Avg	TDs	Avg/Game	Long
SCOTT GUMINA	13	180	13.8	1	20.0	76
BERNARD EUELL	20	155	7.8	0	14.1	19

TACKLES	Total (S-A)	Sk (Yds)	TL (Yds)	Ints
Juan Long	117 (68-49)	1.5 (-17)	7 (-18)	2
DWAYNE CURRY	95 (52-43)	0	5 (-9)	0
Arleye Gibson	89 (46-43)	.5 (-8)	2 (-5)	0
Herman Carroll	80 (47-33)	5 (-45)	6 (-10)	0
WESLEY LEASY	79 (39-40)	3 (-37)	4 (-11)	2

INTERCEPTIONS	No	Yds	TDs	Int/Game	Long
WALT HARRIS	6	59	0	0.5	45
JOHNNIE HARRIS	2	50	0	0.2	30
Juan Long	2	48	0	0.2	45
WESLEY LEASY	2	10	0	0.2	8

Returning Players in All Capitals

Dwayne Curry    Michael Davis    Derrick Taite

1993 Miss. State Team Statistics

	MSU	OPP
FIRST DOWNS	202	215
Rushing	110	93
Passing	83	106
Penalty	9	16
NET YARDS RUSHING	2045	1900
Yards rushing	1791	1535
Yards lost	254	365
Rushing attempts	436	440
Average per rush	4.1	3.5
Average per game	162.8	139.5
NET YARDS PASSING	2141	2327
Average per game	194.6	211.5
Passes attempted	331	331
Passes completed	144	185
Had intercepted	10	15
TOTAL OFFENSIVE YARDS	3932	3862
Average per game	357.5	351.1
Total plays	767	771
Average per play	5.13	5.01
NUMBER PUNTS/YARDS	64/2686	53/2133
Punting average	42.0	40.2
Net punting average	37.8	35.2
PUNT RETURNS/YARDS	33/335	32/267
Punt return average	10.2	8.3
KICKOFF RETURNS/YARDS	36/633	32/781
Kickoff return average	17.6	24.4
PENALTIES/YARDS	77/627	60/444
Penalty yards per game	57.0	40.4
FUMBLES/LOST	20/12	25/14
INTERCEPTION RETURNS/YARDS	15/185	10/109
Interception return average	12.3	10.9
TOUCHDOWNS	27	28
Rushing	12	11
Passing	14	15
Return	1	2
FIELD GOALS MADE/ATTEMPTED	17/23	17/22
KICK EXTRA POINTS MADE/ATTEMPTED	18/18	24/25
SAFETY	0	1
TWO-POINT CONVERSIONS	2-3	0-0
TOTAL POINTS	241	245
Average per game	21.9	22.3

1993 Miss. State Results

3-6-2 Overall • 2-5-1 SEC (5th - Western)

Date	Opponent		Score	Att.
Sept. 4	MEMPHIS STATE	L	35-45	36,669
Sept. 11	LSU [ABC]	L	16-18	33,324
Sept. 25	at Tulane	W	36-10	28,500
Oct. 2	at Florida [JP]	L	24-38	84,738
Oct. 9	at Auburn	L	17-31	84,222
Oct. 16	SOUTH CAROLINA	W	23-0	33,915
Oct. 23	ARKANSAS STATE - HC	T	15-15	33,878
Oct. 30	KENTUCKY	L	17-26	28,607
Nov. 6	at Arkansas (L.R.)	T	13-13	50,075
Nov. 13	at Alabama [ABC]	L	25-36	70,123
Nov. 27	OLE MISS	W	20-13	40,238

1994 SEC Football   121

Jackie Sherrill

HOMETOWN:
Biloxi, Mississippi
(born in Duncan, Oklahoma)

ALMA MATER (YEAR):
Alabama (1966)

PLAYING CAREER:
Three-year Alabama letterman at seven different positions 1963-65.

COACHING CAREER:
Alabama Graduate Assistant 1966; Arkansas Assistant 1967-68; Iowa State Assistant 1968-73; Pittsburgh Assistant 1973-75; Washington State Head Coach 1976; Pittsburgh Head Coach 1977-81; Texas A&M Head Coach 1982-88; Mississippi State Head Coach 1991-present.

COACHING ACHIEVEMENTS:
1979 Eastern Coach of the Year; 1980 Eastern Coach of the Year; 1980 Walter Camp National Coach of the Year; 1985 SWC Coach of the Year; 1985 SWC Champion; 1986 SWC Champion; 1987 SWC Coach of the Year; 1987 SWC Champion.

WIFE:
Peggy Joyce

CHILDREN:
Elizabeth, Kellie, Bonnie, Justin, Braxton Hunter

ASSISTANT COACHES:
BRUCE ARIANS (Virginia Tech 1974)—Offensive Coordinator/Quarterbacks
RICKY BLACK (Mississippi State 1971)—Tight Ends
RICK CHRISTOPHEL (Austin Peay 1975)—Wide Receivers
BILL CLAY (Arkansas 1963)—Defensive Coordinator/Secondary
JIM HELMS (Texas 1967)—Assistant Head Coach/Running Backs
PETE JENKINS (Western Carolina 1963)—Defensive Line
DENVER JOHNSON (Tulsa 1981)—Offensive Line
KEN POPE (Oklahoma 1975)—Outside Linebackers
JIM TOMPKINS (Troy State 1962)—Inside Linebackers

SUPPORT STAFF:
STRATON KARATASSOS (Georgia Southern 1973)—Trainer
DAN AUSTIN (Newberry College 1981)—Strength Coach

Year-By-Year Record

Year	School	Conf.	All	Bowl
1976	Washington St.	2-5 (6th)	3-8	
1977	Pittsburgh		9-2-1	Gator
1978	Pittsburgh		8-4	Tangerine
1979	Pittsburgh		11-1	Fiesta
1980	Pittsburgh		11-1	Gator
1981	Pittsburgh		11-1	Sugar
1982	Texas A&M	3-5 (t6th)	5-6	
1983	Texas A&M	4-3-1 (t3rd)	5-5-1	
1984	Texas A&M	3-5 (7th)	6-5	
1985	Texas A&M	7-1 (1st)	10-2	Cotton
1986	Texas A&M	7-1 (1st)	9-3	Cotton
1987	Texas A&M	6-1 (1st)	10-2-1	Cotton
1988	Texas A&M	6-1	7-5	
1991	Miss. State	4-3 (t4th)	7-5	Liberty
1992	Miss. State	4-4 (3rd-W)	7-5	Peach
1993	Miss. State	2-5-1 (5th-W)	3-6-2	

Overall Record	48-34-2 (.583)	122-61-4 (.663)	16 Years
Miss. State Record	10-12-1 (.456)	17-16-2 (.514)	3 Years
Texas A&M Record	36-17-1 (.676)	52-28-1 (.648)	7 Years
Pittsburgh Record		50-9-1 (.842)	5 Years
Washington St. Record	2-5 (.296)	3-8 (.273)	1 Year
Bowl Record	6-4	(2-1 Texas A&M, 4-1 Pitt, 0-2 MSU)	

Mississippi State

Mississippi State All-Star Candidates

BRIAN ANDERSON
Junior • Center
6-5 • 278 • West Point, Miss.

• Selected as the CommuniGroup Offensive Lineman of the Year, an award given annually to the state of Mississippi's top scholar-lineman.
• Bulldogs' regular center throughout the 1993 season, starting all 11 games.
• A rugged performer who played every snap in six of eight SEC outings last season.
• Named to the SEC Academic Honor Roll with a 3.31 GPA during his sophomore year.

MICHAEL DAVIS
Senior • Running Back
6-1 • 222 • Morton, Miss.

• Enters the 1994 season as the SEC's second-leading returning ball carrier.
• Received honorable mention Football News All-America honors following record-breaking junior season.
• With one year left at MSU, Davis already ranks ninth on MSU's all-time rushing list with 1,792 yards.
• Finished the 1993 campaign as the Bulldog's leading rusher with 883 yards, the most since Walter Packer gained 1,012 yards in 1975.
• Posted a career-high 154 yards rushing on a school-record 40 carries in MSU's season-ending victory over Ole Miss.

DAVIS STATS

Year	Atts	Yds	Avg	TD	Rec	Yds	Avg	TD
1991	70	435	6.2	5	4	20	5.0	0
1992	107	474	4.4	5	8	72	9.0	0
1993	205	883	4.3	7	4	1	0.3	0
Career	382	1792	4.7	17	16	93	5.8	0

DWAYNE CURRY
Sophomore • Middle Linebacker
6-3 • 248 • Pascagoula, Miss.

• Named to the Knoxville-News Sentinel SEC All-Freshman team after standout redshirt freshman season in 1993.
• Despited starting just six games during the 1993 campaign, he finished eighth among all SEC linebackers in total tackles with 95.
• Recorded double figure tackle totals in each of his six straight starting assignments.
• Credited with a career-high 20 total hits against Kentucky, the highest total for a Bulldog since Reggie Stewart made 24 stops against Alabama 1990.

WALT HARRIS
Junior • Cornerback
6-1 • 187 • LaGrange, Ga.

• Tabbed second-team All-SEC by the league's coaches in 1993, becoming one of just three sophomores named to the nine-member first and second team All-SEC secondary.
• Concluded banner sophomore season tied for seventh nationally and third in the SEC with six interceptions, tying the MSU single-season record set by Bill Crick in 1969.
• Finished 12th among conference defensive backs with 61 total tackles.
• Started all 11 games at left cornerback in 1993, leading the Bulldogs in both pass deflections (10) and fumble recoveries (3).

CURRY STATS

Year	Tackles	TFL (Yds)	Sks (Yds)	PBU	CF
1993	95 (52-43)	5 (-9)	0	2	1

HARRIS STATS

Year	Tackles	TFL (Yds)	PBU	INT (Yds)
1992	22 (15-7)	0	5	0
1993	61 (45-16)	1 (-3)	10	6 (59)
Career	83 (60-23)	1 (-3)	15	6 (59)

1994 Mississippi State Roster

No.	Name	Pos.	Ht.	Wt.	Class	Exp.	Hometown (High School/JC)
53	Eric Allen	OL	6-5	250	Fr.	HS	Water Valley, Miss. (Water Valley)
65	Brian Anderson	C	6-5	278	Jr.	2L	Prattville, Ala. (Prattville)
93	Koche Anderson	DT	6-2	276	So.	1L	Canton, Miss. (Canton)
60	Burt Ashley	OG	6-3	277	Fr.	RS	Pontotoc, Miss. (Pontotoc)
55	Benje Bailey	DS	6-4	228	So.	SQ	Jackson, Miss. (Prep)
76	Sam Baker	OG	6-5	264	Fr.	RS	Birmingham, Ala. (Erwin)
9	Andre Bennett	FS	6-0	194	Sr.	3L	Brandon, Miss. (Brandon)
34	Kevin Bouie	RB	6-1	228	Sr.	1L	Pahokee, Fla. (Pahokee/Garden City [KS] CC)
86	Michael Brown	WR	5-10	182	Fr.	RS	Jackson, Miss. (Lanier)
33	Tony Buckhalter	FB	6-0	205	Fr.	HS	Daleville, Ala. (Daleville)
48	Derrick Cagins	DE	6-4	250	Jr.	2L	Columbia, Miss. (East Marion)
70	Matt Caldwell	OT	6-6	303	Jr.	1L	Columbia, Miss. (New Hope)
49	Larry Campbell	OLB	6-3	195	Fr.	HS	Taylorsville, Miss. (Taylorsville)
80	Kenny Causey	WR	6-0	172	So.	1L	Biloxi, Miss. (Biloxi)
11	Darrin Clark	WR	6-1	188	Jr.	1L	Natchez, Miss. (Natchez)
81	Shaston Coleman	WR	6-2	205	Jr.	TR	Ackerman, Miss. (Ackerman/Holmes [MS] CC)
54	Al Cotton	DL	6-6	260	Jr.	TR	Dallas, Texas (Richardson/Tyler [TX] CC)
44	Dwayne Curry	MLB	6-3	248	So.	1L	Pascagoula, Miss. (Pascagoula)
46	Eric Daniel	DB	6-2	180	Fr.	HS	LaGrange, Ga. (LaGrange)
19	Gerald Daniels	WR	5-11	170	So.	1L	Dallas, Texas (DeSoto)
5	Charlie Davidson	CB	5-11	180	Sr.	2L	Dothan, Ala. (Northview)
37	Michael Davis	RB	6-1	222	Sr.	3L	Morton, Miss. (Morton)
30	Conley Earls	MLB	6-1	241	Fr.	RS	Buford, Ga. (Buford)
4	Bernard Euell	WR	5-10	179	Jr.	2L	Jackson, Miss. (Jim Hill)
56	Gregory Favors	OLB	6-3	237	Fr.	RS	Atlanta, Ga. (Southside)
16	Cameron Floyd	WR	6-2	199	Fr.	RS	Pontotoc, Miss. (Pontotoc)
14	Brad Freeman	QB	6-1	190	Fr.	HS	Oxford, Miss. (Oxford)
96	Raymond Gee	DE	6-5	268	Jr.	TR	Cleveland, Miss. (East Side/Delta CC)
47	James Gibson	WR	6-2	202	Sr.	3L	Dothan, Ala. (Dothan)
43	Tyris Gilmore	OLB	6-2	218	Jr.	TR	Alcoa, Tenn. (Alcoa/NE Oklahoma A&M)
87	Lahitia Grant	WR	6-1	184	Fr.	HS	Dora, Ala. (Dora)
31	Nakia Greer	FB	5-10	216	Fr.	RS	Hernando, Miss. (Hernando)
90	James Grier	DT	6-3	324	Fr.	RS	Macon, Ga. (Central)
26	Scott Gumina	SS	6-0	200	Sr.	3L	New Orleans, La. (John Curtis)
3	Johnnie Harris	SS	6-2	197	Sr.	1L	Chicago, Ill. (San Bernardino Valley [CA] CC)
2	Walt Harris	CB	6-1	187	Jr.	2L	LaGrange, Ga. (LaGrange)
76	Melvin Hayes	OT	6-6	328	Sr.	2L	New Orleans, La. (John Curtis)
42	Brandon Hazzard	MLB	6-3	253	So.	1L	Nashville, Tenn. (Antioch)
73	Robert Hicks	OT	6-8	331	Fr.	RS	Atlanta, Ga. (Douglass)
29	James Holloway	FS	6-2	193	Sr.	1L	Prentiss, Miss. (Pearl River [MS] CC)
57	Dan Hoover	C-DS	6-5	260	So.	1L	Fairhope, Ala. (Fairhope)
8	Rodney Hudson	FS	6-0	200	So.	1L	LaGrange, Ga. (LaGrange)
68	Purvis Hunt	OG	6-4	358	Sr.	1L	Jonesboro, La. (Hinds [MS] CC)
36	Robert Issac	RB-KR	5-8	160	Fr.	HS	McComb, Miss. (McComb)
99	Torrence Jackson	DE	6-4	268	Jr.	RS	Pine Bluff, Ark (NE Oklahoma A&M)
72	Jesse James	OT	6-5	316	Sr.	3L	Mobile, Ala. (Williamson)
7	Mike James	OLB	6-1	207	Sr.	1L	Pahokee, Fla. (Garden City [KS] CC)
85	John Jennings	TE	6-4	215	Fr.	HS	Taylorsville, Miss. (Taylorsville)
39	Chris Johnson	DE	6-2	248	Jr.	2L	Columbia, Miss. (East Marion)
17	Chris Jones	WR	6-3	202	Jr.	2L	Tupelo, Miss. (Tupelo)
28	Jeremy Jones	WR-K-P	6-1	188	Fr.	HS	Ashville, Ala. (Ashville)
27	Johnathan Khabeer	DB	5-10	175	Fr.	HS	Atlanta, Ga. (Douglass)
20	Paul Lacoste	MLB	6-2	232	So.	1L	Jackson, Miss. (Prep)
94	Wesley Leasy	DE	6-3	220	Sr.	3L	Greenville, Miss. (Greenville)
41	Michael Lindsey	DE	6-1	265	So.	1L	Vicksburg, Miss. (Vicksburg)
13	Jimmy Lipscomb	CB	5-10	179	So.	1L	Atlanta, Ga. (Douglass)
15	Clay Mack	CB	6-0	190	Jr.	RS	Dallas, Texas (UNLV)
24	Joe Macon	SS	5-10	200	So.	1L	Starkville, Miss. (Starkville)
89	Brandon Mann	TE	6-6	262	Sr.	1L	Rome, Ga. (East Rome)
32	Byron McCall	FB	5-8	222	Sr.	3L	Amory, Miss. (Amory)
52	Henry McCann	OG	6-6	303	So.	1L	Moss Point, Miss. (Moss Point)
6	Fred McCrary	FB	6-0	210	Sr.	3L	Naples, Fla. (Naples)
92	Colby McCullough	DE	6-4	255	So.	1L	Marrero, La. (Shaw)
21	Keffer McGee	RB	6-0	207	Fr.	RS	Crawford, Miss. (West Lowndes)
23	Izell McGill	DB	6-0	160	Fr.	HS	Rex, Ga. (Morrow)
81	Omri Meek	TE	6-1	222	Sr.	RS	Houston, Texas (Yates/Kentucky)
88	Robby Moore	TE	6-3	240	Fr.	HS	Lilburn, Ga. (Parkview)
1	Eric Moulds	WR	6-3	205	Jr.	1L	Lucedale, Miss. (George County)
74	Terrance Mouton	DE	6-4	240	Jr.	TR	San Antonio, Texas (Houston)
98	Jimmie Myles	DT	6-2	310	Sr.	3L	Pascagoula, Miss. (Pascagoula)
64	Toby Myles	OT	6-6	324	Fr.	RS	Jackson, Miss. (Callaway)
84	Alonzo Porter	TE	6-4	259	So.	1L	Starkville, Miss. (Starkville)
35	Tim Rogers	PK	5-10	169	Jr.	TR	Birmingham, Ala. (Mountain Brook/Navy)
22	Andy Russ	PK-P	6-0	186	So.	1L	Nashville, Tenn. (Montgomery Bell Academy)
10	Adam Russell	QB	6-2	193	Fr.	HS	Dora, Ala. (Dora)
95	Corey Sears	DL	6-3	275	Jr.	TR	Universal City, Texas (Navarro [TX] CC)
51	Allan Smith	C	6-3	276	Fr.	RS	Starkville, Miss. (Starkville)
62	Brent Smith	DT	6-6	293	So.	1L	Pontotoc, Miss. (Pontotoc)
67	Cam Smith	OL	6-7	285	Fr.	HS	Cleveland, Miss. (Cleveland)
12	Derrick Taite	QB	6-4	194	So.	1L	Moss Point, Miss. (Moss Point)
18	Shaun Taylor	PK	5-9	170	Sr.	SQ	West Point, Miss. (West Point)
83	Kendell Watkins	TE	6-2	299	Sr.	2L	Jackson, Miss. (Provine)
23	Jim Westbrook	P-H	6-2	175	So.	SQ	Thibodeaux, La. (E.D. White)
82	Jermaine Whipple	WR	6-0	170	Fr.	HS	Warner Robbins, Ga. (Houston County)
25	Andre Williams	WR	6-1	175	Fr.	HS	Houston, Miss. (Houston)
78	Larry Williams	DL	6-3	275	Jr.	TR	Moorhead, Miss. (Delta [MS] CC)
45	Reggie Wilson	OLB	5-11	214	So.	SQ	New Orleans, La. (John Curtis)
66	Jason Wisner	OG	6-3	327	Sr.	2L	Natchez, Miss. (South Natchez)
61	Brian Wright	OT	6-5	300	Jr.	2L	Mary Esther, Fla. (Fort Walton Beach)
40	Torrey Youngblood	OLB	5-10	236	So.	SQ	Biloxi, Miss. (Biloxi)

Numerical Roster

No.	Name	Pos.
1	Eric Moulds	WR
2	Walt Harris	CB
3	Johnnie Harris	SS
4	Bernard Euell	WR
5	Charlie Davidson	CB
6	Fred McCrary	FB
7	Mike James	OLB
8	Rodney Hudson	FS
9	Andre Bennett	FS
10	Adam Russell	QB
11	Darrin Clark	WR
12	Derrick Taite	QB
13	Jimmy Lipscomb	CB
14	Brad Freeman	QB
15	Clay Mack	CB
16	Cameron Floyd	WR
17	Chris Jones	WR
18	Shaun Taylor	PK
19	Gerald Daniels	WR
20	Paul Lacoste	MLB
21	Keffer McGee	RB
22	Andy Russ	PK-K
23	Izell McGill	DB
23	Jim Westbrook	P-H
24	Joe Macon	SS
25	Andre Williams	WR
26	Scott Gumina	SS
27	Johnathan Khabeer	DB
28	Jeremy Jones	WR-K-P
29	James Holloway	FS
30	Conley Earls	MLB
31	Nakia Greer	FB
32	Byron McCall	FB
33	Tony Buckhalter	FB
34	Kevin Bouie	RB
35	Tim Rogers	PK
36	Robert Isaac	RB-KR
37	Michael Davis	RB
39	Chris Johnson	DE
40	Torrey Youngblood	OLB
41	Michael Lindsey	DE
42	Brandon Hazzard	MLB
43	Tyris Gilmore	OLB
44	Dwayne Curry	MLB
45	Reggie Wilson	OLB
46	Eric Daniel	DB
47	James Gibson	WR
48	Derrick Cagins	DE
49	Larry Campbell	OLB
51	Allan Smith	C
52	Henry McCann	OG
54	Al Cotton	DL
55	Benje Bailey	DS
56	Gregory Favors	OLB
57	Dan Hoover	C-DS
60	Burt Ashley	OG
61	Brian Wright	OT
62	Brent Smith	DT
64	Toby Myles	OT
65	Brian Anderson	C
66	Jason Wisner	OG
67	Cam Smith	OL
68	Purvis Hunt	OG
70	Matt Caldwell	OT
72	Jesse James	OT
73	Robert Hicks	OT
74	Terrance Mouton	D
75	Sam Baker	OG
76	Melvin Hayes	OT
78	Larry Williams	DL
80	Kenny Causey	WR
81	Shaston Coleman	WR
81	Omri Meek	TE
82	Jermaine Whipple	WR
83	Kendell Watkins	TE
84	Alonzo Porter	TE
85	John Jennings	TE
86	Michael Brown	WR
87	Lahitia Grant	WR
88	Robby Moore	TE
89	Brandon Mann	TE
90	James Grier	DT
92	Colby McCullough	DE
93	Koche Anderson	DT
94	Wesley Leasy	DE
95	Corey Sears	DL
96	Raymond Gee	DE
98	Jimmie Myles	DT
99	Torrence Jackson	DE

124 Mississippi State

1994 Mississippi State Depth Chart

OFFENSE

Pos	#	Name
WR:	17	CHRIS JONES
	80	Kenny Causey
TE:	83	KENDELL WATKINS
	89	Brandon Mann
LT:	72	JESSE JAMES
	70	Matt Caldwell
LG:	66	JASON WISNER
	59	Brad Ainsworth
C:	65	BRIAN ANDERSON
	57	Dan Hoover
RG:	52	HENRY McCANN
	68	Purvis Hunt
RT:	76	MELVIN HAYES
	61	Brian Wright
WR:	1	Eric Moulds
	4	BERNARD EUELL
QB:	12	Derrick Taite
	11	Darrin Clark
FB:	6	FRED McCRARY
	31	Nakia Greer
RB:	37	MICHAEL DAVIS
	34	Kevin Bouie

DEFENSE

Pos	#	Name
LE:	41	Micheal Lindsey
	99	Torrence Jackson
LT:	98	JIMMIE MYLES
	93	Koche Anderson
RT:	62	Brent Smith
	90	James Grier
RE:	94	WESLEY LEASY
	92	Colby McCullough
OLB:	7	MIKE JAMES
	40	Torrey Youngblood
ILB:	44	DWAYNE CURRY
	20	Paul Lacoste
OLB:	45	Reggie Wilson
	56	Gregory Favors
CB:	2	WALT HARRIS
	13	Jimmy Lipscomb
SS:	3	JOHNNIE HARRIS
	24	Joe Macon
FS:	9	ANDRE BENNETT
	29	James Holloway
CB:	5	CHARLIE DAVIDSON
	15	Clay Mack

SPECIALISTS

Pos	#	Name
PK:	35	Tim Rogers
	18	Shaun Taylor
P:	22	Andy Russ

Returning Starters In All Capitals

1994 Mississippi State Signees

Name	Pos.	Ht.	Wt.	Hometown/High School
Eric Allen	OL	6-5	250	Water Valley, Miss./Water Valley
Tony Buckhalter	FB	6-0	205	Daleville, Ala./Daleville
Larry Campbell	OLB	6-3	195	Taylorsville, Miss./Taylorsville
Shaston Coleman	WR	6-2	205	Ackerman, Miss./Ackerman/Holmes
Al Cotton	DL	6-6	260	Dallas, Texas/Richardson/Tyler
Eric Daniel	DB	6-2	180	LaGrange, Ga./LaGrange
Brad Freeman	QB	6-1	190	Oxford, Miss./Oxford
Raymond Gee	DL	6-5	255	Cleveland, Miss./East Side/Delta
Tyris Gilmore	OLB	6-2	218	Alcoa, Tenn./Alcoa/NE Oklahoma A&M
Lahitia Grant	WR	6-1	184	Dora, Ala./Dora
Robert Issac	RB-KR	5-8	160	McComb, Miss./McComb
John Jennings	TE	6-4	215	Taylorsville, Miss./Taylorsville
Jeremy Jones	WR-K-P	6-1	188	Ashville, Ala./Ashville
Johnathan Khabeer	DB	5-10	175	Atlanta, Ga./Douglass
Izell McGill	DB	6-0	160	Rex, Ga./Morrow
Robby Moore	TE	6-3	240	Lilburn, Ga./Parkview
Terrance Mouton	DL	6-4	240	San Antonio, Texas/St. Gerard/Houston
Stoney Price	OL	6-4	270	Winfield, Ala/Winfield
Curtis Rowe	OLB	6-3	210	Gainesville, Fla./Eastside
Adam Russell	QB	6-2	193	Dora, Ala./Dora
Corey Sears	DL	6-3	275	Universal City, Texas/Judson/Navarro
Cam Smith	OL	6-7	285	Cleveland, Miss./Cleveland
Jermaine Whipple	WR	6-0	170	Warner-Robbins, Ga./Houston County
Andre Williams	WR	6-1	175	Houston, Miss./Houston
Larry Williams	DL	6-3	275	Moorhead, Miss./Gentry/Delta

Eric Moulds

Wesley Leasy

1994 SEC Football

Mississippi State Year-By-Year Records

Year	Coach	SEC	SEC Finish	Overall	Bowls
1895	W.M. Matthews			0-2-0	
1896	J.B. Hildebrand			0-4-0	
1901	L.B. Harvey			2-2-1	
1902	L. Gwin			1-4-1	
1903	Dan Martin			3-0-2	
1904	Dan Martin			2-4-0	
1905	Dan Martin			3-4-0	
1906	Dan Martin			2-2-1	
1907	Fred Furman			6-3-0	
1908	Fred Furman			3-4-0	
1909	W.D. Chadwick			5-4-0	
1910	W.D. Chadwick			7-2-0	
1911	W.D. Chadwick			7-2-1	
1912	W.D. Chadwick			4-3-0	
1913	W.D. Chadwick			6-1-1	
1914	E.C. Hayes			6-2-0	
1915	E.C. Hayes			5-2-1	
1916	E.C. Hayes			4-4-1	
1917	Sid Robinson			6-1-0	
1918	Sid Robinson			3-2-0	
1919	Sid Robinson			6-2-0	
1920	Fred Holtkamp			5-3-0	
1921	Fred Holtkamp			4-4-1	
1922	Dudy Noble			3-4-2	
1923	Earl Able			5-2-2	
1924	Earl Able			5-4-0	
1925	Bernie Bierman			3-4-1	
1926	Bernie Bierman			5-4-0	
1927	J.W. Hancock			5-3-0	
1928	J.W. Hancock			2-4-2	
1929	J.W. Hancock			1-5-2	
1930	Chris Cagle			2-7-0	
1931	Ray Dauber			2-6-0	
1932	Ray Dauber			3-5-0	
1933	Ross McKechnie	1-5-1	12	2-7-1	—
1934	Ross McKechnie	0-5-0	11t	4-6-0	—
1935	Ralph Sasse	2-3-0	9t	8-3-0	—
1936	Ralph Sasse	3-2-0	5	7-3-1	Orange
1937	Ralph Sasse	3-2-0	5	5-4-1	—
1938	Emerson "Spike" Nelson	1-4-0	11	4-6-0	—
1939	Allyn McKeen	3-2-0	4	9-2-0	Orange
1940	Allyn McKeen	4-0-1	2	9-0-1	—
1941	Allyn McKeen	4-0-1	1	8-1-1	—
1942	Allyn McKeen	5-2-0	4	8-2-0	—
1943	NO TEAM				
1944	Allyn McKeen	3-2-0	5	6-2-0	—
1945	Allyn McKeen	2-3-0	7t	6-3-0	—
1946	Allyn McKeen	3-2-0	5	8-2-0	—
1947	Allyn McKeen	2-2-0	4t	7-3-0	—
1948	Allyn McKeen	3-3-0	6t	4-4-1	—
1949	Arthur "Slick" Morton	0-6-0	12	0-8-1	—
1950	Arthur "Slick" Morton	3-4-0	7t	4-5-0	—
1951	Arthur "Slick" Morton	2-5-0	11	4-5-0	—
1952	Murray Warmath	3-4-0	7	5-4-0	—
1953	Murray Warmath	3-1-3	5t	5-2-3	—
1954	Darrell Royal	3-3-0	6t	6-4-0	—
1955	Darrell Royal	4-4-0	6t	6-4-0	—
1956	Wade Walker	2-5-0	8t	4-6-0	—
1957	Wade Walker	4-2-1	3t	6-2-1	—
1958	Wade Walker	1-6-0	12	3-6-0	—
1959	Wade Walker	0-7-0	12	2-7-0	—
1960	Wade Walker	0-5-1	11	2-6-1	—
1961	Wade Walker	1-5-0	10t	5-5-0	—
1962	Paul Davis	2-5-0	9	3-6-0	—
1963	Paul Davis	4-1-2	4	7-2-2	Liberty
1964	Paul Davis	2-5-0	8	4-6-0	—
1965	Paul Davis	1-5-0	9t	4-6-0	—
1966	Paul Davis	0-6-0	9t	2-8-0	—
1967	Charley Shira	0-6-0	9t	1-9-0	—
1968	Charley Shira	0-4-2	9	0-8-2	—
1969	Charley Shira	0-5-0	10	3-7-0	—
1970	Charley Shira	3-4-0	7t	6-5-0	—
1971	Charley Shira	1-7-0	10	2-9-0	—
1972	Charley Shira	1-6-0	9	4-7-0	—
1973	Bob Tyler	2-5-0	8t	4-5-2	—
1974	Bob Tyler	3-3-0	4t	9-3-0	Sun
1975	Bob Tyler	0-6-0	9t	2-9-0	—
1976	Bob Tyler	0-6-0	9t	0-11-0	—
1977	Bob Tyler	0-6-0	9t	0-11-0	—
1978	Bob Tyler	2-4-0	7t	6-5-0	—
1979	Emory Bellard	2-4-0	8	3-8-0	—
1980	Emory Bellard	5-1-0	2t	9-3-0	Sun
1981	Emory Bellard	4-2-0	3	8-4-0	Hall of Fame
1982	Emory Bellard	2-4-0	8	5-6-0	—
1983	Emory Bellard	1-5-0	8	3-8-0	—
1984	Emory Bellard	1-5-0	9t	4-7-0	—
1985	Emory Bellard	0-6-0	9	5-6-0	—
1986	Rockey Felker	2-4-0	7t	6-5-0	—
1987	Rockey Felker	1-5-0	7t	4-7-0	—
1988	Rockey Felker	0-7-0	10	1-10-0	—
1989	Rockey Felker	1-6-0	9	5-6-0	—
1990	Rockey Felker	1-6-0	8	5-6-0	—
1991	Jackie Sherrill	4-3-0	4t	7-5-0	Liberty
1992	Jackie Sherrill	4-4-0	3-W	7-5-0	Peach
1993	Jackie Sherrill	2-5-1	5-W	3-6-2	—

Bowl Results (4-4)

Bowl	Opponent	Result	Date
Orange	Duquesne	L 12-13	1-1-37
Orange	Georgetown	W 14-7	1-1-41
Liberty	North Carolina State	W 16-12	12-21-63
Sun	North Carolina	W 26-24	12-28-74
Sun	Nebraska	L 17-31	12-27-80
Hall of Fame	Kansas	W 10-0	12-31-81
Liberty	Air Force	L 15-38	12-29-91
Peach	North Carolina	L 17-21	1-2-93

Mississippi State

Mississippi State vs. All Opponents

Opponent	W	L	T
Air Force	0	1	0
Alabama	11	64	3
Arkansas	3	0	1
Arkansas State	15	0	1
Army	1	0	0
Auburn	18	47	2
Baylor	0	2	1
Birmingham-Southern	8	0	0
Cal Poly-Pomona	0	1	0
Cal-State Fullerton	2	0	0
Centenary	0	1	2
Chattanooga	4	0	0
Cincinnati	1	1	0
Clemson	0	1	1
Colorado State	2	0	0
Cumberland	2	2	0
Delta State	1	0	0
Detroit	1	0	0
Drake	0	1	0
Drury	1	0	0
Duquesne	3	3	0
Florida	16	30	2
Florida State	2	7	0
Georgetown	1	0	0
Georgia	5	12	0
Georgia Tech	0	2	0
Hardin-Simmons	1	0	0
Haskell Institute	1	0	0
Henderson-Brown	0	1	0
Henderson State	0	1	0
Houston	6	6	0
Illinois	1	1	0
Indiana	0	3	0
Kansas	1	0	0
Kansas State	1	1	0
*Kentucky	8	14	0
Lamar	2	0	0
LSU	32	52	3
Louisiana Tech	5	1	0
Louisville	2	2	0
Loyola (New Orleans)	3	0	0
Marion Institute	4	0	0
Marshall	1	0	0
Maryland	0	1	0
Maryville	0	0	1
Memphis	1	0	0
Memphis State	21	11	0
Mercer	3	0	0
Miami (Florida)	2	3	0
Michigan State	1	2	1
Millsaps	14	2	1
Mississippi	32	52	6
Mississippi College	16	3	0
Missouri	0	2	0
Murray State	1	0	0
Navy	1	0	0
Nebraska	0	1	0
North Carolina	1	1	0
North Carolina State	2	2	0
Northeast Louisiana	2	0	1
North Texas State	6	2	0
Northwest Louisiana	2	0	0
Oklahoma State	1	1	0
Ouachita	3	1	2
Rice	1	0	0
Richmond	2	0	0
Samford	16	1	1
San Francisco	4	0	0
Sewanee	5	1	0
South Carolina	1	1	0

Opponent	W	L	T
Southern Baptist	1	1	0
Southern Mississippi	12	14	1
Southwestern (Memphis)	9	3	0
Southwestern Louisiana	3	0	0
Spring Hill	1	0	0
Syracuse	2	0	0
Tampa	1	1	0
Tennessee	14	22	1
Texas	2	1	0
Texas A&M	2	2	0
Texas Christian	0	0	1
Texas Tech	4	2	1
Transylvania	2	0	1
Trinity	1	0	0
Tulane	26	23	2
Union	4	1	0
Vanderbilt	7	6	2
Washington	0	1	0
Washington (St. Louis)	0	1	0
West Texas State	1	0	0
William and Mary	1	0	0
Xavier (Ohio)	1	0	0

* disagreement between schools about series record

Mississippi State standout Tony James, who helped lead the Bulldogs to the 1991 Liberty Bowl and the 1992 Peach Bowl, holds NCAA career records for total kick returns (199) and total kick return yardage (3,194).

1994 SEC Football

Mississippi State School Records

Individual

Game
Total Offense	408	Dave Marler vs. Alabama	(1978)
Yards Rushing	198	Dennis Johnson vs. Memphis State	(1974)
Rushing Attempts	40	Michael Davis vs. Mississippi	(1993)
Yards Passing	429	Dave Marler vs. Alabama	(1978)
Pass Attempts	53	Joe Reed vs. LSU	(1970)
Pass Completions	32	Tommy Pharr vs. Alabama	(1969)
Yards Receiving	215	David Smith vs. Texas Tech	(1970)
Receptions	14	David Smith vs. Ole Miss	(1969)

Season
Total Offense	2,886	Don Smith	(1985)
Yards Rushing	1,193	Wayne Jones	(1973)
Rushing Attempts	212	Wayne Jones	(1973)
Yards Passing	2,422	Dave Marler	(1978)
Pass Attempts	335	Tony Shell	(1988)
Pass Completions	173	Tommy Pharr	(1968)
Touchdown Passes	15	Don Smith	(1985)
Yards Receiving	1,035	Mardye McDole	(1978)
Receptions	74	David Smith	(1970)
Touchdown Catches	7	Bill Buckley	(1978)
		Mardye McDole	(1978)
		Danny Knight	(1982)
Interceptions	6	Bobby Bethune	(1960)
		Bill Crick	(1969)
		Walt Harris	(1993)
Points	120	Jackie Parker	(1952)

Career
Total Offense	7,097	Don Smith	(1983-86)
Yards Rushing	2,820	Walter Packer	(1973-76)
Rushing Attempts	572	John Bond	(1980-83)
Yards Passing	5,229	Don Smith	(1983-86)
Pass Attempts	738	Don Smith	(1983-86)
Pass Completions	349	Tony Shell	(1988-90)
Touchdown Passes	31	Don Smith	(1983-86)
Yards Receiving	2,214	Mardye McDole	(1977-80)
Receptions	162	David Smith	(1968-70)
Touchdown Catches	14	Bill Buckley	(1971-73)
Interceptions	11	Henry Davison	(1974-77)
		Kenny Johnson	(1976-79)
Points	211	Artie Cosby	(1983-86)

Team

Game
Points	82	vs. Howard	(1910)
Total Offense	596	vs. Florida State	(1978)
Yards Rushing	532	vs. Union	(1941)
Yards Passing	456	vs. Alabama	(1978)
First Downs	32	vs. Memphis State	(1974)
Total Defense	26	vs. Howard	(1963)
Rushing Defense	-21	vs. Southwestern	(1939)
Passing Defense	0	Numerous Times	
		Last: vs. Florida	(1958)

Season
Points	301	(1974)
Total Offense	4,642	(1982)
Yards Rushing	3,135	(1980)
Yards Passing	2,637	(1978)
First Downs	233	(1982)
Fewest Points Allowed	25	(1936)
Total Defense	1,010	(1936)
Rushing Defense	505	(1940)
Passing Defense	325	(1936)
Consecutive Wins	10	(October 19, 1940 to October 4, 1941)

Mardye McDole

Tony Shell

Mississippi State

Mississippi State in the NFL

Jesse Anderson, TE
Tampa Bay Buccaneers 1990-91; Pittsburgh Steelers 1992
Green Bay Packers 1993
Johnny Baker, LB
Houston Oilers 1963-66; San Diego Chargers 1967
Earnest Barnes, DT
Baltimore Colts 1983
Bobby Bethune, DB
San Diego Chargers 1962
Blondy Black, B
Buffalo Bisons 1946; Baltimore Colts 1947
Stan Black, DB
San Francisco 49ers 1977
Richard Blackmore, CB
Philadelphia Eagles 1979-83; San Francisco 49ers 1983
Lamar Blount, E
Baltimore Colts 1947
Ode Burrell, RB
Houston Oilers 1964-69
Jerome Brown, DE
Cleveland Browns 1993
Justin Canale, G
Boston Patriots 1965-68; Cincinnati Bengals 1969
Louis Clark, WR
Seattle Seahawks 1986-92
Keo Coleman, LB
New York Jets 1992
Green Bay Packers 1993
Glen Collins, DT
Cincinnati Bengals 1982-86; San Francisco 49ers 1987
Johnie Cooks, LB
Baltimore Colts 1982-83; Indianapolis Colts 1984-87; New York Giants 1988-90
Elbert Corley, C
Buffalo Bisons 1947; Baltimore Colts 1948
Ray Costict, LB
New England Patriots 1977-79
Willie Daniel, DB
Pittsburgh Steelers 1961-66; Los Angeles Rams 1967-69
Art Davis, B
Pittsburgh Steelers 1956

Harper Davis, HB
Chicago Bears 1950; Green Bay Packers 1951
Jim Eidson, G-C
Dallas Cowboys 1976
Clifton Eley, TE
Minnesota Vikings 1987
Joe Fortunato, LB
Chicago Bears 1955-66
Steve Freeman, DB
Buffalo Bills 1975-86; Minnesota Vikings 1987
Larry Friday, S
Buffalo Bills 1987
Bill Garrett, G
Baltimore Colts 1948-49; Chicago Bears 1950
Charles Gelatka, E
New York Giants 1937-40
Larry Gillard, DE
New York Giants 1978
Tom Goode, C
Houston Oilers 1962-65; Miami Dolphins 1966-69; Baltimore Colts 1970
Jim (Shag) Goolsby, C
Cleveland Rams 1940
Hoyle Granger, RB
Houston Oilers 1966-70, 1972; New Orleans Saints 1971
Michael Haddix, RB
Philadelphia Eagles 1983-88; Green Bay Packers 1990
Clarence Harmon, RB
Washington Redskins 1977-82
Willie Harris, WR
Chicago Bears 1993
Jim Harness, B
Baltimore Colts 1956
Granville Harrison, E
New York Giants 1941; Philadelphia Eagles 1941; Detroit Lions 1942
Kevin Henry, DE
Pittsburgh Steelers 1993
Kent Hull, C
Buffalo Bills 1987-93
Brian Hutson, SS
New England Patriots 1990

Gerald Jackson, S
Kansas City Chiefs 1979
Kirby Jackson, DB
Los Angeles Rams 1987; Buffalo Bills 1989-93
Billy Jefferson, B
Detroit Lions 1941; Philadelphia Eagles 1942
Dennis Johnson, FB-TE
Buffalo Bills 1978-79; New York Giants 1980
Kenneth Johnson, DB
Green Bay Packers 1987-88
Kenny Johnson, DB
Atlanta Falcons 1980-86; Houston Oilers 1986-89
James Jones, RB-KR
Dallas Cowboys 1980-82, 1984-85
Tyrone Keys, LB
Chicago Bears 1983-85; Tampa Bay Bucs 1986-87; San Diego Chargers 1988
D.D. Lewis, LB
Dallas Cowboys 1968, 1970-81
Joe Manley, C-LB
San Francisco 49ers 1953
Mardye McDole, WR
Minnesota Vikings 1981-83
Shorty McWilliams, B
Pittsburgh Steelers 1950
Henry Monroe, CB
Philadelphia Eagles 1979
Tom Neville, T
New England Patriots 1965-77; Denver Broncos 1978; New York Giants 1979
Jack Nix, HB
Cleveland Rams 1940
Walter Packer, RB
Tampa Bay Bucs 1977; Seattle Seahawks 1977
Mike Patrick, P
New England Patriots 1975-78
Aaron Pearson, LB
Kansas City Chiefs 1986-88
Tommy Pharr, S
Buffalo Bills 1970

Bruce Plummer, DB
Denver Broncos 1986-88; Miami Dolphins 1988; Indianapolis Colts 1989; Denver Broncos 1990
Joe Reed, QB
San Francisco 49ers 1972-74; Detroit Lions 1975-79
Alex Sidorik, T
Baltimore Colts 1948-49
Michael Simmons, DE
New Orleans Saints 1989-90
Don Smith, RB
Tampa Bay Buccaneers 1988-89; Buffalo Bills 1990
Truett Smith, QB
Pittsburgh Steelers 1950-51
Billy Stacy, DB
Chicago Cardinals 1959; St. Louis Cardinals 1960-63
Walt Suggs, T
Houston Oilers 1962-71
Pat Swoopes, DT
New Orleans Saints 1987, 1989; Kansas City Chiefs 1991
Bruce Threadgill, S
San Francisco 49ers 1978
John Tripson, T
Detroit Lions 1941
Olanda Truitt, WR
Minnesota Vikings 1993
Jimmy Webb, DT
San Francisco 49ers 1975-80; San Diego Chargers 1981
Greg Williams, DB
Washington Redskins 1982-85
James Williams, LB
New Orleans Saints 1990-93
John Woitt, DB
San Francisco 49ers 1968-69
George Wonsley, RB
Indianapolis Colts 1984-88; New England Patriots 1989
Marc Woodard, OLB
Philadelphia Eagles 1993
Glen Young, WR
Philadelphia Eagles 1983; St. Louis Cardinals 1984; Cleveland Browns 1984-85, 1987-88
Robert Young, DE
Los Angeles Rams 1991-93

D.D. Lewis

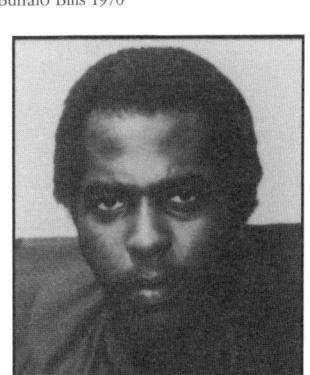

Glen Collins

Johnie Cooks

Kent Hull

1994 SEC Football

Mississippi State Media Information

Mississippi State Assistant Athletic Director/Media & Public Relations
Mike Nemeth

Mississippi State Sports Information
P.O. Box 5308
Miss. State, MS 39762
(601) 325-2703
FAX: (601) 325-2563

Nemeth (Home): (601)323-7780

Football Writers

Don Foster
Starkville Daily News (AM)
Box 1068
Starkville, MS 39759
(601) 323-1642

Henry Matuszak
Columbus Commercial Dispatch (PM)
Box 511
Columbus, MS 39701
(601) 328-2471

Rick Cleveland, Mike Knobler, Donald Dodd
Jackson Clarion-Ledger (AM)
Box 40
Jackson, MS 39205
(601) 961-7294

Wayne Clements
Tupelo Journal (AM)
Box 909
Tupelo, MS 38802
(601) 842-2611

Larry Shoultz
Meridian Star (PM)
Box 1591
Meridian, MS 39301
(601) 693-1551

Tommy Wolfe, Chuck Hathcock
Grenada Sentinel-Star (PM)
Box 907
Grenada, MS 38901
(601) 226-4321

Slim Smith, Wesley Wells
The Sun-Herald (AM)
Box 4567
Biloxi, MS 39535
(601) 896-2352

Bobby Hall, Ron Higgins
Memphis Commercial Appeal (AM)
495 Union Ave.
Memphis, TN 38101
(901) 529-2360

Danny P. Smith
Daily Times Leader
P.O. Box 1176
West Point, MS 39773
(601) 494-1422

Other Daily Newspapers

The Commonwealth (PM)
Box 8050
Greenwood, MS 38930
(601) 453-5312

McComb Enterprise Journal (PM)
Box 910
McComb, MS 39648
(601) 684-2421

Laurel Leader-Call (PM)
Box 728
Laurel, MS 39441
(601) 428-0551

Pascagoula Press (PM)
Box 849
Pascagoula, MS 39568-0849
(601) 762-1111

Brookhaven Daily-Leader (PM)
Box 551
Brookhaven, MS 39601
(601) 833-6961

Clarksdale Press-Register (PM)
Box 1119
Clarksdale, MS 38614
(601) 627-2201

Vicksburg Evening Post (PM)
Box 951
Vicksburg, MS 39180

The Bolivar Commercial (PM)
Drawer 1050
Cleveland, MS 38732
(601) 843-4241

Hattiesburg American (PM)
Box 1111
Hattiesburg, MS 39401
(601) 582-4321

Natchez Democrat (AM)
Box 1447
Natchez, MS 39120
(601) 442-9101

The Delta Democrat-Times (PM)
Box 1618
Greenville, MS 38701
(601) 335-4561

The Daily Corinthian
Box 119
Corinth, MS 38834

Specialty Publications

Joe Dier
Dawgs' Bite
P.O. Drawer 6327
Miss. State, MS 39762
(601) 325-8881

Wire Services

Dan Even, Stephen Hawkins
Associated Press
125 S. Congress, #L170
Jackson, MS 39201
(601) 948-5897

Play-By-Play Broadcasters

Jack Cristil
WTVA-TV
Box 350
Tupelo, MS 38802
(601) 842-7620

John Correro (Sideline)
P.O. Drawer AA
Miss. State, MS 39762
(601) 325-2434

Jim Ellis (Analyst)
Bulldog Sports Network
P.O. Drawer 5327
Miss. State, MS 39762
(601) 325-8950

Stations Carrying Games

Over 50 radio stations with a base carrier. Please mail all releases to: Dixon Williams, TeleSouth Communications, 6310 I-55 North, Jackson, MS 39211. (601) 957-1700.

Television Broadcasters

John Deluca
WCBI-TV
Box 271
Columbus, MS 39701
(601) 245-0133

Will Kollmeyer
WTVA-TV
Box 350
Tupelo, MS 38802
(601) 842-7620

Clay Hall
WLBT-TV
Box 1712
Jackson, MS 39215
(601) 948-3333

Rick Whitlow
WJTV-TV
Box 8887
Jackson, MS 39284
(601) 372-6311

Mike Rowe
WAPT-TV
Box 10297
Jackson, MS 39289
(601) 922-1607

WXVT-TV
3015 E. Reed Rd.
Greenville, MS 38703
(601) 334-1505

Lindsey Hall
WTOK-TV
Box 2988
Meridian, MS 39302
(601) 693-1441

Chuck Stinson
WABG-TV
849 Washington Ave.
Greenville, MS 38701
(800) 634-4493

A.J. Giardina
WLOX-TV
Box 4596
Biloxi, MS 39535
(601) 896-1313

Mitchell Williams
WDAM-TV
Box 16269
Hattiesburg, MS 39404-6269
(601) 544-4730

Charleen McCabe
WHLT-TV
Box 232
Hattiesburg, MS 39401
(601) 545-2077

Ron Thompson
Northland Cable News
300-1/2 S. Jackson St.
Starkville, MS 39759

Radio Stations

Terry O'Neal
WSSO/WMXU-FM
608 Yellowjacket Dr.
Starkville, MS 39759
(601) 323-1230

Jim Scott
WKOR
Box 980
Starkville, MS 39759
(601) 323-4980

Dixon Williams
TeleSouth Communications
6310 I-55 North
Jackson, MS 39211
(601) 957-1700

Jim Buffington
WWZQ-FM
Box 1240
Aberdeen, MS 39730
(601) 369-9672

Bob McRaney
WROB-Radio
P.O. Box 1336
West Point, MS 39773

Campus Media

Sam Cammack
The Reflector
P.O. Drawer X
Mississippi State, MS 39762
(601) 325-2374

Steve Ellis
WMSV-Radio
P.O. Box 6210
Mississippi State, MS 39762
(601) 325-8034

Bennie Ashford
MSU TV Center
P.O. Drawer 6101
Mississippi State, MS 39762
(601) 325-1332

SOUTH CAROLINA

DR. JOHN PALMS
President

DR. SANDRA ROBINSON
Faculty Representative

DR. MIKE McGEE
Athletic Director

University of South Carolina

PRESIDENT:
  Dr. John Palms (The Citadel 1958)
FACULTY REPRESENTATIVE:
  Dr. Sandra Robinson (Marshall 1969)
ATHLETIC DIRECTOR:
  Dr. Mike McGee (Duke 1960)
HEAD COACH:
  Brad Scott (South Florida 1979)
LOCATION: Columbia, South Carolina
FOUNDED: 1801
ENROLLMENT: 25,613
NICKNAME: Gamecocks
COLORS: Garnet and Black
STADIUM: Williams-Brice Stadium (72,400) - Natural

Gamecock Quick Facts

1993 RECORD: 4-7
  (3-4 Home, 1-3 Away)
1993 SEC RECORD (FINISH): 2-6 (t4th Eastern)
BOWL: None
ALL-TIME RECORD: 444-436-43 (.504)
SEC RECORD: 5-11 (.313) - Regular Season Games
SEC CHAMPIONSHIPS: 0
BOWL APPEARANCES: 8
BOWL RECORD: 0-8 (.000)
LAST APPEARANCE: 1988 Liberty Bowl
  (Indiana 34, South Carolina 10)

SOUTH CAROLINA
Team Information

OFFENSIVE SYSTEM: Pro Set

DEFENSIVE SYSTEM: 4-3

LETTERMEN RETURNING: 51
- 24 Offense
- 24 Defense
- 3 Specialist

LETTERMEN LOST: 13
- 5 Offense
- 7 Defense
- 1 Specialists

STARTERS RETURNING: 15
OFFENSE (8)
TE	Boomer Foster	(6-5, 230, Sr.)
OT	Luther Dixon	(6-5, 270, Jr.)
OG	James Dexter	(6-6, 285, Jr.)
C	Vincent Dinkins	(6-2, 288, Sr.)
WR	Toby Cates	(6-0, 193, Sr.)
WR	Chris Alford	(6-2, 180, Jr.)
QB	Steve Taneyhill	(6-5, 200, Jr.)
RB	Brandon Bennett	(6-0, 200, Sr.)

DEFENSE (5)
DE	Stacy Evans	(6-3, 250, Sr.)
NG	Eric Sullivan	(6-3, 280, Jr.)
LB	James Flowers	(6-2, 245, Jr.)
CB	Ron Nealy	(5-10, 170, Jr.)
SS	Tony Watkins	(5-11, 195, Sr.)

SPECIALISTS (2)
PK	Reed Morton	(5-8, 170, So.)
P	Marty Simpson	(6-3, 190, Sr.)

STARTERS LOST: 8
OFFENSE (3)
TE	Mathew Campbell	(6-5, 255, Sr.)
OT	Corey Louchiey	(6-8, 290, Sr.)
RB	Rob DeBoer	(5-10, 205, Sr.)

DEFENSE (5)
DE	Jahmal Pettiford	(6-1, 250)
OLB	Ernest Dixon	(6-2, 240)
ILB	Eric Brown	(6-2, 220)
CB	Frank Adams	(5-8, 165)
FS	Norman Greene	(6-2, 190)

SPECIALISTS (0)

Williams-Brice Stadium (72,400)
Record: 195-131-13 (.594)
First Game: Oct. 6, 1934 — South Carolina 22, VMI 6
Largest Crowd: 75,060 (Sept. 5, 1992)
   Georgia 28, South Carolina 6

1994 South Carolina Schedule

Sept.	3	GEORGIA	COLUMBIA
Sept.	10	ARKANSAS	COLUMBIA
Sept.	17	LOUISIANA TECH	COLUMBIA
Sept.	24	at Kentucky	Lexington, Ky.
Oct.	1	at LSU	Baton Rouge, La.
Oct.	8	EAST CAROLINA	COLUMBIA
Oct.	15	MISSISSIPPI STATE	COLUMBIA
Oct.	22	at Vanderbilt	Nashville, Tenn.
Oct.	29	TENNESSEE	COLUMBIA
Nov.	12	at Florida	Gainesville, Fla.
Nov.	29	at Clemson	Clemson, S.C.

1995 South Carolina Schedule

Sept.	2	at Georgia	Athens, Ga.
Sept.	9	at Arkansas	Fayetteville, Ark.
Sept.	16	LOUISIANA TECH	COLUMBIA
Sept.	23	KENTUCKY	COLUMBIA
Sept.	30	LSU	COLUMBIA
Oct.	7	KENT	COLUMBIA
Oct.	14	at Mississippi State	Starkville, Miss.
Oct.	21	VANDERBILT	COLUMBIA
Oct.	28	at Tennessee	Knoxville, Tenn.
Nov.	11	FLORIDA	COLUMBIA
Nov.	18	CLEMSON	COLUMBIA

"Gamecocks"

South Carolina

1993 S. Carolina Individual Leaders

RUSHING	Atts	Yards	Avg	TDs	Yds/Game
BRANDON BENNETT	193	853	4.4	7	77.5
Rob DeBoer	68	285	4.2	1	25.9
STANLEY PRITCHETT	36	162	4.5	0	14.7
MIKE REDDICK	18	111	6.2	1	10.1
JOE TROUPE	18	78	4.3	0	7.1

PASSING	Atts	Comp	Ints/TDs	Pct	Yds
STEVE TANEYHILL	291	149	14 / 6	.512	1,930
BLAKE WILLIAMSON	34	14	0 / 2	.412	337

RECEIVING	Rec	Yds	Avg	TDs	Yds/Game
TOBY CATES	27	541	20.0	3	49.2
BRANDON BENNETT	26	282	10.8	1	25.6
MIKE REDDICK	23	334	14.5	0	30.4
Rob DeBoer	17	109	6.4	0	9.9
STANLEY PRITCHETT	15	165	11.0	0	15.0

SCORING	G	TDs	PAT	FGs	Tot	Avg
REED MORTON	8	0	18-19	13-19	57	7.1
BRANDON BENNETT	11	8	0	0	48	4.4
TOBY CATES	11	4	0	0	24	2.2
COREY BRIDGES	11	2	0	0	12	1.1

PUNTING	No	Yds	Avg	Long
MARTY SIMPSON	60	2134	35.6	49
DERWIN JEFFCOAT	9	338	37.6	48

KICKOFF RETURNS	No	Yds	Avg	TDs	Avg/Game	Long
BRANDON BENNETT	4	124	31.0	0	11.3	34
Frank Adams	14	291	20.8	0	26.5	57
COREY BRIDGES	7	93	13.3	0	8.5	21

PUNT RETURNS	No	Yds	Avg	TDs	Avg/Game	Long
TOBY CATES	17	100	5.9	0	9.1	20

TACKLES	Total (S-A)	Sk (Yds)	TL (Yds)	Ints
TONY WATKINS	89 (56-33)	2 (-6)	2 (-4)	0
STACY EVANS	75 (48-27)	8 (-44)	12 (-35)	0
Eric Brown	68 (39-29)	1 (-7)	.5 (-1)	1
Ernest Dixon	55 (34-21)	3 (-30)	3 (-6)	0
Jahmal Pettiford	51 (30-21)	4 (-21)	4.5 (-11)	0

INTERCEPTIONS	No	Yds	TDs	Int/Game	Long
Jerry Inman	1	39	0	0.2	39
Mike Landry	1	7	0	0.1	12
Eric Brown	1	10	0	0.1	10

Returning Players in All Capitals

1993 S. Carolina Team Statistics

	USC	OPP
FIRST DOWNS	176	186
Rushing	83	102
Passing	87	69
Penalty	6	15
NET YARDS RUSHING	1371	2010
Yards rushing	1767	2324
Yards lost	396	314
Rushing attempts	409	494
Average per rush	3.4	4.1
Average per game	124.6	182.7
NET YARDS PASSING	2267	1654
Average per game	206.1	150.4
Passes attempted	325	265
Passes completed	163	145
Had intercepted	14	3
TOTAL OFFENSIVE YARDS	3638	3664
Average per game	330.7	333.1
Total plays	734	759
Average per play	4.96	4.83
NUMBER PUNTS/YARDS	69	67
Punting average	35.8	38.0
Net punting average	32.7	34.7
PUNT RETURNS/YARDS	31/218	30/214
Punt return average	7.0	7.1
KICKOFF RETURNS/YARDS	29/541	35/737
Kickoff return average	18.7	21.1
PENALTIES/YARDS	71/570	62/475
Penalty yards per game	51.8	43.2
FUMBLES/LOST	21/11	24/15
INTERCEPTION RETURNS/YARDS	3/61	14/78
Interception return average	20.3	5.6
TOUCHDOWNS	21	25
Rushing	11	18
Passing	8	7
Return	2	0
FIELD GOALS MADE/ATTEMPTED	14/21	14/24
KICK EXTRA POINTS MADE/ATTEMPTED	18/19	20/21
SAFETY	1	0
TWO-POINT CONVERSIONS	0-2	1-4
TOTAL POINTS	188	214
Average per game	17.1	19.5

1993 S. Carolina Results

4-7 Overall • 2-6 SEC (t4th - Eastern)

Sept. 4	at Georgia	W 23-21	84,912
Sept. 11	at Arkansas	L 17-18	47,321
Sept. 18	LOUISIANA TECH	W 34-3	69,208
Sept. 23	KENTUCKY [ESPN]	L 17-21	65,326
Oct. 2	ALABAMA [ESPN]	L 6-17	74,718
Oct. 9	EAST CAROINA	W 27-3	62,307
Oct. 16	at Mississippi State	L 0-23	33,915
Oct. 23	VANDERBILT	W 22-0	58,128
Nov. 30	at Tennessee [JP]	L 3-55	94,791
Nov. 13	FLORIDA [JP]	L 26-37	70,188
Nov. 20	CLEMSON	L 13-16	72,928

Brandon Bennett   **Tony Watkins**   **Steve Taneyhill**

1994 SEC Football

Brad Scott

Year-By-Year Record

Year School   Conf.   All   Bowl

Entering First Season as Head Coach

HOMETOWN:
Arcadia, Florida

ALMA MATER (YEAR):
South Florida (1979)

COACHING CAREER:
DeSoto County H.S. Assistant 1979; Hardee County H.S. Assistant 1980-81; The Citadel Graduate Assistant 1981-82; DeSoto County H.S. Head Coach/Athletic Director 1982-83; Florida State Graduate Assistant 1983-85; Florida State Assistant 1985-90; Florida State Offensive Coordinator 1990-94; South Carolina Head Coach 1994-present.

COACHING ACHIEVEMENTS:
1982 Heartland Conference (H.S.) Coach of the Year.

BORN:
September 30, 1954

WIFE:
Daryle

CHILDREN:
Jeff (12), John (5)

ASSISTANT COACHES:
  WALLY BURNHAM (Samford 1963) -
    Defensive Coordinator/Inside Linebackers
  RICKEY BUSTLE (Clemson 1977) -
    Offensive Coordinator/Quarterbacks
  FRANK HICKSON (Tuskegee 1982) - Running Backs
  BOBBY JOHNS (Alabama 1968) - Secondary
  CHUCK KELLY (Louisiana Tech 1979) - Offensive Line
  BRAD LAWING (Lenoir-Rhyne 1979) - Defensive Line
  MARK SALVA (Florida State 1988) - Offensive Line
  BOB STINCHCOMB (Bethel 1980) -
    Outside Linebackers/Special Teams

SUPPORT STAFF:
  RAY OLIVER (Kansas 1983) - Director of Strength
    and Conditioning
  CLYDE WRENN (N.C. State 1965) - Director of
    Athletics Recruiting

South Carolina

South Carolina All-Star Candidates

BRANDON BENNETT
Senior • Running Back
6-0 • 205 • Taylors, S.C.

• Earned second-team Coaches' All-SEC honors in 1993 after rushing for 853 yards on 193 carries and seven TDs. Ranked sixth in the SEC in rushing (77.5) and in all-purpose yardage (114.7).
• Led USC for the third-straight year in rushing and also scored a team-best eight TDs. Also posted 26 receptions for 282 yards.
• Eclipsed the 100-yard rushing mark four times in 1993 and is currently ranked 10th on the Gamecock all-time rushing list with 2,201 career yards. Became the first player in USC history to accumulate 100 or more yards rushing and receiving in one game (vs. La. Tech/127 rush-129 rec).

BENNETT STATS

Year	Atts	Yds	Avg	TD	Long	Rec	Yds	Avg	TD	Long
1991	154	702	4.6	9	89	16	168	10.5	0	33
1992	149	646	4.3	6	29	22	194	8.8	0	31
1993	193	853	4.4	7	47	26	282	10.8	1	52
Career	496	2,201	4.4	22	89	64	644	10.1	1	52

VINCENT DINKINS
Senior • Center
6-2 • 277 • Columbia, S.C.

• Pre-season All-SEC candidate after starting all 11 games at center in 1993. Projected as the anchor of the Gamecock offensive line.
• Started all 11 games in 1992 at left guard.
• Earned the starting nod at left guard in 1991, but suffered a season-ending injury in practice after the first four games.

STACY EVANS
Senior • Defensive End
6-2 • 262 • Laurens, S.C.

• Earned starting position early in 1993 and quickly emerged as a fierce pass rusher, tallying 75 tackles, a team-best eight sacks and 12 tackles behind the line of scrimmage.
• Named SEC Defensive Player of the Week after recording six tackles, two sacks and three QB pressures in the Gamecocks' 22-0 victory over Vanderbilt.
• Earned second-team All-SEC acclaim in 1993, his rookie season with the Gamecocks.

EVANS STATS

Year	Tackles	TFL	Sacks	FR
1993	75	12	8	2

DAVID TURNIPSEED
Senior • Defensive Tackle
6-4 • 257 • Spartanburg, S.C.

• Earned SEC Defensive Player of the Week for his performance versus Georgia last seasons, posting seven solo tackles, one tackle for loss, and one quarterback pressure. In that victory he also caused a fumble, and blocked a field goal attempt.
• Played in five games, including four starts, last season before missing the remainder of the year due to surgery to repair a torn tendon in his finger.
• Started all 11 games at defensive end in 1992, and registered a career-best 14 tackles versus Kentucky that season.

TURNIPSEED STATS

Year	Tackles	TFL	Sacks	FR
1991	27	2	0	1
1992	57	4	0	0
1993	22	3	2	1
Career	106	9	2	2

1994 SEC Football

1994 South Carolina Roster

No.	Name	Pos.	Ht.	Wt.	Class	Exp.	Hometown (High School/JC)
28	Chris Abrams	DB	6-0	167	So.	1L	Waynesboro, Ga. (Burke)
30	Reggie Alexander	FB	6-0	205	Jr.	1L	Pelham, Ga. (Pelham)
17	Chris Alford	DB	6-0	183	Jr.	2L	McBee, S.C. (McBee)
28	Brian Autry	QB	6-0	180	Fr.	SQ	Columbia, S.C. (Spring Valley)
22	Corey Bell	DB	6-1	185	So.	SQ	Miami, Fla. (Edison)
33	Brandon Bennett	RB	6-0	205	Sr.	3L	Taylors, S.C. (Riverside)
4	Corey Bridges	WR	5-6	166	So.	1L	Newnan, Ga. (Newnan)
98	Quinn Brodie	LB	6-2	233	So.	SQ	Athen, Ga. (Cedar Shoals)
43	Aubrey Brooks	LB	6-0	216	So.	2L	Sumter, S.C. (Sumter)
42	J.J. Brown	DE	6-3	235	Fr.	SQ	Chesterfield, S.C. (Chesterfield)
89	Maynard Caldwell	DE	6-0	233	So.	1L	Rock Hill, S.C. (Northwestern)
45	Hank Campbell	LB	6-0	230	Jr.	1L	Charleston, S.C. (James Island)
95	Freddie Carter	DT	6-2	269	So.	1L	Bessemer City, N.C. (Bessemer City)
12	Toby Cates	WR	6-1	194	Sr.	3L	Inman, S.C. (Chapman)
29	Todd Clemons	WR	5-10	155	Fr.	SQ	Washington, Penn. (Washington)
5	Terry Cousin	DB	5-10	173	So.	1L	Miami, Fla. (Miami Beach)
83	James Cunningham	TE	6-3	240	Jr.	2L	Decatur, Ga. (Henderson)
68	James Dexter	OG	6-6	282	Jr.	2L	Springfield, Va. (W. Springfield)
73	Vincent Dinkins	C	6-2	277	Sr.	3L	Columbia, S.C. (Lower Richland)
54	Luther Dixon	OT	6-4	279	Jr.	2L	Palmetto, Ga. (B.E. Mays)
93	Stacy Evans	DE	6-2	262	Sr.	1L	Laurens, S.C. (N. Greenville JC)
35	James Flowers	DE	6-2	250	Jr.	2L	Macon, Ga. (Southwest)
87	Boomer Foster	TE	6-4	240	Sr.	3L	Jonesboro, Ga. (Jonesboro)
16	Kurt Frederick	WR	6-3	196	Sr.	3L	Tucker, Ga. (Tucker)
59	Derek Gregory	DS	5-11	239	Jr.	2L	Spartanburg, S.C. (Dorman)
55	Earl Guidry	DL	6-1	240	So.	SQ	Ft. Lauderdale, Fla. (Stranahan)
57	Anton Gunn	OG	6-4	260	So.	1L	Virginia Beach, Va. (Kempsville)
9	Terrell Harris	WR	6-0	164	Jr.	2L	Miami, Fla. (Coral Gables)
71	Chuck Henrich	C	6-3	263	Fr.	SQ	Clifton Hgts., Penn. (Upper Darby)
76	Delvin Herring	OG	6-3	320	Jr.	2L	Jacksonville, Fla. (Ribault)
81	Oscar Howard	WR	5-10	168	Fr.	SQ	Columbia, S.C. (Spring Valley)
46	Roderick Howell	TE	6-3	227	Jr.	2L	Carol City, Fla. (Carol City)
63	Ed Hrubiec	OG	6-2	269	So.	1L	Berling, Conn. (Berlin)
7	DeAndre James	DB	5-10	179	So.	1L	Hillcrest, S.C. (Hillcrest)
8	Derwin Jeffcoat	P	6-2	212	Jr.	2L	Pamplico, S.C. (Hanna-Pamplico)
41	Cleon Jones, Jr.	RB	5-10	200	Sr.	2L	Mobile, Ala. (Vigor)
80	Monty Means	WR	6-3	200	Jr.	1L	Union, S.C. (Union)
14	Reed Morton	PK	5-7	176	So.	1L	Irmo, S.C. (Irmo)
3	Ron Nealy	DB	5-9	177	Jr.	2L	Pottstown, Penn. (Glen Mills)
82	Calvin Owens	WR	6-1	175	Fr.	SQ	N. Augusta, S.C. (N. Augusta)
67	Aaron Ponder	OL	6-3	270	Jr.	SQ	Columbia, S.C. (Keenan)
39	Stanley Pritchett	FB	6-1	230	Jr.	2L	Atlanta, Ga. (Frederick Douglas)
25	Mike Reddick	RB	5-10	180	Jr.	2L	Miami, Fla. (Chris. Columbus)
47	Konata Reid	LB	6-4	195	Sr.	3L	Myrtle Beach, S.C. (Myrtle Beach)
20	Reggie Richardson	DB	5-9	172	Jr.	2L	Florence, S.C. (S. Florence)
88	Marcus Robinson	WR	6-4	205	So.	1L	Ft. Valley, Ga. (Peach County)
32	Ric Robinson	DB	5-11	182	Jr.	1L	Stone Mountain, Ga. (Tucker)
58	Chris Rumph	DE	6-3	224	Sr.	3L	St. Matthews, S.C. (Calhoun Co.)
36	Marcus Simmons	RB	5-9	186	Fr.	SQ	Lake City, S.C. (Lake City)
19	Marty Simpson	PK	6-3	186	Sr.	3L	Columbia, S.C. (Spring Valley)
65	Vincent Simpson	OL	6-4	266	Sr.	1L	Greenwood, S.C. (Ga. Military)
64	Elliot Smith	OT	6-5	281	So.	SQ	Estill, S.C. (Estill)
44	Robert Smith	LB	6-4	217	So.	1L	Sumter, S.C. (Sumter)
50	Ronnie Smith	LB	6-0	241	Jr.	2L	Athen, Ga. (Cedar Shoals)
23	Shawn Sterling	DB	6-0	203	So.	SQ	Rock Hill, S.C. (Rock Hill)
51	Romel Stowers	LB	6-0	228	Fr.	SQ	Liberty, S.C. (Pendleton)
62	Eric Sullivan	NG	6-2	269	Jr.	2L	Laurens, S.C. (Laurens)
18	Steve Taneyhill	QB	6-3	205	Jr.	2L	Altoona, Penn. (Altoona)
34	Joe Troupe	RB	5-9	177	So.	1L	Tampa, Fla. (Chamberlain)
91	David Turnipseed	DT	6-4	257	Sr.	3L	Spartanburg, S.C. (Dorman)
79	Kevin Wade	OL	6-5	330	Fr.	SQ	Farmville, N.C. (Farmville Central)
94	Mike Washington	NG	6-1	290	Jr.	2L	Milledgeville, Ga. (Baldwin)
24	Tony Watkins	SS	5-11	200	Sr.	3L	Rock Hill, S.C. (Rock Hill)
75	Randy Wheeler	OT	6-3	279	So.	1L	Hartsville, S.C. (Hartsville)
78	Travis Whitfield	DT	6-4	260	Fr.	SQ	Honea Path, S.C. (Belton)
27	Lee Wiggins	DB	6-0	188	Fr.	SQ	Hartsville, S.C. (Hartsville)
10	Blake Williamson	QB	6-3	206	Jr.	2L	Anderson, S.C. (T.L. Hanna)
49	Benji Young	LB	6-0	193	So.	1L	Rock Hill, S.C. (Northwestern)
97	Damian Younge	DE	6-3	235	So.	SQ	Orangeburg, S.C. (Orangeburg-Wilkinson)

Numerical Roster

No.	Name	Pos.
3	Ron Nealy	CB
4	Corey Bridges	WR
5	Terry Cousin	DB
7	DeAndre James	DB
8	Derwin Jeffcoat	P
9	Terrell Harris	WR
10	Blake Williamson	QB
12	Toby Cates	WR
14	Reed Morton	PK
16	Kurt Frederick	WR
17	Chris Alford	DB
18	Steve Taneyhill	QB
19	Marty Simpson	PK
20	Reggie Richardson	DB
22	Corey Bell	DB
23	Shawn Sterling	DB
24	Tony Watkins	SS
25	Mike Reddick	RB
27	Lee Wiggins	DB
28	Chris Abrams	DB
29	Todd Clemons	WR
30	Reggie Alexander	FB
32	Ric Robinson	DB
33	Brandon Bennett	RB
34	Joe Troupe	RB
35	James Flowers	DE
36	Marcus Simmons	RB
39	Stanley Pritchett	FB
41	Cleon Jones, Jr.	RB
42	J.J. Brown	DE
43	Aubrey Brooks	LB
44	Robert Smith	LB
46	Roderick Howell	TE
47	Konata Reid	LB
49	Benji Young	LB
50	Ronnie Smith	LB
51	Romel Stowers	LB
54	Luther Dixon	OL
55	Earl Guidry	DL
57	Anton Gunn	OL
58	Chris Rumph	DE
59	Derek Gregory	DS
62	Eric Sullivan	NG
63	Ed Hrubiec	OL
64	Elliot Smith	OL
65	Vincent Simpson	DL
67	Aaron Ponder	OL
68	James Dexter	OL
71	Chuck Henrich	OL
73	Vincent Dinkins	C
75	Randy Wheeler	OT
76	Delvin Herring	OL
78	Travis Whitfield	DL
79	Kevin Wade	OL
80	Monty Means	WR
81	Oscar Howard	WR
82	Calvin Owens	WR
83	James Cunningham	TE
87	Boomer Foster	TE
88	Marcus Robinson	WR
89	Maynard Caldwell	DE
91	David Turnipseed	DT
93	Stacy Evans	DE
94	Mike Washington	NG
95	Freddie Carter	DL
97	Damian Younge	DE
98	Quinn Brodie	LB

1994 South Carolina Depth Chart

OFFENSE

QB:	18	STEVE TANEYHILL
	10	Blake Williamson
TB:	33	BRANDON BENNETT
	34	Joe Troupe
FB:	39	Stanley Pritchett
	30	Reggie Alexander
TT:	75	Randy Wheeler
	67	Aaron Ponder
TG:	57	Anton Gunn
	63	Ed Hrubiec
C:	73	VINCENT DINKINS
	71	Chuck Henrich
SG:	68	JAMES DEXTER
	76	Delvin Herring
ST:	54	LUTHER DIXON
	64	Elliott Smith
TE:	87	BOOMER FOSTER
	83	James Cummings
X:	80	Monty Means
	12	TOBY CATES
Z:	4	Corey Bridges
	82	Calvin Owens

DEFENSE

CB:	5	Terry Cousin
	22	Corey Bell
CB:	20	Reggie Richardson
	27	Lee Wiggins
FS:	7	DeAndre James
	17	Chris Alford
SS:	24	TONY WATKINS
	23	Shawn Sterling
ILB:	50	Ronnie Smith
	44	Robert Smith
MLB:	45	Hank Campbell
	51	Romel Stowers
ILB:	43	Aubrey Brooks
	47	Konata Reid
DE:	93	STACY EVANS
	97	Damian Yongue
NG:	62	ERIC SULLIVAN
	94	Mike Washington
DT:	91	David Turnipseed
	95	Freddie Carter
DE:	89	Maynard Caldwell
	58	Chris Rumph

SPECIALISTS

PK:	14	REED MORTON
	19	Marty Simpson
P:	8	Derwin Jeffcoat
	19	MARTY SIMPSON

Returning Starters In All Capitals

1994 South Carolina Signees

Name	Pos.	Ht.	Wt.	Hometown/High School
Reggie Baker	L/LB	6-6	270	Jacksonville, Fla./Raines
Paul Beckwith	L/LB	6-4	255	Palatka, Fla./Palatka
J.J. Brown	L/LB	6-4	235	Chesterfield, S.C./Chesterfield
Shane Burnham	L/LB	6-0	200	Tallahassee, Fla./Lincoln
Jody Caldwell	L/LB	6-3	225	Hartsville, S.C./Hartsville
Zola Davis	B/WR	6-2	195	Charleston, S.C./Burke
Arturo Freeman	B/WR	6-0	180	Orangeburg, S.C./Orangeburg-Wilkinson
Jeff Kilgore	B/WR	5-9	165	Greenville, S.C./J.L. Mann
Jamie Lawrence	L/LB	6-4	220	Columbia, S.C./Heathwood Hall
Shah Mays	B/WR	5-11	155	Tallahassee, Fla./Lincoln
Maurice Miller	L/LB	6-4	260	Cheraw, S.C./Cheraw
Darrel Nicklow	B/WR	5-11	170	Arcadia, Fla./Itawamba CC
Andray Spearman	L/LB	6-4	290	Greenwood, S.C./Greenwood
Keris Sullivan	B/WR	5-8	170	Woodbine, Ga./Camden County
Henry Taylor	L/LB	6-3	240	Barnwell, S.C./Barnwell
Homer Torrance	B/WR	6-2	195	Winter Park, Fla./West Orange
Ben Washington	B/WR	6-1	190	Tallahassee, Fla./Lincoln
Anthony Wright	B/WR	6-3	180	Vanceboro, N.C./West Craven

Tony Watkins

Toby Cates

1994 SEC Football

South Carolina Year-By-Year Records

Year	Coach	SEC	SEC Finish	Overall	Bowls
1892	No Coach			0-1-0	
1893	No Team				
1894	No Coach			0-2-0	
1895	No Coach			2-1-0	
1896	W.H. Whaley			1-3-0	
1897	W. P. Murphy			0-3-0	
1898	W. Wertenbaker			1-2-0	
1899	I. O. Hunt			2-3-0	
1900	I. O. Hunt			4-3-0	
1901	R. W. Dickson			3-4-0	
1902	C. R. Williams			6-1-0	
1903	C. R. Williams			8-2-0	
1904	Christie Benet			5-2-1	
1905	Christie Benet			4-2-1	
1906	(Football banned by trustees)				
1907	Douglas McKay			3-0-0	
1908	Christie Benet			3-5-1	
1909	Christie Benet			2-6-0	
1910	John H. Neff			4-4-0	
1911	John H. Neff			1-4-2	
1912	N. B. Edgerton			5-2-1	
1913	N. B. Edgerton			4-3-0	
1914	N. B. Edgerton			5-5-1	
1915	N. B. Edgerton			5-3-1	
1916	Rice Warren			2-7-0	
1917	Dixon Foster			3-5-0	
1918	Frank Dobson			2-1-1	
1919	Dixon Foster			1-7-1	
1920	Sol Metzger			5-4-0	
1921	Sol Metzger			5-1-2	
1922	Sol Metzger			5-4-0	
1923	Sol Metzger			4-6-0	
1924	Sol Metzger			7-3-0	
1925	Branch Bocock			7-3-0	
1926	Branch Bocock			6-4-0	
1927	Harry Lightsey			4-5-0	
1928	Billy Laval			6-2-2	
1929	Billy Laval			6-5-0	
1930	Billy Laval			6-4-0	
1931	Billy Laval			5-4-1	
1932	Billy Laval			5-4-2	
1933	Billy Laval			6-3-1	—
1934	Billy Laval			5-4-0	—
1935	Don McCallister			3-7-0	—
1936	Don McCallister			5-7-0	—
1937	Don McCallister			5-6-1	—
1938	Rex Enright			6-4-1	—
1939	Rex Enright			3-6-1	—
1940	Rex Enright			3-6-0	—
1941	Rex Enright			4-4-1	—
1942	Rex Enright			1-7-1	—
1943	J. P. Moran			5-2-0	—
1944	William Newton			3-4-2	—
1945	Johnnie McMillan			2-4-3	Gator
1946	Rex Enright			5-3-0	—
1947	Rex Enright			6-2-1	—

Year	Coach	SEC	SEC Finish	Overall	Bowls
1948	Rex Enright			3-5-0	—
1949	Rex Enright			4-6-0	—
1950	Rex Enright			3-4-2	—
1951	Rex Enright			5-4-0	—
1952	Rex Enright			5-5-0	—
1953	Rex Enright			7-3-0	—
1954	Rex Enright			6-4-0	—
1955	Rex Enright			3-6-0	—
1956	Warren Giese			7-3-0	—
1957	Warren Giese			5-5-0	—
1958	Warren Giese			7-3-0	—
1959	Warren Giese			6-4-0	—
1960	Warren Giese			3-6-1	—
1961	Marvin Bass			4-6-0	—
1962	Marvin Bass			4-5-1	—
1963	Marvin Bass			1-8-1	—
1964	Marvin Bass			3-5-2	—
1965	Marvin Bass			5-5-0	—
1966	Paul Dietzel			1-9-0	—
1967	Paul Dietzel			5-5-0	—
1968	Paul Dietzel			4-6-0	—
1969	Paul Dietzel			7-4-0	Peach
1970	Paul Dietzel			4-6-1	—
1971	Paul Dietzel			6-5-0	—
1972	Paul Dietzel			4-7-0	—
1973	Paul Dietzel			7-4-0	—
1974	Paul Dietzel			4-7-0	—
1975	Jim Carlen			7-5-0	Tangerine
1976	Jim Carlen			6-5-0	—
1977	Jim Carlen			5-7-0	—
1978	Jim Carlen			5-5-1	—
1979	Jim Carlen			8-4-0	Hall of Fame
1980	Jim Carlen			8-4-0	Gator
1981	Jim Carlen			6-6-0	—
1982	Richard Bell			4-7-0	—
1983	Joe Morrison			5-6-0	—
1984	Joe Morrison			10-2-0	Gator
1985	Joe Morrison			5-6-0	—
1986	Joe Morrison			3-6-2	—
1987	Joe Morrison			8-4-0	Gator
1988	Joe Morrison			8-4-0	Liberty
1989	Sparky Woods			6-4-1	—
1990	Sparky Woods			6-5-0	—
1991	Sparky Woods			3-6-2	—
1992	Sparky Woods	3-4-0	4th-E	5-6-0	—
1993	Sparky Woods	2-6	t4th-E	4-7-0	—

Bowl Results (0-8)

Bowl	Opponent	Result	Date
Gator	Wake Forest	L 14-26	1-1-46
Peach	West Virginia	L 3-14	12-30-69
Tangerine	Miami-Ohio	L 7-20	12-20-75
Hall of Fame	Missouri	L 14-24	12-29-79
Gator	Pittsburgh	L 9-37	12-29-80
Gator	Oklahoma State	L 14-21	12-28-84
Gator	LSU	L 13-30	12-31-87
Liberty	Indiana	L 10-34	12-28-88

138 South Carolina

South Carolina vs. All Opponents

Opponent	W	L	T
Alabama	0	9	0
Appalachian State	8	1	0
Arkansas	0	2	0
Army	1	2	0
Auburn	1	2	1
Augusta Y	0	1	0
Baylor	1	2	0
Bingham	5	2	1
Camp Blanding	1	0	0
Catholic	1	2	0
Centre	1	2	0
Charleston	7	0	0
Charleston AA	0	1	0
Charleston A. C.	1	0	0
Charleston Coast Guard	1	0	1
Charleston M. C.	1	0	0
Charleston Y	0	2	0
Chicago	1	0	0
Cincinnati	2	0	0
The Citadel	39	7	3
Clemson	33	54	4
Columbia AA	1	0	0
Columbia Y	2	0	0
Cumberland	1	0	0
Davidson	6	13	0
Detroit	1	0	0
Duke	17	24	3
Duquesne	1	1	0
East Carolina	9	2	0
East Tennessee State	1	0	0
Emory and Henry	1	0	0
Erskine	15	1	0
Florida	3	8	3
Florida State	3	15	0
Fordham	0	1	0
Fort Benning (176th Inf.)	0	1	0
Furman	26	20	1
George Washington	1	1	0
Georgetown	0	1	0
Georgia	10	34	2
Georgia College	1	0	0
Georgia M. S.	2	0	0
Georgia Pre-Flight	0	1	0
Georgia Tech	9	12	0
Guilford	4	0	0
Hawaii	0	2	0
Houston	0	2	0
Indiana	0	1	0
Iowa State	1	0	0
Kansas State	2	1	0
Kentucky	1	3	1
Lenoir	1	0	0
Louisiana State	1	12	0
Louisiana Tech	2	0	1
Machinists Mates	1	0	0
Marquette	1	0	1
Maryland	11	17	0
Memphis State	2	2	0
Mercer	1	1	0
Michigan	1	1	0
Miami (Fla.)	5	8	2
Miami (Ohio)	2	3	0
Mississippi	5	4	0
Mississippi State	1	1	0
Missouri	0	1	0
Navy	4	3	0
Nebraska	0	3	0
Newberry	11	1	1
North Carolina	16	34	4
North Carolina M. A.	2	0	0
North Carolina M. C.	0	1	0
North Carolina State	25	25	4
Northwestern	0	1	0
Notre Dame	1	3	0
Ohio University	2	0	0
Oklahoma State	1	1	0
Pacific	2	1	0
Penn State	0	2	0
Pittsburgh	1	3	0
Porter	1	0	0
Presbyterian	12	3	0
Richmond	1	0	0
Ridgewood	0	0	1
St. Albans	1	0	0
Sewanee	2	2	0
Southern California	1	1	0
Southern Illinois	1	0	0
Temple	0	1	0
Tennessee	2	8	2
Texas	1	0	0
Tulane	0	3	0
Tulsa	1	0	0
Vanderbilt	3	0	0
Villanova	1	4	1
Virginia	20	11	1
V.M.I.	1	1	0
Virginia Tech	11	7	2
Washington and Lee	2	3	0
Wake Forest	34	20	2
Welsh Neck	3	0	0
West Virginia	3	7	1
Western Carolina	4	0	0
Western Michigan	1	0	0
Wichita State	1	0	0
Wofford	15	4	0
Xavier (Ohio)	1	1	0

George Rogers, who won the 1980 Heisman Trophy, captured the national rushing title his senior season (1,894) after finishing second in 1979 (1,681).

South Carolina School Records

Individual

Game
Total Offense	428	Todd Ellis vs. Virginia Tech	(1986)
Yards Rushing	278	Brandon Bennett vs. East Tennessee St.	(1991)
Rushing Attempts	39	Ron Bass vs. North Carolina	(1974)
Yards Passing	425	Todd Ellis vs. East Carolina	(1987)
Pass Attempts	53	Todd Ellis vs. Virginia Tech	(1986)
Pass Completions	30	Todd Ellis vs. Appalachian State	(1987)
Yards Receiving	199	Fred Zeigler vs. Virginia	(1968)
Receptions	12	Fred Zeigler vs. Virginia	(1968)

Season
Total Offense	3,016	Todd Ellis	(1986)
Yards Rushing	1,894	George Rogers	(1980)
Rushing Attempts	324	George Rogers	(1980)
Yards Passing	3,020	Todd Ellis	(1986)
Pass Attempts	432	Todd Ellis	(1987)
Pass Completions	241	Todd Ellis	(1987)
Touchdown Passes	20	Todd Ellis	(1986)
Yards Receiving	1,106	Sterling Sharpe	(1986)
Receptions	74	Sterling Sharpe	(1986)
Touchdown Catches	10	Sterling Sharpe	(1986)
Interceptions	9	Bryant Gilliard	(1984)
Points	113	Collin Mackie	(1987)

Career
Total Offense	9,351	Todd Ellis	(1986-89)
Yards Rushing	5,204	George Rogers	(1977-80)
Rushing Attempts	954	George Rogers	(1977-80)
Yards Passing	9,953	Todd Ellis	(1986-89)
Pass Attempts	1,350	Todd Ellis	(1986-89)
Pass Completions	747	Todd Ellis	(1986-89)
Touchdown Passes	49	Todd Ellis	(1986-89)
Yards Receiving	2,497	Sterling Sharpe	(1983, 1985-87)
Receptions	169	Sterling Sharpe	(1983, 1985-87)
Touchdown Catches	17	Sterling Sharpe	(1983, 1985-87)
Interceptions	14	Bo Davies	(1969-71)
Points	330	Collin Mackie	(1987-90)

Team

Game
Points	73	vs. Wichita State	(1980)
Total Offense	636	vs. The Citadel	(1985)
Yards Rushing	474	vs. Presbyterian	(1937)
Yards Passing	425	vs. East Carolina	(1987)
First Downs	33	vs. East Carolina	(1990)
Total Defense	8	vs. Clemson	(1943)
Rushing Defense	-39	vs. Pacific	(1980)
Passing Defense	0	Numerous Times	
		Last: vs. Georgia Tech	(1976)

Season
Points	381	(1984)
Total Offense	5,095	(1984)
Yards Rushing	N/A	
Yards Passing	3,235	(1987)
First Downs	269	(1975 and 1987)
Fewest Points Allowed	27	(1925)
Total Defense	2,000	(1956)
Rushing Defense	1,158	(1987)
Passing Defense	476	(1956)
Consecutive Wins	9	(September 8, 1984 to November 10, 1984)

Sterling Sharpe

Colin Mackie

South Carolina

South Carolina in the NFL

Tommy Addison, LB
Boston Patriots 1960-67

Darrell Austin, OG-C
Denver Broncos 1974
New York Jets 1975-78
Tampa Bay Buccaneers 1979-80

Ryan Bethea, WR
Minnesota Vikings 1988

Harold Blackwell, B
Chicago Cardinals 1945

Robert Brooks
Green Bay Packers 1992-93

Bobby Bryant, DB
Minnesota Vikings 1968-81

Leonard Burton, C
Buffalo Bills 1986-91;
Cleveland Browns 1992

Steve Courson, OG
Pittsburgh Steelers 1977-83
Tampa Bay 1984-85

Larry Craig, QB
Green Bay Packers 1939-49

Leon Cunningham, C
Detroit Lions 1955

Bill Currier, DB
Houston Oilers 1977-79
New England Patriots 1980
New York Giants 1981-85

Sam DeLuca, G-T
Los Angeles Chargers 1960
San Diego Chargers 1961-63
New York Jets 1964-66

Mike Dingle, RB
Cincinnati Bengals 1992

Gerald Dixon, OLB
Cleveland Browns 1992-93

Danny Dyches, C
New York Jets 1971
Buffalo Bills 1972

Ernest Dye, OT
Arizona Cardinals 1993

Brad Edwards, DB
Minnesota Vikings 1988-89
Washington Redskins, 1990-93

Arthur "Dutch" Elston, QB
Cleveland Rams 1942
San Francisco 49ers 1946-48

Billy Gambrell, E
St. Louis Cardinals 1963-68
Detroit Lions 1968-69

Rusty Ganas, DT
Baltimore Colts 1971

Harold Green, RB
Cincinnati Bengals 1990-93

Al Grygo, B
Chicago Bears 1944-45

Rickey Hagood, DL
Seattle Seahawks 1984
San Diego Chargers 1984
Los Angeles Raiders 1985

Elzaphan "Zip" Hanna, G
Washington Redskins 1945

Roy Hart, NG
Seattle Seahawks 1988-90
Los Angeles Raiders 1991
New York Jets 1992

Alex Hawkins, B-E
Baltimore Colts 1959-65, 67
Atlanta Falcons 1966

Ira Hillary, WR
Cincinnati Bengals 1987-89
Minnesota Vikings 1990

Ed Holler, LB
Green Bay Packers 1963-64
Pittsburgh Steelers 1964

John Keenan, G
Washington Redskins 1944-45

James "Blackie" Kincaid, B
Washington Redskins 1954

John Kimpara, T
Los Angeles Chargers 1960

Joe Krivonak, G
Miami Seahawks 1946

Ronnie Lamb, B
Denver Broncos 1968
Cincinnati Bengals 1968-71
Atlanta Falcons 1972

Kevin Long, RB
New York Jets 1977-81

Zion McKinney, FL
Washington Redskins 1980

Bryant "Meatball" Meeks, C
Pittsburgh Steelers 1947-48

Corey Miller, LB
New York Giants 1991-93

Eddie Miller, WR
Indianapolis Colts 1992-93

Bill Miner, G
Chicago Bears 1947-49
New York Giants 1950

Glenn Myers, E
Columbus Bullies 1940

Chris Norman, P
Denver Broncos 1984-87

Andrew Provence, DL
Atlanta Falcons 1983-87
Denver Broncos 1988-90

Dan Reeves, RB
Dallas Cowboys 1965-72

Roy Don "Butch" Reeves, DB
Buffalo Bills 1969

Don Rogers, C
Los Angeles Chargers 1960
San Diego Chargers 1961-64

George Rogers, RB
New Orleans Saints 1981-84
Washington Redskins 1985-87

Ken Roskie, B
San Francisco 49ers 1946
Detroit Lions 1948
Green Bay Packers 1948

Max Runager, P
Philadelphia Eagles 1980-83
San Francisco 49ers 1984-88
Cleveland Browns 1988
Kansas City Chiefs 1989-present

Rusty Russell, OT
Philadelphia Eagles 1984-85

Jay Saldi, TE
Dallas Cowboys, 1976-82
Chicago Bears 1984

Rick Sanford, DB
New England Patriots 1979-85

James Seawright, LB
Buffalo Bills 1985-87

Willie Scott, TE
Kansas City Chiefs 1981-86
New England Patriots 1986-89

Sterling Sharpe, WR
Green Bay Packers 1988-93

Chuck Slaughter, OL
New Orleans Saints 1982

Lou Sossamon, C
New York Yankees 1946-48

Dave Sparks, G
San Francisco 49ers 1951
Washington Redskins 1954

Stan Stasica, B
Miami Seahawks 1948

Calvin Stephens, OL
New England Patriots 1991-93

Bishop Strickland, B
San Francisco 49ers 1951

Bill Troup, QB
Baltimore Colts 1974-78

Alexander Urban, E
Green Bay Packers
1941, 1944-45

Emanual Weaver, DL
Cincinnati Bengals 1982-83

J.R. Wilburn, E
Pittsburgh Steelers 1966-70

Clarence Williams, RB
San Diego Chargers 1977-81
Washington Redskins 1982-83

Johnnie Wright, RB
Baltimore Colts 1981-82

Brad Edwards

1994 SEC Football   141

South Carolina Media Information

South Carolina Assistant Athletic Director/ Media Relations
Kerry Tharp

South Carolina Sports Information
Rex Enright Athletic Center
Rosewood Drive
Columbia, SC 29208
(803) 777-5204
FAX: (803) 777-2967

Tharp (Home): 776-0382

Football Beat Writers
David Newton
The State
Box 1333
Columbia, SC 29202
(803) 771-8470

Rick Scoppe
The Greenville News
248 Ashton Circle
Lexington, SC 29073
(803) 957-6322

Cedric Harmon
Spartanburg Herald
Box 1657
Spartanburg, SC 29304
(803) 582-5673

Bob Lang
The Post-Courier
134 Columbus Street
Charleston, SC 29403
(803) 577-7111

Jim Gilstrap
The Independent-Mail
Box 2507
Anderson, SC 29622
(803) 224-4321

Stan Olson
The Observer
Box 32188
Charlotte, NC 28232
(704) 358-5125

Other Newspapers
Bob Spear, Sports Editor
The State
Box 1333
Columbia, SC 29202
(803) 771-8470

Dan Foster, Columnist
The News
Box 1688
Greenville, SC 29602
(803) 298-4306

Ken Burger, Executive Sports Editor
The Post-Courier
134 Columbus Street
Charleston, SC 29403
(803) 577-7111

Bob Bestler, Sports Editor
The Sun-News
Myrtle Beach, SC 29577
(803) 626-0315

Randy Beard, Sports Editor
The Independent-Mail
Box 2507
Anderson, SC 29622
(803) 224-4321

Dennis Shumate, Sports Editor
The Times & Democrat
211 Broughton Street
Orangeburg, SC 29115
(803) 534-1060

Paul Bowker, Sports Editor
The Herald
Box 11707
Rock Hill, SC 29731
(803) 329-4008

Meri-Jo Borzilleri, Sports Editor
The Island Packet
Box 5727
Hilton Head, SC 29938
(803) 785-4293

Ward Clayton, Sports Editor
The Chronicle-Herald
725 Broad Street
Augusta, GA 30913
(404) 724-0851

Jim Fair, Sports Editor
Spartanburg Herald
Box 1657
Spartanburg, SC 29304

Anthony Stastny, Sports Editor
The Morning News
Box 1088
Savannah, GA 31402
(912) 236-9511

Luther Gaillard, Sports Editor
The Piedmont
Box 1699
Greenville, SC 29602
(803) 298-4202

Wire Service
Pete Iacobelli
Associated Press
Box 101101
Columbia, SC 29202
(803) 799-5510

Radio Network
Liz McMillan
Host Communications
Roast Dormitory
University of South Carolina
Columbia, SC 29208

Bob Fulton (Play-By-Play)
110 Oak Lane
Cayce, SC 29033
(803) 794-0657

Tommy Suggs (Color Analyst)
12 Dill Court
Columbia, SC 29204

Specialty Publications
Dexter Hudson, Editor
Spurs & Feathers
Box 8055
Columbia, SC 29202
(803) 256-1789

Campus Media
Sports Editor
The Gamecock
Drawer A
University of South Carolina
Columbia, SC 29208
(803) 777-7182

Sports Director
WUSC-Radio
Russell House
University of South Carolina
Columbia, SC 29208
(803) 777-4165

Television
Joe Daggett
WIS-TV
1111 Bull Street
Columbia, SC 29202
(803) 758-1288

Terry Chick
WOLO-TV
Box 4217
Columbia, SC 29204
(803) 754-7528

Bob Shields
WLTX-TV
Drawer M
Columbia, SC 29205
(803) 776-9508

Geoff Hart
WYFF-TV
Box 788
Greenville, SC 29602
(803) 240-5264

Pete Yanity
WSPA-TV
Box 1717
Spartanburg, SC 29301
(803) 587-4479

Radio
Jim Powell, Sports Director
WVOC Radio
Box 21567
Columbia, SC 29221
(803) 772-5840

Phil Kornblut
SC Network
3710 Landmark Dr.
Suite 10
Columbia, SC 29204

Teddy Heffner
2700 Bendemeer Dr.
Columbia, SC 29209

TENNESSEE

DR. JOE JOHNSON
President

DR. CARL ASP
Faculty Representative

DOUG DICKEY
Athletic Director

University of Tennessee

PRESIDENT:
  Dr. Joe Johnson (Birmingham Southern 1955)
FACULTY REPRESENTATIVE:
  Dr. Carl Asp (Ohio State 1963)
ATHLETIC DIRECTOR:
  Doug Dickey (Florida 1954)
HEAD COACH:
  Phillip Fulmer (Tennessee 1972)
LOCATION: Knoxville, Tennessee
FOUNDED: 1794
ENROLLMENT: 25,890
NICKNAME: Volunteers
COLORS: Orange and White
STADIUM: Neyland Stadium/Shields-Watkins Field (91,902) - Natural

Volunteer Quick Facts

1993 RECORD: 9-2-1
  (7-0 Home, 2-1-1 Away, 0-1 Neutral)
1993 SEC RECORD (FINISH): 6-1-1 (2nd-Eastern)
  (4-0 Home, 2-1-1 Away)
BOWL: CompUSA Florida Citrus
  Penn State 31, Tennessee 13
ALL-TIME RECORD: 636-277-54 (.686)
SEC RECORD: 223-125-20 (.633) — Regular Season Games
SEC CHAMPIONSHIPS: 11
  (1938, 39t, 40, 46t, 51t, 56, 67, 69, 85, 89t, 90)
BOWL APPEARANCES: 34
BOWL RECORD: 18-16 (.529)
LAST APPEARANCE: 1994 CompUSA Florida Citrus Bowl
  (Penn State 31, Tennessee 13)

TENNESSEE
Team Information

OFFENSIVE SYSTEM: Multiple

DEFENSIVE SYSTEM: 4-3

LETTERMEN RETURNING: 48
- 26 Offense
- 20 Defense
- 2 Specialists

LETTERMEN LOST: 19
- 7 Offense
- 9 Defense
- 3 Specialists

STARTERS RETURNING: 14
OFFENSE (7)
- TE David Horn (6-4, 248, Jr.)
- LT Jason Layman (6-5, 287, Jr.)
- LG Kevin Mays (6-4, 284, Sr.)
- C Bubba Miller (6-1, 285, Jr.)
- RG Jeff Smith (6-3, 310, Jr.)
- RT Leslie Ratliffe (6-7, 302, Jr.)
- FB Mose Phillips (6-0, 221, Sr.)

DEFENSE (5)
- LB Scott Galyon (6-2, 232, Jr.)
- LB Ben Talley (6-3, 239, Sr.)
- FS Jason Parker (6-0, 192, Jr.)
- CB DeRon Jenkins (5-11, 167, Jr.)
- CB Ronald Davis (5-11, 197, Sr.)

SPECIALISTS (2)
- PK John Becksvoort (6-1, 177, Sr.)
- P Tom Hutton (6-1, 195, Sr.)

STARTERS LOST: 10
OFFENSE (4)
- SE Cory Fleming (6-3, 207)
- FLK Craig Faulkner (5-11, 180)
- QB Heath Shuler (6-3, 212)
- TB Charlie Garner (5-10, 187)

DEFENSE (6)
- DE James Wilson (6-3, 251)
- DE Horace Morris (6-3, 230)
- DT Shane Bonham (6-4, 260)
- DT Paul Yatkowski (6-3, 250)
- LB Reggie Ingram (6-2, 235)
- SS Victor Brown (6-1, 205)

SPECIALISTS (0)

Neyland Stadium (91,902)
Record: 343-85-17 (.790)
First Game: Sept. 24, 1921 — Tennessee 27, Emory & Henry 0
Largest Crowd: 97,731 (Sept. 28, 1991)
    Tennessee 30, Auburn 21

1994 Tennessee Schedule

Sept.	3	at UCLA	Pasadena, Calif.
Sept.	10	at Georgia	Athens, Ga.
Sept.	17	FLORIDA	KNOXVILLE
Sept.	24	at Mississippi State	Starkville, Miss.
Oct.	1	WASHINGTON STATE - HC	KNOXVILLE
Oct.	8	ARKANSAS	KNOXVILLE
Oct.	15	ALABAMA	KNOXVILLE
Oct.	29	at South Carolina	Columbia, S.C.
Nov.	12	MEMPHIS	KNOXVILLE
Nov.	19	KENTUCKY	KNOXVILLE
Nov.	26	at Vanderbilt	Nashville

1995 Tennessee Schedule

Sept.	2	EAST CAROLINA	KNOXVILLE
Sept.	9	GEORGIA	KNOXVILLE
Sept.	16	at Florida	Gainesville, Fla.
Sept.	23	MISSISSIPPI STATE	KNOXVILLE
Sept.	30	OKLAHOMA STATE	KNOXVILLE
Oct.	7	at Arkansas	Fayetteville, Ark.
Oct.	14	at Alabama	Birmingham, Ala.
Oct.	28	SOUTH CAROLINA	KNOXVILLE
Nov.	4	SOUTHERN MISSISSIPPI	KNOXVILLE
Nov.	18	at Kentucky	Lexington, Ky.
Nov.	25	VANDERBILT	KNOXVILLE

Tennessee

1993 Tennessee Individual Leaders

RUSHING	Atts	Yds	Avg	TDs	Yds./Game
Charlie Garner	159	1161	7.3	8	105.6
JAMES STEWART	86	537	6.2	9	48.8
AARON HAYDEN	28	217	7.8	1	54.3
MOSE PHILLIPS	40	199	5.0	3	18.1
ERIC LANE	18	134	7.4	1	12.2

PASSING	Atts	Comp	Ints/TDs	Pct	Yds
Heath Shuler	285	184	8/25	.646	2,354
JERRY COLQUITT	26	19	1/4	.731	233
TODD HELTON	9	5	0/2	.556	78

RECEIVING	Rec	Yds	Avg	TDs	Yds/Game
Craig Faulkner	40	680	17.0	6	61.8
Cory Fleming	39	596	15.3	11	54.2
BILLY WILLIAMS	39	513	13.2	5	46.6
JAMES STEWART	12	89	7.4	0	8.1
Charlie Garner	12	81	6.8	0	7.4

SCORING	G	TDs	PAT	FGs	Tot	Avg
JOHN BECKSVOORT	11	0	59-59	12-13	95	8.6
Cory Fleming	11	11	0	0	66	6.0
JAMES STEWART	11	9	0	0	54	4.9
Charlie Garner	11	8	1 2-pt	0	50	4.5
Craig Faulkner	11	6	0	0	36	3.2

PUNTING	No	Yds	Avg	Long
TOM HUTTON	40	1584	39.6	55
Joey Chapman	2	62	31.0	32

KICKOFF RETURNS	No	Yds	Avg	TDs	Avg/Game	Long
BILLY WILLIAMS	13	369	28.4	0	33.5	43
Charlie Garner	6	139	23.2	0	12.6	32
NILO SILVAN	4	87	21.8	0	7.9	30

PUNT RETURNS	No	Yds	Avg	TDs	Avg/Game	Long
SHAWN SUMMERS	18	255	14.2	1	23.2	51
Cory Fleming	14	89	6.4	0	8.1	25
BILLY WILLIAMS	3	15	5.0	0	1.4	20

TACKLES	Total(S-A)	Sk(Yds)	TL(Yds)	Ints
BEN TALLEY	87 (56-31)	4(-47)	7(-20)	0
Reggie Ingram	77 (58-19)	0	2(-5)	0
JASON PARKER	61 (43-18)	0	2(-5)	4
SCOTT GALYON	54 (36-18)	1(-1)	4(-8)	1
RAYMOND AUSTIN	51 (38-13)	2(-14)	2(-12)	1

INTERCEPTIONS	No	Yds	TDs	Int/Game	Long
DeRon Jenkins	5	13	0	0.5	5
JASON PARKER	4	20	0	0.4	15
SHANE BEGNAUD	2	30	0	0.2	28
SHAWN SUMMERS	1	24	0	0.1	24

Returning Players in All Capitals

DeRon Jenkins    **Scott Galyon**    **James Stewart**

1993 Tennessee Team Statistics

	UT	OPP
FIRST DOWNS	258	186
Rushing	137	84
Passing	114	88
Penalty	7	14
NET YARDS RUSHING	2621	1290
Yards rushing	2775	1727
Yards lost	154	437
Rushing attempts	442	433
Average per rush	5.9	3.0
Average per game	238.3	117.3
NET YARDS PASSING	2665	2105
Average per game	242.3	191.4
Passes attempted	320	347
Passes completed	208	167
Had intercepted	9	18
TOTAL OFFENSIVE YARDS	5286	3395
Average per game	480.5	308.6
Total plays	762	780
Average per play	6.9	4.4
NUMBER PUNTS/YARDS	42/1646	67/2604
Punting average	39.2	38.9
Net punting average	37.4	32.1
PUNT RETURNS/YARDS	37/453	18/77
Punt return average	12.2	4.3
KICKOFF RETURNS/YARDS	28/661	59/1222
Kickoff return average	23.6	20.7
PENALTIES/YARDS	73/624	65/516
Penalty yards per game	56.7	46.9
FUMBLES/LOST	17/11	32/15
INTERCEPTION RETURNS/YARDS	18/138	9/36
Int. return average	7.6	4.0
TOUCHDOWNS	62	16
Rushing	27	8
Passing	31	7
Return	2	1
Others	2	0
FIELD GOALS MADE/ATTEMPTED	12/13	11/15
SAFETY	1	0
TWO-POINTS CONVERSIONS	1/3	1/2
TOTAL POINTS	471	144
Average per game	42.8	13.1

1993 Tennessee Results

9-2-1 Overall • 6-1-1 SEC (2nd - Eastern)

Date	Opponent		Score	Attendance
Sept. 4	LOUISIANA TECH	W	50-0	95,106
Sept. 11	GEORGIA [ESPN]	W	38-6	96,228
Sept. 18	at Florida [ABC]	L	34-41	85,247
Sept. 25	LSU [JP]	W	42-20	95,931
Oct. 2	DUKE - HC	W	52-19	96,173
Oct. 9	at Arkansas [JP]	W	28-14	54,120
Oct. 16	at Alabama [ABC]	T	17-17	83,091
Oct. 30	SOUTH CAROLINA [JP]	W	55-3	94,791
Nov. 6	LOUISVILLE [ABC]	W	45-10	94,826
Nov. 20	at Kentucky [ESPN]	W	48-0	57,878
Nov. 27	VANDERBILT [JP]	W	62-14	94,225
Jan. 1	Penn State [ABC]	L	13-31	72,456
	(CompUSA Florida Cirtus Bowl)			

1994 SEC Football

Phillip Fulmer

Year-By-Year Record

Year	School	Conf.	All	Bowl
1992	Tennessee	2-0	4-0	Hall of Fame
1993	Tennessee	6-1-1	9-2-1	Citrus
OVERALL RECORD		8-1-1 (.850)	13-2-1 (.844)	2 Years
Tennessee Record		8-1-1 (.850)	13-2-1 (.844)	2 Years
Bowl Record		1-1	(1-1 Tennessee)	

HOMETOWN:
Winchester, Tennessee

ALMA MATER:
Tennessee (1972)

PLAYING CAREER:
Tennessee offensive guard 1969-71; Alternate captain of 1971 Volunteer squad which posted a 10-2 mark and a Liberty Bowl victory.

COACHING CAREER:
Tennessee Assistant 1972-73; Wichita State Assistant 1974-78; Vanderbilt Assistant 1979; Tennessee Assistant 1980-92; Tennessee Interim Head Coach (four games) 1992; Tennessee Head Coach 1993-present.

BORN:
September 1, 1950

WIFE:
Vicky Morey

CHILDREN:
Phillip Jr. 24, Courtney Lorna 11, Brittany 9, Allison 7

ASSISTANT COACHES:
KIPPY BROWN (Memphis State 1977) - Assistant Head Coach/Receivers
DAVID CUTLIFFE (Alabama 1976) - Offensive Coordinator/Quarterbacks
LARRY MARMIE (Eastern Kentucky 1965) - Defensive Coordinator
MARK BRADLEY (Samford 1969) - Tight Ends
DAN BROOKS (Western Carolina 1976) - Defensive Line
JOHNNY CHAVIS (Tennessee 1979) - Linebackers
STEVE MARSHALL (Louisville 1980) - Offensive Line
RANDY SANDERS (Tennessee 1987) - Running Backs, Recruiting Coordinator
LOVIE SMITH (Tulsa 1979) - Defensive Backs.

SUPPORT STAFF:
MIKE ROLLO (Tennessee 1977) - Trainer
GARY WYANT (Wichita State 1962) - Assistant Athletic Director (Football Operations)
JOHN STUCKY (Kansas State 1970) - Director of Athletic Fitness

Tennessee

Tennessee All-Star Candidates

JOHN BECKSVOORT
Senior • Placekicker
6-1 • 177
Chattanooga, Tenn.

• Named first team All-America by Scripps-Howard and Football Writers, a Lou Groza Award finalist, first team All-SEC by Associated Press and the *Birmingham News* and AT&T Long Distance Award winner in 1993.
• Made 12 of 13 field goals and 59 of 59 extra points as the SEC's leading scorer in 1993 with 95 points.
• Has made 122 straight PATs during his career, which ranks as the second longest streak in SEC history.
• Holds school and SEC record for most PAT kicks attempted and made in a season with 59 in 1993.

BECKSVOORT STATS

Year	FGM	FGA	Pct	Long	PAT	Pct	Pts	Avg
1991	15	21	.714	44	28/28	1.000	73	9.1
1992	16	23	.696	53	35/35	1.000	83	7.5
1993	12	13	.923	51	59/59	1.000	95	8.6
Career	43	57	.754	53	122/122	1.000	251	8.4

BEN TALLEY
Senior • Linebacker
6-3 • 239
Griffin, Ga.

• A defensive mainstay at linebacker who started every contest and was named second team All-SEC last season.
• Led the team in total hits for the second straight season with 87, including 56 primary stops and 31 assists.
• Finished second on the squad in Big Plays with 17, including seven tackles for loss, four sacks, three passes broken up, two fumble recoveries and a caused fumble.
• Tied for sixth in the SEC in tackles among defensive ends and outside linebackers.

TALLEY STATS

Year	Tackles	Sks(Yds)	TFL(Yds)	Int	PBU	FC
1991	9 (4-5)	0	2 (-4)	0	0	0
1992	85 (53-32)	1 (-8)	8 (-27)	2	3	3
1993	87 (56-31)	4 (-47)	7 (-20)	0	3	1
Career	181 (113-68)	5 (-56)	17 (-51)	2	6	4

JASON PARKER
Junior • Safety
6-0 • 192
Garland, Texas

• Named second team All-SEC last season.
• Snared four interceptions and had three pass break ups as the designated quarterback of the Volunteer secondary.
• Finished third on the team in tackles with 61 (43 solo) and registered 11 Big Plays, including one caused fumble, two fumble recoveries and two tackles for loss.
• A two-year starter who manned the free safety position in every game last season and 10 games as a true freshman.

PARKER STATS

Year	Tackles	TFL(Yds)	Int-Yds	PBU	FC	FR
1992	59 (38-21)	2 (-6)	4-55	2	0	2
1993	61 (43-18)	2 (-5)	4-20	3	1	2
Career	120 (81-39)	4 (-11)	8-75	5	1	4

JEFF SMITH
Junior • Offensive Guard
6-3 • 310
Decatur, Tenn.

• Tabbed first team All-SEC by AP and Coaches, third team All-America by AP and sophomore All-America by *Football News*.
• A two-year starter who has shown his versatility over his career by playing both guard spots and center.
• Key figure in UT's offensive line, allowing the Vols to lead the SEC in rushing at 238.2 yards per game and rank 13th nationally.
• SEC Academic Honor Roll performer last season, he helped create line surges that allowed UT offense to generate eight 100-plus yards rushers on the year.

1994 SEC Football

1994 Tennessee Roster

No.	Name	Pos.	Ht.	Wt.	Class	Exp.	Hometown (High School/JC)
58	Brandon Ashley	DE	6-3	261	Fr.	SQ	Dallas, Texas (Carter)
28	Raymond Austin	DB	5-11	181	So.	1L	Lawton, Okla. (Eisenshower)
10	John Becksvoort	PK	6-1	177	Sr.	3L	Chattanooga, Tenn. (Red Bank)
26	Shane Begnaud	DB	6-1	186	So.	1L	Lafayette, La. (Northside)
31	Jim Bencik	WR	5-9	172	So.	SQ	Rochester, Mich. (Adams)
94	Billy Beron	DT	6-3	271	Fr.	SQ	River Ridge, La. (Arch. Rummel)
84	Shane Burton	DE	6-5	272	Jr.	2L	Catawba, N.C. (Bandys)
97	Ryan Collins	LB	6-4	228	Fr.	SQ	New Market, Tenn. (Jefferson Co.)
14	Jerry Colquitt	QB	6-4	208	Sr.	3L	Oak Ridge, Tenn. (Oak Ridge)
1	Ronald Davis	DB	5-11	197	Sr.	3L	Bartlett, Tenn. (Bartlett)
50	Bill Duff	DE/DT	6-3	262	Fr.	SQ	Delran, N.J. (Delran)
36	Tory Edge	DB	5-9	181	Fr.	SQ	Hampton, Va. (Phoebus)
46	John Emery	DE	6-2	253	So.	1L	Norco, La. (Destrehan)
88	Cortney Epps	WR	6-0	190	Fr.	SQ	Dallas, Texas (Carter)
20	Chester Ford	RB	5-11	250	So.	SQ	Danville, Ky. (Danville)
93	Scott Galyon	LB	6-2	232	Jr.	2L	Seymour, Tenn. (Seymour)
51	Brent Gibson	C	6-4	282	So.	1L	Canton, N.C. (Pisgah)
25	Jay Graham	RB	6-0	206	So.	1L	Kannapolis, N.C. (Concord)
53	Mark Graves	C	6-3	269	So.	SQ	Marietta, Ga. (Sprayberry)
8	Mike Grein	QB	6-1	180	Fr.	SQ	Houston, Texas (Nimitz)
24	Aaron Hayden	RB	6-0	214	Sr.	3L	Detroit, Mich. (Mumford)
2	Todd Helton	QB	6-3	194	Jr.	1L	Knoxville, Tenn. (Central)
47	Tyrone Hines	LB	6-2	231	So.	SQ	Brownsville, Tenn. (Haywood Co.)
52	Mark Holland	C	6-3	244	Sr.	2L	Sale Creek, Tenn. (Rhea Co.)
82	David Horn	TE	6-4	248	Jr.	2L	Jonesboro, Ga. (Riverdale)
77	Richard Howard	OG	6-6	313	So.	SQ	Oak Ridge, Tenn. (Oak Ridge)
43	Tom Hutton	P	6-1	195	Sr.	3L	Memphis, Tenn. (Memphis Univ.)
18	DeRon Jenkins	DB	5-11	167	Jr.	2L	St. Louis, Mo. (Ritenour)
45	Nick Jester	LB	6-0	208	Jr.	2L	Delray Beach, Fla. (Atlantic)
38	Greg Johnson	DB	6-0	194	So.	1L	Nashville, Tenn. (Franklin Road Academy)
27	Kendrick Jones	WR	5-8	189	Sr.	3L	Collierville, Tenn. (Collierville)
11	Joey Kent	WR	6-1	184	So.	1L	Huntsville, Ala. (Johnson)
37	Neal Kerney	RB	5-11	205	Sr.	SQ	Kingsport, Tenn. (Sullivan South)
42	George Kidd	LB	6-1	223	Jr.	2L	Milan, Tenn. (Milan)
29	Brent Kilpatrick	WR	6-1	180	Sr.	SQ	Greenback, Tenn. (Greenback)
79	Brad Lampley	OG	6-5	256	Fr.	SQ	Louisville, Ky. (Trinity)
5	Eric Lane	RB	6-0	212	So.	1L	Chestnut Ridge, N.Y. (Bergen Catholic)
66	Jason Layman	OT	6-5	287	Jr.	2L	Sevierville, Tenn. (Sevier Co.)
67	Kevin Mays	OG	6-4	284	Sr.	3L	Kingston, Tenn. (Roane Co.)
71	Bubba Miller	C	6-1	285	Jr.	2L	Franklin, Tenn. (Brentwood Academy)
60	Ralph Nelson	OG	6-0	288	So.	1L	Kingsport, Tenn. (Sullivan South)
9	Tori Noel	DB	6-0	182	So.	1L	Memphis, Tenn. (Melrose)
7	Jason Parker	DB	6-0	192	Jr.	2L	Garland, Texas (North Garland)
73	Trey Peterson	OG	6-3	270	Jr.	1L	New Smyrna Beach, Fla. (New Smyrna Beach)
89	Scott Pfeiffer	TE	6-4	260	So.	1L	St. Louis, Mo. (St. Louis Univ.)
19	Mose Phillips	RB	6-0	221	Sr.	3L	Nashville, Tenn. (Hillsboro)
3	Ronnie Pillow	RB	6-0	195	Fr.	SQ	Columbia, Tenn. (Central)
59	Sam Pinner	OT	6-4	270	Fr.	SQ	Memphis, Tenn. (Bolton)
65	Robert Poole	OG	6-3	304	Fr.	SQ	Birmingham, Ala. (Ensley)
17	Quincy Prigmore	LB	6-1	231	Jr.	2L	Cleveland, Tenn. (Cleveland)
75	Leslie Ratliffe	OT	6-7	302	Jr.	2L	Newport, Ark. (Newport)
68	Patrick Rhodes	OT	6-2	285	So.	SQ	Rocky Face, Ga. (Dalton)
95	Tony Robinson	DE	6-6	243	Fr.	SQ	Memphis, Tenn. (Coffeyville CC)
22	Jesse Sanders	LB	5-11	222	Jr.	2L	Sebring, Fla. (Sebring)
87	John Sartelle	TE	6-4	241	So.	1L	Memphis, Tenn. (Memphis Univ.)
13	Scott Sexton	WR	5-9	173	Sr.	SQ	Knoxville, Tenn. (Carter)
81	Benjie Shuler	WR	6-2	175	So.	1L	Bryson City, N.C. (Swain Co.)
83	Nilo Silvan	WR	5-9	176	Jr.	1L	Covington, La. (St. Paul)
74	Jeff Smith	OG	6-3	310	Jr.	2L	Decatur, Tenn. (Meigs Co.)
33	James Stewart	RB	6-1	218	Sr.	3L	Morristown, Tenn. (West)
98	Cory Stone	DT	6-2	275	Sr.	1L	Memphis, Tenn. (Central)
23	Shawn Summers	DB	5-8	188	Jr.	2L	Oak Ridge, Tenn. (Oak Ridge)
39	Brad Symonds	DB	6-0	188	Sr.	SQ	S. Windsor, Conn. (Windsor)
90	Ben Talley	LB	6-3	239	Sr.	3L	Griffin, Ga. (Griffin)
57	Leland Taylor	DT	6-3	285	So.	1L	Louisville, Ky. (Fairdale)
70	Trey Teague	DT	6-5	281	Fr.	SQ	Jackson, Tenn. (University)
76	Mark Upton	OT	6-3	270	So.	1L	Soddy-Daisy, Tenn. (Soddy-Daisy)
15	Lance Wheaton	QB	5-11	199	Sr.	2L	Kingston, Tenn. (Midway)
64	Steve White	DE	6-2	256	Jr.	2L	Memphis, Tenn. (Westwood)
80	Billy Williams	WR	5-11	174	Sr.	1L	Alcoa, Tenn. (Alcoa)
86	Todd Williams	TE	6-4	234	Sr.	SQ	Dallas, Texas (Highland Park)

Numerical Roster

No.	Name	Pos.
1	Ronald Davis	DB
2	Todd Helton	QB
3	Ronnie Pillow	RB
5	Eric Lane	RB
7	Jason Parker	DB
8	Mike Grein	QB
9	Tori Noel	DB
10	John Becksvoort	PK
11	Joey Kent	WR
13	Scott Sexton	WR
14	Jerry Colquitt	QB
15	Lance Wheaton	QB
17	Quincy Prigmore	LB
18	DeRon Jenkins	DB
19	Mose Phillips	RB
20	Chester Ford	RB
22	Jesse Sanders	LB
23	Shawn Summers	DB
24	Aaron Hayden	RB
25	Jay Graham	RB
26	Shane Begnaud	DB
27	Kendrick Jones	WR
28	Raymond Austin	DB
29	Brent Kilpatrick	WR
31	Jim Bencik	WR
33	James Stewart	RB
36	Tory Edge	DB
37	Neal Kerney	RB
38	Greg Johnson	DB
39	Brad Symonds	DB
42	George Kidd	LB
43	Tom Hutton	P
45	Nick Jester	LB
46	John Emery	DE
47	Tyrone Hines	LB
50	Bill Duff	DE/DT
51	Brent Gibson	C
52	Mark Holland	C
53	Mark Graves	C
57	Leland Taylor	DT
58	Brandon Ashley	DE
59	Sam Pinner	OT
60	Ralph Nelson	OG
64	Steve White	DE
65	Robert Poole	OG
66	Jason Layman	OT
67	Kevin Mays	OG
68	Patrick Rhodes	OT
70	Trey Teague	DT
71	Bubba Miller	C
73	Trey Peterson	OG
74	Jeff Smith	OG
75	Leslie Ratliffe	OT
76	Mark Upton	OT
77	Richard Howard	OG
79	Brad Lampley	OG
80	Billy Williams	WR
81	Benjie Shuler	WR
82	David Horn	TE
83	Nilo Silvan	WR
84	Shane Burton	DE
86	Todd Williams	TE
87	John Sartelle	TE
88	Cortney Epps	WR
89	Scott Pfeiffer	TE
90	Ben Talley	LB
93	Scott Galyon	LB
94	Billy Beron	DT
95	Tony Robinson	DE
97	Ryan Collins	LB
98	Cory Stone	DT

148 Tennessee

1994 Tennessee Depth Chart

OFFENSE

TE:	82	DAVID HORN
	89	Scott Pfeiffer
LT:	66	JASON LAYMAN
	76	Mark Upton
LG:	67	KEVIN MAYS
	73	Trey Peterson
C:	71	BUBBA MILLER
	51	Brent Gibson
RG:	74	JEFF SMITH
	65	Robert Poole
RT:	75	LESLIE RATLIFFE
	65	Robert Poole
FLK:	80	Billy Williams
	83	Nilo Silvan
SE:	11	Joey Kent
	81	Benjie Shuler
QB:	14	Jerry Colquitt
	2	Todd Helton
TB:	33	James Stewart
	24	Aaron Hayden
FB:	19	MOSE PHILLIPS
	5	Eric Lane

DEFENSE

LE:	84	Shane Burton
	95	Tony Robinson
LT:	98	Cory Stone
	70	Trey Teague
RT:	57	Leland Taylor
	94	Billy Beron
RE:	64	Steve White
	46	John Emery
LLB:	42	George Kidd
	22	Jesse Sanders
MLB:	93	SCOTT GALYON
	47	Tyrone Hines
RLB:	90	BEN TALLEY
	45	Nick Jester
LCB:	18	DeRON JENKINS
	23	Shawn Summers
RCB:	1	RONALD DAVIS
	36	Tory Edge
SS:	28	Raymond Austin
	9	Tori Noel
FS:	7	JASON PARKER
	26	Shane Begnaud

SPECIALISTS

PK:	10	JOHN BECKSVOORT
P:	43	TOM HUTTON

Returning Starters In All Capitals

1994 Tennessee Signees

Name	Pos.	Ht.	Wt.	Hometown/High School
Jonathan Brown	L	6-5	245	Tulsa, Okla./Booker T. Washington
Jeff Coleman	L	6-4	237	Gaffney, S.C./Gaffney
Terry Fair	B	5-11	175	Phoenix, Ariz./S. Mountain
Cory Gaines	B	5-11	185	Baton Rouge, La./Catholic
Ron Green	L	6-3	265	Severna Park, Md./Severna Park
Jeff Hall	PK	6-0	182	Winchester/Franklin Co.
Mercedes Hamilton	L	6-4	280	Waynesboro, Ga./Fork Union (Va.) Acad.
Anthony Hampton	B	6-5	210	Englewood, N.J./Dwight Morrow
Steve Johnson	B	5-11	175	Powder Springs, Ga./McEachern
Craig Kyler	B	6-1	185	Baltimore, Md./Balitmore Polytechnic
Mark Levine	B	6-0	185	Dallas, Texas/Skyline
Peyton Manning	QB	6-5	200	New Orleans, La./Isidore Newman
Andy McCullough	B	6-4	210	Dayton, Ohio/Meadowlake
Dustin Moore	B	6-3	220	Greeneville, Tenn./Greeneville
Marcus Nash	B	6-3	190	Tulsa, Okla./Edmond Memorial
Will Newman	L	6-5	295	New Market, Tenn./Jefferson Co.
Jarvis Reado	L	6-6	290	Marrero, La./Archbishop Shaw
Diron Robinson	L	6-4	250	Oklahoma City, Okla./Midwest City
James Smith	B	6-0	180	Bylthe, Calif./Arizona West. College
Maurice Staley	B	6-1	195	Charlotte, N.C./West Charlotte
Branndon Stewart	QB	6-2	210	Stephenville, Texas/Stephenville

Bubba Miller

Billy Williams

1994 SEC Football

Tennessee Year-By-Year Records

Year	Coach	SEC	SEC Finish	Overall	Bowls
1891	None			0-1-0	
1892	None			2-5-0	
1893	None			2-4-0	
1894	No Team				
1895	No Team				
1896	None			4-0-0	
1897	None			4-1-0	
1898	No Team				
1899	J.A. Pierce			5-2-0	
1900	J.A. Pierce			3-2-1	
1901	George Kelley			3-3-2	
1902	H.F. Fisher			6-2-0	
1903	H.F. Fisher			4-5-0	
1904	S.D. Crawford			3-5-1	
1905	J.D. DePree			3-5-1	
1906	J.D. DePree/Roscoe Ward			1-6-2	
1907	George Levene			7-2-1	
1908	George Levene			7-2-0	
1909	George Levene			1-6-2	
1910	Alex Stone			3-5-1	
1911	Z.G. Clevenger			3-4-2	
1912	Z.G. Clevenger			4-4-0	
1913	Z.G. Clevenger			6-3-0	
1914	Z.G. Clevenger			9-0-0	
1915	Z.G. Clevenger			4-4-0	
1916	John R. Bender			8-0-1	
1917	No Team				
1918	No Team				
1919	John R. Bender			3-3-3	
1920	John R. Bender			7-2-0	
1921	M.B. Banks			6-2-1	
1922	M.B. Banks			8-2-0	
1923	M.B. Banks			5-4-1	
1924	M.B. Banks			3-5-0	
1925	M.B. Banks			5-2-1	
1926	Bob Neyland			8-1-0	
1927	Bob Neyland			8-0-1	
1928	Bob Neyland			9-0-1	
1929	Bob Neyland			9-0-1	
1930	Bob Neyland			9-1-0	
1931	Bob Neyland			9-0-1	New York
1932	Bob Neyland			9-0-1	
1933	Bob Neyland	5-2-0	4	7-3-0	—
1934	Bob Neyland	5-1-0	3	8-2-0	—
1935	W.H. Britton	2-3-0	9t	4-5-0	—
1936	Bob Neyland	3-1-2	4	6-2-2	—
1937	Bob Neyland	4-3-0	7	6-3-1	—
1938	Bob Neyland	7-0-0	1	11-0-0	Orange
1939	Bob Neyland	6-0-0	1t	10-1-0	Rose
1940	Bob Neyland	5-0-0	1	10-1-0	Sugar
1941	John Barnhill	3-1-0	2	8-2-0	—
1942	John Barnhill	4-1-0	2t	9-1-1	Sugar
1943	NO TEAM				
1944	John Barnhill	5-0-1	2	7-1-1	Rose
1945	John Barnhill	3-1-0	2	8-1-0	—
1946	Bob Neyland	5-0-0	1t	9-2-0	Orange
1947	Bob Neyland	2-3-0	9t	5-5-0	—
1948	Bob Neyland	2-3-1	8	4-4-2	—
1949	Bob Neyland	4-1-1	3	7-2-1	—
1950	Bob Neyland	4-1-0	2	11-1-0	Cotton
1951	Bob Neyland	5-0-0	1t	10-1-0	Sugar
1952	Bob Neyland	5-0-1	2	8-2-1	Cotton
1953	Harvey Robinson	3-2-1	7	6-4-1	—
1954	Harvey Robinson	1-5-0	11t	4-6-0	—
1955	Bowden Wyatt	3-2-1	4	6-3-1	—
1956	Bowden Wyatt	6-0-0	1	10-1-0	Sugar
1957	Bowden Wyatt	4-3-0	5	8-3-0	Gator
1958	Bowden Wyatt	4-3-0	5	4-6-0	—
1959	Bowden Wyatt	3-4-1	8	5-4-1	—
1960	Bowden Wyatt	3-2-2	5	6-2-2	—
1961	Bowden Wyatt	4-3-0	4t	6-4-0	—
1962	Bowden Wyatt	2-6-0	10	4-6-0	—
1963	Jim McDonald	3-5-0	8	5-5-0	—
1964	Doug Dickey	1-5-1	10	4-5-1	—
1965	Doug Dickey	3-1-2	3t	8-1-2	Bluebonnet
1966	Doug Dickey	4-2-0	5	8-3-0	Gator
1967	Doug Dickey	6-0-0	1	9-2-0	Orange
1968	Doug Dickey	4-1-1	2	8-2-1	Cotton
1969	Doug Dickey	5-1-0	1	9-2-0	Gator
1970	Bill Battle	4-1-0	2	11-1-0	Sugar
1971	Bill Battle	4-2-0	4t	10-2-0	Liberty
1972	Bill Battle	4-2-0	4	10-2-0	Bluebonnet
1973	Bill Battle	3-3-0	4	8-4-0	Gator
1974	Bill Battle	2-3-1	7t	7-3-2	Liberty
1975	Bill Battle	3-3-0	5	7-5-0	—
1976	Bill Battle	2-4-0	8	6-5-0	—
1977	Johnny Majors	1-5-0	8	4-7-0	—
1978	Johnny Majors	3-3-0	4t	5-5-1	—
1979	Johnny Majors	3-3-0	5t	7-5-0	Bluebonnet
1980	Johnny Majors	3-3-0	6	5-6-0	—
1981	Johnny Majors	3-3-0	4t	8-4-0	Garden State
1982	Johnny Majors	3-2-1	5	6-5-1	Peach
1983	Johnny Majors	4-2-0	3t	9-3-0	Citrus
1984	Johnny Majors	3-3-0	5t	7-4-1	Sun
1985	Johnny Majors	5-1-0	1	9-1-2	Sugar
1986	Johnny Majors	3-3-0	6	7-5-0	Liberty
1987	Johnny Majors	4-1-1	3	10-2-1	Peach
1988	Johnny Majors	3-4-0	6t	5-6-0	—
1989	Johnny Majors	6-1-0	1t	11-1-0	Cotton
1990	Johnny Majors	5-1-1	1	9-2-2	Sugar
1991	Johnny Majors	5-2-0	3	9-3-0	Fiesta
1992	Johnny Majors/Phillip Fulmer	5-3-0	3-E	9-3-0	Hall of Fame
1993	Phillip Fulmer	6-1-1	2-E	9-2-1	Citrus

Bowl Results (18-16)

Bowl	Opponent	Result	Date
*New York	New York University	W 13-0	12-5-31
Orange	Oklahoma	W 17-0	1-1-39
Rose	Southern Cal	L 0-14	1-1-40
Sugar	Boston College	L 13-19	1-1-41
Sugar	Tulsa	W 14-7	1-1-43
Rose	Southern Cal	L 0-25	1-1-45
Orange	Rice	L 0-8	1-1-47
Cotton	Texas	W 20-14	1-1-51
Sugar	Maryland	L 13-28	1-1-52
Cotton	Texas	L 0-16	1-1-53
Sugar	Baylor	L 7-13	1-1-57
Gator	Texas A&M	W 3-0	12-28-57
Bluebonnet	Tulsa	W 27-6	12-18-65
Gator	Syracuse	W 18-12	12-31-66
Orange	Oklahoma	L 24-26	1-1-68
Cotton	Texas	L 13-36	1-1-69
Gator	Florida	L 13-14	12-27-69
Sugar	Air Force	W 34-13	1-1-71
Liberty	Arkansas	W 14-13	12-20-71
Bluebonnet	LSU	W 24-17	12-30-72
Gator	Texas Tech	L 19-28	12-29-73
Liberty	Maryland	W 7-3	12-16-74
Bluebonnet	Purdue	L 22-27	12-31-79
Garden State	Wisconsin	W 28-21	12-13-81
Peach	Iowa	L 22-28	12-31-82
Citrus	Maryland	W 30-23	12-17-83
Sun	Maryland	L 27-28	12-22-84
Sugar	Miami-Florida	W 35-7	1-1-86
Liberty	Minnesota	W 21-14	12-29-86
Peach	Indiana	W 27-22	1-2-88
Cotton	Arkansas	W 31-27	1-1-90
Sugar	Virginia	W 23-22	1-1-91
Fiesta	Penn State	L 17-42	1-1-92
Hall of Fame	Boston College	W 38-23	1-1-93
Citrus	Penn State	L 13-31	1-1-94

*not recognized by NCAA

Tennessee vs. All Opponents

Opponent	W	L	T
Air Force	1	0	0
Akron	1	0	0
Alabama	27	41	8
American University	2	0	1
Arkansas	4	1	0
Army	5	2	1
Athens	1	0	0
Auburn	18	22	3
Baylor	0	1	0
Boston College	8	2	0
California	1	1	0
Cal-Santa Barbara	1	0	0
Carson-Newman	12	0	0
Central University	1	0	0
Centre	10	3	2
Cincinnati	4	1	0
Citadel	3	0	0
Clemson	11	5	2
Colorado	0	0	1
Colorado State	4	0	0
Cumberland	1	0	0
Dartmouth	0	1	0
Davidson	1	0	0
Dayton	4	0	0
Duke	13	13	2
Emory & Henry	5	0	0
Florida	15	8	0
Florida State	0	1	0
Fordham	1	1	0
Furman	2	0	0
George Washington	1	0	0
Georgetown	3	0	0
Georgia	11	10	2
Georgia Tech	24	17	2
Hawaii	2	0	0
Houston	1	1	0
Howard	2	0	0
Indiana	1	0	0
Iowa	1	1	0
Iowa State	1	0	0
Kansas	2	0	0
Kentucky	57	23	9
LSU	18	3	3
Louisiana Tech	1	0	0
Louisville	5	0	0
Maryland	5	2	0
Maryville	25	1	1
Memphis State	14	0	0
Mercer	2	1	0
Miami (Fla.)	1	0	0
Minnesota	1	0	0
Mississippi	39	18	1
Mississippi State	22	14	1
Nashville	2	1	1
New Mexico	2	0	0
New York University	1	0	0
North Carolina	20	10	1
North Carolina State	1	1	0
North Texas State	0	1	0
Notre Dame	2	2	0
Oklahoma	1	1	0
Oregon State	1	0	1
Pacific	1	0	0
Penn State	2	2	0
Pittsburgh	0	2	0
Purdue	0	1	0
Rice	2	1	0
Richmond	1	0	0
Rutgers	2	1	0
Sewanee	12	10	0
South Carolina	8	2	2
Southern Cal	0	4	0

Opponent	W	L	T
Southern Methodist	1	0	0
Southern Mississippi	1	0	0
Southwestern	3	0	0
Southern Louisiana	1	0	0
Syracuse	1	0	0
Tampa	2	0	0
Temple	2	0	0
Tennessee-Chattanooga	36	2	2
Tennessee Tech	5	0	0
Texas	1	2	0
Texas A&M	1	0	0
Texas Christian	2	0	0
Texas El Paso	2	0	0
Texas Tech	0	1	0
Transylvania	4	1	0
Tulane	4	1	0
Tulsa	5	0	0
Tusculum	3	0	0
UCLA	5	3	2
Utah	3	0	0
Vanderbilt	56	26	5
Villanova	1	0	0
Virginia	3	1	0
Virginia Military	0	1	0
Virginia Tech	4	2	0
Wake Forest	6	3	0
Washington & Lee	5	0	0
Washington State	3	1	0
Wichita State	1	0	0
William & Mary	1	0	0
Williamsburg	2	0	0
Wisconsin	1	0	0
Wofford	1	0	0

General Robert R. Neyland (kneeling right) guided Tennessee to a 173-31-12 record (1926-34, 36-40, 46-52), including the 1951 National Championship and five SEC titles.

1994 SEC Football

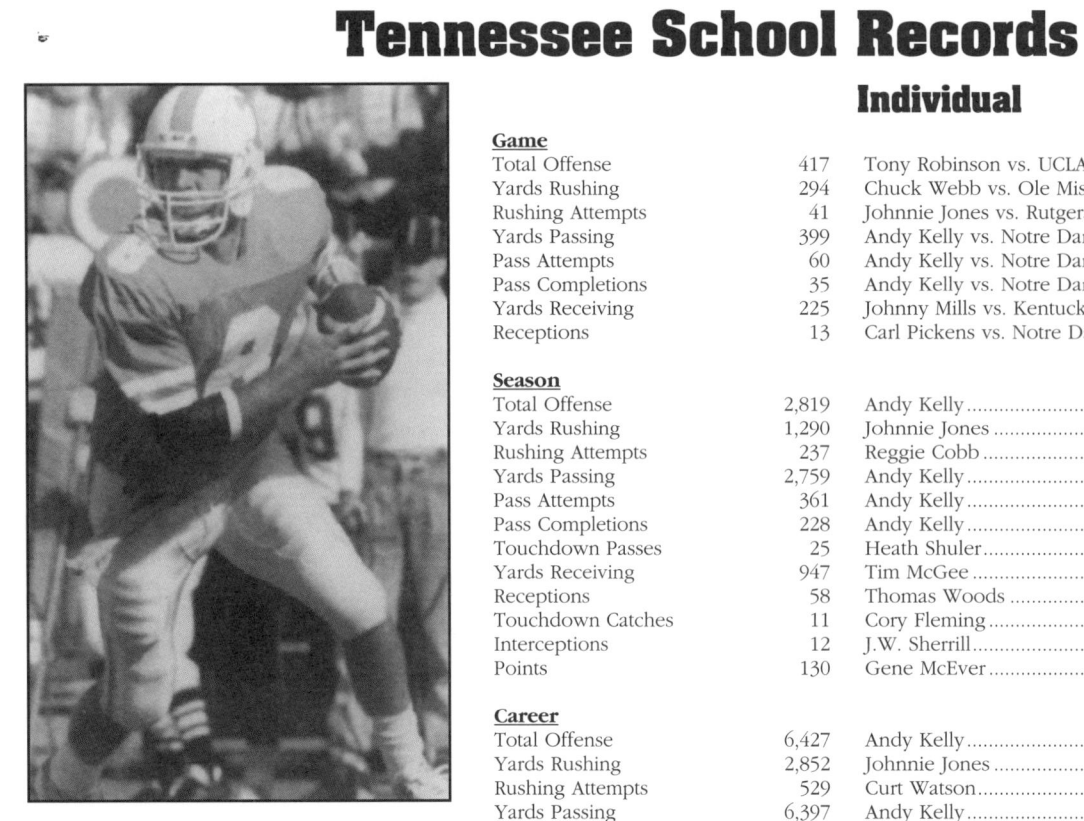

Tennessee School Records

Individual

Game
Total Offense	417	Tony Robinson vs. UCLA	(1985)
Yards Rushing	294	Chuck Webb vs. Ole Miss	(1989)
Rushing Attempts	41	Johnnie Jones vs. Rutgers	(1983)
Yards Passing	399	Andy Kelly vs. Notre Dame	(1990)
Pass Attempts	60	Andy Kelly vs. Notre Dame	(1990)
Pass Completions	35	Andy Kelly vs. Notre Dame	(1990)
Yards Receiving	225	Johnny Mills vs. Kentucky	(1975)
Receptions	13	Carl Pickens vs. Notre Dame	(1990)

Season
Total Offense	2,819	Andy Kelly	(1991)
Yards Rushing	1,290	Johnnie Jones	(1984)
Rushing Attempts	237	Reggie Cobb	(1987)
Yards Passing	2,759	Andy Kelly	(1991)
Pass Attempts	361	Andy Kelly	(1991)
Pass Completions	228	Andy Kelly	(1991)
Touchdown Passes	25	Heath Shuler	(1993)
Yards Receiving	947	Tim McGee	(1985)
Receptions	58	Thomas Woods	(1988)
Touchdown Catches	11	Cory Fleming	(1993)
Interceptions	12	J.W. Sherrill	(1949)
Points	130	Gene McEver	(1929)

Career
Total Offense	6,427	Andy Kelly	(1988-91)
Yards Rushing	2,852	Johnnie Jones	(1981-84)
Rushing Attempts	529	Curt Watson	(1969-71)
Yards Passing	6,397	Andy Kelly	(1988-91)
Pass Attempts	846	Andy Kelly	(1988-91)
Pass Completions	514	Andy Kelly	(1988-91)
Touchdown Passes	36	Andy Kelly	(1988-91)
	36	Heath Shuler	(1991-93)
Yards Receiving	2,042	Tim McGee	(1982-85)
Receptions	124	Thomas Woods	(1986-89)
Touchdown Catches	18	Cory Fleming	(1990-93)
Interceptions	18	Tim Priest	(1968-70)
Points	314	Fuad Reveiz	(1981-84)

Team

Game
Points	68	vs. Tennessee Tech	(1951)
Total Offense	606	vs. Vanderbilt	(1991)
Yards Rushing	513	vs. Washington & Lee	(1951)
Yards Passing	399	vs. Notre Dame	(1990)
First Downs	32	vs. UCLA	(1968)
		vs. Memphis State	(1991)
		vs. Vanderbilt	(1991)
Total Defense	13	vs. Vanderbilt	(1952)
Rushing Defense	-9	vs. Wofford	(1952)
Passing Defense	-3	vs. Kentucky	(1946)

Season
Points	471	(1993)
Total Offense	5,285	(1993)
Yards Rushing	3,068	(1951)
Yards Passing	2,813	(1991)
First Downs	266	(1991)
Fewest Points Allowed	0	(1939)
Total Defense	1,023	(1939)
Rushing Defense	385	(1945)
Passing Defense	392	(1939)
Consecutive Wins	23	(November 25, 1937 to December 9, 1939)

Andy Kelly

Cory Fleming

152 Tennessee

Tennessee in the NFL

Greg Amsler, RB
Phoenix Cardinals 1991; New York Giants 1992
Bill Anderson, E
Washington Redskins 1958-63; Green Bay Packers 1965-66
Pete Athas, CB
New York Giants 1971-75; Minnesota Vikings 1975; Cleveland Browns 1975; New Orleans Saints 1976
Doug Atkins, DE
Cleveland Browns 1953-54; Chicago Bears 1955-66; New Orleans Saints 1967-69
Howard (Screeno) Bailey, T
Philadelphia Eagles 1935
Sam Bartholomew, B
Philadelphia Eagles 1941
Bill Bates, DB
Dallas Cowboys 1983-93
Ed Beard, LB
San Francisco 49ers 1965-73
John Boynton, T
Miami Dolphins 1969
Art Brandau, C
Pittsburgh Steelers 1945-46
Eddie Brown, S
Cleveland Browns 1974-75; Washington Redskins 1975-77; Los Angeles Rams 1978-79
John Bruhin, G
Tampa Bay Buccaneers 1988-91; Philadelphia Eagles 1992
Johnny Butler, B
Philadelphia Eagles 1943, 1945; Pittsburgh Steelers 1943-44; Chicago Cardinals 1944
George Cafego, B
Washington Redskins 1943
Whit Canale, DE
Miami Dolphins 1966; Boston Patriots 1968
Dale Carter, DB
Kansas City Chiefs 1992-93
Bob Cifers, B
Detroit Lions 1944-46; Pittsburgh Steelers 1947-48; Green Bay Packers 1949
Ed Cifers, E
Washington Redskins 1941-42, 1946; Chicago Bears 1947-48
Neil Clabo, P
Minnesota Vikings 1975-77
Boyd Clay, T
Cleveland Rams 1940-42, 1944
Joey Clinkscales, WR
Pittsburgh Steelers 1987-88; Tampa Bay Buccaneers 1988
Mike Cofer, DE
Detroit Lions 1983-93
Reggie Cobb, RB
Tampa Bay Buccaneers 1990-93
Craig Colquitt, P
Pittsburgh Steelers 1978-84
Jimmy Colquitt, P
Seattle Seahawks 1985
Richard Cooper, OT
New Orleans Saints 1989-93
Bernard Dafney, OT
Minnesota Vikings 1993
Ted Daffer, E
Chicago Bears 1954
Antone Davis, OT
Philadelphia Eagles 1991-93
Keith DeLong, LB
San Francisco 49ers 1989-93
Steve DeLong, DE
San Diego Chargers 1965-71; Chicago Bears 1972
Jerry DeLucca, G
Philadelphia Eagles 1959; Boston Patriots 1960-61, 63-64; Buffalo Bills 1962-63
Austin Denney, E
Chicago Bears 1967-69; Buffalo Bills 1970-71
Bob Dobelstein, G
New York Giants 1946-48
David Douglas, T
Cincinnati Bengals 1986-88; New England Patriots 1989-90
Clyde Duncan, WR
St. Louis Cardinals, 1984-85
Frank Emanuel, LB
Miami Dolphins 1966-69; New Orleans Saints 1970
Dick Evey, T
Chicago Bears 1964-69; Los Angeles Rams 1970; Detroit Lions 1971

Beattie Feathers, B
Chicago Bears 1934-37; Green Bay Packers 1940
Richmond Flowers, S
Dallas Cowboys 1969-71; New York Giants 1971-73
Jeff Francis, QB
Los Angeles Raiders 1989; Cleveland Browns 1991
Ken Frost, DT
Dallas Cowboys 1961-62
Jim Gaffney, B
Washington Redskins 1945-46
Greg Gaines, LB
Seattle Seahawks 1981-88
Harry Galbreath, OL
Miami Dolphins 1988-92; Green Bay Packers 1993
Willie Gault, WR
Chicago Bears 1983-87; Los Angeles Raiders 1988-93
Glenn Glass, B
Pittsburgh Steelers 1962-63; Philadelphia Eagles 1964-65; Denver Broncos 1966; Atlanta Falcons 1966
Bob Gordon, B
Chicago Cardinals 1958; Houston Oilers 1960
John Gordy, G
Detroit Lions 1957, 1959-67
Sam Graddy, WR
Denver Broncos 1987-88; Los Angeles Raiders 1989-93
Conrad Graham, DB
Chicago Bears 1973
Ray Graves, C
Philadelphia Eagles 1942-43, 1946; Pittsburgh Steelers 1943
Anthony Hancock, WR
Kansas City Chiefs 1982-86
Alvin Harper, WR
Dallas Cowboys 1991-93
Tracy Hayworth, DE
Detroit Lions 1990-93
Herman Hickman, G
Brooklyn Dodgers 1932-34
Jim Hill, B
Detroit Lions 1951-52; Pittsburgh Steelers 1955
Bill Hillman, B
Detroit Lions 1947
Marion Hobby, DE
New England Patriots 1990-92
Joey Howard, OL
San Diego Chargers 1988-90
William Howard, RB
Tampa Bay Buccaneers 1988-89
Frank Hubbell, DE-TE
Los Angeles Rams 1947-49
Dick Huffman, T
Los Angeles Rams 1947-50
George Hunt, K
Baltimore Colts 1973; New York Giants 1975
Al Hust, E
St. Louis Cardinals 1946
Brian Ingram, LB
New England Patriots 1982-86; San Diego Chargers 1987
Tim Irwin, T
Minnesota Vikings 1981-93
Roland James, CB
New England Patriots 1980-90
Bob Johnson, C
Cincinnati Bengals 1968-79
Dale Jones, LB
Dallas Cowboys 1987
Todd Kelly, DE
San Francisco 49ers 1993
Gene Killian, G
Dallas Cowboys 1974
Steve Kiner, LB
Dallas Cowboys 1970; Boston Patriots 1971, 1973; Houston Oilers 1974-78
Steve Knight, G
Baltimore Colts 1987-88
Karl Kremser, K
Miami Dolphins 1969-70
Hank Lauricella, RB
Dallas Texans 1952
Cotton Letner, LB
Buffalo Bills 1961
Paul Lipscomb, T
Green Bay Packers 1945-49; Washington Redskins 1950-54; Chicago Bears 1954

Mike Lucci, LB
Cleveland Browns 1962-64; Detroit Lions 1965-73
Ron McCartney, LB
Atlanta Falcons 1977-79
J.J. McCleskey, WR
New Orleans Saints 1993
Darris McCord, DE
Detroit Lions 1955-67
Terry McDaniel, DB
Los Angeles Raiders 1988-93
Tim McGee, WR
Cincinnati Bengals 1986-92; Washington Redskins 1993
Raleigh McKenzie, G
Washington Redskins 1985-93
Reggie McKenzie, LB
Los Angeles Raiders 1985-88; Phoenix Cardinals 1989-90
Charles McRae, OT
Tampa Bay Buccaneers 1992-93
Bill Majors, DB
Buffalo Bills 1961
Bobby Majors, S
Cleveland Browns 1972
Mickey Marvin, G
Oakland Raiders 1977-81; Los Angeles Raiders 1982-87
Johnny Michels, G
Philadelphia Eagles 1953-56
Anthony Miller, WR
San Diego Chargers 1988-93
Darrin Miller, LB
Seattle Seahawks 1988-89
Mike Miller, P
New York Giants 1983
Chris Mims, DE
San Diego Chargers 1992-93
Stan Mitchell, RB
Miami Dolphins 1966-70
Jeff Moore, WR
Los Angeles Rams 1980-81
Anthony Morgan, WR
Chicago Bears 1992-93
Stanley Morgan, WR
New England Patriots 1977-89; Indianapolis Colts 1990
Randall Morris, RB
Seattle Seahawks 1984-88
Tom Myslinski, OG
Buffalo Bills 1993
Paul Naumoff, LB
Detroit Lions 1967-78
Ed Nickla, E
Chicago Bears 1959
Bob Petrella, S
Miami Dolphins 1966-71
Gordon Polofsky, G
St. Louis Cardinals 1952-54
Carl Pickens, WR
Cincinnati Bengals 1992-93
Steve Poole, LB
New York Jets 1976
Craig Puki, LB
San Francisco 49ers 1980-81
Bert Rechichar, DB
Baltimore Colts 1953-59; Pittsburgh Steelers 1960; New York Titans 1961
Lloyd Reese, P
Chicago Bears 1946
Fuad Reveiz, PK
Miami Dolphins 1985-89; Minnesota Vikings 1990-93
Jack Reynolds, LB
Los Angeles Rams 1970-80; San Francisco 49ers 1981-84
Larry Robinson, RB
Dallas Cowboys 1973
Roy Rose, E
New York Giants 1936
Al Russas, T
Detroit Lions 1949
Pat Ryan, QB
New York Jets 1978-89; Philadelphia Eagles 1991
Joe Schaffer, HB
Buffalo Bills 1960
Bobby Scott, QB
New Orleans Saints 1973-82
Robert Shaw, C
Dallas Cowboys 1979-82

Horace (Bud) Sherrod, E
New York Giants 1952
Lebron Shields, B
Baltimore Colts 1960; Minnesota Vikings 1961
Marshall Shires, T
Philadelphia Eagles 1945
Len Simonetti, T
Cleveland Browns 1946-48
Kevin Simons, OL
Cincinnati Bengals 1989
Tony Simmons, DE
San Diego Chargers 1985-87
Tommy Sims
Indianapolis Colts 1986
Curt Singer, OL
Washington Redskins 1984; Seattle Seahawks 1986-88; Tampa Bay Buccaneers 1988; New York Jets 1989
Walt Slater, B
Pittsburgh Steelers 1947
Carl Smith, FB
Buffalo Bills 1960
Chuck Smith, DE
Atlanta Falcons 1992-93
Daryle Smith, OL
Dallas Cowboys 1987-89; Cleveland Browns 1989; Philadelphia Eagles 1990-92
Andy Spiva, LB
Atlanta Falcons 1977
Danny Spradlin, LB
Dallas Cowboys 1981-82; Tampa Bay Buccaneers 1983-84; St. Louis Cardinals 1985
Haskel Stanback, RB
Atlanta Falcons 1974-79
Mike Stratton, LB
Buffalo Bills 1962-73; San Diego Chargers 1973
Jack Stroud, G-T
New York Giants 1953-64
Mark Studaway, DL
Houston Oilers 1984; Tampa Bay Bucs 1985
Bob Suffridge, G
Philadelphia Eagles 1941, 1945
Eric Swanson, E
St. Louis Cardinals 1986
Dave Thomas, DB
Dallas Cowboys 1993
Alvin Toles, LB
New Orleans 1985-89
Tom Tracy, B
Detroit Lions 1956-57; Pittsburgh Steelers 1958-63; Washington Redskins 1963-64
Jesse Turnbow, DT
Cleveland Browns 1978
Charles (Pug) Vaughn, B
Detroit Lions 1935; Chicago Cardinals 1936
Hal Wantland, TE
Miami Dolphins 1966
Buist Warren, B
Philadelphia Eagles 1945; Pittsburgh Steelers 1945
Dewey Warren, QB
Cincinnati Bengals 1968
John Warren, P
Dallas Cowboys 1983-84
Jim Weatherford, S
Atlanta Falcons 1969
Herman Weaver, P
Detroit Lions 1970-76; Seattle Seahawks 1977-80
Chuck Webb, RB
Green Bay Packers 1991
Hodges West, T
Philadelphia Eagles 1941
Brad White, DT
Tampa Bay Buccaneers 1981-83; Indianapolis Colts 1984-85
Reggie White, DT
Philadelphia Eagles 1985-91; Green Bay Packers 1993
Ron Widby, P
Dallas Cowboys 1968-71; Green Bay Packers 1972
Bruce Wilkerson, OG
Los Angeles Raiders 1987-93
Darryal Wilson, WR
New England Patriots 1983-84
Carl Zander, LB
Cincinnati Bengals 1985-91

1994 SEC Football

Tennessee Media Information

Tennessee Associate AD/ Media Relations
Haywood Harris

Tennessee Assistant AD/ Sports Information
Bud Ford

Tennessee Sports Information
P.O. Box 15016
Knoxville, TN 37901
(615) 974-1212
FAX (615) 974-1269

Ford (Home): 922-1657

Football Writers
Mike Strange, Jimmy Hyams, Gary Lundy and John Adams
Knoxville News-Sentinel
204 W. Church St.
Knoxville, TN 37901
(615) 521-8136

Joe Biddle, Dana Gelin
Nashville Banner
1100 Broadway
Nashville, TN 37202
(615) 295-8253

Larry Taft
The Tennessean
1100 Broadway
Nashville, TN 37202
(615) 259-8012

Buck Johnson, Larry Fleming
Chattanooga Times
170 E. 10th St.
Chattanooga, TN 37401
(615) 756-1234

Ward Gossett, Roy Exum
Chattanooga News-Free Press
400 E. 11th St.
Chattanooga, TN 37401
(615) 756-6900

Sports Dept.
Bristol Herald-Courier
320 Pierce St.
Bristol, VA 24201
(703) 669-2181

Joe Avento
Johnson City Press
204 W. Main St.
Johnson City, TN 37601
(615) 929-3111

Paul McAfee, Bob Gilbert
Maryville Times
307 E. Harper St.
Maryville, TN 37801
(615) 981-1100

Fred Williams
Citizen-Tribune
P.O. Box 625
Morristown, TN 37814
(615) 581-5630

Mike Blackerby
Oak Ridger
101 E. Tyrone Road
Oak Ridge, TN 37830
(615) 482-1021

Aaron Keen, Editor
Rocky Top Views
304 Rembrandt Drive
Old Hickory, TN 37138
(615) 754-6356

Other Daily Newspapers
Bobby Hall
Memphis Commercial-Appeal
495 Union Ave.
Memphis, TN 38101
(901) 529-2366

Clarksville Leaf-Chronicle
Box 829
Clarksville, TN 37040
(615) 552-1801

George Starr
Cleveland Banner
Box 199
Cleveland, TN 37311
(615) 472-5041

Marion Wilhoite
Columbia Herald
1115 S. Main St.
Columbia, TN 38401
(615) 388-6464

Elizabethton Star
Box 951
Elizabethton, TN 37643
(615) 542-4151

Wayne Phillips
Greeneville Sun
P.O. Box 1630
Greeneville, TN 37744
(615) 638-4181

Dan Morris
Jackson Sun
245 W. Lafayette
Jackson, TN 38301
(901) 427-3333

Ron Bliss
Kingsport News
701 Lynn Garden Drive
Kingsport, TN 37660
(615) 246-8121

Jim Davis
The Mountain Press
111 Commerce
Sevierville, TN 37864
(615) 428-0746

Doug Mead
Asheville Citizen
14 O'Henry Ave.
Asheville, NC 28802

Specialty Publications
Smokey's Tale
Tom Mattingly
P.O. Box 15016
Knoxville, TN 37901
(615) 974-1212

Wire Services
Duncan Mansfield, Tom Sharpe, AP
204 W. Church St.
Knoxville, TN 37901
(615) 522-3963

Play-by-Play Broadcasters
John Ward, Play by Play
Vol Radio Network
12003 Fox Den Road
Concord, TN 37720
(615) 688-3151

Bill Anderson, Color
Vol Network
6423 Deane Hill Dr.
Knoxville, TN 37919
(615) 584-0137

Stations Carrying Games
95 radio stations. For complete information contact Host Communications - Tennessee Division, P.O. Box 11125, Knoxville, TN 37939. Ed Huster - Executive Producer (615) 584-7043

Television Broadcasters
Bob Kesling
WBIR-TV
1513 Hutchinson Ave.
Knoxville, Tn 37917
(615) 637-1702

Jim Wogan
WATE-TV
P.O. Box 2349
Knoxville, TN 37901
(615) 637-9666

Rick Russo
WTVK-TV
P.O. Box 1388
Knoxville, TN 37901
(615) 450-8888

Barry Rice
UTV (University of Tennessee)
Neyland Thompson Sports Complex
Knoxville, TN 37996
(615) 974-7442

Hope Hines
WTVF-TV
474 James Robertson Pkwy.
Nashville, TN 37210
(615) 244-5000

Rudy Kalis
WSMV-TV
5700 Knob Road
Nashville, TN 37209
(615) 749-2244

Steve Phillips
WKRN-TV
441 Murfreesboro Rd.
Nashville, TN 37210
(615) 259-2200

Darrell Patterson
WTVC-TV
410 West 6th St.
Chattanooga, TN 37402
(615) 756-5500

Kevin Billingsley
WDEF-TV
3300 Broad Street
Chattanooga, TN 37408
(615) 267-3392

John Fricke
WRCB-TV
900 Whitehall Rd.
Chattanooga, TN 37405
(615) 266-5039

Brian Moore
WCYB-TV
511 Cumberland St.
Bristol, VA 24201
(703) 669-4161

Dave Weatherly
WBBJ-TV
349 Music St.
Jackson, TN. 38301

Kenny Hawkins
WJHL-TV
338 E. Main St.
Johnson City, TN 37601
(615) 926-2151

Bob Haywood
WKPT-TV
222 Commerce St.
Kingsport, TN 37662
(615) 246-9578

Stan Pamfillis
WLOS-TV
P.O. Box 1250
Asheville, NC 28802
(704) 255-0013

Les Smith
WREG-TV
803 Channel 3 Dr.
Memphis, TN 38103
(901) 577-0117

Glenn Carver
WHBQ-TV
P.O. Box 11407
Memphis, TN 38111
(901) 320-1367

Mike Fleming
WMC-TV
1960 Union Ave.
Memphis, TN 38104
(901) 726-0416

Radio Stations
Mike Keith
WIVK Radio
6711 Kingston Pike
Knoxville, TN 37919
(615) 588-6511

WUTK Radio
P103 Andy Holt Tower
Knoxville, TN 37996
(615) 974-6897

Jeff Jacoby
WMYU-FM
P.O. Box 50730
Knoxville, TN 37920
(615) 691-8080

Campus Media
The Daily Beacon
11 Communications Bldg.
Knoxville, TN 37996-0413
(615) 974-3226

The Volunteer Yearbook
11 Communications Bldg.
Knoxville, TN 37996-0413
(615) 974-3226

Tennessee

VANDERBILT

JOE B. WYATT
Chancellor

DR. TOM BURISH
Faculty Representative

PAUL HOOLAHAN
Athletic Director

Vanderbilt University

CHANCELLOR:
  Joe B. Wyatt (Texas 1956)
FACULTY REPRESENTATIVE:
  Dr. Tom Burish (Notre Dame 1971)
ATHLETIC DIRECTOR:
  Paul Hoolahan (North Carolina 1972)
HEAD COACH:
  Gerry DiNardo (Notre Dame 1975)
LOCATION: Nashville, Tennessee
FOUNDED: 1873
ENROLLMENT: 9,302
NICKNAME: Commodores
COLORS: Black and Gold
STADIUM: Vanderbilt Stadium/Dudley Field (41,000) - Artificial

Commodore Quick Facts

1993 RECORD: 4-7
  (3-3 Home, 1-4 Away)
1993 SEC RECORD/FINISH: 1-7 (6th-Eastern)
  (1-3 Home, 0-4 Away)
BOWL: None
ALL-TIME RECORD: 502-428-50 (.538)
SEC RECORD: 98-259-18 (.286) — Regular Season Only
SEC CHAMPIONSHIPS: 0
BOWL APPEARANCES: 3
BOWL RECORD: 1-1-1 (.500)
LAST APPEARANCE: 1982 Hall of Fame Bowl
  (Air Force 36, Vanderbilt 28)

VANDERBILT
Team Information

OFFENSIVE SYSTEM: I-Bone

DEFENSIVE SYSTEM: 4-3

LETTERMEN RETURNING: 25
- 14 Offense
- 9 Defense
- 2 Specialists

LETTERMEN LOST: 24
- 12 Offense
- 12 Defense
- 0 Specialists

STARTERS RETURNING: 13
- **OFFENSE** (7)
  - OT Owen Neil (6-5, 300, Jr.)
  - C   Richard Saenz (6-4, 275, Sr.)
  - TE Robert Couch (6-6, 290, Jr.)
  - SE Kenny Simon (6-0, 193, Jr.)
  - QB Ronnie Gordon (6-1, 182, So.)
  - FB Royce Love (6-2, 240, Jr.)
  - WB Eric Lewis (6-4, 218, Sr.)
- **DEFENSE** (4)
  - DT James Manley (6-4, 288, Jr.)
  - DT Brian Boykin (6-3, 275, So.)
  - LB Gerald Collins (6-3, 248, Sr.)
  - SS Eric Vance (6-4, 218, So.)
- **SPECIALISTS** (2)
  - PK Steve Yenner (6-0, 171, Sr.)
  - P   Bill Marinagngel (6-2, 212, So.)

STARTERS LOST: 11
- **OFFENSE** (4)
  - OG Ryan Bell (6-3, 275, Sr.)
  - OG Mark Mikesell (6-4, 271, Sr.)
  - OT Eric Dahlberg (6-6, 264, Sr.)
  - TB Tony Jackson (5-8, 176, Sr.)
- **DEFENSE** (7)
  - DE Alan Young (6-4, 244, Sr.)
  - DE John DeWitt (6-4, 242, Sr.)
  - LB Shelton Quarles (6-2, 212, Sr.)
  - LB Rico Francis (6-0, 204, Sr.)
  - CB Robert Davis (5-9, 193, Sr.)
  - CB Byron King (5-11, 193, Jr.)
  - FS Aaron Smith (5-11, 195, Sr.)
- **SPECIALISTS** (0)

Vanderbilt Stadium (41,000)
Record: 32-42-1 (.433)
First Game: Sept. 12, 1981 — Vanderbilt 23, Maryland 17

1994 Vanderbilt Schedule

Sept.	3	WAKE FOREST	NASHVILLE
Sept.	10	at Alabama	Tuscaloosa
Sept.	17	OLE MISS	NASHVILLE
Oct.	1	at Arkansas	Little Rock, Ark.
Oct.	8	at Cincinnati	Cincinnati, Ohio
Oct.	15	at Georgia	Athens, Ga.
Oct.	22	SOUTH CAROLINA	NASHVILLE
Oct.	29	NORTHERN ILLINOIS	NASHVILLE
Nov.	5	at Kentucky	Lexington, Ky.
Nov.	19	FLORIDA	NASHVILLE
Nov.	26	TENNESSEE	NASHVILLE

1995 Vanderbilt Schedule

Sept.	2	ALABAMA	NASHVILLE
Sept.	9	VIRGINIA MILITARY	NASHVILLE
Sept.	16	at Notre Dame	South Bend, Ind.
Sept.	23	TEXAS CHRISTIAN	NASHVILLE
Sept.	30	ARKANSAS	NASHVILLE
Oct.	14	GEORGIA	NASHVILLE
Oct.	21	at South Carolina	Columbia, S.C.
Oct.	28	at Ole Miss	Oxford, Miss.
Nov.	4	KENTUCKY	NASHVILLE
Nov.	18	at Florida	Gainesville, Fla.
Nov.	25	at Tennessee	Knoxville, Tenn.

Vanderbilt

1993 Vanderbilt Individual Leaders

RUSHING	Atts	Yards	Avg	TDs	Yds/Game
Tony Jackson	120	607	5.1	3	55.2
CLIFF DEESE	78	315	4.0	2	35.0
KENNY SIMON	74	292	3.9	1	29.2
JERMAINE JOHNSON	52	207	4.0	2	23.0
ERIC LEWIS	22	174	7.9	1	15.8

PASSING	Atts	Comp	Ints/TDs	Pct	Yds
RONNIE GORDON	98	40	4 / 0	.408	400
CEDRIC DOUGLAS	32	7	2 / 0	.219	88
KENNY SIMON	27	8	7 / 0	.296	58

RECEIVING	Rec	Yds	Avg	TDs	Yds/Game
KENNY SIMON	15	166	11.1	0	16.6
Tony Jackson	9	70	7.8	0	6.4
SANFORD WARE	7	97	13.9	0	8.8
JASON TOMICHEK	7	71	10.1	0	6.5
ERIC LEWIS	6	53	8.8	0	4.8

SCORING	G	TDs	PAT	FGs	Tot	Avg
STEVE YENNER	11	0	15-16	8-14	39	3.5
RONNIE GORDON	8	4	0-0	0-0	24	3.0
Tony Jackson	11	3	0-0	0-0	18	1.6
CLIFF DEESE	9	2	0-0	0-0	12	1.3
JERMAINE JOHNSON	9	2	0-0	0-0	12	1.3

PUNTING	No	Yds	Avg	Long
BILL MARINANGEL	68	2482	35.5	54

KICKOFF RETURNS	No	Yds	Avg	TDs	Avg/Game	Long
Tony Jackson	31	753	24.3	0	68.5	55
KENNY SIMON	3	65	21.7	0	6.5	28
JERMAINE JOHNSON	4	81	20.3	0	7.2	35

PUNT RETURNS	No	Yds	Avg	TDs	Avg/Game	Long
Robert Davis	1	25	25.0	0	2.3	25
Tony Jackson	2	11	5.5	0	1.0	8
Jeff Brothers	13	68	5.2	0	6.2	39

TACKLES	Total (S-A)	Sk (Yds)	TL(Yds)	Ints
Shelton Quarles	99 (70-29)	3 (-10)	7 (-23)	2
GERALD COLLINGS	85 (58-28)	2 (-18)	6 (-31)	0
Rico Francis	66 (48-18)	0	4 (-11)	1
JAMES MANLEY	65 (43-22)	2.5 (-18)	7.5 (-30)	0
Aaron Smith	60 (36-24)	0	2 (-3)	1

INTERCEPTIONS	No	Yds	TDs	Int/Game	Long
Byron King	4	21	0	0.4	21
Shelton Quarles	2	16	0	0.2	16

Returning Players in All Capitals

Ronnie Gordon    **Kenny Simon**    **Steve Yenner**

1993 Vanderbilt Team Statistics

	VU	OPP
FIRST DOWNS	152	201
Rushing	110	88
Passing	25	105
Penalty	17	8
NET YARDS RUSHING	2149	1453
Yards rushing	2590	1763
Yards lost	441	310
Rushing attempts	565	397
Average per rush	3.8	3.7
Average per game	195.4	132.1
NET YARDS PASSING	546	2423
Average per game	49.6	220.3
Passes attempted	157	397
Passes completed	55	174
Had intercepted	13	13
TOTAL OFFENSIVE YARDS	2695	3876
Average per game	245.0	352.4
Total plays	722	715
Average per play	3.7	5.4
NUMBERS PUNTS/YARDS	71/2488	51/1796
Punting average	35.0	35.2
Net Punting average	31.3	33.2
PUNT RETURNS/YARDS	16/104	36/268
Punt return average	6.5	7.4
KICKOFF RETURNS/YARDS	48/1005	20/565
Kickoff return average	20.9	21.7
PENALTIES/YARDS	69/539	59/496
Penalty yards per game	49.0	45.1
FUMBLES/LOST	35/20	22/12
INTERCEPTION RETURNS/YARDS	13/116	13/178
Interception return average	8.9	13.7
TOUCHDOWNS	16	37
Rushing	14	15
Passing	0	16
Return	1	4
Other	1	2
FIELD GOALS MADE/ATTEMPTED	8/13	10/21
SAFETY	1	1
TWO-POINT CONVERSIONS	0	0
TOTAL POINTS	137	290
Average per game	12.5	26.4

1993 Vanderbilt Results

4-7 Overall • 1-7 SEC (6th - Eastern)

Sept. 4	at Wake Forest	W	27-10
Sept. 11	ALABAMA	L	6-17
Sept. 18	at Ole Miss	L	7-49
Oct. 2	AUBURN	L	10-14
Oct. 9	CINCINNATI	W	17-7
Oct. 16	GEORGIA	L	3-41
Oct. 23	at South Carolina	L	0-22
Nov. 6	KENTUCKY	W	12-7
Nov. 13	NAVY	W	41-7
Nov. 20	at Florida	L	0-52
Nov. 27	at Tennessee	L	14-62

1994 SEC Football

Gerry DiNardo

Year-By-Year Record

Year	School	Conf.	All	Bowl
1991	Vanderbilt	3-4 (t6th)	5-6	
1992	Vanderbilt	2-6 (t5E)	4-7	
1993	Vanderbilt	1-7 (6thE)	4-7	
OVERALL RECORD		6-17 (.261)	13-20 (.394)	3 Years
Vanderbilt Record		6-17 (.261)	13-20 (.394)	3 Years
Bowl Record			0-0	

HOMETOWN:
Brooklyn, New York

ALMA MATER:
Notre Dame (1975)

PLAYING CAREER:
Notre Dame Offensive Guard 1972-74 (Three-year starter; Consensus All-America 1974; Coaches' All-America Game 1974)

COACHING CAREER:
Maine Assistant 1975-77; Eastern Michigan Assistant 1978-81; Colorado Assistant 1982-90; Vanderbilt Head Coach 1990-present.

COACHING ACHIEVEMENTS:
1989 Athlon Publication's National Assistant Coach of the Year; 1991 SEC Coach of the Year (AP and TBS); 1991 Kodak Regional Coach of the Year.

BORN:
November 10, 1953

WIFE:
Terri

CHILDREN:
Kate (12)

ASSISTANT COACHES:
RON CASE (Carson-Newman 1973) - Defensive Backs
BILL ELIAS (Massachusetts 1977) - Defensive Ends/Recruiting Coordinator
DON FREASE (Oregon 1972) - Offensive Coordinator/Tight Ends
HAL HUNTER (Northwestern 1981) - Offensive Line
FRED LAMBERT (California State-Hayward 1970) - Running Backs
BOB McCONNELL (Maine 1973) - Wide Receivers
JAPPY OLIVER (Purdue 1978) - Linebackers
CARL REESE (Missouri 1965) - Defensive Coordinator
CHRIS SYMINGTON (Colorado 1988) - Defensive Tackles

SUPPORT STAFF:
CHRIS GAINES (Vanderbilt 1988) - Strength Coach
RICK GEORGE (Illinois 1982) - Associate A.D. for External Operations

Vanderbilt

Vanderbilt All-Star Candidates

GERALD COLLINS
Senior • Linebacker
6-3 • 248 • St. Louis, Mo.

• The anchor of the Vanderbilt defense, he ranked second on the team in tackles last season with 86 total hits (58 solo, 28 assists).
• Recorded six tackles for loss, two quarterback sacks, five passes broken up, two fumble recoveries and one caused fumble in 1993.
• Made a courageous and successful return to football after missing most of the 1992 season with a life-threatening staph infection.

ERIC LEWIS
Senior • Fullback
6-0 • 210 • Oxford, Ala.

• Moved to fullback during spring practice after starting at wingback the last two seasons.
• Versatile performer who is equally adept at rushing, receiving and blocking.
• Rushed for 174 yards on 22 carries last season for a hefty 7.9 yards per carry average.
• Scored game-clinching touchdown against Wake Forest with a 33-yard scoring run.

COLLINS STATS

Year	Tackles(S-A)	Sk(Yds)	TFL(Yds)	Int
1989	5 (1-4)	0	0	0
1990	55 (31-24)	1 (-6)	1 (-4)	0
1991	79 (43-36)	0	1 (-1)	0
1992	10 (5-5)	0	1 (-1)	0
1993	86 (58-28)	2 (-18)	4 (-13)	0
Career	235 (138-97)	3 (-24)	7 (-19)	0

LEWIS STATS

Year	Att	Yds	Avg	TD	Rec	Yds	Avg
1991	22	60	2.7	0	1	5	5.0
1992	39	189	4.8	1	3	24	8.0
1993	22	174	7.9	1	6	53	8.8
Career	83	423	5.1	2	10	82	8.2

VANDERBILT

OWEN NEIL
Junior • Offensive Tackle
6-5 • 300 • Louisville, Ky.

• Keystone of Vanderbilt's offensive line who has emerged as one of the league's top blockers.
• A two-year starter at left tackle, he was named to USA Today's Fabulous Freshman Team and the All-SEC freshman squad in his first year.
• A key factor in helping the Commodores rank second in the SEC in rushing in 1992 and fourth in the league in 1993.

1994 SEC Football

1994 Vanderbilt Roster

No.	Name	Pos.	Ht.	Wt.	Class	Exp.	Hometown (High School/JC)
24	Matt Anderson	SS	5-11	185	Fr.	SQ	Garland, Texas (South Garland)
32	Derrick Atterberry	CB	6-0	170	Jr.	SQ	Dayton, Ohio (Patterson)
12	Gabe Banks	SE	6-0	184	Jr.	2L	Delaware, Ohio (Hayes)
73	Brian Boykin	DT	6-3	275	So.	1L	Birmingham, Ala. (Huffman)
36	Bart Cason	FB	6-1	230	Fr.	SQ	Maywood, Ill. (Nazareth Academy)
40	Gerald Collins	LB	6-3	248	Sr.	3L	St. Louis, Mo. (Roosevelt)
74	Robert Couch	OT	6-6	290	Jr.	1L	Irving, Texas (MacArthur)
33	Cliff Deese	TB	5-8	180	Jr.	2L	Houston, Texas (Westfield)
75	Allen DeGraffenreid	OT	6-5	291	So.	SQ	Dunwoody, Ga. (Dunwoody)
91	Byran DeGraffenreid	DT	6-6	289	Jr.	2L	Dunwoody, Ga. (Dunwoody)
4	Ed DeMesa	QB	5-10	175	Jr.	TR	Vallejo, Calif. (Solano Community College)
49	Jamie Duncan	LB	6-1	224	Fr.	SQ	Wilmington, Del. (Christiana)
10	Jason Ellerbe	SE	6-1	185	Jr.	SQ	Sealy, Texas (Sealy)
1	Charles Fant	WB	6-0	196	Jr.	SQ	Goshen, Ohio (Goshen)
13	DeReal Finklin	CB	5-10	185	So.	1L	Lakewood, N.J. (Lakewood)
67	Tim Fitz	C	6-4	260	Jr.	SQ	Cincinnati, Ohio (Moeller)
9	Marcus Forrest	TB	5-9	185	Fr.	SQ	Aurora, Ill. (Waubonsie Valley)
3	Ronnie Gordon	QB	6-1	182	So.	1L	Albany, Ga. (Dougherty)
23	Darryl Griffin	SE	5-11	197	Jr.	SQ	Chicago, Ill. (Mount Carmel)
54	Darren Hale	K	5-11	165	Jr.	SQ	Lenexa, Kan. (Shawnee Mission West)
34	Carlton Hall	LB	6-1	230	Fr.	SQ	Midwest City, Okla. (Midwest City)
96	Jason Hill	DE	6-4	251	Fr.	SQ	Nashville, Tenn. (Brentwood Academy)
30	Bobby Jackson	SE	5-10	175	So.	SQ	Daytona Beach, Fla. (Father Lopez)
45	Mark Jefcoat	LB	6-2	222	So.	1L	Brandon, Miss. (NW Rankin)
5	Jermaine Johnson	TB	5-7	176	So.	1L	Carrollton, Ga. (Carrollton)
26	Antony Jordon	DB	6-4	215	Fr.	SQ	Sewell, N.J. (Washington Township)
55	Bryan Josey	OT	6-5	293	Jr.	1L	Molino, Fla. (Tate)
85	Bryon Koepke	DE	6-4	250	Jr.	2L	Chicago Heights, Ill. (Mt. Carmel)
16	Eric Lanctot	K	5-7	161	So.	SQ	St. Petersburg, Fla. (Shorecrest)
44	Durego Lewis	FB	6-0	230	So.	SQ	Knoxville, Tenn. (Central)
22	Eric Lewis	WB	6-0	210	Sr.	3L	Oxford, Ala. (Munford)
2	Marcus Lewis	QB	5-10	170	Fr.	SQ	South Fulton, Tenn. (Union City)
48	Royce Love	FB	6-2	240	Jr.	2L	East Chicago, Ind. (Central)
56	James Manley	DT	6-4	288	Jr.	2L	Birmingham, Ala. (Huffman)
29	Bill Marinangel	DB	6-2	212	So.	1L	McHenry, Ill. (McHenry)
84	Bill McDermond	LB	6-2	215	Jr.	SQ	Darnestown, Md. (Wootton)
69	Owen Neil	OT	6-5	300	Jr.	2L	Louisville, Ky. (DeSales)
50	Chad Painter	OG	6-4	290	So.	SQ	Knoxville, Tenn. (Powell)
88	Donald Pitre	SE	6-0	182	So.	SQ	Opelousas, La. (Opelousas)
68	Walter Pitts	LB	6-4	230	So.	SQ	Lexington, S.C. (Heathwood Hall)
76	Robert Reynolds	OT	6-6	303	Jr.	SQ	Louisville, Ky. (Male)
21	Chris Ryals	FS	6-0	180	Jr.	SQ	Cincinnati, Ohio (Moeller)
60	Richard Saenz	C	6-4	275	Sr.	3L	Houston, Texas (Klein Forest)
42	Alex Scarbrough	FB	6-1	190	Jr.	SQ	Birmingham, Ala. (Mountain Brook)
95	Matt Schuckman	DE	6-4	250	So.	SQ	Newton, Kan. (Newton)
87	Tom Sharpe	TE	6-5	240	So.	SQ	Checotah, Okla. (Checotah)
7	Robert Sheffield	CB	6-1	180	Fr.	SQ	Daytona Beach, Fla. (Mainland)
6	Kenny Simon	SE	6-0	193	Jr.	1L	Biloxi, Miss. (Biloxi)
89	Jay Stallworth	TE	6-2	252	Fr.	SQ	Marshall, Texas (Marshall)
79	Rick Stepp	OT	6-4	276	Jr.	SQ	Sarasota, Fla. (Riverview)
66	Tim Storer	OG	6-3	275	So.	SQ	Bartlesville, Okla. (Bartlesville)
62	Bill Sullivan	DT	6-3	251	Sr.	3L	Houston, Texas (Nimitz)
53	David Tandy	OG	6-4	266	Jr.	SQ	Owensboro, Ky. (Owensboro)
83	Jason Tomichek	TE	6-5	260	So.	1L	Nashville, Tenn. (Franklin Road Academy)
19	Eric Vance	FS	6-4	218	So.	1L	Hurst, Texas (L.D. Bell)
64	Jerry Vascocu	OG	6-2	275	Jr.	SQ	Ruston, La. (Cedar Creek)
80	Sanford Ware	SE	5-10	186	Jr.	1L	Clemson, S. C. (Daniel)
72	Bill White	OG	6-3	280	Jr.	TR	Spokane, Wash. (Gavilan College)
46	Kirk Williams	LB	6-0	220	So.	1L	Aurora, Ill. (Waubonsie Valley)
90	Marcus Williams	TE	6-6	234	Fr.	SQ	Glasgow, Ky. (Glasgow)
86	Troy Williams	SE	6-3	210	Fr.	SQ	Bradenton, Fla. (Bradenton Southeast)
77	Chad Wood	C	6-4	260	Fr.	SQ	South Garland, Texas (South Garland)
14	Steve Yenner	K	6-0	171	Jr.	1L	Kalamazoo, Mich. (Grand Rapids Comm. College)
97	Glenn Young	DE	6-4	247	Fr.	SQ	Harper Woods, Mich. (Bishop Gallagher)

Numerical Roster

No.	Name	Pos.
1	Charles Fant	WB
2	Marcus Lewis	QB
3	Ronnie Gordon	QB
4	Ed DeMesa	QB
5	Jermaine Johnson	TB
6	Kenny Simon	SE
7	Robert Sheffield	CB
9	Marcus Forrest	TB
10	Jason Ellerbe	SE
12	Gabe Banks	SE
13	DeReal Finklin	CB
14	Steve Yenner	K
16	Eric Lanctot	K
19	Eric Vance	FS
21	Chris Ryals	FS
22	Eric Lewis	WR
23	Darryl Griffin	SE
24	Matt Anderson	SS
26	Antony Jordan	DB
29	Bill Marinangel	P-DB
30	Bobby Jackson	SE
32	Derrick Atterbury	CB
33	Cliff Deese	TB
34	Carlton Hall	LB
36	Bart Cason	FB
40	Gerald Collins	LB
42	Alex Scarbrough	FB
44	Durego Lewis	FB
45	Mark Jefcoat	LB
46	Kirk Williams	LB
48	Royce Love	FB
49	Jamie Duncan	LB
50	Chad Painter	OG
53	David Tandy	OG
54	Darren Hale	K
55	Bryan Josey	OT
56	James Manley	DT
60	Richard Saenz	C
62	Bill Sullivan	DT
64	Jerry Vascocu	OG
66	Tim Storer	OG
67	Tim Fitz	C
68	Walter Pitts	LB
69	Owen Neil	OT
72	Bill White	OG
73	Brian Boykin	DT
74	Robert Couch	OT
75	Allen DeGraffenreid	OT
76	Robert Reynolds	OT
77	Chad Wood	C
79	Rick Stepp	OT
80	Sanford Ware	SE
83	Jason Tomichek	TE
84	Bill McDermond	LB
85	Bryon Koepke	DE
86	Troy Williams	SE
87	Tom Sharpe	TE
88	Donald Pitre	SE
89	Jay Stallworth	TE
90	Marcus Williams	TE
91	Byran DeGraffenreid	DT
95	Matt Schuckman	DE
96	Jason Hill	DE
97	Glenn Young	DE

Vanderbilt

1994 Vanderbilt Depth Chart

OFFENSE

Pos	#	Name
TE:	83	Jason Tomichek
	90	Marcus Williams
LT:	69	OWEN NEIL
	50	Chad Painter
LG:	77	Chad Wood
	64	Jerry Vascocu
C:	60	RICHARD SAENZ
	67	Tim Fitz
RG:	66	Tim Storer
	53	David Tandy
RT:	55	Bryan Josey
	74	Robert Couch
SE:	6	KENNY SIMON
	80	Sanford Ware
QB:	3	RONNIE GORDON
	2	Marcus Lewis
FB:	22	ERIC LEWIS
	48	Royce Love
TB:	33	Cliff Deese
	48	Royce Love
WB:	12	Gabe Banks
	1	Charles Fant

DEFENSE

Pos	#	Name
LE:	89	Jay Stallworth
	96	Jason Hill
LT:	62	Bill Sullivan
	73	Brian Boykin
RT:	56	JAMES MANLEY
	73	Brian Boykin
RE:	95	Matt Schuckman
	97	Glenn Young
LB:	40	GERALD COLLINS
	46	Kirk Williams
MLB:	34	Carlton Hall
	84	Bill McDermond
LB:	49	Jamie Duncan
	45	Mark Jefcoat
LCB:	7	Robert Sheffield
	32	Derrick Atterberry
SS:	24	Matt Anderson
	21	Chris Ryals
FS:	19	ERIC VANCE
	29	Bill Marinangel
RCB:	13	DeReal Finklin
	32	Derrick Atterberry

SPECIALISTS

Pos	#	Name
KS:	14	STEVE YENNER
	16	Eric Lanctot
P:	29	BILL MARINAGNGEL
	14	Steve Yenner

Returning Starters In All Capitals

1994 Vanderbilt Signees

Name	Pos.	Ht.	Wt.	Hometown/High School
Damien Allen	QB	6-3	180	Strongville, Ohio/Strongville
Jim Anguiano	OL	6-3	265	Grand Prairie, Texas/Grand Prairie
Antony Azama	DB	5-11	168	Daytona Beach, Fla./Mainland
Fred Baker	WR	6-5	210	Soperton, Ga./Treutlen Co.
Rahim Batten	QB	5-10	185	Detroit, Mich./Bishop Gallagher
John Bradley	LB	6-2	217	Mount Airy, N.C./Mount Airy
Richard Calhoun	LB	6-3	215	Troy, Ala./Henderson
Corey Chavous	WR-DB	6-1	191	Aiken, S.C./Silver Bluff
Kenny Christian	DE	6-3	230	Brandon, Miss./Brandon
Ed DeMesa	QB	5-11	170	Vallejo, Cal./Vallejo-Solano JC
Jason Dunnavant	FB	6-2	210	Nashville, Tenn./Battle Ground Academy
O.J. Fleming	WR	6-4	190	Franklin, Tenn./Battle Ground Academy
Will Jacobs	OL	6-5	295	Houston, Texas/Westfield
Matt Linder	WR	6-3	185	Austin, Texas/Westlake
Darweshi Miles	LB	6-1	220	Houston, Texas/Nimitz
Paul Morgan	FB	6-0	230	Courtland, Miss./South Panola
Rosevelt Noble	DB	5-11	190	Kankakee, Ill./Kankakee
Robert Simmons	WR	5-9	180	Evanston, Ill./Evanston Township
Ian Smith	DE	6-4	240	Sewell, N.J./Washington Township
Shawn Stuckey	LB	6-1	220	Daleville Heights, Ala./Daleville
Duane Todd	WR-DB	6-4	200	Lorain, Ohio/Clearview
Bill White	OL	6-3	280	Spokane, Wash./East Valley-Gavilan JC
Marcus Williams	RB-DB	6-1	200	Richardson, Texas/Plano East
Jerimy Wills	QB	6-3	175	Garland, Texas/South Garland
Eric Wissman	TE	6-4	235	Florence, Ala./Bradshaw
Tyrone Yarbrough	RB	5-11	175	Dallas, Texas/Samuell

Cliff Deese

Eric Lewis

1994 SEC Football

161

Vanderbilt Year-By-Year Records

Year	Coach	SEC	SEC Finish	Overall	Bowls
1892	E.N. Beaumont			2-2	
1890	Elliott H. Jones			1-0-0	
1891	Elliott H. Jones			3-1-0	
1892	Elliott H. Jones			4-4-0	
1893	W.J. Keller			6-1-0	
1894	Henry Thornton			7-1-0	
1895	C.L. Upton			5-3-1	
1896	R.G. Acton			3-2-2	
1897	R.G. Acton			6-0-1	
1898	R.G. Acton			1-5-0	
1899	J.L. Crane			7-2-0	
1900	J.L. Crane			4-4-1	
1901	W.H. Watkins			6-1-1	
1902	W.H. Watkins			8-1-0	
1903	J.H. Henry			6-1-1	
1904	Dan McGugin			9-0-0	
1905	Dan McGugin			7-1-0	
1906	Dan McGugin			8-1-0	
1907	Dan McGugin			5-1-1	
1908	Dan McGugin			7-2-1	
1909	Dan McGugin			7-3-0	
1910	Dan McGugin			8-0-1	
1911	Dan McGugin			8-1-0	
1912	Dan McGugin			8-1-1	
1913	Dan McGugin			5-3-0	
1914	Dan McGugin			2-6-0	
1915	Dan McGugin			9-1-0	
1916	Dan McGugin			7-1-1	
1917	Dan McGugin			5-3-0	
1918	Ray Morrison (acting)			4-2-0	
1919	Dan McGugin			5-1-2	
1920	Dan McGugin			5-3-1	
1921	Dan McGugin			7-0-1	
1922	Dan McGugin			8-0-1	
1923	Dan McGugin			5-2-1	
1924	Dan McGugin			6-3-1	
1925	Dan McGugin			6-3-0	
1926	Dan McGugin			8-1-0	
1927	Dan McGugin			8-1-2	
1928	Dan McGugin			8-2-0	
1929	Dan McGugin			7-2-0	
1930	Dan McGugin			8-2-0	
1931	Dan McGugin			5-4-0	
1932	Dan McGugin			6-1-2	
1933	Dan McGugin	2-2-2	6	t4-3-3	—
1934	Dan McGugin	4-3-0	6	6-3-0	—
1935	Ray Morrison	5-1-0	2	7-3-0	—
1936	Ray Morrison	1-3-1	9	3-5-1	—
1937	Ray Morrison	4-2-0	4	7-2-0	—
1938	Ray Morrison	4-3-0	6	6-3-0	—
1939	Ray Morrison	1-6-0	11	2-7-1	—
1940	Red Sanders	1-5-1	11	3-6-1	—
1941	Red Sanders	3-2-0	6	8-2-0	—
1942	Red Sanders	2-4-0	8	6-4-0	—
1943	Herc Alley	0-0-0	-	5-0-0	—
1944	Doby Bartling	0-0-0	-	3-0-1	—

Year	Coach	SEC	SEC Finish	Overall	Bowls
1945	Doby Bartling	2-4-0	9	3-6-0	—
1946	Red Sanders	3-4-0	7	5-4-0	—
1947	Red Sanders	3-3-0	4t	6-4-0	—
1948	Red Sanders	4-2-1	4	8-2-1	—
1949	Bill Edwards	4-4-0	7	5-5-0	—
1950	Bill Edwards	3-4-0	7t	7-4-0	—
1951	Bill Edwards	3-5-0	7	6-5-0	—
1952	Bill Edwards	1-4-1	11	3-5-2	—
1953	Art Guepe	1-5-0	10t	3-7-0	—
1954	Art Guepe	1-5-0	11t	2-7-0	—
1955	Art Guepe	4-3-0	5	8-3-0	Gator
1956	Art Guepe	2-5-0	8t	5-5-0	—
1957	Art Guepe	3-3-1	6t	5-3-2	—
1958	Art Guepe	2-1-3	4	5-2-3	—
1959	Art Guepe	3-2-2	5t	5-3-2	—
1960	Art Guepe	0-7-0	12	3-7-0	—
1961	Art Guepe	1-6-0	12	2-8-0	—
1962	Art Guepe	1-6-0	11	1-9-0	—
1963	Jack Green	0-5-2	10	1-7-2	—
1964	Jack Green	1-4-1	9	3-6-1	—
1965	Jack Green	1-5-0	9t	2-7-1	—
1966	Jack Green	0-6-0	9t	1-9-0	—
1967	Bill Pace	0-6-0	9t	2-7-1	—
1968	Bill Pace	2-3-1	8	5-4-1	—
1969	Bill Pace	2-3-0	7	4-6-0	—
1970	Bill Pace	1-5-0	9	4-7-0	—
1971	Bill Pace	1-5-0	7	4-6-0	—
1972	Bill Pace	0-6-0	10	3-8-0	—
1973	Steve Sloan	1-5-0	10	5-6-0	—
1974	Steve Sloan	2-3-1	7t	7-3-2	Peach
1975	Fred Pancoast	2-4-0	6t	7-4-0	—
1976	Fred Pancoast	0-6-0	9t	2-9-0	—
1977	Fred Pancoast	0-6-0	9t	2-9-0	—
1978	Fred Pancoast	0-6-0	10	2-9-0	—
1979	George MacIntyre	0-6-0	9t	1-10-0	—
1980	George MacIntyre	0-6-0	9t	2-9-0	—
1981	George MacIntyre	1-5-0	10	4-7-0	—
1982	George MacIntyre	4-2-0	3t	8-4-0	Hall of Fame
1983	George MacIntyre	0-6-0	9t	2-9-0	—
1984	George MacIntyre	2-4-0	7t	5-6-0	—
1985	George MacIntyre	1-4-1	7	3-7-1	—
1986	Watson Brown	0-6-0	10	1-10-0	—
1987	Watson Brown	1-5-0	7t	4-7-0	—
1988	Watson Brown	2-5-0	8	3-8-0	—
1989	Watson Brown	0-7-0	10	1-10-0	—
1990	Watson Brown	1-6-0	8t	1-10-0	—
1991	Gerry DiNardo	3-4-0	6t	5-6-0	—
1992	Gerry DiNardo	2-6-0	5t-E	4-7-0	—
1993	Gerry DiNardo	1-7	6-E	4-7-0	—

Bowl Results (1-1-1)

Bowl	Opponent	Result	Date
Gator	Auburn	W 25-13	12-31-55
Peach	Texas Tech	T 6-6	12-28-74
Hall of Fame	Air Force	L 28-36	12-31-82

Vanderbilt vs. All Opponents

Opponent	W	L	T
Air Force	2	3	0
Alabama	18	49	4
Auburn	19	15	1
Arkansas	1	2	0
Army	4	3	0
Baylor	0	2	0
Boston College	0	2	0
Carson-Newman	1	0	0
Central University	13	1	1
Centre College	4	2	1
Chattanooga	17	1	0
Chicago	2	1	0
Cincinnati	3	3	0
Citadel	3	2	0
Clemson	3	1	0
Colgate	1	0	0
Cumberland	6	1	0
Davidson	2	0	0
Duke	2	3	0
Florida	9	16	2
Fordham	0	1	0
Florence State	1	0	0
Furman	1	1	0
George Washington	3	0	0
Georgetown	2	0	0
Georgia	16	36	2
Georgia Tech	15	16	3
Harvard	0	1	0
Henderson-Brown	6	0	0
Indiana	0	2	0
Iowa State	1	1	0
Kansas	1	1	0
Kansas State	1	0	0
Kentucky	33	30	4
Kentucky State	2	0	0
LSU	7	16	1
Louisville	2	0	1
Marquette	1	0	0
Marshall	2	0	0
Maryland	8	4	0
Maryville	6	0	0
Memphis State	7	5	0
Mercer	4	0	0
Miami (Florida)	4	4	0
Miami (Ohio)	1	0	0
Michigan	0	9	1
Middle Tennessee	12	0	0
Milligan	1	0	0
Minnesota	2	2	0
Mississippi	31	35	2
Mississippi State	6	7	2
Missouri	1	2	1
Missouri Mines	1	0	0
Nashville	7	0	1
Navy	2	1	2
North Carolina	5	8	0
North Carolina State	1	0	0
Northwestern	1	0	1
Ohio	1	0	0
Ohio State	1	3	0
Oklahoma	0	2	1
Ouachita	2	0	0
Pennsylvania	0	1	0
Penn State	1	0	0
Princeton	1	1	0
Purdue	2	0	0
Rice	2	1	0
Rose Poly	8	0	0
Rutgers	2	0	0

Opponent	W	L	T
Samford	2	0	0
Sewanee	40	8	4
South Carolina	0	3	0
Southern Methodist	2	2	0
Southwest (Memphis)	7	1	0
Spring Hill	1	0	0
Syracuse	0	2	0
Tampa	3	1	0
Temple	0	1	0
*Tennessee	27	56	5
Tennessee Tech	10	0	1
Texas	8	3	1
Texas Tech	0	0	1
Transylvania	2	0	0
Tulane	17	28	3
UCLA	0	1	0
Union (Tennessee)	3	0	0
Villanova	1	0	0
Virginia	12	7	2
Virginia Military	3	2	0
Virginia Tech	3	6	0
Wake Forest	4	3	0
Washington (St. Louis)	6	3	0
Washington & Lee	2	0	0
West Virginia	1	1	0
William & Mary	4	0	0
Western Kentucky	3	0	0
Yale	1	0	1

* disagreement between schools about series record

Vanderbilt standout Chuck Scott, who earned All-SEC honors as a tight end in 1983 and as a wide receiver in 1984, holds the league's third-highest mark for career touchdown catches with 20.

1994 SEC Football

Vanderbilt School Records

Individual

Game
Total Offense	521	Whit Taylor vs. Tennessee	(1981)
Yards Rushing	321	Frank Mordica vs. Air Force	(1978)
Rushing Attempts	35	Jamie O'Rourke vs. Tulane	(1971)
Yards Passing	464	Whit Taylor vs. Tennessee	(1981)
Pass Attempts	62	John Gromos vs. Alabama	(1989)
Pass Completions	33	Kurt Page vs. Georgia	(1983)
Yards Receiving	222	Clarence Sevillian vs. Tennessee	(1992)
Receptions	17	Keith Edwards vs. Georgia	(1983)

Season
Total Offense	3,034	Kurt Page	(1983)
Yards Rushing	1,103	Corey Harris	(1991)
Rushing Attempts	229	Corey Harris	(1991)
Yards Passing	3,178	Kurt Page	(1983)
Pass Attempts	493	Kurt Page	(1983)
Pass Completions	286	Kurt Page	(1983)
Touchdown Passes	22	Whit Taylor	(1982)
Yards Receiving	1,213	Boo Mitchell	(1988)
Receptions	97	Keith Edwards	(1983)
Touchdown Catches	14	Allama Matthews	(1982)
Interceptions	8	Scott Wingfield	(1973)
		Leonard Coleman	(1982)
Points	90	Jack Jenkins	(1941)

Career
Total Offense	6,727	Whit Taylor	(1979-82)
Yards Rushing	2,632	Frank Mordica	(1976-79)
Rushing Attempts	619	Carl Woods	(1983-86)
Yards Passing	6,307	Whit Taylor	(1979-82)
Pass Attempts	1,016	Whit Taylor	(1979-82)
Pass Completions	555	Whit Taylor	(1979-82)
Touchdown Passes	41	Whit Taylor	(1979-82)
Yards Receiving	2,964	Boo Mitchell	(1985-88)
Receptions	200	Keith Edwards	(1980, 1982-84)
Touchdown Catches	20	Chuck Scott	(1981-84)
Interceptions	15	Leonard Coleman	(1980-83)
Points	192	Ricky Anderson	(1981-84)

Team

Game
Points	105	vs. Bethel	(1912)
Total Offense	798	vs. Northwestern	(1952)
Yards Rushing	606	vs. Tennessee Tech	(1942)
Yards Passing	464	vs. Tennessee	(1981)
First Downs	40	vs. Davidson	(1969)
Total Defense	14	vs. Tennessee Tech	(1941)
Rushing Defense	-15	vs. Louisville	(1941)
Passing Defense	N/A		

Season
Points	514	(1915)
Total Offense	4,570	(1974)
Yards Rushing	2,894	(1974)
Yards Passing	3,299	(1983)
First Downs	237	(1987)
Fewest Points Allowed	8	(1910)
Total Defense	N/A	
Rushing Defense	N/A	
Passing Defense	N/A	
Consecutive Wins	10	(1911-12; Four in 1911, six in 1912)
		(1926-27; Seven in 1926, Three in 1927)

Carl Woods

Frank Mordica

164 Vanderbilt

Vanderbilt in the NFL

Sam Agee, B
Chicago Cardinals 1938-39

Jim Arnold, P
Kansas City Chiefs 1983-85; Detroit Lions 1986-91

Bob Asher, T
Dallas Cowboys 1970; Chicago Bears 1972-75

Lynn Bomar, E
New York Giants 1925-26

Preston Brown, WR-KR
New England Patriots 1980; New York Jets 1983

Tim Bryant, LB
Minnesota Vikings 1987

Wamon Buggs, WR
Green Bay Packers 1982

Leonard Coleman, CB
Indianapolis Colts 1985-87; San Diego Chargers 1988-89

Ken Cooper, C
Baltimore Colts 1949-50

Ben Donnell, DE
Los Angeles Chargers 1960

Chris Gaines, LB
Miami Dolphins 1988

Bob Goodridge, E
Minnesota Vikings 1968

Henry Gude, G
Philadelphia Eagles 1946

Corey Harris, RB
Houston Oilers 1992; Green Bay Packers 1992

Dennis Harrison, DE
Philadelphia Eagles 1978-84; Los Angeles Rams 1985; Atlanta Falcons 1986-87

Larry Hayes, LB
New York Giants 1961; Los Angeles Rams 1962-63

Chip Healy, LB
St. Louis Cardinals 1969-70

Roy Huggins, B
Los Angeles Rams 1944

Mark Ilgenfritz, DE
Cleveland Browns 1974

Jack Jenkins, B
Washington Redskins 1943, 1946-47

Phil King, B
New York Giants 1958-63; Pittsburgh Steelers 1964; Minnesota Vikings 1965-66

Charlie Leyendecker, T
Philadelphia Eagles 1933

Allama Matthews, TE
Atlanta Falcons 1983-86

Rob Monaco, OT
St. Louis Cardinals 1985-86

Tom Moore, B
Green Bay Packers 1960-65; Los Angeles Rams 1966; Atlanta Falcons 1967

Doug Nettles, DB
Baltimore Colts 1974-79; New York Giants 1980

John North, E
Baltimore Colts 1948-50

Carl Parker, WR
Cincinnati Bengals 1988-89

Jim Peebles, E
Washington Redskins 1946-49, 1951

Dick Plasman, E
Chicago Bears 1937-41, 1944; Chicago Cardinals 1946-47

Buford (Baby) Ray, T
Green Bay Packers 1938-48

Tom Redmond, DE
St. Louis Cardinals 1960-65

Herb Rich, B
Baltimore Colts 1950; Los Angeles Rams 1951-53; New York Giants 1954-56

Pat Saindon, G
New Orleans Saints 1986

Alf Satterfield, T
San Francisco 49ers 1947

Chuck Scott, WR
Los Angeles Rams 1985-86; Dallas Cowboys 1987

Ed Smith, LB
Baltimore Colts 1980-81

Ken Stone, DB
Buffalo Bills 1973; Washington Redskins 1973-75; Tampa Bay Buccaneers 1976; St. Louis Cardinals 1977-80

Pat Toomay, DE
Dallas Cowboys 1970-74; Buffalo Bills 1975; Oakland Raiders 1977-79

Bill Wade, QB
Los Angeles Rams 1954-60; Chicago Bears 1961-66

Brenard Wilson, S
Philadelphia Eagles 1979-86

DeMond Winston, LB
New Orleans Saints 1990-93

Will Wolford, OT
Buffalo Bills 1986-92; Indianapolis Colts 1993

Carl Woods, RB
New England Patriots 1987

Corey Harris

Will Wolford

1994 SEC Football

Vanderbilt Media Information

Vanderbilt SID
Rod Williamson

Vanderbilt Sports Information
P.O. Box 120158
Nashville, TN 37212
(615) 322-4121
FAX: (615) 343-7064

Williamson (Home) 794-1839

Football Writers
Mike Organ
The Tennessean (AM)
1100 Broadway
Nashville, TN 37203
(615) 259-8010

Mark McGee
Nashville Banner (PM)
1100 Broadway
Nashville, TN 37203
(615) 259-8252

Other Daily Newspapers
Chattanooga News-Free Press (PM)
400 East 11th
Chattanooga, TN 37402
(615) 756-6900

Chattanooga Times (AM)
P.O. Box 951
Chattanooga, TN 37401
(615) 756-1234

Marion Wilhoite
Columbia Daily Herald
P.O. Box 1425
Columbia, TN 38401
(615) 388-6464

Memphis Commercial Appeal
495 Union Ave.
Memphis, TN 38101
(901) 529-2546

Columnists
David Climer, Jimmy Davy,
Larry Woody
The Tennessean (AM)
1100 Broadway
Nashville, TN 37203
(615) 259-8010

Joe Biddle
Nashville Banner (PM)
1100 Broadway
Nashville, TN 37203
(615) 259-8252

Roy Exum
News-Free Press (PM)
400 East 11th
Chattanooga, TN 37401
(615) 757-6273

Wire Service
Teresa Walker
Associated Press
1100 Broadway
Nashville, TN 37203
(615) 244-2205

Commodore Network
Wes Durham (Play-By-Play)
Vanderbilt Athletic Department
P.O. Box 120158
Nashville, TN 37212
(615) 322-4121

Ralph Miranda (Analyst)
Vanderbilt Athletic Dept.
P.O. Box 120158
Nashville, TN 37212
(615) 322-4727

Stations Carrying Games
Radio—WSM-AM
2644 McGavock Pike
Nashville, TN 37214
(615) 871-6711

Tom Stevens
(Network Coordinator)
Farrell Creative Communications
102 Woodmont Blvd.
Nashville, TN 37205
(615) 383-1988

Television Broadcasters
Steve Phillips, Joe Fisher
WKRN-TV ABC
441 Murfreesboro Road,
Nashville, TN 37210
(615) 248-7239

Rudy Kalis, Garry Gupton
WSMV-TV NBC
P.O. Box 4
Nashville, TN 37202
(615) 353-2231

Hope Hines, Mark Howard
WTVF-TV CBS
474 James Robertson Parkway
Nashville, TN 37219
(615) 248-5285

Radio Stations
Walt Adams
WSM Radio
2644 McGavock Pike
Nashville, TN 37214
(615) 871-6711

George Plaster
WWTN Radio
The Penthouse
1808 West End Building
Nashville, TN 37203
(615) 320-9986

Bob Bell, Bill King
WLAC Radio
10 Music Circle East
Nashville, TN 37203
(615) 256-0555

Jim Fitzgerald
Tennessee Radio Network
621 Mainstream, Suite 230
Nashville, TN 37228
(615) 742-6100

Campus Media
Vanderbilt Hustler (Newspaper)
Box 1504 Station B
Nashville, TN 37235
(615) 322-2424

WRVU Radio
Box 9100 Station B
Nashville, TN 37235
(615) 322-7625

Commodore (Yearbook)
Box 1517 Station B
Nashville, TN 37235
(615) 322-2450

1993 IN REVIEW

The Florida Gators received the 1993 SEC Championship trophy from Commissioner Roy Kramer following their 28-13 victory over Alabama in the second annual title game at Legion Field.

1993 SEC Standings

EASTERN DIVISION	SEC	Pct	All	Pct
*Florida	7-1	.875	11-2	.846
Tennessee	6-1-1	.813	9-2-1	.792
Kentucky	4-4	.500	6-6	.500
Georgia	2-6	.250	5-6	.455
South Carolina	2-6	.250	4-7	.364
Vanderbilt	1-7	.125	4-7	.364

* SEC and Eastern Division Champion

WESTERN DIVISION	SEC	Pct	All	Pct
+Alabama	5-2-1	.688	9-3-1	.731
Arkansas	3-4-1	.438	5-5-1	.500
LSU	3-5	.375	5-6	.455
Ole Miss	3-5	.375	5-6	.455
Miss. State	2-5-1	.313	3-6-2	.364
#Auburn	8-0	1.000	11-0	1.000

+Western Division Champion   #Not eligible for title
Overall record includes bowl games

Non-Conference Record

28-7-1 (.792)

3-2 vs. Atlantic Coast	1-0 vs. Southern
0-1 vs. Big Ten	2-1 vs. Southwest
8-0-1 vs. Big West	12-3 vs. Independents
1-0 vs. Mid-American	1-0 vs. Division I-AA

Division I Non-Conference Records

SOUTHEASTERN	28-7-1	.792
Pacific-10	23-9	.719
Big East	22-9-1	.703
Big Ten	23-10	.697
Atlantic Coast	19-10	.655
Big Eight	21-11-1	.652
Western Athletic	17-19	.472
Southwest	12-18-2	.406
Mid-American	7-19	.269
Big West	12-37-1	.250

1993 SEC Bowl Results

PEACH BOWL • December 31, 1993 • Atlanta, Ga.
Clemson 14, **KENTUCKY 13**

OUTBACK STEAKHOUSE GATOR BOWL • December 31, 1993 • ESPN-TV
ALABAMA 24, North Carolina 10

CompUSA FLORIDA CITRUS BOWL • January 1, 1994 • ABC-TV
Penn State 31, **TENNESSEE 13**

USFG INSURANCE SUGAR BOWL • January 1, 1994 • ABC-TV
FLORIDA 41, West Virginia 7

Returning Statistical Leaders

RUSHING
RB - Moe Williams, Kentucky
1993: 164 for 928; 5.7 avg; 5 TDs; 4-SEC/38-NCAA

PASSING YARDAGE
QB - Eric Zeier, Georgia
1993: 269-425-7; 3,525 yards; 24 TDs; 1-SEC

PASSING EFFICIENCY
QB - Eric Zeier, Georgia
1993: 148.3; 269-425-7; 3,525 yds; 2-SEC/18-NCAA

RECEIVING
WR - Brice Hunter, Georgia
1993: 76 for 970 yds (12.8 avg); 9 TDs; 1-SEC

SCORING
PK - John Becksvoort, Tennessee
1993: 95 pts (59 PAT/12 FG); 1-SEC/10-NCAA

FIELD GOALS
PK - Michael Proctor, Alabama
1993: 1.8 FGPG; 22 of 29 (76%); 1-SEC/1-NCAA

PUNTING
P - Terry Daniel, Auburn
1993: 51 for 2393 yds; 46.9 avg; 1-SEC/2-NCAA

TACKLES
LB - Abdul Jackson, Ole Miss
1993: 140 (65-75); 5 TFL (-19); 1-SEC

INTERCEPTIONS
CB - Alundis Brice, Ole Miss
1993: 7; 0.6 INTPG; 2 TDs; t1-SEC/t2-NCAA

1993 SEC Championship Game

The SEC staged its second annual Championship Football Game on December 4, 1993, with Eastern Division Champion Florida defeating Western Division winner Alabama 28-13 in front of a crowd of 76,345 at Birmingham's Legion Field.

The Gators were led by quarterback Terry Dean, who passed for 256 yards and two touchdowns en route to Championship Game Most Valuable Player honors. After virtually three quarters of neck-and-neck football, and the Gators leading by one, 14-13, Florida was faced with a fourth-and-eight situation. Punter Shayne Edge kept the drive alive with a 20-yard sprint, and on the next play, Dean hit wideout Jack Jackson with a 43-yard strike to give Florida an eight-point cushion. From there, the Florida defense held its ground and the Gators secured the victory.

The victory secured Florida as the host of the USF+G Sugar Bowl. On January 1, 1994, the eighth-ranked Gators defeated West Virginia 41-7 in New Orleans to win their first Sugar Bowl title.

The SEC etched its mark in the college football history books in 1992 with the inaugural game, the first-ever Division IA championship between its two division winners. Alabama defeated Florida in that contest, 28-21, and went on to win the National crown.

1993 SEC Championship

December 4 • Birmingham
Legion Field (76,345)

Scoring

	1	2	3	4	Final
FLORIDA	7	7	7	7	28
ALABAMA	7	3	3	0	13

Team	Time	Scoring Play
UA	10:13	Lynch 1 run (Proctor kick)
		Drive: 71 yards, 8 plays, 4:47
UF	1:02	Houston 13 pass from Dean (Davis kick)
		Drive: 44 yards, 9 plays, 1:43
UA	12:02	Proctor 45 FG
UF	1:10	Dean 2 run (Davis kick)
		Drive: 35 yards, 6 plays, 1:44
UA	2:14	Proctor 25 FG
UF	:28	J. Jackson 43 pass from Dean (Davis kick)
		Drive: 80 yards, 7 plays, 1:46
UF	11:59	Rhett 3 run (Davis kick)
		Drive: 54 yards, 9 plays, 3:22

Statistics

	Alabama	Florida
First Downs	17	20
Rushing Atts. - Net Yds.	40 - 118	31 - 103
Passing	17-29-2	21-38-2
Passing Yards	161	271
Time of Possession	32:17	27:43

Individual Leaders

RUSHING
UA - Palmer (16-93); UF - Rhett (22-88)

PASSING
UA Palmer (8-16-1, 90 yds); UF - Dean (20-37-2, 256 yds)

RECEIVING
UA - Malone (3-37); UF - W. Jackson (9-114)

Most Valuable Player
QB Terry Dean (Florida)

Florida quarterback Terry Dean earned Most Valuable Player honors after converting 20 of 37 passes for 256 yards and two touchdowns.

A crowd of 76,345 gathered at Birmingham's Legion Field for the second annual SEC Football Championship Game.

1994 SEC Football

1993 SEC Team Statistics
(NCAA Ranking in Parentheses)

TOTAL OFFENSE

School	GAMES	PLAYS	YDS	AVG	TD	YDSPG
Tennessee (6)	11	762	5286	6.94	62	480.55
Florida (7)	12	888	5719	6.44	61	476.58
Georgia (19)	11	776	4733	6.10	39	430.27
Auburn (25)	11	800	4620	5.78	45	420.00
Alabama (43)	12	835	4688	5.61	36	390.67
Miss State (58)	11	767	3932	5.13	27	357.45
S Carolina (76)	11	734	3638	4.96	21	330.73
Kentucky (78)	11	759	3620	4.77	26	329.09
Arkansas (89)	11	731	3477	4.76	22	316.09
LSU (90)	11	759	3451	4.55	21	313.73
Ole Miss (92)	11	682	3352	4.91	28	304.73
Vanderbilt (104)	11	721	2682	3.72	16	243.82

RUSHING OFFENSE

School	GAMES	CAR	YDS	AVG	TD	YDSPG
Tennessee (13)	11	442	2621	5.93	27	238.27
Auburn (21)	11	513	2432	4.74	26	221.09
Kentucky (24)	11	545	2315	4.25	17	210.45
Vanderbilt (30)	11	564	2136	3.79	14	194.18
Arkansas (33)	11	498	2123	4.26	14	193.00
Alabama (42)	12	535	2119	3.96	20	176.58
Miss State (51)	11	436	1791	4.11	12	162.82
Ole Miss (68)	11	426	1574	3.69	9	143.09
Florida (74)	12	400	1647	4.12	18	137.25
LSU (77)	11	418	1449	3.47	12	131.73
S Carolina (83)	11	409	1371	3.35	11	124.64
Georgia (93)	11	344	1181	3.43	12	107.36

TOTAL DEFENSE

School	GAMES	PLAYS	YDS	AVG	TD	YDSPG
Ole Miss (1)	11	724	2580	3.56	14	234.55
Alabama (5)	12	738	3104	4.21	19	258.67
Tennessee (13)	11	780	3395	4.35	16	308.64
Auburn (15)	11	698	3432	4.92	24	312.00
S Carolina (28)	11	759	3664	4.83	25	333.09
Florida (30)	12	836	4039	4.83	28	336.58
Kentucky (37)	11	729	3796	5.21	23	345.09
Miss State (40)	11	771	3862	5.01	28	351.09
Vanderbilt (43)	11	715	3876	5.42	37	352.36
Arkansas (45)	11	765	3925	5.13	22	356.82
Georgia (63)	11	785	4190	5.34	37	380.91
LSU (72)	11	734	4353	5.93	41	395.73

RUSHING DEFENSE

School	GAMES	CAR	YDS	AVG	TD	YDSPG
Ole Miss (6)	11	463	1127	2.43	8	102.45
Florida (9)	12	417	1334	3.20	9	111.17
Tennessee (12)	11	433	1290	2.98	8	117.27
Auburn (21)	11	349	1393	3.99	7	126.64
Alabama (25)	12	428	1565	3.66	10	130.42
Vanderbilt (27)	11	397	1453	3.66	15	132.09
Miss State (34t)	11	440	1535	3.49	10	139.55
Kentucky (47)	11	385	1707	4.43	11	155.18
Arkansas (59)	11	463	1853	4.00	11	168.45
S Carolina (67)	11	494	2010	4.07	18	182.73
LSU (81)	11	434	2149	4.95	20	195.36
Georgia (83)	11	488	2161	4.43	21	196.45

PASSING OFFENSE

School	GAMES	ATT	CMP	INT	PCT	YDS	YDS/ATT	TD	YDSPG	INTPA	YDS/CMP
Florida (4)	12	488	284	21	0.58	4072	8.34	41	339.33	4.30	14.34
Georgia (8)	11	432	272	7	0.63	3552	8.22	24	322.91	1.62	13.06
Tennessee (29)	11	320	208	9	0.65	2665	8.32	31	242.27	2.81	12.81
Alabama (45)	12	300	169	16	0.56	2569	8.56	13	214.08	5.33	15.20
S Carolina (50)	11	325	163	14	0.50	2267	6.98	8	206.09	4.31	13.91
Auburn (57)	11	288	174	8	0.60	2188	7.60	15	198.91	2.78	12.57
Miss State (59)	11	331	144	10	0.44	2141	6.47	14	194.64	3.02	14.87
LSU (66)	11	341	161	16	0.47	2002	5.87	9	182.00	4.69	12.43
Ole Miss (78)	11	255	143	14	0.56	1778	6.97	14	161.64	5.49	12.43
Arkansas (97)	11	233	114	10	0.49	1354	5.81	6	123.09	4.29	11.88
Kentucky (99)	11	214	108	11	0.50	1305	6.10	9	118.64	5.14	12.08
Vanderbilt (105)	11	157	55	13	0.35	546	3.48	0	49.64	8.28	9.93

PASSING DEFENSE

School	GAMES	ATT	CMP	INT	PCT	YDS	YDS/ATT	TD	YDSPG	INTPA	YDS/CMP
Alabama (2)	12	310	144	22	0.46	1539	4.96	9	128.25	7.10	10.69
Ole Miss (3)	11	261	117	15	0.45	1453	5.57	5	132.09	5.75	12.42
S Carolina (35)	11	265	145	3	0.55	1654	6.24	7	150.36	1.13	11.41
Georgia (32)	11	297	163	17	0.55	2029	6.83	14	184.45	5.72	12.45
Auburn (9)	11	349	153	15	0.44	2039	5.84	15	185.36	4.30	13.33
Arkansas (34)	11	302	171	13	0.57	2072	6.86	9	188.36	4.30	12.12
Kentucky (11)	11	344	177	20	0.51	2089	6.07	11	189.91	5.81	11.80
Tennessee (5)	11	347	167	18	0.48	2105	6.07	7	191.36	5.19	12.60
LSU (78)	11	300	176	13	0.59	2204	7.35	20	200.36	4.33	12.52
Miss State (52)	11	331	185	15	0.56	2327	7.03	14	211.55	4.53	12.58
Vanderbilt (68)	11	318	174	13	0.55	2423	7.62	16	220.27	4.09	13.93
Florida (39)	12	419	233	16	0.56	2705	6.46	17	225.42	3.82	11.61

*NCAA Ranks Pass Efficiency Defense

SCORING OFFENSE

School	GAMES	PTS	AVG	TD	KXP	OXP	FG	SF
Tennessee (2)	11	471	42.82	62	59	1	12	1
Florida (4)	12	472	39.33	61	53	3	15	1
Auburn (18)	11	353	32.09	45	45	0	12	1
Georgia (28)	11	328	29.82	39	35	1	19	0
Alabama (38)	12	316	26.33	36	32	1	22	0
Ole Miss (66)	11	242	22.00	28	25	0	15	2
Miss State (67)	11	241	21.91	27	18	5	17	0
Kentucky (79)	11	207	18.82	26	22	3	7	1
LSU (88)	11	190	17.27	21	17	1	15	0
S Carolina (89)	11	188	17.09	21	18	0	14	1
Arkansas (98)	11	165	15.00	22	18	0	5	0
Vanderbilt (103)	11	137	12.45	16	15	0	8	1

SCORING DEFENSE

School	GAMES	PTS	AVG	TD	KXP	OXP	FG	SF
Ole Miss (4)	11	142	12.91	14	10	2	14	1
Tennessee (5)	11	144	13.09	16	13	1	11	0
Alabama (6)	12	158	13.17	19	16	1	8	1
Auburn (19)	11	192	17.45	24	20	2	8	0
Kentucky (21)	11	195	17.73	23	18	2	11	1
Arkansas (25)	11	208	18.91	22	20	1	18	0
S Carolina (31)	11	214	19.45	25	20	1	14	0
Florida (33)	12	237	19.75	28	22	1	15	0
Miss State (45)	11	245	22.27	28	24	0	17	1
Georgia (68)	11	289	26.27	37	33	2	10	0
Vanderbilt (69)	11	290	26.36	37	36	0	10	1
LSU (74)	11	308	28.00	41	38	0	8	0

1993 In Review

KICKOFF RETURNS

School	GAMES	NO	YDS	TD	AVG
Tennessee (12)	11	28	661	0	23.61
Florida (22)	12	37	828	1	22.38
Vanderbilt (40)	11	48	1005	0	20.94
Ole Miss (41)	11	37	773	0	20.89
Georgia (52)	11	43	861	0	20.02
Alabama (57)	12	30	589	0	19.63
LSU (60)	11	46	901	0	19.59
S. Carolina (75)	11	29	541	0	18.66
Auburn (81)	11	30	537	0	17.90
Arkansas (82)	11	36	640	0	17.78
Miss State (85)	11	36	633	0	17.58
Kentucky (87)	11	33	577	0	17.48

NET PUNTING

School	PUNTS	AVG	NO RET	YDS RET	NET AVG	TOT YDS
Auburn (7)	51	46.92	26	418	38.73	2393
Florida (9)	44	41.80	20	142	38.50	1839
Alabama (14)	56	43.59	29	311	38.04	2441
Miss State (15)	64	41.97	31	267	37.80	2686
Tennessee (21)	42	39.19	18	77	37.36	1646
LSU (30)	56	39.88	22	166	36.91	2233
Arkansas (49)	56	37.66	20	110	35.70	2109
Kentucky (61)	55	37.25	21	139	34.73	2049
Georgia (70)	48	37.54	32	158	34.25	1802
S Carolina (88)	69	35.83	30	214	32.72	2472
Ole Miss (97)	66	34.18	25	159	31.77	2256
Vanderbilt (99)	70	35.54	36	268	31.71	2488

PUNT RETURNS

School	GAMES	NO	YDS	TD	AVG
LSU (6)	11	20	256	0	12.80
Tennessee (9)	11	37	453	2	12.24
Ole Miss (13)	11	37	420	1	11.35
Georgia (20)	11	25	263	1	10.52
Miss State (21)	11	33	335	1	10.15
Florida (46)	12	35	298	0	8.50
Alabama (47)	12	32	270	0	8.44
Auburn (56t)	11	32	264	0	8.25
S. Carolina (71)	11	31	218	2	7.03
Vanderbilt (78)	11	16	104	0	6.50
Arkansas (86)	11	28	157	0	5.61
Kentucky (94)	11	30	153	0	5.10

QUARTERBACK SACKS

School	G	SCKS	YDS	SCKS/GM
Tennessee	11	38	261	3.45
Arkansas	11	30	194	2.73
Ole Miss	11	29	207	2.64
Alabama	12	31	195	2.58
Vanderbilt	11	28	173	2.55
Florida	12	30	238	2.50
S. Carolina	11	27	163	2.45
Miss State	11	26	165	2.36
Georgia	11	25	124	2.27
Auburn	11	24	141	2.18
Kentucky	11	14	78	1.27
LSU	11	14	110	1.27

FIRST DOWNS PER GAME

School	G	RUSH	RSH/GM	PASS	PASS/GM	PEN	PEN/GM	TOTAL	FD/GM
Florida	12	103	8.58	182	15.17	13	1.08	298	24.83
Tennessee	11	137	12.45	114	10.36	7	0.64	258	23.45
Auburn	11	133	12.09	99	9.00	16	1.45	248	22.55
Georgia	11	77	7.00	139	12.64	16	1.45	232	21.09
Alabama	12	113	9.42	97	8.08	16	1.33	226	18.83
LSU	11	90	8.18	102	9.27	10	0.91	202	18.36
Miss State	11	110	10.00	83	7.55	9	0.82	202	18.36
Arkansas	11	126	11.45	62	5.64	12	1.09	200	18.18
Kentucky	11	121	11.00	56	5.09	15	1.36	192	17.45
Ole Miss	11	88	8.00	83	7.55	9	0.82	180	16.36
S Carolina	11	83	7.55	87	7.91	6	0.55	176	16.00
Vanderbilt	11	109	9.91	25	2.27	17	1.55	151	13.73

FIRST DOWNS ALLOWED PER GAME

School	G	RUSH	RSH/GM	PASS	PASS/GM	PEN	PEN/GM	TOTAL	FD/GM
Alabama	12	91	7.58	73	6.08	6	0.50	170	14.17
Ole Miss	11	75	6.82	67	6.09	22	2.00	164	14.91
Auburn	11	71	6.45	82	7.45	12	1.09	165	15.00
Kentucky	11	89	8.09	85	7.73	8	0.73	182	16.55
Tennessee	11	84	7.64	88	8.00	14	1.27	186	16.91
S Carolina	11	102	9.27	69	6.27	15	1.36	186	16.91
Vanderbilt	11	88	8.00	105	9.55	8	0.73	201	18.27
Florida	12	88	7.33	116	9.67	21	1.75	225	18.75
Miss State	11	93	8.45	106	9.64	16	1.45	215	19.55
Georgia	11	113	10.27	92	8.36	11	1.00	216	19.64
Arkansas	11	115	10.45	101	9.18	7	0.64	223	20.27
LSU	11	122	11.09	90	8.18	18	1.64	230	20.91

THIRD DOWN CONVERSIONS

School	G	CONV	ATT	PCT
Tennessee	11	60	129	0.47
Arkansas	11	77	166	0.46
Florida	12	65	156	0.42
LSU	11	69	169	0.41
Alabama	12	75	188	0.40
Auburn	11	57	146	0.39
Kentucky	11	64	168	0.38
Miss State	11	63	175	0.36
Georgia	11	55	151	0.36
S. Carolina	11	54	163	0.33
Vanderbilt	11	52	167	0.31
Ole Miss	11	43	145	0.30

FOURTH DOWN CONVERSIONS

School	G	CONV	ATT	PCT
Miss State	11	14	19	0.74
Georgia	11	11	17	0.65
Tennessee	11	6	10	0.60
Alabama	12	8	16	0.50
Florida	12	8	17	0.47
LSU	11	6	13	0.46
Arkansas	11	7	16	0.44
Kentucky	11	10	23	0.43
Ole Miss	11	3	7	0.43
Vanderbilt	11	7	17	0.41
Auburn	11	4	10	0.40
S Carolina	11	4	13	0.31

THIRD DOWN CONVERSIONS DEFENSE

School	G	CONV	ATT	PCT
Alabama	12	47	169	0.28
Auburn	11	43	153	0.28
S Carolina	11	53	167	0.32
Vanderbilt	11	46	139	0.33
Florida	12	61	183	0.33
Kentucky	11	50	152	0.33
Ole Miss	11	57	168	0.34
Tennessee	11	64	178	0.36
Arkansas	11	64	155	0.41
LSU	11	66	155	0.43
Georgia	11	73	168	0.43
Miss State	11	73	165	0.44

FOURTH DOWN CONVERSIONS DEFENSE

School	G	CONV	ATT	PCT
Miss State	11	2	9	0.22
Auburn	11	7	20	0.35
Tennessee	11	8	22	0.36
Vanderbilt	11	6	14	0.43
Arkansas	11	8	18	0.44
Ole Miss	11	4	9	0.44
Florida	12	9	18	0.50
Georgia	11	9	18	0.50
Alabama	12	5	10	0.50
Kentucky	11	12	20	0.60
LSU	11	9	14	0.64
S Carolina	11	8	11	0.73

PENALTY YARDS PER GAME

School	G	PEN	YDS	YDS/GM
Kentucky	11	38	320	29.09
Arkansas	11	48	430	39.09
Vanderbilt	11	69	539	49.00
Auburn	11	66	551	50.09
S. Carolina	11	71	570	51.82
LSU	11	67	606	55.09
Tennessee	11	73	624	56.73
Miss State	11	77	627	57.00
Georgia	11	78	631	57.36
Alabama	12	83	702	58.50
Ole Miss	11	81	677	61.55
Florida	12	109	846	70.50

TURNOVER RATIO

School	G	INT	FUM REC	TAKE AWAYS	HAD INT	FUM LOST	TO	DIFF	RATIO
Tennessee (4t)	11	18	15	33	9	11	20	13	1.18
Ole Miss (4t)	11	15	15	30	14	3	17	13	1.18
Georgia (23t)	11	17	9	26	7	12	19	7	0.64
Miss State (23t)	11	15	14	29	10	12	22	7	0.64
Kentucky (28t)	11	20	9	29	11	12	23	6	0.55
Alabama (47t)	12	22	7	29	16	9	25	4	0.33
Auburn (43t)	11	15	10	25	8	14	22	3	0.27
Florida (58)	12	16	14	30	21	9	30	0	0.00
LSU (71t)	11	13	7	20	16	9	25	-5	-0.45
Arkansas (75)	11	13	6	19	10	15	25	-6	-0.55
S Carolina (79t)	11	3	15	18	14	11	25	-7	-0.64
Vanderbilt (84t)	11	13	12	25	13	20	33	-8	-0.73

1994 SEC Football

1993 SEC Individual Statistics

(NCAA Ranking in Parentheses)

RUSHING

Player, Team	G	ATT	YDS	AVG	TD	YDSPG	POS	HT	WT	CL
1 James Bostic, Auburn (13)	11	199	1205	6.1	12	109.6	TB	6-0	224	JR
2 Errict Rhett, Florida (16)	12	247	1289	5.2	11	107.4	RB	5-11	214	SR
3 Charlie Garner, Tenn (17)	11	159	1161	7.3	8	105.6	RB	5-10	187	SR
4 Moe Williams, Kentucky (38)	11	164	928	5.7	5	84.4	TB	6-2	205	FR
5 Michael Davis, Miss St (47)	11	205	883	4.3	7	80.3	RB	6-1	239	JR
6 Brandon Bennett, S Carolina	11	193	853	4.4	7	77.6	RB	6-0	198	JR
7 Terrell Davis, Georgia	11	167	824	4.9	5	74.9	SB	6-1	206	JR
8 Sherman Williams, Alabama	11	168	738	4.4	9	67.1	RB	5-10	193	JR
9 Oscar Malone, Arkansas	9	89	555	6.2	5	61.7	TB	5-9	180	SO
10 Kevin Bouie, Miss State	9	115	505	4.4	3	56.1	RB	6-1	220	JR
11 Jay Johnson, LSU	10	106	558	5.3	6	55.8	TB	5-9	184	SO
12 Tony Jackson, Vanderbilt	11	120	607	5.1	3	55.2	TB	5-8	176	SR

PASSING (Minimum 10 Passes per Game Played)

Player, Team	G	ATT	CMP	CMP PCT	INT	YDS	YDSPG	TD	RATING POINTS	POS	HT	WT	CL
1 Heath Shuler, Tennessee (6)	11	285	184	64.6	8	2354	214.0	25	157.3	QB	6-3	212	JR
2 Eric Zeier, Georgia (18)	11	425	269	63.3	7	3525	320.5	24	148.3	QB	6-2	200	JR
3 Terry Dean, Florida (20)	10	200	118	59.0	10	1651	165.1	17	146.4	QB	6-2	204	JR
4 Danny Wuerffel, Florida (22)	11	273	159	58.2	10	2230	202.7	22	146.1	QB	6-2	201	FR
5 Stan White, Auburn (35)	11	271	164	60.5	8	2057	187.0	13	134.2	QB	6-3	202	SR
6 Jay Barker, Alabama (39)	9	171	98	57.3	7	1525	169.4	4	131.8	QB	6-3	210	JR
7 Lawrence Adams, Ole Miss (45)	11	195	110	56.4	12	1415	128.6	13	127.1	QB	5-10	185	SO
8 Pookie Jones, Kentucky	11	163	85	52.2	7	1071	97.4	8	115.0	QB	6-1	196	JR
9 Todd Jordan, Miss State	11	294	131	44.6	9	1935	175.9	11	106.1	QB	6-4	230	SR
10 Barry Lunney, Jr., Arkansas	11	202	104	51.5	7	1241	112.8	6	106.0	QB	6-2	185	JR
11 Steve Taneyhill, S Carolina	11	291	149	51.2	14	1930	175.5	6	104.1	QB	6-5	208	SO
12 Jamie Howard, LSU	10	248	106	42.7	12	1319	131.9	7	87.1	QB	6-1	195	SO

RECEIVING (By Number of Receptions)

Player, Team	G	REC	YDS	TD	YDSPG	CTPG	AVG	POS	HT	WT	CL
1 Brice Hunter, Georgia	11	76	970	9	88.2	6.9	12.8	WR	6-0	195	SO
2 David Palmer, Alabama	12	61	1000	7	83.3	5.1	16.4	FL	5-9	170	JR
3 Jack Jackson, Florida	12	51	949	11	79.1	4.3	18.6	WR	5-9	167	SO
4 Shannon Mitchell, Georgia	11	49	539	2	49.0	4.5	11.0	TE	6-3	235	SR
5 Willie Jackson, Florida	9	49	675	6	75.0	5.4	13.8	WR	6-1	202	SR
6 Frank Sanders, Auburn	11	48	842	6	76.5	4.4	17.5	WR	6-2	200	JR
7 Chris Doering, Florida	12	43	553	7	46.1	3.6	12.9	WR	6-4	175	SO
8 Craig Faulkner, Tennessee	11	40	680	6	61.8	3.6	17.0	WR	5-11	180	SR
9 Cory Fleming, Tennessee	11	39	596	11	54.2	3.6	15.3	WR	6-3	207	SR
9 Billy Williams, Tennessee	11	39	513	5	46.6	3.6	13.2	WR	5-11	161	JR
9 Jeff Thomas, Georgia	11	39	469	1	42.6	3.6	12.0	SE	6-2	192	JR
12 Hason Graham, Georgia	11	36	699	5	63.5	3.3	19.4	WR	5-11	170	JR

RECEIVING (By Yards per Game)

Player, Team	G	REC	YDS	TD	YDSPG	CTPG	AVG	POS	HT	WT	CL
1 Brice Hunter, Georgia (13)	11	76	970	9	88.2	6.9	12.8	WR	6-0	195	SO
2 David Palmer, Alabama (23)	12	61	1000	7	83.3	5.1	16.4	FL	5-9	170	JR
3 Jack Jackson, Florida (33)	12	51	949	11	79.1	4.3	18.6	WR	5-9	167	SO
4 Frank Sanders, Auburn (34)	11	48	842	6	76.5	4.4	17.5	WR	6-2	200	JR
5 Willie Jackson, Florida (35)	9	49	675	6	75.0	5.4	13.8	WR	6-1	202	SR
6 Hason Graham, Georgia	11	36	699	5	63.5	3.3	19.4	WR	5-11	170	JR
7 Craig Faulkner, Tennessee	11	40	680	6	61.8	3.6	17.0	WR	5-11	180	SR
8 Eddie Small, Ole Miss	11	33	624	6	56.7	3.0	18.9	WR	6-0	200	SR
9 Cory Fleming, Tennessee	11	39	596	11	54.2	3.6	15.3	WR	6-3	207	SR
10 Harrison Houston, Florida	12	35	643	7	53.6	2.9	18.4	WR	5-9	175	SR
11 Chris Jones, Miss State	11	24	541	2	49.2	2.2	22.5	WR	6-3	202	SO
11 Toby Cates, S Carolina	11	27	541	3	49.2	2.5	20.0	WR	6-0	193	JR

FIELD GOALS

Player, Team	G	FGA	FGM	PCT	FGPG	POS	HT	WT	CL
1 Michael Proctor, Alabama (1)	12	29	22	0.76	1.8	K	5-11	183	SO
2 Kanon Parkman, Georgia (3t)	11	27	19	0.70	1.7	PK	5-11	168	SO
3 Tom Burke, Miss State (6t)	11	23	17	0.74	1.6	PK	5-11	156	SR
4 Andre Lafleur, LSU (13)	10	17	14	0.82	1.4	PK	5-11	176	SO
5 Judd Davis, Florida (23t)	12	19	15	0.79	1.3	PK	6-1	185	JR
6 Walter Grant, Ole Miss (26)	10	20	12	0.60	1.2	K	5-7	177	JR
7 John Becksvoort, Tenn (37t)	11	13	12	0.92	1.1	PK	6-1	170	JR
7 Scott Etheridge, Auburn (37t)	11	15	12	0.80	1.1	PK	5-11	156	SR
9 Steve Yenner, Vanderbilt	11	13	8	0.62	0.7	K	6-0	170	JR
10 Juha Leonoff, Kentucky	11	12	5	0.42	0.5	PK	5-10	178	JR
11 Lance Ellison, Arkansas	11	10	4	0.40	0.4	K	6-5	230	JR

PUNTING

Player, Team	G	NO	YDS	AVG	POS	HT	WT	CL
1 Terry Daniel, Auburn (2)	11	51	2393	46.9	P	6-1	226	JR
2 Bryne Diehl, Alabama (7)	12	56	2441	43.6	P	6-3	215	JR
3 Todd Jordan, Miss State (11)	11	56	2403	42.9	QB	6-4	230	SR
4 Shayne Edge, Florida	12	43	1837	42.7	P	5-11	171	JR
5 Scott Holstein, LSU (35)	11	56	2233	39.9	P	6-5	209	SR
6 Tom Hutton, Tennessee (40)	11	40	1584	39.6	P	6-1	193	SR
7 Scot Armstrong, Georgia	11	37	1419	38.4	P	6-2	192	SR
8 Doyle Preston, Arkansas	11	56	2109	37.7	P	6-2	190	SO
9 Bill Marinangel, Vanderbilt	11	68	2482	36.5	WB	6-2	212	FR
10 Daniel Ariza, Kentucky	11	27	976	36.2	P	5-9	178	JR
11 Marty Simpson, S Carolina	10	60	2134	35.6	K/P	6-3	180	JR
12 Chris McCardle, Ole Miss	11	65	2256	34.7	P	5-9	185	SO

PUNT RETURNS (Minimum 1 Punt Return per Game)

Player, Team	G	NO	YDS	AVG	PGM	TD	POS	HT	WT	CL
1 Shawn Summers, Tennessee (2)	11	18	255	14.2	1.6	1	DB	5-8	178	SO
2 Scott Gumina, Miss State (4)	9	13	180	13.9	1.4	1	OLB	6-0	200	JR
3 Eddie Kennison, LSU (6)	11	20	256	12.8	1.8	0	WR	6-1	180	FR
4 Ta'Boris Fisher, Ole Miss (14)	11	29	330	11.4	2.6	1	WR	5-8	165	FR
5 Sorola Palmer, Florida (22t)	10	13	129	9.9	1.3	0	WR	5-10	170	SO
6 Larry Kennedy, Florida (35)	12	19	165	8.7	1.6	0	CB	5-10	184	JR
7 David Palmer, Alabama (47)	12	31	244	7.9	2.6	0	FL	5-9	170	JR
8 Thomas Bailey, Auburn (48)	11	27	210	7.8	2.5	0	WR	6-0	196	JR
9 Bernard Euell, Miss St (49)	11	20	155	7.8	1.8	0	WR	5-10	179	SO
10 Cory Fleming, Tennessee	11	14	89	6.4	1.3	0	WR	6-3	207	SR
11 Toby Cates, S Carolina	11	17	100	5.9	1.6	0	WR	6-0	193	JR
12 Orlando Watters, Arkansas	11	28	157	5.6	2.6	0	CB	5-11	176	SR

KICKOFF RETURNS (Minimum 1 Kickoff Return per Game)

Player, Team	G	NO	YDS	AVG	PGM	TD	POS	HT	WT	CL
1 Billy Williams, Tennessee	11	13	369	28.4	1.2	0	WR	5-11	161	JR
2 Jack Jackson, Florida (5)	12	17	480	28.2	1.4	1	WR	5-9	167	SO
3 Mark Smith, Ole Miss	10	11	290	26.4	1.1	0	QB	5-9	180	SO
4 David Butler, LSU	11	11	270	24.6	1.0	0	WR	5-9	180	SO
5 Tony Jackson, Vanderbilt (23)	11	31	753	24.3	2.8	0	TB	5-8	176	SR
6 Eddie Kennison, LSU (40)	11	18	410	22.8	1.6	0	WR	6-1	180	FR
7 Jerry Jerman, Georgia (48)	10	18	398	22.1	1.8	0	SE	5-10	181	JR
8 David Palmer, Alabama (49)	12	20	439	22.0	1.7	0	FL	5-9	170	JR
9 Orlando Watters, Arkansas	11	18	392	21.8	1.6	0	CB	5-11	176	SR
10 Frank Adams, S Carolina	10	14	291	20.8	1.4	0	CB	5-8	172	SR
11 Hason Graham, Georgia	11	13	261	20.1	1.2	0	WR	5-11	170	JR
12 Joe Woods, Ole Miss	11	12	235	19.6	1.1	0	WR	5-9	160	SO

INTERCEPTIONS

Player, Team	G	NO	YDS	TD	IPG	POS	HT	WT	CL
1 Alundis Brice, Ole Miss (2t)	11	7	98	2	0.6	CB	5-11	180	JR
1 Antonio Langham, Alabama (2t)	11	7	66	1	0.6	CB	6-1	170	SR
3 Orlando Watters, Arkansas (7t)	11	6	185	2	0.6	CB	5-11	176	SR
3 Marcus Jenkins, Kentucky (7t)	11	6	45	0	0.6	SS	6-2	195	SR
3 Walt Harris, Miss State (7t)	11	6	59	0	0.6	CB	6-1	187	SO
6 DeRon Jenkins, Tenn (18t)	11	5	13	0	0.5	DB	5-11	173	SO
6 Anthony Marshall, LSU (18t)	11	5	7	0	0.5	FS	6-2	203	SR
6 Brian Robinson, Auburn (18t)	11	5	131	2	0.5	FS	6-3	194	SO
9 Chris Shelling, Auburn (33t)	11	4	169	1	0.4	CB	5-10	180	JR
9 Tory James, LSU (33t)	11	4	87	0	0.4	CB	6-2	174	SO
9 Byron King, Vanderbilt	11	4	21	0	0.4	CB	5-11	193	JR
9 Jason Parker, Tennessee	11	4	20	0	0.4	DB	6-0	187	SO
13 Willie Gaston, Alabama	12	4	14	0	0.3	CB	5-11	183	JR
13 Michael Gilmore, Florida	12	4	0	0	0.3	FS	5-11	180	JR
13 Tommy Johnson, Alabama	12	4	18	0	0.3	CB	5-10	180	JR

SCORING

Player, Team	G	TD	XP	FG	PTS	PTPG	FGA	XPA	POS	HT	WT	CL
1 John Becksvoort, Tenn (10)	11	0	59	12	95	8.6	13	59	PK	6-1	170	JR
2 Kanon Parkman, Georgia (12)	11	0	35	19	92	8.4	27	36	PK	5-11	168	SO
3 Michael Proctor, Alabama (17)	12	0	31	22	97	8.1	29	31	K	5-11	183	SO
4 Judd Davis, Florida (18t)	12	0	51	15	96	8.0	19	53	PK	6-1	185	JR
5 Scott Etheridge, Auburn (33)	11	0	45	12	81	7.4	15	45	PK	5-11	156	SR
6 James Bostic, Auburn (40t)	11	13	0	0	78	7.1	0	0	TB	6-0	224	JR
7 Tom Burke, Miss State	11	0	18	17	69	6.3	23	18	PK	5-11	156	SR
8 Jack Jackson, Florida	12	12	0	0	72	6.0	0	0	WR	5-9	167	SO
8 Cory Fleming, Tennessee	11	11	0	0	66	6.0	0	0	WR	6-3	207	SR
10 Walter Grant, Ole Miss	10	0	23	12	59	5.9	20	24	K	5-7	177	JR
10 Andre Lafleur, LSU	10	0	17	14	59	5.9	17	19	PK	5-11	176	SO
12 Errict Rhett, Florida	12	11	0	0	66	5.5	0	0	RB	5-11	214	SR

TOTAL OFFENSE

Player, Team	G	CAR	GAIN	LOSS	NET	ATT	YDS	PLAYS	YDS	YD/PL	TDR	YDSPG	POS	HT	WT	CL
1 Eric Zeier, Georgia (3)	11	59	161	204	-43	425	3525	484	3482	7.2	25	316.6	QB	6-2	200	JR
2 Heath Shuler, Tennessee (29)	11	46	137	64	73	285	2353	331	2426	7.3	28	220.6	QB	6-3	212	JR
3 Danny Wuerffel, Florida (40)	11	40	46	135	-89	273	2230	313	2141	6.8	23	194.6	QB	6-2	201	FR
4 Stan White, Auburn (44)	11	79	208	175	33	271	2057	350	2090	6.0	17	190.0	QB	6-3	202	SR
5 Todd Jordan, Miss State	11	42	123	136	-13	294	1935	336	1922	5.7	12	174.7	QB	6-4	230	SR
6 Terry Dean, Florida	10	43	135	111	24	200	1651	243	1675	6.9	19	167.5	QB	6-2	204	JR
7 Jay Barker, Alabama	9	42	87	164	-77	171	1525	213	1448	6.8	5	160.9	QB	6-3	210	JR
8 Steve Taneyhill, S Carolina	11	42	18	214	-196	291	1930	333	1734	5.2	7	157.6	QB	6-5	208	SO
9 Lawrence Adams, Ole Miss	11	108	361	196	165	195	1415	303	1580	5.2	15	143.6	QB	5-10	185	SO
10 Jamie Howard, LSU	10	45	147	147	0	248	1319	293	1319	4.5	7	131.9	QB	6-1	195	SO
11 Barry Lunney, Jr., Arkansas	11	75	248	108	140	202	1241	277	1381	5.0	8	125.6	QB	6-2	185	SO
12 Pookie Jones, Kentucky	11	130	506	218	288	163	1071	293	1359	4.6	14	123.6	QB	6-1	196	JR

ALL-PURPOSE RUNNERS

Player, Team	G	RUSH	REC	PR	KOR	YDS	YDSPG	PLAYS	YDSPL	POS	HT	WT	CL
1 David Palmer, Alabama (7)	12	278	1000	244	439	1961	163.4	154	12.7	FL	5-9	170	JR
2 Tony Jackson, Vanderbilt (24)	11	607	70	11	753	1441	131.0	162	8.9	TB	5-8	176	SR
3 Errict Rhett, Florida (26)	12	1289	271	0	0	1560	130.0	283	5.5	RB	5-11	214	SR
4 Charlie Garner, Tenn (33)	11	1161	81	0	139	1381	125.6	177	7.8	RB	5-10	187	SR
5 Jack Jackson, Florida (38)	12	0	949	0	480	1429	119.1	69	20.7	WR	5-9	167	SO
6 Brandon Bennett, S Car. (45)	11	853	282	0	124	1259	114.5	223	5.7	RB	6-0	198	JR
7 James Bostic, Auburn (48)	11	1205	40	0	0	1245	113.2	209	6.0	TB	6-0	224	JR
8 Eddie Kennison, LSU	11	24	466	256	410	1156	105.1	73	15.8	WR	6-1	180	FR
9 Thomas Bailey, Auburn	11	0	427	210	504	1141	103.7	80	14.3	WR	6-0	196	JR
10 Terrell Davis, Georgia	11	824	161	0	0	985	89.6	179	5.5	SB	6-1	206	JR
11 Brice Hunter, Georgia	11	10	970	0	0	980	89.1	79	12.4	WR	6-0	195	SO
12 Moe Williams, Kentucky	11	928	41	0	0	969	88.1	171	5.7	TB	6-2	205	FR

NOTE: As established by the NCAA, a player must play in 75 percent of the games to be listed in the statistics.

1993 SEC Defensive Leaders

LINEBACKERS

Player, Team	Tackles	Solos	Assists	Sacks	TFLs	INTs
Abdul Jackson, UM	140	65	75	0	5 (-19)	0
Jason Miska, AU	125	68	57	2 (-9)	4 (-6)	0
Ed Robinson, UF	117	59	58	.5 (-11)	5 (-18)	0
Juan Long, MSU	117	68	49	1.5(-17)	7 (-18)	2
Marty Moore, UK	116	81	35	0	3 (-7)	3
Randall Godfrey, UG	114	71	43	1 (-5)	4 (-5)	1
Shelton Quarles, VU	99	70	29	3 (-10)	7 (-23)	2
Dwayne Curry, MSU	95	52	43	0	5 (-9)	0
Gary Abide, UM	93	46	47	4 (-20)	3 (-5)	1
Charlie Clemons, UG	90	50	40	0	2 (-3)	3
Dexter Daniels, UF	86	47	39	.5 (-6)	2 (-10)	1
Gerald Collins, VU	86	58	28	2 (-18)	6 (-31)	0
Wesley Leasy, MSU	79	39	40	3 (-37)	4 (-11)	2
Terry Solomon, AU	77	42	35	1 (-10)	1 (-2)	0
Reggie Ingram, UT	77	58	19	0	2 (-5)	0
Ric. Washington, LSU	73	40	33	0	1 (-1)	0
Michael Rogers, UA	72	49	23	2 (-16)	8 (-17)	0
Robert Deshotel, LSU	68	44	24	3 (-20)	5 (-25)	0
Eric Brown, USC	68	39	29	1 (-7)	.5 (-1)	1
Mike Calais, LSU	67	39	28	0	4 (-6)	0
Rico Francis, VU	66	48	18	0	4 (-11)	1
Whit Marshall, UG	59	34	25	0	1 (-1)	0

ENDS & OUTSIDE LINEBACKERS

Player, Team	Tackles	Solos	Assists	Sacks	TFLs	INTs
Anthony Harris, AU	123	53	70	7 (-32)	8 (-17)	1
Darwin Ireland, AR	93	37	56	1 (-7)	3 (-10)	0
Dewayne Dotson, UM	92	44	48	5 (-36)	10 (-38)	0
Mitch Davis, UG	87	49	38	13 (-74)	6 (-12)	1
Ben Talley, UT	87	56	31	4 (-47)	7 (-20)	0
Cassius Ware, UM	83	57	26	9 (-74)	12 (-58)	1
Herman Carroll, MSU	80	47	33	5 (-45)	6 (-10)	0
Lateef Travis, MSU	78	46	32	4.5 (-45)	9 (-25)	0
Lemanski Hall, UA	76	48	28	2 (-14)	8 (-19)	2
Stacy Evans, USC	75	48	27	8 (-44)	12 (-35)	0
Henry Ford, AR	68	42	26	14 (-85)	23 (-116)	0
Monty Grow, UF	67	37	30	.5 (-11)	4 (-18)	1
Corey White, LSU	64	40	24	3 (-26)	7 (-33)	0
Willie Whitehead, AU	63	31	32	3 (-13)	6 (-33)	0

Kentucky linebacker Marty Moore earned All-SEC honors after finishing the 1993 campaign with 116 tackles and leading the Wildcats to their first bowl appearance since 1984.

Player, Team	Tackles	Solos	Assists	Sacks	TFLs	INTs
Duce Williams, UK	62	45	17	0	3 (-15)	2
Gary Walker, AU	61	38	23	5 (-26)	6 (-19)	0
Ben Hanks, UF	59	32	27	0	4 (-10)	0
Tyrone Chatman, AR	56	28	28	0	2 (-3)	2
Phillip Daniels, UG	56	24	32	3 (-15)	2 (-2)	0
Will Brown, UA	55	33	22	5 (-35)	3 (-6)	0
Ernest Dixon, USC	55	34	21	3 (-30)	3 (-6)	0
Carlo Butler, UG	52	31	21	1 (-5)	2 (-6)	0
Jahmal Pettiford, USC	51	30	21	4 (-21)	4.5 (-11)	0

SECONDARY

Player, Team	Tackles	Solos	Assists	Sacks	TFLs	INTs
Tony Watkins, USC	89	56	33	2 (-6)	2 (-4)	0
Greg Tremble, UG	80	56	24	0	3 (-7)	3
Johnny Dixon, UM	75	49	26	3 (-28)	8 (-22)	2
Brian Robinson, AU	74	43	31	0	1 (-1)	5
Chris Shelling, AU	74	46	28	0	2 (-14)	4
Sam Shade, UA	73	50	23	0	5 (-31)	2
Anth. Marshall, LSU	72	44	28	1 (-6)	1 (-6)	5
Larry Kennedy, UF	67	47	20	0	1 (-1)	0
Marcus Jenkins, UK	67	59	8	0	2 (-2)	6
Lawrence Wright, UF	62	38	24	0	1 (-1)	2
Otis Mounds, AU	61	32	29	0	2 (-6)	1
Walt Harris, MSU	61	45	16	0	1 (-3)	6
Jason Parker, UT	61	43	18	0	2 (-5)	4
Aaron Smith, VU	60	36	24	0	2 (-3)	1
Michael Gilmore, UF	59	33	26	0	0	4
Frankie Luster, MSU	59	37	22	2 (-19)	4 (-8)	1
Byron King, VU	59	36	23	0	2 (-5)	4
Alundis Brice, UM	58	42	16	0	0	7
Orlando Watters, AR	57	40	17	0	3 (-9)	6
Robert Davis, VU	57	43	14	0	1 (-1)	1

DEFENSIVE LINEMEN

Player, Team	Tackles	Solos	Assists	Sacks	TFLs	INTs
Arleye Gibson, MSU	89	46	43	.5 (-8)	2 (-5)	0
Bill Rosenberg, UG	79	35	44	1 (-1)	6 (-10)	0
Mike Pelton, AU	73	42	31	5 (-33)	9 (-26)	0
William Gaines, UF	73	50	23	2.5 (-23)	11.5 (-35)	0
Matt Storm, UG	73	41	32	6 (-31)	2 (-4)	0
Jeremy Nunley, UA	72	41	31	10 (-60)	6 (-14)	0
Damon Primus, AU	72	43	29	5 (-16)	9 (-30)	0
Randy Hart, AU	69	34	35	5 (-9)	3 (-10)	0
Kevin Carter, UF	59	33	26	6.5 (-57)	5 (-16)	0
Ellis Johnson, UF	55	39	16	7 (-47)	8 (-29)	0
Marcus Adair, AR	54	26	28	7 (-57)	11 (-65)	0
James Manley, VU	54	36	18	2.5 (-18)	7.5 (-30)	0
Tim Bowens, UM	53	47	6	6 (-39)	5 (-7)	1
Vernon Wade, AR	49	23	26	2 (-19)	10 (-29)	0
Alan Young, VU	49	28	21	12 (-60)	16 (-68)	0
Paul Yatkowski, UT	47	33	14	2 (-11)	8 (-17)	1
Jon Collins, UK	46	28	8	1 (-4)	5 (-16)	0
Billy Lofton, UK	44	21	23	2 (-6)	1 (-2)	0
Zane Beehn, UK	40	23	17	3 (-23)	7 (-22)	0
Brian Boykin, VU	40	19	21	2 (-8)	6.5 (-19)	0

QUARTERBACK SACKS

Player, Team	Pos.	Sacks	Yards
Henry Ford, AR	DE	14	-85
Mitch Davis, UG	OLB	13	-74
Alan Young, VU	DE	12	-60
Jeremy Nunley, UA	DE	10	-60
Cassius Ware, UM	ILB	9	-74
Stacy Evans, USC	OLB	8	-44
Horace Morris, UT	DE	8	-58
James Wilson, UT	DE	7.5	-54
Marcus Adair, AR	DE	7	-57
Anthony Harris, AU	LB	7	-32
Ellis Johnson, UF	DE	7	-47
Kevin Carter, UF	DE	6.5	-57
Matt Storm, UG	DT	6	-31
Tim Bowens, UM	DT	6	-39

174 1993 In Review

1993 SEC Superlatives

TEAM

POINTS
62 - Tennessee vs. Vanderbilt (62-14)
61 - Florida vs. Southwestern Louisiana (61-14)
58 - Florida vs. LSU (58-3)
56 - Alabama vs. Louisiana Tech (56-3)
55 - Tennessee vs. South Carolina (55-3)
55 - Auburn vs. New Mexico State (61-14)

TOTAL OFFENSE
667 - Georgia vs. So. Miss (123 rush, 544 pass)
642 - Florida vs. USL (130 rush, 512 pass)
631 - S. Carolina vs. La. Tech (281 rush, 350 pass)
619 - Florida vs. Miss. State (170 rush, 449 pass)
579 - Auburn vs. N. Mexico St. (289 rush, 290 pass)
571 - Tennessee vs. Kentucky (280 rush, 291 pass)

RUSHING OFFENSE
431 - Vanderbilt vs. Wake Forest (67 atts; 3 TDs)
412 - Arkansas vs. LSU (56 atts, 5 TDs)
365 - Vanderbilt vs. Navy (75 atts; 5 TDs)
359 - Tennessee vs. Vanderbilt (44 atts; 6 TDs)
348 - Miss. State vs. Tulane (53 atts; 1 TD)

PASSING OFFENSE
544 - Georgia vs. So. Miss (30-47-0; 4 TDs)
512 - Florida vs. USL (34-50-1; 7 TDs)
449 - Florida vs. Miss. St. (27-41-2; 3 TDs)
426 - Georgia vs. Auburn (34-53-2; 3 TDs)
425 - Georgia vs. Kentucky (31-47-1; 3 TDs)

FEWEST POINTS ALLOWED
0 - Tennessee vs. La. Tech (50-0) & vs UK (48-0)
0 - Kentucky vs. Kent (35-0) & Ole Miss (21-0)
0 - Ole Miss vs. Arkansas (19-0) & N. Illinois (44-0)
0 - Florida vs. Vanderbilt (52-0)
0 - Alabama vs. So. Miss (40-0)
0 - Miss. State vs. South Carolina (23-0)
0 - South Carolina vs. Vanderbilt (22-0)

TOTAL DEFENSE
51 - Ole Miss vs. Vanderbilt (32 rush, 19 pass)
84 - So. Carolina vs. Vanderbilt (40 rush, 40 pass)
89 - Florida vs. Arkansas St. (76 rush, 13 pass)
131 - Alabama vs. La. Tech (87 rush, 44 pass)
136 - Miss. State vs. Tulane (-9 rush, 145 pass)

RUSHING DEFENSE
-9 - Miss. State vs. Tulane (24 atts; 0 TDs)
1 - Ole Miss vs. Georgia (26 atts; 0 TDs)
28 - Ole Miss vs. UT-Chattanooga (31 atts; 0 TDs)
28 - Miss. State vs. South Carolina (29 atts; 0 TDs)
32 - Ole Miss vs. Vanderbilt (36 atts; 0 TDs)

PASSING DEFENSE
7 - Auburn vs. Vanderbilt (1-4-1; 0 TDs)
13 - Florida vs. Arkansas State (3-8-0; 0 TDs)
19 - Ole Miss vs. Vanderbilt (1-14-3; 0 TDs)
23 - LSU vs. Arkansas (3-8-1; 0 TDs)
33 - Kentucky vs. Vanderbilt (4-9-1; 0 TDs)
36 - Kentucky vs. East Carolina (5-16-1; 0 TDs)

INDIVIDUAL

RUSH ATTEMPTS (YDS; TDS)
41 - Errict Rhett, Florida vs. Georgia (183; 2)
40 - Michael Davis, Miss. State vs. Ole Miss (154; 1)
34 - Marius Johnson, Arkansas vs. Tulsa (177; 2)
33 - Michael Davis, Miss. State vs. USC (128; 1)

PASS ATTEMPTS
65 - Eric Zeier, Georgia vs. Florida (36-65-1; 386 yards, 2 TDs)
53 - Eric Zeier, Georgia vs. Auburn (34-53-2; 426 yards, 3 TDs)
50 - Danny Wuerffel, Florida vs. Auburn (25-50-2; 386 yards, 3 TDs)
47 - Eric Zeier, Georgia vs. Kentucky (31-47-1; 425 yards, 3 TDs)
47 - Eric Zeier, Georgia vs. So. Miss (30-47-0; 544 yards, 4 TDs)

PASS COMPLETIONS
36 - Eric Zeier, Georgia vs. Florida (36-65-1; 386 yards, 2 TDs)
34 - Eric Zeier, Georgia vs. Auburn (34-53-2; 426 yards, 3 TDs)
31 - Eric Zeier, Georgia vs. Kentucky (31-47-2; 425 yards, 3 TDs)
30 - Eric Zeier, Georgia vs. So. Miss (30-47-0; 544 yds, 4 TDs)
28 - Eric Zeier, Georgia vs. Georgia Tech (28-41-0, 328 yds, 1 TD)
28 - Chad Loup, LSU vs. Arkansas (28-43-2, 339 yds, 1 TD)

PASS RECEPTIONS (YDS; TDS)
15 - Shannon Mitchell, Georgia vs. Fla. (140; 1)
12 - Chris Doering, Florida vs. Miss. State (199; 3)
10 - Brice Hunter, Georgia vs. So. Miss (179; 2)
10 - Hason Graham, Georgia vs. Auburn (175; 1)
10 - Brice Hunter, Georgia vs. Auburn (84; 1)

LONGEST RUSHING TOUCHDOWN
73 - Charlie Garner, Tennessee vs. Alabama
70 - Moe Williams, Kentucky vs. Florida
70 - James Bostic, Auburn vs. Alabama
67 - Brian Steger, Alabama vs. Southern Miss.
66 - Carlton Calvin, Arkansas vs. LSU

LONGEST PASSING TOUCHDOWN
80 - Eric Zeier to Hason Graham, UG vs. TTU
80 - Eric Zeier to Hason Graham, UG vs. Vanderbilt
80 - Lawrence Adams to Eddie Small, UM vs. NIU
77 - Freddie Kitchens to Toderick Malone, UA vs. SM
76 - Eric Zeier to Hason Graham, UG vs. Auburn

LONGEST FIELD GOAL
53 - Steve Yenner, Vanderbilt vs. Auburn
53 - Michael Proctor, Alabama vs. Ole Miss
51 - John Becksvoort, Tennessee vs. La. Tech
50 - Walter Grant, Ole Miss vs. UT-Chattanooga
50 - Tom Burke, Miss. St. vs. Alabama

LONGEST PUNT
71 - Terry Daniel, Auburn vs. Florida
68 - Nicky Nickels, Kentucky vs. Indiana
68 - Bryne Diehl, Alabama vs. Auburn

LONGEST KICKOFF RETURN
100 - Jack Jackson, Florida vs. Miss. State
73 - Jerry Jerman, Georgia vs. Texas Tech

LONGEST PUNT RETURN
77 - Ta'Boris Fisher, Ole Miss vs. Auburn
76 - Scott Gumina, Miss. State vs. Tulane

1994 SEC Football

1993 Top Performances

100-YARD RUSHERS (Attempts-TDs)
196 - Errict Rhett, UF vs. AU (22-1)
186 - Charlie Garner, UT vs. UK (19-1)
183 - James Bostic, AU vs. UG (19-3)
183 - Errict Rhett, UF vs. UG (41-3)
177 - Terrell Davis, UG vs. ARK. (31-0)
177 - Marius Johnson, ARK. vs. Tulsa (34-2)
159 - Moe Williams, UK vs. UG (17-1)
154 - Michael Davis, MSU vs. UM (40-1)
151 - Charlie Garner, UT vs. VU (16-1)
148 - Sherman Williams, UA vs. ARK. (24-1)
147 - James Bostic, AU vs. UA (19-1)
147 - Errict Rhett, UF vs. UT (30-2)
144 - Charlie Garner, UT vs. UA (17-1)
143 - Oscar Malone, ARK. vs. LSU (10-2)
141 - Oscar Malone, ARK. vs. USC (22-1)
140 - James Bostic, AU vs. MSU (20-0)
138 - James Bostic, AU vs. UM (28-1)
136 - Errict Rhett, UF vs. UK (21-0)
132 - Brandon Bennett, USC vs. UK (26-2)
131 - Terrell Davis, UG vs. UT (22-0)
130 - Pookie Jones, UK vs. Kent (16-2)
129 - Charlie Garner, UT vs. Duke (10-1)
129 - Moe Williams, UK vs. ECU (25-0)
128 - Michael Davis, MSU vs. USC (33-1)
127 - Brandon Bennett, USC vs. La. Tech (12-1)
124 - Michael Davis, MSU vs. Tulane (24-1)
124 - Carlton Calvin, ARK. vs. LSU (14-2)
122 - Stephen Davis, AU vs. Samford (18-2)
122 - Errict Rhett, UF vs. MSU (19-1)
120 - Tony Jackson, VU vs. Navy (15-1)
120 - Sherman Williams, UA vs. VU (19-0)
120 - Kevin Bouie, MSU vs. ARK. (25-0)
120 - Errict Rhett, UF vs. USC (29-2)
119 - Aaron Hayden, UT vs. La. Tech (10-0)
118 - Cliff Deese, VU vs. W. Forest (21-1)
116 - James Bostic, AU vs. S. Miss (25-3)
114 - James Stewart, UT vs. USC (9-2)
110 - James Bostic, AU vs. LSU (12-1)
110 - Tony Jackson, VU vs. Wake Forest (14-1)
109 - Moe Williams, UK vs. UF (9-1)
108 - Errict Rhett, UF vs. Ark. St. (16-1)
108 - Brandon Bennett, USC vs. UG (24-1)
107 - Charlie Garner, UT vs. UG (15-1)
106 - Moe Williams, UK vs. LSU (16-1)
106 - Sherman Williams, UA vs. Tulane (17-2)
106 - Marius Johnson, ARK. vs. LSU (19-0)
106 - Sherman Williams, UA vs. USC (23-2)
105 - Kevin Bouie, MSU vs. Tulane (15-0)
105 - Charlie Garner, UT vs. USC (9-1)
104 - Brian Steger, UA vs. SM (7-1)
104 - James Bostic, AU vs. NMSU (11-0)
104 - Jay Johnson, LSU vs. UM (15-2)
104 - Sherman Williams, UA vs. La. Tech (23-3)
102 - Karl Williamson, MSU vs. Tulane (12-0)
102 - Michael Davis, MSU vs. UA (23-0)
102 - Brandon Bennett, USC vs. ECU (31-0)

300-YARD PASSERS (Comp-Att-Int; TDs)
544 - Eric Zeier, UG vs. SM (30-47-0; 4)
449 - Danny Wuerffel, UF vs. MSU (27-41-2; 3)
448 - Terry Dean, UF vs. USL (26-38-0; 6)
426 - Eric Zeier, UG vs. AU (34-53-2; 3)
425 - Eric Zeier, UG vs. UK (31-47-1; 3)
405 - Todd Jordan, MSU vs. UF (24-44-0; 2)
386 - Eric Zeier, UG vs. UF (36-65-1; 2)
386 - Danny Wuerffel, UF vs. AU (25-50-2; 3)
379 - Eric Zeier, UG vs. VU (25-35-0; 4)
370 - Todd Jordan, MSU vs. MSU (23-43-0; 3)
355 - Heath Shuler, UT vs. UF (25-41-1; 5)
339 - Chad Loup, LSU vs. ARK. (28-43-2; 1)
333 - Danny Wuerffel, UF vs. USC (25-37-0; 2)
328 - Eric Zeier, UG vs. Ga. Tech (28-41-0; 1)
317 - Eric Zeier, UG vs. TTU (13-19-0; 4)
312 - Jay Barker, UA vs. UT (22-40-1; 0)
311 - Steve Taneyhill, USC vs. La.Tech (15-32-1; 1)
307 - Heath Shuler, UT vs. ARK. (19-26-1; 1)

100-YARD RECEIVERS (No.-TDs)
217 - David Palmer, UA vs. VU (8-2)
210 - Eddie Small, UM vs. VU (6-2)
199 - Chris Doering, UF vs. MSU (12-3)
195 - Eddie Kennison, LSU vs. USU (6-1)
179 - Brice Hunter, UG vs. SM (10-2)
175 - Hason Graham, UG vs. AU (10-1)
171 - David Palmer, UA vs. MSU (8-1)
167 - Jack Jackson, UF vs. USC (6-1)
153 - Jack Jackson, UF vs. USL (8-3)
144 - Chris Jones, MSU vs. UF (5-1)
140 - Shannon Mitchell, UG vs. UF (15-1)
140 - Billy Williams, UT vs. UF (5-3)
140 - Willie Jackson, UF vs. Fla. St. (7-2)
135 - Eddie Small, UM vs. N. Illinois (5-2)
134 - Frank Sanders, AU vs. ARK (7-0)
131 - Shannon Mitchell, UG vs. UK (7-1)
129 - Brandon Bennett, USC vs. La. Tech (5-1)
129 - David Palmer, UA vs. SM (8-1)
115 - Kenny Causey, MSU vs. UA (7-0)
112 - Harrison Houston, UF vs. USL (4-0)
111 - Harrison Houston, UF vs. Fla. St. (6-0)
109 - Mike Reddick, USC vs. UF (5-0)
109 - Brice Hunter, UG vs. UF (9-1)
108 - Willie Jackson, UF vs. Ark. St. (7-1)
108 - Jack Jackson, UF vs. AU (3-2)
106 - Joey Kent, UT vs. UK (3-2)
106 - Craig Faulkner, UT vs. ARK. (4-1)
106 - Brice Hunter, UG vs. VU (7-1)
105 - Cory Fleming, UT vs. UG (7-2)
105 - Roell Preston, UM vs. UG (3-1)
101 - Hason Graham, UG vs. VU (3-1)
101 - Cory Fleming, UT vs. ARK. (6-0)
100 - Harrison Houston, UF vs. LSU (5-2)

100-YARD RUSHING GAME LEADERS
7 - James Bostic (Auburn)
7 - Errict Rhett (Florida)
6 - Charlie Garner (Tennessee)
5 - Sherman Williams (Alabama)
4 - Brandon Bennett (S. Carolina)
4 - Michael Davis (Miss. State)
4 - Moe Williams (Kentucky)

300-YARD PASSING GAME LEADERS
7 - Eric Zeier (Georgia)
3 - Danny Wuerffel (Florida)
2 - Todd Jordan (Miss. State)
2 - Heath Shuler (Tennessee)

100-YARD RECEIVING GAME LEADERS
3 - Harrison Houston (Florida)
3 - Brice Hunter (Georgia)
3 - Jack Jackson (Florida)
3 - David Palmer (Alabama)
2 - Cory Fleming (Tennessee)
2 - Willie Jackson (Florida)
2 - Shannon Mitchell (Georgia)
2 - Eddie Small (Ole Miss)

SEC in the NFL Draft
April 24-25, 1994

1st Round (6)
3	QB Heath Shuler, Tennessee		Washington Redskins
9	DB Antonio Langham, Alabama		Cleveland Browns
14	OT Bernard Williams, Georgia		Philadelphia Eagles
15	OT Wayne Gandy, Auburn		Los Angeles Rams
20	DT Tim Bowens, Ole Miss		Miami Dolphins
26	DE Henry Ford, Arkansas		Houston Oilers

2nd Round (7)
34	RB Errict Rhett, Florida		Tampa Bay Buccaneers
35	WR Kevin Lee, Alabama		New England Patriots
36	C Kevin Mawae, LSU		Seattle Seahawks
40	WR David Palmer, Alabama		Minnesota Vikings
42	RB Charlie Garner, Tennessee		Philadelphia Eagles
43	OG Isaac Davis, Arkansas		San Diego Chargers
60	DE Jeremy Nunley, Alabama		Houston Oilers

3rd Round (5)
69	TE Harold Bishop, LSU		Tampa Bay Buccaneers
83	RB James Bostic, Auburn		Los Angeles Rams
87	WR Cory Fleming, Tennessee		San Francisco 49ers
93	DT Shane Bonham, Tennessee		Detroit Lions
98	OT Corey Louchiey, S. Carolina		Buffalo Bills

4th Round (3)
109	WR Willie Jackson, Florida		Dallas Cowboys
118	LB Mitch Davis, Georgia		Atlanta Falcons
131	LB DeWayne Dotson, Ole Miss		Dallas Cowboys

5th Round (6)
138	WR Harrison Houston, Florida		Atlanta Falcons
139	OG Anthony Redmon, Auburn		Arizona Cardinals
142	DE Herman Carroll, Miss. State		New Orleans Saints
147	DT William Gaines, Florida		Miami Dolphins
152	LB Horace Morris, Tennessee		New York Jets
159	OT Roosevelt Patterson, Alabama		Los Angeles Raiders

6th Round (1)
172	TE Terry Samuels, Kentucky		Arizona Cardinals

7th Round (4)
204	RB Frank Harvey, Georgia		Arizona Cardinals
207	LB Zane Beehn, Kentucky		San Diego Chargers
220	LB Lemanski Hall, Alabama		Houston Oilers
222	LB Marty Moore, Kentucky		New England Patriots

NFL DRAFT NOTES

SELECTIONS BY CONFERENCE

Conference	Total
Southeastern	32
Pacific-10	25
Big 10	21
Atlantic Coast	19
Big Eight	19
Southwest	16
Big East	14
Western Athletic	13

FIRST ROUND SELECTIONS

Conference	Total
Southeastern	6
Pacific-10	5
Big 10	4
Independants	4
Southwest	3
Atlantic Coast	2
Big Eight	2
Western Athletic	2
Southwestern Athletic	1

SEC SELECTIONS

School	Total	Selections
Alabama	6	9, 35, 40, 60, 159, 220
Tennessee	5	3, 42, 87, 93, 152
Florida	4	34, 109, 138, 147
Auburn	3	15, 83, 139
Georgia	3	14, 118, 204
Kentucky	3	172, 207, 222
Arkansas	2	26, 43
LSU	2	36, 69
Ole Miss	2	20, 131
Miss. State	1	142
S. Carolina	1	98

SEC Presence in the NFL

The 1993 opening day National Football League rosters were highlighted by 178 players form Southeastern Conference schools. All 28 NFL team rosters include at least one player who played college football at an SEC institution. A total of 96 now toil in the National Football Conference (NFC), with a conference-high 11 included on the Philadelphia Eagles' and Green Bay Packers' roster. In addition, 82 players now display their talents in the American Football Conference (AFC), as the Pittsburgh Steelers have a league-high 12 players from SEC institutions.

Florida's Emmit Smith, a first-round draft pick in 1990, earned MVP honors of the 1994 Super Bowl for the Dallas Cowboys.

NFL Players (by school)

Auburn	28	Kentucky	12
Tennessee	28	Ole Miss	12
Alabama	20	Arkansas	7
LSU	20	Miss. State	7
Florida	19	S. Carolina	7
Georgia	14	Vanderbilt	4

1994 SEC Football 177

1993 NCAA Attendance Leaders

	TEAMS	GAMES	ATTENDANCE	AVG PG	CHANGE+ IN AVG		CHANGE+ IN TOTAL	
1. Big Ten (I-A)#	11	68	*4,320,397	63,535	Up	359	Up	150,792
2. Southeastern (I-A)	12	78	*4,897,564	62,789	Down	948	Up	53,550
3. Pacific-10 (I-A)	10	57	2,731,361	47,919	Up	829	Down	94,040
4. Big Eight (I-A)	8	48	2,126,247	44,297	Down	3,531	Down	121,660
5. Atlantic Coast (I-A)	9	54	*2,379,045	44,056	Up	43	Up	46,371
6. Big East (I-A)	8	47	1,787,843	38,039	Down	446	Down	59,426
7. Southwest (I-A)	8	45	1,587,652	35,281	Down	829	Down	109,500
8. Western Athletic (I-A)	10	61	2,109,441	34,581	Down	612	Down	2,146
9. I-A Independents	10	51	1,554,522	30,481	Down	22	Down	303,498
10. Southwestern (I-AA)	8	42	772,714	18,398	Down	2,406	Down	101,058
11. Big West (I-A)#	10	48	*778,224	16,213	Up	929	Up	14,040
12. Mid-American (I-A)	10	51	726,847	14,252	Down	120	Up	22,614
13. Southern (I-AA)	9	51	617,620	12,110	Down	628	Down	82,993
14. Mid-Eastern (I-AA)	7	40	440,012	11,000	Down	867	Down	10,950
15. Ivy Group (I-AA)	8	42	420,915	10,022	Down	28	Up	18,935
16. Big Sky (I-AA)	8	48	460,613	9,596	Up	83	Up	23,021
17. Southland (I-AA)	8	43	403,508	9,384	Down	171	Down	26,463
18. Yankee (I-AA)#	12	67	*550,245	8,213	Down	617	Down	41,355
19. Gateway (I-AA)	7	36	285,921	7,942	Down	704	Down	59,902
20. I-AA Independents#	21	107	*524,308	4,900	Up	528	Up	82,746
21. Ohio Valley (I-AA)	9	49	294,714	6,015	Down	2,052	Down	100,550
22. Patriot (I-AA)	6	29	165,581	5,710	Down	812	Down	36,606
23. Pioneer (I-AA)#	6	32	94,995	2,969	Down	572	Down	14,790
24. Metro Atlantic (I-AA)#	6	29	34,483	1,189	Up	137	Up	5,038
I-A Neutral Sites	5	306,295	61,259	—	—	—	—	
I-AA Neutral Sites	8	291,244	36,406	—	—	—	—	
DIVISION I-A#	106	613	25,305,438	41,281	Up	111	Down	96,608
DIVISION I-AA#	115	623	5,356,873	8,599	Down	1,830	Up	298,918
I-A & I-AA Combined	221	1,236	30,662,311	24,808	Down	2,833	Up	202,310
NCAA DIVISION II#	142	718	2,572,053	3,582	Down	669	Down	161,041
NCAA DIVISION III#	197	934	1,636,270	1,752	Down	132	Down	396,066
ALL NCAA TEAMS	560	2,888	34,870,634	12,074	Down	400	Down	354,797

By percentage of capacity: Div. 1-A 76.69 percent (Southeastern 91.97, Atlantic Coast 86.20, Big Ten 85.94, Big Eight 78.45, Western Athletic 75.38, Big East 72.60, Pacific-10 69.81, Div. 1-A Independents 68.15, Southwest 62.62, Mid-American 53.88, Big West 52.04).

Div. I-AA 48.43 percent (Southern 70.06, Mid-Eastern 64.03, Big Sky 62.41, Southwestern 60.96, Yankee 56.58, Southland 55.47, Metro Atlantic 49.69, Gateway 49.54, Ohio Valley 43.10, Patriot 40.62, Pioneer 31.77, I-AA Independents 30.15, Ivy 27.36).

Did not have same lineup in 1993 as in 1992.   *Record for this conference.
+ The 1993 figures used for comparison reflect changes in conference and division lineups to provide parallel, valid comparisons.

1993 Division I-A School Attendance Leaders

	GAMES	ATTEND.	AVG.	CHANGE			GAMES	ATTEND.	AVG.	CHANGE	
1. Michigan	7	739,620	105,660	Down	207	38. North Caro. St.	6	245,163	40,861	Down	6,296
2. Tennessee	7	667,280	95,326	Down	598	39. Hawaii	8	326,454	40,807	Down	3,625
3. Penn St.	6	564,190	94,032	Down	834	40. California	6	242,798	40,466	Down	15,566
4. Ohio St.	6	553,489	92,248	Down	402	41. Minnesota	6	239,973	39,996	Up	2,088
5. Florida	6	507,072	84,512	Up	708	42. Fresno St.	6	237,214	39,536	Up	4,311
6. Auburn	7	567,506	81,072	Up	8,136	43. Virginia Tech	6	236,484	39,414	Down	5,688
7. Georgia	6	468,457	78,076	Down	5,118	44. Virginia	6	234,000	39,000	Down	4,067
8. Alabama	7	529,765	75,681	Down	1,071	45. Air Force	6	233,157	38,860	Down	1,764
9. Nebraska	7	529,521	75,646	Down	541	46. Louisville	5	188,040	37,608	Up	5,225
10. Wisconsin	5	377,537	75,507	Up	14,129	47. Indiana	7	262,140	37,449	Down	6,018
11. Florida St.	6	443,811	73,969	Up	11,172	48. Missouri	5	186,819	37,364	Down	1,608
12. Washington	6	429,401	71,567	Down	504	49. Maryland	5	186,773	37,355	Up	9,331
13. Iowa	6	410,842	68,474	Up	1,833	50. San Diego St.	7	260,832	37,262	Down	8,463
14. South Caro.	7	472,803	67,543	Up	3,815	51. Oregon	5	183,445	36,689	Up	2,891
15. Clemson	7	467,773	66,825	Down	9,964	52. Iowa St.	6	213,303	35,551	Down	2,031
16. Brigham Young	6	391,219	65,203	Up	124	53. Kansas	6	210,500	35,083	Down	6,834
17. Texas	5	312,201	62,440	Down	5,712	54. Baylor	5	171,910	34,382	Up	2,023
18. Oklahoma	5	310,620	62,124	Down	2,042	55. Army	6	33,802	33,802	Down	1,061
19. Michigan St.	6	368,922	61,487	Up	1,673	56. Boston College	6	199,188	33,198	Up	3,349
20. Louisiana St.	6	361,632	60,272	Down	6,756	57. Mississippi St.	6	199,093	33,182	Down	6,238
21. Texas A&M	6	357,645	59,608	Up	4,201	58. Vanderbilt	6	198,465	33,078	Down	5,100
22. Notre Dame	6	354,450	59,075		0	59. Mississippi	6	196,000	32,667	Down	3,914
23. Southern Cal	5	295,106	59,021	Down	733	60. Texas Tech	5	160,851	32,170	Down	6,812
24. Stanford	7	404,600	57,800	Up	5,733	61. Kansas St.	7	217,739	31,106	Up	3,333
25. West Va.	7	404,500	57,786	Up	8,502	62. Northwestern	6	185,791	30,965	Down	8,402
26. Kentucky	6	312,455	52,076	Down	2,070	63. Rutgers	6	184,258	30,710	Up	1,574
27. Colorado	6	311,370	51,895	Up	2,203	64. Memphis St.	5	151,296	30,259	Down	7,149
28. Arizona St.	6	309,557	51,593	Up	2,699	65. Oregon St.	5	144,481	28,896	Up	779
29. Illinois	6	306,108	51,018	Up	815	66. Washington St.	5	135,931	27,186	Up	1,648
30. Arizona	6	304,564	50,761	Up	3,740	67. East Caro.	5	134,482	26,896	Down	5,918
31. North Caro.	7	340,600	48,657	Up	1,486	68. UTEP	6	133,886	26,777	Up	5,015
32. Syracuse	5	240,320	48,064	Down	1,254	69. Pittsburgh	6	155,818	25,970	Down	5,749
33. Miami (Fla.)	6	287,319	47,887	Down	7,788	70. Texas Christian	6	155,342	25,890	Up	203
34. UCLA	6	281,478	46,913	Up	2,347	71. Navy	5	129,143	25,829	Down	9,280
35. Arkansas	6	260,299	43,383	Down	2,650	72. New Mexico	6	151,844	25,307	Up	6,050
36. Purdue	6	260,285	43,381	Up	5,152	73. Nevada	6	150,883	25,147	Up	3,128
37. Georgia Tech	6	248,127	41,355	Down	1,823	74. Tulsa	5	125,385	25,077	Up	2,649

1993 In Review

THROUGH THE YEARS

Ole Miss quarterback Archie Manning twice earned All-America honors and was named the 1969 SEC Most Valuable Player. Manning, who guided the Rebels to three-straight bowl appearances, set the conference record with 540 yards total offense against Alabama in 1969.

National Champions

Year	Team	Poll
1951	Tennessee	AP, UPI
1957	Auburn	AP
1958	LSU	AP, UPI
1960	Ole Miss	FWAA
1961	Alabama	AP, UPI
1964	Alabama	AP, UPI
1965	Alabama	AP, FWAA
1973	Alabama	UPI
1978	Alabama	AP, FWAA
1979	Alabama	AP, UPI, FWAA
1980	Georgia	AP, UPI, FWAA
1992	Alabama	AP, UPI, USA Today, FWAA

NOTE: Arkansas was named the 1964 FWAA National Champion.

Undefeated and Untied Teams
(Regular Season)

Year	Team	W-L-T	Pts	Opp	Bowl	Opponent	Score
1934	Alabama	9-0-0	287	32	Rose	Stanford	29-13
1937	Alabama	9-0-0	225	20	Rose	California	0-13
1938	Tennessee	10-0-0	276	16	Orange	Oklahoma	17-0
1939	Tennessee	10-0-0	212	0	Rose	Southern Cal	0-14
1940	Tennessee	10-0-0	319	26	Sugar	Boston Coll.	13-19
1945	Alabama	9-0-0	396	66	Rose	Southern Cal	34-14
1946	Georgia	10-0-0	372	100	Sugar	N. Carolina	20-10
1951	Tennessee	10-0-0	373	88	Sugar	Maryland	13-28
1952	Ga. Tech	11-0-0	301	52	Sugar	Mississippi	24-7
1956	Tennessee	10-0-0	268	75	Sugar	Baylor	7-13
1957	Auburn	10-0-0	207	28	(None)		
1958	LSU	10-0-0	275	53	Sugar	Clemson	7-0
1961	Alabama	10-0-0	287	22	Sugar	Arkansas	10-3
1962	Mississippi	9-0-0	230	40	Sugar	Arkansas	17-13
1964	Alabama	10-0-0	223	67	Orange	Texas	17-21
1966	Alabama	10-0-0	267	37	Sugar	Nebraska	34-7
1971	Alabama	11-0-0	362	84	Orange	Nebraska	6-38
1973	Alabama	11-0-0	454	89	Sugar	Notre Dame	23-24
1974	Alabama	11-0-0	318	83	Orange	Notre Dame	11-13
1979	Alabama	11-0-0	359	58	Sugar	Arkansas	24-9
1980	Georgia	11-0-0	316	127	Sugar	Notre Dame	17-10
1982	Georgia	11-0-0	315	133	Sugar	Penn State	23-27
1992	Alabama	12-0-0	332	109	Sugar	Miami	34-13
1993	Auburn	11-0-0	353	192	(None)		

SEC Football Champions

Year	Team	SEC W-L-T	Pct	Overall Records	Pct
1933	Alabama	5-0-1	.917	7-1-1	.833
1934	Tulane	8-0	1.000	10-1	.909
	Alabama	7-0	1.000	10-0	1.000
1935	LSU	5-0	1.000	9-2	.848
1936	LSU	6-0	1.000	9-1-1	.864
1937	Alabama	6-0	1.000	9-1	.900
1938	Tennessee	7-0	1.000	11-0	1.000
1939	Tennessee	6-0	1.000	10-1	.909
	Georgia Tech	6-0	1.000	7-2	.778
	Tulane	5-0	1.000	8-0-1	.944
1940	Tennessee	5-0	1.000	10-1	.909
1941	Miss. State	4-0-1	.900	8-1-1	.850
1942	Georgia	6-1-0	.857	11-1	.917
1943	Georgia Tech	3-0	1.000	7-4	.636
1944	Georgia Tech	4-0	1.000	9-2	.818
1945	Alabama	6-0	1.000	10-0	1.000
1946	Georgia	5-0	1.000	11-0	1.000
	Tennessee	5-0	1.000	9-2	.818
1947	Mississippi	6-1-0	.857	9-2	.818
1948	Georgia	6-0	1.000	9-2	.818
1949	Tulane	5-1-0	.833	7-2-1	.750
1950	Kentucky	5-1-0	.833	11-1	.917
1951	Georgia Tech	7-0	1.000	10-0-1	.958
	Tennessee	5-0	1.000	10-1	.909
1952	Georgia Tech	6-0	1.000	12-0	1.000
1953	Alabama	4-0-3	.786	6-3-3	.625
1954	Mississippi	5-1-0	.833	9-2	.818
1955	Mississippi	5-1-0	.833	10-1	.909
1956	Tennessee	6-0	1.000	10-1	.909
1957	Auburn	7-0	1.000	10-0	1.000
1958	LSU	6-0	1.000	11-0	1.000
1959	Georgia	7-0	1.000	10-1	.909
1960	Mississippi	5-0-1	.917	10-0-1	.955
1961	Alabama	7-0	1.000	11-0	1.000
	LSU	6-0	1.000	10-1	.909
1962	Mississippi	6-0	1.000	10-0	1.000
1963	Mississippi	5-0-1	.917	7-1-2	.800
1964	Alabama	8-0	1.000	10-1	.909
1965	Alabama	6-1-1	.813	9-1-1	.864
1966	Alabama	6-0	1.000	11-0	1.000
	Georgia	6-0	1.000	10-1	.909
1967	Tennessee	6-0	1.000	9-2	.818
1968	Georgia	5-0-1	.917	8-1-2	.818
1969	Tennessee	5-1-0	.833	9-2	.818
1970	LSU	5-0	1.000	9-3	.750
1971	Alabama	7-0	1.000	11-1	.917
1972	Alabama	7-1-0	.875	10-2	.833
1973	Alabama	8-0	1.000	11-1	.917
1974	Alabama	6-0	1.000	11-1	.917
1975	Alabama	6-0	1.000	11-1	.917
1976	Georgia	5-1-0	.833	10-2	.833
	Kentucky	5-1-0	.833	9-3	.750
1977	Alabama	7-0	1.000	11-1	.917
1978	Alabama	6-0	1.000	11-1	.917
1979	Alabama	6-0	1.000	12-0	1.000
1980	Georgia	6-0	1.000	12-0	1.000
1981	Georgia	6-0	1.000	10-2	.833
	Alabama	6-0	1.000	9-2-1	.792
1982	Georgia	6-0	1.000	11-1	.917
1983	Auburn	6-0	1.000	11-1	.917
1984	Vacated				
1985	Tennessee	5-1-0	.833	9-1-2	.833
1986	LSU	5-1-0	.833	9-3	.750
1987	Auburn	5-0-1	.917	9-1-2	.833
1988	Auburn	6-1	.857	10-2	.833
	LSU	6-1	.857	8-4	.667
1989	Tennessee	6-1	.857	11-1	.917
	Alabama	6-1	.857	10-2	.833
	Auburn	6-1	.857	10-2	.833
1990	Tennessee	5-1-1	.786	9-2-2	.769
1991	Florida	7-0	1.000	10-2	.833
1992	Alabama	8-0	1.000	13-0	1.000
1993	Florida	7-1	.875	11-2	.846

180 Through The Years

National Champions

Southeastern Conference teams have won 12 national championships (AP, UPI, Football Writers Association). Alabama headlines the league with seven titles - 1961, 1964, 1965, 1973, 1978, 1979 and 1992. Tennessee was the first conference squad to capture the national crown in 1951. Auburn ruled supreme in 1957, while LSU followed in 1958. Ole Miss stood atop the land in 1960 and Georgia earned the distinction in 1980. Arkansas, which joined the SEC in 1991, captured the 1964 national title (FWAA).

Tennessee Volunteers (10-1) — 1951 (AP, UPI)

Ole Miss Rebels (9-0-1) — 1960 (FWAA)

Auburn Tigers (10-0) — 1957 (AP)

Georgia Bulldogs (12-0) — 1980 (AP, UPI, FWAA)

LSU Tigers (11-0) — 1958 (AP, UPI)

Alabama Crimson Tide (13-0) — 1992 (AP, UPI, USA Today, FWAA)

SEC All-Time Football Standings

(Regular season games against each other, 1933 through 1993)

School	Years	Games	Won-Lost-Tied	Pct.	1993 SEC Record
ALABAMA	60	408	284-103-21	.722	5-2-1
TENNESSEE	60	368	223-125-20	.633	6-1-1
GEORGIA	61	371	212-146-13	.589	2-6
LSU	61	376	202-153-21	.565	3-5
AUBURN	60	387	203-167-17	.547	8-0
OLE MISS	60	363	189-159-15	.541	3-5
FLORIDA	60	359	174-170-15	.506	7-1
ARKANSAS	2	16	6-8-2	.406	3-4-1
KENTUCKY	60	367	117-238-12	.335	4-4
MISSISSIPPI STATE	60	373	116-245-12	.327	2-5-1
SOUTH CAROLINA	2	16	5-11	.313	2-6
VANDERBILT	59	375	98-259-18	.286	1-7

Former Members

GEORGIA TECH	31	194	115- 70- 9	.616
TULANE	33	195	69-113-13	.387
SEWANEE	8	37	0- 37- 0	.000

Note: Sewanee withdrew after the 1940 season, Georgia Tech after 1963 and Tulane after 1965. During World War II Alabama, Auburn, Florida, Kentucky, Ole Miss, Miss. State, Tennessee and Vanderbilt suspended football in 1943; Vanderbilt through '44. Appointed conference games of 1954, '58, '64, '65, '66, '67, '68 and the Alabama-Ole Miss games of 1980 and '81 are not included in these records or total points.

SEC Football Winning Streaks

Wins	School	Years	Streak
28	ALABAMA	1991-93	Final 10 games of 1991 through first five games of 1993
28	ALABAMA	1978-80	Final nine games of 1978 through seventh game of 1980
23	TENNESSEE	1937-39	Final two games of 1937 through tenth game of 1939
20	ALABAMA	1924-26	Final game of 1924 through ninth game of 1926
19	ALABAMA	1961-62	Entire 1961 season through eighth game of 1962
19	LSU	1957-59	Final game of 1957 through seventh game of 1959
18	GEORGIA TECH	1951-53	Final five games of 1951 through first game of 1953
17	AUBURN	1956-58	Final four games of 1956 through third game of 1958
17	GEORGIA	1945-47	Final five games of 1945 through first game of 1947
15	GEORGIA	1979-81	Final game of 1979 through second game of 1981
13	OLE MISS	1955-56	Final nine games of 1955 through fourth game of 1956
13	VANDERBILT	1903-05	Final two games of 1903 through second game of 1905
12	KENTUCKY	1909-10	Last five of 1909 through seventh game of 1910

Listing includes bowl games

* National Record: Oklahoma won 47 straight games from 1953-57

NOTE: Arkansas recorded a 22-game winning streak from November 23, 1963 to January 1, 1966 as a member of the Southwest Conference.

Consecutive SEC Victories

Wins	School	Years	Streak
27	ALABAMA	1976-80	Final four SEC games in 1976 through fourth SEC game of 1980
23	GEORGIA	1980-83	All SEC games in 1980 through fifth SEC game of 1983
20	ALABAMA	1973-75	All SEC games in 1973 through sixth SEC game of 1975
20	TENNESSEE	1937-40	Final two SEC games of 1937 through 1940
18	ALABAMA	1991-93	Second SEC game of 1991 through third SEC game of 1993
14	ALABAMA	1971-72	All SEC games in 1971 through all SEC games of 1972
14	GEORGIA TECH	1950-52	Final SEC game of 1950 through sixth SEC game of 1952
13	LSU	1935-37	All SEC games in 1935 through second SEC game of 1937
13	OLE MISS	1961-63	Final two SEC games of 1961 through fifth SEC game of 1963

Listing includes regular season games only

NOTE: Georgia Tech was a member of the Southeastern Conference from 1933-63.

Intraconference Record
(1933-1992)

	UA W-L-T	AR W-L-T	AU W-L-T	UF W-L-T	UG W-L-T	UK W-L-T	LSU W-L-T	UM W-L-T	MSU W-L-T	USC W-L-T	UT W-L-T	VU W-L-T
UA	—	2-0	29-17-0	11-6-0	22-11-1	19-0-1	26-12-3	14-4-1	49-7-1	2-0	32-21-7	43-10-4
AR	0-2	—	0-1-1		1-1		2-0	0-2	0-1-1	2-0		1-1
AU	17-29-0	1-0-1	—	31-25-2	31-26-3	20-5-1	7-11-1	10-4-0	37-15-2	—	21-17-3	9-6-0
UF	6-11-0		25-31-2	—	24-35-1	26-14-0	19-18-3	7-7-1	28-16-1	2-0	7-10-0	16-9-2
UG	11-22-1	1-1	26-31-3	35-24-2	—	35-9-2	7-11-1	21-10-1	12-4-0	1-1	4-7-1	32-6-1
UK	0-19-1	—	5-20-1	14-26-0	9-36-2	—	12-31-1	12-23-1	12-5-0	2-0	13-45-3	29-19-3
LSU	12-26-3	0-2	11-7-1	18-19-3	10-8-1	31-12-1	—	30-24-4	38-21-1	—	3-16-2	16-5-1
UM	4-14-1	2-0	4-10-0	7-7-1	10-21-1	23-12-1	24-30-4	—	41-15-4	—	18-30-1	35-13-2
MSU	7-49-1	1-0-1	15-37-2	15-28-1	4-12-0	5-12-0	21-38-1	15-41-1	—	0-2	9-14-1	7-4-1
USC	0-2	0-2	—	0-2	1-1	0-2	—	—	0-2	—	1-1	2-0
UT	21-23-7	1-1	17-21-3	10-7-0	7-4-1	45-13-3	16-3-2	30-18-1	14-9-1	1-1	—	49-8-1
VU	10-44-4	—	6-9-0	9-16-2	6-32-1	19-29-3	5-16-1	13-34-2	4-7-1	0-2	8-50-1	—

Sewanee's intraconference record was: Alabama 0-3, Florida 0-5, Georgia Tech 0-2, Kentucky 0-1, Ole Miss 0-4, Miss. State 0-4, Tennessee 0-3, Tulane 0-7 and Vanderbilt 0-8. Georgia Tech's intraconference record was: Alabama 9-17-1, Auburn 18-11-1, Florida 16-5-3, Georgia 16-13-2, Kentucky 11-6-0, LSU 9-5-0, Ole Miss 1-0-0, Tennessee 8-5-1, Tulane 17-3-0, Vanderbilt 8-5-1 and Sewanee 2-0. Tulane's intraconference record was: Alabama 7-14-2, Auburn 11-8-3, Florida 3-5-2, Georgia 4-9-0, Georgia Tech 3-17-0, Kentucky 3-2-0, LSU 5-24-4, Ole Miss 7-16-0, Miss. State 8-11-0, Tennessee 0-2-0, Vanderbilt 11-5-2.

Through The Years

SEC vs. Other Conferences

Conference	W	L	T	Pct.
Atlantic Coast	190	78	9	.702
Big Eight	40	38	6	.512
Big East	1	2	0	.333
Big Ten	31	22	1	.583
Big West (PCAA)	25	0	1	.980
Ivy League	7	3	0	.700
Mid-American	24	7	0	.774
Missouri Valley	50	5	1	.902
Pacific 10	46	20	5	.683
Southern	178	58	10	.744
Southland	12	0	1	.962
Southwest	174	117	16	.593
Western Athletic	24	5	0	.828
Yankee	1	0	0	1.000
TOTALS	**803**	**365**	**50**	**.685**
Independents	683	333	31	.667

Non-Conference Records
(Does not include bowl games)

School	Won	Lost	Tied	Pct.
Alabama	193	49	6	.790
Arkansas	2	4	0	.333
Auburn	181	63	8	.734
Florida	181	89	8	.665
Georgia	211	78	14	.719
Kentucky	175	78	9	.685
LSU	203	70	11	.734
Ole Miss	192	70	8	.726
Miss. State	175	61	8	.734
S. Carolina	4	2	0	.667
Tennessee	220	55	9	.790
Vanderbilt	145	92	9	.608
TOTALS	**1882**	**711**	**90**	**.718**

Most Played SEC Rivalries

Games	Series	Series Record	First Game	Last Game
97	Auburn vs. Georgia	Auburn 46-44-7	1892	1993
90	Auburn vs. Georgia Tech	Auburn 47-39-4*	1892	1987
90	LSU vs. Tulane	LSU 61-22-7**	1893	1987
90	Ole Miss vs. Miss. State	Ole Miss 52-32-6	1901	1993
89	Kentucky vs. Tennessee	Tennessee 57-23-9	1893	1993
#	Tennessee vs. Vanderbilt	(see below)	1896	1993
87	LSU vs. Miss. State	LSU 52-32-3	1896	1993
85	Georgia vs. Georgia Tech	Georgia 47-33-5***	1893	1993
82##	LSU vs. Ole Miss	(see below)	1894	1993
78	Alabama vs. Miss. State	Alabama 64-11-3	1896	1993
76	Alabama vs. Tennessee	Alabama 41-27-8	1901	1993
71	Alabama vs. Vanderbilt	Alabama 49-18-4	1903	1993
###	Florida vs. Georgia	(see below)	1904/1915	1993
70	Auburn vs. Florida	Auburn 38-30-2	1912	1993
68	Ole Miss vs. Vanderbilt	Ole Miss 35-31-2	1894	1993
67	Auburn vs. Miss. State	Auburn 47-18-2	1905	1993
66	Kentucky vs. Vanderbilt	Vanderbilt 33-29-4	1896	1993
64	Ole Miss vs. Tulane	Ole Miss 36-28****	1893	1992
59	Alabama vs. Georgia	Alabama 33-22-4	1895	1991
58	Ole Miss vs. Tennessee	Tennessee 39-18-1	1902	1991
58	Alabama vs. Auburn	Alabama 33-24-1	1893	1993
57	Alabama vs. LSU	Alabama 37-15-5	1895	1993

Note: List includes all games played through the 1993 season between teams that were at one time members of the SEC.

Disagreement in series record. Tennessee records show 87 games (56-26-5 Tennessee), while Vanderbilt records show 88 games (57-27-5 Tennessee).

Disagreement in series record. LSU records show 82 games (46-32-4 LSU), while Ole Miss records show 82 games (47-31-4 LSU).

###Disagreement in series record. Florida records show 71 games (43-26-2 Georgia), while Georgia records show 72 games (44-26-2 Georgia). Game in question is 1904. Florida records show the school fielded its first varsity football team in 1906.

* Since Georgia Tech withdrew from the SEC following the 1963 season, Auburn-Georgia Tech series record is 17-7 (Auburn).

** Since Tulane withdrew from the SEC following the 1965 season, LSU-Tulane series record is 24-4 (LSU).

*** Since Georgia Tech withdrew from the SEC following the 1963 season, Georgia-Georgia Tech series record is 22-8 (Georgia).

Year-By-Year Non-Conference Record

Year	Won	Lost	Tie	Pct.
1933	37	13	4	.722
1934	35	17	2	.667
1935	40	15	1	.723
1936	39	14	6	.712
1937	38	14	4	.714
1938	36	18	0	.667
1939	45	14	2	.754
1930s	**270**	**105**	**19**	**.709**
1940	46	18	0	.719
1941	46	13	0	.780
1942	44	10	3	.798
1943	22	7	0	.759
1944	30	13	1	.693
1945	33	17	0	.660
1946	39	12	1	.760
1947	40	13	1	.750
1948	32	7	4	.791
1949	27	13	4	.659
1940s	**359**	**123**	**14**	**.738**
1950	37	12	2	.745
1951	37	9	1	.798
1952	38	9	1	.802
1953	31	17	1	.643
1954	27	15	2	.636
1955	31	10	1	.750
1956	28	9	3	.738
1957	22	9	2	.697
1958	33	10	0	.767
1959	36	7	1	.830
1950s	**320**	**107**	**14**	**.741**
1960	34	7	1	.821
1961	32	14	1	.691
1962	24	10	9	.663
1963	29	11	2	.714
1964	28	13	1	.679
1965	30	15	1	.663
1966	29	13	2	.682
1967	24	17	2	.581
1968	31	12	1	.716
1969	36	13	0	.735
1960s	**297**	**125**	**20**	**.695**
1970	35	14	1	.710
1971	41	9	0	.820
1972	33	11	0	.750
1973	34	11	3	.740
1974	43	11	3	.781
1975	32	21	1	.602
1976	30	31	1	.587
1977	26	22	1	.541
1978	31	20	2	.604
1979	23	29	1	.443
1970s	**328**	**169**	**13**	**.656**
1980	34	20	0	.630
1981	32	22	1	.591
1982	38	18	1	.675
1983	38	16	3	.693
1984	38	15	3	.705
1985	40	10	5	.773
1986	40	15	2	.719
1987	38	17	2	.684
1988	27	18	0	.600
1989	30	10	0	.750
1980s	**356**	**161**	**17**	**.683**
1990	25	15	1	.623
1991	32	8	0	.800
1992	27	9	0	.750
1993	28	7	1	.792

1994 SEC Football

SEC Annual Football Standings

1933

School	W-L-T	Pct.	Pts.	Opp.	W-L-T	Pts.	Opp.
Alabama	5-0-1	.917	69	15	7-1-1	130	17
LSU	3-0-2	.800	73	20	7-0-3	176	27
Georgia	3-1-0	.750	53	33	8-2-0	148	86
Tennessee	5-2-0	.714	134	37	7-3-0	176	47
Tulane	4-2-1	.643	127	55	6-3-1	160	68
Auburn	2-2-0	.500	40	43	5-5-0	133	104
Mississippi	2-2-1	.500	78	66	6-3-2	167	79
Vanderbilt	2-2-2	.500	56	74	4-3-3	126	107
Florida	2-3-0	.400	58	53	5-3-1	114	53
Kentucky	2-3-0	.400	14	87	5-5-0	91	116
Ga. Tech	2-5-0	.286	62	55	5-5-0	117	63
Miss. State	1-5-1	.214	39	143	2-7-1	69	149
Sewanee	0-6-0	.000	36	158	3-6-0	75	165

1934

School	W-L-T	Pct.	Pts.	Opp.	W-L-T	Pts.	Opp.
Tulane	8-0-0	1.000	148	49	9-1-0	195	69
Alabama	7-0-0	1.000	223	32	9-0-0	287	32
Tennessee	5-1-0	.833	98	32	8-2-0	175	58
LSU	4-2-0	.667	133	41	7-2-2	172	77
Georgia	3-2-0	.600	51	33	7-3-0	141	56
Vanderbilt	4-3-0	.571	66	94	6-3-0	105	100
Florida	2-2-1	.500	52	74	6-3-1	113	110
Mississippi	2-3-1	.417	39	78	4-5-1	114	98
Kentucky	1-3-0	.250	30	73	5-5-0	123	86
Auburn	1-6-0	.143	37	87	2-8-0	58	107
Sewanee	0-4-0	.000	12	105	2-7-0	40	147
Miss. State	0-5-0	.000	6	94	4-6-0	79	126
Ga. Tech	0-6-0	.000	42	125	1-9-0	56	187

Bowls: Rose (Alabama 29, Stanford 13); Sugar (Tulane 20, Temple 14)

1935

School	W-L-T	Pct.	Pts.	Opp.	W-L-T	Pts.	Opp.
LSU	5-0-0	1.000	95	15	9-1-0	221	38
Vanderbilt	5-1-0	.833	103	42	7-3-0	179	68
Mississippi	3-1-0	.750	87	26	9-2-0	292	66
Auburn	5-2-0	.714	118	39	8-2-0	201	46
Alabama	4-2-0	.667	106	48	6-2-1	185	55
Tulane	3-3-0	.500	85	97	6-4-0	156	123
Kentucky	3-3-0	.500	80	68	5-4-0	167	94
Ga. Tech	3-4-0	.429	123	123	5-5-0	162	142
Miss. State	2-3-0	.400	73	63	8-3-0	190	76
Tennessee	2-3-0	.400	34	84	4-5-0	98	155
Georgia	2-4-0	.333	54	81	6-4-0	169	88
Florida	1-6-0	.143	51	134	3-7-0	113	154
Sewanee	0-6-0	.000	0	189	2-7-0	15	228

Bowls: Sugar (TCU 3, LSU 2); Orange (Catholic University 20, Ole Miss 19)

1936

School	W-L-T	Pct.	Pts.	Opp.	W-L-T	Pts.	Opp.
LSU	6-0-0	1.000	143	13	9-0-1	281	33
Alabama	5-0-1	.917	89	29	8-0-1	168	35
Auburn	4-1-1	.750	58	44	7-2-2	160	63
Tennessee	3-1-2	.667	79	25	6-2-2	147	52
Miss. State	3-2-0	.600	101	25	7-2-1	220	25
Georgia	3-3-0	.500	74	133	5-4-1	115	159
Ga. Tech	3-3-1	.500	164	63	5-5-1	251	103
Tulane	2-3-1	.417	73	91	6-3-1	163	117
Vanderbilt	1-3-1	.300	33	59	3-5-1	115	87
Kentucky	1-3-0	.250	13	55	6-4-0	179	84
Florida	1-5-0	.167	40	98	4-6-0	99	125
Mississippi	0-3-1	.125	12	46	5-5-2	150	98
Sewanee	0-5-0	.000	13	211	0-6-1	20	230

Bowls: Bacardi (Auburn 7, Villanova 7); Sugar (Santa Clara 21, LSU 14); Orange (Duquesne 13, Mississippi State 12)

1937

School	W-L-T	Pct.	Pts.	Opp.	W-L-T	Pts.	Opp.
Alabama	6-0-0	1.000	145	20	9-0-0	225	20
LSU	5-1-0	.833	108	21	9-1-0	234	27
Auburn	4-1-2	.714	95	23	5-2-3	121	36
Vanderbilt	4-2-0	.667	80	36	7-2-0	121	42
Miss. State	3-2-0	.600	42	94	5-4-1	119	117
Ga. Tech	3-2-1	.583	64	34	6-3-1	177	54
Tennessee	4-3-0	.571	130	47	6-3-1	189	47
Florida	3-4-0	.429	46	59	4-7-0	86	89
Tulane	2-3-1	.417	66	50	5-4-1	164	69
Georgia	1-2-2	.400	13	50	6-3-2	151	64
Mississippi	0-4-0	.000	14	68	4-5-1	127	106
Kentucky	0-5-0	.000	0	104	4-6-0	93	130
Sewanee	0-6-0	.000	7	204	2-7-0	78	213

Bowls: Rose (California 13, Alabama 0); Orange (Auburn 6, Michigan State 0); Sugar (Santa Clara 6, LSU 0)

1938

School	W-L-T	Pct.	Pts.	Opp.	W-L-T	Pts.	Opp.
Tennessee	7-0-0	1.000	167	9	10-0-0	276	16
Alabama	4-1-1	.750	82	33	7-1-1	149	40
Tulane	4-1-1	.750	107	9	7-2-1	211	53
Mississippi	3-2-0	.600	85	73	9-2-0	232	120
Ga. Tech	2-1-3	.583	47	51	3-4-3	72	84
Vanderbilt	4-3-0	.571	54	49	6-3-0	84	49
Florida	2-2-1	.500	25	54	4-5-1	112	149
Auburn	3-3-1	.500	84	49	4-5-1	110	88
Georgia	1-2-1	.375	39	57	5-4-1	145	143
LSU	2-4-0	.333	58	83	6-4-0	160	89
Miss. State	1-4-0	.200	41	98	4-6-0	123	131
Kentucky	0-4-0	.000	31	105	2-7-0	150	160
Sewanee	0-6-0	.000	9	159	1-8-0	59	213

Bowls: Orange (Tennessee 17, Oklahoma 0)

Through The Years

1939

School	W-L-T	Pct.	Pts.	Opp.	W-L-T	Pts.	Opp.
Tennessee	6-0-0	1.000	120	0	10-0-0	212	0
Ga. Tech	6-0-0	1.000	74	25	7-2-0	129	49
Tulane	5-0-0	1.000	128	26	8-0-1	181	46
Miss. State	3-2-0	.600	47	32	8-2-0	216	32
Mississippi	2-2-0	.500	40	50	7-2-0	230	64
Kentucky	2-2-1	.500	47	58	6-2-1	161	64
Auburn	3-3-1	.500	48	40	5-5-1	71	69
Alabama	2-3-1	.417	53	47	5-3-1	101	53
Georgia	1-3-0	.250	12	35	5-6-0	113	98
LSU	1-5-0	.167	58	109	4-5-0	111	116
Vanderbilt	1-6-0	.143	57	120	2-7-1	96	165
Florida	0-3-1	.125	16	48	5-5-1	78	66
Sewanee	0-3-0	.000	7	117	3-5-0	43	150

Bowls: Orange (Georgia Tech 21, Missouri 7); Rose (Southern Cal 14, Tennessee 0); Sugar (Texas A&M 14, Tulane 13)

1940

School	W-L-T	Pct.	Pts.	Opp.	W-L-T	Pts.	Opp.
Tennessee	5-0-0	1.000	122	12	10-0-0	319	26
Miss. State	4-0-1	.900	88	21	9-0-1	233	51
Mississippi	3-1-0	.750	60	46	9-2-0	251	100
Alabama	4-2-0	.667	89	80	7-2-0	166	80
Auburn	3-2-1	.583	89	70	6-4-1	170	153
LSU	3-3-0	.500	55	82	6-4-0	139	112
Georgia	2-3-1	.417	82	106	5-4-1	209	134
Florida	2-3-0	.400	48	81	5-5-0	136	141
Kentucky	1-2-2	.400	40	79	5-3-2	190	107
Tulane	1-3-0	.250	41	60	5-5-0	144	126
Vanderbilt	1-5-1	.214	55	91	3-6-1	101	98
Ga. Tech	1-5-0	.167	72	93	3-7-0	139	160
Sewanee	0-1-0	.000	0	20	3-5-0	132	125

Bowls: Orange (Mississippi State 14, Georgetown 7); Sugar (Boston College 19, Tennessee 13)

1941

School	W-L-T	Pct.	Pts.	Opp.	W-L-T	Pts.	Opp.
Miss. State	4-0-1	.900	40	7	8-1-1	191	55
Tennessee	3-1-0	.750	61	29	8-2-0	182	73
Alabama	5-2-0	.714	105	51	8-2-0	234	64
Georgia	3-1-1	.700	75	44	8-1-1	279	59
Mississippi	2-1-1	.625	47	45	6-2-1	131	67
Vanderbilt	3-2-0	.600	81	82	8-2-0	260	89
LSU	2-2-2	.500	54	40	4-4-2	119	93
Tulane	2-3-0	.400	93	72	5-4-0	220	95
Ga. Tech	2-4-0	.333	62	96	3-6-0	82	130
Florida	1-3-0	.250	24	42	4-6-0	149	97
Auburn	0-4-1	.100	28	88	4-5-1	123	115
Kentucky	0-4-0	.000	35	109	5-4-0	151	154

Bowls: Cotton (Alabama 29, Texas A&M 21); Orange (Georgia 40, TCU 26)

---

*Appointed Conference Games

While the SEC rule requiring six football games with member schools was in effect, 16 games with outside schools were appointed to serve as conference games to avoid a violation for the members. The won-lost records of these games are included in the annual conference standings, but the results are not included in the conference point totals.

1954—Ole Miss vs. Arkansas, 0-6
1958—Ole Miss vs. Houston, 56-7
1964—Tulane vs. Miami, 0-21
1965—Georgia vs. Clemson, 23-9
  Tennessee vs. S. Carolina, 24-3
1966—Florida vs. Tulane, 31-10
  Georgia vs. N. Carolina, 28-3
  LSU vs. Tulane, 21-7
  Tennessee vs. S. Carolina, 29-17
  Vanderbilt vs. Tulane, 12-13
1967—Georgia vs. Clemson, 24-17
  Vanderbilt vs. Tulane, 14-27
1968—Florida vs. Tulane, 24-3
  LSU vs. TCU, 10-7
  LSU vs. Tulane, 34-10
  Miss. State vs. Tex. Tech, 28-28
  Vanderbilt vs. Tulane, 21-7

1942

School	W-L-T	Pct.	Pts.	Opp.	W-L-T	Pts.	Opp.
Georgia	6-1-0	.857	238	56	10-1-0	367	76
Ga. Tech	4-1-0	.800	89	48	9-1-0	212	73
Tennessee	4-1-0	.800	85	15	8-1-1	245	54
Miss. State	5-2-0	.714	188	62	8-2-0	200	77
Alabama	4-2-0	.667	80	41	7-3-0	209	76
LSU	3-2-0	.600	62	70	7-3-0	192	117
Auburn	3-3-0	.500	79	60	6-4-1	174	133
Vanderbilt	2-4-0	.333	61	113	6-4-0	232	113
Florida	1-3-0	.250	25	121	3-7-0	106	185
Tulane	1-4-0	.200	47	113	4-5-0	121	154
Kentucky	0-5-0	.000	19	101	3-6-1	155	154
Mississippi	0-5-0	.000	33	136	2-7-0	132	163

Bowls: Orange (Alabama 37, Boston College 21); Rose (Georgia 9, UCLA 0); Cotton (Texas 14, Georgia Tech 7); Sugar (Tennessee 14, Tulsa 7)

1943

School	W-L-T	Pct.	Pts.	Opp.	W-L-T	Pts.	Opp.
Ga. Tech	3-0-0	1.000	123	7	7-3-0	280	124
Tulane	1-1-0	.500	27	33	3-3-0	92	94
LSU	2-2-0	.500	68	102	5-3-0	143	144
Georgia	0-3-0	.000	33	109	6-4-0	264	153
Vanderbilt	0-0-0	.000	0	0	5-0-0	145	33

Bowls: Sugar (Georgia Tech 20, Tulsa 18); Orange (LSU 19, Texas A&M 14)

1944

School	W-L-T	Pct.	Pts.	Opp.	W-L-T	Pts.	Opp.
Ga. Tech	4-0-0	1.000	119	13	8-2-0	241	75
Tennessee	5-0-1	.917	120	27	8-0-1	173	48
Georgia	4-2-0	.667	121	103	7-3-0	269	130
Alabama	3-1-2	.667	128	47	5-1-2	246	54
Miss. State	3-2-0	.600	73	59	6-2-0	219	79
LSU	2-3-1	.417	79	80	2-5-1	92	101
Mississippi	2-3-0	.400	59	95	2-6-0	77	178
Tulane	1-2-0	.333	29	72	4-3-0	113	125
Kentucky	1-5-0	.167	59	134	3-6-0	125	147
Florida	0-3-0	.000	18	104	4-3-0	108	136
Auburn	0-4-0	.000	47	118	4-4-0	181	137
Vanderbilt	0-0-0	.000	0	0	3-0-1	67	23

Bowls: Sugar (Duke 29, Alabama 26); Orange (Tulsa 26, Georgia Tech 12); Rose (Southern Cal 25, Tennessee 0)

1945

School	W-L-T	Pct.	Pts.	Opp.	W-L-T	Pts.	Opp.
Alabama	6-0-0	1.000	265	60	9-0-0	396	66
Tennessee	3-1-0	.750	100	25	8-1-0	238	52
LSU	5-2-0	.714	172	80	7-2-0	245	92
Georgia	4-2-0	.667	164	66	8-2-0	294	94
Mississippi	3-3-0	.500	68	112	4-5-0	100	183
Ga. Tech	2-2-0	.500	68	56	4-6-0	157	165
Miss. State	2-3-0	.400	79	96	6-3-0	221	108
Auburn	2-3-0	.400	46	89	5-5-0	172	129
Vanderbilt	2-4-0	.333	40	175	3-6-0	71	215
Florida	1-3-1	.300	32	79	4-5-1	155	100
Tulane	1-3-1	.300	41	113	2-6-1	93	212
Kentucky	0-5-0	.000	38	162	2-8-0	96	217

Bowls: Rose (Alabama 34, Southern Cal 14); Oil (Georgia 20, Tulsa 6)

1994 SEC Football

1946

School	W-L-T	Pct.	Pts.	Opp.	W-L-T	Pts.	Opp.
Georgia	5-0-0	1.000	151	34	10-0-0	372	100
Tennessee	5-0-0	1.000	57	29	9-1-0	175	89
LSU	5-1-0	.833	140	101	9-1-0	240	123
Ga. Tech	4-2-0	.667	128	75	8-2-0	243	108
Miss. State	3-2-0	.600	80	44	8-2-0	271	71
Alabama	4-3-0	.571	85	84	7-4-0	186	110
Vanderbilt	3-4-0	.429	66	43	5-4-0	108	43
Kentucky	2-3-0	.400	50	69	7-3-0	233	97
Tulane	2-4-0	.333	106	110	3-7-0	179	209
Auburn	1-5-0	.167	53	164	4-6-0	132	210
Mississippi	1-6-0	.143	61	130	2-7-0	77	144
Florida	0-5-0	.000	46	140	0-9-0	104	264

Bowls: Sugar (Georgia 20, North Carolina 10); Oil (Georgia Tech 41, St. Mary's 19); Cotton (LSU 0, Arkansas 0); Orange (Rice 8, Tennessee 0)

1947

School	W-L-T	Pct.	Pts.	Opp.	W-L-T	Pts.	Opp.
Mississippi	6-1-0	.857	157	82	8-2-0	256	101
Ga. Tech	4-1-0	.800	88	21	9-1-0	220	35
Alabama	5-2-0	.714	122	61	8-2-0	203	74
Miss. State	2-2-0	.500	54	54	7-3-0	169	89
Georgia	3-3-0	.500	104	81	7-4-0	192	115
Vanderbilt	3-3-0	.500	72	58	6-4-0	182	85
Tulane	2-3-2	.429	88	100	2-5-2	94	192
LSU	2-3-1	.417	95	121	5-3-1	149	161
Kentucky	2-3-0	.400	53	40	7-3-0	151	59
Tennessee	2-3-0	.400	38	93	5-5-0	164	152
Auburn	1-5-0	.167	33	151	2-7-0	78	204
Florida	0-3-1	.125	33	75	4-5-1	125	156

Bowls: Sugar (Texas 27, Alabama 7); Gator (Georgia 20, Maryland 20); Orange (Georgia Tech 20, Kansas 14); Great Lakes (Kentucky 24, Villanova 14); Delta (Ole Miss 13, TCU 9)

1948

School	W-L-T	Pct.	Pts.	Opp.	W-L-T	Pts.	Opp.
Georgia	6-0-0	1.000	175	51	9-1-0	278	100
Mississippi	6-1-0	.857	160	73	8-1-0	226	93
Tulane	5-1-0	.833	124	40	9-1-0	207	60
Vanderbilt	4-2-1	.643	170	67	8-2-1	328	73
Ga. Tech	4-3-0	.571	126	62	7-3-0	226	69
Alabama	4-4-1	.500	153	164	6-4-1	228	170
Miss. State	3-3-0	.500	62	59	4-4-1	103	87
Tennessee	2-3-1	.417	59	77	4-4-2	140	98
Kentucky	1-3-1	.300	60	96	5-3-2	199	128
Florida	1-5-0	.167	78	153	5-5-0	213	206
LSU	1-5-0	.167	52	178	3-7-0	99	271
Auburn	0-7-0	.000	29	228	1-8-1	68	262

Bowls: Orange (Texas 41, Georgia 28)

1949

School	W-L-T	Pct.	Pts.	Opp.	W-L-T	Pts.	Opp.
Tulane	5-1-0	.833	155	61	7-2-1	251	142
Kentucky	4-1-0	.800	126	6	9-2-0	304	53
Tennessee	4-1-1	.750	97	64	7-2-1	214	104
Ga. Tech	5-2-0	.714	134	99	7-3-0	197	129
LSU	4-2-0	.667	122	53	8-2-0	231	74
Alabama	4-3-1	.563	145	96	6-3-1	227	130
Vanderbilt	4-4-0	.500	144	170	5-5-0	177	183
Auburn	2-4-2	.375	114	168	2-4-3	134	188
Mississippi	2-4-0	.333	107	151	4-5-1	246	243
Florida	1-4-1	.250	86	156	4-5-1	180	218
Georgia	1-4-1	.250	47	94	4-6-1	177	134
Miss. State	0-6-0	.000	25	184	0-8-1	38	224

Bowls: Orange (Santa Clara 21, Kentucky 13); Sugar (Oklahoma 35, LSU 0)

1950

School	W-L-T	Pct.	Pts.	Opp.	W-L-T	Pts.	Opp.
Kentucky	5-1-0	.833	157	48	10-1-0	380	62
Tennessee	4-1-0	.800	99	16	10-1-0	315	57
Alabama	6-2-0	.750	214	101	9-2-0	328	107
Tulane	3-1-1	.700	118	66	6-2-1	260	97
Ga. Tech	4-2-0	.667	89	95	5-6-0	182	193
Georgia	3-2-1	.583	65	44	6-2-3	158	65
Miss. State	3-4-0	.429	95	123	4-5-0	169	137
LSU	2-3-2	.429	107	88	4-5-2	165	151
Vanderbilt	3-4-0	.429	128	178	7-4-0	252	216
Florida	2-4-0	.333	90	137	5-5-0	157	181
Mississippi	1-5-0	.167	75	169	5-5-0	207	183
Auburn	0-7-0	.000	17	189	0-10-0	31	255

Bowls: Presidential Cup (Texas A&M 40, Georgia 20); Sugar (Kentucky 13, Oklahoma 7); Cotton (Tennessee 20, Texas 14)

1951

School	W-L-T	Pct.	Pts.	Opp.	W-L-T	Pts.	Opp.
Ga. Tech	7-0-0	1.000	175	41	10-0-1	278	76
Tennessee	5-0-0	1.000	150	61	10-0-0	373	88
LSU	4-2-1	.643	63	71	7-3-1	128	111
Mississippi	4-2-1	.643	181	130	6-3-1	254	157
Kentucky	3-3-0	.500	102	68	7-4-0	294	114
Auburn	3-4-0	.429	101	164	5-5-0	180	212
Vanderbilt	3-5-0	.375	147	167	6-5-0	201	195
Alabama	3-5-0	.375	116	140	5-6-0	263	188
Georgia	2-4-1	.333	73	97	5-5-0	176	184
Florida	2-4-0	.333	88	96	5-5-0	174	131
Miss. State	2-5-0	.286	23	107	4-5-0	82	127
Tulane	1-5-0	.167	40	117	4-6-0	143	172

Bowls: Orange (Georgia Tech 17, Baylor 14); Cotton (Kentucky 20, TCU 7); Sugar (Maryland 28, Tennessee 13)

1952

School	W-L-T	Pct.	Pts.	Opp.	W-L-T	Pts.	Opp.
Ga. Tech	6-0-0	1.000	124	26	11-0-0	301	52
Tennessee	5-0-1	.917	142	36	8-1-1	259	63
Mississippi	4-0-2	.833	122	69	8-0-2	237	96
Alabama	4-2-0	.667	121	85	9-2-0	264	133
Georgia	4-3-0	.571	108	131	7-4-0	226	208
Florida	3-3-0	.500	127	84	7-3-0	290	109
Miss. State	3-4-0	.429	170	172	5-4-0	225	186
Tulane	3-5-0	.375	107	132	5-5-0	188	146
Kentucky	1-3-2	.333	75	121	5-4-2	161	173
LSU	2-5-0	.286	101	138	3-7-0	148	214
Vanderbilt	1-4-1	.250	55	145	3-5-2	151	199
Auburn	0-7-0	.000	75	188	2-8-0	139	208

Bowls: Orange (Alabama 61, Syracuse 6); Gator (Florida 14, Tulsa 13); Sugar (Georgia Tech 24, Ole Miss 7); Cotton (Texas 16, Tennessee 0)

1953

School	W-L-T	Pct.	Pts.	Opp.	W-L-T	Pts.	Opp.
Alabama	4-0-3	.786	91	51	6-2-3	172	124
Ga. Tech	4-1-1	.750	140	44	8-2-1	246	92
Mississippi	4-1-1	.750	129	62	7-2-1	236	113
Kentucky	4-1-1	.750	137	89	7-2-1	201	116
Auburn	4-2-1	.643	136	99	7-2-1	257	138
Miss. State	3-1-3	.643	121	80	5-2-3	196	219
Tennessee	3-2-1	.583	95	80	6-4-1	240	153
LSU	2-3-3	.438	123	138	5-3-3	194	159
Florida	1-3-2	.333	69	79	3-5-2	200	113
Vanderbilt	1-5-0	.167	59	172	3-7-0	131	258
Georgia	1-5-0	.167	71	149	3-8-0	155	250
Tulane	1-5-0	.167	68	196	1-8-1	129	228

Bowls: Cotton (Rice 28, Alabama 6); Gator (Texas Tech 35, Auburn 13); Sugar (Georgia Tech 42, West Virginia 19)

Through The Years

1954

School	W-L-T	Pct.	Pts.	Opp.	W-L-T	Pts.	Opp.
*Mississippi	5-1-0	.833	119	29	9-1-0	283	47
Ga. Tech	6-2-0	.750	145	63	7-3-0	175	91
Florida	5-2-0	.714	94	66	5-5-0	115	128
Kentucky	5-2-0	.714	90	95	7-3-0	151	125
Georgia	3-2-1	.583	40	69	6-3-1	89	89
Auburn	3-3-0	.500	124	54	7-3-0	243	73
Miss. State	3-3-0	.500	58	47	6-4-0	192	120
Alabama	3-3-2	.500	74	74	4-5-2	123	104
LSU	2-5-0	.286	66	115	5-6-0	125	173
Tulane	1-6-1	.188	26	124	1-6-3	46	144
Vanderbilt	1-5-0	.167	68	91	2-7-0	134	169
Tennessee	1-5-0	.167	39	116	4-6-0	105	164

Bowls: Gator (Auburn 33, Baylor 13); Cotton (Georgia Tech 14, Arkansas 6); Sugar (Navy 21, Ole Miss 0)

1955

School	W-L-T	Pct.	Pts.	Opp.	W-L-T	Pts.	Opp.
Mississippi	5-1-0	.833	135	73	9-1-0	251	97
Auburn	5-1-1	.786	123	92	8-1-1	211	98
Ga. Tech	4-1-1	.750	87	33	8-1-1	182	46
Tennessee	3-2-1	.583	74	57	6-3-1	188	92
Vanderbilt	4-3-0	.571	123	66	7-3-0	215	73
Miss. State	4-4-0	.500	120	135	6-4-0	173	142
Kentucky	3-3-1	.500	89	108	6-3-1	178	131
Tulane	3-3-1	.500	101	94	5-4-1	163	136
LSU	2-3-1	.417	106	81	3-5-2	139	149
Florida	3-5-0	.375	77	119	4-6-0	111	126
Georgia	2-5-0	.286	91	123	4-6-0	173	170
Alabama	0-7-0	.000	36	181	0-10-0	48	256

Bowls: Gator (Vanderbilt 25, Auburn 13); Sugar (Georgia Tech 7, Pittsburgh 0); Cotton (Ole Miss 14, TCU 13)

1956

School	W-L-T	Pct.	Pts.	Opp.	W-L-T	Pts.	Opp.
Tennessee	6-0-0	1.000	139	28	10-0-0	268	75
Ga. Tech	7-1-0	.875	211	26	9-1-0	227	33
Florida	5-2-0	.714	124	58	6-3-1	158	98
Mississippi	4-2-0	.667	122	68	7-3-0	207	82
Auburn	4-3-0	.571	108	110	7-3-0	174	117
Kentucky	4-4-0	.500	72	105	6-4-0	119	105
Tulane	3-3-0	.500	56	83	6-4-0	124	123
Vanderbilt	2-5-0	.286	72	91	5-5-0	147	113
Alabama	2-5-0	.286	53	152	2-7-1	85	208
Miss. State	2-5-0	.286	104	119	4-6-0	148	152
LSU	1-5-0	.167	50	158	3-7-0	104	197
Georgia	1-6-0	.143	30	143	3-6-1	66	162

Bowls: Gator (Georgia Tech 21, Pittsburgh 14); Sugar (Baylor 13, Tennessee 7)

1957

School	W-L-T	Pct.	Pts.	Opp.	W-L-T	Pts.	Opp.
Auburn	7-0-0	1.000	90	7	10-0-0	207	28
Mississippi	5-0-1	.917	128	26	8-1-1	232	52
Miss. State	4-2-1	.643	118	81	6-2-1	175	100
Florida	4-2-1	.643	92	70	6-2-1	133	70
Tennessee	4-3-0	.571	82	62	7-3-0	161	75
Vanderbilt	3-3-1	.500	47	81	5-3-2	113	108
LSU	4-4-0	.500	126	76	5-5-0	159	110
Ga. Tech	3-4-1	.438	62	71	4-4-2	75	71
Georgia	3-4-0	.429	72	71	3-7-0	93	150
Tulane	1-5-0	.167	41	135	2-8-0	94	195
Alabama	1-6-1	.188	40	143	2-7-1	69	173
Kentucky	1-7-0	.125	48	120	3-7-0	128	127

Bowls: Sugar (Ole Miss 39, Texas 7); Gator (Tennessee 3, Texas A&M 0)

1958

School	W-L-T	Pct.	Pts.	Opp.	W-L-T	Pts.	Opp.
LSU	6-0-0	1.000	138	23	10-0-0	275	53
Auburn	6-0-1	.929	102	40	9-0-1	173	62
*Mississippi	4-2-0	.667	83	46	8-2-0	215	65
Vanderbilt	2-1-3	.583	45	30	5-2-3	131	71
Tennessee	4-3-0	.571	64	77	4-6-0	77	122
Alabama	3-4-1	.438	63	69	5-4-1	106	75
Kentucky	3-4-1	.438	65	109	5-4-1	136	115
Florida	2-3-1	.417	66	56	6-3-1	171	93
Ga. Tech	2-3-1	.417	53	60	5-4-1	98	91
Georgia	2-4-0	.333	70	64	4-6-0	196	114
Tulane	1-5-0	.167	35	148	3-7-0	195	189
Miss. State	1-6-0	.143	61	123	3-6-0	127	129

Bowls: Gator (Ole Miss 7, Florida 3); Sugar (LSU 7, Clemson 0)

1959

School	W-L-T	Pct.	Pts.	Opp.	W-L-T	Pts.	Opp.
Georgia	7-0-0	1.000	123	53	9-1-0	214	89
LSU	5-1-0	.833	79	23	9-1-0	164	29
Mississippi	5-1-0	.833	184	21	9-1-0	329	21
Alabama	4-1-2	.714	65	45	7-1-2	95	52
Auburn	4-3-0	.571	90	33	7-3-0	174	58
Vanderbilt	3-2-2	.571	57	79	5-3-2	138	106
Ga. Tech	3-3-0	.500	76	69	6-4-0	129	107
Tennessee	3-4-1	.438	60	111	5-4-1	112	118
Florida	2-4-0	.333	60	62	5-4-1	169	107
Kentucky	1-6-0	.143	45	97	4-6-0	140	107
Tulane	0-5-1	.083	39	143	3-6-1	94	176
Miss. State	0-7-0	.000	19	161	2-7-0	96	198

Bowls: Liberty (Penn State 7, Alabama 0); Orange (Georgia 14, Missouri 0); Gator (Arkansas 14, Georgia Tech 7); Sugar (Ole Miss 21, LSU 0)

1960

School	W-L-T	Pct.	Pts.	Opp.	W-L-T	Pts.	Opp.
Mississippi	5-0-1	.917	138	37	9-0-1	266	64
Florida	5-1-0	.833	93	57	8-2-0	144	74
Alabama	5-1-1	.786	81	47	8-1-1	180	53
Auburn	5-2-0	.714	68	52	8-2-0	155	80
Tennessee	3-2-2	.571	85	58	6-2-2	209	79
Georgia	4-3-0	.571	88	95	6-4-0	174	118
Ga. Tech	4-4-0	.500	102	78	5-5-0	118	97
LSU	2-3-1	.417	42	37	5-4-1	105	50
Kentucky	2-4-1	.357	79	81	5-4-1	206	81
Tulane	1-4-1	.250	57	84	3-6-1	132	139
Miss. State	0-5-1	.084	41	96	2-6-1	101	119
Vanderbilt	0-7-0	.000	7	159	3-7-0	74	193

Bowls: Bluebonnet (Alabama 3, Texas 3); Gator (Florida 13, Baylor 12); Sugar (Ole Miss 14, Rice 6)

1961

School	W-L-T	Pct.	Pts.	Opp.	W-L-T	Pts.	Opp.
Alabama	7-0-0	1.000	178	15	10-0-0	287	22
LSU	6-0-0	1.000	143	27	9-1-0	234	50
Mississippi	5-1-0	.833	176	33	9-1-0	326	40
Tennessee	4-3-0	.571	128	114	6-4-0	221	149
Ga. Tech	4-3-0	.571	90	43	7-3-0	162	50
Florida	3-3-0	.500	57	92	4-5-1	97	146
Auburn	3-4-0	.429	94	109	6-4-0	174	137
Kentucky	2-4-0	.333	81	101	5-5-0	138	123
Georgia	2-5-0	.286	60	128	3-7-0	84	177
Miss. State	1-5-0	.167	34	112	5-5-0	111	135
Tulane	1-5-0	.167	20	175	2-8-0	60	225
Vanderbilt	1-6-0	.143	51	163	2-8-0	95	220

Bowls: Sugar (Alabama 10, Arkansas 3); Gator (Penn State 30, Georgia Tech 15); Orange (LSU 25, Colorado 7); Cotton (Texas 12, Ole Miss 7)

*See page 185 "Appointed Conference Games."

1994 SEC Football

1962

School	W-L-T	Pct.	Pts.	Opp.	W-L-T	Pts.	Opp.
Mississippi	6-0-0	1.000	117	19	9-0-0	230	40
Alabama	6-1-0	.857	187	27	9-1-0	272	39
LSU	5-1-0	.833	113	25	8-1-1	162	34
Ga. Tech	5-2-0	.714	141	51	7-2-1	201	83
Florida	4-2-0	.667	106	74	6-4-0	204	132
Auburn	4-3-0	.571	88	134	6-3-1	173	168
Georgia	2-3-1	.417	68	123	3-4-3	109	174
Kentucky	2-3-1	.417	32	54	3-5-2	85	101
Miss. State	2-5-0	.286	60	101	3-6-0	76	132
Tennessee	2-6-0	.250	108	120	4-6-0	179	134
Vanderbilt	1-6-0	.143	34	141	1-9-0	62	215
Tulane	0-7-0	.000	43	228	0-10-0	76	293

Bowls: Orange (Alabama 17, Oklahoma 0); Gator (Florida 17, Penn State 7); Bluebonnet (Missouri 14, Georgia Tech 10); Cotton (LSU 13, Texas 0); Sugar (Ole Miss 17, Arkansas 13)

1963

School	W-L-T	Pct.	Pts.	Opp.	W-L-T	Pts.	Opp.
Mississippi	5-0-1	.917	146	27	7-0-2	207	33
Auburn	6-1-0	.857	119	74	9-1-0	189	103
Alabama	6-2-0	.750	177	63	8-2-0	215	88
Miss. State	4-1-2	.714	96	65	6-2-2	169	82
LSU	4-2-0	.667	78	57	7-3-0	135	98
Ga. Tech	4-3-0	.571	101	76	7-3-0	173	89
Florida	3-3-1	.500	61	71	6-3-1	130	120
Tennessee	3-5-0	.375	85	108	5-5-0	168	121
Georgia	2-4-0	.333	61	95	4-5-1	133	151
Vanderbilt	0-5-2	.143	23	113	1-7-2	73	146
Kentucky	0-5-1	.083	41	109	3-6-1	142	168
Tulane	0-6-1	.071	23	153	1-8-1	43	191

Bowls: Sugar (Alabama 12, Ole Miss 7); Orange (Nebraska 13, Auburn 7); Bluebonnet (Baylor 14, LSU 7); Liberty (Mississippi State 16, North Carolina State 12)

1964

School	W-L-T	Pct.	Pts.	Opp.	W-L-T	Pts.	Opp.
Alabama	8-0-0	1.000	188	60	10-0-0	233	67
Georgia	4-2-0	.667	52	59	6-3-1	123	98
Florida	4-2-0	.667	101	64	7-3-0	181	98
Kentucky	4-2-0	.667	95	97	5-5-0	150	194
LSU	4-2-1	.643	83	70	7-2-1	115	79
Auburn	3-3-0	.500	43	65	6-4-0	123	91
Mississippi	2-4-1	.357	113	104	5-4-1	210	113
Miss. State	2-5-0	.286	82	102	4-6-0	155	143
Vanderbilt	1-4-1	.250	37	67	3-6-1	79	122
Tennessee	1-5-1	.214	32	87	4-5-1	80	121
*Tulane	1-5-0	.167	31	82	3-7-0	79	147

Bowls: Orange (Texas 21, Alabama 17); Sun (Georgia 7, Texas Tech 0); Sugar (LSU 13, Syracuse 10); Bluebonnet (Tulsa 14, Ole Miss 7)

1965

School	W-L-T	Pct.	Pts.	Opp.	W-L-T	Pts.	Opp.
Alabama	6-1-1	.813	161	65	8-1-1	217	79
Auburn	4-1-1	.750	113	115	5-4-1	165	162
Florida	4-2-0	.667	126	76	7-3-0	221	129
*Tennessee	3-1-2	.667	73	40	7-1-2	193	92
Mississippi	5-3-0	.625	129	77	6-4-0	166	108
LSU	3-3-0	.500	144	109	7-3-0	251	157
Kentucky	3-3-0	.500	120	90	6-4-0	202	160
*Georgia	3-3-0	.500	81	90	6-4-0	186	158
Vanderbilt	1-5-0	.167	40	125	2-7-1	85	180
Tulane	1-5-0	.167	37	192	2-8-0	71	268
Miss. State	1-5-0	.167	78	123	4-6-0	202	172

Bowls: Orange (Alabama 39, Nebraska 28); Liberty (Ole Miss 13, Auburn 7); Sugar (Missouri 20, Florida 18); Cotton (LSU 14, Arkansas 7); Bluebonnet (Tennessee 27, Tulsa 6)

1966

School	W-L-T	Pct.	Pts.	Opp.	W-L-T	Pts.	Opp.
Alabama	6-0-0	1.000	149	37	10-0-0	267	37
*Georgia	6-0-0	1.000	104	58	9-1-0	211	89
*Florida	5-1-0	.800	109	68	8-2-0	238	135
Mississippi	5-2-0	.714	116	33	8-2-0	170	46
*Tennessee	4-2-0	.667	101	44	7-3-0	222	87
*LSU	3-3-0	.500	54	73	5-4-1	135	124
Kentucky	2-4-0	.333	65	119	3-6-1	107	196
Auburn	1-5-0	.167	60	127	4-6-0	104	162
Miss. State	0-6-0	.000	45	129	2-8-0	75	176
*Vanderbilt	0-6-0	.000	16	131	1-9-0	72	237

Bowls: Sugar (Alabama 34, Nebraska 7); Orange (Florida 27, Georgia Tech 12); Cotton (Georgia 24, SMU 9); Bluebonnet (Texas 19, Ole Miss 0); Gator (Tennessee 18, Syracuse 12)

1967

School	W-L-T	Pct.	Pts.	Opp.	W-L-T	Pts.	Opp.
Tennessee	6-0-0	1.000	146	68	9-1-0	259	115
Alabama	5-1-0	.833	96	61	8-1-1	188	111
Florida	4-2-0	.667	123	120	6-4-0	201	161
*Georgia	4-2-0	.667	114	53	7-3-0	250	105
Mississippi	4-2-1	.643	120	97	6-3-1	174	151
LSU	3-2-1	.583	155	50	7-3-0	248	114
Auburn	3-3-0	.500	126	79	6-4-0	237	123
Kentucky	1-6-0	.143	65	187	2-8-0	111	230
*Vanderbilt	0-6-0	.000	71	143	2-7-1	165	241
Miss. State	0-6-0	.000	10	168	1-9-0	49	259

Bowls: Cotton (Texas A&M 20, Alabama 16); Liberty (North Carolina State 14, Georgia 7); Sugar (LSU 20, Wyoming 13); Sun (UTEP 14, Ole Miss 7); Orange (Oklahoma 26, Tennessee 24)

1968

School	W-L-T	Pct.	Pts.	Opp.	W-L-T	Pts.	Opp.
Georgia	5-0-1	.917	173	47	8-0-2	282	98
Tennessee	4-1-1	.750	106	68	8-1-1	248	110
Alabama	4-2-0	.667	108	63	8-2-0	174	104
*LSU	4-2-0	.667	64	62	7-3-0	190	144
Auburn	4-2-0	.667	123	75	6-4-0	223	149
*Florida	3-2-1	.583	74	117	6-3-1	151	175
Mississippi	3-2-1	.583	91	115	6-3-1	178	180
*Vanderbilt	2-3-1	.417	40	87	5-4-1	163	147
*Miss. State	0-4-2	.167	60	114	0-8-2	146	260
Kentucky	0-7-0	.000	59	150	3-7-0	141	206

Bowls: Gator (Missouri 35, Alabama 10); Sun (Auburn 34, Arizona 10); Sugar (Arkansas 16, Georgia 2); Peach (LSU 31, Florida State 27); Liberty (Ole Miss 34, Virginia Tech 17); Cotton (Texas 36, Tennessee 13)

1969

School	W-L-T	Pct.	Pts.	Opp.	W-L-T	Pts.	Opp.
Tennessee	5-1-0	.833	174	127	9-1-0	315	165
LSU	4-1-0	.800	162	77	9-1-0	349	91
Auburn	5-2-0	.714	238	123	8-2-0	363	137
Florida	3-1-1	.700	144	112	8-1-1	329	187
Mississippi	4-2-0	.667	178	105	7-3-0	307	140
Georgia	2-3-1	.417	79	97	5-4-1	212	101
Vanderbilt	2-3-0	.400	11	137	4-6-0	242	264
Alabama	2-4-0	.333	121	175	6-4-0	281	221
Kentucky	1-6-0	.143	61	224	2-8-0	104	295
Miss. State	0-5-0	.000	95	231	3-7-0	193	385

Bowls: Liberty (Colorado 47, Alabama 33); Astro-Bluebonnet (Houston 36, Auburn 7); Gator (Florida 14, Tennessee 13); Sun (Nebraska 45, Georgia 6); Sugar (Ole Miss 27, Arkansas 22)

* See page 185 "Appointed Conference Games."

Through The Years

1970

School	W-L-T	Pct.	Pts.	Opp.	W-L-T	Pts.	Opp.
LSU	5-0-0	1.000	144	49	9-2-0	277	96
Tennessee	4-1-0	.800	154	49	10-1-0	336	103
Auburn	5-2-0	.800	247	128	8-2-0	355	149
Mississippi	4-2-0	.667	156	157	7-3-0	285	220
Florida	3-3-0	.500	118	190	7-4-0	224	256
Georgia	3-3-0	.500	131	85	5-5-0	242	153
Alabama	3-4-0	.429	176	151	6-5-0	310	240
Miss. State	3-4-0	.429	72	189	6-5-0	171	264
Vanderbilt	1-5-0	.167	60	159	4-7-0	201	213
Kentucky	0-7-0	.000	72	173	2-9-0	131	233

Bowls: Astro-Bluebonnet (Alabama 24, Oklahoma 24); Gator (Auburn 35; Ole Miss 28); Orange (Nebraska 17, LSU 12); Sugar (Tennessee 34, Air Force 13)

1971

School	W-L-T	Pct.	Pts.	Opp.	W-L-T	Pts.	Opp.
Alabama	7-0-0	1.000	238	45	11-0-0	362	84
Auburn	5-1-0	.833	160	94	9-1-0	313	132
Georgia	5-1-0	.833	200	56	10-1-0	353	112
Mississippi	4-2-0	.667	147	127	9-2-0	322	204
Tennessee	4-2-0	.667	94	76	9-2-0	256	108
LSU	3-2-0	.600	122	61	8-3-0	320	138
Vanderbilt	1-5-0	.167	146	146	4-6-0	136	208
Florida	1-6-0	.143	79	232	4-7-0	174	298
Kentucky	1-6-0	.143	84	186	3-8-0	144	284
Miss. State	1-7-0	.125	80	251	2-9-0	120	311

Bowls: Orange (Nebraska 38, Alabama 6); Sugar (Oklahoma 40, Auburn 22); Gator (Georgia 7, North Carolina 3); Sun (LSU 33, Iowa State 15); Peach (Ole Miss 41, Georgia Tech 18); Liberty (Tennessee 14, Arkansas 13)

1972

School	W-L-T	Pct.	Pts.	Opp.	W-L-T	Pts.	Opp.
Alabama	7-1-0	.875	258	97	10-1-0	393	133
Auburn	6-1-0	.857	120	103	9-1-0	185	138
LSU	4-1-1	.750	114	75	9-1-1	235	121
Tennessee	4-2-0	.667	94	44	9-2-0	273	83
Georgia	4-3-0	.571	82	96	7-4-0	174	163
Florida	3-3-1	.500	121	76	5-5-1	218	144
Mississippi	2-5-0	.286	124	104	5-5-0	192	142
Kentucky	2-5-0	.286	45	141	3-8-0	131	232
Miss. State	1-6-0	.143	81	202	4-7-0	197	254
Vanderbilt	0-6-0	.000	60	161	3-8-0	129	243

Bowls: Cotton (Texas 17, Alabama 13); Gator (Auburn 24, Colorado 3); Astro-Bluebonnet (Tennessee 24, LSU 17)

1973

School	W-L-T	Pct.	Pts.	Opp.	W-L-T	Pts.	Opp.
Alabama	8-0-0	1.000	268	70	11-0-0	454	89
LSU	5-1-0	.833	156	72	9-2-0	258	153
Mississippi	4-3-0	.571	124	137	6-5-0	202	177
Tennessee	3-3-0	.500	127	136	8-3-0	272	219
Florida	3-4-0	.429	82	141	7-4-0	180	171
Kentucky	3-4-0	.429	148	130	5-6-0	226	196
Georgia	3-4-0	.429	128	114	6-4-1	207	150
Auburn	2-5-0	.286	73	140	6-5-0	153	159
Miss. State	2-5-0	.286	133	205	4-5-2	219	255
Vanderbilt	1-5-0	.167	87	181	5-6-0	181	262

Bowls: Sugar (Notre Dame 24, Alabama 23); Sun (Missouri 34, Auburn 17); Tangerine (Miami-Ohio 16, Florida 7); Peach (Georgia 17, Maryland 16); Orange (Penn State 16, LSU 9); Gator (Texas Tech 28, Tennessee 19)

1974

School	W-L-T	Pct.	Pts.	Opp.	W-L-T	Pts.	Opp.
Alabama	6-0-0	1.000	168	50	11-0-0	318	83
Auburn	4-2-0	.667	120	88	9-2-0	260	126
Georgia	4-2-0	.667	155	122	6-5-0	317	264
Kentucky	3-3-0	.500	139	128	6-5-0	248	194
Florida	3-3-0	.500	128	123	8-3-0	251	184
Miss. State	3-3-0	.500	109	121	8-3-0	301	200
Vanderbilt	2-3-1	.417	122	144	7-3-1	307	193
Tennessee	2-3-1	.417	90	144	6-3-2	204	178
LSU	2-4-0	.333	77	91	5-5-1	202	168
Mississippi	0-6-0	.000	65	192	3-8-0	135	241

Bowls: Orange (Notre Dame 13, Alabama 11); Gator (Auburn 27, Texas 3); Sugar (Nebraska 13, Florida 10); Tangerine (Miami-Ohio 21; Georgia 10); Sun (Mississippi State 26, North Carolina 24); Liberty (Tennessee 7, Maryland 3); Peach (Vanderbilt 6, Texas Tech 6)

1975

School	W-L-T	Pct.	Pts.	Opp.	W-L-T	Pts.	Opp.
Alabama	6-0-0	1.000	174	40	10-1-0	361	66
Mississippi	5-1-0	.833	104	78	6-5-0	170	162
Georgia	5-1-0	.833	147	70	9-2-0	289	166
Florida	5-1-0	.833	182	47	9-2-0	302	104
Tennessee	3-3-0	.500	89	110	7-5-0	253	193
Vanderbilt	2-4-0	.333	47	156	7-4-0	119	200
f-LSU	2-4-0	.333	62	128	5-6-0	159	202
f-Auburn	2-4-0	.333	80	138	4-6-1	174	243
Kentucky	0-6-0	.000	59	131	2-8-1	132	188
f-Miss. State	0-6-0	.000	70	116	2-9-0	165	166

f-includes forfeit imposed on Miss. St. by NCAA & SEC
Bowls: Sugar (Alabama 13, Penn State 6); Gator (Maryland 13, Florida 0); Cotton (Arkansas 31, Georgia 10)

1976

School	W-L-T	Pct.	Pts.	Opp.	W-L-T	Pts.	Opp.
Georgia	5-1-0	.833	183	55	10-1-0	324	118
f-Kentucky	5-1-0	.833	84	61	8-3-0	188	151
Alabama	5-2-0	.714	169	99	8-3-0	291	134
Florida	4-2-0	.667	142	159	8-3-0	314	255
f-Mississippi	4-3-0	.571	68	142	6-5-0	153	180
f-LSU	3-3-0	.500	138	118	7-3-1	255	149
f-Auburn	3-3-0	.500	93	146	4-7-0	194	267
Tennessee	2-4-0	.333	104	101	6-5-0	237	162
Vanderbilt	0-6-0	.000	47	167	2-9-0	131	282
f-Miss. State	0-6-0	.000	138	118	0-11-0	269	178

f-Includes forfeit imposed on Miss. St. by NCAA & SEC
Bowls: Liberty (Alabama 36, UCLA 6); Sun (Texas A&M 37, Florida 14); Sugar (Pittsburgh 27, Georgia 3); Peach (Kentucky 21, North Carolina 0)

1977

School	W-L-T	Pct.	Pts.	Opp.	W-L-T	Pts.	Opp.
Alabama	7-0-0	1.000	209	76	10-1-0	345	133
Kentucky	6-0-0	1.000	152	50	10-1-0	252	111
f-Auburn	5-1-0	.833	131	130	6-5-0	204	243
LSU	4-2-0	.667	135	131	8-3-0	375	196
Florida	3-3-0	.500	108	135	6-4-1	251	235
f-Mississippi	3-4-0	.429	145	143	6-5-0	208	196
Georgia	2-4-0	.333	79	132	5-6-0	157	191
Tennessee	1-5-0	.167	112	136	4-7-0	229	229
Vanderbilt	0-6-0	.000	67	172	2-9-0	141	276
f-Miss. State	0-6-0	.000	105	138	0-11-0	193	227

f-Includes forfeit imposed on Miss. State by NCAA & SEC
Bowls: Sugar (Alabama 35, Ohio State 6); Sun (Stanford 24, LSU 14)

1978

School	W-L-T	Pct.	Pts.	Opp.	W-L-T	Pts.	Opp.
Alabama	6-0-0	1.000	204	97	10-1-0	331	161
Georgia	5-0-1	.917	160	90	9-1-1	268	162
Auburn	3-2-1	.583	129	104	6-4-1	238	191
LSU	3-3-0	.500	126	100	8-3-0	264	173
Tennessee	3-3-0	.500	159	139	5-5-1	251	209
Florida	3-3-0	.500	38	104	4-7-0	249	223
Kentucky	2-4-0	.333	123	104	4-6-1	193	189
Mississippi	2-4-0	.333	107	154	5-6-0	181	240
Miss. State	2-4-0	.333	71	137	6-5-0	232	205
Vanderbilt	0-6-0	.000	72	260	2-9-0	164	418

Bowls: Sugar (Alabama 14, Penn State 7); Bluebonnet (Stanford 25, Georgia 22); Liberty (Missouri 20, LSU 15)

1979

School	W-L-T	Pct.	Pts.	Opp.	W-L-T	Pts.	Opp.
Alabama	6-0-0	1.000	185	45	11-0-0	259	58
Georgia	5-1-0	.833	142	94	6-5-0	206	189
Auburn	4-2-0	.667	153	124	8-3-0	330	238
LSU	4-2-0	.667	106	73	6-5-0	241	141
Tennessee	3-3-0	.500	132	143	7-4-0	289	208
Kentucky	3-3-0	.500	116	79	5-6-0	180	143
Mississippi	3-3-0	.500	169	123	4-7-0	251	298
Miss. State	2-4-0	.333	74	92	3-8-0	162	179
Vanderbilt	0-6-0	.000	96	262	1-10-0	179	418
Florida	0-6-0	.000	39	167	0-10-1	106	265

Bowls: Sugar (Alabama 24, Arkansas 9); Tangerine (LSU 34, Wake Forest 10); Bluebonnet (Purdue 27, Tennessee 22)

1980

School	W-L-T	Pct.	Pts.	Opp.	W-L-T	Pts.	Opp.
Georgia	6-0-0	1.000	169	78	11-0-0	316	127
Miss. State	5-1-0	.833	143	104	9-2-0	284	216
*Alabama	5-1-0	.833	178	31	9-2-0	322	96
LSU	4-2-0	.667	138	133	7-4-0	213	193
Florida	4-2-0	.667	102	93	7-4-0	221	166
Tennessee	3-3-0	.500	162	90	5-6-0	256	189
*Mississippi	2-4-0	.333	101	123	3-8-0	263	266
Kentucky	1-5-0	.167	70	161	3-8-0	167	280
Auburn	0-6-0	.000	87	173	5-6-0	235	238
Vanderbilt	0-6-0	.000	51	215	2-9-0	140	352

Bowls: Cotton (Alabama 30, Baylor 2); Tangerine (Florida 35, Maryland 20); Sugar (Georgia 17, Notre Dame 10); Sun (Nebraska 31, Mississippi State 17)

* Alabama-Ole Miss game does not count in standings.

1981

School	W-L-T	Pct.	Pts.	Opp.	W-L-T	Pts.	Opp.
Georgia	6-0-0	1.000	205	62	10-1-0	352	98
*Alabama	6-0-0	1.000	150	70	9-1-1	284	137
Miss. State	4-2-0	.667	122	76	7-4-0	278	137
Florida	3-3-0	.500	145	93	7-4-0	216	140
Tennessee	3-3-0	.500	105	164	7-4-0	211	166
Auburn	2-4-0	.333	87	102	5-6-0	202	222
Kentucky	2-4-0	.333	70	117	3-8-0	186	244
Ole Miss	1-4-1	.250	101	185	4-6-1	169	272
LSU	1-4-1	.250	84	121	3-7-1	167	281
Vanderbilt	1-5-0	.167	108	188	4-7-0	134	284

Bowls: Cotton (Texas 14, Alabama 12); Peach (West Virginia 26, Florida 6); Sugar (Pittsburgh 24, Georgia 20); Hall of Fame (Mississippi State 10, Kansas 0); Garden State (Tennessee 28, Wisconsin 21)

* Alabama-Ole Miss game does not count in standings.

1982

School	W-L-T	Pct.	Pts.	Opp.	W-L-T	Pts.	Opp.
Georgia	6-0-0	1.000	179	73	11-0-0	315	133
LSU	4-1-1	.750	171	92	8-2-1	365	170
Auburn	4-2-0	.667	131	94	8-3-0	241	171
Vanderbilt	4-2-0	.667	135	121	8-3-0	265	206
Tennessee	3-2-1	.583	152	128	6-4-1	259	211
Florida	3-3-0	.500	127	146	8-3-0	272	200
Alabama	3-3-0	.500	146	125	7-4-0	317	201
Miss. State	2-4-0	.333	122	145	5-6-0	352	244
Ole Miss	0-6-0	.000	69	196	4-7-0	208	262
Kentucky	0-6-0	.000	57	169	0-10-1	96	287

Bowls: Liberty (Alabama 21, Illinois 15); Tangerine (Auburn 33, Boston College 26); Bluebonnet (Arkansas 28, Florida 24); Sugar (Penn State 27, Georgia 23); Orange (Nebraska 21, LSU 20); Peach (Iowa 28, Tennessee 22); Hall of Fame (Air Force 36, Vanderbilt 28)

1983

School	W-L-T	Pct.	Pts.	Opp.	W-L-T	Pts.	Opp.
Auburn	6-0-0	1.000	178	96	10-1-0	302	179
Georgia	5-1-0	.833	140	74	9-1-1	264	149
Florida	4-2-0	.667	149	84	8-2-1	290	150
Tennessee	4-2-0	.667	129	114	8-3-0	252	142
Alabama	4-2-0	.667	205	132	7-4-0	338	222
Ole Miss	4-2-0	.667	96	147	6-5-0	176	255
Kentucky	2-4-0	.333	87	151	6-4-1	212	217
Miss. State	1-5-0	.167	118	168	3-8-0	196	279
LSU	0-6-0	.000	112	176	4-7-0	251	253
Vanderbilt	0-6-0	.000	93	165	2-9-0	183	274

Bowls: Sun (Alabama 28, SMU 7); Sugar (Auburn 9, Michigan 7); Gator (Florida 14, Iowa 6); Cotton (Georgia 10, Texas 9); Hall of Fame (West Virginia 20, Kentucky 16); Independence (Air Force 9, Ole Miss 3); Florida Citrus (Tennessee 30, Maryland 23)

1984

School	W-L-T	Pct.	Pts.	Opp.	W-L-T	Pts.	Opp.
#Florida	5-0-1	.917	167	83	9-1-1	341	170
LSU	4-1-1	.750	153	117	8-2-1	305	198
Auburn	4-2-0	.667	109	97	8-4-0	339	239
Georgia	4-2-0	.667	153	116	7-4-0	246	213
Kentucky	3-3-0	.500	95	141	8-3-0	273	202
Tennessee	3-3-0	.500	150	146	7-3-1	300	248
Vanderbilt	2-4-0	.333	160	193	5-6-0	276	277
Alabama	2-4-0	.333	117	134	5-6-0	226	208
Ole Miss	1-5-0	.167	115	148	4-6-1	194	203
Miss. State	1-5-0	.167	85	130	4-7-0	198	230

Bowls: Liberty (Auburn 21, Arkansas 15); Florida Citrus (Georgia 17, Florida State 17); Hall of Fame (Kentucky 20, Wisconsin 19); Sugar (Nebraska 28, LSU 20); Sun (Maryland 28, Tennessee 27)

Championship vacated

1985

School	W-L-T	Pct.	Pts.	Opp.	W-L-T	Pts.	Opp.
Tennessee	5-1-0	.833	170	65	8-1-2	290	133
LSU	4-1-1	.750	104	56	9-1-1	220	113
Alabama	4-1-1	.750	157	117	8-2-1	294	178
Georgia	3-2-1	.583	138	87	7-3-1	284	158
Auburn	3-3-0	.500	139	96	8-3-0	328	172
Ole Miss	2-4-0	.333	115	172	4-6-1	210	276
Vanderbilt	1-4-1	.250	78	191	3-7-1	166	308
Kentucky	1-5-0	.167	76	143	5-6-0	194	211
Miss. State	0-6-0	.000	120	196	5-6-0	257	288
@Florida	5-1-0	.833	105	79	9-1-1	186	162

Bowls: Aloha (Alabama 24, Southern Cal 3); Cotton (Texas A&M 36, Auburn 16); Sun (Georgia 13, Arizona 13); Liberty (Baylor 21, LSU 7); Sugar (Tennessee 35, Miami-Fla. 7)

@Not eligible for championship

Through The Years

1986

School	Conference W-L-T	Pct.	Pts.	Opp.	Overall W-L-T	Pct.	Pts.	Opp.
LSU	5-1-0	.833	156	78	9-2-0	.818	291	155
Auburn	4-2-0	.667	154	72	9-2-0	.818	379	115
Alabama	4-2-0	.667	184	83	9-3-0	.750	323	157
Georgia	4-2-0	.667	136	105	8-3-0	.727	285	206
Ole Miss	4-2-0	.667	126	83	7-3-1	.683	220	150
Tennessee	3-3-0	.500	144	156	6-5-0	.556	272	235
Florida	2-4-0	.333	86	111	6-5-0	.556	223	175
Miss. State	2-4-0	.333	55	177	6-5-0	.556	195	275
Kentucky	2-4-0	.333	91	141	5-5-1	.500	228	207
Vanderbilt	0-6-0	.000	89	208	1-10-0	.091	193	337

Bowls: Sun (Alabama 28, Washington 6); Florida Citrus (Auburn 16, Southern Cal 7); Hall of Fame (Boston College 27, Georgia 23); Sugar (Nebraska 30, LSU 13); Independence (Ole Miss 20, Texas Tech 17); Liberty (Tennessee 21, Minnesota 14)

1987

School	Conference W-L-T	Pct.	Pts.	Opp.	Overall W-L-T	Pct.	Pts.	Opp.
Auburn	5-0-1	.917	172	59	9-1-1	.864	298	116
LSU	5-1-0	.833	159	91	9-1-1	.864	335	171
Tennessee	4-1-1	.750	197	142	9-2-1	.792	395	224
Georgia	4-2-0	.667	157	115	8-3-0	.727	291	187
Alabama	4-2-0	.667	128	106	7-4-0	.636	244	185
Florida	3-3-0	.500	114	96	6-5-0	.545	283	158
Kentucky	1-5-0	.167	123	146	5-6-0	.455	258	185
Vanderbilt	1-5-0	.167	150	239	4-7-0	.364	286	355
Miss. State	1-5-0	.167	82	189	4-7-0	.364	169	259
Ole Miss	1-5-0	.167	108	207	3-8-0	.273	223	309

Bowls: Hall of Fame (Michigan 28, Alabama 24); Sugar (Auburn 16, Syracuse 16); Aloha (UCLA 20, Florida 16); Liberty (Georgia 20, Arkansas 17); Gator (LSU 30, South Carolina 13); Peach (Tennessee 27, Indiana 22)

1988

School	Conference W-L-T	Pct.	Pts.	Opp.	Overall W-L-T	Pct.	Pts.	Opp.
Auburn	6-1-0	.858	148	43	10-1-0	.909	331	79
LSU	6-1-0	.857	132	87	8-3-0	.727	239	181
Georgia	5-2-0	.714	193	125	8-3-0	.727	324	185
Alabama	4-3-0	.571	196	147	8-3-0	.727	288	160
Florida	4-3-0	.571	99	106	6-5-0	.545	254	175
Ole Miss	3-4-0	.429	150	160	5-6-0	.455	221	223
Tennessee	3-4-0	.429	114	171	5-6-0	.455	212	286
Kentucky	2-5-0	.286	122	141	5-6-0	.455	217	208
Vanderbilt	2-5-0	.286	128	178	3-8-0	.273	202	277
Miss. State	0-7-0	.000	98	222	1-10-0	.090	172	332

Bowls: Sun (Alabama 29, Army 28); Sugar (Florida State 13, Auburn 7); All American (Florida 14, Illinois 10); Gator (Georgia 34, Michigan State 27); Hall of Fame (Syracuse 23, LSU 10)

1989

School	Conference W-L-T	Pct.	Pts.	Opp.	Overall W-L-T	Pct.	Pts.	Opp.
Alabama	6-1-0	.857	219	130	10-1-0	.909	332	184
Tennessee	6-1-0	.857	194	155	10-1-0	.909	315	190
Auburn	6-1-0	.857	122	69	9-2-0	.818	253	127
Florida	4-3-0	.571	145	103	7-4-0	.636	261	168
Ole Miss	4-3-0	.571	164	189	7-4-0	.636	267	285
Georgia	4-3-0	.571	139	109	6-5-0	.545	233	179
Kentucky	2-5-0	.286	118	174	6-5-0	.545	212	220
LSU	2-5-0	.286	174	180	4-7-0	.364	295	252
Miss. State	1-6-0	.143	89	153	5-6-0	.455	205	207
Vanderbilt	0-7-0	.000	85	187	1-10-0	.091	162	265

Bowls: Sugar (Miami-Fla. 33, Alabama 25); Hall of Fame (Auburn 31, Ohio State 14); Freedom (Washington 34, Florida 7); Peach (Syracuse 19, Georgia 18); Liberty (Ole Miss 42, Air Force 29); Cotton (Tennessee 31, Arkansas 27)

1990

School	Conference W-L-T	Pct.	Pts.	Opp.	Overall W-L-T	Pct.	Pts.	Opp.
Tennessee	5-1-1	.786	230	106	8-2-2	.750	442	198
Ole Miss	5-2-0	.714	140	119	9-2-0	.818	257	191
Alabama	5-2-0	.714	159	78	7-4-0	.636	253	127
Auburn	4-2-1	.643	170	132	7-3-1	.682	256	193
Kentucky	3-4-0	.429	163	214	4-7-0	.364	228	316
LSU	2-5-0	.286	112	168	5-6-0	.455	183	238
Georgia	2-5-0	.286	122	187	4-7-0	.364	185	293
Miss. State	1-6-0	.143	102	173	5-6-0	.455	207	236
Vanderbilt	1-6-0	.143	140	266	1-10-0	.091	227	457
#Florida	6-1-0	.857	221	116	9-2-0	.818	387	171

\# Not eligible for championship

Bowls: Fiesta (Louisville 34, Alabama 7); Peach (Auburn 27, Indiana 23); Gator (Michigan 35, Ole Miss 3); Sugar (Tennessee 23, Virginia 22)

1991

School	Conference W-L-T	Pct.	Pts.	Opp.	Overall W-L-T	Pct.	Pts.	Opp.
Florida	7-0	1.000	226	74	10-1	.909	361	152
Alabama	6-1	.857	128	101	10-1	.909	294	118
Tennessee	5-2	.714	190	136	9-2	.818	335	221
Georgia	4-3	.571	192	163	8-3	.727	312	204
Miss. State	4-3	.571	145	119	7-4	.636	276	156
LSU	3-4	.429	116	157	5-6	.455	248	263
Vanderbilt	3-4	.429	127	192	5-6	.455	205	267
Auburn	2-5	.286	128	170	5-6	.455	233	214
Ole Miss	1-6	.143	148	189	5-6	.455	242	223
Kentucky	0-7	.000	113	212	3-8	.273	190	268

Bowls: Blockbuster (Alabama 30, Colorado 25); Sugar (Notre Dame 39, Florida 28); Independence (Georgia 24, Arkansas 15); Liberty (Air Force 38, Mississippi State 15); Fiesta (Penn State 42, Tennessee 17)

1992

EASTERN DIVISION

School	Conference W-L-T	Pct.	Pts.	Opp.	Overall W-L-T	Pct.	Pts.	Opp.
Florida	6-2	.750	188	164	8-4	.667	288	267
Georgia	6-2	.750	231	117	9-2	.818	352	141
Tennessee	5-3	.625	205	149	8-3	.727	309	173
South Carolina	3-5	.375	104	194	5-6	.455	160	240
Kentucky	2-6	.250	136	224	4-7	.364	207	280
Vanderbilt	2-6	.250	149	193	4-7	.364	224	277

WESTERN DIVISION

School	Conference W-L-T	Pct.	Pts.	Opp.	Overall W-L-T	Pct.	Pts.	Opp.
Alabama	8-0	1.000	237	78	12-0	1.000	332	109
Ole Miss	5-3	.625	165	147	8-3	.727	230	174
Miss. State	4-4	.500	131	144	7-4	.636	235	176
Arkansas	3-4-1	.438	144	153	3-7-1	.318	172	209
Auburn	2-5-1	.313	132	173	5-5-1	.500	228	205
LSU	1-7	.125	115	201	2-9	.182	175	261

Bowls: Gator (Florida 27, N.C. State 10); Liberty (Ole Miss 13, Air Force 0); Hall of Fame (Tennessee 38, Boston College 23); Florida Citrus (Georgia 21, Ohio State 14); Sugar (Alabama 34, Miami-Fla. 13); Peach (North Carolina 21, Mississisppi State 17)

1993

EASTERN DIVISION

School	Conference W-L-T	Pct.	Pts.	Opp.	Overall W-L-T	Pct.	Pts.	Opp.
Florida	7-1	.875	318	171	11-2	.846	472	237
Tennessee	6-1-1	.813	324	115	9-2-1	.792	471	144
Kentucky	4-4	.500	158	168	6-6	.500	207	195
Georgia	2-6	.250	179	218	5-6	.455	328	289
South Carolina	2-6	.250	114	192	4-7	.364	188	214
Vanderbilt	1-7	.125	52	264	4-7	.364	137	290

WESTERN DIVISION

School	Conference W-L-T	Pct.	Pts.	Opp.	Overall W-L-T	Pct.	Pts.	Opp.
Alabama	5-2-1	.688	176	110	9-3-1	.731	316	158
Arkansas	3-4-1	.438	131	185	5-5-1	.500	165	208
LSU	3-5	.375	128	257	5-6	.455	190	308
Ole Miss	3-5	.375	155	116	5-6	.455	242	142
Miss. State	2-5-1	.313	155	175	3-6-2	.364	241	245
*Auburn	8-0	1.000	228	147	11-0	1.000	353	192

*Not eligible for title

Bowls: Peach (Clemson 14, Kentucky 13); Gator (Alabama 24, North Carolina 10); Citrus (Penn State 31, Tennessee 13); Sugar (Florida 41, West Virginia 7).

1994 SEC Football

National Statistical Champions

TEAM OFFENSE

SCORING
1946   Georgia (37.2 ppg)

TOTAL OFFENSE
1942   Georgia (429.5 yds per game)
1961   Ole Miss (418.7 yds per game)

PASSING OFFENSE
1970   Auburn (288.5 yds per game)

PUNT RETURNS
1991   Alabama (16.8 yds per return)

SCORING DEFENSE
1939   Tennessee (0.0 ppg)
1940   Tennessee (2.6 ppg)
1949   Kentucky (4.8 ppg)
1955   Ga. Tech (4.6 ppg)
1956   Ga. Tech (3.3 ppg)
1957   Aubrn (2.8 ppg)
1959   Ole Miss (2.1 ppg)
1960   LSU (5.0 ppg)
1961   Alabama (2.2 ppg)
1962   LSU (3.4 ppg)
1963   Ole Miss (3.7 ppg)
1966   Alabama (3.7 ppg)
1968   Georgia (9.8 ppg)
1975   Alabama (6.0 ppg)
1979   Alabama (5.3 ppg)
1988   Auburn (7.2 ppg)

RUSHING DEFENSE
1945   Alabama (33.9 ypg)
1957   Auburn (67.4 ypg)
1958   Auburn (79.6 ypg)
1963   Ole Miss (77.3 ypg)
1969   LSU (38.9 ypg)
1970   LSU (52.2 ypg)

TEAM DEFENSE

1988   Auburn (63.2 ypg)
1992   Alabama (55.0 ypg)

TOTAL DEFENSE
1938   Alabama (77.9 ypg)
1945   Alabama (109.9 ypg)
1948   Ga. Tech (151.3 ypg)
1949   Kentucky (153.8 ypg)
1952   Tennessee (166.7 ypg)
1954   Ole Miss (172.3 ypg)
1957   Auburn (133.0 ypg)
1958   Auburn (157.5 ypg)
1961   Alabama (132.6 ypg)
1962   Ole Miss (142.2 ypg)
1964   Auburn (164.7 ypg)
1988   Auburn (218.1 ypg)
1992   Alabama (194.2 ypg)
1993   Ole Miss (234.6 ypg)

PASSING DEFENSE
1950   Tennessee (67.5 ypg)
1953   Alabama (45.6 ypg)
1954   Florida (42.0 ypg)
1957   Ga. Tech (33.4 ypg)
1959   Alabama (45.7 ypg)
1972   Vanderbilt (80.3 ypg)
1990   Alabama (82.47 ypg)

INDIVIDUAL CHAMPIONS

TOTAL OFFENSE
Frank Sinkwich, Georgia, 1942 (2,187 yards)
Travis Tidwell, Auburn, 1946 (1,715 yards)
Pat Sullivan, Auburn, 1970 (285.6 ypg)

RUSHING
Frank Sinkwich, Georgia, 1941 (1,103 yards)
John Dottley, Ole Miss, 1949 (1,312 yards)

PASSING
Johnny Cook, Georgia, 1943 (73 of 157; 1,005 yards)
Travis Tidwell, Auburn, 1946 (79 of 158; 943 yards)
Charley Conerly, Ole Miss, 1947 (133 of 233; 1,367 yards)

PASSING EFFICIENCY
Charlie Connerly, Ole Miss, 1947 (125.8)
Babe Parilli, Kentucky, 1951 (130.8)
Steve Sloan, Alabama, 1965 (153.8)
Dewey Warren, Tennessee, 1966 (142.2)

RECEIVING
Ken Kavanaugh, LSU, 1939 (30 for 467)
Reid Moseley, Georgia, 1944 (32 for 506)
Reid Moseley, Georgia, 1945 (31 for 662)
Barney Poole, Ole Miss, 1947 (52 for 513)
John Carson, Georgia, 1953 (45 for 663)
Bob Goodridge, Vanderbilt, 1967 (79 for 1,114)
Keith Edwards, Vanderbilt, 1983 (97 for 909)

SCORING
Parker Hall, Ole Miss, 1938 (73 pts. on 11 TDs, 7 PATs)
Steve Van Buren, LSU, 1943 (98 pts. on 14 TDs, 14 PATs)
Jackie Parker, Miss. State, 1952 (120 pts. on 16 TDs, 24 PATs)
Garrison Hearst, Georgia, 1992 (126 pts. on 21 TDs)

INTERCEPTIONS
Bobby Wilson, Ole Miss, 1949 (10 for 70 yards)
Hootie Ingram, Alabama, 1952 (10 for 63 yards)
Jeff Hipp, Georgia 1980 (8 for 104)*
Terry Hoage, Georgia, 1982 (12 for 51)
Chris White, Tennessee, 1985 (9 for 168)*

PUNTING
Bobby Cifers, Tennessee, 1942 (42.9 average)
Zeke Bratowski, Georgia, 1953 (42.6 average)
Don Chandler, Florida, 1955 (44.3 average)
Bobby Walden, Georgia, 1958 (45.3 average)
Frank Lambert, Ole Miss, 1964 (44.1 average)

Ron Widby, Tennessee, 1967 (43.8 average)
Jim Miller, Ole Miss, 1977 (45.9 average)
Ricky Anderson, Vanderbilt, 1984 (48.2 average)

PUNT RETURNS
Junie Hovious, Ole Miss, 1940 (15.1 ypr)
Harry Gilmer, Alabama, 1946 (11.8 ypr)
Lee Nalley, Vanderbilt, 1948 (18.4 ypr)
Lee Nalley, Vanderbilt, 1949 (14.2 ypr)
Bill Stacy, Miss. State, 1956 (12.1 ypr)
Scott Woerner, Georgia, 1980 (15.7 ypr)
Glen Young, Miss. State, 1981 (16.2 ypr)
Lionel James, Auburn, 1982 (15.8 ypr)
Ricky Nattiel, Florida, 1984 (15.7 ypr)

KICKOFF RETURNS
Max McGee, Tulane, 1953 (21.8 ypr)
Dan Bland, Miss. State, 1964 (27.9 ypr)
Marcus Rhoden, Miss. State, 1966 (22.0 ypr)
Dale Carter, Tennessee, 1990 (29.8 ypr)

FIELD GOALS
Ed Dyas, Auburn, 1960 (13 of 18)
Al Woodall, Auburn, 1962 (8 of 20)*
Billy Lothridge, Ga. Tech, 1963 (12 of 16)
Doug Moreau, LSU, 1964 (13 of 20)
Kim Braswell, Georgia, 1970 (13 of 17)
Kevin Butler, Georgia, 1981 (19 of 26)*
Philip Doyle, Alabama, 1989 (22 of 25, 2.00 FGPG)*
Philip Doyle, Alabama, 1990 (24 of 29, 2.18 FGPG)
Michael Proctor, Alabama, (22 of 29, 1.8 FGPG)

SCORING (KICKERS)
Hugh Morrow, Alabama, 1945 (46 of 46 PATs)
George Jernigan, Georgia, 1946 (47 of 47 PATs)
Pepper Rodgers, Ga. Tech, 1952 (48 on 36 PATs, 4 FGs)
Paige Cothern, Ole Miss, 1955 (38 on 20 PATs, 6 FGs)
Bob Khayat, Ole Miss, 1958 (34 on 22 PATs, 4 FGs)
Bob Khayat, Ole Miss, 1959 (40 on 25 PATs, 5 FGs)
Ed Dyas, Auburn, 1960 (51 on 12 PATs, 13 FGs)
David Ray, Alabama 1964 (52 on 23 PATs, 12 FGs)

ALL-PURPOSE RUNNING
Parker Hall, Ole Miss, 1938 (129.1 ypg)
*—tied for National Championship

Annual Team Statistical Leaders

SCORING OFFENSE

Year	School	G	Pts	Avg
1933	LSU	10	176	17.6
	Tennessee	10	176	17.6
1934	Alabama	9	287	31.9
1935	Ole Miss	11	292	26.5
1936	LSU	10	281	28.1
1937	Alabama	9	225	25.0
1938	Tennessee	10	276	27.6
1939	Ole Miss	9	230	25.6
1940	Tennessee	10	319	31.9
1941	Georgia	10	279	27.9
1942	Georgia	11	367	33.4
1943	Ga. Tech	10	280	28.0
1944	Georgia	10	269	26.9
1945	Alabama	9	396	44.0
1946	Georgia	10	372	37.2
1947	Ole Miss	10	256	25.6
1948	Vanderbilt	11	328	29.8
1949	Kentucky	11	304	27.6
1950	Kentucky	11	380	34.5
1951	Tennessee	10	373	37.3
1952	Florida	10	290	29.0
1953	Auburn	10	257	25.7
1954	Ole Miss	10	283	28.3
1955	Ole Miss	10	251	25.1
1956	Tennessee	10	268	26.8
1957	Ole Miss	10	232	23.2
1958	LSU	10	275	27.5
1959	Ole Miss	10	329	32.9
1960	Ole Miss	10	266	26.6
1961	Ole Miss	10	326	32.6
1962	Alabama	10	272	27.2
1963	Ole Miss	9	207	23.0
1964	Alabama	10	233	23.3
1965	LSU	10	251	25.1
1966	Alabama	10	265	26.5
1967	Tennessee	10	259	25.9
1968	Georgia	10	282	28.2
1969	Auburn	10	363	36.3
1970	Auburn	10	355	35.5
1971	Alabama	11	362	32.9
1972	Alabama	11	393	35.7
1973	Alabama	11	454	41.3
1974	Alabama	11	318	28.9
1975	Alabama	11	361	32.8
1976	Georgia	11	324	29.5
1977	LSU	11	375	34.1
1978	Alabama	11	331	30.1
1979	Alabama	11	359	32.6
1980	Alabama	11	322	29.3
1981	Georgia	11	352	32.0
1982	LSU	11	365	33.2
1983	Alabama	11	338	30.7
1984	Florida	11	341	31.0
1985	Auburn	11	328	29.8
1986	Auburn	11	379	34.5
1987	Tennessee	12	395	32.9
1988	Auburn	11	331	30.1
1989	Alabama	11	332	30.2
1990	Tennessee	12	440	36.7
1991	Florida	11	361	32.8
1992	Georgia	11	352	32.0
1993	Tennessee	11	471	42.8

SCORING DEFENSE

Year	School	G	Pts	Avg
1933	Alabama	9	17	1.9
1934	Alabama	9	32	3.6
1935	LSU	10	38	3.8
1936	Miss. State	10	25	2.5
1937	Alabama	9	20	2.2
1938	Tennessee	10	16	1.6
1939	Tennessee	10	0	0.0
1940	Tennessee	10	26	2.6
1941	Miss. State	10	55	5.5
1942	Tennessee	10	54	5.4
1943	Ga. Tech	10	124	12.4
1944	Tennessee	9	48	5.3
1945	Alabama	9	66	7.3
1946	Vanderbilt	9	43	4.8
1947	Ga. Tech	10	35	3.5
1948	Tulane	10	60	6.0
1949	Kentucky	11	53	4.8
1950	Tennessee	11	57	5.2
1951	Ga. Tech	11	76	6.9
1952	Ga. Tech	11	52	4.7
1953	Ga. Tech	11	92	8.4
1954	Ole Miss	10	47	4.7
1955	Ole Miss	10	46	4.6
1956	Ga. Tech	10	33	3.3
1957	Auburn	10	28	2.8
1958	LSU	10	53	5.3
1959	Ole Miss	10	21	2.1
1960	LSU	10	50	5.0
1961	Alabama	10	22	2.2
1962	LSU	10	34	3.4
1963	Ole Miss	9	33	3.7
1964	Alabama	10	67	6.7
1965	Alabama	10	79	7.9
1966	Alabama	10	37	3.7
1967	Georgia	10	105	10.5
1968	Georgia	10	98	9.8
1969	LSU	10	91	9.1
1970	LSU	11	96	8.7
1971	Alabama	11	84	7.6
1972	Tennessee	11	83	7.5
1973	Alabama	11	89	8.1
1974	Alabama	11	83	7.5
1975	Alabama	11	66	6.0
1976	Georgia	11	118	10.7
1977	Kentucky	11	111	10.1
1978	Alabama	11	161	14.6
1979	Alabama	11	58	5.3
1980	Alabama	11	96	8.7
1981	Georgia	11	98	8.9
1982	Georgia	11	133	12.1
1983	Tennessee	11	142	12.9
1984	Florida	11	170	15.5
1985	LSU	11	113	10.3
1986	Auburn	11	115	10.5
1987	Auburn	11	116	10.6
1988	Auburn	11	79	7.2
1989	Auburn	11	117	10.6
1990	Alabama	11	127	11.6
1991	Alabama	11	118	10.7
1992	Alabama	12	109	9.1
1993	Ole Miss	11	142	12.9

RUSHING OFFENSE

Year	School	G	Atts	Yds	Game Avg
1948	Tulane	10		2393	239.3
1949	Ole Miss	10	531	2529	252.9
1950	Alabama	11	586	3007	273.4
1951	Tennessee	10	553	3068	306.8
1952	Alabama	11	608	2737	250.6
1953	Auburn	10	467	2255	225.5
1954	Auburn	10	507	2496	249.6
1955	Auburn	10	464	2413	241.3
1956	Auburn	10	515	2760	276.0
1957	Ole Miss	10	582	3063	306.3
1958	Ole Miss	10	503	2096	209.6
1959	Ole Miss	10	528	2394	239.4
1960	Ole Miss	10	475	2283	228.3
1961	Ole Miss	10	472	2362	236.2
1962	Ole Miss	9	467	2153	239.2
1963	LSU	10		2087	208.7
1964	Alabama	10	445	1799	179.9
1965	LSU	10	497	2077	207.7
1966	Georgia	10	515	1953	195.3
1967	LSU	10	554	2361	236.1
1968	Georgia	10	609	1988	198.8
1969	Auburn	10	471	2241	224.1
1970	Tennessee	11	563	2365	215.0
1971	Alabama	11	705	3565	324.1
1972	Alabama	11	704	3332	302.9
1973	Alabama	11	664	4027	366.1
1974	Alabama	11	686	3288	298.9
1975	Florida	11	657	3326	302.4
1976	Georgia	11	693	3075	279.5
1977	LSU	11	674	3352	304.7
1978	Alabama	11	638	3158	287.1
1979	Alabama	11	763	3792	344.7
1980	Alabama	11	632	3381	307.4
1981	Georgia	11	656	3102	282.0
1982	Georgia	11	647	3023	274.8
1983	Auburn	11	600	3231	293.7
1984	Auburn	12	673	3086	257.2
1985	Auburn	11	620	3438	312.5
1986	Alabama	12	585	3167	263.9
1987	Georgia	11	596	3016	274.2
1988	Georgia	11	547	2778	252.5
1989	Tennessee	11	582	2701	245.6
1990	Vanderbilt	11	538	2498	227.1
1991	Alabama	11	557	2772	252.0
1992	Georgia	11	458	2584	234.9
1993	Tennessee	11	442	2621	238.3

PASSING OFFENSE

Year	School	G	Att	Cmp	Yds	Game Avg
1948	Ga. Tech	10	206	112	1746	174.6
1949	Ole Miss	10	149	67	1335	133.5
1950	Kentucky	11	230	125	1714	155.8
1951	Georgia	10	265	121	1618	161.8
1952	Georgia	11	266	134	1878	170.7
1953	Georgia	11	247	118	1575	143.2
1954	Ole Miss	10	175	81	1554	155.4
1955	Georgia	10	145	66	1156	115.6
1956	Ole Miss	10	173	79	1215	121.5
1957	Vanderbilt	10	134	58	776	77.6
1958	Auburn	10	179	86	1211	121.1
1959	Ole Miss	10	170	81	1295	129.5
1960	Kentucky	10			1633	163.3
1961	Ole Miss	10	202	109	1827	182.7
1962	Auburn	10	258	122	1512	151.2
1963	Ole Miss	9	191	103	1506	167.3
1964	Kentucky	10	230	114	1609	160.9
1965	Florida	10	309	158	2033	203.3
1966	Florida	10	328	199	2242	224.2
1967	Florida	10	284	149	1954	195.4
1968	Miss. State	10	342	186	2047	204.7
1969	Florida	10	413	233	3016	301.6
1970	Auburn	10	311	181	2885	288.5
1971	Auburn	10	316	180	2277	227.7
1972	LSU	11	247	125	1701	154.6
1973	Miss. State	11	238	119	1630	148.2
1974	Vanderbilt	11	212	119	1676	152.4
1975	Tennessee	12	211	102	1686	140.5
1976	Florida	11	191	106	1783	162.1
1977	Vanderbilt	11	283	137	1683	153.0
1978	Miss. State	11	311	177	2637	239.7
1979	LSU	11	295	137	2061	187.4
1980	Ole Miss	11	295	164	2045	185.9
1981	Vanderbilt	11	476	269	3036	276.0
1982	Vanderbilt	11	454	252	2837	257.9
1983	Vanderbilt	11	519	296	3299	293.7
1984	Vanderbilt	11	437	246	2920	265.5
1985	Florida	11	304	189	2924	265.8
1986	LSU	11	335	207	2623	235.8
1987	LSU	11	311	187	2554	232.2
1988	Vanderbilt	11	370	202	2652	241.1
1989	LSU	11	327	188	2839	258.1
1990	Florida	11	415	246	3197	290.6
1991	Florida	11	390	235	3393	308.5
1992	Florida	12	503	290	3440	286.7
1993	Florida	12	488	284	4072	339.3

1994 SEC Football 193

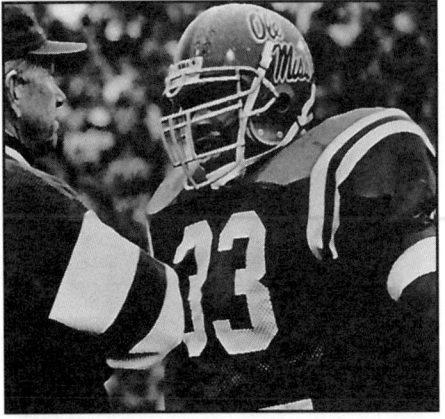

Annual Team Statistical Leaders

TOTAL OFFENSE

Year	School	G	Atts	Yds	Game Avg
1948	Ga. Tech	10	658	3549	354.9
1949	Ole Miss	10	680	3864	386.4
1950	Alabama	11	773	4578	416.2
1951	Ole Miss	10	701	3726	372.6
1952	Ole Miss	10	748	3883	388.3
1953	Auburn	10	607	3398	339.8
1954	Ole Miss	10	664	3875	387.5
1955	Ole Miss	10	609	3396	339.6
1956	Auburn	10	670	3749	374.9
1957	Ole Miss	10	666	3562	356.2
1958	Auburn	10	649	3194	319.4
1959	Ole Miss	10	698	3690	369.0
1960	Ole Miss	10	646	3626	362.6
1961	Ole Miss	10	674	4186	418.6
1962	Ole Miss	9	628	3281	364.5
1963	Ole Miss	9		2944	327.1
1964	Alabama	10	620	3129	312.9
1965	Florida	10	719	3376	337.6
1966	Florida	10	714	3611	361.1
1967	Florida	10	799	3673	367.3
1968	Georgia	10	859	3917	391.7
1969	Florida	10	826	4348	434.8
1970	Auburn	10	684	4850	485.0
1971	LSU	11	832	4263	387.5
1972	Alabama	11	832	4501	409.2
1973	Alabama	11	758	5288	480.7
1974	Vanderbilt	11	825	4570	415.5
1975	Florida	11	796	4460	405.5
1976	Florida	11	737	4400	400.0
1977	Alabama	11	821	4584	416.7
1978	Alabama	11	796	4433	403.0
1979	Alabama	11	875	4715	428.6
1980	Ole Miss	11	829	4286	389.6
1981	Georgia	11	865	4912	446.5
1982	Miss. State	11	771	4642	422.0
1983	Alabama	11	823	4665	424.1
1984	Auburn	12	911	4923	410.2
1985	Auburn	11	808	4594	417.6
1986	Auburn	11	766	4590	417.3
1987	LSU	11	747	4845	440.5
1988	Auburn	11	804	4774	434.0
1989	Alabama	11	888	4778	434.4
1990	Florida	11	855	4978	452.6
1991	Tennessee	11	878	5145	467.7
1992	Georgia	11	732	4954	450.4
1993	Tennessee	11	762	5286	480.6

Ole Miss Linebacker Dewayne Dotson led a Rebel defense that allowed opponents only 234.6 total yards per game in 1993.

RUSHING DEFENSE

Year	School	G	Atts	Yds	Game Avg
1948	Ga. Tech	10		749	74.9
1949	Kentucky	11	455	788	71.6
1950	Tulane	9	373	824	91.5
1951	Ga. Tech	11	477	1164	105.8
1952	Ga. Tech	11	473	1175	106.8
1953	LSU	11	481	1567	142.4
1954	Ole Miss	10	374	901	90.1
1955	Auburn	10	405	1078	107.8
1956	Ga. Tech	10	405	1284	128.4
1957	Auburn	10	390	674	67.4
1958	Auburn	10	370	796	79.6
1959	LSU	10		908	90.8
1960	Ole Miss	10	386	881	88.1
1961	Alabama	10		550	55.0
1962	Alabama	10		588	58.8
1963	Ole Miss	9	316	699	77.7
1964	Auburn	10	354	819	81.9
1965	Florida	10	408	884	88.4
1966	Ole Miss	10	408	741	74.1
1967	Alabama	10	411	940	94.0
1968	Alabama	10	401	849	84.9
1969	LSU	10	353	384	38.4
1970	LSU	11	356	574	52.2
1971	Georgia	11	424	1076	97.8
1972	Alabama	11	459	1263	114.8
1973	Alabama	11	487	1536	139.6
1974	Alabama	11	478	1599	145.4
1975	Alabama	11	460	1037	94.3
1976	LSU	11	504	1568	142.5
1977	Kentucky	11	493	1322	120.2
1978	Alabama	11	485	1540	140.0
1979	Alabama	11	393	1121	101.9
1980	Alabama	11	520	1394	126.7
1981	Georgia	11	391	797	72.5
1982	LSU	11	406	1004	91.3
1983	Tennessee	11	433	1231	111.9
1984	Florida	11	406	1336	121.5
1985	Georgia	11	440	1095	99.5
1986	Auburn	11	409	1325	120.5
1987	Auburn	11	437	1380	125.5
1988	Auburn	11	334	695	63.2
1989	Florida	11	397	975	88.6
1990	Florida	11	386	941	85.6
1991	Florida	11	398	1103	100.3
1992	Alabama	12	395	660	55.0
1993	Ole Miss	11	463	1127	102.5

PASSING DEFENSE

Year	School	G	Att	Cmp	Yds	Game Avg
1948	Tennessee	10	193	77	748	74.8
1949	Tennessee	10	161	64	752	75.2
1950	Tennessee	11	154	65	652	59.2
1951	Vanderbilt	11	125	53	861	78.2
1952	Tennessee	10	116	44	531	53.1
1953	Tennessee	11	148	59	594	54.0
1954	Alabama	11	122	43	504	45.8
1955	Florida	10	92	37	420	42.0
1956	Ole Miss	10	118	48	506	50.6
1957	Ga. Tech	10	73	31	334	33.4
1958	Alabama	10			600	60.0
1959	Alabama	10			636	63.6
1960	Tennessee	10			538	53.8
1961	Ole Miss	10	149	58	649	64.9
1962	Ole Miss	9	146	60	670	74.4
1963	Ole Miss	9	123	47	522	58.0
1964	Florida	10	150	57	640	64.0
1965	Vanderbilt	10	152	78	849	84.9
1966	Alabama	10	208	86	944	94.4
1967	Georgia	10	214	77	947	94.7
1968	Vanderbilt	10	259	117	1293	129.3
1969	Georgia	10	298	117	1357	135.7
1970	Vanderbilt	11	207	108	1376	125.1
1971	Vanderbilt	11	196	89	1035	94.1
1972	Vanderbilt	11	164	61	883	80.3
1973	Florida	11	165	72	938	85.3
1974	Alabama	11	201	82	822	74.7
1975	Auburn	11	150	73	980	89.1
1976	Vanderbilt	11	155	72	892	81.1
1977	Tennessee	11	179	78	1067	97.0
1978	Vanderbilt	11	177	84	1284	116.7
1979	Alabama	11	218	78	860	78.2
1980	Alabama	11	210	93	1093	99.4
1981	Kentucky	11	236	123	1405	127.7
1982	Miss. State	11	236	132	1578	143.5
1983	Florida	11	296	156	1663	151.2
1984	Alabama	11	273	138	1573	143.0
1985	Tennessee	11	299	156	1650	150.0
1986	Tennessee	11	203	99	1248	113.5
1987	Florida	11	269	128	1512	137.5
1988	Florida	11	254	121	1360	123.6
1989	Miss. State	11	288	148	1599	145.4
1990	LSU	11	244	122	1395	126.8
1991	Tennessee	11	244	119	1627	147.9
1992	Alabama	12	330	164	1670	139.2
1993	Alabama	12	310	144	1539	128.3

TOTAL DEFENSE

Year	School	G	Atts	Yds	Game Avg
1948	Ga. Tech	10		1513	151.3
1949	Kentucky	11		1692	153.8
1951	Ga. Tech	11	708	2190	199.0
1950	Kentucky	11	674	1895	172.2
1952	Tennessee	10	578	1667	167.7
1953	Ga. Tech	11	655	2384	216.7
1954	Ole Miss	10	536	1723	172.3
1955	Auburn	10	531	1832	183.2
1956	Ole Miss	10	572	1955	195.5
1957	Auburn	10	529	1330	133.0
1958	Auburn	10	521	1575	157.5
1959	LSU	10	559	1432	143.2
1960	Alabama	10	535	1576	157.6
1961	Alabama	10		1321	132.1
1962	Ole Miss	9	446	1280	142.2
1963	Ole Miss	9	439	1221	135.7
1964	Auburn	10	495	1647	164.7
1965	Florida	10	617	2017	201.7
1966	Alabama	10	544	1741	174.1
1967	Georgia	10	647	2126	212.6
1968	Georgia	10	650	2351	235.1
1969	LSU	10	714	2280	228.0
1970	LSU	11	746	2689	244.5
1971	Alabama	11	663	2417	219.7
1972	Alabama	11	674	2334	212.2
1973	Florida	11	743	2656	241.5
1974	Alabama	11	679	2421	202.1
1975	Alabama	11	677	2046	186.0
1976	LSU	11	702	2564	233.1
1977	Kentucky	11	728	2590	235.5
1978	LSU	11	749	3122	283.8
1979	Alabama	11	611	1981	180.1
1980	Alabama	11	730	2487	226.1
1981	Florida	11	784	2826	256.9
1982	LSU	11	704	2707	246.1
1983	Tennessee	11	756	3069	279.0
1984	Florida	11	738	3325	302.3
1985	Florida	11	726	3111	282.8
1986	Ole Miss	11	777	3145	285.9
1987	Florida	11	744	2956	268.7
1988	Auburn	11	667	2399	218.1
1989	Florida	11	698	2661	241.9
1990	Alabama	11	711	2523	229.4
1991	Tennessee	11	676	3154	286.7
1992	Alabama	12	725	2330	194.7
1993	Ole Miss	11	724	2580	234.6

Through The Years

Annual Individual Statistical Leaders

RUSHING (Ranked on Total Yards)

Year	Player (School)	Atts	Net Yds
1948	Eddie Price, Tulane	188	1178
1949	John Dottley, Ole Miss	208	1312
1950	John Dottley, Ole Miss	191	1007
1951	Hank Lauricella, Tennessee	111	881
1952	Bobby Marlow, Alabama	176	950
1953	Jerry Marchand, LSU	137	696
1954	Joe Childress, Auburn	148	836
1955	Fob James, Auburn	123	879
1956	Tommy Lorino, Auburn	82	692
1957	Jimmy Taylor, LSU	162	762
1958	Billy Cannon, LSU	115	686
1959	Charley Flowers, Ole Miss	141	733
1960	Tom Mason, Tulane	120	663
1961	Mike Fracchia, Alabama	130	652
1962	Larry Dupree, Florida	113	604
1963	Jimmy Sidle, Auburn	185	1006
1964	Don Schwab, LSU	160	683
1965	Steve Bowman, Alabama	153	770
1966	Larry Smith, Florida	162	742
1967	Steve Hindman, Ole Miss	215	829
1968	Rich Pickens, Tennessee	133	736
1969	Doug Mathews, Vanderbilt	167	849

Beginning in 1970, ranked on yards per game

Year	Player (School)	G	Att	Yds	Game Avg
1970	Johnny Musso, Alabama	11	226	1137	103.4
1971	Johnny Musso, Alabama	10	191	1088	108.8
1972	Terry Henley, Auburn	9	216	843	93.7
1973	Sonny Collins, Kentucky	11	224	1213	110.3
1974	Sonny Collins, Kentucky	9	177	970	107.8
1975	Jimmy DuBose, Florida	11	191	1307	118.8
1976	Terry Robiskie, LSU	11	224	1117	101.5
1977	Charles Alexander, LSU	11	311	1686	153.3
1978	Joe Cribbs, Auburn	10	253	1205	120.5
1979	James Brooks, Auburn	11	163	1208	109.8
1980	Herschel Walker, Georgia	11	274	1616	146.9
1981	Herschel Walker, Georgia	11	385	1891	171.9
1982	Herschel Walker, Georgia	11	335	1752	159.3
1983	Johnnie Jones, Tennessee	10	191	1116	111.6
1984	Johnnie Jones, Tennessee	11	229	1290	117.3
1985	Bo Jackson, Auburn	11	278	1786	162.4
1986	Brent Fullwood, Auburn	11	167	1391	126.5
1987	Emmitt Smith, Florida	11	229	1341	121.9
1988	Tim Worley, Georgia	11	191	1216	110.5
1989	Emmitt Smith, Florida	11	284	1599	145.4
1990	Tony Thompson, Tennessee	11	219	1261	105.1
1991	Errict Rhett, Florida	11	224	1109	100.8
1992	Garrison Hearst, Georgia	11	228	1547	140.6
1993	James Bostic, Auburn	11	199	1205	109.6

Tennessee's Johnnie Jones captured the SEC rushing title in 1983 and 1984.

In 1962 Joe Namath of Alabama won the conference passing crown with 1,192 yards.

PASSING (Ranked on Total Yards)

Year	Player (School)	Att.-Comp.-Int	Yards	TDs	Pct.
1948	John Rauch, Georgia	141-71-13	1307	5	50.4
1949	Babe Parilli, Kentucky	150-81-13	1081	8	54.0
1950	Babe Parilli, Kentucky	203-114-12	1627	23	56.1
1951	Babe Parilli, Kentucky	239-136-12	1643	19	56.9
1952	Zeke Bratkowski, Georgia	262-131-16	1824	12	50.0
1953	Zeke Bratkowski, Georgia	224-113-23	1461	6	50.4
1954	Bob Hardy, Kentucky	108-57-11	887	5	52.8
1955	Dick Young, Georgia	97-48-8	875	8	49.5
1956	Raymond Brown, Ole Miss	84-40-8	653	8	47.6
1957	Boyce Smith, Vanderbilt	98-49-10	664	8	50.0
1958	Richie Pettibon, Tulane	125-66-10	728	3	52.8
1959	Jake Gibbs, Ole Miss	94-46-2	755	6	48.9
1960	Fran Tarkenton, Georgia	185-108-12	1189	7	58.4
1961	Pat Trammell, Alabama	133-75-2	1035	8	56.4
1962	Joe Namath, Alabama	146-76-8	1192	13	52.0
1963	Larry Rakestraw, Georgia	209-103-14	1297	7	49.3
1964	Rick Norton, Kentucky	202-106-10	1514	9	52.5
1965	Steve Spurrier, Florida	287-148-13	1893	14	51.6
1966	Steve Spurrier, Florida	291-179-8	2012	16	61.5

*Beginning in 1967, ranked on efficiency rating
(Based on an average of 10 attempts per game)*

Year	Player & School	Att.-Comp.-Int.-Yards	TDs	Pct.	Rating
1967	Ken Stabler, Alabama	178-103-13-1214	9	57.9	116.94
1968	Bubba Wyche, Tennessee	237-134- 7-1539	14	56.5	124.63
1969	Archie Manning, Ole Miss	265-154- 9-1752	14	58.2	135.15
1970	Pat Sullivan, Auburn	281-167-12-2586	17	59.4	148.09
1971	Bert Jones, LSU	119- 66- 4-945	9	55.5	141.43
1972	Bert Jones, LSU	199-103- 7-1446	14	51.8	129.00
1973	Condredge Holloway, Tenn.	154- 89- 4-1450	10	57.8	136.75
1974	Matt Robinson, Georgia	121- 60-10-1317	8	49.6	150.07
1975	Randy Wallace, Tennessee	145- 72-11-1318	8	49.7	133.21
1976	Jimmy Fisher, Florida	146- 83- 8-1511	10	56.8	155.36
1977	Jeff Rutledge, Alabama	107- 64- 5-1207	8	59.8	169.88
1978	Jeff Rutledge, Alabama	140- 73-10-1078	13	52.1	133.05
1979	John Fourcade, Ole Miss	196-115- 9-1521	7	58.7	126.50
1980	Buck Belue, Georgia	156- 77- 5-1314	11	49.3	131.80
1981	Buck Belue, Georgia	188-114- 9-1603	12	60.6	143.70
1982	Alan Risher, LSU	234-149- 8-1834	17	63.7	146.00
1983	Wayne Peace, Florida	292-186-10-2079	10	63.7	128.00
1984	Kerwin Bell, Florida	184- 98- 7-1614	16	53.3	148.00
1985	Daryl Dickey, Tennessee	131- 85- 1-1161	10	64.9	163.10
1986	Tom Hodson, LSU	288-175- 8-2261	19	60.8	142.90
1987	Eric Jones, Vanderbilt	229-139-11-1954	16	60.7	145.80
1988	Reggie Slack, Auburn	279-168-11-2230	9	60.2	130.11
1989	Tom Hodson, LSU	317-183-12-2655	22	57.7	143.41
1990	Mike Healey, Vanderbilt	130- 75- 1-1041	10	57.7	148.80
1991	Shane Matthews, Florida	361-218- 18-3130	28	60.4	148.84
1992	Eric Zeier, Georgia	258-151-12-2248	12	58.5	137.80
1993	Heath Shuler, Tenn.	285-184-8-2354	25	64.6	157.3

1994 SEC Football 195

Annual Individual Statistical Leaders

RECEIVING (Ranked on Total Yards)

Year	Player & School	Rec.	Yds
1948	Bob Walston, Georgia	25	525
1949	Jack Stribling, Ole Miss	22	598
1950	Bucky Curtis, Vanderbilt	27	791
1951	Harry Babcock, Georgia	41	666

Beginning in 1952, ranked on total receptions

Year	Player & School	Rec.	Yds
1952	John Carson, Georgia	32	467
1953	John Carson, Georgia	45	663
1954	Jim Pyburn, Auburn	28	460
1955	Jimmy Orr, Georgia	24	443
1956	Jimmy Phillips, Auburn	23	383
1957	Jimmy Orr, Georgia	16	237
1958	Calvin Bird, Kentucky	21	373
	Pete Abanie, Tulane	21	266
1959	Bobby Towns, Georgia	18	263
1960	Fred Brown, Georgia	31	275
1961	Tom Hutchinson, Kentucky	32	543
1962	Clem Dellenger, Tulane	39	375
1963	Pat Hodgson, Georgia	24	375
1964	Charley Casey, Florida	47	673
1965	Charley Casey, Florida	58	809
1966	Richard Trapp, Florida	63	872
1967	Bob Goodridge, Vanderbilt	79	1114
1968	Sammy Miller, Miss. State	64	909
1969	Carlos Alvarez, Florida	88	1329

Beginning in 1970, ranked on receptions per game

Year	Player & School	G	Rec.	Yds	RPG
1970	David Smith, Miss. State	11	74	987	6.7
1971	Terry Beasley, Auburn	10	55	846	5.5
1972	Bill Buckley, Miss. State	11	47	776	4.3
1973	Bill Buckley, Miss. State	11	41	661	3.7
1974	Lee McGriff, Florida	11	36	698	3.3
1975	Larry Seivers, Tennessee	11	41	840	3.7
1976	Larry Seivers, Tennessee	11	51	737	4.6
1977	Martin Cox, Vanderbilt	11	48	783	4.4
1978	Mardye McDole, Miss. State	11	48	1035	4.4
1979	Preston Brown, Vanderbilt	11	52	786	4.7
1980	Cris Collinsworth, Florida	11	40	599	3.6

RECEIVING (Cont.)

Year	Player & School	G	Rec.	Yds	RPG
1981	Norman Jordan, Vanderbilt	9	49	454	5.4
1982	Allama Matthews, Vanderbilt	11	61	797	5.5
1983	Keith Edwards, Vanderbilt	11	97	909	8.8
1984	Keith Edwards, Vanderbilt	11	60	576	5.5
1985	Everett Crawford, Vanderbilt	10	50	533	5.2
1986	Wendell Davis, LSU	11	80	1244	7.3
1987	Wendell Davis, LSU	11	72	993	6.6
1988	Boo Mitchell, Vanderbilt	11	78	1213	7.1
1989	Brad Gaines, Vanderbilt	11	67	634	6.1
1990	Kirk Kirkpatrick, Florida	11	55	770	5.0
1991	Todd Kinchen, LSU	11	53	855	4.8
1992	Willie Jackson, Florida	12	62	722	5.2
1993	Brice Hunter, Georgia	11	76	970	6.9

TOTAL OFFENSE (Ranked on Total Yards)

Year	Player & School	Rush Yds	Pass Yds	Total
1948	John Rauch, Georgia	-117	1307	1190
1949	John Dottley, Ole Miss	1312	0	1312
1950	Babe Parilli, Kentucky	54	1627	1681
1951	Bill Wade, Vanderbilt	37	1609	1646
1952	Zeke Bratkowski, Georgia	-50	1824	1774
1953	Zeke Bratkowski, Georgia	-45	1461	1416
1954	Bobby Freeman, Auburn	267	865	1132
1955	John Majors, Tennessee	657	476	1133
1956	John Majors, Tennessee	549	552	1101
1957	Ray Brown, Ole Miss	530	308	838
1958	Lloyd Nix, Auburn	283	682	965
1958	Jake Gibbs, Ole Miss	228	755	933
1960	Fran Tarkenton, Georgia	85	1189	1274
1961	Pat Trammell, Alabama	279	1035	1314
1962	Billy Lothridge, Ga. Tech	478	1006	1484
1963	Jimmy Sidle, Auburn	1006	706	1712
1964	Rick Norton, Kentucky	-195	1514	1319
1965	Steve Spurrier, Florida	230	1893	2123
1966	Steve Spurrier, Florida	66	2012	2095
1967	Loran Carter, Auburn	65	1307	1372
1968	Tommy Pharr, Miss. State	239	1838	2085
1969	John Reaves, Florida	-44	2896	2852

Beginning in 1970, ranked on average yards-per-game

Year	Player & School	G	Rush Yds	Pass Yds	Total	Avg
1970	Pat Sullivan, Auburn	10	270	2586	2856	285.6
1971	Pat Sullivan, Auburn	10	84	2012	2096	209.6
1972	Norris Weese, Ole Miss	10	542	917	1459	145.9
1973	Fred Fisher, Vanderbilt	11	373	1450	1823	165.7
1974	Rockey Felker, Miss. State	11	446	1147	1593	144.8
1975	Randy Wallace, Tennessee	12	211	1318	1529	127.4
1976	Jimmy Fisher, Florida	11	288	1511	1799	163.5
1977	Charles Alexander, LSU	11	1686	17	1783	162.1
1978	Dave Marler, Miss. State	11	-31	2422	2391	217.4
1979	John Fourcade, Ole Miss	11	493	1521	2014	183.1
1980	John Fourcade, Ole Miss	11	402	1897	2299	209.0
1981	Whit Taylor, Vanderbilt	9	-65	2318	2253	250.3
1982	Whit Taylor, Vanderbilt	11	198	2481	2679	243.5
1983	Kurt Page, Vanderbilt	11	-144	3178	3034	275.8
1984	Kurt Page, Vanderbilt	11	-64	2405	2341	212.8
1985	Don Smith, Miss. State	11	554	2332	2886	262.4
1986	Don Smith, Miss. State	11	403	2349	2752	213.9
1987	Eric Jones, Vanderbilt	11	665	1954	2619	238.1
1988	Eric Jones, Vanderbilt	11	305	2548	2853	259.4
1989	Tom Hodson, LSU	11	-51	2655	2604	236.7
1990	Shane Matthews, Florida	11	-27	2952	2925	265.9
1991	Shane Matthews, Florida	11	10	3130	3140	285.5
1992	Shane Matthews, Florida	12	-29	3205	3176	264.7
1993	Eric Zeier, Georgia	11	-43	3525	3482	316.6

Vanderbilt quarterback Eric Jones twice led the SEC in total offense (1987 and 1988).

Through The Years

Annual Individual Statistical Leaders

SCORING (Ranked on Total Points)

Year	Player & School	TDs	PATs	FGs	Pts
1933	Beattie Feathers, Tennessee	13	0	0	78
1934	Claude Simons, Tulane	10	9	0	69
1935	Ray Hapes, Ole Miss	12	2	0	74
1936	Bob Davis, Kentucky	11	0	0	66
1937	Pinky Rohm, LSU	9	0	0	54
	Bob Davis, Kentucky	9	0	0	54
1938	Parker Hall, Ole Miss	11	6	0	72
1939	Harvey Johnson, MSU	10	2	0	62
1940	Merle Hapes, Miss. State	12	0	0	72
1941	Jack Jenkins, Vanderbilt	12	15	1	90
1942	Frank Sinkwich, Georgia	16	0	0	96
1943	Steve Van Buren, LSU	14	14	0	98
1944	Tom McWilliams, Miss. State	14	0	0	84
1945	Fred Grant, Alabama	11	0	0	66
1946	Charlie Trippi, Georgia	14	0	0	84
1947	Charlie Conerly, Ole Miss	9	0	0	54
	Bobby Forbes, Florida	9	0	0	54
1948	Joe Geri, Georgia	9	36	0	90
1949	John Dottley, Ole Miss	14	0	0	84
1950	Al Bruno, Kentucky	10	0	0	60
	Wilbur Jamerson, Kentucky	10	0	0	60
	Al Lary, Alabama	10	0	0	60
1951	Hal Payne, Tennessee	14	0	0	84
1952	Jackie Parker, Miss. State	16	24	0	120
1953	Jimmy Wade, Tennessee	12	0	0	72
1954	Joe Childress, Auburn	7	20	1	65
1955	Paige Cothren, Ole Miss	6	20	6	74
1956	Jim Taylor, LSU	8	8	1	59
1957	Jim Taylor, LSU	12	14	0	86
1958	Billy Cannon, LSU	11	8	0	74
1959	Charley Flowers, Ole Miss	11	0	0	66
1960	Tom Mason, Tulane	13	0	0	78
1961	Wendell Harris, LSU	8	28	6	94
1962	Cotton Clark, Alabama	15	2	0	92
1963	Billy Lothridge, Ga. Tech	3	15	12	69
1964	Doug Moreau, LSU	4	10	13	73
1965	Rodger Bird, Kentucky	13	0	0	78
1966	Bobby Etter, Georgia	0	21	12	57
1967	Dicky Lyons, Kentucky	11	4	1	73
1968	Dicky Lyons, Kentucky	11	0	0	66
1969	Tommy Durrance, Florida	18	2	0	110

Beginning in 1970, ranked on points per game

Year	Player & School	G	TDs	PATs	FGs	Pts	Avg
1970	Terry Beasley, Auburn	10	12	0	0	72	7.2
1971	Johnny Musso, Alabama	10	16	0	0	100	10.0
1972	Haskel Stanback, Tennessee	10	13	0	0	78	7.8
1973	Sonny Collins, Kentucky	11	13	1-2pt.	0	80	7.3
1974	Stanley Morgan, Tennessee	11	14	0	0	84	7.6
1975	Kevin McLee, Georgia	10	10	0	0	60	6.0
	Stanley Morgan, Tennessee	10	10	0	0	60	6.0
1976	Terry Robiskie, LSU	11	12	0	0	72	6.5
1977	Charles Alexander, LSU	11	17	2	0	104	9.5
1978	Joe Cribbs, Auburn	10	16	2	0	98	9.8
1979	Joe Cribbs, Auburn	11	15	4	0	94	8.5
1980	Herschel Walker, Georgia	11	15	0	0	90	8.2
1981	Herschel Walker, Georgia	11	20	0	0	120	10.9
1982	Herschel Walker, Georgia	11	17	1-2pt.	0	104	9.5
1983	Bobby Raymond, Florida	11	0	29	20	89	8.1
1984	Bobby Raymond, Florida	11	0	34	23	103	9.4
1985	Bo Jackson, Auburn	11	17	0	0	102	9.3
	Carlos Reveiz, Tennessee	11	0	30	24	102	9.3
1986	William Howard, Tennessee	8	14	1-2pt.	0	86	10.8
1987	Reggie Cobb, Tennessee	12	20	0	0	120	10.0
1988	Tim Worley, Georgia	11	18	0	0	108	9.8
1989	Siran Stacy, Alabama	11	18	0	0	108	9.8
1990	Greg Burke, Tennessee	12	0	50	19	107	8.9
1991	Arden Czyzewski, Florida	11	0	44	11	77	7.0
1992	Garrison Hearst, Georgia	11	21	0	0	126	11.5
1993	John Becksvoort, Tennessee	11	0	59	12	95	8.6

PUNTING (Ranked on Average)

Year	Player & School	Kicks	Yards	Avg
1948	Rip Collins, LSU	66		41.3
1949	Fred Montsdeoca, Florida	62		41.6
1951	Bobby Wilson, Alabama	33		41.9
1952	Rick Casares, Florida	23		41.4
1953	Zeke Bratkowski, Georgia	50		42.6
1954	Don Chandler, Florida	21		42.9
1955	Don Chandler, Florida	22		44.3
1956	Bob Gordon, Tennessee	14		47.1
1957	Bob Gordon, Tennessee	40		42.7
1958	Bobby Walden, Georgia	44		45.3
1959	Bobby Joe Green, Florida	54		44.9
1960	Bobby Walden, Georgia	38	1657	43.6
1961	Hank Lesesne, Vanderbilt	41	1703	41.5
1962	George Canale, Tennessee	53	2218	41.8
1963	Joe Kilgore, Auburn	51	2106	41.3
1964	Frank Lambert, Ole Miss	50	2205	44.1
1965	Richard McGraw, Miss. State	48	2014	42.0
1966	Ron Widby, Tennessee	48	2104	43.8
1967	Eddie Ray, LSU	52	2228	42.8
1968	Julian Fagan, Ole Miss	75	3120	41.6
1969	Spike Jones, Georgia	71	3092	43.5
1970	Frank Mann, Alabama	46	1880	40.9
1971	Greg Gantt, Alabama	47	1967	41.9
1972	Greg Gantt, Alabama	44	1875	42.6
1973	Greg Gantt, Alabama	25	1217	48.7
1974	Neil Clabo, Tennessee	64	2757	43.1
1975	Clyde Baumgarner, Auburn	49	2004	40.9
1976	Craig Colquitt, Tennessee	59	2510	42.5
1977	Jim Miller, Ole Miss	66	3029	45.9
1978	Jim Miller, Ole Miss	76	3283	43.2
1979	Jim Miller, Ole Miss	53	2362	44.6
1980	Jim Arnold, Vanderbilt	72	3180	44.2
1981	Malcolm Simmons, Alabama	60	2637	43.9
1982	Jimmy Colquitt, Tennessee	46	2156	46.9
1983	Paul Calhoun, Kentucky	69	2981	43.2
1984	Ricky Anderson, Vanderbilt	58	2793	48.2
1985	Lewis Colbert, Auburn	57	2610	45.8
1986	Bill Smith, Ole Miss	57	2522	44.3
1987	Matt DeFrank, LSU	33	1373	41.6
1988	Kent Elmore, Tennessee	41	1818	44.3
1989	Rene Bourgeois, LSU	39	1715	44.0
1990	Joey Chapman, Tennessee	45	1885	41.9
1991	Shayne Edge, Florida	46	1991	43.3
1992	Todd Jordan, Miss. State	52	2267	43.6
1993	Terry Daniel, Auburn	51	2393	46.9

Auburn running back Joe Cribbs was the SEC's leading scorer in both 1978 and 1979.

1994 SEC Football

All-Time Television Appearances of SEC Schools

ALABAMA (98-51-5)

Year—Score, Audience (Bowl)
1951— Alabama 13, Tennessee 27
1952— Alabama 3, Georgia Tech 7, National
　　Alabama 61, Syracuse 6, National (Orange)
1953— Alabama 0, Tennessee 0, CBS
　　Alabama 6, Rice 28, National (Cotton)
1954— Alabama 0, Georgia Tech 20, National
1959— Alabama 0, Penn State 7 (Liberty)
1960— Alabama 21, Georgia 6, ABC
　　Alabama 3, Texas 3, National (Bluebonnet)
1961— Alabama 34, Tennessee 3, ABC
　　Alabama 10, Arkansas 3, NBC (Sugar)
1962— Alabama 27, Tennessee 7
　　Alabama 17, Oklahoma 0, NBC (Orange)
1963— Alabama 17, Miami 12, CBS
　　Alabama 12, Ole Miss 7, NBC (Sugar)
1964— Alabama 21, Auburn 14, NBC
　　Alabama 17, Texas 21, NBC (Orange)
1965— Alabama 17, Georgia 18, NBC
　　Alabama 31, LSU 7, NBC
　　Alabama 39, Nebraska 28, NBC (Orange)
1966— Alabama 21, LSU 0, ABC
　　Alabama 31, Auburn 0, ABC
　　Alabama 34, Nebraska 7, ABC (Sugar)
1967— Alabama 21, Ole Miss 7, ABC
　　Alabama 16, Texas A&M 20, CBS (Cotton)
1968— Alabama 9, Tennessee 10, ABC
　　Alabama 14, Miami 6, ABC
　　Alabama 10, Missouri 35, National (Gator)
1969— Alabama 33, Ole Miss 32, ABC
　　Alabama 33, Colorado 47, National (Liberty)
1970— Alabama 23, Ole Miss 48, ABC
　　Alabama 9, LSU 14, ABC
　　Alabama 24, Oklahoma 24, National (Bluebonnet)
1971— Alabama 14, LSU 7, ABC
　　Alabama 31, Auburn 7, ABC
　　Alabama 6, Nebraska 38, NBC (Orange)
1972— Alabama 35, LSU 21, ABC
　　Alabama 13, Texas 17, CBS (Cotton)
1973— Alabama 42, Tennessee 21, ABC

Year—Score, Audience (Bowl)
　　Alabama 21, LSU 7, ABC
　　Alabama 35, Auburn 0, ABC
　　Alabama 23, Notre Dame 24, ABC (Sugar)
1974— Alabama 35, Ole Miss 21, ABC
　　Alabama 30, LSU 0, ABC
　　Alabama 17, Auburn 13, ABC
　　Alabama 11, Notre Dame 13, NBC (Orange)
1975— Alabama 7, Missouri 20, ABC
　　Alabama 28, Auburn 0, ABC
　　Alabama 13, Penn State 6, ABC (Sugar)
1976— Alabama 20, Tennessee 13, ABC
　　Alabama 18, Notre Dame 21, ABC
　　Alabama 36, UCLA 6, National (Liberty)
1977— Alabama 24, Nebraska 31, ABC
　　Alabama 21, Southern Cal 20, ABC
　　Alabama 24, LSU 3, ABC
　　Alabama 35, Ohio State 6, ABC (Sugar)
1978— Alabama 20, Nebraska 3, ABC
　　Alabama 14, Southern Cal 24, ABC
　　Alabama 31, LSU 10, ABC
　　Alabama 14, Penn State 7, ABC (Sugar)
1979— Alabama 30, Georgia Tech 6, ABC
　　Alabama 30, Miami 0, ABC
　　Alabama 24, Arkansas 9, ABC (Sugar)
1980— Alabama 27, Tennessee 0, ABC
　　Alabama 0, Notre Dame 7, ABC
　　Alabama 30, Baylor 2, CBS (Cotton)
1981— Alabama 24, LSU 7, ABC
　　Alabama 31, Penn State 16, ABC
　　Alabama 28, Auburn 17, ABC
　　Alabama 12, Texas 14, CBS (Cotton)
1982— Alabama 42, Penn State 21, ABC
　　Alabama 22, Auburn 23, ABC
　　Alabama 21, Illinois 15, National (Liberty)
1983— Alabama 28, Penn State 34, CBS
　　Alabama 32, LSU 26, ABC
　　Alabama 13, Boston College 20, CBS
　　Alabama 20, Auburn 23, ABC
　　Alabama 28, SMU 7, CBS (Sun)
1984— Alabama 31, Boston College 38, ABC
　　Alabama 6, Georgia Tech 16, WTBS
　　Alabama 14, Georgia 24, ABC
　　Alabama 17, Auburn 15, ABC

Year—Score, Audience (Bowl)
1985— Alabama 20, Georgia 16, ABC
　　Alabama 23, Texas A&M 10, ESPN
　　Alabama 40, Vanderbilt 20, WTBS
　　Alabama 17, Penn State 19, ABC
　　Alabama 14, Tennessee 16, WTBS
　　Alabama 14, LSU 14, ABC
　　Alabama 25, Auburn 23, ABC
　　Alabama 24, Southern Cal 3, NBC (Aloha)
1986— Alabama 16, Ohio State 10, Raycom (Kickoff Classic)
　　Alabama 42, Vanderbilt 10, WTBS
　　Alabama 28, Notre Dame 10, ABC
　　Alabama 56, Tennessee 28, ABC
　　Alabama 3, Penn State 23, ABC
　　Alabama 38, Miss. State 3, WTBS
　　Alabama 10, LSU 14, ESPN
　　Alabama 17, Auburn 21, ABC
　　Alabama 28, Washington 6, CBS (Sun)
1987— Alabama 24, Penn State 13, CBS
　　Alabama 14, Florida 23, WTBS
　　Alabama 41, Tennessee 22, ESPN
　　Alabama 22, LSU 10, ESPN
　　Alabama 0, Auburn 10, CBS
　　Alabama 6, Notre Dame 37, CBS
　　Alabama 24, Michigan 28, NBC (Hall of Fame)
1988— Alabama 31, Kentucky 27, WTBS
　　Alabama 12, Ole Miss 22, WTBS
　　Alabama 8, Penn State 3, CBS
　　Alabama 18, LSU 19, CBS
　　Alabama 10, Auburn 15, CBS
　　Alabama 30, Texas A&M 10, ESPN
　　Alabama 29, Army 28, CBS (Sun)
1989— Alabama 15, Kentucky 3, TBS
　　Alabama 20, Vanderbilt 14, TBS
　　Alabama 47, Tennessee 30, CBS
　　Alabama 17, Penn State 16, CBS
　　Alabama 23, Miss. State 10, TBS
　　Alabama 32, LSU 16, ESPN
　　Alabama 20, Auburn 30, CBS
　　Alabama 25, Miami 33, ABC (Sugar)
1990— Alabama 13, Florida 17, TBS
　　Alabama 16, Georgia 17, ABC
　　Alabama 9, Tennessee 6, ESPN
　　Alabama 0, Penn State 9, ESPN
　　Alabama 22, Miss. State 0, TBS
　　Alabama 16, Auburn 7, CBS
　　Alabama 7, Louisville 34, NBC (Fiesta)
1991— Alabama 0, Florida 35, ESPN
　　Alabama 10, Georgia 0, ABC
　　Alabama 24, Tennessee 19, ABC
　　Alabama 13, Miss. State 7, TBS
　　Alabama 20, LSU 17, ABC
　　Alabama 13, Auburn 6, ESPN
　　Alabama 30, Colorado 25, CBS (Blockbuster)
1992— Alabama 25, Vanderbilt 8, JP Sports
　　Alabama 17, Tennessee 10, ABC
　　Alabama 31, Ole Miss 10, JP Sports
　　Alabama 31, LSU 11, ABC
　　Alabama 30, Miss. State 21, ESPN
　　Alabama 17, Auburn 0, ABC
　　Alabama 28, Florida 21 ABC
　　Alabama 34, Miami 13, ABC (Sugar)
1993— Alabama 17, Vanderbilt 6, JP Sports
　　Alabama 43, Arkansas 3, JP Sports
　　Alabama 17, S. Carolina 6, ESPN
　　Alabama 17, Tennessee 17, ABC
　　Alabama 19, Ole Miss 17, ABC
　　LSU 17, Alabama 13, JP Sports
　　Alabama 36, Miss. State 25, ABC
　　Florida 28, Alabama 13, ABC
　　Alabama 24, N. Carolina 10, TBS (Gator)

The Alabama-Tennessee game on October 20, 1951, was the first televised event in SEC history. The Volunteers posted a 27-13 victory at Birmingham's Legion Field en route to winning the SEC's first national championship with a 10-0 regular-season mark.

198　Through The Years

ARKANSAS (52-59-2)

Year—Score, Audience (Bowl)
1953—Arkansas 0, Ole Miss 28, CBS
    Arkansas 6, Georgia Tech 14, National
1955—Arkansas 10, Rice 0, Regional
    Arkansas 6, SMU 0, Regional
1956—Arkansas 6, TCU 41, National
    Arkansas 0, Texas A&M 27, Regional
1957—Arkansas 7, Rice 13, Regional
1959—Arkansas 12, Texas A&M 7, Regional
    Arkansas 17, SMU 14, Regional
    Arkansas 14, Georgia Tech 7, National (Gator)
1960—Arkansas 24, Texas 23, Regional
    Arkansas 6, Duke 7, National (Cotton)
1961—Arkansas 0, Ole Miss 16, National
    Arkansas 3, Alabama 10, National (Sugar)
1962—Arkansas 13, Ole Miss 17, National (Sugar)
1963—Arkansas 0, Rice 7, Regional
1964—Arkansas 29, TCU 6, Regional
    Arkansas 10, Nebraska 7, CBS (Cotton)
1965—Arkansas 27, Texas 24, NBC
    Arkansas 42, Texas Tech 24, NBC
    Arkansas 7, LSU 14, CBS (Cotton)
1966—Arkansas 12, Texas 7, NBC
1967—Arkansas 12, Texas 21, ABC
    Arkansas 27, Texas Tech 31, ABC
1968—Arkansas 35, SMU 29, ABC
    Arkansas 16, Georgia 2, ABC (Sugar)
1969—Arkansas 35, Texas A&M 13, ABC
    Arkansas 33, Texas Tech 0, ABC
    Arkansas 14, Texas 15, ABC
    Arkansas 22, Ole Miss 27, ABC (Sugar)
1970—Arkansas 28, Stanford 34, ABC
    Arkansas 7, Texas 42, ABC
1971—Arkansas 31, Texas 7, ABC
    Arkansas 18, SMU 13, ABC
    Arkansas 13, Tennessee 14, ABC (Liberty)
1972—Arkansas 15, Texas 35, ABC
1973—Arkansas 6, Oklahoma State 38, ABC
1974—Arkansas 7, Texas 38, ABC
1975—Arkansas 18, Texas 24, ABC
    Arkansas 31, Texas A&M 6, ABC
    Arkansas 31, Georgia 10, CBS (Cotton)
1976—Arkansas 10, Texas A&M 31, ABC
    Arkansas 12, Texas 29, ABC
1977—Arkansas 9, Texas 13, ABC
    Arkansas 17, Texas Tech 14, ABC
    Arkansas 31, Oklahoma 6, NBC (Orange)
1978—Arkansas 21, Texas 28, ABC
    Arkansas 26, Texas A&M 7, ABC
    Arkansas 10, UCLA 10, NBC (Fiesta)
1979—Arkansas 17, Texas 14, ABC
    Arkansas 10, Houston 13, ABC
    Arkansas 9, Alabama 24, ABC (Sugar)
1980—Arkansas 17, Texas 23, ABC
    Arkansas 15, Baylor 42, ABC
    Arkansas 34, Tulane 15, Mizlou (Hall of Fame)
1981—Arkansas 42, Texas 11, ABC
    Arkansas 41, Baylor 39, ESPN
    Arkansas 10, Texas A&M 7, ABC
    Arkansas 27, North Carolina 31, ABC (Gator)
1982—Arkansas 35, TCU 0, ESPN
    Arkansas 38, Houston 3, CBS
    Arkansas 17, SMU 17, ABC
    Arkansas 7, Texas 33, ABC
    Arkansas 28, Florida 24, Mizlou (Bluebonnett)
1983—Arkansas 38, TCU 21, Raycom
    Arkansas 3, Texas 31, ABC
    Arkansas 0, SMU 17, ABC
1984—Arkansas 33, Navy 10, ESPN
    Arkansas 28, Texas A&M 0, Raycom
    Arkansas 28, SMU 31, ESPN
    Arkansas 15, Auburn 21, Raycom (Liberty)
1985—Arkansas 41, TCU 0, Raycom
    Arkansas 57, Houston 27, USA
    Arkansas 20, Baylor 14, Baylor

Year—Score, Audience (Bowl)
    Arkansas 6, Texas A&M 10, ESPN
    Arkansas 18, Arizona State 17, Mizlou (Holiday)
1986—Arkansas 34, TCU 17, Raycom
    Arkansas 21, Texas 14, ESPN
    Arkansas 14, Texas A&M 10, ABC
    Arkansas 8, Oklahoma 42, NBC (Orange)
1987—Arkansas 30, Tulsa 15, Raycom
    Arkansas 7, Miami (Fla.) 51, ESPN
    Arkansas 14, Texas 16, ESPN
    Arkansas 38, Rice 14, Raycom
    Arkansas 38, Hawaii 20, ESPN
    Arkansas 17, Georgia 20, Raycom (Liberty)
1988—Arkansas 31, Texas Tech 10, Raycom
    Arkansas 26, Houston 21, Raycom
    Arkansas 16, Miami (Fla.) 18, CBS
    Arkansas 3, UCLA 17, CBS (Cotton)
1989—Arkansas 20, Texas 24, ABC
    Arkansas 38, Rice 17, Raycom
    Arkansas 19, Baylor 10, ESPN
    Arkansas 23, Texas A&M 22, CBS
    Arkansas 27, Tennessee 31, CBS (Cotton)
1990—Arkansas 17, Ole Miss 21, Raycom
    Arkansas 17, Texas 49, Raycom
    Arkansas 3, Baylor 34, Raycom
1991—Arkansas 3, Miami (Fla.) 31, ABC
    Arkansas 14, Texas 13, Raycom
    Arkansas 5, Baylor 9, ABC
    Arkansas 21, Texas Tech 38, Raycom
    Arkansas 15, Texas A&M 13, ESPN
    Arkansas 15, Georgia 24, ABC (Independence)
1992—Arkansas 3, Georgia 27, JP Sports
    Arkansas 25, Tennessee 24, JP Sports
    Arkansas 3, Miss. State 10, JP Sports
    Arkansas 30, LSU 6 ESPN
1993—Alabama 43, Arkansas 3, JP Sports
    Tennessee 28, Arkansas 14, JP Sports
    Ole Miss 19, Arkansas 0, JP Sports
    Arkansas 42, LSU 24, ESPN

AUBURN (54-45-3)

Year—Score, Audience (Bowl)
1953—Auburn 13, Texas Tech 35, National (Gator)
1954—Auburn 33, Baylor 13, National (Gator)
1955—Auburn 13, Vanderbilt 25, National (Gator)
1958—Auburn 13, Tennessee 0, National
1963—Auburn 7, Nebraska 13, NBC (Orange)
1964—Auburn 14, Alabama 21, NBC
1965—Auburn 28, Florida 17, NBC
    Auburn 7, Ole Miss 13, ABC (Liberty)
1966—Auburn 0, Alabama 31, ABC
1968—Auburn 34, Arizona 10, National (Sun)
1969—Auburn 19, Tennessee 45, ABC
    Auburn 20, LSU 21, ABC
    Auburn 7, Houston 36, National (Bluebonnet)
1970—Auburn 17, Georgia 31, ABC
    Auburn 35, Ole Miss 28, NBC (Gator)
1971—Auburn 10, Tennessee 9, ABC
    Auburn 7, Alabama 31, ABC
    Auburn 22, Oklahoma 40, ABC (Sugar)
1972—Auburn 27, Florida State 14, ABC
    Auburn 27, Georgia 10, ABC
    Auburn 24, Colorado 3, National (Gator)
1973—Auburn 0, Alabama 35, ABC
    Auburn 17, Missouri 34, CBS (Sun)
1974—Auburn 14, Florida 25, ABC
    Auburn 13, Alabama 17, ABC
    Auburn 27, Texas 3, National (Gator)
1975—Auburn 13, Georgia 28, ABC
    Auburn 0, Alabama 28, ABC
1976—Auburn 38, Tennessee 28, ABC
1977—Auburn 21, Ole Miss 15, ABC

Year—Score, Audience (Bowl)
1978—Auburn 29, Tennessee 10, ABC
    Auburn 10, Georgia Tech 24, ABC
1981—Auburn 17, Alabama 28, ABC
1982—Auburn 23, Alabama 22, ABC
    Auburn 33, Boston College 26, National (Tangerine)
1983—Auburn 7, Texas 20, CBS
    Auburn 13, Georgia 7, ABC
    Auburn 23, Alabama 20, ABC
    Auburn 9, Michigan 7, ABC (Sugar)
1984—Auburn 18, Miami 20, KATZ (Kickoff Classic)
    Auburn 27, Texas 35, ESPN
    Auburn 29, Tennessee 10, WTBS
    Auburn 17, Ole Miss 13, WTBS
    Auburn 3, Florida 24, ABC
    Auburn 21, Georgia 12, ESPN
    Auburn 15, Alabama 17, ABC
    Auburn 21, Arkansas 15, National (Liberty)
1985—Auburn 49, Southwestern La. 7, WTBS
    Auburn 20, Tennessee 38, ABC
    Auburn 41, Ole Miss 0, WTBS
    Auburn 59, Florida State 27, WTBS
    Auburn 17, Georgia Tech 14, CBS
    Auburn 24, Georgia 10, ABC
    Auburn 23, Alabama 25, ABC
    Auburn 16, Texas A&M 36, CBS (Cotton)
1986—Auburn 34, Tennessee 8, ABC
    Auburn 31, Vanderbilt 9, WTBS
    Auburn 35, Miss. State 6, ESPN
    Auburn 52, Cincinnati 7, ABC
    Auburn 16, Georgia 20, ESPN
    Auburn 21, Alabama 17, ABC
    Auburn 16, Southern Cal 7, ABC (Citrus)
    Auburn 31, Texas 3, ESPN
1987—Auburn 20, Tennessee 20, WTBS
    Auburn 48, Vanderbilt 15, WTBS
    Auburn 29, Florida 6, ESPN
    Auburn 6, Florida State 34, CBS
    Auburn 27, Georgia 11, ESPN
    Auburn 10, Alabama 0, CBS
    Auburn 16, Syracuse 16, ABC (Sugar)
1988—Auburn 20, Kentucky 10, WTBS
    Auburn 6, LSU 7, ESPN
    Auburn 16, Florida 0, ESPN
    Auburn 38, Tennessee 6, CBS
    Auburn 20, Georgia 10, CBS
    Auburn 15, Alabama 10, CBS
    Auburn 7, Florida State 13, ABC (Sugar)
1989—Auburn 14, Tennessee 21, CBS
    Auburn 24, Kentucky 12, TBS
    Auburn 10, LSU 6, CBS
    Auburn 14, Florida State 22, ESPN
    Auburn 10, Florida 7, ESPN
    Auburn 20, Georgia 3, TBS
    Auburn 30, Alabama 20, CBS
    Auburn 31, Ohio State 14, NBC (Hall of Fame)
1990—Auburn 26, Tennessee 26, ESPN
    Auburn 20, Florida State 17, ESPN
    Auburn 7, Florida 48, ESPN
    Auburn 33, Georgia 10, ESPN
    Auburn 7, Alabama 16, CBS
    Auburn 27, Indiana 23, ABC (Peach)
1991—Auburn 14, Texas 10, ESPN
    Auburn 21, Tennessee 30, ESPN
    Auburn 9, Southern Miss 10, TBS
    Auburn 17, Miss. State 24, ABC
    Auburn 10, Florida 31, ABC
    Auburn 27, Georgia 37, ESPN
    Auburn 6, Alabama 13, ESPN
1992—Auburn 30, LSU 28, JP Sports
    Auburn 9, Florida 24, ABC
    Auburn 10, Georgia 14, ABC
    Auburn 0, Alabama 17, ABC

1994 SEC Football

All-Time Television Appearances of SEC Schools

FLORIDA (48-53-2)

Year—Score, Audience (Bowl)
1958—Florida 3, Ole Miss 7, National (Gator)
1960—Florida 13, Baylor 12, National (Gator)
1962—Florida 17, Penn State 7, National (Gator)
1963—Florida 0, Georgia Tech 9, ABC
1964—Florida 24, SMU 8, ABC
1965—Florida 17, Auburn 28, ABC
Florida 18, Missouri 20, National (Sugar)
1966—Florida 27, Georgia Tech 12, NBC (Orange)
1967—Florida 17, Georgia 16, ABC
Florida 13, Miami (Fla.) 20, ABC
1968—Florida 9, Florida State 3, ABC
1969—Florida 13, Georgia 13, ABC
Florida 14, Tennessee 13, National (Gator)
1970—Florida 7, Tennessee 38, ABC
Florida 24, Georgia 17, ABC
1972—Florida 7, Georgia 10, ABC
1973—Florida 11, Georgia 10, ABC
Florida 7, Miami (Ohio) 16, National (Tangerine)
1974—Florida 25, Auburn 14, ABC
Florida 24, Kentucky 41, ABC
Florida 10, Nebraska 13, ABC (Sugar)
1975—Florida 7, Georgia 10, ABC
Florida 0, Maryland 13, National (Gator)
1976—Florida 27, Georgia 41, ABC
Florida 14, Texas A&M 37, National (Sun)
1977—Florida 24, Miss. State 22, ABC
Florida 22, Georgia 17, ABC
Florida 9, Florida State 37, ABC
1978—Florida 13, Georgia Tech 17, ABC
1979—Florida 10, Georgia 33, ABC
Florida 16, Florida State 27, ABC
1980—Florida 21, Georgia 26, ABC
Florida 7, Miami (Fla.) 31, ABC
Florida 13, Florida State 17, ABC
Florida 35, Maryland 20, National (Tangerine)
1981—Florida 7, Miss. State 28—ABC
Florida 21, Georgia 26, ABC
Florida 6, West Virginia 26, National (Peach)
1982—Florida 17, Southern Cal 9, ABC
Florida 0, Georgia 44, CBS

Year—Score, Audience (Bowl)
Florida 24, Arkansas 28, National (Bluebonnet)
1983—Florida 9, Georgia 10, CBS
Florida 53, Florida State 14, CBS
Florida 14, Iowa 6, National (Gator)
1984—Florida 20, Miami 32, ESPN
Florida 21, LSU 21, WTBS
Florida 24, Auburn 3, ABC
Florida 27, Georgia 0, WTBS
Florida 27, Florida State 17, ABC
1987—Florida 4, Miami 31, WTBS
Florida 24, Alabama 14, WTBS
Florida 10, LSU 13, ESPN
Florida 6, Auburn 29, ESPN
Florida 10, Georgia 23, WTBS
Florida 27, Kentucky 14, WTBS
Florida 14, Florida State 28, CBS
Florida 16, UCLA 20, ABC (Aloha)
1988—Florida 6, LSU 19, CBS
Florida 9, Vanderbilt 24, WTBS
Florida 0, Auburn 16, ESPN
Florida 3, Georgia 26, WTBS
Florida 17, Florida State 52
Florida 14, Illinois 10, ESPN (All-American)
1989—Florida 19, Ole Miss 24, TBS
Florida 7, Auburn 10, ESPN
Florida 10, Georgia 17, TBS
Florida 17, Florida State 24, ESPN
Florida 7, Washington 34, NBC (Freedom)
1990—Florida 17, Alabama 13, TBS
Florida 34, Miss. State 21, TBS
Florida 34, LSU 8, ESPN
Florida 3, Tennessee 45, ESPN
Florida 48, Auburn 7, ESPN
Florida 38, Georgia 7, TBS
Florida 47, Kentucky 15, TBS
Florida 30, Florida State 45, ESPN
1991—Florida 35, Alabama 0, ESPN
Florida 21, Syracuse 38, ABC
Florida 29, Miss. State 7, TBS
Florida 35, Tennessee 18, ESPN
Florida 31, Auburn 10, ABC
Florida 45, Georgia 13, ESPN
Florida 14, Florida State 9, ABC
Florida 28, Notre Dame 39, ABC (Sugar)

Year—Score, Audience (Bowl)
1992—Florida 35, Kentucky 19, JP Sports
Florida 14, Tennessee 31, ABC
Florida 6, Miss. State 30, ESPN
Florida 24, Auburn 9, ABC
Florida 26, Georgia 24, ABC
Florida 14, S. Carolina 9, JP Sports
Florida 41, Vanderbilt 21, JP Sports
Florida 2, Florida State 45, ABC
Florida 21, Alabama 28, ABC
Florida 27, N.C. State 10, TBS (Gator)
1993—Florida 41, Tennessee 34, ABC
Florida 38, Miss. State 24, JP Sports
Florida 58, LSU 3, ESPN
Florida 33, Georgia 26, ABC
Florida 37, S. Carolina 26, JP Sports
Florida 52, Vanderbilt 0, JP Sports
Florida State 33, Florida 21, ABC
Florida 28, Alabama 13, ABC
Florida 41, West Virginia 7, ABC (Sugar)

GEORGIA (72-45-4)

Year—Score, Audience (Bowl)
1959—Georgia 14, Missouri 0, National (Orange)
1960—Georgia 6, Alabama 21, National
1964—Georgia 7, Texas Tech 0, National (Sun)
1965—Georgia 18, Alabama 17, ABC
1966—Georgia 24, SMU 9, CBS (Cotton)
1967—Georgia 16, Florida 17, ABC
Georgia 21, Georgia Tech 14, ABC
Georgia 7, North Carolina St. 14, National (Liberty)
1968—Georgia 17, Tennessee 17, ABC
Georgia 21, Ole Miss 7, ABC
Georgia 2, Arkansas 16, ABC (Sugar)
1969—Georgia 13, Florida 13, ABC
Georgia 6, Nebraska 45, National (Sun)
1970—Georgia 52, South Carolina 34, ABC
Georgia 17, Florida 24, ABC
Georgia 31, Auburn 17, ABC
1971—Georgia 49, Florida 7, ABC
Georgia 28, Georgia Tech 24, ABC
Georgia 7, North Carolina 3, National (Gator)
1972—Georgia 13, Tulane 24, ABC
Georgia 10, Auburn 27, ABC
Georgia 10, Florida 7, ABC
1973—Georgia 10, Florida 11, ABC
Georgia 17, Maryland 16, National (Peach)
1974—Georgia 10, Miami (Ohio) 21, National (Tangerine)
1975—Georgia 10, Florida 7, ABC
Georgia 28, Auburn 13, ABC
Georgia 42, Georgia Tech 26, ABC
Georgia 10, Arkansas 31, CBS (Cotton)
1976—Georgia 41, Clemson 0, ABC
Georgia 41, Florida 27, ABC
Georgia 3, Pittsburgh 27, ABC (Sugar)
1977—Georgia 17, Florida 22, ABC
1978—Georgia 16, Baylor 14, ABC
Georgia 29, Georgia Tech 28, ABC
Georgia 22, Stanford 25, National (Bluebonnet)
1979—Georgia 33, Florida 10, ABC
Georgia 16, Georgia Tech 3, ABC
1980—Georgia 13, South Carolina 10, ABC
Georgia 26, Florida 21, ABC
Georgia 17, Notre Dame 10, ABC (Sugar)
1981—Georgia 53, Vanderbilt 21, ABC
Georgia 26, Florida 21, ABC

On December 5, 1992, Alabama defeated Florida 28-21 in the inaugural SEC Football Championship Game. The contest, which was televised nationally by ABC Sports, drew a 9.8 rating. ABC games during the 1992 season earned a 6.4 national average.

Through The Years

Georgia (continued)
Georgia 44, Georgia Tech 7, ABC
Georgia 20, Pittsburgh 24, ABC (Sugar)
1982—Georgia 13, Clemson 7, ABC
Georgia 29, Miss. State 22, CBS
Georgia 44, Florida 0, CBS
Georgia 23, Penn State 27, ABC (Sugar)
1983—Georgia 19, UCLA 8, ABC
Georgia 10, Florida 9, CBS
Georgia 7, Auburn 13, ABC
Georgia 10, Texas 9, CBS (Cotton)
1984—Georgia 24, Alabama 14, ABC
Georgia 18, Ole Miss 12, WTBS
Georgia 62, Vanderbilt 35, WTBS
Georgia 37, Kentucky 7, WTBS
Georgia 0, Florida 27, WTBS
Georgia 12, Auburn 21, ESPN
Georgia 17, Florida State 17, NBC
(Citrus)
1985—Georgia 16, Alabama 20, ABC
Georgia 17, Baylor 14, WTBS
Georgia 20, Clemson 13, CBS (Sun)
Georgia 26, Kentucky 6, WTBS
Georgia 10, Auburn 24, ABC
Georgia 16, Georgia Tech 20, WTBS0
Georgia 13, Arizona 13, CBS (Sun)
1986—Georgia 28, Clemson 31, ABC
Georgia 31, South Carolina 26, ESPN
Georgia 14, Ole Miss 10, WTBS
Georgia 38, Vanderbilt 16, WTBS
Georgia 20, Auburn 16, ESPN
Georgia 31, Georgia Tech 24, WTBS
Georgia 24, Boston College 27, Mizlou
(Hall of Fame)
1987—Georgia 20, Clemson 21, CBS
Georgia 23, LSU 26, ESPN
Georgia 17, Kentucky 14, WTBS
Georgia 23, Florida 10, WTBS
Georgia 11, Auburn 27, ESPN
Georgia 30, Georgia Tech 16, ESPN
Georgia 20, Arkansas 17, Raycom
(Liberty)
1988—Georgia 28, Tennessee 17, ESPN
Georgia 10, South Carolina 23, WTBS
Georgia 10, Kentucky 16, WTBS
Georgia 26, Florida 3, WTBS
Georgia 10, Auburn 20, CBS
Georgia 24, Georgia Tech 3, WTBS
Georgia 34, Michigan State 27, ESPN
(Gator)
1989—Georgia 15, Baylor 3, TBS
Georgia 14, Tennessee 17, ESPN
Georgia 13, Ole Miss 17, TBS
Georgia 17, Florida 10, TBS
Georgia 3, Auburn 20, TBS
Georgia 18, Syracuse 19, ABC (Peach)
1990—Georgia 17, Alabama 16, CBS
Georgia 12, Ole Miss 28, TBS
Georgia 7, Florida 38, TBS
Georgia 10, Auburn 33, ESPN
Georgia 23, Georgia Tech 40, TBS
1991—Georgia 31, LSU 10, ABC
Georgia 0, Alabama 10, ABC
Georgia 27, Clemson 12, ESPN
Georgia 37, Ole Miss 17, SportSouth
Georgia 49, Kentucky 27, TBS
Georgia 13, Florida 45, ESPN
Georgia 37, Auburn 27, TBS
Georgia 18, Georgia Tech 15, JP Sports
Georgia 24, Arkansas 15, ABC (Independence)
1992—Georgia 31, Tennessee 34, ABC
Georgia 37, Ole Miss 11, ABC
Georgia 27, Arkansas 3, JP Sports
Georgia 30, Vanderbilt 20, JP Sports
Georgia 24, Florida 26, ABC
Georgia 14, Auburn 10, ABC
Georgia 31, Georgia Tech 17, ESPN

Year—Score, Audience (Bowl)
Georgia 21, Ohio State 14, ESPN (Citrus)
1993—S. Carolina 23, Georgia 21, JP Sports
Tennessee 38, Georgia 6, ESPN
Georgia 33, Kentucky 28, JP Sports
Florida 33, Georgia 26, ABC
Georgia 43, Georgia Tech 10, ABC

KENTUCKY (12-34-1)

Year—Score, Audience (Bowl)
1956—Kentucky 6, Georgia Tech 14
1969—Kentucky 30, Indiana 58, ABC
1974—Kentucky 38, Vanderbilt 12, ABC
Kentucky 41, Florida 24, ABC
1975—Kentucky 10, Maryland 10, ABC
1976—Kentucky 14, Maryland 24
Kentucky 21, North Carolina 0, National
(Peach)
1979—Kentucky 10, Indiana 18, ABC
1981—Kentucky 3, Clemson 21, ABC
1983—Kentucky 24, Indiana 13, CBS
Kentucky 26, Tulane 14, CBS
Kentucky 17, Vanderbilt 8, WTBS
Kentucky 0, Tennessee 10, ABC
Kentucky 16, West Virginia 20, National
(Hall of Fame)
1984—Kentucky 30, Tulane 26, WTBS
Kentucky 10, LSU 36, ABC
Kentucky 7, Georgia 37, WTBS
Kentucky 17, Florida 25, WTBS
Kentucky 20, Wisconsin 19, National
(Hall of Fame)
1985—Kentucky 0, LSU 10, ESPN
Kentucky 6, Georgia 26, WTBS
Kentucky 24, Vanderbilt 31, WTBS
Kentucky 0, Tennessee 42, WTBS
1986—Kentucky 34, Vanderbilt 22, WTBS
1987—Kentucky 9, LSU 34, WTBS
Kentucky 14, Georgia 17, WTBS
Kentucky 14, Florida 27, WTBS
1988—Kentucky 10, Auburn 20, WTBS
Kentucky 27, Alabama 31, WTBS
Kentucky 16, Georgia 10, WTBS
1989—Kentucky 3, Alabama 15, TBS
Kentucky 12, Auburn 24, TBS
Kentucky 10, Tennessee 31, ESPN
1990—Kentucky 29, Ole Miss 35, TBS
Kentucky 15, Florida 47, TBS
Kentucky 28, Tennessee 42, TBS
1991—Kentucky 10, Indiana 13, ESPN
Kentucky 26, LSU 29, TBS
Kentucky 27, Georgia 49, TBS
Kentucky 7, Vanderbilt 17, TBS
Kentucky 7, Tennessee 16, TBS
1992—Kentucky 19, Florida 35, JP Sports
Kentucky 13, S. Carolina 9, JP Sports
1993—Kentucky 21, S. Carolina 17, ESPN
Georgia 33, Kentucky 28, JP Sports
Tennessee 48, Kentucky 0, ESPN
Clemson 14, Kentucky 13, ESPN (Peach)

LSU (43-58-6)

Year—Score, Audience (Bowl)
1958—LSU 7, Clemson 0, NBC (Sugar)
1959—LSU 26, Rice 3, NBC
LSU 0, Ole Miss 21, NBC (Sugar)
1960—LSU 6, Ole Miss 6, ABC
1961—LSU 30, North Carolina 0, ABC
LSU 25, Colorado 7, NBC (Orange)
1962—LSU 10, Georgia Tech 7, NBC
LSU 13, Texas 0, CBS (Cotton)
1963—LSU 3, Ole Miss 37, CBS
LSU 7, Baylor 14, National (Bluebonnet)
1964—LSU 3, Tennessee 3, NBC

Year—Score, Audience (Bowl)
LSU 13, Syracuse 10, National (Sugar)
1965—LSU 7, Alabama 31, ABC
LSU 14, Arkansas 7, CBS (Cotton)
1966—LSU 0, Alabama 21, ABC
LSU 17, Miss. State 7, ABC
1967—LSU 13, Ole Miss 13, ABC
LSU 20, Wyoming 13, ABC (Sugar)
1968—LSU 31, Florida State 27, National
(Peach)
1969—LSU 21, Auburn 20, ABC
LSU 23, Ole Miss 26, ABC
1970—LSU 14, Alabama 9, ABC
LSU 61, Ole Miss 17, ABC
LSU 12, Nebraska 17, NBC (Orange)
1971—LSU 7, Alabama 14, ABC
LSU 28, Notre Dame 8, ABC
LSU 33, Iowa State 15, National (Sun)
1972—LSU 21, Alabama 35, ABC
LSU 17, Tennessee 24, National
(Bluebonnet)
1973—LSU 51, Ole Miss 14, ABC
LSU 7, Alabama 21, ABC
LSU 9, Penn State 16, NBC (Orange)
1974—LSU 0, Alabama 30, ABC
1975—LSU 13, Ole Miss 17, ABC
1977—LSU 28, Ole Miss 21, ABC
LSU 3, Alabama 24, ABC
LSU 14, Stanford 24, CBS (Sun)
1978—LSU 30, Ole Miss 8, ABC
LSU 10, Alabama 31, ABC
LSU 15, Missouri 20, National (Liberty)
1979—LSU 19, Florida State 24, ABC
LSU 13, Tulane 24, ABC
LSU 24, Wake Forest 10, National
(Tangerine)
1980—LSU 38, Ole Miss 16, ABC
1981—LSU 7, Alabama 24, ABC
LSU 9, Notre Dame 27, USA
1982—LSU 24, Miss. State 27, CBS
LSU 20, Nebraska 21, NBC (Orange)
1983—LSU 35, Florida State 40, ABC
LSU 6, Tennessee 20, WTBS
LSU 26, Alabama 32, ABC
LSU 20, Tulane 7, WTBS
1984—LSU 21, Florida 21, WTBS
LSU 34, Vanderbilt 27, ESPN
LSU 36, Kentucky 10, ABC
LSU 22, Notre Dame 30, ABC
LSU 10, Nebraska 28, ABC (Sugar)
1985—LSU 10, Kentucky 0, ESPN
LSU 14, Ole Miss 0, WTBS
LSU 14, Alabama 14, ABC
LSU 10, Notre Dame 7, USA
LSU 7, Baylor 21, KATZ (Liberty)
1986—LSU 35, Texas A&M 17, ESPN
LSU 19, Ole Miss 21, ABC
LSU 14, Alabama 10, ABC
LSU 21, Notre Dame 19, ESPN
LSU 15, Nebraska 30, ABC (Sugar)
1987—LSU 17, Texas A&M 3, ESPN
LSU 13, Ohio State 13, CBS
LSU 13, Florida 10, ESPN
LSU 26, Georgia 23, ESPN
LSU 34, Kentucky 9, WTBS
LSU 10, Alabama 22, ESPN
LSU 30, South Carolina 13, CBS (Gator)
1988—LSU 34, Tennessee 9, WTBS
LSU 33, Ohio State 36, ABC
LSU 19, Florida 6, CBS
LSU 7, Auburn 6, ESPN
LSU 31, Ole Miss 20, WTBS
LSU 20, Miss. State 3, WTBS
LSU 18, Alabama 17, CBS
LSU 3, Miami 44, ESPN
LSU 10, Syracuse 23, NBC (Hall of Fame)
(continued)

1994 SEC Football 201

All-Time Television Appearances of SEC Schools

LSU (continued)
1989—LSU 16, Texas A&M 28, ESPN
LSU 21, Florida State 31, ESPN
LSU 16, Auburn 10, CBS
LSU 39, Tennessee 45, TBS
LSU 16, Alabama 32, ESPN
1990—LSU 21, Vanderbilt 24, TBS
LSU 8, Florida 34, ESPN
LSU 3, Florida State 42, TBS
1991—LSU 10, Georgia 31, ABC
LSU 7, Texas A&M 45, Raycom
LSU 29, Kentucky 26, TBS
LSU 16, Florida State 27, ESPN
LSU 17, Alabama 20, ABC
1992—LSU 22, Texas A&M 31, ABC
LSU 28, Auburn 30, JP Sports
LSU 0, Tennessee 20, ESPN
LSU 11, Alabama 31, ABC
LSU 6, Arkansas 30, ESP
1993—Texas A&M 24, LSU 0, ABC
LSU 18, Miss. State 16, ABC
Tennessee 42, LSU 20, JP Sports
Florida 58, LSU 3, ESPN
LSU 17, Alabama 13, JP Sports
Arkansas 42, LSU 24, ESPN

OLE MISS (36-38-2)

Year—Score, Audience (Bowl)
1952—Ole Miss 7, Georgia Tech 24, ABC (Sugar)
1953—Ole Miss 28, Arkansas 0, CBS
1954—Ole Miss 0, Navy 21, ABC (Sugar)
1955—Ole Miss 14, TCU 13, CBS (Cotton)
1957—Ole Miss 39, Texas 7, NBC (Sugar)
1958—Ole Miss 7, Florida 3, CBS (Gator)
1959—Ole Miss 21, LSU 0, NBC (Sugar)
1960—Ole Miss 6, LSU 6, ABC
Ole Miss 14, Rice 6, NBC (Sugar)
1961—Ole Miss 16, Arkansas 0, ABC
Ole Miss 7, Texas 12, CBS (Cotton)
1962—Ole Miss 17, Arkansas 13, NBC (Sugar)
1963—Ole Miss 37, LSU 3, CBS
Ole Miss 7, Alabama 12, NBC (Sugar)
1964—Ole Miss 17, Miss. State 20, NBC
Ole Miss 7, Tulsa 14, CBS (Bluebonnet)
1965—Ole Miss 14, Tennessee 13, NBC
Ole Miss 13, Auburn 7, ABC (Liberty)
1966—Ole Miss 0, Texas 19, ABC (Bluebonnet)
1967—Ole Miss 7, Alabama 21, ABC
Ole Miss 13, LSU 13, ABC
Ole Miss 7, Texas-El Paso 14, National (Sun)
1968—Ole Miss 7, Georgia 21, ABC
Ole Miss 34, Virginia Tech 17, ABC (Liberty)
1969—Ole Miss 32, Alabama 33, ABC
Ole Miss 26, LSU 23, ABC
Ole Miss 27, Arkansas 22, ABC (Sugar)
1970—Ole Miss 48, Alabama 23, ABC
Ole Miss 17, LSU 61, ABC
Ole Miss 28, Auburn 35, NBC (Gator)
1971—Ole Miss 41, Georgia Tech 18, Mizlou (Peach)
1973—Ole Miss 14, LSU 51, ABC
Ole Miss 28, Tennessee 18, ABC
1974—Ole Miss 21, Alabama 35, ABC
1975—Ole Miss 17, LSU 13, ABC
Ole Miss 15, Auburn 21, ABC
Ole Miss 21, LSU 28, ABC
1978—Ole Miss 8, LSU 30, ABC

Year—Score, Audience (Bowl)
1979—Ole Miss 7, Missouri 33, ABC
Ole Miss 15, Tulane 44, ABC
1980—Ole Miss 16, LSU 38, ABC
1982—Ole Miss 10, Vanderbilt 19, CBS
Ole Miss 45, Tulane 14, WTBS
1983—Ole Miss 13, Tennessee 10, WTBS
Ole Miss 3, Air Force 9, Mizlou (Independence)
1984—Ole Miss 13, Auburn 17, WTBS
Ole Miss 12, Georgia 18, WTBS
Ole Miss 24, Miss. State 3, WTBS
1985—Ole Miss 0, Auburn 41, ESPN
Ole Miss 0, LSU 14, WTBS
Ole Miss 14, Notre Dame 37, USA
Ole Miss 14, Tennessee 34, WTBS
1986—Ole Miss 35, Tulane 10, WTBS
Ole Miss 10, Georgia 14, WTBS
Ole Miss 21, LSU 19, ABC
Ole Miss 10, Tennessee 22, WTBS
Ole Miss 24, Miss. State 3, WTBS
Ole Miss 20, Texas Tech 17, Mizlou (Independence)
1988—Ole Miss 22, Alabama 12, WTBS
Ole Miss 20, LSU 31, WTBS
1989—Ole Miss 24, Florida 19, TBS
Ole Miss 17, Georgia 13, TBS
Ole Miss 42, Air Force 29, Raycom (Liberty)
1990—Ole Miss 21, Arkansas 17, Raycom
Ole Miss 35, Kentucky 29, TBS
Ole Miss 28, Georgia 12, TBS
Ole Miss 13, Tennessee 22, CBS
Ole Miss 3, Michigan 35, ESPN (Gator)
1991—Ole Miss 22, Tulane 3, TBS
Ole Miss 17, Georgia 37, SportSouth
1992—Ole Miss 11, Georgia 37, ABC
Ole Miss 10, Alabama 31, JP Sports
Ole Miss 17, Miss. State 10, JP Sports
Ole Miss 13, Air Force 0, ESPN (Liberty)
1993—Ole Miss 19, Arkansas 0, JP Sports
Alabama 19, Ole Miss 14, ABC

MISSISSIPPI STATE (11-26-0)

Year—Score, Audience (Bowl)
1963—Miss. State 16, N.C. State 12, National (Liberty)
1964—Miss. State 20, Ole Miss 17, NBC
1966—Miss. State 7, LSU 17, ABC
1974—Miss. State 26, N. Carolina 24, CBS (Sun)
1977—Miss. State 22, Florida 24, ABC
1980—Miss. State 17, Nebraska 31, CBS (Sun)
1981—Miss. State 28, Florida 7, ABC
Miss. State 3, Missouri 14, ABC
Miss. State 10, Alabama 13, ESPN
Miss. State 10, Kansas 0, Mizlou (Hall of Fame)
1982—Miss. State 22, Georgia 29, CBS
Miss. State 14, Southern Miss 20, ABC
Miss. State 27, LSU 24, CBS
1984—Miss. State 3, Ole Miss 24, WTBS
1986—Miss. State 27, Tennessee 23, WTBS
Miss. State 6, Auburn 35, ESPN
Miss. State 3, Alabama 38, WTBS
Miss. State 3, Ole Miss 24, WTBS
1987—Miss. State 10, Tennessee 38, WTBS
Miss. State 3, LSU 20, WTBS
1989—Miss. State 10, Alabama 23, TBS
1990—Miss. State 7, Tennessee 40, TBS
Miss. State 21, Florida 34, TBS

Year—Score, Audience (Bowl)
Miss. State 0, Alabama 22, TBS
1991—Miss. State 13, Texas 6, TBS
Miss. State 24, Tennessee 26, TBS
Miss. State 7, Florida 29, TBS
Miss. State 24, Auburn 17, ABC
Miss. State 7, Alabama 13, TBS
Miss. State 15, Air Force 38, ESPN (Liberty)
1992—Miss. State 28, Texas 10, ESPN
Miss. State 30, Florida 6, ESPN
Miss. State 10, Arkansas 3, JP Sports
Miss. State 21, Alabama 30, ESPN
Miss. State 10, Ole Miss 17, JP Sports
Miss. State 17, N. Carolina 21, ESPN (Peach)
1993—LSU 18, Miss. State 16, ABC
Florida 38, Miss. State 24, JP Sports
Alabama 36, Miss. State 25, ABC

SOUTH CAROLINA (15-43-0)

Year-Score, Audience (Bowl)
1958—S. Carolina 9, North Carolina 6, ACC Network
1964—S. Carolina 14, N.C. State 17, ABC
1969—S. Carolina 3, West Virginia 14, Mizlou (Peach)
1970—S. Carolina 34, Georgia 52, ABC
1975—S. Carolina 21, N.C. State 28, ABC
S. Carolina 7, Miami (Ohio) 20, Independent (Tangerine)
1976—S. Carolina 27, Georgia Tech 17, ABC
1977—S. Carolina 19, East Carolina 16, ABC
S. Carolina 27, Clemson 31, ABC
1979—S. Carolina 0, N. Carolina 28, ESPN
S. Carolina 13, Clemson 9, ESPN
S. Carolina 14, Missouri 24, Mizlou (Hall of Fame)
1980—S. Carolina 10, Georgia 13, ABC
S. Carolina 9, Pittsburgh 37, ABC (Gator)
1981—S. Carolina 28, Pittsburgh 42, ABC
S. Carolina 20, N.C. State 12, ABC
S. Carolina 13, Clemson 29, ESPN
1982—S. Carolina 18, Georgia 34, USA
S. Carolina 6, Clemson 24, USA
1983—S. Carolina 6, Notre Dame 30, ESPN
S. Carolina 31, N.C. State 17, WTBS
S. Carolina 13, Clemson 22, ESPN
1984—S. Carolina 45, Pittsburgh 21, Katz Sports
S. Carolina 36, Notre Dame 32, Metrosports
S. Carolina 38, Florida State 26, ABC
S. Carolina 21, Navy 38, Metrosports
S. Carolina 22, Clemson 21, ESPN
S. Carolina 14, Oklahoma State 21, ABC (Gator)
1985—S. Carolina 3, Michigan 34, ABC
S. Carolina 7, Pittsburgh 42, ESPN
S. Carolina 14, Florida State 56, ESPN
1986—S. Carolina 14, Miami (Fla.) 34, ESPN
S. Carolina 20, Virginia 30, JP Sports
S. Carolina 26, Georgia 31, ESPN
1987—S. Carolina 21, Nebraska 30, ESPN
S. Carolina 20, Clemson 7, ESPN
S. Carolina 16, Miami (Fla.) 20, ESPN
S. Carolina 13, LSU 30, CBS (Gator)
1988—S. Carolina 23, Georgia 10, WTBS
S. Carolina 20, N.C. State 7, ESPN
S. Carolina 0, Florida State 59, ESPN
S. Carolina 10, Clemson 29, JP Sports
S. Carolina 10, Indiana 34, Raycom (Liberty)
1989—S. Carolina 0, Clemson 45, ESPN
1990—S. Carolina 6, Georgia Tech 27, ESPN
S. Carolina 29, West Virginia 10, ESPN
1991—S. Carolina 21, N.C. State 17, ABC
S. Carolina 10, Florida State 38, JP Sports
(continued)

202 Through The Years

South Carolina (continued)
S. Carolina 24, Clemson 41, JP Sports
1992—S. Carolina 9, Kentucky 13, JP Sports
S. Carolina 24, Tennessee 23, JP Sports
S. Carolina 9, Florida 14, JP Sports
1993—S. Carolina 23, Georgia 21, JP Sports
Kentucky 21, S. Carolina 17, ESPN
Alabama 17, S. Carolina 6, ABC
Tennessee 55, S. Carolina 3, JP Sports
Florida 37, S. Carolina 26, JP Sports
Clemson 16, S. Carolina 13, JP Sports

TENNESSEE (61-45-10)

Year—Score, Audience (Bowl)
1951—Tennessee 27, Alabama 13
1952—Tennessee 0, Texas 16, National (Cotton)
1953—Tennessee 0, Alabama 0, CBS
1956—Tennessee 7, Baylor 13, National (Sugar)
1957—Tennessee 3, Texas A&M 0, National (Gator)
1958—Tennessee 0, Auburn 13, National
1961—Tennessee 3, Alabama 34, ABC
1962—Tennessee 7, Alabama 27
1964—Tennessee 3, LSU 3, NBC
1965—Tennessee 13, Ole Miss 14, NBC
Tennessee 27, Tulsa 6, National (Bluebonnet)
1966—Tennessee 3, Georgia Tech 6, ABC
Tennessee 28, Kentucky 19, ABC
Tennessee 18, Syracuse 12, National (Gator)
1967—Tennessee 24, Georgia Tech 13, ABC
Tennessee 24, Oklahoma 26, NBC (Orange)
1968—Tennessee 17, Georgia 17, ABC
Tennessee 10, Alabama 9, ABC
Tennessee 13, Texas 36, CBS (Cotton)
1969—Tennessee 45, Auburn 19, ABC
Tennessee 13, Florida 14, National (Gator)
1970—Tennessee 38, Florida 7, ABC
Tennessee 34, Air Force 13, ABC (Sugar)
1971—Tennessee 9, Auburn 10, ABC
Tennessee 31, Penn State 11, ABC
Tennessee 14, Arkansas 13, ABC (Liberty)
1972—Tennessee 34, Georgia Tech 3, ABC
Tennessee 24, LSU 17, National (Bluebonnet)
1973—Tennessee 21, Alabama 42, ABC
Tennessee 18, Ole Miss 28, ABC
Tennessee 19, Texas Tech 28, ABC (Gator)
1974—Tennessee 17, UCLA 17, ABC
Tennessee 7, Maryland 3, ABC (Liberty)
1975—Tennessee 28, UCLA 34, ABC
1976—Tennessee 28, Auburn 38, ABC
Tennessee 13, Alabama 20, ABC
1978—Tennessee 10, Auburn 29, ABC
1979—Tennessee 22, Purdue 27, National (Bluebonnet)
1980—Tennessee 0, Alabama 27, ABC
1981—Tennessee 28, Wisconsin 21, National (Garden State)
1982—Tennessee 21, Georgia Tech 31
Tennessee 22, Iowa 28, National (Peach)
1983—Tennessee 20, LSU 6, WTBS
Tennessee 10, Ole Miss 13, WTBS
Tennessee 10, Kentucky 0, ABC
Tennessee 34, Vanderbilt 24, CBS
Tennessee 30, Maryland 23, Mizlou (Citrus)
1984—Tennessee 10, Auburn 29, ABC
Tennessee 29, Vanderbilt 13, WTBS
Tennessee 27, Maryland 28, CBS (Sun)
1985—Tennessee 26, UCLA 26, ABC
Tennessee 38, Auburn 20, ABC

Year—Score, Audience (Bowl)
Tennessee 16, Alabama 14, WTBS
Tennessee 6, Georgia Tech 6, ESPN
Tennessee 34, Ole Miss 14, WTBS
Tennessee 42, Kentucky 0, WTBS
Tennessee 30, Vanderbilt 0, WTBS
Tennessee 35, Miami (Fla.) 7, ABC (Sugar)
1986—Tennessee 23, Miss. State 27, WTBS
Tennessee 8, Auburn 34, WTBS
Tennessee 28, Alabama 56, ABC
Tennessee 13, Georgia Tech 14, WTBS
Tennessee 22, Ole Miss 10, WTBS
Tennessee 21, Minnesota 14, Raycom (Liberty)
1987—Tennessee 23, Iowa 22, ABC (Kickoff Classic)
Tennessee 38, Miss. State 10, WTBS
Tennessee 20, Auburn 20, WTBS
Tennessee 38, California 12, WTBS
Tennessee 22, Alabama 41, ESPN
Tennessee 18, Boston College 20, Jeff Pilot
Tennessee 27, Indiana 22, Mizlou (Peach)
1988—Tennessee 17, Georgia 28, ESPN
Tennessee 9, LSU 34, WTBS
Tennessee 6, Auburn 36, CBS
1989—Tennessee 21, Auburn 14, CBS
Tennessee 17, Georgia 14, ESPN
Tennessee 30, Alabama 47, CBS
Tennessee 45, LSU 39, TBS
Tennessee 31, Kentucky 10, ESPN
Tennessee 17, Vanderbilt 10, TBS
Tennessee 31, Arkansas 27, CBS (Cotton)
1990—Tennessee 31, Colorado 31, NBC
Tennessee 40, Miss. State 7, TBS
Tennessee 26, Auburn 26, ESPN
Tennessee 45, Florida 3, ESPN
Tennessee 6, Alabama 9, ESPN
Tennessee 29, Notre Dame 34, CBS
Tennessee 22, Ole Miss 13, CBS
Tennessee 42, Kentucky 28, TBS
Tennessee 23, Virginia 22, ABC (Sugar)
1991—Tennessee 28, Louisville 11, ESPN
Tennessee 30, UCLA 16, TBS
Tennessee 26, Miss. State 24, TBS
Tennessee 30, Auburn 21, ESPN
Tennessee 18, Florida 35, ESPN
Tennessee 19, Alabama 24, ABC
Tennessee 35, Notre Dame 34, NBC
Tennessee 16, Kentucky 7, TBS
Tennessee 45, Vanderbilt 0, SportSouth
Tennessee 17, Penn State 42, NBC (Fiesta)
1992—Tennessee 34, Georgia 31, ABC
Tennessee 31, Florida 14, ABC
Tennessee 20, LSU 0, ESPN
Tennessee 24, Arkansas 25, JP Sports
Tennessee 10, Alabama 17, ABC
Tennessee 23, S. Carolina 24, JP Sports
Tennessee 38, Boston College 23, ESPN (Hall of Fame)
1993—Tennessee 38, Georgia 6, ESPN
Florida 41, Tennessee 34, ABC
Tennessee 42, LSU 20, JP Sports
Tennessee 28, Arkansas 14, JP Sports
Tennessee 17, Alabama 17, ABC
Tennessee 55, S. Carolina 3, JP Sports
Tennessee 45, Louisville 10, ABC
Tennessee 48, Kentucky 0, ESPN
Tennessee 62, Vanderbilt 14, JP Sports
Penn State 31, Tennessee 13, ABC (Citrus)

VANDERBILT (8-26-1)

Year—Score, Audience (Bowl)
1955—Vanderbilt 25, Auburn 13, National (Gator)
1974—Vanderbilt 12, Kentucky 38, ABC
Vanderbilt 6, Texas Tech 6, National (Peach)
1981—Vanderbilt 21, Georgia 53, ABC
1982—Vanderbilt 19, Ole Miss 10, CBS
Vanderbilt 28, Air Force 36, National (Hall of Fame)
1983—Vanderbilt 24, Tennessee 34, CBS
Vanderbilt 14, Maryland 21, ABC
Vanderbilt 8, Kentucky 17, WTBS
Vanderbilt 30, Tulane 17, WTBS
1984—Vanderbilt 13, Tennessee 29, WTBS
Vanderbilt 35, Georgia 62, WTBS
Vanderbilt 27, LSU 34, ESPN
1985—Vanderbilt 0, Tennessee 30, WTBS
Vanderbilt 31, Kentucky 24, WTBS
Vanderbilt 20, Alabama 40, WTBS
1986—Vanderbilt 10, Alabama 42, WTBS
Vanderbilt 9, Auburn 31, WTBS
Vanderbilt 16, Georgia 38, WTBS
Vanderbilt 22, Kentucky 34, WTBS
1987—Vanderbilt 15, Auburn 48, WTBS
Vanderbilt 24, Rutgers 13, WTBS
1988—Vanderbilt 24, Florida 9, WTBS
1989—Vanderbilt 14, Alabama 20, TBS
Vanderbilt 10, Tennessee 17, TBS
1990—Vanderbilt 24, LSU 21, TBS
1991—Vanderbilt 10, Syracuse 37, Big East Network
Vanderbilt 17, Kentucky 7, TBS
Vanderbilt 0, Tennessee 45, SportSouth
1992—Vanderbilt 8, Alabama 25, JP Sports
Vanderbilt 20, Georgia 30, JP Sports
Vanderbilt 21, Florida 41, JP Sports
1993—Alabama 17, Vanderbilt 6, JP Sports
Florida 52, Vanderbilt 0, JP Sports
Tennessee 62, Vanderbilt 14, JP Sports

Note: Bowl games, even if played on New Year's Day of the following year, are listed for the season the bid was earned.

1994 SEC Football   **203**

National Attendance Leaders

1959
		G	Att.	Avg.
1.	Ohio State	6	495,536	82,589
2.	Michigan	6	456,385	76,064
3.	**LSU**	**7**	**408,727**	**58,390**
4.	Michigan State	5	282,327	56,465
5.	Notre Dame	5	281,153	56,231
6.	Iowa	5	279,400	55,880
7.	Oklahoma	5	275,828	55,166
8.	Illinois	5	270,710	54,142
9.	Minnesota	5	263,983	52,797
10.	Wisconsin	5	254,072	50,814

1960
		G	Att.	Avg.
1.	Ohio State	5	413,583	82,717
2.	Michigan State	4	274,367	68,592
3.	Michigan	6	374,682	62,447
4.	Minnesota	6	344,988	57,498
5.	Notre Dame	5	277,278	55,456
6.	Oklahoma	6	327,217	54,536
7.	**LSU**	**6**	**318,899**	**53,150**
8.	Iowa	5	264,100	52,820
9.	Wisconsin	5	262,082	52,416
10.	Illinois	5	249,218	48,844

1961
		G	Att.	Avg.
1.	Ohio State	5	414,712	82,942
2.	Michigan	7	514,924	73,561
3.	**LSU**	**6**	**381,409**	**63,651**
4.	Minnesota	6	366,491	61,082
5.	Iowa	5	290,250	58,050
6.	Michigan State	5	281,372	56,274
7.	Notre Dame	5	269,066	53,813
8.	Texas	6	321,898	53,650
9.	Washington	6	316,148	52,691
10.	Oklahoma	4	196,450	49,113

1962
		G	Att.	Avg.
1.	Ohio State	6	497,644	82,941
2.	Michigan State	4	272,568	68,142
3.	**LSU**	**6**	**397,701**	**66,284**
4.	Minnesota	6	370,423	61,737
5.	Michigan	5	304,207	60,841
6.	Oklahoma	6	352,817	58,803
7.	Texas	6	345,413	57,569
8.	Iowa	5	281,080	56,216
9.	Wisconsin	6	334,259	55,710
10.	Washington	6	324,468	54,078

1963
		G	Att.	Avg.
1.	Ohio State	5	416,023	83,205
2.	**LSU**	**6**	**396,846**	**66,141**
3.	Michigan State	5	326,597	65,319
4.	Wisconsin	5	306,114	61,223
5.	Michigan	7	424,728	60,675
6.	Texas	6	360,986	60,164
7.	Minnesota	5	290,746	58,149
8.	Iowa	4	230,300	57,575
9.	Washington	5	277,040	55,408
10.	Southern Cal	6	331,062	55,177

1964
		G	Att.	Avg.
1.	Ohio State	7	583,740	83,391
2.	Michigan State	4	284,933	71,233
3.	Michigan	6	388,829	64,805
4.	**LSU**	**6**	**380,687**	**63,448**
5.	Texas	5	309,181	61,836
6.	Wisconsin	5	303,590	60,718
7.	Illinois	4	235,120	58,780
8.	Notre Dame	5	291,826	58,365
9.	Washington	5	280,285	56,057
10.	Minnesota	5	279,822	55,964

1965
		G	Att.	Avg.
1.	Ohio State	5	416,282	83,256
2.	Michigan	6	450,487	80,081
3.	Michigan State	5	346,296	69,259
4.	**LSU**	**7**	**457,733**	**65,390**
5.	Texas	6	362,356	60,393
6.	Notre Dame	5	295,675	59,135
7.	Southern Cal	6	345,872	57,645
8.	Wisconsin	5	282,139	56,428
9.	Washington	6	327,592	54,599
10.	Nebraska	6	321,469	53,578

1966
		G	Att.	Avg.
1.	Ohio State	6	488,399	81,400
2.	Michigan State	6	426,750	71,125
3.	Michigan	6	413,599	68,933
4.	**LSU**	**6**	**386,098**	**64,350**
5.	Nebraska	5	318,822	63,764
6.	Notre Dame	5	295,375	59,075
7.	Southern Cal	5	288,618	57,724
8.	**Alabama**	**8**	**458,451**	**57,306**
9.	Texas	5	283,531	56,706
10.	Washington	5	275,396	55,079

1967
		G	Att.	Avg.
1.	Ohio State	5	383,502	76,700
2.	Michigan	6	447,289	74,548
3.	Michigan State	6	411,916	68,653
4.	**LSU**	**7**	**454,101**	**64,872**
5.	Nebraska	5	321,714	64,343
6.	Southern Cal	5	314,246	62,849
7.	Notre Dame	5	305,375	61,075
8.	Texas	6	364,988	60,831
9.	Purdue	5	300,567	60,113
10.	**Florida**	**6**	**355,496**	**59,249**

1968
		G	Att.	Avg.
1.	Ohio State	6	482,564	80,427
2.	Southern Cal	5	354,945	70,989
3.	Michigan State	6	414,177	69,030
4.	Michigan	6	407,948	67,991
5.	**LSU**	**6**	**396,774**	**66,129**
6.	Nebraska	5	329,836	65,967
7.	Texas	5	316,664	63,333
8.	**Tennessee**	**6**	**373,550**	**62,258**
9.	Purdue	5	305,620	61,124
10.	Notre Dame	6	366,450	61,075

1969
		G	Att.	Avg.
1.	Ohio State	5	431,175	86,235
2.	Michigan	6	428,780	71,463
3.	Michigan State	5	352,123	70,425
4.	Nebraska	6	400,668	66,778
5.	Purdue	5	333,122	66,624
6.	Southern Cal	5	330,714	66,143
7.	**LSU**	**6**	**388,461**	**64,744**
8.	Notre Dame	5	305,375	61,075
9.	**Alabama**	**4**	**242,932**	**60,733**
10.	**Georgia**	**6**	**360,417**	**60,070**

1970
		G	Att.	Avg.
1.	Ohio State	5	432,451	86,490
2.	Michigan	6	476,164	79,361
3.	Purdue	5	340,090	68,018
4.	Nebraska	6	403,277	67,213
5.	Texas	5	327,515	65,503
6.	Michigan State	6	387,051	64,509
7.	Wisconsin	6	377,335	62,889
8.	Stanford	5	313,553	62,711
9.	**LSU**	**7**	**436,823**	**62,403**
10.	Southern Cal	5	307,147	61,429

1971
		G	Att.	Avg.
1.	Ohio State	6	506,699	84,450
2.	Michigan	7	564,376	80,625
3.	Wisconsin	6	408,885	68,148
4.	Nebraska	7	473,346	67,621
5.	**LSU**	**7**	**463,491**	**66,213**
6.	Purdue	5	329,124	65,825
7.	Texas	6	392,844	65,474
8.	**Alabama**	**5**	**313,652**	**62,370**
9.	Stanford	6	371,013	61,836
10.	Michigan State	5	306,162	61,232

1972
		G	Att.	Avg.
1.	Michigan	6	513,398	85,566
2.	Ohio State	6	509,420	84,903
3.	Nebraska	6	456,859	76,143
4.	Wisconsin	6	422,721	70,454
5.	**Tennessee**	**6**	**409,188**	**68,198**
6.	Texas	5	339,368	67,874
7.	**LSU**	**7**	**470,078**	**67,154**
8.	Michigan State	6	398,660	66,443
9.	**Alabama**	**9**	**572,372**	**63,597**
10.	Oklahoma	7	441,988	63,141

1973
		G	Att.	Avg.
1.	Ohio State	6	523,369	87,228
2.	Michigan	7	595,171	85,024
3.	Nebraska	6	456,726	76,121
4.	Southern Cal	6	413,220	68,870
5.	**LSU**	**7**	**474,108**	**67,730**
6.	**Tennessee**	**7**	**460,641**	**65,806**
7.	Texas	6	381,065	63,511
8.	**Alabama**	**5**	**316,548**	**63,310**
9.	Oklahoma	5	309,130	61,826
10.	Michigan State	5	306,542	61,308

1974
		G	Att.	Avg.
1.	Michigan	6	562,105	93,684
2.	Ohio State	6	525,314	87,552
3.	Nebraska	7	534,388	76,341
4.	Wisconsin	5	358,150	71,630
5.	**Tennessee**	**8**	**929,127**	**66,141**
6.	**LSU**	**6**	**395,587**	**65,931**
7.	Michigan State	6	386,237	64,373
8.	Oklahoma	7	442,988	63,284
9.	**Alabama**	**7**	**442,661**	**63,237**
10.	Texas	5	305,834	61,167

1975
		G	Att.	Avg.
1.	Michigan	7	689,146	98,449
2.	Ohio State	6	527,141	87,856
3.	Nebraska	7	533,368	76,195
4.	Wisconsin	6	443,771	73,961
5.	**Tennessee**	**7**	**508,724**	**72,674**
6.	Oklahoma	6	421,421	70,236
7.	Michigan State	6	401,369	66,894
8.	Missouri	5	322,977	64,595
9.	**LSU**	**6**	**386,171**	**64,362**
10.	**Alabama**	**7**	**435,583**	**62,226**

1976
		G	Att.	Avg.
1.	Michigan	7	722,133	103,159
2.	Ohio State	6	526,216	87,702
3.	**Tennessee**	**7**	**564,922**	**80,703**
4.	Nebraska	6	455,856	75,976
5.	Wisconsin	6	425,386	70,897
6.	Oklahoma	6	425,113	70,852
7.	**LSU**	**7**	**452,921**	**64,703**
8.	Missouri	5	317,902	63,580
9.	Texas	5	308,218	61,643
10.	Notre Dame	5	305,375	61,075

Through The Years

1977
		G	Att.	Avg.
1.	Michigan	7	729,418	104,203
2.	Ohio State	6	525,535	87,589
3.	**Tennessee**	7	**582,979**	**83,283**
4.	Nebraska	7	533,054	76,151
5.	Wisconsin	6	436,093	72,682
6.	Oklahoma	6	427,104	71,184
7.	**Alabama**	5	**323,166**	**64,333**
8.	Southern Cal	6	381,958	63,660
9.	**LSU**	7	**445,433**	**63,633**
10.	**Florida**	6	**375,814**	**62,636**

1978
		G	Att.	Avg.
1.	Michigan	6	629,690	104,948
2.	Ohio State	7	614,881	87,840
3.	**Tennessee**	8	**627,881**	**78,422**
4.	Penn State	7	542,144	77,449
5.	Nebraska	6	455,061	75,843
6.	**LSU**	6	**446,392**	**74,398**
7.	Wisconsin	7	500,102	71,443
8.	Oklahoma	6	427,967	71,327
9.	Texas	6	427,755	71,292

1979
		G	Att.	Avg.
1.	Michigan	7	730,315	104,331
2.	Ohio State	7	611,794	87,399
3.	**Tennessee**	6	**512,139**	**85,357**
4.	Penn State	7	541,895	77,414
5.	Michigan State	6	460,135	76,689
6.	Nebraska	6	456,457	76,076
7.	Wisconsin	6	444,075	74,013
8.	**LSU**	7	**507,984**	**72,569**
9.	Oklahoma	6	426,416	71,069
10.	Missouri	6	419,202	69,867

1980
		G	Att.	Avg.
1.	Michigan	6	625,292	104,292
2.	**Tennessee**	8	**709,193**	**88,649**
3.	Ohio State	7	615,746	87,925
4.	Penn State	6	498,268	83,045
5.	Nebraska	7	523,326	76,047
6.	Oklahoma	7	521,144	74,449
7.	**LSU**	6	**444,703**	**74,117**
8.	Wisconsin	6	428,166	71,361
9.	**Alabama**	7	**494,662**	**70,666**
10.	Michigan State	6	420,550	70,092

1981
		G	Att.	Avg.
1.	Michigan	6	632,990	105,498
2.	**Tennessee**	6	**558,996**	**93,166**
3.	Ohio State	6	521,760	86,960
4.	Penn State	6	507,697	84,616
5.	**Georgia**	6	**484,162**	**80,694**
6.	Nebraska	6	457,675	76,279
7.	Oklahoma	6	455,078	75,846
8.	**LSU**	7	**513,850**	**73,407**
9.	Southern Cal	6	432,266	72,044
10.	Wisconsin	7	501,482	71,640

1982
		G	Att.	Avg.
1.	Michigan	6	631,746	105,291
2.	**Tennessee**	6	**561,102**	**93,517**
3.	Ohio State	7	623,154	89,022
4.	Penn State	7	588,287	84,041
5.	**Georgia**	6	**490,080**	**81,680**
6.	**LSU**	7	**537,012**	**76,716**
7.	Nebraska	6	457,614	76,269
8.	Oklahoma	6	456,510	76,085
9.	**Florida**	7	**535,432**	**73,855**
10.	Wisconsin	7	497,280	71,040

1983
		G	Att.	Avg.
1.	Michigan	6	626,916	104,486
2.	**Tennessee**	7	**659,059**	**94,151**
3.	Ohio State	6	534,110	89,018
4.	**Georgia**	7	**574,898**	**82,128**
5.	Penn State	7	572,256	81,751
6.	**LSU**	7	**535,432**	**76,490**
7.	Nebraska	6	458,005	76,334
8.	Oklahoma	6	450,048	75,008
9.	**Auburn**	7	**524,065**	**74,866**
10.	Clemson	7	521,898	74,557

1984
		G	Att.	Avg.
1.	Michigan	7	726,734	103,819
2.	**Tennessee**	7	**654,602**	**93,515**
3.	Ohio State	6	536,691	89,449
4.	Penn State	6	511,638	85,273
5.	Texas	6	475,456	79,243
6.	**LSU**	6	**467,746**	**77,958**
7.	**Georgia**	6	**466,884**	**77,814**
8.	Clemson	6	466,077	77,680
9.	Illinois	6	458,397	76,400
10.	Nebraska	6	457,280	76,213

1985
		G	Att.	Avg.
1.	Michigan	6	602,783	100,464
2.	**Tennessee**	7	**658,690**	**94,099**
3.	Ohio State	6	535,284	89,214
4.	Penn State	6	505,895	84,316
5.	**Georgia**	7	**567,888**	**81,127**
6.	Clemson	6	460,413	76,736
7.	Illinois	6	457,639	76,273
8.	Nebraska	7	531,738	75,963
9.	**LSU**	6	**454,182**	**75,697**
10.	Oklahoma	6	446,656	74,443

1986
		G	Att.	Avg.
1.	Michigan	6	631,261	105,210
2.	**Tennessee**	7	**643,317**	**91,902**
3.	Ohio State	6	536,210	89,368
4.	Penn State	7	595,703	85,100
5.	**Georgia**	6	**477,573**	**79,596**
6.	Clemson	5	397,000	79,400
7.	**LSU**	7	**546,471**	**78,067**
8.	Nebraska	6	456,187	76,031
9.	**Florida**	7	**528,188**	**75,455**
10.	Oklahoma	6	450,500	75,083

1987
		G	Att.	Avg.
1.	Michigan	7	731,281	104,469
2.	**Tennessee**	8	**705,434**	**88,179**
3.	Ohio State	6	511,772	85,295
4.	Penn State	7	590,677	84,382
5.	**Georgia**	6	**476,614**	**79,436**
6.	**Auburn**	7	**551,276**	**78,754**
7.	**LSU**	7	**541,238**	**77,320**
8.	Michigan State	6	462,090	77,015
9.	Nebraska	7	533,107	76,158
10.	Clemson	8	602,526	75,316

1988
		G	Att.	Avg.
1.	Michigan	6	628,806	104,801
2.	**Tennessee**	6	**551,677**	**91,946**
3.	Ohio State	6	516,972	86,162
4.	Penn State	6	504,840	84,140
5.	Clemson	6	490,500	81,750
6.	**Georgia**	6	**481,406**	**80,234**
7.	**LSU**	6	**464,006**	**77,334**
8.	Southern Cal	5	380,315	76,063
9.	Michigan State	6	454,950	75,825
10.	**Florida**	7	**517,019**	**73,860**

1989
		G	Att.	Avg.
1.	Michigan	6	632,135	105,356
2.	**Tennessee**	6	**563,502**	**93,917**
3.	Ohio State	6	511,812	85,302
4.	Penn State	6	501,870	83,645
5.	**Auburn**	7	**577,556**	**82,508**
6.	**Georgia**	6	**489,210**	**81,535**
7.	Clemson	6	472,902	78,817
8.	Nebraska	7	457,788	76,298
9.	**Alabama**	6	**438,258**	**73,043**
10.	Michigan State	6	433,896	72,316

1990
		G	Att.	Avg.
1.	Michigan	6	627,048	104,508
2.	**Tennessee**	7	**666,540**	**95,220**
3.	Ohio State	6	512,094	85,349
4.	Penn State	6	511,224	85,204
5.	**Auburn**	7	**569,975**	**81,425**
6.	**Georgia**	6	**481,038**	**80,173**
7.	Clemson	6	475,176	79,196
8.	Nebraska	7	533,673	76,239
9.	Texas	5	380,035	76,007
10.	**Florida**	7	**526,827**	**75,261**

1991
		G	Att.	Avg.
1.	Michigan	6	632,024	105,337
2.	**Tennessee**	6	**578,389**	**96,398**
3.	Penn State	6	575,077	95,846
4.	Ohio State	7	620,845	88,692
5.	**Florida**	6	**506,729**	**84,455**
6.	**Georgia**	7	**577,922**	**82,560**
7.	**Auburn**	7	**552,155**	**78,879**
8.	Nebraska	7	533,715	76,245
9.	**Alabama**	6	**453,094**	**75,516**
10.	Clemson	7	513,915	73,416

1992
		G	Att.	Avg.
1.	Michigan	6	635,201	105,867
2.	**Tennessee**	6	**575,544**	**95,924**
3.	Penn State	6	569,195	94,866
4.	Ohio State	6	555,900	92,650
5.	**Florida**	7	**586,626**	**83,804**
6.	**Georgia**	6	**499,162**	**83,194**
7.	Clemson	6	460,732	76,789
8.	**Alabama**	7	**537,264**	**76,752**
9.	Nebraska	6	457,124	76,187
10.	**Auburn**	7	**510,549**	**72,936**

1993
		G	Att.	Avg.
1.	Michigan	7	739,620	105,660
2.	**Tennessee**	7	**667,280**	**95,326**
3.	Penn State	6	564,190	94,032
4.	Ohio State	6	553,489	92,248
5.	**Florida**	6	**507,072**	**84,512**
6.	**Auburn**	7	**567,506**	**81,072**
7.	**Georgia**	6	**468,457**	**78,076**
8.	**Alabama**	7	**529,765**	**75,681**
9.	Nebraska	7	529,521	75,646
10.	Wisconsin	5	377,537	75,507

SEC Dominates Top 10

Tennessee, Florida, Auburn, Georgia and Alabama notched NCAA Top 10 attendance totals in 1993, marking the third-straight year the SEC earned five Top 10 showings. Over the last six years, SEC schools have made 27 Top 10 appearances to lead all conferences. The Big 10 is second with 16.

1994 SEC Football

Conference Attendance Leaders

1981

	Team	Games	Attendance	Average
Big 10	10	60	3,818,728	63,645
SEC	**10**	**61**	**3,846,492**	**63,057**
Big 8	8	50	2,559,480	51,190
Pac 10	10	59	2,772,237	46,987
SWC	9	54	2,232,757	41,347
ACC	7	40	1,589,152	39,729
WAC	9	51	1,443,515	28,304

1982

	Team	Games	Attendance	Average
Big 10	10	59	3,935,722	66,707
SEC	**10**	**66**	**4,206,507**	**63,735**
Big 8	8	48	2,377,389	49,529
Pac 10	10	59	2,745,676	46,537
SWC	9	52	2,226,009	42,808
ACC	8	41	1,706,451	41,621
WAC	9	53	1,605,684	30,296

1983

	Teams	Games	Attendance	Pct/Capacity	Average
Big 10	10	59	3,710,931	94.1	67,471
SEC	**10**	**65**	**4,214,702**	**98.5**	**64,842**
Big 8	8	49	2,398,184	85.7	48,943
Pac 10	10	58	2,740,406	72.2	47,248
ACC	8	49	2,087,800	88.6	42,608
SWC	9	56	2,292,540	69.3	40,938
WAC	9	52	1,567,062	62.1	30,136

1984

	Teams	Games	Attendance	Pct/Capacity	Average
Big 10	10	58	3,943,802	94.1	67,997
SEC	**10**	**63**	**4,007,351**	**97.0**	**63,609**
Big 8	8	45	2,247,010	86.7	49,934
Pac 10	10	63	2,976,655	70.7	47,248
ACC	8	46	1,998,274	88.9	43,441
SWC	9	53	2,177,507	70.2	41,085
WAC	9	55	1,741,793	69.6	31,669

1985

	Teams	Games	Attendance	Pct/Capacity	Average
Big 10	10	60	4,015,693	93.9	66,928
SEC	**10**	**63**	**4,017,104**	**95.8**	**63,764**
Pac 10	10	56	2,665,356	72.8	47,596
Big 8	8	54	2,504,509	81.6	46,380
ACC	8	48	2,029,574	86.4	42,283
SWC	9	51	2,077,717	68.8	40,740
WAC	9	55	1,744,123	67.3	31,711

1986

	Teams	Games	Attendance	Pct/Capacity	Average
Big 10	10	61	4,006,845	92.8	65,686
SEC	**10**	**69**	**4,351,832**	**94.3**	**63,070**
Pac 10	10	59	2,856,910	73.0	48,422
Big 8	8	49	2,242,082	80.4	45,757
ACC	8	45	1,848,949	86.3	41,088
SWC	9	53	2,006,663	64.3	37,862
WAC	9	51	1,748,857	74.3	34,291

1987

	Teams	Games	Attendance	Pct/Capacity	Average
Big 10	10	61	3,990,524	90.7	65,418
SEC	**10**	**64**	**4,117,046**	**94.1**	**64,329**
Pac 10	10	57	2,866,723	73.0	50,293
Big 8	8	49	2,182,199	80.2	44,535
ACC	8	47	1,970,198	84.2	41,919
SWC	8	48	1,859,454	65.2	38,739
WAC	9	54	1,927,572	77.0	35,696

1988

	Teams	Games	Attendance	Pct/Capacity	Average
SEC	**10**	**62**	**3,912,241**	**91.3**	**63,101**
Big 10	10	59	3,714,231	88.2	62,953
Pac 10	10	60	3,058,637	74.4	50,977
Big 8	8	49	2,184,333	77.9	44,578
ACC	8	47	1,911,949	84.0	40,680
SWC	8	46	1,774,120	65.4	38,568
WAC	9	54	1,795,735	73.0	33,254

1989

	Teams	Games	Attendance	Pct/Capacity	Average
SEC	**10**	**63**	**4,123,005**	**94.5**	**65,445**
Big 10	10	59	3,492,647	83.5	59,197
Pac 10	10	60	3,006,176	71.1	50,103
Big 8	8	49	2,362,465	84.3	48,214
ACC	8	49	2,010,317	84.3	41,027
SWC	9	51	1,914,608	67.8	37,541
WAC	9	55	1,844,999	71.9	33,545

1990

	Teams	Games	Attendance	Pct/Capacity	Average
SEC	**10**	**66**	**4,215,400**	**93.3**	**63,870**
Big 10	10	60	3,533,504	82.6	58,892
Pac 10	10	58	2,872,173	73.7	49,520
Big 8	8	49	2,257,825	79.9	46,078
ACC	8	47	1,988,781	88.3	42,314
SWC	9	53	2,087,248	69.8	39,382
WAC	9	55	1,784,807	70.6	32,451

1991

	Teams	Games	Attendance	Pct/Capacity	Average
SEC	**10**	**61**	**4,063,190**	**95.5**	**66,610**
Big 10	10	61	3,674,654	83.1	60,240
Pac 10	10	59	2,851,991	70.4	48,339
Big 8	8	49	2,308,238	81.6	47,107
ACC	8	51	2,257,413	89.3	44,263
SWC	9	50	2,062,309	72.8	41,246
Big East	8	47	1,788,611	69.7	38,056
WAC	9	55	1,883,861	73.0	34,252

1992

	Teams	Games	Attendance	Pct/Capacity	Average
SEC	**12**	**76**	**4,844,014**	**93.5**	**63,737**
Big 10	10	60	3,600,410	82.4	60,007
Big 8	8	47	2,247,907	82.3	47,828
Pac 10	10	60	2,825,401	70.8	47,090
ACC	9	53	2,332,674	89.9	44,013
Big East	8	48	1,847,269	70.7	38,485
SWC	8	47	1,697,152	64.1	36,110
WAC	10	60	2,111,587	77.6	35,193

1993

	Teams	Games	Attendance	Pct/Capacity	Average
Big 10	11	68	4,320,397	85.9	63,535
SEC	**12**	**78**	**4,897,564**	**91.9**	**62,789**
Pac-10	10	57	2,731,361	69.8	47,919
Big 8	8	48	2,126,247	78.4	44,297
ACC	9	54	2,379,045	86.2	44,056
Big East	8	47	1,787,843	72.6	38,039
SWC	8	45	1,587,652	62.6	35,281

Through The Years

RECORD BOOK

Herschel Walker, who set 11 NCAA, 16 SEC and 41 school records, won the 1982 Heisman Trophy and led Georgia to the 1980 National Championship and a 33-3 mark during his career.

Southeastern Conference Individual Records
TOTAL OFFENSE

PLAYS

GAME:

- 78—Whit Taylor, Vanderbilt vs. Georgia (20 rushes, 58 passes) 1982
- 73—Eric Zeier, Georgia vs. Florida (8 rushes, 65 passes) 1993
- 69—Archie Manning, Ole Miss vs. Southern Miss (13 rushes, 56 passes).......1969
- 68—John Reaves, Florida vs. Auburn (2 rushes, 66 passes) 1969
- 67—Archie Manning, Ole Miss vs. Alabama (15 rushes, 52 passes)................1969
- 66—Andy Kelly, Tennessee vs. Notre Dame (6 rushes, 60 passes).................1990
- 66—Shane Matthews, Florida vs. Florida State (18 rushes, 48 passes)...........1990
- 64—Whit Taylor, Vanderbilt vs. Tennessee (11 rushes, 53 passes)..................1981
- 62—Bubba Wyche, Tennessee vs. Auburn (17 rushes, 45 passes) 1968
- 62—Archie Manning, Ole Miss vs. Southern Miss (23 rushes, 39 passes).......1968
- 62—Joe Reed, Miss. State vs. LSU (9 rushes, 53 passes)...............................1970
- 62—Larry Ochab, Florida vs. Florida State (8 rushes, 54 passes) 1979
- 62—Whit Taylor, Vanderbilt vs. Florida (15 rushes, 47 passes) 1982
- 62—John Gromos, Vanderbilt vs. Alabama (0 rushes, 62 passes)..................1989
- 62—Stan White, Auburn vs. Tennessee (4 rushes, 58 passes).......................1990

SEASON:

- 559—Whit Taylor, Vanderbilt (153 rushes, 406 passes) 1982
- 553—Kurt Page, Vanderbilt (60 rushes, 493 passes)......................................1983
- 536—Shane Matthews, Florida (74 rushes, 463 passes) 1992
- 504—Eric Jones, Vanderbilt (144 rushes, 360 passes)....................................1988
- 502—Don Smith, Miss. State (190 rushes, 312 passes) 1985
- 484—Eric Zeier, Georgia (59 rushes, 425 passes) 1993
- 460—Tommy Pharr, Miss. State (141 rushes, 319 passes) 1968
- 450—Shane Matthews, Florida (72 rushes, 378 passes) 1990
- 449—Joe Reed, Miss. State (115 rushes, 294 passes) 1970
- 428—John Reaves, Florida (32 rushes, 396 passes) 1969
- 421—Whit Taylor, Vanderbilt (64 rushes, 357 passes) 1981
- 418—Andy Kelly, Tennessee (57 rushes, 361 passes) 1991
- 414—Jeff Wickersham, LSU (68 rushes, 346 passes) 1985
- 413—John Reaves, Florida (37 rushes, 376 passes) 1970
- 412—Steve Spurrier, Florida (125 rushes, 287 passes) 1966
- 411—John Fourcade, Ole Miss (125 rushes, 286 passes)...............................1980
- 411—Jeff Francis, Tennessee (97 rushes, 314 passes) 1988
- 411—Shane Matthews, Florida (50 rushes, 361 passes).................................1991

CAREER:

- 1,481—Stan White, Auburn (250 rushes, 1,231 passes) 1990-93
- 1,397—Shane Matthews, Florida (195 rushes, 1,202 passes) 1989-92
- 1,347—Whit Taylor, Vanderbilt (331 rushes, 1,016 passes) 1979-82
- 1,307—Tommy Hodson, LSU (144 rushes, 1,163 passes) 1986-89
- 1,275—John Fourcde, Ole Miss (456 rushes, 819 passes) 1978-81
- 1,247—Kent Austin, Ole Miss (266 rushes, 981 passes) 1981-85
- 1,239—Wayne Peace, Florida (248 rushes, 991 passes) 1980-83
- 1,238—John Reaves, Florida (110 rushes, 1,228 passes)...............................1969-71
- 1,237—John Bond, Miss. State (572 rushes, 665 passes) 1980-83
- 1,223—Don Smith, Miss. State (485 rushing, 748 passing) 1983-86
- 1,181—Jeff Wickersham, LSU (176 rushes, 1,005 passes) 1982-85
- 1,119—Kerwin Bell, Florida (170 rushes, 949 passes) 1984-87
- 1,106—Eric Zeier, Georgia (137 rushes, 969 passes) 1991-present
- 1,075—Archie Manning, Ole Miss (314 rushes, 761 passes).........................1968-70

YARDS GAINED

GAME:

- 540—Archie Manning, Ole Miss vs. Alabama (104 rushing, 436 passing).......1969
- 527—Eric Zeier, Georgia vs. Southern Mississippi (-17 rushing, 544 passing) 1993
- 521—Whit Taylor, Vanderbilt vs. Tennessee (57 rushing, 464 passing)..........1981
- 457—Scott Hunter, Alabama vs. Auburn (-27 rushing, 484 passing) 1969
- 433—Whit Taylor, Vanderbilt vs. Tennessee (42 rushing, 391 passing) 1982
- 433—Tommy Hodson, LSU vs. Tennessee (-5 rushing, 438 passing) 1989
- 428—Danny Wuerffel, Florida vs. Miss. St. (-21 rushing, 449 passing)............1993
- 423—Eric Zeier, Georgia vs. Kentucky (-2 rushing, 425 passing) 1993
- 419—Eric Zeier, Georgia vs. Florida (33 rushing, 386 passing) 1993
- 418—Terry Dean, Florida vs. SW Louisiana (-30 rushing, 448 passing) 1993
- 417—Tony Robinson, Tennessee vs. UCLA (30 rushing, 387 passing)...........1985
- 414—Larry Rakestraw, Georgia vs. Miami (7 rushing, 407 passing) 1963
- 413—John Darnell, Ole Miss vs. Arkansas State (1 rushing, 412 passing).....1989
- 410—Eric Zeier, Georgia vs. Auburn (-16 rushing, 426 passing) 1993
- 408—Dave Marler, Miss. State vs. Alabama (-21 rushing, 429 passing) 1978

- 407—Andy Kelly, Tennessee vs. Notre Dame (8 rushing, 399 passing)..........1990
- 406—Eric Jones, Vanderbilt vs. Duke (64 rushing, 342 passing) 1987
- 405—Pookie Jones, Kentucky vs. Miss. State (48 rushing, 357 passing)........1992
- 400—Jesse Daigle, LSU vs. Miss. State (6 rushing, 394 passing) 1991
- 395—Todd Jordan, Miss. State vs. Florida (-10 rushing, 405 passing) 1993
- 389—Tony Robinson, Tennessee vs. Florida (18 rushing, 371 passing).........1984
- 386—Andy Kelly, Tennessee vs. Florida (-6 rushing, 392 passing) 1991
- 384—Charles Trippi, Georgia vs. Georgia Tech 1945
- 381—Mike Shula, Alabama vs. Memphis State (14 rushing, 367 passing,) 1985

SEASON:

- 3,482—Eric Zeier, Georgia (-43 rushing, 3,525 passing) 1993
- 3,176—Shane Matthews, Florida (-29 rushing, 3,205 passing) 1992
- 3,140—Shane Matthews, Florida (10 rushing, 3,130 passing) 1991
- 3,034—Kurt Page, Vanderbilt (-144 rushing, 3,178 passing) 1983
- 2,925—Shane Matthews, Florida (-27 rushing, 2,952 passing) 1990
- 2,886—Don Smith, Miss. State (554 rushing, 2,332 passing) 1985
- 2,856—Pat Sullivan, Auburn (270 rushing, 2,586 passing) 1970
- 2,853—Eric Jones, Vanderbilt (305 rushing, 2,548 passing) 1988
- 2,852—John Reaves, Florida (-44 rushing, 2,896 passing) 1969
- 2,819—Andy Kelly, Tennessee (60 rushing, 2,759 passing) 1991
- 2,679—Whit Taylor, Vanderbilt (198 rushing, 2,481 passing) 1982
- 2,619—Eric Jones, Vanderbilt (665 rushing, 1,954 passing) 1987
- 2,604—Tommy Hodson, LSU (-51 rushing, 2,655 passing) 1989
- 2,469—Kerwin Bell, Florida (-218 rushing, 2,687 passing) 1985
- 2,436—Jeff Wickersham, LSU (-106 rushing, 2542 passing) 1983
- 2,431—John Reaves, Florida (-118 rushing, 2,549 passing) 1970
- 2,427—Heath Shuler, Tennessee (73 rushing, 2,354 passing) 1993
- 2,401—John Darnell, Ole Miss (75 rushing, 2,326 passing............................1989
- 2,391—Dave Marler, Mississippi State (-31 rushing, 2,422 passing) 1978
- 2,349—Don Smith, Mississippi State (704 rushing, 1,609 passing) 1986
- 2,341—Kurt Page, Vanderbilt (-64 rushing, 2,405 passing) 1984
- 2,329—Walter Lewis, Alabama (338 rushing, 1,991 passing) 1983
- 2,325—Gary Hollingsworth, Alabama (-54 rushing, 2,379 passing) 1989
- 2,299—John Fourcade, Ole Miss (402 rushing, 1,897 passing) 1980
- 2,289—Jeff Francis, Tennessee (52 rushing, 2,237 passing) 1988
- 2,264—Archie Manning, Ole Miss (502 rushing, 1762 passing) 1969

CAREER:

- 9,241—Shane Matthews, Florida (-46 rushing, 9,287 passing) 1989-92
- 8,938—Tommy Hodson, LSU (-177 rushing, 9,115 passing) 1986-89
- 7,920—Stan White, Auburn (-96 rushing, 8,016 passing) 1990-93
- 7,384—Eric Zeier, Georgia (-373 rushing, 7,757 passing) 1991-present
- 7,213—John Reaves, Florida (-366 rushing, 7,549 passing) 1969-71
- 7,097—Don Smith, Miss. State (1,868 rushing, 5,229 passing) 1983-86
- 7,032—Kerwin Bell, Florida (-533 rushing, 7,585 passing) 1984-87
- 6,946—Wayne Peace, Florida (-260 rushing, 7,206 passing) 1980-83
- 6,901—John Bond, Miss. State (2,280 rushing, 4,621 passing) 1980-83
- 6,843—Pat Sullivan, Auburn (569 rushing, 6,284 passing) 1969-71
- 6,727—Whit Taylor, Vanderbilt (420 rushing, 6,307 passing) 1979-82
- 6,713—John Fourcade, Ole Miss (1,301 rushing, 5,412 passing) 1978-81
- 6,705—Jeff Wickersham, LSU (6,921 rushing, 216 passing) 1982-85
- 6,427—Andy Kelly, Tennessee (30 rushing, 6,397 passing) 1988-91
- 6,240—Eric Jones, Vanderbilt (1,211 rushing, 5,029 passing) 1986-88
- 6,179—Kent Austin, Ole Miss (-5 rushing, 6,184 passing) 1981-85
- 6,008—Kurt Page, Vanderbilt (-225 rushing, 6,233 passing) 1981-84
- 5,900—Jeff Francis, Tennessee (33 rushing, 5,867 passing) 1985-88
- 5,690—Walter Lewis, Alabama (1,433 rushing, 4,257 passing) 1980-83
- 5,576—Archie Manning, Ole Miss (823 rushing, 4,753 passing) 1968-70
- 5,456—Bill Ransdell, Kentucky (-108 rushing, 5,564 passing) 1983-86
- 5,290—Steve Spurrier, Florida (442 rushing, 4,848 passing) 1964-66

YARDS PER GAME

SEASON:

- 316.6—Eric Zeier, Georgia (-43 rush, 3,525 pass, 11 games) 1993
- 285.6—Pat Sullivan, Auburn (270 rush, 2,586 pass, 10 games) 1970
- 285.5—Shane Matthews, Florida (10 rush, 3,130 pass, 11 games) 1991
- 285.2—John Reaves, Florida (-44 rush, 2,896 pass, 10 games) 1969
- 275.8—Kurt Page, Vanderbilt (-144 rush, 3,178 pass, 11 games) 1983
- 262.4—Don Smith, Miss. State (554 rush, 2,332 pass, 11 games) 1985
- 265.9—Shane Matthews, Florida (-27 rush, 2,952 pass, 11 games) 1990
- 264.7—Shane Matthews, Florida (-29 rush, 3,205 pass, 12 games) 1992
- 259.4—Eric Jones, Vanderbilt (305 rush, 2,548 pass, 11 games) 1988

208 Record Book

250.3— Whit Taylor, Vanderbilt (-65 rush, 2,318 pass, 9 games) 1981
243.5— Whit Taylor, Vanderbilt (198 rush, 2,481 pass, 11 games) 1982
238.1— Eric Jones, Vanderbilt (665 rush, 1,954 pass, 11 games) 1987
236.7— Tommy Hodson, LSU (-51 rush, 2,655 pass, 11 games) 1989
226.4— Archie Manning, Ole Miss (502 rush, 1,762 pass, 10 games.................1969
224.5— Kerwin Bell, Florida (-218 rush, 2,687 pass) 1985
221.5— Jeff Wickersham, LSU (-106 rush, 2,542 pass, 11 games) 1983
221.0— John Reaves, Florida (-118 rush, 2,549 pass, 11 games) 1970

CAREER:
264.0— Shane Matthews, Florida (9,241 yards in 35 games) 1989-92
228.1— Pat Sullivan, Auburn (6,844 yards in 30 games) 1969-71
227.6— John Reaves, Florida (7,283 yards in 32 games) 1969-71
223.8— Eric Zeier, Georgia (7,384 yards in 33 games) 1991-present
206.5— Archie Manning, Ole Miss (5,576 yards in 27 games) 1968-70
203.1— Tommy Hodson, LSU (8,938 yards in 44 games) 1986-89
195.0— Eric Jones, Vanderbilt (6,240 yards in 32 games) 1986-88
180.0— Stan White, Auburn (7,920 yards in 44 games) 1990-93
176.4— Jeff Wickersham, LSU (6,705 yards in 38 games) 1982-85
176.3— Steve Spurrier, Florida (5,290 yards in 30 games) 1964-66
173.5— Jeff Francis, Tennessee (5,900 yards in 34 games) 1985-88
170.9— Scott Hunter, Alabama (4,785 yards in 28 games) 1968-70
170.9— Gary Hollingsworth, Alabama (3,759 yards in 22 games) 1989-90
167.4— Kerwin Bell, Florida (7,032 yards in 42 games) 1984-87
166.9— Wayne Peace, Florida (6,946 yards in 41 games) 1980-83
165.6— Heath Shuler, Tennessee (4,472 yards in 27 games) 1991-93
165.0— Don Smith, Miss. State (7,097 yards in 43 games) 1983-86
164.1— Whit Taylor, Vanderbilt (6,727 yards in 42 games) 1979-82
162.6— Kent Austin, Ole Miss (6,179 yards in 38 games) 1981-85
160.4— Tony Robinson, Tennessee (3,529 yards in 22 games) 1982-85

YARDS PER PLAY

GAME: (Min. 10 plays)
21.4— Eagle Day, Ole Miss vs. Villanova (10 for 214) 1954
19.9— Parker Hall, Ole Miss vs. Sewanee (10 for 199) 1938

GAME: (Min. 20 plays)
13.2— Eric Zeier, Georgia vs. Texas Tech (23 for 303) 1993
12.8— Pat Sullivan, Auburn vs. Florida (30 for 384) 1970
12.3— Herschel Walker, Georgia vs. Vanderbilt (23 for 283) 1980
12.3— Eric Zeier, Georgia vs. Kentucky (24 for 294) 1991
11.8— Johnny Dottley, Ole Miss vs. Chattanooga (20 for 235) 1949
11.7— Garrison Hearst, Georgia vs. Vanderbilt (21 for 246).......................1992
10.9— Bert Jones, LSU vs. Auburn (22 for 240) 1972
10.8— John Bond, Miss. State vs. Ole Miss (29 for 314) 1980

GAME: (Min. 40 plays)
10.8— Eric Zeier, Georgia vs. Southern Miss. (49 for 527) 1993
8.8— Eric Zeier, Georgia vs. Kentucky (48 for 423) 1993
8.6— Eric Jones, Vanderbilt vs. Rutgers (43 for 368) 1987
8.4— Larry Rakestraw, Georgia vs. Miami (49 for 414) 1963
8.4— John Darnell, Ole Miss vs. Arkansas State (49 for 413) 1989
8.4— Pookie Jones, Kentucky vs. Miss. State (48 for 405) 1992
8.4— Todd Jordan, Miss. State vs. Florida (47 for 395) 1993

GAME: (Min. 50 plays)
8.14— Whit Taylor, Vanderbilt vs. Tennessee (64 for 521) 1981
8.06— Archie Manning, Ole Miss vs. Alabama (67 for 540) 1969

SEASON: (Min. 300 plays)
8.57— Pat Sullivan, Auburn (333 for 2,856) 1970
7.33— Heath Shuler, Tennessee (331 for 2,427) 1993
7.22— Kerwin Bell, Florida (342 for 2,469) 1985
7.19— Eric Zeier, Georgia (484 for 3,482) 1993
7.17— Scott Hunter, Alabama (301 for 2,157) 1969
6.98— Tommy Hodson, LSU (373 for 2,604) 1989
6.91— Tom Hodson, LSU (321 for 2,219) 1986
6.73— John Bond, Miss. State (327 for 2,200) 1982
6.67— John Reaves, Florida (428 for 2,852) 1969
6.52— Wayne Peace, Florida (301 for 1,963) 1982
6.50— Shane Matthews, Florida (450 for 2,925) 1990
6.42— Eric Jones, Vanderbilt (408 for 2,619) 1987

6.41— Frank Sinkwich, Georgia (341 for 2,187) 1942
6.39— Pat Sullivan, Auburn (328 for 2,096) 1971

CAREER:: (Min. 900 plays)
7.03— Pat Sullivan, Auburn (974 for 6,844) 1969-71
6.68— Eric Zeier, Georgia (1,106 for 7,384) 1991-present
6.61— Shane Matthews, Florida (1,397 for 9,241) 1989-92
6.54— Andy Kelly, Tennessee (982 for 6,427) 1988-91
6.28— Kerwin Bell, Florida (1,119 for 7,032) 1984-87
6.17— Jeff Francis, Tennessee (956 for 5,900) 1985-88
5.94— Eric Jones, Vanderbilt (1,050 for 6,240) 1986-88
5.88— John Reaves, Florida (1,238 for 7,283) 1969-71
5.80— Don Smith, Miss. State (1,223 for 7,097) 1983-86
5.71— Kurt Page, Vanderbilt (1,052 for 6,008) 1981-84
5.68— Jeff Wickersham, LSU (1,181 for 6,705) 1982-85
5.61— Wayne Peace, Florida (1,239 for 6,946) 1980-83
5.58— John Bond, Miss. State (1,237 for 6,901) 1980-83
5.47— Bill Ransdell, Kentucky (996 for 5,456) 1983-86
5.35— Stan White, Auburn (1,481 for 7,920) 1990-93
5.32— Steve Spurrier, Florida (995 for 5,290) 1964-66
5.29— Herschel Walker, Georgia (994 for 5,259) 1980-82
5.27— John Fourcade, Ole Miss (1,275 for 6,713) 1978-81

TOUCHDOWN RESPONSIBILITY

GAME:
7— Showboat Boykin, Ole Miss vs. Miss. State (all rushing) 1951
6— Charles Conerly, Ole Miss vs. Tennessee (2 rushing, 4 passing) 1947
6— Jackie Parker, Miss. State vs. Auburn (3 rushing, 3 passing) 1952
6— Terry Dean, Florida vs. SW Louisiana (all passing) 1993

SEASON:
30— Shane Matthews, Florida (1 rushing, 28 passing, 1 receiving) 1991
28— Babe Parilli, Kentucky (5 rushing, 23 passing) 1950
28— Heath Shuler, Tennessee (3 rushing, 25 passing) 1993
27— Frank Sinkwich, Georgia (17 rushing, 10 passing) 1942
27— Charles Conerly, Ole Miss (9 rushing, 18 passing) 1947
27— Shane Matthews, Florida (4 rushing, 23 passing) 1990
26— Pat Sullivan, Auburn (9 rushing, 17 passing) 1970
25— John Reaves, Florida (1 rushing, 24 passing) 1969
25— Shane Matthews, Florida (2 rushing, 23 passing) 1992
25— Eric Zeier, Georgia (1 rushing, 24 passing) 1993
24— Jackie Parker, Miss. State (16 rushing, 8 passing) 1952
24— Whit Taylor, Vanderbilt (2 rushing, 22 passing) 1982
24— Tommy Hodson, LSU (2 rushing, 22 passing) 1989
23— Archie Manning, Ole Miss (14 rushing, 9 passing) 1969
22— Harry Gilmer, Alabama (9 rushing, 13 passing) 1945
22— Pat Sullivan, Auburn (2 rushing, 20 passing) 1971
22— Parker Hall, Ole Miss (11 rushing, 11 passing) 1938
22— Eric Jones, Vanderbilt (6 rushing, 16 passing) 1987

CAREER:
82— Shane Matthews, Florida (7 rushing, 74 passing, 1 receiving) 1989-92
71— Pat Sullivan, Auburn (18 rushing, 53 passing) 1969-71
71— Tommy Hodson, LSU (2 rushing, 69 passing) 1986-89
60— Frank Sinkwich, Georgia (30 rushing, 30 passing) 1940-42
60— Kerwin Bell, Florida (4 rushing, 56 passing) 1984-87
58— John Reaves, Florida (4 rushing, 54 passing) 1969-71
57— Babe Parilli, Kentucky (7 rushing, 50 passing) 1949-51
56— Archie Manning, Ole Miss (25 rushing, 31 passing) 1968-70
53— Harry Gilmer, Alabama (19 rushing, 29 passing, 2PR, 1 INT. RET,
      1 KOR) 1944-47
52— Herschel Walker, Georgia (49 rushing, 3 receiving) 1980-82
52— Don Smith, Miss. State (21 rushing, 31 passing) 1983-86
51— Stan White, Auburn (11 rushing, 40 passing) 1990-93
50— Dalton Hilliard, LSU (44 rushing, 6 receiving) 1982-85
50— Heath Shuler, Tennessee (14 rushing, 36 passing) 1991-93
47— John Fourcade, Ole Miss (22 rushing, 25 passing) 1978-81
46— Whit Taylor, Vanderbilt (5 rushing, 41 passing) 1979-82
46— Eric Zeier, Georgia (3 rushing, 43 passing) 1991-present
45— Johnny Rauch, Georgia (12 rushing, 33 passing) 1946-48
45— Eric Jones, Vanderbilt (13 rushing, 32 passing) 1986-88

1994 SEC Football

RUSHING

MOST RUSHES

GAME:

47—Herschel Walker, Georgia vs. Florida (192 yards) 1981
43—Charles Alexander, LSU vs. Wyoming (231 yards) 1977
43—Herschel Walker, Georgia vs. South Carolina (219 yards) 1980
42—Johnny Musso, Alabama vs. Auburn (221 yards) 1970
41—Charles Alexander, LSU vs. Tulane (199 yards) 1977
41—Herschel Walker, Georgia vs. Ole Miss (265 yards) 1981
41—Johnnie Jones, Tennessee vs. Rutgers (234 yards) 1983
41—Errict Rhett, Florida vs. Georgia (183 yards) 1993
40—Johnny Dottley, Ole Miss vs. Miss. State (216 yards) 1949
40—Charles Alexander, LSU vs. Florida (156 yards) 1978
40—Michael Davis, Miss. State vs. Ole Miss (154 yards) 1993

SEASON:

385—Herschel Walker, Georgia (1,891 yards) 1981
335—Herschel Walker, Georgia (1,752 yards) 1982
311—Charles Alexander, LSU (1,686 yards) 1977
287—Willie McClendon, Georgia (1,312 yards) 1978
284—Emmitt Smith, Florida (1,599 yards) 1989
281—Charles Alexander, LSU (1,172 yards) 1978
278—Bo Jackson, Auburn (1,786 yards) 1985
274—Herschel Walker, Georgia (1,616 yards) 1980
261—James Brooks, Auburn (1,314 yards) 1980

CAREER:

*994—Herschel Walker, Georgia (5,259 yards) 1980-82
882—Dalton Hilliard, LSU (4,050 yards) 1982-85
873—Errict Rhett, Florida (4,163 yards) 1989-93
855—Charles Alexander, LSU (4,035 yards) 1975-78
777—Sonny Collins, Kentucky (3,835 yards) 1972-75
700—Emmitt Smith, Florida (3,928 yards) 1987-89
657—Joe Cribbs, Auburn (3,368 yards) 1976-79
650—Bo Jackson, Auburn (4,303 yards) 1982-85
639—Neal Anderson, Florida (3,234 yards) 1982-85
638—George Adams, Kentucky (2,648 yards) 1981-84
621—James Brooks, Auburn (3,523 yards) 1977-80

RUSHES PER GAME

SEASON:

35.0—Herschel Walker, (385 in 11 games) 1981
30.4—Herschel Walker, Georgia (335 in 11 games) 1982
28.3—Charles Alexander, LSU (311 in 11 games) 1977
26.1—Willie McClendon, Georgia (287 in 11 games) 1978
25.8—Emmitt Smith, Florida (284 in 11 games) 1989
25.5—Charles Alexander, LSU (281 in 11 games) 1978
25.3—Joe Cribbs, Auburn (253 in 11 games) 1978
25.2—Bo Jackson, Auburn (278 in 11 games) 1985
24.9—Herschel Walker, Georgia (274 in 11 games) 1980
24.0—Terry Henley, Auburn (216 in 9 games) 1972

CAREER:

30.1—Herschel Walker, Georgia (994 in 33 games) 1980-82
22.5—Emmitt Smith, Florida (700 in 31 games) 1987-89
20.0—Dalton Hilliard, LSU (882 in 44 games) 1982-85
19.4—Charles Alexander, LSU (855 in 44 games) 1975-78
19.1—Johnny Musso, Alabama (574 in 30 games) 1969-71
18.9—Sonny Collins, Kentucky (777 in 41 games) 1972-75
18.6—Siran Stacy, Alabama (429 in 23 games) 1989-91
17.9—Errict Rhett, Florida (626 in 35 games) 1989-92
17.6—Kevin McLee, Georgia (562 in 32 games) 1975-77
17.6—Bobby Humphrey, Alabama (615 in 35 games) 1985-88
17.3—Larry Smith, Florida (520 in 30 games) 1966-68
17.2—Joe Cribbs, Auburn (657 in 38 games) 1976-79
17.1—Bo Jackson, Auburn (650 in 38 games) 1982-85
*—NCAA record for three years

YARDS GAINED

GAME:

321—Frank Mordica, Vanderbilt vs. Air Force (22 rushes) 1978
316—Emmitt Smith, Florida vs. New Mexico (31 rushes) 1989
307—Curtis Kuykendall, Auburn vs. Miami (33 rushes) 1944
294—Chuck Webb, Tennessee vs. Ole Miss (35 rushes) 1989
290—Bo Jackson, Auburn vs. SW Louisiana (23 rushes) 985
284—Bobby Humphrey, Alabama vs. Miss. State (30 rushes) 1986
283—Herschel Walker, Georgia vs. Vanderbilt (22 rushes) 1980
267—Bob Davis, Kentucky vs. Washington & Lee 1937
265—Herschel Walker, Georgia vs. Ole Miss (41 rushes) 1981
256—Bo Jackson, Auburn vs. Alabama (20 rushes) 1983
250—Joe Cribbs, Auburn vs. Georgia (34 rushes) 1978
248—Johnnie Jones, Tennessee vs. Vanderbilt (30 rushes) 1983
248—Tony Thompson, Tennessee vs. Miss. State (22 rushes) 1990
246—Bob Davis, Kentucky vs. Maryville 1936
246—Garrison Hearst, Georgia vs. Vanderbilt (21 rushes) 1992
242—Bo Jackson, Auburn vs. Georgia Tech (32 rushes) 1985
241—Randy Baldwin, Ole Miss vs. Tulane (17 rushes) 1990
240—Bo Jackson, Auburn vs. Ole Miss (38 rushes) 1985
239—Charles Trippi, Georgia vs. Florida 1945
238—Herschel Walker, Georgia vs. Florida (37 rushes) 1980
238—Ivy Joe Hunter, Kentucky vs. Vanderbilt (30 rushes) 1986

SEASON:

1,891—Herschel Walker, Georgia (385 rushes) 1981
1,786—Bo Jackson, Auburn (278 rushes) 1985
1,752—Herschel Walker, Georgia (335 rushes) 1982
1,686—Charles Alexander, LSU (311 rushes) 1977
1,616—Herschel Walker, Georgia (274 rushes) 1980
1,599—Emmitt Smith, Florida (284 rushes) 1989
1,547—Garrison Hearst, Georgia (228 rushes) 1992
1,471—Bobby Humphrey, Alabama (236 rushes) 1986
1,391—Brent Fullwood, Auburn (167 rushes) 1986
1.341—Emmitt Smith, Florida (229 rushes) 1987
1,314—James Brooks, Auburn (261 rushes) 1980
1,312—Johnny Dottley, Ole Miss (208 rushes) 1949
1,312—Willie McClendon, Georgia (287 rushes) 1978
1,307—Jimmy Dubose, Florida (191 rushes) 1975

CAREER:

*5,259—Herschel Walker, Georgia (33 games) 1980-82
4,303—Bo Jackson, Auburn (38 games) 1982-85
4,163—Errict Rhett, Florida (48 games) 1989-93
4,050—Dalton Hilliard, LSU (44 games) 1982-85
4,035—Charles Alexander, LSU (44 games) 1975-78
3,928—Emmitt Smith, Florida (31 games) 1987-89
3,835—Sonny Collins, Kentucky (41 games) 1972-75
3,523—James Brooks, Auburn (38 games) 1977-80
3,420—Bobby Humphrey, Alabama (35 games) 1985-88
3,368—Joe Cribbs, Auburn (38 games) 1976-79
3,234—Neal Anderson, Florida (44 games) 1982-85
3,232—Garrison Hearst, Georgia (33 games) 1990-92
3,095—Eddie Price, Tulane (39 games) 1946-49
3,017—Lars Tate, Georgia (42 games) 1984-87
2,904—Harvey Williams, LSU (40 games) 1986-90
2,892—Mark Higgs, Kentucky (42 games) 1984-87
2,852—Johnnie Jones, Tennessee (34 games) 1981-84
2,820—Walter Packer, Miss. State (43 games) 1973-76
2,789—Brent Fullwood, Auburn (39 games) 1983-86
2,741—Johnny Musso, Alabama (30 games) 1969-71
*—NCAA record for three years

YARDS PER GAME

SEASON:

171.9—Herschel Walker, Georgia (1,891 in 11 games) 1981
162.4—Bo Jackson, Auburn (1,786 in 11 games) 1985
159.3—Herschel Walker, Georgia (1,752 in 11 games) 1982
153.3—Charles Alexander, LSU (1,686 in 11 games) 1977
146.9—Herschel Walker, Georgia (1,616 in 11 games) 1980
145.4—Emmitt Smith, Florida (1,599 in 11 games) 1989
140.6—Garrison Hearst, Georgia (1,547 in 11 games) 1992
131.2—Johnny Dottley, Ole Miss (1,312 in 10 games) 1949
126.5—Brent Fullwood, Auburn (1,391 in 11 games) 1986
123.6—Chuck Webb, Tennessee (1,236 in 10 games) 1989
122.6—Bobby Humphrey, Alabama (1,471 in 12 games) 1986
121.9—Emmitt Smith, Florida (1,341 in 11 games) 1987
120.5—Joe Cribbs, Auburn (1,205 in 10 games) 1978
119.5—James Brooks, Auburn (1,314 in 11 games) 1980
119.3—Willie McClendon, Georgia (1,312 in 11 games) 1978

CAREER:

159.4—Herschel Walker, Georgia (5,259 in 33 games) 1980-82
126.7—Emmitt Smith, Florida (3,928 in 31 games) 1987-89
113.2—Bo Jackson, Auburn (4,303 in 38 games) 1982-85
97.9—Garrison Hearst, Georgia (3,232 in 33 games) 1990-92
97.7—Bobby Humphrey (3,420 in 35 games) 1985-88
95.0—Charlie Garner, Tennessee (2,089 in 22 games) 1992-93
93.5—Sonny Collins, Kentucky (3,835 in 41 games) 1972-75
92.7—James Brooks, Auburn (3,523 on 38 games) 1977-80
92.0—Dalton Hilliard, LSU (4,050 on 44 games) 1982-85
91.7—Charles Alexander, LSU (4,935 on 44 games) 1975-78

210 Record Book

91.4—Johnny Musso, Alabama (2,741 on 30 games) 1969-71
89.9—Curtis Kuykendall, Auburn (1,619 on 18 games) 1944-45
88.6—Joe Cribbs, Auburn (3,368 on 38 games) 1976-79
86.7—Errict Rhett, Florida (4,163 on 48 games) 1989-93
86.1—Rodney Hampton, Georgia (2,668 on 31 games) 1987-89
85.3—Bobby Marlow, Alabama (2,560 on 30 games) 1950-52

YARDS PER RUSH
GAME: (Min. 40 rushes)
6.5 — Herschel Walker, Georgia vs. Ole Miss (265 on 41) 1981
5.7 — Johnnie Jones, Tennessee vs. Rutgers (234 on 41) 1983
5.4 — Johnny Dottley, Ole Miss vs. Miss. State (216 on 40) 1949
5.37—Charles Alexander, LSU vs. Wyoming (231 on 43) 1977
5.3 — Johnny Musso, Alabama vs. Auburn (221 on 42) 1970
GAME: (Min. 30 rushes)
10.2— Emmitt Smith, Florida vs. New Mexico (316 on 31) 1989
9.5— Bobby Humphrey, Alabama vs. Miss State (284 on 30) 1986
9.3— Curtis Kuykendall, Auburn vs. Miami (307 on 33) 1944
8.4— Chuck Webb, Tennessee vs. Ole Miss (294 on 35) 1989
8.3— Johnnie Jones, Tennessee vs. Vanderbilt (248 on 30) 1983
7.6— Charles Alexander, LSU vs. Oregon (237 on 31) 1977
7.5— Bo Jackson, Auburn vs. Georgia Tech (242 on 32) 1985
GAME: (Min. 20 rushes)
14.6—Frank Mordica, Vanderbilt vs. Air Force (321 on 22)1978
12.9—Herschel Walker, Georgia vs. Vanderbilt (283 on 22) 1980
12.8— Bo Jackson, Auburn vs. Alabama (256 on 20) 1983
12.6— Bo Jackson, Auburn vs. SW Louisiana (290 on 23) 1985
11.8— Johnny Dottley, Ole Miss vs. Chattanooga (235 on 20) 1949
11.7— Garrison Hearst, Georgia vs. Vanderbilt (246 on 21) 1992
11.3— Tony Thompson, Tennessee vs. Miss. State (248 on 22) 1990
10.5— Johnny Dottley, Ole Miss vs. TCU (230 on 22) 1949
GAME: (Min. 10 rushes)
19.6 — Harvey Williams, LSU vs. Rice (196 on 10) 1987
17.5 — George Canale, Tennessee vs. Chattanooga (175 on 10) 1962
17.45—Billy Baggett, LSU vs. Ole Miss (192 on 11) 1950
16.2— Tony Green, Florida vs. Maryland (162 on 10) 1974
15.2— Johnny Dottley, Ole Miss vs. Boston College (182 on 12) 1950
SEASON: (Min. 200 rushes)
6.8— Garrison Hearst, Georgia (1,547 on 228) 1992
6.4— Bo Jackson, Auburn (1,786 on 278) 1985
6.3— Johnny Dottley, Ole Miss (1,312 on 208) 1949
6.2— Bobby Humphrey, Alabama (1,471 on 236) 1986
5.9— Herschel Walker, Georgia (1,616 on 274) 1980
5.9— Emmitt Smith, Florida (1,341 on 229) 1987
5.9— Chuck Webb, Tennessee (1,236 on 209) 1989
5.8— Tony Thompson, Tennessee (1,261 on 219) 1990
5.6— Johnnie Jones, Tennessee (1,290 on 229) 1984
5.6— Joe Cribbs, Auburn (1,120 on 200) 1979
5.6— Emmitt Smith, Florida (1,599 on 284) 1989
5.4— Charles Alexander, LSU (1,686 on 311) 1977
5.4— Sonny Collins, Kentucky (1,213 on 224) 1973
SEASON: (Min. 100 rushes)
8.3— Brent Fullwood, Auburn (1,391 on 167) 1986
7.9— Hank Lauricella, Tennessee (881 on 111) 1951
7.7— Bo Jackson, Auburn (1,213 on 158) 1983
7.6— Monk Gafford, Auburn (1,004 on 132) 1942
7.5— Bobby Marlow, Alabama (882 on 118) 1950
7.4— James Brooks, Auburn (1,208 on 163) 1979
7.3— Charles Hunsinger, Florida (842 on 115) 1948
7.3— Charlie Garner, Tennessee (1,161 on 159) 1993
CAREER: (MIN. 400 rushes)
6.6— Bo Jackson, Auburn (4,303 on 650) 1982-85
6.3— Bobby Marlow, Alabama (2,560 on 480) 1950-52
6.0— Micheal Haddix, Miss. State (2,558 on 425) 1979-82
6.0— Garrison Hearst, Georgia (3,232 on 543) 1990-92
5.8— Walter Packer, Miss. State (2,820 on 483) 1973-76
5.8— Tony Green, Florida (2,590 on 445) 1974-77
5.7— James Brooks, Auburn (3,523 on 621) 1977-80
5.7— Rodney Hampton, Georgia (2,668 on 472) 1987-89
5.6— Bobby Humphrey, Alabama (3,420 on 615) 1985-88
5.6— Emmitt Smith, Florida (3,828 on 700) 1987-89
5.6— Johnny Davis, Alabama (2,519 on 447) 1974-77
5.5— Johnnie Jones, Tennessee (2,852 on 517) 1981-84
5.3— Herschel Walker, Georgia (5,259 on 994) 1980-82
5.3— Reggie Cobb, Tennessee (2,360 on 445) 1987-89
5.1— Joe Gribbs, Auburn (3,368 on 657) 1976-79

4.9— Sonny Collins, Kentucky (3,835 on 777) 1972-75
4.9— Neal Anderson, Florida (3,234 on 639) 1982-85
4.9— Lars Tate, Georgia (3,017 on 615) 1984-87
4.9— Siran Stacy, Alabama (2,105 on 429) 1989-91
4.9— Harvey Williams, LSU (2,860 on 588) 1986-90
4.8— Frank Mordica, Vanderbilt (2,632 on 546) 1976-79
4.8— Johnny Musso, Alabama (2,741 on 574) 1969-71
4.7— Charles Alexander, LSU (4,035 on 855) 1975-78

TOUCHDOWNS RUSHING
SEASON:
19—Garrison Hearst, Georgia 1992
18—Herschel Walker, Georgia 1981
17—Charles Alexander, LSU 1977
17—Bo Jackson, Auburn 1985
17—Reggie Cobb, Tennessee 1987
17—Tim Worley, Georgia 1988
17—Siran Stacy, Alabama 1989
16—Jackie Parker, Miss. State 1952
16—Johnny Musso, Alabama 1971
16—Joe Cribbs, Auburn 1978
16—Herschel Walker, Georgia 1982
16—Lars Tate, Georgia 1986
16—Tony Thompson, Tennessee 1990
CAREER:
49—Herschel Walker, Georgia 1980-82
44—Dalton Hilliard, LSU 1982-85
43—Bo Jackson, Auburn 1982-85
40—Charles Alexander, LSU 1975-78
36—Lars Tate, Georgia 1984-87
36—Emmitt Smith, Florida 1987-89
34—Johnny Musso, Alabama 1969-71
34—Joe Cribbs, Auburn 1976-79
34—Errict Rhett, Florida 1990-93
33—Bobby Humphrey, Alabama 1985-88
33—Garrison Hearst, Georgia 1990-92
32—Charles Trippi, Georgia 1942, 1945-46
30—Bob Davis, Kentucky 1935-37
30—Neal Anderson, Florida 1982-85
29—Terry Robiskie, LSU 1973-76
29—Tony Nathan, Alabama 1975-78
28—Frank Sinkwich, Georgia 1942-45
28—Siran Stacy, Alabama 1989-91

LONG TOUCHDOWN PLAYS (RUSHING)
GAME:
99—Kelsey Finch, Tennessee vs. Florida 1977
98—Stanley Howell, Miss. State vs. Southern Miss 1979
97—Blondy Black, Miss. State vs. Duquesne 1942
96—Emmitt Smith, Florida vs. Miss. State 1988
96—Chris Anderson, Alabama vs. Temple 1991
95—Harry Gilmer, Alabama vs. Kentucky 1945
94—Jessie Fatherree, LSU vs. Georgia 1935
94—Sal Nicolo, LSU vs. Rice 1952
92—Ralph O'Gwynne, Auburn vs. Loyola 1936
92—Bobby Marlow, Alabama vs. Georgia Tech 1952
91—Harry Jones, Kentucky vs. George Washington 1951
91—Willie Wilder, Florida vs. Miss. State 1976

ALL-PURPOSE YARDS
SEASON:
187.9—Herschel Walker, Georgia (1,891 rush, 84 rec.,
 92 KOR in 11 games) 1981
173.6—Garrison Hearst, Georgia (1,547 rush, 324 rec., 39 KOR) 1992
170.6—Herschel Walker, Georgia (1,752 rush, 89 rec.,
 36 KOR in 11 games) 1982
169.0—Bo Jackson, Auburn (1,786 rush, 73 rec., in 11 games) 1985
168.0—Bobby Humphrey, Alabama (1,471 rush, 201 rec.,
 344 KOR in 12 games) 1986
CAREER:
5,749—Herschel Walker, Georgia (5,249 rush, 243 rec., 247 KOR) 1980-82
5,596—James Brooks, Auburn (3,523 rush, 347 rec., 1,726 KOR) 1977-80
5,393—Errict Rhett, Florida (4,163 rush, 1,230 rec.) 1990-93
5,326—Dalton Hilliard, LSU (4,050 rush, 1,133 rec., 143 KOR) 1982-85
4,958—Bobby Humphrey, Alabama (3,420 rush, 523 rec., 1,015 KOR) 1985-88
4,892—Bo Jackson, Auburn (4,363 rush, 272 rec., 317 KOR) 1982-85

1994 SEC Football

PASSING

ATTEMPTS
GAME:
- 66—John Reaves, Florida vs. Auburn (33 comp., 369 yds.)..................1969
- 66—Eric Zeier, Georgia vs. Florida (36 comp., 386 yards)....................1993
- 62—John Gromos, Vanderbilt vs. Alabma (30 comp., 324 yds.)............1989
- 60—Andy Kelly, Tennessee vs. Notre Dame (35 comp., 399 yards)........1990
- 58—Whit Taylor, Vanderbilt vs. Georgia (27 comp., 257 yds.).............1982
- 58—Stan White, Auburn vs. Tennessee (30 comp., 338 yards)..............1990
- 56—Archie Manning, Ole Miss vs. Southern Miss (30 comp., 369 yds.)..1970
- 56—Kurt Page, Vanderbilt vs. Georgia (33 comp., 303 yards)..............1983
- 56—Bill Ransdell, Kentucky vs. Vanderbilt (30 comp., 322 yds.).........1985
- 56—Andy Kelly, Tennessee vs. Florida (33 comp., 392 yds.)...............1991
- 55—Scott Hunter, Alabama vs. Auburn (30 comp., 484 yds.)..............1969
- 55—Andy Kelly, Tennessee vs. Colorado (33 comp., 368 yds.)............1990
- 54—Larry Ochab, Florida vs. Florida State (22 comp., 270 yds.).........1979
- 53—John Reaves, Florida vs. Tulane (29 comp., 297 yds.).................1969
- 53—John Reaves, Florida vs. N.C. State (21 comp., 214 yds.)............1970
- 53—Joe Reed, Miss. State vs. LSU (24 comp., 248 yds.)....................1970
- 53—Whit Taylor, Vanderbilt vs. Tennessee (29 comp., 464 yds.).........1981
- 53—Eric Zeier, Georgia vs. Auburn (34 comp., 426 yards) 1993

SEASON:
- 493—Kurt Page, Vanderbilt (286 comp., 3,178 yds.)..........................1983
- 463—Shane Matthews, Florida (275 comp., 3,205 yds.).....................1992
- 425—Eric Zeier, Georgia (269 comp., 3,525 yards)............................1993
- 406—Whit Taylor, Vanderbilt (228 comp., 2,481 yds.).......................1982
- 396—John Reaves, Florida (222 comp., 2,896 yds.)..........................1969
- 378—Shane Matthews, Florida (229 comp., 2,952 yds.)....................1990
- 376—John Reaves, Florida (188 comp., 2,549 yds.)..........................1970
- 361—Shane Matthews, Florida (218 comp., 3,130 yds.)....................1991
- 361—Andy Kelly, Tennessee (228 comp., 2,759 yds.).......................1991
- 360—Eric Jones, Vanderbilt (196 comp., 2,548 yds.) 1988
- 357—Whit Taylor, Vanderbilt (209 comp., 2,318 yds.).....................1981
- 356—John Reaves, Florida (193 comp., 2,104 yds.)..........................1971
- 350—Kurt Page, Vanderbilt (203 comp., 2,405 yds.).........................1984
- 346—Jeff Wickersham, LSU (209 comp., 2,145 yds.)........................1985
- 339—Gary Hollingsworth, Alabama (205 comp., 2,379 yds.)............1989
- 338—Stan White, Auburn (180 comp., 2,242 yds.)...........................1990
- 337—Jeff Wickersham, LSU (193 comp., 2,542 yds.)........................1983
- 335—Tony Shell, Miss. State (153 comp., 1,884 yds) 1988
- 320—John Gromos, Vanderbilt (154 comp., 1,744 yds.)....................1989
- 319—Tommy Pharr, Miss. State (173 comp., 1, 838 yds.).................1968
- 317—Tommy Hodson, LSU (183 comp., 2,655 yds.).........................1989
- 317—Stan White, Auburn (158 comp., 1,927 yds.)...........................1991

CAREER:
- 1,231—Stan White, Auburn (659 comp., 8,016 yds.).....................1990-93
- 1,202—Shane Matthews, Florida (722 comp., 9,287 yds.).............1989-92
- 1,163—Tommy Hodson, LSU (674 comp., 9,115 yds.)....................1986-89
- 1,128—John Reaves, Florida (603 comp., 7,549 yds.).....................1969-71
- 1,016—Whit Taylor, Vanderbilt (555 comp., 6,307 yds.) 1979-82
- 1,005—Jeff Wickersham, LSU (587 comp., 6,921 yds.) 1985
- 991— Wayne Peace, Florida (610 comp., 7,206 yds.)....................1980-83
- 981— Kent Austin, Ole Miss (566 comp., 6,184 yds.)....................1981-85
- 969— Eric Zeier, Georgia (579 comp., 7,757 yards) 1991-present
- 949— Kerwin Bell, Florida (549 comp., 7,585 yds.)......................1984-87
- 936— Kurt Page, Vanderbilt (531 comp., 6,233 yds.)....................1981-84
- 846— Andy Kelly, Tennessee (517 comp., 6,397 yds.)..................1988-91
- 819— John Fourcade, Ole Miss (445 comp., 5,412 yds.)...............1978-81
- 817— Pat Sullivan, Auburn (454 comp., 6,284 yds.).....................1969-71
- 816— Bill Ransdell, Kentucky (469 comp., 5,456 yds.).................1983-86
- 809— Mark Young, Ole Miss (410 comp., 4,971 yds.)...................1985-88
- 768— Jeff Francis, Tennessee (476 comp., 5,867 yds.)...................1985-88
- 761— Archie Manning, Ole Miss (395 comp., 4,753 yds.).............1968-70
- 738— Don Smith, Miss. State (342 comp., 5,229 yds.)...................1983-86
- 734— Zeke Bratkowski, Georgia (360 comp., 4,836 yds.)..............1951-53
- 715— Tony Shell, Miss. State (349 comp., 4,292 yds.)..................1988-90
- 714— Kerwin Bell, Florida (409 comp., 5,816 yds.)......................1984-87

COMPLETIONS
GAME:
- 37—Kent Austin, Ole Miss vs. Tennessee (50 atts., 381 yds.)............1982
- 36—Eric Zeier, Georgia vs. Florida (65 atts., 386 yards) 1993
- 35—Andy Kelly, Tennessee vs. Notre Dame (60 atts., 399 yds.) 1990
- 34—Eric Zeier, Georgia vs. Auburn (53 atts., 426 yards) 1993
- 33—Archie Manning, Ole Miss vs. Alabama (52 atts., 436 yds.).......1969
- 33—John Reaves, Florida vs. Auburn (66 atts., 369 yds.).................1969
- 33—John Reaves, Florida vs. Miami (50 atts., 348 yds.)...................1971
- 33—Jeff Wickersham, LSU vs. Miss. State (51 atts., 368 yds.)......... 1983
- 33—Kurt Page, Vanderbilt vs. Georgia (56 atts., 303 yds.)................1983
- 33—Kerwin Bell, Florida vs. Georgia (49 atts., 408 yds.).................1985
- 33—Andy Kelly, Tennessee vs. Colorado (55 atts., 368 yds.)............1990
- 33—Andy Kelly, Tennessee vs. Florida (56 atts., 368 yds.)...............1991
- 32—Tommy Pharr, Miss. State vs. Alabama (49 atts., 258 yds.).......1969
- 32—Kurt Page, Vanderbilt vs. Kentucky (47 atts., 345 yds.)............1983
- 32—Gary Hollingsworth, Alabama vs. Tennessee (46 atts., 379 yds.)...1989
- 32—Shane Matthews, Florida vs. Louisville (46 atts., 317 yds.).......1992
- 31—Kurt Page, Vanderbilt vs. Kentucky (49 atts., 347 yds.)............1984
- 31—Jeff Wickersham, LSU vs. Notre Dame (42 atts., 294 yds.).......1985
- 31—Tommy Hodson, LSU vs. Tennessee (49 atts., 438 yds.)............1989
- 31—Eric Zeier, Georgia vs. Kentucky (47 atts., 425 yards)...............1993

SEASON:
- 286—Kurt Page, Vanderbilt (493 atts., 3,178 yds.).............................1983
- 275—Shane Matthews, Florida (463 atts., 3,205 yds.)......................1992
- 269—Eric Zeier, Georgia (425 atts., 3,525 yds.)................................1993
- 229—Shane Matthews, Florida (378 atts., 2,952 yds.).....................1990
- 228—Whit Taylor, Vanderbilt (406 atts., 2,481 yds.).......................1982
- 228—Andy Kelly, Tennessee (361 atts., 2,759 yds.)..........................1991
- 222—John Reaves, Florida (396 atts., 2,896 yds.)............................1969
- 218—Shane Matthews, Florida (361 atts., 3,130 yds.)......................1991
- 209—Whit Taylor, Vanderbilt (357 atts., 2,318 yds.).......................1981
- 209—Jeff Wickersham, LSU (346 atts., 2,145 yds.)..........................1985
- 205—Gary Hollingsworth, Alabama (339 atts., 2,379 yds.).............1989]
- 203—Kurt Page, Vanderbilt (350 atts., 2,405 yds.)...........................1984
- 196—Eric Jones, Vanderbilt (360 atts., 2,548 yds.)..........................1988
- 193—John Reaves, Florida (356 atts., 2,104 yds.)............................1971
- 193—Jeff Wickersham, LSU (337 atts., 2,542 yds.)..........................1983

CAREER:
- 722—Shane Matthews, Florida (1,202 atts., 9,287 yds.)................1989-92
- 674—Tommy Hodson, LSU (1,163 atts., 9,115 yds.).......................1986-89
- 659—Stan White, Auburn (1,231 atts., 8,016 yds.).........................1990-93
- 610—Wayne Peace, Florida (991 atts., 7,206 yds.)........................1980-83
- 603—John Reaves, Florida (1,128 atts., 7,549 yds.)......................1969-71
- 587—Jeff Wickersham, LSU (1,005 atts., 6,921 yds.)........................1982-85
- 579—Eric Zeier, Georgia (969 atts., 7,757 yards)...................1991-present
- 566—Kent Austin, Ole Miss (981 atts., 6,184 yds.)........................1981-85
- 555—Whit Taylor, Vanderbilt (1,016 atts., 6,307 yds.).................1979-82
- 549—Kerwin Bell, Florida (949 atts., 7,585 yds.)...........................1984-87
- 531—Kurt Page, Vanderbilt (936 atts., 6,233 yds.).........................1981-84
- 517—Andy Kelly, Tennessee (846 atts., 6,377 yds.).......................1988-91
- 476—Jeff Francis, Tennessee (768 atts., 5,867 yds.).......................1985-88
- 469—Bill Ransdell, Kentucky (816 atts., 5,456 yds.).....................1983-86
- 454—Pat Sullivan, Auburn (817 atts., 6,284 yds.).........................1969-71
- 445—John Fourcade, Ole Miss (819 atts., 5,412 yds.)...................1978-81
- 410—Mark Young, Ole Miss (809 atts., 4,971 yds.).......................1985-88
- 409—Kerwin Bell, Florida (714 atts., 5,816 yds.)..........................1984-87
- 395—Archie Manning, Ole Miss (761 atts., 4,753 yds.)................1968-70
- 392—Steve Spurrier, Florida (692 atts., 4,848 yds.).......................1964-66
- 382—Scott Hunter, Alabama (672 atts., 4,899 yds.)......................1968-70
- 381—Alan Risher, LSU (615 atts., 4,585 yds.)...............................1980-82

CONSECUTIVE COMPLETIONS
- 20—Kent Austin, Ole Miss (5 vs. Tulane, 15 vs. Tennessee)..............1982
- 17—Dave Marler, Miss. State (6 vs. Florida State, 11 vs. Tennessee)..............1978
- 16—Steve Spurrier, Florida (9 vs. Florida State, 7 vs. N.C. State) 1966
- 16—Stan White, Auburn vs. New Mexico State 1993
- 15—Kent Austin, Ole Miss (3 vs. Tulane, 12 vs. Vanderbilt) 1985
- 15—Eric Zeier, Georgia vs. Georgia Tech 1993
- 14—Terry Dean, Florida (11 vs. Arkansas State, 3 vs. Kentucky)....................1993
- 14—Chad Loup, LSU vs. Arkansas 1993
- 13—Pat Sullivan, Auburn vs. Georgia Tech 1971
- 13—Kent Austin, Ole Miss vs. Tulane 1982
- 13—Kurt Page, Vanderbilt vs. Tulane...1983

COMPLETION PERCENTAGE
GAME: (Min. 10 comp.)
- 94.7—Kent Austin, Ole Miss vs. Tulane (18 of 19)...............................1982
- 91.7—Nelson Stokley, LSU vs. Miss. State (11 of 12).........................1967
- 91.7—David Rudder, Tennessee vs. Alabama (11 of 12) 1978
- 88.2—Bobby Garner, Ole Miss vs. Memphis State (15 of 17) 1978
- 88.2—Wayne Peace, Florida vs. West Texas State (15 of 17) 1982
- 86.9—Bill Ransdell, Kentucky vs. Florida (20 of 23) 1986
- 86.7—Jake Gibbs, Ole Miss vs. Miss. State (13 of 15) 1960

212 Record Book

86.7—Kevin Dooley, Kentucky vs. Indiana (13 of 15) 1987
86.7—Walter Lewis, Alabama vs. Ole Miss (13 of 15) 1983
86.7—Danny Woodson, Alabama vs. Vanderbilt (13 of 15)..........1991
84.6—Jake Gibbs, Ole Miss vs. Tennessee (11 of 13) 1960
84.6—Harry Gilmer, Alabama vs. Georgia Tech (11 of 13) 1947
82.6—Andy Kelly, Tennessee vs. Ole Miss (19 of 23) 1990
82.6—Eric Zeier, Georgia vs. Kentucky (19 of 23) 1991
81.3—John Bond, Miss. State vs. Tulane (13 of 16) 1982

GAME (Min. 20 comp.)
80.8—Alan Risher, LSU vs. Ole Miss (21 of 26).....................1981
80.0—Alan Cockrell, Tennessee vs. Duke (20 of 25).................1982
77.8—Jeff Francis, Tennessee vs. California (21 of 27)..............1987
77.8—Pat Sullivan, Auburn vs. Florida (21 of 27) 1970
77.8—Eric Zeier, Georgia vs. South Carolina (21 of 27) 1993
76.6—Andy Kelly, Tennessee vs. Auburn (23 of 30) 1991
76.3—Tommy Pharr, Miss. State vs. Florida St. (29 of 38)...........1968
75.9—Scott Hunter, Alabama vs. Ole Miss (22 of 29) 1969
75.7—Andy Kelly, Tennessee vs. Memphis State (28 of 37) 1991
75.0—Babe Parilli, Kentucky vs. North Dakota (21 of 28) 1950
75.0—Wayne Peace, Florida vs. Vanderbilt (28 of 36) 1982

GAME: (Min. 30 comp.)
74.0—Kent Austin, Ole Miss vs. Tennessee (37 of 50) 1982
73.8—Jeff Wickersham, LSU vs. Notre Dame (31 of 42)............1985
73.3—Gary Hollingsworth, Alabama vs. Southern Miss (22 of 30) ...1989
69.6—Gary Hollingsworth, Alabama vs. Tennessee (32 of 46) 1989
68.1—Kurt Page, Vanderbilt vs. Kentucky (32 of 46) 1989
67.3—Kerwin Bell, Florida vs. Georgia (33 of 49) 1985
66.0—Eric Zeier, Georgia vs. Kentucky (31 of 47) 1993
65.3—Tommy Pharr, Miss. State vs. Alabama (32 of 49) 1969
65.2—Jeff Burger vs. Georgia Tech (30 of 46) 1987
64.7—Jeff Wickersham, LSU vs. Miss. State (33 of 51) 1983

SEASON: (Min. 100 comp.)
70.7—Wayne Peace, Florida (174 of 246) 1982
66.7—Jeff Burger, Auburn (178 of 267) 1987
64.6—Heath Shuler, Tennessee (184 of 285) 1993
64.4—Jeff Francis, Tennessee (150 of 233) 1986
63.7—Wayne Peace, Florida (186 of 292) 1983
63.7—Alan Risher, LSU (149 of 234) 1982
63.0—Alan Risher, LSU (150 of 238) 1981
62.5—Kerwin Bell, Florida (180 of 288) 1985
62.2—Walter Lewis, Alabama (102 of 164) 1982
61.7—Tony Robinson, Tennessee (156 of 253) 1984
61.6—Steve Spurrier, Florida (179 of 291) 1966
60.6—Kent Austin, Ole Miss (186 of 307) 1982
60.8—Tom Hodson, LSU (175 of 288) 1986

SEASON: (Min. 200 comp.)
63.3—Eric Zeier, Georgia (269 of 425) 1993
63.2—Andy Kelly, Tennessee (228 of 361) 1991
60.6—Shane Matthews, Florida (229 of 378) 1990
60.4—Jeff Wickersham, LSU (209 of 346) 1985
60.4—Shane Matthews, Florida (218 of 361) 1991
59.4—Shane Matthews, Florida (275 of 463) 1992
58.5—Whit Taylor, Vanderbilt (209 of 357) 1981
58.0—Kurt Page, Vanderbilt (286 of 493) 1983
58.0—Kurt Page, Vanderbilt (203 of 350) 1984

CAREER: (MIN. 300 comp.)
61.98—Jeff Francis, Tennessee (476 of 768) 1985-88
61.95—Alan Risher, LSU (381 of 615) 1980-82
61.6—Wayne Peace, Florida (610 of 991) 1980-83
61.6—Heath Shuler, Tennessee (316 of 513) 1991-93
60.8—Andy Kelly, Tennessee (517 of 846) 1988-91
60.0—Shane Matthews, Florida (722 of 1,202) 1989-92
59.8—Eric Zeier, Georgia (579 of 969) 1991-present
58.4—Jeff Wickersham, LSU (587 of 1005) 1982-85
57.9—Tommy Hodson, LSU (674 of 1,163) 1986-89
57.8—Kerwin Bell, Florida (549 of 1,163) 1984-87
57.7—Kent Austin, Ole Miss (566 of 981) 1981-85
57.5—Bill Ransdell, Kentucky (469 of 816) 1983-86
56.8—Scott Hunter, Alabama (382 of 672) 1968-70
56.7—Kurt Page, Vanderbilt (531 of 936) 1981-84
56.6—Steve Spurrier, Florida (392 of 692) 1964-66
55.9—Babe Parilli, Kentucky (331 of 592) 1949-51
55.6—Pat Sullivan, Auburn (454 of 817) 1969-71
55.6—Gary Hollingsworth, Alabama (345 of 621) 1989-90

YARDS GAINED

GAME:
544—Eric Zeier, Georgia vs. Southern Miss. (30 of 47) 1993
484—Scott Hunter, Alabama vs. Auburn (30 of 55) 1969
464—Whit Taylor, Vanderbilt vs. Tennessee (29 of 53) 1981
449—Danny Wuerffel, Florida vs. Miss. State (27 of 41) 1993
448—Terry Dean, Florida vs. SW Louisiana (26 of 38) 1993
438—Tommy Hodson, LSU vs. Tennessee (31 of 49) 1989
436—Archie Manning, Ole Miss vs. Tennessee (33 of 52) 1969
429—Dave Marler, Miss. State vs. Alabama (28 of 46) 1978
426—Eric Zeier, Georgia vs. Auburn (34 of 53) 1993
425—Eric Zeier, Georgia vs. Kentucky (31 of 47) 1993
412—John Darnell, Ole Miss vs. Arkansas State (23 of 35) 1989
408—Kerwin Bell, Florida vs. George (33 of 49) 1985
407—Larry Rakestraw, Georgia vs. Miami (25 of 38) 1963
405—Todd Jordan, Miss. State vs. Florida (24 of 44) 1993
399—Andy Kelly, Tennessee vs. Notre Dame (35 of 60) 1990
394—Jesse Daigle, LSU vs. Miss State (25 of 44) 1991
392—Andy Kelly, Tennessee vs. Florida (33 of 56) 1991
391—Whit Taylor, Vanderbilt vs. Tennessee (29 of 53) 1982
387—Tony Robinson, Tennessee vs. UCLA (25 of 35) 1985
386—Eric Zeier, Georgia vs. Florida (36 of 65) 1993
386—Danny Wuerffel, Florida vs. Auburn (25 of 50) 1993
385—Bobby Scott, Tennessee vs. Florida (21 of 38) 1970
381—Kent Austin, Ole Miss. vs. Tennessee (37 of 50) 1982
381—Tommy Hodson, LSU vs. Ole Miss (18 of 30) 1989

SEASON:
3,525—Eric Zeier, Georgia (269 of 425) 1993
3,205—Shane Matthews, Florida (275 of 463) 1992
3,178—Kurt Page, Vanderbilt (286 of 493) 1983
3,130—Shane Matthews, Florida (218 of 361) 1991
2,952—Shane Matthews, Florida (229 of 378) 1990
2,896—John Reaves, Florida (222 of 396) 1969
2,759—Andy Kelly, Tennessee (228 of 361) 1991
2,687—Kerwin Bell, Florida (180 of 288) 1985
2,655—Tommy Hodson, LSU (183 of 317) 1989
2,586—Pat Sullivan, Auburn (167 of 281) 1970
2,549—John Reaves, Florida (188 of 376) 1970
2,548—Eric Jones, Vanderbilt (196 of 360) 1988
2,542—Jeff Wickersham, LSU (193 of 337) 1983
2,481—Whit Taylor, Vanderbilt (228 of 406) 1982
2,422—Dave Marler, Miss. State (163 of 287) 1978
2,405—Kurt Page, Vanderbilt (203 of 350) 1984
2,379—Gary Hollingsworth, Alabama (205 of 339) 1989
2,354—Heath Shuler, Tennessee (184 of 285) 1993
2,332—Don Smith, Miss. State (143 of 312) 1985
2,326—John Darnell, Ole Miss (167 of 301) 1989
2,318—Whit Taylor, Vanderbilt (209 of 357) 1981
2,261—Tom Hodson, LSU (175 of 288) 1986
2,248—Eric Zeier, Georgia (151 of 258) 1992
2,242—Stan White, Auburn (180 of 338) 1990
2,241—Andy Kelly, Tennessee (179 of 304) 1990
2,237—Jeff Francis, Tennessee (191 of 314) 1988
2,230—Reggie Slack, Auburn (168 of 279) 1988
2,230—Danny Wuerffel, Florida (159 of 273) 1993
2,188—Scott Hunter, Alabama (157 of 266) 1969

CAREER:
9,287—Shane Matthews, Florida (722 of 1,202) 1989-92
9,115—Tommy Hodson, LSU (674 of 1,163) 1986-89
8,016—Stan White, Auburn (659 of 1,231) 1990-93
7,757—Eric Zeier, Georgia (579 of 969) 1991-present
7,585—Kerwin Bell, Florida (549 of 949) 1984-87
7,549—John Reaves, Florida (603 of 1,128) 1969-71
7,206—Wayne Peace, Florida (610 of 991) 1980-83
6,921—Jeff Wickersham, LSU (587 of 1005) 1982-85
6,397—Andy Kelly, Tennessee (517 of 846) 1988-91
6,307—Whit Taylor, Vanderbilt (555 of 1,016) 1979-82
6,284—Pat Sullivan, Auburn (454 of 817) 1969-71
6,233—Kurt Page, Vanderbilt (531 of 936) 1981-84
6,184—Kent Austin, Ole Miss (566 of 1981) 1981-85
5,867—Jeff Francis, Tennessee (476 of 768) 1985-88
5,564—Bill Ransdell, Kentucky (469 of 816) 1983-86
5,412—John Fourcade, Ole Miss (445 of 819) 1978-81

1994 SEC Football   213

PASSING

TOUCHDOWN PASSES
GAME
- 6—Terry Dean, Florida vs. SW Louisiana 1993
- 5—Babe Parilli, Kentucky vs. Cincinnati 1950
- 5—Babe Parilli, Kentucky vs. North Dakota 1950
- 5—Bill Wade, Vanderbilt vs. Auburn 1950
- 5—Fred Dempsey, Tulane vs. Louisiana College 1952
- 5—John Reaves, Florida vs. Houston 1969
- 5—John Reaves, Florida vs. Vanderbilt 1969
- 5—Gary Hollingsworth, Alabama vs. Ole Miss 1989
- 5—Andy Kelly, Tennessee vs. Vanderbilt 1990
- 5—Shane Matthews, Florida vs. San Jose State 1991
- 5—Heath Shuler, Tennessee vs. Florida 1993

SEASON:
- 28—Shane Matthews, Florida 1991
- 25—Heath Shuler, Tennessee 1993
- 24—John Reaves, Florida 1969
- 24—Eric Zeier, Georgia 1993
- 23—Babe Parilli, Kentucky 1950
- 23—Shane Matthews, Florida 1990
- 23—Shane Matthews, Florida 1992
- 22—Whit Taylor, Vanderbilt 1982
- 22—Tommy Hodson, LSU 1989
- 22—Danny Wuerffel, Florida 1993
- 21—Kerwin Bell, Florida 1985
- 20—Pat Sullivan, Auburn 1971
- 19—Babe Parilli, Kentucky 1951
- 19—Tommy Hodson, LSU 1986
- 18—Charles Conerly, Ole Miss 1947
- 18—Dewey Warren, Tennessee 1966
- 17—Pat Sullivan, Auburn 1970
- 17—John Reaves, Florida 1971
- 17—Alan Risher, LSU 1982
- 17—Terry Dean, Florida 1993

CAREER:
- 74—Shane Matthews, Florida 1989-92
- 69—Tommy Hodson, LSU 1986-89
- 56—Kerwin Bell, Florida 1984-87
- 54—John Reaves, Florida 1969-71
- 53—Pat Sullivan, Auburn 1969-71
- 50—Babe Parilli, Kentucky 1949-51
- 43—Eric Zeier, Georgia 1991-present
- 41—Whit Taylor, Vanderbilt 1979-82
- 40—Stan White, Auburn 1990-93
- 36—Steve Spurrier, Florida 1964-66
- 36—Andy Kelly, Tennessee 1988-91
- 36—Heath Shuler, Tennessee 1991-93
- 35—Mike Shula, Alabama 1983-86
- 35—Kurt Page, Vanderbilt 1981-84
- 34—Wayne Peace, Florida 1980-83
- 33—Johnny Rauch, Georgia 1946-48
- 32—Bobby Scott, Tennessee 1968-70
- 32—Buck Belue, Georgia 1978-81
- 32—Eric Jones, Vanderbilt 1986-88
- 31—Bill Wade, Vanderbilt 1949-51
- 31—Archie Manning, Ole Miss 1968-70
- 31—Alan Risher, LSU 1980-82
- 31—Kent Austin, Ole Miss 1981-85
- 31—Don Smith, Miss. State 1983-86
- 31—Mark Young, Ole Miss 1985-88

INTERCEPTIONS
GAME:
- 9—John Reaves, Florida vs. Auburn (66 atts.) 1969
- 8—Zeke Bratkowski, Georgia vs. Georgia Tech (35 atts.) 1951
- 6—Johnny Rauch, Georgia vs. Chattanooga 1948
- 6—Max Stainbrook, Miss. State vs. Cincinnati (16 atts.) 1949
- 6—Rick Norton, Kentucky vs. LSU 1965
- 6—Bernie Scruggs, Kentucky vs. West Virginia 1969

SEASON:
- 29—Zeke Bratkowski, Georgia (248 atts.) 1951
- 29—Kurt Page, Vanderbilt (493 atts.) 1983
- 23—Zeke Bratkowski, Georgia (224 atts.) 1953
- 21—Dave Bair, Kentucky (164 atts.) 1967
- 21—Loran Carter, Auburn (241 atts.) 1968
- 21—John Reaves, Florida (356 atts.) 1971
- 20—Johnny Cook, Georgia 1943
- 20—John Fourcade, Ole Miss (286 atts.) 1980
- 20—Randy Jenkins, Kentucky (187 atts.) 1982

CAREER:
- 68—Zeke Bratkowski, Georgia (734 atts.) 1951-53
- 59—John Reaves, Florida (1,128 atts.) 1969-71
- 53—Randy Jenkins, Kentucky (716 atts.) 1979-83
- 52—Stan White, Auburn (1,231 atts.) 1990-93
- 47—Loran Carter, Auburn (476 atts.) 1966-68
- 46—Shane Matthews, Florida (1,202 atts.) 1989-92
- 44—Rick Norton, Kentucky (598 atts.) 1963-65
- 44—Kurt Page, Vanderbilt (936 atts.) 1981-84
- 44—Stan White, Auburn (960 atts.) 1990-1992
- 42—Larry Rakestraw, Georgia (514 atts.) 1961-63
- 41—Whit Taylor, Vanderbilt (1,016 atts.) 1979-82
- 41—Tommy Hodson, LSU (1,163 atts.) 1986-89

CONSECUTIVE ATTEMPTS WITHOUT AN INTERCEPTION
- 137—Alan Risher, LSU 1982
- 131—Kent Austin, Ole Miss 1984
- 130—Eric Zeier, Georgia 1993
- 124—Wayne Johnson, Georgia 1988
- 118—Kurt Page, Vanderbilt 1984
- 117—Wayne Peace, Florida 1981
- 116—Mike Healey, Vanderbilt 1990
- 114—Eric Zeier, Georgia 1991
- 110—Don Smith, Miss. State 1985-86
- 105—Bill Ransdell, Kentucky 1985
- 105—Bill Ransdell, Kentucky 1986
- 105—Tommy Hodson, LSU 1987-88
- 104—Steve Spurrier, Florida 1966
- 104—John Fourcade, Ole Miss 1981
- 100—Jeff Rutledge, Alabama 1977-78
- 100—David Smith, Alabama 1988

LOWEST PERCENTAGE OF INTERCEPTIONS
SEASON: (Min. 100 atts.)
- 0.76—Daryl Dickey, Tennessee (1 in 131) 1985
- 0.77—Mike Healey, Vanderbilt (1 in 130) 1990
- 1.27—Randy Campbell, Auburn (2 in 158) 1982
- 1.50—Pat Trammell, Alabama (2 in 133) 1961

SEASON: (Min. 200 atts.)
- 1.39—Eric Zeier, Georgia (4 in 286) 1991
- 1.79—Heath Shuler, Tennessee (4 in 224) 1992
- 1.99—John Fourcade, Ole Miss (5 in 251) 1981
- 2.13—Bill Ransdell, Kentucky (5 in 231) 1985

SEASON: (Min. 300 atts.)
- 1.65—Eric Zeier, Georgia (23 in 969) 1993
- 2.57—Kurt Page, Vanderbilt (9 in 350) 1984
- 2.60—Jeff Wickersham, LSU (9 in 346) 1985
- 2.65—Kent Austin, Ole Miss (8 in 302) 1984
- 2.80—Whit Taylor, Vanderbilt (10 in 357) 1981
- 2.96—Whit Taylor, Vanderbilt (12 in 406) 1982

CAREER: (MIN. 200 atts.)
- 1.67—Randy Campbell, Auburn (5 in 300) 1982-83

CAREER: (MIN. 400 atts.)
- 2.34—Heath Shuler, Tennessee (12 in 513) 1991-93
- 2.95—Condredge Holloway, Tennessee (12 in 407) 1972-74

CAREER: (MIN. 600 atts.)
- 2.37—Eric Zeier, Georgia (23 in 969) 1991-present
- 3.38—Jeff Francis, Tennessee (26 in 768) 1985-88
- 3.68—Kerwin Bell, Florida (35 in 949) 1984-87
- 3.83—Shane Matthews, Florida (46 in 1,202) 1989-92
- 3.88—Jeff Wickersham, LSU (39 in 1,005) 1982-85

LONGEST TOUCHDOWN PASSES
GAME:
- 99—Chris Collinsworth to Derrick Gaffney, Florida vs. Rice 1977
- 96—Kerwin Bell to Ricky Nattiel, Florida vs. Georgia 1984
- 93—Buck Belue to Lindsay Scott, Georgia vs. Florida 1980
- 93—Kyle Morris to Stacey Simmons, Florida vs. Montana State 1988
- 93—Greg Talley to Kevin Maxwell, Georgia vs. Vanderbilt 1989
- 92—Kirby Moore to Randy Wheeler, Georgia vs. Auburn 1965
- 92—Dave Bair to Dicky Lyons, Kentucky vs. Georgia 1968
- 91—Buck Belue to Amp Arnold, Georgia vs. Kentucky 1980
- 90—Frank Sinkwich to Lamar Davis, Georgia vs. Cincinnati 1942
- 90—Jeff Dunn to Pierre Goode, Alabama vs. Tennessee 1987

RECEIVING

CATCHES
GAME:
- 17—Keith Edwards, Vanderbilt vs. Georgia (141 yards) 1983
- 15—Bob Goodridge, Vanderbilt vs. Navy (201 yards) 1967
- 15—Carlos Alvarez, Florida vs. Miami (237 yards) 1969
- 15—Keith Edwards, Vanderbilt vs. Kentucky (147 yards) 1984
- 15—Shannon Mitchell, Georgia vs. Florida (140 yards) 1993
- 14—David Smith, Miss. State vs. Ole Miss (194 yards) 1969
- 14—Wendell Davis, LSU vs. Ole Miss (208 yards) 1986
- 13—Barney Poole, Ole Miss vs. Chattanooga (95 yards) 1969
- 13—Floyd Franks, Ole Miss vs. Alabama (191 yards) 1969
- 13—Brad Gaines, Vanderbilt vs. Georgia (168 yards) 1989
- 13—Brad Gaines, Vanderbilt vs. Memphis State (120 yards) 1989
- 13—Carl Pickens, Tennessee vs. Notre Dame (163 yards) 1990

SEASON:
- 97—Keith Edwards, Vanderbilt (909 yards) 1983
- 88—Carlos Alvarez, Florida (1,329 yards) 1969
- 80—Wendell Davis, LSU (1,244 yards) 1986
- 79—Bob Goodridge, Vanderbilt (1,114 yards) 1967
- 78—Boo Mitchell, Vanderbilt (1,213 yards) 1988
- 76—Brice Hunter, Georgia (970 yards) 1993
- 74—David Smith, Miss. State (987 yards) 1970
- 72—Wendell Davis, LSU (993 yards) 1987
- 70—Chuck Scott, Vanderbilt (971 yards) 1983
- 67—Brad Gaines, Vanderbilt (634 yards) 1989
- 64—Sammy Milner, Miss. State (909 yards) 1968
- 64—Sammy Milner, Miss. State (745 yards) 1969
- 63—Richard Trapp, Florida (872 yards) 1966
- 62—Willie Jackson, Florida (772 yards) 1992
- 61—Allama Matthews, Vanderbilt (797 yards) 1982
- 61—David Palmer, Alabama (1,000 yards) 1993
- 60—Keith Edwards, Vanderbilt (576 yards) 1984

CAREER:
- 200—Keith Edwards, Vanderbilt (1,757 yards) 1980, 1982-84
- 188—Boo Mitchell, Vanderbilt (2,964 yards) 1985-88
- 183—Wendell Davis, LSU (2,708 yards) 1984-87
- 172—Carlos Alvarez, Florida (2,563 yards) 1969-71
- 162—David Smith, Miss. State (2,168 yards) 1968-70
- 162—Willie Jackson, Florida (2,172 yards) 1990-93
- 153—Errict Rhett, Florida (1,230 yards) 1990-93
- 152—Eric Martin, LSU (2,625 yards) 1981-84
- 146—Sammy Milner, Miss. State (1,806 yards) 1968-70
- 145—Chuck Scott, Vanderbilt (2,219 yards) 1982-84
- 143—Everett Crawford, Vanderbilt (1,503 yards) 1984-87
- 141—Terry Beasley, Auburn (2,507 yards) 1969-71
- 132—Richard Trapp, Florida (1,783 yards) 1965-67
- 132—David Bailey, Alabama (1,857 yards) 1969-71
- 132—Martin Cox, Vanderbilt (2,275 yards) 1975-78
- 132—Tony Moss, LSU (2,196 yards) 1986-89
- 131—Lindsay Scott, Georgia (2,098 yards) 1978-81
- 127—Floyd Franks, Ole Miss (1,707 yards) 1968-70

YARDS GAINED
GAME:
- 263—Alexander Wright, Auburn vs. Pacific (5 catches) 1989
- 248—Todd Kinchen, LSU vs. Miss. State (9 catches) 1991
- 237—Carlos Alvarez, Florida vs. Miami (15 catches) 1969
- 225—Johnny Mills, Tennessee vs. Kentucky (7 catches) 1966
- 222—Clarence Sevillian, Vanderbilt vs. Tennessee (6 catches) 1992
- 217—Willie Gault, Tennessee vs. Vanderbilt (4 catches) 1981
- 217—David Palmer, Alabama vs. Vanderbilt (8 catches) 1993
- 215—David Smith, Miss. State vs. Texas Tech (12 catches) 1970
- 210—Eddie Small, Ole Miss vs. Vanderbilt (6 catches) 1993
- 209—Eric Martin, LSU vs. Alabama (8 catches) 1983
- 208—Sammy Milner, Miss. State vs. Texas Tech (9 catches) 1968
- 208—Danny Knight, Miss. State vs. Florida (8 catches) 1982
- 208—Wendell Davis, LSU vs. Ole Miss (14 catches) 1986
- 202—Buck Martin, Georgia Tech vs. Auburn (10 catches) 1951
- 201—Bob Goodridge, Vanderbilt vs. Navy (15 catches) 1967
- 201—Carlos Carson, LSU vs. Rice (5 catches) 1977
- 201—Carl Pickens, Tennessee vs. Kentucky (10 catches) 1990

SEASON:
- 1,329—Carlos Alvarez, Florida (88 catches) 1969
- 1,244—Wendell Davis, LSU (80 catches) 1986
- 1,213—Boo Mitchell, Vanderbilt (78 catches) 1988
- 1,114—Bob Goodridge, Vanderbilt (79 catches) 1967
- 1,064—Eric Martin, LSU (52 catches) 1983
- 1,051—Terry Beasley, Auburn (52 catches) 1970
- 1,035—Mardye McDole, Miss. State (48 catches) 1978
- 1,000—David Palmer, Alabama (61 catches) 1993
- 993—Wendell Davis, LSU (72 catches) 1987
- 987—David Smith, Miss. State (74 catches) 1970
- 975—Chuck Scott, Vanderbilt (54 catches) 1984
- 971—Chuck Scott, Vanderbilt (70 catches) 1983
- 970—Brice Hunter, Georgia (76 catches) 1993
- 967—Wes Chandler, Florida (44 catches) 1976

CAREER:
- 2,964—Boo Mitchell, Vanderbilt (188 catches) 1985-88
- 2,708—Wendell Davis, LSU (183 catches) 1984-87
- 2,625—Eric Martin, LSU (152 catches) 1981-84
- 2,563—Carlos Alvarez, Florida (172 catches) 1969-71
- 2,507—Terry Beasley, Auburn (141 catches) 1969-71
- 2,275—Martin Cox, Vanderbilt (132 catches) 1975-78
- 2,219—Chuck Scott, Vanderbilt (145 catches) 1982-84
- 2,214—Mardye McDole, Miss. State (116 catches) 1977-80
- 2,196—Tony Moss, LSU (143 catches) 1986-89
- 2,172—Willie Jackson, Florida (162 catches) 1990-93
- 2,168—David Smith, Miss. State (162 catches) 1968-70
- 2,098—Lindsay Scott, Georgia (131 catches) 1978-81
- 2,086—Ricky Nattiel, Florida (117 catches) 1983-86
- 2,070—Ozzie Newsome, Alabama (102 catches) 1974-77
- 2,042—Tim McGee, Tennessee (123 catches) 1983-85
- 2,012—J.R. Ambrose, Ole Miss (118 catches) 1984-87

YARDS PER GAME
SEASON:
- 132.9—Carlos Alvarez, Florida (1,329 in 10 games) 1969
- 113.1—Wendell Davis, LSU (1,244 in 11 games) 1986
- 111.4—Bob Goodridge, Vanderbilt (1,114 in 10 games) 1967
- 110.3—Boo Mitchell, Vanderbilt (1,213 in 11 games) 1988
- 105.1—Terry Beasley, Auburn (1,051 in 10 games) 1970
- 97.0—Eric Martin, LSU (1,064 in 11 games) 1983
- 94.5—David Smith, Miss. State (756 in 8 games) 1969
- 94.1—Mardye McDole, Miss. State (1,035 in 11 games) 1978
- 90.9—Sammy Milner, Miss. State (909 in 10 games) 1968
- 89.7—David Smith, Miss. State (987 in 11 games) 1970
- 88.6—Chuck Scott, Vanderbilt (975 in 11 games) 1984
- 88.3—Chuck Scott, Vanderbilt (971 in 11 games) 1983
- 88.2—Brice Hunter, Georgia (970 in 11 games) 1993

CAREER:
- 83.9—Terry Beasley, Auburn (2,507 in 30 games) 1969-71
- 82.6—Carlos Alvarez, Florida (2,563 in 31 games) 1969-71
- 74.8—David Smith, Miss. State (2,168 in 29 games) 1968-70

YARDS PER CATCH
GAME: (Min. 5 catches)
- 52.6—Alexander Wright, Auburn vs. Pacific (5 for 263) 1989
- 40.2—Carlos Carson, LSU vs. Rice (5 for 201) 1977
- 40.0—Pat Coleman, Ole Miss vs. Arkansas State (5 for 200) 1989
- 37.0—Clarence Sevillian, Vanderbilt vs. Tennessee (6 for 222) 1992
- 35.0—Eddie Small, Ole Miss vs. Vanderbilt (6 for 210) 1993
- 32.7—Bucky Curtis, Vanderbilt vs. Alabama (6 for 196) 1950
- 32.5—Eddie Kennison, LSU vs. Utah State (6 for 195) 1993
- 32.2—Larry Seivers, Tennessee vs. N. Texas St. (5 for 161) 1975
- 32.2—Ricky Nattiel, Florida vs. Florida St. (5 for 161) 1985
- 32.1—Johnny Mills, Tennessee vs. Kentucky (7 for 225) 1967
- 32.0—Freddy Weygand, Auburn vs. Georgia Tech (5 for 160) 1984
- 30.0—Andre Hastings, Georgia vs. Tennessee (5 for 150) 1992
- 28.8—Chris Jones, Miss. State (5 for 144) 1993
- 28.6—Pat Coleman, Ole Miss vs. Vanderbilt (5 for 143) 1988
- 27.6—Todd Kinchen, LSU vs. Miss. State (9 for 248) 1991
- 27.2—Tim McGee, Tennessee vs. Auburn (6 for 163) 1985
- 27.1—David Palmer, Alabama vs. Vanderbilt (8 for 217) 1993
- 27.0—Eddie Small, Ole Miss vs. Northern Illinois (5 for 135) 1993
- 26.8—Willie Green, Ole Miss vs. Georgia (6 for 161) 1989
- 26.5—Chuck Scott, Vanderbilt vs. Auburn (6 for 159) 1983
- 26.5—Anthony Miller, Tennessee vs. Alabama (6 for 159) 1986
- 26.4—Eric Hoggatt, Miss. State vs. Florida (5 for 132) 1969
- 26.1—Eric Martin, LSU vs. Alabama (8 for 209) 1983

1994 SEC Football 215

RECEIVING

GAME: (Min. 10 catches)
- 20.2— Buck Martin, Georgia Tech vs. Auburn (10 for 202) 1951
- 20.1— Carl Pickens, Tennessee vs. Kentucky (10 for 201)...............1990
- 19.0— Tim McGee, Tennessee vs. Vanderbilt (10 for 190)................1984
- 18.3— Tyrone Young, Florida vs. Georgia (10 for 183)....................1980
- 17.9— David Smith, Miss. State vs. Texas Tech (12 for 215)............1970
- 17.9— Brice Hunter, Georgia vs. Southern Miss. (10 for 179)..........1993

GAME: (Min. 15 catches)
- 15.8— Carlos Alvarez, Florida vs. Miami (15 for 237).....................1969
- 13.4— Bob Goodridge, Vanderbilt vs. Navy (15 for 201)..................1967

SEASON: (Min. 25 catches)
- 29.3— Bucky Curtis, Vanderbilt (27 for 791)..................................1950
- 25.0— Danny Knight, Miss. State (37 for 924).................................1982
- 24.9— Freddy Weygand, Auburn (32 for 796)..................................1984
- 23.5— Larry Seiple, Kentucky (27 for 635).......................................1966
- 22.3— Andy Hamilton, LSU (39 for 870)...1970
- 22.3— Ozzie Newsome, Alabama (36 for 804)................................1977
- 22.0— Wes Chandler, Florida (44 for 967).......................................1976
- 21.6— Mardye McDole, Miss. State (48 for 1,035).........................1978
- 21.2— Ozzie Newsome, Alabama (25 for 529)................................1976
- 21.2— Clarence Sevillian, Vanderbilt (33 for 701)..........................1992
- 21.1— Ricky Nattiel, Florida (31 for 653)...1985

SEASON: (Min. 50 catches)
- 20.5— Eric Martin, LSU (52 for 1,064)...1983
- 20.2— Terry Beasley, Auburn (52 for 1,051)....................................1970
- 18.6— Jack Jackson, Florida (51 for 949)..1993
- 18.1— Chuck Scott, Vanderbilt (54 for 975)....................................1984
- 17.3— Carl Pickens, Tennessee (53 for 917)....................................1990
- 16.5— Andre Hastings, Georgia (52 for 860)...................................1992
- 16.4— David Palmer, Alabama (61 for 1,000).................................1993
- 16.1— Todd Kinchen, LSU (53 for 855)...1991
- 15.8— Tony Moss, LSU (59 for 934)...1989
- 15.4— Terry Beasley, Auburn (55 for 846).......................................1971
- 15.2— Dennis Homan, Alabama (54 for 820)..................................1967
- 15.1— David Smith, Miss. State (50 for 756)....................................1969
- 15.1— Preston Brown, Vanderbilt (52 for 786)................................1979

SEASON: (Min. 75 catches)
- 15.6— Wendell Davis, LSU (80 for 1,244)...1986
- 15.6— Boo Mitchell, Vanderbilt (78 for 1,213).................................1988
- 15.1— Carlos Alvarez, Florida (88 for 1,329)...................................1969
- 14.1— Bob Goodridge, Vanderbilt (79 for 1,114)............................1967

CAREER: (Min. 50 catches)
- 24.5— Bucky Curtis, Vanderbilt (61 for 1,496)........................1947-50
- 22.6— Wayne Wheeler, Alabama (55 for 1,246).....................1971-73
- 21.9— Danny Knight, Miss. State (81 for 1,773).....................1980-83
- 21.3— Wes Chandler, Florida (92 for 1,963)............................1974-77
- 21.3— Byron Franklin, Auburn (74 for 1,573).........................1977-80

CAREER: (Min. 100 catches)
- 20.3— Ozzie Newsome, Alabama (102 for 2,070)................1974-77
- 20.1— Willie Green, Ole Miss (113 for 2,274)........................1986-89
- 20.0— Andy Hamilton, LSU (100 for 1,995)...........................1969-71
- 19.1— Mardye McDole, Miss. State (116 for 2,214)...............1977-80
- 17.8— Ricky Nattiel, Florida (117 for 2,086)...........................1983-86
- 17.8— Terry Beasley, Auburn (141 for 2,507).........................1969-71
- 17.3— Eric Martin, LSU (152 for 2,625).................................1981-84
- 17.2— Anthony Hancock, Tennessee (106 for 1,826)............1978-81
- 17.2— Martin Cox, Vanderbilt (132 for 2,275).......................1975-78
- 17.2— Carl Pickens, Tennessee (109 for 1,875)......................1989-91
- 17.1— J. R. Ambrose, Ole Miss (118 for 2,012)......................1984-87
- 16.6— Tim McGee, Tennessee (123 for 2,042).......................1983-85
- 16.6— Tony Moss, LSU (132 for 2,196)..................................1986-89
- 16.4— Larry Seivers, Tennessee (117 for 1,924)....................1974-76
- 16.1— Cris Collinsworth, Florida (120 for 1,937).................1977-80
- 16.0— Lindsay Scott, Georgia (131 for 2,098).......................1978-81

TOUCHDOWN CATCHES

GAME:
- 5— Carlos Carson, LSU vs. Rice..1977
- 4— Al Bruno, Kentucky vs. North Dakota..1950
- 4— Buck Martin, Georgia Tech vs. Auburn.....................................1951
- 4— Allama Matthews, Vanderbilt vs. Virginia Tech......................1982
- 4— Alexander Wright, Auburn vs. Pacific.......................................1989
- 4— Tony Moss, LSU vs. Ohio...1989

SEASON:
- 14— Allama Matthews, Vanderbilt (11 games)................................1982

- 12— Carlos Alvarez, Florida (10 games)...1969
- 12— Terry Beasley, Auburn (10 games)..1971
- 12— Carl Parker, Vanderbilt (11 games)...1987
- 11— Terry Beasley, Auburn (10 games)..1970
- 11— Wendell Davis, LSU (11 games)...1986
- 11— Cory Fleming, Tennessee (11 games).......................................1993
- 11— Jack Jackson, Florida (12 games)...1993
- 10— Al Lary, Alabama (10 games)...1950
- 10— Al Bruno, Kentucky (10 games)...1950
- 10— Wes Chandler, Florida (11 games)..1976
- 10— Carlos Carson, LSU (11 games)...1977
- 10— Ernie Mills, Florida (11 games)...1990
- 10— Willie Jackson, Florida (11 games)...1991

CAREER:
- 29— Terry Beasley, Auburn (30 games)......................................1969-71
- 24— Willie Jackson, Florida (37 games)......................................1990-93
- 22— Wes Chandler, Florida (43 games).......................................1974-77
- 20— Chuck Scott, Vanderbilt (33 games)....................................1982-84
- 19— Carlos Alvarez, Florida (31 games).....................................1969-71
- 19— Wendell Davis, LSU (35 games)...1984-87
- 18— Dennis Homan, Alabama (30 games).................................1965-67
- 18— Andy Hamilton, LSU (32 games)..1969-71
- 18— Allama Matthews, Vanderbilt (29 games)..........................1979-82
- 18— Ricky Nattiel, Florida (39 games)...1983-86
- 18— Willie Jackson, Florida (28 games).......................................1990-92
- 18— Cory Fleming, Tennessee (38 games)..................................1990-93
- 17— Ken Kavenaugh, LSU...1937-39
- 17— Bucky Curtis, Vanderbilt (42 games)...................................1947-50
- 17— Steve Meilinger, Kentucky..1951-53

Split end Ozzie Newsome, voted Alabama's Player of the Decade for the 1970s, holds the SEC career mark for average yards per catch at 20.3.

216 Record Book

SCORING

MOST POINTS
GAME:
- 42—Showboat Boykin, Ole Miss vs. Miss. State (7 TDs) 1951
- 30—Bob Davis, Kentucky vs. Maryville (5 TDs) 1936
- 30—Bob Davis, Kentucky vs. Washington & Lee (5 TDs) 1937
- 30—Carlos Carson, LSU vs. Rice (5 TDs) 1977
- 30—Frank Mordica, Vanderbilt vs. Air Force (5 TDs) 1978
- 30—Joe Cribbs, Auburn vs. Vanderbilt (5 TDs) 1978
- 29—Jackie Parker, Miss. St. vs. Arkansas St. (4 TDs, 5 PAT) 1952

SEASON:
- 126—Garrison Hearst, Georgia (21 TDs) 1992
- 120—Jackie Parker, Miss. State (16 TDs, 24 PAT) 1952
- 120—Herschel Walker, Georgia (20 TDs) 1981
- 120—Reggie Cobb, Tennessee (20 TDs) 1987
- 110—Tommy Durrance, Florida (18 TDs, 1 two-point) 1969
- 108—Tim Worley, Georgia (18 TDs) 1988
- 108—Siran Stacy, Alabama (18 TDs) 1989
- 107—Greg Burke, Tennessee (19 FGs, 50 PATs) 1990
- 104—Charles Alexander, LSU (17 TDs, 1 two-point) 1977
- 104—Herschel Walker, Georgia (17 TDs, 1 two-point) 1982
- 104—Bobby Humphrey, Alabama (17 TDs, 1 two-point) 1986
- 103—Bobby Raymond, Florida (23 FGs, 34 PAT) 1984
- 102—Frank Sinkwich, Georgia (17 TDs) 1942
- 102—Bo Jackson, Auburn (17 TDs) 1985
- 102—Carlos Reveiz, Tennessee (24FGs, 30 PAT) 1985
- 102—Lars Tate, Georgia (17 TDs) 1986
- 101—Fuad Reveiz, Tennessee (27 FGs, 20 PAT) 1982
- 100—Johnny Musso, Alabama (16 TDs, 2 two-point) 1971
- 100—Philip Doyle, Alabama (22 FGs, 34 PAT) 1989
- 98—Steve Van Buren, LSU (14 TDs, 14 PAT) 1943
- 98—Joe Cribbs, Auburn (16 TDs, 1 two-point) 1978
- 97—Philip Doyle, Alabama (24 FGs, 25 PAT) 1990
- 97—Michael Proctor, Alabama (22 FGs, 31 PATs) 1993
- 96—Charles Alexander, LSU (16 TDs) 1978
- 96—Dalton Hilliard, LSU (16 TDs) 1982
- 96—Tony Thompson, Tennessee (16 TDs) 1990

CAREER:
- 353—Kevin Butler, Georgia (122 PAT, 77 FGs, 44 games) 1981-84
- 345—Philip Doyle, Alabama (105 PAT, 78 FGs, 1 TD, 43 games) 1987-90
- 314—Herschel Walker, Georgia (52 TDS, 1 two-point, 33 games) 1980-82
- 314—Fuad Reveiz, Tennessee (101 PAT, 71 FGs, 44 games) 1981-84
- 312—Van Tiffin, Alabama (59 FGs, 135 PATs, 44 games) 1983-86
- 302—Dalton Hilliard, LSU (50 TDs, 1 two-point, 44 games) 1982-85
- 292—David Browndyke, LSU (109 PAT, 61 FGs) 1986-89
- 274—Bo Jackson, Auburn (45 TDs, 2 two-point, 38 games) 1982-85
- 269—Rex Robinson, Georgia (101 PAT, 56 FGs, 44 games) 1977-80
- 254—Charles Alexander, LSU (42 TDs, 1 two-point, 44 games) 1975-78
- 251—John Becksvoort, Tennessee (122 PAT, 43 FGs, 33 games) 1991-present
- 246—Joey Worley, Kentucky (57 FGs, 75 PATs) 1984-87
- 242—Bobby Humphrey, Alabama (40 TDs, 1 two-point, 35 games) 1985-88
- 236—Stanley Morgan, Tennessee (39 TDs, 1 two-point, 44 games) 1973-76
- 236—Al Del Greco, Auburn (110 PAT, 42 FGs, 44 games) 1980-83
- 232—Johnny Musso, Alabama (38 TDs, 2 two-point, 30 games) 1969-71

MOST TOUCHDOWNS
GAME:
- *7—Showboat Boykin, Ole Miss vs. Miss. State 1951
- 5—Bob Davis, Kentucky vs. Maryville 1936
- 5—Bob Davis, Kentucky vs. Washington & Lee 1937
- 5—Carlos Carson, LSU vs. Rice 1977
- 5—Frank Mordica, Vanderbilt vs. Air Force 1978
- 5—Joe Cribbs, Auburn vs. Vanderbilt 1978

SEASON:
- 21—Garrison Hearst, Georgia 1992
- 20—Herschel Walker, Georgia 1981
- 20—Reggie Cobb, Tennessee 1987
- 18—Tommy Durrance, Florida 1969
- 18—Tim Worley, Georgia 1988
- 18—Siran Stacy, Alabama 1989
- 17—Frank Sinkwich, Georgia 1942
- 17—Charles Alexander, LSU 1977
- 17—Herschel Walker, Georgia 1982
- 17—Bo Jackson, Auburn 1985
- 17—Bobby Humphrey, Alabama 1986
- 17—Lars Tate, Georgia 1986

*—NCAA record

CAREER:
- 52—Herschel Walker, Georgia (33 games) 1980-82
- 50—Dalton Hilliard, LSU (44 games) 1982-85
- 45—Bo Jackson, Auburn (38 games) 1982-85
- 42—Charles Alexander, LSU (44 games) 1975-78
- 40—Bobby Humphrey, Alabama (35 games) 1985-88
- 39—Stanley Morgan, Tennessee (44 games) 1973-76
- 38—Johnny Musso, Alabama (30 games) 1969-71
- 37—Lars Tate, Georgia (42 games) 1984-87
- 37—Emmitt Smith, Florida (31 games) 1987-89
- 36—Errict Rhett, Florida (48 games) 1990-93
- 35—Garrison Hearst, Georgia 1990-92
- 34—Joe Cribbs, Auburn (38 games) 1976-79
- 32—Charles Trippi, Georgia (30 games) 1942, 1945-1946
- 32—Neal Anderson, Florida (44 games) 1982-85
- 30—Bob Davis, Kentucky (30 games) 1935-37
- 30—Frank Sinkwich, Georgia (28 games) 1940-42
- 30—Garry James, LSU (44 games) 1982-85
- 30—Bobby Marlow, Alabama (34 games) 1950-52
- 29—Harvey Williams, LSU (40 games) 1986-90
- 29—Terry Robiskie, LSU (44 games) 1973-76
- 28—Wes Chandler, Florida (43 games) 1974-77
- 28—Tim Worley, Georgia (26 games) 1985-86; 1988
- 27—Andy Kozar, Tennessee (29 games) 1950-52
- 27—Tommy Durrance, Florida (30 games) 1969-71
- 27—Rodger Bird, Kentucky (30 games) 1963-65
- 27—George Adams, Kentucky (44 games) 1981-84

FIELD GOAL ATTEMPTS
GAME:
- 7—Al Del Greco, Auburn vs. Kentucky (made 6) 1982
- 7—Doug Pelfrey, Kentucky vs. Miss. State (made 5) 1992
- 6—John Riley, Auburn vs. Kentucky (made 4) 1968
- 6—Alan Duncan, Tennessee vs. Kentucky (made 5) 1978
- 6—Rex Robinson, Georgia vs. Georgia Tech (made 3) 1979
- 6—Bobby Raymond, Florida vs. Florida State (made 6) 1983
- 6—Bobby Raymond, Florida vs. Kentucky (made 6) 1984
- 6—David Browndyke, LSU vs. Ole Miss (made 4) 1986
- 6—Philip Doyle, Alabama vs. SW Louisiana (made 6) 1990
- 6—Kanon Parkman, Georgia vs. Florida (made 4) 1993

SEASON:
- 31—Fuad Reveiz, Tennessee (made 27) 1982
- 31—Philip Doyle, Alabama (made 19) 1988
- 29—Greg Burke, Tennessee (made 19) 1990
- 29—Philip Doyle, Alabama (made 24) 1990
- 29—Michael Proctor, Alabama (made 22) 1993
- 28—Kevin Butler, Georgia (made 23) 1984
- 28—Carlos Reveiz, Tennessee (made 24) 1985
- 28—Joe Worley, Kentucky (made 19) 1985
- 28—Scott Etheridge, Auburn (made 22) 1992
- 27—Michael Proctor, Alabama (made 19) 1992
- 27—Chris Gardner, MSU (made 15) 1992
- 27—John Pierce, Kentucky (made 10) 1975
- 27—Kanon Parkman, Georgia (made 19) 1993
- 26—John Riley, Auburn (made 12) 1968
- 26—Dave Marler, Miss. State (made 13) 1978
- 26—Kevin Butler, Georgia (made 19) 1981
- 26—Bobby Raymond, Florida (made 23) 1984
- 26—Jim Von Wyl, Auburn (made 15) 1991

CAREER:
- 105—Philip Doyle, Alabama (made 78) 1987-90
- 98—Kevin Butler, Georgia (made 77) 1981-84
- 95—Fuad Reveiz, Tennessee (made 71) 1981-84
- 87—Van Tiffin, Alabama (made 59) 1983-86
- 85—Joey Worley, Kentucky (made 57) 1984-87
- 84—Rex Robinson, Georgia (made 56) 1977-80
- 81—Artie Cosby, Miss. State (made 48) 1983-86
- 75—David Browndyke, LSU (made 61) 1986-89
- 75—Brian Lee, Ole Miss (made 41) 1989-92
- 69—Al Del Greco, Auburn (made 42) 1980-83
- 66—Steve Crumley, Georgia (made 46) 1985-88
- 65—John Riley, Auburn (made 31) 1967-69
- 63—Brian Clark, Florida (made 43) 1979-81

FIELD GOALS MADE
GAME:
- 6—Al Del Greco, Auburn vs. Kentucky (7 atts.) 1982

1994 SEC Football 217

SCORING

6—Bobby Raymond, Florida vs. Florida State (6 atts.) 1983
6—Bobby Raymond, Florida vs. Kentucky (6 atts.) 1984
6—Philip Doyle, Alabama vs. SW Louisiana (6 atts.) 1990
5—Brian Clark, Florida vs. Ole Miss (5 atts.) 1980
5—Jorge Portela, Auburn vs. Florida (5 atts.) 1977
5—Alan Duncan, Tennessee vs. Kentucky (6 atts.) 1978
5—Fuad Reveiz, Tennessee vs. Memphis State (5 atts.) 1982
5—Fuad Reveiz, Tennessee vs. Kentucky (5 atts.) 1982
5—Brian Lee, Ole Miss vs. Tulane (5 atts.) 1991
5—Doug Pelfrey, Kentucky vs. Miss. State (7 atts.) 1992
5—Scott Etheridge, Auburn vs. LSU (5 atts.) 1992

SEASON:
27—Fuad Reveiz, Tennessee (31 atts.) 1982
24—Carlos Reveiz, Tennessee (28 atts.) 1985
24—Philip Doyle, Alabama (29 atts.) 1990
23—Bobby Raymond, Florida (26 atts.) 1984
23—Kevin Butler, Georgia (28 atts.) 1984
22—Philip Doyle, Alabama (25 atts.) 1989
22—Scott Etheridge, Auburn (28 atts.) 1992
22—Michael Proctor, Alabama (29 atts.) 1993
20—Bobby Raymond, Florida (23 atts.) 1983
20—Fuad Reveiz, Tennessee (23 atts.) 1984

CAREER:
78—Philip Doyle, Alabama (105 atts.) 1987-90
77—Kevin Butler, Georgia (98 atts.) 1981-84
71—Fuad Reveiz, Tennessee (95 atts.) 1981-84
61—David Browndyke, LSU (75 atts.) 1986-89
59—Van Tiffin, Alabama (87 atts.) 1983-86
57—Joey Worley, Kentucky (85 atts.) 1984-87
56—Rex Robinson, Georgia (84 atts.) 1977-80
48—Artie Cosby, Miss. State (81 atts.) 1983-86
46—Steve Crumley, Georgia (66 atts.) 1985-88
46—John Kasay, Georgia (65 atts.) 1987-90
45—Win Lyle, Auburn (59 atts.) 1987-89
43—Bobby Raymond, Florida (49 atts.) 1982-84
43—Brian Clark, Florida (63 atts.) 1979-81
43—John Becksvoort, Tennessee (57 atts.) 1991-present
42—Al Del Greco, Auburn (69 atts.) 1980-83
41—Joel Logan, Miss. State (61 atts.) 1987-90
41—Brian Lee, Ole Miss (75 atts) 1989-92
40—Ricky Anderson, Vanderbilt (57 atts.) 1982-84

LONG FIELD GOALS
GAME:
60—Fuad Reveiz, Tennessee vs. Georgia Tech 1982
60—Kevin Butler, Georgia vs. Clemson 1984
60—Chris Perkins, Florida vs. Tulane 1984
59—Cloyce Hinton, Ole Miss vs. Georgia 1969
59—Kevin Butler, Georgia vs. Ole Miss 1982
58—Allan Leavitt, Georgia vs. Vanderbilt 1976
57—Neil O'Donoghue, Auburn vs. Tennessee 1976

CONSECUTIVE FIELD GOALS
18—Fuad Reveiz, Tennessee 1984
17—Bobby Raymond, Florida 1984

FIELD GOAL PERCENTAGE
SEASON: (Min. 10 made)
100.0—David Browndyke, LSU (14 of 14) 1989
93.3—Mike Conway, LSU (14 of 15) 1978
SEASON: (Min. 20 made)
88.4—Bobby Raymond, Florida (23 of 26) 1984
87.1—Fuad Reveiz, Tennessee (27 of 31) 1982
86.9—Bobby Raymond, Florida (20 of 23) 1983
86.9—Fuad Reveiz, Tennessee (20 of 23) 1984
85.7—Carlos Reveiz, Tennessee (24 of 28) 1985
CAREER: (Min. 25 made)
* 88.0—Bobby Raymond, Florida (43 of 49) 1982-84
82.9—Berj Yepremian, Florida (29 of 35) 1976-78
81.3—David Browndyke, LSU (61 of 75) 1986-89
79.1—Scott Etheridge, Auburn (34 of 43) 1992-93
78.5—Kevin Butler, Georgia (77 of 98) 1981-84
76.3—Win Lyle, Auburn (45 of 59) 1987-89
75.4—John Becksvoort, Tennessee (43 of 57) 1991-present
75.0—Arden Czyzewski, Florida (33 of 44) 1988-91
74.7—Fuad Reveiz, Tennessee (71 of 95) 1981-84

74.3—Philip Doyle, Alabama (78 of 105) 1987-90
71.4—Bobby Etter, Georgia (25 of 35) 1964-66
70.8—John Kasay, Georgia (46 of 65) 1987-90
70.7—Kenny Willis, Kentucky (29 of 41) 1987-89
70.2—Ricky Anderson, Vanderbilt (40 of 57) 1982-84
69.8—Peter Kim, Alabama (37 of 53) 1980-82
69.7—Steve Crumley, Georgia (46 of 66) 1985-88
69.2—Johnny Clark, Vanderbilt (36 of 52) 1986-89
68.9—Alan Duncan, Tennessee (31 of 45) 1978-80
68.3—Brian Clark, Florida (43 of 63) 1979-81

PAT KICKS ATTEMPTED
GAME:
13—Red Lutz, Alabama vs. Delta State (made 11) 1951
11—Bill Davis, Alabama vs. Virginia Tech (made 11) 1973
11—George Jernigan, Georgia vs. Furman (made 10) 1946
10—Bob Gain, Kentucky vs. North Dakota (made 10) 1950
10—Bobby Moreau, LSU vs. Rice (made 10) 1977
SEASON:
59—John Becksvoort, Tennessee (made 59) 1993
58—Hugh Morrow, Alabama (made 46) 1945
54—Leo Costa, Georgia (made 42) 1942
53—Bill Davis, Alabama (made 51) 1973
53—Judd Davis, Florida (made 51) 1993
52—George Jernigan, Georgia (made 47) 1946
50—Bill Davis, Alabama (made 46) 1972
50—Greg Burke, Tennessee (made 50) 1990
49—Chris Knapp, Auburn (made 49) 1986
48—Zack Clinard, Vanderbilt (made 40) 1948
48—Juan Betanzos, LSU (made 47) 1982
45—Arden Czyzewski, Florida (made 42) 1990
45—Scott Etheridge, Auburn (made 45) 1993
44—Mark Lumpkin, LSU (made 38) 1969
44—Gardner Jett, Auburn (made 41) 1970
44—Kim Braswell, Georgia (made 38) 1971
44—Arden Czyzewski, Florida (made 44) 1991
43—George Hunt, Tennessee (made 42) 1970
CAREER:
148—Hugh Morrow, Alabama (made 120) 1944-47
143—Bill Davis, Alabama (made 133) 1971-73
135—Van Tiffin, Alabama (made 135) 1983-86
129—Allan Leavitt, Georgia (made 125) 1973-76
125—Kevin Butler, Georgia (made 122) 1981-84
122—John Becksvoort, Tennessee (made 122) 1991-present
111—George Hunt, Tennessee (made 107) 1969-71
111—Al Del Greco, Auburn (made 110) 1980-83
109—David Browndyke, LSU (made 109) 1986-89
108—Philip Doyle, Alabama (made 105) 1987-90
104—Gardner Jett, Auburn (made 98) 1970-72
104—David Posey, Florida (made 100) 1973-76
103—Fuad Reveiz, Tennessee (made 101) 1981-84
102—Rex Robinson, Georgia (made 101) 1977-80
102—Mark Lumpkin, LSU (made 92) 1968-70

PAT KICKS MADE
GAME:
11—Bill Davis, Alabama vs. Virginia Tech (11 atts.) 1973
11—Red Lutz, Alabama vs. Delta State (13 atts.) 1951
10—Bob Gain, Kentucky vs. North Dakota (10 atts.) 1950
10—Bobby Moreau, LSU vs. Rice (10 atts.) 1977
10—George Jernigan, Georgia vs. Furman (10 atts.) 1946
SEASON:
59—John Becksvoort, Tennessee (59 atts.) 1993
51—Bill Davis, Alabama (53 atts.) 1973
51—Judd Davis, Florida (53 atts.) 1993
50—Greg Burke, Tennessee (50 atts.) 1990
49—Chris Knapp, Auburn (49 atts.) 1986
47—Juan Betanzos, LSU (48 atts.) 1982
47—George Jernigan, Georgia (52 atts.) 1946
46—Bill Davis, Alabama (50 atts.) 1972
46—Hugh Morrow, Alabama (58 atts.) 1945
45—Scott Etheridge, Auburn (45 atts.) 1993
44—Arden Czyzewski, Florida (44 atts.) 1991
43—Leo Costa, Georgia (54 atts.) 1942
42—George Hunt, Tennessee (43 atts.) 1970
42—Arden Czyzewski, Florida (45 atts.) 1990

41—Gardner Jett, Auburn (44 atts.) 1970
41—David Browndyke, LSU (41 atts.) 1987
41—Todd Peterson, Georgia (42 atts.) 1992
CAREER:
135—Van Tiffin, Alabama (made 135) 1983-86
133—Bill Davis, Alabama (143 atts.) 1971-73
125—Allan Leavitt, Georgia (129 atts.) 1973-76
122—Kevin Butler, Georgia (125 atts.) 1981-84
122—John Becksvoort, Tennessee (made 122) 1993
120—Hugh Morrow, Alabama (148 atts.) 1944-47
110—Al Del Greco, Auburn (111 atts.) 1980-83
109—David Browndyke, LSU (109 atts.) 1986-89
107—George Hunt, Tennessee (111 atts.) 1969-71
105—Philip Doyle, Alabama (108 atts.) 1987-90
101—Rex Robinson, Georgia (102 atts.) 1977-80
101—Fuad Reveiz, Tennessee (103 atts.) 1981-84
100—David Posey, Florida (104 atts.) 1973-76

PAT KICKS PERCENTAGE
GAME: (Min. 10 atts.)
100—Bill Davis, Alabama vs. Virginia Tech (11 of 11) 1973
100—Bob Gain, Kentucky vs. North Dakota (10 of 10) 1950
100—Bobby Moreau, LSU vs. Rice (10 of 10) 1977
SEASON: (Min. 30 atts.)
100—Greg Burke, Tennessee (50 of 50) 1990
100—Chris Knapp, Auburn (49 of 49) 1986
100—Arden Czyzewski, Florida (44 of 44) 1991
100—David Browndyke, LSU (41 of 41) 1987
100—Van Tiffin, Alabama (40 of 40) 1983
100—Rex Robinson, Georgia (36 of 36) 1980
100—Peter Kim, Alabama (36 of 36) 1982
100—Greg Burke, Tennessee (36 of 36) 1989
100—John Becksvoort, Tennessee (35 of 35) 1992
100—Alan Duncan, Tennessee (33 of 33) 1979
100—Van Tiffin, Alabama (33 of 33) 1985
100—Steve Crumley, Georgia (33 of 33) 1986
100—Win Lyle, Auburn (32 of 32) 1987
100—Ricky Townsend, Tennessee (31 of 31) 1972
100—Kinney Jordan, Miss. State (31 of 31) 1976
100—Ricky Anderson, Vanderbilt (31 of 31) 1982
100—George Hunt, Tennessee (30 of 30) 1971
100—Carlos Reveiz, Tennessee (30 of 30) 1985
100—John Becksvoort, Tennessee (made 59 of 59) 1993
100—Scott Etheridge, Auburn (45 of 45) 1993
100—Michael Proctor, Alabama (31 of 31) 1993
CAREER: (MIN. 100 atts.)
*100—Van Tiffin, Alabama (135 of 135) 1983-86
*100—David Browndyke, LSU (109 of 109) 1986-89
100—Brian Clark, Florida (62 of 62) 1979-81
99.1—Al Del Greco, Auburn (110 of 111) 1980-83
99.0—Rex Robinson, Georgia (101 of 102) 1977-80

CONSECUTIVE PAT KICKS MADE
135—Van Tiffin, Alabama 1983-86
109—David Browndyke, LSU 1986-89
122—John Becksvoort, Tennessee 1991-present
101—Rex Robinson, Georgia 1977-80
 86—Greg Burke, Tennessee 1989-90
 66—Alan Duncan, Tennessee 1978-80
 65—Bryan Owen, Ole Miss 1986-87
 65—Scott Etheridge, Auburn 1992-93
 64—Joey Worley, Kentucky 1984-87
 63—John Becksvoort, Tennessee 1991-1992
 62—Brian Clark, Florida 1979-81
 61—Allan Leavitt, Georgia 1974-75
 60—George Hunt, Tennessee 1970-71

TOTAL POINTS SCORED BY KICKING
GAME:
23—Bobby Raymond, Florida vs. Florida State (6 FGs, 5 PATs) 1983
19—Bobby Raymond, Florida vs. Kentucky (6 FGs, 1 PAT) 1984
19—Philip Doyle, Alabama vs. SW Louisiana (6 FGs, 1 PAT) 1990
18—Al Del Greco, Auburn vs. Kentucky (6 FGs) 1982
18—Doug Pelfrey, Kentucky vs. Miss. State (5 FGs, 3 PAT) 1992
17—Jorge Portela, Auburn vs. Florida (5 FGs, 2 PATs) 1977
*—NCAA record

17—Alan Duncan, Tennessee vs. Kentucky (5 FGs, 2 PATs) 1978
17—Fuad Reveiz, Tennessee vs. Memphis State (5 FGs, 2 PATs) ..1982
17—David Browndyke, LSU vs. Miss. State (4 FGs, 5 PATs) 1986
SEASON:
107—Greg Burke, Tennessee (19 FGs, 50 PATs) 1990
103—Bobby Raymond, Florida (23 FGs, 34 PATs) 1984
102—Carlos Reveiz, Tennessee (24 FGs, 30 PATs) 1985
101—Fuad Reveiz, Tennessee (27 FGs, 20 PATs) 1982
100—Philip Doyle, Alabama (22 FGs, 34 PATs) 1989
 97—Philip Doyle, Alabama (24 FGs, 25 PATs) 1990
 97—Michael Proctor, Alabama (22 FGs, 31 PATs) 1993
 95—John Becksvoort, Tennessee (12 FGs, 59 PATs) 1993
 94—Michael Proctor, Alabama (19 FGs, 37 PATs) 1992
 94—Kevin Butler, Georgia (19 FGs, 37 PATs) 1981
 92—Kevin Butler, Georgia (23 FGs, 23 PATs) 1984
 92—Kanon Parkman, Georgia (19 FGs, 35 PATs) 1993
 89—Bobby Raymond, Florida (20 FGs, 29 PATs) 1983
 89—Fuad Reveiz, Tennessee (20 FGs, 29 PATs) 1984
 88—Phil Reich, Tennessee (16 FGs, 40 PATs) 1987
 86—Scott Etheridge, Auburn (22 FGs, 20 PATs) 1992
 85—Kevin Butler, Georgia (17 FGs, 34 PATs) 1982
 85—Philip Doyle, Alabama (19 FGs, 28 PATs) 1988
CAREER:
353—Kevin Butler, Georgia (77 FGs, 122 PATs) 1981-84
339—Philip Doyle, Alabama (78 FGs, 105 PATs) 1987-90
314—Fuad Reveiz, Tennessee (71 FGs, 101 PATs) 1981-84
312—Van Tiffin, Alabama (59 FGs, 135 PATs) 1983-86
292—David Browndyke, LSU (61 FGs, 109 PATs) 1986-89
269—Rex Robinson, Georgia (56 FGs, 101 PATs) 1977-80
251—John Becksvoort, Tennessee (43 FGs, 122 PATs) 1991-present
246—Joey Worley, Kentucky (57 FGs, 75 PATs) 1984-87
236—Al Del Greco, Auburn (42 FGs, 110 PATs) 1980-83
218—Steve Crumley, Georgia (46 FGs, 80 PATs) 1985-88
211—Bill Davis, Alabama (26 FGs, 133 PATs) 1971-73
211—Artie Cosby, Miss. State (48 FGs, 67 PATs) 1983-86
209—Allan Leavitt, Georgia (28 FGs, 125 PATs) 1971-73
207—Peter Kim, Alabama (37 FGs, 96 PATs) 1980-82
207—Brian Lee, Ole Miss (41 FGs, 84 PATs) 1989-92
203—George Hunt, Tennessee (32 FGs, 107 PATs) 1969-71

Georgia's Kevin Butler, a two-time All-America selection, is the SEC's all-time leading scorer with 353 points. The talented placekicker also stands second in the league with 77 career field goals.

1994 SEC Football 219

PUNTING

MOST PUNTS

GAME:

- 30—Bert Johnson, Kentucky vs. Washington & Lee 1934
- 23—Bud Walton, Florida vs. Georgia Tech 1938
- 21—Hawk Cavette, Georgia Tech vs. Florida 1938
- 19—Johnny Cain, Alabama vs. Tennessee 1932
- 16—Bob Hardison, Miss. State vs. TCU 1936
- 15—Connie Frederick, Auburn vs. Clemson 1968
- 14—Bill Hartman, Georgia vs. Auburn 1937
- 14—Bobby Collins, Miss. State vs. LSU 1951
- 14—Boyce Smith, Vanderbilt vs. Florida 1958
- 14—Dick McGraw, Miss. State vs. Southern Miss 1967
- 14—John Schaffler, Vanderbilt vs. Louisville 1971
- 14—Craig Colquitt, Tennessee vs. Kentucky 1976

SEASON:

- 101—Ralph Kercheval, Kentucky (4,413 yards for 43.5 avg.) 1933
- 95—Dick McGraw, Miss. State (3,567 yards for 37.5 avg.) 1967
- 92—Dick McGowen, Auburn (3,833 yards for 42.2 avg.) 1939
- 90—Dave Hardt, Kentucky (3,471 yards for 38.6 avg.) 1970
- 83—Bud Walton, Florida (3,002 yards for 36.2 avg.) 1938
- 83—Buster Morrison, Florida (3,187 yards for 38.4 avg.) 1972
- 81—Dixie Howell, Alabama (3,216 yards for 39.7 avg.) 1933
- 81—Al Doggett, LSU (3,147 yards for 38.9 avg.) 1952
- 80—Dave Hardt, Kentucky (3,257 yards for 40.7 avg.) 1969
- 80—Don Golden, Georgia (3,092 for 38.7 avg.) 1972

CAREER:

- 277—Jim Arnold, Vanderbilt (12,171 yards for 43.9) 1979-82
- 266—Jim Miller, Ole Miss (11,549 yards for 43.4 avg.) 1976-79
- 254—Bill Smith, Ole Miss (11,260 for 44.3) 1983-86
- 248—Dave Hardt, Kentucky (9,737 yards for 39.3 avg.) 1968-70
- 244—Lewis Colbert, Auburn (10,179 for 41.7 avg.) 1982-85
- 231—Charles Childers, Ole Miss (9,074 for 39.3 avg.) 1987-90
- 219—David Lawrence, Vanderbilt (9,058 yards for 41.4 avg.) 1989-92
- 217—Dana Moore, Miss. State (8,860 yards for 40.8 avg.) 1979-82
- 215—Jerry Shuford, Vanderbilt (8,393 yards for 39.0 avg.) 1963-65
- 214—Dick McGraw, Miss. State (8,358 yards for 39.1 avg.) 1965-67
- 213—Mike Riley, Miss. State (8,572 for 40.2) 1987-91
- 204—Craig Colquitt, Tennessee (8,662 yards for 42.5 avg.) 1975-77
- 203—Chris Mohr, Alabama (8,636 yards for 42.5 avg.) 1985-88
- 201—Jimmy Colquitt, Tennessee (8,816 yards for 43.9 avg.) 1981-84

YARDS PUNTED

GAME:

- 1,155—Bert Johnson, Kentucky vs. Washington & Lee (30 for 38.5 avg.) 1934
- 914—Johnny Cain, Alabama vs. Tennessee (19 for 48.1 avg.) 1932
- 904—Hawk Cavette, Georgia Tech vs. Florida (21 for 43.9 avg.) 1938
- 899—Bud Walton, Florida vs. Georgia Tech (23 for 39.1 avg.) 1938

SEASON:

- 4,413—Ralph Kercheval, Kentucky (101 for 43.5 avg.) 1933
- 3,883—Dick McGowen, Auburn (92 for 42.2 avg.) 1939
- 3,581—Bill Smith, Ole Miss (79 for 45.3 avg.) 1985
- 3,567—Dick McGraw, Miss. State (95 for 37.5 avg.) 1967
- 3,471—Dave Hardt, Kentucky (90 for 38.6 avg.) 1970
- 3,386—Jim Arnold, Vanderbilt (74 for 45.8 avg.) 1982
- 3,283—Jim Miller, Ole Miss (76 for 43.2 avg.) 1978
- 3,281—Jerry Shuford, Vanderbilt (79 for 41.5 avg.) 1965
- 3,257—Dave Hardt, Kentucky (80 for 40.7 avg.) 1969
- 3,216—Dixie Howell, Alabama (81 for 39.7 avg.) 1933
- 3,187—Buster Morrison, Florida (83 for 38.4 avg.) 1972

CAREER:

- 12,171—Jim Arnold, Vanderbilt (277 for 43.9 avg.) 1979-82
- 11,549—Jim Miller, Ole Miss (266 for 43.4 avg.) 1976-79
- 11,260—Bill Smith, Ole Miss (254 for 44.3) 1983-86
- 10,179—Lewis Colbert, Auburn (244 for 41.7) 1982-85
- 9,737—Dave Hardt, Kentucky (248 for 39.3 avg.) 1968-70
- 9,074—Charles Childers, Ole Miss (231 for 39.3 avg.) 1987-90
- 9,058—David Lawrence, Vanderbilt (219 for 41.4 avg.) 1989-92
- 8,860—Dana Moore, Miss. State (217 for 40.8 avg.) 1979-82
- 8,816—Jimmy Colquitt, Tennessee (201 for 43.9 avg.) 1981-84
- 8,662—Craig Colquitt, Tennessee (204 for 42.5 avg.) 1975-77
- 8,636—Chris Mohr, Alabama (203 for 42.5 avg.) 1985-88
- 8,572—Mike Riley, Miss. State (213 for 40.2) 1987-91
- 8,432—Paul Calhoun, Kentucky (198 for 42.6 avg.) 1981-84
- 8,393—Jerry Shuford, Vanderbilt (215 for 39.0 avg.) 1963-65
- 8,363—Dick McGraw, Miss. State (214 for 39.1 avg.) 1965-67
- 8,269—Julian Fagan, Ole Miss (199 for 41.5 avg.) 1967-69
- 8,220—Dick McGowen, Auburn (194 for 42.4 avg.) 1938-40

PUNTING AVERAGE

GAME: (Min. 2 punts)

- 84.5—Bill Smith, Ole Miss vs. Southern Miss (2 for 169) 1984

GAME (Min. 7 punts)

- 53.1—Jim Arnold, Vanderbilt vs. North Carolina (8 for 425) 1982
- 53.0—Fred Montsdeoca, Florida vs. Alabama (7 for 371) 1949
- 51.3—Billy Cannon, LSU vs. Ole Miss (7 for 359) 1957
- 51.3—Jim Arnold, Vanderbilt vs. Air Force (8 for 410) 1979

GAME (Min. 10 punts)

- 52.0—Ralph Kercheval, Kentucky vs. Cincinnati (10 for 520) 1933
- 48.1—Greg Breland, Ole Miss vs. Missouri (10 for 481) 1974
- 48.1—Johnny Cain, Alabama vs. Tennessee (19 for 914) 1932
- 47.3—Jerry Stovall, LSU vs. Ole Miss (10 for 473) 1960

GAME (Min. 20 punts)

- 43.0—Hawk Cavette, Georgia Tech vs. Florida (21 for 904) 1938

SEASON: (Min. 50 punts)

- 48.2—Ricky Anderson, Vanderbilt (58 for 2,793) 1984
- 46.9—Terry Daniel, Auburn (51 for 2,393) 1993
- 45.9—Jim Miller, Ole Miss (66 for 3,029) 1977
- 45.8—Jim Arnold, Vanderbilt (74 for 3,386) 1982
- 45.8—Lewis Colbert, Auburn (57 for 2,610) 1985
- 45.4—Chip Andrews, Georgia (63 for 2,858) 1984
- 45.3—Charles Conerly, Ole Miss (53 for 2,399) 1946

SEASON: (Min. 75 punts)

- 45.3—Bill Smith, Ole Miss (79 for 3,581) 1985
- 43.2—Jim Miller, Ole Miss (76 for 3,283) 1978
- 42.2—Dick McGowen, Auburn (92 for 3,883) 1939
- 41.6—Julian Fagan, Ole Miss (75 for 3,120) 1968
- 41.5—Jerry Shuford, Vanderbilt (79 for 3,281) 1965

SEASON (Min. 100 punts)

- 43.5—Ralph Kercheval, Kentucky (101 for 4,394) 1933

CAREER: (Min. 100 punts)

- 45.6—Ricky Anderson, Vanderbilt (111 for 5,067) 1983-84
- 44.5—Terry Daniel, Auburn (116 for 5,164) 1992-present
- 44.4—Ray Criswell, Florida (161 for 7,153) 1982-85
- *44.3—Bill Smith, Ole Miss (254 for 11,260) 1983-86
- 43.9—Jim Arnold, Vanderbilt (277 for 12,171) 1979-82
- 43.9—Jimmy Colquitt, Tennessee (204 for 8,662) 1981-84
- 43.6—Greg Gantt, Alabama (116 for 5,095) 1971-73
- 43.4—Jim Miller, Ole Miss (266 for 11,549) 1976-79
- 43.2—Chip Andrews, Georgia (109 for 4,706) 1983-84
- 43.0—Charley Conerly, Ole Miss (110 for 4,731) 1946-47
- 43.0—Paul Calhoun, Kentucky (188 for 8,094) 1982-84
- 42.8—Bobby Walden, Georgia (137 for 5,869) 1958-60
- 42.8—Malcolm Simmons, Alabama (154 for 6,596) 1981-83
- 42.8—Todd Jordan, Miss. State (112 for 4,793) 1989-93
- 42.6—Paul Calhoun, Kentucky (198 for 8,432) 1982-84
- 42.5—Chris Mohr, Alabama (203 for 8,636) 1985-88
- 42.5—Craig Colquitt, Tennessee (204 for 8,662) 1975-77

*NCAA Record (Minimum 250 punts)

220 Record Book

PUNTING

MOST PUNTS, 50 YARDS OR MORE
*86—Bill Smith, Ole Miss 1983-86

MOST CONSECUTIVE GAMES
1 PUNT OF 50 YARDS OR MORE
*32—Bill Smith, Ole Miss 1983-86

MOST GAMES AVERAGING 40
OR MORE YARDS (Minimum 4)
*36—Bill Smith, Ole Miss 1983-86

LONG PUNTS
GAME:
- 92—Bill Smith, Ole Miss vs. Southern Miss 1984
- 89—Dixie Howell, Alabama vs. Tennessee 1933
- 87—Rufus Deal, Auburn vs. Georgia Tech 1939
- 87—Spike Jones, Georgia vs. Auburn 1967
- 85—Greg Gantt, Alabama vs. Miss. State 1971
- 84—Mike Patrick, Miss. State vs. Alabama 1974
- 83—Dixie Howell, Alabama vs. Kentucky 1933
- 83—Billy Mann, Ole Miss vs. Tennessee 1938

PUNT RETURNS

MOST RETURNS
GAME:
- 17—A.B. Stubbs, Miss. State vs. TCU (122 yards) 1936
- 11—Bobby Herrington, Miss. State vs. Southwestern (116 yards) 1933
- 9—Bobby Jordan, Auburn vs. Clemson 1952
- 9—Mike Siganos, Kentucky vs. Tennessee (85 yards) 1976
- 8—Harry Gilmer, Alabama vs. Tennessee 1946
- 8—J.P. Moore, Vanderbilt vs. Florida 1946
- 8—Lee Nalley, Vanderbilt vs. Ole Miss 1948
- 8—Doug Cunningham, Ole Miss vs. Southern Miss (102 yards) 1966
- 8—Thomas Bailey, Auburn vs. Georgia Southern (62 yards) 1991

SEASON:
- 45—Willie Shelby, Alabama (396 yards) 1975
- 43—Lee Nalley, Vanderbilt (791 yards) 1948
- 43—Mike Siganos, Kentucky (308 yards) 1977
- 42—Bobby Majors, Tennessee (437 yards) 1971
- 42—Eddie Brown, Tennessee (429 yards) 1972
- 42—Greg Richardson, Alabama (393 yards) 1986
- 42—Thomas Bailey, Auburn (548 yards) 1991
- 41—Wallace Brown, Florida 1934
- 41—Sammy Grezaffi, LSU (369 yards) 1967
- 40—Mike Siganos, Kentucky (216 yards) 1976
- 40—Tony James, Miss. State (437 yards) 1989

CAREER:
- 125—Greg Richardson, Alabama (1,011 yards) 1983-86
- 121—Tony James, MSU (1,332 yards) 1989-92
- 117—Bobby Majors, Tennessee (1,163 yards) 1969-71
- 113—Mike Siganos, Kentucky (789 yards) 1975-77
- 109—Lee Nalley, Vanderbilt (1,695 yards) 1947-49
- 105—Trey Gainous, Auburn (954 yards) 1983-86
- 97—Thomas Bailey, Auburn (1,012 yards) 1991-present
- 89—Willie Shelby, Alabama (861 yards) 1973-75
- 89—Jimmy Harrell, Georgia (787 yards) 1981-84
- 88—Buzy Rosenberg, Georgia (946 yards) 1970-72
- 88—Scott Woerner, Georgia (1,077 yards) 1977-80
- 85—Tony James, Miss. State (974 yards) 1989-91
- 84—Junie Hovious, Ole Miss (1,142 yards) 1939-41
- 83—Harry Gilmer, Alabama (1,119 yards) 1944-47
- 83—David Palmer, Alabama (889 yards) 1991-93
- 81—Doug Cunningham, Ole Miss (941 yards) 1964-66

YARDS RETURNED
GAME:
- 203—Lee Nalley, Vanderbilt vs. Kentucky (6 returns) 1948
- 202—Buzy Rosenberg, Georgia vs. Oregon State (5 returns) 1971
- 195—Andy Molls, Kentucky vs. Vanderbilt (6 returns) 1981
- 173—Mike Fuller, Auburn vs. Chattanooga (3 returns) 1977
- 169—Norman Jefferson, LSU vs. Ole Miss (7 returns) 1983
- 157—Bobby Herrington, Miss. State vs. Vanderbilt (8 returns) 1933
- 156—Phil Cutchin, Kentucky vs. Georgia (4 returns) 1946
- 149—Tom McWilliams, Miss. State vs. Chattanooga (4 returns) 1946
- 145—Joe Labruzzo, LSU vs. Rice (3 returns) 1965
- 135—Bert Rechichar, Tennessee vs. Wash. & Lee (3 returns) 1950

*—NCAA Record

SEASON:
- *791—Lee Nalley, Vanderbilt (43 returns) 1948
- 539—Pinky Rohm, LSU (35 returns) 1937
- 528—Thomas Bailey, Auburn (42 returns) 1991
- 502—Mike Fuller, Auburn (30 returns) 1974
- 498—Junie Hovious, Ole Miss (36 returns) 1940
- 498—Lee Nalley, Vanderbilt (35 returns) 1949
- 488—Scott Woerner, Georgia (31 returns) 1980
- 473—Jimmy Carter, Auburn (38 returns) 1967
- 464—Lamar Davis, Georgia 1941
- 463—Junie Hovious, Ole Miss (36 returns) 1941
- 457—Bobby Majors, Tennessee (38 returns) 1969

CAREER:
- *1,695—Lee Nalley, Vanderbilt (109 returns) 1947-49
- 1,332—Tony James, MSU (121 returns) 1989-92
- 1,163—Bobby Majors, Tennessee (117 returns) 1969-71
- 1,142—Junie Hovious, Ole Miss (84 returns) 1938-41
- 1,119—Harry Gilmer, Alabama (83 returns) 1944-47
- 1,119—Greg Richardson, Alabama (125 returns) 1983-86
- 1,077—Scott Woerner, Georgia (88 returns) 1977-80
- 1,065—Dicky Lyons, Kentucky (69 returns) 1966-68
- 1,014—Chuck Carswell, Georgia (88 returns) 1988-91
- 1,012—Thomas Bailey, Auburn (47 returns) 1991-present

GAIN PER RETURN
GAME: (Min. 3)
- 57.6—Mike Fuller, Auburn vs. Chattanooga (3 for 173) 1974
- 48.3—Joe Labruzzo, LSU vs. Rice (3 for 145) 1963
- 45.0—Bert Rechichar, Tennessee vs. Wash. & Lee (3 for 135) 1950
- 40.4—Buzy Rosenberg, Georgia vs. Oregon State (5 for 202) 1971
- 37.8—Will Glover, Ole Miss vs. Chattanooga (4 for 151) 1947
- 37.3—Tom McWilliams, Miss. State vs. Chattanooga (4 for 149) .1946
- 35.0—Tony Kotowski, Miss. State vs. Ark. State (3 for 105) 1951
- 33.8—Lee Nalley, Vanderbilt vs. Kentucky (6 for 203) 1948
- 32.5—Andy Molls, Kentucky vs. Vanderbilt (6 for 195) 1981

SEASON: (Min. 10)
- 26.7—Hal Griffin, Florida (10 for 267) 1947
- *25.9—Bill Blackstock, Tennessee (12 for 311) 1951
- 25.2—Ken Phares, Miss. State (10 for 252) 1971
- 23.9—Hal Griffin, Florida (13 for 310) 1946
- 21.7—Marcus Rhoden, Miss. State (19 for 413) 1965
- 20.4—Walter Slater, Tennessee 1941
- 20.0—Gordon Pettus, Alabama (10 for 200) 1948

SEASON: (Min. 20)
- 19.1—Mike Fuller, Auburn (20 for 381) 1973
- 18.4—Rick Kimbrough, Ole Miss (20 for 368) 1973

SEASON: (Min. 40)
- 18.4—Lee Nalley, Vanderbilt (43 for 791) 1948

SEASON: (Min. 50)
- 17.7—Mike Fuller, Auburn (50 for 883) 1973-74
- 15.4—Dicky Lyons, Kentucky (69 for 1,065) 1966-68
- 14.7—Bert Rechichar, Tennessee (55 for 808) 1949-51
- 14.5—Tom McWilliams, Miss. State (55 for 795) 1944, 46-48

1994 SEC Football

PUNT RETURNS

GAIN PER RETURN (Continued)

CAREER: (Min. 100)
- 15.6— Lee Nalley, Vanderbilt (109 for 1,695)..................1947-49
- 11.0—Tony James, MSU (121 for 1,332)..........................1989-92
- 9.9— Bobby Majors, Tennessee (117 for 1,163)................1969-71
- 9.1— Trey Gainous, Auburn (105 for 954).......................1983-86
- 8.1— Greg Richardson, Alabama (125 for 1,011)..............1983-86

PUNT RETURN TOUCHDOWNS

GAME:
- *2— Tommy Casanova, LSU vs. Ole Miss........................1970
- *2— Buzy Rosenberg, Georgia vs. Oregon State.............1971
- *2— David Langner, Auburn vs. Alabama.......................1972
- *2— Mike Fuller, Auburn vs. Chattanooga......................1974

SEASON:
- 3— Pinky Rohm, LSU...1937
- 3— Lee Nalley, Vanderbilt..1948
- 3— Marcus Rhoden, Miss. State......................................1965
- 3— Mike Fuller, Auburn..1974
- 3— David Palmer, Alabama..1991

CAREER:
- 5—Lee Nalley, Vanderbilt..1947-49
- 4—David Palmer, Alabama...1991-1993
- 4—Tom McWilliams, Miss. State.....................................1944-47
- 4—Bobby Majors, Tennessee..1969-71
- 4—Steve Tannen, Florida...1967-69
- 4—Buzy Rosenberg, Georgia..1970-72

LONG PUNT RETURNS

GAME:
- 100—Bert Rechichar, Tennessee vs. Washington & Lee..........1950
- 100—Jim Campagna, Georgia vs. Vanderbilt........................1952
- 98—Ray Hapes, Ole Miss vs. SW Louisiana......................1935
- 97—Hal Griffin, Florida vs. Miami......................................1946
- 97—Dicky Lyons, Kentucky vs. Houston.............................1966
- 96—Ray Hapes, Ole Miss vs. Union...................................1936
- 96—John Hovious, Ole Miss vs. Georgia...........................1940
- 95—Ray Hapes, Ole Miss vs. SW Louisiana.......................1935
- 95—Rab Rodgers, Ole Miss vs. Memphis State.................1935
- 95—Bobby Freeman, Auburn vs. Georgia..........................1953

KICKOFF RETURNS

MOST RETURNS

GAME:
- 7—Doug Matthews, Vanderbilt vs. Florida (168 yards)................1969
- 7—Jeff Peeples, Vanderbilt vs. Ole Miss (138 yards)..................1970
- 7—Willie Gault, Tennessee vs. USC (123 yards).........................1981
- 6—Chuck Boyd, Vanderbilt vs. Alabama....................................1966
- 6—Doug Matthews, Vanderbilt vs. Florida (105 yards)................1967
- 6—Eric Hoggatt, Miss. State vs. Houston (157 yards)..................1969
- 6—David Smith, Miss. State vs. LSU (175 yards)........................1969
- 6—Walter Packer, Miss. State vs. Kentucky (99 yards)................1973
- 6—Rick Kimbrough, Ole Miss vs. Alabama (98 yards).................1974
- 6—Scott Woerner, Georgia vs. Kentucky (190 yards)..................1977
- 6—George Adams, Kentucky vs. Florida (90 yards)....................1984
- 6—George Adams, Kentucky vs. LSU (59 yards)........................1982
- 6—Kurt Johnson, Kentucky vs. LSU (99 yards)..........................1991
- 6—Kurt Johnson, Kentucky vs. Florida (98 yards)......................1991
- 6—Michael Robinson, Miss. State vs. Alabama (150 yards).......1986
- 6—Vincent Brownlee, Ole Miss vs. Georgia (112 yards)..............1991
- 6—Bernard Euell, Miss. State vs. LSU (55 yards).......................1993

SEASON:
- 33—Jeff Peeples, Vanderbilt (646 yards)....................................1970
- 32—Tony Jackson, Vanderbilt (794 yards).................................1992
- 31—Preston Brown, Vanderbilt (536 yards)................................1979
- 31—Tony Jackson, Vanderbilt (753 yards).................................1993
- 29—Kerry Watkins, Florida (666 yards).......................................1986
- 28—Dave Strong, Vanderbilt (577 yards)....................................1967
- 28—Gene Washington, Georgia (669 yards)...............................1974
- 28—Willie Gault, Tennessee (606 yards).....................................1981
- 28—Mark Johnson, Vanderbilt (635 yards).................................1987
- 28—Pat Coleman, Ole Miss (560 yards).....................................1988
- 27—David Smith, Miss. State (590 yards)..................................1968
- 27—James Brooks, Auburn (654 yards).....................................1977
- 27—Lindsay Scott, Georgia (532 yards).....................................1979
- 27—Mark Johnson, Vanderbilt (582 yards).................................1986
- 27—Mark Johnson, Vanderbilt (521 yards).................................1988
- 27—Eddie Myles, Miss. State (535 yards)..................................1988
- 27—Dale Carter, Tennessee (623 yards)....................................1991
- 27—Ronald Davis, Tennessee (570 yards).................................1992

CAREER:
- 107—Mark Johnson, Vanderbilt (2,263 yards)..........................1986-88, 90
- 85—Tony Jackson, Vanderbilt (2,004 yards)............................1989-93

*—NCAA record

- 80—Preston Brown, Vanderbilt (1,497 yards)..........................1976-79
- 78—Willie Gault, Tennessee (1,854 yards)..............................1979-82
- 78—Tony James, Miss. State (1,862 yards)..............................1989-92
- 74—Corey Harris, Vanderbilt (1,614 yards)...............................1988-91
- 74—Kurt Johnson, Kentucky (1,560 yards)................................1989-92
- 71—Gene Washington, Georgia (1,637 yards)..........................1973-76
- 70—Robert Dow, LSU (1,780 yards)..1973-76
- 68—James Brooks, Auburn (1,726 yards).................................1977-80
- 68—John Moore, Miss. State (1,197 yards)..............................1985-89
- 66—Glen Young, Miss. State (1,538 yards)..............................1979-82
- 65—Doug Nettles, Vanderbilt (1,449 yards)..............................1971-73
- 64—Clay Parker, Vanderbilt (1,388 yards).................................1981-83, 85
- 61—Thomas Bailey, Auburn (1,303 yards)................................1991-present
- 60—Walter Packer, Miss. State (1,166 yards)..........................1973-76

YARDS RETURNED

GAME:
- 197—Kerry Goode, Alabama vs. Boston College (4 returns)..........1984
- 196—George Ranager, Alabama vs. Auburn (5 returns)................1969
- 190—Scott Woerner, Georgia vs. Kentucky (6 returns)..................1977
- 175—David Smith, Miss. State vs. LSU (6 returns).......................1969
- 168—Doug Matthews, Vanderbilt vs. Florida (7 returns)................1969
- 166—Roger Gann, Kentucky vs. Indiana (4 returns)......................1969
- 159—Tony Mayes, Kentucky vs. Georgia (5 returns).....................1983
- 159—Tony Lomack, Florida vs. Kentucky (3 returns)....................1989
- 159—Andre Hasting, Georgia vs. Kentucky (3 returns).................1990
- 158—Harry Jones, Kentucky vs. Tennessee (5 returns)................1951
- 157—Eric Hoggatt, Miss. State vs. Houston (6 returns)................1969
- 155—Robert Beaird, Auburn vs. Alabama...................................1965
- 150—Cris Collinsworth, Florida vs. LSU (4 returns).....................1978

SEASON:
- 794—Tony Jackson, Vanderbilt (32 returns)................................1992
- 753—Tony Jackson, Vanderbilt (31 returns)................................1993
- 669—Gene Washington, Georgia (28 returns)............................1974
- 666—Kerry Watkins, Florida (29 returns)......................................1986
- 662—Willie Gault, Tennessee (24 returns)..................................1980
- 654—James Brooks, Auburn (27 returns)....................................1977
- 646—Jeff Peeples, Vanderbilt (33 returns)..................................1970
- 643—Michael Robinson, Miss. State (26 returns).......................1986
- 635—Mark Johnson, Vanderbilt (28 returns)...............................1987
- 623—Dale Carter, Tennessee (27 returns)..................................1991
- 607—Doug Matthews, Vanderbilt (26 returns)............................1969
- 606—Willie Gault, Tennessee (28 returns)..................................1981

KICKOFF RETURNS

CAREER:
- 2,263—Mark Johnson, Vanderbilt (107 returns) 1986-88, 90
- 2,004—Tony Jackson, Vanderbilt (85 returns) 1989-93
- 1,862—Tony James, Miss. State (78 returns) 1989-92
- 1,854—Willie Gault, Tennessee (78 returns) 1979-82
- 1,780—Robert Dow, LSU (70 returns) 1973-76
- 1,726—James Brooks, Auburn (68 returns) 1977-80
- 1,637—Gene Washington, Georgia (71 returns) 1973-76
- 1,614—Corey Harris, Vanderbilt (74 returns) 1988-91
- 1,560—Kurt Johnson, Kentucky (74 returns) 1989-92
- 1,538—Glen Young, Miss. State (66 returns) 1979-82
- 1,497—Preston Brown, Vanderbilt (80 returns) 1976-79
- 1,449—Doug Nettles, Vanderbilt (65 returns) 1971-73
- 1,388—Clay Parker, Vanderbilt (64 returns) 1981-83; 85
- 1,303—Thomas Bailey, Auburn (61 returns) 1991-present
- 1,248—Willie Jackson, Florida (57 returns) 1970-72
- 1,197—John Moore, Miss. State (68 returns) 1985-89
- 1,188—Dicky Lyons, Kentucky (56 returns) 1966-68
- 1,166—Walter Packer, Miss. State (60 returns) 1973-76
- 1,140—Lindsay Scott, Georgia (51 returns) 1978-81

YARDS PER RETURN

SEASON: (Min. 20)
- 27.9—Dan Bland, Miss. State (20 for 558) 1964
- 27.6—Willie Gault, Tennessee (24 for 662) 1980
- 27.5—James Brooks, Auburn (21 for 577) 1979
- 26.5—Lindsay Scott, Georgia (20 for 529) 1978
- 26.0—Robert Dow, LSU, (23 for 598) 1975
- 25.6—Kurt Johnson, Kentucky (21 for 537) 1989
- 25.0—Dan Bland, Miss. State (20 for 499) 1965
- 25.0—Robert Dow, LSU (20 for 499) 1976

SEASON: (Min. 30)
- 24.8—Tony Jackson, Vanderbilt (32 for 794) 1992
- 24.3—Tony Jackson, Vanderbilt (31 for 753) 1993
- 19.6—Jeff Peeples, Vanderbilt (33 for 646) 1970
- 17.3—Preston Brown, Vanderbilt (31 for 536) 1979

CAREER: (Min. 30)
- 27.1—Calvin Bird, Kentucky (37 for 1,001) 1958-60
- 26.6—Dan Bland, Miss. State (42 for 1,118) 1963-65
- 25.7—Dale Carter, Tennessee (44 for 1,130) 1990-91
- 25.4—Doug Cunningham, Ole Miss (35 for 888) 1964-66

CAREER: (min. 50)
- 25.4—Robert Dow, LSU (70 for 1,780) 1973-76
- 25.4—James Brooks, Auburn (68 for 1,726) 1977-80
- 23.9—Tony James, Miss. State (78 for 1,862) 1989-92
- 23.8—Willie Gault, Tennessee (78 for 1,854) 1979-82
- 23.7—Tony James, Miss. State (60 for 1,424) 1989-91
- 23.6—Tony Jackson, Vanderbilt (85 for 2,004) 1989-93
- 23.4—Gene Washington, Georgia (71 for 1,668) 1973-76
- 23.3—Glen Young, Miss. State (66 for 1,538) 1979-82
- 22.5—Harrison Houston, Florida (54 for 1,216) 1990-93
- 22.2—Paul Hofer, Ole Miss (51 for 1,133) 1972-75
- 21.9—Willie Jackson, Florida (57 for 1,248) 1970-72
- 21.8—Corey Harris, Vanderbilt (74 for 1,614) 1988-91
- 21.7—Clay Parker, Vanderbilt (64 for 1388) 1981-83; 85

KICKOFF RETURN TOUCHDOWNS

SEASON:
- 3—Willie Gault, Tennessee 1980

CAREER:
- 4—Willie Gault, Tennessee 1979-82

LONG KICKOFF RETURNS

GAME:
- 100—Pat Reen, Florida vs. Miami 1940
- 100—Jim Burkett, Alabama vs. Duquesne 1949
- 100—Bobby Duke, Alabama vs. Auburn 1953
- 100—Jimmy Burson, Alabama vs. Tennessee-Chattanooga 1960
- 100—Gary Martin, Alabama vs. Miami 1963
- 100—Ray Ogden, Alabama vs. Auburn 1964
- 100—Sammy Grezaffi, LSU vs. Tennessee 1967
- 100—George Ranager, Alabama vs. Auburn 1969
- 100—Vernon Studdard, Ole Miss vs. Alabama 1970
- 100—Willie Shelby, Alabama vs. Kentucky 1973
- 100—Preston Brown, Vanderbilt vs. Ole Miss 1977
- 100—Sam DeJarnette, Auburn vs. Miss. State 1980
- 100—Willie Gault, Tennessee vs. Pittsburgh 1980
- 100—Glen Young, Miss. State vs. LSU 1980
- 100—Eric Martin, LSU vs. Kentucky 1981
- 100—Pierre Goode, Alabama vs. Ole Miss 1988
- 100—Kurt Johnson, Kentucky vs. Georgia 1989

TOTAL KICK RETURNS

MOST RETURNS

SEASON:
- 66—Thomas Bailey, Auburn (42 PR, 24 KOR) 1991
- 61—Tony James, Miss. State (40 PR, 21 KOR) 1989
- 59—Willie Gault, Tennessee (31 PR, 28 KOR) 1981
- 58—Sammy Grezaffi, (41 PR, 17 KOR) 1967
- 55—Willie Shelby, Alabama (45 PR, 10 KOR) 1975
- 54—Tony James, Miss. State (36 PR, 18 KOR) 1992
- 53—Thomas Bailey, Auburn (27 PR, 26 KOR) 1993
- 51—Doug Cunningham, Ole Miss (33 PR, 18 KOR) 1965
- 51—Dale Carter, Tennessee (24 PR, 27 KOR) 1991
- 50—Wayne Swineford, Georgia (34 PR, 16 KOR) 1964
- 50—Bobby Majors, Tennessee (42 PR, 8 KOR) 1971
- 50—Vincent Brownlee, Ole Miss (28 PR, 22 KOR) 1991
- 49—Pat Coleman, Ole Miss (21 PR, 28 KOR) 1988
- 48—Danny Fischer, Ole Miss (35 PR, 13 KOR) 1976
- 47—Preston Brown, Vanderbilt (16 PR, 31 KOR) 1979
- 46—Jake Scott, Georgia (35 PR, 11 KOR) 1969
- 46—Dale Carter, Tennessee (17 PR, 29 KOR) 1990
- 45—Bobby Majors, Tennessee (37 PR, 8 KOR) 1969
- 45—Preston Brown, Vanderbilt (12 PR, 24 KOR) 1977
- 45—Willie Gault, Tennessee (21 PR, 24 KOR) 1980

CAREER:
- *199—Tony James, Miss. State (121 PR, 78 KOR) 1989-92
- 158—Thomas Bailey, Auburn (97 PR, 61 KOR) 1991-present
- 156—Willie Gault, Tennessee (78 PR, 78 KOR) 1979-82
- 139—Preston Brown, Vanderbilt (59 PR, 80 KOR) 1976-79
- 138—Kurt Johnson, Kentucky (64 PR, 74 KOR) 1989-92
- 133—Bobby Majors, Tennessee (117 PR, 16 KOR) 1969-71
- 129—Sammy Grezaffi, LSU (79 PR, 40 KOR) 1965-67
- 125—Dicky Lyons, Kentucky (69 PR, 56 KOR) 1966-68
- 119—Lee Nalley, Vanderbilt (109 PR, 10 KOR) 1947-49
- 116—Doug Cunningham, Ole Miss (81 PR, 35 KOR) 1964-66
- 112—Glen Young, Miss. State (46 PR, 66 KOR) 1979-82
- 112—Willie Goodloe, Ole Miss (64 PR, 48 KOR) 1984-88
- 111—Stanley Morgan, Tennessee (74 PR, 37 KOR) 1973-76
- 107—Mark Johnson, Vanderbilt (0 PR, 107 KOR) 1986-88, 90
- 105—Thomas Bailey, Auburn (70 PR, 35 KOR) 1991-1992
- 97—Dale Carter, Tennessee (53 PR, 44 KOR) 1990-91
- 93—Hal Littleford, Tennessee (79 PR, 14 KOR) 1947-49

MOST RETURN YARDS

GAME:
- 235—Dicky Lyons, Kentucky vs. LSU (4/75 PR, 4/160 KOR) 1967
- 210—Dale Carter, Tennessee vs. Kentucky (4/62 PR, 4/148 KOR) 1990
- 203—Lee Nalley, Vanderbilt vs. Kentucky (6/203 PR) 1948
- 202—Buzy Rosenberg, Georgia vs. Oregon State (5/202 PR) 1971
- 201—Willie Gault, Tennessee vs. Ole Miss (2/115 PR, 3/86 KOR) 1981
- 200—Mike Fuller, Auburn vs. Chattanooga (3/173 PR, 1/27 KOR) 1974

SEASON:
- 1,119—Thomas Bailey, Auburn (42/528 PR, 24/591 KOR) 1991
- 987—Willie Gault, Tennessee (31/381 PR, 28/606 KOR) 1981
- 914—Tony James, Miss. State (40/437 PR, 21/477 KOR) 1989
- 888—Dale Carter, Tennessee (29/381 PR, 17/507 KOR) 1990
- 864—Dicky Lyons, Kentucky (24/390 PR, 18/474 KOR) 1967
- 849—Vincent Brownlee, Ole Miss (28/331 PR, 22/518 KOR) 1991
- 845—Doug Cunningham, Ole Miss (33/395 PR, 18/450 KOR) 1965
- 801—Mike Fuller, Auburn (20/381 PR, 16/420 KOR) 1973
- 796—Tony James, Miss. State (36/358 PR, 18/438 KOR) 1992
- 794—Tony Jackson, Vanderbilt (32/794 KOR) 1992
- 791—Lee Nalley, Vanderbilt (43/791 PR) 1948
- 773—Tony James, Miss. State (23/341 PR, 18/432 KOR) 1990
- 768—Pat Coleman, Ole Miss (21/208 PR, 26/560 KOR) 1988

1994 SEC Football

TOTAL KICK RETURNS

MOST RETURN YARDS (Continued)

SEASON:

- 765— Willie Gault, Tennessee (21/103 PR, 24/662 KOR) 1980
- 764— Dale Carter, Tennessee (24/141 PR, 27/623 KOR) 1991
- 764— Tony Jackson, Vanderbilt (2/11 PR, 31/757 KOR) 1993
- 724— Lee Nalley, Vanderbilt (35/498 PR, 8/226 KOR) 1949
- 718— Kurt Johnson, Kentucky (15/181 PR, 21/537 KOR) 1989
- 714— Glen Young, Miss. State (19/307 PR, 18/407 KOR) 1981
- 714— Thomas Bailey, Auburn (27/210 PR, 26/504 KOR) 1993
- 711— Tony James, Miss. State (22/196 PR, 18/438 KOR) 1991
- 709— Wayne Swineford, Georgia (34/343 PR, 16/366 KOR) 1964
- 703— Dicky Lyons, Kentucky (20/256 PR, 22/447 KOR) 1968
- 703— Kerry Watkins, Florida (6/37 PR, 29/666 KOR) 1986

CAREER:

- *3,194— Tony James, Miss. State (121/1,332 PR, 78/1,862 KOR) 1989-92
- 2,513— Willie Gault, Tennessee (78/659 PR, 78/1,854 KOR) 1979-82
- 2,315— Thomas Bailey, Auburn (97/1,012 PR, 61/1,303 KOR) 1991-1993
- 2,263— Mark Johnson, Vanderbilt (107/2,263 KOR) 1986-88, 90
- 2,253— Dicky Lyons, Kentucky (69/1,065 PR, 56/1,188 KOR) 1966-68
- 2,088— Kurt Johnson, Kentucky (64/528 PR, 74/1,560 KOR) 1989-92
- 2,050— Glen Young, Miss. State (46/512 PR, 66/1,538 KOR) 1979-82
- 2,040— Robert Dow, LSU (37/260 PR, 70/1,780 KOR) 1973-76
- 2,015— Tony Jackson, Vanderbilt (2/11 PR, 85/2,004 KOR) 1989-93
- 1,994— Preston Brown, Vanderbilt (59/497 PR, 80/1,497) 1976-79
- 1,976— Lee Nalley, Vanderbilt (109/1,695 PR, 10/281 KOR) 1947-49
- 1,854— James Brooks, Auburn (15/128 PR, 68/1,726 KOR) 1977-80
- 1,850— Corey Harris, Vanderbilt (32/236 PR, 74/1,614 KOR) 1988-91
- 1,829— Doug Cunningham, Ole Miss (81/941, 35/888 KOR) 1964-66
- 1,738— Mark Johnson, Vanderbilt (82/1,738 KOR) 1986-88
- 1,668— Mike Fuller, Auburn (50/883 PR, 33/785 KOR) 1972-74
- 1,652— Dale Carter, Tennessee (53/522 PR, 44/1,130 KOR) 1990-91
- 1,615— Stanley Morgan, Tennessee (74/852, 37/763) 1973-76
- 1,530— Bobby Majors, Tennessee (117/1,163 PR, 16/367 KOR) 1969-71

YARDS PER RETURN

GAME:

- 50.0— Mike Fuller, Auburn vs. Chattanooga (200 yds., 4 rets.) 1974
- 49.3— Kerry Goode, Alabama vs. Boston Coll. (197 yds., 4 rets.) 1984
- 48.8— Bobby Majors, Tennessee vs. Penn State (195 yds., 4 rets.) 1971
- 40.8— Tony Jackson, Vanderbilt vs. Duke (163 yards, 4 rets.) 1992
- 40.4— Buzy Rosenberg, Georgia vs. Ore. St. (202 yds., 5 rets.) 1971

SEASON: (Min. 20)

- 24.8— Calvin Bird, Kentucky (10/169 PR, 14/426 KOR) 1959
- 24.2— Tony Nathan, Alabama (18/223 PR, 10/212 KOR) 1977
- 20.6— Dicky Lyons, Kentucky (24/390 PR, 18/474 KOR) 1967

CAREER: (Min. 100)

- 21.1— Mark Johnson, Vanderbilt (107/2,263 KOR) 1986-88, 90
- 19.1— Robert Dow, LSU (37/360 PR, 70/1,780 KOR) 1973-76
- 18.4— Glen Young, Miss. State (46/512 PR, 66/1,538 KOR) 1979-82
- 18.0— Dicky Lyons, Kentucky (60/1,065 PR, 56/1,188 KOR) 1966-68
- 17.5— Corey Harris, Vanderbilt (32/236 PR, 74/1,614 KOR) 1988-91
- 16.6— Lee Nalley, Vanderbilt (109/1,695 PR, 10/281 KOR) 1947-49
- 16.1— Willie Gault, Tennessee (78/659 PR, 78/1,854 KOR) 1979-82
- 16.1— Tony James, Miss. State (121/1,332 PR, 78/1,862 KOR) 1989-92

KICK RETURN TOUCHDOWNS

SEASON:

- 5— Pinky Rohm, LSU (3 PR, 2 KOR) 1937

CAREER:

- 6— Lee Nalley, Vanderbilt (5 PR, 1 KOR) 1947-49
- 5— Pinky Rohm, LSU (3 PR, 2 KOR) 1937
- 5— Willie Gault, Tennessee (1 PR, 4 KOR) 1979-82
- 5— Tom McWilliams, Miss. State (4 PR, 1 KOR) 1944-48
- 4— Doug Cunningham, Ole Miss (3 PR, 1 KOR) 1964-66
- 4— Marcus Rhoden, Miss. State (3 PR, 1 KOR) 1964-66
- 4— Bobby Majors, Tennessee (4 PR) 1969-71
- 4— Mike Fuller, Auburn (3 PR, 1 KOR) 1972-74
- 4— Steve Tannen, Florida (4 PR) 1967-69
- 4— David Palmer, Alabama (4 PR) 1991-1992

INTERCEPTIONS

MOST INTERCEPTIONS

GAME:

- 4— Jack Nix, Mississippi State vs. Arkansas 1939
- 3— 36 players; last players:
- Marcus Jenkins, Kentucky vs. Florida 1993
- Will White, Florida vs. Alabama 1990
- Chris Donnelly, Vanderbilt vs. Memphis State 1989
- Shan Morris, Auburn vs. Mississippi State 1988
- Todd Sandroni, Ole Miss vs. Georgia 1988
- Preston Warren, Tennessee vs. Boston College 1988
- Aundray Bruce, Auburn vs. Georgia Tech 1987
- Don Price, Ole Miss vs. Vanderbilt 1986
- Chris White, Tennessee vs. UCLA 1985
- Tom Powell, Auburn vs. Tennessee 1985

SEASON:

- 12— J.W. Sherrill, Tennessee (104 yards) 1949
- 12— Terry Hoage, Georgia (51 yards) 1982
- 10— Bobby Wilson, Ole Miss (70 yards) 1949
- 10— Hootie Ingram, Alabama (163 yards) 1952
- 10— Jake Scott, Georgia (175 yards) 1968
- 10— Bobby Majors, Tennessee (177 yards) 1970
- 10— Ben Smith, Georgia (54 yards) 1989

CAREER:

- 20— Bobby Wilson, Ole Miss (379 yards) 1946-49
- 20— Chris Williams, LSU (91 yards) 1977-80
- 19— Glen Cannon, Ole Miss (180 yards) 1967-69
- 19— Antonio Langham, Alabama (229 yards) 1990-93
- 18— Buddy McClinton, Auburn (251 yards) 1967-69
- 18— Tim Priest, Tennessee (305 yards) 1968-70
- 16— Jake Scott, Georgia (315 yards) 1967-68
- 16— Mike Jones, Tennessee (305 yards) 1967-69
- 16— Harry Harrison, Ole Miss (242 yards) 1971-73
- 16— Jeremiah Castille, Alabama (186 yards) 1979-82
- 16— John Mangum, Alabama (95 yards) 1986-89

YARDS RETURNED

GAME:

- 162— Joe Brodsky, Florida vs. Miss. State (3 int.) 1956
- 155— Greg Long, Kentucky vs. North Texas State (3 int.) 1981

SEASON:

- 244— Joe Brodsky, Florida (5 int.) 1956
- 219— Greg Jackson, LSU (7 int.) 1988
- 197— David Hunter, Kentucky (3 int.) 1968
- 189— Eli Marichich, Georgia (8 int.) 1948
- 177— Bobby Majors, Tennessee (10 int.) 1970
- 176— Greg Long, Kentucky (4 int.) 1981
- 175— Jake Scott, Georgia (10 int.) 1968
- 174— Tim Priest, Tennessee (9 int.) 1970
- 169— Chris Shelling, Auburn (4 int.) 1993
- 168— Chris White, Tennessee (9 int.) 1985
- 163— Hootie Ingram, Alabama (10 int.) 1952
- 160— Bobby Wilson, Ole Miss (5 int.) 1947
- 158— Bobby Luna, Alabama (6 int.) 1953
- 156— David Langner, Auburn (8 int.) 1972

CAREER:

- 379— Bobby Wilson, Ole Miss (20 int.) 1946-49
- 376— Darryl Bishop, Kentucky (14 int.) 1971-73

INTERCEPTIONS

315— Jake Scott, Georgia (16 int.) 1967-68
310— Wilbur Jamerson, Kentucky (11 int.) 1947-50
305— Mike Jones, Tennessee (16 int.) 1967-69
305— Tim Priest, Tennessee (18 int.) 1968-70
303— Scott Woerner, Georgia (13 int.) 1978-80
293— Conrad Graham, Tennessee (15 int.) 1970-72
287— David Langner, Auburn (12 int.) 1971-73
281— Jackie Walker, Tennessee (11 int.) 1969-71

YARDS PER INTERCEPTION

GAME: (Min. 3)

54.0— Joe Brodsky, Florida vs. Miss. State (3/162) 1956
51.7— Greg Long, Kentucky vs. North Texas State (3/155) 1981

SEASON: (Min. 5)

44.8— Joe Brodsky, Florida (5/244) 1956
32.0— Bobby Wilson, Ole Miss (5/160) 1947
31.3— Greg Jackson, LSU (7/219) 1988
29.8— Darryl Bishop, Kentucky (5/149) 1972
29.8— Bobby Wilson, Ole Miss (5/149) 1948
26.8— Harper Davis, Miss. State (5/134) 1948
26.2— Brian Robinson, Auburn (5/131) 1993
25.8— Scott Woerner, Georgia (5/129) 1980
24.6— Darryl Bishop, Kentucky (5/123) 1973
24.2— Jay Chesley, Vanderbilt (5/121) 1974
23.6— Eli Maricich, Georgia (8/189) 1948
21.4— Mike Jones, Tennessee (7/150) 1967
21.2— Dale Carter, Tennessee (5/106) 1990
20.2— Jeremiah Castille, Alabama (5/101) 1981

SEASON: (Min. 10)

17.7— Bobby Majors, Tennessee (10/177) 1970
17.5— Jake Scott, Georgia, (10/175) 1968
16.3— Hootie Ingram, Alabama (10/163) 1952

CAREER: (Min. 10)

28.2— Wilbur Jamerson, Kentucky (11 for 310) 1947-50
26.8— Darryl Bishop, Kentucky (14/376) 1971-73
25.5— Jackie Walker, Tennessee (11/281) 1969-71

*—NCAA record

24.4— Eddie Brown, Tennessee (10/244) 1971-73
23.9— David Langner, Auburn (12/287) 1971-73
23.6— Greg Jackson, LSU (11/260) 1985-88
23.3— Scott Woerner, Georgia (13/303) 1978-80
22.9— Robert Davis, Vanderbilt (10/229) 1990-93
21.0— Lynn Hughes, Georgia (10/210) 1967-68

CAREER: (Min. 15)

19.7— Jake Scott, Georgia (16/315) 1967-68
19.5— Conrad Graham, Tennessee (15/293) 1970-72
19.1— Mike Jones, Tennessee (16/305) 1967-69
19.0— Bobby Wilson, Ole Miss (20/379) 1946-49

INTERCEPTION TOUCHDOWNS

GAME:

*2— Joe Brodsky, Florida vs. Miss. State 1956
*2— Jake Scott, Georgia vs. Kentucky 1968

CAREER:

*5— Jackie Walker, Tennessee (32 games) 1969-71
3— Dallas Owens, Kentucky (44 games) 1974-77
3— Kevin Porter, Auburn (44 games) 1984-87
3— Greg Jackson, LSU (44 games) 1985-88
3— Orlando Watters, Arkansas (34 games) 1991-93

LONG INTERCEPTION RETURNS

GAME:

100— Ray Hapes, Ole Miss vs. Ouachita 1937
100— Bob Davis, Kentucky vs. Washington & Lee 1937
100— Ray Martin, Tennessee vs. Louisville 1953
100— Jackie Simpson, Florida vs. Miss. State 1955
100— Joe Brodsky, Florida vs. Miss. State 1956
100— Charlie Britt, Georgia vs. Florida 1959
100— Louis Guy, Ole Miss vs. Tennessee 1962
100— White Graves, LSU vs. Kentucky 1964
100— Dave Hunter, Kentucky vs. West Virginia 1968
100— Greg Jackson, LSU vs. Mississippi State 1988

Kentucky's Dicky Lyons ran back kicks for a league-record 235 yards vs. LSU in 1967 and tallied the SEC's fourth-best career kick return mark with 2,253 yards.

Bobby Wilson, a standout performer at Ole Miss from 1946-49, owns a share of the SEC career interceptions record with 20. He returned those thefts for a league-record 379 yards.

1994 SEC Football   225

SEC 3,000-Yard Club

Total Yards	Player and School	Games	Rushing Att/Yards	Passing Att/Yards	Receiving Cgt/Yards	Year	TD Rsp.
3,482	Eric Zeier, Georgia	11	59/-43	425/3,525	....	1993	25
3,176	Shane Matthews, Florida	12	73/-29	463/3,205	....	1992	25
3,159	Shane Matthews, Florida	11	50/10	361/3130	1/19	1991	30
3,034	Kurt Page, Vandy	11	60/-144	493/3178	....	1983	16

SEC 2,000-Yard Club

Total Yards	Player and School	Games	Rushing Att/Yards	Passing Att/Yards	Receiving Cgt/Yards	Year	TD Rsp.
2,913	Shane Matthews, Florida	11	72/-27	378/2952	1/-12	1990	27
2,886	Don Smith, MSU	11	190/554	312/2332	....	1985	21
2,856	Pat Sullivan, Aub.	10	52/270	281/2586	....	1970	26
2,853	Eric Jones, Vandy	11	144/305	360/2548	....	1988	16
2,852	John Reaves, Fla.	10	32/-44	396/2896	....	1969	25
2,819	Andy Kelly, Tenn.	11	57/60	361/2759	....	1991	18
2,679	Whit Taylor, Vandy	11	153/198	406/2481	....	1982	24
2,619	Eric Jones, Vandy	11	179/665	229/1954	....	1987	22
2,655	Tommy Hodson, LSU	11	56/-177	317/2,655	....	1989	24
2,469	Kerwin Bell, Fla.	11	54/-218	288/2687	....	1985	21
2,427	Heath Shuler, Tenn.	11	46/73	285/2354	....	1993	28
2,436	Jeff Wickersham, LSU	11	58/-106	337/2542	....	1983	14
2,431	John Reaves, Fla.	11	37/-118	376/2549	....	1970	14
2,401	John Darnell, Miss.	11	110/75	167/2,326	....	1989	12
2,391	Dave Marler, MSU	11	88/-31	287/2422	....	1978	12
2,349	Don Smith, MSU	11	159/740	244/1609	....	1986	16
2,341	Kurt Page, Vandy	11	41/-64	350/2405	....	1984	17
2,329	Walter Lewis, Ala.	11	135/338	256/1991	....	1983	19
2,325	Gary Hollingsworth, Ala.	11	44/-54	339/2,379	....	1989	14
2,299	John Fourcade, Miss.	11	125/402	286/1897	....	1980	19
2,289	Jeff Francis, Tenn.	11	97/52	314/2237	....	1988	15
2,264	Archie Manning, Miss.	10	124/502	265/1762	....	1969	23
2,259	Andy Kelly, Tenn.	12	38/18	304/2241	....	1990	14
2,253	Whit Taylor, Vandy	9	64/65	357/2318	....	1981	15
2,219	Tommy Hodson, LSU	11	33/-42	288/2261	....	1986	19
2,213	Reggie Slack, Aub.	11	39/-17	279/2230	....	1988	11
2,200	John Bond, MSU	11	144/609	183/1591	....	1982	11
2,187	Frank Sinkwich, Ga.	11	175/795	166/1392	....	1942	26
2,157	Scott Hunter, Ala.	10	35/-31	266/2188	....	1969	12
2,141	Danny Wuerffel, Fla.	11	40/-89	273/2230	....	1993	23
2,133	Stan White, Aub.	11	38/-109	338/2,242	....	1990	14
2,117	Eric Zeier, Georgia	11	37/-131	258/2,248	....	1992	12
2,111	Steve Spurrier, Fla.	10	125/230	287/1893	1/-12	1965	16
2,103	Tommy Hodson, LSU	11	22/-22	265/2125	....	1987	15
2,096	Pat Sullivan, Aub.	11	47/84	281/2012	....	1971	22
2,095	Steve Spurrier, Fla.	10	76/66	291/2012	2/17	1966	17
2,090	Wayne Peace, Fla.	11	59/11	292/2079	....	1983	13
2,090	Stan White, Aub.	11	79/33	271/2057	....	1993	17
2,089	Tony Robinson, Tenn.	10	78/126	253/1963	....	1984	17
2,087	Walter Lewis, Ala.	11	143/572	164/1575	....	1982	13
2,084	Jeff Wickersham, LSU	11	68/-61	346/2142	....	1985	6
2,081	Jeff Wickersham, LSU	11	41/-84	312/2165	....	1984	12
2,077	Tommy Pharr, MSU	10	141/239	319/1838	3/8	1968	12
2,039	Kent Austin, Miss.	11	103/150	302/1889	....	1984	8
2,039	Mike Shula, Ala.	11	52/28	229/2009	1/2	1985	18
2,036	Alan Risher, LSU	11	105/202	234/1834	....	1982	21
2,014	John Fourcade, Miss.	11	128/493	196/1521	....	1979	13
2,012	Tommy Hodson, LSU	11	33/-62	293/2074	....	1988	13
2,011	Jimmy Streater, Tenn.	11	146/593	198/1418	....	1978	14

Florida quarterback Shane Matthews, the SEC's career passing leader, became the only player in conference history to throw for 3,000 yards in consecutive seasons.

Vanderbilt's Kurt Page was the first quarterback in SEC history to pass for more than 3,000 yards in a season. He twice led the league in total offense.

226 Record Book

SEC 1,500-Yard Club

Total Yards	Player and School	Games	Rushing Att/Yards	Passing Att/Yards	Receiving Cgt/Yards	Year	TD Rsp.
1,998	Heath Shuler, Tenn.	11	105/286	224/1712	. . . .	1992	21
1,989	Reggie Slack, Aub.	11	55/3	252/1,986	. . . .	1989	14
1,975	Herschel Walker, Ga.	11	385/1891	. . . .	14/84	1981	18
1,963	Alan Cockrell, Tenn.	11	53/58	294/2021	. . . .	1982	13
1,959	Kent Austin, Miss.	11	38/67	307/2026	. . . .	1982	13
1,938	Stan White, Aub.	11	57/3	317/1,927	1/14	1991	12
1,932	Joe Reed, MSU	11	155/316	294/1616	1/1	1970	15
1,922	Todd Jordan, MSU	11	42/-13	294/1935	. . . .	1993	12
1,918	John Bond, MSU	11	164/612	205/1306	. . . .	1983	15
1,893	Wayne Peace, Fla.	11	55/158	246/2053	. . . .	1982	9
1,892	Pat Sullivan, Aub.	10	52/206	257/1686	. . . .	1969	23
1,889	Mark Young, Miss.	11	64/80	312/1969	. . . .	1988	10
1,888	Bo Jackson, Aub.	11	278/1815	1/0	4/73	1985	17
1,886	Jeff Burger, Auburn	11	38/180	267/2066	. . . .	1987	13
1,885	James Jackson, Ga.	10	108/410	181/1475	. . . .	1986	13
1,871	Garrison Hearst, Ga.	11	228/1547	. . . .	22/324	1992	21
1,855	Jeff Francis, Tenn.	10	38/91	233/1946	. . . .	1986	9
1,843	Tony Shell, MSU	11	40/66	293/1909	. . . .	1990	10
1,841	Herschel Walker, Ga.	11	335/1752	. . . .	5/89	1982	17
1,829	Tony Shell, MSU	11	20/55	335/1884	. . . .	1988	13
1,823	Fred Fisher, Vandy	11	130/373	234/1450	. . . .	1973	13
1,816	Frank Sinkwich, Ga.	10	209/1103	115/713	. . . .	1941	18
1,806	Emmitt Smith, Fla.	11	284/1599	. . . .	21/207	1989	15
1,799	Jimmy Fisher, Fla.	11	104/288	146/1511	. . . .	1976	18
1,786	Bobby Scott, Tenn	11	51/89	252/1697	. . . .	1970	17
1,784	Charles Conerly, Miss.	10	104/417	233/1367	. . . .	1947	27
1,783	Charles Alexander, LSU	11	311/1686	1/17	12/80	1977	17
1,781	Don Smith, MSU	10	128/545	176/1236	. . . .	1984	15
1,774	Zeke Bratkowski, Ga.	11	19/50	262/1824	. . . .	1952	13
1,773	Stan White, Aub.	11	76/-17	157/1790	. . . .	1992	8
1,758	Alan Risher, LSU	11	117/22	238/1780	. . . .	1981	8
1,757	Dewey Warren, Tenn.	10	70/41	229/1716	. . . .	1966	23
1,734	Steve Taneyhill, USC	11	42/-196	291/1,930	. . . .	1993	7
1,729	Pookie Jones, Ky.	11	140/295	203/1434	. . . .	1992	8
1,720	Bill Ransdell, Ky.	9	42/24	231/1744	. . . .	1985	5
1,716	Archie Manning, Miss.	10	110/208	263/1510	1/2	1968	13
1,715	Travis Tidwell, Aub.	10	181/772	158/943	. . . .	1946	10
1,712	Jimmy Sidle, Aub.	10	185/1006	136/706	. . . .	1963	15
1,712	John Fourcade, Miss.	11	113/179	137/1533	. . . .	1981	10
1,710	Mike Cavan, Ga.	10	102/91	207/1619	. . . .	1968	13
1,710	William Robinson, MSU	9	154/543	77/1,167	. . . .	1991	13
1,706	Rick Norton, Ky.	10	57/117	214/1823	. . . .	1965	13
1,705	Buck Belue, Ga.	11	67/102	188/1603	. . . .	1981	15
1,693	Wayne Peace, Fla.	11	64/110	273/1803	. . . .	1981	12
1,688	Bill Ransdell, Ky.	11	35/60	266/1748	. . . .	1984	11
1,686	Herschel Walker, Ga.	11	274/1616	. . . .	7/70	1980	15
1,681	Babe Parilli, Ky.	11	31/54	203/1627	. . . .	1950	28
1,675	Terry Dean, Fla.	10	43/24	200/1651	. . . .	1993	19
1,661	Alan Cockrell, Tenn.	11	42/22	243/1683	. . . .	1983	15
1,652	Phil Gargis, Aub.	11	142/534	166/1118	. . . .	1976	16
1,646	Bill Wade, Vandy	11	59/37	223/1609	. . . .	1951	14
1,640	Bill Ransdell, Ky.	11	91/30	256/1610	. . . .	1986	4
1,634	Zeke Bratkowski, Ga.	10	21/56	248/1578	. . . .	1951	5
1,633	Jimmy Streater, Tenn.	9	82/377	161/1256	. . . .	1979	16
1,609	Kerwin Bell, Fla.	11	40/5	184/1614	. . . .	1984	18
1,607	Tommy Pharr, MSU	10	51/4	258/1603	. . . .	1969	12
1,595	Bill Wade, Vandy	11	47/1	177/1596	. . . .	1950	18
1,594	Archie Manning, Miss.	8	80/113	233/1481	. . . .	1970	20
1,593	Rockey Felker, MSU	11	149/446	155/1147	. . . .	1974	15
1,593	Bruce Threadgill, MSU	11	143/274	219/1317	1/2	1977	9
1,585	Kerwin Bell, Fla.	11	42/184	239/1769	. . . .	1987	9
1,582	Jeff Francis, Tenn.	9	43/70	201/1512	. . . .	1987	9
1,582	Condredge Holloway, Tenn.	11	128/433	154/1149	. . . .	1973	14
1,582	Matt Robinson, Ga.	11	99/265	121/1317	. . . .	1974	15
1,580	Lawrence Adams, Miss.	11	108/196	195/1415	. . . .	1993	15
1,579	John Gromos, Vandy	10	43/165	320/1,744	. . . .	1989	10
1,573	Jeff Burger, Aub.	11	26/98	222/1671	. . . .	1986	10
1,572	Mark Young, Miss.	11	53/82	261/1490	. . . .	1987	12
1,571	Mike Wright, Vandy	11	159/188	211/1383	. . . .	1977	8
1,569	John Bond, MSU	11	131/720	133/849	. . . .	1980	10
1,558	Parker Hall, Miss.	11	108/698	99/860	. . . .	1938	21
1,538	David Palmer, Ala.	12	42/278	30/260	61/1,000	1993	9
1,529	Randy Wallace, Tenn.	11	132/211	145/1318	. . . .	1975	11
1,525	Emmitt Smith, Fla.	11	229/1341	. . . .	25/184	1987	13
1,520	Jay Barker, Ala.	13	64/-94	243/1614	. . . .	1992	7
1,518	Jeff Rutledge, Ala.	11	109/311	107/1207	. . . .	1977	12
1,518	Marcus Wilson, Vandy	11	181/488	164/1030	. . . .	1992	12
1,510	Derrick Ramsey, Ky.	11	159/618	156/892	. . . .	1977	19
1,508	Steadman Shealy, Ala.	11	152/791	81/717	. . . .	1979	16
1,502	Bubba Wyche, Tenn.	10	104/37	237/1539	. . . .	1968	15
1,502	Mike Shula, Ala.	12	47/16	235/1486	. . . .	1986	14

LSU's Tommy Hodson, a four-time All-SEC selection, is the only quarterback to pass for more than 2,000 yards in four straight seasons.

Mississippi State quarterback John Bond became only the second player in NCAA history to pass for 4,000 yards and rush for 2,000 yards in a career.

1994 SEC Football

Longest Rushing Touchdowns

Yds.	Player Team and Opponent	Year
99	Kelsey Finch—Tennessee vs. Florida	1977
98	Stanley Howell—Miss. State vs. Sou. Miss.	1979
97	Blondy Black—Miss. State vs. Duquesne	1942
96	Chris Anderson—Alabama vs. Temple	1991
96	Emmitt Smith—Florida vs. Miss. State	1988
95	Jesse Fatherree—LSU vs. Georgia	1935
95	Harry Gilmer—Ala. vs. Kentucky	1945
94	Sal Nicolo—LSU vs. Rice	1952
94	Stacey Simmons—Florida vs. Kentucky	1987
92	Ralph O'Gwynne—Auburn vs. Loyola	1936
92	Bobby Marlow—Alabama vs. Ga.Tech	1950
92	Ray Brown—Miss. vs. Texas	1957
91	Harry Jones—Kentucky vs. George Washington	1951
91	Willie Wilder—Florida vs. Miss. State	1976
90	Guy Miner—LSU vs. Auburn	1936
90	Ken McLean—Florida vs. Georgia	1944
90	Ode Burrell—Miss. State vs. Tulane	1962
90	Fred Collins—Miss. State vs. Ole Miss	1979
89	Harry Robinson—Tulane vs. SMU	1944
89	Johnny Griffith—Georgia vs. Furman	1946
89	Tim Worley—Georgia vs. Florida	1985
88	Adrian Dodson—LSU vs. Tulane	1940
88	Bill Ransdell—Kentucky vs. Xavier	1950
88	Brent Fullwood—Auburn vs. Miss. State	1986
87	Dick Dorsey—Tennessee vs. Va. Tech	1933
87	Bob McCoy—Ga. Tech vs. Citadel	1948
87	Harol Lofton—Miss. vs. Arkansas	1953
87	Kirby Moore—Georgia vs. S. Carolina	1967
87	Billy Jackson—Alabama vs. Florida	1978
87	Lionel James—Auburn vs. Georgia	1982
87	John Bond—Miss. State vs. Auburn	1982
87	Kenny Roberts, Miss. State vs. Vanderbilt	1989
86	J.L. Williams—Florida vs. West Texas State	1982
86	Charlie Trippi—Georgia vs. Ga. Tech	1942
86	Jeff Burkette—LSU vs. Georgia Navy	1942
86	Charlie Smith—Georgia vs. Kentucky	1945
86	Gene Newton—Tulane vs. Miss.	1956
86	Gerry Bussell—Ga. Tech vs. Georgia	1962
86	Calvin Culliver—Alabama vs. Va. Tech	1973
85	Blondy Black—Miss. State vs. S. Francisco	1941
85	Harry Robinson—Tulane vs. Clemson	1944
85	Don Phelps—Kentucky vs. Michigan St.	1946
85	Morris Harrison—Ga. Tech vs. Citadel	1947
85	Billy Mixon—Georgia vs. Boston College	1950
85	Harry Wright—Ga. Tech vs. Davidson	1950
85	Showboat Boykin—Miss. vs. Miss. State	1951
85	Calvin Culliver—Alabama vs. Vanderbilt	1974
85	Walter Packer—Miss. State vs. LSU	1975
85	Joe Cribbs—Auburn vs. Alabama	1977
85	Mark Higgs—Kentucky vs. Utah St.	1987
85	Danny Woodson—Alabama vs. Temple	1991
84	David Brown—Alabama vs. S. Carolina	1942
84	Bobby Lance—Florida vs. Auburn	1954
84	Connie Frederick—Auburn vs. Alabama	1969
84	James Ray—Georgia vs. S. Carolina	1971
84	Don Smith—Miss. State vs. Southern Miss	1984
84	Mark Higgs—Kentucky vs. Vanderbilt	1984
83	Bob Davis—Kentucky vs. Maryville	1936
83	Lowell Tew—Bill Cadenhead—Ala. vs. Ga.	1947
83	Ralph Genito—Kentucky vs. Miami	1948
83	Corky Tharp—Alabama vs. Va. Tech	1952
83	Bobby Humphrey—Alabama vs. Miss. State	1987
82	Bill Crass—LSU vs. Arkansas	1936
82	Houston Patton—Miss. vs. N. Texas St.	1953
82	Bob Kosid—Kentucky vs. Detroit	1963
82	Phil Gargis—Auburn vs. Fla. State	1976
82	Tony Nathan—Alabama vs. Miss. State	1978
82	Tom Venable—Kentucky vs. Bowling Green	1979
81	Joe Kilgrow—Alabama vs. Miss. State	1936
81	Fred Glauden—Tulane vs. Sewanee	1938
81	Hank Lauricella—Tenn. vs. Tenn. Tech	1950
81	Willie McClendon—Georgia vs. S. Carolina	1978
80	Floyd Roberts—Tulane vs. Colgate	1933
80	Rand Dixon—Vanderbilt vs. Cincinnati	1934
80	Howard Bryan—Tulane vs. Georgia	1936
80	Bob Davis—Kentucky vs. Wash. & Lee	1937
80	Frank Chambers—Miss. State vs. Arkansas	1939
80	Frank Chambers—Miss. State vs. Bham-Sou.	1939
80	Herschel Mosley—Alabama vs. Vandy	1939
80	Bobby Landrell—Miss. vs. Arkansas	1941
80	Noah Mullins—Kentucky vs. S'western	1941
80	Eddie Prokop—Ga. Tech vs. N.Carolina	1943
80	Charlie Smith—Georgia vs. UT-Chatt.	1945
80	Travis Tidwell—Auburn vs. Furman	1946
80	Bobby Forbes—Florida vs. Auburn	1947
80	Zealand Thigpen—Vanderbilt vs. LSU	1948
80	Johnny Majors—Tennessee vs. Miss. State	1954
80	Benny Nelson—Alabama vs. Auburn	1963
80	Jack Harper—Florida vs. SMU	1964
80	Barry Cotney—Miss. State vs. Tampa	1965
80	Bruce Kemp—Georgia vs. Tennessee	1968
80	Wallace Clark—Auburn vs. Kentucky	1970
80	James Taylor—Alabama vs. Va. Tech	1973
80	Wilbur Jackson—Alabama vs. Tennessee	1973
80	Ken Northington—Kentucky vs. Vanderbilt	1974
80	Jimmy DuBose—Florida vs. Kentucky	1975
80	Stanley Morgan—Tennessee vs. Kentucky	1975
80	Leon Perry—Miss. vs. Miss. State	1976
80	Len Copeland—Miss. State vs. No. Texas St.	1977
80	James Jones—Miss. State vs. No. Texas St.	1977
80	Jimmy Streater—Tennessee vs. California	1977
80	Tony Green—Florida vs. Miss. State	1977
80	Van Heflin—Vanderbilt vs. Air Force	1979
80	Neal Anderson—Florida vs. Tennessee	1984
80	Tony Thompson—Tennessee vs. Miss. State	1990
80	Frank Harvey—Georgia vs. Florida	1992
79	Ralph O'Gwynne—Auburn vs. Bham-Southern	1936
79	Buddy Banker—Tulane vs. Miss. Coll.	1937
79	Bobby Forbes—Florida vs. N.C. State	1947
79	Charles Hunsinger—Florida vs. Tulsa	1948
79	Bobby Freeman—Auburn vs. Wofford	1951
79	Lauren Hargrove—Georgia vs. Auburn	1951
79	Frank Mordica—Vanderbilt vs. Alabama	1978
79	James Brooks—Auburn vs. Vanderbilt	1979
79	Reggie Cobb, Tennessee vs. Auburn	1989
78	John Hovious—Miss. vs. Tulane	1941
78	W. A. Jones—Tulane vs. Clemson	1944
78	Gordon Pettus—Alabama vs. Kentucky	1945
78	Terry Henley—Auburn vs. Clemson	1970
78	Glynn Harrison—Georgia vs. Ga. Tech	1975
77	Jimmy Fenton—Auburn vs. Bham-Southern	1936
77	Leo Mullins—Florida vs. Stetson	1936
77	Blondy Black—Miss. State vs. S.Francisco	1942
77	Jim Parrott—Kentucky vs. Tennessee	1944
77	Bobby Wilson—Miss. vs. Miss. State	1947
77	Charles Hunsinger—Florida vs. Alabama	1948
77	Harol Lofton—Miss. vs. Miss. State	1952
77	Bill Teas—Ga. Tech vs. LSU	1954
77	Phil King—Vanderbilt vs. Mid.Tenn.	1955
77	Jimmy Sidle—Auburn vs. Florida State	1962
77	Marcus Rhoden—Miss. State vs. Florida	1964
77	Marcus Rhoden—Miss. State vs. Tulane	1964
77	Frank Mordica—Vandy vs. Air Force	1978
77	Tim Worley—Georgia vs. TCU	1988
76	Young Boozer—Alabama vs. Miss. State	1934
76	Tom McWilliams—Miss. State vs. Auburn	1944
76	J.D. Roddam—Alabama vs. Duquesne	1949
76	Jimmy Barton—LSU vs. SE Louisiana	1949
76	Lindy Callahan—Miss. vs. Auburn	1951
76	Bobby Dellinger—Georgia vs. Miami	1952
76	Fob James—Auburn vs. UT-Chatt.	1955
76	Jimmy Dunn—Florida vs. Georgia	1958
76	Rodger Bird—Kentucky vs. LSU	1964
76	Marcus Rhoden—Miss. State vs. LSU	1965
76	Herschel Walker—Georgia vs. Texas A&M	1980
76	Herschel Walker—Georgia vs. S. Carolina	1980
76	Neal Anderson—Florida vs. LSU	1983
76	Mark Higgs—Kentucky vs. Rutgers	1984
76	Bo Jackson—Auburn vs. SW Louisiana	1985
76	Bo Jackson—Auburn vs. Ga. Tech	1985
76	Keith Henderson—Georgia vs. Florida	1985
76	Harvey Williams—LSU vs. Ole Miss	1987
76	Murry Hill—Alabama vs. Kentucky	1988
76	James Joseph—Auburn vs. Kansas	1988
75	Floyd Roberts—Tulane vs. Georgia	1933
75	Floyd Roberts—Tulane vs. Kentucky	1933
75	Floyd Roberts—Tulane vs. Miss.	1933
75	Casey Kimbrell—Auburn vs. Duke	1933
75	Bob Davis—Kentucky vs. Ga. Tech	1935
75	Herbert McAnly—Florida vs. Sewanee	1935
75	Bob Davis—Kentucky vs. Xavier	1936
75	Jim Fordham—Georgia vs. Miami	1938
75	Noah Mullins—Kentucky vs. Xavier	1939
75	Blondy Black—Miss. State vs. Auburn	1941
75	Buster Stephens—Tennessee vs. Florida	1944
75	Roy Bailey—Tulane vs. Vanderbilt	1952
75	Max McGee—Tulane vs. Citadel	1953
75	Gene Etter—Tennessee vs. Miss.	1958
75	Bob Hoover—Florida vs. Texas A&M	1962
75	Lorenzo Hampton—Florida vs. W. Texas St.	1982
75	Gene Jelks—Alabama vs. Vanderbilt	1986
75	Garrison Hearst—Georgia vs. Georgia Southern	1992

Longest Touchdown Pass Plays

Yds.	Passer and Receiver	Team and Opponent	Year
99	Cris Collinsworth to Derrick Gaffney	Florida vs. Rice	1977
96	Kerwin Bell to Ricky Nattiel	Florida vs. Georgia	1984
93	Buck Belue to Lindsay Scott	Georgia vs. Florida	1980
93	Kyle Morris to Stacey Simmons	Florida vs. Montana State	1988
93	Greg Talley to Kevin Maxwell	Georgia vs. Vanderbilt	1989
92	Kirby Moore to Randy Wheeler	Georgia vs. Auburn	1965
92	Dave Bair to Dicky Lyons	Kentucky vs. Georgia	1968
91	Buck Belue to Amp Arnold	Georgia vs. Kentucky	1980
90	Frank Sinkwich to Lamar Davis	Georgia vs. Cincinnati	1942
90	Jeff Dunn to Pierre Goode	Alabama vs. Tennessee	1987
89	Charley Britt to George Guister	Georgia vs. South Carolina	1958
88	Marcus Wilson to Clarence Sevillian	Vanderbilt vs. Tennessee	1992
87	Tom Gray to Bill Fugua	Vanderbilt vs. LSU	1945
87	Albert Elmore to Bobby Luna	Alabama vs. LSU	1954
87	Ray Goff to Gene Washington	Georgia vs. Kentucky	1976
87	Andy Kelly to Carl Pickens	Tennessee vs. Louisville	1991
87	Tommy Pharr to Eric Hoggatt	Mississippi State vs. Florida	1969
86	Matt Robinson to Richard Appleby	Georgia vs. Ole Miss	1974
86	Mike Healey to Clarence Sevillian	Vanderbilt vs. Duke	1991
85	Bill Wade to Bucky Curtis	Vanderbilt vs. Alabama	1950
85	Pat Sullivan to Alvin Bresler	Auburn vs. Ga. Tech	1970
85	Gary Rutledge to Joe Dale Harris	Alabama vs. California	1973
85	Matt Robinson to Gene Washington	Georgia vs. Clemson	1976
85	Terry LeCount to Wes Chandler	Florida vs. LSU	1977
85	Jimmy Streater to Anthony Hancock	Tennessee vs. Vanderbilt	1979
85	Alan Cockrell to Clyde Duncan	Tennessee vs. Vanderbilt	1983
85	Reggie Slack to James Joseph	Auburn vs. Kansas	1988
84	Kyle Morris to Tony Lomack	Florida vs. Louisiana Tech	1989
83	John Rauch to Eli Marichich	Georgia vs. Alabama	1947
83	Bill Stanton to Wm. Earl Morgan	Miss. State vs. Kentucky	1955
83	Glynn Griffing to Chuck Morris	Ole Miss vs. Houston	1961
83	Randy Jenkins to Allan Watson	Kentucky vs. Indiana	1980
83	Kerwin Bell to Ricky Nattiel	Florida vs. Miss. State	1985
82	Bobby Scott to Lester McClain	Tennessee vs. Memphis State	1969
82	Steve Ensminger to Carlos Carson	LSU vs. Georgia	1978
82	Kerwin Bell to Frankie Neal	Florida vs. Florida State	1985
82	John Gromos to Carl Parker	Vanderbilt vs. Virginia Tech	1985
82	Andy Kelly to Alvin Harper	Tennessee vs. Auburn	1990
82	Tom Luke to Tyrone Ashley	Ole Miss vs. Tennessee	1991
81	Merle Hapes to John Hovious	Ole Miss vs. Vanderbilt	1939
81	Dudley Spence to Lee Hayley	Auburn vs. Wofford	1952
81	John Reaves to Jim Yancey	Florida vs. Fla. State	1969
81	Bruce Threadgill to Dennis Johnson	Miss. State vs. Washington	1977
81	Ken Coley to Joey Jones	Alabama vs. Vanderbilt	1981
81	Greg Talley to Arthur Marshall	Georgia vs. William & Mary	1988
80	Tom Hodson to Sam Martin	LSU vs. Rice	1987
80	John Bond to Danny Knight	Miss. State vs. Florida	1982
80	John Bond to Danny Knight	Miss. State vs. Memphis State	1982
80	Maurice Green to Henry Wagnon	Georgia vs. Tulane	1934
80	Ermal Allen to Junior Jones	Kentucky vs. Georgia	1939
80	Frank Sinkwich to Lamar Davis	Georgia vs. Cincinnati	1942
80	Y.A. Tittle to Dan Sandifer	LSU vs. Ga. Tech	1946
80	Norm Stevens to Al Doggett	LSU vs. Kentucky	1952
80	Richard Allen to Ray Brown	Florida vs. Tennessee	1954
80	David Smith to Sammy Milner	Miss. State vs. Texas Tech	1968
80	Pat Sullivan to Terry Beasley	Auburn vs. Florida	1970
80	Gary Rutledge to Wayne Wheeler	Alabama vs. Tennessee	1973
80	Richard Appleby to Gene Washington	Georgia vs. Florida	1975
80	Larry McCrimmon to Felix Wilson	Kentucky vs. Florida	1978
80	Buck Belue to Lindsay Scott	Georgia vs. Ga. Tech	1981
80	Steve Alatorre to Willie Gault	Tennessee vs. Alabama	1981
80	Jeff Wickersham to Eric Martin	LSU vs. Alabama	1983
80	Alan Cockrell to Lenny Taylor	Tennessee vs. Alabama	1983
80	Alan Cockrell to Clyde Duncan	Tennessee vs. Alabama	1983
80	Eric Zeier to Hason Graham	Georgia vs. Texas Tech	1993
80	Eric Zeier to Hason Graham	Georgia vs. Vanderbilt	1993
80	Lawrence Adams to Eddie Small	Ole Miss vs. Northern Illinois	1993
79	Homer Key to Cy Grant	Georgia vs. Ga. Tech	1933
79	Ed Holtsinger to Walter Kilzer	Ga. Tech vs. Auburn	1945
79	Houston Patton to Dave Dickerson	Ole Miss vs. Villanova	1954
79	Ken Stabler to Dennis Homan	Alabama vs. La. Tech	1966
79	Denny Painter to Dave Strong	Vanderbilt vs. Tulane	1969
79	Eric Jones to Rodney Barrett	Vanderbilt vs. Alabama	1988
79	Chad Loup to Todd Kinchen	LSU vs. Texas A&M	1990
78	Jake Gibbs to Bobby Crespino	Ole Miss vs. Vanderbilt	1958
78	Bobby Hunt to Lamar Rawson	Auburn vs. Miami	1959
78	Dave Marler to Mardye McDole	Miss. State vs. Tennessee	1978
78	Alan Cockrell to Willie Gault	Tennessee vs. Auburn	1982
78	Alan Cockrell to Tim McGee	Tennessee vs. Vanderbilt	1983
78	James Jackson to Fred Lane	Georgia vs. Clemson	1986
78	Reggie Slack to Alexander Wright	Auburn vs. Pacific	1989
78	Mike Healey to Mark Johnson	Vanderbilt vs. Army	1990
78	Stan White to Joe Frazier	Auburn vs. Tennessee	1991

Florida All-America wide receiver Cris Collinsworth threw the longest touchdown pass in SEC history with a 99-yarder to Derrick Gaffney against Rice in 1977.

Georgia's Lindsay Scott hauled in a 93-yard touchdown catch versus Florida during the Bulldogs' 1980 national championship season.

1994 SEC Football 229

Longest Kickoff Returns

Yds.	Player — Team and Opponent	Year
100	Howard Bryan—Tulane vs. Ga. Tech	1933
100	Bobby Kellogg—Tulane vs. Ole Miss	1939
100	Pat Reen—Florida vs. Miami	1940
100	Lou Thomas—Tulane vs. N.Carolina	1941
100	Eddie Price—Tulane vs. Alabama	1947
100	Jim Burkett—Alabama vs. Duquesne	1949
100	Bobby Duke—Auburn vs. Ole Miss State	1953
100	Jimmy Burson—Auburn vs. UT-Chatt	1960
100	Gary Martin—Alabama vs. Miami	1963
100	Ray Ogden—Alabama vs. Auburn	1964
100	Sammy Grezaffi—LSU vs. Tennessee	1967
100	George Ranager—Alabama vs. Auburn	1969
100	Vernon Studdard—Ole Miss vs. Alabama	1970
100	Willie Shelby—Alabama vs. Kentucky	1973
100	Preston Brown—Vanderbilt vs. Miss.	1977
100	Sam DeJarnette—Auburn vs. Miss. State	1980
100	Willie Gault—Tennessee vs. Pittsburgh	1980
100	Glen Young—Miss. State vs. LSU	1980
100	Eric Martin—LSU vs. Kentucky	1981
100	Pierre Goode—Alabama vs. Ole Miss	1988
100	Kurt Johnson—Kentucky vs. Georgia	1989
99	Carl Sikes—Miss. State vs. LSU	1933
99	Woodford Dunn—Sewanee vs. UT-Chatt	1940
99	J.W. Brodnax—LSU vs. Florida	1957
99	Lindsay Scott—Georgia vs. LSU	1978
99	Hokie Gajan—LSU vs. Wyoming	1978
99	Kerry Goode—Alabama vs. Boston College	1984
99	Tony Lomack—Florida vs. Kentucky	1989
98	Henry Krouse—Tennessee vs. N.Carolina	1934
98	Billy Chase—Florida vs. Ole Miss	1934
98	Dennis Cross—Miss. State vs. Howard	1936
98	Jerry Stovall—LSU vs. Ga. Tech	1962
98	Doug Kotar—Kentucky vs. Clemson	1971
98	Gary Moore—Tennessee vs. Auburn	1979
97	Lee Nalley—Vanderbilt vs. Florida	1949
97	Benny Nelson—Alabama vs. Vanderbilt	1963
97	Billy Cannon—LSU vs. Texas Tech	1957
97	Cris Collinsworth—Florida vs. LSU	1978
97	Lee Davis—Ole Miss vs. Miss State	1984
97	Tony Jackson—Vanderbilt vs. Duke	1992
96	Ray Hapes—Ole Miss vs. Temple	1936
96	Jim Campagna—Georgia vs. Auburn	1952
96	Spec Kelley—Auburn vs. Miss. State	1938
96	Lamar Davis—Georgia vs. Tulane	1940
96	Charles Hunsinger—Florida vs. Alabama	1948
96	Joe May—LSU vs. Kentucky	1955
96	Mike Fuller—Auburn vs. Georgia	1973
96	Willie Gault—Tennessee vs. LSU	1982
96	Brent Fullwood—Auburn vs. Southern Miss	1984
96	Gene Jelks—Alabama vs. Temple	1986
96	Jerry Bouldin—Miss. State vs. Southern Miss	1989
96	Gene Washington—Georgia vs. Clemson	1973
95	Jesse Fatheree—LSU vs. Auburn	1934
95	Ray Hapes—Ole Miss vs. Miss. State	1935
95	Vassa Cate—Georgia vs. S. Carolina	1939
95	Noah Mullins—Ky. vs. Wash. & Lee	1940
95	Jimmy Nelson—Alabama vs. Howard	1941
95	Blondy Black—Miss. State vs. Miss.	1942
95	Harry Gilmer—Alabama vs. LSU	1944
95	Bob Conway—Alabama vs. LSU	1952
95	Marcus Rhoden—Miss. State vs. Southern Miss.	1966
95	Roger Gann—Kentucky vs. Indiana	1969
95	Willie Gault—Tennessee vs. Vanderbilt	1980
95	Doug Nettles—Vanderbilt vs. Virginia	1969
94	Jack Hudson—Vanderbilt vs. Virginia	1955
94	Mallon Faircloth—Tennessee vs. UT-Chatt	1963
94	James Brooks—Auburn vs. Duke	1980
94	J.R. Ambrose—Ole Miss vs. Vanderbilt	1986
93	Pinky Rohm—LSU vs. NW Louisiana	1937
93	Bill Hartman—Georgia vs. Ga. Tech	1937
93	Jimmy Nelson—Alabama vs. Ga. Tech	1940
93	Pat Reen—Florida vs. Auburn	1940
93	Bubber Ely—Tulane vs. N.Carolina	1941
93	Tom McWilliams—Miss. State vs. Auburn	1944
93	Billy Williamson—Ga. Tech vs. Tennessee	1960
93	Glenn Glass—Tennessee vs. Vanderbilt	1961
93	Gerry Bussell—Ga. Tech vs. Tulane	1962
93	Buddy Seay—Alabama vs. Vanderbilt	1970
93	Tim Worley—Georgia vs. Ole Miss	1988
93	Carl Pickens—Tennessee vs. LSU	1989
92	Don Phelps—Kentucky vs. Ole Miss	1946
92	Butch Wilson—Alabama vs. Auburn	1962
92	Rodger Bird—Kentucky vs. Va. Tech	1963
92	Robert Dow—LSU vs. Utah	1974
92	Rick Neel—Auburn vs. Florida State	1975
92	James Jones—Miss. State vs. Maryland	1979
92	Willie Gault—Tennessee vs. Kentucky	1980
92	Mark Johnson—Vanderbilt vs. Tulane	1987
91	Buster Stephens—Tennessee vs. Kentucky	1944
91	Les Simerville—Ga. Tech vs. Tulane	1957
91	Dale Carter—Tennessee vs. Florida	1990
91	Frank Adams—S. Carolina vs. Louisiana Tech	1992
90	Ray Hapes—Ole Miss vs. Memphis State	1935
90	Jack Hancock—Ga. Tech vs. N.Dame	1940
90	Noah Mullins—Kentucky vs. Geo. Wash.	1940
90	Leslie Dodson—Ole Miss vs. Arkansas	1940
90	Jerome Daly—Ole Miss vs. Miss. State	1942
90	Floyd Reid—Georgia vs. Clemson	1945
90	Billy Ball—Auburn vs. Clemson	1947
90	Tyrone Ashley—Ole Miss vs. Tennessee	1989
90	David Palmer—Alabama vs. LSU	1991
89	John Rauch—Georgia vs. Wake Forest	1945
89	Bobby Forbes—Florida vs. Furman	1947
89	Bobby Gordon—Tennessee vs. UT-Chatt	1957
89	Larry Ellis—Auburn vs. Florida	1966
89	Bo Bowen—Ole Miss vs. Memphis State	1967
89	Bobby Knight—Ole Miss vs. Tampa	1971
89	Andre Hastings—Georgia vs. Kentucky	1990
88	James Pettus—Auburn vs. Kentucky	1959
88	Phil King—Vanderbilt vs. Florida	1957
88	Tom Calvin—Alabama vs. Florida	1949
87	Pay Pelfrey—Auburn vs. La. Tech	1948
87	Ken Konz—LSU vs. Vanderbilt	1948
87	Bill Svoboda—Tulane vs. Alabama	1949
87	Kent Lawrence—Georgia vs. VMI	1966
87	James Otis Doss—Miss. State vs. Kansas St.	1977
86	Pinky Rohm—LSU vs. Loyola	1937
86	Vernon Studdard—Ole Miss vs. UT-Chatt.	1970
86	Gene Washington—Georgia vs. N.C. State	1973
86	Norman Jefferson—LSU vs. Tennessee	1983
85	Gene Littleton—Georgia vs. Citadel	1958
85	Ned Peters—Ole Miss vs. Florida	1935
85	Warren Brunner—Tulane vs. Auburn	1938
85	Lowell Tew—Alabama vs. Miss. State	1945
85	Don Phelps—Kentucky vs. Mich. State	1946
85	Norm Duplain—Miss. State vs. Tulane	1951
85	Stacey Simmons—Florida vs. Ole Miss	1988

230 Record Book

Longest Punts

Yds.	Player	Team and Opponent	Year
92	Bill Smith	Ole Miss vs. Southern Miss	1984
89	Dixie Howell	Alabama vs. Tennessee	1933
*87	Rufus Deal	Auburn vs. Ga. Tech	1939
87	O.J. Key	Tulane vs. Florida	1946
87	Spike Jones	Georgia vs. Auburn	1967
85	Greg Gantt	Alabama vs. Miss. State	1971
84	Mike Patrick	Miss. State vs. Alabama	1974
83	Dixie Howell	Alabama vs. Kentucky	1933
*83	Billy Mann	Miss. vs. Tennessee	1938
82	Bill Hartman	Georgia vs. Tulane	1937
82	Bobby Joe Green	Florida vs. Georgia	1958
82	Mike Patrick	Miss. State vs. Wm. & Mary	1974
82	Jim Miller	Miss. vs. S. Carolina	1976
*82	Buddy Holt	Alabama vs. Vanderbilt	1977
82	Ricky Anderson	Vanderbilt vs. Georgia	1984
81	Monk Gafford	Auburn vs. Clemson	1941
81	Kent Elmore	Tennessee vs. Vanderbilt	1988
80	Dave Davis	Ga. Tech vs. Army	1952
80	Don Golden	Georgia vs. Kentucky	1973
80	Paul Calhoun	Kentucky vs. Indiana	1983
79	Ed Palmer	Tennessee vs. Alabama	1934
79	Johnny Butler	LSU vs. Miss.	1942
79	Alvin Dark	LSU vs. Miss.	1942
79	Charlie Trippi	Georgia vs. Auburn	1945
79	Rip Collins	LSU vs. Boston College	1947
79	Jack Saye	Georgia vs. Florida State	1961
79	Barry Burton	Vanderbilt vs. Georgia	1973
79	Jim Arnold	Vanderbilt vs. Ole Miss	1981
79	Marty Simpson	S. Carolina vs. Vanderbilt	1992
78	Ralph Kercheval	Kentucky vs. Ga. Tech	1933
78	Russ Mosley	Alabama vs. Georgia	1942
78	Tom McWilliams	Miss. State vs. Ark. A&M	1944
78	Billy Murphy	Miss. State vs. Kentucky	1946
78	Bobby Walden	Georgia vs. Citadel	1958
78	Neil Clabo	Tennessee vs. Kentucky	1973
78	Barry Burton	Vanderbilt vs. Kentucky	1975
78	Randy Jenkins	Kentucky vs. Tennessee	1983
77	Lou Thomas	Tulane vs. Georgia	1942
77	John Bruce	Miss. vs. Miss. State	1944
77	Bobby Wilson	Miss. vs. Boston College	1948
77	Zeke Bratkowski	Georgia vs. Auburn	1951
*77	Gerald Burch	Ga. Tech vs. Clemson	1958
77	Bill Schoenrock	Miss. State vs. Tennessee	1959
77	Bill Smith	Ole Miss vs. Southern Miss	1984
77	Lewis Colbert	Auburn vs. SW Louisiana	1985
*76	Beattie Feathers	Tennessee vs. Florida	1933
76	Joe Riley	Alabama vs. Vanderbilt	1936
76	Rip Collins	LSU vs. Vanderbilt	1947
76	Hank Lauricella	Tennessee vs. Alabama	1951
76	Don Chandler	Florida vs. Georgia Tech	1955
76	Jim Miller	Miss. vs. Tulane	1976
76	Shayne Edge	Florida vs. Vanderbilt	1992
*75	Marvin Smith	Miss. vs. Miss. State	1938
75	Hank Lauricella	Tennessee vs. Miss.	1950
75	Lea Paslay	Miss. vs. Miss. State	1953
75	Floyd Teas	Vanderbilt vs. Alabama	1953
75	Julian Fagan	Miss. vs. Memphis St.	1967
75	Bill Hawk	Kentucky vs. Tennessee	1991
*74	Clarence Hapes	Miss. vs. Centenary	1935
*74	Sonny Bruce	Miss. State vs. Tulane	1938
74	Joe Geri	Georgia vs. Florida	1947
74	Bill Majors	Tennessee vs. Auburn	1958
74	Don Golden	Georgia vs. Vanderbilt	1973
74	Joey Chapman	Tennessee vs. Pacific	1990
74	Hank Lesesne	Vanderbilt vs. Kentucky	1960
73	Ray Criswell	Florida vs. LSU	1982
73	Jim Arnold	Vanderbilt vs. Miami	1980
73	Malcolm Simmons	Alabama vs. Ga. Tech	1981
73	Chris Mohr	Alabama vs. Notre Dame	1986
73	Mike Riley	Miss. State vs. Auburn	1991
72	Floyd Teas	Vanderbilt vs. Alabama	1953
72	Herman Weaver	Tennessee vs. Ky.	1967
72	Tom McWilliams	Miss. State vs. Duquesne	1947
71	Charley Conerly	Miss. vs. Vanderbilt	1947
71	Hank Lauricella	Tennessee vs. Miss. State	1951
71	Bobby Gordon	Tennessee vs. Alabama	1957
71	Jerry Shuford	Vanderbilt vs. Alabama	1964
71	Neil Clabo	Tennessee vs. Auburn	1973
71	Craig Colquitt	Tenn. vs. Oregon St.	1977
71	Kevin Kelly	Kentucky vs. Miss. State	1977
71	Jim Miller	Ole Miss vs. Georgia	1977
71	Cody Whitt	Vanderbilt vs. Ole Miss	1977
71	Malcolm Simmons	Alabama vs. Ole Miss	1983
71	Matt DeFrank	LSU vs. Florida	1986
71	Mike Riley	Miss. State vs. Auburn	1989
71	Tom Hutton	Tennessee vs. Kentucky	1992
71	David Lawrence	Vanderbilt vs. Tennessee	1992
71	Terry Daniel	Auburn vs. Miss. State	1993

*In the air

Longest Punt Returns

Yds.	Player	School and Opponent	Year
100	Bert Rechichar	Tenn. vs. Wash. & Lee	1950
100	Jim Campagna	Georgia vs. Vanderbilt	1952
98	Ray Hapes	Miss. vs. SW Louisiana	1935
97	Hal Griffin	Florida vs. Miami	1946
97	Dicky Lyons	Kentucky vs. Houston	1966
96	Ray Hapes	Miss. vs. Union	1936
96	John Hovious	Miss. vs. Georgia	1940
95	Ray Hapes	Miss. vs. SW Louisiana	1935
95	Rab Rodgers	Miss. vs. Memphis State	1935
95	Bobby Freeman	Auburn vs. Georgia	1953
93	Ray Hapes	Miss. vs. Union	1936
93	John McGeever	Auburn vs. Kentucky	1961
92	Herschel Mosley	Alabama vs. Howard	1937
92	Harry Gilmer	Alabama vs. LSU	1947
92	Ken Konz	LSU vs. Tulane	1949
91	Cotton Clark	Alabama vs. Tulsa	1962
90	David Palmer	Alabama vs. LSU	1991
90	Harold Payne	Tennessee vs. Duke	1949
90	Zippy Morocco	Georgia vs. Furman	1950
90	Jake Scott	Georgia vs. Tennessee	1968
90	Craig Burns	LSU vs. Miss. State	1970
90	Ken Phares	Miss. State vs. Lamar	1971
90	Preston Brown	Vanderbilt vs. Arkansas	1978
89	Len Staggs	Miss. vs. LSU	1942
89	Jim Glisson	Tulane vs. LSU	1948
89	Tommy Warner	Tulane vs. Va. Tech	1957
89	Billy Cannon	LSU vs. Miss.	1959
89	Marcus Rhoden	Miss. State vs. Houston	1965
89	Doug Mathews	Vanderbilt vs. Davidson	1968
89	James Owens	Auburn vs. Florida	1970
89	Roland James	Tennessee vs. Vanderbilt	1979
89	Vincent Brownlee	Ole Miss vs. Arkansas	1990
88	Charles Conerly	Miss. vs. Georgia	1942
88	Don Phelps	Kentucky vs. Marquette	1946
88	Lee Nalley	Vanderbilt vs. Miami	1947
88	Lee Nalley	Vanderbilt vs. Kentucky	1948
88	Eli Maricich	Georgia vs. N. Carolina	1949
88	Frank Dowsing	Miss. State vs. Alabama	1971
88	Larry Carter	Kentucky vs. Virginia Tech	1978
87	Hal Griffin	Florida vs. Villanova	1946
87	Charley Horton	Vanderbilt vs. Penn.	1953
87	Johnny Menger	Ga. Tech vs. Auburn	1956
87	John McGeever	Auburn vs. Kentucky	1961
87	Glen Young	Miss. State vs. Vanderbilt	1981
87	Andy Molls	Kentucky vs. Vanderbilt	1981
87	Orlando Watters	Arkansas vs. South Carolina	1992
86	Jerry Nunnally	Georgia vs. Centre	1941
86	Corky Tharp	Alabama vs. Georgia	1953
86	Darrell Cox	Kentucky vs. Florida State	1961
85	Buist Warren	Tennessee vs. Miss.	1938
85	Lamar Davis	Georgia vs. Dartmouth	1941
85	Jimmy Nelson	Alabama vs. Miami	1941
85	Billy Brewer	Miss. vs. UT-Chatt.	1959
85	George Canale	Tenn. vs. N. Carolina	1960
85	Eddie Brown	Tennessee vs. Georgia	1973
84	Loren Broadus	Florida vs. Rollins	1948
84	Norm Hodgins	LSU vs. Rice	1971
84	Willie Shelby	Alabama vs. Washington	1975
84	Preston Brown	Vanderbilt vs. Air Force	1976
83	Dutch Konemann	Ga. Tech vs. Florida	1935
83	George Grandy	Florida vs. Tulane	1966
83	Pat Coleman	Ole Miss vs. Memphis State	1988
83	Thomas Bailey	Auburn vs. Ole Miss	1991
82	Hal Griffin	Florida vs. Kansas State	1947
82	Jim Tait	Miss. State vs. Memphis State	1955
82	Preston Ridlehuber	Georgia vs. Vanderbilt	1965
82	Harvin Clark	Florida vs. Miami	1971
82	Thomas Woods	Tennessee vs. Washington State	1988
81	Johnny Cook	Georgia vs. VMI	1943
81	Steve Van Buren	LSU vs. Georgia	1943
81	David Ray	Vanderbilt vs. Missouri	1958
81	Ken Stone	Vanderbilt vs. UT-Chatt.	1970
81	Trey Gainous	Auburn vs. Tennessee	1983
80	Harvey Johnson	Miss. State vs. Howard	1939
80	Lamar Davis	Georgia vs. Furman	1942
80	Harry Gilmer	Alabama vs. Georgia	1947
80	Jerry Tiblier	Miss. vs. Tennessee	1948
80	Bob Brengle	Tennessee vs. N. Carolina	1954
80	J.B. Davis	Georgia vs. Alabama	1956
80	Sammy Grezaffi	LSU vs. Kentucky	1966

1994 SEC Football

Longest Interception Returns

Yds.	Player — Team and Opponent	Year
100	Ray Hapes—Miss. vs. Ouachita	1937
100	Bob Davis—Kentucky vs. Wash. & Lee	1937
100	Frank Broyles—Ga. Tech vs. Clemson	1944
100	Ray Martin—Tennessee vs. Louisville	1953
100	Jackie Simpson—Florida vs. Miss. State	1955
100	Joe Brodsky—Florida vs. Miss. State	1956
100	Charlie Britt—Georgia vs. Florida	1959
100	Louis Guy—Miss. vs. Tennessee	1962
100	White Graves—LSU vs. Kentucky	1964
100	Dave Hunter—Kentucky vs. West Va.	1968
100	Greg Jackson—LSU vs. Miss. State	1988
99	Bobby Wilson—Miss. vs. Florida	1948
99	Orlando Watters—Arkansas vs. LSU	1993
98	John Liptak—Auburn vs. Georgia	1947
98	John Gamble—Vanderbilt vs. Citadel	1966
98	Scott Woerner—Georgia vs. Clemson	1980
98	Mark McMillian—Alabama vs. UT-Chattanooga	1991
97	Jack Nix—Miss. State vs. Miss.	1938
97	Darryl Bishop—Kentucky vs. Miss. State	1972
96	Corky Tharp—Alabama vs. Tennessee	1954
96	Art Reynolds—Tennessee vs. Memphis St.	1972
96	Calvin Jackson—Auburn vs. Florida	1993
95	Rodger Bird—Kentucky vs. Auburn	1964
95	Larry Buie—Miss. State vs. Florida	1973
95	David Johnson—Kentucky vs. Cincinnati	1986
93	James Stell—LSU vs. NW Louisiana	1937
93	Don Frampton—Kentucky vs. Miss.	1949
92	Clint Castleberry—Ga. Tech vs. Navy	1942
91	Fred Wilcox—Tulane vs. Miss.	1954
91	Greg Long—Kentucky vs. N. Texas St.	1981
90	Roland James—Tennessee vs. Miss.	1978
89	Steve Hughes—Georgia vs. Citadel	1939
89	Jimmy Heidel—Miss. vs. Kentucky	1964
89	Joe Stephen—Kentucky vs. Florida	1969
88	Jimmy Nelson—Alabama vs. Howard	1940
88	James Stuart—Miss. State vs. Murray	1946
88	Charlie Daigle—Tulane vs. SE La.	1951
88	David Langner—Auburn vs. UT-Chatt	1971
87	Ralph Ruch—Sewanee vs. Alabama	1934
87	Duke Warren—Florida vs. Stetson	1935
87	Fred Grant—Alabama vs. Miss. State	1944
87	Joe Gambrell—Alabama vs. SW La.	1946
87	Tommy Warner—Tulane vs. Auburn	1955
87	Joe Burson—Georgia vs. Auburn	1962
86	Danny Byers—Vanderbilt vs. Tennessee	1953
85	Barney Mintz—Tulane vs. Colgate	1935
85	Ben Griffith—Miss. State vs. Bham-Sou.	1939
85	Larry King—LSU vs. Miss. State	1955
85	Gary Adams—Arkansas vs. Auburn	1992
84	Roger Urbano—Tennessee vs. Maryland	1956
84	Dick Kirk—Florida vs. Auburn	1964
83	Danny Jeffries—Tennessee vs. S. Carolina	1971
83	Darryl Bishop—Kentucky vs. Miss. State	1973
82	Jim Loflin-Dan Sandifer—LSU vs. Ala.	1946
81	Lloyd Cheatham—Auburn vs. Bos. Coll.	1939
81	Dallas Owens—Kentucky vs. LSU	1977
80	Dixie Howell—Alabama vs. Vanderbilt	1933
80	Ken Kavanaugh—LSU vs. Holy Cross	1939
80	Joe Jackura—Georgia vs. Alabama	1948
80	John Netoskie—Kentucky vs. Miami	1949
80	Fred Bilyeu—Georgia vs. N. Carolina	1951
80	Steve Higginbotham—Alabama vs. Houston	1970

Longest Fumble-In-Air Returns

Yds.	Player — Team and Opponent	Year
100	Dextar Stanphill—Sewanee vs. Florida	1936
100	Ken Kavanaugh—LSU vs. Rice	1937
98	Millard Morris—Auburn vs. LSU	1934
96	Darrin Miller—Tennessee vs. Iowa	1987
94	George Mathews—Ga. Tech vs. Navy	1946
94	David Ray—Vanderbilt vs. Tulane	1958
91	Gusty Yearout—Auburn vs. Florida	1966
91	Cassius Ware—Ole Miss vs. Auburn	1992
87	Carl Johnson—Tennessee vs. Kentucky	1971
76	Conrad Graham—Tennessee vs. Penn. St.	1971
76	Wayne Williams—LSU vs. Vanderbilt	1992
70	Christie Hauck—Vanderbilt vs. Tulane	1969
70	Brad Armstead—Kentucky vs. Vanderbilt	1992
60	Tim Drinkard—Auburn vs. Alabama	1982
60	Ed Graham—Auburn vs. FSU	1984

Longest Field Goals

Yds.	Player — Team and Opponent	Year
60	Fuad Reveiz—Tennessee vs. Ga. Tech	1982
60	Chris Perkins—Florida vs. Tulane	1984
60	Kevin Butler—Georgia vs. Clemson	1984
59	Cloyce Hinton—Miss. vs. Georgia	1969
59	Kevin Butler—Georgia vs. Ole Miss	1982
58	Cloyce Hinton—Miss. vs. Houston	1970
58	Allan Leavitt—Georgia vs. Vanderbilt	1976
58	Neil O'Donoghue—Auburn vs. Tennessee	1976
57	Jim Gaylor—Tennessee vs. Kentucky	1977
57	Rex Robinson—Georgia vs. S. Carolina	1980
57	Rex Robinson—Georgia vs. Ga. Tech	1980
57	Kevin Butler—Georgia vs. Ga. Tech	1984
57	Van Tiffin—Alabama vs. Texas A&M	1985
57	Bryan Owen—Ole Miss vs. Tulane	1988
56	John Riley—Auburn vs. Tennessee	1969
55	Hawkins Golden—Vanderbilt vs. Tampa	1973
55	Alan Duncan—Tennessee vs. Ga. Tech	1980
55	Brian Clark—Florida vs. Kentucky	1981
55	Fuad Reveiz—Tennessee vs. Kentucky	1982
55	Carlos Reveiz—Tennessee vs. Ga. Tech	1985
55	Win Lyle—Auburn vs. Tennessee	1987
54	Fuad Reveiz—Tennessee vs. Memphis St.	1982
54	Karl Kremser—Tennessee vs. Alabama	1968
54	John Riley—Auburn vs. Kentucky	1969
54	Pete Rajecki—Georgia vs. Miss. State	1970
54	Allan Leavitt—Georgia vs. Alabama	1973
54	Neil O'Donoghue—Auburn vs. Miss. State	1975
54	David Posey—Florida vs. Florida State	1976
54	Berj Yepremian—Florida vs. Utah	1977
54	Ronald Lewis—LSU vs. North Carolina	1985
54	Artie Cosby—Miss. State vs. Memphis State	1985
54	Johnny Clark—Vanderbilt vs. Auburn	1987
53	George Shuford—Tennessee vs. Alabama	1961
53	Don Bright—Tulane vs. Duke	1964
53	Juan Roca—LSU vs. Rice	1972
53	John Williams—Florida vs. Kentucky	1973
53	Allan Leavitt—Georgia vs. Auburn	1974
53	Kinney Jordan—Miss. State vs. Florida	1975
53	Neil O'Donoghue—Auburn vs. Va. Tech	1975
53	Kinney Jordan—Miss. State vs. Louisville	1976
53	Rex Robinson—Georgia vs. Alabama	1977
53	Alan Duncan—Tennessee vs. Duke	1978
53	Kevin Butler—Georgia vs. Miss. State	1983
53	Chris Perkins—Florida vs. Miami	1983
53	Van Tiffin—Alabama vs. Penn State	1984
53	Carlos Reveiz—Tennessee vs. UTEP	1986
53	Philip Doyle—Alabama vs. Temple	1988
53	John Kasay—Georgia vs. Temple	1989
53	Doug Pelfrey—Kentucky vs. Indiana	1991
53	Doug Pelfrey—Kentucky vs. Cincinnati	1991
53	John Becksvoort—Tennessee vs. Arkansas	1992
53	Michael Proctor—Alabama vs. Ole Miss	1993
53	Steve Yenner—Vanderbilt vs. Auburn	1993
52	Durwood Pennington—Georgia vs. Kentucky	1961
52	John Riley—Auburn vs. Tennessee	1969
52	Juan Roca—LSU vs. Wisconsin	1972
52	Juan Roca—LSU vs. Miss. State	1973
52	John Pierce—Kentucky vs. Florida	1974
52	Allan Leavitt—Georgia vs. Auburn	1975
52	Joe Bryant—Kentucky vs. Va. Tech	1977
52	Berj Yepremian—Florida vs. Alabama	1978
52	Mike Woodard—Vanderbilt vs. Miss.	1978
52	Brian Clark—Florida vs. Kentucky	1979
52	Jorge Portela—Auburn vs. Florida	1979
52	Al Del Greco—Auburn vs. Alabama	1980
52	Kevin Butler—Georgia vs. Ole Miss	1981
52	Kevin Butler—Georgia vs. Ga. Tech	1981
52	Rick Strein—Kentucky vs. Kansas	1981
52	Al Del Greco—Auburn vs. Nebraska	1981
52	Fuad Reveiz—Tennessee vs. Miss.	1982
52	Fuad Reveiz—Tennessee vs. Iowa St.	1982
52	Fuad Reveiz—Tennessee vs. LSU	1982
52	Fuad Reveiz—Tennessee vs. Memphis St.	1982
52	Ricky Anderson—Vanderbilt vs. Alabama	1983
52	Carlos Reveiz—Tennessee vs. Wake Forest	1985
52	Van Tiffin—Alabama vs. Auburn	1985
52	David Browndyke—LSU vs. Ole Miss	1986
52	Bryan Young—Ole Miss vs. Arkansas St.	1987
52	Win Lyle—Auburn vs. Tennessee	1987
52	Robert McGinty—Florida vs. Georgia	1987
52	Philip Doyle—Alabama vs. Memphis State	1987
52	Doug Pelfrey—Kentucky vs. Florida	1991
52	Doug Pelfrey—Kentucky vs. LSU	1992
52	Doug Pelfrey—Kentucky vs. Miss. State	1992

Southeastern Conference Team Offense Records
RUSHING

MOST RUSHES
GAME:
- 89— Georgia vs. Kentucky 1967
- 86— Auburn vs. Vanderbilt 1951
- 83— LSU vs. Wyoming 1977
- 82— LSU vs. Florida 1977
- 82— Alabama vs. Baylor 1979
- 82— Auburn vs. Ole Miss 1985
- 80— Ole Miss vs. Miss. State 1949
- 80— Alabama vs. Vanderbilt 1972
- 79— Georgia Tech vs. Sewanee 1935
- 79— LSU vs. Florida 1978
- 78— Vanderbilt vs. Tulane 1971
- 78— Miss. State vs. Louisville 1976

SEASON:
- 763— Alabama (3,792 yards in 11 games) 1979
- 724— Kentucky (2,661 yards in 11 games) 1975
- 707— Alabama (3,082 yards in 11 games) 1981
- 705— Alabama (3,565 yards in 11 games) 1971
- 704— Alabama (3,332 yards in 11 games) 1972
- 697— Alabama (3,268 yards in 11 games) 1977
- 693— Georgia (3,075 yards in 11 games) 1976
- 691— Georgia (3,377 yards in 11 games) 1971
- 686— Alabama (3,288 yards in 11 games) 1974
- 680— Alabama (3,320 yards in 11 games) 1975
- 680— Georgia (3,267 yards in 11 games) 1975

YARDS GAINED
GAME:
- 748— Alabama vs. Virginia Tech (73 rushes) 1973
- 638— Tulane vs. Mississippi College 1937
- 606— Vanderbilt vs. Tennessee Poly 1942
- 565— Auburn vs. Southwestern Louisiana (58 rushes) 1985
- 547— Vanderbilt vs. Air Force (60 rushes) 1978
- 532— Miss. State vs. Union (60 rushes) 1941
- 531— Alabama vs. Ole Miss (73 rushes) 1971
- 515— Ole Miss vs. Auburn (53 rushes) 1951
- 514— Alabama vs. Miss. State (74 rushes) 1986

SEASON:
- 4,027— Alabama (664 rushes in 11 games) 1973
- 3,792— Alabama (763 rushes in 11 games) 1979
- 3,565— Alabama (705 rushes in 11 games) 1971
- 3,438— Auburn (620 rushes in 11 games) 1985
- 3,392— Alabama (704 rushes in 11 games) 1972
- 3,381— Alabama (632 rushes in 11 games) 1980
- 3,352— LSU (674 rushes in 11 games) 1977
- 3,337— Georgia (691 rushes in 11 games) 1971
- 3,326— Florida (657 rushes in 11 games) 1975
- 3,320— Alabama (680 rushes in 11 games) 1975

YARDS PER GAME
- 366.1— Alabama (4,927 in 11 games) 1973
- 344.7— Alabama (3,792 in 11 games) 1979
- 324.1— Alabama (3,565 in 11 games) 1971
- 312.5— Auburn (3,438 in 11 games) 1985
- 307.4— Alabama (3,381 in 11 games) 1980
- 306.8— Tennessee (3,068 in 10 games) 1951
- 306.3— Ole Miss (3,063 in 10 games) 1957
- 304.7— LSU (3,352 in 11 games) 1977
- 303.4— Georgia (3,377 in 11 games) 1971
- 302.9— Alabama (3,332 in 11 games) 1972

YARDS PER RUSH
GAME:
- 10.7— Tennessee vs. Tennessee Tech (44 for 469) 1951
- 10.2— Alabama vs. Virginia Tech (72 for 748) 1973
- 10.1— LSU vs. Rice (43 for 436) 1987
- 9.7— Ole Miss vs. Auburn (53 for 515) 1951
- 9.7— Auburn vs. Vanderbilt (45 for 438) 1979
- 9.7— Auburn vs. Southwestern Louisiana (58 for 565) 1985
- 9.5— Ole Miss vs. Tulane (40 for 380) 1990
- 9.1— Vanderbilt vs. Air Force (60 for 547) 1978

SEASON:
- 6.8— LSU (306 for 2,632) 1945
- 6.1— Alabama (664 for 4,027) 1973
- 5.9— Tennessee (442 for 2,621) 1993
- 5.7— Auburn (579 for 3,279) 1979
- 5.6— Georgia (584 for 3,249) 1985
- 5.6— Georgia (458 for 2,584) 1992
- 5.5— Auburn (620 for 3,438) 1985
- 5.5— Tennessee (553 for 3,068) 1951
- 5.3— Auburn (515 for 2,760) 1956
- 5.3— Ole Miss (582 for 3,063) 1957

PASSING

MOST ATTEMPTS
GAME:
- 66— Florida vs. Auburn (33 comp.) 1969
- 65— Georgia vs. Florida (36 comp.) 1993
- 63— Vanderbilt vs. Alabama (31 comp.) 1989
- 60— Tennessee vs. Notre Dame (35 comp.) 1990
- 58— Vanderbilt vs. Georgia (27 comp.) 1982
- 58— Auburn vs. Tennessee (30 comp.) 1990
- 56— Ole Miss vs. Southern Miss (30 comp.) 1970
- 56— LSU vs. Tulane (26 comp.) 1979
- 56— Vanderbilt vs. Maryland (29 comp.) 1983
- 56— Vanderbilt vs. Georgia (33 comp.) 1983
- 56— Kentucky vs. Vanderbilt (30 comp.) 1985
- 56— Tennessee vs. Florida (33 comp.) 1991

SEASON:
- 519— Vanderbilt (296 comp.) 1983
- 503— Florida (290 comp.) 1992
- 488— Florida (284 comp.) 1993
- 476— Vanderbilt (269 comp.) 1981
- 454— Vanderbilt (252 comp.) 1982
- 437— Vanderbilt (246 comp.) 1984
- 432— Georgia (272 comp.) 1993
- 421— Vanderbilt (201 comp.) 1989
- 415— Florida (246 comp.) 1990
- 413— Florida (233 comp.) 1969

COMPLETIONS
GAME:
- 37— Ole Miss vs. Tennessee (50 atts.) 1982
- 36— Georgia vs. Florida (65 atts.) 1993
- 35— Tennessee vs. Notre Dame (60 atts.) 1990
- 34— Georgia vs. Auburn (53 atts.) 1993
- 34— Florida vs. Southwestern Louisiana (50 atts.) 1993
- 33— Ole Miss vs. Alabama (52 atts.) 1969
- 33— Florida vs. Auburn (66 atts.) 1969
- 33— Vanderbilt vs. Georgia (56 atts.) 1983
- 33— Vanderbilt vs. Kentucky (48 atts.) 1983
- 33— LSU vs. Miss. State (51 atts.) 1983
- 33— Florida vs. Georgia (49 atts.) 1985
- 33— Tennessee vs. Washington State (55 atts.) 1988
- 33— Tennessee vs. Colorado (55 atts.) 1990
- 33— Tennessee vs. Florida (56 atts.) 1991

SEASON:
- 296— Vanderbilt (519 atts.) 1983
- 290— Florida (503 atts.) 1992
- 284— Florida (488 atts.) 1993
- 272— Georgia (432 atts.) 1993
- 269— Vanderbilt (476 atts.) 1981
- 252— Vanderbilt (454 atts.) 1982
- 246— Vanderbilt (437 atts.) 1984
- 246— Florida (415 atts.) 1990

1994 SEC Football

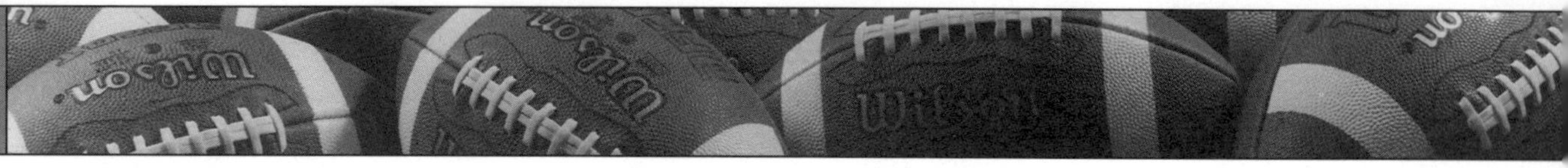

PASSING

COMPLETION PERCENTAGE

GAME: (Min. 20 atts.)

95.0— Ole Miss vs. Tulane (19 of 20) ... 1982
86.9— Kentucky vs. Florida (20 of 23) ... 1986
81.0— Alabama vs. Southern Miss. (21 of 26) ... 1950
81.0— LSU vs. Ole Miss (21 of 24) ... 1981
80.0— Florida vs. West Texas State (20 of 25) ... 1982
80.0— LSU vs. Cal. State-Fullerton (16 of 20) ... 1987

GAME: (Min. 30 atts.)

77.8— Florida vs. Vanderbilt (28 of 36) ... 1982
76.7— Florida vs. Auburn (23 of 30) ... 1982
75.7— Tennessee vs. Memphis State (28 of 37) ... 1991
74.4— Miss. State vs. FSU (29 of 39) ... 1968
74.0— Ole Miss vs. Tennessee (37 of 50) ... 1982
73.8— LSU vs. Notre Dame (31 of 42) ... 1985

SEASON: (Min. 100 atts.)

68.8— Florida (203 of 295) ... 1982

SEASON: (Min. 300 atts.)

65.0— Tennessee (208 of 320) ... 1993
63.0— Georgia (272 fo 432) ... 1993
63.3— Florida (193 of 305) ... 1983
63.1— Tennessee (231 of 366) ... 1991
62.2— Florida (189 of 304) ... 1985
60.7— Florida (199 of 328) ... 1966
60.3— Florida (235 of 390) ... 1991
60.2— Alabama (230 of 382) ... 1989
59.5— Alabama (195 of 328) ... 1969
59.3— Florida (246 of 415) ... 1990
59.1— Ole Miss (215 of 364) ... 1982
58.7— Tennessee (178 of 303) ... 1982
58.2— Auburn (181 of 311) ... 1970
58.2— Florida (284 of 488) ... 1993
57.7— Florida (290 of 503) ... 1992
57.1— LSU (194 of 340) ... 1983

YARDS GAINED

GAME:

544— Georgia vs. Southern Miss. (30 of 47) ... 1993
512— Florida vs. Southwestern Louisiana (34 of 50) ... 1993
484— Alabama vs. Auburn (30 of 55) ... 1969
471— Florida vs. N. Illinois (29 of 45) ... 1991
464— Vanderbilt vs. Tennessee (29 of 53) ... 1981
456— Miss. State vs. Alabama (31 of 53) ... 1978
449— Florida vs. Miss. State (27 of 41) ... 1993
442— Auburn vs. Florida (24 of 34) ... 1970
440— Kentucky vs. Tennessee (28 of 46) ... 1969
438— LSU vs. Tennessee (31 of 49) ... 1989
436— Ole Miss vs. Alabama (33 of 52) ... 1969
426— Georgia vs. Auburn (34 of 53) ... 1993
425— Georgia vs. Kentucky (31 of 47) ... 1993
412— Ole Miss vs. Arkansas State (23 of 35) ... 1989
408— Florida vs. Georgia (33 of 49) ... 1985
407— Georgia vs. Miami (25 of 38) ... 1963
406— Georgia vs. Vanderbilt (28 of 41) ... 1993

SEASON:

4,072— Florida (284 of 488) ... 1993
3,552— Georgia (272 of 432) ... 1993
3,440— Florida (290 of 503) ... 1992
3,393— Florida (235 of 390) ... 1991
3,299— Vanderbilt (296 of 519) ... 1983
3,197— Florida (246 of 415) ... 1990
3,036— Vanderbilt (269 of 476) ... 1981
3,016— Florida (233 of 413) ... 1969
2,924— Florida (189 of 304) ... 1985
2,920— Vanderbilt (246 of 437) ... 1984
2,885— Auburn (181 of 311) ... 1970
2,839— LSU (188 of 327) ... 1989
2,837— Vanderbilt (252 of 454) ... 1982
2,813— Tennessee (231 of 366) ... 1991
2,707— Alabama (195 of 328) ... 1969

YARDS PER GAME

339.3— Florida (4,072 in 12 games) ... 1993
322.9— Georgia (3,552 in 11 games) ... 1993
308.5— Florida (3,393 in 11 games) ... 1991
301.6— Florida (3,016 in 10 games) ... 1969
299.9— Vanderbilt (3,299 in 11 games) ... 1983
290.6— Florida (3,197 in 11 games) ... 1990
288.5— Auburn (2,885 in 10 games) ... 1970
286.7— Florida (3,440 in 12 games) ... 1992
276.0— Vanderbilt (3,036 in 11 games) ... 1981
270.7— Alabama (2,707 in 10 games) ... 1969
265.8— Florida (2,924 in 11 games) ... 1985

YARDS PER ATTEMPT

SEASON:

*13.4— Alabama (94 for 1,261) ... 1973
10.4— Alabama (111 for 1,156) ... 1981
10.2— Georgia (153 for 1,567) ... 1974
9.6— Florida (304 for 2,924) ... 1985
9.4— Auburn (311 for 2,885) ... 1970
9.3— Georgia (162 for 1,506) ... 1948
9.1— Alabama (178 for 1,169) ... 1972
9.1— Alabama (87 for 1,697) ... 1982
9.0— Ole Miss (148 for 1,355) ... 1949
9.0— Ole Miss (202 for 1,827) ... 1961

TOUCHDOWNS

GAME:

8— Kentucky vs. North Dakota ... 1950
7— Alabama vs. Southern Miss ... 1950
7— LSU vs. Ohio ... 1989
7— Florida vs. Southwestern Louisiana ... 1993
6— Ole Miss vs. Houston ... 1960
6— Vanderbilt vs. Virginia Tech ... 1982

SEASON:

32— Florida (11 games) ... 1991
31— Tennessee (11 games) ... 1993
27— Kentucky (11 games) ... 1950
26— Vanderbilt (11 games) ... 1982
26— LSU (11 games) ... 1989
25— Florida (11 games) ... 1990
25— Florida (12 games) ... 1992
24— Florida (10 games) ... 1969
24— Auburn (10 games) ... 1971
24— Florida (11 games) ... 1985
24— Georgia (11 games) ... 1993
23— Georgia (11 games) ... 1942
21— LSU (11 games) ... 1982
21— LSU (11 games) ... 1986
20— LSU (11 games) ... 1971
20— Vanderbilt (11 games) ... 1984

INTERCEPTIONS

GAME:

9— Florida vs. Auburn ... 1969
8— Alabama vs. Tennessee ... 1970
8— Miss. State vs. Alabama ... 1936

SEASON:

35— Georgia (356 atts., 180 comp.) ... 1982
33— Georgia ... 1946
33— Kentucky (227 atts., 110 comp.) ... 1967
32— Georgia (265 atts., 121 comp.) ... 1951
31— Vanderbilt (519 atts., 296 comp.) ... 1983
30— Vanderbilt (254 atts., 90 comp) ... 1972
29— Auburn (151 atts., 63 comp.) ... 1948
28— Kentucky (286 atts., 139 comp.) ... 1982
25— Miss. State (153 atts., 40 comp.) ... 1949
25— Georgia (247 atts., 118 comp.) ... 1953
25— Tulane ... 1958
25— Auburn (286 atts., 126 comp.) ... 1968
25— Alabama (322 atts., 175 comp.) ... 1970
25— Kentucky ... 1980

FEWEST INTERCEPTIONS

GAME: (Min. 35 atts.)

0 interceptions

Kentucky vs. Vanderbilt (56 atts.) ... 1985
Vanderbilt vs. Tennessee (53 atts.) ... 1983
Ole Miss vs. Tennessee (50 atts.) ... 1982
LSU vs. Tennessee (49 atts.) ... 1989
Vanderbilt vs. Ole Miss (47 atts.) ... 1989
Georgia vs. Southern Miss. (47 atts.) ... 1993
South Carolina vs. Vanderbilt (47 atts.) ... 1993
Alabama vs. Tennessee (46 atts.) ... 1989
Florida vs. N. Illinois (45 atts.) ... 1991
LSU vs. Miss. State (44 atts.) ... 1991
Miss. State vs. Memphis State (44 atts.) ... 1993
Miss. State vs. Florida (44 atts.) ... 1993
Vanderbilt vs. Virginia Tech (43 atts.) ... 1982

*—NCAA record

FEWEST INTERCEPTIONS (Continued)
Florida vs. Georgia (42 atts.)..1969
Florida vs. Georgia (42 atts.)..1990
LSU vs. Vanderbilt (42 atts.)..1985
Ole Miss vs. LSU (42 atts.)..1987
Kentucky vs. Ole Miss (42 atts.)..1990
LSU vs. Auburn (42 atts.)..1988
Alabama vs. Miami (41 atts.)..1969
Ole Miss vs. Tulane (41 atts.)..1989
Georgia vs. Vanderbilt (41 atts.).......................................1993
Georgia vs. Georgia Tech (41 atts.)...................................1993
LSU vs. Ohio State (40 atts.)..1988
Tennessee vs. Vanderbilt (38 atts.)...................................1992
Auburn vs. Cal St. Fullerton (37 atts.)...............................1990
Auburn vs. Louisiana Tech (37 atts.).................................1990
Florida vs. Southwestern Louisiana (50 atts.)...................1993
LSU vs. Ole Miss (36 atts.)...1971
LSU vs. Kentucky (35 atts.)..1986
Ole Miss vs. Arkansas State (35 atts.)..............................1989
Vanderbilt vs. Alabama (35 atts.).....................................1990

SEASON: (Min. 100 atts.)
* 0.96%—Alabama (1 in 104)...1980

SEASON: (Min. 150 atts.)
**1.13%—Georgia (4 in 355)..1991
  1.14%—Auburn (2 in 175)..1982
  1.75%—Alabama (3 in 171).......................................1965
  1.82%—Alabama (2 in 111).......................................1981

SEASON: (Min. 200 atts.)
**1.13%—Georgia (4 in 355)..1991
  1.54%—Tennessee (4 in 259)....................................1992
  1.62%—Georgia (7 in 432)..1993
  1.95%—Vanderbilt (5 in 256)....................................1973
  2.63%—Tennessee (7 in 266)....................................1986
  2.65%—Ole Miss (9 in 339).......................................1984
  2.73%—LSU (10 in 366)..1985
  2.94%—Alabama (8 in 235).......................................1985

*—NCAA record for 100 attempts
**—NCAA record for 150 and 200 attempts

TOTAL OFFENSE

MOST PLAYS
GAME:
105— Georgia vs. Kentucky...1967
102— Alabama vs. Miami...1969
101— Auburn vs. Ole Miss...1985
 99— LSU vs. Tulane...1969
 99— Auburn vs. Tennessee...1990
 98— Ole Miss vs. Chattanooga.......................................1951
 98— LSU vs. Tulane...1968
 98— LSU vs. Wyoming..1978
 97— LSU vs. Kentucky..1985
 97— Alabama vs. Tennessee..1989
 95— Ole Miss vs. Chattanooga.......................................1971
 95— Tennessee vs. Miss. State......................................1991

SEASON:
926— Florida (4,679 yards)..1992
911— Auburn (4,923 yards)...1984
888— Florida (5,719 yards)..1993
882— LSU (4,284 yards)...1985
881— Tennessee (4,361 yards).......................................1970
878— Tennessee (5,145 yards).......................................1991
875— Alabama (4,715 yards)..1979
872— LSU (5,542 yards)...1977
865— Georgia (4,912 yards)..1981
864— Alabama (4,354 yards)..1992
860— LSU (4,089 yards)...1969
859— Georgia (3,917 yards)..1968
859— LSU (4,089 yards)...1969
856— LSU (3,942 yards)...1972
855— Florida (4,978 yards)..1990
850— Kentucky (3,217 yards)...1975
849— Ole Miss (4,286 yards)...1980

YARDS GAINED
GAME:
833— Alabama vs. Virginia Tech (748 rushing, 85 passing)..............1973
798— Vanderbilt vs. Davidson (430 rushing, 368 passing)..............1969
774— Florida vs. West Texas State (394 rushing, 380 passing).......1982
746— LSU vs. Rice (502 rushing, 244 passing).................................1977
706— Georgia Tech vs. Citadel..1948
695— Auburn vs. Southwestern Louisiana (565 rushing, 130 passing)....1985
680— Auburn vs. Kansas (309 rushing, 371 passing)...................1988
667— Alabama vs. California (405 rushing, 262 passing)..............1973
667— Georgia vs. Southern Miss. (123 rushing, 544 passing).......1993
664— LSU vs. Rice..1987
654— Georgia vs. Ole Miss...1942
650— LSU vs. Wisconsin...1972
646— Kentucky vs. Tennessee Tech (446 rushing, 200 passing).....1951
644— Alabama vs. LSU (387 rushing, 257 passing)........................1989
642— Florida vs. Southwestern Louisiana (130 rush, 512 pass)....1993
631— South Carolina (281 rushing, 350 passing)...................1993
626— Alabama vs. Penn State (290 rushing, 336 passing)..........1983
626— Georgia vs. William & Mary (372 rushing, 254 passing)....1988
623— Ole Miss vs. Auburn (515 rushing, 108 passing)................1951

SEASON:
5,719— Florida (1,647 rush, 4,072 pass), 12 games..................1993
5,288— Alabama (4,027 rush, 1,261 pass, 11 games)................1973
5,285— Tennessee (2,621 rush, 2,664 pass, 11 games)..............1993
5,145— Tennessee (2,332 rush, 2,813 pass, 11 games)..............1991
5,028— Florida (1,635 rush, 3,393 pass, 11 games)...................1991
4,978— Florida (1,781 rush, 3,197 pass in 11 games)................1990
4,954— Georgia (2,584 rush, 2,370 pass, 11 games)..................1992
4,933— Tennessee (2,468 rush, 2,465 pass in 12 games)...........1990
4,923— Auburn (3,086 rush, 1,837 pass, 11 games)...................1984
4,912— Georgia (3,102 rush, 1,810 pass, 11 games).................1981
4,871— Tennessee (2,652 rush, 2,219 pass, 12 games)..............1987
4,850— Auburn (1,965 rush, 2,885 pass, 10 games)...................1970
4,843— LSU (2,289 rush, 2,554 pass, 11 games).......................1987
4,778— Alabama (2,124 rush, 2,654 pass, 11 games)................1989
4,733— Georgia (1,181 rush, 3,552 pass, 11 games).................1993
4,728— Alabama (3,167 rush, 1,561 pass, 12 games)................1986
4,724— Georgia (1,264 rush, 2,101 pass, 11 games).................1942
4,715— Alabama (3,792 rush, 923 pass, 11 games)...................1979
4,679— Florida (1,239 rush, 3,440 pass, 12 games)...................1992
4,665— Alabama (2,656 rush, 2,009 pass, 11 games)................1983
4,642— Miss. State (2,899 rush, 1,743 pass, 11 games).............1982
4,632— Alabama (2,935 rush, 1,697 pass, 11 games)................1982

YARDS PER GAME
485.0— Auburn (4,850 in 10 games)................................1970
480.7— Alabama (5,288 in 11 games)..............................1973
480.5— Tennessee (5,285 in 11 games)...........................1993
476.6— Florida (5,719 in 12 games).................................1993
467.7— Tennessee (5,145 in 11 games)...........................1991
457.1— Florida (5,028 in 11 games).................................1991
452.6— Florida (4,978 in 11 games).................................1990
450.4— Georgia (4,954 in 11 games)................................1992
446.5— Georgia (4,912 in 11 games)................................1981
440.3— LSU (4,843 in 11 games).......................................1987
434.8— Florida (4,348 in 10 games).................................1969
434.4— Alabama (4,778 in 11 games)..............................1989
434.4— Auburn (4,777 in 11 games)................................1988
430.3— Georgia (4,733 in 11 games)................................1993
429.4— Georgia (4,724 in 11 games)................................1942
428.6— Alabama (4,715 in 11 games)..............................1979
424.1— Alabama (4,665 in 11 games)..............................1983
422.0— Miss. State (4,642 in 11 games)...........................1982
421.7— Alabama (3,795 in 9 games)................................1945
421.1— Alabama (4,632 in 11 games)..............................1982

YARDS PER PLAY
GAME:
11.9— Alabama vs. Virginia Tech (70 for 833).................1973
10.6— Tennessee vs. Louisville (44 for 465)....................1953
10.3— Auburn vs. Kansas (66 for 680)............................1988
10.1— LSU vs. Rice (66 for 664).......................................1987
10.0— Ole Miss vs. Auburn (62 for 623).........................1951
 9.54— Ole Miss vs. Tulane (52 for 496)..........................1990
 9.18— Georgia vs. Tennessee (62 for 569)....................1992
 9.14— Auburn vs. Southwestern Louisiana (76 for 695)..........1985
 8.73— Ole Miss vs. Chattanooga (67 for 585)................1949
 8.69— Vanderbilt vs. Miami (49 for 426).......................1948

1994 SEC Football 235

TOTAL OFFENSE

YARDS PER PLAY (Continued)

SEASON:
- 7.09 —Auburn (4,850 in 648) 1970
- 6.98 —Alabama (5,288 in 758) 1973
- 6.94 —Tennessee (5.285 in 762) 1993
- 6.77 —Georgia (4,954 in 732) 1992
- 6.66 —LSU (3,210 in 482) 1945
- 6.44 —Florida (5,719 in 888) 1993
- 6.38 —Florida (5,028 in 787) 1991
- 6.30 —Auburn (3,491 in 544) 1954
- 6.22 —Ole Miss (4,192 in 674) 1961
- 6.10 —Georgia (4,733 in 11 games) 1993
- 6.02 —Miss. State (4,642 in 771) 1982
- 5.97 —Florida (4,400 in 737) 1976

MOST RUSHING

GAME:
- 28 —Auburn vs. Ole Miss 1985
- 27 —Vanderbilt vs. Davidson 1969
- 27 —Georgia vs. South Carolina 1974
- 27 —LSU vs. Wyoming 1977
- 26 —Alabama vs. Ole Miss 1971
- 26 —Alabama vs. Virginia Tech 1973
- 26 —Miss. State vs. Colorado State 1981
- 26 —Georgia vs. Memphis State 1982

SEASON:
- 213 —Alabama 1979
- 211 —Auburn 1969
- 208 —Auburn 1985
- 192 —Alabama 1973
- 188 —Alabama 1971
- 186 —Georgia 1975
- 186 —LSU 1977
- 179 —Alabama 1977
- 176 —Georgia 1981

MOST PASSING

GAME:
- 21 —LSU vs. Tennessee 1989
- 21 —Georgia vs. Southern Miss. 1993
- 21 —Georgia vs. Florida 1993
- 20 —Kentucky vs. Tennessee 1969
- 20 —Alabama vs. Auburn 1979
- 20 —Vanderbilt vs. Tennessee 1981
- 19 —Georgia vs. Miami 1963
- 19 —Miss. State vs. Alabama 1978
- 19 —Alabama vs. Tennessee 1989
- 19 —Florida vs. Florida State 1990
- 19 —Florida vs. Louisville 1992

SEASON:
- 182 —Florida 1993
- 170 —Florida 1992
- 158 —Vanderbilt 1983
- 153 —Vanderbilt 1981
- 142 —Florida 1990
- 141 —Florida 1991
- 139 —Georgia 1993
- 136 —Florida 1969
- 134 —Vanderbilt 1984
- 134 —Alabama 1989
- 130 —Vanderbilt 1982
- 128 —Vanderbilt 1985
- 126 —Tennessee 1991
- 125 —Florida 1985
- 123 —Florida 1970
- 122 —Alabama 1969
- 122 —LSU 1989

TOTAL

GAME:
- 40 —Vanderbilt vs. Davidson 1969
- 39 —Auburn vs. Ole Miss 1985
- 38 —Vanderbilt vs. Washington & Lee 1952
- 36 —Ole Miss vs. Memphis State 1980
- 35 —LSU vs. Miss. State 1969
- 35 —Ole Miss vs. Chattanooga 1971
- 35 —Georgia vs. Vanderbilt 1981
- 34 —Alabama vs. Penn State 1983
- 34 —Georgia vs. Memphis State 1982

FIRST DOWNS

SEASON:
- 298 —Florida 1993
- 273 —Florida 1990
- 271 —Georgia 1981
- 270 —Florida 1992
- 266 —Tennessee 1991
- 263 —Alabama 1979
- 261 —Tennessee 1987
- 261 —Alabama 1989
- 261 —Florida 1991
- 258 —Tennessee 1993
- 250 —Alabama 1983
- 249 —Alabama 1970
- 248 —Auburn 1993
- 247 —Alabama 1982
- 245 —Ole Miss 1980
- 242 —Tennessee 1990
- 241 —Alabama 1977
- 241 —Alabama 1992
- 239 —Alabama 1972
- 239 —Alabama 1973
- 239 —Tennessee 1989
- 238 —Auburn 1985

Alabama's Steadman Shealy quarterbacked the Tide to an SEC record 213 rushing first downs in 1979. The versatile signal caller led the team in rushing and passing that season.

PUNTING

MOST PUNTS

GAME:

    36—Kentucky vs. Washington & Lee 1934
    23—Florida vs. Georgia Tech 1938
    21—Georgia Tech vs. Florida 1938
    20—Ole Miss vs. LSU 1934
    20—Miss. State vs. TCU 1936
    17—LSU vs. Miss. State 1940
    17—LSU vs. Tennessee 1942
    16—Vanderbilt vs. Louisville 1971

SEASON:

* 139—Tennessee 1937
    112—Auburn 1939
    110—Florida 1937
    101—Kentucky 1933
    96—Ole Miss 1938
    96—Miss. State 1967
    92—Alabama 1941
    92—Alabama 1946
    92—Kentucky 1970
    91—Vanderbilt 1946

YARDS PUNTING

GAME:

    1,386—Kentucky vs. Washington & Lee (36 punts) 1934
    904—Georgia Tech vs. Florida (21 punts) 1938
    899—Florida vs. Georgia Tech (23 punts) 1938
    780—Ole Miss vs. LSU (20 punts) 1934
    666—Miss State vs. TCU (20 punts) 1966
    664—LSU vs. Miss. State (17 punts) 1940

SEASON:

    5,620—Tennessee (139 punts) 1937
    4,844—Auburn (112 punts) 1939
    4,394—Kentucky (101 punts) 1933
    3,745—Ole Miss 1940
    3,581—Ole Miss (79 punts) 1985
    3,567—Miss. State (96 punts) 1967
    3,528—Vanderbilt (78 punts) 1982
    3,471—Kentucky (92 punts) 1970
    3,283—Ole Miss (76 punts) 1978
    3,281—Vanderbilt (80 punts) 1965

PUNTING AVERAGE

GAME: (Min. 10)

    52.0—Kentucky vs. Cincinnati (10 for 520) 1944
    48.1—Ole Miss vs. Missouri (10 for 481) 1973
    47.3—LSU vs. Ole Miss (10 for 473) 1960
    46.6—Alabama vs. Miss. State 1958

GAME (Min. 20)

    43.0—Georgia Tech vs. Florida 1938
    39.1—Florida vs. Georgia Tech (23 for 899) 1938

SEASON:

    47.6—Vanderbilt (59 for 2,810) 1984
    46.9—Auburn (51 for 2,393) 1993
    45.9—Ole Miss (66 for 3,029) 1979
    45.8—Auburn (57 for 2,610) 1985
    45.4—Florida (39 for 1,771) 1983
    45.3—Georgia (44 for 1,994) 1958
    45.1—Tennessee (58 for 2,614) 1982
    45.1—Georgia (64 for 2,885) 1984
    45.0—Tennessee (66 for 2,969) 1977

PUNT RETURNS

MOST RETURNS

GAME:

    20—Miss. State vs. TCU (128 yards) 1936
    13—LSU vs. Tulane (126 yards) 1937
    13—Ole Miss vs. Union (203 yards) 1940
    11—Vanderbilt vs. N.C. State 1946
    10—Alabama vs. Kentucky 1946
    10—Tennessee vs. Tennessee Tech 1947
    10—Alabama vs. Miss. State (59 yards) 1967
    10—Kentucky vs. Tennessee 1976

SEASON:

    71—Alabama (783 yards) 1946
    70—Miss. State (778 yards) 1936
    68—Tennessee (844 yards) 1939
    68—Tennessee (974 yards) 1940
    61—Miss. State (542 yards) 1940
    656—Ole Miss (837 yards) 1940
    655—Vanderbilt (907 yards) 1948
    655—Alabama (438 yards) 1975
    49—Kentucky (314 yards) 1947
    49—Kentucky (450 yards) 1950
    49—Alabama (516 yards) 1973

*—NCAA record

YARDS RETURNED

GAME:

    225—Miss. State vs. Chattanooga (8 returns) 1946
    205—LSU vs. Ole Miss (6 returns) 1970
    204—Alabama vs. LSU (5 returns) 1947
    203—Ole Miss vs. Union (13 returns) 1940
    203—Vanderbilt vs. Kentucky (6 returns) 1948
    202—Georgia vs. Oregon State (5 returns) 1971
    195—Kentucky vs. Vanderbilt (6 returns) 1981
    192—Tennessee vs. Chattanooga 1951

SEASON:

    974—Tennessee (68 returns) 1940
    907—Vanderbilt (55 returns) 1948
    844—Tennessee (68 returns) 1939
    837—Ole Miss (56 returns) 1940
    783—Alabama (71 returns) 1946
    778—Miss. State (70 returns) 1936
    676—Ole Miss (36 returns) 1948
    661—Miss. State (44 returns) 1946
    642—Auburn (40 returns) 1973
    630—Florida (32 returns) 1947

1994 SEC Football

PUNT RETURNS

YARDS PER RETURN

GAME:

40.8—Alabama vs. LSU (5 for 204)	1991
40.4—Georgia vs. Oregon State (5 for 202)	1971
33.8—Vanderbilt vs. Kentucky (6 for 203)	1948
30.0—Miss. State vs. Houston (5 for 150)	1965
28.3—Ole Miss vs. Georgia (7 for 198)	1940
28.1—Miss. State vs. Chattanooga (8 for 255)	1946

SEASON:

20.8—Miss. State (25 for 521)	1971
20.5—Miss. State (22 for 450)	1965
19.7—Florida (32 for 630)	1947
18.8—Ole Miss (36 for 676)	1948
16.6—Auburn (35 for 580)	1974
16.5—Georgia (33 for 544)	1980
16.1—Auburn (40 for 642)	1973
15.8—Auburn (26 for 412)	1982
15.7—LSU (39 for 614)	1970
15.6—LSU (20 for 313)	1963

KICKOFF RETURNS

MOST RETURNS

GAME:

11—Ole Miss vs. Alabama	1989
10—Miss. State vs. Houston	1969
10—Miss. State vs. Tulane	1949
9—Alabama vs. USC	1970
9—Vanderbilt vs. Alabama	1990
9—Vanderbilt vs. Auburn	1990
9—Vanderbilt vs. Tennessee	1993
8—Auburn vs. Alabama	1948
8—Auburn vs. Miss. State	1952
8—Vanderbilt vs. Tennessee	1952
8—Kentucky vs. Florida State	1964
8—Ole Miss vs. LSU	1970
8—Vanderbilt vs. Georgia	1975
8—Vanderbilt vs. Alabama	1979
8—Tennessee vs. USC	1981
8—Kentucky vs. Tennessee	1985
8—Tennessee vs. Alabama	1989
8—Kentucky vs. Florida	1990
8—Vanderbilt vs. Alabama	1991
8—Kentucky vs. Georgia	1991
8—Florida vs. Florida State	1992
8—Vanderbilt vs. Florida	1993

SEASON:

58—Vanderbilt	1990
56—Vanderbilt	1986
56—Vanderbilt	1987
54—Vanderbilt	1979
53—Vanderbilt	1978
53—Miss. State	1988
52—Miss. State	1969
51—Kentucky	1971
51—Florida	1971
50—Miss State	1985
50—Kentucky	1990
49—Miss. State	1970
49—Florida	1992
48—Miss. State	1968
48—Florida	1970
48—Vanderbilt	1980
48—Ole Miss	1989
48—Vanderbilt	1993
47—Miss. State	1973
47—Tennessee	1987

YARDS RETURNED

GAME:

259—Alabama vs. Auburn (8 returns)	1969
250—Alabama vs. Boston College (7 returns)	1984
234—Ole Miss vs. Alabama (11 returns)	1989
227—Miss. State vs. Houston (10 returns)	1969

SEASON:

1,194—Vanderbilt (56 returns)	1987
1,181—Kentucky (51 returns)	1971
1,179—LSU (46 returns)	1948
1,168—Vanderbilt (56 returns)	1986
1,153—Miss. State (52 returns)	1969
1,124—Vanderbilt (58 returns)	1990
1,040—Florida (49 returns)	1992
1,023—Tennessee (42 returns)	1990
1,005—Vanderbilt (48 returns)	1993
999—Vanderbilt (46 returns)	1989
984—Miss. State (48 returns)	1970
975—Miss. State (48 returns)	1968
975—Kentucky (50 returns)	1990
974—Vanderbilt (48 returns)	1980
964—Vanderbilt (54 returns)	1979
952—Miss. State (53 returns)	1988
951—Vanderbilt (43 returns)	1992
948—Miss State (50 returns)	1985
940—Ole Miss (42 returns)	1974
938—Tennessee (47 returns)	1987
934—Florida (51 returns)	1971
932—Ole Miss (48 returns)	1989
924—Miss. State (47 returns)	1973

YARDS PER RETURN

GAME: (Min. 3)

66.7—Kentucky vs. Vanderbilt (3 for 200)	1945
46.0—Miss. State vs. Southern Miss (3 for 138)	1966
45.7—Ole Miss vs. Arkansas (3 for 137)	1940
44.3—Florida vs. Ole Miss (3 for 133)	1988
40.8—Vanderbilt vs. Duke (4 for 163)	1992
39.8—Florida vs. Kentucky (4 for 159)	1989
35.7—Alabama vs. Boston College (7 for 250)	1984
33.5—Miss. State vs. Southern Miss (4 for 134)	1989
32.4—Alabama vs. Auburn (8 for 259)	1969
31.7—Georgia vs. Kentucky (6 for 190)	1977
31.5—Vanderbilt vs. Alabama (6 for 189)	1975
30.9—Tennessee vs. Alabama (6 for 180)	1973

SEASON:

28.8—Miss. State (19 for 547)	1940
27.8—Alabama (19 for 529)	1963
26.6—Georgia	1947
26.4—Alabama (17 for 449)	1964
25.8—Miss. State (21 for 542)	1946
25.6—Tennessee	1946
25.6—Kentucky (24 for 615)	1983
25.6—LSU (46 for 1,179)	1948
25.1—Tennessee (29 for 729)	1980
24.4—Georgia (36 for 879)	1973
24.4—Tennessee (42 for 1,023)	1990
24.3—Kentucky (29 for 705)	1963
24.3—Auburn (27 for 655)	1979

Florida placekicker Bobby Raymond tied the SEC record twice for most field goals in a game with six against Florida State in 1983 and six versus Kentucky in 1984.

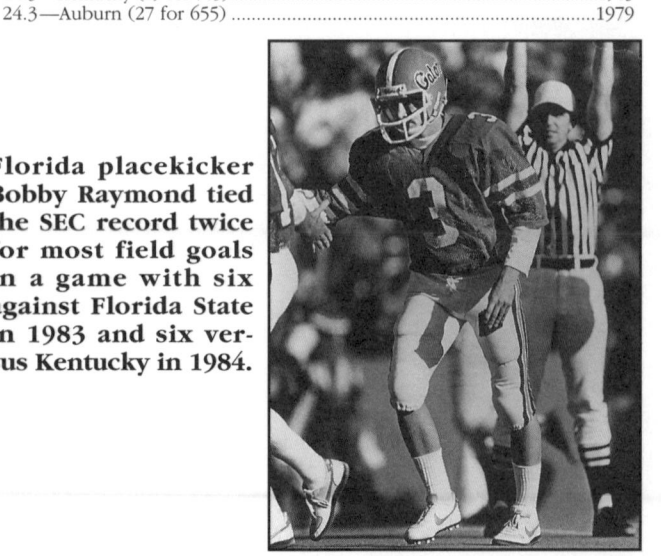

238 Record Book

SCORING

MOST POINTS

GAME:

- 93—LSU vs. Southwestern Louisiana 1936
- 92—Ole Miss vs. West Tennessee Teachers 1935
- 89—Alabama vs. Delta State 1951
- 83—Kentucky vs. North Dakota 1950
- 81—Georgia vs. Mercer 1941
- 77—Alabama vs. Virginia Tech 1973
- 77—LSU vs. Rice 1977
- 77—Florida vs. West Texas State 1982
- 75—Georgia vs. Florida 1942

SEASON:

- 472—Florida (12 games) 1993
- 471—Tennessee (11 games) 1993
- 454—Alabama (11 games) 1973
- 442—Tennessee (12 games) 1990
- 396—Alabama (9 games) 1945
- 395—Tennessee (12 games) 1987
- 393—Alabama (11 games) 1972
- 387—Florida (11 games) 1990
- 380—Kentucky (11 games) 1950
- 379—Auburn (11 games) 1986
- 375—LSU (11 games) 1977
- 373—Tennessee (10 games) 1951
- 372—Georgia (10 games) 1946
- 365—LSU (11 games) 1982
- 363—Auburn (10 games) 1969
- 362—Alabama (11 games) 1971

MOST POINTS TWO TEAMS

- 97—Georgia (62) vs. Vanderbilt (35) 1984
- 94—Alabama (59) vs. Ole Miss (35) 1980

POINTS PER GAME

- 44.0—Alabama (396 in 9) 1945
- 42.8—Tennessee (471 in 11) 1993
- 41.3—Alabama (454 in 11) 1973
- 39.3—Florida (472 in 12) 1993
- 37.3—Tennessee (373 in 10) 1951
- 37.2—Georgia (372 in 10) 1946
- 36.8—Tennessee (442 in 12) 1990
- 36.3—Auburn (363 in 10) 1969
- 35.7—Alabama (393 in 11) 1972
- 35.2—Florida (387 in 11) 1990
- 34.9—LSU (349 in 10) 1969
- 34.5—Kentucky (380 in 11) 1950
- 34.5—Auburn (379 in 11) 1986
- 34.1—LSU (375 in 11) 1977
- 33.3—Ole Miss (333 in 10) 1959

MOST TOUCHDOWNS

GAME:

- 14—Ole Miss vs. West Tennessee Teachers 1935
- 14—LSU vs. Southwestern Louisiana 1936
- 13—Alabama vs. Delta State 1951
- 12—Kentucky vs. North Dakota 1950
- 11—Alabama vs. Virginia Tech 1973
- 11—LSU vs. Rice 1977
- 11—Florida vs. West Texas State 1982

SEASON:

- 62—Tennessee (11 games) 1993
- 61—Alabama (11 games) 1973
- 61—Florida (12 games) 1993
- 58—Alabama (9 games) 1945
- 56—Kentucky (11 games) 1950
- 55—Tennessee (10 games) 1951
- 55—Tennessee (12 games) 1990
- 54—Georgia (10 games) 1946
- 53—Alabama (11 games) 1972
- 51—LSU (11 games) 1977
- 50—Auburn (11 games) 1986
- 49—Florida (11 games) 1990
- 47—Ole Miss (10 games) 1961
- 47—LSU (11 games) 1969
- 47—LSU (11 games) 1982
- 47—Florida (11 games) 1991
- 46—Alabama (11 games) 1975

MOST FIELD GOALS

GAME:

- 6—Florida vs. Kentucky 1984
- 6—Florida vs. Florida State 1983
- 6—Auburn vs. Kentucky 1982
- 5—Auburn vs. Florida 1977
- 5—Tennessee vs. Kentucky 1978
- 5—Florida vs. Ole Miss 1980
- 5—Tennessee vs. Kentucky 1982
- 5—Tennessee vs. Memphis State 1982
- 5—Ole Miss vs. Tulane 1991

SEASON:

- 27—Tennessee 1982
- 25—Florida 1984
- 24—Tennessee 1985
- 23—Georgia 1984
- 23—Florida 1983

MOST PAT KICKS

GAME:

- 11—Kentucky vs. North Dakota 1950
- 11—Alabama vs. Delta State 1951
- 11—Alabama vs. Virginia Tech 1973
- 11—LSU vs. Rice 1977
- 11—Florida vs. West Texas State 1982

SEASON:

- 59—Tennessee 1993
- 53—Tennessee 1990
- 53—Florida 1993
- 51—Alabama 1973
- 49—Auburn 1986
- 47—Georgia 1946
- 47—LSU 1982
- 45—Florida 1991
- 45—Auburn 1993
- 44—Kentucky 1950
- 44—Florida 1990
- 44—Georgia 1992
- 43—LSU 1977
- 42—Tennessee 1971
- 40—Alabama 1983

CONSECUTIVE PAT KICKS

- 199—Alabama (Peter Kim 54, Paul Trodd 4, Terry Sanders 1, Van Tiffin 135, Philip Doyle 5) 1981-87
- 130—Georgia (Rex Robinson 101, Kevin Butler 29) 1977-81
- 122—Tennessee (John Becksvoort 122) 1991-present
- 109—LSU (David Browndyke 109) 1986-1989
- 105—Tennessee (George Hunt 60, Ricky Townsend 45) 1970-73
- 79—Vanderbilt (Johnny Clark 9, Rob Chura 8, Jeff Owen 41, Rob Chura 18, Steve Yenner 3) 1989-93
- 74—Ole Miss (Steve Lavinghouze 59, Hoppy Langley 15) 1975-77

MOST POINTS IN A TIE GAME

- 37-37—Alabama vs. Florida State 1967

1994 SEC Football

Southeastern Conference Team Defense Records
RUSHING DEFENSE

FEWEST RUSHES ALLOWED
GAME:
- 13— Florida vs. Vanderbilt 1983
- 13— Alabama vs. Vanderbilt 1989
- 14— Florida vs. Georgia 1993
- 16— Alabama vs. Davidson 1969
- 16— Alabama vs. Auburn 1969
- 16— Auburn vs. Kansas 1987
- 17— Auburn vs. Ole Miss 1985
- 18— Vanderbilt vs. N.C. State 1946
- 18— Georgia vs. Brigham Young 1982
- 18— LSU vs. Tulane 1985
- 18— Kentucky vs. Georgia 1993
- 20— Alabama vs. Georgia Tech 1979
- 20— Miss. State vs. San Francisco 1946
- 20— Alabama vs. Southern Miss 1989

SEASON:
- 231— Tennessee (9 games) 1945
- 300— Ole Miss (10 games) 1962
- 321— Alabama (10 games) 1961
- 328— Miss. State (10 games) 1936
- 334— Miss. State (10 games) 1946
- 353— LSU (10 games) 1969
- 354— Alabama (10 games) 1964
- 356— LSU (11 games) 1970
- 371— Florida (10 games) 1963
- 372— Ole Miss (10 games) 1964

FEWEST YARDS ALLOWED
GAME:
- Minus 93— Kentucky vs. Kansas State 1970
- Minus 85— Auburn vs. Miami 1968
- Minus 50— LSU vs. Ole Miss 1982
- Minus 49— Alabama vs. Houston 1962
- Minus 49— Georgia vs. VMI 1967
- Minus 43— LSU vs. Mercer 1940
- Minus 39— Kentucky vs. Evansville 1947
- Minus 30— Auburn vs. Tennessee 1957
- Minus 21— Miss. State vs. Southwestern 1939
- Minus 16— Ole Miss vs. Auburn 1992
- Minus 15— Ole Miss vs. Florida 1946
- Minus 14— Florida vs. Auburn 1990
- Minus 11— Kentucky vs. Auburn 1961
- Minus 10— Florida vs. LSU 1985
- Minus 10— Miss. State vs. Florida 1981

SEASON:
- 305— Alabama (9 games) 1938
- 385— Tennessee (9 games) 1945
- 389— LSU (10 games) 1969
- 410— Alabama (9 games) 1945
- 505— Miss. State (10 games) 1940
- 574— LSU (11 games) 1970
- 588— Alabama (10 games) 1962
- 596— Georgia (10 games) 1941
- 610— Ole Miss (9 games) 1962
- 660— Alabama (12 games) 1992
- 664— Miss. State (10 games) 1946
- 674— Auburn (10 games) 1957

FEWEST YARDS PER GAME
- 33.9— Alabama (305 yards in 9 games) 1938
- 38.9— LSU (389 yards in 10 games) 1969
- 42.8— Tennessee (385 yards in 9 games) 1945
- 50.5— Miss. State (505 yards in 10 games) 1940
- 52.2— LSU (574 yards in 11 games) 1970
- 54.2— Georgia (596 yards in 11 games) 1941
- 55.0— Alabama (660 yards in 12 games) 1992
- 58.8— Alabama (588 yards in 10 games) 1962
- 63.2— Auburn (695 yards in 11 games) 1988
- 66.4— Miss. State (664 yards in 10 games) 1946
- 67.4— Auburn (674 yards in 10 games) 1957
- 67.8— Ole Miss (610 yards in 10 games) 1962
- 71.6— Kentucky (788 yards in 11 games) 1949

FEWEST YARDS PER RUSH
GAME:
- Minus 3.95— Kentucky vs. Kansas State (-91 in 23 rushes) 1970
- Minus 1.98— Auburn vs. Miami (-85 yards in 43 rushes) 1968

SEASON:
- 0.95— Alabama (305 yards in 321 rushes) 1938
- 1.09— LSU (384 yards in 353 rushes) 1969
- 1.44— Miss. State (505 yards in 350 rushes) 1940
- 1.61— LSU (574 yards in 356 rushes) 1970
- 1.67— Tennessee (385 yards in 231 rushes) 1945
- 1.67— Alabama (660 yards in 395 rushes) 1992
- 1.73— Kentucky (788 yards in 455 rushes) 1949
- 1.73— Auburn (674 yards in 390 rushes) 1957
- 1.99— Miss. State (664 yards in 334 rushes) 1946
- 2.03— Auburn (796 yards in 392 rushes) 1969
- 2.04— Georgia (797 yards in 391 rushes) 1981

PASSING DEFENSE

FEWEST PASSES
GAME:
- *0— Kentucky vs. Tennessee 1952
- 0— Tennessee vs. Georgia Tech 1977
- 1— Miss. State vs. Union 1942
- 1— Tennessee vs. Miss. State 1950
- 1— Vanderbilt vs. Tennessee 1951

SEASON:
- 73— Georgia Tech (10 games) 1957
- 87— Alabama (10 games) 1955
- 88— Alabama (9 games) 1938
- 92— Florida (10 games) 1955
- 93— Tulane (10 games) 1957
- 96— Kentucky (10 games) 1955
- 102— Miss. State (9 games) 1950
- 103— Miss. State (10 games) 1936
- 103— LSU (10 games) 1955

FEWEST COMPLETIONS
GAME:
Several teams with 0
Last Team: Ole Miss vs. Alabama 1988

SEASON:
- 31— Alabama (9 games) 1938
- 31— Georgia Tech (10 games) 1957
- 33— Tulane (10 games) 1957
- 35— Kentucky (10 games) 1955
- 36— Auburn (11 games) 1936
- 37— Florida (10 games) 1955

PASSING DEFENSE

FEWEST COMPLETIONS (Continued)

37— Kentucky (10 games) 1957
39— Florida (9 games) 1957
40— Miss. State (10 games) 1936
40— Alabama (10 games) 1955
40— LSU (10 games) 1955

LOWEST COMPLETION PERCENTAGE

GAME:

Several teams with 0
Last Team: Ole Miss vs. Alabama 1988

SEASON:

27.1— Auburn (36 of 133) 1950
31.9— Ole Miss (52 of 163) 1950
32.2— Kentucky (37 of 115) 1957
33.1— Ole Miss (44 of 133) 1957
35.2— Alabama (43 of 122) 1954
35.5— Alabama (61 of 172) 1949
35.5— Tulane (33 of 93) 1957
35.6— Kentucky (48 of 135) 1954
35.8— Tulane (67 of 187) 1949
35.8— Alabama (78 of 218) 1979

FEWEST YARDS

GAME:

Minus 10— Auburn vs. Alabama (1 comp.) 1952
Minus 3— Tennessee vs. Kentucky (1 comp.) 1949
Minus 3— Georgia Tech vs. South Carolina (1 comp.) ... 1949
Minus 1— Kentucky vs. LSU 1953
Minus 1— Florida vs. Vanderbilt (1 comp.) 1958

SEASON:

291— Alabama (9 games) 1945
325— Miss. State (10 games) 1936
334— Georgia Tech (10 games) 1957
392— Tennessee (10 games) 1939
412— Tulane (10 games) 1951
457— Alabama (10 games) 1959
477— Florida (9 games) 1957
479— Kentucky (10 games) 1955
500— Ole Miss (10 games) 1957

FEWEST TOUCHDOWNS

SEASON:

*0— Tennessee (10 games) 1939
3— LSU (10 games) 1959

INTERCEPTIONS

GAME:

9— Georgia vs. Presbyterian (42 passes) 1943
9— Auburn vs. Florida (66 passes) 1969
8— Tennessee vs. Alabama (51 passes) 1970
8— Alabama vs. Miss. State (24 passes) 1936
8— LSU vs. Villanova (38 passes) 1951
7— Ole Miss vs. Southwestern 1939
7— Alabama vs. Auburn (24 passes) 1965
7— Ole Miss vs. Houston (31 passes) 1966
7— Kentucky vs. Florida (52 passes) 1993

*—NCAA record

SEASON:

36— Tennessee 1970
35— Georgia 1982
34— Auburn 1969
33— Georgia 1946
30— Tennessee 1969
29— Kentucky 1949
28— Ole Miss 1940
28— Kentucky 1950
27— LSU 1984
27— LSU 1986

INTERCEPTION RETURN YARDS

GAME:

*240— Kentucky vs. Ole Miss (6 ints.) 1949
214— Tennessee vs. South Carolina (5 ints.) 1971

SEASON:

*782— Tennessee (25 ints.) 1971
719— Kentucky (29 ints.) 1949

INTERCEPTION RETURN TOUCHDOWNS

SEASON:

*7— Tennessee 1971
6— Kentucky 1949
4— Tennessee 1990
4— LSU 1991
4— Auburn 1993
3— Miss. State 1948
3— Georgia 1949
3— Georgia 1969
3— Kentucky 1974
3— Florida 1990
3— Alabama 1991
3— Ole Miss 1993

Bobby Majors, a two-time All-SEC defensive back, hauled in 10 interceptions during the 1970 campaign as Tennessee set a conference record with 36 thefts. The following season the Volunteers established a league and national mark by returning seven interceptions for touchdowns.

1994 SEC Football 241

TOTAL DEFENSE

FEWEST PLAYS

GAME:

24—Ole Miss vs. South Carolina	1947
30—Auburn vs. Ole Miss	1985
33—Tennessee vs. Vanderbilt	1946
34—Alabama vs. Southern Miss	1954
35—Miss. State vs. Howard	1963
37—Vanderbilt vs. Chattanooga	1950
37—Miss. State vs. Florida	1956

SEASON:

368—Tennessee	1945
431—Miss. State	1936
439—Ole Miss	1963
470—Miss. State	1950
494—Florida	1957
495—Auburn	1964
506—Auburn	1954
516—Georgia Tech	1955
517—Ole Miss	1959
521—Auburn	1958

FEWEST YARDS

GAME:

Minus 30—Auburn vs. Tennessee	1958
Minus 4—Alabama vs. Houston	1962
0—Ole Miss vs. Sewanee	1938
1—Kentucky vs. Citadel	1949
9—Auburn vs. Ole Miss	1985
13—Tennessee vs. Vanderbilt	1952

SEASON:

596—Alabama (9 games)	1938
1,010—Miss. State (10 games)	1936
1,023—Tennessee (10 games)	1939
1,222—Ole Miss (9 games)	1963
1,236—LSU (10 games)	1937

FEWEST YARDS PER GAME

SEASON:

77.9—Alabama (701 yards in 9 games)	1938
101.0—Miss. State (1,010 yards in 10 games)	1936
102.3—Tennessee (1,023 yards in 10 games)	1939

FIRST DOWNS

FEWEST RUSHING

GAME:

0—Several Teams—Last: Ole Miss vs. South Carolina	1972

SEASON:

24—Alabama (9 games)	1938
34—LSU (10 games)	1969
41—Ole Miss (9 games)	1963
41—LSU (11 games)	1970
43—Auburn (10 games)	1970
46—Alabama (10 games)	1966
49—Auburn (11 games)	1988
52—Alabama (12 games)	1992
53—Florida (10 games)	1963
53—Georgia (10 games)	1968
53—Auburn (10 games)	1969

FEWEST PASSING

GAME:

0—By several teams
Last—Florida vs. Auburn 1989

SEASON:

11—Alabama (9 games)	1938

23—Ole Miss (9 games)	1963
29—Auburn (10 games)	1964
33—Miss. State (10 games)	1963
34—Florida (10 games)	1964
35—LSU (10 games)	1964
35—Vanderbilt (10 games)	1965
37—Georgia Tech (10 games)	1963
38—Auburn (10 games)	1963
38—Vanderbilt (11 games)	1972

FEWEST TOTAL

GAME:

0—Auburn vs. Tennessee	1958

SEASON:

35—Alabama (9 games)	1938
51—Miss. State (10 games)	1936
55—Tennessee (9 games)	1945
68—Miss. State (10 games)	1940
71—Ole Miss (9 games)	1963
79—Ole Miss (9 games)	1962
80—Auburn (10 games)	1964
82—Florida (10 games)	1969
99—Alabama (10 games)	1966

SCORING DEFENSE

FEWEST POINTS

SEASON:

*0—Tennessee (10 games)	1939
17—Alabama (9 games)	1933

*—NCAA record

20—Alabama (9 games)	1937
21—Ole Miss (10 games)	1959
22—Alabama (10 games)	1961
25—Miss. State (10 games)	1936
27—LSU (10 games)	1937
28—Auburn (10 games)	1957
29—LSU (10 games)	1959

242 Record Book

SEC Football Championship Game
• Individual Superlatives •

MOST RUSHING ATTEMPTS:	22 - Errict Rhett, Florida (59 yds.)	12/5/92
	22 - Errict Rhett, Florida (102 yds.)	12/4/93
MOST RUSHING YARDS:	117 - Derrick Lassic, Alabama (21 atts.)	12/5/92
MOST RUSHING TOUCHDOWNS:	2 - Derrick Lassic, Alabama (21 for 117 yds.)	12/5/92
LONGEST RUSH:	25 - Derrick Lassic, Alabama	12/5/92
LONGEST TOUCHDOWN RUSH:	15 - Derrick Lassic, Alabama	12/5/92
MOST PASSING ATTEMPTS:	49 - Shane Matthews, Florida (30 comp.	12/5/92
MOST PASSING COMPLETIONS:	30 - Shane Matthews, Florida (49 atts.)	12/5/92
MOST PASSING YARDS:	287 - Shane Matthews, Florida (30-49, 2 TDs)	12/5/92
MOST PASSING TOUCHDOWNS:	2 - Shane Matthews, Florida	12/5/92
	2 - Terry Dean, Florida	12/4/93
MOST PASSES INTERCEPTED:	2 - Shane Matthews, Florida	12/5/92
	2 - Terry Dean, Florida	12/4/93
LONGEST TOUCHDOWN PASS:	43 - Jack Jackson, Florida (Terry Dean)	12/4/93
MOST PASS RECEPTIONS:	10 - Errict Rhett, Florida (82 yds., 1 TD)	12/5/92
MOST YARDS RECEIVING:	114 - Willie Jackson, Florida (9 rec.)	12/4/93
MOST TOUCHDOWNS RECEIVING:	1 - Curtis Brown, Alabama (1 for 30 yds.)	12/5/92
	1 - Willie Jackson, Florida (9 for 100 yds.)	12/5/92
	1 - Errict Rhett, Florida (10 for 82 yds.)	12/5/92
	1 - Harrison Houston, Florida (2 for 48 yds.)	12/4/93
	1 - Jack Jackson, Florida (4 for 62 yds.)	12/4/93
LONGEST PASS RECEPTION:	43 - Jack Jackson, Florida (Terry Dean)	12/4/93
MOST PUNTS:	10 - Bryne Diehl, Alabama (326 yds.)	12/5/92
BEST PUNTING AVERAGE:	43.6 - Bryne Diehl, Florida (7 for 305 yds.)	12/4/93
LONGEST PUNT:	56 - Bryne Diehl, Alabama	12/4/93
MOST PUNT RETURNS:	5 - Sorola Palmer, Florida (95 yds.)	12/4/93
BEST PUNT RETURN AVERAGE (Min. 3):	19.0 - Sorola Palmer, Florida (5 for 95 yds.)	12/4/93
MOST PUNT RETURN TOUCHDOWNS:	None	
LONGEST PUNT RETURN:	33 - Sorola Palmer, Florida	12/4/93
MOST KICKOFF RETURNS:	5 - Harrison Houston, Florida (71 yds.)	12/5/92
MOST KICKOFF RETURN YARDS:	71 - Harrison Houston, Florida (5 ret.)	12/5/92
BEST KICKOFF RETURN AVERAGE (Min. 3):	14.2 - Harrison Houston, Florida (5 for 71 yds.)	12/5/92
MOST KICKOFF RETURN TOUCHDOWNS:	None	
LONGEST KICKOFF RETURN:	29 - Chris Anderson, Alabama	12/4/93
MOST INTERCEPTIONS:	2 - Tommy Johnson, Alabama (18 yds.)	12/4/93
	2 - Michael Gilmore, Florida (0 yds.)	12/4/93
MOST INTERCEPTION RETURN YARDS:	27 - Antonio Langham, Alabama (1 ret.)	12/5/92
MOST INTERCEPTION RETURN TOUCHDOWNS:	1 - Antonio Langham, Alabama (27 yds.)	12/5/92
LONGEST INTERCEPTION RETURN:	27 - Antonio Langham, Alabama	12/5/92
MOST FIELD GOALS:	2 - Michael Proctor, Alabama (45, 25)	12/4/93
MOST YARDS TOTAL OFFENSE:	274 - Shane Matthews, Florida (-13 rush, 287 pass)	12/5/92
MOST POINTS SCORED:	12 - Derrick Lassic, Alabama (2 rush TDs)	12/5/92
	12 - Errict Rhett, Florida (1 rush, 1 rec. TD)	12/5/92
MOST TOTAL TACKLES:	12 - Chris Donnelly, Alabama (8-4)	12/4/93
MOST FUMBLES CAUSED:	1 - Kevin Carter, Florida	12/4/93
MOST FUMBLES RECOVERED:	1 - Joey Harville, Alabama	12/4/93
MOST QUARTERBACK SACKS:	1 - Nine players	
MOST TACKLES FOR LOSS:	2 - John Copeland, Alabama (-9 yds.)	12/5/92
	2 - Monty Grow, Florida (-15 yds.)	12/4/93
MOST PASS BREAKUPS:	2 - Tommy Johnson, Alabama	12/4/93

Alabama All-America defensive back Antonio Langham returned an interception 27 yards for a score to secure the Crimson Tide's 28-21 win over Florida in the 1992 contest.

Florida's Willie Jackson holds the mark for most yards receiving in the championship game with 114 yards on nine catches versus Alabama in 1993.

1994 SEC Football   243

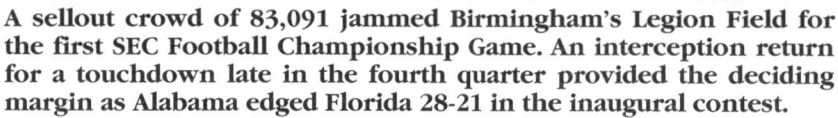

1992 SEC Championship Game
Birmingham, Alabama • Dec. 5
Legion Field
Attendance: 83,091

	1	2	3	4	FINAL
ALABAMA	7	7	7	7	28
FLORIDA	7	0	7	7	21

1993 SEC Championship Game
Birmingham, Alabama • Dec. 4
Legion Field
Attendance: 76,345

	1	2	3	4	FINAL
FLORIDA	7	7	7	7	28
ALABAMA	7	3	3	0	13

A sellout crowd of 83,091 jammed Birmingham's Legion Field for the first SEC Football Championship Game. An interception return for a touchdown late in the fourth quarter provided the deciding margin as Alabama edged Florida 28-21 in the inaugural contest.

SEC Football Championship Game • Team Highs & Lows

POINTS SCORED
- High: 28 - Alabama — 12/5/92
- 28 - Florida — 12/4/93
- Low: 13 - Alabama — 12/4/93

FIRST DOWNS
- High: 22 - Florida (5 rush, 16 pass, 1 penalty) — 12/5/92
- Low: 15 - Alabama (9 rush, 5 pass, 1 penalty) — 12/5/92

RUSHING ATTEMPTS
- High: 41 - Alabama (132 yds., 2 TDs) — 12/5/92
- Low: 30 - Florida (30 yds., 1 TD) — 12/5/92

RUSHING YARDS
- High: 132 - Alabama (41 atts., 2 TDs) — 12/5/92
- Low: 30 - Florida (30 atts., 1 TD) — 12/5/92

PASSING ATTEMPTS
- High: 49 - Florida (30 comp., 287 yds., 2 TDs) — 12/5/92
- Low: 18 - Alabama (10 comp., 154 yds., 1 TD) — 12/5/92

PASSING COMPLETIONS
- High: 30 - Florida (49 atts., 287 yds., 2 TDs) — 12/5/92
- Low: 10 - Alabama (18 atts., 154 yds., 1 TD) — 12/5/92

PASSES HAD INTERCEPTED
- High: 2 - Florida — 12/5/92
- Low: 0 - Alabama — 12/5/92

PASSING YARDAGE
- High: 287 - Florida (30-49-2, 2 TDs) — 12/5/92
- Low: 154 - Alabama (10-18-0, 1 TD) — 12/5/92

TOTAL PLAYS
- High: 79 - Florida (30 rush, 49 pass) — 12/5/92
- Low: 59 - Alabama (41 rush, 18 pass) — 12/5/92

TOTAL OFFENSE
- High: 374 - Florida (103 rush, 271 pass) — 12/4/93
- Low: 279 - Alabama (118 rush, 161 pass) — 12/4/93

AVERAGE GAIN PER PLAY
- High: 5.42 - Florida (69 for 374 yds.) — 12/4/93
- Low: 4.01 - Florida (79 for 317 yds.) — 12/5/92

RETURN YARDS
- High: 95 - Florida (95 PR, 0 INT, 0 FUB) — 12/4/93
- Low: 23 - Florida (23 PR, 0 INT, 0 FUB) — 12/5/92

KICKOFF RETURN YARDS
- High: 94 - Alabama (4 ret.) — 12/4/93
- Low: 14 - Alabama (3 ret.) — 12/5/92

PUNT RETURN YARDS
- High: 95 - Florida (5 ret.) — 12/4/93
- Low: 23 - Florida (4 ret.) — 12/5/92

INTERCEPTION RETURN YARDS
- High: 27 - Alabama (2 ret.) — 12/5/92
- Low: 0 - Florida (0 ret.) — 12/5/92
- 0 - Florida (2 ret.) — 12/4/93

PENALTY YARDAGE
- High: 95 - Florida (13 penalties) — 12/4/93
- Low: 30 - Florida (4 penalties) — 12/5/92

TIME OF POSSESSION
- High: 32:17 - Alabama — 12/4/93
- Low: 27:43 - Florida — 12/4/93

Alabama and Florida have squared off in both editions of the SEC Championship Game. Alabama won the inaugural contest 28-21 in 1992, but Florida prevailed 28-13 in last year's title game.

HONORS

Tennessee quarterback Heath Shuler completed the 1993 season by being named the consensus SEC Player of the Year and finishing second in the Heisman Trophy balloting, the league's highest finish since 1985.

National Football Foundation Hall of Fame

Selected from SEC Member Schools

1994 Inductees

Vince Dooley, Head Coach.................1964-88................Georgia
Tucker Frederickson, Back..................1962-64................Auburn
Ozzie Newsome, Tight End..................1974-77................Alabama

Vince Dooley, Georgia
1994 Inductee

Tucker Frederickson, Auburn
1994 Inductee

Ozzie Newsome, Alabama
1994 Inductee

PLAYERS

Alabama
- *QB A.T.S. (Pooley) Hubert, '25
- *HB Johnny Mack Brown, '25
- *Tackle Fred Sington, '30
- *FB Johnny Cain, '33
- End Don Hutson, '34
- TB Millard (Dixie) Howell, '34
- QB Riley Smith, '35
- Tackle Don Whitmire, '44
- HB Harry Gilmer, '48
- Center Vaughn Mancha, '47
- Center Lee Roy Jordan, '62

Arkansas
- End Wear K. Schoonover, '29
- HB Clyde Scott, '48
- HB Lance Alworth, '61
- OL Loyd Phillips, '66

Auburn
- *HB Jimmy Hitchcock, '32
- Center Walter Gilbert, '36
- QB Pat Sullivan, '72

Florida
- *End Dale Van Sickel, '28
- QB Steve Spurrier, '66
- DL Jack Youngblood, '70

Georgia
- *HB Robert McWhorter, '13
- *End Vernon "Catfish" Smith, '31
- FB Bill Hartman, '38
- HB Frank Sinkwich, '42
- HB Charles Trippi, '46
- QB Fran Tarkenton, '60

Kentucky
- Tackle Bob Gain, '50
- QB Vito "Babe" Parilli, '51
- OL Lou Michaels, '57

LSU
- *QB G.E. (Doc) Fenton, '09
- QB Abe Mickal, '35
- End Gaynell Tinsley, '36
- End Ken Kavanaugh, '39

Mississippi
- Tackle Frank (Bruiser) Kinard, '38
- HB Parker Hall, '39
- HB Doug Kenna, '41
- TB Charley Conerly, '47
- End Barney Poole, '48
- QB Archie Manning, '71

Mississippi State
- Back Jackie Parker, '53

Tennessee
- *Guard Nate Dougherty, '09
- *HB Eugene McEver, '31
- *QB Robert Lee Dodd, '30
- *Guard Herman Hickman, '31
- HB Beattie Feathers, '33
- End Bowden Wyatt, '38
- HB George Cafego, '39
- Guard Robert Suffridge, '40
- Guard Edward Molinski, '40
- HB Hank Lauricella, '52
- End Doug Atkins, '52
- Back Johnny Majors, '57
- Guard Steve DeLong '65
- Center Bob Johnson, '68

Vanderbilt
- *FB John J. Tigert, '04
- *Tackle Josh Cody, '20
- *End Lynn Bomar, '24
- *QB William Spears, '27
- Center Carl Hinkle, '37

COACHES

Name and Alma Mater	School(s)
Bill ALEXANDER (Georgia Tech)	Georgia Tech
*Dana BIBLE (Carson-Newman)	LSU
*Bernie BIERMAN (Minnesota)	Miss. State, Tulane
Frank BROYLES (Georgia Tech)	Missouri, Arkansas
Paul (Bear) BRYANT (Alabama)	Kentucky, Alabama
*Mike DONAHUE (Yale)	Auburn, LSU
Bill EDWARDS (Wittenberg)	Vanderbilt
Ray GRAVES (Tennessee)	Florida
*John HEISMAN (Penn)	Auburn, Georgia Tech
Frank HOWARD (Clemson)	Alabama
Morley JENNINGS (Miss. State)	Baylor
L.M. (Biff) JONES	LSU
Ralph (Shug) JORDAN (Auburn)	Auburn
Charlie McCLENDON (Kentucky)	LSU

Name and Alma Mater	School(s)
Dan McGUGIN (Michigan)	Vanderbilt
Allyn McKEEN (Tennessee)	Mississippi State
Bernie MOORE (Carson-Newman)	LSU
*Ray MORRISON (Vanderbilt)	SMU, Vanderbilt, Temple
Jess NEELY (Vanderbilt)	Southwestern, Clemson, Rice
R.R. NEYLAND (Army)	Tennessee
Darrell ROYAL (Oklahoma)	Miss. State
*Clark SHAUGHNESSY (Minnesota)	Tulane
Francis SCHMIDT	Tulsa, Arkansas, TCU, Ohio State, Idaho
Frank THOMAS (Notre Dame)	Alabama
Thad (Pie) VANN (Ole Miss)	Southern Miss
John VAUGHT (Texas Christian)	Ole Miss
*Wallace WADE (Brown)	Alabama
G.S. (Pop) WARNER (Cornell)	Georgia

*Participated before SEC was organized.

SEC Heisman Trophy Winners

1942 — FRANK SINKWICH
Georgia Halfback

Frank Sinkwich became the first player from the Southeastern area to win the coveted Heisman Trophy, winning the award in 1942, the year he led Georgia to an 11-1 record and a 9-0 victory over UCLA in the Rose Bowl. Sinkwich led the nation in rushing in 1941 and total offense in 1942. His individual performance in the 1942 Orange Bowl (a 40-26 victory over TCU) is still regarded as the best one-man showing in that New Year's Day Classic. Against the Horned Frogs, Sinkwich completed nine of 13 passes for 243 yards and three touchdowns, rushed for 139 yards including a 43-yard TD run, for 382 yards of total offense. Nicknamed "Flatfoot Frankie," Sinkwich received his Heisman Trophy while in his Marine uniform. A long-time businessman in Athens, Sinkwich died Oct. 22, 1990.

SINKWICH STATS

Year	Att	Yds (Rushing)	Avg	TD	Team Record	Att	Comp	Int	Pct	Yds	TD
1940	63	373	5.9	5	5-4-1	44	21	2	.477	226	6
1941	209	1103	5.3	8	9-1-1	115	52	7	.452	713	14
1942	175	795	4.5	17	11-1	166	84	7	.506	1392	10
TOTALS	447	2271	5.1	30		325	157	16	.483	2331	30

1959 — BILLY CANNON
LSU Halfback

A rare combination of strength and speed, LSU's Billy Cannon became the SEC's second Heisman winner in 1959. In the Tigers' heart-stopping 7-3 win over Ole Miss in 1959, Cannon, who ran the 100-yard dash in 9.4 and threw the shot put 54-4 for the LSU track team, entered his name in college football folklore with an 89-yard punt return in the fourth quarter for the winning points. However, it was a dramatic goal line stand in the final seconds with Cannon making the game-saving tackle that preserved the LSU win. Although renowned for his offensive skills, Cannon's contemporaries claim he was a better defender. He also averaged 40.3 yards per punt as a college star. Cannon had a successful 11-year pro career with the Houston Oilers, Oakland Raiders and Kansas City Chiefs. Today, Cannon is a dentist in Baton Rouge.

CANNON STATS

Year	Att	Yds (Rushing)	Avg	Team Record	No	Yds (Receiving)	Avg	TD	No	Yds (Returns)	Avg	TD
1957	105	583	5.5	5-5	11	199	18.1	1	18	382	21.2	1
1958	115	686	5.9	11-0	9	162	18.0	1	12	171	14.3	0
1959	139	598	4.3	9-2	11	161	14.6	0	23	412	17.9	1
TOTALS	359	1867	5.2		31	522	16.8	2	53	965	18.2	2

CAREER PASSING: 12 for 26, 118 yards CAREER PUNTING: 111 for 37.8 average CAREER INTERCEPTIONS: 7 for 165 yards, 1 TD

1966 — STEVE SPURRIER
Florida Quarterback

Another skilled all-around player, Florida's Steve Spurrier earned his Heisman Trophy in 1966, edging Purdue's Bob Griese for the coveted award. In his Gator career, Spurrier completed 392 of 692 for 4,848 yards and 37 touchdowns, while rushing for 442 yards. He led his 1966 Gator team to a 9-2 record, including a 27-12 victory over Georgia Tech in the 1967 Orange Bowl. However, it was the 1966 Sugar Bowl that enhanced Spurrier's image nationwide, when he led a fourth-quarter rally against Missouri which fell two points shy. Trailing 20-0 entering the final period, Spurrier led the Gators to three touchdowns; unfortunately for Florida all three attempts at two point plays were unsuccessful. As a professional, Spurrier played for the San Francisco 49ers, Minnesota Vikings and Tampa Bay Bucs. He now serves as the head coach at his alma mater.

SPURRIER STATS

Year	Att	Comp	Int	Pct	Yds	TD	Team Record
1964	114	65	10	.570	943	6	7-3
1965	287	148	13	.516	1893	14	7-4
1966	291	179	8	.615	2012	16	9-2
TOTALS	692	392	31	.566	4848	36	

SEC Heisman Trophy Winners

1971 — PAT SULLIVAN
Auburn Quarterback

In his brilliant three-year career at Auburn, Pat Sullivan guided an offensive team that averaged 34.4 points and 425.8 yards per game. While a junior, he led the nation in total offense with 285.6 yards per game before going on to win the Heisman his senior year. Sullivan became the first Heisman recipient ever to play at a school where John Heisman (for whom the trophy is named) coached. In his three-year career, Sullivan accounted for 71 touchdowns (18 running and 53 passing) for a then-national record. Winner of the MVP Award in the 1971 Gator Bowl, Sullivan went on to play professionally for the Atlanta Falcons, Washington Redskins and San Francisco 49ers. After serving as president of his own tire company in Birmingham, Ala., and color analyst on the Auburn Radio Network, he returned to Auburn in 1986 to serve as an assistant coach to Pat Dye. He enters his third season as head coach at TCU in 1994.

SULLIVAN STATS

Year	G	Att	Comp	Int	Pct	Yds	TD	Team Record	G	Att	Yds	Avg	TD
1969	10	257	123	16	.479	1686	16	8-3	10	56	205	3.6	7
1970	10	281	167	12	.594	2586	17	9-2	10	52	270	5.1	9
1971	10	281	162	11	.577	2012	20	9-2	10	47	84	1.8	2
TOTALS	30	819	452	39	.552	6284	53		30	155	559	3.6	18

1982 — HERSCHEL WALKER
Georgia Tailback

Georgia's Herschel Walker, third in the Heisman voting in 1980 and second in 1981, continued his progression toward the trophy in 1982, winning easily over Stanford's John Elway. Leading the Bulldogs to a three-year record of 33-3, including a perfect 12-0 National Championship season in 1980, Walker finished third on the all-time rushing list in the NCAA with a three-year total of 5,259 yards, finishing behind Pittsburgh's Tony Dorsett (6,082) and Southern Cal's Charles White (5,598), both of whom needed four years to reach their figures. During his Georgia career, Walker set 10 NCAA records, 15 SEC records, and 30 Georgia records. He also starred at track, running a 10.1 100-meter dash and a 6.18 60-yard dash. Walker is now playing professional football with the Philadelphia Eagles after playing with the Dallas Cowboys, Minnesota Vikings and the New Jersey Generals in the USFL.

WALKER STATS

Year	G	Att	Yds	Avg	YPG	TD	LG	Team Record
1980	11	274	1616	5.9	146.9	15	76	12-0
1981	11	385	1891	4.9	172.0	20	32	10-2
1982	11	335	1752	5.2	159.3	17	59	11-1
TOTALS	33	994	5259	5.3	159.4	52	76	

1985 — BO JACKSON
Auburn Tailback

A gifted athlete, Auburn's Vincent "Bo" Jackson became the sixth SEC player to claim the Heisman Trophy, winning the award over Iowa's Chuck Long in the closest balloting ever. Rarely have the nation's sports fans witnessed such a talented player. He became the Southeastern Conference's first three-sport letterman in two decades, claiming monograms in football, baseball and track.

As a football player, Jackson gained 4,303 yards in his career, averaging 6.6 yards per carry, an SEC record. During his Auburn career, Jackson was MVP in four different bowl games, winning honors for his play in the Tangerine, Sugar, Liberty and Cotton Bowl.

During his Heisman-winning season, Jackson led the SEC in rushing (162.4 yards per game), scoring (102 points), and all-purpose running (169.0 yards per game).

Continuing his multi-sport pursuits as a professional, Jackson plays baseball for the California Angels. He earned MVP honors at the 1990 Major League All-Star Game while playing for the Kansas City Royals. A hip injury ended his football career in 1991 after playing with the Los Angeles Raiders.

JACKSON STATS

Year	G	Att	Yds	Avg	YPG	TD	LG	Team Record
1982	11	127	829	6.5	75.4	9	53	9-3
1983	11	158	1213	7.7	110.3	12	80	11-1
1984	6	87	475	5.5	79.2	5	53	9-4
1985	11	278	1786	6.4	162.4	17	76	8-4
TOTALS	38	650	4303	6.6	113.2	43	80	

CAREER RECEIVING: 26-272 yards (10.5 avg.), 2 TDs, Long 44

SEC in the Heisman Vote

1935
1. Jay Berwanger, Chicago
2. Monk Meyer, Army
3. William Shakespeare, Notre Dame
4. Pepper Constable, Princeton
No player west of the Mississippi was eligible for the trophy this year.

1936
1. Larry Kelley, Yale
2. Sam Francis, Nebraska
3. Ray Buivid, Marquette
4. Sammy Baugh, TCU
5. Clint Frank, Yale
6. Ed Widseth, Minnesota
7. Ace Parker, Duke
8. Fred Vanzo, Northwestern
9. **Gaynell Tinsley, LSU**
10. Alex Wojciechowicz, Fordham

1937
1. Clint Frank, Yale
2. Byron White, Colorado
3. Marshall Goldberg, Pittsburgh
4. Alex Wojciechowicz, Fordham
5. **Joe Kilgrow, Alabama**
6. Sid Luckman, Columbia
7. **Carl Hinkle, Vanderbilt**
8. Vic Bottari, California
9. Sam Chapman, California
10. Brud Holland, Cornell

1938
1. Davey O'Brien, TCU
2. Marshall Goldberg, Pittsburgh
3. Sid Luckman, Columbia
4. Bob MacLeod, Dartmouth
5. Vic Bottari, California
6. Howard Weiss, Wisconsin
7. **George Cafego, Tennessee**
8. Kialdrich, TCU
9. Whitey Beinor, Notre Dame
10. Dean Hill, Duke

1939
1. Nile Kinnick, Iowa
2. Tom Harmon, Michigan
3. Paul Christman, Missouri
4. **George Cafego, Tennessee**
5. John Kimbrough, Texas A&M
6. Kenny Washington, UCLA
7. **Ken Kavanaugh, LSU**
8. Banks McFadden, Clemson
9. Jay Graybeal, Oregon
10. John Schiechl, Santa Clara

1940
1. Tom Harmon, Michigan
2. John Kimbrough, Texas A&M
3. George Franck, Minnesota
4. Frankie Albert, Stanford
5. Paul Christman, Missouri
6. **Bob Suffridge, Tennessee**
7. Charles O'Rourke, Boston College
8. Norman Standlee, Stanford
9. Marshall Robnett, Texas A&M
10. Walt Matuszczak, Cornell

1941
1. Bruce Smith, Minnesota
2. Angelo Bertelli, Notre Dame
3. Frankie Albert, Stanford
4. **Frank Sinkwich, Georgia**
5. Bill Dudley, Virginia
6. Endicott Peabody, Harvard
7. Edgar Jones, Pitt
8. Bob Westfall, Michigan
9. Steve Lach, Duke
10. Jack Crain, Texas

1942
1. **Frank Sinkwich, Georgia**
2. Paul Governali, Columbia
3. **Clint Castleberry, Georgia Tech**
4. Mike Holovak, Boston College
5. Bill Hillenbrand, Indiana
6. Angelo Bertelli, Notre Dame
7. Dick Wildung, Minnesota
8. Gene Fekete, Ohio State
9. Glenn Dobbs, Tulsa
10. Dave Schreiner, Wisconsin

1943
1. Angelo Bertelli, Notre Dame
2. Bob Odell, Pennsylvania
3. Otto Graham, Northwestern
4. Creighton Miller, Notre Dame
5. **Eddie Prokop, Georgia Tech**
6. Bill Hamburg, Navy
7. Bill Daley, Michigan
8. Tony Butkovich, Purdue
9. Jim White, Notre Dame

1944
1. Les Horvath, Ohio State
2. Glenn Davis, Army
3. Felix Blanchard, Army
4. Don Whitmire, Navy
5. Buddy Young, Illinois
6. Bob Kelly, Notre Dame
7. Bob Jenkins, Navy
8. Doug Kenna, Army
9. Bob Feinmore, Oklahoma A&M
10. **Shorty McWilliams, Mississippi State**

1945
1. Felix Blanchard, Army
2. Glenn Davis, Army
3. Bob Feinmore, Oklahoma A&M
4. Herman Wedemeyer, St. Mary's
5. **Harry Gilmer, Alabama**
6. Frank Dancewicz, Notre Dame
7. Warren Amling, Ohio State
8. Pete Pihos, Indiana
9. Clyde Scott, Navy

1946
1. Glenn Davis, Army
2. **Charles Trippi, Georgia**
3. John Lujack, Notre Dame
4. Felix Blanchard, Army
5. Herman Wedemeyer, St. Mary's
6. Arnold Tucker, Army
7. **Harry Gilmer, Alabama**
8. Burr Baldwin, UCLA
9. Bobby Layne, Texas

1947
1. John Lujack, Notre Dame
2. Bob Chappuis, Michigan
3. Doak Walker, SMU
4. **Charley Conerly, Ole Miss**
5. **Harry Gilmer, Alabama**
6. Bobby Layne, Texas
7. Chuck Bednarik, Pennsylvania
8. Bill Swiacki, Columbia

1948
1. Doak Walker, SMU
2. Charlie Justice, North Carolina
3. Chuck Bednarik, Pennsylvania
4. Jackie Jensen, California
5. Stanley Heath, Nevada
6. Norm Van Brocklin, Oregon
7. Emil Sitko, Notre Dame
8. Jack Mitchell, Oklahoma

1949
1. Leon Hart, Notre Dame
2. Charlie Justice, North Carolina
3. Doak Walker, SMU
4. Arnold Galiffa, Army
5. Bob Williams, Notre Dame
6. Eddie LeBaron, College of Pacific
7. Clayton Tonnemaker, Minnesota
8. Emil Sitko, Notre Dame

1950
1. Vic Janowicz, Ohio State
2. Kyle Rote, SMU
3. Red Bagnell, Pennsylvania
4. **Babe Parilli, Kentucky**
5. Bobby Reynolds, Nebraska
6. Bob Williams, Notre Dame
7. Leon Heath, Oklahoma
8. Dan Foldberg, Army

1951
1. Dick Kazmaier, Princeton
2. **Hank Lauricella, Tennessee**
3. **Babe Parilli, Kentucky**
4. Bill McColl, Stanford
5. John Bright, Drake
6. John Karras, Illinois
7. Larry Isbell, Baylor
8. Hugh McElhenny, Washington
9. Ollie Matson, San Francisco

1952
1. Billy Vessels, Oklahoma
2. Jack Scarbath, Maryland
3. Paul Giel, Minnesota
4. Don Moomaw, UCLA
5. John Lattner, Notre Dame
6. Paul Cameron, UCLA
7. Jim Sears, Southern California
8. Don McAuliffe, Michigan State
9. Don Heinrich, Washington

1953
1. John Lattner, Notre Dame
2. Paul Giel, Minnesota
3. Paul Cameron, UCLA
4. Bernie Faloney, Maryland
5. Bob Garrett, Stanford
6. Alan Ameche, Wisconsin
7. J.C. Caroline, Illinois
8. J.D. Roberts, Oklahoma
9. Lamar McHan, Arkansas

1954
1. Alan Ameche, Wisconsin
2. Kurt Burris, Oklahoma
3. Howard Cassady, Ohio State
4. Ralph Guglielmi, Notre Dame
5. Paul Larson, California
6. Dick Moegle, Rice
7. Jack Elena, UCLA
8. George Shaw, Oregon
9. Pete Vann, Army
10. Bob McNamara, Minnesota

1955
1. Howard Cassady, Ohio State
2. Jim Swink, TCU
3. George Welsh, Navy
4. Earl Morrall, Michigan State
5. Paul Hornung, Notre Dame
6. Bob Pellegrini, Maryland
7. Ron Beagle, Navy
8. Ron Kramer, Michigan
9. Bo Bolinger, Oklahoma
10. Jon Arnett, Southern California

1994 SEC Football   249

SEC in the Heisman Vote

1956
1. Paul Hornung, Notre Dame
2. **John Majors, Tennessee**
3. Tom McDonald, Oklahoma
4. Gerry Tubbs, Oklahoma
5. Jimmy Brown, Syracuse
6. Ron Kramer, Michigan
7. Steve Brodie, Stanford
8. Jim Parker, Ohio State
9. Kenny Ploen, Iowa
10. Joe Walton, Pittsburgh

1957
1. John Crow, Texas A&M
2. Alex Karras, Iowa
3. Walt Kowalczyk, Michigan State
4. **Lou Michaels, Kentucky**
5. Tom Forrestal, Navy
6. **Jim Phillips, Auburn**
7. Bob Anderson, Army
8. Dan Currie, Michigan State
9. Clendon Thomas, Oklahoma
10. Lee Grosscup, Utah
11. King Hill, Rice

1958
1. Peter Dawkins, Army
2. Randy Duncan, Iowa
3. **Billy Cannon, LSU**
4. Bob White, Ohio State
5. Joe Kapp, California
6. Bill Austin, Rutgers
7. Bob Harrison, Oklahoma
8. Dick Bass, College of Pacific
9. Don Meredith, SMU
10. Nick Pietrosante, Notre Dame

1959
1. **Billy Cannon, LSU**
2. Richie Lucas, Penn State
3. Don Meredith, SMU
4. Bill Burrell, Illinois
5. **Charles Flowers, Ole Miss**
6. Dean Look, Michigan State
7. Dale Hackbart, Wisconsin
8. Dwight Nichols, Iowa State
9. Monty Stickles, Notre Dame
10. Ron Burton, Northwestern

1960
1. Joe Bellino, Navy
2. Tom Brown, Minnesota
3. **Jake Gibbs, Ole Miss**
4. **Ed Dyas, Auburn**
5. Bill Kilmer, UCLA
6. Mike Ditka, Pittsburgh
7. Tom Matte, Ohio State
8. Dan LaRose, Missouri
9. Purvis Atkins, New Mexico State
10. E.J. Holub, Texas

1961
1. Ernie Davis, Syracuse
2. Bob Ferguson, Ohio State
3. Jimmy Saxton, Texas
4. Sandy Stephens, Minnesota
5. **Pat Trammell, Alabama**
6. Joe Romig, Colorado
7. John Hadl, Kansas
8. Gary Collins, Maryland
9. Roman Gabriel, N.C. State
10. Merlin Olsen, Utah State

1962
1. Terry Baker, Oregon State
2. **Jerry Stovall, LSU**
3. Bob Bell, Minnesota
4. **Lee Roy Jordan, Alabama**
5. George Mira, Miami
6. Pat Richter, Wisconsin
7. George Saimes, Michigan State
8. **Billy Lothridge, Georgia Tech**
9. Ron Vander Kelen, Wisconsin
10. Eldon Fortie, Brigham Young

1963
1. Roger Staubach, Navy
2. **Billy Lothridge, Georgia Tech**
3. Sherman Lewis, Michigan State
4. Don Trull, Baylor
5. Scott Appleton, Texas
6. Dick Butkus, Illinois
7. **Jimmy Sidle, Auburn**
8. Terry Isaacson, Air Force
9. Jay Wilkinson, Duke
10. George Mira, Miami

1964
1. John Huarte, Notre Dame
2. Jerry Rhome, Tulsa
3. Dick Butkus, Illinois
4. Bob Timberlake, Michigan
5. Jack Snow, Notre Dame
6. **Tucker Frederickson, Auburn**
7. Craig Morton, California
8. **Steve DeLong, Tennessee**
9. Cosmo Iacavazzi, Princeton
10. Brian Piccolo, Wake Forest
11. **Joe Namath, Alabama**
12. Gale Sayers, Kansas

1965
1. Mike Garrett, Southern California
2. Howard Twilley, Tulsa
3. Jim Grabowski, Illinois
4. Don Anderson, Texas Tech
5. Floyd Little, Syracuse
6. Steve Juday, Michigan State
7. Tom Nobis, Texas
8. Bob Griese, Purdue
9. **Steve Spurrier, Florida**
10. **Steve Sloan, Alabama**
11. Bill Wolski, Notre Dame
12. Ron Landeck, Princeton
13. Clint Jones, Michigan State
14. Bill Anderson, Tulsa

1966
1. **Steve Spurrier, Florida**
2. Bob Griese, Purdue
3. Nick Eddy, Notre Dame
4. Gary Beban, UCLA
5. Floyd Little, Syracuse
6. Clint Jones, Michigan State
7. Mel Farr, UCLA
8. Terry Hanratty, Notre Dame
9. Loyd Phillips, Arkansas
10. **George Patton, Georgia**
11. Virgil Carter, Brigham Young
12. Wayne Meylan, Nebraska
13. Pete Pifer, Oregon State
14. Len Snow, Georgia Tech

1967
1. Gary Beban, UCLA
2. O.J. Simpson, Southern California
3. Leroy Keyes, Purdue
4. Larry Csonka, Syracuse
5. Kim Hammond, Florida State
6. **Bob Johnson, Tennessee**
7. Granville Liggins, Oklahoma
8. **Dewey Warren, Tennessee**
9. Wayne Meylan, Nebraska
10. Terry Hanratty, Notre Dame
11. **Dennis Homan, Alabama**
12. Paul Toscano, Wyoming
13. Ted Hendricks, Miami
14. Chris Gilbert, Texas

1968
1. O.J. Simpson, Southern California
2. Leroy Keyes, Purdue
3. Terry Hanratty, Notre Dame
4. Ted Kwalick, Penn State
5. Ted Hendricks, Miami
6. Ron Johnson, Michigan
7. Bob Douglas, Kansas
8. Chris Gilbert, Texas
9. Bryan Dowling, Yale
10. Ron Sellers, Florida State
11. Bill Enyart, Oregon State
12. Ed Podolok, Iowa
13. Eugene Morris, West Texas State
14. Paul Gipson, Houston

Tennessee's Johnny Majors, a two-time SEC Most Valuable Player, was the runner-up for the 1956 Heisman Trophy.

250 Honors

1969
1. Steve Owens, Oklahoma
2. Mike Phipps, Purdue
3. Rex Kern, Ohio State
4. **Archie Manning, Ole Miss**
5. Mike Reid, Penn State
6. Mike McCoy, Notre Dame
7. Jim Otis, Ohio State
8. Jim Plunkett, Stanford
9. **Steve Kiner, Tennessee**
10. Jack Tatum, Ohio State
11. Bob Anderson, Colorado
12. Lynn Dickey, Kansas State
13. John Isenbarger, Indiana
14. Bill Cappelman, Florida State

1970
1. Jim Plunkett, Stanford
2. Joe Theismann, Notre Dame
3. **Archie Manning, Ole Miss**
4. Steve Worster, Texas
5. Rex Kern, Ohio State
6. **Pat Sullivan, Auburn**
7. Jack Tatum, Ohio State
8. Ernie Jennings, Air Force
9. Don McCauley, North Carolina
10. Lynn Dickey, Kansas State
11. Ed Marinaro, Cornell
12. Tom Gatewood, Notre Dame
13. Joe Spagnola, Arizona State
14. Dennis Dummitt, UCLA

1971
1. **Pat Sullivan, Auburn**
2. Ed Marinaro, Cornell
3. Gregg Pruitt, Oklahoma
4. **John Musso, Alabama**
5. Lydell Mitchell, Penn State
6. Jack Mildren, Oklahoma
7. Jerry Tagge, Nebraska
8. Chuck Ealey, Toledo
9. Walt Patulski, Notre Dame
10. Eric Allen, Michigan State
11. Bill Taylor, Michigan
12. Bob Moore, Oregon
13. **Terry Beasley, Auburn**
14. Sonny Sixkiller, Washington

1972
1. Johnny Rodgers, Nebraska
2. Gregg Pruitt, Oklahoma
3. Rich Glover, Nebraska
4. **Bert Jones, LSU**
5. **Terry Davis, Alabama**
6. John Hufnagel, Penn State
7. George Amundsen, Iowa State
8. Otis Armstrong, Purdue
9. Don Strock, Virginia Tech
10. Gary Huff, Florida State
11. **John Hannah, Alabama**
12. Tony Adams, Utah State
13. Brad Van Pelt, Michigan State
14. Howard Stevens, Louisville

1973
1. John Cappelletti, Penn State
2. John Hicks, Ohio State
3. Roosevelt Leaks, Texas
4. David Jaynes, Kansas
5. Archie Griffin, Ohio State
6. Randy Gradishar, Ohio State
7. Lucious Selmon, Oklahoma
8. Woody Green, Arizona State
9. Danny White, Arizona State
10. Kermit Johnson, UCLA
11. Tony Dorsett, Pittsburgh
12. Lynn Swann, Southern California
13. Anthony Davis, Southern California
14. **Condredge Holloway, Tennessee**

1974
1. Archie Griffin, Ohio State
2. Anthony Davis, Southern California
3. Joe Washington, Oklahoma
4. Tom Clements, Notre Dame
5. Dave Humm, Nebraska
6. Dennis Franklin, Michigan State
7. Rod Shoate, Oklahoma
8. Gary Scheide, Brigham Young
9. Randy White, Maryland
10. Steve Bartkowski, California
11. Steve Joachim, Temple
12. Fred Solomon, Tampa
13. Tony Dorsett, Pittsburgh
14. Walter Payton, Jackson State

1975
1. Archie Griffin, Ohio State
2. Chuck Muncie, California
3. Ricky Bell, Southern California
4. Tony Dorsett, Pittsburgh
5. Joe Washington, Oklahoma
6. **Jimmy Dubose, Florida**
7. John Sciarra, UCLA
8. Gordon Bell, Michigan
9. Leroy Selman, Oklahoma
10. Gene Swick, Toledo
11. **Leroy Cook, Alabama**
12. Steve Niehaus, Notre Dame
13. Jeff Grantz, South Carolina
14. Nolan Cromwell, Kansas

1976
1. Tony Dorsett, Pittsburgh
2. Ricky Bell, Southern California
3. Rob Lytle, Michigan
4. Terry Miller, Oklahoma State
5. Tom Kramer, Rice
6. Gifford Nielsen, Brigham Young
7. **Ray Goff, Georgia**
8. Mike Voight, North Carolina
9. Joe Roth, California
10. Jeff Dankworth, UCLA
11. Vince Ferragamo, Nebraska
12. **Larry Seivers, Tennessee**
13. Pete Johnson, Ohio State
14. Rick Leach, Michigan

1977
1. Earl Campbell, Texas
2. Terry Miller, Oklahoma State
3. Ken MacAfee, Notre Dame
4. Doug Williams, Grambling College
5. Ross Browner, Notre Dame
6. Guy Benjamin, Stanford
7. Matt Cavanaugh, Pittsburgh
8. Rick Leach, Michigan
9. **Charles Alexander, LSU**
10. **Wes Chandler, Florida**

1978
1. Billy Sims, Oklahoma
2. Chuck Fusina, Penn State
3. Rich Leach, Michigan
4. Charles White, Southern California
5. **Charles Alexander, LSU**
6. Ted Brown, N.C. State
7. Steve Fuller, Clemson
8. Eddie Lee Ivery, Georgia Tech
9. Jack Thompson, Washington State
10. Jerry Robinson, UCLA

1979
1. Charles White, Southern California
2. Billy Sims, Oklahoma
3. Marc Wilson, Brigham Young
4. Art Schlichter, Ohio State
5. Vagas Ferguson, Notre Dame
6. Paul McDonald, Southern California
7. George Rogers, South Carolina
8. Mark Herrmann, Purdue
9. Ron Simmons, Florida State
10. **Steadman Shealy, Alabama**

1980
1. George Rogers, South Carolina
2. Hugh Green, Pittsburgh
3. **Herschel Walker, Georgia**
4. Mark Herrmann, Purdue
5. Jim McMahon, Brigham Young
6. Art Schlichter, Ohio State
7. Neil Lomax, Portland State
8. Jarvis Redwine, Nebraska
9. Ken Easley, UCLA
10. Anthony Carter, Michigan

1981
1. Marcus Allen, Southern California
2. **Herschel Walker, Georgia**
3. Jim McMahon, Brigham Young
4. Dan Marino, Pittsburgh
5. Art Schlichter, Ohio State
6. Darrin Nelson, Stanford
7. Anthony Carter, Michigan
8. Kenneth Sims, Texas
9. Reggie Collier, Southern Mississippi
10. Rich Diana, Yale

1982
1. **Herschel Walker, Georgia**
2. John Elway, Stanford
3. Eric Dickerson, SMU
4. Anthony Carter, Michigan
5. Dave Rimington, Nebraska
6. Todd Blackledge, Penn State
7. Tom Ramsey, UCLA
8. Tony Eason, Illinois
9. Dan Marino, Pittsburgh
10. Mike Rozier, Nebraska
11. Curt Warner, Penn State

LSU running back Charles Alexander, who twice earned All-America honors, also finished in the top 10 Heisman voting on two occasions.

1994 SEC Football   251

SEC in the Heisman Vote

Georgia rover Terry Hoage placed fifth in the 1983 Heisman Trophy balloting, marking the highest finish by an SEC defensive player.

Auburn's Bo Jackson, who rushed for 4,303 yards during his career, is the SEC's most recent Heisman Trophy winner.

1983
1. Mike Rozier, Nebraska
2. Steve Young, Brigham Young
3. Doug Flutie, Boston College
4. Turner Gill, Nebraska
5. **Terry Hoage, Georgia**
6. Napoleon McCallum, Navy
7. Jeff Hostetler, West Virginia
8. Bill Fralic, Pittsburgh
9. **Walter Lewis, Alabama**
10. Boomer Esiason, Maryland

1984
1. Doug Flutie, Boston College
2. Keith Byars, Ohio State
3. Robbie Bosco, Brigham Young
4. Bernie Kosar, Miami
5. Keith Davis, TCU
6. Bill Fralic, Pittsburgh
7. Chuck Long, Iowa
8. Greg Allen, Florida State
9. Jerry Rice, Mississippi Valley
10. Reuben Mayes, Washington State

1985
1. **Bo Jackson, Auburn**
2. Chuck Long, Iowa
3. Robbie Bosco, Brigham Young
4. Lorenzo White, Michigan State
5. Vinnie Testaverde, Miami
6. Jim Everett, Purdue
7. Napolean McCallum, Navy
8. Allen Pinkett, Notre Dame
9. Joe Dudek, Plymouth State
10. Brian McClure, Bowling Green
10. Thurman Thomas, Oklahoma State

1986
1. Vinny Testaverde, Miami
2. Paul Palmer, Temple
3. Jim Harbaugh, Michigan
4. Brian Bosworth, Oklahoma
5. Gordon Lockbaum, Holy Cross
6. **Brent Fullwood, Auburn**
7. **Cornelius Bennett, Alabama**
8. D.J. Dozier, Penn State
9. Kevin Sweeney, Fresno State
10. Chris Spielman, Ohio State

1987
1. Tim Brown, Notre Dame
2. Don McPherson, Syracuse
3. Gordon Lockbaum, Holy Cross
4. Lorenzo White, Michigan State
5. Craig Heyward, Pittsburgh
6. Chris Spielman, Ohio State
7. Thurman Thomas, Oklahoma State
8. Gaston Green, UCLA
9. **Emmitt Smith, Florida**
10. **Bobby Humphrey, Alabama**

1988
1. Barry Sanders, Oklahoma State
2. Rodney Peete, Southern California
3. Troy Aikman, UCLA
4. Steve Walsh, Miami
5. Major Harris, West Virginia
6. Tony Manderich, Michigan State
7. Timm Rosenbach, Washington State
8. Deion Sanders, Florida State
9. Anthony Thompson, Indiana
10. **Derrick Thomas, Alabama**

1989
1. Andre Ware, Houston
2. Anthony Thompson, Indiana
3. Major Harris, West Virginia
4. Tony Rice, Notre Dame
5. Darian Hagan, Colorado
6. Dee Dowis, Air Force
7. **Emmitt Smith, Florida**
8. Percy Snow, Michigan State
9. Ty Detmer, Brigham Young
10. Raghib Ismail, Notre Dame
11. Blair Thomas, Penn State

1990
1. Ty Detmer, Brigham Young
2. Raghib Ismail, Notre Dame
3. Eric Bieniemy, Colorado
4. Shawn Moore, Virginia
5. David Klingler, Houston
6. Herman Moore, Virginia
7. Greg Lewis, Washington
8. Craig Erickson, Miami
9. Darren Lewis, Texas A&M
10. Mike Mayweather, Army

1991
1. Desmond Howard, Michigan
2. Casey Weldon, Florida State
3. Ty Detmer, Brigham Young
4. Steve Emtman, Washington
5. **Shane Matthews, Florida**
6. Vaughn Dunbar, Indiana
7. Jeff Blake, East Carolina
8. Terrell Buckley, Florida State
9. Marshall Faulk, San Diego State
10. Bucky Richardson, Texas A&M

1992
1. Gino Toretta, Miami
2. Marshall Faulk, San Diego State
3. **Garrison Hearst, Georgia**
4. Marvin Jones, Florida State
5. Reggie Brooks, Notre Dame
6. Charlie Ward, Florida State
7. Michael Barrow, Miami
8. Drew Bledsoe, Washington State
9. Glyn Milburn, Stanford
10. **Eric Curry, Alabama**

1993
1. Charlie Ward, Florida State
2. **Heath Shuler, Tennessee**
3. **David Palmer, Alabama**
4. Marshall Faulk, San Diego State
5. Glenn Foley, Boston College
6. LeShon Johnson, Northern Illinois
7. J.J. Stokes, UCLA
8. Tyrone Wheatley, Michigan
9. Trent Dilfer, Fresno State
10. **Eric Zeier, Georgia**

Honors

Award Winners

Outland Trophy

(Honoring the outstanding interior lineman in the United States, selected by the Football Writers Association of America)

Year	Pos	Player, School
1946	T -	George Connor, Notre Dame
1947	G -	Joe Steffy, Army
1948	G -	Bill Fischer, Notre Dame
1949	G -	Ed Bagdon, Michigan State
1950	**T -**	**Bob Gain, Kentucky**
1951	T -	Jim Weatherall, Oklahoma
1952	T -	Dick Modzelewski, Maryland
1953	G -	J.D. Roberts, Oklahoma
1954	G -	Bill Brooks, Arkansas
1955	G -	Calvin Jones, Iowa
1956	G -	Jim Parker, Ohio State
1957	T -	Alex Karras, Iowa
1958	**G -**	**Zeke Smith, Auburn**
1959	T -	Mike McGee, Duke
1960	G -	Tom Brown, Minnesota
1961	T -	Merlin Olsen, Utah State
1962	T -	Bobby Bell, Minnesota
1963	T -	Scott Appleton, Texas
1964	**T -**	**Steve DeLong, Tennessee**
1965	G -	Tommy Nobis, Texas
1966	T -	Loyd Phillips, Arkansas
1967	T -	Ron Yary, Southern Cal
1968	**T -**	**Bill Stanfill, Georgia**
1969	DT-	Mike Reid, Penn State
1970	MG-	Jim Stillwagon, Ohio State
1971	DT-	Larry Jacobson, Nebraska
1972	MG-	Rich Glover, Nebraska
1973	OT-	John Hicks, Ohio State
1974	DE-	Randy White, Maryland
1975	DT-	Lee Roy Selmon, Oklahoma
1976	DE-	*Ross Browner, Notre Dame
1977	DT-	Brad Shearer, Texas
1978	G -	Greg Roberts, Oklahoma
1979	C -	Jim Ritcher, N.C. State
1980	T -	Mark May, Pittsburgh
1981	C -	*Dave Rimington, Nebraska
1982	C -	Dave Rimington, Nebraska
1983	G -	Dean Steinkuhler, Nebraska
1984	DT-	Bruce Smith, Virginia Tech
1985	NG-	Mike Ruth, Boston College
1986	DT-	Jason Buck, Brigham Young
1987	DT-	Chad Hennings, Air Force
1988	**DT-**	**Tracy Rocker, Auburn**
1989	G -	Mohammed Elewonibi, BYU
1990	DT-	Russell Maryland, Miami
1991	DT-	*Steve Emtman, Washington
1992	G-	Will Shields, Nebraska
1993	NG-	Rob Waldrop, Arizona

*Junior

Jim Thorpe Award

First presented in 1986 to honor the nation's best defensive back by the Jim Thorpe Athletic Club of Oklahoma City. The award is named after Jim Thorpe, Olympic champion, two-time consensus All-America halfback at Carlisle and professional football player.

1986	Thomas Everett, Baylor
1987	(tie) Bennie Blades, Miami
	Rickey Dixon, Oklahoma
1988	Deion Sanders, Florida State
1989	Mark Carrier, Southern Cal
1990	Darryll Lewis, Arizona
1991	Terrell Buckley, Florida State
1992	Deon Figures, Colorado
1993	**Antonio Langham, Alabama**

Vince Lombardi/Rotary Award

(Honoring the outstanding college lineman of the year, sponsored by the Rotary Club of Houston)

1970	MG-	Jim Stillwagon, Ohio State
1971	DE-	Walt Patulski, Notre Dame
1972	MG-	Rich Glover, Nebraska
1973	OT-	John Hicks, Ohio State
1974	DT-	Randy White, Maryland
1975	DT-	Lee Roy Selmon, Oklahoma
1976	DT-	Wilson Whitley, Houston
1977	DE-	Ross Browner, Notre Dame
1978	DT-	Bruce Clark, Penn State
1979	G -	Brad Budde, Southern Cal
1980	DE-	Hugh Green, Pittsburgh
1981	DT-	Kenneth Sims, Texas
1982	C -	Dave Rimington, Nebraska
1983	G -	Dean Steinkuhler, Nebraska
1984	DT-	Tony Degrate, Texas
1985	NG-	Tony Casillas, Oklahoma
1986	**LB-**	**Cornelius Bennett, Alabama**
1987	LB-	Chris Spielman, Ohio State
1988	**DT-**	**Tracy Rocker, Auburn**
1989	LB-	Percy Snow, Michigan State
1990	NT-	Chris Zorich, Notre Dame
1991	DT-	Steve Emtman, Washington
1992	LB-	Marvin Jones, Florida State
1993	OT-	Aaron Taylor, Notre Dame

Butkus Award

(Emblematic of the top collegiate linebacker, established by the Downtown Athletic Club of Orlando and named for Hall of Famer Dick Butkus of Illinois)

1985	Brian Bosworth, Oklahoma
1986	Brian Bosworth, Oklahoma
1987	Paul McGowan, Florida State
1988	**Derrick Thomas, Alabama**
1989	Percy Snow, Michigan State
1990	Alfred White, Colorado
1991	Erick Anderson, Michigan
1992	Marvin Jones, Florida State
1993	Trev Alberts, Nebraska

Doak Walker Award

(Presented to the nation's best running back among Division IA juniors or seniors, sponsored by the GTE/Southern Methodist Athletic Forum and named for Doak Walker - SMU's three-time consensus All-America halfback and 1948 Heisman Trophy winner)

1990	Greg Lewis, Washington
1991	Trevor Cobb, Rice
1992	**Garrison Hearst, Georgia**
1993	Byron Morris, Texas Tech

Lou Groza Award

Presented for the first time in 1992 to honor the nation's top collegiate place-kicker. Sponsored by the Palm Beach County Sports Authority in conjuction with the Orange Bowl Committee. The award is named after NFL Hall of Fame kicker Lou Groza.

1992	Joe Allison, Memphis State
1993	**Judd Davis, Florida**

Maxwell Award

(Presented to the nation's outstanding college football player by the Maxwell Football Club of Philadelphia)

1937	HB-	Clint Frank, Yale
1938	QB-	Davey O'Brien, Texas Christian
1939	HB-	Nile Kinnick, Iowa
1940	HB-	Tom Harmon, Michigan
1941	HB-	Bill Dudley, Virginia
1942	QB-	Paul Governali, Columbia
1943	HB-	Bob Odell, Pennsylvania
1944	HB-	Glenn Davis, Army
1945	FB-	Doc Blanchard, Army
1946	**HB-**	**Charley Trippi, Georgia**
1947	HB-	Doak Walker, SMU
1948	C -	Chuck Bednarik, Pennsylvania
1949	E -	Leon Hart, Notre Dame
1950	HB-	Reds Bagnell, Pennsylvania
1951	HB-	Dick Kazmaier, Princeton
1952	HB-	John Lattner, Notre Dame
1953	HB-	John Lattner, Notre Dame
1954	E -	Ron Beagle, Navy
1955	HB-	Howard Cassady, Ohio State
1956	HB-	Tommy McDonald, Oklahoma
1957	T -	Bob Reifsnyder, Navy
1958	HB-	Pete Dawkins, Army
1959	QB-	Rich Lucas, Penn State
1960	HB-	Joe Bellino, Navy
1961	FB-	Bob Ferguson, Ohio State
1962	QB-	Terry Baker, Oregon State
1963	QB-	Roger Staubach, Navy
1964	C -	Glenn Ressler, Penn State
1965	LB-	Tommy Nobis, Texas
1966	LB-	Jim Lynch, Notre Dame
1967	QB-	Gary Beban, UCLA
1968	RB-	O.J. Simpson, Southern Cal
1969	DT-	Mike Reid, Penn State
1970	QB-	Jim Plunkett, Stanford
1971	RB-	Ed Marinaro, Cornell
1972	DB-	Brad VanPelt, Michigan State
1973	RB-	John Cappelletti, Penn State
1974	QB-	Steve Joachim, Temple
1975	RB-	Archie Griffin, Ohio State
1976	RB-	Tony Dorsett, Pittsburgh
1977	DE-	Ross Browner, Notre Dame
1978	QB-	Chuck Fusina, Penn State
1979	RB-	Charles White, Southern Cal
1980	DE-	Hugh Green, Pittsburgh
1981	RB-	Marcus Allen, Southern Cal
1982	**RB-**	**Herschel Walker, Georgia**
1983	RB-	Mike Rozier, Nebraska
1984	QB-	Doug Flutie, Boston College
1985	QB-	Chuck Long, Iowa
1986	QB-	Vinny Testaverde, Miami
1987	QB-	Don McPherson, Syracuse
1988	RB-	Barry Sanders, Oklahoma State
1989	RB-	Anthony Thompson, Indiana
1990	QB-	Ty Detmer, Brigham Young
1991	WR-	Desmond Howard, Michigan
1992	QB-	Gino Torretta, Miami
1993	QB-	Charlie Ward, Florida State

1994 SEC Football

SEC All-Americas

NOTE: First team members only; AP (Associated Press), UP (United Press), INS (International News Service), UPI (United Press-International), NEA (Newspaper Enterprises Association), CP (Central Press), FWAA (Football Writers of America Association), Coaches (American Football Coaches Association), AAB (All-American Board), Camp (Walter Camp), Rice (Grantland Rice), Spt. News (Sporting News), FB News (Football News), FD (Football Digest), QB (Quarterbacker), CBS (Columbia Broadcasting), NBC (National Broadcasting).

Cornelius Bennett
Alabama

ALABAMA

1915—W.T. "Bully" Van de Graff, Tackle
1925—A.T.S. "Pooley" Hubert, QB
1926—Hoyt "Wu" Winslett, End (NCAA Guide)
1929—Tony Holm, FB (NCAA Guide)
1930—Fred Sington, Tackle (AP, UP, INS, NEA, AAB, Rice, Colliers, NY Sun, Coll. Humor)
1931—Johnny Cain, FB (UP, All-American Board)
1932—Johnny Cain, FB (NY Sun, College Humor)
1933—Tom Hupke, Guard (Associated Press)
1934—Don Hutson, End (AP, UP, INS, NEA, Rice, Collier's, NY Sun, CP, NCAA Guide)
Bill Lee, Tackle (AP, UP, INS, CP, Collier's, AAB, College-Humor)
Millard "Dixie" Howell, HB (AP, UP, INS, NEA, Rice, Collier's, NY Sun, NCAA Guide, CP)
1935—Riley Smith, QB (AP, UP, INS, CP, NY Sun, Rice)
1936—Arthur "Tarzan" White, Guard (NCAA Guide)
1937—James Ryba, Tackle (NCAA Guide)
Leroy Monsky, Guard (AP, UP, INS, NEA, AAB, NY Sun, Rose)
Joe Kilgrow, HB (NCAA Guide)
1939—Carey Cox, Center (NCAA Guide)
1941—Holt Rast, End (AP, UP, INS, NEA, AAB, NY Sun, Rice, Collier's)
1942—Don Whitmire, Tackle (NCAA Guide)
Joe Domnanovich, Center (AP, UP, INS, NEA, AAB, Rice, Collier's)

1945—Vaughn Mancha, Center (AP, UP, INS, NEA, AAB, Rice, Collier's)
Harry Gilmer, TB (UPI, Spt. News, Post)
1950—Eddie Salem, HB (AP)
1952—Bobby Marlow, HB (Athletic Pub.)
1954—George Mason, Tackle, (FD)
1961—Billy Neighbors, Tackle (AP, UPI, NEA, CP, FWAA, Coaches, Sp. News, FB News)
1962—Lee Roy Jordan, Center (AP, UPI, NEA, CP, FWAA, Coaches, Time, NY News, CBS)
1964—Dan Kearley, Tackle (Associated Press)
Wayne Freeman, Guard (NEA, NY News)
Joe Namath, QB (Litkenhous)
David Ray, HB (FB News)
1965—Paul Crane, Center (AP, UPI, NEA, FWAA, Coaches, NY News)
Steve Sloan, QB (FB News)
1966—Cecil Dowdy, Guard (AP, UPI, NEA, CP, FWAA, Coaches, NY News)
Ray Perkins, End (AP, NEA, FWAA, Coaches)
Bobby Johns, DB (Central Press)
Richard Cole, Tackle (FB News)
1967—Dennis Homan, Rcv (AP, UPI, CP, FWAA, Coaches, Camp, Time, Spt. News, NY News)
Bobby Johns, DB (UPI, Coaches, Camp, FB News)
Ken Stabler, QB (FB News)
1968—Mike Hall, LB (CP, Camp, FB News)
Sam Gellerstedt, Guard (FB News)
1969—Alvin Samples, Guard (CP, FB News)
1970—Johnny Musso, TB (Camp, FB News)
1971—Johnny Musso, TB (UPI, CP, FWAA), Camp, Coaches, Time, FB News)
John Hannah, Tackle (Coaches)
1972—John Hannah, Guard (AP, UPI, NEA, FWAA, Coaches, Camp, Time, Spt. News, FB News, Gridiron)
Jim Krapf, Center (Coaches)
John Mitchell, End (Coaches)
1973—Buddy Brown, Tackle (AP, UPI, NEA, FWAA, Coaches)
Woodrow Lowe, LB (NEA, FWAA)
Wayne Wheeler, WR (Camp, Spt. News, FB News, Universal Spts.)
1974—Leroy Cook, DE (AP, FWAA)
Woodrow Lowe, LB (UPI, Camp, FB News)
Mike Washington, DB (NEA, Time, FB News)
Sylvester Croom, Center (Coaches)
1975—Leroy Cook, DE (AP, UPI, FWAA, Coaches, Camp, FB News)
Woodrow Lowe, LB (UPI)
1977—Ozzie Newsome, WR (AP, NEA, FWAA, Camp, Coaches, Spt. News, FB News)

1978—Marty Lyons, DT (AP, FWAA, Spt. News, FB News, NEA)
Barry Krauss, LB (Spt. News)
1979—Jim Bunch, OT (AP, Coaches, FWAA)
Don McNeal, DB (NEA, Spt. News)
Dwight Stephenson, Center (FB News)
1980—E.J. Junior, DE (AP, UPI, NEA, FWAA, Coaches, Camp, Spt. News)
Thomas Boyd, LB (Camp)
1981—Tommy Wilcox, DB (AP, UPI, Coaches, Camp, FB News)
Thomas Boyd, LB (NEA, Camp)
1982—Mike Pitts, DE (UPI, Coaches, FB News, FWAA)
Jeremiah Castille, DB (Coaches, Kodak)
Tommy Wilcox, DB (Walter Camp)
1984—Cornelius Bennett, LB (Spt. News, FB News)
1985—Cornelius Bennett, LB (FB News, Camp, Spt. News)
Jon Hand, DT (Spt. News)
1986—Cornelius Bennett, LB (AP, UPI, FB News, Spt. News, Scripps-Howard, Camp, College & Pro Weekly FWAA, Coaches)
Bobby Humphrey, RB (College & Pro Weekly)
Van Tiffin, PK (Scripps-Howard, College & Pro Weekly)
1987—Bobby Humphrey, RB (Camp, Spt. News)
1988—Kermit Kendrick, DB (College & Pro Weekly)
Derrick Thomas, LB (AP, UPI, Coaches, FWAA, Camp, Scripps-Howard, Spt. News, FB News, College & Pro Weekly, Gannett News)
1989—John Mangum, DB (FB News)
Keith McCants, LB (AP, UPI, Coaches, FWAA, Camp, Scripps Howard, Spt. News, FB News)
1990—Philip Doyle, PK (AP, Camp, Coaches, FB News, FWAA, Kodak, Scripps Howard)
1992—John Copeland, DE (AP, Kodak, Camp, FB News, FWAA, Spt. News)
Eric Curry, DE (AP, UPI, Kodak, Camp, Spt. News)
1993—Antonio Langham, DE (AP, UPI, Coaches, Camp, FB News, FWAA, Scripps Howard, Spt. News)
David Palmer, WR (AP, UPI, Coaches, Camp, FB News, FWAA, Spt. News)
Michael Proctor, PK (FB News)

254 Honors

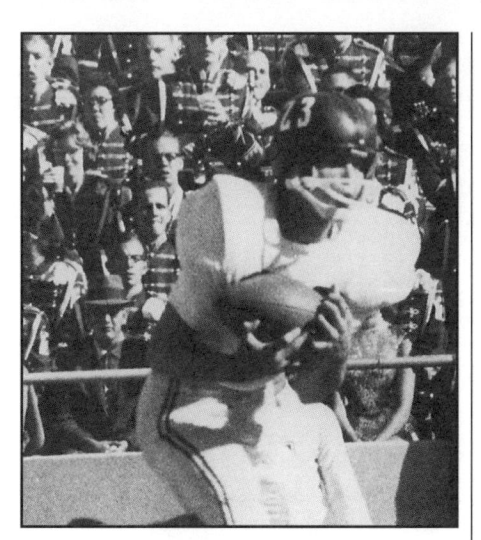

**Lance Alworth
Arkansas**

ARKANSAS

(Editor's Note: Team names are not available for Arkansas All-America players.)
1929—Wear Schoonover, E
1937—Jim Benton, E
1948—Clyde Scott, TB
1954—Bud Brooks, G
1959—Jim Mooty, HB
1960—Wayne Harris, LB
1961—Lance Alworth, HB
1962—Billy Moore, QB
1964—Ronnie Caveness, C
1965—Bobby Crockett, E
Glen Ray Hines, OT
Loyd Phillips, DT
1966—Martine Bercher, S
Loyd Phillips, DT
1968—Jim Barnes, G
1969—Rodney Brand, C
Chuck Discus, E
Cliff Powell, LB
1970—Dick Bumpas, DT
Chuck Discus, E
Bruce James, DE
Bill McClard, PK
1971—Bill McClard, PK
1976—Steve Little, PK
1977—Leotis Harris, G
Steve Little, PK
1978—Dan Hampton, DT
Jimmy Walker, DT
1979—Greg Kolenda, OT
1981—Bruce Lahay, PK
Billy Ray Smith, DE
1982—Steve Korte, OG
Billy Ray Smith, DE
1983—Ron Faurot, DE
1986—Greg Horne, P
1987—Tony Cherico, NG
1988—Wayne Martin, DT
Kendall Trainor, PK
1989—Jim Mabry, OT

AUBURN

1932—Jimmy Hitchcock, HB (NCAA Guide)
1937—Walter Gilbert, Center
1942—Ray (Monk) Gafford, HB (NCAA Guide)
1944—Caleb (Tex) Warrington, Center (NCAA Guide)
1949—Travis Tidwell, QB (Williamson)
1954—Jim Pyburn, End (Athletic Pub.)
1955—Frank D'Agostino, Tackle (AP, Collier's, NY News, Hearst)
Joe Childress, FB (FWAA)
Fob James, HB (INS, Movietone News)
1957—Jimmy Phillips, End (AP, UPI, INS, NEA, CP, FWAA-Look, Coaches, Hearst, Spt. News, Today, NBC)
1958—Zeke Smith, Guard (AP, NEA, CP, FWAA-Look, Time)
Jackie Burkett, Center (Coaches, Time)
1959—Zeke Smith, Guard (Coaches, Time)
Ken Rice, Tackle, (NEA, FWAA-Look)
1960—Ken Rice, Tackle (AP, UPI, CP, FWAA-Look, Coaches, Time, Spt. News, NBC)
Ed Dyas, FB (FWAA-Look)
1963—Jimmy Sidle, QB (AP, FWAA-Look, FB News)
1964—Tucker Frederickson, FB (AP, NEA, CP, FWAA-Look, Time, NY News, Spt. News)
1965—Jack Thornton, Tackle (NEA)
Billy Cody, LB (FB News)
1967—Freddie Hyatt, End (FB News)
1968—Dave Campbell, Tackle (NEA)
1969—Buddy McClinton, Safety (AP, UPI, CP, FWAA-Look, Coaches, FB News, Camp)
1970—Larry Willingham, DB (UPI, NEA, CP, FWAA-Look, Coaches, Spt. News, FB News, Time)
Terry Beasley, End/Flanker (FB News)
Pat Sullivan, QB (FB News)
1971—Pat Sullivan, QB (AP, UPI, NEA, CP, FWAA, Coaches, Camp, Spt. News, FB News, Time)
Terry Beasley, WR (AP, UPI, NEA, CP, FWAA, Coaches, Camp, Spt. News, FB News, Time)
1973—Steve Taylor, Center (Universal Spt.)
1974—Ken Bernich, LB (AP, Coaches, Camp)
Mike Fuller, Safety (FB News)
1976—Neil O'Donoghue, PK (Spt. News)
1981—Keith Uecker, OT (Mizlou)
1983—Bo Jackson, RB (AP, UPI, Coaches, FWAA, FB News)
1984—Gregg Carr, LB (AP, UPI, Coaches, FB News, Camp)
1985—Bo Jackson, RB (AP, UPI, FB News, Camp, Coaches, Scripps-Howard, FWAA, Spt. News, College & Pro Weekly, Scripps-Howard)
Lewis Colbert, P (Coaches, Spt. News)
Ben Tamburello, C (FB News)
1986—Brent Fullwood, TB (AP, UPI, FB News, Spt. News, Scripps-Howard, Camp, College & Pro Weekly, FWAA, Coaches)
Ben Tamburello, C (AP, UPI, Spt. News, Scripps-Howard, Camp, College & Pro Weekly, FWAA, Coaches)
1987—Aundray Bruce, OLB (Coaches, Camp, Scripps-Howard, UPI, Spt. News)
Tracy Rocker, DT (Camp, FWAA, Scripps-Howard, FB News, UPI, College & Pro Weekly)
Stacy Searels, OT (FB News, AP)
Kurt Crain, LB (AP)
1988—Tracy Rocker, DT (AP, UPI, Coaches, FWAA, Camp, Scripps-Howard, Spt. News, FB News, College & Pro Weekly, Gannett)
Walter Reeves, TE (Spt. News)
Benji Roland, NG (Spt. News)
1989—Ed King, OG (AP, FWAA, FB News, Scripps-Howard, Camp)
Craig Ogletree, LB (Spt. News)
1990—Ed King, OG (AP, Camp, Coaches, FB News, FWAA, Scripps Howard)
David Rocker, DL (Camp, Coaches)
1993—Terry Daniel, P (AP, Coaches, Camp, FB News, FWAA, Spt. News
Wayne Gandy, OT (AP, UPI, FWAA, Scripps Howard, Spt. News

**Ed King
Auburn**

1994 SEC Football 255

SEC All-Americas

Louis Oliver
Florida

FLORIDA

1928—Dale Van Sickel, End (AP, NEA, Rice)
1952—Charles LaPradd, Tackle (AP, NY News)
1956—John Barrow, Guard (FWAA-Look)
1958—Val Heckman, Tackle (FWAA-Look)
1954—Larry DuPree, HB (Coaches)
   Dennis Murphy, Tackle (FB News)
1965—Charles Casey, End (AP, Coaches)
   Steve Spurrier, QB (FWAA-Look)
   Lynn Mathews, End (NEA)
   Bruce Bennett, DB (UPI)
   Larry Gagner, Guard (NBC, FB News)
1966—Steve Spurrier, QB (AP, UPI, FWAA-Look, NEA, Coaches, Spt. News, FB News, Time, CP, NBC, NY News)
   Bill Carr, Center (Time, FB News)
1968—Guy Dennis, Guard (UPI, NY News, Camp)
   Larry Smith, FB (Spt. News, FB News)
1969—Carlos Alvarez, End/Flanker (UPI, NEA, Coaches, FB News, NY News, Camp)
   Steve Tannen, Sideback (FB News, Time)
1970—Jack Youngblood, End (CP, FWAA-Look, Spt. News, FB News, Time)
1971—John Reaves, QB (Time)
1974—Ralph Ortega, LB (Time, Spt. News)
   Burton Lawless, Guard (NEA)
1975—Sammy Green, LB (AP, NEA, FWAA)
1976—Wes Chandler, SE (NEA, FB News)
1977—Wes Chandler, WR (UPI, NEA, Spt. News, FB News)
1980—David Little, LB (AP, FWAA, FB News)
   Cris Collinsworth, WR (NEA)
1982—Wilber Marshall, LB (AP, FWAA)
1983—Wilber Marshall, LB (Camp, UPI, Coaches, FB News)
1984—Lomas Brown, OT (AP, Coaches, FWAA-Look, Camp, Spt. News)
   Alonzo Johnson, LB (Spt. News)
1985—Alonzo Johnson, LB (FB News, Scripps-Howard, College & Pro Weekly)
   Jeff Zimmerman, OG (FB News, Camp, Spt. News)
1986—Jarvis Williams, DB (FB News)
   Jeff Zimmerman, OG (Camp)
1987—Jarvis Williams, DB (Camp, College & Pro Weekly)
   Louis Oliver, DB (Spt. News)
   Clifford Charlton, OLB (Spt. News)
1988—Trace Armstrong, DT (Spt. News)
   Louis Oliver, DB (AP, Coaches, Camp, Scripps-Howard, College & Pro Weekly)
1989—Emmitt Smith, RB (AP, UPI, Coaches, Camp, FWAA, FB News, Scripps-Howard, Spt. News)
1990—Huey Richardson, LB (AP, FB News)
   Will White, DB (FWAA)
1991—Brad Culpepper, DT (AP, FB News, Coaches, Scripps Howard)
1993—Judd Davis, PK (UPI)
   Errict Rhett, RB (FB News)

GEORGIA

1913—Bob McWhorter, HB (Parke Davis, NY Herald)
1923—Joe Bennett, Tackle (NEA, Billy Evans)
1927—I.M. (Chick) Shiver, End (AP, Rice)
   Tom A. Nash, End (AAB)
1930—Herb Maffett, End (NY Post)
   Ralph (Red) Maddox, Guard (NS)
1931—Vernon (Catfish) Smith, End (AP, Rice)
1937—William Hartman, Jr., AA Board of FB)
1941—Frank Sinkwich, HB (AP, UP, CP, AAB, Colliers, Look, Liberty, Esquire, Post, Time, Spt. News)
1942—Frank Sinkwich, HB (AP, UP, INS, NEA, CP, Colliers, Look, Liberty, Esquire, Post, Time, Spt. News)
   George Poschner, End (Look)
1945—Mike Castronis, Tackle (NS)
1946—Charley Trippi, TB (AP, UP, INS, NEA, Colliers, Life, Look, Post)
   Herb St. John, Guard (NCAA Guide)
1947—Dan Edwards, End, (Coaches)
1948—John Rauch, QB (Rice, AAB)
1953—Johnny Carson, End (FWAA, Paramont News)
1959—Pat Dye, Guard (FB News)
1960—Pat Dye, Guard (FB News)
1964—Jim Wilson, Tackle (AP, NEA, FWAA-Look)
   Ray Rissmiller, Tackle (Time, Spt. News)
1965—George Patton, Tackle (AP, FWAA-Look, FB News)
1966—George Patton, Tackle (AP, CP, NY News, FB News)
   Edgar Chandler, Guard (NEA)
1967—Edgar Chandler, Guard (AP, UPI, NEA, CP, FWAA-Look, Coaches, Camp, Time, Spt. News, FB News, NY News)
1968—Bill Stanfill, Tackle (AP, UPI, CP, FWAA-Look, Coaches, Spt. News, FB News, NY News, Camp, Time)
   Jake Scott, Safety (AP, UPI, NEA, FWAA-Look, Coaches, FB News, NY News, Camp)
1969—Steve Greer, Guard (FB News, Sports Extra)
   Tommy Lyons, Center (Sports Extra)
1970—Tommy Lyons, Center (Sports Extra)
1971—Royce Smith, Guard (AP, UPI, NEA, CP, FWAA, Coaches, Camp, Spt. News, FB News, Time)
1974—Craig Hertwig, Guard (AP)
1975—Randy Johnson, Guard (AP, UPI, Coaches, Camp)
1976—Joel Parrish, Guard (UPI, FWAA, Coaches, Camp, FB News)
   Mike Wilson, Tackle (AP, NEA)
1977—George Collins, Guard (Spt. News)
1980—Herschel Walker, RB (AP, UPI, NEA, FWAA, Coaches, Camp, Spt. News)
   Rex Robinson, PK (UPI, NEA, FWAA, Camp, FB News)
   Scott Woerner, DB (UPI, Coaches, Camp, FB News)
1981—Herschel Walker, RB (AP, UPI, NEA, FWAA, Coaches, Camp, Spt. News, FB News)
1982—Herschel Walker, RB (AP, UPI, Coaches, FB News, FWAA, Camp)
   Terry Hoage, R (AP, UPI, Coaches, Camp)
   Jimmy Payne, T (Camp)

Garrison Hearst
Georgia

256 Honors

1983—Terry Hoage, R (Camp, Coaches, FB News, FWAA, Spt. News, UPI)
Kevin Butler, PK (FB News)
Freddie Gilbert, DT (UPI)
1984—Kevin Butler, PK (UPI, FWAA-Look, FB News, Coaches, Camp)
Jeff Sanchez, S (UPI, Coaches, FB News)
1985—John Little, R (FB News)
Peter Anderson, C (Coaches, AP, UPI, Spt. News, College & Pro Weekly)
1986—John Little, R (FB News, Camp, College & Pro Weekly)
Wilbur Stozier, T (FB News)
1988—Troy Sadowski, TE (Camp)
Todd Wheeler, C (College & Pro Weekly)
Tim Worley, RB (Coaches, FWAA, Camp, Scripps-Howard, Gannett News)
1992—Garrison Hearst, RB (AP, UPI, Kodak, Camp, FB News, FWAA, Spt News)
1993—Bernard Williams, OT (FB News)

KENTUCKY

1942—Clyde Johnson, Tackle (AP)
1949—Bob Gain, Tackle (All-Players, NY Sun, NEA)
1950—Bob Gain, Tackle (AP, UPI, INS, NEA, CP, FWAA-Look, AAB, NY News, FD, Par. News)
Vito (Babe) Parilli, QB (AP, INS, Colliers, NY News, Spt. News, Par. News, AAB)
1951—Vito (Babe) Parilli, QB (UP, INS, NEA, CP, AAB, NY News, All-Players, Par. News, Grid. News, QB, Farley, Husing)
Doug Moseley, Center (AP, FWAA-Look)
1952—Steve Meilinger, End (AP, NEA, All-Players)
1953—Steve Meilinger, End (NEA, Colliers, AAB, Williamson)

Steve Meilinger
Kentucky

1955—Howard Schnellenberger, End (AP)
1956—Lou Michaels, Tackle (UP, NA, Colliers, NY News)
1957—Lou Michaels, Tackle (AP, NEA, FWAA-Look, Coaches, Hearst, CP, NY News, Spt. News)
1961—Irv Goode, Center (Time)
1963—Hershel Turner, Tackle (Time)
1965—Sam Ball, Tackle (UPI, NEA, FWAA-Look, Coaches, Time, Spt. News)
Rodger Bird, HB (Time, NBC)
Rick Norton, QB (Time, NBC)
1974—Elmore Stephens, TE (Time)
Rick Nuzum, Center (NEA)
1976—Warren Bryant, Tackle (Coaches Camp)
1977—Art Still, End, (AP, UPI, NEA, Coaches, FWAA, Camp, Spt. News, FB News)
1989—Mike Pfeifer, OT (FB News)

LSU

1935—Gaynell Tinsley, End (AP)
1936—Gaynell Tinsley, End (AP)
1939—Ken Kavanaugh, End (AP)
1951—George Tarasovic, Center (NEA)
1954—Sid Fournet, Tackle (Look, FWAA, NEA, UPI, AP, Williamson, INS)
1957—Jimmy Taylor, FB (FWAA-Look)
1958—Max Fugler, Center (FWAA-Look, NBC)
Billy Cannon, HB (AP, UPI, NEA, CP, Coaches, Spt. News, NY News, FWAA-Look, Time, NBC, Leahy)
1959—Billy Cannon, HB (AP, UPI, NEA CP, Coaches, FWAA-Look, Spt. News, NY News, NBC, Hearst)
1961—Roy Winston, Guard (AP, UPI, NEA, CP, FWAA-Look, Coaches, NY News, Spt. News, Time)
1962—Jerry Stovall, HB (AP, UPI, NEA, CP, FWAA-Look, Coaches, NY News, Spt. News, Time, CBS)
Fred Miller, Tackle (FWAA-Look)
1963—Billy Truax, End (FB News)
1964—Remi Prudhomme, Tackle (NEA, NY News, FB News)
1965—George Rice, Tackle (Time, Spt. News)
Doug Moreau, End (FB News)
1967—John Garlington, End (Coaches)
1969—George Bevan, LB (FWAA-Look, Coaches)
Tommy Casanova, DB (FB News)
1970—Mike Anderson, LB (AP, UPI, CP, FWAA-Look, Coaches, FB News, Time)
Tommy Casanova, DB (AP, Coaches)
1971—Tommy Cassanova, DB (UPI, CP, FWAA, Camp, FB News, Time)
Ronnie Estay, Tackle (Coaches)
1972—Bert Jones, QB (UPI, NEA, Coaches, Time, Spt. News)
Warren Capone, LB (FWAA)
1973—Tyler Lafauci, Guard (AP, NEA, Camp)
Warren Capone, LB (FWAA, Coaches)
1974—Mike Williams, DB (Coaches, Spt. News, Time)
1977—Charles Alexander, RB (UPI, Coaches, FWAA, Camp)

Nacho Albergamo
LSU

1978—Charles Alexander, RB (Coaches, FWAA, Camp, Spt. News, NEA)
Robert Dugas, OT (FB News)
1982—James Britt, DB (NEA)
Al Richardson, LB (FB News)
1983—Eric Martin, SE (Spt. News)
1984—Lance Smith, OT (UPI, Coaches, FB News)
1985—Michael Brooks, LB (AP, Scripps-Howard, College & Pro Weekly)
1986—Wendell Davis, SE (Spt. News, College & Pro Weekly, FWAA)
1987—Wendell Davis, WR (Coaches, FWAA, Scripps-Howard, FB News, UPI, College & Pro Weekly)
Nacho Albergamo, C (Coaches, Camp, AP, UPI, College & Pro Weekly)
1988—Greg Jackson, DB (Gannett News)

1994 SEC Football 257

SEC All-Americas

Charley Conerly
Ole Miss

OLE MISS

1936—Frank (Bruiser) Kinard, Tackle (NS, AAB)
1937—Frank (Bruiser) Kinard, Tackle (UP, INS, NEA, NY News, Par. News, Fox-Movietone)
1938—Parker Hall, HB (AP, UP, NY Sun, (Brooklyn Eagle, Williamson)
1947—Charley Conerly, TB (UP, INS, NEA, FWAA-Look, All-Players, PIC, Houlgate, Williamson)
Barney Poole, End (UP, Coaches, AAB, PIC, QB, NY News, Par. News, Houlgate, Williamson)
1948—Barney Poole, End (AP, INS, All-Players, Houlgate, Williamson, Fraley, Bill Stern)
1952—Kline Gilbert, Tackle (AP, FWAA-Look, FB Digest)
Jimmy Lear, QB (Red Grange)
1953—Crawford Mims, Guard, (AP, UP, NEA, FWAA-Look, Colliers, NBC, FD, Spt. News, Williamson)
1954—Rex Boggan, Tackle (AP)
1956—Paige Cothren, FB (College Editors)
1957—Jackie Simpson, Guard (Coaches, FWAA-Look)
1959—Charles Flowers, FB (AP, UPI, NEA, CP, FWAA-Look, Coaches, NBC, Spt. News, NY News)
Marvin Terrell, Guard (FWAA-Look)
1960—Jake Gibbs, QB (AP, UPI, NEA, CP, FWAA-Look, Coaches, NY News, Spt. News, NBC)
1961—Billy Ray Adams, FB (FWAA-Look)
Jim Dunaway, Tackle (FB News)
Treva Bolin, Guard (Time)
Doug Elmore, QB (CP)
1962—Jim Dunaway, Tackle (NEA, UPI, NY News, Time, CBS, Spt. News, FB News)
Glynn Griffing, QB (FWAA-Look)

1963—Kenny Dill, Center (FWAA-Look, FB News)
1964—Allen Brown, End (AP, Time, Spt. News)
Stan Hindman, Guard (Time, NBC, Spt. News, FB News)
Billy Clay, DB (Spt. News)
1967—Jim Urbanek, Tackle (FB News)
1969—Archie Manning, QB (FB News)
Glenn Cannon, Safety (Coaches, Spt. News, Time)
1970—Archie Manning, QB (FB News)
1973—Harry Harrison, DB (NEA)
1979—Jim Miller, Punter (UPI, NEA, FWAA, Camp, Spt. News)
1984—Freddie Joe Nunn, DE (UPI, FB News)
1985—Bill Smith, P (FB News, FWAA, College & Pro Weekly)
1986—Bill Smith, P (FB News, Camp, College & Pro Weekly)
1988—Wesley Walls, TE (AP)
1992—Everett Lindsay, OT (AP, FWAA)

MISSISSIPPI STATE

1940—Erwin (Buddy) Elrod, End (NCAA Guide)
1951—Joe Fortunato, FB (Athletic Pub.)
1953—Jackie Parker, QB (FWAA-Look)
1954—Hal Easterwood, Center (FWAA-Look)
1955—Scott Suber, Guard (NEA)
Art Davis, HB (FWAA-Look)
1967—D.D. Lewis, LB (NEA, NY News)
1972—Frank Dowsing, DB (FB News)
1974—Jimmy Webb, DE (Coaches, Camp)
1976—Stan Black, Safety (NEA)
1980—Mardye McDole, WR (Spt. News)
1981—Johnnie Cooks, LB (AP, NEA, FWAA, Spt. News, FB News)
Glen Collins, DT (Spt. News)
1982—Wayne Harris, OG (Spt. News, Mizlou)

Jackie Parker
Mississippi State

Del Wilkes
South Carolina

SOUTH CAROLINA

1954—Frank Mincevich, G (FWAA)
1969—Warren Muir, FB (Coaches)
1970—Dick Harris, DB (Coaches, FB News)
1972—John LeHeup, DT (Coaches)
1978—Rick Sanford, DB (Spt. News)
1979—George Rogers, RB (AP)
1980—George Rogers, RB (AP, UPI, Coaches, FB News, Spt. News, Camp, FWAA)
1982—Andrew Provence, DT (Spt. News)
1984—Del Wilkes, OG (AP, Camp, Coaches)
James Seawright, LB (AP, FWAA)
1986—Sterling Sharpe, WB (FWAA, Spt. News)

258 Honors

**Reggie White
Tennessee**

TENNESSEE

1929—Gene McEver, HB (UP, NEA)
1930—Bobby Dodd, QB (NEA, Rice)
1931—Herman Hickman, Guard (Rice)
1933—Beattie Feathers, HB (AP, UP, Rice)
1938—Bowden Wyatt, End (UP, INS, Rice)
Bob Suffridge, Guard (UP)
1939—George Cafego, HB (INS)
Bob Suffridge, Guard (UP, INS)
Ed Molinski, Guard (Rice)
Abe Shires, Tackle (INS)
1940—Bob Suffridge, Guard (AP, UP, INS, Rice)
Bob Foxx, HB (INS)
1944—Bob Dobelstein, Guard (NY Sun)
1946—Dick Huffman, Tackle (AP, Rice)
1950—Ted Daffer, Guard (Colliers)
Bud Sherrod, End (NEA)
1951—Hank Lauricella, HB (AP, UP, NEA, INS, CP, FWAA-Look, Colliers, AAB, NY News, All-Players, QB, Par. News, Fraley, Husing)
Ted Daffer, Guard (INS, NEA, NY News)
Bill Pearman, Tackle (AP, NEA, FWAA-Look, NY News)
1952—Doug Atkins, Tackle (INS, AAB, NY News)
John Michels, Guard (AP, UP, NEA, FWAA-Look, AAB, QB, NY News, All-Players)
1954—Darris McCord, Tackle (FWAA-Look)
1956—Johnny Majors, HB (AP, UP, INS, NEA, FWAA-Look, Colliers, Hearst, Spt. News, NY News, NBC, Leahy)
Kyle (Buddy) Cruze, End (FWAA-Look)
1957—Bill Johnson, Guard (NEA, FWAA-Look)
1963—Steve DeLong, Guard (FWAA-Look, FB News)
1964—Steve DeLong, Guard (AP, NEA, FWAA-Look, NY News, NBC, Time, Spt. News, FB News)
1965—Frank Emanuel, LB (AP, NEA, FWAA-Look, Time, Spt. News, FB News)
1966—Paul Naumoff, LB (AP, UPI, FWAA-Look, Coaches, FB News)
Austin Denney, End (NEA)
Ron Widby, Punter (Spt. News)
Bob Johnson, Center (FB News)
1967—Bob Johnson, Center (AP, UPI, NEA, FWAA-Look, Coaches, Time, Spt. News, NY News)
Al Dorsey, DB1 (UPI, NY News, FB News)
Richmond Flowers, WB (FB News)
1968—Charley Rosenfelder, Guard (AP, UPI, NEA, CP, FWAA-Look, Coaches, NY News, Camp)
Steve Kiner, LB (AP, CP, FWAA-Look, FB News)
Jim Weatherford, DB (Coaches)
1969—Chip Kell, Guard (AP, UPI, CP, FWAA-Look, Coaches, FB News, NY News, Camp)
Steve Kiner, LB (AP, UPI, NEA, CP, FWAA-Look, Coaches, FB News, NY News, Spt. News, Camp, Time)
Jack Reynolds, LB (FB News)
1970—Chip Kell, Guard (AP, UPI, NEA, CP, FWAA-Look, Coaches, FB News)
Jackie Walker, LB (NEA, FB News)
1971—Bobby Majors, DB (AP, UPI, NEA, CP, FWAA, Time, Coaches, Camp, Spt. News, FB News)
Jackie Walker, LB (UPI, CP, FWAA, Camp, FB News)
1972—Jamie Rotella, LB (UPI, Coaches, FB News)
Conrad Graham, DB (UPI, FB News)
Ricky Townsend, PK (FWAA)
1973—Eddie Brown, DB (FB News)
Ricky Townsend, PK (FWAA)
1975—Larry Seivers, End (AP, FWAA, FB News)
1976—Larry Seivers, End (AP, UPI, NEA, Coaches, Camp, Spt. News, FB Today)
1979—Roland James, DB (UPI, NEA, Coaches, FWAA, Camp, Spt. News, FB News)
1982—Willie Gault, WR (NEA, FWAA)
1983—Reggie White, DT (Camp, Coaches, FB News, FWAA, AP, UPI, Spt. News)
Jimmy Colquitt, P (Camp)
1984—Bill Mayo, OG (UPI, FB News, Camp)
1985—Tim McGee, WR (AP, UPI, Coaches, College & Pro Weekly)
Chris White, S (Scripps-Howard)
1987—Harry Galbreath, OG (Spt. News)
1988—Keith Delong, LB (AP, UPI, Spt. News, Gannett News)
1989—Eric Still, OG (AP, UPI, Coaches, Camp, FWAA, Scripps-Howard, Spt. News)
1990—Antone Davis, OT (AP, Camp, Coaches, FB News, FWAA, Scripps Howard)
1991—Dale Carter, DB (AP, Camp, FB News, FWAA, Scripps Howard)
Carl Pickens, WR (Coaches, FB News, Scripps Howard)
1993—John Becksvoort, PK (FWAA, Scripps Howard)

VANDERBILT

1911—Ray Morrison, QB (NY World)
1923—Lynn Bomar, End (Camp, Frank Menke)
1924—H.C. (Hek) Wakefield, End (NS, Lawrence Perry, Billy Evans)
1927—Bill Spears, QB (AP, NEA)
1928—Dick Abernathy, End (CP)
1929—John "Bull" Brown, Guard (Coaches)
1932—Pete Gracey, Center (UP)
1937—Carl Hinkle, Center (AP, Rice, Liberty)
1941—Bob Gude, Center, (Paramount News)
1950—Bucky Curtis, End (INS, FWAA-Look)
1958—George Deiderich, Guard (AP, FWAA-Look, Coaches)
1968—Chip Healy, LB (CP)
1969—Bob Asher, Tackle (NEA, CP)
1972—Ken Stone, DB (Gridiron)
1974—Barry Burton, TE (FB News)
1982—Jim Arnold, P (AP, UPI, FWAA, Coaches, FB News)
Allama Matthews, TE (FB News)
1983—Chuck Scott, TE (Spt. News)
1984—Ricky Anderson, P (AP, UPI, Coaches Football Writers, FB News, Camp)
1987—Chris Gaines, LB (Coaches)

**Ricky Anderson
Vanderbilt**

1994 SEC Football 259

SEC Academic All-Americas
First-Team Selections

1954— Harold Easterwood, C, Miss. State
1955— George Walker, QB, Arkansas
1956— Charles Rader, T, Tennessee
1957— Jerry Ford, C, Arkansas
Gerald Nesbitt, FB, Arkansas
Jim Phillips, E, Auburn
Bill Johnson, G, Tennessee
1959— Wayne Harris, C, Arkansas
Jackie Burkett, C, Auburn
Mickey Mangham, E, LSU
Charles Flowers, FB, Ole Miss
Robert Khayat, G, Ole Miss
1960— Joe Paul Alberty, FB, Arkansas
Ed Dyas, B, Auburn
Fran Tarkenton, B, Georgia
Charles Strange, C, LSU
1961— Tommy Brooker, E, Alabama
Pat Trammell, B, Alabama
Lance Alworth, HB, Arkansas
Billy Joe Booth, T, LSU
Doug Elmore, QB, Ole Miss
1964— Gaylon McCollough, C, Alabama
Ken Hatfield, HB, Arkansas
1965— Dennis Homan, SE, Alabama
Steve Sloan, QB, Alabama
Jack Brasuell, HB, Arkansas
Jim Lindsey, WB, Arkansas
Randy Stewart, C, Arkansas
Bill Cody, LB, Auburn
Charles Casey, E, Florida
Bob Etter, PK, Georgia
Stan Hindman, G, Ole Miss
Mark Gentry, T, Tennessee
1966— Bob Etter, PK, Georgia
Lynn Hughes, DB, Georgia
Mac Haik, SE, Ole Miss

1967— Bob Childs, LB, Alabama
Steve Davis, PK, Alabama
Donnie Sutton, FL, Alabama
Bob Johnson, C, Tennessee
1968— Bob White, PK, Arkansas
Bill Stanfill, DE, Georgia
Steve Hindman, TB, Ole Miss
Jim Burns, DB, Vanderbilt
1969— Bill Burnett, TB, Arkansas
Terry Stewart, DB, Arkansas
Buddy McClinton, DB, Auburn
Carlos Alvarez, SE, Florida
Julian Fagan, P, Ole Miss
1970— Johnny Musso, TB, Alabama
Tim Priest, DB, Tennessee
1971— Johnny Musso, TB, Alabama
Carlos Alvarez, SE, Florida
Tom Nash, T, Georgia
Mixon Robinson, DE, Georgia
Jay Michaelson, PK, LSU
1972— Frank Dowsing, B, Miss. State
1973— Randy Hall, DT, Alabama
Tyler Lafauci, OG, LSU
Joe Winkler, DB, LSU
Jimmy Webb, DT, Miss. State
1974— Randy Hall, DT, Alabama
Bobby Davis, LB, Auburn
Tom Ranieri, G, Kentucky
Brad Davis, RB, LSU
Greg Markow, DE, Ole Miss
Doug Martin, WR, Vanderbilt
1975— Danny Ridgeway, PK, Alabama
Chuck Fletcher, T, Auburn
Damon Regen, LB, Vanderbilt
1976— Chris Vacarella, WB, Auburn
David Posey, PK, Florida

Will Coltharp, DE, Miss. State
1977— Wes Chandler, WR, Florida
Jeff Lewis, LB, Georgia
Robert Dugas, T, LSU
Robert Fabris, SE, Ole Miss
George Plasketes, DE, Ole Miss
Greg Martin, PK, Vanderbilt
1978— Mark Keen, C, Kentucky
Jim Kovach, LB, Kentucky
1979— Major Ogilvie, RB, Alabama
Brad Shoup, DB, Arkansas
1980— Cris Collinsworth, WR, Florida
Ken Toler, WR, Ole Miss
Tim Irwin, OT, Tennessee
1982— Terry Hoage, DB, Georgia
Mike Terry, DE, Tennessee
1983— Terry Hoage, DB, Georgia
Phil Roach, WR, Vanderbilt
1984— Gregg Carr, LB, Auburn
Juan Carlos Betanzos, PK, LSU
1985— Ken Pietrowiak, C, Kentucky
Danny Hoskins, OG, Ole Miss
Jeff Noblin, DB, Ole Miss
1986— Nacho Albergamo, C, LSU
Danny Hoskins, OG, Ole Miss
Jeff Noblin, DB, Ole Miss
1987— Danny Hoskins, OG, Ole Miss
Mark Fryer, OT, South Carolina
1988— Wesley Walls, TE, Ole Miss
Mark Fryer, OT, South Carolina
1989— Todd Sandroni, DB, Ole Miss
Bo Russell, DB, Miss. State
1991— Brad Culpepper, DT, Florida
Joe Reaves, LB, South Carolina
1992— Todd Peterson, PK, Georgia
1993— Michael Gilmore, DB, Florida

Harold Easterwood
Mississippi State

Carlos Alvarez
Florida

Todd Sandroni
Ole Miss

National Football Foundation Scholar-Athlete Awards

For the college senior in NCAA District III who is outstanding in football ability and performance, in academic application and achievement, and in campus leadership and example.

Year	Name	Pos.	School	Major
1959	Neyle Sollee	FB	Tennessee	Engineering
1960	Ed Dyas	FB	Auburn	pre-Medicine
1961	Wade Butcher	E	Vanderbilt	Electrical Engineering
1965	John Cochran	LB	Auburn	Space Engineering
1966	Bobby Etter	PK	Georgia	Mathematics
	Stanley Juk	DB	South Carolina	Chemistry
1967	Tommy Lawhorne	LB	Georgia	Medicine
	Bob Johnson	C	Tennessee	Engineering
1968	Billy Payne	E	Georgia	Political Science
	Steve Hindman	TB	Ole Miss	Medicine
1969	Tim Callaway	MG	Georgia	Business
	Terry Stewart	S	Arkansas	Chemical Engineering
1970	Tommy Lyons	C	Georgia	Psychology
	Don Denbo	G	Tennessee	Medicine
1971	Tom Nash	T	Georgia	Mathematics
	Johnny Musso	HB	Alabama	pre-Law
1972	Frank Dowsing	DB	Miss. State	pre-Medicine
1973	Norris Weese	QB	Ole Miss	Accounting
1974	William R. Cregar	FB	South Carolina	Biology
	Randy Hall	DT	Alabama	pre-Medicine
	Doug Martin	WR	Vanderbilt	Physics/Economics
1975	Dick Lawrence	OT	Ole Miss	Business
1976	John R. Busby	S	Arkansas	pre-Medicine
	Darrell Carpenter	DT	Florida	Business
	Mike Mauck	DB	Tennessee	pre-Dental
1977	Jeff Lewis	LB	Georgia	pre-Law
1978	William Bradford Shoup	DB	Arkansas	pre-Medicine
	Robert Dugas	OT	LSU	pre-Medicine
	Jim Kovach	LB	Kentucky	Medicine
1979	Steadman Shealy	QB	Alabama	Physical Education
	Leon Shadowen	OG	Kentucky	Accounting/pre-Law
1982	Gordon Beckham	QB	South Carolina	English
	James Britt	CB	LSU	Accounting
1983	Terry Hoage	DB	Georgia	Genetics
1984	Gregg Carr	LB	Auburn	Engineering
	Gary Rolle	WR	Florida	Zoology
1985	Kent Austin	QB	Ole Miss	pre-Law
1986	Jeff Noblin	S	Ole Miss	pre-Medicine
1987	Nacho Albergamo	C	LSU	pre-Medicine
	Danny Hoskins	OG	Ole Miss	Engineering
1988	Wesley Walls	TE	Ole Miss	Engineering
1989	Andy McCarroll	LB	Vanderbilt	English
	Bo Russell	DB	Miss. State	General Business
1990	Sol Graves	QB	LSU	Zoology/pre-Medicine
1991	Brad Culpepper	DT	Florida	History

CFA Academic Achievement Award Winners

The College Football Association Academic Achievement Award is presented annually by the Touchdown Club of Memphis, Tenn., to the school with the highest graduation rate among members of its football team.

Kentucky captured the SEC's first award in 1989 by graduating 90 percent of its incoming class of 1983. UK reported that 18 of 20 football players who began classes in 1983 completed degree requirements.

Half of the league's member institutions have earned honorable mention distinction since 1987, including Florida, Kentucky, Ole Miss, Mississippi State, Tennessee and Vanderbilt. In 1994 Kentucky, Mississippi State and Vanderbilt received honorable mention status for registering graduation reports of 70 percent or higher.

According to CFA survey results, the overall graduation rate of its member schools has shown a significant increase in the last several years. In 1986 the CFA membership graduated 41.6 percent of its football players, compared to a rate of 57.9 percent in 1994.

A complete listing of Academic Achievement winners follows:

Year	School	Honorable Mention (SEC Only)
1981	Duke	
1982	Notre Dame	
1983	Notre Dame	
1984	Notre Dame Duke	
1985	Virginia	
1986	Virginia	
1987	Duke	Vanderbilt
1988	Notre Dame	Kentucky, Vanderbilt
1989	**Kentucky**	Tennessee, Vanderbilt
1990	Duke	Vanderbilt
1991	Notre Dame	Kentucky, Tennessee, Vanderbilt
1992	Boston College Texas Christian	Florida, Miss. State, Vanderbilt
1993	Duke	Kentucky, Ole Miss, Miss. State, Tennessee
1994	Duke	Kentucky, Miss. State, Vanderbilt

CFA Honorees

1991 Scholar-Athlete Team

Offense
OL-Cal Dixon, Florida
OL-Greg Lahr, Kentucky

Defense
DL-Brad Culpepper, Florida
DL-Scott Wharton, LSU
LB-Daniel Boyd, Miss. State

1992 Scholar-Athlete Team

Offense
OL-Alec Millen, Georgia
PK-Doug Pelfrey, Kentucky

Defense
DL-Owen Kelly, Arkansas
LB-Daniel Boyd, Miss. State
LB-Dean Wells, Kentucky

1993 Scholar-Athlete Team

Offense
OL-Chris Oliver, Arkansas
QB-Eric Zeier, Georgia

Defense
LB-Marty Moore, Kentucky
DB-Michael Gilmore, Florida

1993 Goodworks Team

DL-Travis Jones, Georgia
DL-Kevin Carter, Florida

Note: The teams were selected by a College Football Association panel, which included faculty, athletic administrators, football coaches, academic advisors and sports information directors. Criteria for selection include: cumlative GPA between 3.0 and 4.0; junior athletic standing; completion of 50 percent of degree requirement; one full year completed at nominating institution and starter or meaningful reserve.

Nashville Banner Awards
SEC Most Valuable Player

1933—HB Beattie Feathers, Tennessee
1934—TB Dixie Howell, Alabama
1935—E Willie Geny, Vanderbilt
1936—C Walter Gilbert, Auburn
1937—C Carl Hinkle, Vanderbilt
1938—HB George Cafego, Tennessee
1939—E Ken Kavanaugh, LSU
1939—WB Bob Foxx, Tennessee
1940—E Erwin Elrod, Miss. State
1941—FB Jack Jenkins, Vanderbilt
1942—TB Frank Sinkwich, Georgia
1943—No Selection Made
1944—HB Tom McWilliams, Miss. State
1945—TB Harry Gilmer, Alabama
1946—HB Charley Trippi, Georgia
1947—TB Charley Conerly, Ole Miss
1948—QB John Rauch, Georgia
1949—QB Travis Tidwell, Auburn
1950—QB Babe Parilli, Kentucky
1951—QB Bill Wade, Vanderbilt
1952—QB Jackie Parker, Miss. State
1953—QB Jackie Parker, Miss. State
1954—HB Art Davis, Miss. State
1955—TB John Majors, Tennessee
1956—TB John Majors, Tennessee
1957—T Lou Michaels, Kentucky
1958—HB Billy Cannon, LSU
1959—HB Billy Cannon, LSU
1960—QB Jake Gibbs, Ole Miss
1961—QB Pat Trammell, Alabama
1962—HB Jerry Stovall, LSU
1963—QB Jimmy Sidle, Auburn
1964—FB Tucker Frederickson, Auburn
1965—QB Steve Sloan, Alabama
1966—QB Steve Spurrier, Florida
1967—E Bob Goodridge, Vanderbilt
1968—S Jake Scott, Georgia
1969—QB Archie Manning, Ole Miss
1970—QB Pat Sullivan, Auburn
1971—TB Johnny Musso, Alabama
1972—QB Terry Davis, Alabama
1973—TB Sonny Collins, Kentucky
1974—QB Rockey Felker, Miss. State
1975—FB Jimmy DuBose, Florida
1976—QB Ray Goff, Georgia
1977—TB Charles Alexander, LSU
1978—TB Willie McClendon, Georgia
1979—RB Joe Cribbs, Auburn
1980—RB Herschel Walker, Georgia
1981—RB Herschel Walker, Georgia
1982—RB Herschel Walker, Georgia
1983—DT Reggie White, Tennessee
1984—QB Kerwin Bell, Florida
1985—RB Bo Jackson, Auburn
1986—LB Cornelius Bennett, Alabama
1987—WR Wendell Davis, LSU
1988—DT Tracy Rocker, Auburn
1989—RB Emmitt Smith, Florida
1990—QB Shane Matthews, Florida
1991—QB Shane Matthews, Florida
1992—RB Garrison Hearst, Georgia
1993—QB Heath Shuler, Tennessee

Birmingham Quarterback Club Awards
SEC Most Valuable Players

1942—H-Ray (Monk) Gafford, Auburn
1948—L-Billy Healy, Ga. Tech; B-John Rauch, Georgia
1949—L-Bob Gain, Kentucky; B-Travis Tidwell, Auburn
1950—L-Ted Daffer, Tennessee; B-Babe Parilli, Kentucky
1951—L-Ray Beck, Ga. Tech; B-Hank Lauricella, Tennessee
1952—L-George Morris, Ga. Tech; B-Bobby Marlow, Alabama
1953—L-Harold Easterwood, Miss. State; B-Jackie Parker, Miss. State
1954—L-Sid Fournet, LSU; B-Joe Childress, Auburn
1955—L-Scott Suber, Miss. State; B-Charlie Horton, Vanderbilt
1956—L-Lou Michaels, Kentucky; B-Johnny Majors, Tennessee
1957—L-Jimmy Phillips, Auburn; B-Jimmy Taylor, LSU
1958—L-Zeke Smith, Auburn; B-Billy Cannon, LSU
1959—L-Marvin Terrell, Ole Miss; B-Tom Moore, Vanderbilt
1960—L-Billy Shaw, Ga. Tech; B-Ed Dyas, Auburn
1961—L-Billy Neighbors, Alabama; B-Pat Trammell, Alabama
1962—L-Lee Roy Jordan, Alabama; B-Jerry Stovall, LSU
1963—L-Whaley Hall, Ole Miss; B-Jimmy Sidle, Auburn
1964—L-Steve DeLong, Tennessee; B-Tucker Frederickson, Auburn
1965—L-Paul Crane, Alabama; B-Steve Sloan, Alabama
1966—L-Ray Perkins, Alabama; B-Steve Spurrier, Florida
1967—L-Bob Johnson, Tennessee; B-Ken Stabler, Alabama
1968—L-Bill Stanfill, Georgia; B-Jake Scott, Georgia
1969—L-Mike Kolen, Auburn; B-Archie Manning, Ole Miss
1970—L-Chip Kell, Tennessee; B-Pat Sullivan, Auburn
1971—L-Terry Beasley, Auburn; B-Pat Sullivan, Auburn, and Johnny Musso, Alabama
1972—L-John Hannah, Alabama; B-Terry Davis, Alabama
1973—L-Buddy Brown, Alabama; B-Wilbur Jackson, Alabama
1974—L-Leroy Cook, Alabama; B-Mike Fuller, Auburn
1975—L-Randy Johnson, Georgia; B-Richard Todd, Alabama
1976—L-Joel Parrish, Georgia; B-Terry Robiskie, LSU
1977—L-Ozzie Newsome, Alabama; B-Derrick Ramsey, Kentucky
1978—L-Marty Lyons, Alabama; B-Joe Cribbs, Auburn
1979—L-Dwight Stephenson, Alabama; B-Joe Cribbs, Auburn
1980—L-E. J. Junior, Alabama; B-Herschel Walker, Georgia
1981—L-Johnie Cooks, Miss. State; B-Buck Belue, Georgia
1982—L-Willie Gault, Tennessee; B-Herschel Walker, Georgia
1983—L-Reggie White, Tennessee; B-Randy Campbell, Auburn
1984—L-Gregg Carr, Auburn; B-Paul Ott Carruth, Alabama
1985—L-Jon Hand, Alabama; B-Bo Jackson, Auburn
1986—L-Cornelius Bennett, Alabama; B-Brent Fullwood, Auburn
1987—L-Curt Crain, Auburn; B-Eric Jones, Vanderbilt
1988—L-Tracy Rocker, Auburn; B-David Smith, Alabama
1989—L-Eric Still, Tennessee; B-Gary Hollingsworth, Alabama
1990—L-Antone Davis, Tennessee; B-Philip Doyle (PK), Alabama
1991—L-Brad Culpepper, Florida; B-Corey Harris, Vanderbilt
1992—L-John Copeland, Alabama; B-Shane Matthews, Florida
1993—L-Tobie Sheils, Alabama; B-Stan White, Auburn

Birmingham Touchdown Club Awards
Most Valuable Senior

1976—DE Art Still, Kentucky
1977—TB Willie McClendon, Georgia
1978—QB Jeff Rutledge, Alabama
1979—QB Steadman Shealy, Alabama
1980—DB Scott Woerner, Georgia
1981—LB Johnie Cooks, Miss. State
1982—QB Whit Taylor, Vanderbilt
1983—QB Walter Lewis, Alabama and DT Reggie White, Tennessee
1984—PK Kevin Butler, Georgia
1985—RB Bo Jackson, Auburn
1986—LB Cornelius Bennett, Alabama
1987—WR Wendell Davis, LSU
1988—DT Tracy Rocker, Auburn and LB Derrick Thomas, Alabama
1989—QB Reggie Slack, Auburn
1990—RB Tony Thompson, Tennessee and PK Philip Doyle, Alabama
1991—QB Andy Kelly, Tennessee
1992—DE John Copeland, Alabama
1993—QB Stan White, Auburn

Honors

Jacobs Award
Outstanding SEC Blocker

1935— Riley Smith, Alabama
1936— Billy May, LSU
1937— Leroy Monsky, Alabama
1938— Sam Bartholomew, Tennessee
1939— Sam Bartholomew, Tennessee
1940— Lloyd Cheatham, Auburn
1941— Jack Jenkins, Vanderbilt
1942— Jack Jenkins, Vanderbilt
1943— John Steber, Ga. Tech
1944— Billy Bevis, Tennessee
1945— Billy Bevis, Tennessee
1946— Hal Self, Alabama
1947— Buddy Bowen, Ole Miss
1948— Truitt Smith, Miss. State
1949— Butch Avinger, Alabama
1950— Butch Avinger, Alabama
1951— Jimmy Hahn, Tennessee
1952— John Michels, Tennessee
1953— Crawford Mims, Ole Miss
1954— Charles Evans, Miss. State
1955— Paige Cothren, Ole Miss
1956— Stockton Adkins, Tennessee
1957— Stockton Adkins, Tennessee
1958— J. W. Brodnax, LSU
1959— Jim Cartwright, Tennessee
1960— Jim Cartwright, Tennessee
1961— Billy Neighbors, Alabama
1962— Butch Wilson, Alabama
1963— Tucker Frederickson, Auburn
1964— Tucker Frederickson, Auburn
1965— Hal Wantland, Tennessee
1966— Cecil Dowdy, Alabama
1967— Bob Johnson, Tennessee
1968— Brad Johnson, Georgia
1969— Chip Kell, Tennessee
1970— Chip Kell, Tennessee
1971— Royce Smith, Georgia
1972— John Hannah, Alabama
1973— Buddy Brown, Alabama
1974— Sylvester Croom, Alabama
1975— Randy Johnson, Georgia
1976— Warren Bryant, Kentucky
1977— Bob Cryder, Alabama
1978— Robert Dugas, LSU
1979— Dwight Stephenson, Alabama
1980— Nat Hudson, Georgia
1981— Wayne Harris, Miss. State
1982— Wayne Harris, Miss. State
1983— Guy McIntyre, Georgia
1984— Lomas Brown, Florida
1985— Peter Anderson, Georgia
1986— Wes Neighbors, Alabama
1987— Harry Galbreath, Tennessee
1988— Howard Cross, Alabama
1989— Eric Still, Tennessee
1990— Antone Davis, Tennessee
1991— Cal Dixon, Florida
1992— Everett Lindsay, Ole Miss
1993— Tobie Sheils, Alabama

Originated by Dr. W. P. Jacobs of Clinton, S.C., selected by poll of SEC coaches.

Atlanta Touchdown Club Awards

SEC Player of the Year

1939— HB Howard Ector, Ga. Tech
1940— G Bob Suffridge, Tennessee
1941— TB Frank Sinkwich, Georgia
1942— HB Monk Gafford, Auburn
1943— HB Eddie Prokop, Ga.Tech
1944— QB Frank Broyles, Ga.Tech

SEC Back of the Year

1945— QB Harry Gilmer, Alabama
1946— HB Charley Trippi, Georgia
1947— TB Charley Conerly, Ole Miss
1948— QB John Rauch, Georgia
1949— QB Travis Tidwell, Auburn
1950— QB Babe Parilli, Kentucky
1951— QB Bill Wade, Vanderbilt
1952— QB Zeke Bratkowski, Georgia
1953— QB Jackie Parker, Miss. State
1954— QB Bobby Freeman, Auburn
1955— HB Fob James, Jr., Auburn
1956— TB Johnny Majors, Tennessee
1957— FB Jimmy Taylor, LSU
1958— HB Billy Cannon, LSU
1959— QB Francis Tarkenton, Georgia
1960— QB Jake Gibbs, Ole Miss
1961— QB Pat Trammell, Alabama
1962— QB Glynn Griffing, Ole Miss
1962— HB Jerry Stovall, LSU
1963— QB Billy Lothridge, Ga. Tech

Southeast Area Back

1964— FB Tucker Frederickson, Auburn
1965— QB Steve Sloan, Alabama
1966— FLK Ray Perkins, Alabama
1967— QB Ken Stabler, Alabama
1968— FLK Ron Sellers, Florida State
1969— QB Archie Manning, Ole Miss
1970— QB Pat Sullivan, Auburn
1971— HB Johnny Musso, Alabama
1972— HB Terry Henley, Auburn
1973— QB Gary Rutledge, Alabama
1974— QB Rockey Felker, Miss. State
1975— QB Jeff Grantz, South Carolina
1975— QB Jeff Grantz, South Carolina
1976— QB Ray Goff, Georgia
1976— QB Ray Goff, Georgia
1977— QB Steve Fuller, Clemson
1978— TB Willie McClendon, Georgia
1978— TB Eddie Lee Ivery, Ga. Tech

1979— RB Joe Cribbs, Auburn
1980— OB George Rogers, South Carolina
    DB Scott Woerner, Georgia
1981— QB Buck Belue, Georgia
    DB Jeff Davis, Clemson
1982— OB Herschel Walker, Georgia
    DB Terry Hoage, Georgia
1983— OB Bo Jackson, Auburn
    DB Terry Hoage, Georgia
1984— OB Robert Lavette, Ga. Tech
    DB Knox Culpepper, Georgia
1985— OB Bo Jackson, Auburn
    DB Ted Roof, Ga. Tech
1986— OB Brent Fullwood, Auburn
    DB John Little, Georgia
1987— OB Sterling Sharpe, South Carolina
    DB Gene Jelks, Alabama
1988— DB Andre Thomas, Ga. Tech
    OB Steve Walsh, Miami
1989— OB Rodney Hampton, Georgia
    DB John Mangum, Alabama
1990— OB Shawn Moore, Virginia
    DB Efrum Thomas, Alabama
1991— QB Shane Matthews, Florida
    DB—Dale Carter, Tennessee
1992— OB Terry Kirby, Virginia
    DB Ray Buchanan, Louisville
1993— DB Charlie Ward, Florida State
    DB Bracey Walker, North Carolina

SEC Lineman of the Year

1945— C Paul Duke, Ga. Tech
1946— C Paul Duke, Ga. Tech
1947— T Bobby Davis, Ga. Tech
1948— G Bill Healy, Ga. Tech
1949— T Bob Gain, Kentucky
1950— C Bob Bossons, Ga. Tech
1951— T Lum Snyder, Ga. Tech
1952— C George Morris, Ga. Tech
1953— E John Carson, Georgia
1954— C Larry Morris, Ga. Tech
1955— G Franklin Brooks, Ga.Tech
1956— G John Barrow, Florida
1957— T Lou Michaels, Kentucky
1958— G Zeke Smith, Auburn
1959— C Maxie Baughan, Ga.Tech
1960— G Pat Dye, Georgia
1961— G Roy Winston, LSU
1962— C Lee Roy Jordan, Alabama
1963— C Kenny Dill, Ole Miss

Southeast Area Lineman

1964— E Fred Biletnikoff, Florida State
1965— E Charlie Casey, Florida
1966— C Jim Breland, Ga. Tech
1967— T Edgar Chandler, Georgia
1968— T Bill Stanfill, Georgia
1969— G Steve Greer, Georgia
1970— T Rock Perdoni, Ga. Tech
1971— G Royce Smith, Georgia
1972— G John Hannah, Alabama
1973— G Buddy Brown, Alabama
1974— T Craig Hertwig, Georgia
1975— G Randy Johnson, Georgia
1975— E Leroy Cook, Alabama
1976— G Joel Parrish, Georgia
1976— T Mike Wilson, Georgia
1977— E Ozzie Newsome, Alabama
1978— LB Barry Krauss, Alabama
1979— DT Jim Stucky, Clemson
1980— OL Nat Hudson, Georgia
    DL E.J. Junior, Alabama
1981— OL Lee North, Tenneseee
    DL Johnie Cooks, Miss. State
1982— OL Allama Matthews, Vanderbilt
    DL Ramsey Dardar, LSU
1983— OL Phillip Ebinger, Duke
    DL Reggie White, Tennessee
1984— OL Bill Mayo, Tennessee
    DL Gregg Carr, Auburn
1985— OL Peter Anderson, Georgia
    DL Jon Hand, Alabama
1986— OL John Davis, Ga. Tech
    DL Dale Jones, Tennessee
1987— OL Stacy Searels, Auburn
    DL Paul McGowan, Florida State
1988— DL Tracy Rocker, Auburn
    OL Todd Wheeler, Georgia
1989— OL Michael Tanks, Florida State
    DL Greg Mark, Miami
1990— OL Stacy Long, Clemson
    DL Huey Richardson, Florida
1991— OL Jeb Fletch, Clemson
    DL Marco Coleman, Georgia Tech
1992— OL Tom Scott, East Carolina
    DL Eric Curry, Alabama
1993— OL Wayne Gandy, Auburn
    LB Mitch Davis, Georgia

1994 SEC Football   263

Associated Press All-SEC Teams

1933
First Team
E— Graham Batchelor, Ga.
T— Jack Torrance, LSU
G— LeRoy Moorehead, Ga.
C— Sheriff Maples, Tenn.
G— Tom Hupke, Ala.
T— Bob Tharpe, Ga. Tech
E— Gump Ariail, Aub.
B— Ripper Williams, Aub.
B— Beattie Feathers, Tenn.
B— Dixie Howell, Ala.
B— Ralph Kercheval, Ky.

Second Team
E— Jimmy Slocum, Ga. Tech
T— Bill Lee, Ala.
G— J.B. Ellis, Tenn.
C— Homer Robinson, Tul.
G— Boots Chambless, Aub.
T— Hal Starbuck, Fla.
E— Joe Rupert, Ky.
B— Rand Dixon, Vandy
B— Floyd Roberts, Tul.
B— Cy Grant, Ga.
B— Jack Phillips, Ga. Tech

Third Team
E— Don Hutson, Ala.
T— Clyde Williams, Ga. Tech
G— Sam Brown, Vandy
C— Welcome Shearer, Fla.
G— Dave Wilcox, Ga. Tech
T— Jesse Flowers, Miss.
E— Bart Herrington, Miss.
B— Casey Kimbrell, Aub.
B— Homer Key, Ga.
B— R.H. Herrington, MSU
B— George Chapman, Ga.

1934
First Team
E— Don Hutson, Ala.
T— Justin Rukas, LSU
G— Murray Warmath, Tenn.
C— Homer Robinson, Tul.
G— Charlie Marr, Ala.
T— Bill Lee, Ala.
E— Bennie Fenton, Aub.
B— Dixie Howell, Ala.
B— Bert Johnson, Ky.
B— Abe Mickal, LSU
B— Claude Simons, Tul.

Second Team
E— Paul Bryant, Ala.
T— C.W. Williams, Ga. Tech
G— John Brown, Ga.
C— John McKnight, Ga.
G— George Tessier, Tul.
T— Howard Bailey, Tenn.
E— Gene Rose, Tenn.
B— Rand Dixon, Vandy
B— Charlie Vaughan, Tenn.
B— Julius Brown, Fla.
B— Joe Demyanovich, Ala.

Third Team
E— Joe Rupert, Ky.
T— William Stark, Fla.
G— Buck Brown, LSU
C— Walter Gilbert, Aub.
G— Mike Welch, Aub.
T— Rannie Throgmorton, Vandy
E— Willie Geny, Vandy
B— Riley Smith, Ala.
B— Jess Fatherree, LSU
B— Shorty Roberts, Ga. Tech
B— George Chapman, Ga.

1935
First Team
E— Gaynell Tinsley, LSU
T— Haygood Paterson, Aub.
G— Frank Johnson, Ga.
C— Walter Gilbert, Aub.
G— J.M. Fitzsimmons, Ga. Tech
T— James Whatley, Ala.
E— Willie Geny, Vandy
B— Riley Smith, Ala.
B— Ike Pickle, MSU
B— Jess Fatherree, LSU
B— Bill Crass, LSU

Second Team
E— Gene Rose, Tenn.
T— Sterling Richardson, Miss.
G— Sam Brown, Vandy
C— Kavanaugh Francis, Ala.
G— Frank Gantt, Aub.
T— Justin Rukas, LSU
E— Chuck Gelatka, MSU
B— Rand Dixon, Vandy
B— Bob Davis, Ky.
B— Rab Rodgers, Miss.
B— Abe Mickal, LSU

Third Team
E— Paul Bryant, Ala.
T— Stanley Nevers, Ky.
G— Willie Stone, MSU
C— Marvin Stewart, LSU
G— Arthur White, Ala.
T— Rannie Throgmorton, Vandy
E— Warren Barrett, LSU
B— Barney Mintz, Tul.
B— Ray Hapes, Miss.
B— Billy Chase, Fla.
B— Dutch Konemann, Ga. Tech

1936
First Team
E— Gaynell Tinsley, LSU
T— Frank Kinard, Miss.
G— Arthur White, Ala.
C— Walter Gilbert, Aub.
G— Wardell Leisk, LSU
T— Rupert Colmore, Sew.
E— Joel Eaves, Aub.
B— Joe Riley, Ala.
B— Phil Dickens, Tenn.
B— Howard Bryan, Tul.
B— Dutch Konemann, Ga. Tech

Second Team
E— Perron Shoemaker, Ala.
T— William Moss, Tul.
G— Dewitt Weaver, Tenn.
C— Marvin Stewart, LSU
G— J.M. Fitzsimmons, Ga. Tech
T— Stanley Nevers, Ky.
E— Otis Maffett, Ga.
B— Walter Mayberry, Fla.
B— Joe Kilgrow, Ala.
B— Clarence Hapes, Miss.
B— Pat Coffee, LSU

Third Team
E— Chuck Gelatka, MSU
T— Paul Carroll, LSU
G— Frank Gantt, Aub.
C— Carl Hinkle, Vandy
G— Pete Tinsley, Ga.
T— Alex Lott, MSU
E— Dick Plasman, Vandy
B— Billy May, LSU
B— Bill Crass, LSU
B— Bob Davis, Ky.
B— Wilton Kilgore, Aub.

1937
First Team
E— Bill Jordan, Ga. Tech
T— Frank Kinard, Miss.
G— Leroy Monsky, Ala.
C— Carl Hinkle, Vandy
G— Ralph Sivell, Aub.
T— Eddie Gatto, LSU
E— Erwin Warren, Ala.
B— Fletcher Simms, Ga. Tech
B— Joe Kilgrow, Ala.
B— Walter Mayberry, Fla.
B— Bill Hartman, Ga.

Second Team
E— Ralph Wenzel, Tul.
T— Torrance Russell, Aub.
G— Ed Merlin, Vandy
C— Quinton Lumpkin, Ga.
G— Ed Sydnor, Ky.
T— Buford Ray, Vandy
E— Perron Shoemaker, Ala.
B— George Cafego, Tenn.
B— Pinky Rohm, LSU
B— Bob Davis, Ky.
B— Charles Holm, Ala.

Third Team
E— Bowden Wyatt, Tenn.
T— Ben Friend, LSU
G— Norman Hall, Tul.
C— Jack Chivington, Ga. Tech
G— Pete Tinsley, Ga.
T— Jim Ryba, Ala.
E— Ken Kavanaugh, LSU
B— Lunsford Hollins, Vandy
B— Jim Fenton, Aub.
B— Dutch Konemann, Ga. Tech
B— Guy Milner, LSU

1938
First Team
E— Bowden Wyatt, Tenn.
T— Eddie Gatto, LSU
G— Jimmy Brooks, Ga. Tech
C— Quinton Lumpkin, Ga.
G— Bob Suffridge, Tenn.
T— Torrance Russell, Aub.
E— Ken Kavanaugh, LSU
B— George Cafego, Tenn.
B— Parker Hall, Miss.
B— Warren Brunner, Tul.
B— Charles Holm, Ala.

Second Team
E— Ralph Wenzel, Tul.
T— Maurice Holdgraf, Vandy
G— John Goree, LSU
C— Jack Chivington, Ga. Tech
G— Milton Howell, Aub.
T— Ray Miller, Tul.
E— Marvin Franklin, Vandy
B— Vic Bradford, Ala.
B— Spec Kelly, Aub.
B— Dave Zoeller, Ky.
B— Lee Coffman, Tenn.

Third Team
E— Perron Shoemaker, Ala.
T— Malcolm Gray, MSU
G— Ed Molinski, Tenn.
C— Sherman Hinkebein, Ky.
G— Frank Koesis, Fla.
T— Walter Merrill, Ala.
E— Bill McCubbin, Ky.
B— Kimble Bradley, Miss.
B— Babe Wood, Tenn.
B— Jim Fordham, Ga.
B— Bert Marshall, Vandy

1939
First Team
E— Bob Ison, Ga. Tech
T— Harley McCollum, Tul.
G— Ed Molinski, Tenn.
C— James Rike, Tenn.
G— John Goree, LSU
T— Marshall Shires, Tenn.
E— Ken Kavanaugh, LSU
B— George Cafego, Tenn.
B— Bob Foxx, Tenn.
B— Bob Kellogg, Tul.
B— Bill Schneller, Miss.

Second Team
E— Ralph Wenzel, Tul.
T— John Eibner, Ky.
G— Bob Suffridge, Tenn.
C— John Goolsby, MSU
G— Milton Howell, Aub.
T— Fred Davis, Ala.
E— Erwin Ford, MSU
B— Sam Bartholomew, Tenn.
B— John Hovious, Miss.
B— Dick McGowen, Aub.
B— Howard Ector, Ga. Tech

Third Team
E— Harold Newman, Ala.
T— Clark Goff, Fla.
G— Tom O'Boyle, Tul.
C— Winkey Autrey, Miss.
G— Neil Cavette, Ga. Tech
T— Walter Merrill, Ala.
E— Bill McCubbin, Ky.
B— Buck Murphy, Ga. Tech
B— Junius Plunkett, Vandy
B— Jack Nix, MSU
B— Fred Gloden, Tul.

1940
First Team
E— Erwin Elrod, MSU
T— Marshall Shires, Tenn.
G— Bob Shuffridge, Tenn.
C— Bob Gude, Vandy
G— Hunter Corhern, MSU
T— Fred Davis, Ala.
E— Holt Rast, Ala.
B— Bob Foxx, Tenn.
B— John Hovious, Miss.
B— Jimmy Nelson, Ala.
B— Dick McGowen, Aub.

Second Team
E— Edward Cifers, Tenn.
T— Charles Dufour, Tul.
G— Ed Molinski, Tenn.
C— Bert Ackermann, Tenn.
G— Ed Hickerson, Ala.
T— John Tripson, MSU
E— Bob Ison, Ga. Tech
B— Harvey Johnson, MSU
B— John Butler, Tenn.
B— Jim Thibaut, Tul.
B— Merle Hapes, Miss.

Third Team
E— Forrest Ferguson, Fla.
T— John Eibner, Ky.
G— Julius Battista, Fla.
C— Warren Averitte, Ala.
G— John Goree, LSU
T— John Barrett, LSU
E— Harold Newman, Ala.
B— Charles Ishmael, Ky.
B— Johnny Bosch, Ga. Tech
B— Rufus Deal, Aub.
B— Billy Jefferson, MSU

1941
First Team
E— Holt Rast, Ala.
T— Ernest Blandin, Tul.
G— John Wyhonic, Ala.
C— Bob Gude, Vandy
G— Homer Hazel, Miss.
T— Don Edmiston, Tenn.
E— Bill Eubanks, Miss.
B— Jack Jenkins, Vandy
B— Frank Sinkwich, Ga.
B— Jimmy Nelson, Ala.
B— Merle Hapes, Miss.

Second Team
E— Forrest Ferguson, Fla.
T— Bill Arnold, MSU
G— Jack Tittle, Tul.
C— Bernie Lipkis, LSU
G— Oscar Britt, Miss.
T— Charles Sanders, Ga. Tech
E— George Webb, Ga. Tech
B— Lloyd Cheatham, Aub.
B— John Hovious, Miss.
B— Blondy Black, MSU
B— Walt McDonald, Tul.

Third Team
E— Bill Hornick, Tul.
T— Milton Hull, Fla.
G— Walter Ruark, Ga.
C— Ray Graves, Tenn.
G— George Hecht, Ala.
T— Chet Kozel, Miss.
E— George Poschner, Ga.
B— Cliff Kimsey, Ga.
B— Tom Harrison, Fla.
B— Bob Glass, Tul.
B— Noah Mullins, Ky.

1942
First Team
E— George Poschner, Ga.
T— Clyde Johnson, Ky.
G— Harvey Hardy, Ga. Tech
C— Joe Domnanovich, Ala.
G— Walter Ruark, Ga.
T— Don Whitmire, Ala.
E— Albert Hust, Tenn.
B— Jack Jenkins, Vandy
B— Monk Gafford, Aub.
B— Clint Castleberry, Ga. Tech
B— Frank Sinkwich, Ga.

Second Team
E— Martin Comer, Tul.
T— Mitchell Olenski, Ala.
G— Raymond Ray, MSU
C— George Manning, Ga. Tech
G— George Hecht, Ala.
T— Denver Crawford, Tenn.
E— Bob Patterson, MSU
B— Walt McDonald, Tul.
B— Blondy Black, MSU
B— Russ Craft, Ala.
B— Bob Cifers, Tenn.

Third Team
E— Sam Sharpe, Ala.
T— Gene Ellenson, Ga.
G— Oscar Britt, Miss.
C— Jim Talley, LSU
G— Curtis Patterson, MSU
T— Dick Huffman, Tenn.
E— Jack Marshall, Ga. Tech
B— Lou Thomas, Tul.
B— Alvin Dark, LSU
B— Lamar Davis, Ga.
B— Bernie Rohling, Vandy

1943
First Team
E— Phil Tinsley, Ga. Tech
T— Joe Hartley, LSU
G— John Steber, Ga. Tech
C— Buddy Gatewood, Tul.
G— Gatson Bourgeois, Tul.
T— Bill Chambers, Ga. Tech
E— Ray Olsen, Tul.
B— Joe Renfroe, Tul.
B— Eddie Prokop, Ga. Tech
B— Johnny Cook, Ga.
B— Steve Van Buren, LSU

Second Team
E— Charles Webb, LSU
T— Fred Roseman, Tul.
G— Carl Janneck, LSU
C— George Manning, Ga. Tech
G— Frank Beall, Ga. Tech
T— George Jones, Tul.
E— Walt Kilzer, Ga. Tech
B— Leonard Finley, Tul.
B— Harry Robinson, Vandy
B— Charlie Smith, Ga.
B— Mickey Logan, Ga. Tech

Third Team
E— Jim Wilson, Ga. Tech
T— W.N. Smith, Ga. Tech
G— Mike Castronis, Ga.
C— Ed Clauch, LSU
G— Charley Hoover, Ga. Tech
T— Ralph Hunt, LSU
E— Ken Tarzetti, Tul.
B— Bobby Hague, Ga.
B— William Jones, Tul.
B— Joe Nagata, LSU
B— Frank Broyles, Ga. Tech
(Only Four Teams Played Due to the War)

1944
First Team
E— Phil Tinsley, Ga. Tech
T— Hillery Horne, MSU
G— Herb St. John, Ga.
C— Tex Warrington, Aub.
G— Bob Dobelstein, Tenn.
T— Wash Serini, Ky.
E— Ray Olsen, Tul.
B— Buster Stephens, Tenn.
B— Tom McWilliams, MSU
B— William Jones, Tul.
B— Frank Broyles, Ga. Tech

Second Team
E— Ralph Jones, Ala.
T— Andy Perhach, Ga.
G— Maurice Furchgott, Ga. Tech
C— Vaughn Mancha, Ala.
G— Gaston Bourgeois, Tul.
T— Dub Garrett, MSU
E— Reid Moseley, Ga.
B— Harry Gilmer, Ala.
B— Allen Bowen, Ga. Tech
B— Bill Bevis, Tenn.
B— Curtis Kuykendall, Aub.

Third Team
E— Bill Hildebrand, MSU
T— Tom Whitley, Ala.
G— Roland Phillips, Ga. Tech
C— Russ Morrow, Tenn.
G— Gerald Bertucci, LSU
T— Mike Castronis, Ga.
E— Bob McCain, Miss.
B— Norman Klein, Ky.
B— Bobby Forbes, Fla.
B— George Mathews, Ga. Tech
B— Gene Knight, LSU

1945
First Team
E— Rebel Steiner, Ala.
T— Tom Whitley, Ala.
G— Bob Dobelstein, Tenn.
C— Vaughn Mancha, Ala.
G— Felix Trapani, LSU
T— Bobby Davis, Ga. Tech
E— Bill Hidebrand, MSU
B— Harry Gilmer, Ala.
B— Harper Davis, MSU
B— Charley Trippi, Ga.
B— Gene Knight, LSU

Second Team
E— Reid Mosely, Ga.
T— Wash Serini, Ky.
G— Jack Green, Ala.
C— Paul Duke, Ga. Tech
G— Gaston Bourgeois, Tul.
T— Mike Castronis, Ga.
E— Clyde Lindsey, LSU
B— Curtis Kuykendall, Aub.
B— Buster Stephens, Tenn.
B— George Mathews, Ga. Tech
B— Lowell Tew, Ala.

Third Team
E— Buddy Pike, Tenn.
T— Jack White, Fla.
G— George Hills, Ga. Tech
C— Hugh Bowers, Tul.
G— Herb St. John, Ga.
T— Dub Garrett, MSU
E— Walt Kilzer, Ga. Tech
B— Bill Bevis, Tenn.
B— Jim Cason, LSU
B— Bill Fuqua, Vandy
B— Graham Bramlett, MSU

1946
First Team
E— Wallace Jones, Ky.
T— Bobby Davis, Ga. Tech
G— Herb St. John, Ga.
C— Paul Duke, Ga. Tech
G— Wren Worley, LSU
T— Dick Huffman, Tenn.
E— Ray Poole, Miss.
B— Charley Trippi, Ga.
B— Harry Gilmer, Ala.
B— Frank Broyles, Ga. Tech
B— Tom McWilliams, MS

Second Team
E— Frank Hubbell, Tenn.
T— Dub Garrett, MSU
G— Bill Healy, Ga. Tech
C— Vaughn Mancha, Ala.
G— Tex Robertson, Vandy
T— Ed Champagne, LSU
E— Joe Tereshinski, Ga.
B— Charley Conerly, Miss.
B— Travis Tidwell, Aub.
B— John Rauch, Ga.
B— Y.A. Tittle, LSU

Third Team
E— Broughton Williams, Fla.
T— Alf Saterfield, Vandy
G— Gaston Bourgeois, Tul.
C— Jay Rhodemyre, Ky.
G— Mike Harris, MSU
T— Jack Bush, Ga.
E— Ted Cook, Ala.
B— Dan Sandifer, LSU
B— Pat McHugh, Ga. Tech
B— Harper Davis, MSU
B— Walter Slater, Tenn.

1947
First Team
E— Barney Poole, Miss.
T— Bobby Davis, Ga. Tech
G— John Wozniak, Ala.
C— Jay Rhodemyre, Ky.
G— Bill Healy, Ga. Tech
T— Dub Garrett, MSU
E— Dan Edwards, Ga.
B— Charles Conerly, Miss.
B— Harry Gilmer, Ala.
B— Rip Collins, Ky.
B— Tom McWilliams, MSU

Second Team
E— John North, Vandy
T— Bill Erickson, Miss.
G— Herb St. John, Ga.
C— Vaughn Mancha, Ala.
G— Tex Robertson, Vandy
T— Wash Serini, Ky.
E— Abner Wimberly, LSU
B— John Rauch, Ga.
B— Bobby Forbes, Fla.
B— Lowell Tew, Ala.
B— Y.A. Tittle, LSU

Third Team
E— Rebel Steiner, Ala.
T— Charles Compton, Ala.
G— Wren Worley, LSU
C— Louis Hook, Ga. Tech
G— Leo Yarutis, Ky.
T— Denver Crawford, Tenn.
E— George Brodnax, Ga. Tech
B— Bobby Berry, Vandy
B— Harper Davis, MSU
B— Allen Bowen, Ga. Tech
B— Eddie Price, Tul.

1948
First Team
E— Barney Poole, Miss.
T— Paul Lea, Tul.
G— Bill Healy, Ga. Tech
C— John Clark, Vandy
G— Jimmy Crawford, Miss.
T— Norman Meseroll, Tenn.
E— George Brodnax, Ga. Tech
B— John Rauch, Ga.
B— Charles Hunsinger, Fla.
B— Tom McWilliams, MSU
B— Eddie Price, Tul.

Second Team
E— Abner Wimberly, LSU
T— Porter Payne, Ga.
G— Ken Cooper, Vandy
C— Hal Herring, Aub.
G— Dennis Doyle, Tul.
T— Robert Gain, Ky.
E— Jim Powell, Tenn.
B— Farley Salmon, Miss.
B— Hal Littleford, Tenn.
B— Herb Rich, Vandy
B— Frank Ziegler, Ga. Tech

Third Team
E— Wallace Jones, Ky.
T— Dutch Cantrell, Vandy
G— Homer Hobbs, Ga.
C— Ed Clauch, LSU
G— Jim Vugrin, Ga. Tech
T— Clay Matthews, Ga. Tech
E— Dick Sheffield, Tul.
B— Harper Davis, MSU
B— Bob McCoy, Ga. Tech
B— Bill Cadenhead, Ala.
B— Joe Geri, Ga.

1994 SEC Football 265

Associated Press All-SEC Teams

1949
First Team
E— Bud Sherrod, Tenn.
T— Bob Gain, Ky.
G— Allen Hover, LSU
C— Harry Ulinski, Ky.
G— Ed Holdnak, Ala.
T— Paul Lea, Tul.
E— Sam Lyle, LSU
B— Eddie Price, Tul.
B— Travis Tidwell, Aub.
B— John Dottley, Miss.
B— Charles Hunsinger, Fla.
Second Team
E— Bob Walston, Ga.
T— Tom Coleman, Ga. Tech
G— Dennis Doyle, Tul.
C— Jerry Taylor, MSU
G— Jimmy Crawford, Miss.
T— Ray Collins, LSU
E— Jack Stribling, Miss.
B— Babe Parilli, Ky.
B— Jimmy Jordan, Ga. Tech
B— Herb Rich, Vandy
B— Zollie Toth, LSU
Third Team
E— Bucky Curtis, Vandy
T— Marion Campbell, Ga.
G— Mike Mizerany, Ala.
C— Jimmy Kynes, Fla.
G— Ted Daffer, Tenn.
T— Carl Copp, Vandy
E— Dick Harvin, Ga. Tech
B— Don Phelps, Ky.
B— Floyd Reid, Ga.
B— Butch Avinger, Ala.
B— Lee Nalley, Vandy

1950
First Team
E— Bucky Curtis, Vandy
T— Bob Gain, Ky.
G— Mike Mizerany, Ala.
C— Pat O'Sullivan, Ala.
G— Ted Daffer, Tenn.
T— Paul Lea, Tul.
E— Bud Sherrod, Tenn.
B— Babe Parilli, Ky.
B— John Dottley, Miss.
B— Ed Salem, Ala.
B— Ken Konz, LSU
Second Team
E— Al Lary, Ala.
T— Bill Pearman, Tenn.
G— Rocco Principle, Ky.
C— Doug Moseley, Ky.
G— Bill Wannamaker, Ky.
T— Russ Faulkinberry, Vandy
E— Al Bruno, Ky.
B— Haywood Sullivan, Fla.
B— Bill Wade, Vandy
B— Bill Leskovar, Ky.
B— Hank Lauricella, Tenn.
Third Team
E— John Weigle, Ga. Tech
T— Marion Campbell, Ga.
G— Tom Banks, Aub.
C— Bob Bossons, Ga. Tech
G— Pat James, Ky.
T— Charles LaPradd, Fla.
E— Bill Stribling, Miss.
B— Billy Mixon, Ga.
B— Butch Avinger, Ala.
B— Wilbur Jamerson, Ky.
B— Bobby North, Ga. Tech

1951—Offense
First Team
E— Harry Babcock, Ga.
T— Lum Snyder, Ga. Tech
G— John Michels, Tenn.
C— Doug Moseley, Ky.
G— Gene Donaldson, Ky.
T— Bob Werckle, Vandy
E— Steve Meilinger, Ky.
B— Hank Lauricella, Tenn.
B— Babe Parilli, Ky.
B— Bill Wade, Vandy
B— Darrell Crawford, Ga. Tech
Second Team
E— Buck Martin, Ga. Tech
T— Jerome Helluin, Tul.
G— Ed Bauer, Aub.
C— Carroll McDonald, Fla.
G— Sid Fournet, LSU
T— Jim MacKenzie, Ky.
E— Ben Roderick, Vandy
B— Bobby Marlow, Ala.
B— Bert Rechichar, Tenn.
B— Andy Kozar, Tenn.
B— Zeke Bratkowski, Ga.
Third Team
E— Lee Hayley, Aub.
T— Hal Miller, Ga. Tech
G— Ed Duncan, Aub.
C— Bob Davis, Tenn.
G— Jerry Watford, Ala.
T— Ray Potter, LSU
E— Warren Virgets, LSU
B— Leon Hardeman, Ga. Tech
B— Hal Payne, Tenn.
B— Haywood Sullivan, Fla.
B— Jimmy Lear, Miss.

1951—Defense
First Team
E— Doug Atkins, Tenn.
T— Lamar Wheat, Ga. Tech
G— Ted Daffer, Tenn.
C— George Tarasovic, LSU
G— Ray Beck, Ga. Tech
T— Bill Pearman, Tenn.
E— Harold Maxwell, Miss.
B— Bobby Marlow, Ala.
B— Bert Rechichar, Tenn.
B— Claude Hipps, Ga.
B— Joe Fortunato, MSU
Second Team
E— Bobby Flowers, Fla.
T— Charlie LaPradd, Fla.
G— Joe D'Agostino, Fla.
C— Ralph Carrigan, Ala.
G— Jess Richardson, Ala.
T— Billy Pyron, MSU
E— Red Lutz, Ala.
B— George Morris, Ga. Tech
B— Vince Dooley, Aub.
B— Jim Roshto, LSU
B— Gordon Polofsky, Tenn.
Third Team
E— Jesse Yates, LSU
T— Marion Campbell, Ga.
G— Art Kleinschmidt, Tul.
C— Larry Morris, Ga. Tech
G— John Cheadle, Vandy
T— Bill Turnbeugh, Aub.
E— Bob Fry, Ky.
B— Emery Clark, Ky.
B— Mickey Lakos, Vandy
B— Jim Barton, LSU
B— Bobby Wilson, Ala.

1952—Offense
First Team
E— Harry Babcock, Ga.
T— Kline Gilbert, Miss.
G— John Michels, Tenn.
C— Pete Brown, Ga. Tech
G— Jerry Watford, Ala.
T— Hal Miller, Ga. Tech
E— Steve Meilinger, Ky.
B— Jackie Parker, MSU
B— Leon Hardemann, Ga. Tech
B— Bobby Marlow, Ala.
B— Andy Kozar, Tenn.
Second Team
E— Buck Martin, Ga. Tech
T— Jim Haslam, Tenn.
G— Jake Shoemaker, Ga. Tech
C— Bo Reid, MSU
G— Al Robelot, Tul.
T— Travis Hunt, Ala.
E— Ben Roderick, Vandy
B— Zeke Bratkowski, Ga.
B— Rick Casares, Fla.
B— Corky Tharp, Ala.
B— Joe Fortunato, MSU
Third Team
E— Lee Hayley, Aub.
T— Bob Fry, Ky.
G— Jerry May, Miss.
C— Larry Stone, Vandy
G— Ed Gossage, Ga. Tech
T— Dewayne Douglas, Fla.
E— Jeff Knox, Ga. Tech
B— Jimmy Lear, Miss.
B— Buford Long, Fla.
B— Billy Teas, Ga. Tech
B— Max McGee, Tul.

1952—Defense
First Team
E— Sam Hensley, Ga. Tech
T— Charlie LaPradd, Fla.
G— Joe D'Agostino, Fla.
LB— George Morris, Ga. Tech
LB— Larry Morris, Ga. Tech
G— Francis Holohan, Tenn.
T— Doug Atkins, Tenn.
E— Mack Franklin, Tenn.
HB— Bobby Moorhead, Ga. Tech
HB— Cecil Ingram, Ala.
S— Art Decarlo, Ga.
Second Team
E— Joe O'Malley, Ga.
T— Bill Burnbeaugh, Aub.
G— Crawford Mims, Miss.
LB— Ralph Carrigan, Ala.
LB— Tommy Adkins, Ky.
G— Orville Vereen, Ga. Tech
T— Ed Culpepper, Ala.
E— Bob Hines, Vandy
HB— Charles Ware, Fla.
HB— Bobby Jordan, Aub.
S— George Brancato, LSU
Third Team
E— Jim Mask, Miss.
T— Paul Miller, LSU
G— Chris Filipkowski, Ga.
LB— Arlen Jumper, Fla.
LB— Bill Barbish, Tenn.
G— Tony Sardisco, Tul.
T— Bob Sherman, Ga. Tech
E— Roger Rotroff, Tenn.
HB— Charlie Brannon, Ga. Tech
HB— Charley Oakley, LSU
S— Don Gleisner, Vandy

1953
First Team
E— John Carson, Ga.
T— Sid Fournet, LSU
G— Crawford Mims, Miss.
C— Larry Morris, Ga. Tech
G— Ray Correll, Ky.
T— Frank D'Agostino, Aub.
E— Jim Pybrun, Aub.
B— Jackie Parker, MSU
B— Corky Tharp, Ala.
B— Steve Meilinger, Ky.
B— Glenn Turner, Ga. Tech
Second Team
E— Roger Rotroff, Tenn.
T— Bob Fisher, Tenn.
G— Joe D'Agostino, Fla.
C— Ralph Carrigan, Ala.
G— George Atkins, Aub.
T— Bob Sherman, Ga. Tech
E— Joe Tuminello, LSU
B— Zeke Bratkowski, Ga.
B— Leon Hardeman, Ga. Tech
B— Jimmy Wade, Tenn.
B— Ralph Paolone, Ky.
Third Team
E— Mack Franklin, Tenn.
T— Tom Morris, MSU
G— Al Robelot, Tul.
C— Hal Easterwood, MSU
G— Pete Williams, Vandy
T— Dan Hunter, Fla.
E— Sam Hensley, Ga. Tech
B— Bobby Freeman, Aub.
B— Bill Teas, Ga. Tech
B— Hal Lofton, Miss.
B— Jerry Marchand, LSU

1954
First Team
E— Jim Pyburn, Aub.
T— Sid Fournet, LSU
G— Bobby Goodall, Vandy
C— Hal Easterwood, MSU
G— Franklin Brooks, Ga. Tech
T— Rex Reed Boggan, Miss.
E— Henry Hair, Ga. Tech
B— Bob Hardy, Ky.
B— Arthur Davis, MSU
B— Tom Tracy, Tenn.
B— Joe Childress, Aub.
Second Team
E— Joe Tuminello, LSU
T— Darris McCord, Tenn.
G— Don Shea, Ga.
C— Larry Morris, Ga. Tech
G— Bryan Bunthorne, Tul.
T— Frank D'Agostino, Aub.
E— Joe O'Malley, Ga.
B— Eagle Day, Miss.
B— Allen Muirhead, Miss.
B— Corky Tharp, Ala.
B— Mal Hammack, Fla.
Third Team
E— Howard Schnellenberger, Ky.
T— George Mason, Ala.
G— George Atkins, Aub.
C— Steve DeLaTorre, Fla.
G— Bill Dooley, MSU
T— Pud Mosteller, Ga.
E— Ray Brown, Fla.
B— Bobby Freeman, Aub.
B— Charley Horton, Vandy
B— Jimmy Thompson, Ga. Tech
B— Bobby Garrard, Ga.

266 Honors

1955
First Team
E— Joe Tuminello, LSU
T— Frank D'Agostino, Aub.
G— Scott Suber, MSU
C— Steve DeLaTorre, Fla.
G— Franklin Brooks, Ga. Tech
T— Earl Leggett, LSU
E— Howard Schnellenberger, Ky.
B— Johnny Majors, Tenn.
B— Fob James, Aub.
B— Charley Horton, Vandy
B— Paige Cothren, Miss.

Second Team
E— Joe Stephenson, Vandy
T— M.L. Brackett, Aub.
G— Tony Sardisco, Tul.
C— Gene Dubisson, Miss.
G— Buddy Alliston, Miss.
T— Charles Rader, Tenn.
E— Jimmy Phillips, Aub.
B— Bob Hardy, Ky.
B— George Volkert, Ga. Tech
B— Art Davis, MSU
B— Joe Childress, Aub.

Third Team
E— Nick Germanos, Ala.
T— Jim Barron, MSU
G— Larry Frank, Vandy
C— Bob Scarbrough, Aub.
G— Bryan Bunthorne, Tul.
T— Lou Michaels, Ky.
E— Roy Wilkins, Ga.
B— Eagle Day, Miss.
B— Jackie Simpson, Fla.
B— Billy Kinard, Miss.
B— Ronnie Quillian, Tul.

1956
First Team
E— Buddy Cruze, Tenn.
T— Lou Michaels, Ky.
G— John Barrow, Fla.
C— Don Stephenson, Ga. Tech
G— John Gordy, Tenn.
T— Billy Yelverton, Miss.
E— Ron Bennett, MSU
B— Billy Stacy, MSU
B— Johnny Majors, Tenn.
B— Paige Cothren, Miss.
B— Ken Owen, Ga. Tech

Second Team
E— Jimmy Phillips, Aub.
T— J.T. Frankenberger, Ky.
G— Allen Ecker, Ga. Tech
C— Dave Kuhn, Ky.
G— Paul Ziegler, LSU
T— Dalton Truax, Tul.
E— Jerry Nabors, Ga. Tech
B— Gene Newton, Tul.
B— Tommy Lorino, Aub.
B— Paul Rotenberg, Ga. Tech
B— Ronny Quillian, Tul.

Third Team
E— Roger Urbano, Tenn.
T— Carl Vereen, Ga. Tech
G— Ernest Danjean, Aub.
C— Jerry Stone, Miss.
G— Charles Duck, Miss.
T— Art Demmas, Vandy
E— John Wood, LSU
B— Toppy Vann, Ga. Tech
B— Phil King, Vandy
B— Jimmy Rountree, Fla.
B— Bob Dougherty, Ky.

1957
First Team
E— Jimmy Phillips, Aub.
T— Lou Michaels, Ky.
G— Bill Johnson, Tenn.
C— Don Stephenson, Ga. Tech
G— Jackie Simpson, Miss.
T— Gene Hickerson, Miss.
E— Jerry Wilson, Aub.
B— Billy Stacy, MSU
B— Bobby Gordon, Tenn.
B— Jim Rountree, Fla.
B— Jimmy Taylor, LSU

Second Team
E— Bob Laws, Vandy
T— Charlie Mitchell, Fla.
G— Billy Rains, Ala.
C— Jackie Burkett, Aub.
G— George Deiderich, Vandy
T— Ben Preston, Aub.
E— Jerry Nabors, Ga. Tech
B— Ray Brown, Miss.
B— Phil King, Vandy
B— Bobby Cravens, Ky.
B— Billy Atkins, Aub.

Third Team
E— Don Fleming, Fla.
T— Nat Dye, Ga.
G— Zeke Smith, Aub.
C— Jack Benson, MSU
G— Cicero Lucas, Ga.
T— Sam Latham, MSU
E— John Benge, MSU
B— Boyce Smith, Vandy
B— Tommy Lorino, Aub.
B— Billy Lott, Miss.
B— Theron Sapp, Ga.

1958
First Team
E— Jerry Wilson, Aub.
T— Don Fleming, Fla.
G— Vel Heckman, Fla.
C— Cleve Wester, Aub.
G— Zeke Smith, Aub.
T— George Deiderich, Vandy
E— Jackie Burkett, Aub.
B— Waren Rabb, LSU
B— Billy Cannon, LSU
B— John Robinson, LSU
B— Charlie Flowers, Miss.

Second Team
E— Larry Grantham, Miss.
T— Billy Hendrix, LSU
G— Nat Dye, Ga.
C— Charles Strange, LSU
G— Don Cochran, Ala.
T— Jack Benson, MSU
E— Max Fugler, LSU
B— Richie Petibon, Tul.
B— Tom Moore, Vandy
B— Bobby Cravens, Ky.
B— Theron Sapp, Ga.

Third Team
E— Dave Hudson, Fla.
T— Gerald Burch, Ga. Tech
G— Dave Sington, Ala.
C— Bob Lindon, Ky.
G— Bobby Urbano, Tenn.
T— Larry Kahlden, LSU
E— Max Baughan, Ga. Tech
B— Billy Stacy, MSU
B— Tommy Lorino, Aub.
B— Floyd Faucette, Ga. Tech
B— J.W. Brodnax, LSU

1959
First Team
E— Larry Grantham, Miss.
T— Jimmy Vickers, Ga.
G— Ken Rice, Aub.
C— Joe Schaffer, Tenn.
G— Marvin Terrell, Miss.
T— Zeke Smith, Aub.
E— Maxie Baughan, Ga. Tech
B— Francis Tarkenton, Ga.
B— Billy Cannon, LSU
B— Tom Moore, Vandy
B— Charles Flowers, Miss.

Second Team
E— John Brewer, Miss.
T— Mickey Mangham, LSU
G— Larry Wagner, Vandy
C— Toby Deese, Ga. Tech
G— Don Cochran, Ala.
T— Pat Dye, Ga.
E— Tom Goode, MSU
B— Jake Gibbs, Miss.
B— Calvin Bird, Ky.
B— Bobby Walden, Ga.
B— Ed Dyas, Aub.

Third Team
E— Dave Hudson, Fla.
T— LaVelle White, MSU
G— Lynn LeBlanc, LSU
C— Danny Royal, Fla.
G— Billy Roland, Ga.
T— Bob Talamini, Ky.
E— Jackie Burkett, Aub.
B— Bobby Hunt, Aub.
B— Johnny Robinson, LSU
B— Lamar Rawson, Aub.
B— Taz Anderson, Ga. Tech

1960
First Team
E— Johnny Brewer, Miss.
T— Tom Hutchinson, Ky.
G— Ken Rice, Aub.
C— Billy Shaw, Ga. Tech
G— Vic Miranda, Fla.
T— Richard Price, Miss.
E— Tom Goode, MSU
B— Jake Gibbs, Miss.
B— Tom Mason, Tul.
B— Francis Tarkenton, Ga.
B— Ed Dyas, Aub.

Second Team
E— Pat Patchen, Fla.
T— Gerald Burch, Ga. Tech
G— Billy Wilson, Aub.
C— Bob Benton, Miss.
G— Pat Dye, Ga.
T— Roy Winston, LSU
E— Charles Strange, LSU
B— Larry Libertore, Fla.
B— Fred Brown, Ga.
B— Billy Williamson, Ga. Tech
B— James Anderson, Miss.

Third Team
E— Ralph Smith, Miss.
T— Mike Lasorsa, Tenn.
G— Pete Case, Ga.
C— Jim Beaver, Fla.
G— Billy Neighbors, Ala.
T— Lloyd Hodge, Ky.
E— Mike Lucci, Tenn.
B— Phil Nugent, Tul.
B— Jim Cartwright, Tenn.
B— Leon Fuller, Ala.
B— Don Goodman, Fla.

1961
First Team
E— Tom Hutchinson, Ky.
T— Dave Edwards, Aub.
G— Billy Neighbors, Ala.
C— Jim Dunaway, Miss.
G— Roy Winston, LSU
T— Dave Watson, Ga. Tech
E— Mike Lucci, Tenn.
B— Pat Trammell, Ala.
B— Billy Ray Adams, Miss.
B— Wendell Harris, LSU
B— Mike Fracchia, Ala.

Second Team
E— Ralph Smith, Miss.
T— Johnny Baker, MSU
G— Billy Booth, LSU
C— Pete Case, Ga.
G— Harold Ericksen, Ga. Tech
T— Rodney Guillot, LSU
E— Lee Roy Jordan, Ala.
B— Doug Elmore, Miss.
B— Jerry Stovall, LSU
B— Mallon Faircloth, Tenn.
B— Bill McKenny, Ga.

Third Team
E— Gene Sykes, LSU
T— Tommy Brooker, Ala.
G— Jim Beaver, Fla.
C— Ernie Colquett, Tul.
G— Billy Ray Jones, Miss.
T— Howard Benton, MSU
E— Wayne Frazier, Aub.
B— Hank Lesesne, Vandy
B— Billy Williamson, Ga. Tech
B— Don Goodman, Fla.
B— Earl Gros, LSU

1962
First Team
E— Tom Hutchinson, Ky.
T— Johnny Baker, MSU
G— Fred Miller, LSU
C— Junior Hawthorne, Ky.
G— Rufus Guthrie, Ga. Tech
T— Don Dickson, Miss.
E— Lee Roy Jordan, Ala.
B— Jerry Stovall, LSU
B— Glynn Griffing, Miss.
B— Billy Lotridge, Ga. Tech
B— Larry Dupree, Fla.

Second Team
E— Billy Martin, Ga. Tech
T— Clem Dellenger, Tul.
G— Jim Dunaway, Miss.
C— Frank Lasky, Fla.
G— Robbie Hucklebridge, LSU
T— Steve DeLong, Tenn.
E— Dennis Gaubatz, LSU
B— Larry Rakestraw, Ga.
B— Joe Namath, Ala.
B— Cotton Clark, Ala.
B— Darrell Cox, Ky.

Third Team
E— Richard Williamson, Ala.
T— Sam Holland, Fla.
G— Larry Stallings, Ga. Tech
C— Ernie Colquette, Tul.
G— Larry Travis, Fla.
T— Dave Watson, Ga. Tech
E— Jim Price, Aub.
B— Lindy Infante, Fla.
B— Mike McNames, Ga. Tech
B— Chuck Morris, Miss.
B— Louis Guy, Miss.

1994 SEC Football

Associated Press All-SEC Teams

1963

First Team
- E— Billy Martin, Ga. Tech
- E— Allen Brown, Miss.
- T— Whaley Hall, Miss.
- T— Tommy Nevile, MSU
- G— Steve DeLong, Tenn.
- G— Rob Hucklebridge, LSU
- C— Kenny Dill, Miss.
- B— Billy Lothridge, Ga. Tech
- B— Jimmy Sidle, Aub.
- B— Benny Nelson, Ala.
- B— Larry Dupree, Fla.

Second Team
- E— Billy Traux, LSU
- E— Howard Simpson, Aub.
- T— Ray Rissmiller, Ga.
- T— Dennis Murphy, Fla.
- G— Stan Hindman, Miss.
- G— Pat Watson, MSU
- C— Dave Simmons, Ga. Tech
- B— Larry Rakestraw, Ga.
- B— Ode Burrell, MSU
- B— Tucker Frederickson, Aub.
- B— Perry Lee Dunn, Miss.

Third Team
- E— Pat Hodgson, Ga.
- E— Clem Dellenger, Tul.
- T— Mike Calamari, Tul.
- T— Ralph Pere, LSU
- G— Al Lewis, Ala.
- G— Bill Van Dyke, Aub.
- C— Bill Cody, Aub.
- B— Joe Namath, Ala.
- B— Larry Rawson, Aub.
- B— Don Schwab, LSU
- B— Hoyle Granger, MSU

NOTE: The Associated Press began naming first and second teams for both offense and defense in 1964.

1964
OFFENSE

First Team
- E— Doug Moreau, LSU
- E— Charley Casey, Fla.
- T— Jim Wilson, Ga.
- T— George Rice, LSU
- G— Wayne Freeman, Ala.
- G— Larry Gagner, Fla.
- C— Richard Granier, LSU
- QB—Joe Namath, Ala.
- H— Roger Bird, Ky.
- H— Mike Dennis, Miss.
- F— Steve Bowman, Ala.

Second Team
- E— Tommy Inman, MSU
- E— Tommy Tolleson, Ala.
- T— Ray Rissmiller, Ga.
- T— Gary Hart, Vandy
- G— Stan Hindman, Miss.
- G— Justin Canale, MSU
- C— Gaylon McCollough, Ala.
- QB—Jim Weatherly, Miss.
- H— Larry Dupree, Fla.
- H— Marcus Rhoden, MSU
- F— Hoyle Granger, MSU

DEFENSE

First Team
- E— Rick Kestner, Ky.
- E— Allen Brown, Miss.
- T— Jack Thornton, Aub.
- T— Dan Kearley, Ala.
- G— Steve DeLong, Tenn.
- G— Bill Richburg, Fla.
- LB—Mike Vincent, LSU
- LB—Bill Cody, Aub.
- DB—Tucker Frederickson, Aub.
- DB—Bruce Bennett, Fla.
- DB—Wayne Swinford, Ga.

Second Team
- E— Lynn Matthews, Fla.
- E— Barry Wilson, Ga.
- T— George Patton, Ga.
- T— Tommy Neville, MSU
- G— Leon Verriere, Tul.
- G— Pat Watson, MSU
- LB—Frank Emanuel, Tenn.
- LB—Paul Crane, Ala.
- DB—Allen Trammell, Fla.
- DB—Dave Malone, Vandy
- DB—Steve Sloan, Ala.

1965
OFFENSE

First Team
- E— Tommy Tolleson, Ala.
- E— Charles Casey, Fla.
- T— Sam Ball, Ky.
- T— Dave McCormick, LSU
- G— Stan Hindman, Miss.
- G— Larry Beckman, Fla.
- C— Paul Crane, Ala.
- QB—Steve Spurrier, Fla.
- B— Steve Bowman, Ala.
- B— Roger Bird, Ky.
- B— Mike Dennis, Miss.

Second Team
- E— Barry Brown, Fla.
- E— Pat Hodgson, Ga.
- T— Jim Harvey, Miss.
- T— Andy Gross, Aub.
- G— Doug Davis, Ky.
- G— Bobby Gratz, Tenn.
- C— Forrest Blue, Aub.
- QB—Steve Sloan, Ala.
- B— Hoyle Granger, MSU
- B— Larry Seiple, Ky.
- B— Joe Labruzzo, LSU

DEFENSE

First Team
- E— Creed Gilmer, Ala.
- E— Bobby Frazier, Tenn.
- T— Jack Thornton, Aub.
- T— Jim Urbanek, Miss.
- G— George Patton, Ga.
- LB—Frank Emanuel, Tenn.
- LB—Bill Goss, Tul.
- LB—Bill Cody, Aub.
- B— Bobby Johns, Ala.
- B— Bruce Bennett, Fla.
- B— Lynn Hughes, Ga.

Second Team
- E— Lynn Mathews, Fla.
- E— Lane Wolbe, Vandy
- T— George Rice, LSU
- T— Dick Lemay, Vandy
- G— Grady Bolton, MSU
- LB—Tom Fisher, Tenn.
- LB—Mike McGraw, Ky.
- LB—Tim Bates, Ala.
- B— Marv Cornelius, MSU
- B— Terry Beadles, Ky.
- B— Bobby Beaird, Aub.

1966
OFFENSE

First Team
- E— Johnny Mills, Tenn.
- E— Ray Perkins, Ala.
- T— Cecil Dowdy, Ala.
- T— Edgar Chandler, Ga.
- G— Bob Johnson, Tenn.
- G— Don Hayes, Ga.
- C— Bill Carr, Fla.
- QB—Steve Spurrier, Fla.
- RB—Larry Smith, Fla.
- RB—Doug Cunningham, Miss.
- FL—Richard Trapp, Fla.

Second Team
- E— Austin Denny, Tenn.
- E— Wayne Cook, Ala.
- T— Jerry Duncan, Ala.
- T— Bubba Hampton, MSU
- G— Jim Benson, Fla.
- G— Scott Hall, Vandy
- C— Chuck Hinton, Miss.
- QB—Dewey Warren, Tenn.
- RB—Ronnie Jenkins, Ga.
- RB—Charlie Fulton, Tenn.
- FL—Freddie Hyatt, Aub.

DEFENSE

First Team
- E— John Garlington, LSU
- E— Larry Kohn, Ga.
- T— George Patton, Ga.
- T— Jim Urbanek, Miss.
- G— Jimmy Keyes, Miss.
- LB—Paul Naumoff, Tenn.
- LB—George Bevan, LSU
- LB—D.D. Lewis, MSU
- B— Lynn Hughes, Ga.
- B— Bobby Johns, Ala.
- B— Gerry Warfield, Miss.

Second Team
- E— Jeff Van Note, Ky.
- E— Jerry Richardson, Miss.
- T— Bill Stanfill, Ga.
- T— Richard Cole, Ala.
- G— Bobby Morel, Tenn.
- LB—Gusty Yearout, Aub.
- LB—Doug Archibald, Vandy
- LB—Chip Healy, Vandy
- B— Dicky Lyons, Ky.
- B— Jerry Davis, Ky.
- B— Sammy Grezaffi, LSU

1967
OFFENSE

First Team
- E— Dennis Homan, Ala.
- E— Bob Goodridge, Vandy
- T— Edgar Chandler, Ga.
- T— John Boynton, Tenn.
- G— Guy Dennis, Fla.
- G— Charles Rosenfielder, Tenn.
- C— Bob Johnson, Tenn.
- QB—Ken Stabler, Ala.
- RB—Larry Smith, Fla.
- FL—Richard Trapp, Fla.
- FB—Ronnie Jenkins, Ga.
- PK—Wayne Barfield, Fla.

Second Team
- E— Freddie Hyatt, Aub.
- E— Mac Haik, Miss.
- T— Alan Bush, Miss.
- T— Elliott Gammage, Tenn.
- G— Bruce Stevens, Ala.
- G— Don Hayes, Ga.
- C— Barry Wilson, LSU
- QB—Nelson Stokley, LSU
- RB—Steve Hindman, Miss.
- FL—Richmond Flowers, Tenn.
- FB—Walter Chadwick, Tenn.
- PK—Karl Kremser, Tenn.

DEFENSE

First Team
- E— John Garlington, LSU
- E— Mike Ford, Ala.
- T— Bill Stanfill, Ga.
- T— Jim Urbanek, Miss.
- G— Gusty Yearout, Aub.
- G— Mike Hall, Ala.
- LB—D.D. Lewis, MSU
- LB—Jimmy Keyes, Miss.
- DB—Albert Dorsey, Tenn.
- DB—Sammy Grezaffi, LSU
- DB—Jack Scott, Ga.
- P— Eddie Ray, LSU

Second Team
- E— Jerry Richardson, Miss.
- E— Nick Showalter, Tenn.
- T— Charlie Collins, Aub.
- T— Glenn Higgins, MSU
- G— Don Giordano, Fla.
- G— Dan Sartin, Miss.
- LB—Steve Kiner, Tenn.
- LB—Robert Margeson, Aub.
- DB—Buddy McClinton, Aub.
- DB—Tommy James, Miss.
- DB—Mike Jones, Tenn.
- P— Julian Fagan, Miss.

1968
OFFENSE

First Team
- E—Dennis Hughes, Ga.
- E—Tim Christian, Aub.
- T—David Rholetter, Ga.
- T—Bill Fortier, LSU
- G—Charles Rosenfelder, Tenn.
- G—Alvin Samples, Ala.
- C—Chip Kell, Tenn.
- QB—Tommy Pharr, MSU
- HB—Dicky Lyons, Ky.
- FL—Sammy Milner, MSU
- FB—Richard Pickens, Tenn.
- PK—John Riley, Aub.

Second Team
- E—Ken DeLong, Tenn.
- E—Donnie Sutton, Ala.
- T—Bob Asher, Vandy
- T—Jerry Gordon, Aub.
- G—Guy Dennis, Fla.
- G—Johnny McDonald, Aub.
- C—Godfrey Zaundrecher, LSU
- QB—Mike Cavan, Ga.
- HB—Richmond Flowers, Tenn.
- FL—Kent Lawrence, Ga.
- FB—Larry Smith, Fla.
- PK—Jim McCoullough, Ga.

DEFENSE

First Team
- E—Billy Payne, Ga.
- E—Mike Ford, Ala.
- T—Bill Stanfill, Ga.
- T—David Campbell, Aub.
- G—Sam Gellerstedt, Ala.
- LB—Steve Kiner, Tenn.
- LB—Mike Hall, Ala.
- LB—Mike Kolen, Aub.
- DB—Jake Scott, Ga.
- DB—Buddy McClinton, Aub.
- DB—Glenn Cannon, Miss.
- P—Spike Jones, Ga.

Second Team
- E—Neal McMeans, Tenn.
- E—Dick Palmer, Ky.
- T—Dick Williams, Tenn.
- T—Randy Barron, Ala.
- G—David Roller, Ky.
- LB—Mike Anderson, LSU
- LB—Frank Trapp, Miss.
- LB—Happy Dicks, Ga.
- DB—Steve Tannen, Fla.
- DB—Gerry Kent, LSU
- DB—Jim Weatherford, Tenn.
- P—Julian Fagan, Miss.

1969
OFFENSE

First Team
- E—Carlos Alvarez, Fla.
- E—Sammy Milner, MSU
- T—Bob Asher, Vandy
- T—Danny Ford, Ala.
- G—Chip Kell, Tenn.
- G—Alvin Samples, Ala.
- C—Tom Banks, Aub.
- B—Archie Manning, Miss.
- B—John Reaves, Fla.
- B—Curt Watson, Tenn.
- B—Eddie Ray, LSU

Second Team
- E—Floyd Franks, Miss.
- E—Terry Beasley, Aub.
- T—Mac Steen, Fla.
- T—Richard Cheek, Aub.
- G—Don Williams, Fla.
- G—Skip Jernigan, Miss.
- C—Mike Bevans, Tenn.
- B—Pat Sullivan, Aub.
- B—Johnny Musso, Ala.
- B—Tommy Durrance, Fla.
- B—Connie Frederick, Aub.

DEFENSE

First Team
- E—Louis Faber, Miss.
- E—David Ghesquiere, Fla.
- T—David Roller, Ky.
- T—Steve Greer, Ga.
- LB—Steve Kiner, Tenn.
- LB—George Bevan, LSU
- LB—Mike Kolen, Aub.
- LB—Jack Reynolds, Tenn.
- DB—Buddy McClinton, Aub.
- DB—Glenn Cannon, Miss.
- DB—Tommy Casanova, LSU

Second Team
- E—Dick Palmer, Ky.
- E—Neal Dettmering, Aub.
- T—Buz Morrow, Miss.
- T—Frank Yanossy, Tenn.
- LB—Larry Thomas, Miss.
- LB—Chip Wisdom, Ga.
- LB—Joe Federspiel, Ky.
- LB—Bob Strickland, Aub.
- DB—Tim Priest, Tenn.
- DB—Steve Tonnen, Fla.
- DB—Larry Willingham, Aub.

1970
OFFENSE

First Team
- SE—Terry Beasley, Aub.
- TE—Jim Yancey, Fla.
- T—Worthy McClure, Miss.
- T—Royce Smith, Ga.
- G—Chip Kell, Tenn.
- G—Skip Jernigan, Miss.
- C—Mike Bevans, Tenn.
- QB—Pat Sullivan, Aub.
- RB—Johnny Musso, Ala.
- RB—Curt Watson, Tenn.
- FL—David Smith, MSU
- PK—Gardner Jett, Aub.

Second Team
- SE—David Bailey, Ala.
- TE—Jim Poole, Miss.
- T—John Hannah, Ala.
- T—Danny Speigner, Aub.
- G—Mike Demarie, LSU
- G—Jimmy Speigner, Aub.
- C—Tommy Lyons, Ga.
- QB—Archie Manning, Miss.
- RB—Art Cantrelle, LSU
- RB—Randy Reed, Miss.
- FL—Floyd Franks, Miss.
- PK—Kim Braswell, Ga.

DEFENSE

First Team
- E—Jack Youngblood, Fla.
- E—Dennis Coleman, Miss.
- T—John Sage, LSU
- T—Dave Roller, Ky.
- LB—Mike Anderson, LSU
- LB—Jackie Walker, Tenn.
- LB—Bobby Strickland, Aub.
- B—Tommy Casanova, LSU
- B—Bobby Majors, Tenn.
- B—Larry Willingham, Aub.
- B—Buzy Rosenberg, Ga.
- P—Steve Smith, Vandy

Second Team
- E—Dave Hardt, Ky.
- E—Chuck Heard, Ga.
- T—Ronnie Estay, LSU
- T—Larry Brasher, Ga.
- LB—Chip Wisdom, Ga.
- LB—Fred Brister, Miss.
- LB—Chuck Dees, MSU
- B—Tim Priest, Tenn.
- B—Craig Burns, LSU
- B—Ray Heidel, Miss.
- B—Ken Phares, MSU
- P—Frank Mann, Ala.

1971
OFFENSE

First Team
- SE—Terry Beasley, Aub.
- TE—David Bailey, Ala.
- LT—Jim Krapf, Ala.
- RT—Tom Nash, Ga.
- LG—Royce Smith, Ga.
- RG—John Hannah, Ala.
- C—Kendall Keith, Ga.
- QB—Pat Sullivan, Aub.
- RB—Johnny Musso, Ala.
- RB—Art Cantrelle, LSU
- FL—Andy Hamilton, LSU
- PK—George Hunt, Tenn.

Second Team
- SE—Dick Schmalz, Aub.
- TE—Carlos Alvarez, Fla.
- LT—Eric Hoggat, MSU
- RT—Danny Speigner, Aub.
- LG—Fred Abbott, Fla.
- RG—Mike Demarie, LSU
- C—Bill Emendorfer, Tenn.
- QB—Jimmy Grammer, Ala.
- RB—John Reaves, Fla.
- RB—Curt Watson, Tenn.
- FL—Andy Johnson, Ga.
- PK—Jay Michaelson, LSU

DEFENSE

First Team
- LE—Robin Parkhouse, Ala.
- RE—Bob Brown, Aub.
- LT—Ronnie Estay, LSU
- RT—Elmer Allen, Miss.
- LB—Joe Federspiel, Ky.
- LB—Bob Nettles, Tenn.
- LB—Tom Surlas, Ala.
- BK—Bobby Majors, Tenn.
- BK—Steve Higginbotham, Ala.
- BK—Frank Dowsing, MSU
- BK—Buzy Rosenberg, Ga.
- P—David Beverly, Aub.

Second Team
- LE—Mixon Robinson, Ga.
- RE—George Abernathy, Vandy
- LT—Chuck Heard, Ga.
- RT—Tommy Yearout, Aub.
- LB—Chip Wisdom, Ga.
- LB—Jeff Rouzie, Ala.
- LB—Jackie Walker, Tenn.
- BK—Paul Dongieux, Miss.
- BK—Johnny Simmons, Aub.
- BK—Conrad Graham, Tenn.
- BK—Ken Stone, Vandy
- P—Greg Gantt, Ala.

1972
OFFENSE

First Team
- WR—Bill Buckley, MSU
- WR—Wayne Wheeler, Ala.
- TE—Butch Veazey, Miss.
- T—Mac Lorendo, Aub.
- T—Don Leathers, Miss.
- G—John Hannah, Ala.
- G—Bill Emendorfer, Tenn.
- C—Jim Krapf, Ala.
- QB—Terry Davis, Ala.
- RB—Nat Moore, Fla.
- RB—Terry Henley, Aub.
- PK—Ricky Townsend, Tenn.

Second Team
- WR—Gerald Keigley, LSU
- WR—Walter Overton, Vandy
- TE—Brad Boyd, LSU
- T—Paul Parker, Fla.
- T—L.T. Southall, Vandy
- G—Tyler Lafauci, LSU
- G—Art Bressler, Miss.
- C—Chris Hammond, Ga.
- QB—Bert Jones, LSU
- RB—Haskel Stanback, Tenn.
- RB—Steve Bisceglia, Ala.
- PK—Gardner Jett, Aub.

DEFENSE

First Team
- E—Danny Sanspree, Aub.
- E—John Mitchell, Ala.
- T—John Wood, LSU
- T—John Wagster, Tenn.
- LB—Jamie Rotella, Tenn.
- LB—Warren Capone, LSU
- LB—Fred Abbott, Fla.
- B—Bobby McKinney, Ala.
- B—Conrad Graham, Tenn.
- B—Ken Stone, Vandy
- B—Dave Beck, Aub.
- P—Greg Gantt, Ala.

Second Team
- E—Ricky Browne, Fla.
- E—John Croyle, Ala.
- T—Skip Kubelius, Ala.
- T—Benny Sivley, Aub.
- LB—Ken Bernich, Aub.
- LB—John David Calhoun, MSU
- LB—Art Reynolds, Tenn.
- B—Daryl Bishop, Ky.
- B—Jim Revels, Fla.
- B—Ken Phares, MSU
- B—Mike Williams, LSU
- P—Rusty Jackson, LSU

1994 SEC Football 269

Associated Press All-SEC Teams

1973
OFFENSE
First Team
WR—Wayne Wheeler, Ala.
TE—Brad Boyd, LSU
T—Buddy Brown, Ala.
T—Tyler Lafauci, LSU
G—Mac McWhorter, Ga.
G—Art Bressler, Miss.
C—Steve Taylor, Aub.
QB—Condredge Holloway, Tenn.
RB—Sonny Collins, Ky.
RB—Wayne Jones, MSU
RB—Wilbur Jackson, Ala.
PK—Hawkins Golden, Vandy

Second Team
WR—Lee McGriff, Fla.
TE—Butch Veazey, Miss.
T—Harvey Sword, Ky.
T—Richard Brooks, LSU
G—Lee Gross, Aub.
G—Burton Lawless, Fla.
C—Jimmy Ray Stephens, Fla.
QB—Gary Rutledge, Ala.
RB—Brad Davis, LSU
RB—Haskel Stanback, Tenn.
RB—Paul Hofer, Miss.

DEFENSE
First Team
E—Ricky Browne, Fla.
E—Binks Miciotto, LSU
T—Mike Raines, Ala.
T—Benny Sivley, Aub.
LB—Warren Capone, LSU
LB—Woodrow Lowe, Ala.
LB—Ralph Ortega, Fla.
B—Eddie Brown, Tenn.
B—Mike Washington, Ala.
B—Jim Revels, Fla.
KR—Mike Fuller, Aub.
P—Greg Gantt, Ala.

Second Team
E—Mike Dubose, Ala.
E—Jimmy Webb, MSU
T—David Hitchcock, Fla.
T—Ben Williams, Miss.
G—Danny Jones, Ga.
LB—Jim Stuart, Miss.
LB—Ken Bernich, Aub.
LB—Bo Harris, LSU
B—Darryl Bishop, Ky.
B—Harry Harrison, Miss.
B—Mike Williams, LSU

1974
OFFENSE
First Team
WR—Lee McGriff, Fla.
TE—Barry Burton, Vandy
T—Craig Hertwig, Ga.
T—Warren Bryant, Ky.
G—Gene Moshier, Vandy
G—John Rogers, Ala.
C—Lee Gross, Aub.
QB—Rockey Felker, MSU
RB—Sonny Collins, Ky.
RB—Glynn Harrison, Ga.
RB—Walter Packer, MSU
PK—Mark Adams, Vandy

Second Team
WR—Gene Washington, Ga.
TE—Richard Appleby, Ga.
T—Chuck Fletcher, Aub.
T—Paul Parker, Fla.
G—Burton Lawless, Fla.
G—Sam Nichols, MSU
C—Rick Nuzum, Ky.
QB—Mike Fanuzzi, Ky.
RB—Willie Shelby, Ala.
RB—Stanley Morgan, Tenn.
RB—Jamie O'Rourke, Vandy
RB—Horace King, Ga.

DEFENSE
First Team
E—Leroy Cook, Ala.
E—Rusty Deen, Aub.
T—Jimmy Webb, MSU
T—Steve Cassidy, LSU
LB—Ken Bernich, Aub.
LB—Glenn Cameron, Fla.
LB—Woodrow Lowe, Ala.
B—Mike Washington, Ala.
B—Ricky Davis, Ala.
B—Mike Fuller, Aub.
B—Jay Chesley, Vandy
P—Neil Clabo, Tenn.

Second Team
E—Mike Dubose, Ala.
E—David McKnight, Ga.
T—Ben Williams, Miss.
T—Robert Pulliam, Tenn.
LB—Ralph Ortega, Fla.
LB—Sylvester Boler, Ga.
LB—Harvey Hull, MSU
LB—Tom Galbierz, Vandy
B—Jim McKinney, Aub.
B—Mike Williams, LSU
B—Steve Curnutte, Vandy
B—Wayne Fields, Fla.
P—John Tetterson, Ky.

1975
OFFENSE
First Team
SE—Larry Seivers, Tenn.
TE—Barry Burton, Vandy
T—Warren Bryant, Ky.
T—Mike Williams, Fla.
G—Randy Johnson, Ga.
G—David Gerasimchuck, Ala.
C—Richard Keys, MSU
QB—Richard Todd, Ala.
RB—Jimmy DuBose, Fla.
RB—Glynn Harrison, Ga.
RB—Sonny Collins, Ky.
PK—David Posey, Fla.

Second Team
SE—Rick Kimbrough, Miss.
SE—Jeff Gilligan, Aub.
TE—Tommy West, Tenn.
T—Mike Wilson, Ga.
T—Chuck Fletcher, Aub.
G—Gerald Loper, Fla.
G—Sam Nichols, MSU
C—Robbie Moore, Fla.
QB—Don Gaffney, Fla.
RB—Walter Packer, MSU
RB—Johnny Davis, Ala.
RB—Stanley Morgan, Tenn.
RB—Kevin McLee, Ga.
PK—Mark Adams, Vandy

DEFENSE
First Team
E—Leroy Cook, Ala.
E—Kenny Bordelon, LSU
T—Bob Baumhower, Ala.
T—Steve Cassidy, LSU
T—Rick Telhiard, Aub.
MG—Ben Williams, Miss.
LB—Sammy Green, Fla.
LB—Conley Duncan, Ala.
LB—Andy Spiva, Tenn.
B—Mike Mauck, Tenn.
B—Wayne Rhodes, Ala.
B—Jay Chesley, Vandy
P—Clyde Baumgartner, Aub.

Second Team
E—Gary Turner, Miss.
E—Ron McCartney, Tenn.
T—Darrell Carpenter, Fla.
T—Lawrence Johnson, Miss.
MG—Harvey Hull, MSU
LB—Ben Zambiasi, Ga.
LB—Jim Kovach, Ky.
LB—Ray Costict, MSU
B—Henry Davis, Fla.
B—Bill Krug, Ga.
B—Stan Black, MSU
P—Bill Farris, Miss.

1976
OFFENSE
First Team
WR—Larry Seivers, Tenn.
WR—Wes Chandler, Fla.
TE—Ozzie Newsome, Ala.
T—Mike Wilson, Ga.
T—Warren Bryant, Ky.
G—Joel Parrish, Ga.
G—Dave Gerasimchuk, Ala.
C—Richard Keys, MSU
QB—Ray Goff, Ga.
RB—Terry Robiskie, LSU
RB—Kevin McLee, Ga.
PK—Allen Leavitt, Ga.

Second Team
WR—Gene Washington, Ga.
WR—Stanley Morgan, Tenn.
TE—Jimmy Stephens, Fla.
T—K.J. Lazenby, Ala.
T—Bobby Dugas, LSU
T—Davis Forrester, Fla.
G—Sam Nichols, MSU
G—David Ostrowski, Aub.
C—Robbie Moore, Fla.
QB—Phil Gargis, Aub.
RB—Johnny Davis, Ala.
PB—Dennis Johnson, MSU
PK—Neil O'Donoghue, Aub.

DEFENSE
First Team
E—Lew Sibley, LSU
E—Art Still, Ky.
T—Charles Hannah, Ala.
T—A.J. Duhe, LSU
MG—Harvey Hull, MSU
LB—Ben Zambiasi, Ga.
LB—Ray Costict, MSU
LB—Andy Spiva, Tenn.
DB—Stan Black, MSU
DB—Bill Krug, Ga.
DB—Clinton Burrell, LSU
P—Craig Colquitt, Tenn.

Second Team
E—Paul Harris, Ala.
E—Jeff McCollum, Aub.
T—Bob Baumhower, Ala.
T—Darrell Carpenter, Fla.
LB—Kem Coleman, Miss.
LB—Freddie Smith, Aub.
LB—Jon Streete, LSU
LB—Jim Kovach, Ky.
B—Bernard Wilson, Vandy
B—Alvin Cowans, Fla.
B—Mike Siganos, Ky.
B—Charlie Moss, Miss.
P—Clyde Baumgartner, Aub.

1977
OFFENSE
First Team
WR—Wes Chandler, Fla.
WR—Martin Cox, Vandy
TE—Ozzie Newsome, Ala.
T—Robert Dugas, LSU
T—Jim Bunch, Ala.
G—Tom Dornbrook, Ky.
G—Lynn Johnson, Aub.
C—Dwight Stephenson, Ala.
QB—Derrick Ramsey, Ky.
RB—Charles Alexander, LSU
RB—Johnny Davis, Ala.
PK—Jorge Portella, Aub.

Second Team
WR—Dave Trosper, Ky.
WR—Carlos Carson, LSU
TE—Curtis Weathers, Miss.
T—Mark Trogdon, MSU
T—Brent Watson, Tenn.
G—George Collins, Ga.
G—Randy White, Miss.
C—Robert Shaw, Tenn.
QB—Jeff Rutledge, Ala.
RB—Tony Nathan, Ala.
RB—Tony Green, Fla.
PK—Berj Yepremian, Fla.

DEFENSE
First Team
E—Art Still, Ky.
E—George Plasketes, Miss.
T—Larry Gillard, MSU
T—Ronnie Swoopes, Ga.
MG—Scott Hutchinson, Fla.
LB—Ben Zambiasi, Ga.
LB—Freddie Smith, Aub.
LB—Ed Smith, Vandy
LB—Scott Brantley, Fla.
DB—Mike Siganos, Ky.
DB—Dallas Owens, Ky.
DB—James McKinney, Aub.
P—Craig Colquitt, Tenn.

Second Team
E—Wayne Hamilton, Ala.
E—John Adams, LSU
T—Marty Lyons, Ala.
T—Jerry Blanton, Ky.
MG—Richard Jaffe, Ky.
LB—Kem Coleman, Miss.
LB—Charlie Williams, Fla.
LB—Barry Krauss, Ala.
DB—Mike Tucker, Ala.
DB—Bill Krug, Ga.
DB—Brenard Wilson, Vandy
P—Jim Miller, Miss.

Honors

1978
OFFENSE

First Team
WR—Mardye McDole, MSU
WR—Cris Collinsworth, Fla.
T—Robert Dugas, LSU
T—Mike Burrow, Aub.
G—Mike Brock, Ala.
G—Mack Guest, Ga.
C—Robert Shaw, Tenn.
C—Dwight Stephenson, Ala.
QB—Dave Marler, MSU
RB—Charles Alexander, LSU
RB—Willie McClendon, Ga.
RB—Joe Cribbs, Aub.
PK—Berj Yepremian, Fla.

Second Team
WR—Martin Cox, Vandy
TE—Reggie Harper, Tenn.
T—Don Swafford, Fla.
T—Tom Woodroof, Vandy
G—Tom Kearns, Ky.
G—Matt Brasewell, Ga.
C—Jay Whitley, LSU
QB—Jeff Rutledge, Ala.
RB—Tony Nathan, Ala.
RB—Frank Mordica, Vandy
RB—James Jones, MSU
PK—Rex Robinson, Ga.

DEFENSE

First Team
E—John Adams, LSU
E—E.J. Junior, Ala.
T—Marty Lyons, Ala.
T—Frank Warren, Aub.
LB—Scot Brantley, Fla.
LB—Barry Krauss, Ala.
LB—Ricky McBride, Ga.
LB—Jim Kovach, Ky.
B—Roland James, Tenn.
B—Murray Legg, Ala.
B—Chris Williams, LSU
P—Jim Miller, Miss.

Second Team
E—Michael Dupree, Fla.
E—Lyman White, LSU
T—Tyrone Keys, MSU
T—George Atiyeh, LSU
MG—Richard Jaffe, Ky.
LB—Johnie Cooks, MSU
LB—David Little, Fla.
LB—Randy Sittason, Vandy
B—Willie Teal, LSU
B—Larry Carter, Ky.
B—Clifford Toney, Ala.
P—Skip Johnston, Aub.

1979
OFFENSE

First Team
SE—Preston Brown, Vandy
TE—Reggie Harper, Tenn
T—Jim Bunch, Ala.
T—Matt Braswell, Ga.
G—Mike Brock, Ala.
G—Ray Donaldson, Ga.
C—Dwight Stephenson, Ala.
QB—Steadman Shealy, Ala.
RB—James Brooks, Aub.
RB—Joe Cribbs, Aub.
FLK—Cris Collinsworth, Fla.
PK—Rex Robinson, Ga.

Second Team
WR—Mardye McDole, MSU
WR—Felix Wilson, Ky.
T—George Stephenson, Aub.
T—Buddy Aydelette, Ala.
T—Tim Irwin, Tenn.
G—Tom Kearns, Ky.
G—Alan Hartlein, MSU
C—John Ed Bradley, LSU
QB—John Fourcade, Miss.
RB—Frank Mordica, Vandy
RB—Major Ogilvie, Ala.
FB—Steve Whitman, Ala.
PK—Jorge Portela, Aub.

DEFENSE

First Team
E—E.J. Junior, Ala.
E—Lyman White, LSU
T—Frank Warren, Aub.
T—David Hannah, Ala.
MG—Richard Jaffe, Ky.
LB—Freddie Smith, Aub.
LB—Thomas Boyd, Ala.
DB—Roland James, Tenn.
DB—Don McNeal, Ala.
DB—Scott Woerner, Ga.
DB—Willie Teal, LSU
P—Jim Miller, Miss.

Second Team
E—John Adams, LSU
E—Wayne Hamilton, Ala.
T—Byron Braggs, Ala.
T—Tyrone Keys, MSU
MG—George Atiyeh, LSU
LB—Craig Puki, Tenn.
LB—David Little, Fla.
DB—James McKinney, Aub.
DB—Chris Williams, LSU
DB—Kenny Johnson, MSU
DB—Larry Carter, Ky.
DB—Tommy Wilcox, Ala.
P—Jim Arnold, Vandy
P—Skip Johnston, Aub.

1980
OFFENSE

First Team
WR—Cris Collinsworth, Fla.
WR—Mardye McDole, MSU
TE—Chris Faulkner, Fla.
T—Tim Irwin, Tenn.
T—Alan Massey, MSU
G—Tim Morrison, Ga.
G—Wayne Harris, MSU
C—Ken Roark, Ky.
QB—Buck Belue, Ga.
RB—Herschel Walker, Ga.
RB—James Brooks, Aub.
PK—Rex Robinson, Ga.

Second Team
WR—Anthony Hancock, Tenn.
WR—Byron Franklin, Aub.
WR—Ken Toler, Miss.
TE—Reggie Harper, Tenn.
T—George Stephenson, Aub.
T—Nat Hudson, Ga
G—Ken Hammond, Vandy
G—Chris Cottam, Miss.
C—Lee North, Tenn.
QB—John Fourcade, Miss.
RB—Billy Jackson, Ala.
RB—Major Ogilvie, Ala.
PK—Alan Duncan, Tenn.

DEFENSE

First Team
E—E.J. Junior, Ala.
E—Lyman White, LSU
T—Frank Warren, Aub.
T—Eddie Weaver, Ga.
MG—Jim Noonan, Tenn.
LB—David Little, Fla.
LB—Thomas Boyd, Ala.
LB—Johnie Cooks, MSU
DB—Tommy Wilcox, Ala.
DB—Scott Woerner, Ga.
DB—Chris Williams, LSU
DB—Jeff Hipp, Ga.
P—Jim Arnold, Vandy

Second Team
E—Tyrone Keys, MSU
E—Tim Golden, Fla.
T—Glen Collins, MSU
T—David Galloway, Fla.
MG—Warren Lyles, Ala.
LB—Randy Scott, Ala.
LB—Andrew Coleman, Vandy
LB—Al Richardson, LSU
DB—Clifford Toney, Aub.
DB—Ricky Tucker, Ala.
DB—Tim Groves, Fla.
P—Mark Dickert, Fla.

1981
OFFENSE

First Team
WR—Lindsay Scott, Ga.
WR—Wamon Buggs, Vandy
TE—Malcolm Scott, LSU
T—Keith Uecker, Aub.
T—Pat Phenix, Miss.
G—Wayne Harris, MSU
G—Ken Hammond, Vandy
C—Lee North, Tenn.
QB—Buck Belue, Ga.
RB—Herschel Walker, Ga.
RB—James Jones, Fla.
PK—Brian Clark, Fla.

Second Team
WR—Orlando McDaniel, LSU
WR—Anthony Hancock, Tenn.
TE—Jerry Price, MSU
T—Bob Cayavec, Ala.
T—Loie Hudgins, Vandy
G—Jimmy Harper, Ga.
G—Doug Vickers, Ala.
C—Steve Mott, Ala.
C—Joe Happe, Ga.
QB—Whit Taylor, Vandy
RB—Michael Haddix, MSU
RB—Ronnie Stewart, Ga.
PK—Kevin Butler, Ga.

DEFENSE

First Team
E—Billy Jackson, MSU
E—Mike Pitts, Ala.
T—David Galloway, Fla.
T—Glen Collins, MSU
T—Jimmy Payne, Ga.
MG—Warren Lyles, Ala.
LB—Johnie Cooks, MSU
LB—Wilber Marshall, Fla.
LB—Danny Skutack, Aub.
DB—Tommy Wilcox, Ala.
DB—Jeremiah Castille, Ala.
DB—Andy Molls, Ky.
P—Jim Arnold, Vandy

Second Team
E—Don Fielder, Ky.
E—Steve Bearden, Vandy
T—Donnie Humphrey, Aub.
T—Edmund Nelson, Aub.
MG—Eddie Weaver, Ga.
LB—Fernando Jackson, Fla.
LB—Tommy Thurson, Ga.
LB—Robbie Jones, Ala.
LB—Al Richardson, LSU
DB—Thomas Boyd, Ala.
DB—Tony Lilly, Fla.
DB—Bill Bates, Tenn.
DB—Bob Harris, Aub.
P—Jimmy Colquitt, Tenn.

1982
OFFENSE

First Team
WR—Willie Gault, Tenn.
TE—Allama Matthews, Vandy
T—Joe Beazley, Ala.
T—Lance Smith, LSU
G—Wayne Harris, MSU
G—David Jordan, Aub.
C—Wayne Radloff, Ga.
QB—Whit Taylor, Vandy
RB—Herschel Walker, Ga.
RB—James Jones, Fla.
RB—Dalton Hilliard, LSU
PK—Fuad Reveiz, Tenn.

Second Team
WR—Danny Knight, MSU
TE—Malcolm Scott, Vandy
IL—Pat Arrington, Aub.
IL—Pat Phenix, Miss.
IL—Dan Fike, Fla.
IL—Guy McIntyre, Ga.
C—Steve Mott, Ala.
QB—Alan Risher, LSU
RB—Lionel James, Aub.
RB—Bo Jackson, Aub.
RB—Michael Haddix, MSU
PK—Kevin Butler, Ga.

DEFENSE

First Team
E—Mike Pitts, Ala.
E—Freddie Gilbert, Ga.
T—Ramsey Dardar, LSU
T—Doug Smith, Aub.
MG—Dowe Aughtman, Aub.
LB—Wilber Marshall, Fla.
LB—Al Richardson, LSU
LB—Tommy Thurson, Ga.
B—Terry Hoage, Ga.
B—Jeremiah Castille, Ala.
B—James Britt, LSU
B—Jeff Sanchez, Ga.
P—Jim Arnold, Vandy

Second Team
E—Mike Cofer, Tenn.
E—Steve Bearden, Vandy
T—Jackie Cline, Ala.
T—Andre Townsend, Miss.
LB—Gregg Carr, Aub.
LB—Chris Martin, Aub.
B—Tommy Wilcox, Ala.
B—Bob Harris, Aub.
B—Manuel Young, Vandy
B—Tony Lilly, Fla.
B—Andy Molls, Ky.
P—Jimmy Colquitt, Tenn.

1994 SEC Football

Associated Press All-SEC Teams

1983
OFFENSE

First Team
WR—Dwayne Dixon, Fla.
WR—Eric Martin, LSU
TE—Chuck Scott, Vandy
T—Pat Arrington, Auburn
T—Guy McIntyre, Ga.
G—Mike Adcock, Ala.
G—David Jordan, Aub.
C—Phil Bromley, Fla.
QB—Walter Lewis, Ala.
RB—Bo Jackson, Aub.
RB—Johnnie Jones, Tenn.
RB—Ricky Moore, Ala.
PK—Kevin Butler, Ga.

Second Team
WR—Joey Jones, Ala.
TE—Clarence Kay, Ga.
T—Lomas Brown, Fla.
T—Winford Hood, Ga.
G—John Hunt, Fla.
G—Bill Mayo, Tenn.
C—Glenn Streno, Tenn.
QB—Wayne Peace, Fla.
RB—Neal Anderson, Fla.
RB—Keith Edwards, Vandy
RB—Lionel James, Aub.
PK—Van Tiffin, Ala.

DEFENSE

First Team
E—Steve Bearden, Vandy
E—Freddie Gilbert, Ga.
T—Doug Smith, Aub.
T—Reggie White, Tenn.
MG—Dowe Aughtman, Aub.
LB—Gregg Carr, Aub.
LB—Billy Jackson, MSU
LB—Wilber Marshall, Fla.
DB—Leonard Coleman, Vandy
DB—Terry Hoage, Ga.
RDB—Tony Lilly, Fla.
P—Paul Calhoun, Ky.

Second Team
E—Emanuel King, Ala.
E—Gerald Robinson, Aub.
T—Donnie Humphrey, Aub.
T—Andre Townsend, Miss.
MG—Tim Newton, Fla.
LB—Knox Culpepper, Ga.
LB—Tommy Thurson, Ga.
LB—Alvin Toles, Tenn.
DB—Kerry Baird, Ky.
DB—Liffort Hobley, LSU
DB—David King, Aub.
P—Ray Criswell, Fla.

1984
OFFENSE

First Team   **Second Team**
WR—Chuck Scott, Vandy
TE—Jim Popp, Vandy
T—Lomas Brown, Fla.
T—Lance Smith, LSU
G—Jeff Lott, Aub.
G—Bill Mayo, Tenn.
C—Phil Bromley, Fla.
QB—Tony Robinson, Tenn.
RB—Johnnie Jones, Tenn.
RB—Dalton Hilliard, LSU
RB—George Adams, Ky.
PK—Kevin Butler, Ga.

WR—Eric Martin, LSU
TE—Jeff Parks, Aub.
T—Rob Monaco, Vandy
T—Crawford Ker, Fla.
G—Jeff Zimmerman, Fla.
G—Pete Anderson, Ga.
C—Wes Neighbors, Ala.
QB—Kerwin Bell, Fla.
RB—Neal Anderson, Fla.
RB—John L. Williams, Fla.
FL—Tim McGee, Tenn.
PK—Fuad Reveiz, Tenn.

DEFENSE

First Team
E—Freddie Joe Nunn, Miss.
E—Gerald Robinson, Aub.
TT—Ben Thomas, Aub.
T—Jon Hand, Ala.
MG—Tim Newton, Fla.
LB—Gregg Carr, Aub.
LB—Alonzo Johnson, Fla.
LB—Cornelius Bennett, Ala.
LB—Knox Culpepper, Ga.
DB—Jeff Sanchez, Ga.
DB—Paul Calhoun, Ky.
DB—Liffort Hobley, LSU
P—Ricky Anderson, Vandy

Second Team
E—Michael Brooks, LSU
E—Kenny Sims, Ga.
T—Pat Swoopes, MSU
T—Karl Jordan, Vandy
MG—Harold Hallman, Aub.
LB—Shawn Burks, LSU
LB—Cam Jacobs, Ky.
LB—Aaron Pearson, MSU
DB—Manuel Young, Vandy
DB—David King, Aub.
DB—Jeffery Dale, LSU
P—Bill Smith, Miss.

1985
OFFENSE

First Team
WR—Tim McGee, Tenn.
WR—Al Bell, Ala.
TE—Jim Popp, Vandy
OT—Will Wolford, Vandy
OT—Steve Wallace, Aub.
OG—Jeff Zimmerman, Fla.
OG—Bruce Wilkerson, Tenn.
OC—Peter Anderson, Ga.
QB—Kerwin Bell, Fla.
RB—Bo Jackson, Aub.
RB—Dalton Hilliard, LSU
RB—Neal Anderson, Fla.
PK—Carlos Reveiz, Tenn.

Second Team
WR—J.R. Ambrose, Miss.
TE—Jeff Parks, Aub.
OT—Stacy Searels, Aub.
OT—Curt Gore, LSU
OG—Rusty Brown, MSU
OG—Jim Reichwein, Ky.
OC—Ben Tamburello, Aub.
QB—Mike Shula, Ala.
RB—John L. Williams, Fla.
RB—Garry James, LSU
RB—Brent Fullwood, Aub.
PK—Van Tiffin, Ala.

DEFENSE

First Team
DE—Greg Waters, Ga.
WDE—Roland Barbay, LSU
DT—Gerald Williams, Aub.
DT—Jon Hand, Ala.
OMG—Harold Hallman, Aub.
LB—Michael Brooks, LSU
LB—Cornelius Bennett, Ala.
LB—Alonzo Johnson, Fla.
LB—Dale Jones, Tenn.
DB—Chris White, Tenn.
DB—Tom Powell, Aub.
DB—John Little, Ga.
P—Lewis Colbert, Aub.

Second Team
DE—Brian Williams, Ky.
DE—Karl Wilson, LSU
DT—Pat Swoopes, MSU
DT—Keith Williams, Fla.
NG—Curt Jarvis, Ala.
LB—Aaron Pearson, MSU
LB—Shawn Burks, LSU
LB—Wayne Davis, Ala.
DB—Russell Hairston, Ky.
DB—Freddie Robinson, Ala.
DB—Jarvis Williams, Fla.
P—Bill Smith, Miss.

1986
OFFENSE

First Team
WR—Wendell Davis, LSU
WR—Ricky Nattiel, Florida
TE—Carl Parker, Vandy
OT—Stacy Searels, Aub.
OT—Wilbur Strozier, Ga.
OG—Eric Andolsek, LSU
OG—Bill Condon, Ala.
C—Ben Tamburello, Aub.
QB—Tommy Hodson, LSU
QB—Don Smith, MSU
RB—Brent Fullwood, Aub.
RB—Bobby Humphrey, Ala.
PK—Van Tiffin, Ala.

Second Team
WR—J.R. Ambrose, Miss.
WR—Al Bell, Ala.
TE—Brian Kinchen, LSU
OT—Bruce Wilkerson, Tenn.
OT—Jeff Zimmerman, Fla.
OG—Harry Galbreath, Tenn.
OG—John Hazard, LSU
C—Wes Neighbors, Ala.
QB—Kerwin Bell, Fla.
RB—William Howard, Tenn.
RB—Lars Tate, Ga.
PK—Joe Worley, Ky.

DEFENSE

First Team
DE—Karl Wilson, LSU
DE—Aundray Bruce, Aub.
DT—Tracy Rocker, Aub.
DT—Keith Williams, Fla.
NG—Henry Thomas, LSU
LB—Cornelius Bennett, Ala.
LB—Kurt Crain, Aub.
LB—Clifford Charlton, Fla.
DB—John Little, Ga.
DB—Freddie Robinson, Ala.
DB—Adrian White, Fla.
P—Bill Smith, Miss.

Second Team
DE—Roland Barbay, LSU
DE—Dale Jones, Tenn.
DT—Mike Fitzsimmons, Miss.
DT—Henry Harris, Ga.
NG—Curt Jarvis, Ala.
LB—Toby Caston, LSU
LB—John Brantley, Ga.
LB—Jeff Herrod, Miss.
DB—Kevin Porter, Aub.
DB—Jarvis Williams, Fla.
DB—Jeff Noblin, Miss.
P—Cris Carpenter, Ga.

1987
OFFENSE

First Team
WR—Wendell Davis, LSU
WR—Lawyer Tillman, Aub.
TE—Walter Reeves, Aub.
OL—Kim Stephens, Ga.
OL—Stacy Searels, Aub.
OL—Harry Galbreath, Tenn.
OL—Eric Andolsek, LSU
C—Nacho Albergamo, LSU
QB—Tommy Hodson, LSU
RB—Bobby Humphrey, Ala.
RB—Emmitt Smith, Fla.
PK—Win Lyle, Aub.

Second Team
WR—J.R. Ambrose, Ole Miss
WR—Carl Parker, Vandy
TE—Brian Kinchen, LSU
OL—David Williams, Fla.
OL—Bill Condon, Ala.
OL—Greg Kunkel, Ky.
OL—Dermontti Dawson, Ky.
C—Daryl Holt, Vandy
QB—Jeff Burger, Aub.
RB—Mark Higgs, Ky.
RB—Reggie Cobb, Tenn.
RB—Lars Tate, Ga.
PK—David Browndyke, LSU

DEFENSE

First Team
T—Tracy Rocker—Aub.
T—Rhondy Weston, Fla.
DE—Clifford Charlton, Fla.
DE—Aundray Bruce, Aub.
LB—Kurt Crain, Aub.
LB—John Brantley, Ga.
LB—Chris Gaines, Vandy
LB—Derrick Thomas, Ala.
DB—Kevin Porter, Aub.
DB—Louis Oliver, Fla.
DB—Terry McDaniel, Tenn.
P—Matt DeFrank, LSU

Second Team
DT—Nate Hill, Aub.
DT—Jerry Reese, Ky.
NG—Willie Wyatt, Ala.
DE—Ron Sancho, LSU
DE—Randy Rockwell, Ala.
LB—Jeff Herrod, Ole Miss
LB—Kelly Ziegler, Tenn.
LB—Keith DeLong, Tenn.
DB—Chris Carrier, LSU
DB—Jarvis Williams, Fla.
DB—John Mangum, Ala.
DB—Todd Sandroni, Ole Miss
P—Bob Garmon, Tenn.

272 Honors

1988
OFFENSE

First Team
WR—Boo Mitchell, Vandy
WR—Tony Moss, LSU
TE—Wesley Walls, Miss.
OT—Jim Thompson, Aub.
OT—David Williams, Fla.
OG—Rodney Garner, Aub.
OG—Larry Rose, Ala.
C—Todd Wheeler, Ga.
QB—Reggie Slack, Aub.
RB—Tim Worley, Ga.
RB—Emmitt Smith, Fla.
PK—David Browndyke, LSU

Second Team
WR—Thomas Woods, Tenn.
TE—Walter Reeves, Aub.
TE—Troy Sadowski, Ga.
OT—Scott Adams, Ga.
OT—Ralph Norwood, LSU
OG—Ruffin Rodrigue, LSU
OG—Eric Still, Tenn.
C—John Hudson, Aub.
QB—Jeff Francis, Tenn.
QB—Tom Hodson, LSU
QB—Eric Jones, Vandy
RB—Stacy Danley, Aub.
RB—Eddie Fuller, LSU
RB—Rodney Hampton, Ga.
RB—Murry Hill, Ala.
PK—John David Francis, Fla.

DEFENSE

First Team
DT—Trace Armstrong, Fla.
DT—Tracy Rocker, Aub.
MG—Benji Roland, Aub.
LB—Keith DeLong, Tenn.
LB—Randy Holleran, Ky.
LB—Quentin Riggins, Aub.
OLB—Ron Sancho, LSU
OLB—Derrick Thomas, Ala.
DB—Greg Jackson, LSU
DB—Stevon Moore, Miss.
DB—Louis Oliver, Fla.
P—Brian Shulman, Aub.

Second Team
DT—Oliver Barnett, Ky.
DT—Rhondy Weston, Fla.
MG—Darrell Phillips, LSU
LB—Chris Chenault, Ky.
LB—Terrie Webster, Ga.
LB—James Williams, MSU
OLB—Eric Hill, LSU
OLB—Richard Tardits, Ga.
DB—Kermit Kendrick, Ala.
DB—Todd Sandroni, Miss.
DB—Ben Smith, Ga.
DB—Preston Warren, Tenn.
P—Chris Mohr, Ala.

1989
OFFENSE

First Team
WR—Tony Moss, LSU
TE—Lamonde Russell, Ala.
OT—Mike Pfeifer, Ky.
OT—Terrill Chatman, Ala.
OG—Eric Still, Tenn.
OG—Ed King, Aub.
C—Roger Shultz, Ala.
QB—Gary Hollingsworth, Ala.
RB—Emmitt Smith, Fla.
RB—Chuck Webb, Tenn.
RB—Siran Stacy, Ala.
PK—Philip Doyle, Ala.

Second Team
WR—Thomas Woods, Tenn.
WR—Willie Green, Miss.
TE—Jessee Anderson, MSU
OT—Curt Mull, Ga.
OT—John Durden, Fla.
OT—Charles McRae, Tenn.
OG—Joel Mazzella, Ky.
OG—Ricky Byrd, MSU
C—John Hudson, Aub.
QB—Tom Hodson, LSU
RB—Rodney Hampton, Ga.
RB—Alfred Rawls, Ky.
PK—David Browndyke, LSU

DEFENSE

First Team
DT—Oliver Barnett, Ky.
DT—Bill Goldberg, Ga.
DT—David Rocker, Aub.
MG—Willie Wyatt, Ala.
OLB—Craig Ogletree, Aub.
OLB—Marion Hobby, Tenn.
ILB—Keith McCants, Ala.
ILB—Quentin Riggins, Aub.
DB—Ben Smith, Ga.
DB—John Mangum, Ala.
DB—Richard Fain, Fla.
DB—Efrum Thomas, Ala.
P—Mike Riley, MSU

Second Team
DT—Karl Dunbar, LSU
DT—Fernando Horn, Aub.
MG—Kelvin Pritchett, Miss.
OLB—Huey Richardson, Fla.
OLB—Morris Lewis, Ga.
ILB—James Williams, MSU
ILB—DeMond Winston, Vandy
DB—Preston Warren, Tenn.
DB—John Wiley, Aub.
DB—Bo Russell, MSU
DB—Chauncey Bourgeois, LSU
P—Rene Bourgeois, LSU

1990
OFFENSE

First Team
WR—Carl Pickens, Tenn.
WR—Todd Kinchen, LSU
TE—Kirk Kirkpatrick, Fla.
T—Antone Davis, Tenn.
T—Rob Selby, Aub.
G—Ed King, Aub.
G—Ricky Byrd, MSU
C—Roger Shultz, Ala.
QB—Shane Matthews, Fla.
RB—Tony Thompson, Tenn.
RB—Randy Baldwin, Miss.
PK—Philip Doyle, Ala.

Second Team
WR—Alvin Harper, Tenn.
WR—Ernie Mills, Fla.
TE—Rodney Jackson, Ky.
TE—Lamonde Russell, Ala.
T—Charles McRae, Tenn.
T—Terrill Chatman, Ala.
G—Chris Bromley, Fla.
G—Joel Mazzella, Ky.
C—Blake Miller, LSU
C—Kevin Brothen, Vandy
QB—Andy Kelly, Tenn.
RB—Al Baker, Ky.
RB—Harvey Williams, LSU
PK—John Kasay, Ga.

DEFENSE

First Team
E—Huey Richardson, Fla.
E—George Thornton, Ala.
T—David Rocker, Aub.
T—Kelvin Pritchett, Miss.
LB—Randy Holleran, Ky.
LB—Reggie Stewart, MSU
LB—John Sullins, Ala.
DB—Dale Carter, Tenn.
DB—Efrum Thomas, Ala.
DB—Will White, Fla.
DB—Richard Fain, Fla.
DB—Chris Mitchell, Miss.
P—David Lawrence, Vandy

Second Team
E—Mark Murray, Fla.
E—Rod Keith, Vandy
T—Marc Boutte, LSU
T—Brad Culpepper, Fla.
T—Robert Stewart, Ala.
NG—Robert Tate, Aub.
LB—Godfrey Myles, Fla.
LB—Tim Paulk, Fla.
LB—Morris Lewis, Ga.
LB—Earnest Fields, Tenn.
DB—John Wiley, Aub.
DB—Corey Barlow, Aub.
DB—Derriel McCorvey, LSU
P—Mike Riley, MSU

1991
OFFENSE

First Team
WR—Carl Pickens, Tenn.
WR—Todd Kinchen, LSU
TE—Tyji Armstrong, Miss.
T—John James, MSU
T—Kevin Mawae, LSU
G—Hesham Ismail, Fla.
G—Tom Myslinski, Tenn.
C—Cal Dixon, Fla.
QB—Shane Matthews, Fla.
RB—Errict Rhett, Fla.
RB—Corey Harris, Vandy
PK—Doug Pelfrey, Ky.

Second Team
WR—Willie Jackson, Fla.
WR—Andre Hastings, Ga.
TE—Pat Akos, Vandy
OL—Everett Lindsay, Miss.
OL—Eddie Blake, Aub.
OL—Bob Meeks, Aub.
OL—Mark White, Fla.
C—Kevin Brothen, Vandy
QB—Andy Kelly, Tenn.
RB—Siran Stacy, Ala.
RB—Garrison Hearst, Ga.
PK—Arden Czyewski, Fla.

DEFENSE

First Team
DE—Chuck Smith, Tenn.
DE—Chris Mims, Tenn.
DT—Brad Culpepper, Fla.
DT—Tony McCoy, Fla.
NG—Robert Stewart, Ala.
LB—Tim Paulk, Ga.
LB—John Sullins, Ala.
LB—Dwayne Simmons, Ga.
LB—Keo Coleman, MSU
DB—Dale Carter, Tenn.
DB—Corey Barlow, Aub.
DB—Will White, Fla.
P—Shane Edge, Fla.

Second Team
DE—John Copeland, Ala.
DE—Eric Curry, Ala.
DT—Marc Boutte, LSU
DT—Joey Couch, Ky.
NG—Nate Williams, MSU
LB—Daniel Boyd, MSU
LB—Darrel Crawford, Aub.
LB—Darryl Hardy, Tenn.
LB—Ephesians Bartley, Fla.
DB—Antonio Langham, Ala.
DB—Chuck Carswell, Ga.
DB—George Teague, Ala.
P—David Lawrence, Vandy

Florida defensive tackle Brad Culpepper, a National Football Foundation Scholar Athlete, received AP All-SEC honors in 1990 and 1991.

1994 SEC Football 273

Associated Press All-SEC Teams

Ole Miss tackle Everett Lindsay, who earned All-America and consensus All-SEC accolades, helped guide the Rebels to a 9-3 record in 1992.

Arkansas defensive end Henry Ford, a first-round selection in the 1994 NFL Draft, was tabbed All-SEC after leading the league with 14 sacks last season.

1992
OFFENSE

First Team
WR—Andre Hastings, Ga.
WR—Willie Jackson, Fla.
TE—Pat Akos, Vandy
OL—Everett Lindsay, Miss.
OL—Alec Millen, Ga.
OL—John James, MSU
OL—Mike Stowell, Tenn.
C—Tobie Shiels, Ala.
QB—Shane Matthews, Fla.
RB—Garrison Hearst, Ga.
RB—Cory Philpot, Miss.
PK—Scott Etheridge, Aub.

Second Team
WR—Willie Harris, MSU
TE—Kirk Botkin, Ark.
OL—Todd Perry, Ky.
OL—Kevin Mawae, LSU
OL—Chris Gray, Aub.
OL—Ernest Dye, USC
OL—Jim Watson, Fla.
C—Lee Ford, MSU
QB—Eric Zeier, Ga.
RB—James Bostic, Aub.
RB—Errict Rhett, Fla.
RB—Derrick Lassic, Ala.
PK—Michael Proctor, Ala.
PK—Doug Pelfrey, Ky.

DEFENSE

First Team
DE—John Copeland, Ala.
DE—Eric Curry, Ala.
DT—Chad Brown, Miss.
OLB—Todd Kelly, Tenn.
OLB—Mitch Davis, Ga.
ILB—Daniel Boyd, MSU
ILB—Carlton Miles, Fla.
DB—George Teague, Ala.
DB—Antonio Langham, Ala.
DB—Greg Tremble, Ga.
DB—Jeff Brothers, Vandy
P—Pete Raether, Ark.
P—Todd Jordan, MSU

Second Team
DL—Bo Davis, LSU
DL—Gary Rogers, Vandy
DL—Willie Whitehead, Aub.
DL—Kevin Carter, Fla.
LB—Karekin Cunningham, Aub.
LB—Dewayne Dotson, Miss.
LB—Antonio London, Ala.
LB—Lemanski Hall, Ala.
LB—Marty Moore, Ky.
DB—Kelvin Knight, MSU
DB—Danny Boyd, Miss.
DB—Will White, Fla.
P—Terry Daniel, Aub.

1993
OFFENSE

First Team
WR—David Palmer, Ala.
WR—Brice Hunter, Ga.
TE—Shannon Mitchell, Ga.
OT—Wayne Gandy, Aub.
OT—Reggie Green, Fla.
OG—Jim Watson, Fla.
OG—Jeff Smith, Tenn.
C—Tobie Shiels, Ala.
QB—Heath Shuler, Tenn.
RB—Errict Rhett, Fla.
RB—James Bostic, Aub.
PK—John Becksvoort, Tenn.

Second Team
WR—Jack Jackson, Fla.
WR—Cory Fleming, Tenn.
TE—Kirk Botkin, Ark.
OT—Bernard Williams, Ga.
OT—Jason Odom, Fla.
OG—Ryan Bell, Vandy
OG—Anthony Redmon, Aub.
C—Kevin Mawae, LSU
QB—Eric Zeier, Ga.
RB—Charlie Garner, Tenn.
RB—Moe Williams, Ky.
PK—Scott Etheridge, Aub.
PK—Michael Proctor, Ala.

DEFENSE

First Team
DE—Henry Ford, Ark.
DE—Jeremy Nunley, Ala.
DT—Williams Gaines, Fla.
DT—Arleye Gibson, MSU
LB—Dewayne Dotson, Ole Miss
LB—Cassius Ware, Ole Miss
LB—Mitch Davis, Ga.
LB—Marty Moore, Ky.
DB—Antonio Langham, Ala.
DB—Alundis Brice, Ole Miss
DB—Calvin Jackson, Aub.
P—Terry Daniel, Aub.

Second Team
DE—James Wilson, Tenn.
DE—Alan Young, Vandy
DT—James Gregory, Ala.
DT—Tim Bowens, Ole Miss
LB—Lemanski Hall, Ala.
LB—Abdul Jackson, Ole Miss
LB—Ernest Dixon, USC
LB—Ben Talley, Tenn.
DB—Johnny Dixon, Ole Miss
DB—Marcus Jenkins, Ky.
DB—Anthony Marshall, LSU
DB—Jason Parker, Tenn.
P—Shayne Edge, Fla.

274 Honors

United Press International All-SEC Teams

1950
First Team
E—Bucky Curtis, Vandy
E—Al Lary, Ala.
T—Bob Gain, Ky.
T—Paul Lea, Tul.
G—Ted Daffer, Tenn.
G—Mike Mizerany, Ala.
C—Bob Bossons, Ga. Tech
B—Babe Parilli, Ky.
B—Hank Lauricella, Tenn.
B—Eddie Salem, Ala.
B—John Dottley, Miss.

Second Team
E—Bud Sherrod, Tenn.
E—John Weigle, Ga. Tech
T—Bob Werckle, Vandy
T—Bill Pearman, Tenn.
G—Bill Wannamaker, Ky.
G—Rocco Principe, Ga.
C—Pat O'Sullivan, Ala.
B—Haywood Sullivan, Fla.
B—Bill Wade, Vandy
B—Ken Konz, LSU
B—Bill Leskovar, Ky.

Third Team
E—Ben Zaranka, Ky.
E—Bill Stribling, Miss.
T—Jack Stroud, Tenn.
T—Marion Campbell, Ga.
G—Tom Banks, Aub.
G—Pat James, Ky.
C—Doug Moseley, Ky.
B—Clarence Avinger, Ala.
B—Billy Mixon, Ga.
B—Bobby Marlow, Ala.
B—Bill Jamerson, Ky.

1951
First Team
E—Ben Roderick, Vandy
E—Steve Meilinger, Ky.
T—Bill Pearman, Tenn.
T—Lamar Wheat, Ga. Tech
G—Ted Daffer, Tenn.
G—Ray Beck, Ga. Tech
C—Doug Moseley, Ky.
B—Babe Parilli, Ky.
B—Hank Lauricella, Tenn.
B—Bobby Marlow, Ala.
B—Darrell Crawford, Ga. Tech

Second Team
E—Red Lutz, Ala.
E—Buck Martin, Ga. Tech
T—Bob Werckle, Vandy
T—Charles LaPradd, Fla.
G—Sid Fournet, LSU
G—Ed Bauer, Aub.
C—Gordon Polofky, Tenn.
B—Bill Wade, Vandy
B—Andy Kozar, Tenn.
B—Bert Rechichar, Tenn.
B—Leon Hardeman, Ga. Tech

Third Team
E—Harry Babcock, Ga.
E—Lee Hayley, Aub.
T—Jerome Helliun, Tul.
T—Billy Pyron, MSU
G—John Ignarski, Ky.
G—John Michels, Tenn.
C—Ralph Carrigan, Ala.
B—Haywood Sullivan, Fla.
B—Zeke Bratkowski, Ga.
B—Jimmy Lear, Miss.
B—Hal Payne, Tenn.

1952
First Team
E—Buck Martin, Ga. Tech
E—Steve Meilinger, Ky.
T—Charlie LaPradd, Fla.
T—Doug Atkins, Tenn.
G—John Michels, Tenn.
G—Joe D'Agostino, Fla.
C—George Morris, Ga. Tech
B—Jackie Parker, MSU
B—Leon Hardeman, Ga. Tech
B—Bobby Marlow, Ala.
B—Andy Kozar, Tenn.

Second Team
E—Harry Babcock, Ga.
E—Ben Roderick, Vandy
T—Hal Miller, Ga. Tech
T—Kline Gilbert, Miss.
G—Crawford Mims, Miss.
G—Orrville Vereen, Ga. Tech
C—Pete Brown, Ga. Tech
B—Jimmy Lear, Miss.
B—Zeke Bratkowski, Ga.
B—Joe Fortunato, MSU
B—Rick Casares, Fla.

Third Team
E—Jimmy Mask, Miss.
E—Roger Rotroff, Tenn.
T—Bill Turnbeaugh, Aub.
T—Paul Miller, LSU
G—Jerry Watford, Ala.
G—Ed Gossage, Ga. Tech
C—Larry Morris, Ga. Tech
B—Bill Krietemeyer, Vandy
B—Corky Tharp, Ala.
B—Buford Long, Fla.
B—Max McGee, Tul.

1953
First Team
E—John Carson, Ga.
E—Jim Pyburn, Aub.
T—Sid Fournet, LSU
T—Bill Fisher, Tenn.
G—Crawford Mims, Miss.
G—Joe D'Agostino, Fla.
C—Larry Morris, Ga. Tech
B—Zeke Bratkowski, Ga.
B—Corky Tharp, Ala.
B—Jackie Parker, MSU
B—Steve Meilinger, Ky.

Second Team
E—Sam Hensley, Ga. Tech
E—Roger Rotroff, Tenn.
T—Ed Culpepper, Ala.
T—George Mason, Ala.
G—Ray Correll, Ky.
G—Orrville, Vereen, Ga. Tech
C—Hal Easterwood, MSU
B—Jimmy Wade, Tenn.
B—Leon Hardeman, Ga. Tech
B—Bill Teas, Ga. Tech
B—Glenn Turner, Ga. Tech

Third Team
E—Mack Franklin, Tenn.
E—Bud Wlllis, Ala.
T—Frank D'Agostino, Aub.
T—Bob Sherman, Ga. Tech
G—George Atkins, Aub.
G—Al Robelot, Tul.
C—Ralph Carrigan, Ala.
B—Tommy Lewis, Ala.
B—Bobby Freeman, Aub.
B—Jerry Marchand, LSU
B—Hal Lofton, Miss.

1954
First Team
E—Jim Pyburn, Aub.
E—Henry Hair, Ga. Tech
T—Sid Fournet, LSU
T—Darris McCord, Tenn.
G—Franklin Brooks, Ga. Tech
G—Bobby Goodall, Vandy
C—Larry Morris, Ga. Tech
B—Eagle Day, Miss.
B—Tom Tracy, Tenn.
B—Arthur Davis, MSU
B—Corky Tharp, Ala.

Second Team
E—Bradley Mills, Ky.
E—Joe O'Malley, Ga.
T—Frank D'Agostino, Aub.
T—Rex Reed Boggan, Miss.
G—Bill Dolley, MSU
G—Andy Sardisco, Tul.
C—Hal Easterwood, MSU
B—Bob Hardy, Ky.
B—Joe Childress, Aub.
B—Charley Horton, Vandy
B—Allen Muirhead, Miss.

Third Team
E—Dave Dickerson, Miss.
E—Joe Tuminello, LSU
T—Sid Youngleman, Ala.
T—George Mason, Ala.
G—Don Shea, Ga.
G—George Atkins, Aub.
C—Steve DeLaTorre, Fla.
B—Bobby Freeman, Aub.
B—Bobby McCool, Miss.
B—Jackie Simpson, Fla.
B—Jimmy Thompson, Ga. Tech

1955
First Team
E—Joe Tuminello, LSU
E—Howard Schnellenberger, Ky.
T—Earl Leggett, LSU
T—Frank D'Agostino, Aub.
G—Franklin Brooks, Ga. Tech
G—Scott Suber, MSU
C—Steve DeLaTorre, Fla.
B—Eagle Day, Miss.
B—Johnny Majors, Tenn.
B—Fob James, Aub.
B—Joe Childress, Aub.

Second Team
E—Nick Germanos, Ala.
E—Jimmy Phillips, Aub.
T—Charles Rader, Tenn.
T—M.L. Brackett, Aub.
G—Andy Sardisco, Tul.
G—Larry Frank, Vandy
C—Jimmy Morris, Ga. Tech
B—Bob Hardy, Ky.
B—Charley Horton, Vandy
B—Art Davis, MSU
B—Ronnie Quillian, Tul.

Third Team
E—Roy Wilkins, Ga.
E—Joe Stephenson, Vandy
T—Jim Barron, MSU
T—Carl Vereen, Ga. Tech
G—Bryan Bunthorpe, Tul.
G—Buddy Alliston, Miss.
C—Gene Dubisson, Miss.
B—Wade Mitchell, Ga. Tech
B—Jackie Simpson, Fla.
B—George Volkert, Ga. Tech
B—Paige Cothren, Miss.

1956
First Team
E—Buddy Cruze, Tenn.
E—Ron Bennett, MSU
T—Lou Michaels, Ky.
T—John Gordy, Tenn.
G—John Barrow, Fla.
G—Allen Ecker, Ga. Tech
C—Don Stephenson, Ga. Tech
B—Billy Stacy, MSU
B—Johnny Majors, Tenn.
B—Phil King, Vandy
B—Paige Cothren, Miss.

Second Team
E—Jimmy Phillips, Aub.
E—Roger Urbano, Tenn.
T—Billy Yelverton, Miss.
T—Carl Vereen, Ga. Tech
G—Ernie Danjean, Aub.
G—Jimmy Johnson, Ga. Tech
C—Bubba Howe, Tenn.
B—Gene Newton, Tul.
B—Jackie Simpson, Fla.
B—Paul Rotenberry, Ga. Tech
B—Ronny Quillian, Tul.

Third Team
E—Roy Wilkins, Ga.
E—Bob Laws, Vandy
T—Earl Leggett, LSU
T—J.T. Frankenberger, Ky.
G—Charles Duck, Miss.
G—Tony Cushenberry, Ga.
C—Dave Kuhn, Ky.
B—Wade Mitchell, Ga. Tech
B—Tommy Lorino, Aub.
B—George Volkert, Ga. Tech
B—Ken Owen, Ga. Tech

1957
First Team
E—Jimmy Philips, Aub.
E—Jerry Wilson, Aub.
T—Lou Michaels, Ky.
T—Gene Hickerson, Miss.
G—Bill Johnson, Tenn.
G—George Deiderich, Vandy
C—Don Stephenson, Ga. Tech
B—Billy Stacy, MSU
B—Bobby Gordon, Tenn.
B—Ray Brown, Miss.
B—Jimmy Taylor, LSU

Second Team
E—Jerry Nabors, Ga. Tech
E—Dan Pelham, Fla.
T—Charlie Mitchell, Fla.
T—Jack Benson, MSU
T—Ben Preston, Aub.
G—Jackie Simpson, Miss.
G—Billy Rains, Ala.
C—Jackie Burkett, Aub.
B—Phil King, Vandy
B—Billy Cannon, LSU
B—Jim Rountree, Fla.
B—Billy Atkins, Aub.

Third Team
E—Bob Laws, Vandy
E—Don Williams, Miss.
T—Al Aucoin, LSU
T—Jim Smelcher, Tenn.
G—Zeke Smith, Aub.
G—Tim Baker, Aub.
C—Jimmy Dodd, MSU
B—Boyce Smith, Vandy
B—Tommy Lorino, Aub.
B—Bobby Cravens, Ky.
B—Tommy Bronson, Tenn.

1994 SEC Football 275

United Press International All-SEC Teams

1958
First Team
E—Jerry Wilson, Aub.
E—Don Fleming, Fla.
T—Vel Heckman, Fla.
T—Cleve Wester, Aub.
G—Zeke Smith, Aub.
G—George Deiderich, Vandy
C—Max Fugler, LSU
B—Richie Petibon, Tul.
B—Billy Cannon, LSU
B—Tom Moore, Vandy
B—Theron Sapp, Ga.

Second Team
E—Larry Grantham, Miss.
E—Billy Hendrix, LSU
T—Pat Dye, Ga.
T—Dave Sington, Ala.
G—Jack Benson, MSU
G—Bobby Urbano, Tenn.
C—Jackie Burkett, Aub.
B—Billy Stancy, MSU
B—Bobby Cravens, Ky.
B—Bobby Franklin, Miss.
B—Charlie Flowers, Miss.

(NO THIRD TEAM)

Lee Roy Jordan
Alabama

Jerry Stovall
LSU

1959
First Team
E—Dave Hudson, Fla.
E—Jimmy Vickers, Ga.
T—Joe Schaffer, Tenn.
T—Ken Rice, Aub.
G—Marvin Terrell, Miss.
G—Zeke Smith, Aub.
C—Jackie Burkett, Aub.
B—Fran Tarkenton, Ga.
B—Billy Cannon, LSU
B—Tom Moore, Vandy
B—Charlie Flowers, Miss.

Second Team
E—Gerald Burch, Ga. Tech
E—Larry Grantham, Miss.
T—Charles Strange, LSU
T—Walter Suggs, MSU
G—Don Cochran, Ala.
G—Pat Dye, Ga.
C—Maxie Baughan, Ga. Tech
B—Bobby Hunt, Aub.
B—Johnny Robinson, LSU
B—Jake Gibbs, Miss.
B—Warren Rabb, LSU

Third Team
E—Mickey Mangham, LSU
E—Cotton Letner, Tenn.
T—Larry Wagner, Vandy
T—Billy Shaw, Ga. Tech
G—Richard Price, Miss.
G—Ed McCreedy, LSU
C—Tom Goode, MSU
B—Billy Majors, Tenn.
B—Charley Britt, Ga.
B—Calvin Bird, Ky.
B—Ed Dyas, Aub.

1960
First Team
E—Johnny Brewer, Miss.
E—Pat Patchen, Fla.
T—Ken Rice, Aub.
T—Billy Shaw, Ga. Tech
G—Vic Miranda, Fla.
G—Pat Dye, Ga.
C—Tom Goode, MSU
B—Ed Dyas, Aub.
B—Tom Mason, Tul.
B—Fran Tarkenton, Ga.
B—Jake Gibbs, Miss.

Second Team
E—Gerald Burch, Ga. Tech
E—Cotton Letner, Tenn.
T—Billy Wilson, Aub.
T—Walter Suggs, MSU
G—Richard Price, Miss.
G—Billy Neighbors, Ala.
C—Charles Strange, LSU
B—Larry Libertore, Fla.
B—Fred Brown, Ga.
B—Glenn Glass, Tenn.
B—Billy Williamson, Ga. Tech

Third Team
E—Mickey Mangham, LSU
E—Tom Hutchinson, Ky.
T—Bob Benton, Miss.
T—Ed Nutting, Ga. Tech
G—Edward McCreedy, LSU
G—Lloyd Hodge, Ky.
C—Cody Binkley, Vandy
B—James Anderson, Miss.
B—Calvin Bird, Ky.
B—Don Goodman, Fla.
B—Chick Graning, Ga. Tech

1961
First Team
E—Tom Hutchinson, Ky.
E—Dave Edwards, Aub.
T—Billy Neighbors, Ala.
T—Jim Dunaway, Miss.
G—Roy Winston, LSU
G—Dave Watson, Ga. Tech
C—Lee Roy Jordan, Ala.
B—Pat Trammell, Ala.
B—Billy Ray Adams, Miss.
B—Jerry Stovall, LSU
B—Mike Fracchia, Ala.

Second Team
E—Johnny Baker, MSU
E—Ralph Smith, Miss.
T—Pete Case, Ga.
T—Jim Beaver, Fla.
G—Rufus Guthrie, Ga. Tech
G—Bookie Bolin, Miss.
C—Mike Lucci, Tenn.
B—Doug Elmore, Miss.
B—Wendell Harris, LSU
B—Billy Williamson, Ga. Tech
B—Bill McKenny, Ga.

Third Team
E—Tommy Brooker, Ala.
E—Dave Gash, Ky.
T—Billy Wilson, Aub.
T—Billy Booth, LSU
G—Billy Ray Jones, Miss.
G—Gus Gonzales, Tul.
C—Irvin Goode, Ky.
B—Mallon Faircloth, Tenn.
B—Jerry Woolum, Ky.
B—Don Goodman, Fla.
B—Bobby Hunt, Aub.

1962
First Team
E—Tom Hutchinson, Ky.
E—Billy Martin, Ga. Tech
T—Jim Dunaway, Miss.
T—Fred Miller, LSU
G—Dave Watson, Ga. Tech
G—Rufus Guthrie, Ga. Tech
C—Lee Roy Jordan, Ala.
B—Jerry Stovall, LSU
B—Billy Lothridge, Ga. Tech
B—Glynn Griffing, Miss.
B—Larry Dupree, Fla.

Second Team
E—Johnny Baker, MSU
E—Mickey Babb, Ga.
T—Anton Peters, Fla.
T—Junior Hawthorne, Ky.
G—Don Dickson, Miss.
G—Bill Van Dyke, Aub.
C—Dennis Gaubatz, LSU
B—Joe Namath, Ala.
B—Cotton Clark, Ala.
B—Larry Rakestraw, Ga.
B—Mallon Faircloth, Tenn.

Third Team
E—Richard Williamson, Ala.
E—Ted Davis, Ga. Tech
T—Don Estes, LSU
T—Joe Baughan, Aub.
G—Larry Travis, Fla.
G—Pat Watson, MSU
C—Jim Price, Aub.
B—Mike McNames, Ga. Tech
B—Darrell Cox, Ky.
B—Louis Guy, Miss.
B—Jimmy Burson, Aub.

1963
First Team
E—Billy Martin, Ga. Tech
E—Billy Truax, LSU
T—Herschel Turner, Ky.
T—Whaley Hall, Miss.
G—Steve DeLong, Tenn.
G—Stan Hindman, Miss.
C—Pat Wilson, MSU
B—Jimmy Sidle, Aub.
B—Billy Lothridge, Ga. Tech
B—Benny Nelson, Ala.
B—Larry Dupree, Fla.

Second Team
E—Allen Brown, Miss.
E—Howard Simpson, Aub.
T—Tommy Neville, MSU
T—Ray Rissmiller, Ga.
G—Bob Hucklebridge, LSU
G—Bill Van Dyke, Aub.
C—Kenny Dill, Miss.
B—Larry Rakestraw, Ga.
B—Ode Burrell, MSU
B—Joe Namath, Ala.
B—Perry Lee Dunn, Miss.

Third Team
E—Tommy Inman, MSU
E—Ted Davis, Ga. Tech
T—Dennis Murphy, Fla.
T—Mike Calamari, Tul.
G—Jack Katz, Fla.
G—Remi Prudhomme, LSU
C—Ruffin Rodrigue, LSU
B—Tucker Frederickson, Aub.
B—Danny LeBlanc, LSU
B—Sonny Fisher, MSU
B—Hoyle Granger, MSU

1964
First Team
E—Rick Kestner, Ky.
E—Allen Brown, Miss.
T—Jim Wilson, Ga.
T—Ray Rissmiller, Ga.
G—Steve DeLong, Tenn.
G—Remi Prudhomme, LSU
C—Pat Watson, MSU
B—Tucker Frederickson, Aub.
B—Rodger Bird, Ky.
B—Joe Namath, Ala.
B—Larry Dupree, Fla.

Second Team
E—Charley Casey, Fla.
E—Doug Moreau, LSU
T—Dan Kearley, Ala.
T—Tommy Neville, MSU
G—Stan Hindman, Miss.
G—Wayne Freeman, Ala.
C—Gaylon McCollough, Ala.
B—Steve Sloan, Ala.
B—Hoyle Granger, MSU
B—Mike Dennis, Miss.
B—Jim Weatherly, Miss.

Third Team
E—Tommy Tolleson, Ala.
E—Tommy Inman, MSU
T—Dennis Murphy, Fla.
T—George Rice, LSU
G—Bill Richbourg, Fla.
G—Justin Canale, MSU
C—Ruffin Rodrigue, LSU
B—Joe LeBruzzo, LSU
B—Steve Spurrier, Fla.
B—Steve Bowman, Ala.
B—David Ray, Ala.

Honors

1965

OFFENSE
E—Charles Casey, Fla.
E—Rick Kestner, Ky.
T—Sam Ball, Ky.
T—Dave McCormick, LSU
G—Stan Hindman, Miss.
G—Larry Beckman, Fla.
C—Paul Crane, Ala.
B—Steve Spurrier, Fla.
HB—Rodger Bird, Ky.
HB—Mike Dennis, Miss.
FB—Steve Bowman, Ala.

DEFENSE
E—Bobby Frazier, Tenn.
E—Creed Gilmer, Ala.
T—Jim Urbanek, Miss.
T—George Patton, Ga.
G—Larry Gagner, Fla.
LB—Frank Emanuel, Tenn.
LB—Bill Cody, Aub.
LB—Bill Goss, Tul.
B—Bobby Johns, Ala.
B—Lynn Hughes, Ga.
S—Bruce Bennett, Fla.

1966

OFFENSE
E—Ray Perkins, Ala.
E—Austin Denney, Tenn.
T—Cecil Dowdy, Ala.
T—Edgar Chandler, Ga.
G—Jim Benson, Fla.
G—Johnny Calvert, Ala.
C—Bill Carr, Fla.
TB—Larry Smith, Fla.
QB—Steve Spurrier, Fla.
WB—Richard Trapp, Fla.
FB—Ronnie Jenkins, Ga.

DEFENSE
E—Jerry Richardson, Miss.
E—Mike Robichaux, LSU
T—George Patton, Ga.
T—Jim Urbanek, Miss.
G—Gusty Yearout, Aub.
LB—Paul Naumoff, Tenn.
LB—D.D. Lewis, MSU
LB—Chip Healy, Vandy
HB—Bobby Johns, Ala.
HB—Dicky Thompson, Ala.
S—Lynn Hughes, Ga.

1967

OFFENSE
SE—Dennis Homan, Ala.
TE—Bob Goodridge, Vandy
LT—Edgar Chandler, Ga.
RT—John Boynton, Tenn.
LG—Guy Dennis, Fla.
RG—Bruce Stephens, Ala.
C—Bob Johnson, Tenn.
QB—Ken Stabler, Ala.
TB—Larry Smith, Fla.
FL—Richard Trapp, Fla.
FB—Dicky Lyons, Ky.

DEFENSE
E—John Garlington, LSU
E—Larry Kohn, Ga.
T—Bill Stanfill, Ga.
T—Jim Urbanek, Miss.
MG—Gusty Yearout, Aub.
LB—D.D. Lewis, MSU
LB—Jimmy Keyes, Miss.
LB—Mike Hall, Ala.
HB—Albert Dorsey, Tenn.
HB—Bobby Johns, Ala.
S—Sammy Grezaffi, LSU

1968

OFFENSE
SE—Tim Christian, Aub.
TE—Ken DeLong, Tenn.
LT—Bill Fortier, LSU
RT—David Rholetter, Ga.
LG—Charles Rosenfelder, Tenn.
RG—Guy Dennis, Fla.
C—Tom Banks, Aub.
QB—Loran Carter, Aub.
RB—Dicky Lyons, Ky.
RB—Larry Smith, Fla.
FL—Sammy Milner, MSU

DEFENSE
E—Mike Ford, Ala.
E—Billy Payne, Ga.
T—Bill Stanfill, Ga.
T—David Campbell, Aub.
MG—Sam Gellerstedt, Ala.
LB—Mike Hall, Ala.
LB—Steve Kiner, Tenn.
LB—Mike Kolen, Aub.
HB—Jim Weatherford, Tenn.
HB—Steve Tannen, Fla.
S—Jake Scott, Ga.

1969

OFFENSE
SE—Sammy Milner, MSU
TE—Ken DeLong, Tenn.
LT—Bob Asher, Vandy
RT—Mac Steen, Fla.
LG—Alvin Samples, Ala.
RG—Chip Kell, Tenn.
C—Godfrey Zaunbrecher, LSU
QB—Archie Manning, Miss.
RB—Tommy Durrance, Fla.
RB—Curt Watson, Tenn.
FL—Carlos Alvarez, Fla.

DEFENSE
LE—Louis Farber, Miss.
RE—David Roller, Ky.
LT—Frank Yanossy, Tenn.
RT—David Campbell, Aub.
MG—Steve Greer, Ga.
LB—Steve Kiner, Tenn.
LB—Mike Kolen, Aub.
LB—George Bevan, LSU
HB—Buddy McClinton, Aub.
HB—Tommy Casanova, LSU
S—Glenn Cannon, Miss.

1970

OFFENSE
SE—Terry Beasley, Aub.
TE—Jim Poole, Miss.
LT—Worthy McClure, Miss.
RT—Tom Nash, Ga.
LG—Chip Kell, Tenn.
RG—Skip Jernigan, Miss.
C—Tommy Lyons, Ga.
QB—Pat Sullivan, Aub.
QB—Archie Manning, Miss.
RB—Johnny Musso, Ala.
RB—Curt Watson, Tenn.
FL—David Smith, MSU

DEFENSE
LE—Dennis Coleman, Miss.
RE—Jack Youngblood, Fla.
LT—Dave Roller, Ky.
RT—John Sage, LSU
LB—Jackie Walker, Tenn.
LB—Mike Anderson, LSU
LB—Bob Strickland, Aub.
DB—Larry Willingham, Aub.
DB—Tim Priest, Tenn.
DB—Bobby Majors, Tenn.
DB—Tommy Casanova, LSU

1971

OFFENSE
SE—Terry Beasley, Aub.
TE—Jim Poole, Miss.
LT—John Hannah, Ala.
RT—Tom Nash, Ga.
LG—Royce Smith, Ga.
RT—Mike Demarie, LSU
C—Jimmy Grammer, Ala.
QB—Pat Sullivan, Aub.
RB—Johnny Musso, Ala.
RB—Curt Watson, Tenn.
FL—Dick Schmalz, Aub.

DEFENSE
LE—Robin Parkhouse, Ala.
RE—Mixon Robinson, Ga.
LT—Ronnie Estay, LSU
RT—Tommy Yearout, Aub.
LB—Jackie Walker, Tenn.
LB—Chip Wisdom, Ga.
LB—Joe Federspiel, Ky.
DB—Bobby Majors, Tenn.
DB—Buzy Rosenberg, Ga.
DB—Tommy Casanova, LSU
DB—Steve Higginbotham, Ala.

1972

OFFENSE
SE—Wayne Wheeler, Ala.
TE—Burney Veazey, Miss.
OT—Mac Lorendo, Aub.
OT—Buddy Brown, Ala.
OG—John Hannah, Ala.
OG—Bill Emendorfer, Tenn.
C—Jim Krapf, Ala.
QB—Bert Jones, LSU
QB—Terry Davis, Ala.
RB—Terry Henley, Aub.
RB—Nat Moore, Fla.
WB—Gerald Keigley, LSU

DEFENSE
DE—Danny Sanspree, Aub.
DE—John Mitchell, Ala.
DT—John Wood, LSU
DT—Benny Sivley, Aub.
LB—Jamie Rotella, Tenn.
LB—Fred Abbott, Fla.
LB—Chuck Strickland, Ala.
DB—Conrad Graham, Tenn.
DB—Dave Beck, Aub.
HB—Frank Dowsing, MSU
HB—Bobby McKinney, Ala.

1973

OFFENSE
SE—Wayne Wheeler, Ala.
T—Steve Sprayberry, Ala.
G—Tyler Lafauci, LSU
C—Steve Taylor, Aub.
G—Art Bressler, Miss.
T—Buddy Brown, Ala.
TE—Butch Veazey, Miss.
QB—Condredge Holloway, Tenn.
RB—Sonny Collins, Ky.
RB—Wilbur Jackson, Ala.
RB—Brad Davis, LSU

DEFENSE
L—Jimmy Webb, MSU
L—Jim McCollum, Ky.
L—Benny Sivley, Aub.
L—Ben Williams, Miss.
LB—Warren Capone, LSU
LB—Woodrow Lowe, Ala.
LB—Ralph Ortega, Fla.
B—Eddie Bown, Tenn.
B—Darryl Bishop, Ky.
B—David Langner, Aub.
B—David McMakin, Ala.

1974

OFFENSE
SE—Lee McGriff, Fla.
T—Craig Hertwig, Ga.
G—Mickey Marvin, Tenn.
C—Sylvester Croom, Ala.
G—Randy Johnson, Ga.
T—Warren Bryant, Ky.
TE—Barry Burton, Vandy
QB—Rockey Felker, MSU
RB—Sonny Collins, Ky.
RB—Willie Shelby, Ala.
RB—Stanley Morgan, Tenn.

DEFENSE
E—Leroy Cook, Ala.
T—Jimmy Webb, MSU
T—Ben Williams, Miss.
E—Preston Kendrick, Fla.
LB—Woodrow Lowe, Ala.
LB—Ken Bernich, Aub.
LB—Ralph Ortega, Fla.
DB—Mike Washington, Ala.
DB—Randy Talbot, Fla.
DB—Mike Fuller, Aub.
DB—Ricky Davis, Ala.

1994 SEC Football 277

United Press International All-SEC Teams

1975

OFFENSE
- SE—Larry Seivers, Tenn.
- TE—Barry Burton, Vandy
- T—Warren Bryant, Ky.
- T—Mike Williams, Fla.
- G—Randy Johnson, Ga.
- G—Mickey Marvin, Tenn.
- C—Richard Keys, MSU
- QB—Richard Todd, Ala.
- RB—Jimmy DuBose, Fla.
- RB—Sonny Collins, Ky.
- RB—Glynn Harrison, Ga.

DEFENSE
- E—Leroy Cook, Ala.
- E—Ron McCartney, Tenn.
- T—Steve Cassidy, LSU
- T—Bob Baumhower, Ala.
- MG—Ben Williams, Miss.
- LB—Woodrow Lowe, Ala.
- LB—Conley Duncan, Ala.
- LB—Sammy Green, Fla.
- DB—Jay Chesley, Vandy
- DB—Tyrone King, Ala.
- DB—Alan Pizzitola, Ala.

1976

OFFENSE
- WR—Larry Seivers, Tenn.
- TE—Ozzie Newsome, Ala.
- T—Mike Wilson, Ga.
- T—Warren Bryant, Ky.
- G—Joel Parrish, Ga.
- G—Mickey Marvin, Tenn.
- C—Richard Keys, MSU
- QB—Ray Goff, Ga.
- RB—Terry Robiskie, LSU
- RB—Kevin McLee, Ga.
- RB—Stanley Morgan, Tenn.

DEFENSE
- E—Dicky Clark, Ga.
- E—Art Still, Ky.
- T—Bob Baumhower, Ala.
- T—A.J. Duhe, LSU
- MG—Harvey Hull, MSU
- LB—Andy Spiva, Tenn.
- LB—Ben Zambiasi, Ga.
- LB—Ray Costict, MSU
- DB—Bill King, Ga.
- DB—Stan Black, MSU
- DB—Alvin Cowans, Fla.

1977

OFFENSE
- WR—Wes Chandler, Fla.
- TE—Ozzie Newsome, Ala.
- T—Jim Bunch, Ala.
- T—Robert Dugas, LSU
- G—Craig Duhe, LSU
- G—George Collins, Ga.
- C—Robert Shaw, Tenn.
- QB—Derrick Ramsey, Ky.
- RB—Charles Alexander, LSU
- RB—Johnny Davis, Ala.
- RB—Tony Green, Fla.
- PK—Jorge Portella, Aub.

DEFENSE
- E—Art Still, Ky.
- E—George Plasketes, Miss.
- T—Larry Gillard, MSU
- T—Dennis Harrison, Vandy
- MG—Scott Hutchinson, Fla.
- LB—Freddie Smith, Aub
- LB—Ben Zambiasi, Ga.
- LB—Scott Brantley, Fla.
- DB—Bill Krug, Ala.
- DB—Mike Kramer, Ala.
- DB—Mike Siganos, Ky.
- P—Jim Miller, Miss.

1978

OFFENSE
- WR—Mardye McDole, MSU
- WR—Cris Collinsworth, Fla.
- T—Robert Dugas, LSU
- T—Jim Bunch, Ala.
- G—Dan Fowler, Ky.
- G—Matt Braswell, Ga.
- C—Dwight Stephenson, Ala.
- QB—Dave Marler, MSU
- RB—Charles Alexander, LSU
- RB—Willie McClendon, Ga.
- RB—Joe Cribbs, Aub.
- PK—Rex Robinson, Ga.

DEFENSE
- E—Wayne Hamilton, Ala.
- E—John Adams, LSU
- T—Marty Lyons, Ala.
- T—Charlie Cage, Miss.
- MG—Richard Jaffe, Ky.
- LB—Barry Krauss, Ala.
- LB—Scot Brantley, Fla.
- LB—Jim Kovach, Ky.
- DB—Roland James, Tenn.
- DB—Chris Williams, LSU
- DB—James McKinney, Aub.
- P—Jim Miller, Miss.

1979

OFFENSE
- WR—Preston Brown, Vandy
- FL—Cris Collinsworth, Fla.
- T—Jim Bunch, Ala.
- T—George Stephenson, Aub.
- G—Mike Brock, Ala.
- G—Matt Braswell, Ga.
- C—Dwight Stephenson, Ala.
- QB—Jimmy Streater, Tenn.
- RB—Joe Cribbs, Aub.
- RB—James Brooks, Aub.
- RB—Major Ogilvie, Ala.
- PK—Rex Robinson, Ga.

DEFENSE
- E—E.J. Junior, Ala.
- E—John Adams, LSU
- T—David Hannah, Ala.
- T—Benjy Thibodeaux, LSU
- MG—Richard Jaffe, Ky.
- LB—Thomas Boyd, Ala.
- LB—Freddie Smith, Aub.
- LB—Craig Puki, Tenn.
- DB—Jim Bob Harris, Ala.
- DB—Roland James, Tenn.
- DB—Scott Woerner, Ga.
- P—Jim Miller, Miss.

1980

OFFENSE
- WR—Cris Collinsworth, Fla.
- TE—Chris Faulkner, Fla.
- T—Tim Morrison, Ga.
- T—Tim Irwin, Tenn.
- G—George Stephenson, Aub.
- G—Nat Hudson, Ga.
- C—Lee North, Tenn.
- QB—John Fourcade, Miss.
- RB—Herschel Walker, Ga.
- RB—James Brocks, Aub.
- FL—Mardye McDole, MSU
- PK—Rex Robinson, Ga.

DEFENSE
- E—E.J. Junior, Ala.
- E—Lyman White, LSU
- T—Byron Braggs, Ala.
- T—Jimmy Payne, Ga.
- MG—Jim Noonan, Tenn.
- LB—Thomas Boyd, Ala.
- LB—David Little, Fla.
- LB—Johnie Cooks, MSU
- DB—Scott Woerner, Ga.
- DB—Jeff Hipp, Ga.
- DB—Jim Bob Harris, Ala.
- P—Jim Arnold, Vandy

1981

OFFENSE
- WR—Wamon Buggs, Vandy
- TE—Bart Krout, Ala.
- T—Keith Uecker, Aub.
- T—Bob Cayavec, Ala.
- G—Wayne Harris, MSU
- G—Ken Hammond, Vandy
- C—Lee North, Tenn.
- QB—Buck Belue, Ga.
- RB—Herschel Walker, Ga.
- RB—James Jones, Fla.
- FL—Lindsay Scott, Ga.
- PK—Kevin Butler, Ga.

DEFENSE
- E—Billy Jackson, MSU
- E—David Galloway, Fla.
- T—Eddie Weaver, Ga.
- T—Glen Collins, MSU
- MG—Warren Lyles, LSU
- LB—Johnie Cooks, MSU
- LB—Thomas Boyd, Ala.
- LB—Danny Skutack, Aub.
- DB—Tommy Wilcox, Ala.
- DB—Jim Bob Harris, Ala.
- DB—Rob Fesmire, MSU
- P—Jim Arnold, Vandy

1982

OFFENSE
- WR—Willie Gault, Tenn.
- TE—Allama Matthews, Vandy
- T—Jimmy Harper, Ga.
- T—Pat Phenix, Miss.
- G—Wayne Harris, MSU
- G—Steve Mott, Ala.
- C—Wayne Radloff, Ga.
- QB—Whit Taylor, Vandy
- RB—Herschel Walker, Ga.
- RB—Bo Jackson, Aub.
- FL—Danny Knight, MSU
- PK—Fuad Reveiz, Tenn.

DEFENSE
- E—Mike Pitts, Ala.
- E—Billy Jackson, MSU
- E—Freddie Gilbert, Ga.
- T—Jimmy Payne, Ga.
- NG—Ramsey Dardar, LSU
- LB—Wilber Marshall, Fla.
- LB—Al Richardson, LSU
- LB—Tommy Thurson, Ga.
- DB—Terry Hoage, Ga.
- DB—Jeff Sanchez, Ga.
- DB—Jeremiah Castille, Ala.
- P—Jim Arnold, Vandy

1983

OFFENSE
- WR—Dwayne Dixon, Fla.
- TE—Chuck Scott, Vandy
- T—Pat Arrington, Aub.
- T—Guy McIntyre, Ga.
- G—David Jordan, Aub.
- G—Bill Mayo, Tenn.
- C—Glenn Streno, Tenn.
- QB—Walter Lewis, Ala.
- RB—Bo Jackson, Aub.
- RB—Johnnie Jones, Tenn.
- RB—Ricky Moore, Ala.
- PK—Kevin Butler, Ga.

DEFENSE
- DL—Dowe Aughtman, Aub.
- DL—Freddie Gilbert, Ga.
- DL—Donnie Humphrey, Aub.
- DL—Doug Smith, Aub.
- DL—Reggie White, Tenn.
- LB—Billy Jackson, MSU
- LB—Wilber Marshall, Fla.
- LB—Tommy Thurson, Ga.
- DB—Leonard Coleman, Vandy
- DB—Terry Hoage, Ga.
- DB—David King, Aub.
- P—Ricky Anderson, Vandy

1984

OFFENSE
- WR—Chuck Scott, Vandy
- WR—Eric Martin, LSU
- OL—Lomas Brown, Fla.
- OL—Lance Smith, LSU
- C—Phil Bromley, Fla.
- OL—Rob Monaco, Vandy
- OL—Bill Mayo, Tenn.
- QB—Kurt Page, Vandy
- RB—Johnnie Jones, Tenn.
- RB—Dalton Hilliard, LSU
- RB—George Adams, Ky.
- PK—Kevin Butler, Ga.

DEFENSE
- DL—Jon Hand, Ala.
- DL—Pat Swoopes, MSU
- DL—Tim Newton, Fla.
- DL—Gerald Robinson, Aub.
- DL—Freddie Joe Nunn, Miss.
- LB—Knox Culpepper, Ga.
- LB—Alonzo Johnson, Fla.
- LB—Gregg Carr, Aub.
- DB—Paul Calhoun, Ky.
- DB—Jeff Sanchez, Ga.
- DB—David King, Aub.
- DB—Liffort Hobley, LSU
- P—Ricky Anderson, Vandy

1985

OFFENSE
- WR—Tim McGee, Tenn.
- WR—Albert Bell, Ala.
- OL—Bruce Wilkerson, Tenn.
- OL—Jeff Zimmerman, Fla.
- OC—Wes Neighbors, Ala.
- OL—Will Wolford, Vandy
- OL—Steve Wallace, Aub.
- QB—Mike Shula, Ala.
- QB—Kerwin Bell, Fla.
- RB—Bo Jackson, Aub.
- RB—Dalton Hilliard, LSU
- RB—Neal Anderson, Fla.
- PK—Carlos Reveiz, Tenn.

DEFENSE
- DL—Pat Swoopes, MSU
- DL—Gerald Williams, Aub.
- DL—Jon Hand, Ala.
- DL—Steve Wade, Vandy
- DL—Curt Jarvis, Ala.
- LB—Cornelius Bennett, Ala.
- LB—Alonzo Johnson, Fla.
- LB—Michael Brooks, LSU
- DB—Chris White, Tenn.
- DB—John Little, Ga.
- DB—Tom Powell, Aub.
- DB—Tony Flack, Ga.
- P—Bill Smith, Miss.

1986

OFFENSE
- WR—Wendell Davis, LSU
- WR—Ricky Nattiel, Fla.
- OL—Bruce Wilkerson, Tenn.
- OL—Jeff Zimmerman, Fla.
- OL—Stacy Searels, Aub.
- OL—Wilbur Strozier, Ga.
- C—Ben Tamburello, Aub.
- QB—Don Smith, MSU
- RB—Brent Fullwood, Aub.
- RB—Bobby Humphrey, Ala.
- RB—Lars Tate, Ga.
- PK—Van Tiffin, Ala.

DEFENSE
- DL—Tracy Rocker, Aub.
- DL—Curt Jarvis, Ala.
- DL—Henry Thomas, LSU
- DL—Henry Harris, Ga.
- DL—Keith Williams, Fla.
- LB—Dale Jones, Tenn.
- LB—Cornelius Bennett, Ala.
- LB—Aundray Bruce, Aub.
- DB—Jarvis Williams, Fla.
- DB—Freddie Robinson, Ala.
- DB—John Little, Ga.
- P—Bill Smith, Miss.

1987

OFFENSE
- WR—Wendell Davis, LSU
- WR—Layer Tillman, Aub.
- OL—Bill Condon, Ala.
- OL—Stacy Searels, Aub.
- OL—Harry Galbreath, Tenn.
- OL—Eric Andolsek, LSU
- C—Nacho Albergamo, LSU
- QB—Tommy Hodson, LSU
- RB—Bobby Humphrey, Ala.
- RB—Emmitt Smith, Fla.
- RB—Lars Tate, Ga.
- PK—David Browndyke, LSU

DEFENSE
- L—Tracy Rocker, Aub.
- L—Jeff Roth, Fla.
- L—Mark Hovanic, Tenn.
- L—Willie Wyatt, Ala.
- L—Jerry Reese, Ky.
- LB—Clifford Charlton, Fla.
- LB—Aundray Bruce, Aub.
- LB—Chris Gaines, Vandy
- DB—Kevin Porter, Aub.
- DB—Louis Oliver, Fla.
- DB—Kermit Kendrick, Ala.
- P—Brian Shulman, Aub.

1988

OFFENSE
- WR—Boo Mitchell, Vandy
- WR—Tony Moss, LSU
- OL—Ralph Norwood, LSU
- OL—Larry Rose, Ala.
- OL—Jim Thompson, Aub.
- OL—David Williams, Fla.
- C—Todd Wheeler, Ga.
- QB—Reggie Slack, Aub.
- RB—Stacy Danley, Aub.
- RB—Emmitt Smith, Fla.
- RB—Tim Worley, Ga.
- PK—David Browndyke, LSU

DEFENSE
- DL—Trace Armstrong, Fla.
- DL—Bill Goldberg, Ga.
- DL—Tracy Rocker, Aub.
- DL—Benji Roland, Aub.
- DL—Ron Stallworth, Aub.
- LB—Keith DeLong, Tenn.
- LB—Richard Tardits, Ga.
- LB—Derrick Thomas, Ala.
- DB—Greg Jackson, LSU
- DB—Louis Oliver, Fla.
- DB—Lee Ozmint, Ala.
- P—Brian Shulman, Aub.

1989

OFFENSE
- WR—Tony Moss, LSU
- WR—Lamonde Russell, Ala.
- OL—Ed King, Aub.
- OL—Mike Pfeifer, Ky.
- OL—Eric Still, Tenn.
- OL—Terrill Chatman, Ala.
- C—Roger Shultz, Ala.
- QB—Tommy Hodson, LSU
- RB—Emmitt Smith, Fla.
- RB—Rodney Hampton, Ga.
- RB—Siran Stacy, Ala.
- PK—David Browndyke, LSU

DEFENSE
- DL—Oliver Barnett, Ky.
- DL—Marion Hobby, Tenn.
- DL—David Rocker, Aub.
- DL—Tony Bennett, Miss.
- DL—Willie Wyatt, Ala.
- LB—Keith McCants, Ala.
- LB—Huey Richardson, Fla.
- LB—DeMond Winston, Vandy
- DB—Ben Smith, Ga.
- DB—John Mangum, Ala.
- DB—John Wiley, Aub.
- P—Kent Elmore, Tenn.

1990

OFFENSE
- WR—Ernie Mills, Fla.
- WR—Carl Pickens, Tenn.
- OL—Terrill Chatman, Ala.
- OL—Antone Davis, Tenn.
- OL—Cal Dixon, Fla.
- OL—Ed King, Aub.
- C—Roger Shultz, Ala.
- QB—Shane Matthews, Fla.
- RB—Randy Baldwin, Miss.
- RB—Tony Thompson, Tenn.
- RB—Harvey Williams, LSU
- PK—Philip Doyle, Ala.

DEFENSE
- DL—Marc Boutte, LSU
- DL—Kelvin Pritchett, Miss.
- DL—David Rocker, Aub.
- DL—George Thornton, Ala.
- LB—Tim Paulk, Fla.
- LB—Huey Richardson, Fla.
- LB—John Sullins, Ala.
- DB—Dale Carter, Tenn.
- DB—Efrum Thomas, Ala.
- DB—Will White, Fla.
- DB—John Wiley, Aub.
- P—Joey Chapman, Tenn.

UPI discontinued naming its All-SEC team following the 1990 season.

Auburn's Tracy Rocker, who won the 1988 Outland Trophy and Lombardi Award, was a two-time UPI All-SEC honoree.

1994 SEC Football 279

Coaches' All-SEC

1984

OFFENSE
WR—Chuck Scott, Vandy
WR—Eric Martin, LSU
*TE—Jim Popp, Vandy
*TE—Corwyn Aldredge, MSU
OT—Lomas Brown, Fla.
OT—Lance Smith, LSU
OG—Bill Mayo, Tenn.
OG—Jeff Lott, Aub.
C—Phil Bromley, Fla.
QB—Kurt Page, Vandy
RB—Dalton Hilliard, LSU
RB—Johnnie Jones, Tenn.
PK—Kevin Butler, Ga.

DEFENSE
DE—Freddie Joe Nunn, Miss.
DE—Alonzo Johnson, Fla.
DT—Jon Hand, Ala.
DT—Ben Thomas, Aub.
DG—Tim Newton, Fla.
LB—Gregg Carr, Aub.
*LB—Cornelius Bennett, Ala.
*LB—Knox Culpepper, Ga.
DB—Jeff Sanchez, Ga.
DB—Paul Calhoun, Ky.
DB—Liffort Hobley, LSU
DB—Jeffery Dale, LSU
P—Ricky Anderson, Vandy

1985

OFFENSE
WR—Tim McGee, Tenn.
WR—Al Bell, Ala.
TE—Jim Popp, Vandy
OL—Will Wolford, Vandy
OL—Jeff Zimmerman, Fla.
OL—Bruce Wilkerson, Tenn.
OL—Steve Wallace, Aub.
C—Peter Anderson, Ga.
QB—Mike Shula, Ala.
RB—Bo Jackson, Aub.
RB—Dalton Hilliard, LSU
PK—Carlos Reveiz, Tenn.

DEFENSE
L—Jon Hand, Ala.
L—Gerald Williams, Aub.
L—Roland Barbay, LSU
L—Greg Waters, Ga.
G—Harold Hallman, Aub.
LB—Michael Brooks, LSU
LB—Alonzo Johnson, Fla.
LB—Cornelius Bennett, Ala.
LB—Dale Jones, Tenn.
DB—Chris White, Tenn.
DB—Tom Powell, Aub.
DB—John Little, Ga.
DB—Norman Jefferson, LSU
DB—Freddie Robinson, Ala.
P—Bill Smith, Miss.

1986

OFFENSE
WR—Wendell Davis, LSU
WR—Ricky Nattiel, Fla.
TE—Brian Kinchen, LSU
OL—Eric Andolsek, LSU
OL—Bruce Wilkerson, Tenn.
OL—Jeff Zimmerman, Fla.
OL—Wilbur Strozier, Ga.
*C—Wes Neighbors, Ala.
*C—Ben Tamburello, Aub.
*QB—Don Smith, MSU
*QB—Tommy Hodson, LSU
RB—Brent Fullwood, Aub.
RB—Bobby Humphrey, Ala.
PK—Van Tiffin, Ala.

DEFENSE
L—Tracy Rocker, Aub.
L—Henry Thomas, LSU
L—Roland Barbay, LSU
LB—Jeff Herrod, Miss.
LB—Toby Caston, LSU
OLB—Cornelius Bennett, Ala.
*OLB—Aundray Bruce, Aub.
*OLB—Dale Jones, Tenn.
DB—Stevon Moore, Miss.
DB—Freddie Robinson, Ala.
DB—Jarvis Williams, Fla.
*DB—Adrian White, Fla.
*DB—Jeff Noblin, Miss.
P—Bill Smith, Miss.

1987

OFFENSE
WR—Wendell Davis, LSU
WR—Lawyer Tillman, Aub.
*TE—Howard Cross, Ala.
*TE—Walter Reeves, Aub.
OL—Kim Stephens, Ga.
OL—Stacy Searels, Aub.
OL—Harry Galbreath, Tenn.
OL—Eric Andolsek, LSU
C—Nacho Albergamo, LSU
*QB—Jeff Burger, Aub.
*QB—Tommy Hodson, LSU
RB—Bobby Humphrey, Ala.
RB—Emmitt Smith, Fla.
PK—Win Lyle, Aub.

DEFENSE
T—Tracy Rocker, Aub.
T—Jerry Reese, Ky.
G—Darrell Phillips, LSU
LB—Kurt Crain, Aub.
LB—John Brantley, Ga.
OLB—Aundray Bruce, Aub.
OLB—Derrick Thomas, Ala.
DB—Kevin Porter, Aub.
DB—Louis Oliver, Fla.
DB—Jarvis Williams, Fla.
DB—Chris Carrier, LSU
P—Brian Shulman, Aub.

1988

OFFENSE
WR—Boo Mitchell, Vandy
WR—Tony Moss, LSU
TE—Wesley Walls, Miss.
OL—Ralph Norwood, LSU
OL—David Williams, Fla.
*OL—Larry Rose, Ala.
*OL—Eric Still, Tenn.
*OL—Jim Thompson, Aub.
C—Todd Wheeler, Ga.
QB—Tommy Hodson, LSU
RB—Tim Worley, Ga.
*RB—Eddie Fuller, LSU
*RB—Emmitt Smith, Fla.
PK—David Browndyke, LSU

DEFENSE
T—Trace Armstrong, Fla.
T—Tracy Rocker, Aub.
*MG—Bill Goldberg, Ga.
*MG—Darrell Phillips, LSU
*MG—Jeff Roth, Fla.
LB—Keith DeLong, Tenn.
LB—Quentin Riggins, Aub.
OLB—Eric Hill, LSU
OLB—Derrick Thomas, Ala.
DB—Carlo Cheattom, Aub.
DB—Louis Oliver, Fla.
DB—Todd Sandroni, Miss.
DB—Ben Smith, Ga.
P—Brian Shulman, Aub.

1989

OFFENSE
WR—Tony Moss, LSU
WR—Willie Green, Miss.
TE—Lamonde Russell, Ala.
OL—John Durden, Fla.
OL—Ed King, Aub.
OL—Eric Still, Tenn.
*OL—Terrill Chatman, Ala.
*OL—Antone Davis, Tenn.
*OL—Mike Pfeifer, Ky.
C—John Hudson, Aub.
QB—Gary Hollingsworth, Ala.
RB—Emmitt Smith, Fla.
RB—Chuck Webb, Tenn.
PK—Philip Doyle, Ala.

DEFENSE
DT—Oliver Barnett, Ky.
DT—Marion Hobby, Tenn.
MG—Willie Wyatt, Ala.
ILB—Keith McCants, Ala.
ILB—Quentin Riggins, Aub.
OLB—Huey Richardson, Fla.
*OLB—Tony Bennett, Miss.
*OLB—Craig Ogletree, Aub.
DB—Richard Fain, Fla.
DB—John Mangum, Ala.
DB—Ben Smith, Ga.
DB—Efrum Thomas, Ala.
P—Kent Elmore, Tenn.

*Tied for the position

Ben Smith, who led the SEC with 10 interceptions in 1989 and went on to become a first-round NFL draft pick, twice earned Coaches' All-SEC honors during his career at Georgia.

1990

OFFENSE
WR—Todd Kinchen, LSU
WR—Carl Pickens, Tenn.
TE—Kirk Kirkpatrick, Fla.
OL—Terrill Chatman, Ala.
OL—Antone Davis, Tenn.
OL—Ed King, Aub.
*OL—Charles McRae, Tenn.
*OL—Rob Selby, Aub.
*C—Blake Miller, LSU
*C—Roger Shultz, Ala.
QB—Shane Matthews, Fla.
RB—Randy Baldwin, Miss.
RB—Tony Thompson, Tenn.
PK—Phillip Doyle, Ala.

DEFENSE
DL—Kelvin Pritchett, Miss.
DL—David Rocker, Aub.
DL—George Thornton, Ala.
ILB—Randy Holleran, Ky.
ILB—John Sullins, Ala.
OLB—Godfrey Myles, Fla.
OLB—Huey Richardson, Fla.
DB—Dale Carter, Tenn.
DB—Richard Fain, Fla.
DB—Efrum Thomas, Ala.
DB—Will White, Fla.
P—David Lawrence, Vandy

1991

OFFENSE
WR—Todd Kinchen, LSU
WR—Carl Pickens, Tenn.
TE—Victor Hall, Aub.
OL—Eddie Blake, Aub.
OL—Hesham Ismail, Fla.
OL—Tom Myslinski, Tenn.
*OL—John James, MSU
*OL—Kevin Mawae, LSU
C—Cal Dixon, Fla.
QB—Shane Matthews, Fla.
RB—Corey Harris, Vandy
RB—Siran Stacy, Ala.
PK—Arden Czyzewski, Fla.

DEFENSE
DL—Brad Culpepper, Fla.
DL—Robert Stewart, Ala.
DL—Nate Williams, MSU
ILB—Tim Paulk, Fla.
ILB—Dwayne Simmons, Ga.
OLB—Ephesians Bartley, Fla.
OLB—Darryl Hardy, Tenn.
DB—Corey Barlow, Aub.
DB—Dale Carter, Tenn.
DB—Jeremy Lincoln, Tenn.
DB—Will White, Fla.
P—Shayne Edge, Fla.

1992

OFFENSE—First Team
WR—Andre Hastings, Ga.
WR—Willie Jackson, Fla.
TE—Kirk Botkin, Ark.
OL—Everett Lindsay, Miss.
OL—Ernest Dye, USC
OL—Mike Stowell, Tenn.
OL—John James, MSU
C—Tobie Sheils, Ala.
QB—Shane Matthews, Fla.
RB—Garrison Hearst, Ga.
RB—James Bostic, Ala.
PK—Scott Etheridge, Aub.

DEFENSE—First Team
DL—Eric Curry, Ala.
DL—John Copeland, Ala.
DL—Todd Kelly, Tenn.
ILB—Derrick Oden, Ala.
ILB—James Willis, Aub.
*OLB—Mitch Davis, Ga.
*OLB—Lemanski Hall, Ala.
DB—Antonio Langham, Ala.
DB—George Teague, Ala.
DB—Will White, Fla.
DB—Johnny Dixon, Miss.
P—Todd Jordan, MSU

OFFENSE—Second Team
WR—Eddie Small, Miss.
WR—Willie Harris, MSU
TE—Pat Akos, Vandy
OL—Chris Gray, Aub.
OL—Alec Millen, Ga.
OL—George Wilson, Ala.
OL—Kevin Mawae, LSU
C—Lee Ford, MSU
QB—Eric Zeier, Ga.
RB—Derrick Lassic, Ala.
RB—Cory Philpot, Miss.
PK—Doug Pelfrey, Ky.

DEFENSE—Second Team
DL—Chad Brown, Miss.
DL—Greg Jackson, Ga.
*DL—Jerome Brown, MSU
*DL—Gary Rogers, Vandy
ILB—Daniel Boyd, MSU
*ILB—Dewayne Dotson, Miss.
*ILB—Carlton, Miles, Fla.
OLB—Marc Woodard, MSU
OLB—Karekin Cunningham, Aub.
DB—Jeff Brothers, Vandy
DB—Frank Adams, USC
DB—Danny Boyd, Miss.
*DB—Tony Watkins, USC
*DB—Orlando Watters, Ark.
P—Pete Raether, Ark.

*Tied for the position

1993

OFFENSE—First Team
WR—David Palmer, Ala.
WR—Cory Fleming, Tenn.
TE—Shannon Mitchell, Ga.
OL—Wayne Gandy, Aub.
OL—Bernard Williams, Ga.
OL—Jeff Smith, Tenn.
OL—Reggie Green, Fla.
C—Tobie Sheils, Ala.
QB—Heath Shuler, Tenn.
RB—Errict Rhett, Fla.
RB—James Bostic, Aub.
PK—Michael Proctor, Ala.

DEFENSE—First Team
DL—Henry Ford, Ark.
DL—William Gaines, Fla.
DL—Jeremy Nunley, Ala.
OLB—Dewayne Dotson, Ole Miss
OLB—Ernest Dixon, USC*
OLB—Lemanski Hall, Ala.*
ILB—Marty Moore, Ky.
ILB—Randall Godfrey, Ga.
DB—Antonio Langham, Ala.
DB—Marcus Jenkins, Ky.
DB—Orlando Watters, Ark.
DB—Johnny Dixon, Ole Miss
P—Terry Daniel, Aub.

OFFENSE—Second Team
WR—Brice Hunter, Ga.
WR—Jack Jackson, Fla.
TE—Harold Bishop, LSU
OL—Jason Odom, Fla.
OL—Ryan Bell, Vandy
OL—Isaac Davis, Ark.
OL—Anthony Redmon, Aub.
C—Kevin Mawae, LSU
QB—Eric Zeier, Ga.
RB—Charlie Garner, Tenn.
RB—Brandon Bennett, USC
PK—John Becksvoort, Tenn.

DEFENSE—Second Team
DL—Stacy Evans, USC
DL—Alan Young, Vandy
DL—James Wilson, Tenn.
OLB—Mitch Davis, Ga.
OLB—Cassius Ware, Ole Miss
ILB—Abdul Jackson, Ole Miss
ILB—Juan Long, MSU
DB—Alundis Brice, Ole Miss
DB—Chris Shelling, Aub.
DB—Calvin Jackson, Aub.
DB—Walt Harris, MSU*
DB—Jason Parker, Tenn.*
P—Shayne Edge, Fla.

All-America and All-SEC honorees Eric Curry (80) and John Copeland (94) anchored the NCAA's top-ranked defense which led the Crimson Tide to the 1992 National Championship.

1994 SEC Football 281

Academic All-SEC Teams

1954

Pos.	Player and School	GPA
E	Jimmy Long, Aub.	B+
E	Bill Sennett, Ga. Tech	B+
T	Charles Rader, Tenn.	A-
T	Bill Wheeler, Ky.	B+
G	Len Spadifino, Ga.	B+
G	Pete Williams, Vandy	B+
C	Hal Easterwood, MSU	B+
QB	Wade Mitchell, Ga. Tech	A-
HB	Dave Middleton, Aub.	A-
HB	Bob Davis, Fla.	B+
FB	Bob Clements, Ga.	B+

1955

Pos.	Player and School	GPA
E	Curtis Lynch, Ala.	B+
E	Ron Bennett, MSU	B+
T	Bill Wheeler, Ky.	B+
T	Charles Rader, Tenn.	A+
G	Len Spadifino, Ga.	A+
G	Bob Scarbrough, Aub.	A+
C	Jim Cunningham, Vandy	B+
QB	Wade Mitchell, Ga. Tech	A+
HB	Fob James, Aub.	B+
HB	Joe Childress, Aub.	B+
FB	Don Hunt, Vandy	B+

1956

Pos.	Player and School	GPA
E	Ron Bennett, MSU	B+
E	Kyle Cruze, Tenn.	B+
T	Charles Rader, Tenn.	A-
T	J.T. Frankenberger, Ky.	B+
G	Lucian Tatum, Vandy	A-
G	Allen Ecker, Ga. Tech	B+
C	Jimmy Dodd, MSU	A+
QB	Wade Mitchell, Ga. Tech	A+
HB	Leroy Reed, Miss.	A-
HB	George Whitton, Ga.	A+
FB	Dickie Mattison, Ga. Tech	B+

1957

Pos.	Player and School	GPA
E	Jimmy Phillips, Aub.	B+
E	Jim Urbaniak, Ky.	A+
T	Bill Johnson, Tenn.	B+
T	Al Aucoin, LSU	B+
G	Jimmy Dodd, MSU	A-
G	Foster Watkins, Ga. Tech	A-
C	Jack Benson, MSU	B+
QB	Lloyd Nix, Aub.	B+
HB	Leroy Reed, Miss.	A-
HB	Jimmy Orr, Ga.	B+
FB	Stockton Adkins, Tenn.	B+

1958

Pos.	Player and School	GPA
E	Mickey Mangham, LSU	B+
E	Murray Armstrong, Tenn.	A+
T	Dave Sington, Ala.	B+
T	Charles Strange, LSU	B+
G	Billy Grover, Vandy	A-
G	Zeke Smith, Aub.	B+
C	Ben Donnell, Vandy	B+
QB	Lloyd Nix, Aub.	A+
HB	Floyd Faucette, Ga. Tech	B+
HB	Tommy Lorino, Aub.	B+
FB	Charles Flowers, Miss.	B+

1959

Pos.	Player and School	GPA
E	Mickey Mangham, LSU	B+
E	Lewis Akin, Vandy	B+
T	Charles Strange, LSU	B+
T	Robert Khayat, Miss.	B+
G	Pat Dye, Ga.	A-
G	Don Cochran, Ala.	B+
C	Jackie Burkett, Aub.	B+
QB	Fran Tarkenton, Ga.	B+
HB	Floyd Faucette, Ga. Tech	B+
HB	Tom Moore, Vandy	B+
FB	Charles Flowers, Miss.	B+

1960

Pos.	Player and School	GPA
E	Pat Patchen, Fla.	B+
E	Mickey Mangham, LSU	B+
T	Walter Suggs, MSU	B+
T	Joe LeSage, Tul.	B+
G	Wayne Grubb, Tenn.	B+
G	Treva Bolin, Miss.	B+
C	Charles Strange, LSU	B+
QB	Fran Tarkenton, Ga.	B+
HB	Leon Fuller, Ala.	B+
HB	James Anderson, Miss.	B+
FB	Ed Dyas, Aub.	A-

1961

Pos.	Player and School	GPA
E	Tommy Brooker, Ala.	A-
E	Wade Butcher, Vandy	B+
T	Larry Stallings, Ga. Tech	B+
T	Billy Booth, LSU	B+
G	Bruce Mattox, Tenn.	B+
G	Billy Ray Jones, Miss.	B+
C	Wayne Frazier, Aub.	A+
QB	Pat Trammell, Ala.	A+
HB	Doug Elmore, Miss.	B+
HB	Lee Welch, MSU	B+
FB	Tommy Neck, LSU	B+

1962

Pos.	Player and School	GPA
E	Bill Battle, Ala.	B+
E	Bobby Flurry, LSU	A-
T	Larry Stallings, Ga. Tech	B+
T	Winky Giddens, Aub.	B+
G	Bruce Mattox, Tenn.	B+
G	Larry Travis, Fla.	B+
C	Jule Crocker, Vandy	B+
QB	Charlie Furlow, MSU	B+
HB	Louis Guy, Miss.	B+
HB	Billy Knowles, Ga.	B+
FB	David Rawson, Aub.	A-

1963

Pos.	Player and School	GPA
E	Danny Neuman, LSU	B+
E	Frank Sexton, Ga. Tech	B+
T	Cecil Ford, Miss.	B+
T	Tom Ballard, Ga. Tech	A+
G	Jack Katz, Fla.	B+
G	Pat Watson, MSU	B+
C	Gaylon McCollough, Ala.	B+
QB	Rick Norton, Ky.	B+
HB	Billy Edge, Aub.	B+
HB	Billy Knowles, Ga.	B+
FB	Fred Roberts, Miss.	A+
PK	Tim Davis, Ala.	B+

1964

First Team

Pos.	Player and School	GPA
E	Rick Kestner, Ky.	B+
E	George Norwicki, Ga.	B+
T	Ron Durby, Ala.	A-
T	Conrad Meyer, Tul.	B+
G	Bill Richbourg, Fla.	B+
G	Pat Watson, MSU	B+
C	Gaylon McCollough, Ala.	B+
QB	Steve Sloan, Ala.	B+
HB	Mike Dennis, Miss.	B+
HB	Lance Spalding, Vandy	B+
FB	Steve Bowman, Ala.	B+
LB	Bill Goss, Tul.	B+
LB	Bill Cody, Aub.	B+
S	White Graves, LSU	B+
P	Frank Lambert, Miss.	A+
PK	Bob Etter, Ga.	A-

Second Team

Pos.	Player and School	GPA
E	John Andrighetti, Ky.	B+
E	Bobby Carollo, MSU	A+
T	Bubba Hampton, MSU	B+
T	John Whatley, Fla.	A-
G	Stan Hindman, Miss.	B+
G	Wilford Fuqua, Vandy	B+
C	Norbert Ackerman, Tenn.	A-
QB	Pat Hunnicutt, Ga.	B+
HB	Billy Edge, Aub.	B+
HB	Billy Sumrall, Miss.	B+
FB	John Cochran, Aub.	A+

1965

Offense

Pos.	Player and School	GPA
E	Charles Casey, Fla.	B+
E	Steve Skupas, Vandy	B+
T	Conrad Meyer, Tul.	B+
T	John Watley, Fla.	A-
G	Stan Hindman, Miss.	B+
G	Bubba Hampton, MSU	A-
C	Ray Bedingfield, Miss.	B+
QB	Steve Sloan, Ala.	B+
HB	Charles Fulton, Tenn.	B+
HB	Dennis Homan, Ala.	B+
FB	Dave Wells, Miss.	B+
PK	Bob Etter, Ga.	A+

Defense

Pos.	Player and School	GPA
E	Bobby Carollo, MSU	A-
E	Marvin McQueen, Miss.	B+
T	Mack Gentry, Tenn.	B+
T	Fred Corley, MSU	B+
MG	John Cochran, Aub.	A-
LB	Bill Goss, Tul.	B+
LB	Bill Cody, Aub.	B+
R	Phil Brooks, Vandy	B+
HB	Charles L. Moore, LSU	B+
HB	Tommy Luke, Miss.	B+
S	Lynn Hughes, Ga.	B+
P	Steve Davis, Ala.	A+

1966

Offense

Pos.	Player and School	GPA
E	Mack Haik, Miss.	B+
E	Jack Coons, Fla.	B+
T	Byrd Williams, Ala.	B+
T	Doug Splane, Fla.	B+
G	Jim Benson, Fla.	B+
G	Bubba Hampton, MSU	B+
C	Bob Johnson, Tenn.	A-
QB	Kirby Moore, Ga.	B+
TB	Frank Canterbury, Ala.	A-
FB	Graham McKeel, Fla.	B+
FB	Dennis Homan, Ala.	B+
PK	Bob Etter, Ga.	A+

Defense

Pos.	Player and School	GPA
E	Marvin McQueen, Miss.	B+
E	Al Griffin, Aub.	B+
T	Charles Collins, Aub.	B+
T	Paige Cutcliffe, Fla.	B+
MG	Fred Corley, MSU	B+
LB	Tommy Lawhorne, Ga.	A+
LB	Bob Childs, Ala.	B+
R	Jerry Joseph, LSU	B+
HB	Bobby Beaird, Aub.	A+
HB	Jerry Warfield, Ky.	B+
S	Lynn Hughes, Ga.	A-
P	Steve Davis, Ala.	A-

1967

Offense

Pos.	Player and School	GPA
SE	Joe Jacobs, Ky.	B+
TE	Jack Coons, Fla.	B+
T	Bill Payne, Ga.	A-
T	Hugh Adama, MSU	B+
G	Jerry Guillot, LSU	A+
G	Ted Carmical, MSU	A-
C	Bob Johnson, Tenn.	B+
QB	Kirby Moore, Ga.	B+
TB	Steve Hindman, Miss.	A+
FB	Graham McKeel, Fla.	A-
WB	Charley Fulton, Tenn.	B+
PK	Steve Davis, Ala.	A-

Defense

Pos.	Player and School	GPA
E	Vic Dingus, Tenn.	B+
E	Frank Trapp, Miss.	B+
T	Charles Collins, Aub.	B+
T	Jack Dyer, LSU	A+
MG	Gusty Yearout, Aub.	B+
LB	Tommy Lawhorne, Ga.	A+
LB	Bob Childs, Ala.	B+
LB	Calvin Harrison, MSU	B+
HB	George Davison, Aub.	A-
HB	Donnie Sutton, Ala.	B+
S	Jake Scott, Ga.	B+
P	Julian Fagan, Miss.	A-

1968

Offense

Pos.	Player and School	GPA
SE	David Smith, MSU	B+
TE	Al Giffin, Aub.	B+
T	Alvin Samples, Ala.	B+
T	Jerry Guillot, LSU	B+
G	Ted Carmical, MSU	B+
C	Bruce Yawn, Ga.	B+
C	Bill Nelson, MSU	A+
QB	Scott Hunter, Ala.	B+
TB	Steve Hindman, Miss.	A+
FB	Ed Morgan, Ga.	B+
WB	Dave Strong, Vandy	B+
PK	John Riley, Aub.	B+

Defense

Pos.	Player and School	GPA
E	Billy Payne, Ga.	A-
E	Mike Ford, Ala.	B+
T	Bill Stanfill, Ga.	B+
T	Hugh Adams, MSU	B+
G	John Sage, LSU	B+
LB	Bob Childs, Ala.	B+
LB	Happy Dicks, Ga.	B+
R	Wayne Owen, Ala.	B+
HB	Tim Priest, Tenn.	B+
HB	John Burns, Vandy	B+
S	Donnie Sutton, Ala.	A-
P	Julian Fagan, Miss.	A-

282 Honors

1969

Offense

Pos.	Player and School	GPA
E	Carlos Alvarez, Fla.	B+
E	Lonny Myles, LSU	B
T	Mac Steen, Fla.	B
T	Danny Ford, Ala.	B
G	Don Denbo, Tenn.	A
G	Alvin Samples, Ala.	B+
C	Tommy Lyons, Ga.	B+
QB	Scott Hunter, Ala.	B
TB	Johnny Musso, Ala.	B
FB	Roger Gann, Ky.	A
WB	Dave Strong, Vandy	B
PK	John Riley, Aub.	B

Defense

Pos.	Player and School	GPA
E	Vic Dingus, Tenn.	B+
E	Noel Stahl, Vandy	B+
T	Claude Herard, Miss.	A
T	Lee Daniel, Ga.	B
1G	Tim Callaway, Ga.	B+
LB	Joe Blount, Miss.	B
LB	Jim Nelson, MSU	B+
R	Mike Dean, Ala.	B
HB	Tim Priest, Tenn.	B+
HB	James Earley, LSU	B+
S	Buddy McClinton, Aub.	B+
P	Julian Fagan, Miss.	A+

1970

Offense

Pos.	Player and School	GPA
SE	Carlos Alvarez, Fla.	3.21
TE	Jim Cunningham, Vandy	2.00
T	Tom Nash, Ga.	3.90
T	Dave Hanson, Ky.	3.68
G	Don Denbo, Tenn.	3.39
G	Carey Varnado, Ala.	2.64
C	Tommy Lyons, Ga.	3.72
QB	Neb Hayden, Ala.	2.11
TB	Johnny Musso, Ala.	2.33
FB	Bill Young, Vandy	2.15
FL	Dave Hunter, Ky.	3.00

Defense

Pos.	Player and School	GPA
E	Dennis Coleman, Miss.	3.67
E	Neal Dettmering, Aub.	2.34
T	John Sage, LSU	3.10
T	Ronnie Estay, LSU	3.20
LB	Marrell Jerkins, Aub.	2.06
LB	Rick Muench, Ky.	4.00
LB	Lloyd Frye, LSU	3.30
HB	Tim Priest, Tenn.	3.26
HB	Frank Dowsing, MSU	3.00
S	Bill Norsworthy, LSU	3.80
S	John Burns, Vandy	2.45

1971

Offense

Pos.	Player and School	GPA
SE	Carlos Alvarez, Fla.	3.80
TE	Jim Yancey, Fla.	3.76
T	Tom Nash, Ga.	3.90
T	Charles Stuart, LSU	3.60
G	Jimmy Rosser, Ala.	2.20
G	Joe Edwards, MSU	3.25
C	Jim Krapf, Ala.	2.17
QB	Pat Sullivan, Aub.	2.20
TB	Johnny Musso, Ala.	2.13
FB	Tommy Lowry, Aub.	2.10
WB	Lee Clymer, Ky.	3.17
PK	Jay Michaelson, LSU	3.40

Defense

Pos.	Player and School	GPA
E	Mixon Robinson, Ga.	3.66
E	Reggie Dill, Miss.	3.16
T	Chuck Heard, Ga.	3.19
T	Tommy Butaud, LSU	3.70
LB	Lloyd Frye, LSU	3.20
LB	Rick Muench, Ky.	3.84
LB	Jim Nelson, MSU	3.03
R	Mike Neel, Aub.	2.22
HB	Ken Phares, MSU	3.60
HB	Doug Sorenson, Fla.	3.59
S	Frank Dowsing, MSU	3.07

1972

Offense

Pos.	Player and School	GPA
SE	Doug Martin, Vandy	2.33
TE	Chuck Williamson, LSU	3.33
T	John Gregory, Miss.	3.00
T	L.T. Southall, Vandy	2.00
G	Loyd Daniel, LSU	3.00
G	Mac McWhorter, Ga.	3.00
C	Jim Krapf, Ala.	2.03
QB	Norris Weese, Miss.	3.70
RB	Chris Linderman, Aub.	2.02
RB	Brad Davis, LSU	3.00
WB	Chip Howard, Tenn.	3.11

Defense

Pos.	Player and School	GPA
E	Len Ellspermann, Ga.	3.00
E	Tom Lusk, Ala.	2.11
T	Benny Sivley, Aub.	2.11
T	Tommy Butaud, LSU	3.10
LB	Jamie Rotella, Tenn.	3.00
LB	Fred Abbott, Fla.	3.40
LB	Pepper Rutland, LSU	3.10
R	Mike Neel, Aub.	2.35
HB	Frank Dowsing, MSU	3.78
HB	Dave Beck, Aub.	2.00
HB	Ken Phares, MSU	4.00
P	Buster Morrison, Fla.	3.22

1973

Offense

Pos.	Player and School	GPA
E	Tommy Strahan, MSU	3.60
E	Doug Martin, Vandy	2.91
T	Greg Fountain, MSU	3.07
T	Tom Strickland, LSU	3.60
G	Tyler Lafauci, LSU	3.70
G	Mac McWhorter, Ga.	3.13
C	Logan Killen, LSU	3.30
QB	Norris Weese, Miss.	3.72
TB	Larry Kramer, Miss.	3.06
FB	Vince Kendrick, Fla.	3.32
WB	Bill Buckley, MSU	3.00
WB	Rick Kimbrough, Miss.	3.57

Defense

Pos.	Player and School	GPA
E	Jimmy Webb, MSU	3.75
E	Greg Markow, Miss.	3.70
T	Benny Sivley, Aub.	2.41
T	Randy Hall, Ala.	2.88
LB	Bill Luka, Aub.	2.33
LB	Bobby Davis, Aub.	2.76
R	Joe Winkler, LSU	4.00
HB	Jim Revels, Fla.	3.24
HB	David McMakin, Ala.	2.22
S	Harry Harrison, Miss.	3.14
S	Eddie Brown, Tenn.	3.30

1974

Offense

Pos.	Player and School	GPA
E	Doug Martin, Vandy	3.00
E	Rick Kimbrough, Miss.	3.00
T	Greg Phillips, Tenn.	3.27
T	Larry Thompson, MSU	3.21
G	Richard Clippard, Miss.	3.27
G	John MacNeill, Miss.	3.77
C	Jimmy Kynes, Fla.	3.10
QB	Kenny Lyons, Miss.	3.57
RB	Brad Davis, LSU	3.20
RB	Rick Neel, Aub.	3.13
WB	Dale Fair, Tenn.	2.03
P	Buster Morrison, Fla.	3.00

Defense

Pos.	Player and School	GPA
E	Ron Daily, LSU	3.30
E	Greg Markow, Miss.	4.00
T	Randy Hall, Ala.	3.63
T	Jimmy Webb, MSU	3.51
NG	Tom Ranieri, Ky.	3.65
LB	Bobby Davis, Aub.	2.39
LB	Jim Kovach, Ky.	3.30
CB	Bruce Evans, Aub.	2.76
CB	Jimmy Knecht, LSU	3.70
S	Alan Pizzitola, Ala.	3.04
S	Scott Wingfield, Vandy	2.00

1975

Offense

Pos.	Player and School	GPA
E	Bill Small, Miss.	3.54
E	Bruce Hemphill, LSU	3.50
T	Chuck Fletcher, Aub.	3.00
T	Matt Gossage, Vandy	2.75
G	Hugh Hendrix, Ga.	3.00
G	Gerald Loper, Fla.	3.30
C	Greg Bienvenu, LSU	3.20
QB	Robert Fraley, Ala.	2.83
RB	Glynn Harrison, Ga.	3.33
RB	Kevin McLee, Ga.	3.50
WB	Chris Vacarella, Aub.	2.41
PK	Allan Leavitt, Ga.	3.00
PK	Danny Ridgeway, Ala.	2.76

Defense

Pos.	Player and School	GPA
E	Will Colthrap, MSU	3.54
E	Dicky Clark, Ga.	3.00
T	Steve Cassidy, LSU	3.00
T	A.J. Duhe, LSU	3.20
NG	Tom Ranieri, Ky.	3.08
LB	Calvin Hymel, MSU	3.15
LB	Jim Kovach, Ky.	3.58
LB	Damon Regen, Vandy	2.75
CB	Clinton Burrell, LSU	3.30
CB	Rick Neel, Aub.	2.22
S	Mike Mauck, Tenn.	3.58
P	Bill Farris, Miss.	3.54

1976

Offense

Pos.	Player and School	GPA
SE	Gavin Rees, MSU	3.28
TE	Dick Hayley, Aub.	2.37
T	Bill Evans, Aub.	3.00
T	Brent Watson, Tenn.	3.36
G	Ed Smolder, Ky.	3.81
G	Roy Stuart, LSU	3.00
C	Sid Smith, Ala.	2.37
QB	Matt Robinson, Ga.	3.00
RB	Kevin McLee, Ga.	3.50
RB	Terry Robiskie, LSU	3.00
WB	Chris Vacarella, Aub.	2.80
PK	David Posey, Fla.	3.70

Defense

Pos.	Player and School	GPA
E	Dicky Clark, Ga.	3.00
E	Will Colthrap, MSU	3.77
T	Darrell Carpenter, Fla.	3.40
T	Dennis Harrison, Vandy	2.00
NG	Tim English, Vandy	3.00
LB	Jim Kovach, Ky.	3.81
LB	George Stuart, Miss.	3.06
LB	Ben Zambiasi, Ga.	3.00
CB	Johnny Henderson, Ga.	3.00
CB	Mike Leonard, LSU	3.60
S	Ronnie Barber, LSU	3.10
P	Rod Nelson, Ala.	2.27

1977

Offense

Pos.	Player and School	GPA
SE	Robert Fabris, Miss.	4.00
FL	Gavin Rees, MSU	3.23
TE	Dick Hayley, Aub.	2.81
T	Robert Dugas, LSU	3.70
T	Brent Watson, Tenn.	3.41
G	Lou Green, Ala.	2.06
G	Chris Rich, LSU	3.23
C	Marvin Trott, Aub.	2.43
QB	Jeff Pyburn, Ga.	3.38
RB	Wes Chandler, Fla.	3.13
RB	James Jones, MSU	3.05
PK	Greg Martin, Vandy	4.00

Defense

Pos.	Player and School	GPA
E	George Plasketes, Miss.	3.50
E	Wayne Hamilton, Ala.	2.07
T	Dennis Harrison, Vandy	3.00
T	Melvin Flourney, Fla.	3.38
LB	Jeff Lewis, Ga.	4.00
LB	Steve Ripple, LSU	3.01
LB	Freddie Smith, Aub.	2.44
DB	Jeff Gray, Aub.	2.42
DB	Gary Jones, Miss.	3.08
DB	Chip Linebarrier, Tenn.	3.23
DB	Mike Tucker, Ala.	2.50
P	Kevin Kelly, Ky.	3.00

1978

Offense

Pos.	Player and School	GPA
E	Dick Hayley, Aub.	2.25
E	Mark Hodge, Ga.	3.28
T	Robert Dugas, LSU	3.61
T	Chris Rich, LSU	3.20
G	Tommy Woodroof, Vandy	2.23
G	Murray Whitaker, Miss.	3.49
C	Jay Whitley, Ky.	3.00
QB	Jeff Pyburn, Ga.	3.07
B	Cris Collingsworth, Fla.	3.14
B	Steadman Shealy, Ala.	2.25
B	David Rudder, Tenn.	3.17
PK	Jorge Portela, Aub.	2.22

Defense

Pos.	Player and School	GPA
DL	Bob Grefseng, Miss.	3.62
DL	Craig Roberts, Ky.	3.66
DL	Tim English, Vandy	2.54
DL	Kenny Cole, Vandy	2.57
LB	Jim Kovach, Ky.	3.60
LB	Randy Sittason, Vandy	2.06
LB	Steve Dennis, Ga.	3.25
R	Chris Welton, Ga.	3.61
DB	Jeff Gray, Aub.	2.54
DB	Greg Gaines, Tenn.	3.01
DB	Henry Monroe, MSU	3.25
P	Roger Alsup, Vandy	2.05

1994 SEC Football 283

Academic All-SEC Teams

1979

Offense
Pos.	Player and School	GPA
C	John Ed Bradley, LSU	3.00
OG	Gary Bramblett, Ala.	3.31
CB	James Britt, LSU	3.30
QB	Dwayne Brown, MSU	3.65
FLK	Cris Collinsworth, Fla.	3.06
PK	Alan Duncan, Tenn.	3.17
OT	Brad Everett, Aub.	2.00
OT	Tim Irwin, Tenn.	3.17
OG	Mike Jester, Tenn.	3.25
FS	Ken Luke, Aub.	2.27
PK	Jorge Portela, Aub.	2.20

Defense
Pos.	Player and School	GPA
QB	Jeff Pyburn, Ga.	3.34
SE	Jay Russell, Ga.	3.06
LB/C	Gilbert Sellers, Aub.	2.36
OG	Leon Shadowen, Ky.	3.79
QB	Steadman Shealy, Ala.	3.56
OG	Jim Subers, Fla.	3.50
SE	Ken Toler, Miss.	3.35
QB	Charlie Trotman, Aub.	2.00
OG	Tom Tully, LSU	3.02
DE	Joe Voor, Fla.	3.10
OG	Tommy Woodroof, Vandy	3.40

1980

Offense
Pos.	Player and School	GPA
SE	Brian Atkins, Aub.	3.01
DB	Greg Bell, Ga.	3.17
DE	Vernon Blackard, Aub.	3.20
OG	Gary Bramblett, Ala.	2.24
DB	James Britt, LSU	3.52
QB	Dwayne Brown, MSU	3.66
FL	Cris Collinsworth, Fla.	3.10
DB	Mark Dorminey, Aub.	3.61
PK	Alan Duncan, Tenn.	3.10
OT	Tim Irwin, Tenn.	3.25
DE	Bill Gault, MSU	3.28
SE	Spencer Jackson, Fla.	3.14
DB	Ken Luke, Aub.	3.39

Defense
Pos.	Player and School	GPA
QB	Robby Mink, MSU	3.10
OG	Dan Plonk, Fla.	3.18
FL	Tracy Porter, LSU	3.20
C	John Redmond, Fla.	3.01
LB	Frank Ros, Ga.	3.03
C	Gilbert Sellers, Aub.	3.93
OG	Jim Skuthan, Aub.	3.54
TE	Flavious Smith, Vandy	2.15
OG	Jim Subers, Fla.	3.43
DT	Benjy Thibodeaux, LSU	3.03
SE	Ken Toler, Miss.	3.53
RV	Chris Welton, Ga.	3.31

1981

Offense
Pos.	Player and School	GPA
WR	Spencer Jackson, Fla.	3.21
WR	Broughton Lang, Fla.	3.22
T	Warren Gray, Ga.	3.00
T	Bob Smith, LSU	3.00
G	David Koch, LSU	3.00
G	Dan Plonk, Fla.	3.05
C	Joey Hancock, Vandy	3.05
B	Wayne Peace, Fla.	3.12
B	Gene Lang, LSU	3.23
B	Walter Lewis, Ala.	2.00
B	Breck Tyler, Miss.	3.68
PK	Brian Clark, Fla.	3.44

Defense
Pos.	Player and School	GPA
E	Scott Riley, Aub.	3.13
E	Mike Terry, Tenn.	3.01
T	Keith Martin, Ky.	3.16
T	Dan Dickerson, Aub.	3.06
G	Robin Fisher, Fla.	3.15
G	Vernon Blackard, Aub.	3.04
LB	Gregg Carr, Aub.	3.08
LB	Terry Hoage, Ga.	3.62
DB	Mark Dorminey, Aub.	3.07
DB	Vito McKeever, Fla.	3.19
DB	Johnny Burrow, Miss.	3.33
P	Alan Bollinger, Aub.	3.19

1982

Offense
Pos.	Player and School	GPA
SE	Phil Roach, Vandy	3.17
TE	Rob Mangas, Ky.	3.81
OL	Tracy Turner, Aub.	3.06
OL	Dan Plonk, Fla.	3.02
OL	Jon Moyle, Fla.	3.07
OL	Mike McQueen, Ala.	3.22
OL	Alan Partin, Miss.	4.00
B	Alan Risher, LSU	3.25
B	Whit Taylor, Vandy	3.49
B	Wayne Peace, Fla.	3.01
B	Kent Austin, Miss.	3.63
PK	Juan Betanzos, LSU	3.37

Defense
Pos.	Player and School	GPA
DL	John Clemens, Vandy	3.00
DL	Mike Terry, Tenn.	4.00
DL	Billy Jackson, MSU	3.00
DL	Keith Martin, Ky.	3.10
DL	Vernon Blackard, Aub.	3.03
LB	Scott Schroeder, Ky.	3.00
LB	Gregg Carr, Aub.	3.15
R	Terry Hoage, Ga.	3.85
CB	James Britt, LSU	3.50
CB	Johnny Burrow, Miss.	3.44
S	Mark Dorminey, Aub.	3.02
S	Rocky Colburn, Ala.	2.02
P	Jim Broadway, Ga.	3.57

1983

Offense
Pos.	Player and School	GPA
WR	Phil Roach, Vandy	3.50
WR	Gary Rolle, Fla.	3.90
L	Ron Bojalad, Ky.	3.00
L	Warren Gray, Ga.	3.06
L	Kenneth Leikam, MSU	3.12
L	Mike McQueen, Ala.	2.84
L	Jon Moyle, Fla.	3.30
TE	Chuck Scott, Vandy	3.03
QB	Kent Austin, Miss.	3.60
QB	Walter Lewis, Ala.	2.00
RB	Neal Anderson, Fla.	3.00
RB	Ed Graham, Aub.	3.35
RB	Steve Hendrix, Miss.	4.00
PK	Juan Bentazos, LSU	3.53

Defense
Pos.	Player and School	GPA
L	Keith Martin, Ky.	3.30
L	Benton Red, Miss.	3.00
LB	Gregg Carr, Aub.	3.72
LB	John Fritchie, LSU	3.54
LB	Billy Jackson, MSU	3.00
LB	Dwayne Nesmith, Miss.	3.86
LB	Scott Schroeder, Ky.	3.05
DB	Rocky Colburn, Ala.	2.00
DB	Terry Hoage, Ga.	3.71
DB	Raymond McKenna, MSU	3.24
DB	Bruce Vaughn, Fla.	3.20
P	Tim Cutts, MSU	3.15
P	Malcolm Simmons, Ala.	2.71

SEC Academic Honor Roll

In 1984 the SEC developed the Academic Honor Roll. The new format was adopted to recognize those athletes who had a 3.0 GPA (cumulative or during the past year) and earned a letter during the current season.

1984

Name and School	Pos.	GPA
Todd Roper, Ala.	LB	3.10
Gregg Carr, Aub.	LB	3.47
Kyle Collins, Aub.	RB	3.08
Yann Cowart, Aub.	C	3.00
Jeff Parks, Aub.	TE	3.15
Edward Graham, Aub.	RB	3.48
Tracy Turner, Aub.	OT	3.65
Ricky Nattiel, Fla.	WR	3.00
Bill Nelson, Fla.	LB	3.18
Chris Perkins, Fla.	PK	3.12
Gary Rolle, Fla.	WR	3.68
Scott Trimble, Fla.	OT	3.02
Brett Wiechmann, Fla.	WR	3.61
John Little, Ga.	R	3.11
Jeff Sanchez, Ga.	S	3.29
Brian Davis, Ky.	DE	3.06
Gordon Jackson, Ky.	DB	3.36
Matthew Lucas, Ky.	TE	3.00
Ken Pietrowiak, Ky.	C	3.32
Jim Reichwein, Ky.	OG	3.08
Gary Sexton, Ky.	S	3.09
Mark Wheeler, Ky.	TE	3.06
Brian Williams, Ky.	DE	3.04
Juan Carlos Betanzos, LSU	PK	3.40
John Hazard, LSU	T	3.30
Brian Kinchen, LSU	TE	3.25
Keith Melancon, LSU	OG	3.23
Kent Austin, Miss.	QB	3.49
Danny Hoskins, Miss.	OG	3.78
Ricky Lindstrom, Miss.	LB	3.28
Jeff Noblin, Miss.	FS	3.67
Benton Reed, Miss.	DT	3.07
R.J. McKenna, MSU	FS	3.05
John McAdams, Tenn.	DT	3.11
David Moon, Tenn.	OT	3.11
Tom Burson, Vandy	S	3.25
Bob Illes, Vandy	TE	3.75
Steve McCoy, Vandy	LB	3.00
Chuck Scott, Vandy	FLK	3.46
Wade Smith, Vandy	C	3.24
John Bell Whitesell, Vandy	RB	3.63
Craig Yokely, Vandy	DB	3.76

1985

Name and School	Pos.	GPA
Todd Roper, Ala.	LB	3.00
Russ Carreker, Aub.	LB	3.37
Kyle Collins, Aub.	RB	3.01
Yann Cowart, Aub.	G	3.28
Jeff Parks, Aub.	TE	3.48
Robert Shuler, Aub.	OT	3.44
Jimmie Warren, Aub.	DB	3.08
Rowland Cummings, Fla.	LB	3.14
Bret Wiechmann, Fla.	WR	3.27
Mike Brown, Ga.	R	3.00
John Little, Ga.	R	3.04
Andy Loy, Ga.	DE	3.14
Paul Messer, Ga.	SN	3.35
Chris Derry, Ky.	FB	3.15
Kevin Dooley, Ky.	QB	3.10
Eric Haas, Ky.	S	3.90
Richard Ledford, Ky.	WR	3.04
Matt Lucas, Ky.	TE	3.01
Ken Pietrowiak, Ky.	C	3.29

284 Honors

1985 (continued)

Name and School	Pos.	GPA
Bill Ransdell, Ky.	QB	3.07
James Reichwein, Ky.	RG	3.09
Gary Sexton, Ky.	S	3.17
Tom Wilkins, Ky.	DG	3.07
Nacho Albergamo, LSU	C	3.25
Keith Melancon, LSU	G	3.50
Jeff Wickersham, LSU	QB	3.20
Jud Alexander, Miss.	OG	3.02
Kent Austin, Miss.	QB	3.53
Bob Cheatham, Miss.	OT	3.15
Danny Hoskins, Miss.	OG	3.67
Jeff Noblin, Miss.	FS	3.71
Benton Reed, Miss.	DT	3.02
Jay Schimmel, Miss.	OT	3.53
Marvell McKelphin, MSU	FB	3.04
Scott Wilbanks, MSU	OG	3.29
Troy Hale, Tenn.	WR	3.10
Randy Sanders, Tenn.	QB/H	3.15
Tom Fitz, Vandy	FLK	3.82
Alan Herline, Vandy	PK	3.15
Mark Herrmann, Vandy	OT	3.21
Jeff Holt, Vandy	SS	3.09
Richard Stahl, Vandy	LB	3.45
Brent Turner, Vandy	LB	3.28
Mark Wracher, Vandy	QB	3.11
Craig Yokley, Vandy	CB	3.69

1986

Name and School	Pos.	GPA
Joe Godwin, Ala.	LB	3.42
Kermit Kendrick, Ala.	FS	3.04
Greg Richardson, Ala.	WR	3.00
Ricky Thomas, Ala.	SS	3.31
Russ Carreker, Aub.	LB	3.38
Yann Cowart, Aub.	G	3.19
Gary Kelley, Aub.	DE	3.00
Patrick Mote, Aub.	C	3.05
Tom Powell, Aub.	S	3.04
Ben Tamburello, Aub.	C	3.08
Walter Byrd, Fla.	LB	3.13
Robert Lasky, Fla.	DL	3.11
Ricky Nattiel, Fla.	WR	3.02
Joey Nicoletto, Fla.	LB	3.32
John Spierto, Fla.	DB	3.04
Bret Wiechmann, Fla.	WR	3.48
Rusty Beasley, Ga.	CB	3.11
Rick Fromm, Ga.	S	3.58
Steve Harmon, Ga.	S	3.25
Kim Stephens, Ga.	G	3.36
Todd Williams, Ga.	QB	3.11
Kevin Dooley, Ky.	QB	3.00
John Groves, Ky.	FB	3.14
Scott Haire, Ky.	G	3.00
Tim Jones, Ky.	WR	3.00
Ken Lange, Ky.	C	3.00
Matt Lucas, Ky.	TE	3.06
Larry Smith, Ky.	LB	3.16
Joe David Turner, Ky.	G	3.00
Tom Wilkins, Ky.	G	3.02
Nacho Albergamo, LSU	C	3.40
Jamie Bice, LSU	SS	3.17
Keith Melancon, LSU	G	3.24
Danny Hoskins, Miss.	G	3.65
Jeff Noblin, Miss.	S	3.68
Bryan Owen, Miss.	PK	3.06
Jay Schimmel, Miss.	T	3.33
Wesley Walls, Miss.	DE	3.46

Name and School	Pos.	GPA
Asa Bennett, MSU	S	3.18
Louis Clark, MSU	R	3.25
Kirby Jackson, MSU	CB	3.03
Stacy "Bo" Russell, MSU	B	3.43
Carl Terrell, MSU	TE	3.02
Jed Dance, Tenn.	L	3.14
Charles Davis, Tenn.	S	3.52
Troy Hale, Tenn.	WR	3.17
Stanley Jones, Tenn.	DB	3.05
Anthony Nelson, Tenn.	DB	3.07
Pete Panuska, Tenn.	RB	3.06
Randy Sanders, Tenn.	QB	3.08
Eric Still, Tenn.	G	3.69
Tom Fitz, Vandy	SE	3.66
John Fouts, Vandy	DT	3.15
Chris Gaines, Vandy	LB	3.09
Alan Herline, Vandy	K	3.28
Brent Turner, Vandy	LB	3.40
Mark Wracher, Vandy	QB	3.00

1987

Name and School	Pos.	GPA
Larry Abney, Ala.	B	3.04
Doug Allen, Ala.	FB	3.12
John Mangum, Ala.	CB	3.18
David Smith, Ala.	QB	3.08
Win Lyle, Aub.	K	3.24
Chris Birch, Fla.	G	3.09
Dale Cole, Fla.	T	3.09
Doug Evans, Fla.	T	3.05
Richard Fain, Fla.	DB	3.07
Joey Nicoletto, Fla.	LB	3.21
Louis Oliver, Fla.	S	3.36
Huey Richardson, Fla.	LB	3.22
Cedric Smith, Fla.	FB	3.22
Joe Vorwerk, Fla.	LB	3.13
Charlie Wright, Fla.	G	3.28
Kevin Brown, Ga.	RB	3.00
Mike Brown, Ga.	R	3.24
Will Colley, Ga.	L	3.25
Mark Lewis, Ga.	C	3.67
George Mrvos, Ga.	C	3.46
Kim Stephens, Ga.	G	3.55
Richard Tardits, Ga.	DE	3.27
Mark Vincent, Ga.	CB	3.16
Kevin Dooley, Ky.	QB	3.01
Mark Higgs, Ky.	RB	3.16
Jim Hill, Ky.	C	3.26
Tim Jones, Ky.	R	3.12
Brad Myers, Ky.	C	3.52
Mike Robinson, Ky.	DE	3.58
Ken Willis, Ky.	K	3.36
Nacho Albergamo, LSU	C	3.44
Jamie Bice, LSU	S	3.32
Sol Graves, LSU	QB	3.70
Robert Cagle, Miss.	G	3.52
Shawn Cobb, Miss.	LB	3.42
John Darnell, Miss.	QB	3.03
Butch Davenport, Miss.	CB	3.04
Sonny Harbuck, Miss.	G	3.19
Danny Hoskins, Miss.	G	3.97
Greg Lee, Miss.	TE	3.19
Bryan Owen, Miss.	K	3.08
Todd Sandroni, Miss.	S	3.82
Jay Schimmel, Miss.	T	3.42
Wesley Walls, Miss.	DE	3.39
Deron Zeppelin, Miss.	TE	3.91
Asa Bennett, MSU	S	3.32

Name and School	Pos.	GPA
Scott Berry, MSU	C	3.12
Chris Correro, MSU	S	3.25
Tony Robertson, MSU	T	3.51
Stacy "Bo" Russell, MSU	S	3.57
Stan Sims, MSU	G	3.32
Albert Williams, MSU	B	3.20
Kelly Days, Tenn.	DB	3.10
Keith DeLong, Tenn.	LB	3.04
Terry McDaniel, Tenn.	CB	3.00
Randy Sanders, Tenn.	QB	3.29
Eric Still, Tenn.	G	3.41
Kelly Ziegler, Tenn.	LB	3.13
John Clark, Vandy	PK	3.24
Thomas Fitz, Vandy	WR	3.61
John Fouts, Vandy	G	3.16
Andy McCarroll, Vandy	FB	3.74
Charles Pierson, Vandy	G	3.53
Torrey Price, Vandy	CB	3.13
Brent Turner, Vandy	LB	3.42
DeMond Winston, Vandy	DE	3.50

1988

Name and School	Pos.	GPA
Murry Hill, Ala.	RB	3.23
John Mangum, Ala.	DB	3.17
Chris Mohr, Ala.	P	3.28
Darryl Pickett, Ala.	LB	3.05
Mike Ramil, Ala.	DL	3.17
David Smith, Ala.	QB	3.42
Mike Smith, Ala.	DB	3.29
Lorenzo Ward, Ala.	DB	3.12
Mike Zuga, Ala.	C	3.36
James Clemmer, Aub.	DB	3.04
John Clemmer, Aub.	LB	3.14
Win Lyle, Aub.	PK	3.39
Gregory Staples, Aub.	DB	3.08
Shayne Wasden, Aub.	WR	3.30
Owen Bartruff, Fla.	LB	3.26
Brad Culpepper, Fla.	DL	3.42
Cal Dixon, Fla.	OL	3.11
Anthony Leon, Fla.	DB	3.57
Louis Oliver, Fla.	DB	3.21
Herbert Perry, Fla.	QB	3.20
Huey Richardson, Fla.	LB	3.22
Jeff Roth, Fla.	DL	3.05
Cedric Smith, Fla.	RB	3.10
John Spierto, Fla.	DB	3.31
Charlie Wright, Fla.	OL	3.35
Christopher Broom, Ga.	TE	3.54
R. Melvin Henderson, Ga.	OG	3.25
Mark Lewis, Ga.	KS	3.93
Richard Tardits, Ga.	LB	3.74
Craig Benzinger, Ky.	LB	3.00
Chuck Broughton, Ky.	QB	3.00
Mike Cahill, Ky.	LB	3.70
Doug Houser, Ky.	DL	3.11
Mike Meiners, Ky.	DL	3.00
Todd Meyer, Ky.	DB	3.11
Jeff Nelson, Ky.	P	3.42
Mike Pfeifer, Ky.	OL	3.44
Walter "Bo" Smith, Ky.	OL	3.79
Tim Smith, Ky.	RB	3.33
Ken Willis, Ky.	PK	3.06
Jamie Bice, LSU	DB	3.40
Jay Egloff, LSU	FB	3.33
Solomon Graves, LSU	QB	3.56
Robert Cagle, Jr., Miss.	OL	3.19
Shawn Cobb, Miss.	LB	3.45

1994 SEC Football 285

SEC Academic Honor Roll

1988 (Continued)

Name and School	Pos.	GPA
Jay Hopson, Miss.	DB	3.37
Ronnie McKinney, Miss.	RB	3.31
Dawson Pruett, Miss.	OL	3.29
Todd Sandroni, Miss.	DB	3.53
Darryl Smith, Miss.	DL	3.10
Wesley Walls, Miss.	TE	3.39
Deron Zeppelin, Miss.	TE	3.65
Asa Bennett, MSU	DB	3.20
Jerry Bouldin, MSU	WR	3.00
Chris Correro, MSU	LB	3.33
Heath Jackson, MSU	LB	3.00
John McCulland, MSU	OL	3.09
Tony Robertson, MSU	C	3.60
Bo Russell, MSU	DB	3.48
Roger Simpson, MSU	OL	3.61
Eric Underwood, MSU	QB	3.03
Albert Williams, MSU	DB	3.17
Chris Benson, Tenn.	WR	3.02
Lee England, Tenn.	WR	3.01
Adam Epstein, Tenn.	PK	3.80
James McBrayer, Tenn.	TE	3.00
Thomas Myslinski, Tenn.	OG	3.09
Ray Robinson, Tenn.	C	3.02
Randall Sanders, Tenn.	QB	3.38
Eric Still, Tenn.	OG	3.36
Preston Warren, Tenn.	DB	3.12
Johnny Clark, Vandy	K	3.18
Kevin Dowling, Vandy	OT	3.11
Tom Fitz, Vandy	FL	3.60
John Fouts, Vandy	OG	3.04
John Gromos, Vandy	QB	3.50
Andrew McCarroll, Vandy	FB	3.72
John Newman, Vandy	TB	3.23
Charles Pierson, Vandy	OG	3.54
Brent Turner, Vandy	DE	3.34
Joel Walker, Vandy	DE	3.47
DeMond Winston, Vandy	LB	3.31

1989

Name and School	Pos.	GPA
Jeff Dunn, Ala.	QB	3.40
Johnny Howard, Ala.	OG	3.00
John Mangum, Ala.	DB	3.11
John Clemmer, Aub.	LB	3.39
Win Lyle, Aub.	PK	3.66
Brad Culpepper, Fla.	MG	3.28
Cal Dixon, Fla.	C	3.06
John Durden, Fla.	OT	3.08
John David Francis, Fla.	PK	3.28
Huey Richardson, Fla.	LB	3.15
Cedric Smith, Fla.	FB	3.15
Chuck Wabbersen, Fla.	RB	3.17
Chris Broom, Ga.	TE	3.30
Jimps Cole, Ga.	SN	3.11
Virgil Cole, Ga.	DT	3.00
Lee Fincher, Ga.	P	3.19
John Kasay, Ga.	PK	3.13
Craig Benzinger, Ky.	LB	3.50
Darren Bilberry, Ky.	FB	3.00
Chuck Broughton, Ky.	QB	3.00
Tom Crumrine, Ky.	OT	3.44
Doug Houser, Ky.	DT	3.00
Bill Hulette, Ky.	OG	3.00
Mike Knox, Ky.	FB	3.56
Greg Lahr, Ky.	OT	3.76
Freddie Maggard, Ky.	QB	3.30
Mike Meiners, Ky.	DG	3.08
Andy Murray, Ky.	FB	3.14
Todd Perry, Ky.	OT	3.56
Mike Pfeifer, Ky.	OT	3.89
Ron Robinson, Ky.	FS	3.43
Dean Wells, Ky.	LB	3.32
Ken Willis, Ky.	PK	3.16
Tony Zigman, Ky.	LB	3.25
Paul Ernst, LSU	TE	3.34
Jay Egloff, LSU	FB	3.33
Solomon Graves, LSU	QB	3.65
Oliver Lawrence, LSU	LB	3.00
John Morgan, LSU	OL	3.10
Reginald Walker, LSU	LB	3.10
Scott Wharton, LSU	NG	3.62
Shawn Cobb, Miss.	LB	3.37
John Darnell, Miss.	QB	3.00
Chauncey Godwin, Miss.	DB	3.11
Jay Hopson, Miss.	DB	3.40
Lee Lott, Miss.	OT	3.23
Tom Luke, Miss.	QB	3.40
Gerald McAllister, Miss.	DB	3.06
Ronnie McKinney, Miss.	RB	3.15
Jack Muirhead, Miss.	LB	3.17
Dawson Pruett, Miss.	C	3.50
Camp Roberts, Miss.	TE	3.07
Todd Sandroni, Miss.	DB	3.56
Trea Southerland, Miss.	DB	3.38
Scott Swatzell, Miss.	RB	3.54
Deron Zeppelin, Miss.	OG	3.57
Chris Correro, MSU	DB	3.50
Chris Firle, MSU	WR	3.51
Terry High, MSU	DB	3.00
Dewayne King, MSU	LB	3.17
Bill Knight, MSU	DL	3.14
Joel Logan, MSU	PK	3.03
Stephen McMullan, MSU	C	3.19
Tony Robertson, MSU	LB	3.42
Bo Russell, MSU	DB	3.57
Tony Shell, MSU	QB	3.23
Eric Underwood, MSU	QB	3.04
Albert Williams, MSU	DB	3.11
Sam Wright, MSU	TE	3.12
Chris Benson, Tenn.	WR	3.20
Kent Elmore, Tenn.	P	3.00
Lee England, Tenn.	WR	3.20
Eric Still, Tenn.	OG	3.30
John Clark, Vandy	PK	3.19
John Gromos, Vandy	QB	3.42
Brett Hayes, Vandy	WB	3.15
Mark Kubow, Vandy	TE	3.24
Andrew McCarroll, Vandy	LB	3.76
John Newman, Vandy	DL	3.07
Charles Pierson, Vandy	OG	3.52
Joel Walker, Vandy	DE	3.24
DeMond Winston, Vandy	LB	3.06

1990

Name and School	Pos.	GPA
David Bonamy, Ala.	SE	3.03
Scott Etter, Ala.	QB	3.30
Hamp Greene, Ala.	PK	3.26
Johnny Howard, Ala.	T	3.11
Stan Moss, Ala.	P	3.10
Mike Smith, Ala.	CB	3.08
William Swinney, Ala.	WR	3.05
Tank Williamson, Ala.	P	3.28
George Wilson, Ala.	G	3.11
Pedro Cherry, Aub.	WR	3.48
Clayton Davis, Aub.	TE	3.31
Roy Hunter, Aub.	DB	3.08
Danny Ledbetter, Aub.	LB	3.04
Chad Muilenburg, Aub.	FB	3.11
Dale Overton, Aub.	WR	3.03
Shayne Wasden, Aub.	WR	3.38
Michael Brown, Fla.	DB	3.42
Michael Cohen, Fla.	QB	3.52
Brad Culpepper, Fla.	DT	3.21
Calvert Dixon, Fla.	C	3.00
Jerry Odom, Jr., Fla.	LB	3.01
Huey Richardson, Fla.	DE	3.10
Cornell B. Tinner, Fla.	SS	3.07
Chuck Wabberson, Fla.	RB	3.35
Brian Bowers, Ga.	PK	3.56
Chris Broom, Ga.	TE	3.50
Torrey Evans, Ga.	LB	3.11
Preston Jones, Ga.	QB	3.00
John Kasay, Ga.	PK	3.33
Scott Rissmiller, Ga.	T	3.13
Bill Rosenberg, Ga.	G	3.07
Greg Talley, Ga.	QB	3.33
Richard Turner, Ga.	FS	3.28
George Wynn, Ga.	CB	3.10
Jim Graves, Ky.	LB	3.09
Ryan Hockman, Ky.	QB	3.09
Randy Holleran, Ky.	LB	3.00

Vanderbilt linebacker DeMond Winston, an All-SEC performer in 1989, was three-time member of the Academic Honor Roll.

286 Honors

1990 (Continued)

Name and School	Pos.	GPA
Bill Hulette, Ky.	G	3.00
Greg Hunt, Ky.	FL	3.00
Larry Jackson, Ky.	SS	3.53
Greg Lahr, Ky.	T	3.66
Freddie Maggard, Ky.	QB	3.63
Joel Mazzella, Ky.	G	3.09
Todd Perry, Ky.	G	3.28
Brad Smith, Ky.	QB	3.33
Dean Wells, Ky.	LB	3.29
Gary Willis, Ky.	CB	3.18
Paul Ernst, LSU	TE	3.41
Solomon Graves, LSU	QB	3.65
Mike Hewitt, LSU	LB	3.14
Chad Loup, LSU	QB	3.13
John Morgan, LSU	DT	3.33
Scott Wharton, LSU	NG	3.46
Brian Cagle, Miss.	DT	3.16
Shawn Cobb, Miss.	LB	3.33
Clifton Dew, Miss.	C	3.22
Chauncey Godwin, Miss.	CB	3.24
Jody Hill, Miss.	LB	3.17
James Hopson, Miss.	SS	3.25
Brian Lee, Miss.	PK	3.22
Thomas Luke, Miss.	QB	3.35
Monty Perry, Miss.	G	3.15
Dawson Pruett, Miss.	C	3.50
Todd Sandroni, Miss.	FS	3.53
Thomas Southerland, Miss.	SS	3.59
Scott Swatzell, Miss.	RB	3.21
Daniel Boyd, MSU	LB	3.36
Chris Firle, MSU	WR	3.46
Tony Robertson, MSU	T	3.38
Rodney Whitlock, MSU	C	3.41
Albert Williams, MSU	SS	3.06
Roderick Lewis, Tenn.	DB	3.06
Charles Longmire, Tenn.	WR	3.02
Charles McRae, Tenn.	T	3.18
Robert Todd, Tenn.	T	3.05
Kevin Wendelboe, Tenn.	KS	3.28
Robert Chura, Vandy	KS	3.18
Thor Erikson, Vandy	G	3.00
Brett Hayes, Vandy	WB	3.22
Hubert Jordan, Vandy	C	3.00
Jeffery Owen, Vandy	P-KS	3.38
Royce Risser, Vandy	LB	3.43
Joel Walker, Vandy	DT	3.57
Joel Weingart, Vandy	DB	3.27

1991

Name and School	Pos.	GPA
David Bonamy, Ala.	SE	3.00
Hamp Greene, Ala.	PK	3.26
Matt Hammond, Ala.	T	3.00
Johnny Howard, Ala.	T	3.05
Tobie Sheils, Ala.	C	3.04
Tank Williamson, Ala.	P	3.12
George Wilson, Ala.	G	3.04
Chris Jones, Aub.	SS	3.00
Chad Muilenburg, Aub.	FB	3.11
Richard Shea, Aub.	DT	3.22
Chris Bilkie, Fla.	FB	3.12
Norman Bolduc, Fla.	WR	3.13
Michel Cohen, Fla.	QB	3.40
Brad Culpepper, Fla.	DT	3.34
Terry Dean, Fla.	QB	4.00
Steve Dee, Fla.	WR	3.09
Cal Dixon, Fla.	C	3.00
Jim Franklin, Fla.	TE	3.03

Name and School	Pos.	GPA
Michael Gilmore, Fla.	FS	3.91
Matt Hurbanis, Fla.	LB	3.64
Kris Lay, Fla.	DB	3.57
David Swain, Fla.	DE	3.22
Scot Armstrong, Ga.	P	3.00
Preston Jones, Ga.	QB	3.09
Alec Millen, Ga.	OT	3.35
Steve Moore, Ga.	WR	3.15
Todd Peterson, Ga.	PK	3.48
Scott Rissmiller, Ga.	SN	3.40
Jack Swan, Ga.	C	3.00
Greg Talley, Ga.	QB	3.30
George Wynn, Ga.	DB	3.17
Mark Askin, Ky.	T	3.00
Chip Garner, Ky.	C	3.09
Jim Graves, Ky.	LB	3.13
Bill Hawk, Ky.	P	3.00
Ryan Hockman, Ky.	QB	3.10
Larry Jackson, Ky.	ROV	3.09
Greg Lahr, Ky.	T	3.72
Freddie Maggard, Ky.	QB	3.41
Doug Pelfrey, Ky.	PK	3.15
Todd Perry, Ky.	G	3.04
Brad Smith, Ky.	QB	3.18
Derrick Thomas, Ky.	DE	3.14
Jeff Weihe, Ky.	T	3.25
Dean Wells, Ky.	LB	3.40
Gary Willis, Ky.	DB	3.14
Harold Bishop, LSU	TE	3.20
Mike Blanchard, LSU	OL	4.00
Mike Hewitt, LSU	LB	3.30
Chap Loup, LSU	QB	3.30
Michael Marix, LSU	SN	3.10
Derriel McCorvey, LSU	SS	3.00
John Morgan, LSU	DT	3.10
Jason Rector, LSU	DB	3.60
Brad Strohm, LSU	QB	3.10
Pedro Suarez, LSU	PK	3.00
Reggie Walker, LSU	LB	3.10
Scott Wharton, LSU	NG	3.30
Chauncey Godwin, Miss.	CB	3.00
David Harris, Miss.	DT	3.32
James Hopson, Miss.	SS	3.31
Brian Lee, Miss.	PK	3.16
Robert Little, Miss.	WR	3.24
Tom Luke, Miss.	QB	3.35
Thomas Southerland, Miss.	CB	3.31
Rogers Stephens, Miss.	PK	3.14
Scott Swatzell, Miss.	RB	3.41
J. Abner White, Miss.	C	3.64
Dan Boyd, MSU	LB	3.27
Chris Firle, MSU	WR	3.31
Terry High, MSU	RB	3.00
Armandos Fisher, Tenn.	LB	3.24
Kyle Heran, Tenn.	LB	3.25
Craig Martin, Tenn.	C	3.25
Thomas Myslinski, Tenn.	G	3.11
Robert Todd, Tenn.	TE	3.09
Kevin Wendleboe, Tenn.	KS	4.00
Derrick Gragg, Jr., Vandy	SE	3.08
Jeffrey Owen, Vandy	PK	3.35
David Risser, Vandy	LB	3.65
Alan Young, Vandy	LB	3.49

1992

Name and School	Pos.	GPA
Hamp Greene, Ala.	PK	3.20
Alvin Hope, Ala.	CB	3.04
Martin Houston, Ala.	FB	3.15
Johnny Howard, Ala.	OT	3.03
Stan Moss, Ala.	P	3.07
Myron Pope, Ala.	TE	3.06
Bart Pritchett, Ala.	NT	3.10
Tobie Sheils, Ala.	C	3.05
Dabo Swinney, Ala.	SE	3.08
Jeff Wall, Ala.	H	3.08
George Wilson, Ala.	OG	3.01
Owen Kelly, Ark.	NG	3.48
Chris Oliver, Ark.	OT	3.71
Todd Wright, Ark.	PK	3.23
Todd Boland, Aub.	C	3.14
Sean Carder, Aub.	WR	3.23
Terry Daniel, Aub.	P	3.12
Chris Gray, Aub.	OT	3.05
Clay Helton, Aub.	QB	3.02
Shawn Malone, Aub.	TE	3.63
Chris Bilkie, Fla.	FB	3.03
Michel Cohen, Fla.	QB	3.51
Kendall Cook, Fla.	PK	3.08
Terry Dean, Fla.	QB	3.97
Michael Gilmore, Fla.	FS	3.87
Earl Higgs, Fla.	RB	3.15
Jeremy Kennedy, Fla.	TE	3.23
Matthew Kockevar, Fla.	DB	3.00
Ron Perez, Fla.	P	3.19
David Swain, Fla.	OG	3.11
Brian White, Fla.	PK	3.50
Scot Armstrong, Ga.	P	3.08
Damon Evans, Ga.	SE	3.33
Torrey Evans, Ga.	LB	3.01
Bobby Greene, Ga.	SE	3.23
Al Jackson, Ga.	SS	3.14
Preston Jones, Ga.	QB	3.14

Mississippi State's Daniel Boyd, a three-time SEC Academic Honor Roll member, earned All-SEC honors and helped lead the Bulldogs to the Peach Bowl in 1992.

1994 SEC Football 287

SEC Academic Honor Roll

1992 (Continued)

Name and School	Pos.	GPA
Alec Millen, Ga.	OT	3.24
Todd Peterson, Ga.	PK	3.47
Jason Pickett, Ga.	LB	3.42
Scott Rissmiller, Ga.	SN	3.46
Bill Rosenberg, Ga.	OG	3.03
Jack Swan, Ga.	OG	3.22
Chris Wilson, Ga.	CB	3.03
Eric Zeier, Ga.	QB	3.00
Brad Armstead, Ky.	FS	3.00
Mark Askin, Ky.	OT	3.03
Andy Britt, Ky.	OG	3.00
Mark Chatmon, Ky.	SE	3.06
Dude Harper, Ky.	C	3.10
Ryan Hockman, Ky.	QB	3.53
Cale Langford, Ky.	SE	3.11
Marty Moore, Ky.	LB	3.69
David Parks, Ky.	OG	3.00
Doug Pelfrey, Ky.	PK	3.41
Don Robinson, Ky.	DB	3.11
Reggie Smith, Ky.	LB	3.23
Dean Wells, Ky.	DL	3.30
Mike Blanchard, LSU	C	4.00
Mike Garrett, LSU	FL	3.10
Frank Godfrey, LSU	C	3.10
Mike Hewitt, LSU	LB	3.18
Chap Loup, LSU	QB	3.60
Kevin Mawae, LSU	OT	3.00
Derriel McCorvey, LSU	SS	3.00
John Morgan, LSU	DT	3.50
Gary Pegues, LSU	CB	3.00
David Harris, Miss.	DT	3.20
Joel Jordan, Miss.	OG	3.33
Brian Lee, Miss.	PK	3.40
Franz Lorio, Miss.	C	3.06
Greg Morris, Miss.	WR	3.48
Lynn Ross, Miss.	LB	3.34
Trea Southerland, Miss.	SS	3.59
Rogers Stephens, Miss.	PK	3.23
Jeff Artigues, MSU	KS	3.25
Daniel Boyd, MSU	LB	3.27
Darrin Clark, MSU	WB	3.00
Greg Jones, MSU	TE	3.07
Kelvin Knight, MSU	FS	3.16
Marc Woodard, MSU	LB	3.00
Luther Dixon, USC	OL	3.00
Chuck Driggers, USC	OL	3.04
Troy Duke, USC	DE	3.00
Boomer Foster, USC	TE	3.57
Ben Hogan, USC	LB	3.40
Corey Louchiey, USC	OT	3.09
Michael Muse, USC	OL	3.18
Antoine Rivens, USC	OG	3.17
Marty Simpson, USC	PK	3.39
John Becksvoort, Tenn.	KS	3.38
David Bennett, Tenn.	DB	3.50
Jason Epstein, Tenn.	KS	3.91
Tom Hutton, Tenn.	P	3.19
Cleon Mitchell, Tenn.	RB	3.02
Robert Todd, Tenn.	TE	3.57
Rob Chura, Vandy	KS	3.28
Eric Dahlberg, Vandy	OT	3.31
Eric Lewis, Vandy	FB	3.34
Nizam Walter, Vandy	SS	3.17
Eric Weir, Vandy	SE	3.83

1993

Name and School	Pos.	GPA
Jay Brannen, Ala.	OLB	3.12
Shannon Brown, Ala.	DE	3.06
Lorenzo Cole, Ala.	FL	3.00
John Clay, Ala.	OG	3.22
Matt Hammond, Ala.	OT	3.00
Jason Jack, Ala.	QB	3.42
Jackson Lowery, Ala.	SS	3.11
Kareem McNeal, Ala.	OT	3.13
Josh Niblett, Ala.	QB	3.31
Matt Pine, Ala.	SN	3.00
Tobie Sheils, Ala.	C	3.09
Matt Wethington, Ala.	PK	3.35
Mike Cherry, Ark.	QB	3.44
Brad Hogan, Ark.	OLB	3.72
Barry Lunney, Ark.	QB	3.11
Chris Oliver, Ark.	OT	3.69
Vernon Wade, Ark.	DT	3.33
Todd Boland, Aub.	OT	3.08
James Bryan, Aub.	FB	3.43
John Franklin, Aub.	OT	3.02
Stan White, Aub.	QB	3.04
Sean Carder, Aub.	WR	3.36
James Bates, Fla.	ILB	3.16
Chris Bilkie, Fla.	FB	3.20
Judd Davis, Fla.	PK	3.06
Terry Dean, Fla.	QB	3.88
Michael Gilmore, Fla.	DB	3.63
Jeff Mitchell, Fla.	OG	3.17
David Nabavi, Fla.	WR	3.06
Jason Odom, Fla.	OT	3.27
Scott Perry, Fla.	DE	3.66
David Swain, Fla.	OL	3.47
Adam Whitehurst, Fla.	QB	3.01
Lawrence Wright, Fla.	FS	3.06
Danny Wuerffel, Fla.	QB	3.88
Robert Greene, Ga.	SE	3.49
Danny Ledbetter, Ga.	DT	3.38
Christopher McCranie, Ga.	CB	3.22
Will Muschamp, Ga.	SS	3.08
Brett Pellock, Ga.	P	3.89
Eric Zeier, Ga.	QB	3.02
Mark Askin, Ky.	OT	3.21
Tim Calvert, Ky.	SE	3.60
Brent Claiborne, Ky.	PK	3.31
Trent Digiuro, Ky.	OG	3.00
Dude Harper, Ky.	C	3.30
Chad Hayes, Ky.	FB	3.20
Cale Langford, Ky.	CB	3.50
Rob Manchester, Ky.	SS	3.00
Ray McLaurin, Ky.	TB	3.00
Marty Moore, Ky.	LB	3.50
Darren Murray, Ky.	FB	3.00
David Parks, Ky.	OL	3.29
Mike Schellenberger, Ky.	LB	3.89
Jeff Speedy, Ky.	QB	3.34
Michael Blanchard, LSU	C	4.00
John Booker, LSU	DE	3.40
Mike Hewitt, LSU	OLB	3.44
Chad Loup, LSU	QB	3.56
John Malagarie, LSU	DT	3.03
David Harris, Ole Miss	DT	3.25
Paul Head, Ole Miss	QB	3.53
Franz Lorio, Ole Miss	C	3.00
Michael Lowery, Ole Miss	FS	3.22
Greg Morris, Ole Miss	WR	3.63
Sean O'Malley, Ole Miss	NG	3.00
Deano Orr, Ole Miss	FB	3.00
David Vinson, Ole Miss	C	3.00
Kyle Wicker, Ole Miss	LB	3.54
Trey Wicker, Ole Miss	DE	3.17
Brian Anderson, MSU	C	3.31
Darrin Clark, MSU	WR	3.09
Scott Gumina, MSU	OLB	3.28
Juan Long, MSU	ILB	3.03
Brian Wright, MSU	OT	3.64
Boomer Foster, USC	TE	3.18
Corey Louchiey, USC	OT	3.09
Bru Pender, USC	WR	3.10
Marty Simpson, USC	PK	3.21
Blake Williamson, USC	QB	3.17
Shane Bonham, Tenn.	DT	3.31
Scott Galyon, Tenn.	LB	3.03
Mark Holland, Tenn.	C	3.00
Tom Hutton, Tenn.	P	3.10
Ralph Nelson, Tenn.	DT	3.02
Heath Shuler, Tenn.	QB	3.11
Nilo Silvan, Tenn.	WR	3.00
Jeff Smith, Tenn.	OG	3.04
Mark Upton, Tenn.	DG	3.76
Paul Yatkowski, Tenn.	DT	3.24
Robert Couch, Vandy	OT	3.25
Tor Dixon, Vandy	CB	3.23
Eric Lewis, Vandy	WB	3.31
Chris Ryals, Vandy	FS	3.46
Aaron Smith, Vandy	SS	3.12
Nizam Walter, Vandy	SS	3.09

South Carolina offensive tackle Corey Louchiey, a third-round pick in the 1994 NFL Draft, was named to the SEC Academic Honor Roll in 1992 and 1993.

288 Honors

SEC All-Freshman Teams
(Sponsored by Knoxville News-Sentinel)

1986
OFFENSE:
*QB - Tommy Hodson, LSU
RB - Harvey Williams, LSU
RB - Octavius Gould, Florida
RB - James Joseph, Auburn
REC - Terrence Cleveland, Tennessee
REC - Willie Green, Ole Miss
OL - Mike Zuga, Alabama
OL - Andy Anderson, Alabama
OL - John Hudson, Auburn
OL - Burr Seaver, Vanderbilt
PK - David Browndyke, LSU
RS - T.D. Woods, Tennessee

DEFENSE:
DL - Demond Winston, Vanderbilt
DL - Andy Dotson, Georgia
DL - Darryl Smith, Ole Miss
DL - Vic Adams, Kentucky
LB - Vantriese Davis, Alabama
LB - Pat Moore, Florida
LB - Jesse Anderson, Miss. State
LB - Milton Gordon, Tennessee
DB - Don Price, Ole Miss
DB - Asa Bennett, Miss. State
DB - Torrey Price, Vanderbilt
DB - Ron Robinson, Kentucky
P - Tommy Parks, Miss. State
* - Freshman of the Year

1987
OFFENSE:
WR - Ernie Mills, Florida
WR - Alvin Harper, Tennessee
OL - Tony Robertson, Miss. State
OL - Roger Shultz, Alabama
OL - Dawson Pruett, Ole Miss
OL - Terrill Chatman, Alabama
OL - Robbin Perry, Tennessee
QB - Jeff Dunn, Alabama
*RB - Emmitt Smith, Florida
RB - Reggie Cobb, Tennessee
RB - Rodney Hampton, Georgia
PK - Phillip Doyle, Alabama

DEFENSE:
DL - Charles McRae, Tennessee
DL - Cedric Moore, Vanderbilt
DL - Robert Lenoir, Alabama
DL - Robert Young, Miss. State
LB - Robert Stewart, Alabama
LB - Mark Murray, Florida
LB - Huey Richardson, Florida
DB - Todd Sandroni, Ole Miss
DB - Kelly Days, Tennessee
DB - Chris Tolbert, Kentucky
DB - Eddie Myles, Miss. State
P - Charles Childers, Ole Miss
* - Freshman of the Year

1988
OFFENSE:
WR - Arthur Marshall, Georgia
WR - Shayne Wasden, Auburn
OL - Greg Lahr, Kentucky
OL - Kenny Stewart, Miss. State
OL - Bobby Craycraft, Vanderbilt
OL - John Fisher, Tennessee
OL - Ed King, Auburn
QB - Kyle Morris, Florida
RB - Willie McClendon, Florida
RB - Kevin Turner, Alabama
RB - Henry Love, Auburn
P - Mike Riley, Miss. State

DEFENSE:
DL - Jerry Bell, Kentucky
DL - Rod Keith, Vanderbilt
DL - Shazzon Bradley, Tennessee
LB - Tim Paulk, Florida
LB - Earnest Fields, Tennessee
LB - Melvin Hawkins, Miss. State
LB - Anthony Judge, Auburn
DB - Chuck Carswell, Georgia
DB - Bill Fitzpatrick, Vanderbilt
DB - Chauncey Godwin, Ole Miss
DB - Charles Gardner, Alabama
PK - Chip McCallum, Tennessee
RS - Vince Fuller, LSU

1989
OFFENSE:
WR - Clarence Sevillian, Vanderbilt
WR - Kurt Johnson, Kentucky
OL - Jack Swan, Georgia
OL - John James, Miss. State
OL - Byron Jordan, Miss. State
OL - Everett Lindsay, Ole Miss
OL - Chuck Bradley, Kentucky
QB - Donald Douglas, Florida
RB - Chuck Webb, Tennessee
RB - Kenny Roberts, Miss. State
RB - Darrell Williams, Auburn
PK - Brian Lee, Ole Miss
RS - Tony James, Miss. State

DEFENSE:
DL - George Brown, Georgia
DL - Rodney Stowers, Miss. State
DL - Mike Gandolfo, Vanderbilt
LB - Marc Woodard, Miss. State
LB - Alan Young, Vanderbilt
LB - Nigel Ventress, LSU
LB - David Walkup, LSU
DB - Chris Donnelly, Vanderbilt
DB - Carl Pickens, Tennessee
DB - Mike Jones, Georgia
DB - Will White, Florida
P - David Lawrence, Vanderbilt

1990
OFFENSE:
WR - Andre Hastings, Georgia
WR - Marcus Carter, LSU
TE - Shannon Mitchell, Georgia
OL - Anthony Redmon, Auburn
OL - Kevin Mawae, LSU
OL - Clint Conlee, Ole Miss
OL - Shea Bell, Miss. State
OL - Matt Hammond, Alabama
QB - Stan White, Auburn
*RB - Garrison Hearst, Georgia
RB - Errict Rhett, Florida
FB - Terry Samuels, Kentucky
RS - Chris Anderson, Alabama

DEFENSE:
DL - Willie Jennings, Georgia
DL - Bernard Williams, Georgia
DL - Jeremy Nunley, Alabama
#LB - James Willis, Auburn
LB - Roovelroe Swan, LSU
LB - Shelton Quarles, Vanderbilt
LB - Ed Robinson, Florida
DB - Anthony Marshall, LSU
DB - Ralph Thompson, Georgia
DB - Robert Davis, Vanderbilt
DB - Aaron Smith, Vanderbilt
P - Joey Chapman, Tennessee
* - Freshman of the Year (Offense)
# - Freshman of the Year (Defense)

1991
OFFENSE:
WR - David Palmer, Alabama
WR - Aubrey Hill, Florida
OL - Jon Stevenson, Alabama
OL - Steve Roberts, Georgia
OL - Mark Askin, Kentucky
OL - Richard Saenz, Vanderbilt
*QB - Eric Zeier, Georgia
RB - James Stewart, Tennessee
RB - Aaron Hayden, Tennessee
RB - Joe Frazier, Auburn
FB - Michael Davis, Miss. State
PK - John Becksvoort, Tennessee
RS - Thomas Bailey, Auburn

DEFENSE:
DL - William Crowell, LSU
DL - Damon Betz, Kentucky
DL - Ellis Johnson, Florida
DL - Kevin Carter, Florida
LB - Michael Rogers, Alabama
LB - Damon Ward, Georgia
DB - Melvin Johnson, Kentucky
DB - Ivory Hilliard, LSU
DB - Rodney Young, LSU
DB - Fred Smith, Auburn
DB - Larry Kennedy, Florida
P - Shayne Edge, Florida
* - Freshman of the Year

1992
OFFENSE:
WR - Jack Jackson, Florida
OL - Jeff Smith, Tennessee
OL - Bubba Miller, Tennessee
OL - Reggie Green, Florida
OL - Owen Neil, Vanderbilt
*QB - Steve Taneyhill, S. Carolina
RB - Cliff Deese, Vanderbilt
RB - Oscar Malone, Arkansas
FB - Royce Love, Vanderbilt
PK - Michael Proctor, Alabama
PRS - Shawn Summers, Tennessee
KORS - David Butler, LSU

DEFENSE:
DL - Johnie Church, Florida
DL - Eric Sullivan, S. Carolina
DL - Jeff Kaiser, Georgia
DL - David Barnard, Florida
OLB - Ben Hanks, Florida
OLB - James Gillyard, LSU
#ILB - Randall Godfrey, Georgia
ILB - Anthony Harris, Auburn
DB - Michael Lowery, Ole Miss
DB - Jason Parker, Tennessee
DB - David Snardon, Kentucky
* - Freshman of the Year (Offense)
# - Freshman of the Year (Defense)

1993
OFFENSE:
WR - Ta'Boris Fisher, Ole Miss
WR - Joey Kent, Kentucky
WR - Kenny Causey, Miss. State
OL - Willie Anderson, Auburn
OL - John Harrison, S. Carolina
OL - Ben Bordelon, LSU
OL - Adam Meadows, Georgia
C - Don Struebing, Arkansas
*QB - Danny Wuerffel, Florida
RB - Moe Williams, Kentucky
Athlete - Eddie Kennison, LSU

DEFENSE:
DL - Leland Taylor, Tennessee
DL - Cameron Davis, Florida
DL - Walter Rouse, Georgia
LB - Mike Calais, LSU
LB - Darren Hambrick, Florida
LB - Dwayne Curry, Miss. State
LB - Mark Smith, Arkansas
DB - Lawrence Wright, Florida
DB - Anthone Lott, Florida
DB - Raymond Austin, Tennessee
DB - Eric Vance, Vanderbilt
Sp. Teams - Terry Cousin, S. Carolina
PK - Reed Morton, S. Carolina
*-Freshman of the Year

1994 SEC Football 289

SEC Players of the Week

1985

Date	Offensive	Defensive
Sept. 6	Bo Jackson, Aub.	Cornelius Bennett, Ala.
Sept. 13	Tony Robinson, Tenn.	Chris White, Tenn.
		Cedric Corse, MSU
Sept. 20	Mike Shula, Ala.	John Little, Ga.
Sept. 27	Kerwin Bell, Fla.	Darrin Miller, Tenn.
Oct. 4	Bo Jackson, Aub.	Alonzo Johnson, Fla.
Oct. 11	Jeff Wickersham, LSU	Mike Velotta, Ky.
Oct. 18	Bo Jackson, Aub.	Michael Brooks, LSU
Oct. 25	Kent Austin, Miss.	Greg Waters, Ga.
	Mike Shula, Ala.	
Nov. 2	Gene Jelks, Ala.	Alonzo Johnson, Fla.
Nov. 9	Keith Henderson, Ga.	Greg Waters, Ga.
	Everett Crawford, Vandy	
Nov. 16	Bo Jackson, Aub.	Michael Brooks, LSU
Nov. 23	Jeff Wickersham, LSU	Ron Sancho, LSU
		Henry Thomas, LSU
Nov. 30	Daryl Dickey, Tenn.	Kelly Ziegler, Tenn.

1986

Date	Offensive	Defensive
Aug. 30	Kerwin Bell, Fla.	Ricky Thomas, Ala.
Sept. 6	Don Smith, MSU	Jeff Noblin, Miss.
Sept. 13	Don Smith, MSU	Michael Brooks, LSU
Sept. 20	Bobby Humphrey, Ala.	Cornelius Bennett, Ala.
Sept. 27	Brent Fullwood, Aub.	Aundray Bruce, Aub.
		Mike Fitzsimmons, Miss.
Oct. 4	Al Bell, Ala.	Greg Jackson, LSU
Oct. 11	Brent Fullwood, Aub.	Toby Caston, LSU
Oct. 18	Bobby Humphrey, Ala.	Kurt Crain, Aub.
Oct. 25	Wendell Davis, LSU	Don Price, Miss.
	Brent Fullwood, Aub.	
Nov. 1	Kerwin Bell, Fla.	Keith Williams, Fla.
	Bobby Humphrey, Ala.	Howard Moss, Miss.
Nov. 8	Ivy Joe Hunter, Ky.	Clifford Charlton, Fla.
		Gregg Jackson, LSU
Nov. 15	Tom Hodson, LSU	Steve Boswell, Ga.
	Bill Ransdell, Ky.	
Nov. 22	Tom Hodson, LSU	Jeff Herrod, Miss.
	Wendell Davis, LSU	
Nov. 29	Brent Fullwood, Aub.	Kurt Crain, Aub.
	Lars Tate, Ga.	

1987

Date	Offensive	Defensive
Aug. 30	Reggie Cobb, Tenn.	Kelly Ziegler, Tenn.
Sept. 5	Lars Tate, Ga.	Nate Hill, Aub.
Sept. 12	Bobby Humphrey, Ala.	Derrick Thomas, Ala.
Sept. 19	Emmitt Smith, Fla.	Louis Oliver, Fla.
		Jeff Herrod, Miss.
Sept. 26	Bobby Humphrey, Ala.	Richard Tardits, Ga.
	Eric Jones, Vandy	Keith DeLong, Tenn.
Oct. 3	Rodney Hampton, Ga.	Kurt Crain, Aub.
		Chris Gaines, Vandy
		Ron Sancho, LSU
Oct. 10	Mark Higgs, Ky.	
	Jeff Burger, Aub.	
Oct. 17	Jeff Dunn, Ala.	Aundray Bruce, Aub.
	Tom Hodson, LSU	
Oct. 24	John Darnell, Miss.	Terrie Webster, Ga.
Oct. 31	Wendell Davis, LSU	Kurt Crain, Aub.
	Eric Jones, Vandy	
Nov. 7	Bobby Humphrey, Ala.	Ben Smith, Ga.
	Eric Jones, Vandy	
Nov. 14	Jeff Burger, Aub.	Keith DeLong, Tenn.
Nov. 21	Harvey Williams, LSU	Cedric Corse, MSU
Nov. 27-28	Stacy Danley, Aub.	Kurt Crain, Aub.

1988

Date	Offensive	Defensive
Sept. 3	Rodney Hampton, Ga.	Ron Sancho, LSU
Sept. 10	Boo Mitchell, Vandy	James Williams, MSU
Sept. 17	Tim Worley, Ga.	LSU Team
Sept. 24	Emmitt Smith, Fla.	Tracy Rocker, Aub.
Oct. 1	Tim Worley, Ga.	Richard Fain, Fla.
		Derrick Thomas, Ala.
Oct. 8	Boo Mitchell, Vandy	Tony Bennett, Miss.
Oct. 15	Tony Shell, MSU	Keith DeLong, Tenn.
Oct. 22	Alfred Walls, Ky.	Derrick Thomas, Ala.
	Mark Young, Miss.	
Oct. 29	Eddie Fuller, LSU	Quentin Riggins, Aub.
	David Smith, Ala.	
Nov. 5	Tim Worley, Ga.	Demetrius Douglas, Ga.
		Randy Holleran, Ky.
Nov. 12	Reggie Slack, Aub.	Brian Smith, Aub.
Nov. 19	Jeff Francis, Tenn.	Keith DeLong, Tenn.
Nov. 25-26	Mark Young, Miss.	Ron Stallworth, Aub.
Dec. 1	David Smith, Ala.	Derrick Thomas, Ala.

1989

Date	Offensive	Defensive
Sept. 2	Kenny Roberts, MSU	Tony Bennett, Miss
Sept. 9	Alexander Wright, Aub.	Chauncey Godwin, Miss.
Sept. 16	Siran Stacy, Ala.	Lamar Rogers, Aub.
	John Darnell, Miss.	
Sept. 23	Emmitt Smith, Fla.	Efrum Thomas, Fla.
Sept. 30	Reggie Cobb, Tenn.	Marion Hobby, Tenn.
Oct. 7	Gary Hollingsworth, Ala.	Huey Richardson, Fla.
Oct. 14	John Darnell, Miss.	Oliver Lawrence, LSU
	Emmitt Smith, Fla.	
Oct. 21	Emmitt Smith, Fla.	Keith McCants, Ala.
	Siran Stacy, Ala.	
Oct. 28	Rodney Hampton, Ga.	Ben Smith, Ga.
	Tom Hodson, LSU	
Nov. 4	Tom Hodson, LSU	Quentin Riggins, Aub.
Nov. 11	Ala. Offensive Line	Oliver Barnett, Ky.
Nov. 18	Chuck Webb, Tenn.	John Wiley, Aub.
Nov. 25	Tom Hodson, LSU	James Williams, MSU
	Chuck Webb, Tenn.	
Dec. 2	Alexander Wright, Aub.	Keith McCants, Ala.

1990

Date	Offensive	Defensive
Sept. 1	Tavio Henson, Tenn.	Joey Couch, Ky.
Sept. 8	Tony Thompson, Tenn.	Mike Hewitt, LSU
Sept. 15	James Joseph, Aub.	Will White, Fla.
Sept. 22	Marcus Wilson, Vandy	Chris Mitchell, Miss.
Sept. 29	Randy Baldwin, Miss.	Derriel McCorvey, LSU
	Todd Kinchen, LSU	
	Stan White, Aub.	
Oct. 6	Philip Doyle, Ala.	Walter Tate, Aub.
Oct. 13	Randy Baldwin, Miss.	Dale Carter, Tenn.
Oct. 20	Harvey Williams, LSU	George Teague, Ala.
		George Thornton, Ala.
Oct. 27	Al Baker, Ky.	Reggie Stewart, MSU
Nov. 3	Randy Baldwin, Miss.	Ephesians Bartley, Fla.
		Huey Richardson, Fla.
Nov. 10	Shane Matthews, Fla.	Tim Paulk, Fla.
Nov. 17	Shane Matthews, Fla.	Reggie Stewart, MSU
Nov. 24	Andy Kelly, Tenn.	Earnest Fields, Tenn.
	Carl Pickens, Tenn.	
Dec. 1	Tony Thompson, Tenn.	Efrum Thomas, Ala.

Honors

1991

Date	Offensive	Defensive
Aug. 31	Brian Lee, Miss.	Chad Brown, Miss.
Sept. 7	Shane Matthews, Fla.	Daniel Boyd, MSU
Sept. 14	Errict Rhett, Fla.	Darrell Crawford, Aub.
Sept. 21	Andy Kelly, Tenn.	Robert Stewart, Ala.
		Ricardo Washington, LSU
Sept. 28	Andy Kelly, Tenn.	Brad Culpepper, Fla.
	Carl Pickens, Tenn.	
Oct. 5	Eric Zeier, Ga.	Dwayne Simmons, Ga.
	Russ Shows, Miss.	
Oct. 12	Sleepy Robinson, MSU	Larry Kennedy, Fla.
Oct. 19	Corey Harris, Vandy	Antonio London, Ala.
Oct. 26	Eric Zeier, Ga.	Daniel Boyd, MSU
Nov. 2	Willie Jackson, Fla.	Tim Paulk, Fla.
Nov. 9	Shane Matthews, Fla.	Darryl Hardy, Tenn.
Nov. 16	Todd Kinchen, LSU	Don Robinson, Ky.
Nov. 23	Sleepy Robinson, MSU	Shon Walker, Tenn.
Nov. 30	Garrison Hearst, Ga.	Darren Mickell, Fla.
		Harvey Thomas, Fla.

1992

Date	Offensive	Defensive
Sept. 5	Michael Proctor, Ala.	Cassius Ware, Miss.
Sept. 12	Eric Rhett, Fla.	Orlando Watters, Ark.
Sept. 19	Garrison Hearst, Ga.	Dean Wells, Ky.
Sept. 26	Eric Zeier, Ga.	Tim Cromartie, Aub.
Oct. 3	Cory Philpot, Miss.	Daniel Boyd, MSU
Oct. 10	Todd Wright, Ark.	Kelvin Knight, MSU
Oct. 17	Garrison Hearst, Ga.	John Copeland, Ala.
Oct. 24	Jay Barker, Ala.	Greg Tremble, Ga.
Oct. 31	Shane Matthews, Fla.	Hank Campbell, USC
Nov. 7	Chris Anderson, Ala.	Carlton Miles, Fla.
Nov. 14	Garrison Hearst, Ga.	George Teague, Ala.
Nov. 21	Shane Matthews, Fla.	Jason Parker, Tenn.
Nov. 28	Garrison Hearst, Ga.	Chad Brown, Miss.

1993

Date	Offensive	Defensive
Sept. 4	James Bostic, Aub.	David Turnipseed, USC
Sept. 11	David Palmer, Ala.	Marty Moore, Ky.
Sept. 18	Stan White, Aub.	Dewayne Dotson, Miss.
Sept. 25	Heath Shuler, Tenn.	Cassius Ware, Miss.
Oct. 2	Danny Wuerffel, Fla.	Darwin Ireland, Ark.
Oct. 9	Eric Zeier, Ga.	Chris Shelling, Aub.
Oct. 16	Stan White, Aub.	Juan Long, MSU
Oct. 23	David Palmer, Ala.	Stacy Evans, USC
Oct. 30	Errict Rhett, Fla.	Brian Robinson, Aub.
Nov. 6	Terry Dean, Fla.	Ivory Hilliard, LSU
Nov. 13	James Bostic, Aub.	Lemanski Hall, Ala.
Nov. 20	Charlie Garner, Tenn.	Jason Miska, Aub.
Nov. 27	Eric Zeier, Ga.	Orlando Watters, Ark.

Heisman Trophy finalists David Palmer (Alabama) and Heath Shuler (Tennessee) both received SEC Player of the Week honors during the 1993 season.

All-Time SEC Team

The All-Time SEC Team for the first 50 years (1933-82) was selected by the SEC Skywriters.

First Team Offense

Pos.	Player, School	Yrs.
QB	Archie Manning, Ole Miss	1968-70
HB	Charlie Trippi, Georgia	1942, 1945-46
HB	Billy Cannon, LSU	1957-59
HB	Herschel Walker, Georgia	1980-82
WR	Don Hutson, Alabama	1932-34
WR	Terry Beasley, Auburn	1969-71
TE	Ozzie Newsome, Alabama	1974-77
L	John Hannah, Alabama	1970-72
L	Bruiser Kinard, Ole Miss	1935-37
C	Dwight Stephenson, Alabama	1977-79
L	Bob Suffridge, Tennessee	1938-40
L	Billy Neighbors, Alabama	1959-61
PK	Kevin Butler, Georgia	1981-84

First Team Defense

Pos.	Player, School	Yrs.
L	Doug Atkins, Tennessee	1950-52
L	Bill Stanfill, Georgia	1966-68
L	Jack Youngblood, Florida	1968-70
L	Lou Michaels, Kentucky	1955-57
L	Gaynell Tinsley, LSU	1934-36
LB	Lee Roy Jordan, Alabama	1960-62
LB	Jack Reynolds, Tennessee	1967-69
LB	D.D. Lewis, Miss. State	1965-67
DB	Tucker Frederickson, Auburn	1962-64
DB	Jake Scott, Georgia	1967-68
DB	Tommy Casanova, LSU	1969-71
DB	Don McNeal, Alabama	1977-79
DB	Jimmy Patton, Ole Miss	1953-55
P	Bobby Walden, Georgia	1958-60

COACH: Paul "Bear" Bryant, Alabama and Kentucky

Second Team Offense

Pos.	Player, School	Yrs.
QB	Kenny Stabler, Alabama	1965-67
QB	Charlie Conerly, Ole Miss	1942, 1946-47
HB	Frank Sinkwich, Georgia	1940-42
HB	Joe Cribbs, Auburn	1976-79
HB	Steve Van Buren, LSU	1941-43
WR	Wes Chandler, Florida	1974-77
WR	Barney Poole, Ole Miss	1942, 1947-48
TE	Jim Phillips, Auburn	1955-57
L	William Bryant, Kentucky	1975-77
L	Stan Hindman, Ole Miss	1963-65
C	Bob Johnson, Tennessee	1965-67
L	Zeke Smith, Auburn	1957-59
L	Roy Winston, LSU	1959-61
L	Gene Hickerson, Ole Miss	1955-57
PK	Fuad Reveiz, Tennessee	1981-84

Second Team Defense

Pos.	Player, School	Yrs.
L	Art Still, Kentucky	1975-77
L	Fred Miller, LSU	1960-62
L	Marty Lyons, Alabama	1976-78
L	Steve DeLong, Tennessee	1962-64
LB	Jackie Burkett, Auburn	1957-59
LB	Wilber Marshall, Florida	1980-82
LB	Larry Grantham, Ole Miss	1957-59
LB	Paul Naumoff, Tennessee	1964-66
LB	Mike Kolen, Auburn	1967-69
DB	Jerry Stovall, LSU	1960-62
DB	Roland James, Tennessee	1977-79
DB	Mike Washington, Alabama	1972-74
DB	Bill Stacy, Miss. State	1955-57
P	Herman Weaver, Tennessee	1967-69

COACH: Bob Neyland, Tennessee

1994 SEC Football

Southeast Area All-Time Team

1869-1919 Team

Pos.	Player, School	Final Year
E	James "Red" Roberts, Centre	1921
E	Bob Blake, Vanderbilt	1907
*T	Josh Cody, Vanderbilt	1917
T	W. F. "Bully" Van de Graff, Alabama	1915
G	N. W. "Nate" Dougherty, Tennessee	1909
G	W. E. "Frog" Metzger, Vanderbilt	1911
C	J. N. "Stein" Stone, Vanderbilt	1907
QB	Ray Morrison, Vanderbilt	1911
HB	A. R. "Buck" Flowers, Ga. Tech	1920
HB	Bob McWhorter, Georgia	1913
FB	"Indian Joe" Guyon, Ga. Tech	1918
P	J. F. "Jenks" Gillem, Sewanee	1912
PK	James "Red" Weaver, Centre	1920
PK	Ray Morrison, Vanderbilt	1911

1920-1969 Team

Pos.	Player, School	Final Year
*E	Don Hutson, Alabama	1934
E	Lyon Bomar, Vanderbilt	1923
E	Gaynell Tinsley, LSU	1936
E	Ron Sellar, Florida State	1968
*T	Frank "Bruiser" Kinard, Ole Miss	1937
T	Fred Sington, Alabama	1930
*G	Bob Suffridge, Tennessee	1940
G	Herman Hickman, Tennessee	1931
G	Bill Healey, Ga. Tech	1948
C	Lee Roy Jordan, Alabama	1962
QB	Steve Spurrier, Florida	1966
QB	Vito "Babe" Parilli, Kentucky	1951
HB	Charley Trippi, Georgia	1946
HB	Billy Cannon, LSU	1959
FB	Frank Sinkwich, Georgia	1942
P	Ralph Kercheval, Kentucky	1933
PK	Bobby Etter, Georgia	1966
PK	Lee Nalley, Vanderbilt	1949

*Also elected to All-Time All-America

Quarter-Century All-SEC Team (1950-1974)

A Bicentennial Project of the Birmingham QB Club

Offense

Pos.	Player, School	Final Year
E	Terry Beasley, Auburn	1971
E	Steve Meilinger, Kentucky	1953
T	Bob Gain, Kentucky	1950
T	John Hannah, Alabama	1972
G	Stan Hindman, Ole Miss	1965
G	Ted Daffer, Tennessee	1951
C	Bob Johnson, Tennessee	1967
QB	Archie Manning, Ole Miss	1970
RB	Billy Cannon, LSU	1959
RB	Johnny Musso, Alabama	1971
RB	John Majors, Tennessee	1956
PK	George Hunt, Tennessee	1971

Defense

Pos.	Player, School	Final Year
E	Jack Youngblood, Florida	1970
E	Jim Phillips, Auburn	1957
T	Lou Michaels, Kentucky	1957
T	Bill Stanfill, Georgia	1968
MG	Zeke Smith, Auburn	1959
LB	Lee Roy Jordan, Alabama	1962
LB	Larry Morris, Georgia Tech	1954
LB	Jackie Burkett, Auburn	1959
DB	Jake Scott, Georgia	1968
DB	Tommy Casanova, LSU	1971
DB	Tucker Frederickson, Auburn	1964
P	Bobby Walden, Georgia	1960

Player Of The Quarter Century

| DE | Doug Atkins, Tennessee | 1952 |

25-Year All-SEC Team (1961-85)

The 25-year All-SEC team was chosen for the Lakeland (Fla.) Ledger by a select group who have followed SEC football during the past 25 years. The team is as follows:

Offense

Pos.	Player, School	Final Year
WR	Cris Collinsworth, Florida	1980
WR	Wes Chandler, Florida	1976
TE	Ozzie Newsome, Alabama	1977
OL	John Hannah, Alabama	1972
OL	Bob Johnson, Tennessee	1967
OL	Warren Bryant, Kentucky	1976
OL	Billy Neighbors, Alabama	1961
OL	Dwight Stephenson, Alabama	1979
QB	Archie Manning, Ole Miss	1970
RB	Herschel Walker, Georgia	1982
RB	Bo Jackson, Auburn	1985
PK	Kevin Butler, Georgia	1984

Defense

Pos.	Player, School	Final Year
DL	Bill Stanfill, Georgia	1968
DL	Art Still, Kentucky	1977
DL	Jack Youngblood, Florida	1970
DL	E.J. Junior, Alabama	1980
DL	Steve DeLong, Tennessee	1964
LB	Lee Roy Jordan, Alabama	1962
LB	D.D. Lewis, Miss. State	1967
LB	Wilber Marshall, Florida	1983
DB	Tommy Casanova, LSU	1971
DB	Terry Hoage, Georgia	1983
DB	Jake Scott, Georgia	1968
DB	Tucker Frederickson, Auburn	1964
DB	Scott Woerner, Georgia	1980
P	Jim Arnold, Vanderbilt	1982

COACH: Paul "Bear" Bryant, Alabama

BEST TEAM: 1979 Alabama—(12-0), SEC and National Champions

1980s All-SEC Team

The 1980s All-SEC Team was selected by media representatives across the seven-state region in conjunction with the 1990 SEC Football Fans' Guide.

Offense

Pos.	Player, School	Final Year
WR	Willie Gault, Tennessee	1982
TE	Wesley Walls, Ole Miss	1988
OL	Guy McIntyre, Georgia	1983
OL	Will Wofford, Vanderbilt	1985
OL	Ben Tamburello, Auburn	1986
OL	Wes Neighbors, Alabama	1986
OL	Eric Still, Tennessee	1989
QB	Tommy Hodson, LSU	1989
RB	Herschel Walker, Georgia	1982
RB	Bo Jackson, Auburn	1985
RB	Emmitt Smith, Florida	1989
PK	Kevin Butler, Georgia	1984

Defense

Pos.	Player, School	Final Year
DL	E.J. Junior, Alabama	1980
DL	Reggie White, Tennessee	1983
DL	Tracy Rocker, Auburn	1988
DL	Freddie Joe Nunn, Ole Miss	1984
LB	Derrick Thomas, Alabama	1988
LB	Cornelius Bennett, Alabama	1986
LB	Keith McCants, Alabama	1989
DB	Terry Hoage, Georgia	1983
DB	Louis Oliver, Florida	1988
DB	Scott Woerner, Georgia	1980
DB	Ben Smith, Georgia	1989
P	Bill Smith, Ole Miss	1986

1970s All-SEC Team

The 1970s All-SEC team was selected by the SEC Skywriters in 1980.

Offense

Pos.	Player, School	Final Year
E	Ozzie Newsome, Alabama	1977
E	Wes Chandler, Florida	1976
E	Terry Beasley, Auburn	1971
L	John Hannah, Alabama	1972
L	Warren Bryant, Kentucky	1976
L	Royce Smith, Georgia	1971
L	Tyler Lafauci, LSU	1973
L	Buddy Brown, Alabama	1973
C	Dwight Stephenson, Alabama	1979
QB	Archie Manning, Ole Miss	1970
RB	Sonny Collins, Kentucky	1975
RB	Charles Alexander, LSU	1978
RB	Joe Cribbs, Auburn	1979
PK	Rex Robinson, Georgia	1980

Defense

Pos.	Player, School	Final Year
E	Leroy Cook, Alabama	1975
L	Bob Baumhower, Alabama	1976
L	Frank Warren, Auburn	1979
L	Marty Lyons, Alabama	1978
L	A.J. Duhe, LSU	1976
E	Art Still, Kentucky	1977
LB	Warren Capone, LSU	1973
LB	Woodrow Lowe, Alabama	1975
LB	Karry Krauss, Alabama	1978
DB	Mike Fuller, Auburn	1974
DB	Tommy Casanova, LSU	1971
DB	Bobby Majors, Tennessee	1971
DB	Don McNeal, Alabama	1979

COACH: Paul "Bear" Bryant, Alabama

BEST TEAM: 1979 Alabama - (12-0), SEC and National Champions

1960s All-SEC Team

The 1960s All-SEC team was selected by the SEC Skywriters in 1970.

Offense

Pos.	Player, School	Final Year
E	Dennis Homan, Alabama	1967
E	Ray Perkins, Alabama	1966
E	Charlie Casey, Florida	1965
L	Billy Neighbors, Alabama	1961
L	Stan Hindman, Ole Miss	1965
L	Edgar Chandler, Georgia	1966
L	Roy Winston, LSU	1961
C	Bob Johnson, Tennessee	1967
QB	Archie Manning, Ole Miss	1970
QB	Kenny Stabler, Alabama	1967
RB	Tommy Mason, Tulane	1960
RB	Larry Smith, Florida	1966
PK	Karl Kremser, Tennessee	1967

Defense

Pos.	Player, School	Final Year
L	Bill Stanfill, Georgia	1968
L	Fred Miller, LSU	1962
L	Jim Dunaway, Ole Miss	1962
L	Steve DeLong, Tennessee	1964
LB	D.D. Lewis, Miss. State	1967
LB	Lee Roy Jordan, Alabama	1962
LB	Paul Crane, Alabama	1965
LB	Jack Reynolds, Tennessee	1969
DB	Tucker Frederickson, Auburn	1964
DB	Jerry Stovall, LSU	1962
DB	Jake Scott, Georgia	1968
DB	Glenn Cannon, Ole Miss	1969
P	Herman Weaver, Tennessee	1969

Honors

BOWLS & POLLS

Florida running back Errict Rhett received the 1994 Miller-Digby Award, given to the USF+G Insurance Sugar Bowl MVP, after rushing for 105 yards and three touchdowns in the Gators' 41-7 win over West Virginia.

1994-95 Bowl Directory

LAS VEGAS BOWL III
December 15 — Las Vegas, Nevada
6:00 p.m. (PST) — ESPN

Executive Director: Rick Rogers
PR Director: Suzy Abrams
Address: 2225-E Renaissance Dr.
Las Vegas, NV 89119
Phone: (702) 795-4616
Stadium: Sam Boyd Silver Bowl
(32,000)

Matchup: Big West (1) vs.
MAC (1)
Last Year: Utah State 42,
Ball State 33
SEC Appearances: 0
Last SEC Appearance: NA

JOHN HANCOCK BOWL
December 30 — El Paso, Texas
12:30 p.m. (MST) — CBS

Executive Director: Tom Starr
Address: 4100 Rio Bravo
Suite 303
El Paso, TX 79902
Phone: (915) 533-4416
Stadium: Sun Bowl Stadium (51,270)

Matchup: Coalition Team vs.
Coalition Team
Last Year: Oklahoma 41,
Texas Tech 10
SEC Appearances: 15
Last SEC Appearance: Dec. 24, 1988
Alabama 29, Army 28

JEEP EAGLE ALOHA BOWL
December 25 — Honolulu, Hawaii
3:30 p.m. (EST) — ABC

Executive Director: Marcia Cherner-Klompus
PR Director: Leonard Klompus
Address: 1110 University Avenue
Suite 403
Honolulu, HA 96826
Phone: (808) 947-4141
Stadium: Aloha Stadium (50,000)

Matchup: Big Eight (3) vs.
At Large Team
Last Year: Colorado 41,
Fresno State 30
SEC Appearances: 2
Last SEC Appearance: Dec. 25, 1987
UCLA 20, Florida 16

THRIFTY CAR RENTAL HOLIDAY BOWL
December 30 — San Diego, California
5:00 p.m. (PST) — ESPN

Executive Director: John Reid
PR Director: Bruce Binkowski
Address: 9449 Friars Road, Gate P
San Diego, CA 92108
Phone: (619) 283-5808
Stadium: Jack Murphy Stadium
(61,000)

Matchup: WAC Champ vs.
Big Ten (3)
Last Year: Ohio State 28, BYU 21
SEC Appearances: 0
Last SEC Appearance: NA

POULAN WEED EATER INDEPENDENCE BOWL
December 27 — Shreveport, Louisiana
7:00 p.m. (CST) — ESPN

Executive Director: Glen Krupica
Address: P.O. Box 1723
Shreveport, LA 71166-1723
Phone: (318) 221-0712
Stadium: Independence Stadium
(50,459)

Matchup: At Large Team vs.
At Large Team
Last Year: Virginia Tech 45,
Indiana 20
SEC Appearances: 3
Last SEC Appearance: Dec. 29, 1991
Georgia 24, Arkansas 15

BUILDERS SQUARE ALAMO BOWL
December 31 — San Antonio, Texas
7:00 p.m. (CST) — ESPN

Executive Director: Derrick Fox
PR Director: Bob Gennarelli
Address: The Alamodome
100 Montana
3rd Floor
San Antonio, TX 78203
Phone: (210) 226-2695
Stadium: The Alamodome (65,000)

Matchup: SWC (3) vs.
Pac-10 (4)
Last Year: California 37, Iowa 3
SEC Appearances: 0
Last SEC Appearance: NA

WEISER LOCK COPPER BOWL
December 29 — Tucson, Arizona
6:00 p.m. (MST) — ESPN

Executive Director: Larry Brown
Address: 440 S. Williams Boulevard
Suite 100
Tucson, AZ 85711
Phone: (602) 790-5510
Stadium: Arizona Stadium (57,000)

Matchup: Big Eight (4) vs.
At Large Team
Last Year: Kansas State 52,
Wyoming 17
SEC Appearances: 0
Last SEC Appearance: NA

ST. JUDE LIBERTY BOWL
December 31 — Memphis, Tennessee
7:00 p.m. (CST) — ESPN

Managing Partner: Steve Ehrhart
PR Director: Mike McCormick
Address: 3767 New Getwell
Memphis, TN 38118-6013
Phone: (901) 795-7700
Stadium: Liberty Bowl (62,132)

Matchup: At Large Team vs.
At Large Team
Last Year: Louisville 18,
Michigan State 7
SEC Appearances: 19
Last SEC Appearance: Dec. 31, 1992
Ole Miss 13, Air Force 0

FREEDOM BOWL
December 29 — Anaheim, California
6:00 p.m. (PST) — Raycom

Executive Director: Don Andersen
PR Director: Charlotte Governale
Address: 2000 S. State College Blvd.
Anaheim, CA 92806
Phone: (714) 254-3050
Stadium: Anaheim Stadium (69,000)

Matchup: PAC 10 (3) vs.
WAC (2)
Last Year: Southern Cal 28,
Utah 21
SEC Appearances: 1
Last SEC Appearance: Dec. 30, 1989
Washington 34, Florida 7

PEACH BOWL
January 1 — Atlanta, Georgia
8:00 p.m. (EST) — ESPN

Executive Director: Robert Dale Morgan
PR Director: Ross Bartow
Address: P.O. Box 1336
Atlanta, GA 30301
Phone: (404) 586-8500
Stadium: Georgia Dome (71,000)

Matchup: SEC (4) vs. ACC (3)
Last Year: Clemson 14, Kentucky 13
SEC Appearances: 12
Last SEC Appearance: Dec. 31, 1993
Clemson 14, Kentucky 13

Bowls & Polls

OUTBACK STEAKHOUSE GATOR BOWL
January 1 — Gainesville, Florida
7:30 p.m. (EST) — TBS

Executive Director: Rick Catlett
PR Director: Cheri Smallenberger
Address: 4080 Woodcock Drive
Suite 130
Jacksonville, FL 32207
Phone: (904) 396-1800
Stadium: Ben Hill Griffin Stadium
(83,000)

Matchup: SEC (3) vs.
Coalition Team
Last Year: Alabama 24,
North Carolina 10
SEC Appearances: 31
Last SEC Appearance: Dec. 31, 1993
Alabama 24,
North Carolina 10

HALL OF FAME BOWL
January 2 — Tampa, Florida
11:00 a.m. (EST) — ESPN

Executive Director: James P. McVay
PR Director: Mike Schulze
Address: 4511 N. Himes Avenue
Suite 260
Tampa, FL 33614
Phone: (813) 874-2695
Stadium: Tampa Stadium (74,296)

Matchup: ACC (4) vs.
Big Ten (4)
Last Year: Michigan 42,
N.C. State 7
SEC Appearances: 5
Last SEC Appearance: Jan. 1, 1993
Tennessee 38,
Boston College 23

MOBIL COTTON BOWL CLASSIC
January 2 — Dallas, Texas
Noon (CST) - NBC

General Manager: Rick Baker
PR Director: Charlie Fiss
Address: P.O. Box 569420
Dallas, TX 75356-9420
Phone: (214) 634-7525
Stadium: Cotton Bowl (71,456)

Matchup: SWC Champ vs.
Coalition Team
Last Year: Notre Dame 24,
Texas A&M 21
SEC Appearances: 22
Last SEC Appearance: Jan. 1, 1990
Tennessee 31, Arkansas 27

CompUSA FLORIDA CITRUS BOWL
January 2 — Orlando, Florida
1:00 p.m. (EST) — ABC

Executive Director: Charles H. Rohe
PR Director: Dylan Thomas
Address: 1 Citrus Bowl Place
Orlando, FL 32805
Phone: (407) 423-2476
Stadium: Florida Citrus Bowl (70,000)

Matchup: SEC (2) vs.
Big Ten (2)
Last Year: Penn State 31,
Tennessee 13
SEC Appearances: 10
Last SEC Appearance: Jan. 1, 1994
Penn State 31,
Tennessee 13

CARQUEST BOWL
January 2 — Miami, Florida
1:30 p.m. (EST) - CBS

Executive Director: Brian Flajole
PR Director: Mike Ballweg
Address: 915 Middle River Drive
Suite 120
Ft. Lauderdale, FL 33302
Phone: (305) 564-5000
Stadium: Joe Robbie Stadium (73,000)

Matchup: SEC (5) vs.
Big East (3)
Last Year: Boston College 31,
Virginia 13
SEC Appearances: 1
Last SEC Appearance: Dec. 28, 1991
Alabama 30, Colorado 25

IBM OS/2 FIESTA BOWL
January 2 — Tempe, Arizona
2:30 p.m. (MST) — NBC

Executive Director: John Junker
PR Director: Shawn Schoeffler
Address: 20 S. Ash Avenue
Tempe, AZ 85281
Phone: (602) 350-0900
Stadium: Sun Devil Stadium (74,865)

Matchup: Coalition Team vs.
Coalition Team
Last Year: Arizona 29,
Miami 0
SEC Appearances: 2
Last SEC Appearance: Jan. 1, 1992
Penn State 42, Tennessee 17

ROSE BOWL
January 2 — Pasadena, California
2:00 p.m. (PST) — ABC

Executive Director: John H.B. French
PR Director: Bill Flinn
Address: 391 S. Orange Grove Blvd.
Pasadena, CA 91184
Phone: (818) 449-4100
Stadium: Rose Bowl (103,956)

Matchup: Big Ten Champ vs.
Pac-10 Champ
Last Year: Wisconsin 21, UCLA 16
SEC Appearances: 9
Last SEC Appearance: Jan. 1, 1946
Alabama 34, Southern Cal 14

FEDERAL EXPRESS ORANGE BOWL
January 1 — Miami, Florida
8:00 p.m. (EST) — NBC

Executive Director: Keith Tribble
PR Director: Lisa Franson
Address: 601 Brickell Key Drive
Suite 206
Miami, FL 33131
Phone: (305) 371-4600
Stadium: Orange Bowl (75,000)

Matchup: Big Eight Champ vs.
Coalition Team
Last Year: FSU 18, Nebraska 16
SEC Appearances: 29
Last SEC Appearance: Jan. 1, 1983
Nebraska 21, LSU 20

USF+G INSURANCE SUGAR BOWL
January 2 — New Orleans, Louisiana
7:30 p.m. (CST) — ABC

Executive Director: Troy Mathieu
PR Director: Jeff Hundley
Address: 1500 Sugar Bowl Drive
New Orleans, LA 70112
Phone: (504) 525-8573
Stadium: Louisiana Superdome (73,520)

Matchup: SEC Champ vs.
Coalition Team
Last Year: Florida 41,
West Virginia 7
SEC Appearances: 58
Last SEC Appearance: Jan. 1, 1994
Florida 41,
West Virginia 7

BOWL COALITION INFORMATION

Sugar, Cotton and Orange bowls will select, in order of the rank of their host teams, from a pool of five teams: Notre Dame, ACC Champion, Big East Champion, and two at-large teams (ACC, Big East, Big Eight, Pac-10 and SWC). Fiesta Bowl will choose from the remaining pool of teams. The Gator (one team) and Hancock (two teams) bowls will select the three remaining teams.

1994 SEC Football

SEC Composite Bowl Record

School	W-L-T	Pct.	Last Appearance
Alabama	26-17-3	.598	1993 Gator Bowl
Arkansas	9-15-3	.389	1991 Independence Bowl
Auburn	12-9-2	.565	1990 Peach Bowl
Florida	10-11-0	.476	1994 Sugar Bowl
Georgia	15-13-3	.532	1993 Florida Citrus Bowl
Kentucky	5-3-0	.625	1993 Peach Bowl
LSU	11-16-1	.411	1989 Hall of Fame Bowl
Ole Miss	14-11-0	.560	1992 Liberty Bowl
Mississippi State	4-4-0	.500	1993 Peach Bowl
South Carolina	0-8-0	.000	1988 Liberty Bowl
Tennessee	18-16-0	.529	1994 Florida Citrus Bowl
Vanderbilt	1-1-1	.500	1982 Hall of Fame Bowl
Totals			
Current Members	116-101-10	.513	
Former Members	11-6-0	.647	
OVERALL	127-107-10	.541	
Vs. Non-Conference	119-99-10	.544	

Note: Totals do not include Arkansas and South Carolina appearances prior to joining the SEC.

All-Time Bowl Appearances

School	Appearances
1. **Alabama**	46
2. Southern Cal	36
3. Texas	34
Tennessee	**34**
5. Nebraska	32
6. **Georgia**	**31**
Oklahoma	31
8. Penn State	30
9. **LSU**	**29**
10. **Arkansas**	**27**
11. Ohio State	26
12. Georgia Tech	25
Michigan	25
Ole Miss	**25**
15. **Auburn**	**23**
16. Florida State	22
17. **Florida**	**21**
Texas A&M	21
Washington	21
20. Miami (Florida)	20
21. Clemson	19
Missouri	19
Notre Dame	19
Texas Tech	19
UCLA	19

All-Time Bowl Victories

School	Victories
1. **Alabama**	26
2. Southern Cal	23
3. Oklahoma	20
4. **Tennessee**	**18**
Penn State	18
6. Georgia Tech	17
7. Texas	16
8. **Georgia**	**15**
9. **Ole Miss**	**14**
Nebraska	14
11. Florida State	13
Notre Dame	13
13. **Auburn**	**12**
Clemson	12
Michigan	12
Ohio State	12
Washington	12
18. **LSU**	**11**
Texas A&M	11
20. **Florida**	**10**
Miami (Florida)	10
UCLA	10
23. Arizona State	9
Arkansas	**9**
Oklahoma State	9

SEC Bowl Notes

• At least half of the SEC's membership participated in a bowl game in 11 of the last 13 seasons. Overall, the SEC has posted a nation-high 244 bowl invitations, 83 more than the second place Southwest Conference. Only four times since 1980 has a conference produced more bowl teams in a given year that the SEC.

• Alabama and Georgia, as well as former SEC member Georgia Tech, are three of only four schools to win all four major bowl games (Rose, Sugar, Orange and Cotton). Notre Dame is the only other school to complete the grand slam. Alabama, which holds the national record for most bowl appearances (46), most victories (26) and consecutive appearances (26) is the only school to win each of the majors at least twice.

• The SEC has had seven bowl teams in a season on three occasions. Most recently, the conference was represented by seven teams following both the 1982 and 1983 seasons, in addition to the 1974 campaign.

1983	1982	1974
Alabama-Sun	Alabama-Liberty	Alabama-Orange
Auburn-Sugar	Auburn-Tangerine	Auburn-Gator
Florida-Gator	Florida-Bluebonnet	Florida-Sugar
Georgia-Cotton	Georgia-Sugar	Georgia-Tangerine
Kentucky-Hall of Fame	LSU-Orange	Miss. State-Sun
Ole Miss-Independence	Tennessee-Peach	Tennessee-Liberty
Tennessee-Citrus	Vanderbilt-Hall of Fame	Vanderbilt-Peach

• On eight different occasions, current members of the SEC have competed against one another in bowl games. Ole Miss leads the pack with five bowls against conference foes and Auburn is next with three. Florida, LSU and Tennessee have each squared off against SEC teams twice, while Alabama and Vanderbilt have once. A complete list of SEC vs. SEC bowl games follows:

1955 Gator Bowl- Vanderbilt 25, Auburn 13
1958 Gator Bowl- Ole Miss 7, Florida 3
1960 Sugar Bowl- Ole Miss 21, LSU 0
1964 Sugar Bowl- Alabama 12, Ole Miss 7
1965 Liberty Bowl - Ole Miss 13, Auburn 7
1969 Gator Bowl- Ole Miss 14, Tennessee 13
1971 Gator Bowl- Auburn 35, Ole Miss 28
1972 Bluebonnet Bowl - Tennessee 24, LSU 17

• During the decade of the 1980s the SEC was the only conference to have every member participate in a bowl game. In addition, nine of the league's 10 schools played in at least two postseason events. Overall the SEC led all conferences during the decade with 56 bowl appearances. The Big Ten was second with 45 as the Southwest and Pac Ten tied for third with 35. The Big Eight (31), Atlantic Coast (25) and Western Athletic (21) rounded out the list.

• During the decade of the 1980s the SEC also posted more bowl victories than any other conference. Member institutions won 29 bowl games, while the Pac Ten and Big Ten followed with 22 and 21 respectively. Other victory totals during the decade were as follows: Atlantic Coast (15), Big Eight (13), Southwest (13) and Western Athletic (nine).

SEC BOWL REVENUE DISTRIBUTION

(A) For bowl games providing receipts which result in a balance of less than $2,000,000 (two million), the participating institution shall retain the first $500,000 plus 20 percent of the balance. The remainder shall be remitted to the Commissioner and will be divided into 13 equal shares with two shares to the Conference and one share to each of the other 11 institutions. (Participating institution does not share in the distribution of shares.)

(B) For bowl games providing receipts which result in a balance of more than $2,000,000 (two million), the participating institution shall retain the first $700,000 plus 20 percent of the balance. The remainder shall be remitted to the Commissioner and will be divided into 13 equal shares with two shares to the Conference and one share to each of the other 11 institutions. (Participating institution does not share in the distribution of shares.)

Bowls & Polls

Bowl Games of SEC Members
(Listed by Schools)

ALABAMA
(Won 26, lost 17, tied 3)

1-1-26	Rose Bowl	20	Washington	19
1-1-27	Rose Bowl	7	Stanford	7
1-1-31	Rose Bowl	24	Washington State	0
1-1-35	Rose Bowl	29	Stanford	13
1-1-38	Rose Bowl	0	California	13
1-1-42	Cotton Bowl	29	Texas A&M	21
1-1-43	Orange Bowl	37	Boston College	21
1-1-45	Sugar Bowl	26	Duke	29
1-1-46	Rose Bowl	34	Southern Cal	14
1-1-48	Sugar Bowl	7	Texas	27
1-1-53	Orange Bowl	61	Syracuse	6
1-1-54	Cotton Bowl	6	Rice	28
12-9-59	Liberty Bowl	0	Penn State	7
12-17-60	Bluebonnet Bowl	3	Texas	3
1-1-62	Sugar Bowl	10	Arkansas	3
1-1-63	Orange Bowl	17	Oklahoma	0
1-1-64	Sugar Bowl	12	Ole Miss	7
1-1-65	Orange Bowl	17	Texas	21
1-1-66	Orange Bowl	39	Nebraska	28
1-2-67	Sugar Bowl	34	Nebraska	7
1-1-68	Cotton Bowl	16	Texas A&M	20
12-28-68	Gator Bowl	10	Missouri	35
12-13-69	Liberty Bowl	33	Colorado	47
12-31-70	Bluebonnet Bowl	24	Oklahoma	24
1-1-72	Orange Bowl	6	Nebraska	38
1-1-73	Cotton Bowl	13	Texas	17
1-1-74	Sugar Bowl	23	Notre Dame	24
1-1-75	Orange Bowl	11	Notre Dame	13
12-31-75	Sugar Bowl	13	Penn State	6
12-20-76	Liberty Bowl	36	UCLA	6
1-2-78	Sugar Bowl	35	Ohio State	6
1-1-79	Sugar Bowl	14	Penn State	7
1-1-80	Sugar Bowl	24	Arkansas	9
1-1-81	Cotton Bowl	30	Baylor	2
1-1-82	Cotton Bowl	12	Texas	14
12-29-82	Liberty Bowl	21	Illinois	15
12-24-83	Sun Bowl	28	SMU	7
12-28-85	Aloha Bowl	24	Southern Cal	3
12-25-86	Sun Bowl	28	Washington	6
1-2-88	Hall of Fame Bowl	24	Michigan	28
12-29-88	Sun Bowl	29	Army	28
1-1-90	Sugar Bowl	25	Miami	33
1-1-91	Fiesta Bowl	7	Louisville	34
12-28-91	Blockbuster Bowl	30	Colorado	25
1-1-93	Sugar Bowl	34	Miami	13
12-31-93	Gator Bowl	24	North Carolina	10

ARKANSAS
(Won 9, lost 15, tied 3)

1-1-34	Dixie Bowl	7	Centenary	7
1-1-47	Cotton Bowl	0	LSU	0
1-1-48	Dixie Bowl	21	William & Mary	19
1-1-55	Cotton Bowl	6	Georgia Tech	14
1-2-60	Gator Bowl	14	Georgia Tech	7
1-1-61	Cotton Bowl	6	Duke	7
1-1-62	Sugar Bowl	3	Alabama	10
1-1-63	Sugar Bowl	13	Ole Miss	17
1-1-65	Cotton Bowl	10	Nebraska	7
1-1-66	Cotton Bowl	7	LSU	14
1-1-69	Sugar Bowl	16	Georgia	2
1-1-70	Sugar Bowl	22	Ole Miss	27
12-20-71	Liberty Bowl	13	Tennessee	14
1-1-76	Cotton Bowl	31	Georgia	10

1-2-78	Orange Bowl	31	Oklahoma	6
12-25-78	Fiesta Bowl	10	UCLA	10
1-1-80	Sugar Bowl	9	Alabama	24
12-27-80	Hall of Fame Bowl	34	Tulane	15
12-28-81	Gator Bowl	27	North Carolina	31
12-31-82	Bluebonnet Bowl	28	Florida	24
12-27-84	Liberty Bowl	15	Auburn	21
12-22-85	Holiday Bowl	18	Arizona State	17
1-1-87	Orange Bowl	8	Oklahoma	42
12-29-87	Liberty Bowl	17	Georgia	20
1-2-89	Cotton Bowl	3	UCLA	17
1-1-90	Cotton Bowl	27	Tennessee	31
12-29-91	Independence Bowl	15	Georgia	24

AUBURN
(Won 12, lost 9, tied 2)

1-1-37	Rhumba Bowl	7	Villanova	7
1-1-38	Orange Bowl	6	Michigan State	0
1-1-54	Gator Bowl	13	Texas Tech	35
12-31-54	Gator Bowl	33	Baylor	13
12-31-55	Gator Bowl	13	Vanderbilt	25
1-1-64	Orange Bowl	7	Nebraska	13
12-18-65	Liberty Bowl	7	Ole Miss	13
12-28-68	Sun Bowl	34	Arizona	10
12-31-69	Bluebonnet Bowl	7	Houston	36
1-2-71	Gator Bowl	35	Ole Miss	28
1-1-72	Sugar Bowl	22	Oklahoma	40
12-30-72	Gator Bowl	24	Colorado	3
12-29-73	Sun Bowl	17	Missouri	34
12-30-74	Gator Bowl	27	Texas	3
12-18-82	Tangerine Bowl	33	Boston College	26
1-2-84	Sugar Bowl	9	Michigan	7
12-27-84	Liberty Bowl	21	Arkansas	15
1-1-86	Cotton Bowl	16	Texas A&M	36
1-1-87	Citrus Bowl	16	Southern Cal	7
1-1-88	Sugar Bowl	16	Syracuse	16
1-2-89	Sugar Bowl	7	Florida State	13
1-1-90	Hall of Fame Bowl	31	Ohio State	14
12-29-90	Peach Bowl	27	Indiana	23

FLORIDA
(Won 10, lost 11)

1-1-53	Gator Bowl	14	Tulsa	13
12-27-58	Gator Bowl	3	Ole Miss	7
12-31-60	Gator Bowl	13	Baylor	12
12-28-62	Gator Bowl	17	Penn State	7
1-1-66	Sugar Bowl	18	Missouri	20
1-2-67	Orange Bowl	27	Georgia Tech	12
12-27-69	Gator Bowl	14	Tennessee	13
12-22-73	Tangerine Bowl	7	Miami (Ohio)	16
12-31-74	Sugar Bowl	10	Nebraska	13
12-29-75	Gator Bowl	0	Maryland	13
1-2-77	Sun Bowl	14	Texas A&M	37
12-20-80	Tangerine Bowl	35	Maryland	20
12-31-81	Peach Bowl	6	West Virginia	26
12-31-82	Bluebonnet Bowl	24	Arkansas	28
12-30-83	Gator Bowl	14	Iowa	6
12-25-87	Aloha Bowl	16	UCLA	20
12-29-88	All-American Bowl	14	Illinois	10
12-30-89	Freedom Bowl	7	Washington	34
1-1-92	Sugar Bowl	28	Notre Dame	39
12-31-92	Gator Bowl	27	N.C. State	10
1-1-94	Sugar Bowl	41	West Virginia	7

1994 SEC Football

Bowl Games of SEC Members
(Listed by Schools)

GEORGIA
(Won 15, lost 13, tied 3)

1-1-42	Orange Bowl	40	TCU	26
1-1-43	Rose Bowl	9	UCLA	0
1-1-46	Oil Bowl	20	Tulsa	6
1-1-47	Sugar Bowl	20	North Carolina	10
1-1-48	Gator Bowl	20	Maryland	20
1-1-49	Orange Bowl	28	Texas	41
12-9-50	Presidential Bowl	20	Texas A&M	40
1-1-60	Orange Bowl	14	Missouri	0
12-26-64	Sun Bowl	7	Texas Tech	0
12-31-66	Cotton Bowl	24	SMU	9
12-16-67	Liberty Bowl	7	N.C. State	14
1-1-69	Sugar Bowl	2	Arkansas	16
12-20-69	Sun Bowl	6	Nebraska	45
12-31-71	Gator Bowl	7	North Carolina	3
12-28-73	Peach Bowl	17	Maryland	16
12-20-74	Tangerine Bowl	10	Miami (Ohio)	21
1-1-76	Cotton Bowl	10	Arkansas	31
1-1-77	Sugar Bowl	3	Pittsburgh	27
12-31-78	Bluebonnet Bowl	22	Stanford	25
1-1-81	Sugar Bowl	17	Notre Dame	10
1-1-82	Sugar Bowl	20	Pittsburgh	24
1-1-83	Sugar Bowl	23	Penn State	27
1-2-84	Cotton Bowl	10	Texas	9
12-22-84	Citrus Bowl	17	Florida State	17
12-28-85	Sun Bowl	13	Arizona	13
12-23-86	Hall of Fame Bowl	24	Boston College	27
12-29-87	Liberty Bowl	20	Arkansas	17
1-1-89	Gator Bowl	34	Michigan State	27
12-30-89	Peach Bowl	18	Syracuse	19
12-29-91	Independence Bowl	24	Arkansas	15
1-1-93	Citrus Bowl	21	Ohio State	14

KENTUCKY
(Won 5, lost 3)

12-6-47	Great Lakes Bowl	24	Villanova	14
1-2-50	Orange Bowl	13	Santa Clara	21
1-1-51	Sugar Bowl	13	Oklahoma	7
1-1-52	Cotton Bowl	20	TCU	7
12-31-76	Peach Bowl	21	North Carolina	0
12-22-83	Hall of Fame Bowl	16	West Virginia	20
12-29-84	Hall of Fame Bowl	20	Wisconsin	19
12-31-93	Peach Bowl	13	Clemson	14

LSU
(Won 11, lost 16, tied 1)

1-1-36	Sugar Bowl	2	TCU	3
1-1-37	Sugar Bowl	14	Santa Clara	21
1-1-38	Sugar Bowl	0	Santa Clara	6
1-1-44	Orange Bowl	19	Texas A&M	14
1-1-47	Cotton Bowl	0	Arkansas	0
1-2-50	Sugar Bowl	0	Oklahoma	35
1-1-59	Sugar Bowl	7	Clemson	0
1-1-60	Sugar Bowl	0	Ole Miss	21
1-1-62	Orange Bowl	25	Colorado	7
1-1-63	Cotton Bowl	13	Texas	0
12-21-63	Bluebonnet Bowl	7	Baylor	14
1-1-65	Sugar Bowl	13	Syracuse	10
1-1-66	Cotton Bowl	14	Arkansas	7
1-1-68	Sugar Bowl	20	Wyoming	13
12-30-68	Peach Bowl	31	Florida State	27
1-1-71	Orange Bowl	12	Nebraska	17
12-18-71	Sun Bowl	33	Iowa State	15
12-30-72	Bluebonnet Bowl	17	Tennessee	24
1-1-74	Orange Bowl	9	Penn State	16
12-31-77	Sun Bowl	14	Stanford	24
12-23-78	Liberty Bowl	15	Missouri	20
12-22-79	Tangerine Bowl	34	Wake Forest	10
1-1-83	Orange Bowl	20	Nebraska	21
1-1-85	Sugar Bowl	10	Nebraska	28
12-27-85	Liberty Bowl	7	Baylor	21
1-1-87	Sugar Bowl	15	Nebraska	30
12-31-87	Gator Bowl	30	South Carolina	13
1-2-89	Hall of Fame Bowl	10	Syracuse	23

OLE MISS
(Won 14, lost 11)

1-1-36	Orange Bowl	19	Catholic U.	20
1-1-49	Delta Bowl	13	TCU	9
1-1-53	Sugar Bowl	7	Georgia Tech	24
1-1-55	Sugar Bowl	0	Navy	21
1-2-56	Cotton Bowl	14	TCU	13
1-1-58	Sugar Bowl	39	Texas	7
12-27-58	Gator Bowl	7	Florida	3
1-1-60	Sugar Bowl	21	LSU	0
1-2-61	Sugar Bowl	14	Rice	6
1-1-62	Cotton Bowl	7	Texas	12
1-1-63	Sugar Bowl	17	Arkansas	13
1-1-64	Sugar Bowl	7	Alabama	12
12-19-64	Bluebonnet Bowl	7	Tulsa	14
12-18-65	Liberty Bowl	13	Auburn	7
12-17-66	Bluebonnet Bowl	0	Texas	19
12-30-67	Sun Bowl	7	UTEP	14
12-14-68	Liberty Bowl	34	Virginia Tech	17
1-1-70	Sugar Bowl	27	Arkansas	22
1-2-71	Gator Bowl	28	Auburn	35
12-30-71	Peach Bowl	41	Georgia Tech	18
12-10-83	Independence Bowl	3	Air Force	9
12-20-86	Independence Bowl	20	Texas Tech	17
12-28-89	Liberty Bowl	42	Air Force	29
1-1-91	Gator Bowl	3	Michigan	35
12-31-92	Liberty Bowl	13	Air Force	0

MISSISSIPPI STATE
(Won 4, lost 4)

1-1-37	Orange Bowl	12	Duquesne	13
1-1-41	Orange Bowl	14	Georgetown	7
12-21-63	Liberty Bowl	16	N.C. State	12
12-28-74	Sun Bowl	26	North Carolina	24
12-27-80	Sun Bowl	17	Nebraska	31
12-31-81	Hall of Fame Bowl	10	Kansas	0
12-29-91	Liberty Bowl	15	Air Force	38
1-2-93	Peach Bowl	17	North Carolina	21

SOUTH CAROLINA
(Lost 8)

1-1-46	Gator Bowl	14	Wake Forest	26
12-30-69	Peach Bowl	3	West Virginia	14
12-20-75	Tangerine Bowl	7	Miami (Ohio)	20
12-29-79	Hall of Fame Bowl	14	Missouri	24
12-29-80	Gator Bowl	9	Pittsburgh	37
12-28-84	Gator Bowl	14	Oklahoma State	21
12-31-87	Gator Bowl	13	LSU	30
12-28-88	Liberty Bowl	10	Indiana	34

298 Bowls & Polls

TENNESSEE
(Won 18, lost 16)

Date	Bowl	Score	Opponent	Score
12-5-31	New York Bowl*	13	NYU	0
1-1-39	Orange Bowl	17	Oklahoma	0
1-1-40	Rose Bowl	0	Southern Cal	14
1-1-41	Sugar Bowl	13	Boston College	19
1-1-43	Sugar Bowl	14	Tulsa	7
1-1-45	Rose Bowl	0	Southern Cal	25
1-1-47	Orange Bowl	0	Rice	8
1-1-51	Cotton Bowl	20	Texas	14
1-1-52	Sugar Bowl	13	Maryland	28
1-1-53	Cotton Bowl	0	Texas	16
1-1-57	Sugar Bowl	7	Baylor	13
12-28-57	Gator Bowl	3	Texas A&M	0
12-18-65	Bluebonnet Bowl	27	Tulsa	6
12-31-66	Gator Bowl	18	Syracuse	12
1-1-68	Orange Bowl	24	Oklahoma	26
1-1-69	Cotton Bowl	13	Texas	36
12-27-69	Gator Bowl	13	Florida	14
1-1-71	Sugar Bowl	34	Air Force	13
12-20-71	Liberty Bowl	14	Arkansas	13
12-30-72	Bluebonnet Bowl	24	LSU	17
12-29-73	Gator Bowl	19	Texas Tech	28
12-16-74	Liberty Bowl	7	Maryland	3
12-31-79	Bluebonnet Bowl	22	Purdue	27
12-13-81	Garden State Bowl	28	Wisconsin	21
12-31-82	Peach Bowl	22	Iowa	28
12-17-83	Citrus Bowl	30	Maryland	23
12-22-84	Sun Bowl	27	Maryland	28
1-1-86	Sugar Bowl	35	Miami	7
12-29-86	Liberty Bowl	21	Minnesota	14
1-2-88	Peach Bowl	27	Indiana	22
1-1-90	Cotton Bowl	31	Arkansas	27
1-1-91	Sugar Bowl	23	Virginia	22
1-1-92	Fiesta Bowl	17	Penn State	42
1-1-93	Hall of Fame Bowl	38	Boston College	23
1-1-94	Citrus Bowl	13	Penn State	31

VANDERBILT
(Won 1, lost 1, tied 1)

Date	Bowl	Score	Opponent	Score
12-31-55	Gator Bowl	25	Auburn	13
12-28-74	Peach Bowl	6	Texas Tech	6
12-31-82	Hall of Fame Bowl	28	Air Force	36

* not recognized by NCAA

Bowl Games of Former SEC Members
(Listed by Schools)

GEORGIA TECH
(Won 10, lost 5)

Date	Bowl	Score	Opponent	Score
1-1-40	Orange Bowl	21	Missouri	7
1-1-43	Cotton Bowl	7	Texas	14
1-1-44	Sugar Bowl	20	Tulsa	18
1-1-45	Orange Bowl	12	Tulsa	26
1-1-47	Oil Bowl	41	St. Mary's	19
1-1-48	Orange Bowl	20	Kansas	14
1-1-52	Orange Bowl	17	Baylor	14
1-1-53	Sugar Bowl	24	Ole Miss	7
1-1-54	Sugar Bowl	42	West Virginia	19
1-1-55	Cotton Bowl	14	Arkansas	6
1-2-56	Sugar Bowl	7	Pittsburgh	0
12-29-56	Gator Bowl	21	Pittsburgh	14
1-2-60	Gator Bowl	7	Arkansas	14
12-30-61	Gator Bowl	15	Penn State	30
12-22-62	Bluebonnet Bowl	10	Missouri	14

TULANE
(Won 1, lost 1)

Date	Bowl	Score	Opponent	Score
1-1-35	Sugar Bowl	20	Temple	14
1-1-40	Sugar Bowl	13	Texas A&M	14

Conference Bowl Appearances
(Using Actual Conference Alignments)

Conference	Appearances	W-L-T	Pct.
Southeastern	244	127-107-10	.541
Southwest	161	67-85-9	.444
Pacific-10	147	78-63-6	.551
Big Eight	123	60-62-1	.492
Big Ten	113	52-60-1	.465
Atlantic Coast	78	38-38-2	.500
Western Athletic	52	21-30-1	.413
Mid-American	40	20-19-1	.513
Big West	16	9-6-1	.594
Big East	9	5-4-0	.556

Ole Miss coach John Vaught closed his 25-year career by leading the Rebels to 14-straight bowl games en route to establishing a then national record of 15 consecutive postseason appearances.

1994 SEC Football

Results of Major Bowl Games

ROSE BOWL
Pasadena*

1- 1-02—Michigan 49, Stanford 0
1- 1-16—Washington State 14, Brown 0
1- 1-17—Oregon 14, Pennsylvania 0
1- 1-18—Mare Island 19, Camp Lewis 7
1- 1-19—Great Lakes 17, Mare Island 0
1- 1-20—Harvard 7, Oregon 6
1- 1-21—Carolina 28, Ohio State 0
1- 2-22—Wash. & Jeff. 0, California 0
1- 1-23—Southern Cal 14, Penn State 3
1- 1-24—Navy 14, Washington 14
1- 1-25—Notre Dame 27, Stanford 10
1- 1-26—**Alabama 20, Washington 19**
1- 1-27—**Alabama 7, Stanford 7**
1- 2-28—Stanford 7, Pittsburgh 6
1- 1-29—Georgia Tech 8, California 7
1- 1-30—Southern Cal 47, Pittsburgh 14
1- 1-31—**Alabama 24, Washington State 0**
1- 1-32—Southern Cal 21, Tulane 12
1- 2-33—Southern Cal 35, Pittsburgh 0
1- 1-34—Columbia 7, Stanford 0
1- 1-35—**Alabama 29, Stanford 13**
1- 1-36—Stanford 7, SMU 0
1- 1-37—Pittsburgh 21, Washington 0
1- 1-38—**California 13, Alabama 0**
1- 2-39—Southern Cal 7, Duke 3

Georgia sophomore halfback Charley Trippi was named Rose Bowl MVP for his 115-yard rushing performance in the Bulldogs' 9-0 victory over UCLA in 1943.

1- 1-40—**Southern Cal 14, Tennessee 0**
1- 1-41—Stanford 21, Nebraska 13
1- 1-42—Oregon State 20, Duke 16
1- 1-42—(at Durham)
1- 1-43—**Georgia 9, UCLA 0**
1- 1-44—Southern Cal 29, Washington 0
1- 1-45—**Southern Cal 25, Tennessee 0**
1- 1-46—**Alabama 34, Southern Cal 14**
1- 1-47—Illinois 45, UCLA 14
1- 1-48—Michigan 49, Southern Cal 0
1- 1-49—Northwestern 20, California 14
1- 2-50—Ohio State 17, California 14
1- 1-51—Michigan 14, California 6
1- 1-52—Illinois 40, Stanford 7
1- 1-53—Southern Cal 7, Wisconsin 0
1- 1-54—Michigan State 28, UCLA 20
1- 1-55—Ohio State 20, Southern Cal 7
1- 2-56—Michigan State 17, UCLA 14
1- 1-57—Iowa 35, Oregon State 19
1- 1-58—Ohio State 10, Oregon 7
1- 1-59—Iowa 38, California 12
1- 1-60—Washington 44, Wisconsin 8
1- 2-61—Washington 17, Minnesota 7
1- 1-62—Minnesota 21, UCLA 3
1- 1-63—Southern Cal 42, Wisconsin 37
1- 1-64—Illinois 17, Washington 7
1- 1-65—Michigan 34, Oregon State 7
1- 1-66—UCLA 14, Michigan State 12
1- 2-67—Purdue 14, Southern Cal 13
1- 1-68—Southern Cal 14, Indiana 3
1- 1-69—Ohio State 27, Southern Cal 16
1- 1-70—Southern Cal 10, Michigan 3
1- 1-71—Stanford 27, Ohio State 17
1- 1-72—Stanford 13, Michigan 12
1- 1-73—Southern Cal 42, Ohio State 17
1- 1-74—Ohio State 42, Southern Cal 21
1- 1-75—Southern Cal 18, Ohio State 17
1- 1-76—UCLA 23, Ohio State 10
1- 1-77—Southern Cal 14, Michigan 6
1- 2-78—Washington 27, Michigan 20
1- 1-79—Southern Cal 17, Michigan 10
1- 1-80—Southern Cal 17, Ohio State 16
1- 1-81—Michigan 23, Washington 6
1- 1-82—Washington 28, Iowa 0
1- 1-83—UCLA 24, Michigan 14
1- 2-84—UCLA 45, Illinois 9
1- 1-85—Southern Cal 20, Ohio State 17
1- 1-86—UCLA 45, Iowa 28
1- 1-87—Arizona State 22, Michigan 15
1- 1-88—Michigan State 20, Southern Cal 17
1- 2-89—Michigan 22, Southern Cal 14
1- 1-90—Southern Cal 17, Michigan 10
1- 1-91—Washington 46, Iowa 34
1- 1-92—Washington 34, Michigan 14
1- 1-93—Michigan 38, Washington 31
1- 1-94—Wisconsin 21, UCLA 16

*Held at Tournament Park, 1902-22; at Rose Bowl since 1923.

ORANGE BOWL
Miami

1- 1-35—Bucknell 26, Miami (Fla.) 0
1- 1-36—**Catholic U. 20, Ole Miss 19**
1- 1-37—Duquesne 13, Mississippi State 12
1- 1-38—**Auburn 6, Michigan State 0**
1- 2-39—**Tennessee 17, Oklahoma 0**
1- 1-40—Georgia Tech 21, Missouri 7
1- 1-41—**Mississippi State 14, Georgetown 7**
1- 1-42—**Georgia 40, TCU 26**

1- 1-43—**Alabama 37, Boston College 21**
1- 1-44—**LSU 19, Texas A&M 14**
1- 1-45—**Tulsa 26, Georgia Tech 12**
1- 1-46—Miami (Fla.) 13, Holy Cross 6
1- 1-47—**Rice 8, Tennessee 0**
1- 1-48—**Georgia Tech 20, Kansas 14**
1- 1-49—**Texas 41, Georgia 28**
1- 2-50—Santa Clara 21, **Kentucky 13**
11-1-51—Clemson 15, Miami (Fla.) 14
1- 1-52—**Georgia Tech 17, Baylor 14**
1- 1-53—**Alabama 61, Syracuse 6**
1- 1-54—Oklahoma 7, Maryland 0
1- 1-55—Duke 34, Nebraska 7
1- 2-56—Oklahoma 20, Maryland 6
1- 1-57—Colorado 27, Clemson 21
1- 1-58—Oklahoma 48, Duke 21
1- 1-59—Oklahoma 21, Syracuse 6
1- 1-60—**Georgia 14, Missouri 0**
1- 2-61—Missouri 21, Navy 14
1- 1-62—**LSU 25, Colorado 7**
1- 1-63—**Alabama 17, Oklahoma 0**
1- 1-64—Nebraska 13, **Auburn 7**
1- 1-65—Texas 21, **Alabama 17**
1- 1-66—**Alabama 39, Nebraska 28**
1- 2-67—**Florida 27, Georgia Tech 12**
1- 1-68—**Oklahoma 26, Tennessee 24**
1- 1-69—Penn State 15, Kansas 14
1- 1-70—Penn State 10, Missouri 3
1- 1-71—**Nebraska 17, LSU 12**
1- 1-72—**Nebraska 38, Alabama 6**
1- 1-73—Nebraska 40, Notre Dame 6
1- 1-74—**Penn State 16, LSU 9**
1- 1-75—**Notre Dame 13, Alabama 11**
1- 1-76—Oklahoma 14, Michigan 6
1- 1-77—Ohio State 27, Colorado 10
1- 2-78—Arkansas 31, Oklahoma 6
1- 1-79—Oklahoma 31, Nebraska 24
1- 1-80—Oklahoma 24, Florida State 7
1- 1-81—Oklahoma 18, Florida State 17
1- 1-82—Clemson 22, Nebraska 15
1- 1-83—**Nebraska 21, LSU 20**
1- 2-84—Miami (Fla.) 31, Nebraska 30
1- 1-85—Washington 28, Oklahoma 17
1- 1-86—Oklahoma 25, Penn State 10
1- 1-87—Oklahoma 42, Arkansas 8
1- 1-88—Miami (Fla.) 20, Oklahoma 14
1- 2-89—Miami (Fla.) 23, Nebraska 3
1- 1-90—Notre Dame 21, Colorado 6
1- 1-91—Colorado 10, Notre Dame 9
1- 1-92—Miami (Fla.) 22, Nebraska 0
1- 1-93—Florida State 27, Nebraska 14
1- 1-94—Florida State 18, Nebraska 16

SUGAR BOWL
New Orleans*

1- 1-35—**Tulane 20, Temple 14**
1- 1-36—**TCU 3, LSU 2**
1- 1-37—**Santa Clara 21, LSU 14**
1- 1-38—**Santa Clara 6, LSU 0**
1- 2-39—TCU 15, Carnegie Tech 7
1- 1-40—**Texas A&M 14, Tulane 13**
1- 1-41—**Boston College. 19, Tennessee 13**
1- 1-42—Fordham 2, Missouri 0
1- 1-43—**Tennessee 14, Tulsa 7**
1- 1-44—**Georgia Tech 20, Tulsa 18**
1- 1-45—**Duke 29, Alabama 26**
1- 1-46—Oklahoma State 33, State Mary's 13
1- 1-47—**Georgia 20, North Carolina 10**
1- 1-48—**Texas 27, Alabama 7**

300   Bowls & Polls

1- 1-49—Oklahoma 14, North Carolina 6
1- 2-50—**Oklahoma 35, LSU 0**
1- 1-51—**Kentucky 13, Oklahoma 7**
1- 1-52—**Maryland 28, Tennessee 13**
1- 1-53—**Georgia Tech 24, Ole Miss 7**
1- 1-54—**Georgia Tech 42, West Virginia 19**
1- 1-55—**Navy 21, Ole Miss 0**
1- 2-56—**Georgia Tech 7, Pittsburgh 0**
1- 1-57—**Baylor 13, Tennessee 7**
1- 1-58—**Ole Miss 39, Texas 7**
1- 1-59—**LSU 7, Clemson 0**
1- 1-60—**Ole Miss 21, LSU 0**
1- 2-61—**Ole Miss 14, Rice 6**
1- 1-62—**Alabama 10, Arkansas 3**
1- 1-63—**Ole Miss 17, Arkansas 13**
1- 1-64—**Alabama 12, Ole Miss 7**
1- 1-65—**LSU 13, Syracuse 10**
1- 1-66—**Missouri 20, Florida 18**
1- 2-67—**Alabama 34, Nebraska 7**
1- 1-68—**LSU 20, Wyoming 13**
1- 1-69—**Arkansas 16, Georgia 2**
1- 1-70—**Ole Miss 27, Arkansas 22**
1- 1-71—**Tennessee 34, Air Force 13**
1- 1-72—**Oklahoma 40, Auburn 22**
12-31-72—Oklahoma 14, Penn State 0
12-31-73—**Notre Dame 24, Alabama 23**
12-31-74—**Nebraska 13, Florida 10**
12-31-75—**Alabama 13, Penn State 6**
1- 1 -77—**Pittsburgh 27, Georgia 3**
1- 2 -78—**Alabama 35, Ohio State 6**
1- 1 -79—**Alabama 14, Penn State 7**
1- 1 -80—**Alabama 24, Arkansas 9**
1- 1 -81—**Georgia 17, Notre Dame 10**
1- 1 -82—**Pittsburgh 24, Georgia 20**
1- 1 -83—**Penn State 27, Georgia 23**
1- 2 -84—**Auburn 9, Michigan 7**
1- 1 -85—**Nebraska 28, LSU 10**
1- 1 -86—**Tennessee 35, Miami 7**
1- 1 -87—**Nebraska 30, LSU 15**
1- 1 -88—**Auburn 16, Syracuse 16**
1- 2 -89—**Florida State 13, Auburn 7**
1- 1 -90—**Miami 33, Alabama 25**
1- 1 -91—**Tennessee 23, Virginia 22**
1- 1 -92—**Notre Dame 39, Florida 28**
1- 1 -93—**Alabama 34, Miami 13**
1- 1 -94—**Florida 41, West Virginia 7**
*Held at Tulane Stadium, 1935-74; at Superdome since 1975.

JOHN HANCOCK BOWL
El Paso*
(Sun Bowl 1936-88)
1- 1-36—Hardin-Simmons 14, New Mexico State 14
1- 1-37—Hardin-Simmons 34, Texas-El Paso 6
1- 1-38—West Virginia 7, Texas Tech 6
1- 2-39—Utah 26, New Mexico 0
1- 1-40—Catholic U. 0, Arizona State 0
1- 1-41—Western Reserve 26, Arizona State 13
1- 1-42—Tulsa 6, Texas Tech 0
1- 1-43—2nd Air Force 13, Hardin-Simmons 7
1- 1-44—Southwestern Texas 7, New Mexico 0
1- 1-45—Southwestern Texas 35, New Mexico 0
1- 1-46—New Mexico 34, Denver 24
1- 1-47—Cincinnati 18, Virginia Tech 6
1- 1-48—Miami (O.) 13, Texas Tech 12
1- 1-49—West Virginia 21, Texas-El Paso 12
1- 2-50—Texas-El Paso 33, Georgetown 20
1- 1-51—West Texas State 14, Cincinnati 13
1- 1-52—Texas Tech 25, Pacific 14
1- 1-53—Pacific 26, Southern Miss 7
1- 1-54—Texas-El Paso 37, Southern Miss 14
1- 1-55—Texas-El Paso 47, Florida State 20

1- 2-56—Wyoming 21, Texas Tech 14
1- 1-57—Geo Washington 13, Texas-El Paso 0
1- 1-58—Louisville 34, Drake 20
12-31-58—Wyoming 14, Hardin-Simmons 6
12-31-59—New Mexico State 28, North Texas State 8
12-31-60—New Mexico State 20, Utah State 13
12-30-61—Villanova 17, Wichita State 9
12-31-62—West Texas State 15, Ohio U. 14
12-31-63—Oregon 21, SMU 14
12-26-64—**Georgia 7, Texas Tech 0**
12-31-65—Texas-El Paso 13, TCU 12
12-24-66—Wyoming 28, Florida State 20
12-30-67—**Texas-El Paso 14, Ole Miss 7**
12-28-68—**Auburn 34, Arizona 10**
12-20-69—**Nebraska 45, Georgia 6**
12-19-70—Georgia Tech 17, Texas Tech 9
12-18-71—**LSU 33, Iowa State 15**
12-30-72—North Carolina 32, Texas Tech 28
12-29-73—**Missouri 34, Auburn 17**
12-28-74—**Mississippi State 26, North Carolina 24**
12-26-75—Pittsburgh 33, Kansas 19
1- 2-77—**Texas A&M 37, Florida 14**
12-31-77—**Stanford 24, LSU 14**
12-23-78—Texas 42, Maryland 0
12-22-79—Washington 14, Texas 7
12-27-80—**Nebraska 31, Mississippi State 17**
12-26-81—Oklahoma 40, Houston 14
12-25-82—North Carolina 26, Texas 10
12-24-83—**Alabama 28, SMU 7**
12-22-84—**Maryland 28, Tennessee 27**
12-28-85—**Georgia 13, Arizona 13**
12-25-86—**Alabama 28, Washington 6**
12-25-87—Oklahoma State 35, West Virginia 33
12-24-88—**Alabama 29, Army 28**
12-30-89—Pittsburgh 31, Texas A&M 28
12-31-90—Michigan State 17, Southern Cal 16
12-31-91—UCLA 6, Illinois 3
12-31-92—Baylor 20, Arizona 15
12-24-93—Oklahoma 41, Texas Tech 10
*Held at UTEP's Kidd Field, 1936-62;
at Sun Bowl since 1963.

COTTON BOWL
Dallas
1- 1-37—TCU 16, Marquette 6
1- 1-38—Rice 28, Colorado 14
1- 2-39—State Mary's 20, Texas Tech 13
1- 1-40—Clemson 6, Boston College 3
1- 1-41—Texas A&M 13, Fordham 12
1- 1-42—**Alabama 29, Texas A&M 21**
1- 1-43—**Texas 14, Georgia Tech 7**
1- 1-44—Texas 7, Randolph Field 7
1- 1-45—Oklahoma State 34, TCU 0
1- 1-46—Texas 40, Missouri 27
1- 1-47—**Arkansas 0, LSU 0**
1- 1-48—SMU 13, Penn State 13
1- 1-49—SMU 21, Oregon 13
1- 2-50—Rice 27, North Carolina 13
1- 1-51—**Tennessee 20, Texas 14**
1- 1-52—**Kentucky 20, TCU 7**
1- 1-53—**Texas 16, Tennessee 0**
1- 1-54—**Rice 28, Alabama 6**
1- 1-55—**Georgia Tech 14, Arkansas 6**
1- 2-56—**Ole Miss 14, TCU 13**
1- 1-57—TCU 28, Syracuse 27
1- 1-58—Navy 20, Rice 7
1- 1-59—TCU 0, Air Force 0
1- 1-60—Syracuse 23, Texas 14
1- 2-61—Duke 7, Arkansas 6
1- 1-62—**Texas 12, Ole Miss 7**
1- 1-63—**LSU 13, Texas 0**
1- 1-64—Texas 28, Navy 6

1- 1-65—Arkansas 10, Nebraska 7
1- 1-66—**LSU 14, Arkansas 7**
12-31-66—**Georgia 24, SMU 9**
1- 1-68—**Texas A&M 20, Alabama 16**
1- 1-69—**Texas 36, Tennessee 13**
1- 1-70—Texas 21, Notre Dame 17
1- 1-71—Notre Dame 24, Texas 11
1- 1-72—Penn State 30, Texas 6
1- 1-73—**Texas 17, Alabama 13**
1- 1-74—Nebraska 19, Texas 3
1- 1-75—Penn State 41, Baylor 20
1- 1-76—**Arkansas 31, Georgia 10**
1- 1-77—Houston 30, Maryland 21
1- 2-78—Notre Dame 38, Texas 10
1- 1-79—Notre Dame 35, Houston 34
1- 1-80—Houston 17, Nebraska 14
1- 1-81—**Alabama 30, Baylor 2**
1- 1-82—**Texas 14, Alabama 12**
1- 1-83—SMU 7, Pittsburgh 3
1- 2-84—**Georgia 10, Texas 9**
1- 1-85—Boston College 45, Houston 28
1- 1-86—**Texas A&M 36, Auburn 16**
1- 1-87—Ohio State 28, Texas A&M 12
1- 1-88—Texas A&M 35, Notre Dame 10
1- 2-89—UCLA 17, Arkansas 3
1- 1-90—**Tennessee 31, Arkansas 27**
1- 1-91—Miami 46, Texas 3
1- 1-92—Florida State 10, Texas A&M 2
1- 1-93—Notre Dame 28, Texas A&M 3
1- 1-94—Notre Dame 24, Texas A&M 21

Kentucky quarterback Babe Parilli earned Cotton Bowl MVP honors in 1952. In that game Parilli threw for 85 yards and two touchdowns to lead the Wildcats to a 20-7 victory over TCU.

1994 SEC Football

Results of Major Bowl Games

Auburn freshman quarterback Stan White won Peach Bowl MVP honors after scoring on the game's last play to give the Tigers a 27-23 win over Indiana in 1990.

GATOR BOWL
Jacksonville
1- 1-46—Wake Forest 26, South Carolina 14
1- 1-47—Oklahoma 34, N.C. State 13
1- 1-48—**Maryland 20, Georgia 20**
1- 1-49—Clemson 24, Missouri 23
1- 2-50—Maryland 20, Missouri 7
1- 1-51—Wyoming 20, Washington & Lee 7
1- 1-52—Miami (Fla.) 14, Clemson 0
1- 1-53—**Florida 14, Tulsa 13**
1- 1-54—**Texas Tech 35, Auburn 13**
12-31-54—**Auburn 33, Baylor 13**
12-31-55—**Vanderbilt 25, Auburn 13**
12-29-56—Georgia Tech 21, Pittsburgh 14
12-28-57—Tennessee 3, Texas A&M 0
12-27-58—**Ole Miss 7, Florida 3**
1- 2-60—**Arkansas 14, Georgia Tech 7**
12-31-60—Florida 13, Baylor 12
12-30-61—Penn State 30, Georgia Tech 15
12-29-62—Florida 17, Penn State 7
12-28-63—North Carolina 35, Air Force 0
1- 2-65—Florida State 36, Oklahoma 19
12-31-65—Georgia Tech 31, Texas Tech 21
12-31-66—**Tennessee 18, Syracuse 12**
12-30-67—**Penn State 17, Florida State 17**
12-28-68—**Missouri 35, Alabama 10**
12-27-69—**Florida 14, Tennessee 13**
1- 2-71—**Auburn 35, Ole Miss 28**
12-31-71—**Georgia 7, North Carolina 3**
12-30-72—**Auburn 24, Colorado 3**
12-29-73—**Texas Tech 28, Tennessee 19**
12-30-74—**Auburn 27, Texas 3**
12-29-75—**Maryland 13, Florida 0**
12-27-76—Notre Dame 20, Penn State 9
12-30-77—Pittsburgh 34, Clemson 3
12-29-78—Clemson 17, Ohio State 15
12-28-79—North Carolina 17, Michigan 15
12-29-80—Pittsburgh 37, South Carolina 9
12-28-81—North Carolina 31, Arkansas 27
12-30-82—Florida State 31, West Virginia 12
12-30-83—**Florida 14, Iowa 6**
12-28-84—Oklahoma State 21, South Carolina 14
12-30-85—Florida State 34, Oklahoma State 23
12-27-86—Clemson 27, Stanford 21
12-31-87—**LSU 30, South Carolina 13**
1- 1-89—**Georgia 34, Michigan State 27**
12-30-89—Clemson 27, West Virginia 7
1- 1-91—Michigan 35, Ole Miss 3
12-29-91—Oklahoma 48, Virginia 14
12-31-92—**Florida 27, N.C. State 10**
12-31-93—**Alabama 24, North Carolina 10**

FLORIDA CITRUS BOWL
Orlando
(Tangerine Bowl 1947-82)
1- 1-47—Catawba 31, Maryville 6
1- 1-48—Catawba 7, Marshall 0
1- 1-49—Murray State 21, Sul Ross State 21
1- 2-50—State Vincent 7, Emory & Henry 6
1- 1-51—Morris Harvey 35, Emory & Henry 14
1- 1-52—Stetson 35, Arkansas State 20
1- 1-53—East Texas State 33, Tenn. Tech 0
1- 1-54—East Texas State 7, Arkansas State 7
1- 1-55—Neb.-Omaha 7, Eastern Kentucky 6
1- 2-56—Juniata 6, Missouri Valley 6
1- 1-57—West Texas State 20, Southern Miss 13
1- 1-58—East Texas State 10, Southern Miss 9
12-27-58—East Texas State 26, Missouri Valley 7
1- 1-60—Middle Tennessee 21, Presbyterian 12
12-30-60—Citadel 27, Tennessee Tech 0
12-29-61—Lamar 21, Middle Tennessee 14
12-22-62—Houston 49, Miami (0.) 21
12-28-63—Western Ky. 27, Coast Guard 0
12-12-64—East Carolina 14, Massachusetts 13
12-11-65—East Carolina 31, Maine 0
12-10-66—Morgan State 14, West Chester 6
12-16-67—Tenn.-Martin 25, West Chester 8
12-27-68—Richmond 49, Ohio U. 42
12-26-69—Toledo 56, Davidson 33
12-28-70—Toledo 40, William & Mary 12
12-28-71—Toledo 28, Richmond 3
12-29-72—Tampa 21, Kent State 18
12-22-73—**Miami (O.) 16, Florida 7**
12-21-74—**Miami (O.) 21, Georgia 10**
12-20-75—Miami (O.) 20, South Carolina 7
12-18-76—Oklahoma State 49, Brigham Young 21
12-23-77—Florida State 40, Texas Tech 17
12-23-78—N.C. State 30, Pittsburgh 17
12-22-79—**LSU 34, Wake Forest 10**
12-20-80—Florida 35, Maryland 20
12-19-81—Missouri 19, Southern Miss 17
12-18-82—**Auburn 33, Boston College 26**
12-17-83—**Tennessee 30, Maryland 23**
12-22-84—**Georgia 17, Florida State 17**
12-28-85—Ohio State 10, Brigham Young 7
1- 1-87—**Auburn 16, Southern Cal 7**
1- 1-88—Clemson 35, Penn State 10
1- 2-89—Clemson 13, Oklahoma 6
1- 1-90—Illinois 31, Virginia 21
1- 1-91—Georgia Tech 45, Nebraska 21
1- 1-92—California 37, Clemson 13
1- 1-93—**Georgia 21, Ohio State 14**
1- 1-94—**Penn State 31, Tennessee 13**

BLUEBONNET BOWL
Houston*
12-19-59—Clemson 23, TCU 7
12-17-60—**Texas 3, Alabama 3**
12-16-61—Kansas 33, Rice 7
12-22-62—Missouri 14, Georgia Tech 10
12-21-63—**Baylor 14, LSU 7**
12-19-64—**Tulsa 14, Ole Miss 7**
12-18-65—**Tennessee 27, Tulsa 6**
12- 7-66—**Texas 19, Ole Miss 0**
12-23-67—Colorado 31, Miami (Fla.) 21
12-31-68—SMU 28, Oklahoma 27
12-31-69—**Houston 36, Auburn 7**
12-31-70—**Alabama 24, Oklahoma 24**
12-31-71—Colorado 29, Houston 17
12-30-72—**Tennessee 24, LSU 17**
12-29-73—Houston 47, Tulane 7
12-23-74—N.C. State 31, Houston 31
12-27-75—Texas 38, Colorado 21
12-31-76—Nebraska 27, Texas Tech 24
12-31-77—Southern Cal 47, Texas A&M 28
12-31-78—**Stanford 25, Georgia 22**
12-31-79—**Purdue 27, Tennessee 22**
12-31-80—North Carolina 16, Texas 7
12-31-81—Michigan 33, UCLA 14
12-31-82—**Arkansas 28, Florida 24**
12-31-83—Oklahoma State 24, Baylor 14
12-31-84—West Virginia 31, TCU 14
12-31-85—Air Force 24, Texas 16
12-31-86—Baylor 21, Colorado 9
12-31-87—Texas 32, Pittsburgh 27
*Held at Rice Stadium, 1959-67 and 1985; at Astrodome, 1968-84, 86-87.

LIBERTY BOWL
Memphis*
12-19-59—**Penn State 7, Alabama 0**
12-17-60—Penn State 41, Oregon 12
12-16-61—Syracuse 15, Miami (Fla.) 14
12-15-62—Oregon State 6, Villanova 0
12-21-63—**Mississippi State 16, N.C. State 12**
12-19-64—Utah 32, West Virginia 6
12-18-65—**Ole Miss 13, Auburn 7**
12-10-66—Miami (Fla.) 14, Virginia Tech 7
12-16-67—**N.C. State 14, Georgia 7**
12-14-68—**Ole Miss 34, Virginia Tech 17**
12-13-69—**Colorado 47, Alabama 33**
12-12-70—Tulane 17, Colorado 3
12-20-71—**Tennessee 14, Arkansas 13**
12-18-72—Georgia Tech 31, Iowa State 30
12-17-73—N.C. State 31, Kansas 18
12-16-74—**Tennessee 7, Maryland 3**
12-22-75—Southern Cal 20, Texas A&M 0
12-20-76—**Alabama 36, UCLA 6**
12-19-77—Nebraska 21, North Carolina 17
12-23-78—**Missouri 20, LSU 15**
12-22-79—Penn State 9, Tulane 6
12-27-80—Purdue 28, Missouri 25
12-30-81—Ohio State 31, Navy 28
12-29-82—**Alabama 21, Illinois 15**
12-29-83—Notre Dame 19, Boston College 18
12-27-84—**Auburn 21, Arkansas 15**
12-27-85—**Baylor 21, LSU 7**
12-29-86—**Tennessee 21, Minnesota 14**
12-29-87—**Georgia 20, Arkansas 17**
12-28-88—Indiana 34, South Carolina 10
12-28-89—**Ole Miss 42, Air Force 29**
12-27-90—Air Force 23, Ohio State 11
12-29-91—**Air Force 38, Mississippi State 15**
12-31-92—**Ole Miss 13, Air Force 0**
12-28-93—Louisville 18, Michigan State 7
*Held at Philadelphia 1959-63; at Atlantic City 1964; at Memphis since 1965.

302 Bowls & Polls

PEACH BOWL
Atlanta
12-30-68—**LSU 31, Florida State 27**
12-30-69—West Virginia 14, South Carolina 3
12-30-70—Arizona State 48, North Carolina 26
12-30-71—**Ole Miss 41, Georgia Tech 18**
12-29-72—N.C. State 49, West Virginia 13
12-28-73—**Georgia 17, Maryland 16**
12-28-74—**Vanderbilt 6, Texas Tech 6**
12-31-75—West Virginia 13, N.C. State 10
12-31-76—**Kentucky 21, North Carolina 0**
12-31-77—N.C. State 24, Iowa State 14
12-25-78—Purdue 41, Georgia Tech 21
12-31-79—Baylor 24, Clemson 18
1- 2-81—Miami (Fla.) 20, Virginia Tech 10
12-31-81—**West Virginia 26, Florida 6**
12-31-82—**Iowa 28, Tennessee 22**
12-30-83—Florida State 28, North Carolina 3
12-31-84—Virginia 27, Purdue 24
12-31-85—Army 31, Illinois 29
12-31-86—Virginia Tech 25, N.C. State 24
1- 2-88—**Tennessee 27, Indiana 22**
12-31-88—N.C. State 28, Iowa 23
12-30-89—Syracuse 19, Georgia 18
12-29-90—**Auburn 27, Indiana 23**
1- 1-92—East Carolina 37, N.C. State 34
1- 2-93—**North Carolina 21, Mississippi State 17**
12-31-93—**Clemson 14, Kentucky 13**

FIESTA BOWL
Tempe
12-27-71—Arizona State 45, Florida State 38
12-23-72—Arizona State 49, Missouri 35
12-21-73—Arizona State 28, Pittsburgh 7
12-28-74—Oklahoma State 16, Brigham Young 6
12-26-75—Arizona State 17, Nebraska 14
12-25-76—Oklahoma 41, Wyoming 7
12-25-77—Penn State 42, Arizona State 30
12-25-78—Arkansas 10, UCLA 10
12-25-79—Pittsburgh 16, Arizona 10
12-26-80—Penn State 31, Ohio State 19
1- 1-82—Penn State 26, Southern Cal 10
1- 1-83—Arizona State 32, Oklahoma 21
1- 2-84—Ohio State 28, Pittsburgh 23
1- 1-85—UCLA 39, Miami (Fla.) 37
1- 1-86—Michigan 27, Nebraska 23
1- 2-87—Penn State 14, Miami (Fla.) 10
1- 1-88—Florida State 31, Nebraska 28
1- 2-89—Notre Dame 34, West Virginia 21
1- 1-90—Florida State 41, Nebraska 17
1- 1-91—**Louisville 34, Alabama 7**
1- 1-92—**Penn State 42, Tennessee 17**
1- 1-93—Syracuse 26, Colorado 22
1- 1-94—Arizona 29, Miami (Fla.) 0

INDEPENDENCE BOWL
Shreveport
12-13-76—McNeese State 20, Tulsa 16
12-17-77—Louisiana Tech 24, Louisville 14
12-16-78—East Carolina 35, Louisiana Tech 13
12-15-79—Syracuse 31, McNeese State 7
12-13-80—Southern Miss 16, McNeese State 14
12-12-81—Texas A&M 33, Oklahoma State 16
12-11-82—Wisconsin 14, Kansas State 3
12-10-83—**Air Force 9, Ole Miss 3**
12-15-84—Air Force 23, Virginia Tech 7
12-21-85—Minnesota 20, Clemson 13
12-20-86—**Ole Miss 20, Texas Tech 17**
12-12-87—Washington 24, Tulane 12
12-23-88—Southern Miss 38, Texas-El Paso 18
12-16-89—Oregon 27, Tulsa 24
12-15-90—Louisiana Tech 34, Maryland 34
12-29-91—**Georgia 24, Arkansas 15**

12-31-92—Wake Forest 39, Oregon 35
12-31-93—Virginia Tech 45, Indiana 20

ALL AMERICAN BOWL
Birmingham
(Hall of Fame Classic 1977-84)
12-22-77—Maryland 17, Minnesota 7
12-20-78—Texas A&M 28, Iowa State 12
12-29-79—Missouri 24, South Carolina 14
12-27-80—Arkansas 34, Tulane 15
12-31-81—**Mississippi State 10, Kansas 0**
12-31-82—**Air Force 36, Vanderbilt 28**
12-22-83—**West Virginia 20, Kentucky 16**
12-29-84—**Kentucky 20, Wisconsin 19**
12-31-85—Georgia Tech 17, Michigan State 14
12-31-86—Florida State 27, Indiana 13
12-22-87—Virginia 22, Brigham Young 16
12-29-88—**Florida 14, Illinois 10**
12-28-89—Texas Tech 49, Duke 21
12-28-90—N.C. State 31, Southern Miss 27

HOLIDAY BOWL
San Diego
12-22-78—Navy 23, Brigham Young 16
12-21-79—Indiana 38, Brigham Young 37
12-17-82—Brigham Young 46, SMU 45
12-18-81—Brigham Young 38, Washington State 36
12-17-82—Ohio State 47, Brigham Young 17
12-23-83—Brigham Young 21, Missouri 17
12-21-84—Brigham Young 24, Michigan 17
12-22-85—Arkansas 18, Arizona State 17
12-30-86—Iowa 39, San Diego State 38
12-30-87—Iowa 20, Wyoming 19
12-30-88—Oklahoma State 62, Wyoming 14
12-29-89—Penn State 50, Brigham Young 39
12-29-90—Texas A&M 65, Brigham Young 14
12-30-91—Iowa 13, Brigham Young 13
12-30-92—Hawaii 27, Illinois 17
12-30-93—Ohio State 28, Brigham Young 21

GARDEN STATE BOWL
East Rutherford
12-16-78—Arizona State 34, Rutgers 18
12-15-79—Temple 28, California 17
12-14-80—Houston 35, Navy 0
12-13-81—**Tennessee 28, Wisconsin 21**

CALIFORNIA (RAISIN) BOWL
Fresno
12-19-81—Toledo 27, San Jose State 25
12-18-82—Fresno State 29, Bowling Green 28
12-17-83—N. Illinois 20, Cal State Fullerton 13
12-15-84—UNLV 30, Toledo 13
12-14-85—Fresno State 51, Bowling Green 7
12-31-86—San Jose State 37, Miami (O.), 7
12-12-87—Eastern Michigan 30, San Jose State 27
12-10-88—Fresno State 35, Western Michigan 30
12- 9-89—Fresno State 27, Ball State 6
12- 8-90—San Jose State 48, Central Michigan 24
12-14-91—Bowling Green 28, Fresno State 21

ALOHA BOWL
Honolulu
12-25-82—Washington 21, Maryland 20
12-26-83—Penn State 13, Washington 10
12-27-84—SMU 27, Notre Dame 20
12-28-85—**Alabama 24, Southern Cal 3**
12-27-86—Arizona 30, North Carolina 21
12-25-87—**UCLA 20, Florida 16**
12-25-88—Washington State 24, Houston 22
12-25-89—Michigan State 33, Hawaii 13
12-25-90—Syracuse 28, Arizona 0
12-25-91—Georgia Tech 18, Stanford 17
12-25-92—Kansas 23, BYU 20
12-25-93—Colorado 41, Fresno State 30

FREEDOM BOWL
Anaheim
12-26-84—Iowa 55, Texas 17
12-30-85—Washington 20, Colorado 17
12-30-86—UCLA 31, Brigham Young 10
12-30-87—Arizona Stae 33, Air Force 28
12-29-88—Brigham Young 20, Colorado 17
12-30-89—**Washington 34, Florida 7**
12-29-90—Colorado State 32, Oregon 31
12-30-91—Tulsa 28, San Diego State 17
12-29-92—Fresno State 24, Southern Cal 7
12-30-93—Southern Cal 28, Utah 21

CHERRY BOWL
Pontiac
12-22-84—Army 10, Michigan State 6
12-21-85—Maryland 35, Syracuse 18

HALL OF FAME BOWL
Tampa
12-23-86—**Boston College 27, Georgia 24**
1- 2-88—**Michigan 28, Alabama 24**
1- 2-89—**Syracuse 23, LSU 10**
1- 1-90—**Auburn 31, Ohio State 14**
1- 1-91—Clemson 30, Illinois 0
1- 1-92—Syracuse 24, Ohio State 17
1- 1-93—**Tennessee 38, Boston College 23**
1- 1-94—Michigan 42, N.C. State 7

COPPER BOWL
Tucson
12-31-89—Arizona 17, N.C. State 10
12-31-90—California 17, Wyoming 15
12-31-91—Indiana 24, Baylor 0
12-29-92—Washington State 31, Utah 28
12-29-93—Kansas State 52, Wyoming 17

CARQUEST BOWL
Hollywood (Fla.)
(Blockbuster Bowl 1990-93)
12-28-90—Florida State 24, Penn State 17
12-28-91—**Alabama 30, Colorado 25**
1- 1-93—Stanford 24, Penn State 3
1- 1-94—Boston College 31, Virginia 13

ALAMO BOWL
San Antonio
12-31-93—California 37, Iowa 3

LAS VEGAS BOWL
Las Vegas
12-17-93—Utah State 42, Ball State 33

PRESEASON BOWLS
KICKOFF CLASSIC
East Rutherford
1983—Nebraska 44, Penn State 6
1984—**Miami 20, Auburn 18**
1985—Brigham Young 28, Boston College 14
1986—**Alabama 16, Ohio State 10**
1987—**Tennessee 23, Iowa 22**
1988—Nebraska 23, Texas A&M 14
1989—Notre Dame 36, Virginia 13
1990—Southern Cal 34, Syracuse 16
1991—Penn State 34, Georgia Tech 22
1992—Iowa 24, N.C. State 14
1993—Florida State 42, Kansas 0

DISNEYLAND PIGSKIN CLASSIC
Anaheim
1990—**Tennessee 31, Colorado 31**
1991—Florida State 44, Brigham Young 28
1992—Stanford 10, Texas A&M 7
1993—North Carolina 31, Southern Cal 9

Bowl Most Valuable Players
(year listed actual year the game was played)

SUGAR BOWL
Alabama
Mike Fracchia, B, 1962
Tim Davis, PK, 1964
Kenny Stabler, QB, 1967
Richard Todd, QB, 1975
Jeff Rutledge, QB, 1978
Barry Krauss, LB, 1979
Major Ogilvie, RB, 1980
Derrick Lassic, RB, 1993
Auburn
Bo Jackson, RB, 1984
Florida
Steve Spurrier, QB, 1966
Errict Rhett, RB, 1994
Georgia
Herschel Walker, RB, 1981
Kentucky
Walt Yowarsky, T, 1951
LSU
Billy Cannon, B, 1959
Doug Moreau, SE, 1965
Glenn Smith, RB, 1968
Ole Miss
Raymond Brown, QB, 1958
Bobby Franklin, QB, 1960
Jake Gibbs, QB, 1961
Glynn Griffing, QB, 1963
Archie Manning, QB, 1970
Tennessee
Bobby Scott, QB, 1971
Daryl Dickey, QB, 1986
Andy Kelly, QB, 1991

ORANGE BOWL
Alabama
Lee Roy Jordan, C-LB, 1963
Joe Namath, QB, 1965
Steve Sloan, QB, 1966
Leroy Cook, DE, 1975 (Defense)
Florida
Larry Smith, RB, 1967

COTTON BOWL
Alabama
Warren Lyles, NG, 1981 (Line)
Auburn
Bo Jackson, RB, 1986 (Offense)
Georgia
Kent Lawrence, RB, 1966 (Back)
John Lastinger, QB, 1984 (Back)
Kentucky
Babe Parilli, QB, 1952 (Back)
LSU
Lynn Amedee, QB, 1963 (Back)
Joe Labruzzo, RB, 1966 (Back)
Dave McCormick, OT, 1966 (Line)
Ole Miss
Eagle Day, QB, 1956 (Back)
Buddy Alliston, G, 1956 (Line)
Tennessee
Andy Kozar, RB, 1951 (Back)
Bud Sherrod, E, 1951 (Line)
Chuck Webb, RB, 1990
Carl Pickens, DB, 1990

ROSE BOWL
Alabama
Johnny Mack Brown, B, 1926
Fred Pickhard, T, 1927
John Campbell, B, 1931
Dixie Howell, B, 1935
Harry Gilmer, B, 1946

Georgia
Charley Trippi, B, 1943

GATOR BOWL
Alabama
Mike Hall, LB, 1968 (losing team)
Brian Burgdorf, QB, 1993 (winning team)
Auburn
Vince Dooley, B, 1954 (losing team)
Joe Childress, RB, 1954 (winning team)
Joe Childress, RB, 1955 (losing team)
Pat Sullivan, QB, 1971 (winning team)
Wade Whatley, QB, 1972 (winning team)
Phil Gargis, QB, 1974 (winning team)
Florida
Papa Hall, B, 1953 (winning team)
Dave Hudson, E, 1958 (losing team)
Larry Libertore, QB, 1960
  (winning team)
Tommy Shannon, QB, 1962
  (winning team)
Mike Kelley, LB, 1969
  (winning team)
Tony Lilly, DB, 1983
  (winning team)
Georgia
Wayne Johnson, QB, 1989
  (winning team)
LSU
Wendell Davis, WR, 1987
  (winning team)
Tom Hodson, QB, 1987
  (winning team)
Ole Miss
Bobby Franklin, QB, 1958
  (winning team)
Archie Manning, QB, 1971
  (losing team)
Tennessee
Bobby Gordon, RB, 1957
  (winning team)
Dewey Warren, QB, 1966
  (winning team)
Curt Watson, RB, 1969 (losing team)
Haskel Stanback, RB, 1973
  (losing team)
Vanderbilt
Don Orr, B, 1955 (winning team)

LIBERTY BOWL
Alabama
Jeremiah Castille, CB, 1982 (MVP)
Barry Krauss, LB, 1976 (MVP)
Auburn
Tom Bryan, RB, 1965 (MVP)
Bo Jackson, RB, 1984 (MVP)
Kevin Porter, CB, 1984 (Defense)
Georgia
Kent Lawrence, RB, 1967 (Back)
Edgar Chandler, OG, 1967 (Line)
LSU
Charles Alexander, RB, 1978 (Back)
Benjy Thibodeaux, DT, 1978 (Line)
Norman Jefferson, DB, 1985 (Back)
Michael Brooks, LB, 1985 (Line)
Ole Miss
Charles Hinton, C, 1965 (Offense)
Lee Garner, LB, 1965 (Defense)
Steve Hindman, RB, 1968 (MVP)
Worthy McClure, OT, 1968
  (Offense)

Robert Bailey, MM, 1968 (Defense)
Randy Baldwin, RB, 1989
Jeff Carter, DB, 1989
Cassius Ware, LB, 1992
Mississippi State
Ode Burrell, RB, 1963 (MVP)
Kenny Roberts, RB, 1991
Keo Coleman, LB, 1991
Tennessee
Mike Gayles, RB, 1974 (Offense)
Jeff Francis, QB, 1986 (MVP)
Joey Clinkscales, WR, 1986
  (Offense)
Dale Jones, OLB, 1986 (Defense)

CITRUS BOWL
Auburn
Randy Campbell, QB, 1982 (MVP)
Mark Dorminey, DB, 1982 (Defense)
Brent Fullwood, RB, 1987 (Offense)
Aundray Bruce, DE, 1987 (Defense)
Florida
Cris Collinsworth, SE, 1980 (MVP)
David Galloway, DT, 1980
  (Defense)
Georgia
James Jackson, QB, 1984 (MVP)
Lars Tate, RB, 1984 (Offense)
Kevin Harris, CB, 1984 (Defense)
Garrison Hearst, TB, 1993
LSU
David Woodley, QB, 1979 (MVP)
Benjy Thibodeaux, DT, 1979
  (Defense)
Jerry Murphree, SB, 1979 (Offense)
Tennessee
Johnnie Jones, RB, 1983 (MVP)
Alvin Toles, LB, 1983 (Defense)

PEACH BOWL
Auburn
Stan White, QB, 1990
Kentucky
Rod Stewart, FB, 1976 (Offense)
Mike Martin, LB, 1976 (Defense)
Pookie Jones, QB, 1993 (Offense)
Zane Beehn, DE, 1993 (Defense)
LSU
Mike Hillman, QB, 1968 (Offense)
Ole Miss
Norris Weese, QB, 1971 (Offense)
Crowell Armstrong, LB, 1971
  (Defense)
Tennessee
Reggie Cobb, RB, 1988 (Offense)
Vanderbilt
Dennis Harrison, DT, 1974
  (Defense)

SUN BOWL
Alabama
Walter Lewis, QB, 1983 (MVP)
Wes Neighbors, C, 1983 (Line)
Cornelius Bennett, LB, 1986 (MVP)
David Smith, QB, 1988 (MVP)
Derrick Thomas, LB, 1988
  (Defense)
Auburn
Buddy McClinton, DB, 1968 (MVP)
David Campbell, DT, 1968 (Line)

LSU
Bert Jones, QB, 1971 (MVP, Back)
Andy Hamilton, WR, 1971 (Line)
Charles Alexander, RB, 1977 (Back)
Mississippi State
Terry Vitrano, RB, 1974 (MVP)
Georgia
Preston Ridlehuber, QB, 1964 (MVP)
Peter Anderson, C, 1985 (Line)
Tennessee
Carl Zander, LB, 1984 (Defense)

ALL AMERICAN BOWL
(Hall of Fame Bowl 1977-84)
Florida
Emmitt Smith, RB, 1988 (MVP)
Kentucky
George Adams, RB, 1983
  (losing team)
Mark Logan, RB, 1984
  (winning team)
Mississippi State
John Bond, QB, 1981
  (MVP & Offense)
Johnie Cooks, LB, 1981 (Defense)
Vanderbilt
Whit Taylor, QB, 1982 (losing team)

INDEPENDENCE BOWL
Georgia
Andre Hastings, FLK, 1991 (Offense)
Torrey Evans, ILB, 1991 (Defense)
Ole Miss
Andre Townsend, DT, 1983 (Defense)
Mark Young, QB, 1986 (MVP)

ALOHA BOWL
Alabama
Gene Jelks, RB, 1985 (Offense)
Cornelius Bennett, LB, 1985
  (Defense)

HALL OF FAME
Auburn
Reggie Slack, QB, 1990
Georgia
James Jackson, QB, 1986 (Offense)
Tennessee
Heath Shuler, QB, 1993

BLOCKBUSTER BOWL
Alabama
David Palmer, WR, 1991

GARDEN STATE BOWL
Tennessee
Steve Alatorre, QB, 1981

DELTA BOWL
Ole Miss
Charley Conerly, QB, 1948

PRESIDENTIAL CUP
Georgia
Zippy Morocco, B, 1950

All-Time Final Associated Press Poll

Rank	Team	Points	Top 20	Top 10	Top 5	1st	2nd
1.	Notre Dame	638.5	42	34	22	8	5
2.	Oklahoma	573.5	41	29	24	6	3
3.	Michigan	557	41	32	13	1	2
4.	**ALABAMA**	**545**	**39**	**29**	**17**	**6**	**2**
5.	Ohio State	461	37	21	13	3	4
6.	Nebraska	448	34	23	9	2	1
7.	Southern Cal	407	34	20	11	3	4
8.	Texas	397.5	30	19	15	2	1
9.	**TENNESSEE**	**382**	**31**	**17**	**10**	**1**	**4**
10.	Penn State	361	29	19	12	2	2
11.	UCLA	303	27	14	8	0	1
12.	**AUBURN**	**274**	**24**	**13**	**6**	**1**	**0**
13.	Miami (Florida)	266	18	12	8	4	2
14.	**ARKANSAS**	**263**	**23**	**13**	**3**	**0**	**1**
15.	**LSU**	**260**	**23**	**14**	**5**	**1**	**1**
16.	**GEORGIA**	**248**	**20**	**13**	**7**	**1**	**1**
17.	Michigan State	247	19	12	7	1	4
18.	Washington	212	18	10	4	0	2
19.	Texas A&M	211	18	10	2	1	0
20.	Florida State	209	13	9	6	1	2
21.	**OLE MISS**	**202.5**	**18**	**10**	**4**	**0**	**2**
22.	Pittsburgh	199	16	10	6	2	1
23.	Georgia Tech	192.5	17	9	5	0	2
24.	Clemson	179	18	6	1	1	0
25.	Army	173	13	8	6	2	2
26.	Minnesota	161	12	9	5	4	0
27.	Iowa	154	14	8	3	0	1
28.	**FLORIDA**	**153**	**14**	**6**	**3**	**0**	**0**
29.	Navy	141.5	11	8	7	0	1
30.	Colorado	133	13	4	3	1	0
31.	Duke	130	16	5	2	0	1
32.	Wisconsin	129	10	7	2	0	1
33.	Maryland	127.5	14	5	3	1	0
34.	California	123	10	5	4	0	1
35.	Syracuse	120.5	10	5	2	1	0
36.	Arizona State	116.5	11	6	2	0	1
37.	Illinois	115	10	6	3	0	0
38.	Southern Methodist	113	11	6	3	0	1
39.	Missouri	112.5	12	6	1	0	0
40.	North Carolina	108	13	5	1	0	0
41.	Houston	106.5	12	5	2	0	0
42.	Stanford	106	11	5	1	0	1
43.	Purdue	100.5	12	5	1	0	0
44.	Texas Christian	87	8	4	1	1	0
45.	West Virginia	78	11	3	1	0	0
46.	Boston College	77	7	3	2	0	0
47.	Brigham Young	76	9	2	1	1	0
48.	Baylor	68.5	10	1	0	0	0
49.	Northwestern	67	6	4	0	0	0
50.	Rice	66	8	4	1	0	0
51.	Pennsylvania	60	7	3	0	0	0
52.	Oklahoma State	59	6	2	1	0	0
53.	Fordham	58	6	2	1	0	0
54.	**KENTUCKY**	**56**	**8**	**2**	**0**	**0**	**0**
55.	Santa Clara	55.5	6	2	0	0	0
56.	Oregon State	53	5	3	0	0	0
57.	Tulsa	47	6	1	1	0	0
58.	North Carolina State	46	8	0	0	0	0
59.	Texas Tech	44	5	0	0	0	0
60.	Cornell	43	5	1	1	0	0
61.	Air Force	42	4	2	0	0	0
62.	Kansas	40	4	1	0	0	0
63.	Indiana	38	5	2	2	0	0
64.	**MISSISSIPPI STATE**	**36.5**	**7**	**1**	**0**	**0**	**0**
65.	Dartmouth	35	5	1	0	0	0
	Princeton	35	4	2	0	0	0
67.	Iowa Pre-Flight	34	2	2	1	0	1
	Yale	34	4	0	0	0	0
69.	Arizona	33	5	1	0	0	0
70.	Miami (Ohio)	32	4	1	0	0	0
71.	Tulane	31.5	6	1	1	0	0
72.	Duquesne	31	3	2	0	0	0
73.	Wyoming	29	3	1	0	0	0
74.	Washington State	27	6	0	0	0	0
75.	Holy Cross	26.5	5	1	0	0	0
76.	Villanova	26	3	1	0	0	0
77.	**SOUTH CAROLINA**	**22**	**3**	**0**	**0**	**0**	**0**
	March Field	22	2	2	0	0	0
79.	Bainbridge NTS	20	2	1	1	0	0
	Virginia	20	4	0	0	0	0
81.	Great Lakes	19	2	1	0	0	0
82.	Randolph Field	18	1	1	1	0	0
	William & Mary	18	3	0	0	0	0
	East Carolina	18	2	1	0	0	0
85.	Toledo	16	2	0	0	0	0
86.	Carnegie Tech	15	1	1	0	0	0
	Louisville	15	2	0	0	0	0
88.	St. Mary's (California)	14	1	1	0	0	0
89.	Del Monte P-F	13	1	1	0	0	0
	Pacific	13	2	1	0	0	0
91.	Oregon	12	1	1	0	0	0
92.	Rutgers	11	3	0	0	0	0
	Utah State	11	1	1	0	0	0
94.	Virginia Tech	10	2	0	0	0	0
95.	**VANDERBILT**	**9**	**1**	**0**	**0**	**0**	**0**
96.	Georgetown	8	1	0	0	0	0
97.	Norman P-F	7.5	1	0	0	0	0
98.	San Francisco	7	1	0	0	0	0
99.	Hawaii	6	1	0	0	0	0
	Kansas State	6	1	0	0	0	0
101.	Boston University	5	1	0	0	0	0
	El Toro Maines	5	1	0	0	0	0
	San Diego State	5	1	0	0	0	0
104.	George Washington	4	1	0	0	0	0
	Hardin-Simmons	4	1	0	0	0	0
	New Mexico State	4	1	0	0	0	0
	Temple	4	1	0	0	0	0
	Wake Forest	4	2	0	0	0	0
109.	Colorado College	3	1	0	0	0	0
	Fort Pierce	3	1	0	0	0	0
	Washington & Lee	3	1	0	0	0	0
112.	Columbia	2	2	0	0	0	0
	Delaware	2	1	0	0	0	0
	Fresno State	2	0	0	0	0	0
	Iowa State	2	1	0	0	0	0
	Lafayette	2	1	0	0	0	0
	Louisville	2	0	0	0	0	0
	St. Mary's P-F	2	1	0	0	0	0
118.	Marquette	1	1	0	0	0	0
	Ohio University	1	1	0	0	0	0
	Second Air Force	1	1	0	0	0	0
	Virginia Military	1	1	0	0	0	0

NOTE: Poll was compiled by Charles Woodroof, former SEC Assistant Director of Media Relations. The AP (Writers and Broadcasters) Poll began in 1936. From 1936 to 1961 the wire service ranked 20 teams. From 1962 to 1967 only 10 teams were recognized. From 1968 to 1988 AP again resumed its Top 20 before expanding to 25 teams in 1989. Points were awarded based on a team's finish in the final AP poll each year. Points were awarded on a 20-19-18-17-16-15-14-13-12-11-10-9-8-7-6-5-4-3-2-1 basis from 1936 to 1988, and a 25-24-23-22-21-20-19-18-17-16-15-14-13-12-11-10-9-8-7-6-5-4-3-2-1 basis for 1989 to 1993.

1994 SEC Football

Associated Press Final Rankings

1936
1. Minnesota
2. **LSU**
3. Pittsburgh
4. **Alabama**
5. Washington
6. Santa Clara
7. Northwestern
8. Notre Dame
9. Nebraska
10. Pennsylvania
11. Duke
12. Yale
13. Dartmouth
14. Duquesne
15. Fordham
16. TCU
17. **Tennessee**
18. Arkansas
    Navy
20. Marquette

1937
1. Pittsburgh
2. California
3. Fordham
4. **Alabama**
5. Minnesota
6. Villanova
7. Dartmouth
8. **LSU**
9. Notre Dame
10. Santa Clara
11. Nebraska
12. Yale
13. Ohio State
14. Holy Cross
    Arkansas
16. TCU
17. Colorado
18. Rice
19. N. Carolina
20. Duke

1938
1. TCU
2. **Tennessee**
3. Duke
4. Oklahoma
5. Notre Dame
6. Carnegie Tech
7. Southern Cal
8. Pittsburgh
9. Holy Cross
10. Minnesota
11. Texas Tech
12. Cornell
13. **Alabama**
14. California
15. Fordham
16. Michigan
17. Northwestern
18. Villanova
19. Tulane
20. Dartmouth

1939
1. Texas A&M
2. **Tennessee**
3. Southern Cal
4. Cornell
5. **Tulane**
6. Missouri
7. UCLA
8. Duke
9. Iowa
10. Duquesne
11. Boston Coll.
12. Clemson
13. Notre Dame
14. Santa Clara
15. Ohio State
16. **Ga. Tech**
17. Fordham
18. Nebraska
19. Oklahoma
20. Michigan

1940
1. Minnesota
2. Stanford
3. Michigan
4. **Tennessee**
5. Boston Coll.
6. Texas A&M
7. Nebraska
8. Northwestern
9. **Miss. State**
10. Washington
11. Santa Clara
12. Fordham
13. Georgetown
14. Pennsylvania
15. Cornell
16. SMU
17. Hdn-Simmons
18. Duke
19. Lafayette

1941
1. Minnesota
2. Duke
3. Notre Dame
4. Texas
5. Michigan
6. Fordham
7. Missouri
8. Duquesne
9. Texas A&M
10. Navy
11. Northwestern
12. Oregon St.
13. Ohio State
14. **Georgia**
15. Pennsylvania
16. **Miss. State**
17. **Ole Miss**
18. **Tennessee**
19. Wash. State
20. **Alabama**

1942
1. Ohio State
2. **Georgia**
3. Wisconsin
4. Tulsa
5. **Ga. Tech**
6. Notre Dame
7. **Tennessee**
8. Boston Coll.
9. Michigan
10. **Alabama**
11. Texas
12. Stanford
13. UCLA
14. Wm. & Mary
15. Santa Clara
16. **Auburn**
17. Wash. State
18. **Miss. State**
19. Minnesota
    Holy Cross
    Penn State

1943
1. Notre Dame
2. Iowa P-F
3. Michigan
4. Navy
5. Purdue
6. Great Lakes
7. Duke
8. Del Monte P-F
9. Northwestern
10. March Field
11. Army
12. Washington
13. **Ga. Tech**
14. Texas
15. Tulsa
16. Dartmouth
17. Bainbridge NTS
18. Colorado Coll.
19. Pacific
20. Pennsylvania

1944
1. Army
2. Ohio State
3. Randolph Fld.
4. Navy
5. Bainbridge NTS
6. Iowa P-F
7. Southern Cal
8. Michigan
9. Notre Dame
10. March Field
11. Duke
12. **Tennessee**
13. **Ga. Tech**
    Norman P-F
15. Illinois
16. El Toro Mns.
17. Great Lakes
18. Fort Pierce
19. St. Mary's P-F
20. 2nd Air Force

1945
1. Army
2. **Alabama**
3. Navy
4. Indiana
5. Okla. State
6. Michigan
7. St. Mary's (Cal.)
8. Pennsylvania
9. Notre Dame
10. Texas
11. Southern Cal
12. Ohio State
13. Duke
14. **Tennessee**
15. **LSU**
16. Holy Cross
17. Tulsa
18. **Georgia**
19. Wake Forest
20. Columbia

1946
1. Notre Dame
2. Army
3. **Georgia**
4. UCLA
5. Illinois
6. Michigan
7. **Tennessee**
8. **LSU**
9. N. Carolina
10. Rice
11. Ga. Tech
12. Yale
13. Pennsylvania
14. Oklahoma
15. Texas
16. Arkansas
17. Tulsa
18. N.C. State
19. Delaware
20. Indiana

1947
1. Notre Dame
2. Michigan
3. SMU
4. Penn State
5. Texas
6. **Alabama**
7. Pennsylvania
8. Southern Cal
9. N. Carolina
10. **Ga. Tech**
11. Army
12. Kansas
13. **Ole Miss**
14. Wm. & Mary
15. California
16. Oklahoma
17. N.C. State
18. Rice
19. Duke
20. Columbia

1948
1. Michigan
2. Notre Dame
3. N. Carolina
4. California
5. Oklahoma
6. Army
7. Northwestern
8. **Georgia**
9. Oregon
10. SMU
11. Clemson
12. **Vanderbilt**
13. Tulane
14. Mich. State
15. **Ole Miss**
16. Minnesota
17. Wm. & Mary
18. Penn State
19. Cornell
20. Wake Forest

1949
1. Notre Dame
2. Oklahoma
3. California
4. Army
5. Rice
6. Ohio State
7. Michigan
8. Minnesota
9. **LSU**
10. Pacific
11. **Kentucky**
12. Cornell
13. Villanova
14. Maryland
15. Santa Clara
16. N. Carolina
17. **Tennessee**
18. Princeton
19. Mich. State
20. Missouri
    Baylor

1950
1. Oklahoma
2. Army
3. Texas
4. **Tennessee**
5. California
6. Princeton
7. **Kentucky**
8. Mich. State
9. Michigan
10. Clemson
11. Washington
12. Wyoming
13. Illinois
14. Ohio State
15. Miami, Fla.
16. **Alabama**
17. Nebraska
18. Wash. & Lee
19. Tulsa
20. **Tulane**

1951
1. **Tennessee**
2. Mich. State
3. Maryland
4. Illinois
5. **Ga. Tech**
6. Princeton
7. Stanford
8. Wisconsin
9. Baylor
10. Oklahoma
11. TCU
12. California
13. Virginia
14. S. Francisco
15. **Kentucky**
16. Boston U.
17. UCLA
18. Wash. State
19. Holy Cross
20. Clemson

1952
1. Mich. State
2. **Ga. Tech**
3. Notre Dame
4. Oklahoma
5. Southern Cal
6. UCLA
7. **Ole Miss**
8. **Tennessee**
9. **Alabama**
10. Texas
11. Wisconsin
12. Tulsa
13. Maryland
14. Syracuse
15. **Florida**
16. Duke
17. Ohio State
18. Purdue
19. Princeton
20. **Kentucky**

1953
1. Maryland
2. Notre Dame
3. Mich. State
4. Oklahoma
5. UCLA
6. Rice
7. Illinois
8. **Ga. Tech**
9. Iowa
10. W. Virginia
11. Texas
12. Texas Tech
13. **Alabama**
14. Army
15. Wisconsin
16. **Kentucky**
17. **Auburn**
18. Duke
19. Stanford
20. Michigan

1954
1. Ohio State
2. UCLA
3. Oklahoma
4. Notre Dame
5. Navy
6. **Ole Miss**
7. Army
8. Maryland
9. Wisconsin
10. Arkansas
11. Miami (Fla.)
12. W. Virginia
13. **Auburn**
14. Duke
15. Michigan
16. Va. Tech
17. Southern Cal
18. Baylor
19. Rice
20. Penn State

1955
1. Oklahoma
2. Mich. State
3. Maryland
4. UCLA
5. Ohio State
6. TCU
7. **Ga. Tech**
8. **Auburn**
9. Notre Dame
10. **Ole Miss**
11. Pittsburgh
12. Michigan
13. Southern Cal
14. Miami (Fla.)
15. Miami (Ohio)
16. Stanford
17. Texas A&M
18. Navy
19. W. Virginia
20. Army

306 Bowls & Polls

1956
1. Oklahoma
2. **Tennessee**
3. Iowa
4. **Ga. Tech**
5. Texas A&M
6. Miami (Fla.)
7. Michigan
8. Syracuse
9. Mich. State
10. Oregon St.
11. Baylor
12. Minnesota
13. Pittsburgh
14. TCU
15. Ohio State
16. Navy
17. Geo. Wash.
18. Southern Cal
19. Clemson
20. Colorado

1957
1. **Auburn**
2. Ohio State
3. Mich. State
4. Oklahoma
5. Navy
6. Iowa
7. **Ole Miss**
8. Rice
9. Texas A&M
10. Notre Dame
11. Texas
12. Ariz. State
13. **Tennessee**
14. **Miss. State**
15. N.C. State
16. Duke
17. **Florida**
18. Army
19. Wisconsin
20. VMI

1958
1. **LSU**
2. Iowa
3. Army
4. **Auburn**
5. Oklahoma
6. Air Force
7. Wisconsin
8. Ohio State
9. Syracuse
10. TCU
11. **Ole Miss**
12. Clemson
13. Purdue
14. **Florida**
15. S. Carolina
16. California
17. Notre Dame
18. SMU
19. Okla. State
20. Rutgers

1959
1. Syracuse
2. **Ole Miss**
3. **LSU**
4. Texas
5. **Georgia**
6. Wisconsin
7. TCU
8. Washington
9. Arkansas
10. **Alabama**
11. Clemson
12. Penn State
13. Illinois
14. Southern Cal
15. Oklahoma
16. Wyoming
17. Notre Dame
18. Missouri
19. **Florida**
20. Pittsburgh

1960
1. Minnesota
2. **Ole Miss**
3. Iowa
4. Navy
5. Missouri
6. Washington
7. Arkansas
8. Ohio State
9. **Alabama**
10. Duke
11. Kansas
12. Baylor
13. **Auburn**
14. Yale
15. Mich. State
16. Penn State
17. N. Mex. St.
18. **Florida**
19. Syracuse
    Purdue

1961
1. **Alabama**
2. Ohio State
3. Texas
4. **LSU**
5. **Ole Miss**
6. Minnesota
7. Colorado
8. Mich. State
9. Arkansas
10. Utah State
11. Missouri
12. Purdue
13. **Ga. Tech**
14. Syracuse
15. Rutgers
16. UCLA
17. Rice
    Penn State
    Arizona
20. Duke

1962
1. Southern Cal
2. Wisconsin
3. **Ole Miss**
4. Texas
5. **Alabama**
6. Arkansas
7. **LSU**
8. Oklahoma
9. Penn State
10. Minnesota
Only 10 ranked

1963
1. Texas
2. Navy
3. Illinois
4. Pittsburgh
5. **Auburn**
6. Nebraska
7. **Ole Miss**
8. **Alabama**
9. Oklahoma
10. Mich. State
Only 10 ranked

1964
1. **Alabama**
2. Arkansas
3. Notre Dame
4. Michigan
5. Texas
6. Nebraska
7. **LSU**
8. Oregon St.
9. Ohio State
10. Southern Cal
Only 10 ranked

1965
1. **Alabama**
2. Mich. State
3. Arkansas
4. UCLA
5. Nebraska
6. Missouri
7. **Tennessee**
8. **LSU**
9. Notre Dame
10. Southern Cal
Only 10 ranked

1966
1. Notre Dame
2. Mich. State
3. **Alabama**
4. **Georgia**
5. UCLA
6. Nebraska
7. Purdue
8. Ga. Tech
9. Miami (Fla.)
10. SMU
Only 10 ranked

1967
1. Southern Cal
2. **Tennessee**
3. Oklahoma
4. Indiana
5. Notre Dame
6. Wyoming
7. Oregon St.
8. **Alabama**
9. Purdue
10. Penn State
Only 10 ranked

1968
1. Ohio State
2. Penn State
3. Texas
4. Southern Cal
5. Notre Dame
6. Arkansas
7. Kansas
8. **Georgia**
9. Missouri
10. Purdue
11. Oklahoma
12. Michigan
13. **Tennessee**
14. SMU
15. Oregon St.
16. **Auburn**
17. **Alabama**
18. Houston
19. **LSU**
20. Ohio

1969
1. Texas
2. Penn State
3. Southern Cal
4. Ohio State
5. Notre Dame
6. Missouri
7. Arkansas
8. **Ole Miss**
9. Michigan
10. **LSU**
11. Nebraska
12. Houston
13. UCLA
14. **Florida**
15. **Tennessee**
16. Colorado
17. W. Virginia
18. Purdue
19. Stanford
20. **Auburn**

1970
1. Nebraska
2. Notre Dame
3. Texas
4. **Tennessee**
5. Ohio State
6. Ariz. State
7. **LSU**
8. Stanford
9. Michigan
10. **Auburn**
11. Arkansas
12. Toledo
13. Ga. Tech
14. Dartmouth
15. Southern Cal
16. Air Force
17. Tulane
18. Penn State
19. Houston
20. Oklahoma
    Ole Miss

1971
1. Nebraska
2. Oklahoma
3. Colorado
4. **Alabama**
5. Penn State
6. Michigan
7. **Georgia**
8. Ariz. State
9. **Tennessee**
10. Stanford
11. **LSU**
12. **Auburn**
13. Notre Dame
14. Toledo
15. **Ole Miss**
16. Arkansas
17. Houston
18. Texas
19. Washington
20. Southern Cal

1972
1. Southern Cal
2. Oklahoma
3. Texas
4. Nebraska
5. **Auburn**
6. Michigan
7. **Alabama**
8. **Tennessee**
9. Ohio State
10. Penn State
11. **LSU**
12. N. Carolina
13. Ariz. State
14. Notre Dame
15. UCLA
16. Colorado
17. N.C. State
18. Louisville
19. Wash. State
20. Ga. Tech

1973
1. Notre Dame
2. Ohio State
3. Oklahoma
4. **Alabama**
5. Penn State
6. Michigan
7. Nebraska
8. Southern Cal
9. Ariz. State
    Houston
11. Texas Tech
12. UCLA
13. **LSU**
14. Texas
15. Miami (Ohio)
16. N.C. State
17. Missouri
18. Kansas
19. **Tennessee**
20. Maryland
    Tulane

1974
1. Oklahoma
2. Southern Cal
3. Michigan
4. Ohio State
5. **Alabama**
6. Notre Dame
7. Penn State
8. **Auburn**
9. Nebraska
10. Miami (Ohio)
11. N.C. State
12. Mich. State
13. Maryland
14. Baylor
15. **Florida**
16. Texas A&M
17. **Miss. State**
    Texas
19. Houston
20. **Tennessee**

1975
1. Oklahoma
2. Ariz. State
3. **Alabama**
4. Ohio State
5. UCLA
6. Texas
7. Arkansas
8. Nebraska
9. Penn State
10. Penn State
11. Texas A&M
12. Miami (Ohio)
13. Maryland
14. California
15. Pittsburgh
16. Colorado
17. Southern Cal
18. Arizona
19. **Georgia**
20. W. Virginia

1994 SEC Football 307

Associated Press Final Rankings

1976
1. Pittsburgh
2. Southern Cal
3. Michigan
4. Houston
5. Oklahoma
6. Ohio State
7. Texas A&M
8. Maryland
9. Nebraska
10. **Georgia**
11. **Alabama**
12. Notre Dame
13. Texas Tech
14. Okla. State
15. UCLA
16. Colorado
17. Rutgers
18. **Kentucky**
19. Iowa State
20. **Miss. State**

1977
1. Notre Dame
2. **Alabama**
3. Arkansas
4. Texas
5. Penn State
6. **Kentucky**
7. Oklahoma
8. Pittsburgh
9. Michigan
10. Washington
11. Ohio State
12. Nebraska
13. Southern Cal
14. Florida State
15. Stanford
16. San Diego St.
17. N. Carolina
18. Ariz. State
19. Clemson
20. BYU

1978
1. **Alabama**
2. Southern Cal
3. Oklahoma
4. Penn State
5. Michigan
6. Clemson
7. Notre Dame
8. Nebraska
9. Texas
10. Houston
11. Arkansas
12. Mich. State
13. Purdue
14. UCLA
15. Missouri
16. **Georgia**
17. Stanford
18. N.C. State
19. Texas A&M
20. Maryland

1979
1. **Alabama**
2. Southern Cal
3. Oklahoma
4. Ohio State
5. Houston
6. Florida State
7. Pittsburgh
8. Arkansas
9. Nebraska
10. Purdue
11. Washington
12. Texas
13. BYU
14. Baylor
15. N. Carolina
16. **Auburn**
17. Temple
18. Michigan
19. Indiana
20. Penn State

1980
1. **Georgia**
2. Pittsburgh
3. Oklahoma
4. Michigan
5. Florida State
6. **Alabama**
7. Nebraska
8. Penn State
9. Notre Dame
10. N. Carolina
11. Southern Cal
12. BYU
13. UCLA
14. Baylor
15. Ohio State
16. Washington
17. Purdue
18. Miami (Fla.)
19. **Miss. State**
20. SMU

1981
1. Clemson
2. Texas
3. Penn State
4. Pittsburgh
5. SMU
6. **Georgia**
7. **Alabama**
8. Miami (Fla.)
9. N. Carolina
10. Washington
11. Nebraska
12. Michigan
13. BYU
14. Southern Cal
15. Ohio State
16. Arizona State
17. W. Virginia
18. Iowa
19. Missouri
20. Oklahoma

1982
1. Penn State
2. SMU
3. Nebraska
4. **Georgia**
5. UCLA
6. Ariz. State
7. Washington
8. Clemson
9. Arkansas
10. Pittsburgh
11. **LSU**
12. Ohio State
13. Florida State
14. **Auburn**
15. Southern Cal
16. Oklahoma
17. Texas
18. N. Carolina
19. W. Virginia
20. Maryland

1983
1. Miami (Fla.)
2. Nebraska
3. **Auburn**
4. **Georgia**
5. Texas
6. **Florida**
7. BYU
8. Michigan
9. Ohio State
10. Illinois
11. Clemson
12. SMU
13. Air Force
14. Iowa
15. **Alabama**
16. W. Virginia
17. UCLA
18. Pittsburgh
19. Boston Coll.
20. E. Carolina

1984
1. BYU
2. Washington
3. **Florida**
4. Nebraska
5. Boston Coll.
6. Oklahoma
7. Okla. State
8. SMU
9. UCLA
10. Southern Cal
11. S. Carolina
12. Maryland
13. Ohio State
14. **Auburn**
15. **LSU**
16. Iowa
17. Florida State
18. Miami (Fla.)
19. **Kentucky**
20. Virginia

1985
1. Oklahoma
2. Michigan
3. Penn State
4. **Tennessee**
5. **Florida**
6. Texas A&M
7. UCLA
8. Air Force
9. Miami (Fla.)
10. Iowa
11. Nebraska
12. Arkansas
13. **Alabama**
14. Ohio State
15. Florida State
16. BYU
17. Baylor
18. Maryland
19. Ga. Tech
20. **LSU**

1986
1. Penn State
2. Miami (Fla.)
3. Oklahoma
4. Ariz. State
5. Nebraska
6. **Auburn**
7. Ohio State
8. Michigan
9. **Alabama**
10. **LSU**
11. Arizona
12. Baylor
13. Texas A&M
14. UCLA
15. Arkansas
16. Iowa
17. Clemson
18. Washington
19. Boston Coll.
20. Virginia Tech

1987
1. Miami (Fla.)
2. Florida State
3. Oklahoma
4. Syracuse
5. **LSU**
6. Nebraska
7. **Auburn**
8. Mich. State
9. UCLA
10. Texas A&M
11. Okla. State
12. Clemson
13. **Georgia**
14. **Tennessee**
15. S. Carolina
16. Iowa
17. Notre Dame
18. Southern Cal
19. Michigan
20. Ariz. State

1988
1. Notre Dame
2. Miami (Fla.)
3. Florida State
4. Michigan
5. **W. Virginia**
6. UCLA
7. Southern Cal
8. **Auburn**
9. Clemson
10. Nebraska
11. Okla. State
12. Arkansas
13. Syracuse
14. Oklahoma
15. **Georgia**
16. Wash. State
17. **Alabama**
18. Houston
19. **LSU**
20. Indiana

1989
1. Miami (Fla.)
2. Notre Dame
3. Florida State
4. Colorado
5. **Tennessee**
6. **Auburn**
7. Michigan
8. Southern Cal
9. **Alabama**
10. Illinois
11. Nebraska
12. Clemson
13. Arkansas
14. Houston
15. Penn State
16. Mich. State
17. Pittsburgh
18. Virginia
19. Texas Tech
20. Texas A&M
21. W. Virginia
22. BYU
23. Washington
24. Ohio State
25. Arizona

1990
1. Colorado
2. Ga. Tech
3. Miami (Fla.)
4. Florida State
5. Washington
6. Notre Dame
7. Michigan
8. **Tennessee**
9. Clemson
10. Houston
11. Penn State
12. Texas
13. **Florida**
14. Louisville
15. Texas A&M
16. Mich. State
17. Oklahoma
18. Iowa
19. **Auburn**
20. Southern Cal
21. **Ole Miss**
22. BYU
23. Virginia
24. Nebraska
25. Illinois

1991
1. Miami (Fla.)
2. Washington
3. Penn State
4. Florida State
5. **Alabama**
6. Michigan
7. **Florida**
8. California
9. E. Carolina
10. Iowa
11. Syracuse
12. Texas A&M
13. Notre Dame
14. **Tennessee**
15. Nebraska
16. Oklahoma
17. **Georgia**
18. Clemson
19. UCLA
20. Colorado
21. Tulsa
22. Stanford
23. BYU
24. N.C. State
25. Air Force

1992
1. **Alabama**
2. Florida State
3. Miami
4. Notre Dame
5. Michigan
6. Syracuse
7. Texas A&M
8. **Georgia**
9. Stanford
10. **Florida**
11. Washington
12. **Tennessee**
13. Colorado
14. Nebraska
15. Wash. State
16. **Ole Miss**
17. N.Carolina State
18. Ohio State
19. N. Carolina
20. Hawaii
21. Boston Coll.
22. Kansas
23. **Miss. State**
24. Fresno State
25. Wake Forest

1993
1. Florida State
2. Notre Dame
3. Nebraska
4. **Auburn**
5. **Florida**
6. Wisconsin
7. West Virginia
8. Penn State
9. Texas A&M
10. Arizona
11. Ohio State
12. **Tennessee**
13. Boston College
14. **Alabama**
15. Miami
16. Colorado
17. Oklahoma
18. UCLA
19. North Carolina
20. Kansas State
21. Michigan
22. Virginia Tech
23. Clemson
24. Louisville
25. California

Alabama coach Paul "Bear" Bryant led the Crimson Tide to five No. 1 finishes in the AP poll.

Bowls & Polls

SEC Teams Ranked No. 1
(Week By Week AP Poll)

1939
Oct. 24 Tennessee
Oct. 31 Tennessee
Nov. 7 Tennessee
Nov. 14 Tennessee

1942
Nov. 3 Georgia
Nov. 10 Georgia
Nov. 17 Georgia

1951
Oct. 23 Tennessee
Oct. 30 Tennessee
Nov. 6 Tennessee
Nov. 20 Tennessee
Nov. 27 Tennessee
Dec. 4 Tennessee
National Champ — Tennessee

1956
Nov. 13 Tennessee

1957
Nov. 26 Auburn
Dec. 3 Auburn
National Champ _ Auburn

1958
Oct. 7 Auburn
Oct. 28 LSU
Nov. 4 LSU
Nov. 11 LSU
Nov. 18 LSU
Nov. 25 LSU
Dec. 2 LSU
National Champ — LSU

1959
Sept. 22 LSU
Sept. 29 LSU
Oct. 6 LSU
Oct. 13 LSU
Oct. 20 LSU
Oct. 27 LSU
Nov. 3 LSU

1960
Sept. 20 Ole Miss
Sept. 27 Ole Miss
Oct. 11 Ole Miss

1961
Oct. 10 Ole Miss
Nov. 21 Alabama
Nov. 28 Alabama
Nov. 5 Alabama
National Champ — Alabama

1962
Sept. 25 Alabama
Oct. 9 Alabama
Nov. 13 Alabama

1964
Dec. 1 Alabama
National Champ — Alabama

1965
Dec. 4 Alabama
National Champ — Alabama

1973
Nov. 27 Alabama
Dec. 4 Alabama

1978
Sept. 12 Alabama
Sept. 19 Alabama
Dec. 4 Alabama
National Champ — Alabama

1979
Oct. 16 Alabama
Oct. 23 Alabama
Oct. 30 Alabama
Nov. 6 Alabama
Nov. 13 Alabama
Nov. 20 Alabama
Nov. 27 Alabama
Dec. 3 Alabama
National Champ — Alabama

1980
Sept. 16 Alabama
Sept. 23 Alabama
Sept. 30 Alabama
Oct. 7 Alabama
Oct. 14 Alabama
Oct. 21 Alabama
Oct. 28 Alabama
Nov. 11 Georgia
Nov. 18 Georgia
Nov. 25 Georgia
Dec. 2 Georgia
Dec. 9 Georgia
National Champ — Georgia

1982
Nov. 9 Georgia
Nov. 16 Georgia
Nov. 23 Georgia
Nov. 30 Georgia
Dec. 7 Georgia

1985
Sept. 10 Auburn
Sept. 17 Auburn
Sept. 24 Auburn
Nov. 5 Florida

1992
National Champ — Alabama

NOTE: Arkansas was No. 1 in AP Poll of the week of Oct. 19, 1965.

UPI Final Rankings

1950
1. Oklahoma
2. Texas
3. **Tennessee**
4. California
5. Army
6. Michigan
7. **Kentucky**
8. Princeton
9. Mich. State
10. Ohio State
11. Illinois
12. Clemson
13. Miami (Fla.)
14. Wyoming
15. Washington
    Baylor
17. **Alabama**
18. Wash. & Lee
19. Navy
20. Nebraska
    Wisconsin
    Cornell

1951
1. **Tennessee**
2. Mich. State
3. Illinois
4. Maryland
5. **Ga. Tech**
6. Princeton
7. Stanford
8. Wisconsin
9. Baylor
10. TCU
11. Oklahoma
12. California
13. Notre Dame
14. S.Francisco
14. Purdue
14. Wash.State
17. Holy Cross
17. UCLA
    Kentucky
20. Kansas

1952
1. Mich.State
2. **Ga. Tech**
3. Notre Dame
4. Oklahoma
4. Southern Cal
6. UCLA
7. **Ole Miss**
8. **Tennessee**
9. **Alabama**
10. Wisconsin
11. Texas
12. Purdue
13. Maryland
14. Princeton
15. Ohio State
15. Pittsburgh
17. Navy
18. Duke
19. Houston
    Kentucky

1953
1. Maryland
2. Notre Dame
3. Mich.State
4. UCLA
5. Oklahoma
6. Rice
7. Illinois
8. Texas
9. **Ga. Tech**
10. Iowa
11. **Alabama**
12. Texas Tech
13. W.Virginia
14. Wisconsin
15. **Kentucky**
16. Army
17. Stanford
18. Duke
19. Michigan
20. Ohio State

1954
1. UCLA
2. Ohio State
3. Oklahoma
4. Notre Dame
5. Navy
6. **Ole Miss**
7. Army
8. Arkansas
9. Miami (Fla.)
10. Wisconsin
11. Southern Cal
    Maryland
    Ga. Tech
14. Duke
15. Michigan
16. Penn State
17. SMU
18. Denver
19. Rice
20. Minnesota

1955
1. Oklahoma
2. Mich State
3. Maryland
4. UCLA
5. Ohio State
6. TCU
7. **Ga. Tech**
8. **Auburn**
9. **Ole Miss**
10. Notre Dame
11. Pittsburgh
12. Southern Cal
13. Michigan
14. Texas A&M
15. Army
16. Duke
17. W.Virginia
18. Miami (Fla.)
19. Iowa
20. Navy
    Stanford
    Miami (Ohio)

1956
1. Oklahoma
2. **Tennessee**
3. Iowa
4. **Ga. Tech**
5. Texas A&M
6. Miami (Fla.)
7. Michigan
8. Syracuse
9. Minnesota
10. Mich.State
11. Baylor
12. Pittsburgh
13. Oregon State
14. TCU
15. Southern Cal
16. Wyoming
17. Yale
18. Colorado
19. Navy
20. Duke

1957
1. Ohio State
2. **Auburn**
3. Mich.State
4. Oklahoma
5. Iowa
6. Navy
7. Rice
8. **Ole Miss**
9. Notre Dame
10. Texas A&M
11. Texas
12. Ariz.State
13. Army
14. Duke
    Wisconsin
16. **Tennessee**
17. Oregon
18. Clemson
    UCLA
20. N.C.State

1958
1. **LSU**
2. Iowa
3. Army
4. **Auburn**
5. Oklahoma
6. Wisconsin
7. Ohio State
8. Air Force
9. TCU
10. Syracuse
11. Purdue
12. Ole Miss
13. Clemson
14. Notre Dame
15. **Florida**
16. California
17. Northwestern
18. SMU
(only 18 teams received votes)

1959
1. Syracuse
2. **Ole Miss**
3. **LSU**
4. Texas
5. **Georgia**
6. Wisconsin
7. Washington
8. TCU
9. Arkansas
10. Penn State
11. Illinois
12. Southern Cal
13. **Alabama**
14. Penn State
15. Oklahoma
    Northwestern
16. Mich.State
18. Wyoming
19. **Auburn**
    Missouri

1994 SEC Football   **309**

UPI Final Rankings

1960
1. Minnesota
2. Iowa
3. **Ole Miss**
4. Missouri
5. Washington
6. Navy
7. Arkansas
8. Ohio State
9. Kansas
10. **Alabama**
11. Duke
    Baylor
    Mich. State
14. **Auburn**
15. Purdue
16. **Florida**
17. Texas
18. Yale
19. N. Mex. St.
    Tennessee

1961
1. **Alabama**
2. Ohio State
3. **LSU**
4. Texas
5. **Ole Miss**
6. Minnesota
7. Colorado
8. Arkansas
9. Mich. State
10. Utah State
11. Purdue
    Missouri
13. **Ga. Tech**
14. Duke
15. Kansas
16. Syracuse
17. Wyoming
18. Wisconsin
19. Miami (Fla.)
    Penn State

1962
1. Southern Cal
2. Wisconsin
3. **Ole Miss**
4. Texas
5. **Alabama**
6. Arkansas
7. Oklahoma
8. **LSU**
9. Penn State
10. Minnesota
11. **Ga. Tech**
12. Missouri
13. Ohio State
14. Duke
15. Washington
16. Northwestern
    Oregon State
18. Ariz. State
    Illinois
    Miami (Fla.)

1963
1. Texas
2. Navy
3. Pittsburgh
4. Illinois
5. Nebraska
6. **Auburn**
7. **Ole Miss**
8. Oklahoma
9. **Alabama**
10. Mich. State
11. **Miss. State**
12. Syracuse
13. Ariz. State
14. Memphis St.
15. Washington
16. Penn State
    Southern Cal
    Missouri
19. N. Carolina
20. Baylor

1964
1. **Alabama**
2. Arkansas
3. Notre Dame
4. Michigan
5. Texas
6. Nebraska
7. **LSU**
8. Oregon St.
9. Ohio State
10. Southern Cal
11. Florida State
12. Syracuse
13. Princeton
14. Penn State
    Utah
16. Illinois
    New Mexico
18. Tulsa
    Missouri
20. **Ole Miss**
    Mich. State

1965
1. Mich. State
2. Arkansas
3. Nebraska
4. **Alabama**
5. UCLA
6. Missouri
7. **Tennessee**
8. Notre Dame
9. Southern Cal
10. Texas Tech
11. Ohio State
12. **Florida**
13. Purdue
14. **LSU**
15. **Georgia**
16. Tulsa
17. **Ole Miss**
18. **Kentucky**
19. Syracuse
20. Colorado

1966
1. Notre Dame
2. Mich. State
3. **Alabama**
4. **Georgia**
5. UCLA
6. Purdue
7. Nebraska
8. Ga. Tech
9. SMU
10. Miami (Fla.)
11. **Florida**
12. **Ole Miss**
13. Arkansas
14. **Tennessee**
15. Wyoming
16. Syracuse
17. Houston
18. Southern Cal
19. Oregon State
20. Va. Tech

1967
1. Southern Cal
2. **Tennessee**
3. Oklahoma
4. Notre Dame
5. Wyoming
6. Indiana
7. **Alabama**
8. Oregon State
9. Purdue
10. UCLA
11. Penn State
12. Syracuse
13. Colorado
14. Minnesota
15. Florida State
16. Miami (Fla.)
17. N.C. State
18. **Georgia**
19. Houston
20. Ariz. State

1968
1. Ohio State
2. Southern Cal
3. Penn State
4. **Georgia**
5. Texas
6. Kansas
7. **Tennessee**
8. Notre Dame
9. Arkansas
10. Oklahoma
11. Purdue
12. **Alabama**
13. Oregon State
14. Florida State
15. Michigan
16. SMU
17. Missouri
18. Ohio U.
    Minnesota
20. Houston
    Stanford

1969
1. Texas
2. Penn State
3. Arkansas
4. Southern Cal
5. Ohio State
6. Missouri
7. **LSU**
8. Michigan
9. Notre Dame
10. UCLA
11. **Tennessee**
12. Nebraska
13. **Ole Miss**
14. Stanford
15. **Auburn**
16. Houston
17. **Florida**
18. Purdue
    San Diego St.
    W. Virginia

1970
1. Texas
2. Ohio State
3. Nebraska
4. **Tennessee**
5. Notre Dame
6. **LSU**
7. Michigan
8. Ariz. State
9. **Auburn**
10. Stanford
11. Air Force
12. Arkansas
13. Houston
14. Dartmouth
15. Oklahoma
16. Colorado
17. Ga. Tech
    Toledo
19. Penn State
20. Southern Cal

1971
1. Nebraska
2. **Alabama**
3. Oklahoma
4. Michigan
5. **Auburn**
6. Ariz. State
7. Colorado
8. **Georgia**
9. **Tennessee**
10. **LSU**
11. Penn State
12. Texas
13. Toledo
14. Houston
15. Notre Dame
16. Stanford
17. Iowa State
18. N. Carolina
19. Florida State
20. Arkansas
    Ole Miss

1972
1. Southern Cal
2. Oklahoma
3. Ohio State
4. **Alabama**
5. Texas
6. Michigan
7. **Auburn**
8. Penn State
9. Nebraska
10. **LSU**
11. **Tennessee**
12. Notre Dame
13. Ariz. State
14. Colorado
15. N. Carolina
16. Louisville
17. UCLA
    Wash. State
19. Utah State
20. San Diego St.

1973
1. **Alabama**
2. Oklahoma
3. Ohio State
4. Notre Dame
5. Penn State
6. Michigan
7. Southern Cal
8. Texas
9. UCLA
10. Ariz. State
11. Nebraska
    Texas Tech
13. Houston
14. **LSU**
15. Kansas
    Tulane
17. Miami (Ohio)
18. Maryland
19. San Diego St.
20. **Florida**

1974
1. Southern Cal
2. **Alabama**
3. Ohio State
4. Notre Dame
5. Michigan
6. **Auburn**
7. Penn State
8. Nebraska
9. N.C. State
10. Miami (Ohio)
11. Houston
12. **Florida**
13. Maryland
14. Baylor
15. Texas A&M
    Tennessee
17. **Miss. State**
18. Mich. State
19. Tulsa
(Only 19 rated)

1975
1. Oklahoma
2. Ariz. State
3. **Alabama**
4. Ohio State
5. UCLA
6. Arkansas
7. Texas
8. Michigan
9. Nebraska
10. Penn State
11. Maryland
12. Texas A&M
13. Arizona
14. Pittsburgh
15. California
16. Miami (Ohio)
17. Notre Dame
18. W. Virginia
19. **Georgia**
20. Southern Cal

LSU coach Charlie McClendon led the Tigers to a 137-59-7 mark from 1962-79, including eight UPI Top 20 finishes.

310   Bowls & Polls

1976
1. Pittsburgh
2. Southern Cal
3. Michigan
4. Houston
5. Ohio State
6. Oklahoma
7. Nebraska
8. Texas A&M
9. **Alabama**
10. **Georgia**
11. Maryland
12. **Notre Dame**
13. Texas Tech
14. Okla. State
15. UCLA
16. Colorado
17. Rutgers
18. Iowa State
19. Baylor
    Kentucky

1977
1. Notre Dame
2. **Alabama**
3. Arkansas
4. Penn State
5. Texas
6. Oklahoma
7. Pittsburgh
8. Michigan
9. Washington
10. Nebraska
11. Florida State
12. Ohio State
    Southern Cal
14. N. Carolina
15. Stanford
16. North Texas
    BYU
18. Ariz. State
19. San Diego St.
    N.C. State

1978
1. Southern Cal
2. **Alabama**
3. Oklahoma
4. Penn State
5. Michigan
6. Notre Dame
7. Clemson
8. Nebraska
9. Texas
10. Arkansas
11. Houston
12. UCLA
13. Purdue
14. Missouri
15. **Georgia**
16. Stanford
17. Navy
18. Texas A&M
19. Ariz. State
    N.C. State

1979
1. **Alabama**
2. Southern Cal
3. Oklahoma
4. Ohio State
5. Houston
6. Pittsburgh
7. Nebraska
8. Florida State
9. Arkansas
    Purdue
11. Washington
12. BYU
13. Texas
14. N. Carolina
15. Baylor
16. Indiana
17. Temple
18. Penn State
19. Michigan
20. Missouri

1980
1. **Georgia**
2. Pittsburgh
3. Oklahoma
4. Michigan
5. Florida State
6. **Alabama**
7. Nebraska
8. Penn State
9. N. Carolina
10. Notre Dame
11. BYU
12. Southern Cal
13. Baylor
14. UCLA
15. Ohio State
16. Purdue
17. Washington
18. Miami (Fla.)
19. **Florida**
20. SMU

1981
1. Clemson
2. Pittsburgh
3. Penn State
4. Texas
5. **Georgia**
6. **Alabama**
7. Washington
8. N. Carolina
9. Nebraska
10. Michigan
11. BYU
12. Ohio State
13. Southern Cal
14. Oklahoma
15. Iowa
16. Arkansas
17. **Miss. State**
18. W. Virginia
19. Southern Miss.
20. Missouri

1982
1. Penn State
2. SMU
3. Nebraska
4. **Georgia**
5. UCLA
6. Ariz. State
7. Washington
8. Arkansas
9. Pittsburgh
10. Florida State
11. **LSU**
12. Ohio State
13. N. Carolina
14. **Auburn**
15. Michigan
16. Oklahoma
17. **Alabama**
18. Texas
19. W. Virginia
20. Maryland

1983
1. Miami (Fla.)
2. Nebraska
3. **Auburn**
4. **Georgia**
5. Texas
6. **Florida**
7. BYU
8. Ohio State
9. Michigan
10. Illinois
11. SMU
12. **Alabama**
13. UCLA
14. Iowa
15. Air Force
16. W. Virginia
17. Penn State
18. Okla. State
19. Pittsburgh
20. Boston Coll.

1984
1. BYU
2. Washington
3. Nebraska
4. Boston Coll.
5. Okla. State
6. Oklahoma
7. **Florida**
8. SMU
9. Southern Cal
10. UCLA
11. Maryland
12. Ohio State
13. S. Carolina
14. **Auburn**
15. Iowa
16. **LSU**
17. Virginia
18. West Virginia
19. **Kentucky**
    Florida State

1985
1. Oklahoma
2. Michigan
3. Penn State
4. **Tennessee**
5. Air Force
6. UCLA
7. Texas A&M
8. Miami (Fla.)
9. Iowa
10. Nebraska
11. Ohio State
12. Arkansas
13. Florida State
14. **Alabama**
15. Baylor
16. Fresno State
17. BYU
18. Ga. Tech
19. Maryland
20. **LSU**

1986
1. Penn State
2. Miami (Fla.)
3. Oklahoma
4. Nebraska
5. Ariz. State
6. Ohio State
7. Michigan
8. **Auburn**
9. **Alabama**
10. Arizona
11. **LSU**
12. Texas A&M
13. Baylor
14. UCLA
15. Iowa
16. Arkansas
17. Washington
18. Boston Coll.
19. Clemson
20. Florida State

1987
1. Miami (Fla.)
2. Florida State
3. Oklahoma
4. Syracuse
5. **LSU**
6. Nebraska
7. **Auburn**
8. Mich. State
9. Texas A&M
10. Clemson
11. UCLA
12. Okla. State
13. **Tennessee**
14. **Georgia**
15. S. Carolina
16. Iowa
17. Southern Cal
18. Michigan
19. Texas
20. Indiana

1988
1. Notre Dame
2. Miami (Fla.)
3. Florida State
4. Michigan
5. W. Virginia
6. UCLA
7. **Auburn**
8. Clemson
9. Southern Cal
10. Nebraska
11. Okla. State
12. Syracuse
13. Arkansas
14. Oklahoma
15. **Georgia**
16. Wash. State
17. **Alabama**
    N.C. State
19. Indiana
20. Wyoming

1989
1. Miami (Fla.)
2. Florida State
3. Notre Dame
4. Colorado
5. **Tennessee**
6. **Auburn**
7. **Alabama**
8. Michigan
9. Southern Cal
10. Illinois
11. Clemson
12. Nebraska
13. Arkansas
14. Penn State
15. Virginia
16. Texas Tech
    Mich. State
18. BYU
19. Pittsburgh
20. Washington

1990
1. Ga. Tech
2. Colorado
3. Miami (Fla.)
4. Florida State
5. Washington
6. Notre Dame
7. **Tennessee**
8. Michigan
9. Clemson
10. Penn State
11. Texas
12. Louisville
13. Texas A&M
14. Mich. State
15. Virginia
16. Iowa
17. BYU
    Nebraska
19. **Auburn**
20. San Jose St.
21. Syracuse
22. Southern Cal
23. **Ole Miss**
24. Illinois
25. Va. Tech

1991
1. Washington
2. Miami (Fla.)
3. Penn State
4. Florida State
5. **Alabama**
6. Michigan
7. **Florida**
8. California
9. E. Carolina
10. Iowa
11. Syracuse
12. Notre Dame
13. Texas A&M
14. **Tennessee**
15. Nebraska
16. Oklahoma
17. Clemson
18. Colorado
19. UCLA
20. **Georgia**
21. Tulsa
22. Stanford
23. N.C. State
24. BYU
25. Ohio State

1992
1. **Alabama**
2. Florida State
3. Miami
4. Notre Dame
5. Michigan
6. Syracuse
7. Texas A&M
8. **Georgia**
9. Stanford
10. **Florida**
11. Washington
12. **Tennessee**
13. Colorado
14. Nebraska
15. Wash. State
16. **Ole Miss**
17. N. C. State
18. N. Carolina
19. Ohio State
20. Hawaii
21. Boston Coll.
22. Kansas
23. Fresno State
24. Penn State
25. **Miss. State**

1993
1. Florida State
2. Notre Dame
3. Nebraska
4. **Florida**
5. Wisconsin
6. Texas A&M
7. Penn State
8. West Virginia
9. Ohio State
10. Arizona
11. Boston College
12. **Tennessee**
13. **Alabama**
14. Miami
15. Oklahoma
16. Colorado
17. UCLA
18. Kansas State
19. Michigan
20. North Carolina
21. Virginia Tech
22. Louisville
23. Clemson
24. California
25. Southern Cal

Note: The AFCA poll was conducted by USA Today/CNN beginning in 1991. Beginning in 1991, the UPI Poll was decided by a vote of sportswriters.

1994 SEC Football   311

USA Today/CNN Final Rankings

1982
1. Penn State
2. SMU
3. Nebraska
4. **Georgia**
5. UCLA
6. Arizona State
7. Pittsburgh
8. Arkansas
9. Clemson
10. Washington
11. **LSU**
12. Florida State
13. Ohio State
14. Southern Cal
15. Oklahoma
16. **Auburn**
17. West Virginia
18. Maryland
19. North Carolina
20. Texas
21. Michigan
22. **Alabama**
23. Tulsa
24. Iowa
25. **Florida**

1983
1. Miami (Fla.)
2. **Auburn**
3. Nebraska
4. **Georgia**
5. Texas
6. BYU
7. Michigan
8. Ohio State
9. **Florida**
10. Clemson
11. Illinois
12. SMU
13. **Alabama**
14. Air Force
15. West Virginia
16. Iowa
17. **Tennessee**
18. UCLA
19. Pittsburgh
20. Penn State
21. Oklahoma
22. Boston College
23. Oklahoma State
24. Maryland
25. East Carolina

1984
1. BYU
2. Washington
3. **Florida**
4. Nebraska
5. Oklahoma
6. Boston College
7. Oklahoma State
8. SMU
9. Maryland
10. South Carolina
11. Southern Cal
12. UCLA
13. **LSU**
14. Ohio State
15. **Auburn**
16. Miami (Fla.)
17. Florida State
18. Virginia
19. **Kentucky**
20. Iowa
21. West Virginia
22. Army
23. **Georgia**
24. Air Force
25. Notre Dame

1985
1. Oklahoma
2. Penn State
3. Michigan
4. **Tennessee**
5. **Florida**
6. Miami (Fla.)
7. Air Force
8. Texas A&M
9. UCLA
10. Iowa
11. Nebraska
12. **Alabama**
13. Ohio State
14. Florida State
15. Arkansas
16. BYU
17. Maryland
18. Georgia Tech
19. Baylor
20. **Auburn**
21. **LSU**
22. Army
23. Fresno State
24. **Georgia**
25. Oklahoma State

1986
1. Penn State
2. Miami (Fla.)
3. Oklahoma
4. Nebraska
5. Arizona State
6. Ohio State
7. **Auburn**
8. Michigan
9. **Alabama**
10. **LSU**
11. Arizona
12. Texas A&M
13. UCLA
14. Baylor
15. Boston College
16. Iowa
17. Arkansas
18. Clemson
19. Washington
20. Virginia Tech
21. Florida State
22. Stanford
23. **Georgia**
24. N. C. State
25. San Diego State

1987
1. Miami (Fla.)
2. Florida State
3. Oklahoma
4. Syracuse
5. Nebraska
6. **LSU**
7. **Auburn**
8. Michigan State
9. Texas A&M
10. UCLA
11. Clemson
12. Oklahoma State
13. **Georgia**
14. **Tennessee**
15. Iowa
16. Notre Dame
17. Southern Cal
18. South Carolina
19. Michigan
20. Texas
21. Pittsburgh
22. Indiana
23. Penn State
24. Ohio State
25. **Alabama**

1988
1. Notre Dame
2. Miami (Fla.)
3. Florida State
4. UCLA
5. Michigan
6. West Virginia
7. Southern Cal
8. Nebraska
9. **Auburn**
10. Clemson
11. Oklahoma State
12. Syracuse
13. Oklahoma
14. Arkansas
15. Washington State
16. **Georgia**
17. **Alabama**
18. N.C. State
19. Houston
20. Indiana
21. Wyoming
22. **LSU**
23. Colorado
24. Southern Miss
25. BYU

1989
1. Miami (Fla.)
2. Notre Dame
3. Florida State
4. Colorado
5. **Tennessee**
6. **Auburn**
7. Southern Cal
8. Michigan
9. **Alabama**
10. Illinois
11. Nebraska
12. Clemson
13. Arkansas
14. Houston
15. Penn State
16. Virginia
17. Michigan State
18. Texas Tech
19. Pittsburgh
20. Texas A&M
21. West Virginia
22. BYU
23. Syracuse
24. Ohio State
25. Washington

1990
1. Colorado
2. Georgia Tech
3. Miami (Fla.)
4. Florida State
5. Washington
6. Notre Dame
7. **Tennessee**
8. Michigan
9. Clemson
10. Texas
11. Penn State
12. Houston
13. **Florida**
14. Louisville
15. Michigan State
16. Texas A&M
17. Oklahoma
18. Iowa
19. **Auburn**
20. BYU
21. **Ole Miss**
22. Southern Cal
23. Nebraska
24. Illinois
25. Virginia

1991
1. Washington
2. Miami (Fla.)
3. Penn State
4. Florida State
5. **Alabama**
6. Michigan
7. California
8. **Florida**
9. East Carolina
10. Iowa
11. Syracuse
12. Notre Dame
13. Texas A&M
14. Oklahoma
15. **Tennessee**
16. Nebraska
17. Clemson
18. UCLA
19. **Georgia**
20. Colorado
21. Tulsa
22. Stanford
23. BYU
24. Air Force
25. N.C. State

1992
1. **Alabama**
2. Florida State
3. Miami
4. Notre Dame
5. Michigan
6. Texas A&M
7. Syracuse
8. **Georgia**
9. Stanford
10. Washington
11. **Florida**
12. **Tennessee**
13. Colorado
14. Nebraska
15. N. C. State
16. **Ole Miss**
17. Washington State
18. North Carolina
19. Ohio State
20. Hawaii
21. Boston College
22. Fresno State
23. Kansas
24. Penn State
25. Wake Forest

1993
1. Florida State
2. Notre Dame
3. Nebraska
4. **Florida**
5. Wisconsin
6. West Virginia
7. Penn State
8. Texas A&M
9. Arizona
10. Ohio State
11. **Tennessee**
12. Boston College
13. **Alabama**
14. Oklahoma
15. Miami
16. Colorado
17. UCLA
18. Kansas State
19. Michigan
20. Virginia Tech
21. North Carolina
22. Clemson
23. Louisville
24. California
25. Southern Cal

COACHES

Coach Terry Bowden received consensus 1993 National Coach of the Year honors after guiding Auburn to an 11-0 record in his first season at the helm of the Tiger program.

SEC Coaches' Records

ALABAMA

Coach	Tenure	Conference W-L-T	Overall W-L-T
E.B. Beaumont	1892	—	2-2-0
Eli Abbott	1893-95, 1902	—	7-12-0
Otto Wagonhurst	1896	—	2-1-0
Allen McCants	1897	—	1-0-0
W.A. Martin	1899	—	3-1-0
M. Griffin	1900	—	2-3-0
M.H. Harvey	1901	—	2-1-2
W.B. Blount	1903-04	—	10-7-0
Jack Leavenworth	1905	—	6-4-0
J.W.H. Pollard	1906-09	—	20-4-5
Guy Lowman	1910	—	4-4-0
D.V. Graves	1911-14	—	21-12-3
Thomas Kelly	1915-17	—	17-7-1
Xen C. Scott	1919-22	—	29-9-3
Wallace Wade	1923-30	—	61-13-3
Frank Thomas	1931-46	59-16-6	115-24-7
Harold (Red) Drew	1947-54	33-21-7	54-29-7
J. B. Whitworth	1955-57	3-18-1	4-24-2
Paul (Bear) Bryant	1958-82	137-28-5	232-46-9
Ray Perkins	1983-86	14-9-1	32-15-1
Bill Curry	1987-89	14-6-0	26-10-0
Gene Stallings	1990-93	24-5-1	40-9-1

ARKANSAS

Coach	Tenure	Conference W-L-T	Overall W-L-T
John C. Futrall	1894-96	—	5-2-0
B.N. Wilson	1897-98	—	4-1-1
Colbert Searles	1899-1900	—	5-2-2
Charles Thomas	1901-02	—	9-8-0
D.A. McDaniel	1903	—	3-4-0
A.D. Brown	1904-05	—	6-9-0
F.C. Longman	1906-07	—	5-8-3
Hugo Bezdek	1908-12	—	29-13-1
E.T. Pickering	1913-14	—	11-7-0
T.T. McConnell	1915-16	1-3-0	8-6-1
Norman Paine	1917-18	0-2-1	8-3-1
J.B. Craig	1919	1-2-0	3-4-0
G.W. McLaren	1920-21	4-1-1	8-5-3
Francis Schmidt	1922-28	14-13-2	42-20-3
Fred Thomsen	1929-41	26-42-3	56-61-1
George Cole	1942	0-6-0	3-7-0
John Tomlin	1943	1-4-0	2-7-0
Glen Rose	1944-45	3-7-1	8-12-1
John Barnhill	1946-49	10-13-1	22-17-3
Otis Douglas	1950-52	4-14-0	9-21-0
Bowden Wyatt	1953-54	7-5-0	11-10-0
Jack Mitchell	1955-57	8-9-1	17-12-1
Frank Broyles	1958-76	91-35-5	144-58-5
Lou Holtz	1977-83	37-18-1	60-21-2
Ken Hatfield	1984-89	36-10-0	55-17-1
Jack Crowe	1990-91	6-10-0	9-15-0
Joe Kines#	1992	3-4-1	3-6-1
Danny Ford	1993	3-4-1	5-5-1

#Interim head coach after first game of 1992 season.
*Southwest Conference 1915-1991

AUBURN

Coach	Tenure	Conference W-L-T	Overall W-L-T
Dr. George Petrie	1892	—	2-2-0
G.H. Harvey, D.M. Balliet	1893	—	3-0-2
F.M. Hall	1894	—	1-3-0
John Heisman	1895-99	—	12-4-2
Billy Watkins	1900-01	—	6-3-1
R.S. Kent	1902	—	2-2-1
Mike Harvey	1902	—	0-2-0
Billy Bates	1903	—	4-3-0
Mike Donahue	1904-06, 1908-22	—	99-35-5
W.S. Kienholz	1907	—	6-2-1
Boozer Pitts	1923-24; 1927	—	7-11-6
Dave Morey	1925-27	—	10-10-1
George Bohler	1928-29	—	3-11-0
John Floyd	1929	—	0-4-0
Chet Wynne	1930-33	2-2-0	22-15-2
Jack Meagher	1934-42	26-25-7	48-37-10
Carl Voyles	1944-47	4-17-0	15-22-0
Earl Brown	1948-50	2-18-2	3-22-4
Ralph (Shug) Jordan	1951-75	98-63-4	176-83-6
Doug Barfield	1976-80	15-14-1	29-25-1
Pat Dye	1981-92	48-27-1	99-39-4
Terry Bowden	1993	8-0-0	11-0-0

FLORIDA

Coach	Tenure	Conference W-L-T	Overall W-L-T
Jack Forsythe	1906-08	—	14-6-2
G.E. Pyle	1909-13	—	26-7-3
Charles McCoy	1914-16	—	9-10-0
A.L. Busser	1917-19	—	7-8-0
William Kline	1920-22	—	19-8-2
Gen. VanFleet	1923-24	—	12-3-4
H.L. Sebring	1925-27	—	17-11-2
Charles Bachman	1928-32	—	27-18-3
D.K. (Dutch) Stanley	1933-35	5-11-1	14-13-2
Josh Cody	1936-39	6-14-2	17-24-2
Tom Lieb	1940-45	5-15-1	20-26-1
Ray (Bear) Wolf	1946-49	2-17-2	13-24-2
Bob Woodruff	1950-59	29-32-2	54-41-6
Ray Graves	1960-69	36-19-3	70-31-4
Doug Dickey	1970-78	28-28-1	58-42-2
Charley Pell	1979-84	14-16-1	33-26-2
Galen Hall*	1984-88	24-14-0	37-16-1
Gary Darnell#	1989	2-2-0	3-4-0
Steve Spurrier	1990-93	26-4-0	39-10-0

*Replaced Charley Pell after third game of the 1984 season
#Interim head coach after fifth game of 1989 season

Frank Thomas Alabama **Doug Barfield** Auburn **Ray Graves** Florida

Coaches

GEORGIA

Coach	Tenure	Conference W-L-T	Overall W-L-T
Dr. Charles Herty	1892	—	1-1-0
Ernest Brown	1893	—	2-2-1
Robert Winston	1894	—	5-1-0
Glenn "Pop" Warner	1895-96	—	7-4-0
Charles McCarthy	1897-98	—	6-3-0
Gordon Saussy	1899	—	2-3-1
E.E. Jones	1900	—	2-4-0
Billy Reynolds	1901-02	—	5-7-3
M.M. Dickinson	1903, 1905	—	4-9-0
Charles A. Barnard	1904	—	1-5-0
W.S. Whitney	1906-07	—	6-7-2
Branch Bocock	1908	—	5-2-1
J. Coulter, Frank Dobson	1909	—	1-4-2
W.A. Cunningham	1910-19	—	43-18-9
H.J. Stegeman	1920-22	—	20-6-3
George Woodruff	1923-27	—	30-16-1
Harry Mehre	1928-37	12-12-2	59-34-6
Joel Hunt	1938	1-2-1	5-4-1
Wallace Butts	1939-60	67-60-5	140-86-9
Johnny Griffith	1961-63	6-12-1	10-16-4
Vince Dooley	1964-88	105-41-4	201-77-10
Ray Goff	1989-93	18-19-0	34-24-0

KENTUCKY

Coach	Tenure	Conference W-L-T	Overall W-L-T
Unknown	1891	—	1-1-0
A.M. Miller	1892	—	2-4-1
John A. Thompson	1892-93	—	5-2-1
W.P. Finney	1894	—	5-2-0
Charles Mason	1895	—	4-5-0
Dudley Short	1896	—	3-6-0
Lyman B. Eaton	1897	—	2-4-0
W.R. Bass	1898-99	—	12-2-2
W.H. Kiler	1900-01	—	6-12-1
E.W. McLeod	1902	—	3-5-1
C.A. Wright	1903	—	7-1-0
F.E. Schact	1904	—	15-4-1
J. White Guyn	1906-08	—	17-7-1
R. Sweetland	1909-10, 1912	—	23-5-0
P.P. Douglass	1911	—	7-3-0
Alpha Brumage	1913-14	—	11-5-0
J.J. Tigert	1915-16	—	10-2-3
S.A. Boles	1917	—	3-5-1
Andy Gill	1918-19	—	5-5-1
W.J. Juneau	1920-22	—	13-10-2
J. Winn	1923	—	4-3-2
Fred J. Murphy	1924-26	—	12-14-1
Harry Gammage	1927-33	2-3-0	32-25-5
Chet Wynne	1934-37	5-14-0	20-19-0
A.D. Kirwan	1938-44	4-22-3	24-28-4
Bernie Shively	1945	0-5-0	2-8-0
Paul (Bear) Bryant	1946-53	22-18-4	60-23-5
Blanton Collier	1954-61	21-34-3	41-36-3
Charlie Brandshaw	1962-68	12-30-2	25-41-4
John Ray	1969-72	4-24-0	10-33-0
Fran Curci	1973-81	25-30-0	47-51-2
Jerry Claiborne	1982-89	13-37-0	41-46-3
Bill Curry	1990-93	9-21-0	17-28-0

LSU

Coach	Tenure	Conference W-L-T	Overall W-L-T
Dr. Charles E. Coates	1893	—	0-1-0
Albert P. Simmons	1894-95	—	5-1-0
Allen W. Jeardeau	1896-97	—	7-1-0
Edmond A. Chavanne	1898, 1900	—	3-2-0
John P. Gregg	1899	—	3-2-0
W.S. Boreland	1901-03	—	15-7-0
D.A. Killian	1904-06	—	8-6-2
Edgar R. Wingard	1907-08	—	17-3-0
Joe G. Pritchard	1909	—	4-1-0
John W. Mayhew	1910	—	3-6-0
James K. Dwyer	1911-13	—	16-7-2
E.T. McDonald	1914-16	—	14-7-1
Dana X. Bible	1916	—	1-0-2
Wayne Sutton	1917	—	3-5-0
Irving R. Pray	1916, 1919, 1922	—	11-9-0
Branch Bocock	1920-21	—	11-4-2
Mike Donahue	1923-27	—	23-19-3
Russ Cohen	1928-31	—	23-13-1
Biff Jones	1932-34	7-2-2	20-5-6
Bernie H. Moore	1935-47	23-28-4	83-39-6
Gaynell Tinsley	1948-54	17-25-6	35-34-6
Paul F. Dietzel	1955-61	26-16-2	46-23-3
Charlie McClendon	1962-79	62-38-0	137-59-7
Jerry Stovall	1980-83	9-13-2	22-21-2
Bill Arnsparger	1984-86	13-3-2	26-8-2
Mike Archer	1987-90	15-12-0	27-18-1
Curley Hallman	1991-93	7-18-0	12-21-0

OLE MISS

Coach	Tenure	Conference W-L-T	Overall W-L-T
Dr. A.L. Bondurant	1893	—	4-1-0
C.D. Clark	1894	—	6-1-0
H.L. Fairbanks	1895	—	2-1-0
J.W. Holister	1896	—	1-2-0
T.G. Scarbrough	1898	—	1-1-0
W.H. Lyon	1899	—	3-4-0
Z.N. Estes, Jr.	1900	—	0-3-0
Daniel Martin, William Shibley	1901	—	2-4-0
Daniel Martin	1902	—	4-3-0
Mike Harvey	1903-04	—	6-4-1
T.S. Hammond	1906	—	4-2-0
Frank Mason	1907	—	0-6-0
Frank Kyle	1908	—	3-5-0
Dr. N.P. Stauffer	1909-11	—	17-7-2
Leo DeTray	1912	—	5-3-0
William Driver	1913-14	—	11-7-2
Fred Robbins	1915-16	—	5-12-0
C.R. (Dudy) Noble	1917-18	—	2-7-1
R.L. Sullivan	1919-21	—	11-13-0
R.A. Cowell	1922-23	—	8-11-1
Chester Barnard	1924	—	4-5-0
Homer Hazel	1925-29	—	21-22-3
Ed. L. Walker	1930-37	7-13-3	38-38-8
Harry Mehre	1938-45	15-17-1	39-26-1
Harold (Red) Drew	1946	1-6-0	2-7-0
John Vaught	1947-70, 73	106-41-10	190-60-12
Billy Kinard	1971-73	6-7-0	16-9-0
Ken Cooper	1974-77	12-14-0	21-23-0
Steve Sloan	1978-82	8-18-1	20-34-1
Billy Brewer	1983-93	33-41-0	67-55-3

1994 SEC Football

SEC Coaches' Records

MISSISSIPPI STATE

Coach	Tenure	Conference W-L-T	Overall W-L-T
Dr. Charles Herty	1892	—	1-1-0
W.M. Matthews	1895	—	0-2-0
J.B. Hildebrand	1896	—	0-4-0
L.B. Harvey	1901	—	2-2-1
L. Gwinn	1902	—	1-4-1
Dan Martin	1903-06	—	10-11-3
Fred Furman	1907-08	—	9-7-0
W.D. Chadwick	1909-13	—	29-12-2
E.C. Hayes	1914-16	—	15-8-2
Sid Robinson	1917-19	—	15-5-0
Fred Holtkamp	1920-21	—	9-7-1
C.R. (Dudy) Noble	1922	—	3-4-2
Earl Able	1923-24	—	10-6-2
Bernie Bierman	1925-26	—	8-8-1
J.W. Hancock	1927-29	—	8-12-4
Chris Cagle	1930	—	2-7-0
Ray Dauber	1931-32	—	5-11-0
Ross McKechnie	1933-34	1-10-1	7-12-1
Ralph Sasse	1935-37	8-7-0	20-10-2
Emerson (Spike) Nelson	1938	1-4-0	4-6-0
Allyn McKeen	1939-48	29-16-2	65-19-3
Arthur (Slick) Morton	1949-51	5-15-0	8-18-1
Murray Warmath	1952-53	6-5-3	10-6-3
Darrell Royal	1954-55	7-7-0	12-8-0
Wade Walker	1956-61	8-30-2	22-32-2
Paul Davis	1962-66	9-22-2	20-28-2
Charley Shira	1967-72	5-32-1	16-45-2
Bob Tyler	1973-78	7-30-0	21-44-2
Emory Bellard	1979-85	15-27-0	37-42-0
Rockey Felker	1986-90	5-23-0	21-34-0
Jackie Sherrill	1991-93	10-12-1	17-16-2

SOUTH CAROLINA

Coach	Tenure	Conference W-L-T	Overall W-L-T
W.A. Whaley	1896	—	1-3-0
W.P. Murphy	1897	—	0-3-0
W. Wertenbaker	1898	—	1-2-0
I.O. Hunt	1899-90	—	6-6-0
B.W. Dickson	1901	—	3-4-0
C.R. Williams	1902-03	—	14-3-0
Christie Benet	1904-05, 1908-09	—	14-15-3
Douglas McKay	1907	—	3-0-0
John H. Neff	1910-11	—	5-8-2
N.B. Edgerton	1912-15	—	19-13-3
Rice Warren	1916	—	3-6-0
Dixon Foster	1917, 1991	—	4-12-1
Frank Dobson	1918	—	2-1-1
Sol Metzger	1920-24	—	26-18-2
Branch Bocock	1925-26	—	13-7-0
Harry Lightsey	1927	—	4-5-0
Billy Lavall	1928-34	5-3-0	39-26-6
Don McCallister	1935-37	5-11-1	13-20-1
Rex Enright	1938-42, 1946-55	36-43-3	64-69-7
J.P. Moran	1943	2-1-0	5-2-0
William Newton	1944	1-3-0	3-4-2
Johnnie McMillan	1945	0-3-2	2-4-3
Warren Giese	1956-60	19-15-1	28-21-1
Marvin Bass	1961-65	13-18-1	17-29-4
Paul Dietzel	1966-74	18-10-1	42-53-1
Jim Carlen	1975-81	—	45-36-1
Richard Bell	1982	—	4-7-0
Joe Morrison	1983-88	—	39-28-2
Sparky Woods	1989-93	5-11-0	24-28-3

*Southern Conference 1933-52; Atlantic Coast Conference 1953-70

TENNESSEE

Coach	Tenure	Conference W-L-T	Overall W-L-T
J.A. Pierce	1899-1900	—	8-4-1
George Kelley	1901	—	3-3-2
H.F. Fisher	1902-03	—	10-7-0
S.D. Crawford	1904	—	3-5-1
J.D. DePree	1905-06	—	4-11-3
George Levene	1907-09	—	15-10-3
Andrew A. Stone	1910	—	3-5-1
Z.G. Clevenger	1911-15	—	26-15-2
John R. Bender	1916-20	—	18-5-4
M.B. Banks	1921-25	—	27-15-3
Robert R. Neyland	1926-34, 36-40, 46-52	62-15-5	173-31-12
W.H. (Bill) Britton	1935	2-3-0	4-5-0
John H. Barnhill	1941-45	15-3-1	33-6-0
Harvey L. Robinson	1953-54	4-7-1	10-10-1
Bowden Wyatt	1955-62	29-23-4	49-29-4
Jim McDonald	1963	3-5-0	5-5-0
Doug Dickey	1964-69	21-10-4	46-15-4
Bill Battle	1970-76	22-18-1	59-22-4
Johnny Majors	1977-92	57-40-3	115-62-8
Phillip Fulmer#	1992-93	8-1-1	13-2-1

#Interim head coach for four games of 1992 season.

VANDERBILT

Coach	Tenure	Conference W-L-T	Overall W-L-T
Elliott H. Jones	1890-92	—	8-5-0
W.J. Keller	1893	—	6-1-0
Henry Thornton	1894	—	7-1-0
C.L. Upton	1895	—	5-3-1
R.G. Acton	1896-1898	—	10-7-3
J.L. Crane	1899-1900	—	11-6-1
W.H. Watkins	1901-02	—	14-2-1
J.H. Henry	1903	—	6-1-1
Dan McGugin	1904-17, 19-34	6-5-2	197-55-19
Ray Morrison	1935-39	15-15-1	25-20-2
H.R. (Red) Sanders	1940-42, 46-48	16-20-2	36-22-2
E.H. (Herc) Alley	1943	0-0-0	5-0-0
Doby Bartling	1944-45	2-4-0	6-6-1
W.M. (Bill) Edwards	1945-52	11-17-1	21-19-2
Arthur L. Guepe	1953-62	18-43-6	39-54-7
Jack Green	1963-66	2-19-3	7-29-4
Bill Pace	1967-72	5-27-1	22-38-3
Steve Sloan	1973-74	3-8-1	12-9-1
Fred Pancoast	1975-78	2-22-0	13-31-0
George MacIntyre	1979-85	8-33-1	25-52-1
Watson Brown	1986-90	4-29-0	10-45-0
Gerry DiNardo	1991-93	6-17-0	13-20-0

Emory Bellard Miss. State

Bill Battle Tennessee

Bill Pace Vanderbilt

Coaches

SEC Coach Of The Year

National Coach of the Year

1942—Bill Alexander, Georgia Tech (AFCA)
1956—Bowden Wyatt, Tennessee (AFCA)
1958—Paul Dietzel, LSU (AFCA, FWA)
1961—Paul "Bear" Bryant, Alabama (AFCA)
1970—Charlie McClendon, LSU (AFCA)
1971—Paul "Bear" Bryant, Alabama (AFCA)
1973—Paul "Bear" Bryant, Alabama (AFCA)
1980—Vince Dooley, Georgia (AFCA, FWA, WC)
1982—Jerry Stovall, LSU (WC)
1992—Gene Stallings, Alabama (AFCA, FWA, WC)
1993—Terry Bowden, Auburn (AFCA, FWA, WC)

AFCA—American Football Coaches Association
FWA—Football Writers of America
WC—Walter Camp

AP SEC Coach of the Year

1946—Wally Butts, Georgia
1947—John Vaught, Ole Miss
1948—John Vaught, Ole Miss
1949—Gaynell Tinsley, LSU
1950—Paul Bryant, Kentucky
1951—Bob Neyland, Tennessee
1952—Bobby Dodd, Georgia Tech
1953—Ralph Jordan, Auburn
1954—John Vaught, Ole Miss
1955—John Vaught, Ole Miss
1956—Bowden Wyatt, Tennessee
1957—Ralph Jordan, Auburn
1958—Paul Dietzel, LSU
1959—Paul Bryant, Alabama
1960—John Vaught, Ole Miss
1961—Paul Bryant, Alabama
1962—John Vaught, Ole Miss
1963—Paul Davis, Miss. State
1964—Paul Bryant, Alabama
1965—Paul Bryant, Alabama
1966—Vince Dooley, Georgia
1967—Doug Dickey, Tennessee
1968—Vince Dooley, Georgia
1969—Charlie McClendon, LSU
1970—Charlie Shira, Miss. State
1971—Paul Bryant, Alabama
1972—Ralph Jordan, Auburn
1973—Paul Bryant, Alabama
1974—Steve Sloan, Vanderbilt
1975—Ken Cooper, Ole Miss
1976—Vince Dooley, Georgia
1977—Fran Curci, Kentucky
1978—Paul Bryant, Alabama
1979—Paul Bryant, Alabama
1980—Vince Dooley, Georgia
1981—Paul Bryant, Alabama
1982—Jerry Stovall, LSU
1983—Billy Brewer, Ole Miss
  Jerry Claiborne, Kentucky
1984—Galen Hall, Florida
1985—Johnny Majors, Tennessee
1986—Bill Arnsparger, LSU
1987—Pat Dye, Auburn
1988—Pat Dye, Auburn
1989—Bill Curry, Alabama
1990—Steve Spurrier, Florida
1991—Gerry DiNardo, Vanderbilt
1992—Gene Stallings, Alabama
1993—Terry Bowden, Auburn

UPI SEC Coach of the Year

1960—John Vaught, Ole Miss
1961—Paul Bryant, Alabama
1962—John Vaught, Ole Miss
1963—Ralph Jordan, Auburn
1964—Paul Bryant, Alabama
1965—Paul Bryant, Alabama
1966—Vince Dooley, Georgia
1967—Doug Dickey, Tennessee
1968—Vince Dooley, Georgia
1969—Charlie McClendon, LSU
1970—Charlie McClendon, LSU
1971—Paul Bryant, Alabama
1972—Ralph Jordan, Auburn
1973—Paul Bryant, Alabama
1974—Paul Bryant, Alabama
1975—Ken Cooper, Ole Miss
1976—Vince Dooley, Georgia
1977—Paul Bryant, Alabama
1978—Paul Bryant, Alabama
1979—Paul Bryant, Alabama
1980—Charley Pell, Florida
1981—Paul Bryant, Alabama
1982—George MacIntyre, Vanderbilt
1983—Pat Dye, Auburn
1984—Galen Hall, Florida
1985—Johnny Majors, Tennessee
1986—Billy Brewer, Ole Miss
1987—Bill Curry, Alabama
1988—Pat Dye, Auburn
1989—Bill Curry, Alabama
1990—Steve Spurrier, Florida
NOTE: Discontinued following 1990 season

Nashville Banner SEC Coach of the Year

1935—Jack Meagher, Auburn
1936—Bob Neyland, Tennessee
1937—Ray Morrison, Vanderbilt
1938—Bob Neyland, Tennessee
1939—Bill Alexander, Georgia Tech
1940—Allyn McKeen, Miss. State
1941—Red Sanders, Vanderbilt
1942—Wally Butts, Georgia
1943—No Selection Made
1944—John Barnhill, Tennessee
1945—Frank Thomas, Alabama
1946—Wally Butts, Georgia
1947—John Vaught, Ole Miss
1948—Henry Frnka, Tulane
1949—Gaynell Tinsley, LSU
1950—Bob Neyland, Tennessee
1951—Bobby Dodd, Georgia Tech
1952—Harold Drew, Alabama
1953—Ralph Jordan, Auburn
1954—Blanton Collier, Kentucky
1955—Art Guepe, Vanderbilt
1956—Bowden Wyatt, Tennessee
1957—Wade Walker, Miss. State
1958—Paul Dietzel, LSU
1959—Wally Butts, Georgia
1960—Ray Graves, Florida
1961—Paul Bryant, Alabama
1962—John Vaught, Ole Miss
1963—Ralph Jordan, Auburn
1964—Paul Bryant, Alabama
1965—Doug Dickey, Tennessee
1966—Vince Dooley, Georgia
1967—Doug Dickey, Tennessee
1968—Vince Dooley, Georgia
1969—Charlie McClendon, LSU
1970—Charlie McClendon, LSU
1971—Paul Bryant, Alabama
1972—Ralph Jordan, Auburn
1973—Paul Bryant, Alabama
1974—Paul Bryant, Alabama
1975—Ken Cooper, Ole Miss
1976—Vince Dooley, Georgia
1977—Paul Bryant, Alabama
1978—Vince Dooley, Georgia
1979—Paul Bryant, Alabama
1980—Vince Dooley, Georgia
1981—Paul Bryant, Alabama
1982—George MacIntyre, Vanderbilt
1983—Pat Dye, Auburn
1984—Bill Arnsparger, LSU
1985—Johnny Majors, Tennessee
1986—Bill Arnsparger, LSU
1987—Pat Dye, Auburn
1988—Pat Dye, Auburn
1989—Bill Curry, Alabama
1990—Billy Brewer, Ole Miss
1991—Steve Spurrier, Florida
1992—Gene Stallings, Alabama
1993—Terry Bowden, Auburn

SEC Championship Coaches

Paul "Bear" Bryant (14)—Kentucky (1) 1950; Alabama (13) 1961-64-65-66-71-72-73-74-75-77-78-79-81
Johnny Vaught (6)—Ole Miss 1947-54-55-60-62-63
Vince Dooley (6)—Georgia 1966-68-76-80-81-82
Bob Neyland (5)—Tennessee 1938-39-40-46-51
Frank Thomas (4)—Alabama 1933-34-37-45
Wally Butts (4)—Georgia 1942-46-48-59
Pat Dye (4)—Auburn 1983-87-88-89
Bill Alexander (3)—Georgia Tech 1939-43-44
Johnny Majors (3)—Tennessee 1985-89-90
Steve Spurrier (2)—Florida 1991-93
Bernie Moore (2)—LSU 1935-36
Paul Dietzel (2)—LSU 1958-61
Doug Dickey (2)—Tennessee 1967-69
Bobby Dodd (2)—Georgia Tech 1951-52
Ted Cox (1)—Tulane 1934
Red Dawson (1)—Tulane 1939
Allyn McKeen (1)—Mississippi State 1941
Henry Frnka (1)—Tulane 1949
Red Drew (1)—Alabama 1953
Bowden Wyatt (1)—Tennessee 1956
Ralph Jordan (1)—Auburn 1957
Charlie McClendon (1)—LSU 1970
Fran Curci (1)—Kentucky 1976
Bill Arnsparger (1)—LSU 1986
Mike Archer (1)—LSU 1988
Bill Curry (1)—Alabama 1989
Gene Stallings (1)—Alabama 1992

NOTE: Includes ties

1994 SEC Football

Winningest SEC Coaches
ALL GAMES AT SEC INSTITUTIONS
(By Victories)

Paul "Bear" Bryant
Kentucky/Alabama

Wallace Butts
Georgia

	Wins	Coach (Schools)	Seasons	W-L-T
1.	292	Paul "Bear" Bryant (Kentucky/Alabama)	UK 1946-53	60-23-5
			UA 1958-82	232-46-9
2.	201	Vince Dooley (Georgia)	1964-88	201-77-10
3.	197	Dan McGugin (Vanderbilt)	1904-17; 1919-34	197-55-19
4.	190	John Vaught (Ole Miss)	1947-70; 1973	190-60-12
5.	176	Ralph "Shug" Jordan (Auburn)	1951-75	176-83-6
6.	173	Robert Neyland (Tennessee)	1926-34; 1936-40; 1946-52	173-31-12
7.	140	Wallace Butts (Georgia)	1939-60	140-86-9
8.	137	Charlie McClendon (LSU)	1962-79	137-59-7
9.	122	Mike Donahue (Auburn/LSU)	AU 1904-06; 1908-22	99-35-5
			LSU 1923-27	23-19-3
10.	115	Johnny Majors (Tennessee)	1977-92	115-62-8
	115	Frank Thomas (Alabama)	1931-46	115-24-7
12.	104	Doug Dickey (Tennessee/Florida)	UT 1964-69	46-15-4
			UF 1970-78	58-42-2
13.	99	Pat Dye (Auburn)	1981-92	99-39-4
14.	98	Harry Mehre (Georgia/Ole Miss)	UG 1928-37	59-34-6
			UM 1938-45	39-26-1
15.	83	Bernie Moore (LSU)	1935-47	83-39-6
16.	70	Ray Graves (Florida)	1960-69	70-31-4
17.	67	Billy Brewer (Ole Miss)	1983-present	67-55-3
18.	65	Allyn McKeen (Mississippi State)	1939-48	65-19-3
19.	61	Wallace Wade (Alabama)	1923-30	61-13-3
20.	59	Bill Battle (Tennessee)	1970-76	59-22-4
21.	56	Harold "Red" Drew (Ole Miss/Alabama)	UM 1946	2-7-0
			UA 1947-54	54-29-7
22.	54	Bob Woodruff (Florida)	1950-59	54-41-6

Minimum 50 Victories

(By Percentage)

Robert Neyland
Tennessee

Dan McGugin
Vanderbilt

	Pct	Coach (Schools)	Seasons	W-L-T
1.	.829	Robert Neyland (Tennessee)	1926-34; 1936-40; 1946-52	173-31-12
2.	.812	Wallace Wade (Alabama)	1923-30	61-13-3
3.	.811	Frank Thomas (Alabama)	1931-46	115-24-7
4.	.797	Paul "Bear" Bryant (Kentucky/Alabama)	UK 1946-53	60-23-5
			UA 1958-82	232-46-9
5.	.7644	Allyn McKeen (Mississippi State)	1939-48	65-19-3
6.	.7639	G.E. Pyle (Florida)	1909-13	26-7-3
7.	.762	Dan McGugin (Vanderbilt)	1904-17; 1919-34	197-55-19
8.	.748	John Vaught (Ole Miss)	1947-70; 1973	190-60-12
9.	.722	John Heisman (Auburn)	1895-99	12-4-2
10.	.718	Bill Battle (Tennessee)	1970-76	59-22-4
11.	.715	Vince Dooley (Georgia)	1964-88	201-77-10
12.	.711	Pat Dye (Auburn)	1981-92	99-39-4
13.	.698	W.D. Chadwick (Mississippi State)	1909-13	29-12-2
14.	.694	Galen Hall (Florida)	1984-88	37-16-1
15.	.692	Charlie McClendon (LSU)	1962-79	137-59-7
16.	.686	Ray Graves (Florida)	1960-69	70-31-4
17.	.685	Mike Donahue (Auburn/LSU)	AU 1904-06; 1908-22	99-35-5
			LSU 1923-27	23-19-3
18.	.679	W.A. Cunningham (Georgia)	1910-19	43-18-9
19.	.675	Ralph "Shug" Jordan (Auburn)	1951-75	176-83-6
20.	.672	Bernie Moore (LSU)	1935-47	83-39-6
21.	.660	Paul Dietzel (LSU)	1955-61	46-23-3
22.	.649	George Woodruff (Georgia)	1923-27	30-16-1
23.	.643	Johnny Majors (Tennessee)	1977-92	115-62-8
24.	.641	Doug Dickey (Tennessee/Florida)	UT 1964-69	46-15-4
			UF 1970-78	58-42-2
25.	.633	M.B. Banks (Tennessee)	1921-25	27-15-3
26.	.628	Z.G. Clevenger (Tennessee)	1911-15	26-15-2
27.	.622	Bowden Wyatt (Tennessee)	1955-62	49-29-4
28.	.617	H.R. "Red" Sanders (Vanderbilt)	1940-42; 1946-48	36-22-2
29.	.615	Harry Mehre (Georgia/Ole Miss)	UG 1928-37	59-34-6
			UM 1938-45	39-26-1
30.	.615	Wallace Butts (Georgia)	1939-60	140-86-9
31.	.601	Harold "Red" Drew (Ole Miss/Alabama)	UM 1946	2-7-0
			UA 1947-54	54-29-7

Minimum Five Years And .600 Winning Percentage

Coaches

Winningest SEC Coaches
SEC REGULAR-SEASON GAMES
(By Victories)

	Wins	Coach (Schools)	Seasons	W-L-T
1.	159	Paul "Bear" Bryant (Kentucky/Alabama)	UK 1946-53	22-18-4
			UA 1958-82	137-28-5
2.	106	John Vaught (Ole Miss)	1947-70; 1973	106-41-10
3.	105	Vince Dooley (Georgia)	1964-88	105-41-4
4.	98	Ralph "Shug" Jordan (Auburn)	1951-75	98-63-4
5.	67	Wallace Butts (Georgia)	1939-60	67-60-5
6.	62	Charlie McClendon (LSU)	1962-79	62-38-0
	62	Robert Neyland (Tennessee)	1926-34; 1936-40; 1946-52	62-15-5
8.	59	Frank Thomas (Alabama)	1931-46	59-16-6
9.	57	Johnny Majors (Tennessee)	1977-92	57-40-3
10.	50	Doug Dickey (Tennessee/Florida)	UT 1964-69	21-10-4
			UF 1970-78	28-28-1
11.	48	Pat Dye (Auburn)	1981-92	48-27-1
12.	36	Ray Graves (Florida)	1960-69	36-19-3
13.	34	Harold "Red" Drew (Ole Miss/Alabama)	UM 1946	1-6-0
			UA 1947-54	33-21-7
14.	33	Billy Brewer (Ole Miss)	1983-present	33-41-0
15.	29	Allyn McKeen (Mississippi State)	1939-48	29-16-2
	29	Bob Woodruff (Florida)	1950-59	29-32-2
	29	Bowden Wyatt (Tennessee)	1955-62	29-23-4
18.	27	Harry Mehre (Georgia/Ole Miss)	UG 1928-37	12-12-2
			UM 1938-45	15-17-1
	27	Steve Spurrier (Florida)	1990-present	27-4-0
20.	26	Paul Dietzel (LSU)	1955-61	26-16-2
	26	Jack Meagher (Auburn)	1934-42	26-25-7
22.	25	Fran Curci (Kentucky)	1973-81	25-30-0
23.	24	Gene Stallings (Alabama)	1990-present	24-5-1
24.	23	Bernie Moore (LSU)	1935-47	23-28-4
25.	22	Bill Battle (Tennessee)	1970-76	22-18-1
26.	21	Blanton Collier (Kentucky)	1954-61	21-34-5

Minimum 20 Victories

(By Percentage)

	Pct	Coach (Schools)	Seasons	W-L-T
1.	.787	Robert Neyland (Tennessee)	1926-34; 1936-40; 1946-52	62-15-5
2.	.765	Frank Thomas (Alabama)	1931-46	59-16-6
3.	.764	Paul "Bear" Bryant (Kentucky/Alabama)	UK 1946-53	22-18-4
			UA 1958-82	137-28-5
4.	.713	Vince Dooley (Georgia)	1964-88	105-41-4
5.	.707	John Vaught (Ole Miss)	1947-70; 1973	106-41-10
6.	.657	Ray Graves (Florida)	1960-69	36-19-3
7.	.6383	Allyn McKeen (Mississippi State)	1939-48	29-16-2
8.	.6381	Pat Dye (Auburn)	1981-92	48-27-1
9.	.632	Galen Hall (Florida)	1984-88	24-14-0
10.	.620	Charlie McClendon (LSU)	1962-79	62-38-0
11.	.614	Paul Dietzel (LSU)	1955-61	26-16-2
12.	.606	Ralph "Shug" Jordan (Auburn)	1951-75	98-63-4
13.	.585	Johnny Majors (Tennessee)	1977-92	57-40-3
14.	.560	Doug Dickey (Tennessee/Florida)	UT 1964-69	21-10-4
			UF 1970-78	28-28-1
15.	.554	Bowden Wyatt (Tennessee)	1955-62	29-23-4
16.	.551	Harold "Red" Drew (Ole Miss/Alabama)	UM 1946	1-6-0
			UA 1947-54	33-21-7
17.	.549	Bill Battle (Tennessee)	1970-76	22-18-1
18.	.527	Wallace Butts (Georgia)	1939-60	67-60-5
19.	.517	Doug Barfield (Auburn)	1976-80	15-14-1
20.	.509	Jack Meagher (Auburn)	1934-42	26-25-7
21.	.500	Ray Morrison (Vanderbilt)	1935-39	15-15-1

Minimum Five Years And .500 Winning Percentage

Vince Dooley
Georgia

John Vaught
Ole Miss

Ralph "Shug" Jordan
Auburn

Charlie McClendon
LSU

1994 SEC Football

Winningest Division IA Coaches
(By Victories)

ALL-TIME (Minimum 175)

1. PAUL "BEAR" BRYANT [Alabama 1936]..................323
   (Maryland 1945; Kentucky 1946-53; Texas A&M 1954-57; Alabama 1958-82)
2. AMOS ALONZO STAGG [Yale 1888]..................314
   (Springfield 1890-91; Chicago 1892-1932; Pacific 1933-46)
3. GLENN "POP" WARNER [Cornell 1895]..................313
   (Georgia 1895-96; Cornell 1897-98, 1904-06; Carlisle 1899-1903, 1907-13; Pittsburgh 1915-23; Stanford 1924-32; Temple 1933-38)
4. JOE PATERNO [Brown 1951]..................257
   (Penn State 1966-present)
5. BOBBY BOWDEN [Samford 1953]..................239
   (Samford 1959-62; West Virginia 1970-75; Florida State 1976-present)
6. WOODROW "WOODY" HAYES [Denison 1935]..................238
   (Dennison 1946-48; Miami-Ohio 1949-50; Ohio State 1951-78)
7. GLENN "BO" SCHEMBECHLER [Miami-Ohio 1951]..................234
   (Miami-Ohio 1963-68; Michigan 1969-89)
8. JESS NEELY [Vanderbilt 1924]..................207
   (Rhodes 1924-27; Clemson 1931-39; Rice 1940-66)
9. TOM OSBORNE [Hastings 1959]..................206
   (Nebraska 1973-present)
10. WARREN WOODSON [Baylor 1924]..................203
    (Central Arkansas 1935-39; Hardin-Simmons 1941-42, 1946-51; Arizona 1952-56; New Mexico State 1958-67; Trinity 1972-73)
11. VINCE DOOLEY [Auburn 1954]..................201
    (Georgia 1964-88)
    EDDIE ANDERSON [Notre Dame 1922]..................201
    (Loras 1922-24; DePaul 1925-31; Holy Cross 1933-38, 1950-64; Iowa 1939-42, 1946-49)
13. HAYDEN FRY [Baylor 1951]..................200
    (Southern Methodist 1962-72; North Texas State 1973-1978; Iowa 1979-present)
14. DANA BIBLE [Carson-Newman 1912]..................198
    (Mississippi College 1913-15; LSU 1916; Texas A&M 1917, 1919-28; Nebraska 1929-36; Texas 1937-46)
15. DAN McGUGIN [Michigan 1904]..................197
    (Vanderbilt 1904-17, 1919-34)
    LaVELL EDWARDS [Utah State 1952]..................197
    (Brigham Young 1972-present)
17. FIELDING "HURRY UP" YOST [Lafayette 1897]..................196
    (Ohio Wesleyan 1897; Nebraska 1898; Kansas 1899; Stanford 1900; Michigan 1901-23, 1925-26)
18. HOWARD JONES [Yale 1908]..................194
    (Syracuse 1908; Yale 1909, 1913; Ohio State 1910; Iowa 1916-23; Duke 1924; Southern Cal 1925-40)
19. LOU HOLTZ [Kent 1959]..................193
    (William & Mary 1969-71; North Carolina State 1972-75; Arkansas 1977-83; Minnesota 1984-85; Notre Dame 1986-present)
20. JOHN VAUGHT [Texas Christian 1933]..................190
    (Ole Miss 1947-70, 1973)
21. JIM SWEENEY [Portland 1951]..................186
    (Montana State 1963-67; Washington State 1968-75; Fresno State 1976-present]
22. JOHN HEISMAN [Brown 1890]..................185
    (Oberlin 1892, 1894; Akron 1893; Auburn 1895-99; Clemson 1900-03; Georgia Tech 1904-19; Pennsylvania 1920-22; Washington & Jefferson 1923; Rice 1924-27)
23. DARRELL ROYAL [Oklahoma 1950]..................184
    (Mississippi State 1954-55; Washington 1956; Texas 1957-76)
24. GIL DOBIE [Minnesota 1902]..................180
    (North Dakota State 1906-07; Washington 1908-16; Navy 1917-19; Cornell 1920-35; Boston College 1936-38)
    CARL SNAVELY [Lebanon Valley 1915]..................180
    (Bucknell 1927-33; North Carolina 1934-35, 1945-52; Cornell 1936-44; Washington (Mo.) 1953-58)
26. JERRY CLAIBORNE [Kentucky 1950]..................179
    (Virginia Tech 1961-70; Maryland 1972-81; Kentucky 1982-89)
27. BEN SCHWARTZWALDER [West Virginia 1933]..................178
    (Muhlenberg 1946-48; Syracuse 1949-73)
28. RALPH "SHUG" JORDAN [Auburn 1932]..................176
    (Auburn 1951-75)
    FRANK KUSH [Michigan State 1953]..................176
    (Arizona State 1958-79)
    DON JAMES [Miami-Florida 1954]..................176
    (Kent 1971-74; Washington 1975-92)
    JOHNNY MAJORS [Tennessee 1957]..................176
    (Iowa State 1968-72; Pittsburgh 1973-76, 1993-present; Tennessee 1977-92)

OTHER COACHES AT SEC SCHOOLS
(Minimum 150)

32. ROBERT NEYLAND [Army 1916]..................173
    (Tennessee 1926-34, 1936-40, 1946-52)
35. WALLACE WADE [Brown 1917]..................171
    (Alabama 1923-30; Duke 1931-41)
T40. BOBBY DODD [Tennessee 1931]..................165
    (Georgia Tech 1945-66)
46. FRANCIS SCHMIDT [Nebraska 1914]..................158
    (Tulsa 1919-21; Arkansas 1922-28; Texas Christian 1929-33; Ohio State 1934-40; Idaho 1941-42)
T49. RAY MORRISON [Vanderbilt 1912]..................155
    (Southern Methodist 1915-16, 1922-34; Vanderbilt 1918, 1935-39; Temple 1940-48; Austin 1949-52)
T52. PAT DYE [Georgia 1962]..................153
    (East Carolina 1974-79; Wyoming 1980; Auburn 1981-92)

[Alma Mater]
(Coaching Tenure)

ACTIVE (Minimum 100)
(Minimum five years as Division IA head coach; Record at four-year colleges only)

1. JOE PATERNO (Penn State)..................257
2. BOBBY BOWDEN (Florida State)..................239
3. TOM OSBORNE (Nebraska)..................206
4. HAYDEN FRY (Iowa)..................200
5. LaVELL EDWARDS (Brigham Young)..................197
6. LOU HOLTZ (Notre Dame)..................193
7. JIM SWEENEY (Fresno State)..................186
8. JOHNNY MAJORS (Pittsburgh)..................176
9. BILL MALLORY (Indiana)..................156
   DON NEHLEN (West Virginia)..................156
11. AL MOLDE (Western Michigan)..................152
12. JIM WACKER (Minnesota)..................150
13. TERRY DONAHUE (UCLA)..................139
14. GEORGE WELSH (Virginia)..................135
15. JOHN COOPER (Ohio State)..................126
16. BILLY BREWER (Ole Miss)..................124
17. JACKIE SHERRILL (Mississippi State)..................122
18. KEN HATFIELD (Rice)..................113
19. HERB DEROMEDI (Central Michigan)..................110
20. LARRY SMITH (Missouri)..................110

Less Than Five Years In Division IA
(Includes record at all four-year colleges)

CHRIS AULT (Nevada)..................145
JIM HESS (New Mexico State)..................126

320   Coaches

Winningest Division IA Coaches
(By Percentage)

ALL-TIME (Minimum .750)
(Minimum 10 years as Division I head coach; Record at four-year colleges only)

		Yrs	Won	Lost	Tied	Pct
1.	KNUTE ROCKNE [Notre Dame 1914]	13	105	12	5	.881
	(Notre Dame 1918-30)					
2.	FRANK LEAHY [Notre Dame 1931]	13	107	13	9	.864
	(Boston College 1939-40; Notre Dame 1941-43, 1946-53)					
3.	GEORGE WOODRUFF [Yale 1889]	12	142	25	2	.846
	(Pennsylvania 1892-1901; Illinois 1903; Carlisle 1905)					
4.	BARRY SWITZER [Arkansas 1960]	16	157	29	4	.837
	(Oklahoma 1973-88)					
5.	PERCY HAUGHTON [Harvard 1899]	13	96	17	6	.832
	(Cornell 1899-1900; Harvard 1908-16; Columbia 1923-24)					
6.	BOB NEYLAND [Army 1916]	21	173	31	12	.829
	(Tennessee 1926-34, 1936-40; 1946-52)					
7.	FIELDING "HURRY UP" YOST [Lafayette 1897]	29	196	36	12	.828
	(Ohio Wesleyan 1897; Nebraksa 1898; Kansas 1899; Stanford 1900; Michigan 1901-23, 1925-26)					
8.	CHARLES "BUD" WILKINSON [Minnesota 1937]	17	145	29	4	.826
	(Oklahoma 1947-63)					
9.	JOHN "JOCK" SUTHERLAND [Pittsburgh 1918]	20	144	28	14	.812
	(Lafayette 1919-23; Pittsburgh 1924-38)					
10.	TOM OSBORNE [Hastings 1959]	21	206	47	3	.811
	(Nebraska 1973-present)					
11.	BOB DEVANEY [Alma 1939]	16	136	30	7	.806
	(Wyoming 1957-61; Nebraska 1962-72)					
12.	FRANK THOMAS [Notre Dame 1923]	19	141	33	9	.795
	(Chattanooga 1925-28; Alabama 1931-42, 1944-46)					
13.	HENRY WILLIAMS [Yale 1891]	23	141	34	12	.786
	(Army 1891; Minnesota 1900-21)					
	JOE PATERNO [Brown 1950]	28	257	69	3	.786
	(Penn State 1966-present)					
15.	GIL "GLOOMY GIL" DOBIE [Minnesota 1902]	33	180	45	15	.781
	(North Dakota State 1906-07; Washington 1908-16; Navy 1917-19; Cornell 1920-35; Boston College 1936-38)					
16.	PAUL "BEAR" BRYANT [Alabama 1936]	38	323	85	17	.780
	(Maryland 1945; Kentucky 1946-53; Texas A&M 1954-57; Alabama 1958-82)					
17.	FRED FOLSOM [Dartmouth 1895]	19	106	28	6	.779
	(Colorado 1895-99, 1901-02, 1908-15; Dartmouth 1903-06)					
18.	GLENN "BO" SCHEMBECHLER [Miami-Ohio 1951]	27	234	65	8	.775
	(Miami-Ohio 1963-68; Michigan 1969-89)					
19.	HERBERT "FRITZ" CRISLER [Chicago 1922]	18	116	32	9	.768
	(Minnesota 1930-31; Princeton 1932-37; Michigan 1938-47)					
20.	CHARLEY MORAN [Tennessee 1898]	18	122	33	12	.766
	(Texas A&J 1909-14; Centre 1919-23; Bucknell 1924-26; Catawba 1930-33)					
21.	WALLACE WADE [Brown 1917]	24	171	49	10	.765
	(Alabama 1923-30; Duke 1931-41, 1946-50)					
22.	FRANK KUSH [Michigan State 1953]	22	176	54	1	.764
	(Arizona State 1958-79)					
23.	DAN McGUGIN [Michigan 1904]	30	197	55	19	.762
	(Vanderbilt 1904-17, 1919-34)					
24.	JIMMY CROWLEY [Notre Dame 1925]	13	78	21	10	.761
	(Michigan State 1929-32; Fordham 1933-41)					
25.	ANDY SMITH [Penn State 1905]	17	116	32	13	.761
	(Pennsylvania 1909-12; Purdue 1913-15; California 1916-25)					
26.	WOODROW "WOODY" HAYES [Denison 1935]	33	238	72	10	.759
	(Denison 1946-48; Miami-Ohio 1949-50; Ohio State 1951-78)					
27.	EARL "RED" BLAIK [Miami-Ohio 1918, Army 1920]	25	166	48	14	.759
	(Dartmouth 1934-40; Army 1941-58)					

OTHER COACHES AT SEC SCHOOLS (Minimum .700)

		Yrs	Won	Lost	Tied	Pct
28.	DARRELL ROYAL [Oklahoma 1950]	23	184	60	5	.749
	(Missssissippi State 1954-55; Washington 1956; Texas 1957-76)					
29.	JOHN VAUGHT [Texas Christian 1933]	25	190	61	12	.745
	(Ole Miss 1947-70, 1973)					
30.	DANNY FORD [Alabama 1970]	13	101	34	5	.739
	(Clemson 1978-89; Arkansas 1993-present)					
40.	GLENN "POP" WARNER [Cornell 1895]	44	313	106	32	.729
	(Georgia 1895-96; Cornell 1897-98, 1904-06; Carlisle 1899-1903, 1907-14; Pittsburgh 1915-23; Stanford 1924-32; Temple 1933-38)					
43.	FRANCIS SCHMIDT [Nebraska 1914]	24	158	57	11	.723
	(Tulsa 1919-21; Arkansas 1922-28; Texas Christian 1929-33; Ohio State 1934-40; Idaho 1941-42)					
46.	VINCE DOOLEY [Auburn 1954]	25	201	77	10	.715
	(Georgia 1964-88)					
47.	DANA BIBLE [Carson-Newman 1912]	33	198	72	23	.715
	(Mississippi College 1913-15; LSU 1916; Texas A&M 1917, 1919-28; Nebraska 1929-36; Texas 1937-46)					
48.	BOBBY DODD [Tennessee 1931]	22	165	64	8	.713
	(Georgia Tech 1945-66)					
49.	JOHN HEISMAN [Brown 1890, Pennsylvania 1892]	38	185	70	17	.711
	(Oberlin 1892, 1894; Akron 1893; Auburn 1895-99; Clemson 1900-03; Georgia Tech 1904-19; Pennsylvania 1920-22; Washington & Jefferson 1923; Rice 1924-27)					
51.	HENRY "RED" SANDERS [Vanderbilt 1927]	15	102	41	3	.709
	(Vanderbilt 1940-42, 1946-48; UCLA 1949-57)					
52.	PAT DYE [Georgia 1962]	19	153	62	5	.707
	(East Carolina 1974-79; Wyoming 1980; Auburn 1981-92)					
57.	FRANK BROYLES [Georgia Tech 1947]	20	149	62	6	.700
	(Missouri 1957; Arkansas 1958-76)					
58.	LAWRENCE "BIFF" JONES [Army 1917]	14	87	33	15	.700
	(Army 1928-29; LSU 1932-34; Oklahoma 1935-36; Nebraska 1937-41)					

[Alma Mater]
(Coaching Tenure)

ACTIVE
(Minimum five years as Division IA head coach; Record at four-year colleges only)

		Yrs	Won	Lost	Tied	Pct	Bowls W-L-T
1.	TOM OSBORNE (Nebraska)	21	206	47	3	.811	8-13-0
2.	R.C. SLOCUM (Texas A&M)	5	49	12	1	.793	1-4-0
3.	JOHN ROBINSON (Southern Cal)	8	75	19	2	.792	5-1-0
4.	JOE PATERNO (Penn State)	28	257	69	3	.786	15-8-1
5.	BOBBY BOWDEN (Florida State)	28	239	78	3	.752	13-3-1
6.	DANNY FORD (Arkansas)	13	101	34	5	.739	6-2-0
7.	DENNIS ERICKSON (Miami)	12	103	38	1	.729	5-4-0
8.	LaVELL EDWARDS (Brigham Young)	22	197	73	3	.727	5-12-1
9.	STEVE SPURRIER (Florida)	7	59	23	1	.717	2-2-0
10.	LOU HOLTZ (Notre Dame)	24	193	84	6	.693	10-6-0
11.	GARY GIBBS (Oklahoma)	5	38	17	2	.684	2-0-0
12.	TERRY DONAHUE (UCLA)	18	139	63	8	.681	8-3-1
13.	JACKIE SHERRILL (Miss. State)	16	122	61	4	.663	6-4-0
14.	JOHN COOPER (Ohio State)	17	126	63	6	.662	3-5-0
15.	HERB DEROMEDI (Central Michigan)	16	110	55	10	.657	0-1-0
16.	KEN HATFIELD (Rice)	15	113	62	3	.643	4-6-0
17.	AL MOLDE (Western Michigan)	23	152	87	8	.632	3-6-0
18.	DON NEHLEN (West Virginia)	23	156	91	8	.627	3-5-0
19.	FISHER DeBERRY (Air Force)	10	76	46	1	.622	4-3-0
20.	JOHN RALSTON (San Jose State)	14	88	56	4	.608	2-2-0
21.	JOHNNY MAJORS (Pittsburgh)	26	176	113	10	.605	9-7-0
22.	BOB WAGNER (Hawaii)	7	51	33	2	.604	1-1-0
23.	BILL McCARTNEY (Colorado)	12	82	54	5	.599	2-6-0
24.	BILL MALLORY (Indiana)	24	156	108	4	.589	4-6-0
25.	RAY GOFF (Georgia)	5	34	24	0	.586	2-1-0

OTHER COACHES AT SEC SCHOOLS

		Yrs	Won	Lost	Tied	Pct	W-L-T
32.	BILLY BREWER (Ole Miss)	20	124	95	6	.564	4-3-0
38.	GENE STALLINGS (Alabama)	10	58	51	1	.532	3-1-0
41.	CURLEY HALLMAN (LSU)	6	35	32	0	.522	1-0-0
50.	BILL CURRY (Kentucky)	14	74	81	4	.478	2-3-0

Less Than Five Years In Division IA (IA Yrs)
(Includes record at all four-year colleges)

	Yrs	Won	Lost	Tied	Pct	W-L-T
MARK DUFFNER (Maryland) (2)	8	65	22	1	.744	0-0-0
DENNIS FRANCHIONE (New Mexico) (2)	11	89	32	2	.732	6-5-0*
CHRIS AULT (Nevada) (1)	17	145	58	1	.713	9-8-0*
PAUL PASQUALONI (Syracuse) (3)	8	60	25	1	.703	*2-1-0
TERRY BOWDEN (Auburn) (1)	10	75	36	1	.674	*2-4-0

* Includes record in NCAA and/or NAIA championships.

1994 SEC Football

SEC Licensing Program

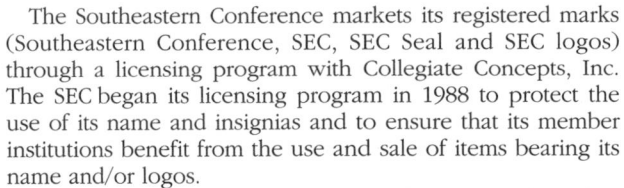

The Southeastern Conference markets its registered marks (Southeastern Conference, SEC, SEC Seal and SEC logos) through a licensing program with Collegiate Concepts, Inc. The SEC began its licensing program in 1988 to protect the use of its name and insignias and to ensure that its member institutions benefit from the use and sale of items bearing its name and/or logos.

The program also ensures that manufacturers and retailers market only the highest-quality merchandise using the conference name and logos. The SEC has joined a consortium of universities throughout the country to bring about consistency in the marketplace for officially-licensed collegiate products.

In addition to the SEC, Collegiate Licensing of Atlanta administers the programs for more than 100 universities and 10 bowls, including the USF&G Sugar Bowl. The objectives of the consortium are to assure that the names and logos of the members are protected and that the members receive their fair share of revenues generated and that, alumni, students and supporters can easily recognize authorized merchandise.

Consumers can tell if the merchandise is authorized by looking for the label which says, "Officially Licensed Collegiate Products."

Corporate Marketing Program

Several of the nation's most prestigious corporations have joined with the Southeastern Conference in supporting intercollegiate athletics.

Begun in 1988, the SEC Corporate Marketing Program allows these corporations to join with the conference as partners in furthering the role of athletics in higher education.

Each member of the SEC corporate marketing team shows its commitment to the future of intercollegiate athletics with contributions to SEC Drug Education programs, SEC Youth Clinics, SEC Scholarship Programs and SEC Academic Enhancement Programs.

The corporations also conduct consumer promotions designed to increase public awareness of the member institutions of the SEC, which in turn supports increased ticket sales and high television and radio ratings.

In addition to the broad spectrum of benefits provided by these contributions, each SEC institution is a direct beneficiary of the program.

Current Corporate Marketing partners with the SEC include Buffalo Rock (Dr. Pepper), First Alabama Bank, Gatorade, General Mills, Golden Flake Snack Foods, Hardee's, HealthSouth, Russell Athletic, Texaco and Toyota.